MORE PRAISE FOR JOAN COLLINS

PAST IMPERFECT

"Vastly amusing reading."
—*SCREEN INTERNATIONAL*

"Compelling."
—*DAILY TELEGRAPH*

"Promises to go straight up the Bestseller List."
—*EVENING NEWS*

PRIME TIME

"This book has everything!"
—*THE NEW YORK DAILY NEWS*

"A sizzling inside look at the broadcasting game in Hollywood . . ."
—*THE LOS ANGELES DAILY NEWS*

"You'll have nothing but a good time celebrity spotting . . ."
—*GLAMOUR*

LOVE AND DESIRE AND HATE

". . . A must for Collins collectors."
—*SAN FRANCISCO CHRONICLE*

"Joan Collins dishes up a tasty read . . ."
—*PUBLISHERS WEEKLY*

". . . Definitely a page turner."
—*HOUSTON CHRONICLE*

Three Complete Bestsellers
Joan Collins

Three Complete Bestsellers
Joan Collins

Her Autobiography
Past Imperfect
and Two Novels
Prime Time
Love and Desire and Hate

WINGS
New York • Avenel, New Jersey

This 1994 edition is published by Wings Books,
distributed by Random House Value Publishing, Inc.,
40 Engelhard Avenue, Avenel, New Jersey 07001,
by arrangement with Simon & Schuster, Inc.

Random House
New York • Toronto • London • Sydney • Auckland

Printed and bound in the United States of America

Library of Congress Cataloging-in-Publication Data

Collins, Joan, 1933–
[Selections.   1994]
Three complete books / Joan Collins.
      p.   cm.
Contents: Past imperfect—Prime time—Love and desire and hate.
ISBN 0-517-10074-6
1. Motion picture industry—Fiction. 2. Collins, Joan, 1933– . 3. Motion picture actors and actresses—Great Britain—Biography. I. Collins, Joan, 1933– Past imperfect. 1994. II. Collins, Joan, 1933– Prime time. 1994. III. Collins, Joan, 1933– Love & desire & hate. 1994. IV. Title.
PR6053.O426A6   1994

823'.914—dc20   94-6605
                                                                                                          CIP

8 7 6 5 4 3 2 1

Contents

PAST IMPERFECT

AN AUTOBIOGRAPHY

Acknowledgments

Grateful thanks to Judy Bryer and Barry Langford, who painstakingly deciphered the hieroglyphics; Michael Korda, my editor, and Dan Green, for giving me the carrot and the stick; George Christy, who insisted I should publish it in America.

For my beautiful children,
Tara, Sacha and Katyana.
They are the past, the present and,
especially, the future.
And for my mother, Elsa.
I wish she could be here
to share it all with me.

❖ *Prologue* ❖

I HAVE ALWAYS LIVED my life with enthusiasm and pleasure. True, I have also made mistakes, for some of which I have paid dearly, but I endeavor to learn from my mistakes, and use them to take a better, more controlled step into the future.

Today I am trying to remain balanced and in control of my destiny, in spite of the extraordinary things that have happened to me in the past three years. Success, it has been said, makes strange bedfellows . . . success can create monsters . . . the price one pays for success is living with the inevitability of failure. I strongly believe, though, that "the person who has never made a mistake is the person who has never accomplished much."

Being always true to my nature, I have never believed that there was "just one reason" for doing anything. In 1977, when I decided to write my autobiography, I did so for three very basic reasons. First, to set the record straight about a lot of the rubbish and gossip that had been written about me. The second reason was to crow a bit. "Hey, look at me! What a helluva life, eh, folks!" It was a way of showing off all my real qualities (good, bad and indifferent) to the possible censure, yet hopeful approbation of my readers—not to mention those closest to me . . . family, friends, and old school chums. And last, but naturally by no means least . . . money. I needed it then and it was not to be sneezed at. Thus PAST IMPERFECT was published in England in 1978 to a stream of outrage from critics and members of the British press. That a *woman* could be so outrageous as to have lived a controversial and sexually liberated life, and *then* have the temerity to shamelessly publish and be damned with it, was more than they could abide, and I was soundly trounced in print—and brutally insulted on TV talk shows.

Interest in America was kindled by the autobiography, but, mortified and upset by my countrymens' wrath, I declined all offers from American publishers. If the British people, who had watched my progress from a 16-year-old movie starlet through the ups and downs of a more than checkered career, through marriages, relationships, and children, could be so outraged, I could only expect to be slaughtered outright in the United States.

Although I had won a certain success in American movies in the late 50s and 60s, I was certainly not a household name in 1978. So I continued to work on movies, TV, and the stage, and was content, quite genuinely, to leave my career where it was—in England. And then three years later, in 1981, came *Dynasty*. If ever one event were to change one's life, without a shadow of a doubt, *Dynasty* sent me soaring, and totally altered my world. The impact of both the show and my character—Alexis Morell Carrington Colby—on American viewers was enormous. Both the public and the media immediately took a fancy to Alexis, realizing perhaps that beneath that dastardly exterior beat a heart of—well, if not gold, at least silver plate.

With the success of *Dynasty*, and my success as Alexis, people started asking me about my past—and PAST IMPERFECT. When was it going to be published? Was it really too shocking for the American public to read? Rumors flew. Had it been banned in the U.S. because of its explicit sexual passages, racy situations, and risqué language? No, no, no, this was not true at all, but I realized I needed to set the record straight. Eventually, after extensive talks with my own conscience, then with Simon and Schuster, I decided to re-write and edit the English edition of PAST IMPERFECT, update it, and publish it in the U.S. Let the chips and the critical barbs fall where they may!

Again this was done for several reasons—the main one *now* being that I wanted the American public to get to know, and perhaps understand, something of the real Joan Collins, not the Machiavellianly cunning bitch who paraded in exaggerated finery across their TV screens every Wednesday night.

I also realize how many young people are extremely interested in an acting career, and hope my experiences might offer some insights into how—and how *not*—to manage that career. And last but by no means least, I have always felt that a woman's place is *not* always in the home and by the kitchen stove. I'm not knocking the millions of women who generally enjoy and obtain satisfaction from being homemakers. But there are many women who, like me, have strong ambitions and desires to make it in a man's world, to fulfill themselves in careers without the help of a man or the advantage of being one. I also feel that I've been somewhat of a pioneer in the women's movement for sexual freedom, sexual equality, and sexual liberation, and *certainly* a pioneer in abolishing those "ageism" taboos and attitudes toward women which have permeated both my life and the lives of millions of other women.

The hardcover edition of PAST IMPERFECT was published by Simon and Schuster in the spring of 1984. It was received favorably by the critics and extremely well by the public, who sent it spinning into the *New York Times* bestseller list for more than three months, where it eventually became Number 2, much to my satisfaction, and to the surprise of certain English critics who had so castigated the original.

As a result of my overactive work schedule, which includes not only acting in and fulfilling my obligations to *Dynasty,* but also other involvements (not to mention my desire to spend time with my family and friends), I have been continually frustrated in never having enough time to really write and express myself as I would like. But I don't believe in "ghost writers." This is all my own work, cross my heart, and it is *not* Alexis speaking now! My time for writing is usually stolen time: in bed at night when everyone in the house is asleep, on planes, under the hairdryer at the studio, on the set or in my dressing room in between takes, in a limousine going to work, sitting on the sofa while Katie watches *The Brady Bunch.* My yellow legal pad is never far away.

My concentration, alas, is never one hundred percent, but I have done my best not only to tell my tale as concisely and with as much detail as possible, but to try and make it interesting—and, hopefully, amusing. I've attempted to take you, the reader, into my confidence, and to have you understand who the person known as Joan Collins really is. I hope I have succeeded. And I hope that you will enjoy my life and my story as much as I have enjoyed living it and writing it.

California
December 1984

❧ *One* ❧

My FIRST RECORDED PUBLIC appearance is a photograph of my mother and father and Lew Grade at a charity ball seven hours before I was born.

Apart from a slightly panicky look in my mother's eyes, no one could even tell that she was about to deliver her firstborn. She is smoothly blond, soignée and flanked by the two young dinner-jacketed men.

My father, Joe Collins, and Lew Grade were at that time partners in the theatrical agency Collins and Grade. They had the suitably smug expressions of men about to become father and godfather for the first time. Although Lord Lew Grade (as he is today) never became my official godfather, he and my parents were then, and for many years to come, so close, both in business and in their personal lives, that he was "Uncle Lew" to me, and he took a personal interest in me when I was a child. Mummy and Daddy were bridesmaid and best man when he married a lovely young singer, Kathleen Moody, during the war—and until Mummy's death in 1962, she and Kathy were the closest of friends, although the business relationship between my father and Lew had long been dissolved.

I was in awe of my father for so many years that it is even now hard to write about him without the feeling he may get cross with me. Throughout years of analysis and soul-searching, with intellectual and emotional knowledge of myself and my relationships, Daddy had always been a frightening figure rather than a father figure. There is no doubt that some of my quests for the eternal love of impossible men were to capture Daddy, for there is no doubt that I had his love for at least the first five or six years of my life.

I was born in a Bayswater nursing home in north London on May 23, sometime between the end of the Great Depression and the beginning of the war. "Any woman who would reveal her age would reveal anything." Thus spake Oscar Wilde. And I agree with him.

According to my parents and relatives I was the world's most adorable-looking baby—but lacked the personality to match. Gemini children are mercurial and moody, charming and delightful one minute, totally impossible the next . . . and I was a typical Gemini. My baby looks were so appealing that my ever vigilant mother had a printed sign, "Please Do Not Kiss Me" displayed in my pram whenever we took our morning strolls.

Beautiful bonny babies must have been rare in north London then, for Mummy was often fighting off women begging to kiss, hold or adopt me. I was so overprotected that my mother even put ice cream in the oven for a few minutes before I ate it so the chill should be off!

It was an idyllic infancy and early childhood. We lived in a flat in Maida Vale three or four blocks from Regent's Park. Daddy worked at the agency with Lew, and adored Baby Joan and Mummy. One of the reasons I was called Joan was because they had wanted a boy, to have been called Joe, Jr., no doubt, and my name was the closest feminine equivalent. Throughout my first fifteen years, whenever my mother called out "Joe," I would often answer.

My adoration for my father was intense. At nursery school I told the other kids that my father was the tallest and handsomest man in the world. Handsome he was, with jet-black curly hair, which he would slick flat to his head with three layers of Brylcreem, dark-brown flashing eyes and a finely chiseled profile. Tall? Well, hardly. One day I realized to my disappointment that my father was only about five feet ten. There is a yellowing photograph in an old family album that epitomizes for me the idealistic father-daughter relationship and is my favorite picture of him and me. I am four or five years old, gap-toothed, large bow in hair and wearing a pretty sunsuit. We are in some faraway summer vacationland. I am sitting on the grass, legs neatly crossed, and smiling fit to burst. He is suntanned, curly-haired and smiling, gray-flanneled and sports-coated, holding in his hand a huge fishing net with which he is about to "catch" the little girl who sits trusting and happy, secure in the love of her handsome father.

My mother was gorgeous too. Blond and blue-eyed, she had the perfect Anglo-Saxon looks to complement my father's darkly Jewish ones. She was as fair as he was dark, and as gentle and kind as he could be stern and strict; my memories of my mother have become fonder through the years. I was always stronger than she and it irritated me that she seemed to adore being a slave to my father. When Joe became angry, we all fled. His raised voice made us nervous. But on looking back, I can see that one of the many qualities that made my mother love him so much was his outrageous sense of humor. He was always cracking jokes, and with his many friends often around, the flat would echo with their laughter.

I was sent to dancing school before I was three. Throughout the rest of my childhood I attended nine or ten different dancing academies as well as thirteen different schools. Before I was even old enough to go to kindergarten I would spend part of each morning listening avidly to the radio, dancing and whirling and humming to the early morning radio programs, while my mother did the housework. In the days before the radio became one continuous DJ program, the variety was infinite, and I would dance spiritedly to marches, classical music, brass bands, Strauss waltzes and, best of all, jazz. And sing too. I had aspirations as a singer, as well as an actress and I knew most of the words to every popular song ever written until the advent of Beatlemania.

Each Sunday we would get into the car and go for a long drive. There was usually a new car each year—impeccably tuned. The boredom of those endless drives lives with me still. To this day, I'd rather go on a plane, train or helicopter than drive anywhere for longer than two hours. We would drive through the unspoiled English countryside to Brighton, where Daddy's mother lived, or to Bognor, where Mummy's mother lived, or to Devon or Sussex or Kent, where nobody we even knew lived, and to relieve the boredom of the drives, I would sing and sing and sing.

Even as a tiny girl my interest in movies, dancing and theater was enormous. My fantasies took over completely, giving me fodder for my bedtime thoughts.

My father was second-generation show business. He was born in Port Elizabeth, South Africa, in 1902, to a successful theatrical agent, Will Collins, and a saucy soubrette and dancer, Henrietta Collins. Hetty must have been an early emancipated woman since she continued dancing with her sister act "The Three Cape Girls" until a month or so before Joe's birth. Considering it was still the Victorian Age, this showed a remarkable lack of concern for convention, something I obviously inherited from her. Photographs of her—hand on hip or posed in a daring cancan costume—show a beautiful, strong-featured young brunette with a willful look about her and a twinkle in her eye.

I remember Grandma Hetty as a lovely, effervescent gutsy lady, who taught me to dance and do the "splits" and high kicks, and was always full of life, laughter and fun up until her death. She encouraged me in my youthful aspirations as singer-dancer-actress. She regaled me with stories of backstage life, and made it sound wonderfully exciting—a world peopled with clowns, dancing and make-believe. I could almost smell the greasepaint and the musty, dank backstage odor of the scenery when she talked.

She had two other children, Lalla and Pauline. My father, the only boy, was spoiled rotten as a child. Both his sisters adored him, as did Hetty, as subsequently did my mother, Elsa, and eventually, of course, me and my sister Jackie, and my half-sister, Natasha. He had a long line of women all competing for his favors. And there's no doubt about it, he was a handsome devil whom women found irresistible.

Both of Hetty's daughters went into the theatrical world—Pauline became a theatrical agent and Lalla, the blond beauty of the family, became a dancer and one of "Cochran's Young Ladies."

Our apartment was always full of amusing and gregarious people whom Daddy represented—comedians, singers, dancers, conjurers and ventriloquists. A veritable procession of outgoing personalities congregated there. Daddy often played cards with them until the early hours; he played a formidable game of poker, which I learned from "kibitzing" over his shoulder.

All of these fascinating people, perhaps to ingratiate themselves with my father to get more work, or maybe because they believed it, would compliment me on my cute little nose, eyes or personality, and usually ended their remarks with "Of course you really *must* go on the stage."

So the seed was planted, and I started to dream my dreams of becoming an actress.

Daddy was proud of me then, there was no doubt of that. He liked the fact that I was cute, bubbly and captivating, and he agreed with his friends that I did indeed have the makings of an actress, although he himself did not advocate the theater as a suitable profession for young girls, knowing the difficulties and rejection so many of them suffered.

I can't pinpoint exactly when I stopped being Daddy's little darling. It could have been when little baby Jackie arrived to take some of the attention away from me. It could have been that with the coming of the London blitz we were speedily packed off to safer pastures in Brighton, Ilfracombe or Bognor, leaving Daddy alone in London to fend for himself. Oh, how my mother worried about him! But he had to stay in the city. There was a huge demand for variety shows and entertainment during the war, and he was putting his comedians, ventriloquists and dancers to work.

The war years are a hazy blur of evacuation to new places—boarding with strange people in even stranger houses and, horror of horrors, *constant* new schools. Shyness, something I had never suffered from previously, suddenly descended on me along with insecurities and doubts. New children at school whispering and giggling in the corner at the nervous new girl made me feel an outsider. I retreated more and more into a fantasy world of dolls, cinema, books and film magazines. Over all of it was a nagging feeling of rejection. I felt that if Daddy *really* loved me he would be with me in all those unfamiliar places.

It was a gypsylike existence. When the blitz and the bombings eased up, we returned to London for a few weeks or months. When the air raids started again, we were awakened in the middle of the night by Mummy and our nanny, bundled into "siren suits" and down to the basement of our block of flats, where we fitfully slept the night away, the sounds of distant exploding bombs and antiaircraft fire echoing through the dark and smelly air-raid shelter.

I was too young to understand how dangerous it really was, or how terrified was my poor mother. With a baby and a small girl to contend with, she was petrified that anything would befall us. Her ambivalent feelings of wanting to be with my father, and yet having to expose her children to peril to do so, must have caused her anguish. So after a short or a long time in London, off we'd go again, to yet another sanctuary, and another new school, and another painful time of trying to make new friends again. And that was the beginning of my gypsy life.

At the age of thirteen I was awkward, spotty, gawky, shy, boy-hating and introverted.

Convinced I didn't have any charms to capture my father's affection as

I had when I was a toddler, and with the added horror of a baby brother, Bill, the family's new darling, I decided that there was only one way to regain his affection and make things the way they were: I decided to try as hard as possible to act and look like a boy! The imminent onset of puberty was a disaster I was convinced couldn't *possibly* happen to me. Girls at school would discuss in hushed tones the horrors of the "curse." I searched the library in vain for an explanation of this, but with nothing forthcoming from my parents, my vivid imagination could only fear the worst.

I accompanied my father to his favorite football games every Saturday afternoon, freezing bravely in boyish corduroy trousers, jumper and brightly striped football scarf, waving my ratchet and jumping up in hysterical joy every time somebody scored a goal, trying hard to please him. I actually loathed football. I couldn't comprehend the fascination of twenty-two unkempt, dirty men kicking a ball around a muddy field, while thousands of raucous blokes in caps and mufflers cheered and screamed. My hatred of football also extended to other active sports, with the exception of swimming, at which I was fair. My performance at netball, lacrosse and tennis was atrocious. However, I feigned enormous enthusiasm for soccer and listened with phony fascination to the Saturday evening football results, hoping to impress my father.

Of course it didn't work. Bill, at two or three, was far more fascinating than gawky me. He pushed his toy cars and trucks happily around on the carpet, watched fondly by my parents, while I glowered jealously at him, stuffed myself frustratedly with sausage rolls and biscuits, and reaffirmed silently to myself my vow to become an actress.

The word "love" was an enigma to me for many years. In spite of two years of analysis and a weekend session at Actualizations, a workshop to explore human potential, my quests for love, although seemingly successful at the time, would leave me two or three years later with the question in my mind as to whether or not I had really loved that man as much as I thought I had at the time.

In the time that I spent at the Royal Academy of Dramatic Art, between the ages of fifteen and a half and sixteen and a half, I discovered the opposite sex for the first time and fell "in love" many times. Much of the time I should have spent studying was squandered in dithering daydreams about the current beloved. Some of these flirtations lasted as long as three or four months, some only three or four days—but they were all platonic. For this was the flirty fifties and God forbid a well brought up half-Jewish girl would do anything as gravely taboo as "go all the way." There were only stolen kisses under the lamppost, furtive hand-holding at the movies, and whispered undying protestations of love in the austere corridors of the Royal Academy.

It was unthinkable for a young girl to sleep with a boy then. General knowledge of sexual practices, not to mention birth control, was skimpy and vague. It was an accepted fact between both sexes that you petted and necked, kissed and cuddled, but, as far as the girls were concerned, you saved your virginity for the marital bed.

I was popular. David McCallum, who was in my class, told me that I was the first girl he and the other boys in class noticed. I suddenly became aware of my sex appeal. It was a novelty to be able to attract young men. However, my interest in them bloomed and faded as fast as the summer flowers; when I lost interest in one, I immediately focused my attention on another. This little game continued in different fashion for many years. It was a classic. A girl with a father complex, looking for affirmation of her desirability by enticing hard-to-get males.

The ones who flocked after *me* were of no interest, and this pattern continued more or less for years. I have always, with few exceptions, chosen the "love object," been the pursuer, won the heart and ended the game. My span of interest and involvement lengthened as I became more mature, and from the brief mad weekly crushes at RADA to my seven-month first marriage to Maxwell Reed, and thence to deeper and more involved affairs, they have successively lasted for longer and longer periods of time.

Most of the men and boys I chose were difficult, unattainable, moody, unpredictable, sometimes unable to love or to be giving and that was *always* what intrigued me. Not for me to be wooed and won; I was the wooer, and in being so I was wounded many times.

But I also was working hard at RADA. Determined to succeed in my profession, I had already been discovered. A modeling agency came to RADA to choose a girl for photographic modeling in women's magazines. I was the lucky one, and even with the miserly salaries paid to a model, I was then able to buy better tickets to the theater and movies, to which I went two or three times a week, to buy some new clothes and occasionally even take a taxi.

I modeled for the illustrations of love stories in women's magazines. In one I was a terrified teenager in a yellow turtleneck about to be raped by a madman in a haunted house. In another, a heartbroken teenager sobbing into her pillow when she discovers she is pregnant. Although not exactly svelte, I modeled teenage clothes for the pages of *Woman* and *Woman's Own*. There was no such thing as a totally teen-oriented market in the early 1950s. Mass-market jeans and casual wear were not the vogue, so the clothes I wore in the photos were frumpy and unflattering. My usual attire was tight jeans and workmen's plaid shirts bought from men's stores. With these I featured giant gypsy gold earrings, flat ballet shoes and a black polo-necked sweater, a hand-me-down from my sophisticated Aunt Lalla. This was an avant-garde costume then. With my exotic makeup—eyes rimmed with black pencil à la the top models of the day— two-inch-thick black eyebrows à la Elizabeth Taylor, my favorite actress, and long, straight bangs and a ponytail, I was the focus of attention wherever I went. Leslie Bricusse—then a student at Cambridge—remembers seeing me at a pub in King's Road, and although he didn't meet me, my outré image stuck with him.

A national magazine did a photo story on jazz clubs, and my picture appeared in print with my partner, with the caption "The couple who dress '*très* Jazz.' " I was unnamed and unknown in the photo. It was only my outrageous outfit that caused me to be noticed.

Jazz clubs and dancing were now my favorite relaxation. Three nights a week, two or three girlfriends and I would sit in smoky dives and listen ecstatically to "Humph," Humphrey Lyttleton's Dixieland Band, which played at 100 Oxford Street, or would go to outlying suburbs to catch other of our favorites: George Melly, Sidney Bechet and Claude Luter. "Humph" was my favorite, and I sat mesmerized for hours as his trumpet played ragtime and jazz from an era that fascinated me—the twenties— "When the Saints Go Marching In," "Jelly Roll Blues," "Hotter Than That," and dozens of others. I danced nonstop for endless hours in the steamy cellar on Oxford Street.

Suddenly my career started to happen. One day the phone rang and someone with a charming voice introduced himself as Bill Watts, a well-known agent, whose specialty was representing pretty young girls. He had seen my pictures in *Woman's Own* and thought I was a possibility for films.

I met him at his office in Mayfair. The walls were completely covered with photos of starlets in bathing suits and various stages of undress. He took me to lunch at a four-star restaurant, and over the shrimp cocktail and chicken vol-au-vent told me that I had "definite film potential." "But I want to be a *serious* actress," I said seriously. "Film stars can't act. They are just discovered behind soda fountains or cosmetic counters. I want to finish my next year at RADA, do several seasons in rep, and then, hopefully, get to the West End. Films are not for me." I sipped some white wine, gazing at him challengingly.

My views were heavily colored by RADA's attitude toward the movie medium. They thought that art was possible only in the theater, and the emphasis was heavily on having a melodic voice, the correct vowels and articulation, wonderfully theatrical gestures and the proper classical attitudes. I quote one of my report cards from RADA: "With so much in her favor this student is hampered by the weakness of her voice. She seems to lack the confidence to project and make use of the amount of voice she does possess. If she will make up her mind to cast away all fear and self-consciousness and *speak out* she will find her confidence increasing, and the unsure element in her acting will disappear. Otherwise it is 'the Films' for her and that would be such a pity." Oh what irony!

Although I worked at it diligently, my voice production and projection were constantly criticized by the teachers at RADA, and instead of gaining confidence and improving I became even more inhibited. We had endless elocution classes. Any dialect was taboo. An Albert Finney or a Michael Caine wouldn't have stood a chance to grow as an actor until he learned to speak with a conformist, aristocratic accent. We were supposed to speak and act as though we were from the same cookie cutter; consequently our true personalities and abilities were never really able to unfold. I was trying to talk and behave on stage like someone else— Claire Bloom or Vivien Leigh.

So I was snobbish about "the films" and it was only the persuasiveness of Bill Watts and his insistence that doing a few movie roles would only enhance my ability and not hinder it that made me sign with his agency.

He worked fast. Within a week I was being considered for the leading role in a film called *Lady Godiva Rides Again,* about the rise and fall of a beauty queen. I tested at Shepperton with several up-and-coming starlets. The makeup man and the hairdresser who painted and coiffed me for Lady Godiva had learned their craft in the dark ages. A thick layer of orange pancake was applied to my cherubic face. "She's moon-faced," they said to each other laconically. Dark-brown shading was plastered on my cheeks, pale-blue eyeshadow on my lids, and away with the doe eyes and the two-inch eyebrows. Carmine lipstick completed the look. A cross between a teenage Joan Crawford and an albino.

No wonder I didn't get the lead. For consolation, I was awarded a supporting role as one of the contestants and spent three freezing days in a black, boned bathing suit shivering in Folkestone Town Hall, along with other runners up, among them Jean Marsh, who went on to bigger and better things with her portrayal of the maid Rose in "Upstairs Downstairs" and the TV series "Nine to Five."

Filming was uncomfortable and boring. Up at 5 A.M. in the pitch-dark, herded around like cattle by a harassed assistant director, either freezing to death or boiling under the arch lights and listening to an incomprehensible jargon from the crew: "It's a dolly shot," "Save the baby," "Trim the arc," "Where's the Chippy?" "Turn over," "Action" . . . little did I realize that this was the dialogue I was destined to hear throughout my career.

Two weeks later, Bill got me a slightly better role as a Greek maid in a forgettable film called *The Woman's Angle* starring Lois Maxwell, later Miss Moneypenny in the James Bond films. The money was princely—fifty pounds. It helped me buy more imitation-gold earrings and polo-neck sweaters, and the publicity helped me become even more of a minor celebrity at RADA, where my amorous adventures were gossiped about.

I now had a double life: aspiring film starlet and dedicated drama student, and the British press were cottoning on to me fast: "Britain's Best Bet Since Jean Simmons" . . . "She has the come-hither eyes of Ava Gardner, the sultry look of Lauren Bacall, a Jane Russell figure, and more sex appeal at her age than any other film actress I've met," raved *Reveille,* the workingman's favorite paper.

But RADA did not approve. "What's all this filming nonsense?" boomed Sir Kenneth Barnes, the austere and forbidding principal, as he blocked my way one morning with his Hitchcockian build. "It's nothing serious, sir," I ventured timidly, trying to get by his bulk. "I'm just doing it to make some extra pocket money." "Well just don't get carried away by it, my dear," he said pontifically. "When all is said and done there is only one thing that matters, and that's the *theatah.*" "Right, sir," I agreed and scampered away to cut a class in favor of a photo session at the *Daily Mirror.* RADA was becoming a drag. I was fed up with being told my voice was too small and breathy, my performances dull, and my projection too inhibited. In the plays we performed I was being given the roles of the sixty-year-old aunt or the crazy Scandinavian maid—a form of revenge by the teachers who disliked my everything, I thought.

At the film studios they told me I was gorgeous and sexy. Actors and crew flirted with me and made me feel that I was talented and wonderful. Bill Watts was my strongest supporter. Of all the agents I have had, he is without a doubt the one who not only believed in my ability, but went out on a limb to tell everyone how much potential I had. It was his gutsy belief in me that got me over my debilitating self-consciousness about my voice and personality and made me realize that I had much more to offer than the teachers at RADA believed.

I took stock of myself. I couldn't possibly believe the "Baby Ava Gardner" nonsense that the newspapers were spouting. I looked in the mirror and saw a big-eyed, round-faced, slightly spotty young girl, with long, thin brownish hair—the bane of my life—and eight pounds overweight. And still a virgin. "Life is a constant diet," I groaned, pushing away the potatoes and reaching for the Lucky Strikes. I drank too much—straight gin usually—smoked too much to look sophisticated, and stayed up too late. I either read avidly until three or four in the morning or danced and dated, so I had deep, dark circles under my eyes. I decided to start a beauty regimen from which I have seldom deviated and went on the first of three hundred or so diets. "If I'm England's answer to Marilyn Monroe—" I gritted my teeth as I brushed my hair with a hundred strokes each night—"I might as well start trying to act the part. And if I get rid of my virginity, that may get rid of my spots too."

I was enjoying my days at the studio—the camaraderie and rapport that exists among the members of a film unit. I usually gravitated to the crew. Their humor and wit appealed to me far more than the boring talk of box-office grosses and script problems that producers and directors indulged in.

On most of the movies I made on location—*Island in the Sun, Seawife, The Bravados, Our Girl Friday*—I would normally be found sharing my box lunches with the hairdresser and the camera crew rather than with the other actors. Although I like actors, I resented the fact that the leading man in a movie usually took it as his prerogative to try to have an affair with the leading lady, and some became quite offended when their advances were rejected. Basically I am a down-to-earth person who likes to "send things up"—something that film crews, particularly in England, also love to do.

It was time for my first important film role and the beginning of what was to become a series of teenage delinquent and "bad girl" roles. The part of Lil in *Judgment Deferred,* a low-budget thriller made at Southall studios, was described in the script as "an exacting and emotional role of a one-time beautiful young girl, a convict's daughter, ruined by the colorful and dangerous crowd in which she has sought pleasure." The *Evening News* review said, "Although so young for her emotional role, Joan comes through with flying colors!" Apparently Basil Dearden and Michael

Relph felt so too—for soon after completing *Judgment Deferred* I went to Ealing Studios, home of the money-making comedies starring Alec Guinness, to make a screen test for Norma, the runaway juvenile delinquent in *I Believe in You.*

Dearden and Relph were a hot team as director and producer. They had a string of successful credits, among them *The Blue Lamp* and *Kind Hearts and Coronets,* and whoever got the part of Norma was, according to Bill Watts, bound to become a star.

I had already made some tests for other films, but they were all unsuccessful for me, usually due to my youth or sultry "foreign" looks. English roses were still big in Britain. The test with Dirk Bogarde was the most thrilling. I wore a pink "baby doll" nightgown and Dirk and I slithered around on a vast satin double bed, indulging in much cinematic kissing. Dirk was attractive and fun, but far too old for me. I had become involved with a fellow RADA student, John Turner. It had lasted several months, something of a record for me. Although we spent nights together when circumstances permitted, he was too much of a gentleman to take advantage of my by now encumbering virginity. Since I had no idea how to seduce him, we kept it a little bit less than platonic.

My picture appeared on the front page of *Reveille*—my first cover! I was thrilled, more so when I was recognized while making a tour of the jewelry counter at Woolworth's looking for more plastic bangles to add to my collection. Even though I was becoming known and in demand, I was making not much more than twenty pounds a week. One doesn't shop at Dior on that kind of money.

Although we were well off, Daddy wasn't lavish with money. Mummy had to save out of the housekeeping to buy herself little extras. Although she was always well dressed and bejeweled, I know how persuasive she had to be with my father to get the things she wanted. I vowed at an early age that my desires for material things would never depend on the whims of a man. It was extremely important to me to become financially independent as soon as possible. In fact, throughout my entire life, through three marriages and all my relationships with men, I have always bought all my own clothes, furs, most of my jewelry, and paid my own bills.

Summer vacation started. One of my girlfriends at RADA became pregnant and had the most horrific abortion at the hands of a back-street butcher. My other girlfriends and I thought that was the wages of sin. I made yet a third test for *I Believe in You.* One of the producers was hot and heavy for me. I got the message loud and clear that if I was "nice" to him, the part would be mine. Since I was not about to be "nice" even to those I was madly in love with, the thought of the sweaty embraces of this (to me) elderly gent was quite appalling. He was somewhere between thirty-five and forty-five with long greasy hair, a florid complexion and a tendency to sweat profusely, especially when he came near me. I declined his advances with as much grace as I could while he drove me home in his Jaguar after the test, and I gloomily realized that I had probably blown the part—if not the producer! For the first time the specter of the casting couch started to raise its ugly head—the favors of pretty young things were to be used as barter to help them up the ladder of fame and fortune. If I was not to take advantage of these opportunities there were plenty of other girls who would be only too delighted to oblige.

I had to make a decision, which I made—and I have *never* gone against that original decision. I would not be "nice to," "sleep with" or even kiss anyone for a job or a part no matter how tempting the role that was offered.

Several years later, when Buddy Adler, who was head of 20th Century-Fox, to whom I was under contract, asked me in his own home if I would like to be the biggest star on the lot, I said "Yes of course." "All you have to do—" and he smiled suavely as he maneuvered me across the lac-quered dance floor of his Beverly Hills mansion—"is be nice to me, and the best parts at the studio are yours." "What do you mean exactly by 'be nice,' Mr. Adler?" a worldly and sophisticated twenty-two-year-old Joan asked warily.

"Listen, honey—" he held me closer in the dance and whispered in my ear—"you're a beautiful girl and I'm not exactly an ugly old man—in fact a lot of women find me very attractive!" He smiled conspiratorially. I looked at him. Six feet, mahogany-tanned, silver hair, and at least old enough to be my father. "We'll see each other a couple of times a week, you can still have your own life, and I'll have mine, of course." He glanced over at his attractive blond wife, Anita Louise. "And you'll have your pick of scripts."

"Mr. Adler." I moved away frostily. "I came here with my agent, Jay Kanter. Why don't we discuss the deal with him?" He looked surprised and then he laughed. "Honey, you have quite a sense of humor." "You bet I have," I muttered to myself, as I went to regale Jay with this sweet story, "and my sense of humor is about all you'll ever get from me."

One of the current crop of contractees was very nice to Mr. Adler, and she landed a lot of the roles I really wanted.

But at seventeen I wasn't as sure of myself as at twenty-two. Con-vinced that by my coolness to the producer I would not get to play Norma, I left for a vacation in Cannes with my sister, Jackie, and my Aunt Lalla and threw myself into getting tanned and terrific in a bikini. Sidney Bechet and Claude Luter were playing in Juan les-Pins and I was able to continue my favorite sport—dancing—when the telegram arrived. "Dear Joan, thought you would like to know you have got the part signed Basil Dearden." I was ecstatic. This was a major film studio and the chance to play with some fine actors: Celia Johnson, Cecil Parker, Harry Fowler and Laurence Harvey. Bill Watts called me: "Come home, all is forgiven," he joked. "You start shooting in two weeks."

The costumes I wore in *I Believe in You* were shabby and tarty. An-thony Mendleson, the costume designer, believed in realism, so we toured the secondhand clothing shops in the East End until we finally found the appropriate clothes. I was convinced I would pick up a social disease from trying them on. Some of them still bore the distinctive odors of their original owners, but the final effect was splendidly sleazy. For the opening scene I wore a brown sateen dress with a low neck and short puffy sleeves. It was ten years old and had probably been worn by its owner for a great deal of that time. It went to the dry cleaner's three times before we got rid of the fragrance. My long hair, which was drenched with olive oil to make it lank and greasy, flopped sadly on my shoulders. I wore vermilion lipstick, rhinestone earrings and down-at-the-heels ankle strap shoes. I looked like a pathetic little cockney tart. Dearden and Relph were pleased as punch.

When not on call I posed for innumerable publicity pictures: romping with puppies and kittens, in shortie nighties, in bikinis, in shorts and the ubiquitous black polo-neck shirt. Nobody realizes how exhausting photographic modeling can be. Sitting or standing with a frozen smile or a sultry sulk on one's face for hours and hours under hot uncomfortable lights, wearing ridiculous outfits and trying to look as if this was a joyful or significant experience takes an enormous amount of discipline and concentration. I soon learned how to cope with it, and it became the kind of discipline that has stood me in good stead all my life.

I became a mini-celebrity, opening fetes and attending garden parties and premieres, all for the great God. Publicity!

The first day on *I Believe in You* we shot my most difficult scene. Cecil Parker, as a truant officer, finds me hiding in his apartment, having escaped from reform school. I had to cry hysterically, which I did, over and over and over again. At the end of the day I had cried for sixty different takes. Sometimes the tears were real, and sometimes the makeup man blew crystals in my eyes, which left them red-rimmed for the next twenty-four hours. Basil Dearden seemed satisfied with my performance, but he was somewhat austere, and since I had always had enormous difficulty in communicating with older men, my shyness and nervousness and desire to excel in this film made me a bumbling and respectful servant to him. I could never call him Basil as the crew did. He was, throughout the eight weeks of shooting, "Mr. Dearden."

Celia Johnson was a gifted, sensitive actress whose most memorable film performance was in Noel Coward's *Brief Encounter* with Trevor Howard. She was extremely kind and thoughtful toward me, helpful and patient. She played my probation officer, and our scenes together were really enjoyable and a wonderful learning experience.

And then there was Larry, Laurence Harvey—or to give him his full Lithuanian name, Larushka Skikne. He was flamboyant, eccentric, gifted, extroverted; he swore wittily; smoked endlessly; drank white wine incessantly; drove dashing cars; wore elegant and expensive suits; told fabulously amusing, naughty stories; and I became instantly smitten. He epitomized a lifestyle to which I knew I could become accustomed: the rich, fast life of fine restaurants, international travel, sophisticated parties and scintillating conversation. He took me under his wing. "I'm going to educate you, little girl," he told me, sipping a vintage claret at La Rue, while a tinkling piano in the background played Gershwin medleys. Elegant women in black strapless cocktail dresses flirted delicately with suave, lounge-suited men, and red-coated waiters hovered discreetly.

"Living well is the best revenge" was Larry's policy. And he certainly did. He tried to teach me some dress sense to make the most of my rather gauche appearance. He tried to educate me about wine and the mysteries of a French menu. He taught me to smoke with elan and swear like a trooper and a lady, but he refused to teach me about life's greatest mystery. Sex. He had a zest for living that was unparalleled and thrilling, and I wanted him to be my first lover. I was convinced he was the one I had been saving myself for.

I didn't know it but he was living with Hermione Baddeley, a middle-aged character actress not noted for her beauty. So when he asked me to a party at her house, I innocently and enthusiastically accepted. Immediately we arrived she approached me, saying, "So this is the one you're seeing, Larry, is it? This is 'the new Jean Simmons.'" She gave me a sarcastic look up and down, not missing a detail of my less-than-expert outfit, her red curls bobbing, a cigarette hanging from carmine lips. "Let me tell you something, my dear, Jean has absolutely nothing to worry about. You don't have her looks, you don't have her talent—and you certainly don't have half the overblown things the newspapers have been saying you have." I burst into tears and rushed to the front door to escape her tirade. "That's right, leave," she called. "No guts, that's the trouble with you young ones today—no guts at all!"

Larry caught up with me in Park Lane and tried to smooth things over. "Don't worry, darling, she doesn't mean it. Come back to the party—I really want you two to be friends." "Oh, Larry," I sobbed, "I'm so humiliated—I can't face that woman—please take me home." But the party had more interest for Larry than I did. He quickly plonked me in a cab, gave the driver a pound, me a paternal kiss on the forehead, told me he loved me and scooted back to Totie's.

I should have realized then and there that Larry really loved only himself. But I saw him through rose-colored glasses. I went home and cried myself to sleep. My fragile ego had again been crumpled. If a woman as talented and important as Hermione Baddeley thought I was untalented and unattractive, maybe I really was. I was quick to believe the worst about myself—especially if disapproval came from someone I respected. Highly sensitive to criticism, I seemed to spend my life trying to do everything to please everybody. Consequently, not only did I not please myself, but I was so busy being what the other person wanted me to be that I almost assumed another identity. This was especially true when I was with my more neurotic boyfriends. I became a non-person, a willing slave—my moods matched theirs. If they wanted to be quiet, I was silent as a mouse. If they wanted to tell funny stories, I would laugh and be a wide-eyed audience. But other than Larry, boys were seldom in my thoughts these days as I plunged into the exciting life of a rising young movie star.

❖ *Two* ❖

THE J. ARTHUR RANK Organization was the most powerful and prolific filmmaker of the 1950s and 1960s. For several years it had placed young actors and actresses under contract for between twenty and fifty pounds a week and "groomed" them for stardom. This grooming was somewhat like going back to drama school but with enormous emphasis on such important acting assets as charm, posture, elegance and a nice smile. A "charm school" had been formed but was now disbanded, and dozens of eager young thespians had received the dubious benefits of what that had offered. Among them had been Honor Blackman, Petula Clark and Maxwell Reed.

Maxwell Reed was my childhood fantasy hero. From the time I first saw him on the screen, smoldering on a Sicilian island with Patricia Roc in *The Brothers,* to the night that Larry Harvey introduced us at La Rue, I had had a tremendous schoolgirl crush on him. I had also adored Montgomery Clift, Gene Kelly and Richard Widmark, but Max epitomized all my adolescent fantasies. He looked divine gazing out of the cover of *Picturegoer* in 1949, black brooding eyes, thick wavy black hair, lips cruel, thick and wet, in anticipation of Margaret Lockwood or Phyllis Calvert. "You'll probably marry him one day" said Diana, my closest school chum, confidently. "He's so gorgeous, almost as handsome as Gregory Peck."

"Oh, he's much better-looking than Gregory Peck," I said, as I lovingly Scotch-taped his smoldering countenance to the inside of my desk. "But I'm never going to get married, you dope. I'm going to be a famous and brilliantly successful actress and have lots of lovers."

My fascination with Maxwell Reed had never waned. When I looked up at all six feet four and a half of him that autumn night in La Rue, my heart leaped into my mouth and the back of my knees went weak. There he was in a white-on-white shirt, white tie with the biggest knot I'd ever seen outside the Duke of Windsor's, navy blue pinstripe suit with the widest shoulders and the narrowest pegtop trousers—and mirror-polished black "winkle-picker" shoes.

He was my schoolgirl dream come to life, and he smiled at me so sexily that I blushed from head to toe. He had an American accent, which was quite odd for a man from South London. He bought me a whiskey and Coke and chatted lightly about Hollywood, from whence he had just returned after starring in a Universal swashbuckler with Ann Blyth, who, he told me, was over the hill now since she was pushing twenty-five.

I was heavily impressed. This was the real thing—a real live handsome famous film star, and he was actually flirting with *me!* I felt inadequate, stupid and badly dressed. I was earning thirty pounds a week on *I Believe in You* and starting to invest some of it in a suitable wardrobe, but my sense of style was still underdeveloped in spite of Larry's tutoring. I was wearing an unflattering green-and-gold brocade dress with puffed sleeves and a Peter Pan collar, black patent high-heeled shoes, and imitation pearl earrings. This was hardly what Ava Gardner would have worn, but dressing well takes time, energy and money. and I had little of any of these. Nevertheless, Max seemed to like what he saw, and after he ditched the girl he had arrived with, he joined us for drinks. He and Larry had recently made a movie together and were friends.

I had an early call at Ealing. Since I didn't drive and couldn't afford to hire a car, I would have to rise at 4:30 A.M. to get to the studio by six-thirty, but this did not detract from my enjoyment of this scintillating evening. I smoked half a pack of Lucky Strikes, drank too many whiskeys and Coke and tried to be witty, pretty and wise. I didn't want him to know I was only seventeen. I thought a thirty-three-year-old man would have no interest in a girl of that age, especially a virgin to boot. How naive.

At seven-thirty the next morning the phone rang in the makeup department. It was he. In a sultry American-cockney accent, he drawled, "Hi, baby, how's it going?" We chatted for a few minutes and then he asked me out. I instantly accepted. I knew it would cause trouble at home if he came to pick me up. Going out with Larry, who was only in his twenties, had driven my parents mad at first until they realized that he was a gentleman and could be trusted with their precious daughter, but a man in his thirties—a man with a reputation as a womanizer (and, as I found out later, a pimp)—this my parents would never accept. I arranged to meet him the following Sunday outside the Bayswater Road tube station.

I was in an agony of indecision for the next two days as to what to wear—casual or formal? Jeans or brocade dress? My choices were limited but going out with such a famous actor and man of the world was a definite sartorial challenge.

I finally chose, for safety, my "uniform" of the day: a tight black gabardine skirt with slits up the side, a sleeveless, low-necked black sweater cinched in by a wide black patent-leather belt that accentuated my twenty-two-inch waist, black stockings, three bangles instead of the usual ten; and my smallest gold gypsy earrings completed what I thought of as a sophisticated look. My toilette took three hours. I was terribly nervous, almost as nervous as I was before the first day's filming of *I Believe in You*.

Would I be interesting enough to hold his attention for the evening? Would he think I was too immature and be bored by my conversation? Where were we going to go? If we went to any restaurant or club in the West End or Soho, someone would be bound to see us together and report back to Daddy, who had friends at every spot in town. Certainly, whenever I had ever gone somewhere with Larry. it had been reported back to them by some spy.

I was so nervous I smoked eight Lucky Strikes just while applying makeup. In any case my hands were shaking so much I could hardly get it on. My mother bade me a fond and approving "Goodnight, have a good time, darling." I had told her I was going to a party with Larry and then to a club so she would not worry. I knew Larry was seeing Totie that evening and I doubted that he would phone. All I had to worry about now were my looks, my personality, my figure and my conversation, all of which I was convinced were way below par.

I took the tube to Bayswater Station—a major mistake, as I got leered at and leched at all the way in my provocative outfit. I arrived at my destination in a frenzy of nerves and fifteen minutes early.

He arrived twenty minutes late, by which time I was convinced he would never appear and I would have to go and drown my sorrows at a nearby pub.

As I peeked in my compact for the three-hundredth time, lo and behold, a gigantic sleek, powder-blue American Buick drew up to the curb, and there he was!

"Get in, baby," he drawled, not bothering to get out to open the door. I had become so used to Larry's impeccable manners that I was slightly taken aback for a second, but I jumped in obediently and we drove off into the London traffic.

He was casually dressed in a black open-necked shirt and black trousers and a belt with an ornate buckle and he wore a massive gold chain around his tanned neck. He seemed friendly and glad to see me. We smoked Chesterfields and drove through Hyde Park. I had never been in an American car before and was interested in the gadgets in the interior. Larry drove an elegant old Bentley, and the other boys I had dated either had no car or drove battered MGs or Triumphs. "Bill would really love this car," I trilled, referring to my seven-year-old brother.

"He's mad for cars." I realized how boring that must have sounded and cast desperately around for some wittier dialogue. He gave me a sleepy-eyed Robert Mitchum look. "Oh, yeah, we must give the kid a ride one day." How considerate, I thought, film stars are human beings after all. There was some more silence, and I smoked furiously while thinking of a suitable subject. A tongue-tied, seventeen-year-old virgin, I thought bitterly, he must be so bored.

We had been driving for about twenty minutes and I paid no attention to where we were going, but suddenly I realized that we had been driving round Hyde Park all the time. "Where are we going?" I ventured to say. He shot me another Mitchum look. "You'll see, baby, it'll be a surprise."

I sat back expectantly. I liked surprises and he probably knew some exciting clubs and dives. In the 1950s London had many clubs that were situated in unusual places: lofts, cellars, in apartment buildings and in houses, so when we drew up outside an old Georgian house in Hanover Square, I did not find this strange. "What's this place?" I said gaily. "The Country Club—baby, come on up." We walked up four flights of stairs past empty office suites and at the top came to a door which he unlocked with a key.

I was slightly puzzled because there were no sounds of conversation or music, but when the door opened it all became horribly clear.

Up yet another flight of stairs, these carpeted in thick crimson carpet, and we entered what was obviously somebody's apartment—and when I took a good look through my starry eyes, I realized from the eight-by-ten glossies it was Max's. Instant panic gripped me—this was very tricky. This was no fellow drama student. This was not polite, gentlemanly John Turner, who would never take advantage of my innocence; or urbane, sophisticated Larry Harvey, to whom sexual matters were unimportant. We hadn't even had dinner and Max had brought me to his flat already. I tried to hide my panic by examining some of the interesting pieces of furniture and objects scattered around. The flat was decorated in medieval-Spanish-Hollywood style. There was a lot of crimson velvet and gold braid, purple silk lampshades on six-masted schooner lamps, some carved-wood thronelike chairs and three or four Impressionist oil paintings. Oh, my God, there was also, I saw out of the corner of my eye, a sort of sofa bed against the far wall, in front of the TV, which appeared to be covered in a zebra-skin rug and three thousand velvet cushions. My parents' shocked expressions seemed to gaze out at me from the black TV screen.

"I'm going to have a bath," Maxwell Reed said casually, as if this was a perfectly ordinary thing to do on your first date. "Do you want a whiskey and Coke, baby?" I nodded numbly. I needed a drink desperately. His having a bath would give me a chance to think about this situation, which seemed to be fraught with dangerous possibilities. He was obviously going to try and seduce me. The flat was an absolute love nest. Subdued lighting, sexy paintings, everything seemed designed to set the scene for a spree—which I just might have been ready for after a few days of getting to know each other—but I had only just met this man.

All of my mother's dire prophecies came flooding into my mind: "Men only want *one thing*." She had drummed that into me since I was twelve, when I had asked her what the word "fuck" meant. I had seen it written on railway-carriage walls and toilets. I had gone to the Public Library and looked it up in every dictionary I could find, but apparently there was no such word. We were walking down Oxford Street on a Saturday morning when I asked the question and my mother threw a mini-fit, pushed me against the wall of Dolcis' shoe shop and hissed at me vehemently, "Don't you *ever* say that word—that's a *terrible* word. I told your father that if he ever said that word I would *divorce* him." So that was the end of finding out at twelve what the word "fuck" meant.

Maxwell interrupted my thoughts. He pressed into my hand an immense red Venetian goblet full to the brim with my favorite drink, Scotch and Coke, and into the other a slim book in a plain brown cover. "Make yourself at home, baby, and have a read while I have a bath," he said, sitting me down in a purple velvet chair. "I won't be long." He disappeared smoothly, leaving me to my sordid thoughts. I took a huge swallow of the drink, which tasted slightly different from the usual

Scotch-and-Coke mix, but different brands of whiskey had different tastes. I didn't worry about it too much. I had other things to think about.

I opened the book and gasped. It was an illustrated volume of extremely explicit and detailed drawings of men and women having sex. I had never seen anything like this before and my mind boggled at some of the different and peculiar positions they were in. I finished the drink and started to feel very strange indeed, and then nothing—total oblivion—I was out.

I came to, to find Max and me entwined on the sofa. I was feeling violently ill. "I'm going to be sick," I gasped. "I'll get the bucket again," he said.

Again! I thought through waves of nausea. "Again—have I been sick before, then?" I lay back, drained, on the zebra-skin rug, with the realization that I had finally "done it" but that I had not even been conscious of it. Max turned on the television set. The screen was dark. "Telly's finished for the night," he said, passing me a Chesterfield. "What do you mean— what time is it?" I cried. If TV had closed down for the night, that meant it was after 11 P.M. and I had been here for over three hours. Doing what? Oh, God, I couldn't even remember.

I passed out again and came to with him trying to kiss me. "I can't! Oh, please stop it!" I tried to say, the nausea rising uncontrollably— "Please, please, don't—I'm going to be sick again." I staggered weakly away from the couch and the debris and tried to find the bathroom.

My favorite black sweater was ripped and lying on the floor, next to a crumpled heap of clothes. My stockings were torn and the clasp had been ripped off my bra. Max turned and smiled at me lazily when I returned from repairing what I could salvage of myself and patted the couch. "Come over here, kid," he said, "and lie down. I think we both got a little more than we expected."

"What did you expect?" I moaned as I fell exhausted onto the couch.

"Well, I gave you a bit of a Mickey Finn to make you feel sexy." He smiled, inhaling deeply. I listened, horrified. "Larry told me that he hadn't had you, and that you were a virgin, but I didn't really believe him —gorgeous little seventeen-year-old birds like you don't stay virgins for long in this business, baby. Did you like it?" He turned to me. I looked at him dumbly. *Like* it? I *hated* it. From what I could remember, it was horrible, degrading and demeaning—and even worse than my mother had led me to expect. Were there actually women who *liked* doing this sort of thing? No wonder some of them got paid for it. It was all too ghastly, and in my weakened state I drifted off into a drugged sleep.

He was starting again, but I felt nothing—not even pain. I just lay there while he continued to—what?—well, no wonder "fuck" was considered a dirty word.

I came to again to find him making me drink some strong coffee. Now I felt awful and used and exhausted.

"Come on, kid," he urged, "gotta get you home to Mummy and Daddy. Are you working tomorrow?" I nodded numbly—I had a 6 A.M. call. Help!

"It's after three," he said. "Come on, girl, up and at 'em." Sheer terror gripped me now. My parents would wait up for me even though they pretended to be asleep. As soon as the clock struck two and I wasn't home. Mummy would be pacing.

Max helped me into my torn and tattered finery. The stockings were a write-off so I didn't even bother to put them back on. My face was a disaster. I stared at it in horror in my compact mirror—mascara-stained cheeks, caked foundation and smeared lipstick. I lurched into the bath-room and washed everything off with soap and water and then shakily applied some lipstick and tried to comb my hair. I couldn't think about what had happened. I still felt incredibly ill and I was petrified thinking about my parents' reactions.

He guided my wobbly legs down the endless flights of stairs. We said little. He kept giving me his laconic Robert Mitchum look as he drove me home to Harley House, which was only about seven minutes' drive from Hanover Square.

"Stop before you come to the entrance," I whispered nervously as we approached the grim Victorian outlines of the flats. "I'll get out here." He leaned over me to open the door. "Will I see you again, baby?" he said, putting his hand on my knee. "Of course," I gulped, nervously pushing his hand away. "I'll give you a ring in a couple of days," he said, kissed me perfunctorily on the cheek and zoomed off into the deserted street.

I staggered into Harley House, hearing voices raised and the phone ringing even before I put my key in the door.

We had lived in this huge basement flat for several years. It looked out on to busy Marylebone Road and got very little daylight, but it was big and spacious enough for three kids and was behind Regent's Park. I opened the heavy oak door and my mother rushed forward and grabbed my arm. "Your father's furious with you!" she cried. "Where have you been? I've called everyone, and *why* are you home so late?" I looked at the grandfather clock in the hall. It was indeed now half-past three and I would have to be up in an hour to take the train to Ealing. "I've been to a party with Larry," I said feebly, trying to muster up some power in my voice.

"Your mother called Laurence Harvey," said my father coming out of the bedroom and tying the knot in his red-and-blue-striped dressing gown. "He said he had not seen you tonight, and did not know where you were—so where *have* you been?"

When my father shouted at me like that my stomach went cold and I got a weak feeling in the back of my knees. He truly scared me to death when he was so angry. He had never actually hit any of us, or used any physical violence at all, but his temper was so strong and his anger so fierce that when he threatened to "beat the daylights out of you," al-though he actually never did, it was a threat that we kids thought could come true if we behaved badly enough. I think now that it would have been better if he had occasionally hit us—because it couldn't have hurt us as much as the constant threat that he *might*

"Larry was terribly worried," said Mummy, trying to smooth things over as usual. "He called some of the people at the studio to see if you were with them, but they didn't know where you were either." "So where were you?" said Daddy. "You'd better tell us, or you'll be standing here all night."

I looked at the clock and for one wild moment felt like shrieking at them, "I've been drugged and raped and abused by a thirty-three-year-old degenerate film star and I *hated* it. You were right, Mummy—it is horrible and vile and I'll never, ever do it again—*ever*. I promise."

But my courage was waning. I tried histrionics and hysterics which sometimes worked. I needed to lie down, have a bath and collect my thoughts before I left in forty-five minutes for the two-hour trip to the studio. Time was running out. "I went to Beryl's father's pub," I sobbed in my mother's arms. "And we had a few drinks and went over to Wood Green jazz club. We met some friends from RADA and went back to their flat to play some records. I was having so much fun I didn't realize the time. I'm sorry." My shoulders were racked with sobs as my mother rocked me gently. My crying had become real. I was extremely upset, and I felt abused and dirty.

This garbled explanation seemed to satisfy my father. He barked a few more terse sentences about ". . . get to bed—you look like hell" and went back to his own bed. Mummy walked me back to my room. I badly wanted to tell her what had happened. I needed comfort and advice—I needed to be mothered, in fact—but I could never trust my mother completely because she sometimes repeated what I said or did, either to my father or one of her girl friends. Besides, if I told her, she would be absolutely horrified and convinced yet again that "Men only want one thing" and would forbid me to ever see Max again. I needed time to think.

I kissed her goodnight and ran a bath. I scrubbed thoroughly, washed my hair, cleaned my teeth for ten minutes, put on jeans, sweater and duffle coat and, after making a strong cup of instant coffee, slipped out of the front door and into the dark and silent streets of Marylebone Road. I walked swiftly for five minutes to Baker Street. In the fifties, a girl could walk around London streets in the dark and not be concerned about muggers or rapists. Since I had been raped once that evening anyway, the odds were against it.

I sat in the railway carriage and looked at my face in the compact mirror. I tried to analyze if I had changed. A workman in paint-stained overalls was staring at me. I wonder if he can tell, I thought to myself, that I'm not a virgin. My face looked the same—the circles under the eyes were darker but that was lack of sleep. I looked young and vulnerable. But I felt I had ended a chapter of my life. I didn't feel like a girl any more. On the other hand, I didn't feel like a woman either.

There was no such thing as "the Pill" yet. I needed to talk to a woman to find out what I had to do. I spoke to Ursula Howells, an actress in *I Believe in You*, about my experience. She was sympathetic and concerned —especially about my becoming pregnant. Horrors! That hadn't even occurred to me. But since it seemed there was nothing I could do about it now, like Scarlett in *Gone With the Wind,* I would have to "think about that tomorrow." Visions of my RADA girlfriend butchered by an abortionist crossed my mind and I shuddered with fear.

I worked hard all day. At the end of the day I went to wardrobe where I was outfitted in a delicious gold lamé dress once worn by Audrey Hepburn, and the publicity boys took me to Ciro's Club, where *Photoplay* magazine was holding its annual Christmas party, although it was still only autumn. Many stars were there, among them Anthony Steel (who had that summer followed my sister, Jackie, and myself all through the streets of Cannes), Kenneth More and Kay Kendall. I had gone out with Steel a couple of times and he seemed quite nice but drank too much. Besides, I didn't really like older men.

Max was turning out to be the exception, however. He had, to my surprise, called me at the studio in the afternoon and asked if I was free for dinner that night. Confused as ever, I accepted. After the party I went to meet him at the Caprice, an exclusive theatrical restaurant. Why did I go to meet him with the ghastly events of last night still fresh in my mind? I was probably flattered that he still wanted to see me after having "had his way with me," as my mother would have put it. And I wanted to prove to myself that I was not just a sex object to be used and discarded at a man's whim. I didn't want to be rejected by him after he had seduced me and I didn't feel like rejecting him. After all, he was a *star!* The only way to win was to play the game to the hilt, and so I tried to pretend that last night had not really happened.

I also apportioned some of the blame to myself—one of my more naive traits. I shouldn't have dated him in the first place. When I saw I was in his apartment I should have got the hell out of there. I could twist this incident in my mind to such an extent that the whole thing became my fault totally. But most of all I was still curious about him as a person, an actor and someone I had admired for a long time. Since our conversation last night had been negligible, I was determined to start afresh. And I was definitely *not* going to the "Country Club" again.

The studio had given me a special coiffure, and I thought I looked grown-up and glamorous. I was aware we made an arresting couple; many people in the restaurant stared at us. He was witty that evening, telling jokes and anecdotes about his life in the merchant navy, his days with the Rank Organization and his recent trip to Hollywood. There had been some talk of me going there to do a movie with Bob Hope, but unfortunately it didn't happen, as the producers thought I was much too young to play opposite Bob—although I did appear with him and Bing Crosby several years later in the last of the "Road" pictures, *The Road to Hong Kong.*

Max had a good sense of humor—his saving grace and a trait which has always appealed to me strongly—and I was in fits of laughter all night. The previous night was not mentioned. It was almost as though it hadn't happened. I was confused, yet happy. He took me home and acted in a very gentlemanly way as he kissed me chastely goodnight on the cheek. I think he was feeling some self-recriminations but we avoided the subject.

We started seeing each other, and he did not approach me sexually for some time—as though to atone for his fault.

During the next month we dated each other constantly. I became involved—in fact, we fell in love, but it was tough because he was exceedingly moody. We had days of light-hearted fun, boating, going to movies and theaters and dancing all night—and then for three or four days he would be in a black mood, surly and vile, snarling, cruel, sadistic and sarcastic. It was hard for me to understand these sudden changes of mood, but I put up with them, as I had strong guilt feelings about his having "deflowered me." And also because my childhood dream was coming true—I was dating a famous, handsome movie star—Maxwell Reed. As far as sex went in our relationship, I gritted my teeth and tolerated it. In fact, I found it really boring, without a flicker of pleasure, just as I had been warned by my mother.

In the days before *Cosmopolitan* magazine told you how to have the most thrilling sexual adventures, before Masters and Johnson published their theories on multiple orgasm and sexual freedom, before the sexual revolution of the sixties, sex was something a girl just did not discuss or think about too much. I realize now that Max was a far from considerate lover. And since there were certain things he liked to do which hurt and revolted me, I merely tolerated the sex because I thought I was in love with him, and because I genuinely thought that this was the way things were *supposed* to be. It was a man's sport—and a woman's chore. Luckily for me the couch on which we usually made love faced the TV set, which was always turned on—even if I wasn't—so I was able to concentrate on something else. It was ironic that at this time I was being hailed as "Britain's Best Bet for Stardom." I was considered the sexiest girl in England. I was Britain's Marilyn Monroe, Sophia Loren and Brigitte Bardot. But none of this idolatry went to my head. I remained insecure and dumb and frigid.

I was still filming *I Believe in You,* going to jazz clubs, visiting RADA to see my friends, going to the theater, doing interviews and publicity and seeing Max two or three times a week. I was very busy whirling, with little time to think.

I have always been able to do two or three times the amount of activities the average person can do. I have enormous energy and wake up practically every day excited about just being alive. This was now a frenetic and exciting period for me. J. Arthur Rank was becoming interested in signing me to a seven-year exclusive contract. They had seen the rushes of *I Believe in You* and liked what they saw. Hollywood had made a couple of nibbles—I was getting warm.

Eventually my parents found out that I had been seeing Maxwell Reed; they were appalled. Max smoothly assured them that he was only educating me in the myriad problems of stardom, that he was my mentor, not my lover, and that our relationship was totally platonic. Incredibly, they believed him. He was the most convincing liar I had ever seen.

After a few months he wanted me to move in with him. The idea was rather appealing. His apartment was cozy, and I was fed up with the endless rules and regulations I had to conform to at home. I had to be home at one o'clock every night or there had better be a good reason why not. But living together seemed premature. Although Max had told me he loved me, I knew there was something vitally wrong with the relationship. I didn't know whether I loved *him* or loved the idea of togetherness. I adored his sense of humor, his looks, his fame. But there was a dark side that I feared and loathed. Maybe I can cope with it, I thought confidently.

He started to suffer severe back pains, and sometimes he would be doubled up in agony. For some reason he blamed me for causing this. He had started talking to me about marriage seriously now, since living together was out of the question because of my moralistic parents, but I was still resistant and unsure. And as I learned later, the more resistant and hard to get a woman is, the more a man wants her—something I'm sure my mother did try to tell me.

One day he was in such severe pain that after the doctor examined him he was sent immediately to the hospital. The next day I was told that Max had slipped a disc and would have to have an operation. After the operation he found he had a total loss of feeling in his lower body—the whole area had become completely numb. In a way, this was poetic justice since I always felt the same way.

The doctors assured him it was temporary—that a few nerve endings had been severed during the operation and that in a few months the nerves would heal, but it put him into the blackest and foulest of moods and he consistently accused me of causing his injury. Since I never instigated lovemaking and, in fact, went to lengths to avoid it, this was farcical. But I was the villainess and the cause of his problems. Not to mention his sudden lack of film offers. As I became "hot," he became "cold."

My guilt got worse as he ranted and raved and screamed at me because he had not made a film for several months. He was short of cash. Suddenly, for every possible thing that went wrong, I became the scapegoat.

He definitely wanted to marry me even more now, but I felt more dubious as to the likely longevity of our marriage. I was still only seventeen and extremely immature mentally and emotionally in spite of my physical appearance. My emotions veered between ecstasy and misery, with very little gray area. There is a fine line between love and hate, and I was treading it with Max. Confusion, guilt and uncertainty were my day-to-day companions now. Because of his disability, Max could only get aroused by sadism. I was so frightened of him I went along with the beatings and the perversions he thought up. He insisted I pose for some nude Polaroid photographs which he thought might turn him on. My pity for him was intense—and my guilt—but now a new sinister element entered our relationship. The more he hurt me physically, the more excited he became. I tolerated it because I hoped it would only be temporary and that when he regained his feelings he would stop. He kept telling me how much he desired me and how difficult it was for him and how I must understand his problems. A woman's lot is to suffer. Thus spake my female ancestors.

My contract with the J. Arthur Rank Organization was signed. I was the first actress Rank had put under contract for over a year. They started to build me up. Every day I did some sort of publicity, and every other day the papers had something to say about me, good, bad or sarcastic.

The Rank contract was probably based a lot on my personal reviews for *I Believe in You*. Although some of the critics were lukewarm toward the movie, most of them had high praise for my potential. Jympson Harmon, one of the top critics, wrote in his review, "Joan Collins makes a tremendous impression as the wayward girl. She has a dark luscious kind of beauty which puts her in the Jane Russell class, but Joan already seems to be an actress of greater ability. On the showing of this first big film part, she looks like the most impressive recruit to British films for many a moon." And *News of the World* raved, "A dozen of my darkest red roses to Joan Collins. Fire and spirit in her acting and that odd combination of allure and mystery that spells eventual world stardom."

This was heady stuff for a teenager. It seems ironic that my very earliest reviews were far more favorable than those in my later years. It's as if the critics said later, "Oh, yeah—she looks good but what else is in the package?" Certainly, on viewing again some of my films and remembering the ghastly reviews I got, I felt that in a way I became the critics' whipping boy. Max had started kidding me about how, with my looks and youth, he and his friends could make a fortune if I would become a high-class courtesan. They were constantly cracking lewd jokes about sex. In fact, sex and women made up 90 percent of the subject matter of conversation between Max and his friends, and usually discussed in derogatory fashion. I knew they had little or no respect for women and were the epitome of what my mother had always described—the men who want only "one thing."

Since neither Max nor I had a film at the moment, we decided to appear together at the Q Theatre in *The Seventh Veil* in the roles portrayed on the screen by James Mason and Ann Todd. Max played the part of the sadistically cruel piano teacher. He played it with so much authenticity that in one of the scenes where he is terrorizing me, he threw me across the stage with such violence and ferocity that I was black and blue for three days. The sadomasochism obviously appealed because we immediately started rehearsing yet another similar story: A "young frightened girl, intimidated but mesmerized by an attractive, sadistic older man"—absolutely the basis of *our* relationship. This one was called *Jassy*, freely adapted from the film of the same name with Margaret Lockwood and again, James Mason.

I was mad about the theater and was only regretful that these were only one-week gigs, but my reviews were excellent, and I started looking for a suitable property to do in the West End.

Finally Max went to my parents to ask for my hand in marriage.

Although my father had suspected this, I think he was amazed that it was actually happening. The four of us sat self-consciously in the living room of our Harley House flat. Dinner was over. The television sound had been turned down, although the black-and-white picture flickered on. Max and I perched on the green velvet Knowle sofa sipping tea from Mummy's best pink china.

When he wanted to, Max could charm the birds out of the trees. A typical actor. My mother was already won over, but Daddy was a harder nut. He disapproved of Max's flashy West End image, he disapproved of the age difference, he disapproved totally of everything the man represented, and would absolutely not allow me to get married at such a tender age to such an unsuitable man. "Well, then," I said, finally asserting myself in their conversation, "if you won't let me marry him, I'll go and live with him."

My parents stared at me in alarm. "You must be out of your mind," my father said. "What would people think? Can you imagine what our friends would say? It would be the talk of London. You absolutely *cannot* live together, I will not allow it!"

"You can't stop me," I said defiantly. "We love each other, Joe," said Max smoothly. "And we want to be together—what can we do?"

Both my parents looked bemused. I think Mummy was secretly thrilled by the romance of it all, but didn't dare come around until my father did first.

"All right," said Daddy, puffing vehemently on a Player's. "All right, but I'll tell you something—and I mean it." He looked at me and I got that funny feeling in the back of my knees again. "This marriage had better last, because if it doesn't—" he stared at me hard—"I never want to speak to you again." I looked at Mummy. She looked away. I looked at the walls and mantelpiece and sideboard in the room. They were covered with photographs of me and my brother, Bill, and sister, Jackie. They certainly loved their kids, but wasn't this a funny way of showing it? Was my darling Daddy serious about disowning me if my marriage failed?

"That's all. That's it," said my father and he leaned over and turned up the sound on the TV. "Make us another cup of tea, Elsa." End of subject.

Max and I left as soon as possible and went to the Mandrake Club, where we celebrated our engagement with Pimm's Number 1. I was outwardly happy—I would get away from home and have some freedom. But my mind was a turmoil of doubts.

One of Max's favorite slogans was "Hate is akin to love." It seemed weird to me, but maybe it might explain my ambivalent feelings toward him. He was not at all good for my fragile ego. Although he thought I was beautiful, he was consistently belittling my conversation, my acting ability and my personality. He advised me often to "cash in on all you have going for you *now* as by the time you're twenty-three you'll be old and washed up." Twenty-three was apparently the cutoff point for Max and his cronies to be attracted to a girl. Anyone older than that was "an old scrubber" in whom they had no interest whatsoever.

We married the day after my eighteenth birthday, at the registry office, Caxton Hall, in a blaze of publicity. I had spent most of the previous week sobbing myself to sleep each night. The thought of getting married terrified me. Suddenly I didn't want to leave the safety and security of the cozy flat where I had spent so much of my childhood. I was scared of my father but I was even more frightened of Max. I had lost eight pounds, and in my white-and-gold wedding dress I looked tiny. I heard some women in the crowd say I was *too* skinny! I'd achieved something I had been trying to do for years without succeeding. Misery must be good for svelteness.

We drove in the Buick to Cannes for our honeymoon. I always became drowsy on long car trips and wanted to sleep. Max pinched and yelled at me to "wake up!" I tried to keep my eyes open by looking at the pictures and the articles that had appeared about us on our wedding day. How happy we seemed. How grownup and assured I looked, as if I married a film star every year. I read with interest a particular story that was printed in the *Daily Mirror*.

"I shall do no cooking or cleaning!" the headline shrieked, shocked that a young bride should be so untraditional as to not get kicks from wearing a frilly apron and cooking tasty meals for her husband. "Her ideas of marriage are honestly unconventional," scolded the article. "She doesn't want to have children for seven or eight years at least—and she wants to keep on acting all the time."

These were revolutionary ideas for the fifties. Women were made to feel guilty if they did not adore housework and want a houseful of kids. My sights were set a little higher. Even though I had chosen to marry so young, I did not feel I had to conform to the usual patterns a wife was supposed to follow.

The honeymoon was a nightmare. Max suddenly became extraordinarily jealous of any man's notice of me. However, the wealthier a man was, the less jealous he became, and he often suggested that we could make some money by "being nice to that chap." But when a couple of young, obviously not rich French photographers came to take photos of me on the beach, Max took me back to our cramped beach hut on the Carlton Beach and slapped my face so hard I felt my teeth would fall out.

"You belong to me now," he screamed so loudly that I knew the ladies sipping afternoon tea on the Carlton Terrace could hear. "So don't be looking at other men—ever—unless they're the ones *I* choose!" The veins stood out on his neck and his eyes bulged in a frenzy. He looked mad. I pressed myself against the wall of the hut. In my pink gingham bikini I felt vulnerable and terrified of the man I married. His hair was dyed black and permed. He had shown me how he did it in the sink at his flat. His eyebrows and eyelashes were heavily mascaraed. Today he was not wearing makeup, because we were on the beach—but he often did. He wore a pair of tiny white shorts and black thong sandals that laced up to mid-calf; three large gold medallions hung around his neck. He got more wolf whistles in the South of France than I did.

Thank God I'm going to start work next week, I thought fervently.

Rank, having put me under contract for fifty pounds a week, had immediately loaned me out to Columbia to play in Boccaccio's *Decameron Nights*, to be made in Madrid and Segovia. It would be my first American film, and I was full of enthusiasm.

Max decided to stay in Cannes and enjoy himself for another week. He had met a millionaire who was talking movie deals, so he was happy. And when he was happy he was nice to me and didn't hit or otherwise hurt me, and then *I* was happy.

Decameron Nights starred Joan Fontaine and Louis Jourdan and consisted of three or four episodes of Boccaccio's stories. I played Joan Fontaine's handmaiden in one segment and in another had tender love scenes with Louis Jourdan. This role was much smaller than my role in *I Believe in You*. But Rank had insisted I do the film, otherwise they would release me from my contract. There were not many roles for sexy-looking teenagers, and Rank was getting a good loan-out price for me, too, none of which I received, however. I just got fifty pounds a week, and Rank got about $25,000. The director, Hugo Fregonese, was cold and treated us casually. Segovia was smelly and dirty and the hotel where we stayed a veritable doss house.

As soon as Max arrived, a week later, we started fighting again. I became petulant, bad-tempered, and unpopular, and was glad to return to London and start another movie.

Cosh Boy was the story of a group of youths who spent their time getting their kicks by robbing and beating up people—rather like today's muggers. I played Renee, the innocent young girlfriend of the leading boy, James Kenney. We had a love scene in the garden of a deserted house, which by today's standards was tame enough to be in a Disney film. After the seduction I become pregnant and try to commit suicide. It was a shopgirl's melodrama and the public loved it. But the simulated sex scenes were so steamy that it became Britain's first X-rated film. The director, Lewis Gilbert, who later did many of the James Bond films, was adorable and lovely to work with. And Max finally got a job and left for Jersey to make *Sea Devils* for Raoul Walsh. It was just the sort of pirate potboiler he loved, especially since he played the "heavy" against Rock Hudson.

We did another play at the Q Theatre, *The Skin of Our Teeth*, by Thornton Wilder, one of the American classics. My part was Sabina, the mischievous vamp, which had originally been played by Vivien Leigh. I was delighted that finally I was going to play a classic role in a great play.

The Q Theatre specialized in revivals. Although it was a small, intimate theater, it nevertheless put on excellent productions and it was considered a coup to play there. Although too young for the role of sixty-year-old Mr. Antrobus, Max put on a ton of makeup, grayed his tinted black hair and played the part quite well. When he stopped posturing, posing and using a phony American accent, he was a reasonable actor. We had just finished a film together for Rank, *The Square Ring*, again directed by Basil Dearden. I played a cameo role as Max's girlfriend, and

Max wasted much time accusing me of upstaging him. Since I was still inexperienced in film acting, I had no idea how to do a lot of things, let alone upstage anyone. I became uneasy during our scenes together for fear I was displeasing him.

The reviews for *The Skin of Our Teeth* were excellent and I enjoyed it more than any film I had made so far. I wanted to do more theater, but first I had to make a strong dramatic film for Rank. *Turn the Key Softly* was the tale of one day in the lives of three women just released from prison. It was an authentic, raw film, so authentic, in fact, that the opening scenes of Yvonne Mitchell, Kathleen Harrison and me being released from prison were shot in Holloway Women's Prison.

I played a young prostitute, in the clink for shoplifting, who tries to keep on the straight and narrow but is tempted by the bright lights and glamour of the West End. We shot on actual locations around London in the dead of winter. It was bitterly cold and I was fitted out in my usual sleaze: tight black satin skirt, slit to the thigh, black stockings, ankle-strap shoes, a flimsy, low-cut Lurex sweater and a yellow short-sleeved jacket. I was blue with cold for most of the time and started thinking longingly of sunkissed California, from where Bill Watts was getting regular calls about my availability.

Due to Rank's giving me a tremendous publicity buildup, I became known as "Britain's Best Bad Girl," and I had hardly any time for myself. At night, exhausted from shooting, I would return to our flat in Hanover Square and attempt to cook dinner and do housework before I flopped exhausted into bed. For, contrary to my brave statements in the *Daily Mirror,* Max was a true male chauvinist and expected his hot dinners every night. My mother had not educated me in the culinary arts because I had always had so many projects going after school that she was loath to take me away from them. Besides my voracious reading (at least seven or eight books a week) I spent a great deal of time writing to film stars for their autographed photos, or cutting and pasting pictures of stars into great scrapbooks. Cooking was too boring to contend with, and besides, I thought I would never need to do it. But Max liked his meat and potatoes, and it was he who taught me the rudiments of cooking. However, if it didn't turn out to his satisfaction, he would sling the whole plate of food across the room.

There was a mirror above the kitchen sink, and sometimes I looked at my bedraggled reflection as I was washing up and compared it with the provocative and alluring face adorning magazines and newspapers. They seemed like two different people—the glamour girl and this pale, pathetic waif. The irony, too, was that Max, due to his work or his disability, didn't want sex very much—a pleasing fact to me—but the public was being fooled when they saw my sexy photos about what I must really be like. I was a celibate sex kitten! My marriage was a fiasco. I lived in fear of Max's moods and rages, but I didn't have the guts to get out. When I wasn't working I rushed to voice classes, dance classes, acting classes—anything to get away from him.

After finishing *Turn the Key Softly* I had several meetings with the

Italian film director Renato Castellani. He was about to make a film of *Romeo and Juliet* and the Rank Organization decided that I would be the perfect Juliet! This did not thrill either Signor Castellani or me. I did not think I was the Juliet type—I had always preferred parts with more meat on their bones, such as Sabina in *The Skin of Our Teeth,* or Cleopatra, or Katherine in *Taming of the Shrew.* I did not see myself as an innocent fourteen-year-old virgin, which was how Castellani wanted the part played. Rank was adamant. He must test me, so test me he did. At least two or three times.

The final test at Pinewood was with Laurence Harvey, who had been signed for Romeo. We were still friendly, but even he agreed that I was too sophisticated-looking for their version of Juliet. Signor Castellani came to me before the last test and gave me his ultimatum. "You will havva the nose job," he said in his heavily accented English. "I will havva the what?" I said incredulously. "Giulietta she hassa the Roman nose! You havva the nose it goes up—is not aristocratic—you go to the good plastic surgeon—he make-a the Roman nose—you be Giulietta!"

"Oh *no*—you've got to be kidding," I wailed, then broke into hysterical laughter. A nose job to get a part? No way. Besides, I liked my nose— hadn't one of the papers said that the three prettiest noses in Britain belonged to Vivien Leigh, Jean Simmons and Joan Collins? I drew the line. Bill Watts was summoned, and amidst much Italian screaming and yelling and my hysterics and total refusal to get the nose job, Rank reluctantly backed down and an unknown actress was signed for Juliet.

Although I'd been been under contract for some months, Rank still didn't have much idea what to do with me. When in doubt they sent me to the Stills Gallery. So, when Noel Langley and George Minter approached them about a loan-out to star in Langley's own novel, *Our Girl Friday,* they allowed me to do it. It was an absolutely gorgeous part. And funny, too. My yen to play comedy was developing. The script was hilarious and the three actors who were in it were important stars. I played Sadie, a willful, spoiled brat of a girl on a holiday cruise with her parents. Their ship is wrecked and Sadie and the three men manage to reach a deserted island where they live together for many months.

Kenneth More played Pat Plunket, the ship's colorful Irish stoker with a fondness for liquor and an eye for the ladies. Kenneth had recently had a huge success in *Genevieve* and had become a big star. George Cole played Carrol, a cynical journalist who hated Sadie, and Robertson Hare —one of the greatest farce actors in England—played Professor Gibble, a prim and proper old economics professor.

This motley group assemble on the island, realize that it's uninhabited and are appalled—one girl on a desert island with three men! A situation fraught with peril for them all, but with amusement for the audience, we hoped. We shot on the island of Majorca. I was given the opportunity to look desirable and wholesome for a change and to wear some pretty clothes, which became skimpier as time and the ravages of desert-island life progressed. The film was a minor hit in England and then in

America, where the title was changed to *The Adventures of Sadie*. My performance started to seriously interest the heads of several studios—among them Darryl Zanuck, the head of production at Fox.

Edward Leggevie, an executive at Fox in London, asked if I would be interested in the idea of going to Hollywood under contract to Fox. Would I? My heart leaped at the idea. I was getting sick of doing endless tests for parts that I didn't get—sick of the snide remarks the press were making about me. "Let's have an end to the puppy fat stars," said Logan Courtney. "She strains to look like Marilyn Monroe," said Donald Zec (a total lie). "Too much publicity and not enough performances," sneered another. Working nonstop (five films and four plays in one-and-a-half years) I thought this most unfair. But the press always managed to make out that I was a total playgirl even if I was working constantly—possibly because of my later cavalier attitude toward negative media criticism. By this time my marriage was so intolerable that I would do *anything* to get away from London. The location in Majorca was wonderful. I felt 100 percent free for the first time ever. But I needed more freedom. I called on the support of my loyal and trustworthy Bill Watts. He promised to find me a play to go on tour. To escape from Maxwell Reed.

The Praying Mantis was a new play—not a particularly good one, but I didn't care. I had to get away. The Rank Organization gave me a bonus of nine hundred pounds—a fortune! They had probably made over seventy-five thousand pounds on me from the various loan-outs, but I was still making only one hundred pounds a week. In *The Praying Mantis* I played a young Byzantine empress who, after making love to her men, sends them away to be executed. Hence the title, from the insect of the same name.

The director, Esme Percy, was a touch grand. He had been a well-known actor, but now was well over sixty and possibly bitter over the passing of the years. He told me condescendingly that I looked like "an expensive toy," a compliment not guaranteed to bring out the best of one's acting talents, particularly in a less than mediocre play.

We played a week at the Q Theatre to lukewarm reviews and houses, and then went on tour for three weeks to Brighton, Wimbledon and Folkestone. In spite of the lousy play and unenthusiastic audiences, I still completely relished it. For the first time I felt I was achieving what I originally wanted to do—to become an actress and not a movie starlet. I felt tremendous freedom on the stage. The inhibitions I had in front of the camera disappeared. I loved the rapport and jokes among the actors. I loved the old drafty dressing rooms with the musty mothball smells of a thousand ancient costumes and stale greasepaint. Our troupe would sit for hours after the show in seedy pubs and even seedier digs, talking about acting, about our lives and aspirations—gossiping, drinking, playing cards and judging ourselves and each other. I knew I was accepted for what I really was: an immature girl trying to learn to act, to grow up, improve herself, in a glare of publicity, with faults, weaknesses and insecurities about herself. But I also knew I had humor and guts and intelligence. I didn't have to play the sexy starlet with Fanny, Jimmy and Ian. We were family and we formed the closest of bonds—we were all just actors. Although the play flopped, this did not deter me from doing another, and on returning to London, I immediately started rehearsals for *Claudia and David,* a funny, tender romantic American comedy about a slightly scatty child bride and her husband.

During this time Max was traveling to and from Rome trying to get work. On one of his trips back he suggested we go to our favorite restaurant-nightclub in London, Les Ambassadeurs.

Les Ambassadeurs was terribly chic. All the visiting American actors and producers and directors made it their home away from home. The club itself was in a beautiful old Georgian house in Hamilton Terrace. The furnishings were subdued and impeccable, the food excellent, and the music, although slightly tame for my jazz-oriented taste, was gay and danceable.

I sat drinking Pimm's, deep in thought about *Claudia and David;* Max was chatting to an elderly Arabian gentleman on the banquette next to him. I ignored them. Max had a habit of gravitating toward rich, elderly men who usually lusted after me. They talked animatedly for a long time.

I was intrigued watching Linda Christian and Edmund Purdom doing the cha-cha when Max pulled my arm and introduced me to the gentleman. "This is Sheik Abdul Ben Kafir," he said. I nodded coldly to this aged roué, who smiled excitedly and looked me up and down. I was wearing a low-cut white chiffon blouse and a green velvet skirt, and I was starting to get a vague idea of what this was all about from the expectant look on the Arab's fat face.

"Excuse me, Sheik," said Max smoothly. "Back in a minute. Going to take little Joanie for a trot around the dance floor." He pulled me onto the floor and to the strains of "From This Moment On" we danced. "Ten thousand pounds," said Max, his face aglow with pride. "He'll pay you ten thousand pounds for *one night!*—and I can even watch!"

"I beg your pardon, Max," I said as coldly as I could, fear gripping the pit of my stomach. "Are you *seriously* suggesting I go to bed with that disgusting old man for *money?*"

"You bloody little idiot," he snarled, whirling me to the far end of the floor. "Ten grand! Tax free! Do you realize what we can do with that sort of money? We can go to Hollywood. We can have a holiday in Florida. We can even buy a cottage in the country. You better start cashing in on what you've got, girl—doing plays at the Q for ten quid a week is *not* going to make us rich in our old age."

I started to protest but he wouldn't listen and squeezed my arms tighter and tighter, until I felt tears welling up. I forced myself not to cry. "One night, baby—that's all. One night with Abdul and we can say 'Fuck you' to all of 'em, be off to Hollywood—What do you say, baby?"

I looked at Abdul nodding and smiling at me over his champagne goblet. His pendulous jowls were wobbling. I looked at my handsome, *loathsome* husband and the tears flooded. "Never," I screamed, turning the heads of Linda and Edmund, who were dancing right behind us. "I will never, ever, ever do that. Never in a million years, Max. Take your sheik and go to hell, both of you." I couldn't control myself any more. The place had become cathedral quiet at my outburst. I rushed from the club, grabbed a cab and went home. It was the final straw. I couldn't take it for another minute. I didn't care if my father disowned me for not making the marriage work. I didn't care if Max made good his oft repeated threat to "have some of the *boys* carve your pretty little face up with a razor if you ever leave me"—nothing mattered any more except saving my self-respect and my sanity.

I went home to Mummy.

❧ *Three* ❧

WE TRIED A BRIEF reconciliation but it was hopeless. Not only did I not love him any more—I disliked him intensely. His ailment hadn't improved and his sexual tendencies were increasingly sadistic and perverted. My parents were glad to have me home again—my father seemed to have forgotten his promise to disown me—and I moved back happily into the familiar back bedroom.

The meetings between my agent and the Fox representatives had heated up and negotiations began to buy my contract outright from Rank. I left for Rome to play wicked Princess Nellifer in a lavish Biblical epic, *Land of the Pharaohs*. It was my first big American film, with an international cast headed by Jack Hawkins. Directed by Howard Hawks, one of the most famous of the Hollywood directors, it was written by an imposing duo—William Faulkner and Harry Kurnitz. Although they slaved away, writing and rewriting daily, it was, in spite of their efforts, a hokey script with some impossible dialogue, made even worse by the fact that they tried to "Biblicize" it.

I was incredibly lucky to get this break and I knew it. I plunged feverishly into an endless series of photo tests, costume fittings, hair and makeup tests. Nellifer was Egyptian, exotic and simmeringly evil, and a multitude of excitable costume designers, blasé hairdressers and enthusiastic makeup men strove to turn a gauche girl only three years out of school into a sultry, wicked Egyptian goddess. My hair was the despair of the brittle, hawk-eyed American hairdresser. Long, thin and stringy, it conformed not at all to the "luxuriantly cascading abundant tresses" attributed to the princess in the script. After my countless brief encounters with every piece of fake hair in Rome, the hairdresser was by now my least favorite person in the world. She constantly lamented my lack of locks.

"We'll just have to call you old pinhead," she sneered jovially, stabbing my skull once more with her three-inch steel hairpins. She finally found a wig we both liked. Waist-length, it contained the life savings of the hair of twelve Italian nuns. It was so heavy that when I moved my head it was if in slow motion. To keep it stuck to my scalp we used 47 bobby pins, 92 sharp hairpins and half a bottle of toupee glue.

When, as often happens today, *Land of the Pharaohs* is shown on the late show and I get praise for my appearance. I smile when I think of the agony I endured at the hands of that hairdresser. Not to mention the complex I had for years because of the "old pinhead" line. Although I have a small head, it is not deformed, as I was led to believe then; I thought I was a bit of a freak in the skull department, thanks to her.

Rome was exciting. "La Dolce Vita" was in full swing. Down the Via Veneto strolled household-name American actors and actresses escaping their taxes by taking eighteen months out of the States. Gorgeous raven-haired Italian starlets sat sipping cappuccino at the sidewalk cafés, waiting to be discovered. Everyone was alive and gay. It was summer and I found a new romance.

Sydney Chaplin was the second son of Charlie Chaplin. Twenty-eight years old, he was very tall, very dark and quite handsome, with black curly hair flecked with gray, and amused brown eyes. He had an outrageous and scurrilous wit. He was so originally hilarious that he made me literally weep with laughter.

Every day we started laughing and didn't stop until the early hours of the morning, when we would stagger out of Victor's Club, the Number One, or whatever disco or club we hit upon that night, and giggle all the way back to the sedate Hotel de La Ville, where most of the international cast stayed during the filming of *Land of the Pharaohs.*

There had been an absence of laughter and gaiety in the latter months of my life with Maxwell Reed. Sydney was like ice water in the desert. He filled a tremendous need in my life to have fun; to enjoy my flaming youth and to be nonconformist as far as the "establishment" went. I didn't deliberately set out to shock people, but Syd gave not a single damn about what the world thought of him. Since I was a chameleon where men were concerned, I too adopted his "screw you" attitude toward his fellow man.

After two weeks of staying up till dawn and listening to Sydney enthrall a roomful of people with his crazy monologues and outrageous jokes, we finally laughed our way into bed—where we proceeded to become, if possible, even *more* hysterical. Someone said to me once, after literally chasing me around my living room for half an hour with me evading this humorist's clutches till, weak with laughter, I managed to usher him to the door, "Well, I may not be much of a lover, but I'm a funny fuck!" Although this was not strictly true of Syd, nevertheless we often ended our nights by my breaking up and him doing a comedy routine. *Nothing* was to be taken seriously, and after a year of torment with Max that was OK by me.

His favorite expression was "motherfucker"—usually shortened to "mother," and his vocabulary was so sprinkled with four-letter words that it was always slightly surprising to play in a scene with him and hear

normal dialogue come out of his mouth. Sometimes in our scenes together I would have to dig my nails into the palms of my hands to stop
giggling. To Syd, life was one great big ball. He loved to drink, to dance,
to gamble, to joke and to play. He didn't take acting seriously. It was just
a way to make some bread. I had thought that he would surely have been
wealthy, as his father was a multimillionaire—but that was not the case.
He had a small allowance but not enough to lead the crazy playboy
existence he desired. He owned two expensive sports cars, a red Ferrari
and a blue Alfa-Romeo, and he lived out of two alligator suitcases.

We would drive back from the beach at Ostia or Fregene in the early
hours at 125 miles an hour, the convertible top down, the warm wind
whipping my hair wildly, and the trees above us melting into a ceiling of
green leaves—laughing all the way. It was a miracle we were never killed.
We gave a new meaning to the word reckless. We lived life in the fast
lane—Zelda and Scott reincarnated.

The part of Princess Nellifer necessitated many changes of wardrobe,
each one more exotic or revealing than the last. The seamstresses at
Scalera Studios were hard at it, sewing hundreds of yards of gold lamé,
silver brocade, chiffon, silk and gold braid into elaborate costumes that I
would wear when I became the Egyptian Queen. My opening outfit was
somewhat simpler. I wore a gold mesh bra and a long purple brocade
skirt which sat low on my hips. Over this was a velvet cloak in which
when I was presented as a gift to the Pharaoh, I would be wrapped.

However, my naked navel presented a problem. It was the mid-fifties.
Censorship was severe. If the Hays Office thought a scene or a costume
too risqué, it was cut, and thousands of dollars of valuable footage went
down the drain.

My outfit was as Egyptian-authentic as the Italian designer could make
it, but my navel was a no-no as far as the censor was concerned. "Cover it
up," said Howard Hawks testily when I presented myself to him for final
approval on this costume. "Find a way to cover it up. The censor thinks
navels are obscene," he snorted despairingly, and went back to his scene.
The designer, Mayo, an excitable Latin, shrugged. *"Il censore è matto—
completamente matto—ma cosa facciamo adesso?"*

"How about a Band-Aid?" I joked. "Or some Plasticine inside it. We'll
get some Plasticine and dye it to match my stomach, and then I'll be
navel-less, just like a big doll!"

They looked at me pityingly—English humor does not appeal to
Italians. "Aha!" Mayo suddenly shrieked, jumping up and down excitedly.
"Mettiamo un bottone in sua piccola bucca!" My Italian was scratchy, but
roughly translated this meant "Let's put a button in her little hole!" They
scurried to their treasure chests and pulled out dozens of buttons—silver,
gold, emerald and finally a ruby. Mayo tried to insert the ruby while I
squirmed uncomfortably. *"Bella!"* said Mayo proudly. *"Molto bella! Cara
*—you think so too?"

I looked in the mirror at the little ruby twinkling brightly in the middle
of my stomach and burst into laughter. With that the ruby exploded out
of its place and disappeared under a sewing machine. *"Chè cosa?"* said

Mayo angrily. "We must put the sticky stuff—we stuff it in hard and it stay there. *Bellissimo—un effetto bellissimo.*" I endured a tube of Johnson's liquid adhesive poured into my navel, and there the ruby stayed, proud and glistening, defying the censor. I thought it looked infinitely more obscene and erotic with the shiny stone drawing attention to what was meant to be unobtrusive, but everyone seemed satisfied, and shooting commenced.

However, several weeks in Sydney's company, scoffing fettuccine and lasagne at Alfredo's and Il Piccolo Mondo and drinking quantities of red wine and crême de menthe had added about eight pounds to my already voluptuous figure. When it came time to do a retake of the first scene I was embarrassed. *Zaftig* was an understatement. I knew Howard Hawks hated plump ladies (he had discovered, or sponsored, Lauren Bacall, Lizabeth Scott and Angie Dickinson, none of them exactly blimps), I endeavored to hold my stomach in tightly during the scene, but each time I squeezed in my muscles, out plopped the dreaded red stone!

Howard Hawks was going crazy.

"For God's sakes—get some airplane glue. Get anything to keep the damned thing in place." And then accusingly to me: "You've gained weight. I told you last week in the rushes you looked *fat*. Have you been dieting?"

"All I've eaten for two days is three hard-boiled eggs, Mr. Hawks," I lied feverishly, thinking of the vast amount of spaghetti Bolognese and zabaglione I had consumed at Alfredo's last night.

"Well you better cut it down to two hard-boiled eggs," he said crustily. "Princess Nellifer should not look as though she is four months pregnant." He stormed off, leaving me properly chastened. He was right. Here I was playing the best role of my career and I was goofing off. Too many late nights and too much pasta and wine do not a love affair with the camera make. I vowed to discipline myself.

I was playing the role of a lifetime—being directed by one of the world's greatest movie directors, working with some of the finest actors around, and I was acting and behaving like a stupid schoolgirl. I was wrong and knew it. I quit drinking, banished pasta from my mind, and was in bed at ten o'clock each night with a copy of *Land of the Pharaohs* in front of me.

But it was not easy, with Syd. When I stayed in and went to bed early he went out with his gang anyway, and since I was infatuated with him I wanted to be where the action was—and that was with him.

I was staying at the Hotel de la Ville, a popular watering hole for French and Italian actors and directors. On my second day, while enjoying a drink on the terrace with Christian Marquand and Dewey Martin, one of the stars of *Pharaohs*, a vision appeared.

"Who is *that?*" breathed Dewey in awe, as the most gorgeous girl I had ever seen walked to the bar.

"Ah, *elle s'appelle Brigitte Bardot, une nouvelle jeune vedette du cinéma, et une amie de moi,*" said Christian. "*Bonsoir,* Roger."

Bardot's escort, a young intense man with a shock of black hair and sharp features, shook hands with Christian hurriedly, gave me the once-over and hastened to the bar where Bardot, to whom he was then married, was getting more than admiring glances from every man in the place.

She was about my age and was indeed delicious. An enviable, petite beauty wearing her soon-to-be-famous pink-and-white tight-waisted gingham peasant dress with the extremely low neckline, her masses of blond hair looking as if she had just tumbled out of bed, and the eyes and lips that every man desired.

And every woman wanted to look like her. I even whipped over to a dressmaker the very next day to have the pink-and-white gingham dress copied!

Although we never met again I remained a fan of Bardot's. Not particularly for her acting—although I thought she had a lot more talent than her sexuality allowed her to show—but for her free and honest approach to love, men and sex. I was also interested through the years to see her ever changing parade of lovers and husbands, and I admired her self-admitted freedom from sexual taboos. I was shocked, however, to read this quote in a magazine recently from this liberated, emancipated lady:

I have to accept old age, right? It is horrible, you rot, you fall to pieces, you stink. It scares me more than anything else. There's a beach not far away but I never go during the day. I am 48 and not so pretty. I wouldn't inflict this sight on anyone any more.

Sad words from anyone, but particularly sad from such a dazzling woman who, had she only felt more secure about things other than just her physical attributes, should realize she is in her prime.

Sydney had gained a few pounds too, and as the time drew near to start our love scenes together, we both made a concerted effort to cut calories and get in shape. His costumes were even more "kitsch" than mine. He wore a small beige felt skullcap which was cunningly cut out to reveal his ears—not his best feature—a long loincloth of an ornate fabric, and a vast neckpiece of gold and ebony; also curious pointed slippers and two large gold slave bracelets on his upper arms, which, due to the amount of food we were consuming, made the flesh squash out above and below in a most unattractive fashion. I was wearing a pink chiffon gown, low-cut and heavily embroidered with crystals, and on my upper arm a tight silver-and-ruby bracelet, around which flesh also bulged. Thank God I wasn't wearing the ruby in my navel too.

When Sydney and I met at 8:30 A.M. on the sound stage at Scalera Studios, we took one look at each other and burst out laughing. "Is this how Theda Bara started?"

"More like Ma and Pa Kettle meet the motherfucking Pharaoh," said Syd, tripping over his pointed sandals and getting entangled in his maxi-skirt.

"Quiet, now hold it down," called the assistant director, and we started blocking the scene when Trenah (Syd) declares his love for Princess Nellifer:

Actors have two dreaded nightmares: One is to appear on stage and forget one's dialogue; the other is to be unable to speak the dialogue because of an uncontrollable urge to laugh. The latter nightmare happened to Sydney and me that day. It was truly ghastly because however hard we forced ourselves not to break up, one or the other of us would at one point or another in the scene start to collapse into giggles. The angrier Howard Hawks became the more we laughed. I was actually terrified and upset after this occurred four or five times, but it didn't help. One look at Syd's earnest face, with his ears sticking out of the weird hat, and I was convulsed. I would try not to break up completely, but Syd saw the strain in my face and that would set him off. It was like an hysterical bad dream. It was also catching. Half the crew were starting to giggle, and it was when we caught sight of the overly serious and cross faces of Howard and the more somber crew members that we all broke up over and over again.

Eventually Howard stopped shooting and bawled Sydney and me out vehemently in front of the entire crew. He sent us home and lectured us sternly to stop behaving like children or our careers would be finished before they got started. He brought us down to earth with a big bang.

This time I really decided to pull myself together—to lose the excess pounds and take my work more seriously. I realized I was losing face and that my behavior was becoming terribly unprofessional.

I had tried to file for a divorce in London before leaving for Rome, but one could not file unless the marriage had existed for three years or more. All I had was an unofficial separation from Max, who was also in Rome at the time working on *Helen of Troy*, another historical and hysterical soap opera.

I was sunbathing on the beach at Fregene one day when I felt a shadow looming over me. I looked up. There he was. Tanned, dyed black hair and small white shorts, and an ominous look on his face. "I want to talk to you." I was surrounded by friends who tried to get rid of him, but he was insistent. "You better come and talk to me now or I'll make a scene right here," he said menacingly. I reluctantly followed him to the beach bar. "Do you remember the photographs I took of you?" he said casually, offering me a cigarette.

I did remember them. It is not an uncommon occurrence for husbands to take nude photos of their wives. Some of our friends did, and although he had coaxed me into posing for them with assurances that he would never show them to a soul, I had been uneasy at the time. The pictures were fairly tame as far as I remembered. I wore the bottom half of a bikini and was posed, bored and sulky, on the zebra-skin sofa. Tame stuff by today's standards. "So what about them?" I said brazening it out.

"I've got a good offer from one of the Italian magazines to buy them from me. They'll pay me a lot of money and I need it." He smiled his Mitchum smile. I looked at him numbly. He surely had to be the lowest form of human life. How could I have ever married such a vile creep? Just looking at him filled me with revulsion.

"So what do you want from me?" I said.

"All the rings I gave you when we were married," he said smoothly. "Wedding, engagement and the topaz."

"You're welcome to them," I said icily. "I'll have someone bring them to your hotel."

"And the check," he said, blocking me as I tried to get back to the beach. "Don't forget to sign it."

I couldn't believe he was serious. In the past month he had sent several crazy letters to me professing his love, and in one of them he had enclosed a blank check from my personal account and asked me to sign it.

"You know I don't have much money," I protested. "There's only a couple of hundred pounds in my account, that's all."

"The check and the rings at my hotel tomorrow night, or the magazine gets the pictures. *Ciao*, kid," and he sauntered off to the bar. I was furious. The man had no ethics at all. He was a street fighter. Maybe I should become one too. I told my mother, who was staying with me. She had grown to hate Max as much as I. I had revealed to her some of the horrors I had been through. We discussed our strategy with Eddie Fowlie, the special-effects man on *Pharaohs* and a friend, who had also been on *Our Girl Friday*. He agreed to take the rings and the blank check to Max at the Residence Palace Hotel the next night.

I didn't have much choice. The money wasn't important and the rings had no sentimental value, but it would have been complete disaster for my career had those nude photos appeared in print. Rumors had been circulating that nude pictures of Marilyn Monroe had been printed some time ago on a girlie calendar.

The world was puritanical and quick to condemn any public figures whose morals were less than faultless. I was worried that if a whiff of this possible scandal reached the ears of 20th Century-Fox, who were in final negotiations with Rank to buy my contract, my Hollywood career would be finished before it had barely begun.

Mummy and I sat in a nearby café compulsively drinking cappuccino and brandy while Eddie went to pick up the photos from Max. He returned triumphantly with a large, sealed manila envelope. I opened the envelope and out fell twelve eight-by-ten glossy pinup pictures from Rank!

"That rotten bastard!" I was so furious I didn't even censor my language in front of my mother. "Of all the lowdown, filthy, lying tricks. He's still got the goddamned pictures." Mummy and Eddie looked at each other helplessly. "I'm going to go and punch him out," said Eddie. But my mother laid a restraining hand on him. "No, let me talk to him first." She strode to the phone. I knocked back a brandy and wondered from where my mother—Mrs. Gentle-Meek-and-Mild, usually—had unearthed this ferocious streak.

When Mummy came back she was trembling with fury. "He told me the photographs are in London in a safety-deposit box," she said, her voice shaking. I was proud of her; she didn't assert herself too often, but there she was—a tigress protecting her cub.

"I called him all the names under the sun, but he said he wants to keep them to remember you by." I passed her my brandy.

"Oh, charming," I said bitterly. "He can show them to all his dirty old Arabian millionaires and tell them what they've missed."

"Anyway," said Mummy, smiling bravely, "he's promised *me* that he will not sell them to any publications, so I suppose we'll just have to take his word for it."

"His *word*—ha!" I threw down another brandy. "He doesn't know the meaning of honor and ethics." Mummy patted my hand comfortingly.

"Never mind, darling. I'm sure we've heard the last of him this time." I nodded weakly but I had a nasty suspicion that the last chapter on Maxwell Reed had yet to be written.

"Three hundred and fifty dollars a week," announced John Shepbridge, his eyes glowing with excitement. "What do you think of that, Joanie? That is terrific for the first year." "Not much," I said diffidently. I sat across from "Goulash," as he was affectionately known, sitting behind his highly polished walnut desk in his London house at 16 South Audley Street. The weak London sun seeped through the tiny Georgian latticed windows and reflected off the silver and porcelain objects scattered tastefully around his office-living room. We were meeting to discuss my deal with Fox. Rank had accepted the fifteen thousand pounds that Fox had offered to buy my contract from them, and Goulash, who was a senior executive of the Famous Artists Agency, was now negotiating my salary terms.

My dream was about to be realized. I was going to Hollywood under an exclusive seven-year contract with 20th Century-Fox. It was an offer not to be sneezed at, but I was sneezing. The reason for my lack of enthusiasm was at this minute in Paris, probably languishing in some bistro or boîte, consuming quantities of vodka and playing the pinball machines.

Goulash looked at me, a flicker of annoyance crossing his face. "What did you say, dear?"

"Three hundred and fifty dollars a week is not that much money, Goulash. *You* know that and I know that. Now if Fox is willing to pay Rank so much money for me, I'm quite sure they will be willing to pay me more as a contract player. I was thinking of, say, twelve hundred and fifty a week."

I had read in a magazine that $1,250 a week was a reasonable salary for a young contract player, and if one settled for less than that, the studios thought of you more as a feature or bit player and it was harder to obtain leading roles. Although I would have sold my soul to go to Hollywood, I had ambivalent feelings at the moment because of my crush on Sydney.

"You're crazy," said Goulash angrily, his Hungarian blood rising to the occasion. "They will never go for that. Never. *Never.* You're totally *unknown* in the States. Why should they pay you three times as much as they usually do? Crazy—crazy." He stomped around his desk angrily mumbling to himself.

"What am I going to tell Charlie?" he said. "He's been talking about you to Darryl for three months now. It's because of *him* you're getting this deal. He's going to be furious."

Charlie was Charles K. Feldman, top executive agent at Famous Artists and a wheeler-dealer to be reckoned with. I knew that because of his influence with Darryl Zanuck, head of production at Fox, who trusted Feldman's enthusiasm for me, I was being offered this contract. I also shrewdly realized that the chances of my getting the better roles at Fox and not being just another two-bit contract player would be enhanced by getting a large weekly salary rather than what was virtually a pittance. (Studio grips earned more than $350 a week.) It was a calculated gamble, and if I lost I could always go back to Syd in Paris, or work in Rome, where I had been getting movie offers.

"I'm very appreciative of all that you and Charlie have done for me," I said formally. "But it's my life and my decision. I want twelve hundred and fifty a week, and if I don't get it—forget it." I got up to leave. "Darling Goulash—I'm leaving for Paris tonight. I'll be at the Hotel Trémoille. Let me know what happens." I kissed him goodbye and he raised his eyebrows in a gesture of resignation.

"Crazy little girl," he said. "You can always find a good *shtup,* but a good contract is a once-in-a-lifetime thing. I hope you're not blowing your career, Joanie."

"I'm not," I said confidently. "Let me quote Joan Crawford: 'You can't cuddle up to a career at night.' " (I had just read that in *Photoplay* and thought it quite profound.) *"Ciao,* Goulash." I walked into South Audley Street feeling grownup and confident. I was not yet twenty-one, but I knew what I wanted—and I was *not* going to sell myself short this time.

As soon as I arrived in Paris, Sydney and I took off in the Ferrari with his friend Adolph Green for a trip to Vevey, Switzerland, to visit Syd's father, Charlie Chaplin. Adolph was squashed in the tiny back seat and we had a hair-raising trip over the snowy, winding mountain roads. I was excitedly looking forward to meeting Syd's family and especially the legendary Charlie.

The house was set in a secluded area, just outside the tiny picturesque village of Vevey, which looked like every postcard of Switzerland. It was an imposing two-story mansion with an apparently endless series of rooms. The rooms were necessary because there seemed to be an endless series of children and nannies, maids, gardeners and secretaries. Although the senior Chaplin had a reputation for being penurious, his lifestyle was lavish. Beyond the rolling green lawns and flower beds was a beautiful lake where all the kids and Charlie and his lovely black-haired, madonnalike wife, Oona, swam and sunbathed. I liked being around this happy family atmosphere, and although Charlie reminded me somewhat of my father, very much the patriarch, strict and authoritarian, he was also warm and human, funny and, strangely, extremely shy.

Although over sixty, Charlie was still busy siring babies. They ranged in age from Charlie, Jr., who was about thirty, to the newest baby of only a few months old. I admired Oona for her lovely maternal calmness, and, playing with her babies, I felt for the very first time a slight flicker of maternal instinct. "What a crazy idea," I said to myself, dismissing it instantly and putting down baby, who was in the process of covering his entire face with nourishing Swiss chocolate. "I've got years to go before I even think about having kids—got my whole life ahead yet. Kids! Ugh! *Quel horreur!*"

Sydney and I stayed with his family for three days, and another side of his personality revealed itself. He was much more subdued around Charlie, not nearly as bawdy, and didn't want any "romantic interludes" in the same house as his father.

"But why?" I whispered. "His room is miles away." "I don't know, for Christ's sakes," he whispered angrily. "I just feel funny about it—can't you understand that?" "I guess so," I said, imagining my reactions in the same situation. "But since they know we have the same room, do you think they imagine we're playing gin rummy all night? And from the number of kids they have, I bet *they* don't play cards too often."

I remembered Syd regaling me with stories about him, his brother and his ex-stepmother, Paulette Goddard. Charlie, Jr., and Syd were about thirteen and fourteen years old, Paulette not more than a dozen years older. Sometimes in the morning the boys would jump into Paulette's silken-covered bed with her and share her toast and coffee while she read her mail and talked on the phone. She would tease and cuddle the adolescent boys, and, though Sydney assured me it was all very innocent, it struck me as odd, to say the least.

In any event, I couldn't understand the great unwillingness on Syd's part to sully the Swiss sheets. Maybe he was a genuine prude—people who swore a lot often were.

In Paris, it was a fun time again; up all night at Jimmy's nightclub or L'Éléphant Blanc, or our favorite restaurant, Moustache. The owner, a huge man with a fine hairy upper lip, was a friend, and we spent wonderfully convivial evenings there. I took long walks through Paris and along the Seine while Syd played golf. I loved exploring the sophisticated Right Bank boutiques, and the tiny cluttered antique and book shops. We rode on the *bateau mouche* on the Seine, spent a day at the Louvre and fell in love with the city. When we weren't exploring, we played Sinatra records and cards, pinball machines in overheated cafés, and drank Beaujolais and laughed and nightclubbed all night. It was good to be alive, young and carefree.

I was still playing the waiting game with Fox. When Goulash called to tell me not only that Fox had accepted my terms, but that they wanted me in California almost immediately, I was thrilled—but dismayed.

Sydney and I sat in a tiny restaurant in Montmartre. The candlelight flickered on the red-checkered tablecloth and the air was thick with the smell of Gauloises and garlic. I was leaving the next day for London to pack and depart for the States. He tried to comfort me as I sobbed into my wine. We thought we loved each other. We would be together soon, he tried to assure me. As soon as he knew about a job that he was hoping for, he would join me in Los Angeles. Not to worry, it would all work out in the end. I hoped he was right.

In London I was surrounded by family and friends, photographers coming over to take pictures, and dressmakers bringing new finery. I was caught up in a whirl of activity and excitement. In the pre-jet days a trip to the States was a major event. To get to New York alone took over ten hours. Today I make a minimum of eight or nine trips a year between L.A. and London and think nothing of it. Finally, amidst tears, laughter and sadness I said goodbye. I hugged my little brother, Bill, whom I felt I hardly knew, kissed my teenage sister, Jackie—we had just started to become close and now I was leaving—a big hug for Daddy and, finally, my darling mother, whom I was beginning to understand and love more and more. She was trying desperately not to cry—and so was I. We were surrounded by reporters and photographers trying to get a human-interest photo story on "Britain's Bad Girl Goes to Hollywood."

Every two or three minutes we heard the sound of a plane taking off. I clutched my brand-new ankle-length mink coat tightly around me and tried to be brave. "I'll write you every week," I said, my voice breaking. "And I'll come and visit as often as I can—it's only a little over five thousand miles from L.A. to London after all." Five thousand miles seemed like a million in the days before transatlantic jets, but I had to say something. The flight was called and I was off, leaving the family and friends I knew and loved, leaving cold, austerity-ridden England: the English country lanes; the pubs; the theater; the jazz clubs; the Sunday papers; everything that was familiar.

My whole life was being left behind and I was going to a strange new country. To a totally different environment. To meet and work with people I didn't know and to start a new life. In Hollywood.

❧ *Four* ❧

"THEY'RE GOING TO LOVE you in Hollywood," Goulash had told me confidently. "They love English girls. You'll be a smash."

I thought ruefully about his words as I sat in my hideous orange-and-yellow hotel room in Beverly Hills for the seventh consecutive night, alone, gazing at an unusual personality on television called Liberace. The days were so full I didn't have time to think. 20th Century-Fox was a hive of activity and I was running from wardrobe department to hairdressing

to stills gallery for a never-ending succession of photographs and interviews. I met every producer and casting director on the lot and didn't
remember any of their names. I sat in the bustling, hustling commissary
at lunchtime eating a new delicacy called "tuna salad" and observed,
wide-eyed, the comings and goings of the stars.

Fox had a huge list of contract players, all of whom were either working in the many films that were in production or were on the lot doing
what I was doing, which was getting their faces in front of as many
directors and producers as possible who were preparing projects. They
included Susan Hayward, Rita Moreno, Sheree North, Debra Paget, Jeff
Hunter, Barbara Rush, Robert Wagner, Gene Tierney, Joanne Woodward, even Clifton Webb—and many more. I hopefully looked each day
for Fox's top star, Marilyn Monroe, but she preferred to lunch in the
seclusion of her dressing-room.

Although Fox was making many movies, its box-office returns for the
past couple of years had been less than brilliant. Zanuck did not have as
much control as he had when the studio was making such blockbusters as
Gentleman's Agreement, A Letter to Three Wives and *All About Eve,* and
although they had made the first CinemaScope film, *The Robe,* a few
years before, things were soggy at the box office. Their films with Marilyn
Monroe, queen of the lot and America's number one pinup, usually made
a profit, but of late Miss Monroe had been giving them problems by
refusing to make such epics as *The Lady in Pink Tights,* and had been
going on suspension and to the Actors Studio in New York. Fox was
starting to groom two young actresses, Jayne Mansfield and Sheree
North, to take her place. They didn't take disobedience from anyone—
not even Marilyn.

Goulash's words seemed anything but prophetic as I sat miserably
alone night after night. The phone rang with invitations to dinner from
men I had heard of but did not know—Nick Hilton, Bob Neal, Greg
Bautzer—but I was always a one-man woman. Faithful to Sydney. I
waited hopefully for him to arrive.

The vastness and variety of Los Angeles astounded me. The place
sprawled on endlessly. Fashionable Beverly Hills, gracious Bel Air,
swinging, youthful Westwood, seedy Hollywood, and the endless suburban fringes with quaint names like Pomona, Orange County, West
Covina, Redlands, Santa Ana, Anaheim—it seemed bigger than *England!*
Each area had a character of its own, and after I rented a car I explored
each of them diligently. I had never seen so many drugstores and gas
stations in my life—but these all looked alike.

The only people I knew socially were the makeup man from *Land of
the Pharaohs* and my agents, and although they were very kind, and I
went to dinner at their houses, I was lonely and homesick. I had not yet
found friends of my own. The social structure of Hollywood and Beverly
Hills was based on dozens of varied cliques. Some people belonged to
one clique and some overlapped and belonged to several. Three or four
or five hundred people made up the social center of Hollywood then, and
I didn't know one of them.

✧   ✧   ✧

I was cast in *The Virgin Queen,* a highly colored and fictionalized account of Queen Elizabeth's supposed romance with Sir Walter Raleigh. The redoubtable and legendary Bette Davis played Queen Elizabeth for the second time, as she had had a huge success in *Elizabeth and Essex* some years back with Errol Flynn. Richard Todd played Raleigh and I played Elizabeth's innocent lady-in-waiting Beth Throgmorton, in love with Raleigh and pregnant by him, much to Good Queen Bess's chagrin. Again I seemed to be playing a wayward girl, but instead of having to wear the sleazy costumes of *Cosh Boy* and *I Believe in You,* I was exquisitely dressed in beautiful Elizabethan laces and farthingales.

Painstaking effort and attention to detail went into the design and construction of these costumes. The wardrobe department at Fox was humming day and night with dozens of seamstresses, tailors, milliners and dressmakers making each creation a vision of perfection. I don't think even in the highest-fashion houses of Paris has there ever been so much time and attention to detail lavished on clothing as there was at the major film studios during their heyday. Each costume was a work of art. One dress was completely embroidered in thousands of tiny seed pearls over rare Belgian lace. Each pearl was sewn on by hand. The workmanship that went into inside seams was as careful as that lavished on the visible parts. For some outfits I would have six or seven complete fittings, and I would stand for hours while every seam was measured to an exact eighth of an inch—God help me if I put on a pound or two at lunch. The waist seams would be snipped and unpicked painstakingly and the dress would be refitted all over again. After I endured this agony a couple of times, I bought a scale and started watching my weight like a hawk. I was impatient at fittings and would yawn, stretch, scratch and fidget to the despair of these dedicated seamstresses.

Bette Davis awed me, and I avoided her off the set whenever possible. I had been warned she did not take kindly to young pretty actresses, and she lashed out at me a couple of times. She had a scathing wit and was not known for mincing words, and I thought it best to keep a low profile around her. I was still insecure about my work. My reviews from the British films constantly emphasized my looks and sex appeal, and this seemed the only aspect of me that the magazine writers and reporters were interested in talking about. My measurements, my love life, and what I ate for breakfast were of far more interest to them than my brain, my approach to my craft, and what I thought of the State of the Union.

I had been warned by the vast publicity department that I should not talk about anything controversial (politics, religion, capital punishment, etc.). There was a morals clause in my contract which guaranteed that if I did anything to invoke the wrath of the Daughters of the American Revolution, the members of the John Birch Society or any other of the dozens of anti-anything organizations that proliferated in America at that time, I would be in trouble. America was in a time of prosperity but, living in the aftermath of the Joe McCarthy hearings, everyone attempted to be good, clean, upstanding, patriotic and loyal to America, with no whiff of communist leanings or subversive activities or sexual aberrations to sully their records.

Sydney finally arrived, and we rented a small, antiseptic furnished apartment on Beverly Glen Boulevard, just four minutes from Fox, and set up house together. Living together openly was considered terribly daring, especially since I was still married, so we tried to keep it as quiet as possible, especially from the Snoop Sisters, the gossip columnists Hedda Hopper and Louella Parsons.

I worked hard on *The Virgin Queen.* On my days off I would have to learn horseback riding, a frightening experience, as horses petrified me. There were also constant fittings, lunch interviews with every magazine in the U.S.A., and photo sessions, which went on endlessly.

It couldn't have been easy for Syd. He was living with a girl who not only was paying the rent but also was busy working all the time. He was not. There wasn't much on the horizon for him, so he threw himself into golf, cards and television—in that order. The only thing he didn't throw himself into too often was me.

He'd changed. Maybe it was being away from his beloved Europe and his cronies. America did not suit him. There were no cozy corner cafés to pass the time of day sipping coffee and telling bawdy stories. No friendly neighborhood bistros full of hearty red-faced, black-bereted men knocking back absinthe and playing the pinball machines. No Ferrari. No nightclubs to sit in until five in the morning, with the action still going strong. Add to this no work, and no wonder a sullen despondency suddenly settled on my handsome, usually laughing and happy lover.

All day, if he wasn't at the golf or tennis or bridge clubs, he was glued to The Box. "Milton Berle," "I Love Lucy," "Dragnet," "Ed Sullivan"— he watched them all, even the soap operas and the children's programs. TV bored me stiff. It had been useful to watch in London as an alternative to Max's unromantic interludes, but I would much rather go to a movie and be enveloped in wide-screen, color and CinemaScope than concentrate on a flickering black-and-white screen.

Life was an adventure, and although I was still shy and reticent with people I didn't know, I wanted to live it to the hilt.

Sydney was part of Gene Kelly's set. They were among the more stimulating and intellectual people in Hollywood. They included Harry Kurnitz, one of the writers on *Land of the Pharaohs,* one of the most amusing men who ever lived; Stanley Donen, who had directed many of MGM's more successful musicals; Adolph Green and Betty Comden, playwrights who had had many smash musical successes on Broadway and were now writing musicals at MGM; George Englund, a producer, and his actress wife, Cloris Leachman; Oscar Levant, a great wit and a great pianist; and Betsy Blair. Gene's wife, an actress and a very bright lady indeed. All of these people intimidated the hell out of me and although they couldn't have been more friendly, I felt like an outsider.

It was only three years since I had made my first film in England and now I was part of a Hollywood group, but I felt inferior to them in every way. They played volleyball, which, on the rare occasions when I attempted to play, ended up with me spraining a finger or breaking a nail. They played charades with skill and expertise. And they conversed with wit and wisdom. I loved hanging out at the Kelly's Cape Cod-style house on Rodeo Drive, and I observed and absorbed all I could. I wanted to expand my knowledge, which I felt was limited, having left the last of many schools at fifteen. I wanted to learn, to experience more of the world of art, literature and music, and to be able to converse easily and knowledgeably with this, to me, highly civilized group. I was conscious of my lack of higher education. I wanted to belong, but I felt like a child whose nose was pressed against the candystore window—a babe in the Hollywoods.

One Saturday night at the Kellys' I noticed a rather nondescript blond girl sitting on the sofa near the bar. Nobody was paying any attention to her so I wandered over and started a conversation. It was unusual for me to find someone shyer than myself. She wore a white knitted silky dress, rather low-cut, and sleeveless, and no bra, which was frightfully daring in the mid-fifties. Her short blond hair was combed carelessly. She had little makeup on her averagely pretty face. It was hard to realize that this was Marilyn Monroe in the flesh! She appeared to be at the party without a date, but her mentor, Milton Greene, was lurking in the background.

She seemed glad that someone was talking to her and we discussed astrology and found out that we were both born under the sign of Gemini —"the terrible twins." She admired my hair, which I wore long and straight, with bangs, to the despair of the hairdressing department at Fox which was always trying to persuade me to cut it in a fashionable bubble cut. It was fascinating to talk to the world-famous Monroe—legendary sex symbol and idol of millions. She seemed a pretty but shy girl, with some complexes and a distrust of people. She left the party early, and I wondered if we would ever bump into each other on the Fox lot. But Marilyn was so insulated from the outside world at the studio that I never did see her again.

She had been supposed to star at Fox in a film about the Stanford White-Harry K. Thaw-Evelyn Nesbit triangle, one of the great scandals of the turn of the century, but she had refused to do it—probably wisely, since Evelyn was supposed to be seventeen or eighteen years old and Marilyn, although marvelous-looking, was around thirty. The studio was going ahead with the movie which was to be called *The Girl in the Red Velvet Swing* and there was much rivalry on the lot as to who would get the plum role of Evelyn Nesbit.

Terry Moore, Debra Paget and several others were tested, and as soon as I completed *The Virgin Queen,* so was I. I didn't hold out much hope of getting the part because it was essential that the girl be American and I still had a strong British accent. I worked on an American accent studiously before the test and waited for the result, which was not long in coming. I read the announcement in the *Hollywood Reporter* one morning and almost choked to death on my bagel. "Collins to play Nesbit" blazed across page one. I was jubilant. To play the leading female role in what was to be one of Fox's most extravagant productions was some achievement for an English girl who had been under contract less than four months.

I was plunged into frantic preparations. Evelyn had started in the chorus at the Floradora Theater so there were two lavish production numbers to learn, and although I had taken dancing classes since childhood, competing with professionals and performing strenuous dances like the cakewalk and cancan were exhausting. We rehearsed the dances in the morning, and after a quick lunch break, I would have to be at wardrobe to fit some of the twenty-seven costumes I was to wear. Then work for two hours on my accent, with Jeff Hunter, a contract actor who had been assigned for some curious reason to be my vocal coach. It was hard to get rid of my clipped British delivery, and I realized that if the accent was going to be authentic at all I would have to adopt it for everyday life too. I started talking with a sort of mid-Atlantic drawl, which reverted to clipped English whenever I returned to England. The word I was never able to master, however, was "girl." The "rl" sound was impossible for me to say with the right drawl. So Jeff and I went through the script substituting whenever possible synonyms for any word ending in "rl"—not an easy task.

Richard Fleischer, a director who had been recently successful at Fox, was directing, and Ray Milland and Farley Granger were to play Stanford White, the architect, and Harry K. Thaw, the dissolute playboy, respectively. If I thought I had been busy before, it was nothing to what happened now. The publicity department had instructions to fill the newspapers and magazines with stories and photos of me. After all, I was still relatively unknown, and Fox wanted to be sure my name was familiar to the American public before *Swing* was released. Now I didn't even have lunch hours to myself. Fox insisted that articles and photos of me were to appear in all the major fan magazines. America was saturated with me.

In print I came out sounding like a cross between Dame Edith Evans and Rita Hayworth. "She thinks America is cool, crazy and jolly good," enthusiastically bannered *Photoplay* and *Modern Screen;* "The Lady Is Dangerous," shrieked *Motion Picture*. Various epithets were attached to me: "Bundle from Britain," "Electric and Elusive," "Cool, Cool Collins," "A Bohemian at Heart," "Global Glamour Girl," and my particular favorite, from the Italian magazine *Oggi:* "The Pouting Panther!"

I was maligned, scorned, criticized, lied about, and my fairly normal mode of living was considered scandalous and disgraceful. All of a sudden I found myself with a reputation as a raving sexpot, swinger and home wrecker, whom Beverly Hills wives were supposed to live in fear of in case I cast my green "orbs" in the direction of their men. Ninety-nine percent of this was total fabrication. I was outspoken, yes. Never a diplomat, I have always found it easier to tell the truth than beat around the bush; but the outrageous stories that proliferated about me surprised even the publicity department. I got an instant reputation as a free-living, free-loving rebel, and it was hard for me to handle.

✿   ✿   ✿

The electric, elusive bundle from Britain, Hollywood's gain and England's loss, bounced into the tiny apartment after work one evening and excitedly started getting dressed for the first press screening of *The Virgin Queen.*

"The bathroom's all yours now," I yelled to Syd, who was lying on the orange living-room couch engrossed in "The Mouseketeers."

"Aw, honey, I'm really beat. I don't think I can make it," he called, not raising his eyes from Annette Funicello's ears.

"Beat? Beat from what?" I angrily surveyed myself in the bedroom mirror as I towel-dried my hair.

He was always beat lately. He played golf from noon till five, hung out and drank with the guys and played poker all night—for stakes he could ill afford. The life and soul of every party we attended, at home he went into a morose depression. Whatever had happened to the jokes and the laughter when we were alone together? "Oh, Sydney must be so much *fun* to be with all the time," trilled a blond starlet as we combed our locks together in the powder room of a Bel Air house, while he was at the bar wowing them with his gags. Sure, I thought bitterly. Only if he has an audience of more than one.

Recently we had adopted a new friend, as bitingly humorous and witty as Sydney but in a slightly more reserved way. Having him around guaranteed that there was never a dull moment, and for the past few weeks the three of us had been inseparable. His name was Arthur Loew, Jr., and he was the scion of one of the royal families of the motion-picture industry. His grandfather, Marcus Loew, had founded Metro-Goldwyn-Mayer studios, and his maternal grandfather, Adolph Zukor, was one of the oldest, most respected and most successful industry figures. Arthur dabbled in writing and producing features at MGM, but his heart was not truly in it, and he was considered to be a rich playboy, squiring beautiful starlets to premieres and parties and living the good life.

I liked him a lot, and so did Sydney, so when Syd suggested that I go to the screening with Arthur, my anger was slightly mollified. Recently I had confided in Arthur some of Syd's and my problems, and he had been a sympathetic listener.

After the screening we went to dinner at a La Cienega steakhouse, and there on the red leather brass-buttoned banquette, drinking whiskey sours and chain-smoking Chesterfields, I started to feel an empathy with Arthur. He was extremely sensitive, an attribute he covered up with his flippant jokes and casual attitudes. He well understood Sydney's dilemma: an out-of-work actor being practically supported by a young, fast-rising actress, and the insurmountable problems we faced.

Sydney and I had never been strong on communicating with each other. Deep feelings were not discussed between us. We never even argued. Our relationship, which had been great fun at the beginning, had disintegrated badly because of a lack of communication. If I found eight pairs of slacks and ten sweaters and dozens of old socks on a chair for weeks, the pile growing and growing, I would not bother to make waves by mentioning it, even if it irritated me. A chasm had developed. I tried to make him hustle to get jobs, but he was self-admittedly bone-lazy and would not go out of his way to grasp opportunities. In a town where opportunities must be grabbed as soon as they appear, this left him sitting by the phone waiting for it to ring—a deadly situation for any actor.

Arthur and I talked on and on. I felt I hadn't really *talked* to anyone for months. I had listened and learned and gossiped and small-talked, but it was unusual to be having a serious conversation about feelings and emotions. Arthur was in analysis and had been for a few years. Although not yet thirty, and wealthy, he had suffered continually during his life. His parents had been divorced several times each, and although close to his mother, Mickey Loew, his great affinity was with his uncle Gerald, who lived in Arizona. "One day I'll give up all this producing bullshit and have a farm in Arizona and raise cattle," he announced prophetically. How boring, I thought to myself. "What fun," I said.

The ending for Syd and me was almost as scruffy as the last part of our relationship had been.

Deep into principal photography on *The Girl in the Red Velvet Swing* I was unable to go with him one Friday to the Racquet Club in Palm Springs where we were spending the weekend. Being of a kind nature, I lent him my car, with the proviso that he meet me at the airport in Palm Springs on Saturday afternoon after I had finished that morning's shooting.

Arriving at Palm Springs airport in sweltering weather, I found no sign of Syd, no messages, no car and no taxis available either. Fuming, I called the Racquet Club. No answer from his room. Eventually a cab appeared, and sweating and hot we drove to the club. The desk clerk informed me that Mr. Chaplin was in the bar. Oh, really, I thought. How typical.

In the bar a pretty sight greeted my eyes. Syd, Gene Kelly, Greg Bautzer, Jack Cushingham and a few other cronies had decided to imbibe after-lunch liquors. They thought it would be fun to sample the bartender's selection alphabetically. Accordingly they had gone from Amaretto to brandy to creme de menthe to Drambuie, and were obviously now on to V for vodka, when I appeared, flushed and furious, in blue jeans.

"Sydney Chaplin," I hissed, "I let you borrow my car, I paid to fly on a bumpy two-engine plane to this godforsaken hole for aging tennis bums to meet you for a relaxing weekend, and you don't even *meet the plane!*" My voice started rising to a crescendo, much to the embarrassment of Greg and Co. Syd, smashed as he was, managed to look sheepish, but, unable to answer me, he picked up his Smirnoff and downed it in a gulp.

"Fuck you, Sydney," I screamed. "Fuck you. Fuck you. Fuck you. Fuck you!"

The select members of the Racquet Club looked aghast at such foul language coming from the lips of such a dainty English girl. Sydney turned slowly on his barstool to face me and staggered to his feet.

"And fuck you too," he blurted out before keeling over, and was only saved from hitting the linoleum by his friend John.

"Well, that," I enunciated clearly in my best Royal Academy of Dramatic Art diction, "will be the last time you will *ever* fuck me again, Sydney." And it was.

Arthur Loew and I fell in love—or did we fall in "like"? It seems to me that in the halcyon days of youth, saying "I love you" was akin to saying "Pass the salt." The feelings I had had for Syd for nearly a year were transferred to Arthur.

I am a strong advocate of monogamy—sequentially, that is. I think it is very hard to stay madly in love for any length of time, be it three months, three years or fifteen years. Eventually a time will come when the thrill is gone; and if there is not something infinitely stronger than romantic sexual attraction, the relationship will flounder. Only a true basis of compatibility can surmount the vagaries of a fickle heart.

With Arthur's encouragement I threw myself into thrice-weekly analysis to try and find out what and who I was. At the same time I was trying to fulfill myself as an actress and was caught up in the merry-go-round of being made into a "star." I started to hate the word "star." It denoted being untouchable. Stars are perfect. They are revered and worshipped. They must always look and act and dress as if they are not mortal. Watching the careers of Elizabeth Taylor and Brigitte Bardot, I have felt pity and sympathy for women who cannot even go to the corner drugstore without causing a riot, whose every move is tabloid fodder. Who can live a normal life with the harness of stardom around her neck? To have the constant pressure of having to live up to the box-office returns of your last picture? To have every line and wrinkle in your face eagerly awaited by avid gossip columnists? To be surrounded by yes-men and pressures that a "civilian" would find hard to understand is unhealthy and poisonous to the mind and spirit.

It takes a very strong character indeed to become a star, remain a star, and still be a real person. Paul Newman is one of the few people I know who is unaffected by his nearly thirty years of stardom. But there are dozens, believing in their invulnerability and their publicity, who have fallen from the grace of the public to become bitter, sad and pathetic people—seeking solace in drink, drugs or frantic sexual activity.

I realized in analysis that that was not my goal. Above the title—below the title—it wasn't important. I wanted to work, I wanted to *live*, and I wanted to enjoy my life and my work without obligations to a public whose fickleness stars lived in fear of.

I took a small apartment on Olive Drive off the Sunset Strip, conveniently located. It was close to Ciro's and the Mocambo nightclubs, our stomping grounds, and a stone's throw from Arthur Loew's house on Miller Drive. I worked practically every day and every Saturday morning on *Swing*, so there was no time to play. I was determined to give a good performance as Evelyn Nesbit, but I found that a great deal more emphasis than I wanted was being attached to my physical appearance. Granted, Evelyn was the original "Gibson Girl" and one of the great beauties from an age in which great beauties abounded, but I felt that the constant scrutiny of a corps of makeup men, hairdressers, costume designers, lighting directors, cameramen and even the director, Richard Fleischer, was beginning to inhibit me.

I was supposed to look exquisite in every frame of the film, which entailed being combed, sprayed, kiss-curled, powdered and lip-glossed before and after every single take. If I moved too violently and a stray lock fell out of place I would hear "Cut" and the wrecking crew would leap to my person. If my smile became too broad, there would be the dreaded word again: "Cut. Joanie, baby, don't smile so wide, you're showing your gums," or "The light's reflecting off her teeth." "Joanie, a little less *grin*, sweetheart—you look like you're catching flies with that smirk." If I did not hit my mark *exactly*, the key light would be a millimeter off, meaning my face would not be perfectly lit. "Cut. Let's go again." I was frightened to breathe too hard in case they complained about my chest moving too much.

Added to this were the costumes, which, although breathtakingly gorgeous to look at, were agony to wear. I wore an authentic corset that laced my waist into the fashionable hour-glass figure of the 1900s. On top of this went several lace petticoats with millions of ruffles, a camisole and then one of the twenty-seven gowns, all of which had more tiny bones in them than a sardine. The collars had little bones or stays in them so that if I moved my head at too much of an angle I would get stabbed in the throat. On my head sat an enormous black wig, beautiful but heavy, secured with ninety hairpins and stuck to my forehead and the side of my face with glue. Sometimes on top of this hair would rest a gigantic hat covered with peacock or ostrich feathers, or an abundance of flowers on trailing ribbons, and the hat was secured to the wig with several lethal hatpins. To dress and arrange the wig alone took an hour and a half each morning—and then another forty-five minutes for makeup and body makeup, which was applied to every inch of skin the camera might possibly glimpse. Add to this the extremely hot lights, and the presence of the *real* Evelyn Nesbit Thaw on the set, watching me like a hawk, and I was understandably a nervous wreck.

Mrs. Thaw was a lady in her seventies, and any vestige of the great beauty she had once possessed was long gone, except for her luxuriant gray hair. I scrutinized her features to find some residue of her looks but to no avail. She was fond of the gin bottle and ate violet-scented cashews to disguise the smell. They didn't. Closer than a foot from her face, and I became dizzy from the fumes.

She constantly told me how much I reminded her of herself when she was a young girl and the toast of New York. She showed me fabulous paintings and photographs of herself from that era. I found this extremely depressing. To have been one of the world's great beauties and to end one's days a penniless, garrulous old woman was a horrible twist of fate.

To be born physically perfect is akin to being born rich and then to gradually become poorer with age. I felt thankful that I did not think myself particularly beautiful, and would, perhaps, with maturity, be able to develop the inner me rather than the exterior which was currently being so overemphasized.

On days when I was not on call I threw on old jeans and a shirt, left off the makeup completely, and, in fact, barely bothered to brush my hair, and I wandered around the supermarkets, the five-and-tens and the drugstores—places I loved. England had been so austere; America was like a great candy store. The studio was not thrilled to see their rising glamour girl looking like a fugitive from Bucks County, and the awesome Hedda Hopper severely censured me in print for "looking like she combs her hair with an eggbeater." Dick Fleischer, coming across me lolling with a group of girlfriends in the commissary one day in blue jeans and makeupless, threw up his hands in mock horror, exclaiming, "My God, I didn't recognize you. You look so ugly!" This caused me in my oversensitive state to cry. I seemed to be going from the sublime to the ridiculous. I achieved the dubious reputation of being a rebel, a swinger and a noncomformist in the days before it was fashionable to be so. I couldn't get it together to look chic and smart when I wasn't working—I just wanted to be me.

Anyone whose mode of dress was in any way unkempt was considered bohemian and a bit strange. Marlon Brando and James Dean were the foremost exponents of the new antiestablishment attitude. Both were greatly admired on the one hand, but on the other they contended with much disapproval.

Jimmy Dean was a fascinating young man who had become a giant star with his first movie, *East of Eden*. He played to perfection the brooding troubled boy in competition with his more favored brother, and questing for the truth about his relationship with his mother. The young people of the fifties immediately adopted him as their symbol, and his star ascended rapidly. He made *Rebel Without a Cause*, which was written by Arthur's cousin, Stewart Stern, and immediately after that was completed, starred in the mammoth production of *Giant*.

It was during the filming of *Giant* that I first met him. It was a brief meeting at a small dinner party in the Valley. I was particularly mesmerized by his eyes, which were a deep, piercing blue and could change instantly from a look of sullen brooding to an expression of extreme mischievousness. He was quite short for a film actor and had longish, blond wavy hair. He seemed terribly shy and clutched the hand of his girlfriend, a gorgeous Swiss starlet under contract to Paramount called Ursula Andress. She had a fabulous body and the shortest haircut I had ever seen. They made a striking couple, both wearing white T-shirts and Levi's.

We often saw him at the home of Oscar Levant. On one occasion Oscar remarked after viewing me in a rather low-cut blouse (I was still wearing those bangs that almost covered my eyes), "I have now seen every part of Joan's anatomy except her forehead!"

James Dean and Oscar Levant, although total opposites, got along famously. Each relished the other's unusualness. Arthur and I would drop by the Levants' after dinner and sit until the early hours talking and laughing with them.

A group of us had dinner one night at Don the Beachcomber's, a Polynesian restaurant in Hollywood noted for its incredibly strong rum-based drinks. After three or four Navy Grogs I was feeling daring, so when Jimmy asked who would like a drive in his brand-new silver Porsche I cheerfully volunteered. Arthur, who usually indulged most of my whims with good grace, pulled me aside and told me not to drive with Jimmy. "He drives like a maniac," he said earnestly. "And after four of those Zombies, or whatever the hell it was we've been drinking, it's too dangerous."

"Oh don't be such a stick-in-the-mud," I giggled. "Come on, Jimmy. Let's race them to Oscar's house." We jumped into his shiny new Porsche. The interior was cramped and it smelled of new leather, but it was indeed a beauty. Jimmy threw the shift into first gear and with the gearbox protesting violently we screeched into the Hollywood Boulevard traffic. During the ten minutes it took us to get to Beverly Hills, I sobered up rapidly. He certainly did drive fast, even recklessly, but with the summer wind blowing through the open windows and the radio blaring, it was exhilarating.

"Don't you think we should slow down?" I said nervously, as we sped down the Strip at about seventy miles an hour, dodging in and out of the after-dinner traffic. He gave me one of his mischievous, brooding looks. "Chicken?" he asked. "What, me? Oh, no. I'd just like to live to be twenty-one." I gulped nervously, hoping a cop car would miraculously appear. "The thing about these cars is that they're fail-safe," he said, expertly overtaking a bleached blonde in a Cadillac and sliding in just a car's length behind a slow-moving Ford. "These cars are made like tanks. They have the best engine and the best transmission, they're totally safe."

He talked on about the merits of his baby until we screeched to a stop in front of the Levants'. "Well, thanks a lot, Jimmy," I said descending on trembling legs. "If I ever need a quick ride to the airport, I'll call on you."

"Do that." He lit up a cigarette and smiled at me sleepily, amused by my timorousness. "Let's go see Oscar." I followed him into the house, making a mental note never to get in a moving vehicle with him again. When Arthur arrived fifteen minutes later, I told him he was right about Jimmy's driving. "He's going to kill himself one of these days if he continues to drive like that!" he said.

A couple of months later I was in New York at the Plaza Hotel for promotions on *Virgin Queen*. The doorbell rang insistently and woke me up. It was only eight o'clock, and I grumpily trundled to the door. "It's me, Arthur," said a strained voice. I opened up. Ashen-faced, he handed me *The New York Times* and then sat down heavily on the sofa. I read unbelievingly: "James Dean dies in automobile accident." He was killed in the silver Porsche. He was twenty-four.

✳   ✳   ✳

One Friday night Arthur and I walked into Chasen's, one of my favorite restaurants. No work tomorrow, so I could go on a two-day eating binge. I was looking forward to having the hashed-in-cream potatoes Chasen's is renowned for. Maybe even a soufflé for dessert. A headline caught my eye on the front page of the *Los Angeles Times,* stacked neatly on the steps outside the restaurant: "Actor sues actress for $1,250 support per month," screamed the banner.

"Oh, darling, buy the paper. I wonder who it is?" I chirped.

We sat in our booth and I scanned the paper. My face stared out at me smiling broadly from column two.

"Oh, my God!" I howled, to the surprise of the headwaiter, who was smiling and taking our order for drinks. He raised his eyebrows fractionally, ignoring the outburst.

"Christ, that rotten bastard has gone and sued me. What am I going to *do?*"

Arthur grabbed the paper and read the article out loud. "Actor Maxwell Reed announced from London today that he was suing his wife, actress Joan Collins, for $1,250 per month. 'I know this is unusual,' said Reed, 'but I have not worked in over a year and am practically destitute. My wife has been in Hollywood for the past nine months. She is making a lot of money and I think she owes me something.' "

We looked at each other. He smiled and patted my hand.

"Poor baby," he said playfully. "Didn't your mummy tell you that all men are rotten?" When things got rough, Arthur joked, but I was not in the mood for jokes. Being sued for alimony is a fairly common occurrence for men—but I had never heard of a woman being sued before.

My parents had been sending me various stories that had been appearing in the English press about Max. They were all based on the same sniveling premise: "I found her. I made her a success. I loved her. She left me—to go to Hollywood. Now I can't get a job."

One particularly revolting story featured a picture of Max trying to look humble in a forty-five-dollar cashmere sweater and heavily mascaraed eyebrows, clutching a large photo of me to his breast and complaining about his love for me and his poverty—and he wondered why no one would employ him! It was nauseating, but I was so busy, I had no time to think of divorce plans. Again, like Scarlett O'Hara, I decided to "think about that tomorrow."

Nothing, however, could put me off food, and we ate heartily while discussing strategy. At the end of the evening my face felt very hot, and hivelike bumps had broken out over my back and shoulders. Peculiar, I thought, probably nerves—and dismissed it from my mind.

I started shooting what I consider to be my first "grown-up" role. In other films I had played girls—wayward, spoiled, delinquent or sexy. Nevertheless they were juvenile-type parts. But the part of Crystal in *The Opposite Sex,* a remake of *The Women,* was definitely not a girl. She was all woman—and all bitch. Sexy, conniving and shrewd, she was the embryo Alexis.

The Women had been a big success in the 1930s, with Joan Crawford as Crystal. The cast had included Norma Shearer, Paulette Goddard, Joan Fontaine and Rosalind Russell.

MGM, who had borrowed me from Fox for this part, was gathering an equally prestigious cast for the latest version: June Allyson, the darling of the Metro lot; Ann Sheridan, the ex-"Oomph Girl"; Ann Miller; Dolores Gray; Carolyn Jones; and many others were cast in this updated version of ladies in the jungle warfare of sex, men, husband-snatching, gossip, back-biting and bitchery. Crystal is the biggest bitch of them all—and loves it. She is a showgirl who has an affair with June Allyson's husband and flaunts it to the world.

Although the part was not that large, it was flashy and juicy, and I had some good scenes. June confronts me in my dressing room and accuses me of the affair. I nonchalantly continue with removing my brief stage costume and changing into street clothes while she addresses me and progressively becomes more angry. June was a tiny lady, about five feet two in heels. She was famous for her cute blond bob and her Peter Pan collars. She was petite, delicate and ladylike, so I was not concerned about the fact that she had to slap my face after the following dialogue:

JUNE: "By the way, if you're dressing for Steven, I wouldn't wear that. He doesn't like anything quite so obvious."

CRYSTAL: "When Steven doesn't like what I wear I take it off!" . . . And June hauled off and belted me. This little lady with her tiny hands had a punch like Muhammad Ali! I felt as if a steamroller had hit me. Something fell from my face and hit the floor with a loud clatter—my teeth? Oh, God, no. Please don't let her have knocked out my *teeth!* My head was ringing, as the slap had connected with my ears. and I couldn't hear a thing. Stars danced before my eyes and I staggered to a chair and collapsed.

"Cut—cut, for Christ's sake, cut!" screamed director David Miller.

"What the *hell's* going on here?" June burst into tears and collapsed into another chair. Makeup men and dressers rushed to the set with smelling salts and succor.

I put my hands tentatively to my mouth. Thank God, a full set of teeth still, but what flew off me? The wardrobe lady solved the mystery, retrieving the long rhinestone earrings which the force of June's slap had sent spinning. But any more shooting was out of the question. On each of my cheeks was forming the perfect imprint of a tiny hand! Branded, if not for life, for the two or three days it took for the welts to go down. June was desperately sorry, and it took longer to calm her down than it did me. Luckily, when they saw the scene on rushes it was unnecessary to reshoot the slap—it had complete authenticity!

The first day of shooting of *The Opposite Sex* at MGM I sat in the large airy makeup-and-hairdressing room and observed wide-eyed the gossipy bustling scene. Sydney Guilaroff, Metro's reigning hairdresser, was in the process of cutting a shoulder-length wig for me. This necessitated a "test" after each trim to get the right chic-yet-sexy look for Crystal. From a long wig, throughout seven or eight haircuts, Sydney finally ended up with giving me a sleek bob.

Sitting in the makeup chair next to me was June Allyson, having a minimal amount of makeup applied to her retroussé nose and pert features. Next to June sat Elizabeth Taylor. Gorgeous and exotic. She was excitedly showing everyone photos of her children.

The biggest star of the Metro lot sat quietly on the side waiting her turn for the makeup man's magic. Grace Kelly. Exquisite. Breeding and class emanating from her aristocratic face and bearing. She was then twenty-six years old—the Princess of Hollywood. Having made several extremely successful films, she was—oh, foolish girl, thought I—giving it all up for the love of handsome Prince Rainier, monarch of Monaco.

This fairytale wedding, which had captured the imagination of the world, was now imminent. Grace sat quietly in plain gray slacks and nondescript blouse going over lists with her secretary, oblivious to the makeup and hair people who bustled around her. She was truly serene even then, and one of the most ravishing women I had ever seen.

I had a number of physical problems on *The Opposite Sex*. A long bathtub scene entailed Crystal's sitting in an ornate marble bathtub, covered with bubbles, talking on the telephone to her boyfriend, and having a conversation with Dolores Gray and a little girl. David Miller believed in endless rehearsals, and we rehearsed for two days, with me immersed in real bubbles. Since bubbles do not last very long, the prop men had to keep adding to the water a mixture of dishwashing detergent and Lux soap flakes.

At the end of the first day my nether regions were pink and puffy. At the end of the second day they were sore and swollen. On the third day, when we finally started to shoot, I was a mass of tender raw flesh. It was agony to sit down, and when the detergent-filled water touched my body, I felt like Joan of Arc burning at the stake. The misery on my face was evident. Something had to be done. The studio doctor was called to give me pain-killing injections, and the prop department evolved an ingenious contraption to prevent my delicate blistered body from touching the water. To the onlooker viewing the scene, here was a glamorous creature chatting cattily on the phone, luscious bubbles caressing her body. Underneath the bubbles, however, was a sheet of strong plywood with a hole cut in to fit my body, and the bubbles were on top of the plywood. Underneath the plywood I was encased in Vaseline and bandages, and on top of this an attractive pair of men's long johns from the gentlemen's wardrobe department. Over this was a large rubber sheet in case any sneaky bubbles managed to slither through the armor. I sat on several cushions, and all in all was feeling no pain and relishing the comparative comfort of these appliances.

Then a young man burst onto the set in the middle of a scene.

"Joan Collins?" he asked accusingly.

"Er, yes—er, maybe," I said nervously, signaling to the assistant director to remove this madman before he did me some injury.

"Cut—cut," yelled David. "What the hell's going on around here? Who is this jerk?"

"Sign here, please," said the jerk, handing me a summons from my ever-dependable husband, Maxwell Reed. I read it unbelievingly while three assistant directors gave the smirking, successful process server the bum's rush.

Maxwell Reed was taking me to court and insisting that I pay him the $1,250 a month he had demanded for support. It was an injunction from a Los Angeles Court judge. I had to do something. And fast.

Fred Leopold was an attorney who specialized in divorce cases. (He later became Mayor of Beverly Hills.) He advised me to pay up. I had a seven-year contract starting at $1,250 a week for the first year and escalating to $5,000 for the seventh year. He told me that if I did not make a deal with Max now, he could wait two or three years and get even more money from me in the future.

I was furious. His allegation that he had "discovered" me and sent me to Hollywood was totally false. I thought I had escaped his vindictiveness but I still sometimes awoke in the middle of the night with the terrifying nightmare again: "One day you'll think you're safe, baby. But one night you'll walk around a dark corner and one of the 'boys' will come and carve that pretty little face of yours up until no one will ever want to look at you again."

I woke in a cold sweat. It was chilling and not beyond the realm of possibility that he would do this ghastly thing to me. God knows he knew enough petty criminal types around London. And now he had come here, to Los Angeles. To try to find work—and to get money from me.

For safety I moved into Arthur's house on Miller Drive. Fred Leopold advised me strongly against it, but I was scared, and I needed someone to be there when I woke up with nightmares.

The divorce cost me over $10,000—an utter fortune for me. I had to get an advance in salary from Fox, for I did not have that kind of money even though I did not live lavishly. Leopold had persuaded Max to accept a lump sum of $4,250, after convincing him and his lawyers that I was not as wealthy as they expected. I also gave him all the money in our joint bank account in London—about $1,400—and I had over $4,000 in legal fees to pay—his and mine. The judge in Los Angeles Superior Court seemed surprised at this settlement and cross-examined me on the stand for ten minutes as to why I was paying this supposedly healthy, reasonably young man such a grand sum. I prayed that the divorce would be granted and that I would be finished with Maxwell Reed forever. The judge, reluctantly, it seemed, granted it. I walked out of the courtroom a free woman—older, wiser, poorer, and with a growing distrust of and hostility toward men.

My mother's words were always in the back of my mind. "Men only want one thing. Men will use a girl, then toss her away when they are tired of her."

Although part of me realized that this was ridiculous, another part of me said, "She's right. Mummy is *right*. Look at how my father treated her. Look at how Max abused you. Sydney didn't really care for you—what about *him?*"

I looked at Arthur, sprawled out on the comfortable sofa of his ranch-style house high in the Hollywood Hills. He was just like the others. He had me. I lived with him. I bought all my own clothes (although he had given me a few pieces of jewelry). I paid for my airfare when I went to London. I was young, beautiful, desirable, successful. Why should he have all of this for nothing? He was young, rich and good-looking, tall, blond, thin, with an aquiline nose—and a terrific sense of humor. I liked him. We had fun together. I wasn't "in love," because ours was not a passionate relationship, but I felt great affection for him.

He had recently finished producing a film starring Paul Newman called *The Rack.* Newman was talking to Arthur now. The two of them lolled on the sofa drinking beer and telling jokes like schoolboys. The house was full of friends, as it was most nights. Arthur ran an open house and there were always eight or ten people for dinner. I was leaving for London in a week to start another film. The gossip columnists had even started hinting that we were on the verge of matrimony.

After all the guests departed, I broached the subject.

"Do you think we ought to date other people while I'm gone?" I said, casually pouring two cognacs into large snifters and handing him one. He looked at me quizzically. "Whom do you have in mind, Richard Burton?" Burton was to be my co-star in *Seawife.*

"Burton's married," I said briskly. "No, I mean three months is a long time to be apart."

"But I'm going to visit you in Jamaica," he interrupted.

"I know that," I said. "How do you feel about me going out with other men, then?"

"I'd rather you didn't," he said flatly, drinking the cognac and preparing to end the conversation.

"Well, then what are you going to do about it, Arthur? If you don't want me to date other guys?"

"I just don't know if I can be faithful to you for that length of time." The words tumbled unselfconsciously from his lips.

I looked at him with growing consternation. "You mean you want to fuck around?"

"Spoken like the Queen of England," he said dryly. "No, my dear, I don't *want* to fuck around, as you so beautifully put it, but if, in the twelve weeks of our separation, a lady should appear who should—how shall I say—arouse my libido, I might, just might, find the temptation alluring enough to—well, yes, fuck around." He drained his glass and looked at me, his boyish face challenging. "It doesn't mean I don't love you, baby."

"Yeah, what's a fuck between friends," I said sarcastically, pulling my fingers away from his. "Don't you have any *control?*"

"I'll tell you what." He pulled my rigid body toward him and put his arms around my shoulders. "Let's play it by ear. If we can be faithful to each other during the time you're away, then I think we should get engaged when you come back." I moved my face quickly so that his lips connected with my ear.

"OK." I jumped up and ground my cigarette out violently. "That's a terrific idea, Arthur. You try to be faithful to me, and I—" I looked him straight in the eye—"I will *try* to be faithful to you. And now I'm going to bed."

I walked upstairs, seething with rage. How dare he put me on trial. *Men.* Who did he think he *was?* Another phrase of my father's flitted through my thoughts: "Why buy the cake when you can have a slice for free?"

I felt angry. I hurt and I wanted him to hurt too.

Fox was about to film *Seawife,* from a best-selling novel, *Sea Wyf and Biscuit,* about a nun wrecked on a desert island with three men. I had already made *Our Girl Friday,* which also had a girl stuck on an island with three men, but for me to play a nun was not only the biggest acting challenge I had yet faced but also to many people one of the worst pieces of miscasting since Lana Turner played a vestal virgin.

Roberto Rossellini, the volatile and talented Italian film director, famous not only for having directed the touching *Open City,* but also for his volcanic affair and subsequent marriage to Ingrid Bergman, had chosen me as his "face of innocence," after seeing one reel of *The Girl in the Red Velvet Swing.* He obviously realized that, behind the wigs, costumes and plastic facade I presented in that film, there was a naïve and vulnerable young girl. Rossellini was a stubborn, opinionated genius who had total autonomy over all his productions. This was to be his first American film and he was determined to do it his way.

Fox was agreeable to practically all his demands except for one thing. They absolutely would not allow Richard Burton, who played "Biscuit," to kiss "Seawife," the nun. Rossellini thought this was an essential part of the story and was insistent on the love scene.

Although Fox, around the same time, was making another nun film with sexual overtones, *Heaven Knows Mr. Allison,* starring Deborah Kerr and Robert Mitchum, nonetheless they were strongly opposed to there being any hint of sex between Burton and me on the screen. For one thing, they would never get a seal of approval from the censor, and for another, every Catholic women's group in America would be up in arms, probably boycotting *all* their movies. So they were understandably worried about Signor Rossellini's preoccupation with the kissing scene.

That was the least of my worries as I arrived in London to face a barrage of press people splitting their sides with laughter at the thought of "Britain's Bad Girl" playing a nun.

"Sister Sizzle," giggled Donald Zee in the *Daily Mirror.*

"Is *this* the face of innocence?" jeered the *Daily Express,* under a two-column picture of me with a ruby in my navel and a come-hither look in my eye. All the old labels were pulled out: "Torrid Baggage"; "Coffee Bar Jezebel"; and the press had a field day with this excruciatingly funny piece of show-biz news. The more I tried to be serious and mature in the countless interviews I gave, the more the press sent me up. It was infuriating because I really did believe that I was good casting for *Seawife*. Without makeup and with my hair cropped short and unstyled, I did have a trusting, innocent look, and I resented the attitude that the newspapers were taking toward me.

Before I left California, Arthur had christened the movie "I Fucked a Nun!"

I spent the two weeks of preproduction in London reading every book on Catholicism I could. I visited a group of nuns in a small convent in Chelsea. I spent many hours talking with them, observing their attitudes, manners and bearing. They were a delightful group of women and girls, with a wonderful inner glow and beauty that emanated from them. Some even had a wicked and wild sense of humor, and many of my preconceived notions of nuns as "holier-than-thou goody-goodies" were shattered. They were real, warm, vibrant human beings who were happier and more at peace with themselves than many of the people I knew. I went to Catholic church and immersed myself in the peace and energy that seemed to glow there.

We made the usual makeup and costume tests. With my scrubbed face, short no-style hair and nun's habit, it looked very much as if Rossellini's intuition had been right and I did have the "face of innocence."

Meanwhile, there were two scripts to study: one, the Fox-approved script, without any intimations of sex and love between Biscuit and Seawife, and the other, Rossellini's infinitely more interesting story of a young novice nun, who had not yet taken her final vows, finding her emotions deeply disturbed by an extended period of time on a deserted island with an attractive and compassionate man. And in the latter script the two do indeed have a "romantic involvement" which would necessitate some torrid love scenes.

Rossellini had left for location scouting in Jamaica after our initial brief meeting and film test in London. There he remained with script number two, which he was now adamant was the only one he would shoot.

When the cast and crew arrived in Jamaica, we found that Signor Rossellini was incommunicado in his suite at the Jamaica Inn. We unpacked and waited for the first day's shooting to commence. We had been hearing rumbles of major rows going on between Fox brass back in L.A. and Rossellini. The assistant directors kept on saying we would be shooting tomorrow or the day after, but days went by with nothing happening. Everyone sat around swimming, drinking rum punches, playing poker and gossiping about each new event. We were having a relaxing holiday in the sun, all expenses paid by Fox.

Four days later a call sheet was pushed under the door of my suite: "Title of Production 'Seawife'—1st Day's Shooting—Exterior Shipwreck —Director, Bob McNaught."

"Bob McNaught! Who the hell is he?"

I rushed next door to the Burtons' suite to find out what was going on. Richard was sitting with his pretty Welsh wife, Sybil, drinking tea and playing Scrabble. He seemed not at all perturbed by my agitation and confirmed what I and the rest of the crew had feared. Fox would not back down on their watered-down script and Rossellini would not back down on his torrid version. It was a total impasse. Rossellini was fired, and instead of spending the time and money to import another director from London or America, Fox was putting the director's reins in the hands of Bob McNaught, who was listed on the unit list as "Production Manager."

A production manager was going to direct *Seawife!* I was horrified. I had been looking forward to being directed in this role by the fabulous, talented Rossellini, whose ability to get magnificent performances from his cast and to bring magic to the screen was legendary. What a bummer! What chance did I stand now of giving a good performance. Although I was fairly confident of my ability to play the role, I knew that I needed the extra impetus that only a really good director can give to an actor to make my performance come believably alive—particularly because I knew so many people were waiting for me to fall flat on my face. And what of Bob McNaught? The poor man would have so many problems with just the mechanics and technicalities of everyday filming, I felt sure there would be little time to give me the support and help I needed.

Bob turned out to be a nice, stolid, middle-aged Englishman, eminently more suited to dealing with the mill on and one major and minor details of managing a production than directing one.

The picture thus became just another run-of-the-mill program filler. Burton didn't give a damn. This was the last of his multiple picture deals with Fox, and he didn't particularly like the script or his role. He had a "take the money and run" attitude toward it, which I found depressing. Already a millionaire, he had cleverly set up all sorts of tax havens and was one of the very first actors to take up residence in Switzerland. Although a successful film actor, his true love was still the theater, and he was longing to get back to New York, where he was about to do a play.

Burton was then about thirty-three years old, with thick, light-brown hair, intense, strong features and eyes of a piercingly hypnotic greenish-blue. His voice was magnificent—deep, resonant—a voice made to declaim *Hamlet* and indeed all of Shakespeare's plays. His skin left a lot to be desired, however. Due to years of working in the coal mines of Wales, his back and shoulders were deeply pitted and rutted with pimples, blackheads and what looked like small craters.

I had admired him for years, and as a schoolgirl had stood outside the Queen's Theatre on Shaftesbury Avenue to get his autograph after seeing his performance in Jean Anouilh's *Ring Around the Moon*. I had watched him, mesmerized by his voice and talent, from high up in the "Gods," and thought him so handsome and talented that I wrote off for an autographed photo, which duly arrived personally signed: "Thank you for your letter. Best wishes, Richard Burton." This treasured memento went into my autograph book along with other trusty favorites. And now, here I was acting opposite this paragon of theatrical proficiency.

His reputation as a lady's man had also preceded him. Although married, rumors of his affairs were discussed knowingly and openly, and he lost no time in making known his intentions toward me. A few days after filming had commenced, we took a swim together during the lunch hour to a small diving raft a few hundred yards from shore. I wore a bikini and presented a wholesome and well-scrubbed look. I lay on my back on the raft, eyes closed, and feeling the hot Jamaican sun absorbing the salt water from my skin. I was feeling happy. I was enjoying the film, and Bob McNaught was OK. Not an innovative director, but not too bad either. The crew was fun, mostly English, and I had been spending a lot of time with them playing poker and giggling at their typically English humor. Arthur had written me several letters, professing undying adoration and "fidelity," and missing me madly, and I was in the sun all the time. I was an avid sun worshipper and I was working on my tan when I felt fingers stroking my wet hair.

"Did anyone ever tell you you look pretty with short hair?" he said, casually moving his hand to my neck.

"Yes," I said, firmly removing the roving hand and squinting up at the greenish eyes, now a foot from mine. "Mr. Rossellini thought I looked adorable with short hair. And so does Arthur, my *boyfriend.*" That should stop him.

"Ah, yes, of course, you go out with the heir to the Loew millions, don't you?" he said, amused and not at all deterred by my evasive tactics.

"Yes. He's very *jealous.* Gets homicidal if he thinks anyone is messing around with his property." I peeked through my wet lashes to see if he had taken the implication.

"My dear, what the eye does not see the heart does not grieve for," he breathed in his most Shakespearean tones and pressed his salty lips to my firmly closed ones. I gritted my teeth and let him kiss me. There is nothing more off-putting to a man than to kiss a girl who won't respond.

"Why don't you relax?" he whispered, his hand fiddling with the ties on my bikini top. "None of the crew can see us."

"I am relaxed," I said gaily. "Relaxed and lying in the sun and thinking about *Arthur!*"

He laughed and lay back on the raft. He was quite attractive . . . if you ignored the spots. But Mrs. Burton was languishing in her suite at the hotel, and I was not interested in an involvement with a married Don Juan.

He looked at me and we both smiled.

"I'll get you yet, Miss Collins," he said lightly, then cleverly realizing that now was not the time, proceeded to tell me in detail about his seductions and conquests of all the actresses he had worked with on stage and screen.

"How fascinating," I breathed during this lengthy saga of lust and intrigue on sets and in dressing rooms and elegant boudoirs. "They *always* succumbed to you finally?"

"Always," he said triumphantly. "Even if—" looking meaningful— "they were not receptive at the outset."

"Well, it should be interesting to see what happens now," I said, noticing that the third assistant was signaling to us frantically from the beach.

"You have eight more weeks on location with me, but I never have liked being part of a collection."

I dived into the warm Caribbean ocean and swam rapidly back to where the crew were assembling for the next setup. He followed, joking and talking, until we got to shore. It was amusing. The great Richard Burton, not only a womanizer but a scalp collector to boot! It would give me the greatest pleasure to *not* be another one on his belt.

He soon found other ladies to console himself with. Some were reasonably attractive and some were, to put it bluntly, dogs! I glimpsed an almost toothless and middle-aged Jamaican maid leaving his quarters early one morning with a satisfied gleam in her eye. When I questioned him about her later in the day he freely admitted he had dallied with her. We were lying side by side on our stomachs in the warm sand waiting for the crew to set up.

"Richard, I do believe you would screw a snake if you had the chance." I laughed unbelievingly.

"Only if it was wearing a skirt, darling," he countered smoothly. "It would have to be a female snake."

I still wrote to Arthur and he to me. According to his letters he was a paragon of fidelity and spent all his evenings either watching TV or going to dinner with his friends Stewart Stern, Paul Newman or George Englund. I didn't believe him; I felt it unlikely that he would write and tell me of his affairs if he was having them.

He arrived in a blaze of hilarity and jokes the last week of shooting in Jamaica. The first night we had dinner with a group from the film, and Arthur was so wildly funny and entertaining that he had everyone, including me, in stitches the whole time. During the week he visited we spent very little time alone and had no time to talk about anything.

"Where's Joan?" said Bob McNaught one day.

"She's laying Loew," said the unit wit, and everyone collapsed with laughter.

We were coming to the culmination of the film, which necessitated some difficult and emotional scenes for me. I was involved in my role and concentrating on it. The weather turned rainy and everyone was getting edgy. They wanted to finish the picture and get the hell off this island and back to England. Eight weeks is a long time to be away from home, and the first halcyon weeks of the location had worn off for the crew and the actors. They wanted their fish and chips for lunch and their *Daily Mirror*, their football on the "telly" and their warm beer in the pubs. Bored already with the rum punches and the rice and jumbo shrimp— Englishmen need England—anxious faces scanned the sky each morning for the dreaded drops of rain that might delay our departure for the homeland.

At last we finished, and I bade a tearful goodbye to Arthur. I was going to London for several more weeks of shooting and post-production, and he to Los Angeles. I was genuinely miserable on the plane to London. I cared about him, even if it was not a passionate and exciting romance. We had not communicated any of our private thoughts and feelings during the week we had been together. No deep communication at all. It was just one big laugh all the time, and I felt sad for us.

It was summertime, but England was predictably cold, wet and rainy. I happily moved in again to the back bedroom at Harley House, luxuriating in my mother's attention. On the days when I wasn't shooting she brought me scrambled eggs and tea in bed in the morning and we would sit and gossip. We became closer than we had at any time that I could remember during my childhood. I felt like a child again in those familiar surroundings. Although Jackie had taken my room when I went to Hollywood, my mother had put back many of my possessions, since Jackie was now in Los Angeles, living in my apartment.

All my old scrapbooks of movie stars were still on the bookshelves. I spent hours looking at all the magazine pictures I had painstakingly pasted in so long ago. What was ironic was that so many of the stars I had admired I had now either worked with or had met socially. There was Maxwell Reed, lids lowered, cigarette in hand, glowering sexily. I shuddered and quickly turned the page. There was Richard Burton, young and innocent, in *The Last Days of Dolwyn,* his first film—not so young and innocent now, I thought. There was chirpy cockney schoolboy Anthony Newley (whom I would marry a few years later) in *Oliver Twist* and *Vice Versa* and *The Huggets.* And there were others I had finally met: Elizabeth Taylor, Gene Kelly, Humphrey Bogart, Montgomery Clift—all staring and smiling from my make-believe paper world. It seemed long ago and yet it was only a few short years.

Arthur had written me:

"I wish I were able to tell you and show you how much I really love you but somehow when we are together I have great trouble in letting my hair down and seem to be flip all the time rather than warm. It seems during my stay in Jamaica that my main task was to entertain the crew rather than be close to you. Anyway, from now on I am really going to try and *force* myself to show you how I feel toward you . . ."

I felt sorry that he was unable to show his love for me and sadness that *I* was stupid enough to choose to love a man who had to *force* himself to show his feelings. We were now shooting *Seawife* at Elstree in the huge water-filled tank that was on stage, filming the shipwreck scenes and the night scenes on the raft. It was miserably cold and uncomfortable, but every evening after work I would adjourn with the crew to the pub across the road, drink gin and tonic and eat sausage rolls. It was convivial, and I enjoyed everyone's company and humor a lot. I found myself wanting more and more to stay home at night with my parents. Although Jackie was in Hollywood, my eleven-year-old brother, Bill, was home, and I suddenly found I really liked family life.

Because I was now a sophisticated divorcee, a well-known actress, and over twenty-one, my father was far more lenient with me, and I was free to come and go as I pleased. For the first time in my life, I had no one to answer to. No more "Where have you been?" "Who with?" "What time will you be home?"

I had my own space—I could think and breathe freely. My parents were so glad to have me back that I could have stayed out all night and they wouldn't have cared.

I borrowed a friend's flat in Eaton Terrace and stayed there sometimes alone, reading, studying my script and thinking about my life. I didn't fancy this life of a "star" much—and I didn't want to marry Arthur either. My one taste of marriage had been such a disaster. I decided to take each day as it came—let the chips fall where they may. The one thing I really loved more than anything else was working; *that* I needed, and after *Seawife* I wanted to do better scripts and get better roles. Men I could live without right now.

I had a few weeks off after *Seawife* and then had to leave again for the West Indies to shoot *Island in the Sun.* Arthur wasn't thrilled with the fact that I was going on location again after nearly three months of being apart. But I had no choice. I was under contract to Fox and they had the right to do with me as they wished for forty weeks of the year.

Island in the Sun was based on a best-selling book by Alec Waugh, with a highly topical theme. Darryl Zanuck himself was going to produce it and had chosen an exciting cast for this story of tension between blacks and whites in the West Indies.

There were fourteen stars, among them James Mason, Joan Fontaine, Harry Belafonte, Dorothy Dandridge, Stephen Boyd and Michael Rennie. It promised to be a highly explosive and controversial film. It would be the first American film to show love scenes between blacks and whites. Already the censor was getting nervous.

I flew back to Los Angeles for a few weeks and picked up several awards for being "The Most Promising Actress," "The Face of the Year" or "Favorite Newcomer" from various exhibitors and magazines, all of which prompted me to comment, "I'm afraid I'll be a has-been before I finish being promising." Then it was back on the plane and off to Barbados in the British West Indies.

The main theme of *Island* was miscegenation. Several interwoven stories all concerned the racial issue, a hot and taboo subject in the late fifties. I played a girl who discovers that her grandmother was black, thus giving her "colored blood," the euphemism then for being one-quarter black. The subject—that of black and white people of both sexes becoming involved with one another and falling in love—was considered so shocking and outrageous that there was a tremendous outcry when Darryl Zanuck announced he was making the novel into a movie. Many states instantly announced that they would never allow it to be shown. Controversy raged; Mr. Zanuck and Robert Rossen were often closeted in their tiny hotel rooms trying to placate some of the more stringent censorship demands.

There was a great similarity between the locations of *Seawife* and *Island in the Sun*—the same tropical days and romantic nights. *Island in the Sun* is still talked about as being one of the most enjoyable locations ever among the British film units. It has become almost legendary. We had an enormous crew, including a second unit. Over one hundred technical men and women converged on the tiny island. Robert Rossen, the

American director, working again after years of being on McCarthy's blacklist, and most known for the award-winning *All the King's Men,* was a hard taskmaster and a tough man, but a complete professional, and he expected total support and obedience from his actors and crew. He was such a martinet that one day he called "Action!" while I was still behind a palm tree putting on my gloves. He chastised me strongly for not being ready when he was ready to shoot. This little confrontation has lived with me to this day and is one of the many reasons why I am always on time, know my lines, and am as disciplined professionally as I can be.

The producer, the cigar-chomping, diminutive Darryl Zanuck, had been instrumental in my coming to Fox. An immensely powerful force in motion pictures, his weak spot was women. Throughout the years he had had a series of affairs with some talented, and not so talented, actresses. His present mistress was absent from this location and he had recently cast his eyes in my direction. Giving new meaning to the word "predatory," he had grabbed me one afternoon in the corridor of the hotel, pressed me against the wall, cigar still firmly clamped between his fingers and tried to convince me of his endurance, prowess and endowments as one of the world's best lovers.

"You've had nothing until you've had me," he muttered, his breath reeking of cigar smoke, as he tried to press gray-moustached lips to mine. "I've got the biggest and the best. I can go all night and all day."

I tried to wriggle free. Though shorter than me, he was powerful in body as well as presence, and I was pinned like a beetle to a board. My struggles would not stop his torrent of lust.

"Why do you waste your time with these boys?" he croaked hoarsely as I skewered my face away from his. "These Arthur Loews and Nicky Hiltons don't know how to please you. You need a real man."

Oh, my God. He was actually giving me the oldest line in the business. I wondered how to get out of this without having to knee him in the groin. Luckily Dorothy Dandridge and a makeup man came walking down the corridor and I made my escape, vowing to keep out of Mr. Z's way in the future.

A tight schedule we were not on. Because of the position of the sun, we finished work by four o'clock every day. The rest of the time we did as we pleased. I always liked to play games, and an endless series of card and party games began: charades, Monopoly, Scrabble and, of course, poker—Gin and Liar's Poker Dice. It was an ongoing party. Each night ended with all of us taking a dip in the warm Caribbean after dozens of Planter's Punches and dancing till we dropped, to the music of exciting steel bands. Although we all boozed, none of us ever felt tired or hung over. Cast and crew alike operated at peak proficiency. The crew were like my brothers; I loved them all.

I had noticed Harry Belafonte immediately, of course, admired his stunning physical appearance. Cast and crew had gathered together at the hotel for a cocktail party during the first week of filming. We would all get to know each other, hopefully like each other, and probably form close attachments which would usually last for as long as the shooting of the movie. Actors are fickle folk. Although closeness develops fast when thrown together on location, it does not always linger longer than the final "Cut." D.C.O.L. "Doesn't count on location" was a well-known phrase.

I had been chatting with Joan Fontaine, whom I knew from *Decameron Nights,* and had observed him from afar. Tall, dark and handsome was an understatement. About six feet one, he had black close-cropped hair, and his skin was the color of caramels. His body was slim and muscular, clothed in tight ivory-colored pants and a bright red shirt open to the navel. He laughed a lot, I noticed, as he, James Mason and Dorothy Dandridge were involved in animated discussion—full, deep-throated laughter that seemed to come right from his gut as he threw back his head and guffawed lustily. The West Indian waiters, running about with trays of rum punches and platters of fried shrimp and other delicacies of the island, smiled every time they caught sight of him. To them, he was a local boy who had made good, and even though he was not from Barbados his songs were indigenous to all parts of the West Indies. He was a folk hero.

He caught my eyes, smiled, and wandered over to us.

"Hi!" he said, extending his hand with a lazy smile.

Joan Fontaine said a brisk hello and I stood slightly tongue-tied, unusual for me, while she and he discussed their roles in the movie.

I gazed at his warm brown eyes and aristocratic nose. He was indeed gorgeous—as women from coast to coast had been discovering for the past several years. In concert, nightclubs and records his fame was spreading rapidly. His sex appeal made women of all ages go weak at the knees, and I, never one to let male beauty go unappreciated, got his message. But I was cautious about men who were overly conscious of their sexual power. My strict and old-fashioned upbringing also made me wary of the ramifications that any involvement with a black man could bring. The pages of *Confidential* were filled with innuendos about celebrities involved in relationships with other races. It was not the thing to do. I started to move away, but he took my arm and looked into my eyes.

"Where are you going?" he asked, his eyes shining with interest and amusement.

"Oh—I—said I'd have dinner with some of the camera boys." I stammered, aware of heat from his hand on my bare arm. He glanced over to where three or four of the English camera crew, mates of mine from *Seawife,* were grouped, observing us with amusement and waiting for developments, which from the look of it seemed inevitable. His grip on my arm did not lessen, and he looked at them and then back to me with even more amusement. My, he was sure of himself.

"An appointment you cannot break?" his voice was husky, sexy and confident.

"That's right," I said lightly, my eyes locked in his as I removed his persuasive fingers from my rather too receptive flesh. "We're having dinner and then playing poker."

"Poker—aahh. Of course. You English ladies always like to play games."

The innuendo was there. He knew and I knew. Even Joan Fontaine knew as she drifted away in a sea of chiffon.

"Well, then, I'll let you go—for now," he said meaningfully, bestowing on me a dazzling and promise-filled smile. I felt my face blushing under its suntan. "Since I don't play games—another time, then." And he smoothly glided off, catlike and elegant, leaving the blushing schoolgirl standing somewhat off balance.

I joined my British compatriots, who went to some lengths to let me know that this fabulous man was considered to be a ladies' man par excellence, and gossip had it that one of his ambitions was to be able to make love to as many beautiful women as he could possibly find. Cheap crew talk, I thought. Though my heart beat a little faster when I thought of him, I realized it was a no-no situation.

Although Belafonte and I had no scenes together, everyone was in the same hotel, so our paths crossed often. At breakfast, lunch and dinner— there he was. Smiling, confident—sexy. Throwing me glances and waiting for *me* to make the move.

For a week I kept out of his way, until the following Sunday when Zanuck arranged a festive brunch for the cast and crew. A hundred and fifty of us gathered around the tables groaning with Caribbean goodies, and I was seated next to him. His proximity and poise made me so nervous that I couldn't eat and I started to chain-smoke.

"You've been avoiding me, Joan Collins," he said, nonchalantly spooning up papaya and melon. "Have the poker games been that exciting?"

"I'm on a winning streak," I said offhandedly, lighting yet another cigarette with shaking hands.

"Allow me," he said, removing the cigarette from my lips and dumping it in the ashtray. I realized that I had lit the wrong end and the singed filter was on fire. Not exactly sophisticated behavior.

From an adjoining table the camera boys were enjoying the whole scene. Damn them, I thought. Interfering busybodies. I didn't belong to them. They were looking out for me as if I were Little Red Riding Hood with the Big Bad Wolf. I decided to enjoy Belafonte's engaging company and ignore the boys and their sniggers.

He was a spirited conversationalist. Warm and articulate, funny; and so engrossed were we in talking that the heaping plates of chicken gumbo, fried shrimp, lobsters, brown rice and exotic fruits were barely touched. Although the chat was light, the undercurrent of mutual attraction was heavy. Darryl Zanuck sat opposite us, chomping on an immense cigar, wearing little blue-and-white-striped shorts and matching shirt, open to show a protruding, gray-haired belly. He occasionally shot us penetrating looks as if questioning whether or not this conversation was innocent. But I gave him my sweetest, most innocent smile to assure him that all was aboveboard.

One thing I gathered from lunching with my handsome friend—he was smart and he was cool. He was no Zanuck who had to press his advances on a woman. Why should he? Women flocked to *him*. I watched them in the hotel lobby, going dithery and weak as they gazed at his sensual frame clad as usual in tight pants and shirt open to the waist, and not at all oblivious to the effect he had on them. He also knew that the entire cast and crew were waiting to see what, if any, developments were about to happen between him and me. Since I did not wish to be the object of gossip during the movie, I didn't relish the idea of the whole world's knowing about an event which to me should be private, so I decided that this tropical, romantic island was neither the time nor the place for us. I stopped thinking about him and returned to the poker table. And he, taking my cue, did not pursue it either.

Toward the end of his shooting—he was to be finished before the rest of us as he had a concert tour—we took a walk along the beach one night. There had been yet another party at the hotel and we had both gone outside for some air. It was hot and the moon was silver and full. I was wearing a bare-shouldered white cotton *broderie anglaise* dress that showed off my deep tan. I took off my sandals to walk where the ocean lapped at the sand. He was also in white, trousers and shirt, and in the silvery light shimmering on our faces, we seemed the same color.

I was sad that he was leaving. Although we had spent little time together, it was only because circumstances and morals decreed that it was "wrong" for us to have anything other than the most casual acquaintanceship. He was a sensitive and bright man. What difference did it make if he was black, white or blue?

"I suppose I won't see you again," I said after we had walked silently along the surf for a while. He didn't answer, but he stopped and looked up at the sky for a while with a faraway incense look on his face. I knelt down to pick up some of the little shells that had scattered like uncut gems over the sand. He was still looking out toward the ocean, the moon making his face into a carved bronze statue and the warm wind blowing the white cotton shirt out from his body. There was something so atavistic and powerful about him, and his silence seemed so full of secret meaning that I felt like an intruder. I continued picking up shells until he suddenly turned, his mood changing—laughing, joking—and pulled me up to stand beside him.

"Look." He pointed to the moon. "Two hundred billion years or more it's been there—what does it matter about us?" He turned to look at me and put his hands on each side of my head and said, "I'll be in Los Angeles in April. At the Grove. Come there." It was neither an invitation nor a command. It was a fact. I would be there.

And I was. His opening night at the Coconut Grove was jam-packed. Half the celebrities in Los Angeles had come to see the magnetic personality and performance of this man who was becoming famous throughout America. He was the first man ever to sell over one million LPs. Not for nothing was he called "King of the Calypso." He had recently broken all records at a huge sports stadium in New York and was fast becoming one of the first black film idols. He had been mesmerizing audiences of every type from true folk-music aficionados to smitten teenagers and matrons to music critics and intellectuals with his honey-voiced and spirited renditions of calypso folk songs and spiritual jazz performed with guts, emotion and honesty.

The Coconut Grove had been built during the peak glamour era of the movies, the 1920s. Gable and Lombard had romanced there. Crawford, Harlow, Bogart, all of the great movie stars had wined and dined, brawled and romanced in its splendid environs. It now had the aura of faded glory. If one looked too closely, the paint was peeling off the walls and the fringe was falling off the pink lampshades that cast flattering soft lights on the jaded faces of those who frequented it now. For the age of the nightclub was fast disappearing as the disco started to take hold. But tonight the giant fake palm trees were magnificently flashy and the atmosphere had an electric anticipatory mood. And so did I.

I had been invited by the studio to attend. I had never seen Belafonte perform before more than just a few people, casually, at some of our gatherings in the West Indies. I was eager to see him. And he did not disappoint. As the stage went dark, a spotlight was turned on, and to the calypso rhythm of his theme song he strolled on—casual, confident—singing, dancing, with a slightly arrogant self-assured style—wholly original.

"If you see me you'll love me" seemed to be his attitude, and so certain was he of his sexuality and magnetism that most of the women there were more than overcome. I sat enthralled, in my low-cut black satin dress, my hair a concoction of curls and bows, a white mink stole gracefully slipping off my shoulders to show cleavage, and with my new diamond earrings from Asprey's flashing—a present to myself. I looked fetching and knew it. And he knew it too as our eyes connected during his act.

The show over, the applause and encores still echoing, an elite group of invitees trekked through the corridors of the old Ambassador Hotel to the "star's dressing room," which is really the star's hotel room, since the management was too cheap to supply both. He was lionized. Bouffant-haired matrons gushed and squealed around him, elbowing each other to get closer. Sharply dressed and sharp-talking guys hovered, ready to talk deals if only they could get to him through the throbbing female hordes.

A waiter passed Dom Perignon which I sipped, sitting in the background, not about to join the gushing group around him. He looked over at me and smiled.

I raised my glass in a silent salute. It was obviously going to be a long party and I didn't feel like sticking around for the grand finale. When my group was ready to leave I went over to him for the *de rigueur* kiss on each cheek and the "Goodbye, darling, you were divine" routine, which I sincerely meant. We exchanged a last lingering look. It was only in the eyes, but it was high voltage. I was silent on the way back to my small apartment. My thoughts were on him, and what might have been.

The Arthur Loew relationship had lasted for nearly fifteen months, but was cooling off now. Although we still saw each other we dated others.

I wanted more than a semi-platonic relationship. I realized that sex was quite important to me. Many people thought it was shocking for a woman to admit she enjoyed making love and that she thought it a perfectly natural thing to do.

Jayne Mansfield tried to change that in a somewhat different way. Arriving under contract to Fox around the same time that I did, she plunged into the publicity machine where Marilyn Monroe left off. An unbelievable figure—40—18—36. Long platinum-blond hair, baby-blue eyes and a talent for gathering personal publicity out of practically everything she did. She starred in several forgettable films but became the American workingman's number one turn-on.

Fox had the brilliant idea of co-starring her and me in a film together. It was a serious and seamy John Steinbeck novel called *The Wayward Bus*. For this true slice of Americana in the raw, they unbelievably imported a young French director from Paris. For the role of the sluttish, nagging, alcoholic wife who runs the tacky diner where the bus makes pit stops, they chose me. I was extremely pleased at the chance to play a character role and not just be the pretty wallpaper. The studio was happy with my performances in *Seawife* and *Island in the Sun* and was giving me a meaty part that showed its confidence in me was growing.

I had to be aged for the role of the drunken wife. Bags and circles were applied under my eyes; my hair, still short from *Seawife,* was a snarled and tangled mess; and I played most of the film in a stained dressing gown. It was challenging to be able to work on a character totally unlike myself. All my personal characteristics, from accent to walk, had to be changed. In *Seawife* I had been able to use parts of myself that were never revealed in films before—innocence and vulnerability, which were in my own makeup. I was surprised Fox had not given this role to Joanne Woodward, their resident young character actress. Surprised, but glad, I threw myself into the movie with tremendous enthusiasm.

Unfortunately, the director, Victor Vicas, was so unfamiliar with the American way of life and so petrified of making mistakes that it was difficult for him to bring Steinbeck's grimly realistic story to life. The film was reviewed unfavorably and it bombed at the box office. I, however, received favorable comments and good reviews. I hoped that this would bring me better and more fulfilling roles and not just "pretty-pretty" ones. Some people seemed amazed at my performance: "But you were *good!*" they would say, the surprise thinly disguised in their voices. Or "I didn't know you could *act,* Joanie baby."

I gritted my teeth, smiling politely. I was gaining more confidence in my ability, but I still constantly had to prove it to others. This continued for several years. Directors, actors or crew members often came up to me with surprised smiles to tell me how good I was, as though they never expected it. I found it galling.

I was still treated by many people like a brainless starlet whose main talent was to go partying and who built a career based on looks and sex appeal. Now I know, since my career has continued for over thirty years, that this isn't true. There are any number of young actresses who flowered and bloomed in the first flush of stardom for a few years only to fall into total obscurity. There are very few so-called beauties or glamour girls who have sustained a career for over three decades. This is a business of survival. To survive you have to work at your craft and become good. You don't get charity jobs.

I was also chastised and criticized for wanting to enjoy my personal life. If I want to go traveling or to parties or discos, who is to say I am inferior to Miss X, who stays at home at night with a boiled egg and a copy of Stanislavsky, and is maybe not a "10"? It has always been easier to be considered a serious actress if you are not good-looking. Beauty is definitely an asset at the beginning of a career. I know it was basically my looks that got me to Hollywood; but after a few years looks are, in fact, a hindrance in advancing a career. It is hard for people to accept beauty and a good actress in the same package.

However, I was not about to go to seed and fall apart physically just to prove I could act, and in fact, I won't ever do that. I enjoy being attractive and dressing well, and it amuses me to see that some people are resentful of how I look.

"How do you *do* it?" they ask bitchily, trying to look behind my ears for some telltale scars; or, "What are you doing to yourself? You've got some magic secret for staying young—tell me what it is."

The truth is, there's no secret. You get the face that you deserve, eventually. I believe in enjoying the life you have as much as possible, in living without envy, frustration and bitterness toward others—and in trying to be happy and worry-free. (Not an easy goal in my life.) A little narcissism is not a bad thing either. It was Gore Vidal who said, "A narcissist is someone better-looking than yourself." True!

I would like to have had some magical prophetic man or woman in my life who became my mentor and helped and guided me through the difficulties of my career. Unfortunately, they did not appear. I went through the jungle alone. Not for me a Carlo Ponti, Roger Vadim or Dino de Laurentiis to help guide me. Not even a trusty agent or manager has gone the distance, with the exception of Bill Watts.

With three films under my belt in less than a year, I took off for Acapulco for a rest. Arthur and I had come to a final parting of the ways on New Year's Eve.

We were dancing at the Charles Lederers' New Year's Eve party. The music was soft and romantic, but we were not. We were having another peevish row, quietly, so that the imposing array of distinguished guests could not overhear our heated discussion. They could not have failed to hear the following dazzling dialogue:

Arthur: "You are a fucking bore."

Me: "And you are a boring fuck." And that was the end of that.

I stayed in Acapulco for four weeks, tanning and learning to water-ski.

I started dating Nicky Hilton, a playboy and first husband of Elizabeth Taylor and the son of Conrad Hilton of the huge hotel chain. Nicky was good-looking in a dissolute and rakish way. Dark hair, dark eyes, he enjoyed a reputation as one of Hollywood's swingingest playboys.

Although he had his own office and was assistant to his father in the hotel business, he preferred to spend his time with girls, at the racetrack and nightclubbing. Since I was not in the mood for serious involvement, and neither was he, he divided his time between Natalie Wood and me for several months, which suited me fine.

Nicky was a devout Catholic in spite of his prolific womanizing. He kept a rosary on the bedside table, which featured an amazing array of pill bottles in all shapes and sizes, girlie magazines, pornographic books, bottles of Coca-Cola, a crucifix, and a gun. He enjoyed filling the gun with blanks and firing it repeatedly at the ceiling in the middle of the night, to the horror of his neighbors on Doheny Drive, who would call the police in a frenzy of fear.

Although only in his early thirties, he appeared as if he had seen and done everything. He had been everywhere, could get practically any girl he wanted and was completely jaded. He had a Southern drawl and was racially bigoted.

Rich men's sons have a hard road to hoe. It is almost the equivalent of being a beautiful girl. You are born with everything. You don't have to do a thing for yourself. It's all there: the money, the power, the girls, the fast cars and the fast life. Arthur learned that his money did not make for happiness. He moved to a ranch in Arizona where he completely changed his lifestyle. He raised cattle, married and found himself. And Syd Chaplin got his act together and made a success on Broadway for a few years.

Alas, poor Nicky did not find a way out, and a few years later he was dead from a drug overdose.

❧ *Five* ❧

"CAN YOU BE READY to leave for Tokyo in three days?" My agent's voice, crisp and businesslike on the phone, woke me from a dreamless sleep. My cocoon of pillows and sheets was rumpled and my mouth was dry from too many cigarettes.

"Damn." I fumbled for the Visine eyedrops among the bedside-table junk. A glass of water fell off the cluttered table that held scripts, magazines, vitamins, a clock, Kleenex, a photo of my parents in an antique silver frame, diamond earrings and pearls tossed carelessly about, and an overflowing ashtray.

I pushed the ashtray under the pile of magazines—the smell was vile at that time of the morning—I tried to collect my thoughts as the Visine did its job on my eyes.

"Three days—that's impossible. I can't be ready in time," I croaked, pulling the sheet around my shoulders and wishing someone would bring me some fresh orange juice, coffee and raisin toast. Oh, for a live-in housekeeper. Alas, my business manager convinced me I couldn't really afford one, although I was earning two thousand dollars a week, had starred in half a dozen movies, and appeared regularly on the covers of magazines worldwide. I was a commodity now, a young, sexy, salable commodity, and my studio employers took full advantage of this fact and were pushing me into film after film—movies unfortunately noted more for their visual beauty and scenic splendor than for their integrity or realism.

My agent was sympathetic but firm. I must report to the Fox wardrobe department at eleven, hair department at one-thirty—and visit the insurance doctor at three for whatever shots I might need for Japan and for his verification that I was healthy. Then, in the two and a half days that would be left prior to my departure, I had to organize the bits and pieces of my own life as well as I could. It was par for the course. I didn't have much to say in the direction my career went. If I ever rebelled, I was put on suspension. No work. No money. Not even another studio was allowed to employ me. And TV was considered lower than low. I was fairly frugal. The apartment on Shoreham Drive—furnished in white-beige-and-pink Sears Roebuck starlet style—cost two hundred fifty dollars a month. I either ate out or was on a diet so my fridge contained cottage cheese, a few bottles of white wine and little else. The freezer, however, was full of Will Wright's ice cream in every different flavor for the odd afternoons when I threw caution to the wind and indulged in an ice-cream fit. I had a car befitting my starlet status. A flashy pink Thunderbird, which certainly got attention when I zipped along Sunset Boulevard well over the speed limit, with the radio blaring Latin American music. My closet contained a large selection of Saks and Magnin's lowest-cut dresses, a white mink stole, a black mink coat, a white sheared-beaver coat and a blue fox hat which I had bought in an abandoned moment and had never worn. I was sartorially prepared for any eventuality. Of material possessions other than these I had none. No paintings or even lithographs graced my walls—I had not yet discovered my passion for collecting Art Deco and Art Nouveau objects. And of emotional involvements I also had none, although my date book was filled.

I lay back on the Porthault pillows—another indulgence, but I liked to wake up in a field of flowers—and thought about Japan. With the memory of two recent locations still lingering, I was not keen on a trip so soon. But I decided I had better think positively and make the best of it. I had never been to the Orient—it could be an exciting experience.

I had never in my life seen such a horde of fans as greeted Robert Wagner, Edmond O'Brien and myself on our arrival at Tokyo airport. Literally thousands of yelling and screaming excited Japanese of all ages whipped themselves into a frenzy at the sight of us. It was quite overwhelming and rather frightening. Even Robert ("R.J.") Wagner, a movie star since his teens, was bowled over by it. The Japanese have always been eager movie fans, and a million flashbulbs on a million Nikon cameras seemed to explode in front of us as we forced our way through the *extremely* polite throngs. The Japanese are so polite and well-mannered that they apologize profusely while shoving you violently at the same time.

On the way to our hotel in the Ginza district I saw dozens of movie theaters literally festooned with giant multicolored blowups of the stars who were appearing in the movies. John Wayne's face in vivid colors one hundred feet high, with slightly slanted eyes, was some sight to behold. But although I enjoyed the ancient charms of Japan I was lonely and miserable.

The script of the film was really awful. Called *Stopover Tokyo*, I immediately dubbed it *Stop Overacting!* R.J., though friendly and nice, was newly engaged to Natalie Wood and spent most of his off-set time with his parents in his suite or calling Natalie in Los Angeles. His phone bill must have been astronomical since he called at least once a day. The crew, with whom I usually hung out on location, were all men well over fifty, who threw themselves into the male-oriented Japanese society with gusto. They frequented the geisha houses where they were treated like lords, fawned over and adored by the geishas—small-boned, tiny creatures, seemingly from another century in their gorgeous, brightly colored kimonos and obis, their miniature feet padding softly in white cotton tabis, their faces masked by white powder, carmine lips and intricate eye makeup, and their heads crowned with enormously heavy glossy black wigs. I did not envy the life of a Japanese woman. Most were still virtually chattels to their men, men who spent practically every night out with other men frolicking at the baths, the geisha houses and the restaurants, where it was taboo for women to join in the festivities. On the few occasions when I did accompany some of the crew to the restaurants and clubs, I felt gawky and gauche next to these exquisite little women, and the men made no secret of their preference for the Oriental female.

"A bunch of women haters," I muttered to my companion, the unit hairdresser, as we sat in the hotel dining room eating teriyaki and fried rice unenthusiastically and feeling bored and despondent. One of the camera crew, a huge beefy Southern redneck, middle-aged and dressed in a hideous plaid shirt, Stetson hat and checked trousers, with his gross paunch hanging over his belt, had dropped by our table with his tiny beautiful geisha to lay a bit of his newfound philosophy on us.

"You Western gals should take a few lessons from these Oriental ladies," he said, his saki-drenched breath causing us to stop eating. "Now little Tamiko here—she *really* knows how to treat a man right. Don't you, Tamiko?"

Tamiko nodded and smiled subserviently at this lout, and I felt disgusted that Japanese women thought themselves so inferior to even the most loathsome of the male sex.

Women's liberation was a glimmer on the horizon. But at least that glimmer was becoming stronger. I considered myself by now to be an emancipated and free woman. If I chose to sleep with whom I wanted, and when I wanted, however, I sometimes became the butt of jokes, crude remarks and a general attitude among some people that I was no better than I should be, or a "tramp." It was considered shocking to be free in sexual attitudes. My proclivity for taking as lovers men who were interesting, young and good-looking did not endear me to a whole section of men in the movie business—producers, directors, heads of studios and big-wigs in general—because I would never have anything to do with *them* at all. The thought of going to bed with some old, fat, ugly or rich man for a job or to do myself some good careerwise was revolting. *That* to me was being a tramp. If I wanted to bed down with three men a week whom I genuinely fancied and liked, I would. It was my life and the time had come to get rid of guilts and live it for *myself*.

However, in Japan there was *no one* I felt even faintly attracted to and I spent most of my free time with the hairdresser, reading, trying to study the ghastly script in my hotel room, or sight-seeing.

One evening the phone rang. It was a man called Charles. We'd met once in Los Angeles and when he invited me to dinner I accepted. A new face was more than welcome in my life. I had killed more time having an elaborate wardrobe made, choosing from the profusion of glorious fabrics —silks, brocades and chiffon—that Japan had to offer. I had to buy five more suitcases to cart home this loot. There were enough cocktail dresses and evening gowns all copied from *Vogue* and *Harper's Bazaar* to keep me dressed differently every night for a year.

For my night out with Charles I wore a pink-and-gold brocade che-ongsam—a high-necked Chinese-style dress, tightly fitted, with a skirt slit to the thigh—quite appropriate for anywhere we might go, be it a quiet bistro or a nightclub. However, I was not prepared for what Charles— tall, dark and quite elegant—suggested we do after dinner. We went to what appeared to be an attractive, dimly lit nightclub—small, very small —and we sat on thick soft cushions on the floor close to a stage that was rather too tiny for dancing.

It was a live sex show—an erotic fantasy! To start with, an amazingly beautiful and nubile young girl cavorted naked on stage. She had shaved her pubic hair and spent much time massaging herself with a long rounded object. After a while two equally sexy young men joined her, and the girl, truly one of the greatest contortionists I have ever seen, knelt and arched her back and bent her head to a 90-degree angle while one of the men made love to her with rabbit rapidity and the other had the most expert fellatio performed on him. I sat there stunned. I could not believe the scene before me. All of this was done in silence, except for some mysterious lute music emanating from an unknown source and the irregular breathing of my escort.

"God! Fantastic!" Charles whispered, his hand landing light as a butterfly's wings on my thigh. "What do you think?" he breathed, nuzzling my left ear, obviously getting wildly aroused.

"I wonder if she can cook," I whispered back, gently removing his hand.

"Who cares," he mumbled as another couple joined the threesome on the stage and proceeded to arrange themselves in every conceivable position. They looked like the "Snake Pit" and I started to giggle furiously—

especially when I caught sight of all the tourists' rapt horny faces in the audience. The more vigorously the performers writhed the more amused I became. To me there was nothing erotic or exciting in this flagrant exhibitionism. Always romantic, I thought the kiss between Montgomery Clift and Elizabeth Taylor in *A Place in the Sun* infinitely more sexy.

Charles, his ardor whetted by this display, thought otherwise, and I pleaded every known combination of female ailments at the entrance to my hotel room before I gracefully got rid of him. Maybe there was something wrong with me if I found a group-sex scene which people paid money to watch such a turn-*off*. Charles was an attractive man. In my circumstances, stuck in Japan for five weeks, celibate and bored, it was curious that his taking me to a supposedly stimulating show had had the reverse effect on me. Most women would probably have leaped into bed with him and made love imaginatively and passionately for hours, turned on by what they had seen. Somehow I felt that both sexes were demeaning themselves by these acts. They were being used, and their degradation was much more apparent than any enjoyment they were probably simulating.

Sex is certainly not a spectator sport, I thought as I got into my lonely bed for the thirty-fifth consecutive night. Charles probably thinks I'm a total square—and I drifted off into a sleep filled with writhing nests of vipers and boa constrictors.

❖ *Six* ❖

IF I THOUGHT I had been in love before, those feelings paled in comparison with my infatuation with George Englund. I had known him, his wife and their rapidly increasing family ever since I had met him at Gene Kelly's house soon after I arrived in America. He had gone to military academy with Sydney Chaplin and was a close friend of Arthur Loew's. His wife, Cloris Leachman, who in the 1970s would become a popular television star playing the role of Phyllis on "The Mary Tyler Moore Show," was an actress, pretty, friendly and neurotic, who dedicated her life and herself to George and the rearing of their three children.

Our friends were mutual. As a foursome with Sydney we'd gone to Palm Springs and Tijuana together, and although I knew that George and Cloris bickered a lot I thought their marriage was OK as most marriages go—not tremendous but not at breaking point either. I was aware of him as an intelligent, attractive man with a fabulous sense of humor—but that was all. Married men were a no-no in my book, especially if I was pally with their wives. It was not cricket.

When I mentioned that I was going to Chicago and New York on promotions for *Stopover Tokyo,* George told me he would be in New

York at the same time and perhaps we'd get together for dinner one night, our schedules permitting. We were, coincidentally, staying at the same hotel, the Plaza. When he came to pick me up that night I was unaware that I was embarking on one of the most traumatic, emotional and unsettling periods of my life.

In retrospect I don't think the highs balanced the lows, but when one is madly, passionately, blindly in love, all reason evaporates. On our first date we went to the Little Club for dinner. He was dressed impeccably as always in a dark blue suit from a Savile Row tailor, a pale blue Turnbull and Asser silk shirt and a Cardin tie. He had a reputation for being very well dressed, and sartorially he could not be faulted. Aside from his clothes, he was devastatingly good-looking. Six feet two, green-eyed, with light brown hair, going ever so *slightly* thin on top—about the only flaw I noticed as I became increasingly aware of him as more than a friend during dinner. He had a wicked wit and a superb mastery of the English language. Indeed he was the perfect advocate of the adage Why use a short word when a six-syllable one will do? Words and phrases I seldom heard outside the New Oxford Dictionary tumbled effortlessly from his lips. He was smart as a whip, and we seemed to spark each other's funnybone too, for he laughed at me as much as I laughed at him.

Ahhh, laughter—one of the greatest aphrodisiacs in the world! He ordered a Mouton-Rothschild '53 with our beef Wellington, and after dinner we drank Calvados and listened to the 30's-style music as the pianist played a selection of what suddenly became my favorite tunes. It was too romantic to be true. The wine, the superb dinner, the intimate velvet banquette where we sat next to each other, George's hand on mine, the Gershwin and Cole Porter songs, some of which he sang softly (he knew the words to even the most obscure songs—there was no end to his talents).

We walked hand in hand after dinner through the empty New York streets with the steam rising from the sidewalks, back to the Plaza, and as he accompanied me to my room my heart was pounding. Was it possible to fall in love over *dinner* with someone you had thought of only as a friend for two years? Apparently it was, and I was hopelessly—helplessly—hooked.

For three days I thought of nothing else. Every possible moment we could share away from my schedule of TV, radio and newspaper interviews, and he from his business meetings, we spent together. We passed a frosty autumnal Sunday walking starry-eyed through Central Park. I was besotted beyond belief and refused to think of the insurmountable problems of his wife and three boys, aged six, four and two.

He assured me over and over again that the marriage was and had been in deep and serious trouble for several years, and that they were only staying together for the sake of the kids. Despite its being such a cliché, it was said so convincingly that I completely believed him. His influence over me was so strong that he could have demanded I skate naked in Rockefeller Center and I would have happily done so. I became truly the Trilby to his Svengali.

On our last evening in New York we went back to the Little Club, which I would forever think of as "our place." I wore a beige suit and a green felt "Garbo" hat. I had just read *The Green Hat* and rather fancied myself as its star-crossed heroine. I sniffled through cocktails, started to cry during dinner, and wept profusely during dessert and coffee. I was feeling guilty now about our situation but I knew I couldn't and wouldn't give him up. Little did I know I was beginning twenty-one months of the most intense misery of my life.

My best friend was Caprice Caprone Yordan, an exquisitely elegant and witty, sophisticated black-haired beauty, married to Philip Yordan, a prolific writer-producer of epic films, usually set in Spain or Africa. Cappy and I shared practically every intimate secret of our lives with each other, and since Philip was constantly working, she had time to kill. She lived in a rambling old Spanish hacienda on Benedict Canyon, and spent her days entertaining her myriad friends, dispensing advice and worldly wisdom with a strong dose of astrology thrown in.

"Guess who I've fallen in love with," I blurted out. It was the morning after I had arrived in L.A., and I rushed over to her house to find her languishing elegantly in bed surrounded by satin-and-lace pillows, a wicker breakfast tray full of tea and croissants, English jams and marmalade and with eleven books on astrology spread over her pink satin coverlet.

"I hope he's rich," said Cappy. "It's about time you found a rich one."

"Not only is he not rich—but he's married." I despaired. "You know I don't care about money but the wife situation is a disaster." I gloomily devoured a croissant with honey while Cappy surveyed me disapprovingly. She was like my big sister. She knew the way my mind worked.

"Married and *poor*—wonderful. You've done it again, my darling. Enough guessing games—who is he and what's his sign?" She pulled one of the astrology books toward her and looked at me questioningly.

"George Englund," I blurted out. "I'm *madly* in love with him—and he with me, so he says." A wave of doubt engulfed me momentarily. I gave Cappy his birth date and waited expectantly for her verdict.

"Oh, you fool," said Cappy. "Not only is he a Cancer—" she consulted her book and frowned—"but he'll hang on to you *forever* and never let you go. His wife will never let *him* go either. *What* are you letting yourself in for, Joanie?"

"It's too late now," I groaned, grabbing another croissant for succor. "I can't give him up. It's ghastly. It's as though he's put a spell on me—what am I going to *do*, Cappy? I simply cannot stop thinking about him *all day long!* This has never happened to me before—Oh, God!"

She looked at me pityingly and did some quick calculations on a pad. "He's perfect for you, of course," she said as she finished her calculations and I finished her breakfast. "His moon and his Venus are in the same house as yours, and all your other signs are totally compatible. You're a perfect match for each other. But darling, he will *never* leave the wife and those kids. He's a *Cancer*, for goodness' sake—*the crab*—my God, his claws won't ever release *anything!* And his wife thinks so too," she said, pushing the books away. "You know she worships the ground he walks on. The best thing for you is to get back to work as quickly as possible and forget him."

I tried halfheartedly to heed my learned friend's advice, but now that I wanted and needed to work, suddenly I went through a dry spell. Although Fox paid me handsomely each week, they did not have any properties suitable for me at the moment. However there was a strong rumor on the lot that they were considering making yet another version of *Cleopatra* and that I was being touted as first choice to play the fabled queen.

Meanwhile, George and I saw each other four or five times a week. We lunched at out-of-the-way restaurants—usually near the airport, where the sound of jet engines often drowned our conversation—or he came to my little apartment for dinner. I never really knew until the last minute when or if I would see him, as he had about forty-seven different projects going at the same time and was wheeling and dealing in all channels. Although I went out on "dates," which I kept platonic, I would never commit my evenings until I knew if he was available. It was hell. I was "back street wife" personified. The worst times were when he said he would be over at eight and didn't show up until ten or eleven and sometimes not at all—only a hurried phone call: "Sorry, babe—can't make it tonight. Have to catch you tomorrow."

I would go to bed forlorn and miserable, trying to understand his problems and trying not to become upset. As the weeks passed and his promises of "trial separations" from his wife came to nothing I began to get immensely depressed.

I tried to become interested in other men, much to his chagrin, but no one could hold a candle to his charm, his wit, his looks or his personality, and I never even tried to find out how they compared in the other departments. After the misery of two days of not seeing him, a few hours in his company with his incredible mind bewitching me with his humor— everything seemed worth it.

He was extraordinarily jealous of me. Cancer crab with claws out. Whenever I dated someone he considered a possible rival, he would cross-question me afterward for hours. We had vicious fights culminating in blissful making-up sessions.

His best friend at the time was Marlon Brando, who was almost as great an admirer of George as I was. George inspired people to worship him. He was confident, clever and so aggressively charming that most people found him irresistible.

Marlon adored him, he emulated his vocabulary and mannerisms, his prowess at storytelling, his slightly superior attitude toward others not on his wavelength. Sometimes I found it hard to tell the difference between the two voices on the telephone. Often Marlon would "beard" for us when we went to restaurants, theaters or screenings. A photograph was taken of the three of us at the theater. When it was printed, luckily only Marlon and I were in it. "Marlon does the town with British actress," crowed the New York tabloids. "Brando and Joan step out together." "We're just extremely good friends," said Miss Collins with originality.

I was conscious of the fact that I had left school at the age of fifteen and that my vocabulary consisted of about twenty thousand words fewer than these two together. They managed to combine the exuberant enthusiasm of two schoolboys at a baseball game with the sophistication of scholarly professors. Their humor and whimsicality fed off each other and they would spark each other to new heights of erudite and enlightening prose.

Marlon had an insatiable curiosity about people. What made them tick? What did they think about the world and other people, what were their feelings, observations, needs? At any gathering Marlon would usually gravitate to the quietest, and what to the unpracticed eye appeared the dullest, person in the room, and engage that person in animated and spirited conversation for hours. He was a master at making the shrinking violet bloom and the wallflower leave the wall. His interest was genuine. He really *was* interested in that pimpled, bespectacled young woman whose manner bespoke the library rather than the boudoir. He would draw her out slowly, painstakingly, with questions asked with intelligence and such obvious concern that the girl would flower before our eyes. He would not, or would rarely, converse with the more secure, flamboyant party-going types—he preferred to find his own party fodder. Deeply engrossed, eyeball to eyeball, hunched in the farthest corner of the room, oblivious to the madding crowd, Marlon and his newfound interest would sit engrossed in each other's company for hours.

This amused George, who would make jokes about Marlon's proclivity for turning on the ugliest girl in the room. "Hey Bud," he teased, as Brando hove into view after a two-hour marathon chat with a mousy little Pasadena housewife type, flustered, breathless and glowing from her encounter with the star—"If you play your cards right I think you may get her!"

Marlon would grin, unable to resist the blandishment of George's forceful personality. His quest was for truth. To find the person behind the mask, the real feelings behind the facade. When he turned his piercing blue eyes on his target, no third degree was necessary. People who had held themselves tightly in check for years would open the floodgates of confession and emotion to Brando. One of the greatest qualities of his acting is that he brings an amazing realism, truth and authenticity to whatever part he plays. In the late 1950s few, if any, actors brought these attributes to their film roles. With the exception of James Dean and Montgomery Clift, intensity and depth of feeling were not inherent in actors of the fifties and sixties—indeed they were almost frowned on as the more fashionable attributes of handsomeness, charm and virility were in favor.

Today Al Pacino, Robert de Niro and Richard Gere carry on where Brando pioneered. The age of the "personality" actor is ending, and a breed of thinking and feeling individuals has appeared, to whom the words "movie star" are anathema, and whose egos are sublimated to the personalities of the characters they are portraying.

Marlon's curiosity extended not only to people he met at parties but also to the content of his friends' refrigerators. To say he was fond of food is an understatement. Food seemed to be sucked down his throat as though by some invisible vacuum. Once we discussed the merits and disadvantages of having a "vomitorium" built into one's house, as in Roman times—a room where after two or three courses of excessive wining and dining, a well-to-do Roman of his day would excuse himself and retire to this quaintly but appropriately named room and relieve his congested stomach by way of an old-fashioned vomit. He would then return to the dining room to indulge in another four or five courses—tripping to the vomitorium whenever the need arose.

The advantages of such a custom to those of us (among them me) who like to eat were obvious. Marlon did sometimes practice this odd method of weight watching while dieting for a role to get down to fighting weight, but I never could. Ah, the joys of being able to indulge in a four-course meal with appropriate wines and liqueurs and having no telltale aftereffects to show up on the scales next day.

George and I caught Marlon red-handed one night at my apartment spooning up the last dregs of a quart of Will Wright's peach-vanilla ice cream while two empty quart containers on the side testified to his healthy appetite.

Caught like a seven-year-old, spoon in mouth, his aplomb never faltered and he managed to give the impression of *savoir-faire* with a trickle of ice cream dribbling down his T-shirt.

George was *everything* I had ever wanted in a man. Except for the fact that he was married, he was perfect in every way. Although his treatment of me was often casual indifference, somehow I accepted it. If love is blind, in my case this was utterly true. I saw George through a rich haze of rose-colored spectacles.

"I am divorcing Cloris," he announced definitively one afternoon three or four months after our liaison had begun. "We will still live together for a while for the sake of the children—occupying separate bedrooms, of course," he added hastily, seeing the sparks appearing in my eyes.

At last! Subconsciously my desire to get Daddy away from Mummy was finally being fulfilled in this relationship. To celebrate his new freedom we flew to Eleuthera, one of the most remote and romantic islands in the Caribbean, where there was nothing but green frothy sea, white sand and a cool blue alcove of a suite. But George was unsatisfied—edgy, upset and remote.

"Why?" I wailed, sitting on the gorgeous golden white beach—an uninhabited vista of paradise to the north, south, east and west of us. "*Why* do you have to think of Cloris and the children *now?*" I threw myself onto the powdery sand in my white bikini and started to sob. I wondered *how* he could *possibly*—viewing my lithe, suntanned body, my face recently described as the world's most beautiful, not to mention all the clever things he'd taught me to say and do—could he *possibly* think of wife and kiddies now? What did I *lack* that I seemed to leave him so unfulfilled? Although I was leaning heavily on my shrink three times a week, I was unable to see that the lacks were not in me alone. George's insurmountable guilt at leaving his wife and three children was fueled by his obsession with me. Our island paradise became a disaster area. Feuding and fighting, we flew back to the States after only three days in Heaven, and I commenced living "back street wife" again.

"Dollink, I know a vonderful man who is *mad* about you." Zsa Zsa Gabor bit crisply into a shrimp and surveyed me shrewdly. "Vat you vant with this—this—son of a bitch married idiot. Dollink, vat he give you?" We sat lunching at Romanoff's, Zsa Zsa dispensing her worldly advice, diamonds glinting in the noonday sun, and I, dark glasses covering the ravages of last night's crying, trying to join in the fun and games of a girls' lunch.

Last night I had operated on a hunch. At eleven, as the dreary prime time ended and the news started, it came to me in a blinding flash that there was no "spare bedroom" at the Englunds' house! Without thinking, I jumped into my car and zoomed over to Westwood. I carefully cruised the alley behind the two-story white house and observed the action. The house had three bedrooms and six occupants—George and Cloris, their three sons and a housekeeper. It was so obvious. Their three sons in one room, the housekeeper in another, Mr. and Mrs. in the master bedroom. I knew the lay of the land, and as if to prove me right, I saw the two leading actors in my soap opera enter the bedroom and indulge in animated discussion as they proceeded to disrobe. Horrified, I gunned my engine and hastily turned into Wilshire Boulevard. I made a U-turn, zombielike, from Wilshire and Westwood Boulevard and cruised the alley more slowly and surely, and more observantly. Yes, it was he. No mistaking that six-foot-two tanned and terrific body—clad now only in blue undershorts as he discussed some subject animatedly with her—wearing an expensive orange Juel Park nightgown—which he could ill afford— and, with shoes off, a good ten inches shorter than he. My most ghastly suspicions were verified. He had lied to me. The bastard was cheating on me—with his wife!

There was no "spare bedroom" while they discussed their upcoming divorce. There was a cozy queen-sized bed and a thirty-two-year-old man and woman with three children and seven years of marriage behind them, off to bed together.

I pressed my foot on the accelerator as hard as I could and zoomed off blinded by tears. At Sunset Boulevard the C.H.I.P.S. got me. Leaving the apartment hurriedly, I had no identification—nor even any money on me.

"OK, lady—where's your I.D.?" said the gum-chewing middle-aged cop testily, oblivious to my bleary-eyed and obviously distressed appearance. I thought it best to turn on my most upper-class British accent as fast as possible. "I'm awfully sorry, officer—but I *cahnt* seem to remember putting it in my reticule when I left my flat."

I realized "reticule" was going a bit far—a Victorian word he probably had never heard of—but "flat" hit the spot, and I knew Americans were slightly in awe of aristocratic up-market British diction. He was no exception. Instead of calling in to his headquarters, as he should have done when finding someone driving over the limit—in which event I would have been computer-checked and they would have found I had a dozen unpaid traffic tickets which *could* necessitate spending the night in jail—he gallantly offered to escort me on his motorcycle back to my "flat" while I retrieved my driver's license from my "reticule."

"Oh, you American policemen are so wonderful," I gushed admiringly, and he, by now mindful of the tears drying on my cheeks and feeling perhaps a bit sorry for a British damsel in distress, left me to my misery.

So I listened to Zsa Zsa at lunch—grimly—more determined than ever to try and break off this disastrous affair with George.

"Dollink, he's vonderful," said Zsa Zsa, tossing her blond and beautifully coiffed curls, her doll-like blue eyes glistening with evangelical fervor at the thought of playing Cupid. I usually avoided blind dates like the plague. Men who were interested in meeting well-known actresses were usually creeps—but I let her have her say while munching my way through as much lunch, and as many glasses of wine, as possible, to dull the pain.

"His name is Rafael Trujillo—you've heard of him, of course?" She looked at me questioningly. I shook my head, mouth full of spinach and bacon salad. Zsa Zsa sighed. Women like Zsa Zsa always seemed to know intimately every head of state, prime minister and tycoon of all the minor countries of the world. Since my involvement with George and my constant sessions with the analyst, my enthusiasm for current world events had waned, and I had not even read *Time* magazine lately. If I had, I would certainly have heard about the Trujillos. Zsa Zsa painstakingly started to fill me in, and I listened halfheartedly.

"His father, of course, is the President of the Dominican Republic and —" she bent forward conspiratorially—"he has sometimes been known as *El Jefe,* 'the chief,' and 'The Caligula of the Caribbean.' " Now I remembered reading about him. Although he had successfully lifted his country from a depressed economic state, in which it had been when he assumed control and took over the government in 1930, he had never tolerated any opposition to his regime and suppressed dissent with arrests, tortures and executions. He guarded his country with a curtain of fear, terrorizing and exploiting his frightened people.

Everything of value in his country belonged either to him or his family. It had become a police state, in which his glassy-eyed photograph appeared in every public building. Major buildings and streets were renamed for him, and he awarded himself numerous titles of importance—he had come a long way from being one of eleven children in a poor peasant family. All in all a very unsavory character indeed, the Idi Amin of his day. A holiday in the Dominican Republic would be at the bottom of my list of favorite places to visit.

But dismissing my protestations about the father's injustices with an airy wave, Zsa Zsa proceeded to fill me in on the son. He was a polo-playing friend of Zsa Zsa's close friend Porfirio Rubirosa. He had recently finished an army stint at Fort Leavenworth in Kansas and now, therefore, had the title of "General" Rafael Trujillo. 'And . . ." Zsa Zsa finished triumphantly, "he's twenty-nine years old—unmarried, *very* handsome, very rich and dying to meet you. Vat do you say, dollink?" I considered carefully while devouring chicken pancakes. Well, why not? Even if his father was the Great Dictator, it didn't necessarily mean the son had to be a baddie too.

"Will you come along too?" I asked Zsa Zsa, who was now surveying me like a mother hen looking at her first new laid egg.

"Oh, dollink—I can't—I can't get to Palm Beach right now. I'm doing a show."

"Palm Beach?" I gasped. "You didn't say anything about Palm Beach. I mean, this is Beverly Hills—I'm not going four thousand miles for a *blind date.*"

"But, dollink," she wheedled, "his boat is there now. He has to be in Palm Beach for the next ten days on business—he can't get here. Surely, dollink—" she lowered her voice conspiratorially and bent her blond head coyly closer to mine—I could smell Arpège and observe that she wore navy blue mascara on her false lashes—"surely you can leave this awful George for a couple of days." She smiled mysteriously and leaned back to sip some more Chablis, her mission, if not accomplished, at least message delivered.

"No way, Zsa Zsa." I lit a cigarette and shook my head violently. "I'm not going all those miles for a date with a guy I don't even *know*—however cute and rich he may be."

"But dollink, you told me you were going to be in New York next week for the opening of your movie. Palm Beach is next *door* practically. He'll send his plane for you, naturally." She continued her argument through the raspberries and ice cream but I was unenthusiastic about the idea. Besides I had to get back to the apartment. George was coming over at three-thirty, and even though he was always late, nevertheless I was always there. Today I had things to discuss.

I dashed back to Shoreham Drive. It was a beautiful sunny Californian afternoon but I felt chilly. He arrived at four. Handsome and tanned as ever wearing an immaculate Prince of Wales plaid suit, which on any other man would have looked tacky and on him looked like a cover of *Gentleman's Quarterly*. His socks matched his tie, I noticed, and the new shoes obviously cost plenty. I tried to remember a present, card, or even a flower he had ever bought me and realized he had never brought me anything but himself. I wondered if that was supposed to suffice.

Our usual afternoon ritual was to chat, kiss, and take it from there. Today I was in the mood only for the first item on the agenda. I needed a drink. To broach this tricky subject was not going to be easy. He accepted the vodka and tonic I handed him and sat opposite me in the armchair, jacket off, leaning back, arms behind head—surveying me with benign satisfaction and a faint smile. I was his property, his little princess in an ivory tower in the hills of Hollywood. Behind him the afternoon sun glinted on his shiny shoes, his gold cuff links and, it gave me a moment of satisfaction to note, his slightly receding hairline. Serves him right, I thought to myself bitterly. I hope it all falls out *soon.* I downed the vodka in one great gulp and came right out with it.

"You told me that you and Cloris sleep in separate rooms, but I don't believe you." I stared at him, hoping against hope he would come up with a good story and that it had all been just a figment of my imagination.

He stared back. He downed his vodka, a look of pain across his face. He lit a cigarette. My God, he never *smoked!* What was going on? OK, George, admit it. *Admit* you slept with your wife. Come out with all the old clichés: *She* was there, you weren't. I thought about you all the time. I only did it once. She tried, but I couldn't do it. . . . Say *something,* but don't sit here at half past four in the afternoon looking like a death in the family and smoking cigarettes. Admit it—tell me—I'll cry a bit and then we'll make up. These thoughts raced through my head as he continued to stare and smoke.

"Cloris is pregnant," he said flatly. "We only did it once, believe me, Joanie, and she's goddamn pregnant again." I stared at him numbly. Pregnant—it wasn't possible—or was it? She already had three kids, with about two years between each one.

"How . . . I mean why? When?" I could barely speak. There was a lump in my throat the size of a fist that only vodka would make go away. I silently filled our empty glasses with straight Smirnoff while he filled me in on the details.

One afternoon seven or eight weeks previously when he had been in my apartment, she had suddenly started knocking on the front door and screaming, "George is here—I know he's here—make him come out." We sat fearfully up in bed, he motioning me to shut up as I attempted to go to the door and assure her that George was not in my apartment. After five or ten minutes the neighbors complained and she left. I was in a mild state of shock for I was not aware that anyone other than Cappy Yordan and Marlon knew about our affair. But rumors in Hollywood are like the jungle drums and obviously word had reached her that his Cadillac was parked on Shoreham Drive several times a week. At that time—according to him—they *were,* in fact, occupying separate bedrooms. He slept in the study on a couch because they were going through some sort of tacit separation while he was trying to sort out his very mixed-up emotions and feelings about me. When he returned that evening she threw everything she had at him—tears, hysteria, even suicide threats. To protect me, and prove to her that he was *not* involved with me, he had slept with her—just that once—and this was the result.

"So now you'll be the father of four," I said, my voice sounding as if it came from my boots. I picked up the vodka bottle and drank it all down —about a quarter of a fifth—and then hurled it across the room at him with all the force I could muster. It crashed into the window behind his head and glass flew everywhere. He jumped up, amazed. I took an ashtray and threw it at another pane in the middle of the bay window, then a glass, a pillow—anything I could lay my hands on, while sobbing and screaming at him hysterically, "That's *my* baby she's having—mine— how could you make *another* child with her? How could you, you bastard?" I threw myself about the room, all reason gone. He tried to calm me. He knew I detested physical violence, had never hit anyone in my life, and that this outbreak was the signal that I was going over the top.

I wouldn't let him touch me. My lungs were raw from yelling and screaming. All the pent-up months of patience, hope, of putting up with his lateness, his lies and his deceptions, were unleashed. If I had had a gun I might even have killed him—a true *crime passionel*. I never knew I possessed such feelings of rage. The dam burst but a tiny objective part of me watched the proceedings with great interest. As an actress I would be able to call on this experience for the future. "Well done," said the little voice admiringly. "What a great performance, dear." The grief, rage and passion that overcame me at four o'clock on a hot sunny afternoon in North Hollywood was never matched in my life—until my daughter Katyana was hit by a car and hovered between life and death in an intensive care unit some twenty years later.

Hours later he left. To his credit he saw me through the tempest and to the shore of oblivion—sleep. As he tiptoed out of the apartment at nine o'clock he left a groggy, helpless wreck lying in bed exhausted, overwrought, filled still with rage and an atavistic desire for revenge.

The next afternoon I called Zsa Zsa. "I'm leaving for New York tomorrow," I said crisply. "Tell your friend Mr. Trujillo to call me at the Plaza."

She had not been too wrong about Trujillo. He was good-looking in a glossy black-haired, olive-skinned Latin way. His manners were impeccable and his admiration for me was apparent. We dined on his palatial 350-foot yacht, the *Angelica,* surrounded by the trappings of wealth that only the very richest can afford. The vast table was set with a hand-embroidered white organdy cloth; the dishes were gold, as was the flatware; the glasses at each place setting were of the most beautiful pale-amber Venetian glass; flowers were everywhere—orchids, lilies and lush tropical plants. There was caviar in profusion, vintage wines and exquisite food. It was a balmy beautiful night in Palm Beach. The moon was full and reflecting on the water which lapped gently at the boat.

Apart from a crew of about eight, not counting the band, there were a few people there—Palm Beach socialites, his equerry and some aides from the Dominican Republic. The talk was frothy—the usual jet-set chat about parties and places and people. Some of them I knew, some of them I didn't. I didn't really care. It was good once again to be in the company of a man who obviously found me thrilling and paid me lavish compliments. Your word is my command seemed to be his attitude. What a change from trying so hard to please George and not succeeding.

We had coffee and cognac on the upper deck where, on the distant shore silhouetted against the navy-blue sky, the palm trees waved lazily in the breeze and the calypso songs brought back memories of locations in the Caribbean. We danced, and I felt lightheaded, lighthearted and more than a little drunk. I had not slept the previous night—thoughts of George's impending fatherhood tormented me. I wanted to go back to the hotel at Palm Beach and sleep for a week. I was tired and told "Ramfis" so, but he insisted that I stay the night in the luxurious stateroom that had been prepared for me.

So why not? I was young, footloose and fancy free. My love affair and my commitment to George still occupied all my thoughts but it was doomed. Why not stay the night with this attractive strange gentleman who treated me like a piece of rare crystal? I had never before slept with anyone unless totally carried away by passion or love. This time my motivation was mental and physical exhaustion, mixed with gratitude for a consolation missing from my life for months. I had been completely faithful to George for over a year, but he had not to me, so this, finally, would be how our affair would end. On a beautiful boat, on a perfect Florida night, with the son of the President of the Dominican Republic.

Autumn came to New York, and it was a frenzy. Interviews, photo sessions, press luncheons and guest shots on TV. *Stopover Tokyo* opened to mediocre-to-lousy reviews. Most of the movies I was making at Fox seemed to get poor reviews, and I would get comments like: "Joan Collins seems to be an actress with more talent than she is able to show in the purely decorative roles she has been playing."

In the half-dozen years my fledgling career had spanned, I had appeared in fifteen films, in some of which I had starred. I had worked with some fine actors and excellent directors. Basil Dearden, who directed *I Believe in You*, was noted for his down-to-earth realism and for bringing a feeling of actuality to all of his film characters. My role of Norma in *I Believe in You* was, I think, one of my better acting jobs in all my early movies. Although it was my first major role, I had yet to experience the agonizing self-consciousness that the early Hollywood years instilled in me, and because of the scruffy way Dearden wanted me to look, I didn't care about my appearance at all. In *I Believe in You* that wasn't important. I was not yet aware of how an early "leap to fame" can leave you up for grabs by every critic around, professional or amateur.

Because of my youth and inexperience, my early films were judged, and fiercely so, on my meager acting talent which, I admit, was somewhat limited then. But to have one's mistakes lambasted and criticized constantly while trying to learn one's profession under the scrutiny of Hollywood moguls, gossips and critics, could be, and *has* been, the finish of many a fledgling career. Self-consciousness is *death* for a performer, but one of the hardest things to overcome on the screen.

I was lucky enough (or stupid enough) not to let the torrent of adverse criticism affect me too deeply, when many more faint-hearted than I might have contemplated ending it all.

I plodded on, appearing in turkey after turkey, gritting my teeth and learning at least *something* from my every movie, play and TV appearance.

Sometimes it was tough to experiment, to try out new ideas as an actor, to stretch. Sometimes I tried and failed dismally, as in *The Good*

Die Young. Lewis Gilbert, a fine and sensitive director, cast me wrongly, I felt, as Richard Basehart's bourgeois sweet and long-suffering wife— the archtypical girl next door role. This was not only wrong for me, as I was only nineteen, considerably younger than Basehart, but I did not have the emotional range or experience to portray the suffering the girl was meant to be feeling.

I was much better in *Our Girl Friday*—young, spoiled, rebellious and playing comedy, for which I felt I had a flair even then.

If I had to advise any young actor or actress about to embark on a career today I would strongly advocate *learning* before plunging into actual performances. Two or three years at a really good drama school is essential, I think. Studying as many great movie actors as possible during this time is a benefit that my generation was not lucky enough to have.

One can now see on TV reruns every day the movie greats of all time: Spencer Tracy, Katharine Hepburn, Barbara Stanwyck, James Cagney, John Garfield, Claudette Colbert, Humphrey Bogart, Bette Davis, Cary Grant, Henry Fonda, Joan Crawford, James Stewart, Carole Lombard . . . the list is endless. And one can learn so much from them. What an opportunity to learn from masters!

I think it is a great pity too that the repertory theater, as I knew it, is no longer with us. For an actor to play dozens of diversified roles in a season is the most wonderful training of all. I cherish the six weeks I spent at Maidstone Repertory Theatre in England during my summer vacation from RADA.

I was lucky enough to be hired at three pounds ten a week—the equivalent of fifteen dollars then—as third assistant stage manager. This was about as low on the totem pole as one could get. The job necessitated being prompter for all the six plays that were staged there, as well as learning at least four of the roles as an understudy. We did the usual repertory fare—*French Without Tears, An Ideal Husband, Private Lives,* and such. I never got to even understudy Amanda, but I have yearned to play her ever since, and one day I *will!*

I regret really that I had so much success so young, and that it all came to me with relative ease. I realize my good fortune in being able to drop out of the "stardom" race for many years, years in which I grasped the opportunity to find out what the hell I was doing actingwise, how and why, and to take stock of myself objectively both as an actress and a woman.

Of course there are so-called "natural" actors, but experience and technique are absolute necessities for sustaining a career, and one can never, ever stop learning. I love the quote by Laurence Olivier in his autobiography about the start of his career. It goes something like: "Most people become actors to express themselves. I began for the simple reasons I wanted to show off!" How true in so many cases.

Land of the Pharaohs gave me my first opportunity to portray clichéd Hollywood glamour and out-and-out villainy, with which, on the screen, I was to become strongly associated. *The Bitch, The Vamp, The Sex Goddess, The Femme Fatale*—all of these labels could be used to describe many of the characters I have portrayed in the more than fifty films I have made.

Since it should, I hope, be apparent from this book that I really am none of these (although there is a part of me that *could* be), perhaps one could say that my acting teeth were sharpened on such films as *The Opposite Sex, Rally Round the Flag, Boys, Up in the Cellar, Alfie Darling, The Bawdy Adventures of Tom Jones, The Moneychangers* and, of course, *The Stud* and *The Bitch*. In all of these I played a vamp or a villainess, as I did in many TV shows.

However in the following movies I played more-or-less "nice girl" roles: *The Virgin Queen, The Girl in the Red Velvet Swing, Seawife, Island in the Sun, Stopover Tokyo, The Bravados, Seven Thieves, Esther and the King, The Road to Hong Kong, The Executioner, Quest for Love* and *The Devil Within Her.*

Alexis in "Dynasty" put the stamp firmly on my villainess image, and it's a hard one to shake. Not that, at the moment, that is my desire. In spite of all her villainy and plotting and scheming, I quite like her!

It was party time in New York. By now the New Yorkers had returned to their favorite haunts, "21," Pavillon, El Morocco and the Little Club, back from their summers in St. Tropez, the Hamptons and the Greek islands.

Around my neck I now sported a dazzling diamond necklace from Van Cleef and Arpels, a gift from Trujillo, which had arrived the day after I returned to New York from Palm Beach. It was an exquisitely beautiful choker in the shape of several flowers consisting of about twenty-five carats, and although I had tried to contact Trujillo to return it, his aides informed me he had returned to Santo Domingo and would be most offended if his "token of esteem" was returned. It would be "an insult," they informed me frostily.

When I phoned Cappy Yordan in Beverly Hills, she was horrified at the thought that I should return it, and so was Zsa Zsa. "Dollink, from him, he is so rich it is like sending a basket of flowers," she scoffed. So I kept it. If you've got it, flaunt it, was one of Cappy's philosophies. So I did.

It was the first piece of valuable jewelry I had ever received. Arthur Loew, with the family millions, had given me little gold pins and rings with a few quarter-carat diamonds strewn around, and Nicky Hilton was not noted for his largesse with women. It's a pity, I thought, that the one piece of jewelry of any value was given to me by a man with whom I had a relationship of no value to me. True, he was nice, charming and handsome, but I had no desire to see him again.

My week's whirl of publicity work ended when I was called back to Los Angeles to start another picture. Nicky Hilton, whom I had started seeing again, and Peter Theodoracopolis, another man I had been dating, had almost come to blows over me one night at the Plaza, and it was time to get out of town and get down to work.

George Englund was out of my system now, I thought. But I was wrong.

One red rose and a note, "Forgive Me. G.," was delivered the day after I got home. I didn't need to know who it was from. I tried to pretend that I didn't care as I sped to the studio to fit costumes for *Rally Round the Flag, Boys* but I couldn't deny that I was exceptionally cheery and full of *joie de vivre*. Was it only because of the note?

My message service called me as I sat in consultation with Charles Le Maire, who was designing the clothes for *Rally*.

"Mr. Cunningham's called you three times today," said Teddy, at the answering service, who knew how many times I would casually ask when I checked in, "Has Mr. Cunningham called?" and how disappointed I was if the answer was negative. Mr. Cunningham was George's telephone alias.

My heart skipped a tiny beat. The mind is controllable but not the heart—mine certainly wasn't.

"If he calls again tell him I'm in wardrobe," I said, and went back to discussing the dresses with Charles, trying to concentrate. Ten minutes later George called. "Before you say anything," he said hastily, "I just want to say three things—I love you, I miss you, and how the fuck is Peter, Theodore, whatever-the-fuck-his-name-is?" I giggled. I couldn't help it.

"We're just good friends," I laughed, fingering the antique diamond brooch that Peter had given me as a parting gift. Suddenly the men I met had become Santa Claus. George didn't have to beg terribly hard for me to agree to see him. He whetted my appetite by telling me he had portentous news of great benefit to both of us. But I insisted we meet at La Scala. Since I considered our affair over, what was there to hide?

"Cloris lost the baby," he said flatly. "It happened a couple of days after you went to New York. We had a lot of fights—heavy ones." He paused to sip his vodka. I hung on his words.

"We've decided to definitely get a divorce. I've consulted a lawyer and . . ." He took another sip. I leaned forward, not really believing what I was hearing.

". . . And I've moved into the Beverly Comstock, on Wilshire—'The boulevard of broken dreams' "—he referred to the fact that there were dozens of hotels along Wilshire in the Westwood area where newly separated or divorced men went to sort out their lives while their lawyers fought it out with their wives for custody of their property, houses, Cadillacs, paintings and children. The wives usually got it all anyway—unlike my farcical divorce settlement with Maxwell Reed. That section of Wilshire Boulevard, which also housed a lot of stewardesses, models and actresses, had become known as a swinging singles paradise.

"So where do I fit into all this?" I asked.

"With me you fit in, of course. I mean I love you. Do you still love me?" My look should have told him that. "And when it's all over maybe we can . . ." He took another drink—this seemed hard for him to get out—but I had to hear it. "D'you fancy being stepmother to three boys?"

It was too much to take. He had finally decided to commit himself. I was the happiest girl in the world. We ordered a bottle of Dom Perignon to celebrate—and while we drank it he informed me that his lawyers had advised him that he must not be seen publicly with a woman alone— particularly me—since Cloris was considering naming me as correspondent. In the unenlightened days of 1958, scandal could still be ruinous to an actor's or an actress's reputation and career. I had as much to lose as he. We agreed on complete discretion until his divorce was final.

We started going to obscure restaurants at the beach and in the Valley. Sometimes we would double date with Marlon Brando and his pretty and dynamic Puerto Rican girlfriend Rita Moreno—an actress usually typecast in "spitfire" roles, and a faithful worshipper at Marlon's shrine. She adored him, but he treated her in a rather cavalier manner, never letting her know where she stood in their stormy affair, which lasted on and off for eight years and culminated in her taking a near-fatal overdose of pills. I sympathized with her. Marlon, too, was having marital problems with his estranged Indian wife, Anna Kashfi. I don't think Marlon ever went out with a blonde—he loved exotic women. Marlon and George were preparing to make a film together called *The Ugly American*. I hoped that George might find a feeling of nepotism in his heart and would cast me in the role of Marlon's wife.

Alas, it was not to be. But I was finally playing a role I really liked and had fun with: witty, outrageous Angela in *Rally Round the Flag, Boys*. Fox had originally wanted Jayne Mansfield to play the sexy young vamp, living in a small town, married to a boring businessman, who tries to seduce Paul Newman away from Joanne Woodward. Joanne and Paul had insisted to director Leo McCarey that Mansfield was far too tarty and obvious for Angela, that the character should have a touch of class and an impish sense of humor, and they persuaded him to cast me. They were good friends and I appreciated their loyalty. Few actors go out of their way to try and get a role for a friend, but the Newmans have always been generous and supportive in their relationships with people they care about. The picture was a happy experience—although again, like most of my movies, neither a critical nor a financial success. Leo McCarey was a famous and beloved director who had made such films as *Going My Way* with Bing Crosby, for which he won an Oscar. But now he was old, seemingly feeble, and had lost the zest and comic flair which had flourished in the thirties. Why did I always seem to work with famed directors who were on their last legs careerwise?

My love life was lyrical now, working with the Newmans was a treat, and finally I was allowed to express my comedic talents, which had been lying dormant since *Skin of Our Teeth*. Critically this turned out to be my most favorable film. I received excellent reviews, expressing surprise an attractive woman should be funny too. I was able to be inventive in ways I had not been allowed before. The laughing scene, where Paul and I get drunk together while I try to teach him how to do the cha-cha, had some hysterically funny moments. We had to laugh all day—take after take— from dawn till dusk. Mascara ran endlessly down my cheeks, and it got so that just the sight of each other would set us off. "Angela—I'd know that face anywhere," groaned Paul between gasps of laughter as he came face to face with my rear end. I was doubled over on the floor, gasping for air, and when he said the line I deflated like a balloon and fell flat on my face. Another cut, and Paul was swinging literally from the chandelier back and forth while I hung onto a pillar for support, weak from laughing. We became so carried away that we couldn't stop even when we sat on canvas chairs between takes and tried to be coherent. It was catching. The crew were laughing helplessly too. Everyone was having a wonderful time. Pity it didn't work that well on the CinemaScope screen.

In the five and a half years I was contracted to Fox, and in fact for several years before and after my tenure there, their record at the box office was appalling. And artistically it was even worse. The studio that had turned out such hits as *Gentleman's Agreement, Grapes of Wrath, Razor's Edge* and *Letter to Three Wives* now turned out things like *The Girl Can't Help It*, with Jayne Mansfield, and *How to Be Very, Very Popular* with Sheree North. Depressing. Especially for the stockholders. Zanuck was less and less involved in the everyday production. Buddy Adler was head of the studio now, and everything he did turned to dross. At this time the studio was deciding to make an expensive blockbuster— *Cleopatra*, the story of the *femme fatale* of all time. In first position for the role of the fascinating Serpent of the Nile was the contender from Great Britain—the "pouting panther" herself—J. Collins. However, the studio, and Walter Wanger, the producer, would not accept me as I was. Grooming had to take place. I had to learn to walk and talk and move like an Egyptian queen. Specialists in the art of walking and deportment (what have I been doing so wrong all these years, pray?) were called in to turn this sow's ear into a silk purse. My body must be slimmed down. At one hundred and twenty pounds I was too curvy for Cleo, so they told me.

I dieted; I exercised; I sat for hours in the makeup and hairdressing rooms while makeup man Whitney Snyder applied unusual and elaborate designs on my face. "I know she had slanted eyes but this is *ridiculous.*" I gazed into a pair of astonished green eyes outlined from nose to temple in black and purple eyeliner; silver sequins outlined the liner, and a glistening blue-black wig cascaded to my shoulders. No less astounding was my costume for the test I was about to make.

A pleated toga of pale violet chiffon stopped at thigh level. Silver sandals laced to the knee—causing me to worry about early varicose veins. A teeny weeny silver bikini bra from which hung baubles, bangles and bric-a-brac of various hues of purple and silver. A giant collar of amethyst and silver inhibited my vocal cords and made moving my head an effort. Immense silver earrings jangled to and fro and constantly tangled themselves in the wig.

The costume was finished off with arm bracelets from wrist to elbow of sturdy sterling silver, nine or ten large rings all representing snakes, and a billowing cloak of purple velvet and silver lamé. This was attached to the giant collar and was so long that if I misjudged my step I would trip and almost strangle myself. In this sensuous, enticing gear I hobbled to Stage 16 to try and act some of the most appalling dialogue ever written opposite an actor who, though obviously chosen for his looks and virility, had as much acting talent as Minnie Mouse—maybe less.

I tried hard. Walter Wanger and Co. persevered. If the first test wasn't too good, maybe it was because the costuming was wrong. Test again— and we did. Three tests, in three outrageous outfits, I made for the coveted role. How I ached to play her. Shaw's Cleopatra had been my test piece for the RADA entrance exam and I knew it was a role suited to me. Naturally they were considering other actresses too, and naturally eventually the casting couch reared its all too ugly head. Spyros Skouras, an elderly Greek gentleman, was the chairman of the board of directors at Fox. He had much to say about the casting of Cleo and he said it. To me and often. Phone calls, suggestions and skittish forays around his desk. He should know better, I thought, as I skipped out of his clutches. He's old enough to be my grandpa.

But with typical Greek tenacity he continued his entreaties and persuasions. An eye for an eye, a tooth for a tooth—a screw for a part. No thank you very much, Mr. Grandfatherly Greek—I have my hands full at home. I tried to be as graceful about it as I could in the circumstances. Greeks don't take kindly to rejection, but he still persisted in calling me often to tell me what a terrible career mistake I was making by my unreceptiveness toward him.

This did not help my relationship with George, who now spent several nights a week at my apartment, considered me his property, and heard the phone conversations. He became enraged at the ancient Greek's audacity. Stupidly I had told him about the young Greek, Peter, and endured several hours of tongue lashing. I had hidden the little diamond anchor he'd given me, and when Peter came out for a visit I hastily sent him back to jet-set land. But George's jealousy was boundless. Too broad a smile at the delivery boy and his dander was up, and off he went again: "Why did you . . . ?" "How could you . . . ?" "Why can't you . . . ?" I knew his dialogue inside out and it was making me a nervous wreck. I started to get occasional attacks of hives, especially after I ate lobster or shrimp. After several tests my doctor discovered I was allergic to shellfish and must stop eating it completely. Quite a blow. I liked it, but my reactions had been getting worse each time I ate it, and Doctor Sellars had warned me that these allergies could become dangerous.

At the end of the shooting of *Rally Round the Flag, Boys* I gave a small dinner party. Although I went to many parties I was not accustomed to giving them. Most of the people who crowded into my tiny and modest apartment were, I thought, used to a more lavish setting for their revels. I fluttered insecurely around trying to be the perfect hostess to people like Milton Berle, Paul Newman, Joanne Woodward, Sammy Davis, Stanley and Marion Donen and about twenty others, and imbibing quite a lot of wine.

La Scala was doing the catering, and I had chosen the menu with care. But not quite enough thought had gone into my choice. After a heaping plate of cioppino I started to feel my cheeks flaming and large welts appeared on my neck and shoulders. "Gosh, you look like a suet pudding!" laughed one of my English girlfriends. I rushed to the bathroom mirror and saw a flushed and swollen face and startled green eyes set in a sea of broken red capillaries and puffed-up eyelids. Dr. Sellars had told me to call him at any hour if this allergy came upon me. The hour had come. I leaped to the phone in the bedroom. Sammy Davis was on it talking earnestly with his hand over his ear to shut out the babble of voices around him. "Kim, baby, you know I care—I don't give a damn what the papers say, baby . . ." I interrupted him in mid-Kim. "Sam— I've *got* to use the phone—please." He didn't hear my frenzied plea and continued his soliloquy . . . "Of course not, baby—how can that bastard Harry push you around like that? . . ."

"Sammy, *please!*" He looked up and gasped, "What happened to your face?" I grabbed the phone from him, yelled a breathless "Sorry, Kim!" and dialed Al Sellars. A group of concerned onlookers had gathered to observe my transformation from dazzling hostess to Dracula. I felt hives swelling like tomatoes all over my face as I breathlessly explained to Sellars my predicament. "Get over here immediately," he said authoritatively.

"I'll drive you," said an anxious Stanley Donen. "Quickly!" I yelped, my desire to escape from my own party and the anxious stares of the guests uppermost in my mind. I grabbed a scarf and we rushed down the stairs, my breathing already starting to feel strange and forced.

Stanley drove fast and erratically through semi-deserted Sunset Boulevard. My face felt as if it was being blown up by a bicycle pump. I shot a feverish glance into the rear-view mirror. "Oh, my *God!* Stanley, don't look at me!" I threw the scarf over what was the most grotesque sight I had ever seen. My face had become the size of a football, and it was getting bigger by the second, and turning purplish red. My eyes were disappearing into the rapidly swelling surrounding tissue. My lips were bananas, so thick I couldn't talk, and worst of all, I realized that I could not get enough air into my throat to breathe properly. It too was swelling rapidly. I was choking for breath.

"Jesus H. Christ!" Stanley's look of frozen horror and his sudden acceleration to one hundred miles an hour and through all the red lights was proof enough of my plight. I couldn't speak—I could hardly breathe. I lay back with the scarf over my face so no one could glimpse this horror, and realized I was probably dying.

"I'm dying . . ." I gasped.

"You'll make it, kid—you'll make it." Stanley's desperate voice was reassuring, but his face, a study in paralyzed fear, was not. At the same time as I was facing death, the little voice in the back of my head was telling me to keep the scarf over my head so no one would have to see how hideous I had become. "Live fast, die young and have a good-looking corpse." It was a Bogart line from *Knock on Any Door*. I had done the first, was about to do the second, but the last was by now far beyond me.

I hope they cremate me before anyone can see what I look like, I thought hazily and then fainted, right into the loving arms of the most beautiful sight I'd ever seen—a nurse. As I was wheeled through the corridor—yes, the wheelchair had been waiting, too—Sellars pumped an injection into my arm and I heard through a haze his Dr. Kildare voice saying ". . . Probably have to give her a tracheotomy." That's all I need, I thought. A tube through my throat. That should photograph attractively —if I live to ever appear on the silver screen again.

The prognosis seemed unlikely. My face was like a revolting barrage balloon floating above me, alien from my body, which felt like ten thousand mosquitoes had just lunched on it. As I was propelled through the hygienic corridors of the Roxbury Medical Center a few passers-by observed this pathetic creature obviously in final death throes and her entourage. A solicitous nurse pumping adrenalin into her arm, calm yet concerned doctor taking her pulse, a frantic-looking tousle-haired film director, and the creature herself, oblivious to her imminent death, concerned only with keeping her ghastly visage far from the madding crowd.

Magically, my body responded instantly to the adrenalin injection the nurse had administered in the lobby. By the time we reached the doctor's office, I could at least breathe a little easier and the dirigible that used to be my face was deflating slightly.

Death did not claim this young victim just yet. My astrologer had told me that I would always "be saved at the eleventh hour," whether from financial ruin, certain death or bad emotional involvements. I was just happy to get my face back. Stanley Donen couldn't get over the fact that at death's door my main concern had been that I should not let anyone see my ugliness. Such is the vanity and insecurity of a young actress under contract to a studio whose entire emphasis throughout her working day is placed on the illusion of retaining perfection of face and body at all times. I couldn't let myself look awful in front of somebody else, even if I was at death's door.

George came back from his nineteenth trip to the Orient, location scouting, and we rather daringly decided to attend a large industry party together.

In the beautiful private room upstairs at Romanoff's all was glitter, glamour and glib talk. *Le tout* Hollywood was there. Everyone from Buddy Adler to Darryl F. Zanuck had put on his best bib and tucker and —to hell with early calls—decided to party.

I wore the Trujillo necklace. It looked divine with the white strapless silk dress and diamond earrings, which I had bought myself from my *Island in the Sun* expense money while in London. Clever kid, living at home and not having to pay those hotel bills. Much smarter to blow the money at Cartier than the Connaught.

George and I made an attractive couple, and by now several people at the party knew of our relationship. I was so happy to be out with him, to feel as though we belonged together. Soon—he had assured me only yesterday—we would be married, a thought too exciting to contemplate without chills running up and down my spine. It was a delicious evening. To be out with the man I loved, publicly for once, to be able to dance with him, touch him, look into his eyes, talk to him and not have to pretend to be enjoying the company of someone else.

"Is that the necklace Trujillo gave you?" I couldn't believe my ears. One of my girlfriends, the only one other than Zsa Zsa and Cappy who knew of it, had plopped herself down next to us as George and I were having a tête-à-tête on a banquette. She was somewhat the worse for wine.

"N-n-no—it's wardrobe," I stammered, noticing out of the corner of my eye George's nostrils flare suspiciously.

"It looks *just* like the one you described to me," she tattled on, squinting close to get a good look.

"Mmm—yes, well they really are doing good things with costume jewelry these days, aren't they?" Her husband mercifully appeared to whisk her onto the dance floor, and I turned, flushing hotly, face to face with George's angry brown eyes.

"Trujillo?" His questioning and menacing tone sent shivers down my spine of a different kind from those I was experiencing only a few minutes ago.

"Trujillo who, may I ask?" His tone became even more menacing and his hand, which had been gently on my knee, now turned into a vice. There was no possible denial—my flaming cheeks and blazing diamonds were proof enough. I was undone, unfaithful to my unfaithful lover— bad, bad girl. I falteringly, stammeringly, haltingly told him all. He extracted every detail from me, his face a mask of rage which he was trying extremely hard and unsuccessfully to control. My tactless friend had realized her *faux pas* and was grimacing "I'm sorrys" at me across the room. By now the nearest onlookers were riveted to our obvious discussion.

"Slut," he whispered savagely into my ear. "You're worse than a street-corner harlot." His fingers gripped my knee even harder and I winced, tears of pain and humiliation squeezing themselves from under my carefully painted eyelids and making little gray streams down pink cheeks. With an uncontrollable epithet bursting from his lips, he ripped the necklace from around my throat and flung it savagely across the room, to the astonishment of several observant ladies to whom diamonds have always been a girl's best friend. And he was off and away, leaving me to grovel for the broken baubles on hands and knees in front of *tout* Hollywood.

A few girlfriends joined in the hunt for those tiny carats—so precious and so useless—but which certain women could not do without. I was not joining their ranks. The insurance alone on this bauble was preposterous, and George's attitude and my humiliation did not seem enough of a price to pay for the privilege of parading this bit of chemical junk around the "A" party circuit. I knew a lot of the older wives of men in the business— producers, directors and executives—did not approve of me. They felt I was a threat to them because of my so-called "loose" morals. Because, strangely enough, with the paradoxical double standard of the day it was considered "OK" for a girl to sleep around with casting directors, producers, agents, to get on and up the ladder. But going to bed with men because it was enjoyable branded one as cheap and frivolous. So, no doubt, some of those ladies contemplating this sad little scene at Romanoff's restaurant were smugly thinking that I was getting what I deserved. Having an affair with a married man, indeed. Serves her right.

We stayed until two-thirty piecing together the bits of necklace on a table like some glittering jigsaw puzzle. It had shattered into about a hundred and fifty pieces—but none of the diamonds themselves were lost, and although the necklace was in pieces it was not irreparable. The waiters joined the treasure hunt and finally we retrieved it all. "Into the vault with this as soon as it's fixed," I said grimly. "It's more trouble than it's worth."

George and I made up, of course. It seemed half of our relationship was making up. We both apologized. He for making a nasty spectacle of me, I for being a faithless sex fiend when his wife was pregnant. For a few weeks all was sweetness and light until suddenly the papers got the goods on Trujillo.

"Gifts for the Girls" screamed the tabloid headlines. "Diamonds for Kim Novak and Joan Collins," yelled the tabloids. " 'Say it again and I'll sue,' " said Zsa Zsa. The yellow presses were running at full speed to print startling and colorful stories of sex, sin and costly baubles in Hollywood.

It started when Congress, while voting on foreign aid to the Dominican Republic, was asked by a Congressman if the Republic really *needed* help. It had been discovered that the young Trujillo, with a wife and six children, appeared to have lined his pockets with over six million dollars which could only have come from American aid, and had proceeded to lavish gifts on various well-known film actresses. The catalogue was impressive. To Zsa Zsa Gabor: 1 Empress Chinchilla Coat—value $8,500; 1 Mercedes-Benz—value $5,500. To Kim Novak (whom he now professed to love and hoped to marry in spite of the six children): 1 diamond-and-pearl ring—value $3,500; 1 pair of diamond earrings—value $1,500; 1 Mercedes-Benz (he obviously liked that car)—$8,500. And—in spite of some weak "No comment" and halfhearted denials to the press—Collins finally admitted all: 1 diamond necklace—value $10,000.

Zsa Zsa sprang fiercely to Trujillo's defense, and even more fiercely to her own when the Congressman accused her of being "the most expensive courtesan since Madame de Pompadour." Zsa Zsa with her typical Hungarian wit countered: "I was born in the wrong century—I would have made a bum of Madame de Pompadour." One up to Hungary.

Miss Novak also jumped to his defense. Photos of their hand-holding had been appearing in the tabloids. "He is a wonderful gentleman and an honor to his great father who is doing a world of good for his country. He is a real goodwill ambassador." So much for Poland.

The British contingent, after grudgingly admitting the existence of the trinket, categorically refused to discuss the man and his affairs at all. I desperately wanted my name out of the headlines, and revealing nothing was the surest way of achieving that.

But the publicity rekindled George's anger and jealousy. There were more scenes, more tears, more making up. I started getting minor allergic reactions again. "It's nervous tension," said my doctor. "Get out of town for a while until this blows over."

I went to New York to do the Steve Allen television show. Walking down Madison Avenue one fine afternoon I stumbled upon an intriguing shop. "Jolie Gabor Jeweler" it was called.

The boutique was filled to overflowing with authentic-looking jewelry. The jewels were in fact paste—glass and rhinestones, but so cleverly designed that they looked like the most expensive diamonds, emeralds, pearls and rubies. The shop had many photographs of the three Gabor girls and Mama, looking delicious and wearing Jolie's jewelry creations, which she designed herself. Madame Gabor, Senior, was there that afternoon in person. A vision in pale beige crepe and pearls, smelling wonderful and looking like a younger, more glamorous Barbara Cartland. By contrast, in my gray pleated skirt, loafers and black polo-neck sweater I looked like a college girl.

Madame Gabor obviously didn't think someone dressed as I was would do anything more than browse, so when I pointed to a "diamond" necklace in one of the showcases, she showed it to me with a marked lack of enthusiasm.

"For your mother, dear?" she inquired in her Zsa Zsa-like husky Hungarian voice.

"No, for me," I said excitedly examining the necklace. It was incredible. It was practically identical to the one Trujillo had given me. An idea had formulated in my mind.

"How much is this?"

"One hundred and twenty-five dollars," said Madame Gabor, quite surprised to see this student type willing to pay that much for something that would be out of place at Vassar. Without makeup and simply dressed, I could easily pass for seventeen or eighteen.

"I'm a friend of your daughter's," I explained as I scribbled the check and showed her my I.D.

"Ah, of course!" She smiled, no longer surprised. With Zsa Zsa anything was possible, and who knew what possibilities lay behind my baggy clothes and innocent face?

"I wish you much success with it, dollink," she said, giving me the package. "It vil look vunderful on you. With the right outfit, of course," she added hastily.

"Thank you, Madame," I trilled, tripping into the Madison Avenue sunshine. George had a surprise in store for him.

We had a romantic candlelit dinner *à deux* at a cozy bistro on the beach at Malibu. It was a perfect California night—a little chilly, but the moon was a miniature crescent, the sea dark and calm, and the beach pebbles crushed softly beneath our feet as we walked hand in hand along the shore. I had drunk a bottle of Liebfraumilch singlehandedly and was feeling rather giddy. We were celebrating our first anniversary of on-and-off togetherness. Ups and downs seemed to be my destiny and I was adapting to them like a trouper. He wasn't an easy man. Fascinating yes, witty and good-looking certainly, but his tempers, his jealousy and his ambivalent attitude toward his divorce proceedings did not make me feel secure. I *still* never knew where I really stood with him. I was about to play a trump card.

"Darling," I cooed, "I know how upset you have been about the diamond necklace." I put my fingers to his mouth to stop his retort. "No, don't say anything, darling. I realize it was an idiotic thing to do, to accept a gift from someone I had—er—hardly known." Again he started to speak but I stopped him. "So, because I love you so much, I'm going to do something that I hope will stop us from bringing this subject up *ever* again."

I brought out the necklace from my bag. The diamonds glittered in the moonlight and I dangled them in front of his eyes. "George, my darling, look, your love means more to me than all the diamond necklaces in the world—" and with that I hurled Jolie Gabor's $125 masterpiece into the waves, where it sank instantly.

He looked at me in stunned amazement. "Jesus, babe, you just threw ten thousand dollars to the sharks."

"I know," I said softly and serenely. "Oscar time," said my inner voice. "Because I love you so much I don't want anything like this to ever come between us again."

He seemed truly moved by this noble gesture and gathered me into a passionate embrace. I felt it was a devious and underhand ploy—one I was not proud of—but I hoped that this would close the Trujillo chapter forever.

It did. But when, a week later, I found him locked in another passionate embrace in a car on Beverly Drive, with the blond wife of one of TV's handsomest Italian singers, I knew that I was dicing with disaster.

I walked into his office the next day, unannounced, and confronted him. He denied it. He was a brilliant liar (I'd heard him with his wife), and he almost convinced me. But not quite. I called the singer's wife in Palm Springs: "You're playing it too close to home, my dear," I said icily. "Lay off George Englund or I'll tell your husband, I swear I will." She spluttered and cried and finally admitted it was true, and I hung up, disgusted. Was I becoming a hard, bitter bitch? Or were circumstances just ganging up on me to turn me into one?

The phone rang. My agent.

"Can you ride a horse?" he inquired.

"Of course not," I replied warily. "They scare me to death."

"You'll have to learn then," he said. "You've been cast opposite Peck in a Western to shoot in two weeks' time in Mexico. Get your ass down to the Fox ranch in Santa Monica tomorrow morning at nine o'clock. You leave for Mexico in ten days so you'd better learn fast."

"But I'm *terrified* of horses," I bleated piteously. "What happens if I can't learn to ride?"

"You'll go on suspension again, and I know you can't afford that," he said crisply. "Get it together, kid." And he hung up.

I lay back on the bed and gazed at the California "cottage-cheese"-

style ceiling, a fixture in most West Hollywood apartments. A Western! Me! The British Bombshell in the saddle—what a joke. But at least it would get me out of town, and away from him. He had a hold on me like Svengali had on Trilby. I knew it, I hated it and loved it: Was I becoming a total masochist? My analyst assured me I was still looking to conquer Daddy and that the George and Cloris situation represented this, but I felt that there was more in it than that. George's attraction was so strong that I knew it couldn't just be a father fascination. When things were going well with us I felt so completely *right* with him, infinitely more than I had ever felt with anyone else before. It was total "oneness." The kind I never could believe existed.

I believe that loving someone, whether it be a lover, parent or friend, is accepting them for the way they really are and not trying to change or shape them into a behavior image of what *you* want them to be. Loving is being happy that the other person is doing something that is making him happy, even if it means that you cannot always be together. Therefore I let George do whatever he wanted. He was still so full of doubts and guilt about his divorce—fine, I would understand and try and help him, support him, and not to make him feel more guilt-ridden by bringing *our* relationship problems into an already difficult situation. He felt a need to see other women occasionally because he'd been trapped in his marriage for so long and had gone straight from that into an affair with me, with never a chance to look around to see where the action was—well, that was a harder pill to swallow, but I understood that too. I tried like hell to understand, because I loved him so much that that was all that mattered. My own pride and self-confidence was on the wane. Being an understanding mistress to a mixed-up and often thoughtless lover was taking its toll. But I was resilient, persistent and tough, and I hung on in. Looking back, he obviously didn't love me enough. But I loved him too much to give him up.

On the occasions that we have bumped into each other throughout the years, he has always been enormously flattering and ruefully reflective about the fact that "if only" I had been more patient and understanding we would have ended up together. I wonder. There is a limit to anyone's patience and understanding.

Brooding endlessly about my romantic problems, my rear end hurting violently from two weeks of riding practice, I flew to a primitive little village on the outskirts of Morelia in Mexico for *The Bravados*. On location again. My God, did I ever seem to spend more than two or three months in one place without whisking off to foreign parts? My astrologer Ben Gary's words about my gypsy life came back again as I looked around the dank and insect-ridden little adobe hut that was to be my home for the next seven weeks.

The Bravados had a good script, a fairly good director, blustering, blunt Henry King, and an excellent cast: Gregory Peck, Henry Silva, Stephen Boyd, Albert Salmi and Lee Van Cleef. However, I was not cast to advantage as an arrogant, tough, hard-riding American ranch owner. I was meant to look as if I'd been born in the saddle and as though I and the horse were bonded to each other. Instead I felt I looked out of place and awkward, and I certainly did.

I had dutifully spent every morning for the past two weeks in comfortable jeans and T-shirt riding, with Henry, Albert and Stephen, stiffly round and round the Fox ranch on a docile nag called Dulcie, who had a temperament like an old shoe, and whose age seemed to put her in the running for the glue factory. Now, dressed in stiff black jodhpurs, narrow boots constricting my feet so that all circulation immediately left my toes, a ruffled white shirt, black gauntlet gloves and a black Stetson slanted sharply over my eyes (over a heavy wig of course), I was shown the horse I would ride in the picture. Imagine a diesel engine attached to a dragon, and that was Pancho. A black stallion, in his prime. Glossy, glistening, beautiful and *dangerous!* I could feel his animal energy palpitating beneath me as four husky handlers forced me protestingly into the saddle.

Pancho, of course, knew I was nervous. Scared shitless was more like it. I leaned over and patted his nose tentatively to let him know I cared. I offered him two large lumps of sugar. He practically took off my hand. I wrenched it back, startled. He was snorting and tossing his great black mane. His hooves were doing a tap dance on the grass. This baby wanted to *go.* He was about to show this crew of strange people lolling about moving arc lamps and cameras who was the boss. I already knew. I leaned over and whispered to the handlers and my riding instructor to stay nearby at all times. Pancho pricked up his ears, half turned his head and neighed jeeringly. He had heard me. I swear that horse *knew* how scared I was.

"Nothing to worry about, honey." My tough, tobacco-chewing teacher, fifty years in the saddle, patted the horse's rump and gave me a reassuring wink. "It's safe as houses if you'll just *relax*—I told you a thousand times. *Relax,* honey, Pancho can feel your tension."

"Please stay near me, *all* of you, until Henry calls 'Action,' " I hissed to the four laconic, weathered old ranch hands, all highly amused by this nervous English lass sitting petrified in the saddle of Mexico's wickedest horse.

As shooting progressed, Pancho and I became even less close. As soon as he sensed me in the vicinity he reared up. His eyes rolled around in his head, and he bared his yellow teeth in a sadistic smile to welcome me to his back. I had begged for a double for the long shots, and finally Henry King, a stickler for realism and a man who couldn't fathom how anyone couldn't *adore* horses, let alone be frightened of them, had grudgingly agreed. However, I think his motives were more for artistic than altruistic reasons. I had put on about ten pounds in two weeks. A mixture of terror and boredom had driven me into the arms of the great pacifier Food! Every night the hotel served pecan pie, my favorite dish. Every night I would persuade the jovial Mexican cook, who loved my appreciation of his food, to give me the left-over pies. I took them to my lonely prefabricated, Holiday Inn-Mexican-style hotel room with the single fifteen-watt light bulb, put on the record player and gorged. To the sentimental ballads of Sinatra, Tony Bennett and Johnny Mathis I devoured slice after slice of pie until, like some early Roman glutton, I fell into an exhausted nightmare sleep, filled with grinningly ghoulish red-eyed fearsome horses, ready to eat me along with their bale of hay. The next morning I'd stuff what remained of the pie in my bag with the script and finish it off as a little midmorning snack. After ten days of this gluttony, the wardrobe woman unsuccessfully tried to zip me into the pants which, tight before, now fitted like a sausage skin. This necessitated her constantly having to reinforce the splitting seams. She asked me if I was pregnant! I wasn't, but looking at my once slim waist, which had gone from twenty-two to twenty-seven inches in less than a fortnight, I could see where she and the rest of the crew might imagine I was three months gone. Round, chubby cheeks hid my once photogenic cheekbones, and my bosoms could rival Mansfield's.

My midnight feasts did not go unnoticed. The director decided to use my riding double as often as possible, hoping that this would relax me and keep me away from the pecan pie. They even got a double for Pancho! As though to prove me right about horses being dangerous, and out of pique at having been thwarted of his fun every morning by terrifying me when I mounted him, Pancho, in retaliation, kicked up his heels one day at my riding instructor. He broke the poor man's ankle in three places, and from then on everyone had a healthy respect for this noble, cunning beast.

I gave up pecan pie and started playing cards at night, and developed a sudden newfound equestrian skill in the saddle of my friendlier new horse, Adonis. I started to do most of the riding myself. Gregory Peck and I had a scene where we had been riding together for three days searching for a kidnapped girl. The hairdresser insisted on setting my wig each night till it was pin-curl perfect, and then glumly watched me as I pushed dirt and twigs through it and messed it up as much as I could. I rubbed mud and dirt in my face and scrubbed off as much globby makeup as I could. "That girl's going to ruin her career," said the hairdresser bitterly to the makeup artiste, as she watched her attractive hairstyle being destroyed. I tore bits and strands out to look as though I'd really been riding for three days. I still looked like a Hollywood actress sitting fully made up on a prop horse, with tight jodhpurs and a wig. Realism was an unfashionable word in 1959. Actresses were supposed to be goddesses. Untouchable. Plastic. As pristine as a box of candy. I'm sure that the public's notion of beautiful movie stars who can't act is partly the result of overzealousness on the part of the costumer, hairdresser and makeup department. Everyone looked like a store-window mannequin. I managed in *The Bravados* to look fairly unpresentable, but by today's movie standards I was still ridiculously well groomed.

I had not exchanged many words with Gregory Peck until we came to the scene where he and I ride together fast and expertly for days. He was quite shy and did not socialize with the cast, spending his time with Veronique, his attractive French wife. The cast and I were in awe of him.

He was a very big star and seemed rather austere, aloof and uninterested in the rest of us.

He was a wonderful-looking man, tall and rangy, with a classically handsome profile and a strongly carved nose. His aloofness, I found out when we rode for so long, was a form of shyness. He was basically not at ease around new people. I found he had a wonderful sense of humor, and, knowing my fear of riding, he was considerate toward me. But on the last day he teased me unmercifully by riding so fast that I was sore for a week. "Come on, Collins!" he yelled as we cantered faster and faster beside a deep canyon that I knew with a sickening lurch meant plunging to certain death if Adonis placed a hoof wrong. "They say you English women can ride," Peck said mock-scornfully, digging his spurs in and making his mount fly even faster. "Let's see you show 'em *all*, Collins— show 'em you're a real horsewoman, will you?" He galloped even faster. The wind almost took off my Stetson and I jammed it down like Greg's until it covered my eyes. It was enormously exhilarating. I felt in command of that three hundred pounds of sinew and muscle beneath me; I wasn't afraid at all, in fact it was a wonderful, free and joyous feeling I had of space, power and purity.

The camera car was hard put to keep up with us. They hadn't expected Greg to gallop so fast, and even less expected that I would be right alongside him, urging my horse to ever greater speed. Even when Henry yelled "Cut," we continued galloping faster and faster into the distance. I was laughing now and so was Greg, as we heard the assistant director plaintively calling us back to our positions. We reined in the horses. I amazed myself with my newfound expertise and galloped back.

"Thank you, Greg," I yelled over my shoulder. Now I was outracing him!

"For what?" he called back.

"For curing me of my fear of horses—you really did it. I'm not scared anymore."

"Don't mention it, ma'am." He smiled gallantly.

I am still not an enthusiast about horses but thanks to Gregory Peck I can at least get on one now without becoming a nervous wreck.

❖ *Seven* ❖

I SAT IN LA Scala with Barbara and Mort Viner, feeling despondent. My relationship with George had been dragging on for over a year. In spite of six or seven separations, he had eventually always returned to Cloris. He was separated from her now and had promised me that when he returned from the Orient he would definitely divorce her. I felt cynical about it. My love had turned to resignation. There were so many obstacles to overcome; nothing ever seemed to go the way George said it would.

I had been in trouble with Fox several times in the past year for turning down scripts that I thought were wrong for me, and I had gone on suspension. I had spent the early part of 1959 extensively preparing to play Cleopatra, but in spite of several tests I wasn't holding much hope for it now. I was drowning my sorrows in Chianti and cannelloni when I became aware of a young man staring at me from the opposite table.

I returned his gaze, which was becoming rather bold. He raised his glass and smiled. I looked away. Flirting with attractive strangers in restaurants can get one into trouble, and I had other things on my mind. I couldn't resist another look when Barbara said, "That boy who's looking at you is Shirley MacLaine's brother, Warren something or other." I looked over and studied him covertly. He was about twenty-one or twenty-two. Blondish slightly curly hair, worn rather longer than was fashionable, a square-cut Clark Kent type of jaw with a Kirk Douglas dimple in the chin—rather small greenish eyes, but a cute turned-up nose and a sensual mouth. From where I sat it looked as though he suffered from a problem I had once had—*spots!* He wore a blue Brooks Brothers shirt and a tweed jacket. All in all, he looked rather appealing and vulnerable, and my interest was somewhat piqued.

"Who's the girl he's with?" I asked Mort, who knew everyone. "Henry Fonda's daughter, Jane," he said. "She's out here to make some basketball picture with Tony Perkins. It's her first movie." "Are they an item?" I asked casually, sipping my drink. Mort looked at me, amused. "Interested, are you?" "Oh, Mort, really, can't I even ask about somebody without the world thinking I fancy them?"

I had only to look at a man these days and people would start surmising I was having a flirt. Because of my secret affair I had been dating a lot, and the gossip columns were full of my supposed "latest loves." What they didn't know was that my dates were a cover-up.

"She's quite pretty," I said taking a look at Jane. "A bit full in the face. I wonder how she'll photograph." "They're working on her cheekbones," said Barbara. "She goes to that woman in the Valley, she does wonders with problem areas." I looked at Jane Fonda. She was pretty in a fresh, scrubbed, wholesome way, and she had long, fair, thick hair. She bore a strong resemblance to her father, Henry. She was hanging onto Warren's every word. They made the perfect all-American couple. I turned back to my cannelloni and continued talking about other things. Out of the corner of my eye I saw Warren looking me over occasionally, but I didn't return his glances.

I thought nothing more of Mr. Beatty. I was busy rehearsing every day at Fox with Candy Barr. I was playing a stripper in *Seven Thieves* and I was lucky enough to have Candy, who was about the best stripper in America, as my teacher. For two or three hours every day she taught me how to move and dance, bump and grind, and strip. How to peel off my gloves, dress and stockings in the most provocative and sexy manner.

How to turn men on in an overt and truly sensual fashion. She taught me more about sensuality than I had learned in all my years under contract. Candy was a down-to-earth girl with an incredibly gorgeous body and an angelic face. She had recently been sentenced to a long jail term for possession of a tiny amount of marijuana. From her ebullient attitude one would never guess this was hanging over her. She was amusing and gay and we had great fun together choreographing my sensuous strip-teases.

Needless to say, Stage 6 at Fox, where we rehearsed, suddenly became the most popular spot on the Fox lot. It was amazing how many agents, writers, producers and crew members used Stage 6 as a shortcut to Stage 5 or Stage 4, or even the commissary. They would linger and watch while Candy put me through my paces. Actually we rather enjoyed getting an honest audience reaction, and the guys were certainly appreciative. But she was a hard taskmaster, so when John Foreman called and asked me to a party at Debbie Power's house, I tried to beg off, exhausted from all the bumping and grinding. Stripping may look easy, but to do it expertly is physically demanding.

John was insistent, so reluctantly I agreed. I didn't feel like getting dressed up. I was getting bored with having to look like a glamour queen every time I went out. The studio frowned on my Bohemian hippie look. I was trying halfheartedly to be chic, but not succeeding very well, because I had recently made Louella Parsons' "10 Worst Dressed Women" list. I think I'll live up to that tonight, I thought—and took from my wardrobe a pair of gray flannel boy's Bermuda shorts, long gray socks, sneakers and a green Brooks Brothers shirt. I scraped my hair into a ponytail and left off the makeup. I liked the look. A cross between Jackie Cooper and Betty Coed.

Debbie Power was the widow of Tyrone Power. Rumors abounded that she was about to marry my ex-boyfriend, Arthur Loew. Her house, in the flats of Beverly Hills, was filled with people when we arrived. The usual mob doing the usual things—drinking, gossiping, talking box-office grosses, whiling away another forgettable evening. I wandered around chatting to a few people and wishing I hadn't come. My outfit caused a few amused remarks. It didn't bother me. I liked being outrageous sometimes, although at other times I felt like being extremely conventional. Gemini coming out again.

"That piano player is really good," I said to John. "Who is he?" John, who was tall, craned his neck above the crowd and said, "I think it's Shirley MacLaine's brother, Warren something-or-other." Aha, there he is again, I thought. Even if he didn't make it as an actor, he was a superb pianist and could definitely make a living in a cocktail lounge if need be. He was doing imitations of various pianistic styles: Errol Garner, George Shearing, Oscar Peterson. It was clever and I drew closer to watch and listen. He noticed I was there and smiled, but he appeared totally absorbed in his music. John and I left after a couple of hours and Warren was still immersed in his piano playing.

The next day was Sunday, gorgeous and sunny. I drove to the beach for my tan and then came back to go to a cocktail party for songwriter Jimmy McHugh. Gardner McKay was my date. When I checked my answering service, there were six messages to call Warren Beatty at the Chateau Marmont. Surprise! We had not exchanged a word and yet he had managed to get my number. Immediately I hung up, the phone rang, and a soft voice said, "Hi, did you get my message?" He didn't say who he was, and I admired his assurance that I would know his voice.

"Yes, I did," I said crisply. "You can't be a poor actor. It costs twenty-five cents a call from the Chateau." He chuckled and said, "Do you want to have dinner tonight?" I thought swiftly. The party was from five-thirty to seven-thirty and although Gardner probably thought I would have dinner with him, nevertheless I had not actually said I would. Gardner, a black-haired six-foot-four actor at Fox, was, according to *Life* magazine, the handsomest man in America. We had been going out in a platonic way for a few months. Fox was pleased to have two of its stars "dating" and we went to various industry functions with their approval.

"OK. I have to go somewhere first. I'll meet you in Beverly Hills." I didn't want him coming to the house and bumping into Gardner.

"Eight o'clock at the corner of Rodeo and Santa Monica," he said. "I can hardly wait." Strangely enough, neither could I. This was odd. Somebody I hadn't met—hadn't spoken to—and I was excited at the thought of having dinner with him.

Rushing home after the party—I pleaded exhaustion and an early call to Gardner—I ripped off the black faille cocktail dress and the flowered organdy hat and jumped into a pair of jeans and a shirt. I brushed my hair and took off some of my makeup. Warren was obviously slightly younger than I. I didn't want to look too done up.

He was waiting at Rodeo and Santa Monica in a rented Chevy. I locked my rented yellow Ford and joined him.

"Hi," we said simultaneously and looked at each other. "Do you like Mexican?" he said, after we had each taken a good look. "Mexican what?" I asked, coming down to earth. He was better looking than I remembered. True, he had a few spots—probably left over from adolescence, which couldn't have been too far behind him—but his eyes, although small, were clear greenish-blue, and I noticed that his hands were beautiful.

"Food, of course," he said as we moved into the Santa Monica traffic. "I thought we'd go to the Casa Escobar—they make terrific Margaritas."

"Sounds good," I said gaily.

Over dinner and Margaritas we couldn't stop talking—or looking. He was in Hollywood hopefully to start his movie career. He had done stock, a lot of TV, and had made a few tests—the usual things young actors do —and was hoping to get the lead in Willian Inge's new play *A Loss of Roses*. He was an Aries and was, curiously, born on March 30—the same date as Sydney Chaplin. I gravitated toward Aries men. Having recently become interested in astrology, I realized that my sign of Gemini had certain compatible signs. These were Aries, Libra, Gemini and Aquarius.

We talked and laughed until past midnight. He dropped me at my car and said he would follow me home to see that I arrived safely.

My Shoreham Drive apartment was about half a mile from his hotel. As I drove through the deserted Beverly Hills streets, I wondered if I should ask him up for a nightcap. I realized what this meant. I was not an innocent virgin. Asking him up for a drink could be construed as an invitation to other things. I was still in love, albeit unhappily, with George. If I asked Warren up, I was taking one giant step.

I liked Warren. I liked his mind. I liked his humor, his conversation—and his physical packaging.

My mind was buzzing with indecisive ifs and buts, pros and cons. As I drove into the underground garage he decided for me. "I'm coming up," he announced, pulling his car in behind mine, "for coffee"—and the die was cast.

We became inseparable. Apart from physical attraction, we seemed to have everything in common. We would stay up all night talking, laughing, discussing, and I would stagger wearily to the studio in the morning to work on *Seven Thieves*. He would call me eighteen times a day. We couldn't bear to be apart. Every second we could be together we were. He hung around the set for hours. We drove to the beach and gazed at the ocean and each other; we went to piano bars to listen to music. Sometimes he played. He played magnificently—after acting, the piano was his main passion. We played poker with my friends, who were all surprised by this sudden romance. "Don't you think he's a touch young for you?" said Cappy one afternoon, after Warren and I had been entwined on a beach chair all day. "He looks about seventeen—and how can you stand those *spots?*"

"Oh, Cappy, for goodness sake, he's not that young. He's twenty-two and I'm only a couple of years older. Don't you see he's the best thing that's happened to me? I've got to get George out of my system and Warren is really helping me to do that."

"But, darling," she said, "he's penniless, he's an unsuccessful, unknown actor, and he's probably using you to get ahead." Dear Cappy! She usually called the shots right—but I ignored her remarks this time, although her advice had usually been on the nose.

"For once in my life, someone is trying to make me happy. Someone is caring about how *I* feel, someone is taking an interest in my mind, in my work, and helping me over my insecurities. It doesn't matter that he's poor and not successful. He's a terrific actor and he's going to make it. You can bet on it." Cappy looked dubious. "Have you told George?" she asked. We were primping in her lavish dressing room.

"Oh, Cappy. I don't know how to tell him," I groaned. "He's in Hong Kong with Marlon. Every time he's phoned, I've been out."

"You must send him a cable," she said firmly. "It's only fair to him. You've been seeing no one else but this Warren for three weeks now. You know George will find out as soon as he gets here. Send it now."

I sat down and reluctantly composed a "Dear John" cable. Although Warren and I were in the midst of a flaming love affair, it was still very hard for me to break off with my married lover after nearly a year and a half of being together. He had treated me callously, I knew—but I also empathized with his marriage problems and the three kids. I understood his problems only too well—that was *my* problem!

"Can't see you any more," I wrote, "In love with someone else—very sorry—love JC." "How's that?" I said, showing it to Cappy.

"Awful," she said, "but better than nothing. Send it."

George returned from the Orient two days later and immediately called. He was charming and persuasive. He couldn't believe I had fallen for someone else. Not after all we had meant to each other. He would definitely and absolutely get the divorce immediately and then we would be together forever. I had heard this line so many times, but he was my weakness and he knew how to manipulate me. He persuaded me to meet him for a drink the following afternoon at the Cock and Bull, an English-style pub on the Strip.

"At least you owe it to me to say goodbye properly," he said, "and not just a damn 'Dear John' telegram."

I told Warren I was meeting George.

"How long will it take?" he asked petulantly. "Oh, just forty-five minutes or an hour," I said airily. "Just to end it civilly, like friends—we owe it to each other."

"You'll probably realize it's him you love and not me," he said moodily, doodling on a piece of paper and fiddling with the phone. He *loved* the telephone. He made twenty to thirty calls a day, often to the same people three or four times.

"I won't," I said, putting my arms around him. "I know I won't. You don't have a thing to worry about."

I left him doodling on his pad, the phone, like some extra part of his body, hanging from his ear, and went to meet George. He was tanned from his trip and beautifully turned out in a beige suit, pale green shirt and a dark green tie. He looked great. I felt sick. I was about to kiss off a year and a half of my life. I was about to get rid of Daddy! I was about to say goodbye to fifteen months of misery, unhappiness, jealousy and hysteria, but also to closeness, intellectual stimulation and, at times, more joy than I'd ever had before.

He ordered Pimm's for us and got down to business. He already knew all about Warren. "He's just a kid," he said. "How can you, a sophisticated woman, be interested in a *kid?*" I started to protest that Warren was twenty-two, but he went on, "Listen, Joanie, I know how tough it's been for you this past year. I know I've been a shit and I understand this little fling of yours had to come. I understand it and I forgive it, and I'll forget it ever happened if you just end it now and come back to me. . . ."

He went on in this vein, ordering more Pimm's and talking in his clever and fascinating way. I began to waver. Maybe he was right. George was a man—a grownup—Warren was a boy. George knew about life, and although Warren was clever and bright and razor-sharp, he was still inexperienced, naive and gauche. My good intentions started to falter. I was so weak. So stupid. After all the lies and promises George had made to me, I was starting to believe him again.

I looked at my watch. Eight o'clock. We had been there for three hours. "I've got to go." I got up hurriedly and he threw a ten-dollar bill on the table and followed me to the parking lot. He grabbed my shoulders as I stood trying to open my car door. "I'm going to give you a week to decide," he said, conceding heavily. "You're a smart girl, you're *not* going to throw your life away on an out-of-work actor who's probably only using you." He bent down and kissed me. A fervent kiss. It felt good. Too good.

"Goodbye," I said faintly as I stumbled into the driver's seat, trembling violently. Oh, God—could I love two men?

"I'll call you tomorrow—I know it's not easy, babe, but don't forget what we had and what we *can* have when I get the divorce."

I pulled away into the Sunset Strip traffic in a turmoil. Warren was not in the apartment. He arrived five minutes later. Furious. "I saw you," he said, ripping off his glasses and jacket, throwing them on the sofa. "I saw you necking in the parking lot." He tried to look menacing and walked toward me. He tripped over a stool—without his glasses he was practically blind.

"We weren't," I said helplessly, and more than a little drunk. "He kissed me goodbye, that's all."

"Oh, sure," he sneered. He had been driving around and around the Cock and Bull for two hours, steaming with jealousy. We fought all night. Yelling, crying, recriminations and declarations of a passion neither of us was really positive about. We ran the gamut of emotions as only actor and actress can. My indecisiveness drove him mad, but it drove *me* mad, too. I wanted to do the right thing for me, but I was so unsure. Did I really love Warren? Enough to end it with George?

The next day I had an early call on *Seven Thieves* to shoot a scene in the Monte Carlo Casino with Rod Steiger. I was a wreck. I had hardly slept and my eyes were swollen from crying. The makeup man, used to the overly developed emotions of actresses, did his magic tricks and I was poured into a tight black satin evening dress, hair swept into a chignon and diamonds in my ears. I looked nearly new, but I couldn't play the scene. I kept blowing my lines—something I *never* did. Henry Hathaway, the director, became furious with me. The angrier he became, the more I blew my lines, until finally I broke down completely and left the set in tears. Rod came to console me. He was a kind and considerate actor—hard to reach on a personal level but wonderful to work with. Very giving.

Warren came for lunch in the commissary and we again hashed over our problems. I told him I was going to see my analyst at five-thirty and that I would try to sort things out.

On the familiar brown couch I tried to be analytical about my problem. I owed nothing to nobody. I should not go to George just because of my "investment" of time, but only if he could make me truly happy—which most of the time he had not managed to do. If Warren made me happy I should be with him. An hour backward, forward, inside out—get rid of my father—for that's what the married man represented. But to chuck out that year and a half when attainment was so close? Or was it? George had lied to me so often—maybe this was another lie. Finally I made a decision. I left Dr. Greenleigh's office and walked, elated, down Bedford Drive to my car. A tap on the shoulder. It was George. Full of confidence and vigor from the hour of uninterrupted soul searching, I told him, "I love you. A lot. I probably always will. You're the brightest, cleverest man I know, but you haven't made me happy. I want and *need* happiness now. I want to be with Warren—he loves me, and we're good for each other now. Please don't try to stop me." He pleaded and remonstrated, but I wouldn't listen. "I hope we can always be friends," I said, meaning it, and walked away.

That night Warren and I celebrated our commitment to each other with his sister, Shirley MacLaine, at La Scala. We had been together nearly a month and everything was blissful.

He left the following week for New York to start rehearsals for Inge's *A Loss of Roses,* with Carol Haney and Betty Field. It was a wonderful break for him. One for which he had been waiting for months. Inge's plays were always critical and commercial successes and Warren's part—that of a tormented young man with a slight Oedipus complex who falls in love with a much older woman—was meaty enough to guarantee he would be noticed and hopefully discovered for films. For, unlike me, Warren's first love and preference was for movies rather than theater.

Inge's plays included *Bus Stop, Come Back Little Sheba, Picnic* and *Dark at the Top of the Stairs,* all major dramatic works which had earned him accolades as one of America's most important playwrights. Warren was nervous and excited about the assignment and he plunged into rehearsals with enthusiasm and optimism. I stayed in Hollywood to finish *Seven Thieves* and then planned to join him. We talked on the phone constantly. I watched him in a TV show called "The Affairs of Dobie Gillis"—he was quite good. He had talent and looks and blinding ambition. I felt he was bound to succeed.

In November, *Seven Thieves* was finished and I caught the midnight plane to Washington, where *A Loss of Roses* had just opened to less than rave reviews. I was tired. Apart from shooting, the strip sequences for *Seven Thieves* were arduous. I had also been cramming in photographic and wardrobe tests for the next film I was supposed to start—D.H. Lawrence's *Sons and Lovers.*

We stayed at the Willard Hotel in Washington. I met his parents, who lived in nearby Arlington. They were kind, humorous people whom I liked instantly. I could see from whom Warren and Shirley had inherited their intelligence and good manners.

As Warren was busy rehearsing all day and performing at night, I had time to myself—something I relished. I took long walks and read, went to the Smithsonian, and thought about our relationship and what I wanted from it. I didn't know—I was happy just taking each day as it came.

Warren and I seemed to be good for each other. We didn't want marriage. I didn't want babies. I just wanted to live and enjoy my life.

When the final script of *Sons and Lovers* arrived, Warren decided I shouldn't do it. Not only did he think the story was unappealing, but he did not want me to go to England and leave *him!* Had the film been a comedy, I would probably have done it anyway. I had been nagging Fox to let me do more comedy roles, but apart from *Rally Round the Flag, Boys,* the funny parts went to other actresses. So I rebelled, realizing this would mean a suspension of salary. Once again! The previous year I had refused two roles, one in *The Last Wagon* and the other in *Madison Avenue.* Both turned out to be flops, but for the duration of the shooting of these films I not only did not get paid but could not accept another job. Since I was by now earning $2,500 a week, forty weeks a year, this financial sacrifice was not easy, but I was becoming discontented with not having any decisive say in my career. Now Warren—the bossy Aries side of him coming out—was making career decisions for me.

I was a "utility infielder." If Fox couldn't get Susan Hayward or Gene Tierney for the role, they'd use me. I was usually cast at the last minute in decorative and unrewarding roles. My agent would call and tell me to get over to wardrobe right away. Once there, old Lana Turner or Maureen O'Hara costumes were refitted and refurbished to fit me and off I would go, to Tokyo, Mexico or wherever the wind blew me, my second-hand finery following. I was not stretching myself at all as an actress and Warren understood this more than anyone.

Jerry Wald, the producer of *Sons and Lovers,* had promised various script changes that would have made my role in *Sons and Lovers* more palatable and interesting. When I read the final script these changes had not been made. Warren encouraged me to walk out of the film. His motives were not exactly selfless. He needed me with him—he was getting lots of publicity over our relationship and it was a tricky time of his life. With me in England he would feel forlorn and lonely. "Don't go, Butterfly," he begged. "Don't leave your Bee." I moved back to New York with him, into the Blackstone Hotel, and *A Loss of Roses* opened. It was not Inge's greatest work. The critics were unkind, but Warren's personal reviews were good and everyone thought he was excellent as the sensitive boy. Interest was stirring for him in Hollywood. The play ran for only three weeks but after it closed we stayed on in New York seeing friends and plays, going to the Harwyn Club—an upmarket Manhattan boite where they let us eat free because of the publicity they got from our going there—arguing and making up, neither of us earning a bean, broke, but loving life and each other a lot.

We moved back to California at the beginning of 1961. We rented a small studio apartment at the Chateau Marmont and started looking for work. Financially I was in good shape again. My suspension from *Sons and Lovers* had ended and I was back on salary and preparing to test for another Western epic called *Big River, Big Man.*

Warren coached me for this test. He was an excellent director and a patient teacher, with an intense and intellectual approach to exploring the depths and details of a characterization.

The endlessly sunny winter and spring California days passed quickly. We spent a lot of time at the Aware Inn, eating health-burgers and drinking carrot juice. Warren was a health freak and was now trying to persuade me to stop both drinking and smoking. After we ate we would walk to Turner's drugstore and flick though a pyramid of movie magazines looking for pictures of us together. The movie magazines loved the "new twosome."

Warren was heavily involved in trying to get the lead in Elia Kazan's *Splendor in the Grass,* again written by his friend William Inge. This necessitated his making three hundred and fifty phone calls a day—two hundred and fifty to his agent, twenty-five to Bill Inge—who was doing all he could to get Kazan to test Warren—twenty-five to me, wherever I was (although when I was working or doing an interview, he was never far away), and the rest to his by now numerous friends and business acquaintances. He was never happier than when he was on the phone, and he didn't need a phone book to remember the important numbers he constantly called. Ten years later, meeting him at a party he said, "CR ——do you remember what that was?" I didn't but he told me it was the telephone number of the apartment on Shoreham Drive where I lived when we met.

Telephoning, however, was secondary to his main passion, which was making love—and he was also able to accept phone calls at the same time. I had heard that men were at their sexual peak between the ages of seventeen and twenty-three. If Warren was anything to go by, this was true. I had never known anyone like him before. It was exciting for the first few months, but after a while I found myself feeling like an object.

One Sunday morning, exhausted, I left him sleeping soundly—another thing he did well—and staggered upstairs to visit an actress girlfriend from New York. She had been happily married for several years to a handsome superstar and idol of millions. "I don't think I can last much longer," I said, lighting a much needed cigarette—frowned upon by Warren. "He never *stops*—it must be all those vitamins he takes."

She smiled warmly, dispensing coffee and sisterly advice. "Just like my husband," she said.

"After all the years you've been together!" I said incredulously.

"Oh, yes. In fact it gets better."

"Better—oh, God. Please." I leaned back and took a drag on the cigarette. "In a few years, I'll be worn out."

"Take my advice, Joan," said my friend. "Don't reject him. If you do, he may find it necessary to go out with other women."

"Perish the thought," I said jealously. But her warning lingered in the back of my mind and we continued with his favorite occupation whenever it suited him. Of course, the inevitable happened.

"I think I'm pregnant," I said coming into the kitchen one day, where he was preparing one of his health concoctions in the blender. He stopped slicing bananas and pouring wheat germ, took off his glasses and stared at me. Without his glasses he was quite myopic, and I wondered why he didn't want to see me. "Pregnant?" he said in his puzzled little-boy voice. "How did that happen?"

"The butler did it," I said sarcastically, "or maybe it's an immaculate conception."

"This is terrible," he said, putting his glasses back on and looking at me as if for the first time. "Terrible!" He threw down seven or eight vitamin E tablets.

"I know," I said in a small voice. "I'm sorry." Not only did I feel awful about it, but I remembered what happened to my girlfriend at RADA who had gone to a butcher of an abortionist in a London back street and almost died. She would never be able to have children. I did not want that to happen to me. Although I wasn't prepared for motherhood, nevertheless I felt that one day, if my maternal instincts rose, I wanted to have my options open.

We sat on the faded red sofa in the living room, I with a stiff vodka, he with his health drink, and discussed what to do. Abortion was a dirty word in the early 1960s. In fact, so was sex. Even living together as Warren and I did was considered risqué. Abortions of a kind were of course available. I had recently gone to Tijuana, the tacky Mexican border town, accompanying a girlfriend and her married lover. I had listened, horrified, to her screams of agony as a Mexican "doctor" performed the operation *without* an anesthetic.

I shuddered at the memory, downing my vodka. We could get married, of course. But I was not in favor of "shotgun" weddings. The few times we had discussed marriage we had both decided that we were too immature to make it work. Besides which, he was practically penniless, exceedingly ambitious, and to get tied down in marriage at the age of twenty-two was totally impractical. So marriage was out. And having a baby was *definitely* out. So there was only one solution.

He called a friend in New York. We had heard that the abortion could be done in clinical circumstances there without risk to health. I would not consider a Tijuana-type deal. The friend arranged it. Warren had to go to New York to start preparing for *Splendor in the Grass* and I followed a few days later.

Early that morning I woke up trembling with my oldest and most frightening nightmare. It was as terrifying as ever. I was walking alone up a very dark and winding staircase. The stairs creaked and the wind howled outside. In the distance I heard dogs barking and an owl hooting, and then silence—only my footsteps, which went faster and faster up the crumbling stone stairs. Rats and mice scurried ahead of me, their tiny, furry bodies brushing my bare legs. Suddenly I heard breathing. "It" was behind me. "It" was getting closer. I ran faster and faster up the endless stairs, hearing the breathing getting closer all the time. And then I came to the top of the stairs to a door that said "Doctor." I rapped furiously. The footsteps were gaining behind me. Slowly the door opened. A grinning old man stood there, his white apron covered with blood, a bloody knife in his hand. He came toward me to take me by the hand. Behind me I heard the moans of a woman. I stepped back. A hand grabbed my arm and swung me backward. "I've got you at last, little girl," screamed Maxwell Reed dementedly, his face a mask of cruelty, his eyes those of a madman. "Now you'll really get cut up and carved up, and no one will ever look at you again!" He raised the bloody knife in his hand to bring it slashing to my face. I screamed.

"What is it, what's the matter?" said Warren, groggy with sleep, as I sat up sobbing, the vivid dream still gripping me.

"I can't go through with it," I sobbed. "I can't, I can't. Please don't make me go there, Warren, I'm scared—I'll have the baby—we'll get it adopted—but I can't go there." He comforted me as I sobbed hysterically. It was true. It is an ironic fact of life that the metabolic and hormonal changes that women go through when pregnant bring them closer each day to a protective feeling toward life inside them. I had been feeling—perish the thought—broody for a couple of weeks now, almost accepting what was happening to me, and now that it was going to be taken from me, I wanted to keep it.

"Butterfly, we *can't*, we can't do it," he said helplessly, trying to comfort me. "Having a baby now will wreck both of our careers—you know it will."

He was right, and I knew it. Ingrid Bergman, a far bigger star than I, had almost wrecked hers by having an out-of-wedlock child by Rossellini. It was a very serious and far-reaching step. There had been rumors of various actresses throughout the years who had disappeared for several months, and a few months after their reappearance had "adopted" a tiny baby, but it was all extremely hush-hush. With the eyes of the gossip columnists on us, nagging in print for us to "tie the knot," it would have been an impossibility. So I dried my tears, putting his ambition and my career first, and mooched about the hotel room until dusk, when it was time to drive to New Jersey.

I wore thick black stockings, a sweater and a full plaid skirt. "Don't wear slacks," I had been told by a sterile, sibilant voice over the telephone when I received my instructions. My eyes, which were swollen and red from crying, were covered by my biggest black sunglasses, and a head scarf covered my untidy hair. I did not wish to be recognized by anyone.

I chain-smoked as Warren drove a rented station wagon to Newark. We spoke little. He glanced at me with concern several times. I wished I could have kept the baby. Practically, though, I knew it was impossible. But the fact that he would not even *consider* that possibility hurt me terribly. He was a man. He took none of the responsibility for me becoming pregnant. That was the woman's department. But pre-Pill, however careful one was, accidents happened, and *she* was the one to face the emotional upheaval that pregnancy causes—and then the unbearably ambivalent feelings it generates.

I tried to convince myself that we were doing the right thing as we entered the Holland Tunnel and Warren started consulting a piece of paper on which were written the directions. I had just turned twenty-six.

I had a thriving career, which, if not exactly to my liking as far as the roles I was playing were concerned, was still lucrative and rewarding in many ways. A baby would change all that. I would have to stop working. Fox would suspend me. I might lose my figure. I might be a lousy mother. He and I were not suited to each other in the long run. Was our love just a physical thing? I didn't seem to be able to be with *any* man for a long period of time. We were both selfish, careless, argumentative, combative and just plain immature. It was stupid to think otherwise. Thus I convinced myself—while my mind shrieked "No!"

I dried my eyes and blew my nose as the car drew to a halt in front of an ominous-looking maroon high-rise apartment building.

"We're—um—here," said my gallant lover, nervously wiping his glasses on the sleeve of his tweed jacket. I noticed his face was covered with perspiration. He was probably more scared than I was. We looked at each other and I swallowed hard. "If anything goes wrong . . ." I started to say, but he interrupted me, almost screaming, "Nothing's going to go wrong—*nothing*. He's the best around. Don't even *think* about *that*, Butterfly."

He was close to tears himself. My maternal instinct went into comforting him, and hand in hand we walked to the green-paint-peeling elevator.

I awoke to hear someone pounding on the door.

"Are you still there?" yelled a coarse voice. I looked at my watch. It was one o'clock in the afternoon. I pulled the covers back over my head and tried to sleep again. The voice kept on yelling.

"Open up in there. I'se gotta clean the room."

"Oh, go to hell," I yelled back. "I don't want it cleaned. Leave me alone."

The voice sniffed, "If that's what you all want, you just go ahead and sleep all day, see if ah care." It shuffled down the corridor and left me in peace.

I tried to go back to sleep. Warren had gone to rehearsal and I didn't want to think about what had happened last night. It was too vivid and too painful. We must get out of this fleabag hotel and find an apartment, I thought, as I drifted back to sleep again.

The next day I felt much better and full of energy again. I pushed the horrifying abortion out of my head. Done. Over. Forgotten. That was yesterday—no point in brooding about it, and—oh, good—I didn't feel maternal any more. Not even to Warren. I called a house agent and went apartment hunting in New York. It was a beautiful, clear, crisp day. A rare day in New York. Newborn—I felt newborn myself, as though a great weight had been lifted and I could get back to living again.

As I rummaged through the drawers to find sweater and stockings, I noticed my jewelry case under the sweater. I opened it up and looked at the diamond necklace. It was scrunched up with some junk jewelry, some Greek worry beads—could've used those a couple of nights ago—and gold chains. I put on the gold chains and slid the leather box back under the pile of sweaters. That necklace. What trouble it had caused me.

Much more trouble than it was worth. I toyed with the idea of putting it in the hotel safe, then forgot about it as the phone rang and the switchboard announced that the real estate agent was downstairs.

Two nights later, dressing to go to El Morocco, I looked for the necklace. Gone. Probably stolen by the maid, angry because she couldn't make up the room. "I think real jewelry is a drag," I announced bravely to Warren, as I heaped on some imitation pearls and waited for the police to arrive. "I really don't care if I ever have expensive jewelry again."

We moved to a tiny apartment on Fifth Avenue. It was furnished in blue-and-white chintz, English antiques, and had bad plumbing. Warren started filming *Splendor in the Grass* with Natalie Wood.

I had known Natalie Wood since I first arrived in Hollywood in the mid-fifties. She was already a star. Although only sixteen, she was starring opposite Jimmy Dean in *Rebel Without a Cause* and was big at the box office. Throughout the fifties and sixties we consecutively or successively dated some of the same men, and we eventually became good friends when our dating whirl stopped. We sent each other flowers and telegrams at the births of our respective children and exchanged long letters when she was in California and I in London. We "did" Rodeo Drive and the boutiques of Beverly Hills after long lunches at the Bistro or the Polo Lounge, and we spent hours on the phone with each other.

She always dressed and behaved like the ultimate star. Spending money with abandon on clothes, furs and jewelry, she was never to be seen in the same outfit twice. Although Natalie was popular both with the young social set in Hollywood and the older group, she was incredibly insecure as a person and about her physical attributes. She always wore high-heeled shoes to maximize her height, and she always wore a thick gold bracelet to cover a slightly protruding bone in her wrist, which was hardly noticeable.

At a dinner party one night, Natalie inadvertently performed one of the most extraordinarily vain gestures I have ever seen. Upon sitting down at the elegant table, she picked up one of the gleaming, polished Georgian knives and, holding it close to her face, examined her lipstick and teeth as though gazing into a compact! Mesmerized by this display of narcissism, I determined to use it as a piece of theatrical business one day. My chance came a few years later while appearing in an Orson Welles television production, *The Dinner Party,* and I was commended by the director for an excellent piece of business!

Natalie and I had a slight falling out in the summer of 1969 in St. Tropez. We were both in between husbands and were staying at a tiny hotel on the beach. We had dined with the usual large group of sun-tanned Riviera playboys and models at L'Escale, and then drifted on to the open-air discotheque Byblos. There were some cute guys in the group, none of whom were averse to pretty actresses. Natalie and I agreed that we would neither of us go home without the other in tow.

"Promise me you won't go yet," she called, as she was whisked onto the dance floor to dance to the romantic ballad "Monia," sung by Peter Holm. Shortly thereafter I, too, hit the dance floor with a would-be beau to the trendy beat of the Beatles chanting "I'm a Loser," and we discoed for an hour. Coming back to our table I found that Natalie had left. No goodbye, no "Sorry Joan, just couldn't resist Jean Pierre or Francois or whomever. I'll see you tomorrow." Not even a message. I was angry, and I had been saddled with a bunch of people I had little in common with. Earlier in the evening we had had drinks with Roger Vadim and his wife, Jane Fonda, but they were not into the disco life since she was pregnant.

I left a note under Natalie's door telling her I felt abandoned and that she had broken a promise. Instead of an apology, she didn't speak to me for three years! It was only the intervention of a mutual friend, Asa Maynor, that eventually got us back together, via a series of lunches. We renewed our friendship, and nothing was ever mentioned of the incident that had caused the rift. Natalie hated confrontations and always felt she was right in her opinions. Those who cared about her did it her way, otherwise they were *out* of her group.

While Warren was filming *Splendor in the Grass,* I went to Berlitz every day and took Italian lessons preparatory to leaving the following month for Italy to film *Esther and the King.* I was unhappy about leaving and so was he, but I was not about to let him interfere with my career again. Not only did I need money, but *Sons and Lovers* had turned out to be a good picture, infinitely better than most of the stuff I had done at Fox. Mary Ure, who had played my role, was nominated for an Oscar the following year. I deeply regretted having turned it down thanks to Warren's insistence. His career was now well and truly off the ground, while mine was stagnating in a stew of forgettable films. I was now getting toward not only the end of my seven-year tenure at Fox, but I had also passed my first quarter century—an age that young actresses had learned to dread ever since the studios had decreed back in the dark ages of moviemaking that twenty-seven was the end of beauty, freshness and youth. New faces were on the horizon. Younger than mine. Fresher. My career was in the doldrums and I knew it. Nine mediocre films in five years are no guarantee of eternal longevity at the box office. As these realizations began to crystallize, I tried even harder, through the efforts of my lawyer, to get out of the remaining eighteen months of my contract. I wanted to be free to accept some of the interesting independent films that were being made in the early sixties. But no, it was not to be. . . .

I had now been on suspension so many times that Fox thought I was crazed. In five years, five suspensions. Is this a record? I wondered as I sat on the set of New York Filmway's studios and watched Elia Kazan direct Warren and Natalie in a scene.

He was a sympathetic, sensitive, brilliant director. Lauded, and rightly so, for a multitude of great movies: *Streetcar Named Desire, Viva Zapata, On the Waterfront, East of Eden* and many more. He had discovered Marlon Brando and James Dean. Would Warren be next? I wondered as I saw "Gadge," his arms around his two young stars, patiently talking, explaining, extracting from them every nuance of thought, meaning and expression for the scene. Warren was very lucky to have Kazan as his first director. Maybe he really would become a big star.

I thought back to what my astrologer, Ben Gary, had said recently, when he had done my chart in conjunction with Warren's. Ben was a psychic astrologer and his predictions had always been uncannily accurate. "You know Warren's birthday is March thirtieth, the same as Sydney Chaplin's," said Ben triumphantly. "He's got all the usual Aries traits," continued Ben. "The ram, of course." I nodded agreement on that. "The ram is the first sign in the zodiac—it represents birth. 'I want' is the Aries credo; they usually get what they want."

"Hmmm, Maxwell Reed was an Aries too," I remembered. "And so was Hitler."

Ben fixed me with his beady eyes and I shut up. "He is stubborn and aggressive, but he is unyielding in his ambition and because of his tremendous drive and energy will have an early and immense success." I listened carefully as Ben continued. "However, after a short period of success, he will go into a dry period for a couple of years, make several career mistakes, but finally will become a major star again—probably in the late sixties. He's very sexual, you know—" he looked at me questioningly. I looked demure. "Most Aries are, of course. Ruled by their cock. How delightful for you, my dear."

"Sometimes," I said cryptically. "What else? Go on, Ben—what about us?" He consulted the hieroglyphics on his chart, peering through his nearsighted eyes and taking a long draught of beer. "You have an affinity for Aries men, you know, my dear—you'll probably marry at least one more of them. But it won't be him!"

"It won't?" I said disappointedly. "Why not?"

"He will not marry for a long time," said my soothsayer. "Probably not until he's forty-five or older. I do see many, many women, though."

"Terrific," I said gloomily. "Are they around him now?"

"No, dear, now he only needs you—later he will need . . ." He pored again over the chart and paused, making little notations with red pencil on the indecipherable squiggles on the paper. "He will need a constant inflation of his ego—one woman will not suffice to satisfy him sexually."

"So where does that leave me?" I asked, trying to look over his shoulder at the squiggles.

"Ah, my dear—you have only just begun to live your life."

This is encouraging, I thought. I seem to have lived so much already.

"You have only just begun your career, which will last for a very, very long time and you will reap the rewards when you are in your forties."

"Forties!" I gasped. "That's ancient, Ben!"

"You are a late bloomer, dear," he admonished. "You are going to surprise a lot of people when you are much older. There will be other men in your future. You will be married again within two years to a . . ." He squinted at his squiggles again, ". . . a writer—no, a producer or director, also an actor. A very multi-faceted man—he does many things."

I giggled and looked over at Cappy sitting on the couch. I believed in astrology, but I couldn't take it completely seriously. However, it was fascinating to hear one's future, even if one took it with a pinch of salt. "This marriage will last six or seven years," continued Ben. "From it will come two or three children—two of them probably twins, or very close in age. Shortly thereafter you'll marry again . . ." he stared at the paper thoughtfully. "It's hard to see that far. I think he is a businessman— maybe an executive in some company."

"Rich?" I said hopefully.

"My dear, you never fall for rich men," said Ben, fixing me with a steely glare. "Your heart rules your head. You will always make enough money to take care of yourself. You will continue working for a very long time—your career will have many ups and downs but you were born under a lucky star. You are truly a survivor."

Ben's prophecies for himself came ominously true several years later. He had always foreseen that he would die when he was thirty-two. On his thirty-second birthday he shut himself in his house with a close friend to take care of his needs. He was ultra-careful. He did not touch anything electrical or mechanical, not even a telephone or a fridge. He insulated himself from anything that could cause him physical harm. A year later he was dead. From malnutrition. His diet of beer, pretzels and potato chips had finally caught up with him.

As of this writing *all* of his prophecies for me have come true.

"I feel like having some chopped liver," said Warren, looking up from studying his script. It was three o'clock on Saturday afternoon. We had only recently finished lunch.

"It's in the refrigerator," he said, going back to his script. "I got it yesterday at Reuben's." I opened the fridge and got the white plastic carton. "Did you find it?" he yelled from the living room. "Yes," I shouted. "What do you think of it?" I opened it slightly. "Umm—smells delicious," I said.

"Does it fit?" he called.

"Fit? Fit where, on a bagel?"

The man was obviously working too hard. "Well, try it on," he said anxiously, appearing in the doorway of the kitchen. "Oh—" he looked sheepishly at my surprised face. "Oh, you haven't found it yet." I followed his eyes to the carton of chopped liver and looked at it more carefully. Stuck in the middle of it was a gold ring encrusted with diamonds *and* pearls. "Oh, darling—it's beautiful," I cried, extracting it from the liver and wiping it off so I could see it in its full glory. "Absolutely beautiful—what's it for?"

"It's your engagement ring, dummy," he said, grinning like a Cheshire cat. "I figured, since you're going away soon and we'll be separated we should um, well, um, you know . . ." He shuffled embarrassedly. Took the glasses off. Put them on again. Grabbed a couple of Vitamin C tablets and crunched them. "Get—well, engaged. What do you think?" He looked anxious.

"I think it's a great idea—just terrific," I squealed happily. "Are you sure you really want to—I mean you're not just doing this to make me feel secure, are you?"

"No, Butterfly, I'm not—you know I don't do anything unless I want to . . . and . . . um . . . well . . . um . . . I guess I want to. We . . . er, could get married at the end of the year." He took his glasses off again and we burst out laughing.

The fact that Warren may have bought me the ring out of a strong guilt feeling because of the abortion crossed my mind. I put it on the third finger of my left hand and left it there for a long, long time. I wore it all the way through *Esther and the King* since it fitted in with the Biblical costumes.

That night we celebrated our engagement by dining at Danny's Hide-away and then going to hear Bobby Short at the Carlyle. I flashed my left hand casually wherever we went, and within a week the columnists were pleased to announce that we had officially become engaged at last.

I was dismal about going to Rome. Although it was my favorite city in the world, I was desolate at leaving Warren, and so was he. He was jealous at the thought of me being around other men. *Especially* Italian men. I tried to convince him not to worry, that I would be fidelity personified—but Aries men are exceedingly possessive, jealous and stubborn, and he would not be convinced.

At Fiumicino airport I was greeted by Raoul Walsh, the roistering one-eyed director, bearing pink roses, also by my Italian agent, two Italian actors from the film, two producers from the film, a bunch of staring tourists and twenty paparazzi.

I was surprised at the number of paparazzi, those Italian photographers who make their living from photographing celebrities outside restaurants, at airports, shopping along the Via Veneto and, oh, major coup, coming out of a lover's apartment after a "romantic interlude." Some do have ethics and respect for people's privacy; others are scavengers feeding on tidbits of celebrities' love lives. One of their favorite tricks is to incite an actor to such extreme rage that he will attempt to either smash the photographer or the camera. These photos—the more irate the actor the better—are usually worth several hundred lire, and will garner a two-page spread in *Tempo, Gente* or *Oggi*.

I was quite popular in Italy, and the number of photographers proved that they still liked me although I hadn't set foot in that country since *Land of the Pharaohs,* five years previously.

Instead of staying in a hotel, where I might get lonely and tempted to accept dinner invitations, Warren had insisted that I stay with Marion Donen in her apartment. Immediately after I arrived, he started bombarding me with telegrams and letters protesting love, fidelity and commitment forever. When we talked on the phone, he sounded so forlorn and depressed that I decided that I would surprise him and fly to New York the following weekend. Twelve days after leaving New York I was back again. I had not yet started shooting the movie and he was over the moon to see me. Not many fiancées fly more than eight thousand miles for three days. He should be *deeply* thrilled. We spent the weekend, what was left of it, in our apartment. Monday and Tuesday I watched him filming again and Tuesday night I was back on Alitalia to the Eternal City. Exhausted but happy.

We had decided to marry in January. I wanted my dress designed in London. I called my English dressmakers, told them to start making up some designs, and started filming *Esther and the King*.

It was an awful film. It was full of pseudo-Biblical banal Hollywood dialogue and, with the exception of Richard Egan, Denis O'Dea and myself, an all-Italian cast who spoke their dialogue in Italian, to which we replied in English! There were also a Spanish and a French actor who spoke their lines in Spanish and French respectively. It was a veritable League of Nations.

It really was terrible stuff. Warren had advised me not to do it. He suggested that I behave so badly when I was in Rome that they would fire me, but atrocious as the film was, my professionalism got the better of me and I tried to do the best I could with the part of the simpering heroine.

Warren's first letter contained some jocular rules and regulations on "How to make a Biblical film." They included:

1. It is always best to try to show as much emotion in all scenes as possible. It is generally best if the actor cries in each scene, taking special pains not to be out of control or realistic to the extent that members of the crew or other actors will be made to feel embarrassed. All gestures and facial expressions should be worked out in front of a large mirror. These should not be deviated from. Remember that the audience is not involved until the actor cries. Be very careful not to let the mascara run.

2. In doing Biblical pictures it is best to try to imagine how Jesus Christ would have said the necessary lines and done the prescribed movements and then to emulate His work.

3. Never change the words in a movie script. These have been written by great creative forces.

4. Do not challenge the director, or especially the producer. These are dedicated men.

5. Do not tire yourself out with thinking about the script between takes or at night away from the set. This destroys spontaneity.

I was still trying to renegotiate my contract with Fox to have some freedom to accept outside offers. But for some reason they wouldn't let me go, although they were dropping other contract players like hot potatoes.

Every night I was in bed reading, or had early dinner with Marion or my agent. I was bored and miserable, hating the movie and missing Warren. I constantly wore, besides the flashy engagement ring, a tiny gold butterfly that he had given me, from my favorite jeweler, Buccellati.

I visited London one weekend and started choosing wedding dress fabrics. Warren's phone calls and letters became more intense and desperate every day: "Can't wait to see you in dress" was the gist of most of them, and "Missing you more than I can bear."

Eventually I could stand it no more. After a pleading consultation with the production manager, he allowed me to fly to New York again for the weekend. Three and a half weeks after I left for Italy, an exhausted wreck deplaned at Idlewild airport on Saturday night and left again on Monday night.

In those forty-eight hours Warren and I did nothing but fight. He was convinced I was having an affair. Nothing I did or said could persuade him otherwise. The fact that I had flown those more than eight thousand miles twice in five weeks just to see him should have been proof enough to him that I loved him. Apparently it wasn't. His insecurities got the better of him, and I became the butt of them. Could it be, I wondered on the plane back to Rome, that *he* was the one who had been unfaithful? And with his co-star Natalie Wood? They had certainly seemed more than close when I observed them at work. My suspicions were now aroused.

Sullen and angry, I returned to the awful film. I mouthed pious and pontificating language while I seethed with rage inside. How dare he treat me as if I were his piece of private property with "For Warren's personal use only" stamped in large letters all over the packaging? I had spent three thousand dollars on air fares alone, never mind the massive phone bills.

He yelled at me for something I hadn't done—maybe I *should* do it. He probably was. With Natalie Wood yet. "Ruled by the cock," Ben had said. Oh, God!

I started returning the flirtatious glances and remarks of a young Italian actor on the movie, Gabriele Tinti.

I always had a penchant for Italian men. I like their appreciation, often verbalized, of women, I like their attitude toward life. I even like the way they dress! This year everyone, including the young actor, wore black shirts open to the waist, a plethora of gold amulets and charms around the neck (to ward off evil, to make them more virile, or just to glisten on a tanned chest) and white cotton or linen pants. Quite a devastating look when teamed with black curly hair, sparkling white teeth in a brown and unbelievably handsome face and amazing slanted green eyes. As I thought of pimply, bespectacled, white-faced Warren, seriously emoting his way through his first movie role and getting angry at *me* all the time, Gabriele was a welcome change.

We launched into what the Italians call a "flirt." My mother and brother, Bill, were by now staying with me, so I was chaperoned at all times, which suited me fine. This was to be a "flirt" and nothing more, since my deep-down monogamous instincts and loyalty to Warren won out over the Italian's passion. But oh, what sitting and hand-holding in a corner of the studio and being told one was *bellissima,* and *meravigliosa, simpatica, più bella del mondo* could do for one's slightly fractured ego. Not to mention the boost in the arm it gave my Italian vocabulary.

Although I wouldn't go out with Gabriele officially, since I was *fidanzata* to Warren, I spent half an hour a night on the phone listening to his protestations of *amore.* Somehow, in Italian the words had far more meaning, although I could not take them seriously. Italian men love to use flowery phrases to their women—just as Englishmen court a woman between going to soccer matches and boozing it up with their mates at the pub. It's all part of the international mating call of men. One must read between the lines (or lack of them) to understand what the man is really *saying.* But when all was said and done I was in love with Warren. This "flirt" was my usual immature way of getting some sort of revenge for the pain he caused me.

Warren's suspicions solidified when he tried to phone for an hour one evening, with the line constantly busy. His suspicions would only be assuaged by another visit from me, which I dutifully and foolishly made. This accomplished nothing more than to alienate the producer and director of *Esther,* get myself splashed all over the New York and English tabloids, including the front page of the *Daily News* as a runaway, renegade actress, and generally achieve nothing more than a temporary truce in our battles. Warren never visited me in Rome. He sent me a telegram on the first anniversary of our meeting: "My life began one year ago." Letters and phone calls and cables continued, but the quality of the relationship started deteriorating.

The phone in the rented house of Sunset Plaza Drive rang, waking me out of a deep sleep. I picked it up, noticing it was barely nine o'clock. Our friends knew better than to call before ten.

"Joanie, it's me," said the anxious voice of my agent. "Can you be packed and ready to leave for London by the end of the day?"

"Oh, no, not again!" I sat up and searched fruitlessly for my eyedrops. "I've only been home a couple of weeks, whatever is all the rush for?"

"It's Elizabeth. They think she's dying. They want you to replace her in *Cleopatra,*" he said tersely.

Dying! Liz Taylor—God, I *don't* believe it—this is a ghastly joke. My eyes snapped open. I nudged Warren awake.

"It's not a joke, sweetheart," the agent went on. "I wish it was. She's so ill they don't think she's going to make it. All the sets are finished at Pinewood. The cast and crew are already on payroll. It's costing them thousands of dollars a day while she's in the clinic. If she dies they've got to start shooting with a new Cleopatra within three days. Fox are way over budget already. They can't afford to screw around any more."

I listened horrified. I couldn't believe the heartlessness of the Fox moguls. All that mattered to them was money—and power, of course. This was all dollars and cents. What did they care if Elizabeth Taylor was dying of pneumonia? All that mattered was that the show must go on. Get someone, anyone, to take her place. Alter her costumes, put her wigs and makeup on the replacement—lights, camera, action—instant Cleopatra—just like Nescafé. It was awful. It was Hollywood. Except that it was happening in London and Elizabeth was fighting for her life in the

London clinic across the street from Harley House where I had spent so much of my life.

I looked at Warren, who had awakened and was trying to listen to what was going on. "I can't—I couldn't do it—I know Elizabeth . . . I would feel too *ghoulish* stepping into her shoes like this." It was true—my whole body had turned to goose bumps during this conversation. However desperately I had wanted the part in *Cleopatra* last year, the thought of finally playing it because the favored choice had died was appalling.

"Sweetheart—don't get so emotional," said my agent, trying to calm me down. "Let's hope she doesn't die—on the other hand, think of your *career!* This is Fox's biggest movie of the year—it's going to cost over six million. It'll make you a Big Star. Besides which, if you don't do it, you'll go on suspension again," he said flatly. "I'll call you in a couple of hours after the next medical report." He hung up and I stared at the receiver numbly.

"What do you think?" said Warren, getting up and jumping into his jeans.

"It's horrible," I said lying back with my arms folded behind my neck and staring at the ceiling, "really horrible."

"It's show biz, baby," said he, pulling a crumpled blue Brooks Brothers shirt out of the eternally half-unpacked suitcase lying open on the floor. "As in there's no biz like it." He looked at me seriously, his unspectacled eyes squinting slightly. "I think it's horrible too!"

"God, I hope she doesn't die," I said.

"She won't," he said confidently, going out to the kitchen to squeeze fresh orange juice and take the fifteen mysterious vitamins he fortified himself with. "She's got nine lives, that woman. Don't worry about it, Butterfly. All you'll have to worry about is making breakfast." He disappeared into the kitchen.

I refused to pack as much as a powder puff until I heard any official news. On the other hand, my agent had told me not to leave the house and to be instantly available. I prowled around unhappily, chain-smoking, biting my nails and fervently wishing for Elizabeth's recovery. We talked on the phone to friends who had the "inside" track on her condition. All the radio and TV news reports seemed to differ. Some said she had pneumonia, others, a chest infection. Some said three doctors were in attendance, some said there were nine doctors, including the Queen's personal physician.

I imagined myself in Elizabeth's place. Hovering between life and death in a sterile hospital room, tubes in my throat and in my arms—what must she be thinking? Did she live her life fully enough? Or did she feel cheated of many more decades? Did she know she was possibly dying? Or was she doped up?

The last time I had seen her she was married to the English actor Michael Wilding, and Arthur Loew and I had dinner with them at LaRue in Hollywood. She was extraordinarily beautiful: deep blue eyes, hundreds of black eyelashes, and a heart-shaped face. She was down to earth.

We chattered and gossiped animatedly all evening, practically ignoring Michael and Arthur. She was dying? It seemed unbelievable.

At six o'clock my agent phoned, gave me permission to go out to dinner but to leave a message on the service where I could be reached. Warren and I munched on a nut, celery and carrot salad at the Aware Inn and gloomily discussed the situation. The next morning my agent called bright and early.

"Good morning, sweetheart," he said cheerily. "You're off the hook. Liz is going to make it."

I heaved a deep sigh of relief. "Good," I breathed. "She does have nine lives after all."

Warren went to London to make *The Roman Spring of Mrs. Stone* opposite Vivien Leigh. I went too, but for a twofold purpose. My mother had been operated on for a malignancy and I wanted to be close to her. My sister Jackie got married amidst great pomp and ceremony. I had tried to dissuade her from this marriage as she was very young, and my own mistake was still fresh in my memory. But she did it anyway.

Warren and I were not getting along. The idea of marriage no longer seemed appealing to either of us. The beige chiffon wedding dress lay carefully packed in tissue paper in my closet in Hollywood and I moved once more into Harley House in the bedroom recently vacated by Jackie.

We were spending less time together. He had recently done his two or three weeks reserve duty at George Air Force Base in Victorville. While at the base, he had bombarded me with telegrams and phone calls in L.A. expressing his misery, loneliness and undying love. So why did he fight with me and harass me all the time when we were together?

Many of his messages stressed how much he was longing to see me in the wedding dress, so, being unable to resist him when he was enchantingly persuasive, I jumped on a plane and went to spend the weekend near him at the Apple Valley Inn, a sweet, rundown hotel in Victorville close to George Air Force Base.

Being in the service definitely did not agree with Warren. He was upset, nervous, depressed and argumentative. Furious that he had to take precious time from his burgeoning career to dedicate to his country. After the initial elation of our first glorious meeting, our relationship once again deteriorated into petty fights and arguments, culminating with me getting on a plane and away from Victorville and back to L.A. as fast as possible.

We seemed to argue about anything and everything. Since Maxwell Reed, and maybe even *because* of him, I have never been the type of woman who is subservient to a man. I believed in total equality in all things and would not tolerate the idea that women were inferior to men. Consequently I was over-aggressive sometimes when it wasn't necessary. Warren, being insecure and aggressive and determined to always get his own way no matter what, and I made a volatile combination. I would not give in to his often very childish demands, and he wanted his own way all the time. I had finally been released from my Fox contract after six years of slavery, and was eager to accept some of the tempting offers I was receiving, but as soon as he read the scripts he would contemptuously throw them aside.

"It's crap, sweetheart, junk—you can't do it."

"But darling, it's seventy-five thousand dollars," I demurred—and the row would start. True, he was a perfectionist, but he had been spoiled by his first film's being of high artistic caliber, and now he wouldn't settle for anything less—and he thought I shouldn't either. Unfortunately, 90 percent of the films made are *not* of high artistic caliber. I had made eighteen movies. Of those eighteen, maybe only two or three had some artistic merit. But acting is a business as well as an art. Sitting around waiting for the phone to ring and my agent to come up with the plum role of the decade was not likely to happen in the foreseeable future. Bakers bake, writers write and actors act. I wanted to work. To practice my craft until the day when, and if, a wonderful and fulfilling role would come along. Meanwhile Warren threw the scripts I was offered into the wastepaper basket.

I went to see a producer about a part I really wanted. He sat behind his giant mahogany desk, his five feet five inches elevated by an extremely high-legged chair, and surveyed me through a haze of cigar smoke.

"You've been around awhile now, dear," he said. "How old are you?"

"I'm twenty-six," I said.

"Twenty-six . . . hmmmmm . . . y'know, that's not young in this business any more, dear."

I was speechless. Not young in the business any more! What cheek! This elderly asshole—fifty if he's a day, telling *me* that twenty-six is not young any more. That epitomized the attitude that pervaded Hollywood at that time.

Discovered at sixteen—Hollywood star at twenty—washed up at twenty-six, I thought despondently. No wonder Daddy wanted me to become a secretary. I surveyed my face in my compact mirror as the elevator glided me smoothly away from this repulsive man. Not over the hill quite yet: I had my own hair and teeth and no wrinkles. What a stupid jerk, I thought, angrily shutting the compact and striding out onto Sunset Boulevard. Trying to make me feel insecure, and angry because he tried to seduce me once in New York and I had rejected him.

"Men. They only want one thing," said a tiny voice in the back of my mind. "They use you. They abuse you. They're all a bunch of bastards."

I sat in Warren's canvas chair on a dark and dank stage at Elstree Studios outside London and watched Warren, dressed and made up like a young Italian gigolo, make love to Vivien Leigh. Vivien was a beautiful woman in her late forties. As the aging Mrs. Stone, an American lady looking for love and companionship in Rome, she was cast perfectly. The great beauty of her early films was no longer much in evidence. Her life, never very happy, was compounded by ill health and drinking, and she looked tired and older than her years. "Beauty is a gift. You should not destroy it," someone said to me once at a party, as I downed a vodka and tonic. Looking at Vivien, and how her lifestyle had taken its toll on her looks, I hastily ground out my cigarette and vowed to take better care of myself. She did not take kindly to me, Miss Leigh, but she certainly did to Warren. He, never one to miss an opportunity, was his most beguiling and adorable self around her.

"Why do you spend so much money on clothes?" she asked me sharply at lunch in the studio restaurant one day. "It's an *absolute* waste of good money. Why, I've never seen you in the same outfit twice." She looked at me accusingly. "And what is that you are wearing today? It looks like a man's suit."

"It is," said I, digging into my steak-and-kidney pie. "It was made for me." Men's suits for women were unusual in the early 1960s. London had not yet become the trend-setting fashion capital of the world, and ladies wore skirts in England.

"You should spend your money on jewelry, my dear," said Vivien, elegantly lifting a glass of wine with her be-ringed and braceleted hand and scrutinizing me disapprovingly. "Jewelry is such a *good* investment. Why, with good jewelry—some pearls and rings, or an attractive brooch —you could wear a little black dress every day and look marvelous."

A little black dress every day. How boring, I thought, looking at War- ren devouring his fish and chips, and apparently oblivious to this catty exchange. He looked devastatingly handsome. There was little trace of the spotty boy I had first seen sixteen months ago.

His hair had been darkened for the part of the Italian gigolo. He had a deep tan, which, although it was out of a bottle, looked as if it came straight from Portofino. He wore a beautifully cut beige silk suit from Brioni, a cream crepe de chine shirt from Battaglia, and a brown-and- beige Saint Laurent tie. No wonder half the females in the restaurant were tripping over themselves to get a glimpse of him. The Warren Beatty sex-symbol image was beginning to emerge. Women adored him. He was loving every minute of it.

"What do you think, Warren darling?" asked Vivien, lightly resting her aristocratic hand on his arm and fluttering her beautiful pale blue eyes.

"Um, I think she looks cute," said Warren, giving me a sly wink. "No use trying to get Joanie to change her way of dressing. She does what she wants. You look like—umm—a little man," he said fondly. I raised my eyes heavenward and observed Vivien's eyelashes batting in his direction. I was not above having a touch of the green-eyed monster myself, so I gave him a swift kick under the table and he quickly went back to his fish and chips. Vivien gave me a sharp look. She was a perceptive lady and *she* knew that *I* knew that she fancied Warren. Whether this May-December flirtation was ever consummated I do not know. Warren was getting plenty of opportunities to be unfaithful if he chose to do so. Women were going gaga at the sight of this vision and he was pleased and flattered by their attentions.

I was worried about my mother. After the operation to remove the malignancy, she seemed in good health and spirits, but the surgery had been debilitating and upsetting to her. With Jackie married and out of the house, I again became the resident daughter, which made her extremely happy.

She worried about me. Would I ever settle down like Jackie and find a man to make me happy? She adored Warren—most women did: he charmed them all—but she was aware of our bickering and realized he was not really the kind of man who could make a woman happy forever. I knew marriage with Warren was not the answer, but I still loved him. Since I found it hard to make major decisions in my life, I continued to let the relationship drift along.

Warren had rented Peter Glenville's house in a charming square near Harrod's for the duration of filming. He was up at dawn every morning, so I preferred to luxuriate in my old familiar bed in Harley House every morning and have Mummy bring me tea, toast, marmalade and mother-and-daughter chat.

Warren and I took a trip to Paris one weekend to visit Joanne Woodward and Paul Newman, who were filming there. We took long walks along the Seine, browsed through the book-stalls and the endless art galleries, and whiled away happy hours in the cafés. I toyed with the idea of buying some paintings. After six years in Hollywood, making a healthy salary, I had almost no possessions except clothes, hundreds of books, a stereo and thousands of records. Not a chair, a teapot or a lampshade had I ever purchased. I had been encouraged by my business manager always to rent furnished apartments and to lease a car while my money was "invested" for me. I had nothing, which meant I was free to go where the wind blew me. And the wind was still blowing in Warren's direction. I knew little about art, but looking at some of Vasarely's abstract lithographs, I found the idea of spending a ton of money on these funny squares and triangles rather formidable.

The Newmans took us one evening to the Carousel, a gay nightclub in Montmartre. It specialized in beautiful young men and boys dressed in women's clothing who sang, danced and mimed on the tiny stage. The club was packed, mostly with tourists, but also with a sprinkling of the *haut monde* and a large group of homosexuals. All eyes focused on our table as Newman, of the fabled blue eyes, and Beatty, not so famous but with a definite aura about him, sat and sipped Poire William, a particularly potent liqueur made from pears.

The "girls" who performed were gorgeous. Divine creatures, each with her hairstyle, makeup and clothes patterned after a particular movie star. There was Marilyn Monroe—Ava Gardner—Audrey Hepburn—each one a vision, and each one more breathtaking than the last. Joanne and I began to feel rather ordinary next to all this glamour. The "girls" performed especially for our table. "Diamonds Are a Girl's Best Friend," huskily sang a vision in red lame and feathers as "she" slithered her boa invitingly over Warren's shoulder blades. *"Je t'aime, je t'aime,"* intoned a masculine but soft voice, looking into the eyes of Paul, "her" makeup so fastidiously applied that it must have taken hours.

Paul and Warren grinned sheepishly at all this attention, while Joanne and I giggled. The songs were performed for our two men, the suggestive glances and gestures directed toward them.

"We should take lessons in sex appeal from this bunch," I said to Joanne. During the finale a dozen pairs of false bosoms and false eyelashes shook and batted triumphantly from the stage as they performed their final number with bobbing ostrich feathers, beehive hairdos, and slit skirts, cleverly covering their strategic areas.

The "proprietress" came up to us after the show. "The ladies would like to 'ave you visit zem backstage—oui?" she breathed. An ancient crone in a three-foot-high red wig and black sequins who on close inspection proved to have a heavy five o'clock shadow under her pancake makeup.

"Oh, c'mon, let's," I giggled, the Poire having loosened my inhibitions.

"Um—er—do ya think we should?" said Warren, nervously glancing at the crone, whose vast false bust was resting on the shoulder of his best blue suit, while she gazed smolderingly into his eyes.

"Yes, yes. I want to see them up close. Come *on*—don't be square."

The two men reluctantly trailed behind us while Joanne and I followed "Madame" backstage to the dressing room. We walked in. Squeals and shrieks of joy from the assembled gentlemen—or ladies. It was hard to tell. Some had on full makeup but had taken off their hairpieces to reveal short-cropped hair. Some were in elaborate underwear with lace and frills and garter belts that would not have been out of place in *Playboy*. One or two had removed their lower garments, revealing that they definitely were not female.

The smell of perfume and powder was intense, as was another, subtler scent that would become more familiar as the decade progressed. They passed a joint to me but I refused. I was trying to drink it all in: the drying stockings; the photos of Jean-Paul Belmondo and Marlon Brando taped to the mirrors; the high-pitched girlish chattering. But these were men, some more gorgeous than many women I knew.

Strangely it was not Paul and Warren whom they oohed and aahed excitedly over. It was Joanne and me!

"Your 'air—eet ees so beautiful," crooned the Monroe look-alike to Joanne. " 'Ow you get that colaire—ees natural, *non?*" "*Mais oui—naturellement c'est naturel,*" indignantly said "Jayne Mansfield," running her fingers through Joanne's bob, as Joanne tried to suppress a smile.

"Ooh—*regardez—regardez les* lashes," said a "Sophia Loren" pointing at my eyelashes. Three or four of them descended on me, avidly discussing my lashes.

"On ze *bottom*—oh, *c'est très, très originale,*" said "Sophia," her eyes staring into mine. " 'Ow you do eet?"

I explained how I sometimes stuck fake eyelashes on my bottom lids— a fashion trend in London. They listened enthralled.

Our dresses, jewelry and hair were examined and fingered. The two men stood forgotten in the corner of the cramped dressing room watching amusedly while Joanne and I were plied with questions about our looks. Eventually we escaped, laughing hysterically, into the Place Pigalle, and strolled over to a nearby bar. The evening was unforgettable for giving me the worst hangover I have ever experienced in my life. On waking, my head felt like a balloon. A sledgehammer was inside it pounding so hard I thought it would explode.

"It's the Poire!" said Warren who, although not a drinker, had done his share that night. "It's ninety proof."

"Oh, God," I gasped, catching a glimpse of my dissipated white face in the mirror. "If the 'girls' could only see me now!"

"Somehow I think that tonight in Montmartre there will be two new stars," said Warren. "Joanne Woodward and Joan Collins starring at the Carousel—authentic down to the last bottom eyelash."

After Warren finished filming *The Roman Spring of Mrs. Stone* we returned to Los Angeles and my house on Sunset Plaza Drive—and the smog and the rows. We argued so much and over such mundane and petty things that the last few months of our relationship are a hazy blur. My mother came to visit with fifteen-year-old Bill, who tended to hero-worship Warren.

"Why did you let them come?" Warren hissed at me loud enough for Mummy, who was sunbathing in the garden, to overhear. "We never have any privacy now—ever." He rummaged through his usual messy suitcase, which was lying on the floor with his shirts and jeans falling out of it, and glared at me accusingly.

I glared back. "She's my *mother*," I said flatly. "I pay most of the rent on this house, and I have every right to have her visit, so stop being such a rat."

My eyes filled with tears. I didn't let him know how much he hurt me by his antagonism toward Mummy. I tried to never let him know he hurt me now. I felt terrible about her recent illness. I wanted to try and be the perfect daughter to her and make her happy as I hadn't done since I was a child. My sister was pregnant now, and Mummy was thrilled, hinting strongly that it was time I took a turn in that direction.

It was obvious I had to be the one to end it with Warren. He seemed content to let it drift sloppily along. What happened to the glorious romantic fun we used to have? Why did all of my relationships with men turn sour? Was it my fault? Was I too strong? Or was I too weak? Or was it—and this I knew deep down to be the truth—that I really *wanted* only the neurotic ones, the men unable truly to love, truly to support and truly to give. Only by gaining the love of one of these impossible men could I prove to myself that I was a worthy person.

Finally I accepted an offer from Norman Panama and Mel Frank to go to London to play opposite Bob Hope and Bing Crosby in *The Road to Hong Kong*.

"It's crap," said Warren, throwing the script to the floor. "Crap! Why do you need to do it?"

I looked at him. "Two reasons," I said simply. "For the money—and to get away from you."

We stared at each other for a long time. It was the end, and we knew it. We held each other tightly. Nearly two years of loving and fighting had passed. He had become a man and almost a star, and I had marked time.

It was time to move on.

❖ *Eight* ❖

THE SIXTIES WERE YOUTH. They were freedom and "flower power." They were "doing your own thing"; "letting it all hang out," and throwing convention to the winds. Nowhere epitomized the Swinging Sixties more than London. It was the place to be, and that's where I was. The decade was young, there was excitement in the air, a feeling of vibrancy and great expectations in people's attitudes. Optimism, originality and enthusiasm were the *modus operandi* of the day. Everyone seemed young, enthusiastic and fresh.

The "Mersey Beat" was starting to drift down from Liverpool, where four mopheaded youths in their early twenties were getting started and a new kind of music was beginning to be heard. They called themselves "The Beatles." Discotheques were sprouting all over England. The youth culture happened with a vengeance. Mary Quant had burst upon the scene with the miniskirt. Girls, and women too, were showing more and more legs. Although there was a war in Vietnam, it was a great time—a wonderful time to be young.

I sat in the White Elephant, one of the most fashionable of London's new restaurants, and observed the scene at lunch. Half of Hollywood seemed to be there making deals, setting up pictures or just sitting there. Many American movie people had decided to leave smog-ridden, heavily taxed Los Angeles and move to tranquil, civilized nonfoggy (thanks to the Clean Air Act in the mid-1950s) London. The restaurant was abuzz with conversation and activity. Crystal sconces glittered; the Italian waiters moved swiftly from table to table. "Cubby" Broccoli, the American producer, stopped by my table to chat. He told me he was producing a film based on Ian Fleming's James Bond spy stories, and they were off to the Caribbean soon. I wished him luck and watched as he said hello to two young men seated at a nearby table.

"That's Tony Newley," said my girlfriend. "You know, the fellow who's just had a big success with that new show *Stop the World—I Want to Get Off.*"

Ah, yes. I remembered reading the reviews when it had opened a few weeks previously. The critics had been harsh, but very intrigued by this practically one-man show in which Newley, in white clown-type makeup and baggy pants, played an amalgam of Everyman. He also directed it and wrote the book, music and lyrics with Leslie Bricusse, who, my friend informed me, was the man lunching with him.

Newley looked familiar. I stared, trying to remember where I had seen that face before. Then it came to me. He was Artful Dodger in David Lean's film of *Oliver Twist*. He was about fourteen then, but still had the same cheeky Cockney face, darting intelligent eyes and strong Romanesque nose. He was now in his late twenties, I thought, satanic and intense looking, with thick dark brown hair and beautifully expressive hands that he used constantly in the conversation. He met my glance and a flicker of recognition crossed his face. I looked away. I was heavily off men right now. Besides, glances in restaurants had caused me trouble before.

I thought no more about him until Robert Wagner, who was also making a movie in London, called and said he had tickets for *Stop the World* and invited me to go. R.J. and I had been friends since the disastrous *Stopover Tokyo*, and since his separation from Natalie Wood we had gone out together several times in London.

The newspapers and gossip magazines jumped on this hot "new twosome" immediately. Numerous articles appeared to the effect that we were "consoling" each other while Natalie and Warren were now dating openly. These reports were fairly irksome. Enough that Warren and I had ended our relationship with honesty and objectivity, trying to remain friends, but to have the eager eyes of the yellow press announcing avidly that Natalie and Warren had been carrying on a passionate affair while she was still married to R.J. and Warren was engaged to me was aggravating, although I knew there might have been some truth to it.

However, Warren, ever quick to make hay while the sun shone, had not found it disadvantageous to his burgeoning career to be dating Natalie, a major star, and since he was fond of seeing himself in photographs with well-known actresses, it served him well. As one wit remarked, "I knew Warren before he only bedded household names." While their relationship developed, R.J.'s and mine did not. Although he was very attractive, I was still neurotic enough to be truly interested only in complex, difficult men—and R.J. was gentle and sweet and too nice for me. We were—hello cliché!—"just good friends." The tabloid-reading public, however, found it hard to believe that an attractive man and woman could merely be friends. Consequently there was plenty of gossip and speculation about our friendship.

I was completely enthralled by *Stop the World—I Want to Get Off*. It was one of the most brilliant, creative and excitingly original shows I had ever seen, made all the more so by the magical presence of Tony Newley. His was a *tour de force*, bravura performance, and although many of the critics belittled it, his talent was the maypole from which the ribbons and form of the musical flowed.

The premise of the show was simple. It was the story of "Littlechap," a sort of Everyman of the world, alternately bumptious and vulnerable, belligerent and sensitive, aging from brash youth to elder statesman, and in between running a veritable gamut of emotional highs and lows, punctuated by show-stopping songs that culminated in the classic "What Kind of Fool Am I?"

At the end of the show I was drained but exhilarated. I hadn't witnessed anything in the theater that had moved me so much for ages. Not only the show, which I had been informed was autobiographical in flavor, but by Newley himself.

"Let's go backstage and say hello," I suggested to R.J., as the cast took their final bows to tumultuous applause. He, as impressed with the show as I was, agreed, and we made our way through the labyrinthine musty back corridors of the Queen's Theatre to Newley's dressing room. A gruff, heavyset man greeted us suspiciously, asked our names and told us rather uncharmingly to wait, as the "young master" was removing his makeup.

R.J. and I raised our eyebrows at each other at this rather grand epithet, used previously, I recall, only by Noel Coward himself. We waited. And waited. And waited. After twenty minutes of staring at the seedy, cracked and waterlogged walls of this far from elegant anteroom, and without being offered so much as a glass of water, my Gemini impatience got the better of me and we decided to leave.

"We're going," I called to a shabby green velvet curtain that separated the waiting room from the star's dressing area.

"Oh—hang on a minute, love. Just putting on me drawers," called a voice in a beguiling Cockney accent. The curtain drew back with a flourish and there stood Littlechap in the flesh. Little he was—at least not very tall. Thin as a rail, white as a sheet, blue of eye and black of hair— and rather sexy. He was toweling traces of white pancake from behind his ears, and his intelligent, deepset eyes were still encircled by the heavy black eyeliner he wore in the show.

"How d'ja do. How d'ja do, sorry to keep you waiting. This muck takes forever to scrub off." We shook hands and R.J. and I gushed how much we *loved* the show, and how wonderful he was. He seemed genuinely pleased to hear this and listened with deep interest to our comments.

The heavyset man hovered disapprovingly in the background, fiddling about with stuff on the dressing table, making it obvious we were not at all welcome.

"Well we better take off and get something to eat," said R.J., intercepting a basilisk stare from the vigilante at the dressing table.

"Why don't we have a bite together?" said Tony. "Unless you two have other plans?"

"No, no, come on—come with us," said I, my interest in "young master" Newley slightly piqued.

"Shall we go to the Trat?" said Tony, putting an old green tweed jacket on top of his baggy gray flannels and black polo neck. "I usually have a table there."

"Sounds good," said R.J., and after Tony bade his surly retainer a brusque "Ta-ta, Ter," we crossed Shaftesbury Avenue to the stylish new Italian bistro, the Trattoria Terrazza. We were greeted effusively by Mario and Franco, who led us down the tiny winding staircase to a marble-floored, white-stucco-painted room hung with Chianti bottles and humming with conversation. In fact, the acoustics at the Trat were such that conversation had to be conducted three pitches above normal level.

This, added to the proximity of the tiny tables to each other, the excitable Italian waiters—who occasionally burst into either song or rage (a trolley laden with desserts was constantly getting in the way of one of the waiters, who would angrily ram it against the patrons' tables)—and the appetizing smells made the evening quite stimulating.

"What will you have, pretty lady?" said Mr. Newley, frowning at the wine list. "Pretty lady"!—an effusive compliment for an Englishman, I thought.

"Verdicchio, please," I said—and we plunged into animated conversation.

We had many friends in common, and the talk flowed easily, punctuated by Tony's sudden bursts of staccato laughter. He had a keen Cockney humor, which I appreciated I was able to slip easily into the vernacular of London slang or Beverly Hills small talk, having spent all my adult life between these two opposite poles. Two hours and several bottles of Verdicchio later we bade each other fond farewells outside the restaurant and went our respective ways home. It had been a stimulating evening. Tony was bright, amusing and attractive, intelligent and likable.

Joyce Blair came to lunch at Shepperton a few days later and I was surprised to hear, "Whatever did you do to Tony? He fancies you like mad."

I sprawled on the couch in my portable dressing room and peeled an apple.

"What did he say, then?"

"Oh, you know. The usual. How fantastic you look and what a great body. All that sort of thing."

"Oh, did he say anything about my mind?"

Joyce giggled. "I think old Tone's a bit of a male chauvinist. He didn't mention your mind. He thought you were funny, though."

"Oh, goody," I said sarcastically, taking a bite from the apple. "That must mean that he *does* think I've got a mind."

"I'll tell you something about Tone," said Joyce, leaning forward confidentially. "He's a super person—really super—I mean we were at Aida Foster's together so we've known each other since we were kids and I've always adored him, but do you know—" she lowered her voice and leaned forward even more—"do you know that he's *never* been in love?"

I stopped in mid-munch. "Never?" I said incredulously. "What is he—gay?"

"No, no. He loves ladies. No, he's just never been able to fall in love with anyone. Can you imagine, darling, twenty-nine and never been in love. Awful, isn't it?"

"*Very* interesting," I said, studying my apple core. "Is that where the song comes from at the end? You know, the fool song?"

"Yes, yes," she said excitedly. "Those lyrics are *exactly* the story of his life. What kind of fool am I, who never fell in love, it seems that I'm the only one that I have been thinking of."

"Oh, please, save us from *that,*" I said, throwing the apple core in the wastebasket. A man who has *never* been in love. How sad—but how challenging. I looked at Joyce and she looked back mischievously.

"Oh, no, dear. I'm *not* interested in making him change his ways," I said hastily.

"Well, a little lunch wouldn't hurt," she said lightly. "He called me yesterday, drove me *mad* for your number. I finally agreed that I might be able to persuade you to have lunch with him—and me too, of course," she added quickly, seeing my dubious look. "Oh, come on, darling. Whatever can happen at *lunch?*"

"You'd be surprised," I said, finding myself, against my will, intrigued by this ambiguous Newley character. I stood up to get ready for the scene. We looked at each other and I smiled at Joyce.

Never been in love, eh? Well, we'll see about that.

I found myself thinking about Anthony Newley during the next twenty-four hours. I was, for nearly the first time in my life, absolutely free of all emotional entanglements. I had no roots; no home; no husband, lover or parents to answer to; no children to look after; no studio contractual obligations. I could do what I liked, when I liked. It was bliss. If I wanted to fly to Paris or Rome for the weekend, all I had to do was pack a bag and jump on a plane. This feeling of total freedom and disencumbrance was so heady and refreshing after my disciplined childhood, disastrous marriage, studio contracts with Rank and Fox, who had controlled my every career move, and then, total involvements sequentially with Sydney, Arthur, George and Warren, that I almost didn't know how to handle it.

I was like a bird that had just learned to fly. The world was mine and I intended to keep it that way for a while.

Occasionally I would get a flicker of envy as I would see some cherubic infant being fondled by its loving mother. Feeling "broody" came upon me now and then, but I pushed these strange maternal feelings away without stopping to analyze and dissect them. I had felt a sense of loss since the abortion. Sometimes when I saw a tiny baby I would automatically calculate what age mine would have been had I had it. But, as with all my deep and subliminal feelings, I would not allow myself to dwell on them. Life was gay. Life was fun. Life was for doing and seeing and going places. There was no time for ruminative self-pity or unhappiness. I wanted to live to the hilt. In doing so, however, I lost touch with a certain basic reality. Never stopping to analyze my constant mistakes, I blindly rushed in where angels feared to tread . . . and Tony Newley was no exception.

Any woman with any horse sense does not fall in love with a man who openly proclaims to the world in song and verse that he is unable to love. She might like him. She might admire his talent and personality—but if she is smart she will not get involved in a relationship with "doomed" written all over it.

Poles apart—we were worlds apart. He was a Libra, quiet, intellectual, home-based, deeply involved in his work and himself. His capacity for *joie de vivre* was not great. He was uncomfortable and out of place except with close, old friends, and in familiar surroundings. He hated to travel—disliked new things. He was nothing like my father, yet the feelings he generated in me, as in all the men to whom I became deeply attached, were exactly those of that little Joan of so long ago, trying to make Daddy love her. I was everything that he shouldn't want in a woman: Gemini—mercurial, moody, exuberant, inexhaustible, extroverted, highly energized and quick-tempered—thinking only of today, dismissing yesterday and letting tomorrow take care of itself.

But despite our different lifestyles and personalities, we became involved. It did not, of course, happen to us simultaneously. First I became infatuated and then persuaded him to feel the same way. Three weeks after our first meeting we became lovers. Not long after that he *professed* to love me.

So, now that I had won his hard-earned "love," what did I intend to do? Was I going to play the little woman role and cook liver and bacon every lunchtime for him at Leslie and Evie Bricusse's flat in Stanmore? Was I going to sit night after night applauding wildly in the stalls as he performed, reveling in the adulation of his enthusiastic audiences? I didn't really know. I was playing it one day at a time.

My mother was dying. I knew she was dying—so did Daddy and Jackie. Only sixteen-year-old Bill was protected from the truth, although with the wisdom of adolescence he no doubt suspected. The final illness came upon her so swiftly that it took us all by surprise.

After a brief period of hospitalization she came back to Harley House to spend her last days with the family. I had to be there. I could not face the fact that she was dying. I refused to believe it. Even now I cannot really believe she is gone. Her photographs are with me all the time: her always smiling, happy face, with the fair curly hair, sparkling blue eyes and high cheekbones, which last I inherited from her, as well as her tremendous *joie de vivre*.

Unfortunately my mother was the product of a strict Victorian authoritarian upbringing. She was nervous about her intellectual capabilities and consequently had a tendency to sometimes play the "dumb blonde" role. She so adored my father that she even gave up all her own friends when they first married and his friends became hers. He was sometimes critical of her and seemed to never let her be her own person and enjoy herself. He, being a male chauvinist before we even knew the meaning of the phrase, ruled the roost totally. His word was law, and woe betide any of us who disobeyed it.

"I pay the bills around here," he would roar if anyone even dared remonstrate or argue with him. "If you're so clever, you make the money to support us all. Then I'll listen to you."

He would shout at Mummy often. It is from him that I inherited *my* impatience and tendency to fly off the handle at petty irritations. But it didn't matter how much he yelled at her—she *adored* him! I could never understand how she could be so warm and loving to someone who sometimes treated her so badly, even though during my early adult life I obviously did the same with my men. Her mentality was such that she believed in the superiority of the male, but at the same time acknowledged men as "the enemy."

She was filled with a host of misconceptions and superstitions that she drummed into me at an early age. I painstakingly exorcised them on the analyst's couch years later. A lot of these adages I deliberately set out to disprove as soon as I became aware of the male sex. *But,* there is a lingering residue of her teachings bouncing around in the subconscious somewhere that agrees with a lot of her philosophies: "Men are no good." "They only want *one thing* from a woman." "He'll have *no respect* for you if you let him *have his way* with you." "Nice girls don't let men *touch them* unless they are married." And so on, and so on . . .

She was not alone in her viewpoints. Millions of women in the 1930s, 1940s and 1950s felt the same way and brought up their little girls to feel the same guilts and unclean feelings about their sexuality. Hopefully, today my generation of women have been able to learn from the sexual revolution of the sixties, and from their own ashamed and furtive early years, how *not* to indoctrinate *their* children.

Be that as it may, I loved my mother, and it was unbearable to know that she was leaving us. Her forte, of course, was motherhood. The kind of mothering that keeps you home from school if you wake up with so much as a sneeze; that sees that you get three good nourishing meals a day, plus at least ten hours sleep; that makes sure all the doors and windows are locked and that there is a light on in the hallway when you go to sleep, in case you get frightened during the night. And who, after nagging you to pick up your dirty clothes, will sigh heavily and pick them up for you. We were taken care of very well. Even during the years of rationing during the war we always had meat, eggs, sugar, and sometimes even candy.

Mummy had her reward from Jackie: a beautiful little baby girl, Tracy, a few months old and the apple of her eye. "If only Joan would get married and settle down," she would say wistfully to Jackie, as they played each afternoon with Tracy in the photograph-laden living room of Harley House. The room was now an absolute shrine to the Collins sisters. Literally hundreds of pictures of us hung on the walls, clustered on the mantelpiece, sideboard and TV. She certainly was proud of her children, and I felt guilty that I had not been able to be closer to her in the past few years.

I refused to leave England and go back to the States while Mummy was so sick. We had taken her to many different doctors and specialists, but the prognosis was always pessimistic. We were told she had only a few months to live, and I was determined to be with her as much as I could.

✿   ✿   ✿

The Road to Hong Kong was finished. It had been fun. I liked Bob Hope immensely. He was the consummate comedian: confident, aggressive, always completely in command and never at a loss for a joke or a quip. He was consistently charming, warm, and down to earth. He was also a Gemini.

Bing Crosby, on the other hand, was a different breed: offhand, grumpy and vague. He appeared to me always as an old man acting very young, or a young man who looked old. His face was like a piece of crumpled tissue paper and I never felt his eyes when he looked at me. They looked *through* me. He did not endear himself to the crew, and he had the revolting habit of spitting on the set or wherever he happened to be. We spent days shooting on stage that had sawdust on the floor, and he would clear his throat and aim a great wad of pipe spit on the piles of sawdust scattered around, to the chagrin of the tiny Cockney in charge of sweeping the set.

"Blimey if I 'as to clean up any more of that old geezer's spittle, I'm goin' to ram it dahn 'is bleedin' throat, I swear I will," he muttered furiously, as he collected the debris in his spade and deposited it in a bucket. Crosby puffed away on his pipe, oblivious to all the activity going on around him. We were standing in the middle of the set getting the final light checks for our love scene, and Bing had spat at least three times that morning.

"How'd you like to have to kiss him?" I whispered to the little Cockney as he angrily brushed at the sawdust around my feet. "Ooohh, you poor little darlin'. I'd rather kiss Hitler," said he, and sniffing disgustedly he walked away.

I arranged my face into the correct loving expression to gaze into Crosby's bland blue eyes and smell his rancid breath and wondered again how people could think an actress's life was just a bowl of cherries.

Tony—Tony Newley—I was obsessed by his outrageous talent, by his brilliant performances. He astounded me with his virtuosity. I and many other people, including himself, thought he was a genius. But geniuses are complicated. And being infatuated with one wasn't a bowl of cherries, either, for although professing love for me, *he* was also interested in a young blonde, in the cast of *Stop the World*. This had been gathering momentum ever since rehearsals had first commenced in April, and various difficulties of consummation only increased Tony's interest.

Blissfully involved in the first passionate throes of an exciting romance with an exciting man, working hard on *Hong Kong*, and devoting what time I had left to spending it with my ailing mother, I had blinkers on as far as another girl in his life was concerned. It wasn't really until six years later, when he wrote, produced, directed and starred in an autobiographical film called *Can Hieronymus Merkin Ever Forget Mercy Humppe and Find True Happiness?* that the full extent of his infatuation with the girl was crystallized for me.

But these were the days and months of what to me has always been the best time of a relationship. The beginning. I was well aware of the familiar pattern and how things started to wear off. I knew I expected too much from men. I expected them to be perfect. I couldn't seem to cope with human frailties and idiosyncrasies. Certainly I was not perfect myself. So was it asking too much to demand faultlessness from others? But now I was giving Tony the benefit of the doubt and making myself well aware of all his failings and foibles before I committed myself. I had decided he would make a fine father for the children I felt I was now ready to have. All I had to do was convince *him*.

I threw myself into the role of "camp follower" with a vengeance. I turned down all movie offers to the despair of my agents who, after working hard to get me out of Fox, now could not cash in on the money I could be making. I devoted myself to being the perfect wife. I cooked. I cleaned. I shopped. Culinary arts I did not know I possessed suddenly blossomed in me. Sausages and Mash, Toad-in-the-Hole, Shepherd's Pie, Irish Stew, Bread-and-Butter Pudding, Rhubarb and Custard—I became an expert in these simple English dishes, and a regular customer at the supermarket on Marylebone Road.

I had competition for his attention though. His mother, Grace, his manager, Terry, and various others all vied with me and each other to be close to him.

His mother worshipped the ground he walked on. She was a sweet birdlike little woman who had given birth to him illegitimately and had been made to pay the price for this (then) outrageous transgression. She had brought him up practically singlehandedly, and she lavished all of her love, attention and adoration on him. He took this as his due. Although she had married, finally, during the war, nevertheless each day she appeared regularly at his cozy, shabby little flat off Earl's Court Road to make his breakfast. She then stayed for the rest of the day doing the housework and just being in his orbit.

I first met her one wintry Monday morning when the door to Tony's bedroom opened at nine o'clock and a perky little face, not unlike his, but crowned with a mass of gray curls, said "Good morning, son, what would you like for your breakfast today? I've got some lovely kippers, or I'll do you some bacon and eggs and fried bread. Or would you rather have some nice porridge, seeing as how it's such a nasty cold day?"

She did not acknowledge that there was another person in the bed with him, and after he had placed his order for porridge, she scampered away without so much as a glance in my direction.

"Do you think I could have a cup of tea?" I asked meekly of the "young master," who seemed not at all surprised by this unusual confrontation—or lack of it.

"Oh—Flower, of course. Mum—Mum," he called, and the little lady scuttled back in again, gray curls bobbing, and wiping her hands on her apron.

"Yes, son," she said nervously, glancing at me.

"Mum. This is Joanie, and she'd like a cup of tea."

"If it's not too much trouble," I said hastily, trying to look innocent and beguiling.

"No—no. Not at all. How do you like it—er—Joanie?"

"Oh. Two lumps please." I smiled sweetly, hoping she would think what a delightful daughter-in-law I would make. "I'll come and help you make the porridge if you like."

"No—no. That's all right. Not to bother, dear. I'll do it." And she quickly disappeared again, no doubt thinking what loose morals the girls of today's generation had. Later Grace and I became friends and, in fact, some of the feelings that I had for my own mother were transferred to her. But at the beginning she was wary of any woman that Tony became involved with.

I instantly became great friends with Tony's best friend and collaborator, Leslie Bricusse, and his beautiful wife, Evie. It was rare to have a four-sided friendship in which any combination of the individuals got along like a house on fire, but the four of us did. At Leslie's and my urging, one cold December weekend we forced Tony on a plane to Paris and away from his ever-present entourage, to sample some of the delights of another environment. He needed a lot of persuasion. It was hard for him to leave the comfort and security of his snug flat in London for "foreign parts," even for two days, and Gallic cooking did not agree with his sensitive stomach. But I was determined to make him get away from his hermitlike existence and get used to some of the better things in life.

One of the songs in the show epitomized the renaissance that Tony was experiencing with his newfound success and acclaim. It was called "I Wanna Be Rich."

> *"I wanna be rich*
> *And live in L.A.,*
> *Go crazy at nighttime*
> *And sleep in the day,*
> *An Italian car*
> *As long as the street,*
> *And the local broads will arrive in hordes,*
> *It'll knock 'em off their feet.*
> *I wanna be famous*
> *And be in the news,*
> *And date a T.V. star*
> *Whenever I choose,*
> *Give me half a chance to lead a dance*
> *And make my pitch*
> *And I'll be dirty rotten filthy stinking* RICH." ©

I fitted well into the "go out with a T.V. star" line. Tony was starting to acclimatize himself to a more sybaritic life as he became more successful.

Leslie and Tony's idol was the Scandinavian filmmaker Ingmar Bergman. So admiring were they of his work that they adopted part of his name and incorporated it into their own names. The still refer to each other by these nicknames to this day. Newley became New*berg*, and Bricusse became Brick*man*. Our sons, who today are great friends, also now call each other Newberg and Brickman.

The four of us had wonderful times and a great kinship. I relied heavily on the camaraderie of this four-sided relationship to help me through the dark days of my mother's failing health and death. Her death, early one May morning in 1962, was almost a relief, as she had been in great pain. She must have known what was happening although we all desperately tried to keep her from knowing the truth.

A few days before she died I sat at her bedside gossiping and telling her jokes, hoping to make her forget her pain. Suddenly she took my hand and looked me in the eye and with great lucidity asked, "What are you going to do with your life? It's time you settled down. You're not going to be young and beautiful forever, you know."

My mother rarely confronted me with this kind of probing question. She had let me live my own life for a long time now. I was taken aback at this, for her, frank approach.

"Well, Tony and I will probably get married—when he gets his divorce," I said, crossing my fingers and sounding confident.

"Ah—I'm glad, darling. He seems good for you. He's stopped you from gadding about." She closed her eyes and breathed deeply and I thought she had gone to sleep. I gently withdrew my hand from hers, but as I did she opened her eyes and looked at me with such love in her face that I could hardly keep from crying.

"You'd be a marvelous mother, darling," she whispered. "I hope you have a baby one day. I hope you have one soon." She closed her eyes again and I gazed at her, the tears streaming down my face. I mentally kicked myself for the fact that there was no way now that she could ever hold a child of mine in her arms. It was too late. I knew it was only a matter of days. My tears fell on her hand and she opened her eyes and smiled at me.

"You're so easily led," she whispered. "And you're so strong too. It makes it difficult for you, difficult." Her voice trailed off and she closed her eyes and murmured as she drifted off to sleep, "I hope you have a child soon. Have it soon, darling. . . ." She loosened her hand in mine and slept. Her hand was so thin and vulnerable, the blue veins standing up like tiny rivers on the frail white skin. My mother. The only person really in my life who had ever cared about me. She was going. And I could do nothing to save her. I went to my room and sobbed for two hours. I then made a resolution. If I did nothing else, I was going to try to do something to please her and make her happy. Although I did not believe in an afterlife, in some way I knew that if and when I had a child she would know about it and be happy.

I cried all my tears for Mummy that evening. When Daddy came into my room at six-thirty the next morning and said, "She's gone," I had already faced the loss and the tears had been shed. But the resolution remained. I had an ambition and a goal now. For her. And I was going to make it happen—come what may.

✿   ✿   ✿

I rented yet another house in Los Angeles. Tony and the Bricusses came to visit for two weeks. Cordell Mews was nestled in the Hollywood Hills behind the fabled Doheny Estates. It was a tiny house, eclectically furnished in chinoiserie and Melrose Avenue pseudo-English antiques. The master bedroom featured a giant bed with an ornately scalloped gold-painted headboard. Tony took one look at the Hollywoodian masterpiece and fell on it gasping for breath. "Ha, ha!" we all shrieked. "What a sense of humor the young master does have." Unfortunately he was not being humorous—a flu bug had attacked him even as he had surveyed the palaces of the affluent during the drive to the house, and he was seized with simultaneous headache, stomachache, throat ache and muscle ache.

"Oh, God, Flower—I'm so sorry," he moaned, as Evie and I scurried about bringing him aspirin and hot lemon and honey—his staple drink, which usually warded off attacks on his ever delicate throat.

"Never mind, darling." I bustled, doing my Florence Nightingale impression. "It's just jet lag. You'll be up and about tomorrow."

"Please God," he groaned pitifully, and sank back onto the carefully arranged pillows we had surrounded him with to protect his head from the wooden monstrosity looming behind him.

"I think I'll have a little kip," he said, putting large wads of pink waxy substance in his ears and placing a black eye mask over his feverish eyes. He wore pajamas—the only man I had ever met, other than my father, who did so—and arranged a decrepit old camel-colored scarf around his neck. He pulled the covers up to his nose and fell instantly asleep. He was, enviably, always able to fall asleep any time, anywhere. I looked at him snoring and tiptoed out to join Leslie and Evie in the living room. What a start to a romantic, whirlwind holiday.

I had planned dinner on the patio, where we could look at the twinkling lights of Los Angeles spread out like a sequined shawl and listen to the newest Sinatra and Mathis records on the excellent stereo system. I had prepared my favorite dish, *Pomme Paysanne*, which I had been introduced to by Laurence Harvey. Actually "Peasant Potato" was the pseudonym for a large baked potato filled with fresh sevruga caviar, butter and sour cream. Even with caviar at fifty dollars an ounce, I had not stinted myself or my guests. I managed to eat several ounces and two potatoes trying to get over my disappointment at Tony's indisposition.

One could not be downhearted for too long, however, around Leslie and Evie. They were young, fun and in love. Evie, with her flawless olive skin, huge dark eyes, lustrous black hair and hourglass figure, was one of the warmest, kindest and funniest girls I knew. She still is. And Leslie, with his Cambridge-fair, typically English looks, owllike glasses and biting humor, was stimulating and witty enough to make me forget Tony wheezing away in the huge "Hollywood" bed. They are two of my closest friends to this day.

Leslie was a great planner. That evening, after several bottles of white wine, we plotted and planned our two-week vacation every minute from dawn to dusk. It was organized with soldierlike precision. Leslie was a grabber of life, and each new day was an adventure to be discovered and savored and enjoyed to the utmost. So he and I had a lot in common. We both had new Polaroid cameras, which we used constantly. Because of the Bricusses, I saw Los Angeles and California through new eyes, discovering places and things about the city that I had not seemed to be aware of before. Life became a constant photo call. Not the boring, uncomfortable sessions in the sterile portrait gallery at the studios but spur-of-the-moment funny photos snapped wherever and whenever.

"Quick, get the Polaroid. Tony's drowning," someone would squeal and off we'd go. Snap—tear—count to ten—pull—*voilà!*

"Oh, it's good of you, Evie"—"Oh, no, I look *awful*—but you look *great!*"

The coffee table was heaped with dozens of pictures. Mugging it up outside Dino's on the Strip, Tony wielding a large comb and trying to look like Kookie "Lend me your comb" Byrnes. There we were at Disneyland, surrounded by Mickey Mouse and Donald Duck, and falling down with laughter. There were Evie and I in the bathroom, in the process of teasing our hair to immense beehives fourteen or sixteen inches high, wearing bras and tights, caught open mouthed with surprise. There was Tony by the swimming pool in Palm Springs wearing football boots, drooping black socks and long gray shorts, lifting with mock effort a huge pair of dumbbells.

There we were, the four of us, clustered around Sammy Davis, Jr., in his dressing room in Vegas, our faces full of admiration, for there was a mutual exchange of hero worship between Tony and Sammy. Sammy often "did" Tony in his act, and was Newley's and Bricusse's first and biggest booster in the States. He, not Tony, had the first big hit with "What Kind of Fool Am I?" Quite a few Newley-Bricusse songs were getting air play now in the States, especially on KLAC. We would often hear the strident Cockney tones boom forth with "Yes, We Have No Bananas," and "Pop Goes the Weasel," but he was still a virtual unknown as far as most of America was concerned.

Leslie had the incredible knack of combining extremely hard, prolific work with a large measure of holidays, vacations and pleasure trips. He could make a simple outing to the zoo a gala event. He was able to turn the most mundane situation into a great adventure. It is a priceless gift, and he has managed through the years to continue doing it, juggling his and Evie's and their son Adam's lives and balancing them with their several homes all over the world, and their dozens of friends. Wherever "Brickman" goes there is always instant action.

All too soon the brief vacation drew to a close. Time for them to return to London and for Tony to start *Stop the World* again for a few months until they would bring the show to New York for a fall season under the auspices of the "King of the Broadway Producers," David Merrick. During his summer break Tony was also going to star in a very demanding role in a movie called *The Small World of Sammy Lee,* while also working with Leslie on two future projects for musicals—*Noah* and *Mr. Fat and Mr. Thin.* On top of that he was appearing in three or four TV specials, his own TV show—called "The Johnny Darling Show"—and cutting at least two or three records. I realized that for the next few months the boy was going to be very, very busy indeed. How I was going to fit into his crammed schedule was a puzzlement. I allied my fortunes with those of the Bricusses. We planned at least three trips during the spring and summer. I had made my own mind up as far as Tony was concerned. I had decided to marry him, and I had made it clear to him that this was what I wanted from our relationship. Having already been married and still only separated from Ann Lynn, he was ambivalent and dreaded another marriage, but he was also terrified of losing me. His feelings vacillated back and forth like a yo-yo. One day totally enamored he could not consider life without me. The next, careless indifference. Adamant that he would be a disaster as a husband and that we were from two different worlds . . . "What can a rich, young, beautiful film star see in a married Cockney, half-Jewish git?" he would ask me ruefully, sitting behind his shabby, top-heavy dressing table backstage at the Queen's Theatre, in his ancient moth-eaten navy blue dressing gown from Marks and Spencer, a brown hairnet scraping his heavy wavy hair off his white forehead, while he scrubbed the cold cream around and around until his black-and-white makeup turned into gray mud.

"I'm half Jewish too, Newberg, don't you forget it. A half-Jewish princess from Bayswater via Sunset Boulevard. I think we make a great combination." I put my head close to his and we studied ourselves in the fly-specked mirror. "If our children have my looks and your brains there'll be no stopping them. It will be an *unbeatable* combination!" He smiled faintly.

"Ah, Flower, you always look on the bright side, don't you?"

"You bet," I said optimistically. "But wouldn't it be awful if the children had your looks and my brains!"

Tony had started divorce proceedings against Ann Lynn, from whom he had been separated for three years. The English courts were notoriously long-winded as far as divorces were concerned, unlike the States, where divorce is as easy to get as a cold. I knew it would be a long and difficult time but I felt confident we were going to win.

While Tony was rehearsing in New York for *Stop the World,* the Bricusses and I spent a week in Jamaica. It had been five or six years since *Seawife.* I revisited the beaches and lagoons with nostalgic interest. Leslie and Evie thought the idea of Tony and me married was super. Even when we sat one evening listening to the ominous tones of the radio announcing that President Kennedy was going to stand firm and not allow Russian bases on Cuba (we were holidaying right in the middle of the Cuban missile crisis!) I was still preoccupied with Tony. We realized that Jamaica was rather too close to Cuba for comfort and that even getting *out* of Jamaica and back to the States might be a trifle dangerous. We flew back to New York.

Tony met us at the airport, thrilled to see me, but at the Philadelphia opening he was cool. First-night nerves, the Bricusses assured me. He's scared; everything is on the line now. But things weren't the same between us. He confessed he was having a fling with the young blonde from *Stop the World*. He realized that she was in every way wrong—but what could he do? The flesh is weak. I knew that. We decided to separate. Heavy-hearted, I flew back to Los Angeles carrying a French poodle named Ladybird that Tony had given me. Now she seemed destined to be my life's companion. I had promised the Bricusses and Tony that whatever personal problems we had, I would definitely attend the first night of *Stop the World* in New York. A week later I flew back and stayed at the Drake Hotel. I was fulfilling my duties as a friend, but I couldn't fight Tony any more. If he preferred another girl to me, that was the end as far as I was concerned. I had offers of movies in Hollywood and Italy and I must get on with my life. Now I could reap the rewards for the years I had spent doing Fox's potboilers.

After the opening of *Stop the World* we went back to Tony's suite at the Navarro and waited for the reviews. They were not good. The critics, although admiring Tony's immense talent and the Bricusse-Newley score, which was magnificent, did not like the show. They felt it was self-indulgent and pretentious. Paul and Joanne Newman had come in from Connecticut, and with Michael Lipton—Tony's best friend—the Bricusses and a few other close mates, we sat reading the scathing reviews by Bosley Crowther and Walter Kerr and felt the kiss of death on the show.

The Newley relationship was over. This was it. Finished. Done with. Goodbye baby and amen. Another year down the tube. We all said tearful goodbyes to each other in the early hours. Leslie and Tony were convinced that Merrick, on the strength of the appalling reviews, would take the show off and that they would go back to London and start writing another one. I was going to accept one of the movie roles. Preferably one that would be ten thousand miles away from Tony. Gloom was rampant.

The next morning, however, an amazing thing happened. There were lines around the block outside the theater. Hundreds of people waiting to buy tickets for *Stop the World*. This time the word of mouth of the public proved stronger than the critics' scathing words. The show became an instant hit.

I was thrilled for Tony, and Leslie and Evie, who were also staying at the Drake Hotel. I had a celebration drink with the Bricusses in the bar a couple of nights later, while Leslie excitedly told me about the great audiences and standing ovations they had been having. "He still loves you, Joanie," said Evie sympathetically. "He really *needs* you. He's miserable without you."

"That's too bad," I said calmly, watching my date for the evening come in. "He's got another girlfriend now and I'm not a groveler, Evie, you know that."

"We certainly *all* know *that*, Jace," said Brickman as the young man came over to our table and sat down and had a drink with us.

I introduced them to Terence Stamp, who was extremely handsome. He had just had a critical success in William Wyler's film *The Collector*, with Samantha Eggar, and having just played the title role in *Billy Budd* for Peter Ustinov, was in New York doing publicity and movie promotion.

"See you later," I said after twenty minutes as Terry and I got up and left for our dinner. Evie shot me a knowing and penetrating look. "He's gorgeous," she whispered to me. "Tony will be *livid* when he hears." He had no right to be livid even if I was subconsciously going out with this very attractive man to make him jealous.

Terry was a Cockney boy, full of whimsical Cockney assurance. His success had not gone to his head and he found all the fuss and hullabaloo "a bit embarrassing." He and Michael Caine had shared a flat when they were penniless actors a few years previously. Now Michael's career was taking off, too. It was the time of the English actor. Albert Finney, Alan Bates, Peter Cook and Dudley Moore, Peter Sellers and now Terence Stamp and Tony Newley were taking America by storm. England was where the action was, and suddenly anything and anyone British had enormous appeal.

Terry was also staying at the Drake Hotel, which certainly made life less complicated. Tony called me three times later that night. I didn't return his calls. I was trying to get over him, and I wasn't going to jump through his hoop whenever he decided to set it up. After a dozen or so phone calls during the next two days in which he begged me to meet him to "talk about things," we met on neutral ground. A bench in Central Park. It was a cold, blustery November day. The trees in the park were stark and bare of leaves. A few brave people walked around with dogs and bundled-up children. We sat huddled on a hard bench. The collar of his navy blue raincoat was turned up, and he wore his usual woolly scarf to protect his valuable vocal cords. He came to the point quickly. He wanted me back. Under any circumstances. Whatever I wanted was fine by him. Anything.

What did I want? Looking at his sad, pale face with the permanently ingrained pained expression I felt compassion and love for him. "I don't think you *really* love me, Tony," I said carefully. "I think you're fascinated with me, infatuated, call it what you will, but I don't truly think it's love, do you?"

"I don't know, Flower. I don't know what the bloody word *means*, for Christ's sake." He got up and strode up and down the path, the wind whipping his thick dark hair, his face a mask of agonized concentration. "I've been miserable the last couple of days. *Miserable*. You've been running around New York with Terry Stamp—oh, yes, all of my friends told me about it." He smiled bitterly. "I think, I really feel, I can't live without you now, Flower." He sat down next to me and put his arms around my shoulders. I was shivering. Whether from the cold or the emotion I didn't know.

"What about the young blonde?" I said evenly. "A month ago it was she whom you couldn't give up. How do you feel about *her* now?"

"I can't deny it, Flower—I can't deny I find her very attractive, but . . ." He paused, groping for words, his dark blue eyes searching my face as though hoping to find the answer there. ". . . I'll really try and truly love you—if you try and help me to. Can you help me, Flower?" I didn't know the answer to that one. I didn't know where altruism ended and ego began. But I knew what *I* wanted and needed out of life now. I wanted to marry and have a child. If it wasn't Tony, it would be someone else eventually. I was in love with Tony but I'd been in love before. Love was like measles. You could get it again.

I told him that if he truly wanted to be with me, then we would have to marry. "Otherwise I'm leaving for Rome next week to do a movie," I said flatly. "You can't keep turning me on and off like a tap." I had been an actress for over ten years now. I wanted to be a wife and mother. I wanted to have children, settle down. Give up this life of furnished apartments and hotel rooms, locations and airports, living out of suitcases. Stop the World—I Want to Get *On*. I want roots. I want to belong. I want to buy my own furniture, get my books and records out of storage, make a nest.

I told him all this and he understood. And he agreed. A week later we moved into a huge unfurnished penthouse apartment on Sixty-third Street. He started immediate divorce proceedings and we haunted Bloomingdale's and furniture stores on Third Avenue for furniture for our nest.

Six weeks later I was pregnant.

The good years had begun.

◆ *Nine* ◆

Tara Cynara Newley was born at Mount Sinai Hospital in New York on October 12, 1963. She was without a doubt the most beautiful creature I had ever set eyes on from her perfectly shaped pink head, with just the tiniest blond fuzz on it, to her enormous blue eyes, rosebud lips and perfect little body. She was so infinitely precious and wonderful that I sat and stared at her in wonderment for hours. She was mine. Ours. Our baby daughter. Tony had wanted a daughter. I didn't mind as long as it was a healthy baby, but I was overjoyed to see his reaction to this gorgeous elf.

I had her by natural childbirth, having done all the right things while I was pregnant: vitamins, rest, tons of milk and eggs and fresh vegetables; natural childbirth classes; special breathing exercises so that she wouldn't have to have any medication or anesthetic while she was experiencing the trauma of birth.

Joanne Woodward had told me I *must* nurse her myself. Although I loved the symbolism of the whole thing, Mother Earth incarnate, I wasn't too sure whether I could really handle it. Having gained thirty-two pounds, I was eager to shed them and get back into my clothes again. Nursing entails drinking two or three quarts of milk or beer a day to keep everything on tap, so to speak. The nurse on my floor was surprised at what I was doing. "We haven't had a mother do that for years—except in the wards, of course," she added hastily. The wards were where the poor Puerto Rican and black women from Harlem were delivered.

I was on the third floor, where the private rooms were. They were occupied by lovely young creatures having their first, second or maximum third child, who would never consider defiling their svelte figures by anything as barbaric as breastfeeding. I was trying hard to do it success-fully.

It was 1963 and a whole movement was afoot to popularize not only natural childbirth but the natural way of feeding the child too. I gritted my teeth. I was quite a curiosity on the third floor as nurses and interns would pop in to see how the movie star was coping with her young. It was a source of much amusement to them' and to some of my friends.

"Joanie, I just can't watch this—it's too disgusting," said horrified Sue Mengers, an agent friend noted for her outspokenness.

When Tara was three days old the hospital sent us home. None of this languishing about in bed eating grapes and being waited on hand and foot applied any more to modern-day obstetrics. Drop the kid and go home was the new method. As Chinese peasant women in the rice pad-dies did.

I called Joanne. The baby was screaming her head off. I was in agony. I had bosoms the size of watermelons and the consistency of granite, and a four-day-old infant starving to death. "I cannot do it, Joanne!" I cried. "This is for mammals and peasants, it's not happening. Tara is *dying* of malnutrition."

"Don't worry," said the calm and assuring tones of my friend. "It's always like this, the fourth day is the worst. Perseverance—I know it hurts but believe me it will be worth it in the end—you'll see."

She persuaded me for forty-five minutes, while I rocked the squalling, and by now terrifying, babe in my arms, the slightest move her little head made against my chest causing me to wince in agony.

"Give it twelve more hours," pleaded Joanne. "I promise you it will get better—I've done it myself with Nell and Melissa. Don't give up on it, my dear—it's worth it." I had a sleepless night. But suddenly the next morning I was the perfect advertisement for Madonna and Child, propped up in bed behind my flowered pillow, hair flowing, along with everything else. Pleased as punch and twice as frisky. What a great feel-ing of achievement. It infinitely surpassed anything I had ever done on the screen.

Tara bloomed. When she was six weeks old she had her first checkup with the pediatrician. "What have you been feeding this baby? She's enormous," said the doctor in surprise, bending over the bonny gurgling princess, already aware of what was going on around her.

I noticed as we drove home in a cab through the crowded New York streets that many people were behaving strangely. Cars had pulled over to the sidewalk. People were standing about in clusters looking depressed and unhappy. I leaned over to the driver. "What's happening? Is there something going on somewhere?"

"Beats me, lady," he drawled in the charming way New York cab drivers have.

As soon as I opened the apartment door I heard our cleaning lady weeping loudly. It sounded like a wake. Tony strode out of the study and beckoned me in. He looked somber and on the brink of tears. The television was on full blast and an ashen-faced announcer was reading a news report.

"Jack Kennedy's been shot, they think he's dying," said Tony.

"Oh, no—oh, God—it's not possible." I sank onto the sofa, the little pink bundle cooing placidly in my arms. We listened and watched in stunned horror for the rest of the day. It wasn't possible that J.F.K., this extraordinary man—a symbol to the world over that America was trying hard to create integration and to erase poverty and unemployment, who was endeavoring to make the nation truly a democracy, who really cared about people—had been assassinated. Friends came over. None of us could do anything other than watch the box, still unable to believe what had happened.

"Shit," said Tony, angrily switching off. "Let's get out of here, Flower —I want to go back to England."

He wrote a song about that terrible day on November 22, 1963. We were both tremendous admirers of the Kennedy family, especially of the President. Tony's homesickness for England probably had a lot to do with his decision to leave the States. He had never felt as though he really belonged in America. Though he was idolized each night by throngs in the audience and the hordes of fans who waited backstage for a glimpse of him, he still felt more his own man in England. He wanted to live in a little hut on the coast of Cornwall, and he would often talk nostalgically of his hut. It had no water or electricity, was in the remotest part of the coast overlooking the fierce coastline, and was made of tin! Probably left over from World War I.

I, more pragmatic about amenities, did not indulge in his enthusiasm for the little hut. But the assassination brought home to him all the things he disliked about New York. He wanted out.

The show was to close soon after Christmas. We were going home again. Who says you can't?

We arrived in Paris on a frosty February day in 1964. We had to wait until the tax year ended on April 6 to enter England. We decided to stay in Paris for a couple of months, where Tony could relax and start writing his new show. It was sad getting rid of our apartment in New York. It had been my very first proper home. The first place for which I had actually bought wallpaper and carpets, had chosen, albeit not terribly tastefully, lamps, sofas and tables, and tentatively started my hand at interior decoration, which was to become a minor passion in my life and, in view of the future moves, a necessity.

What to do with all of this stuff? Records, books, photographs, scrapbooks, junk and mementoes. "Sell it or ship it," said Tony, leaving *me* with the problem of how to do that. I had called my agent in Los Angeles and told him I was going to England "indefinitely" and that I wouldn't be available for work. He hadn't been pleased when, six months earlier, he had excitedly phoned to say that he had a firm offer for me to play Jean Harlow in the movie of Harold Robbins' sexy book *The Carpetbaggers*.

"It's a wonderful part, honey, a terrific role—and the money is great. They really want you."

"Would they really want me if they knew I was six months' pregnant?"

"Joanie . . . What?" My agent was understandably annoyed. Actresses who got pregnant were a nuisance.

"All the time and effort we spent getting you out of Fox—you can't blow that, sweetheart. Not now—it's finally paying off for you."

"It's too late," I said, surveying my bump. "I would look awful in white bias-cut satin."

"You're crazy," he said grimly. "Crazy. You're too young to give up your career. You've worked too hard to pay your dues—it could be really happening for you now, sweetheart. Don't you *care* about working any more?"

"Yes, I *do* care," I answered truthfully. "But my personal life, Tony, Tara and our happiness have to come first. Right now my life is with Tony, and wherever he goes Tara and I go too."

I thought about this as I wheeled Tara in her chic French pram down the boulevards of Paris each morning. After a breakfast of hot croissants and coffee, Tony would settle down to write for three or four hours, and Tara and I would take our morning constitutional. I felt very much the young bourgeois housewife as I sat in the Bois de Boulogne with the other mothers and babies feeding the pigeons and watching the older children on the swings.

Sometimes we would parade down the Champs Élysées and Tara and I would look at the giant movie posters outside the cinemas. *Road to Hong Kong* had just opened, and there was a painting of me fifteen feet high outside one of the theaters. Bouffant hair, glistening red lips and eyes painted an unimaginable shade of grassy green. How far away that life seemed to be already. Pushing the baby carriage in a camel coat, sensible shoes and headscarf, with hardly any makeup, I was unrecognizable as that movie queen up on the billboards. I was, however, for the first time in years, extremely contented.

Tara brought me infinite joy. I had eschewed the idea of a nanny—I wanted to look after my four-month-old infant myself. Although we lived in a suite at the Hotel Grand Point, nevertheless I still had to make and mix her formula myself. I'd stopped nursing her at three months. I washed her clothes by hand, played with her, bathed her and did all the other dozens of things a tiny baby needs. I didn't want anybody else to do this for her. She was my baby and I was going to do right by her.

One night Tony woke me up with a sharp nudge. "What's all that commotion?" I said sleepily. "Sounds like a drunken orgy next door."

"Sounds like they're breaking all the glass and windows in the place," he said, jumping out of bed in his blue and white striped pajamas. "I'll see what's happening." He opened the door of our bedroom, which led to the hall, and recoiled coughing violently. The hall was filled with smoke. He banged the door shut and turned to me, trying to keep the panic off his face. "I think there's a fire," he said quietly.

"Oh, God . . . Tara." My knees turned to water. I leaped from the bed and rushed across the living room which separated her bedroom from ours. It was almost impossible to breathe in her room. Thick black acrid smoke everywhere. I could barely see. "My baby!" I screamed, fearing the worst. She was lying in her cot, gazing with surprised blue eyes at this interesting substance floating around her room. Another minute and she could have suffocated. I grabbed her and fled back to our bedroom.

Tony was talking to the concierge on the phone. "There's a fire . . . um . . . *oui, un feu* . . . er . . . Oh, Christ . . . *un grand feu ici*— help us, *s'il vous plaît.*" His calmness hid the panic he was trying to cover. His atrocious French was not an asset. I heard the concierge yelling excitedly.

I looked outside. It was not a reassuring sight. We were seven floors up. In the street stood a lonely fire truck surrounded by five incompetent firemen lackadaisically trying to connect the hose pipe to a nearby water pump. A knot of mildly interested Frenchmen, obviously on their way home from the local bordello, as it was four in the morning, stood idly by smoking Gauloises and offering advice. Some of them chuckled occasionally. Several people were hanging out of the windows above and below us and screaming frantically. Flames were shooting up from the top of the building, and smoke spiraled from the top floor—the ninth. We were on number seven. The people on the eighth were understandably hysterical. Of the people on the ninth, there seemed no evidence. Dead? Or escaped? A middle-aged German, naked except for a string vest and green socks, was on the balcony immediately above us, jumping up and down and yelling incoherently. I couldn't help a hysterical giggle at the fact that he was so unaware of his nudity—he seemed even more bizarrely naked because of his vest and socks.

I realized I myself was only wearing a see-through short nightgown and nothing underneath. I grabbed a pair of jeans, a sweater and slippers and thrust Tara into Tony's hands. "I must get her bottles." I dashed into the living room, where smoke was seeping in below the door, and snatched three bottles of formula from the fridge. I took my mink from the closet and my jewelry box from the desk. Although frightened to death, I still felt we would be saved at the eleventh hour. Finally finding all this happiness and then getting fried to death in a second-class hotel in Paris could not be my destiny. Or could it? Tony thrust the baby into my arms again and jumped onto the balcony like Errol Flynn. "Where are you going?" I screamed. Was my bridegroom about to commit suicide, or was he going to scramble to safety alone—leaving me holding the baby? I stood shaking helplessly on the tiny balcony watching him maneuver round the side of the hotel to where the smoke seemed less dense. I was suddenly very alone and very frightened. "Help! Help! Please help us!" I screamed.

A small crowd had now gathered in the Champs Élysées to watch with laconic interest sixty people die horribly. They ignored me. The firemen were still fiddling about with the nozzle of their equipment, and my opinion of the French plummeted. What disorganization. They couldn't even get the bloody water connected. We could all go up in flames and they would still be messing about. *"Au secours! Au secours!"* I yelled, hoping that French would do more good than English. Maybe the reason they were so indifferent to our plight was because they knew the hotel was full of German tourists. A *petite* revenge for their occupation. Maybe if they saw a poor young Frenchwoman clutching her tiny babe, a future president of the Republic *peut-être*, they might get their act together and put out this *fucking* fire.

The smoke was getting denser. Sparks were falling on us. A woman on the ninth floor let out a horrifying scream. No wonder—her hair was on fire! It was too, too horrible. A nightmare from which surely I must finally awake. After what seemed a year, Tony scrambled back along the balconies, disheveled, his face blackened from soot and his hands cut and bleeding.

"The fire's in the elevator shaft," he breathed shakily, gasping for air. He was not much of an athlete. "It's on the top floor and burning downward—we've *got* to get out of here, Flower!"

"I know, but how?" I wailed. Tara started to cry. The three of us held on tight together. Horror stories of mutilated bodies found in burned-out buildings filled my mind. I could hear screams, and breaking glass—cries and groans from the floors above us. I saw the headlines on the *Evening Standard* placards in London. "Famous Stars and Baby Die in Paris Hotel Fire!" That would sell a few papers. Everyone would want to know who the stars were and how horribly they died. Circulation would soar.

We stood there trapped. If *we* were too young to die, what about Tara? Four months old—what a tragedy. I tried to imagine my whole life passing through my mind. Wasn't that what supposedly happened when people knew they were doomed? I couldn't think of anything except that my baby's life hadn't even begun yet.

And then—the door to the bedroom burst open and two burly firemen appeared in masks and heavy asbestos gloves. It was the most glorious sight I had ever seen. They yelled at us in French.

One of them grabbed Tara and gestured us to follow him as he crawled on all fours down the corridor. They dampened towels from a bucket of water, and made us cover our heads with them. The floor was burning hot, and acrid smoke filled my lungs even with the wet towels.

The ceiling was an ominous red, and bits of plaster and ash fell on us like confetti. The noise was horrifying. In a dream I crawled behind the huge garlic-smelling fireman, who was clutching my most precious possession, Tara. We reached the stairs which were next to the lift. *"Allez! Allez-vous!"* said the fireman, pushing us to the stairs. I looked up the lift shaft and saw the whole top in flames. I had never "allezed" anywhere as fast as we whisked down those seven flights.

Saved at the eleventh hour. Ben Gary was right again.

I never again have stayed in any hotel room without checking thoroughly to see that the fire escape was within immediate access. Once burned, twice shy—you better believe it!

We left immediately for Switzerland. It was unthinkable to stay in the suite. Everything was blackened by smoke, there was no hot water or electricity. The management begged us to be patient—normal service would be resumed shortly; but the event was so awful that we wanted out.

St. Moritz in early March was just coming to the end of the season. It was the most exclusive, elegant and glamorous ski resort of the international set. The Palace Hotel was where the *haut monde* congregated. My best friend Cappy was now married to Andrea Badrutt, the owner of the Palace Hotel. Cappy had become the doyen and social arbiter of the St. Moritz social calendar. She knew everyone and everyone knew her. Niarchos, Onassis, Agnelli, Thyssen, Von Opel, Gunther Sachs, Charles Clore. The cream of the jet set was partaking of the pleasures of the Palace—probably the least of which was skiing. Intrigue, romance, big business, deception, seduction—all took place, and had for dozens of years, beneath the portals of this magnificent hotel. Set in the middle of the quaint village of St. Moritz, where the simple villagers rubbed shoulders with international playboys and princes, the atmosphere was at once deliciously decadent and jolly healthy.

Into this hothouse atmosphere, redolent of sex, sin and sport, arrived one deranged-looking British actress—grubby and unkempt from twenty-four hours on the train, one Cockney genius, already with a sore throat and incipient flu, who absolutely loathed anything to do with high society, and one adorable female baby—good as gold and who never cried, probably because she hardly ever left her mother's side.

I took Tara everywhere. To lunch at the Palace Grill, where Madame Dewi Sukarno, elegance personified in the simplest of underplayed après-ski clothes, would lunch with Madame Badrutt, a vision in sable ski hat and velvet trousers, Baroness Thyssen (the former model Fiona Campbell-Walter), lustrous red tumbling curls and beautifully cut shirts and jodhpurs—and me. I had not come prepared for the joys of skiing and had to make do with some itchy polo-necked sweaters, tight jeans and a John Lennon black leather cap. Not at all what the *haut monde* would consider *haute couture*. My clothes were liberally sprinkled with baby food and crumbs, since, parked on my lap or nearby on her portable chair, little Tara would sit and gurgle happily away. The ladies and the staff did not exactly approve. The atmosphere was far too refined to have children around, let alone babies, who were usually seen by their parents only between four and five in the afternoon for nursery tea.

"Joanie—you can't go on like this," said Cappy. "You can't go walking about St. Moritz with that baby slung on your back like some African peasant woman. Get a nanny, for goodness' sake, dear."

"I don't *need* a nanny," I said defensively, spooning up a trickle of cereal oozing from Tara's mouth and realizing that it was time to change her diaper again. "What's the *point*, Cappy, in having a child if you don't take care of it yourself?" Tara burped happily in agreement, and beat a little tattoo with her messy spoon on my grubby sweater.

"Look at you!" said Cappy. "Look at your hands—you've *ruined* them by washing her clothes, and whatever else it is you wash." She glanced distastefully at the beautifully decorated marble bathroom now festooned with drying diapers and tiny garments of all descriptions. "The role of hausfrau does not become you," she said sternly. "Neither does this role of camp follower to your husband. You must settle down, darling. Buy a house, get some roots, and you should get back to *work*."

"I know we need roots," I said ruefully. "But we can't go back to England until April because of Tony's tax situation, and honestly, Cappy, I *enjoy* looking after the baby—I really do. And as for work—who needs all that waiting around on sets all day? I've done it since I was sixteen. It's fantastic to be free." I picked Tara up and threw her expertly over my shoulder to burp her, then placed her on the bed to change her.

"I find this delightful domesticity a little hard to take," said Cappy, glancing in the mirror at her patrician features and elegant body, fetchingly clad in gray fox hat and coordinated pale gray ski clothes. "I don't exactly consider you free, dear. At least I hope you can get a baby sitter tonight so you can come to my party at the Corviglia Club."

"Darling, I promise you I will not arrive at your party embarrassing you with egg yolk down my dress and dishwasher hands." I was able to make the transformation from harassed housewife during the day to soignée sophisticate at night with little effort. Geminis thrive on changing roles. It was much more fun to be the perfect mother all day and a vision of glamour by night. But I could never come close to Cappy in the glamour department. She was truly always a vision of beauty, coordination and sophisticated elegance. Years later I based my visual interpretation of Alexis Carrington Colby in *Dynasty* on Caprice Caprone Yordan Badrutt. She was one of the most elegant and stylish beauties who ever lived. And infinitely nicer than Alexis!

John Crosby of the *Herald Tribune* wrote an article about me in St. Moritz called "A Most Peculiar Mother."

St. Moritz—There's a very peculiar mother here named Mrs. Anthony Newley, otherwise known as Joan Collins, a movie star of some renown, who takes care of her own baby!

In this citadel of the rich, this is a throwback to primitive

behavior patterns almost unknown in these parts since they introduced the Roman alphabet.

Other mothers in St. Moritz, who are barely on a first-name basis
with their babies, stare at Miss Collins in considerable awe:
"Washes her own bottles" they whisper to each other. "You know,
the things they feed the baby with."

"All the women here think I'm mad," said Miss Collins. "If they
have one child, they have one nurse, two children, two nurses.
Three children, three nurses" . . . Joan Collins's peculiar behavior
started in Paris when she assumed executive control over Tara
Cynara, washing bottles, changing nappies and all the other unnatural practices for mothers.

On April 7, 1964, Tony and I, and all the other British performers,
writers, sportsmen and others who had gone non-resident for a year,
returned to London. We rented Keith Michell's house in Hampstead and
Tony and Leslie Bricusse plunged feverishly into writing a new show, *The
Roar of the Greasepaint, The Smell of the Crowd.* Evie had just given
birth to a little boy, Adam, my godson, and the six of us were now playing
"Happy Families" together. Except I hardly ever saw my husband. He
was enslaved by his work. He scribbled away morning, noon and night,
with little time for much else. Although I now hired a housekeeper, I was
still preoccupied with the baby and my newfound domesticity. I spent
days looking for houses in the country, but near enough to London, and
finally found a wonderful house at Elstree, full of character and charm,
an old Edwardian mansion with three stories, stables, grounds—just right
for the large family we planned on having. I was expecting another baby,
and although I thought it was rather too hot on the heels of Tara, nevertheless I was completely happy and busy as a little bee.

Friars' Mead, the house was called, and it needed a monstrous amount
of renovation and decoration to make it habitable. It had cost the astronomical sum, in those 1964 preinflation days, of twenty thousand pounds.
Tony thought this was far too expensive, but I had convinced him it was
worth it as we now planned on living in England forever. The days were
full. Playing with Tara, who was becoming more adorable all the time,
consultations with architects and Robin Guild, our interior designer, and
shopping, for wallpapers, fabrics and furniture for this new home. Goodbye Gucci suitcases—hello roots. At *last!*

Tony moaned about the cost of everything. His humble background
had not accustomed him to the fact that things cost money, but he was
learning to like the better things in life, not all of which are free, unfortunately, and I was an expert teacher. My own bank balance, however, was
diminishing rapidly. Always used to making money, I was equally used to
spending it. Tony was not financially secure, certainly not in the league of
being able to fully support a wife who was used to buying her clothes at
St. Laurent and Thea Porter.

✦ ✦ ✦

When an offer materialized for me to go to Rome and star opposite Vittorio Gassman in an Italian comedy, Tony persuaded me to do it. I had just lost the baby I was expecting and was feeling rather blue. Tony was on the road in Manchester and Birmingham, on out-of-town tryouts for *The Roar of the Greasepaint, The Smell of the Crowd.* Leslie, Evie, Tara, Adam and I were of course all there, too.

Tara was one year old when I left for Portofino, Lugano and Rome to make *La Conguintura.* It was the first separation since our marriage. I was very unhappy about it. Although fairly pleased with the idea of getting back to work again, and realizing that to live the life I had been accustomed to for the past several years I needed money, nevertheless I had a foreboding that even with Tony's protestations of "Yes, Flower, do it—you know it'll be good for you. You know you love to work," he did not really mean it. Deep down I think he wanted a wife who would stay at home, cook and take care of the family's needs.

La Conguintura turned out to be one of the most successful movies I made. At least in Italy. It was number eight at the Italian box office the following year. Unfortunately, it was never shown in England or America. A pity, because I was doing my favorite thing, comedy. Tara had a wonderful time on location. She even appeared in a scene in her pram when Gassman trips over her in a mad dash around the hotel in Lugano. Tony, Evie and Leslie all came to Portofino after the London opening of *Greasepaint.* Their faces told the sad story.

Disaster had struck. The critics had given the show every nasty epithet in the book. A lot of love, care, time and talent had gone into it. Tony was upset, not only because of *Greasepaint.* He had discovered that his tax structure was such that it was impossible for him to live permanently in England without paying 90 percent of his income to the government. To top it all, David Merrick, having come to Manchester to see the show, had made an offer they could not refuse. Tony was to play Mr. Thin in *Greasepaint* on Broadway.

Joan, the camp follower immediately did all the right things. Sold the beautiful house at Elstree—we had not even moved in yet. My dream house at last. I begged Tony not to sell it—I would pay the twenty thousand pounds to keep it, but he was adamant, and so was his tax adviser. Neither of us could own property in the U.K. Even though I had been a resident of America for seven years, it could seriously disrupt him taxwise if we kept it.

Out came the twenty Gucci cases, and once more, amidst poignant farewells to our friends and family, we flew to New York. I was pregnant again and liked getting on planes less and less. I was deeply upset by this latest move. This time we moved into a furnished apartment on 72nd Street. With Tony's mother, Grace, now as nanny-cum-housekeeper, I once again found myself living in someone else's house surrounded by someone else's possessions, plus several families of giant cockroaches. At thirty I still owned *nothing* except clothes, books and records. Would I ever have roots?

❂   ❂   ❂

Alexander Anthony Newley was born on September 8, 1965. In the same hospital and in the same room as his sister Tara. It was unbelievably thrilling that I now had a boy too. He was exactly what we wanted. We were now a complete family unit. Indestructible. I was totally involved with my all-consuming role of wife and mother.

Things were going well for us. *The Roar of the Greasepaint,* starring Tony and with Cyril Ritchard playing the other part, had opened to mixed reviews, but praise for Tony's performance was high. He had developed a big following and was a major draw on Broadway now. Our living arrangements, however, were less than satisfactory. That summer we had rented a house on Long Island where I lazed around happily playing with Tara, swimming, sunbathing and barbecuing for the cast on weekends. Tony would leave for the theater around four, and I would have the rest of the day and evening to read, write, think and generally be a placid, bovine lump. My friends were amazed at my transformation. From an energetic, volatile, vigorous creature, who was only happy doing things, going and being where the action was, I had turned into Mother Earth, happy to laze away the days. The high spot of my week was a visit to the local supermarket, wheeling baby Tara in the basket.

A week before Sacha was born, we moved into Paul and Joanne Newman's apartment on Seventy-second Street and Fifth Avenue. It was a beautiful, airy, tastefully furnished apartment, filled with early American furniture and English antiques—a tribute to Joanne's good taste. I had visited her in the hospital a couple of months previously. Her third baby, Claire, was born three months before Sacha. Now my fear of flying had become an obsession.

We were in Toronto, Canada, on tour with the show. I preferred to take the overnight train to New York and back rather than spend two hours in a plane. We had had a bad experience on a short jaunt from Boston to Cleveland in a blinding snowstorm. As the jet, its wheels already descended, was coming in for a landing, two hundred yards from the runway it suddenly zoomed back into the air again. My stomach gave a sickening lurch. The cabin crew went green. I asked one of them what happened. She replied shakily, "Probably something on the runway."

"Probably something on the runway!" What, pray, I wondered, could that something be? Another plane? A stewardess taking an afternoon stroll? A stray dog? It was too horrible to contemplate that one hundred tons of metal carrying sixty or seventy human beings could be wiped out by "something on the runway." When the plane finally landed, I decided never to fly again unless there was absolutely no other alternative. Now with Sacha's arrival and Tony playing to full houses each night, I hoped that there would be no plane trips in the immediate future.

If having one baby and taking care of it alone was novel and fun, suddenly two little babies, one a few days old and one twenty-two months old, both in diapers, became much too hard to handle. I hired a German nanny—Renata. She arrived with excellent references a few days before the new baby was expected.

The hospital, as before, briskly sent me home when Sacha was only three days old. They obviously believed that the more kids you had the less time you deserved for lying about. With terse instructions to "get into bed and take it easy for at least a week" I entered purgatory. As soon as twenty-two-month-old Tara, the pampered and adorable apple of her parents' eyes, got a glimpse of brand-new, excitingly different and magnificently masculine Sacha she smiled, stroked him and begged to be allowed to play with him.

But as soon as he was settled comfortably on my lap in bed, propped up against the Porthault sheets, she flew into a raging fury. She wanted to be where he was. When I held him, she wanted to be held, when I changed him, she wanted to be changed. Her potty training of the past six months went to pot. I couldn't let Sacha sleep in a crib in our room as I had done with Tara, because *she* wanted to be allowed to sleep there too! So he slept downstairs with her and Renata. My German treasure obviously was stone deaf, for the babies could cry and scream all night and she would not be roused. Staggering downstairs at ten or eleven at night, Tony at the theater, Renata dead to the world, I could carry baby Sacha and drag little Tara by the hand up to my bedroom and try to placate them both. Tara got a cookie, Sacha got Mummy, if he was lucky. I was so exhausted he sometimes had to settle for a bottle. At 3 or 4 A.M. the same thing, and again at nine or ten in the morning. The only time Renata was conscious, it seemed, was between eleven in the morning and nine at night. The poor girl needed her sleep—but so did I, and all this traipsing up and down the stairs was a strain. After a week, I woke up one morning feeling like death. The doctor, on examining me, came right to the point.

"You're lucky," he said. "A few years ago this disease carried them off like flies, in the wards."

"What disease?" I said weakly. I had never felt worse.

"Puerperal fever—or childbed fever as it's called now," he said briskly, injecting me with some wonder drug. "Yes, it's a terrible thing, my dear —*was* a terrible thing, I should say, only ten percent survived. We don't see much of it nowadays—only—" he looked at me suspiciously—"with those mothers who *do too much*. Have you been doing too much, young woman?" I nodded weakly. "Keep the children away from her. It can be dangerous to the baby," he told Tony. "We need to get a nurse for her and a new nanny for the children, no doubt." He had caught a glimpse of frail, white-faced Renata, hovering on the landing, clutching a whimpering Tara by the hand. And Sacha's demanding yells for lunch were issuing from the downstairs bedroom.

The new nanny turned out to be a capable treasure, and I was able to relax more. We became friends with a girl who had become the toast of New York in *Funny Girl*, Barbra Streisand, and her husband, Elliott Gould. Elliott was an actor who was finding it hard to get work. His wife's astonishingly sudden and well-deserved success had not rubbed off on him. He was in the unenviable position of being "Mr. Streisand" to the hordes of fans who clustered around the stage door each night and inundated Barbra with their idolatry. She did not take too kindly to giving autographs. She would sweep disdainfully through the crowds to the waiting limousine and rarely deign to scribble her signature.

We had seen her only a year and a half earlier at the Blue Angel, where she was starting out. The magnificence of her vocal talent and originality as a performer took New York by storm instantly. She became a "must see" for anyone and everyone. Barbra and Tony developed a mutual-admiration society. They were similar in temperament—highstrung, hard-working, dedicated to perfecting their craft. We often dined together, talking, laughing and joking late into the night. She had an eloquent Romanesque nose, bouffant hair and porcelain skin, and with her way of dressing, sometimes quaint and kinky, sometimes in the highest of *haute couture* clothes, she was an imposing and unusual-looking woman, in addition to having that exceptional, extraordinary talent. She was about to make her first movie, *Funny Girl.* She questioned me at length about makeup techniques and matters pertaining to motion pictures. Barbra was like Marlon Brando with her thirst for knowledge. Her mind was a sponge—it soaked up everything. She had an intense desire to learn and improve herself in every way.

I found these qualities admirable and enviable. My mind was more like a sieve—the more that went in, the more went instantly out with the vegetable water. Although I was an avid reader and went often to the theater, concerts and movies I still, due to my mercurial tendencies, was hard pushed to remember anything I had read, seen or listened to for more than a couple of weeks afterward. I could learn an entire script in an hour—memorize it by heart—and a month later I couldn't remember a line.

Negotiations had begun for Tony to appear in a major musical for my old alma mater, 20th Century-Fox. It was to be a lavish, mammoth spectacle for which Leslie Bricusse was writing the book and lyrics. *Dr. Doolittle* was adapted from the children's book by Hugh Lofting. Rex Harrison would play Doolittle. Tony was excited about being in such an important production. He was interested in becoming a film star now. He vowed that *Greasepaint* would be the last time he would appear on the stage.

We took the train to California. It took three days. Tony wrote and I stared at the scenery and played with the kids. Tara loved dashing through the carriages and stopping at all the stations to buy souvenirs. At two and a half she was a tiny, beautiful little girl. Bright and funny.

In L.A. Tony was perfectly content to reside in the rented house that Leslie Bricusse had found for us. I wasn't. I insisted we *must* have our own home. We could not continue to dash all over the globe, with two children, seventy-four suitcases, a nanny, a mother-in-law and crates of books, records and junk. Not to mention all of our stuff still in storage.

We started house-hunting in Beverly Hills. Tony was working on another project. Tara started nursery school and Sacha was well taken care of by Rosie, our new nanny. I suddenly started feeling rather useless. I began thinking about acting again. My career—which with the exception of the Italian film had been sublimated for over three years— started to have new meaning for me. Maybe this was because I was living in Hollywood again, where everyone eats, sleeps and breathes motion pictures. Television was a major industry force now, instead of the poor relation to the movies it had been during my Fox days. The William Morris Agency contacted me. Would I be interested in doing some guest shots on TV in various dramatic shows? Why not indeed? I looked as good as, if not better than, when I had arrived in Hollywood a decade previously. Certainly I was a better and more experienced actress. If I was going to continue acting at all I had better start now by stretching myself and accepting some of these roles—even if I considered them somewhat unrewarding.

It's so easy not to work, to let things slide and 'think about that tomorrow.' One day tomorrow arrives, and it's too late, baby. Much too late. Industry people have memories as short as matchsticks. I had made a series of mediocre films a few years ago and then evaporated to virtual retirement as far as they were concerned. It wasn't going to be particularly easy to get back into anything like the position I had had before. A whole new generation of actresses was on the scene—Candice Bergen, Julie Christie, Faye Dunaway, Raquel Welch, Samantha Eggar, Barbra Streisand. These were the stars of the mid-to-late sixties. As far as the American public was concerned I was practically unknown.

"Who's that pretty girl?"

"Oh, that's Anthony Newley's wife—didn't she used to be an actress?"

"Oh, yeah—Joan something-or-other. Whatever happened to her?" Such is life in the tropics of Hollywood.

Luckily, stardom had never been something I strove for. It was acting I enjoyed. The creation, portrayal and characterization of another person. I loved wandering on the back lots in the studios, awed by incredible and beautifully detailed sets that still remained standing after decades.

Tony and I lunched at the Fox commissary. I was amazed at what had happened to the giant back lot I knew. It had been sold for an astronomical fee—no doubt to pay back to the stockholders some of Fox's debts, a few of which surely must have arisen from the turkeys I had appeared in. I felt the urge to work become stronger. I knew my energy and enthusiasm should be channeled into some sort of creative direction. If not acting, then interior designing or writing. Much as I adored my children, I realized that I was not the sort of woman to whom home, hearth and family was the be-all and end-all of feminine existence. Tony, while not discouraging me, was totally absorbed in writing his new show. It was preferable to him to have me occupied and out of the way so that he could concentrate on his work. Tara and Sacha had Rosie Riggs, their fresh-faced English nanny, to look after them and I realized that the day-to-day grind of cooking, washing up and changing diapers was no longer as enthralling as it had been.

Oh, fickle Gemini! Only another of the same sign can truly understand the vagaries of the Mercury-ruled mind: the compulsion to do too much; to take on too many projects; to be able to do six things at once and still have time for one more; the way the mind flitters like a butterfly from one subject to another, from one project to another, never alighting long enough to put down roots.

We are the "butterfly" sign of the zodiac. Youthful in spirit, and often in body, we are open to the new, the unusual, the unexpected. Routine is the kiss of death for the Mercury-ruled sign. Much as I hated to admit it, I still needed the stimulation, joy and excitement that I received from acting.

The signs had been in the air for some time that things were not going well with the marriage. As a way of coping with many things that upset me, I did my Scarlett O'Hara act and thought about it "tomorrow." It certainly was an excellent device for me to avoid dealing with the realities of misery and disappointment and unhappiness. By putting off the moment when I had to analyze and evaluate a particular situation, I successfully managed to never have to think about it at all. Even the most traumatic experience of my life—the death of my mother—I did not completely realize and mourn for until several years later.

It was, and is, of course, a great way of getting through life as happily as possible, and for an actress whose lot is often heartbreak, rejection and frustration, it's a way of keeping sane. But marital problems must be sorted out. Festering sores should be discussed, however painful. Tony's offhand attitude, not wanting to rock the boat and to keep things on an even keel, my "keep it under for another day" attitude, guaranteed that important issues in our marriage were deeply buried.

We did talk. We discussed, sorted out, even argued in a mild way, but Tony hated it. We never dug deep enough to explore our most intimate psyches, secrets and emotional problems. In the end this lack of communication began corroding our marriage.

One night, crossing the street in the pouring rain with my sister Jackie, we almost got hit by a bus. Tony had darted ahead of us. When, later, I told him off, he sulked. Making no waves became the *modus operandi* of our marriage.

Whenever I asserted myself he called me bossy, masculine and ball-breaking. He could not seem to understand that my feelings and ideas had value. Each time we disagreed, the gulf between us widened.

Finally we bought a house in California. Once more the lure of the palm trees and the sweet smell of success beckoned us to tinsel town. I finally attempted to put down those longed-for roots and make a permanent home for us and our two children.

Tara was now three, and I desperately wanted her to have some stability in her life. Born in New York, she had spent more than half her short life in hotel rooms all over America on the never-ending *Greasepaint* tour. Rented houses and apartments everywhere from London to Paris, Rome, Portofino, Lugano, Liverpool, St. Moritz had been her life. Her passport looked like that of an international playgirl. I was determined she should have what most other little girls of her age had. Her own room in which she could play with her toys, secure in the knowledge that this was her *home*. The security that she would stay there, hopefully, for a long, long time. Sacha, at eighteen months, was still too young to feel the effects of the constant changing of scenery, but I knew that he, the most gorgeous hunk of blond curly-haired baby boy, needed his security too.

Hollywood in the late sixties had not changed much from the time I had first arrived. The same lavish and star-studded parties were still being given by the ever diminishing ranks of the movie moguls. Darryl F. Zanuck was gone. Fox was desperately trying to get itself back on its feet after horrendous losses over the past several years. Spyros Skouras, the wily old Greek, was dead; so was Lew Shreiber, my mentor and father confessor during my contract days. Harry Cohn, feared head of Columbia Studios, who ruled the lives of Rita Hayworth and Kim Novak with a rod of iron, was long gone. His place had been taken by a group of corporate executives to whom the word "creative" was anathema.

Bob Evans, under contract to Fox at the same time as I, had taken over the reins at Paramount Studios. He proved to be infinitely better at running a studio than he had ever been as an actor.

Jack Warner was still the boss at Warner Brothers, which was in the process of changing its name to The Burbank Studios. So many independent productions—both TV and motion picture—used the Burbank lot that they changed the name to a more nonspecific one, so as not to invite petty jealousies from other independent studios.

Universal, home of the tacky sand and sin pictures, was now the biggest force in television production. Strongly controlled by the redoubtable Lew Wasserman, former president of MCA and a shrewd and clever businessman to boot, Universal Inc. had amalgamated with the octopus-like MCA agency, which at one time seemed to represent 90 percent of the top theatrical talent in America.

The contract star system had virtually finished, the only exception being likely prospects for TV series at salaries of around two hundred dollars a week. The big superstars were commanding gigantic amounts of money for their movies. Paul Newman, Steve McQueen, Barbra Streisand, Clint Eastwood, Charles Bronson were superstars on a level not seen previously, and their agents now had unprecedented power at the studios. And what do you know? Even Warren Beatty was having a phenomenal success with *Bonnie and Clyde* which he had starred in and produced. He was well on his way to his first million. After Warren's initial impact with *Splendor in the Grass*, he had made a series of indifferent films. Now he was on the crest of superstardom, as well as becoming the most famous stud in the Western Hemisphere. The shyly myopic, pimply-faced, skinny boy who had caused much mirth among my acquaintances when our romance had first started was now a handsome, mysterious, charismatic, sexy movie star, and a brilliant producer too. He had become irresistible to throngs of females. No woman, it was rumored, could resist those greenish-blue, shortsighted eyes. His charm and success with females of all ages had become legendary, and his prowess between the sheets was the subject of much Hollywood tittle-tattle. Although he had always had a "live-in lady" in his life, he apparently was able to cram in an endless amount of extracurricular activity and was on his way to becoming the successor to Errol Flynn as a ladies' man and lover par excellence.

"I must be the only woman in L.A. and New York that Warren hasn't tried to *shtup*," said my agent, Sue Mengers, laughingly. It seemed to be true, although Warren was clever enough never to admit his conquests.

So much of what my astrologer, Ben Gary, had predicted was coming true. Warren's fast rise to fame, fade-out for a few years and then superstardom. My marriage to "actor or writer or director" Newley—he was all of those. And two children: Tara petite, Sacha husky, almost the same size, and who, since I often dressed them alike, were often mistaken for twins. The gypsylike existence Ben had predicted for me had also come true. I didn't want to think about his last prediction, however—that my marriage would last for only seven years. We were barely making it through the fourth.

❧ *Ten* ❧

THE DAISY WAS A Beverly Hills discotheque that overnight became a mecca for everyone in town. Perhaps they were trying to compete with the Swinging Sixties scene in London. As miniskirts rode thigh-high and men's hair began to hang over the collar, dancing frenzy gripped Hollywood the likes of which had not been seen since Joan Crawford Charleston'd her way to fame in the 1920s movie *Our Dancing Daughters*.

Every night the Daisy was jammed with the beautiful people, the trying to be beautiful people, and the not so beautiful people in Hollywood. Stars, starlets, agents, writers, producers and producers' wives all crammed onto the dance floor to "Let it all hang out" (and it often did) or to sit and observe. A sort of madness gripped everyone. Outrageous clothes and extroverted behavior had become the norm. No dinner party was complete without a trip to the Daisy afterward. Everyone was doing the Monkey, the Funky Chicken. It was sheer madness—but lots of fun.

Even Tony would occasionally accompany me there, although he was now busy rehearsing for his role in *Dr. Doolittle* and also writing a new script tentatively based (yet again!) on the story of his life. On the evenings at home he would immediately return to his study after dinner to work on his script. We had virtually no communication; he was wrapped up in his work, and although he told me he loved me, I was dubious.

I was not happy. The beautiful house in Beverly Hills, complete with pool and all mod cons, and the two gorgeous children, the light of my life, couldn't make up for the emptiness I felt. When I managed to extract conversation from Tony about our marital problems he would become irritated and talk about the immense problem he *himself* had in loving and giving fully. Yes, he loved me in his own way—but who was I to him? An attractive stranger who shared his bed, mothered his children, and sat once a fortnight at the head of his dinner table.

When we gave dinner parties I was never sure he would attend. We had a sit-down dinner for fourteen in honor of Peter Sellers, which I had spent a week organizing. Tony pleaded a stomachache and stayed in the bedroom, leaving thirteen for dinner, and me getting fiercely drunk in front of a monosyllabic Sellers.

Tony didn't like dinners or parties anyway, even though they were part of the Hollywood social scene. Often I would go to them with a platonic friend or a married couple or a glamorous gay. I loved dancing, especially at the Daisy.

A young man asked me to dance. He looked vaguely familiar: brawny, blond, tall, a face like a handsome boxer. He looked as though he might get his nose broken one day, or maybe some of those perfect white teeth. He was obviously an actor, although tight blue jeans and a shirt open to well-muscled chest didn't necessarily mean in Hollywood that he was. Physical perfection was the achievement of all in Beautiful Beverly Hills —agents, writers, producers. The gyms were full of them flexing well-tanned biceps and heaving their way through fifty sit-ups a day. The hair stylists couldn't keep up with the demand for the romantically tousled long-haired look, copied from swinging London.

Ryan O'Neal had it going for him in the looks department and he wasn't lacking in charm and humor. Or the sex-appeal department. He was the first man I'd found attractive for a long time. So we kept on dancing for an energetic hour or so. Mick Jagger was singing "I can't get no satisfaction." It sounded like the title song for my marriage.

The fact that I was married didn't seem to faze Ryan. He wanted my telephone number, which I wouldn't give him. Tony would just love that. But Tony must have subconsciously realized that letting me go out alone two or three nights a week to the Daisy was asking for eventual trouble. A nun I had never been—only in the movies.

Ryan was funny and endearing. He had an open, boyish personality and a droll self-mocking attitude toward himself. He was part Irish—with a name like O'Neal what else?—married and divorced and had, like me, two children, Tatum and Griffin, the same age and sex as Tara and Sacha. But attractive as he was, my marriage vows still meant a lot to me. I was not about to open up this can of beans, however inviting the label.

The next afternoon, idly flipping channels to find cartoons for the kiddies, I came across him again, being boyish and sincere with Mia Farrow in the soap opera "Peyton Place." I watched with interest. He definitely had star quality. It flashed across the screen, along with sizzling sex appeal, even with the banal plots and dialogue of "Peyton Place." I switched the channel to the cartoons the children were clamoring for. He was forbidden fruit.

I hankered to play the main female role in *Dr. Doolittle*—that of the haughty British belle who falls for the Cockney-Irish charms of Newley. Although this was a Fox film produced by our friend Arthur Jacobs, they didn't think I was right and the part went to Samantha Eggar.

My Hollywood movie career appeared to be fading fast. Although I received scripts from England, Italy and Spain, I could not land a decent film role in the States. I had been away too long and was no longer a new face. Thank you, Warren. Thank you, Tony. She gave it all up for love. What kind of fool was I? Television offers, however, came aplenty. I had my pick of the top shows and I accepted most of them. Now I could be a wife, a mother and an actress all at once. A neat little package deal. I was trying to please Tony but I really wasn't pleasing myself because guesting on episodic TV shows was not tremendously fulfilling either.

The truth was I enjoyed working—why did I feel pangs of guilt when I admitted it? Why wasn't I just content, like most of the young Beverly Hills matrons I knew, to be a faithful wife (albeit ignored) and a dutiful mother? Content to run the house with my trusty Portuguese couple, to lie by the pool and ruin my skin and then go to the facialist and the dermatologist to repair it, go to the analyst, the hairdresser, the manicurist, the gynecologist, the numerologist, the group-therapy session, the tennis lessons, the tap-dancing classes, the kaffee klatches, the hen-party lunches, the backgammon games, the beach and the gym? Young Beverly Hills matrons had a *slew* of things to do with their day. Why was I so discontented?

Apart from the above there was always shopping—a major occupation for a California lady of leisure. God forbid one didn't pop into Saks or Magnin's at least once a week to blow thirty or forty dollars on some new lipsticks and skin lotions, meander upstairs to Lingerie and buy a few cute robes at eighty or ninety dollars apiece, and top it off with a bauble or two from the cut-price jewelers on Beverly Drive. A solid-gold "his 'n hers" key for "their" house, a solid-gold ankh for good luck, very popular that year, everyone was wearing them, or the latest rip-off from Tiffany's —whatever it was. Money was spent like water. Certainly the average net nut of the moderately wealthy was close to a quarter of a million dollars a year. This went through their wives' sieves as fast as it came in. The men dropped dead of heart attacks and stress younger and younger, while their widows pushed, pulled, tucked, trimmed and taped (no one over sixty-five ever looked a day over forty), collected the insurance money and paid it out over and over again to Saks, Magnin's and the Rodeo Drive boutiques.

I could never understand why everyone had such huge closets overflowing with finery never worn. The usual invitation was "Come to dinner casual or informal." If a brave hostess had the temerity to suggest, "Come to dinner—black tie," there were moans and groans of anguished protest. It was a paradox. Why did they buy all these clothes if they never wore them? Everyone looked more or less the same. The teens, the twenties and the actresses wore jeans and T-shirts, the thirties and forties wore linen pants and silk shirts, the over forties *haute couture* or poly-ester and dacron permapress pants suits with coordinated accessories.

I surveyed my large closet, full of the latest fashions from London. I didn't need a thing. I had everything to wear. I didn't want to learn to play tennis, backgammon or tap dancing. I didn't intend to ruin my skin at the beach or the pool, didn't need the analyst and the gynecologist and didn't believe in numerology or group-therapy sessions. Girls' lunches I liked, but once or twice a week was enough. I wanted to work—I needed the roar of the greasepaint—the lights, the cameras, the action! It was in my blood.

So I worked. "The Man from U.N.C.L.E." with my ex-classmate from RADA, David McCallum; and "Batman" and "The Bing Crosby Special," and "Mission: Impossible" with stalwart Martin Landau and impeccably groomed Barbara Bain. And "Star Trek." "The City on the Edge of For-ever" became one of the most popular episodes. As Edith Keeler, a young mission worker for down-and-out men in New York in the Depres-sion, I try to prove to the world that Hitler was a nice guy. Bill Shatner as Captain Kirk falls in love with Edith, and Mr. Spock—he of the ears—allows her to get run over by a truck lest her teachings lead the world to total destruction.

In the evenings I came home and frolicked with the children, who were totally endearing. Tony and I gazed somberly at each other across our Wedgwood dinner service.

One night I got out all the letters we had written to each other and reread them. My letters were full of love, compassion and understanding. "Please try and understand me," I cried out in red ink on Beverly Hills Hotel notepaper. "The only thing I want is for us to be together—to communicate with each other—I understand your problems—I want to help you—I love you."

Try as I might, the contact and the communication weren't there. Had they ever truly been?

I gazed at my perfectly made up face in the dressing-table mirror. Porcelain skin, helped along by Revlon and Clinique; arresting green eyes, all the better for double sets of eyelashes from the Eyelure com-pany; and a weak chin. I narrowed my eyes and surveyed my chin. Yes, it was definitely the chin of a coward and a weakling; a person unable to make decisions, solve problems or keep the love of her husband. I slammed the makeup drawer shut and stalked into Tony's study. He was curled up on the sofa, wearing his usual black sweater and gray flannels, a plaid blanket covering him up to the chin.

"We're late," I said sternly, as he looked wearily up from the script of *Dr. Doolittle* he was studying. "We're late for Arthur's party." Since Ar-thur was Arthur P. Jacobs, the producer of *Dr. Doolittle*, I expected him to attend this one.

"Sorry, Flower," he said, a smile attempting to flit across his face and failing. "I'm beat. Why don't you call Brickman and Eve and go with them?" He sighed and turned back to his script. The troubles of the world seemed to sit on his shoulders recently. I couldn't understand why. He was starring in an important film and had many good offers lined up.

"OK," I said flatly, not showing any of the emotion that he detested. "Arthur won't be pleased, you know. After all, you are one of his stars. Rex and Samantha and Dick Fleischer will be there. Are you sure you're too tired?"

"I'm exhausted, luv." He rubbed his eyes and yawned as though to emphasize his fatigue. His face did look white and strained.

"Go on, Flower, have a good time. I'll see you in the morning." He gave another sigh—I knew he wanted to be alone. We brushed cheeks. He went back to his script and I went to make my by now inevitable phone call to the Bricusses to pick me up.

After Arthur's party, it was disco time. I hadn't been to the Daisy for several weeks, but even the usual excitement that the place generated couldn't get me out of my depressed lethargy. I gloomily sipped a Brandy Alexander and surveyed the frenetic scene. Legs, legs, legs—a veritable forest of them, kicking and stomping and pirouetting to the latest Beatles and Stones and Supremes discs. With every song that was played I seemed to be able to find some special meaning in its title—"Can't Buy Me Loove," sang McCartney and Lennon, their young voices cascading in a crescendo, and "She Loves You"; and I cynically yeah yeah'd myself into my third Brandy Alexander.

She loves *you* all right, I thought cynically, although it's evaporating rapidly these days. As if to answer my thoughts, Tony's voice crooned over the sound system the words to his most famous song, and the one which made me realize now what he was all about:

> What kind of fool am I
> Who never fell in love
> It seems that I'm the only one
>   that I have been thinking of,
> What kind of man is this?
> An empty shell
> A lonely cell in which an empty
>   heart must dwell.
> What kinds of lips are these
> That lied with every kiss
> That whispered empty words of love
> That left me alone like this
> Why can't I fall in love?
> Like any other man?
> And maybe then I'll know
> What kind of fool I am? ©

My eyes misted. The words applied to Tony totally. I had *known* it, though. He had warned me he was incapable of love, but I had thought my love could change that. What kind of fool was I?

"Like to dance?" Ryan stood there looking arrogant and nervous at the same time. I got up.

"Sure."

"Haven't seen you around lately."

We gyrated in front of each other amidst the flashing lights and the flashing legs.

"I've been working a lot," I explained, becoming caught up in the music and the dancing. It started to blow the blues away. Jagger was suggestively intoning "Under My Thumb." He was good. Ryan looked *very* good. He had enormous energy. Although he had to be on the set of "Peyton Place" at seven in the morning he wasn't concerned about his beauty sleep.

He was an Aries. They were compatible with Gemini because of their vitality and spark. Sydney—Max—Warren. Aries men were my weak spot.

We danced on until closing time. The ridiculously early California licensing laws dictated that all drinks must be off the table by one forty-five. He insisted on driving me home but I was nervous in his car. God forbid Tony looked out the window and saw his dutiful wife arriving home at two in the morning with a good-looking actor.

"Give me your number," he urged as we approached the driveway. "We can have lunch or tea. English ladies always have tea, don't they?" His blue eyes twinkled. He was definitely adorable. But trouble. Trouble I did not need.

I took *his* number and promised to call him sometime.

"Promise!" He leaned over the steering wheel to kiss me, which I avoided by stumbling hastily out of the car.

"I promise, I promise," I whispered, hoping that my Portuguese couple hadn't seen us.

"I'll be waiting then," he called. His sports car made a 100-degree turn, and with a screech of brakes he zoomed off down the hill.

I didn't call. I couldn't. I wasn't a teenager calling a boy for an innocent date. He knew what it meant if I called him. I knew too. I was Sadie, Sadie, married lady now, and even if it wasn't a wonderful marriage and my husband slaved over a hot script all day, I still wanted my marriage to work.

Tony went to New York for a few days and I went to work at Universal, guesting on "Run for Your Life," with Ben Gazzara. It was the usual cops-and-robbers shoot-'em-up TV trash, and I played the usual glamorous villainess. The spy with a heart of brass.

Tara came to visit one day. She watched a scene in which Gazzara tells me off angrily for not being a good enough spy. Suddenly her baby voice piped up indignantly, "Don't you talk to my Mummy like that, you naughty rude man!" Ben and the crew broke up—Tara was showing her mettle at an early age.

Ryan showed up and insisted on buying me lunch at a Chinese restaurant on Ventura Boulevard. For forty-five minutes he was captivating, witty and triumphant that we were lunching at last. He was enormously appealing in a roguish way. Not to be taken seriously, but he had all the sparkle that was lacking in Tony's personality. He positively glittered with exuberance and enthusiasm.

"What about dinner?" he said as we drove through the gates of Lew Wasserman's big black glass film factory.

"Never," I said faintly and unconvincingly.

"What are you doing tomorrow?" He never gave up. I liked that. His butterfly net was always out.

"Tomorrow's my birthday. Tony's coming back from New York. We'll probably celebrate with a hot dog in front of the TV set," I said firmly, surprised by the bitterness in my voice.

"I'll call and wish you Happy Birthday then." I jumped out and went back to Ben Gazzara and Co. feeling lighthearted.

Tony did not make it back in time for my birthday. The meetings in New York were taking longer than expected. He sent a huge bunch of flowers and a regretful phone call.

"Happy Birthday, English lady—where's your husband taking you tonight?" said the husky familiar voice, the sound of which always brought a smile to my face. I certainly didn't want the crew of "Run for Your Life" to notice that.

"He's not," I said simply. "He's stuck in the Big Apple, with only his record producer for company."

"Oh, you poor kid," he clucked sympathetically. "Well, er, we wouldn't want you to be alone on your birthday, would we?"

"No, we wouldn't." There was a pregnant pause. I suddenly decided what I wanted for my birthday present. A girl should get what she deserves on her birthday. And she did.

A few weeks later my sister Jackie married for the second time—Oscar Lerman, an American businessman. Her first husband had died in tragic circumstances and I really hoped that now she would find the happiness she truly deserved. Certainly it had eluded me most of my life. Oh, yes, there had been passion and infatuation and what, for months or sometimes years, I had thought was love. As I stood behind Jackie and Oscar at the simple wedding ceremony at our house I realized definitively that nobody had ever really loved the real me. They had professed their love, but when the chips were down, none of it meant a damn thing. But *I* had chosen these men, and I'd usually picked Mr. Wrong.

I knew why, now—that was the irony of it. I *had* to pick the toughest ones—those who couldn't, wouldn't, or didn't know *how* to commit. *Why* did I constantly make the same mistake? To get Daddy, obviously. Because he had always been undemonstrative. I never felt he loved or cared about me enough. If I could get a difficult man to fall in love with me, *then* I could say to my seven-year-old self, "Wow! I'm a worthwhile person at last. Daddy loves me, and I've *got* him!"

If I had guts I'd end my marriage. Tony's love for me was not based on reality. He professed love when I was being a good little, sweet little,

home-loving obedient Joanie—Flower. But if I showed any of the other
sides, the strong side, the ambitious side, the assertive side, the argumentative side, he couldn't *stand* me—and he admitted it. It was the same
with the other men I'd loved. Total adoration when I was behaving myself and no understanding at all when I wasn't what they expected me to
be.

I knew I had my faults. But show me a faultless person and I'll show
you a dull one.

I decided to go back into analysis and try to sort myself out again.

Tony left for England and *Dr. Doolittle* locations. I stayed on in Beverly Hills for a few weeks. I was enjoying being with Ryan. He had a tiny
apartment on Doheny Drive and the afternoons flew by.

Several people suspected our relationship by now. Although we had
been discreet, we had often been in each other's company. We even went
to dinner with the newlywed Lermans. I realized I was playing a dangerous game when I read the blind item in a gossip column one morning:

Mr. X, talented British-born performer, seems unaware that his
sexy actress wife Mrs. X is doing more than just polishing her dance
steps with handsome Mr. Z, up and coming star of one of America's
favorite soap operas. . . .

Oh, God—if the columnist knew about it, that meant it was almost in
public domain. I didn't relish at all Tony's becoming the town cuckold,
with all the sniggering innuendos.

I packed my bags, and flew to join him in London with my children
and the nanny. My little fling was over. I had to now work out whether
there was any hope or life left in our marriage before the rot really set in
—for the sake of our precious children.

Rumblings had obviously reached Tony about Ryan. He had, in fact,
brought Tatum and Griffin up to our house to swim several times with
Tara and Sacha. He did tricks with them in the pool. People weren't
blind. We'd been seen together often enough. Tony wasn't stupid. Suddenly he obviously realized my dissatisfaction and the possibility of losing
me. He was aware I was attractive to men, more now than in my Rank
and Fox days, because I had gained an aura of sophistication. He made a
genuine effort to become the loving husband he had been at the beginning of our marriage, and we sailed happily through the next year on
more-or-less calm water.

The following year, along with Paul Newman, Sammy Davis, Peter
Lawford, Ronnie Buck and two or three other businessmen, Tony and I
went into the discotheque business. The Factory became an overnight
sensation. It was on the top floor of an old abandoned factory on Robertson Drive, in Hollywood, and decorated in a melange of Art Deco, Art
Nouveau, English antiques, stained-glass windows and flashing disco
lights. With a live band augmenting the recorded sounds, it was flashy,
fun and fabulous. Opening night, the club was jammed with major stars

and celebrities. The huge dance floor was packed with dozens of the most famous people in Hollywood. Word gets around fast and even at three hundred and fifty dollars a membership, everyone wanted to join. Night after night the most illustrious and glamorous people—some of whom had never even set foot in a disco before—sat and stared at the incredible goings-on. Marlon Brando came. So did Barbra Streisand, Steve Mc-Queen, Loretta Young, Liza Minnelli, Dean Martin, Peter Sellers, Bobby Kennedy, Vanessa Redgrave, everyone who meant anything at that time —a Who's Who couldn't do it justice. Tony and I spent practically every night there. He even got to like dancing.

We couldn't believe how quickly the success of the Factory happened. But just as quickly as it started, it faded. Too much too soon. Goodbye Sweet Factory. In a little less than a year its vogue had passed, just like many a Hollywood career—and Tony and I were back in London again.

Tony was achieving his life's desire to write, direct and star in an erotic musical-comedy-fantasy, based on his life story. It was succinctly called *Can Hieronymus Merkin Ever Forget Mercy Humppe and Find True Happiness?* This was an avant-garde satirical Fellini-esque movie about a successful actor-director (Newley-Merkin) who, at the age of thirty-eight sits, miserable and bitter, on the beach outside his Beverly Hills mansion screening a montage of film clips from his life, while showing them to his two tiny children and his old Cockney mother. His main fantasy in the film revolves around a deliciously nubile blonde, Mercy Humppe, for whom he has been searching all his life. He considers her his suppressed desire and the penultimate sexual object. She is a slave to his whims. He is desperately torn between his love for her and for the beautiful, head-strong raven-haired Polyester Poontang (guess who?) who becomes the mother of his two children and puts up with his philandering with every Jane, June and Jenny who crosses his path, or, as they were more poeti-cally named in the film, Filigree Fondle, Trampolina Wham Bang, and Maidenhair Fern!

Incredibly, I decided I had to play the part of Ms. Poontang. Who other than I could play it better? Since our two children—now four and two and a half—had been cast at the insistence of Tony as his children in the film, Thumbelina and Thaxted, I would have to be in London and Malta in any case for four or five months, being a stage mama. Universal thought it a great idea and I got the part, for which I was paid the princely sum of two thousand pounds!

Tony wrote a song for Polyester to sing to Hieronymus. It was a cute song. He even dedicated it to me, since it was based completely on our relationship. Before I sing the song there is a symbolic scene where the two meet for the first time. Polyester looks at the mask (Newley-Merkin's alter ego) and says:

POLYESTER (*sympathetic as she looks at* THE MASK)
Typical Libra. You bruise so easily!
HIERONYMUS (leering to *himself*)
Typical Gemini . . . you gonna get it.

(They stare at each other in a kind of mutual fascination.)
POLYESTER
You realize, of course, we have absolutely nothing in common . . .
    And POLYESTER *sings,*

How did you get into my horoscope
You funny irascible lovable dope.
Isn't it clear from the stars that you haven't a hope with me?
Anyone else would have known in advance,
Libra and Gemini haven't a chance.
Anyone else would have seen at a glance it could never be—
Chalk and Cheese—we're as different as Chalk and Cheese.
Were there ever two people more out of step before
More unalike if you please
Souls apart, we are opposite, poles apart.
When I think about me and you saying, how do you do?
Maybe it wasn't so smart.
Me, I'm bright, got a groovy scene.
I like to be where it's at!
You're up-tight as a tambourine
What kind of music is that?
Chalk and Cheese—who would ever blend things like these?
On the other hand people say love is here to stay
Hurray for the birds and the bees!
I'm a fool maybe—but I don't mind chalk with my cheese.

I performed this little ditty clad in a clinging white Grecian gown, while Tony (talk about upstaging) wore nothing except a giant toy key sticking out of the bottom of his spine! He was playing his alter ego, and an actor stood next to him, his face covered by a pink mask on which no features were shown, and dressed in Tony's clothes. A motley selection of hankies and camera tape covered Tony's full frontal which, although never actually revealed to the camera in this scene, one could catch glimpses of later in the sensuous graphic underwater love scenes with the virginal Miss Humppe. This part was played by flaxen-haired *Playboy* centerfold Connie Kreski, after a search rivaling that of the quest for Scarlett O'Hara.

Tony and Connie became extremely close on this movie. Since she was a novice to films, he obviously had to coach her a lot, and they spent many an hour together on and off the set rehearsing their scenes.

She, however, was not the only pebble on the beaches of Malta. Women featured heavily in Hieronymus Merkin's life, and there were dozens and dozens of girls to be interviewed, talked to, rehearsed, prepared and built up for the many roles in the film.

I had a sick, horrible feeling when I first read the script of *H.M.* Tony seemed to have spelled out the death of our marriage with this totally revealing picture of his life.

Hieronymus has a sidekick producer and mentor—Good Time Eddie Filth (Milton Berle), who encourages him in his philanderings. Newley-Merkin has a scene where he sits on top of the mountain having the following dialogue with God:

There has never been a woman who commanded a moment of my regard after I'd made love to her. I realize I have no respect for women—I really believe I hate them, and take my revenge in sex. The ritual murder, forever stabbing and reopening the divine wound.

After this speech, Good Time Eddie, dressed as Satan, officiates at a ceremony in which dozens of robed candle-holding monks surround an altar bed on which lies a naked woman. Hieronymus is ceremoniously derobed and mounts the altar and the girl to ritual moans.

The finale of the movie finds Hieronymus at dawn, still on the beach, surrounded by his paraphernalia—skips, wardrobe hampers, sky-high cans of film and scrapbooks, mementos of his career, and his whirring projector. The two kids are asleep on Grandma's knee. Hieronymus sings a plaintive ballad summing up his misery and disillusionment with life. It was called "I'm All I Need":

> *I'm all I need, if I got me—I got rainbows*
> *If I got me—just you see how the rain goes away*
> *'Cos I've got somebody who cares*
> *Someone who likes my company*
> *While I've got me—I've got a sky full of bluebirds*
> *When did you see someone as lucky as me?*

He continues in this vein. As the song finishes, a squad car approaches on the beach and disgorges two Los Angeles cops and a distraught Polyester-Joan, who has been calling throughout the movie for her husband.

She rushes toward him, gathering Thaxted-Sacha in her arms and Thumbelina-Tara by her tiny hands, and a torrent of words pour out. "Darling, are you *crazy?* . . . Have you been here all night? . . . I've been calling . . . didn't you hear me calling? I didn't know what to think. I called the police. Your agent called the police. I called the hospital. You do this sort of thing, you do it all the time. You don't think and you don't care. Well I've had enough. I'm taking the children—yes I am —I'm taking them back to Europe and this time I mean it. This time *I really do mean it*—I really do."

Exit Polyester-Joan, sobbing hysterically, with Thaxted-Sacha and Thumbelina-Tara, leaving Hieronymus-Newley unmoved and slightly puzzled.

The playing of this scene affected me so violently that during and after each take a positive torrent of real tears burst forth—all the anguish I had been concealing for six years. It was true. Our marriage was badly cracked, and when I finally saw the film in a private screening room in London a few months later I knew there was no hope for us ever to live as husband and wife again.

◄*Eleven*►

"THIS IS RON KASS."

My heart said, "Oh, nice!" It had done so before, of course, so I was used to it. The man sitting on the couch in my living room in London was an extremely attractive American. He was tall, with fair hair worn, happily, somewhat shorter than in the current vogue for shoulder-length locks, amazing green eyes in a deeply tanned face, sensual mouth and a warm, open and endearing smile. He was sartorially perfect in a beige suit and black sweater—dressed, I guessed correctly, by the tailor Doug Hayward. Doug had been a close friend of Tony's and mine ever since Evie Bricusse and I used to go with our respective husbands to his tailor shop, then in shabby Shepherd's Bush. Now he was the top tailor of the Swinging Sixties London set. He had a chic shop in Mount Street, near Park Street, where Tony and I were temporarily living while he cut and edited *Hieronymus Merkin*. And hello, hello! a mere two blocks away from elegant South Street, where Ron resided. We were all within a stone's throw of each other, were we of a mind to throw stones, which indeed I was not after meeting the attractive Mr. Kass.

We had dinner at the Club dell' Aretusa, the fashionable Italian restaurant-disco on King's Road, where rock stars rubbed shoulders with MPs, and debutantes, models, managers, photographers and actresses hung out. It was wall-to-wall "in" and lots of fun. Anybody who was anybody was usually there each night.

Evie Bricusse was Doug's "date" for the evening, I was with Tony, and Ron was alone. He was recently separated from his wife of several years. She and their three sons were living in Lugano while he was in London, managing director and president of Apple Records, the Beatles' recording company.

It was a fairly sparkling evening at Aretusa. Michael Caine was there with Bianca Jagger. So was Jean Shrimpton, London's top model, with Cockney photographer David Bailey, the hottest photographer in England. The Swinging Sixties were regretfully drawing to a close, but many of the people who had made them swing were at Aretusa that night. Bailey dropped by the table. He wanted to arrange to take a picture of Tony and me for his book to commemorate the dizzy decade. Seven years after publication, nearly all the couples Bailey pictured in *Goodbye Baby and Amen* were divorced or separated, some by tragic circumstances— Susan Hampshire and her French husband, Dudley Moore and Suzy

Kendall, and Roman Polanski and gorgeous, ill-fated Sharon Tate among them.

Tony was not unaware of the interested looks I was trying not to exchange with Ron, but shortly after dinner he excused himself and telling me to "have a good time, Flower," went home to work.

Doug, Evie, Ron and I sat sipping Sambuca in the discotheque. I was attracted to Ron, not only for his warmth and easy personality but also for the energy and enthusiasm that emanated from him. He was an Aries. Not only that, his birth *date*, March 30, was exactly the same day as Sydney Chaplin's and Warren Beatty's! Surely the chances of that were two million to one.

We started to see each other. Just for lunch or tea at first. I was treading extremely warily. Aside from the physical attraction, I felt that Ron was a man who could be a friend. I could talk with him about any subject under the sun. We exchanged ideas, explored each other's minds. He was mature, although only thirty-three, and had an enormous zest for life. Here at last was a man who was a match for my physical energy and stamina. Seemingly indefatigable, he ran the Beatles' company, jumped regularly on a jet to New York, Rome or Geneva at least twice a week and was able to stay up until three or four feeling no jet lag even after a sixteen-hour day.

He was a doer and an organizer, as well as a very dominant male. He was also the first man I had become involved with who was not either an actor, a producer, or a playboy. He was substance. He was, in fact, a supervisor, businessman and executive with a Bachelor of Science degree in business (as a graduate of UCLA business school), an Associate of Arts degree in music, and had a keen and intelligent mind. He always knew what he wanted and he usually got it. And what he wanted was me.

But married butterflies who had difficulty in making decisions are not so easily caught, and our relationship had stormy waters to ride. He was the first man I had ever met who thought of me first and himself second. This was an exceptionally novel experience for me. Ron literally swept me off my feet. Try as I did to stem the tide, I found myself becoming more and more attracted to him, not only in an emotional and supportive way but in the need we discovered in each other as human beings and friends. I grew to lean on him and depend on his advice more and more.

Because Tony was still completely enmeshed in his work I was able to see Ron often. Since Tony never asked where I went, I had considerable freedom. Tara and Sacha were now both at school, and my supply of American TV shows was not in evidence, so Ron and I managed to spend much time discovering each other. And the more I discovered, the more I liked. We did not launch into a flaming affair immediately. Perhaps now I was finally realizing that here was the man I had been searching for all my life. I wanted to be very careful. I didn't want to injure our blossoming friendship and love by jumping instantly into bed. So we lunched at the Connaught, had tea at Claridge's, met for drinks at Trader Vic's and bided our time.

I went to Trieste to make an "intellectual" film. At least, my Italian agent had assured me it was an intellectual film. "Not much money, *cara*, but aah—the *prestige!*" The director was a dedicated Communist, the crew numbered a mere seventeen; my salary was minimal, and I was not allowed to smile once in the film, since the director considered smiling a cheap and shallow Hollywood device.

"Do you see smiles in a Bergman film?" he roared. "Or an Antonioni film? Maybe you have only *one* smile in my film, when you are very, *very* sad."

I played a desolate young widow who becomes involved in a love affair with a seventeen-year-old boy. For this I had to do my first nude scene, which made me very nervous. It was nearly 1970. Nudity on the screen was suddenly fashionable, all the rage, yes, sir. No more ruby in the navel, flower in the too-plunging neckline. Goodbye, chaste kiss and fade-out to the sound of sensual violins. Hello, take off your bra and jump into the sack or the sofa or the back of a truck—wherever it would be the most "artistic" to shoot the scene. Our director finally decided, after mulling it over for days, that our love scene would perhaps play better in bed. Thus, one freezing winter afternoon in Trieste, a town on the border between Italy and Yugoslavia and one of the most dismal and depressing cities I had ever stayed in, I took off my all for "art."

Mathieu Carrière, the twenty-year-old actor playing the boy, was not quite as nervous as I, perhaps because he was allowed to keep his shorts on. I wore a vast assortment of tights, socks and leg warmers to keep out the freezing air (Michael Caine told me he wore Wellington boots for his love scenes in bed in *Alfie*). I still had to be bare above the waist, however. The director had assured me repeatedly that this was an "art" film. He was not interested in showing anything as vulgarly commercial as a nipple, but he just needed the two bodies in the throes of sexual passion anyway—so throb we must. I decided to cleverly camouflage the basic bits of my anatomy with camera tape. Camera tape, unlike ordinary sticky tape, is very strong. It is used to attach weights to cameras, and has a thousand and one other uses in the studio. Italian camera tape is bright blue. In my dressing room I carefully attached a neat X of camera tape in the middle of each breast. Great ad for Blue Cross, I thought, surveying my surrealistic image in the mirror.

Mathieu arrived with a bottle of brandy, thoughtfully sent by the director to "warm us up"—whether for the love scene or to keep out the bitter cold we knew not. Half a bottle of brandy later I found myself drunk and panicky, tucked in between the sheets with young Monsieur Carrière who was, if anything, even drunker and more panicked than I. Peering hopefully at us behind the hand-held camera was moustachio'd *Il Regista* himself, sizzling with artistic fervor. The Italian crew lounged nonchalantly about, pretending indifference to the simulated coupling they were about to see. I kept on my robe, while the director tried to get the perfect angle for this piece of celluloid passion. Mathieu appeared to have fallen asleep—it was comfortable in the bed and a tiny snore escaped from his beatifically smiling countenance. I nudged him awake. We clutched each other stolidly. Two great hunks of flesh, neither of us about to do anything remotely sensual until the magic word *"Azione!"* was screamed. It is always screamed by Italian film directors. The director feels that this electric word will galvanize his cast into dynamic performances.

"Va bene—va bene. Allora, Joan." He turned to me. "Take off the roba."

"Shit," I muttered. The moment of truth had come. What the hell was I doing here, thousands of miles from my loved ones, making a lousy uncommercial Italian art film which no one would probably see anyway? Lying in bed with a young lad barely past puberty, with blue camera tape covering my chest. Oh, the degradation! I bravely ripped off the robe and threw myself onto Mathieu's scrawny chest to cover my by now embarrassing blue crosses.

"OK. O.K. *Azione!"* screamed the director excitedly. The whirring cameras could not keep up with the sound of his yelled instruction. *"Kees —beeg beeg kees."* I pressed myself even more fervently to Mathieu and we locked lips and simulated lust. "More *sexy!"* roared Romano. "You *woman,* he *boy*—ees veree veree beeg *thrill* for you." God, this was like making silent movies. Sound was not a big issue in Italian pictures; everything was dubbed later. Our director was going a bit far, even so. His vocal efforts were causing me to giggle. I tried to prevent it by biting my lip, and found Mathieu's there instead.

Squirm, squirm—wriggle, wriggle—pant, pant—we wrestled around on the bed. I felt as passionate as a cat on a cold tin roof. To top it off, my suppressed giggles caused me to get hiccups. I was determined to keep my back to the camera all the time but the staccato heaving of my shoulders every three seconds made the director furiously yell *"Cut!"* We disengaged lips—a thin line of saliva connected us—I disconnected it, giggled and hiccuped. Mathieu was dissolved in hysterical drunken laughter. We disengaged arms. I tried to back off from his chest and found I couldn't. The edge of one of my blue crosses had attached itself to Mathieu's chest. We were Siamese twins. Like courting couples who are found locked in the throes of sexual embrace and who, unable to separate, have to be taken to the hospital while they put them under a cold shower and administer nonstimulating drugs to cool their ardor. Mathieu, aware of what had happened, became even more hysterical with laughter and, hiccuping wildly, so did I. The crew were puzzled until they saw what had happened, and guffaws abounded. But the director remained aloof and cold. He hated people to smile, let alone laugh. The wardrobe lady eventually separated us and I put on my robe and staggered, still hiccuping, to my dressing room to recuperate.

"We will shoot the rest of the scene tomorrow," said the director coldly, "when you 'ave both *sobered up.*" He stalked off briskly, moustache bristling.

After downing a double espresso I proceeded to try and remove the tape. It was stuck solid as a rock. It would not budge. Alarmed at the thought of permanently blue breasts I rushed back to the hotel and, after soaking in a hot bath for an hour, attempted to pull off the offending tape. The agony was such that after it was finally removed, and my bosoms were raw from the pulling, I vowed, to hell with false modesty— in the future if I had to do any nude scenes they would be *au naturel*.

Tony and I by now had an unspoken "arrangement." He went his way and I went mine. I was in a tremendous dilemma. I wanted to be with Ron, I felt he was the man I had been searching for—he combined the qualities of leadership, dominance and intelligence with love, warmth, communication and compassion. I still loved Tony, but in a completely different way. I felt sadness for him and for his inability to give himself totally to anything except his work. And he was also the father of my children. This was my biggest problem. I dreaded having to break up the children's secure and happy home. To take away their roots, which I had fought hard to get for them. Every time I made the decision to separate from Tony, I changed my mind again because of the pain and hurt it would bring my children, who were the most important entities in my life. How could I ruin their innocent lives? It would be selfish and rotten of me. At the same time, I realized that living in a house without real love was probably much worse for them. I agonized for months, completely torn, completely unable to decide one way or another. I hated myself for being so weak, for not being able to take the decisive initiative and end the marriage. Meanwhile I juggled my quadruple lives and tried to put on a happy face.

I had always had a hankering to be a singer. At one time I took singing lessons in Hollywood before auditioning for a Broadway musical. Luckily I didn't get it since it closed after three performances. My voice was quite good but weak (rather like my character). I had crooned a passable duet with Bing Crosby in *Road to Hong Kong*, called "Let's Not Be Sensible," by my Oscar-winning friend Sammy Cahn, and I had also sung the notorious "Chalk and Cheese" opposite my naked husband in *Hieronymus*. Now Tony's record company in London had approached him about producing and writing an album on which I would perform. The irony of this close working relationship commencing at about the same time our marriage was going down the drain did not escape us.

We were in the process of an amicable "trial separation" although still residing in the same house "for the sake of the children." I had told him about Ron, and I knew about Connie Kreski and various others. We were going to attempt to get through this exceedingly difficult period as normally as possible. It was naive of us to think it could be so.

The album was to be called tentatively *And She Sings Too!* and would feature on the sleeve a photo of me looking beguilingly sexy. My voice was sort of breathy and girlish. Streisand definitely did not have to worry. Tony wrote a song which he gave me. I sang it for the album. It was a hard-driving rock song, better performed by someone with the vocal strength of Petula Clark. It was called "Why Do You Try and Change Me?" and it said it *all* about our marriage.

You tell me you love me
But if you love me Baby
Why do you try and change me?
I don't want to change you baby
You know you have faults as well
I accept them 'cos I really love you.
You can lead a horse to water
But you'll never ever alter me.
I'm free—I'm me . . .
Life is a Mardi Gras and I refuse to miss the party.
I want to dance the night away—
You want to keep me home a perfect little household pet.
But I don't want to be your mother
Take me as a friend and lover
That's the only way I want us to be.
Strange, when I think at first
You seemed to be so mad about me
Why should you suddenly complain?
If you go on and on insisting that I do things your way
You are going to drive me from you
After everything we've gone through
Tell me what you want
I wish that you'd say.
Didn't I change my name for you?
Didn't I play the game for you?
Didn't I make it wild for you?
Didn't I make a child for you?
Take me the way I am or leave me alone
Didn't I stay at home for you?
Didn't I give up Rome for you?
What do I have to do to show you I care?©

I awoke at six o'clock with a distinct feeling of foreboding. I was having a dream of such reality that I forced myself to awake from it. Could it be true? I had to find out immediately and the only way to do that was to make a phone call to Brazil. To Rio de Janeiro, where Ron had gone for the annual song festival. He had wanted me to go with him and I had been sorely torn. For weeks I anguished about the ramifications a trip to Rio would bring. I wanted to go. Traveling—experiencing new places, sounds, vibrations, meeting new people—was one of my greatest pleasures, and Rio had always been one of the places I wanted to visit. To go with Ron would be an extra bonus. But although Tony was aware of my relationship with Ron, it simply wasn't cricket to openly attend a highly publicized music festival, at which the press of the world would be, with my lover. I was quite popular in Latin America. If we went to the festival together it was tantamount to taking an ad in *Variety*.

But reason prevailed. I needed time—time to think about my children, and what divorcing their father could do to them. I couldn't decide.

I knew what I wanted: I wanted Ron. But I was still trying to have my cake and eat it too, a practical impossibility.

I drove later that morning to Ron's rented house on Coldwater Canyon to phone him in Rio. When his voice came through, faint and surprised, yet happy to hear from me, I didn't beat about the bush. The dream was too vivid in my mind.

"Who's this dark-haired twenty-six-year-old socialite you've been going out with?" I said sharply. Diplomacy and tact were never my strong points.

"Whaat?" His voice from a distance of more than six thousand miles sounded fuzzily amazed. "How do you know about her? Who told you?"

It was true then. My dream was a reality. "I just know, that's all," I battled on bravely. "How long has it been going on?"

"My God, Joan." He was the only man who had ever called me by my proper name. A good sign—maybe he saw the real me, and not some plaything or imaginary goddess. I had always been Honey, Sweetheart, Babe, Joanie-bird, Butterfly, Flower, or Jaycee before Ron.

"It hasn't really been 'going on.' I met this girl—she's a lovely girl—" I gritted my teeth. "But we haven't got really involved or anything—yet."

Yet! Yet! Oh, I was such a fool, an absolute fool. I had let this extremely handsome man of thirty-four go off to Rio telling him that, after over a year of knowing each other, I "had to have more time to think things over" and expecting him to stay faithful to me. He was only human. And he was a man.

I realized that I was close to losing the one man who had really understood me and with whom I had true communication.

We talked for an hour. An hour in which I finally resolved my horribly ambivalent feelings and faced up to what losing Ron meant. I knew now what I wanted, needed, and what he wanted too. We had to be together. It was the only way.

If anyone imagines that divorce for an actor or actress is easy, let them think again. This parting was infinitely more horrible than my divorce from Maxwell Reed had been. I really did still care about Tony. My conscience was deeply affected by what I was doing to my two innocent children. But the sparks of love between Tony and me were not enough to rekindle our marriage. We liked and respected each other, but living together any more was out of the question. The split was amicable. Painful, hurtful, but amicable. I wasn't the right woman for him and he knew it. We had been staying together for the children's sake for far too long. Even they, at the tender ages of six and a half and four and a half, were aware of it.

The beautiful house on Summit Drive went on the market. I took no alimony—only a property settlement derived mostly from the sale of the house—which was soon bought by Sammy Davis, Jr. We agreed on a sum for the children's support. They were my responsibility now, and since I had let my career take a secondary position for seven years, the prospects of my earning enough money again to support them were dim, to say the least.

Ron already had a wife and three kids in Lugano to whom he had to pay alimony and child support. I could hardly ask him to support my children as well.

My marriage to Tony had lasted seven years, just as uncannily true as Ben Gary had predicted.

I assured Tony that he could see the children whenever he wished. The last thing I ever wanted was to have them hurt or used as a pawn in the marital upheavals, as I had seen so many selfish spouses do.

I returned yet again, bags, baggage, furniture and children, to my beloved London.

Ron was now president of MGM records and Robins Feist and Miller Music Publishing Company. He had plush offices in New York and spent much time commuting between continents. I refused, for the children's sake, to move into Ron's Mayfair townhouse with him, and instead took a cramped and overpriced furnished flat around the corner. I plunged into getting the children settled in new schools, trying to set up my career once again in a different country and generally sorting out all our lives. I was in love with Ron, although we fought a lot. We both always said what was on our minds. It was instant combustibility. But at least it was honest. I felt that at last I had found true, dedicated and supportive love in Ron. However, I did not wish to traumatize the children even more by a new "Daddy" suddenly appearing on the scene. My main concern was to take care of their needs and adjust them as well as I could to their new and strange life. London life is very different from sunny Beverly Hills, where most families have a swimming pool in their backyard.

It was the spring of 1970. Ron bought me a new minicar. I raced around London hunting again for a suitable house. Ron wanted us to marry, but I was convinced that, as Oscar Wilde said, "One should always be in love—that is why one should never marry." Two attempts at marriage had made me realize I wasn't very good at it. And it was too soon.

Luckily I was able to start working in films immediately. I made several in quick succession. In the early part of the 1970s I made *Three in the Cellar* in New Mexico, before I left for England. It was a comedy—a rather abortive one. I played Larry (J.R.) Hagman's wife. J.R. and Alexis in the same movie! I had known Larry since I was at RADA. He was Mary Martin's son, then appearing on stage in *South Pacific* with her. (He was in the chorus.) We dated a couple of times casually, little dreaming that some thirty years later we would be the reigning villains on TV. He was very different from his J.R. image—quiet, shy and self-effacing. I made *Quest for Love* and *Revenge* for Rank at Pinewood Studios, my old stamping grounds. Over fifteen years had passed since the "coffee bar Jezebel" had crossed those hallowed portals to portray wayward teenagers and sexy delinquents. Now I played leading ladies, sometimes if I was lucky with a touch of humor or evil thrown in. None of these films were by any means either box-office bonanzas or works of art, but an actor acts and a baker bakes and I needed the bread.

Then came a quick series of horror films which were euphemistically referred to as "psychological melodramas": *Fear in the Night, Tales from the Crypt, Dark Places* and *Tales that Witness Madness.* I became known by the British press as Queen of the Horror Films—a title I didn't particularly relish. But I was resilient. A survivor. I considered myself lucky to be working so much after such a long period away from the British screen, particularly since I was well into my thirties. The critics were sometimes kind. "Miss Collins—an actress always better than her material," said the *Evening Standard*—and "Joan Collins is an actress who only improves . . . and brings beauty, luminosity, and compelling charm to the screen." How nice!

I had always thought that if my acting career collapsed I might become a casting director. I could see the potential in some unknown actor or actress and say "There's a future star." It first happened at MGM while making *The Opposite Sex.* A young guy, about my age, who worked in the mail room and sometimes delivered my fan letters, used to whistle at me as I sailed by in my tight-waisted Helen Rose creations to the commissary for lunch. One day I stopped to chat. He was cute—boyish, with black curly hair, wide blue eyes, a sense of humor and a certain offbeat sex appeal. He must have had a lot of confidence in himself for he asked me for a date, which I refused. He told me he was an actor, and his name was Jack Nicholson.

In 1972 Ron and I finally found the perfect London house we had been searching for. It was, from the outside, a rather ordinary looking semidetached 1930s house, not unlike forty or fifty others on the same avenue, but it was exactly what we wanted. A warm family home into which Ron, Tara, Sacha and I happily moved, and with the added excitement of a new addition expected to our already large family. Ron's three husky young sons—David, Robert and Jonathan—visited us each summer and at Christmas time at our house in Marbella. When baby Katyana arrived we had a his, hers and theirs brood.

Ron and I sat with friends Paul Wasserman—Ron's best friend—Peter Kameron, and Burt and Maxine Kamerman in Mr. Chow's ten days before the baby was due. We doodled possible names on the paper tablecloth. Ron desperately wanted a girl—after three boys, who wouldn't? Pete was sure it would be a girl. Pete was one of Ron's closest friends. He had given up most of his material possessions and had spent several years traveling the world and searching for the truth. A true guru!

He had just returned from a trip to India and meeting with that extraordinary Indian, Saha Baba, a holy man held in the highest esteem. Pete had a small phial of gray dust, and he dabbed some of it on my forehead and cheekbones. It was a substance that Saha Baba had created himself—out of thin air, literally—and it had, so I was told, powerful properties. Pete was a great believer in getting your "karma" right.

After he applied the ashes he told me that the baby would be a blessed child, possessed of immense personal magnetism, intelligence, beauty and luck. "You'll have her tomorrow," he said gravely, convinced it was a girl.

"Nonsense—it's not due for at least ten days," laughed Ron. We wrote down some names—mostly Russian, from his ancestry, for his original family name was Kaschinoff—Tatiana, Katya, Katyana. I wanted something completely original but with a Russian flavor. Four hours later, after consuming an immense Chinese meal, and Ron consuming a powerful sleeping pill, I went into labor. Unable to rouse Ron from a deep sleep I poured three cups of strong coffee down his throat before he could get himself together enough to drive me to the nursing home!

I was having this child, again by natural childbirth, helped along by Ron's encouragement, and a fierce Scrabble game which lasted almost until the birth.

When James Schneider, my obstetrician, said excitedly, "It's a girl!" I argued with him. "You're just saying that to make Ron happy," I said. "He always gets what he wants and you don't want to disappoint him." Ron was at the birth, beside himself with joy. Katyana Kennedy Kass brought us even closer together.

I was extremely concerned about the effect a new baby would have on Tara and Sacha. It hadn't been easy for them adjusting to a new country, new friends, new house, new school, new stepfather. I remembered how horrible I had felt attending all those different schools and having to make new friends when I was a child. But they adored Katy and seemed to adjust to their new situation.

Katy was born on June 20, 1972. Being a Gemini too, she and I probably understand each other better than anyone else in the world.

I was now in what without a doubt was the happiest time of my life. If one can measure the highs and lows of one's life, the years between 1970 and 1975 were almost perfect. I loved my husband. I adored my children. I was happy living in England with my family and working on some things I really enjoyed.

Buzz Kulik, who had directed me a few years earlier in a ghastly potboiler, *Warning Shot*, with David Janssen, asked me to play Lorraine Sheldon in *The Man Who Came to Dinner*.

This was a prestigious NBC Hallmark Hall of Fame two-hour special and, although shot in England, it was to be shown in America for Thanksgiving.

Lorraine was a wonderful part based on the character of Gertrude Lawrence. Flamboyant and eccentric, it was the sort of part I had been wanting to sink my teeth into. Finally a decent role. I hoped it was not going to be a flash in the pan, after which I'd drift back into my usual wallpaper parts or horror films.

Buzz gathered an excellent cast. Lee Remick was to play Maggie, Sheridan Whiteside's loyal secretary, immortalized in the screen version by Bette Davis. Marty Feldman played the mad Groucho Marx character, Don Knotts the catatonically shy doctor, Peter Haskell the journalist, and last but definitely not least, Orson Welles himself as Sheridan Whiteside. *The* man who came to dinner.

He comes to the house of a respectable middle-aged Connecticut couple, breaks his leg, and stays, creating havoc, turmoil, and humor. It is a marvelous comedy. Sheridan Whiteside is one of the best (and longest) comedy roles ever written for an actor. He dominates every scene, is bitingly witty, ruthless, scheming and hilarious. Hallmark felt they had a major coup in getting this giant of the entertainment world to grace them with his august presence. He was treated like an emperor.

We rehearsed for three weeks, during which time Mr. Welles consumed vast quantities of burgundy-colored liquid from teacups and read every one of his lines from massive cue cards three feet by three feet which were held in place by two wide-eyed nervous students from RADA.

I felt like a wide-eyed nervous girl from RADA myself in the intimidating presence of Welles. He was immense, literally and figuratively, and frightening. His reputation for not letting anyone get the better of him preceded him. I practically curtsied and would have pulled my forelock reverently if I had one, such was the awe he instilled in us. After all, he was the boy wonder of the movies who, at the age of twenty-five, had made *Citizen Kane,* one of the greatest movies of all time. Awesome Orson I called him. I was playing a poised, sophisticated actress, whom nothing fazed, but I had to steel my nerves while working with his mightiness.

He was rehearsing a long speech to me one afternoon. I was standing on my mark when he suddenly ended the speech with, "And I can't read the rest of the lines because *Miss Collins* is standing in front of the damn cue cards!"

"But I'm on my mark, Orson," I muttered feebly, catching a sympathetic grimace from Lee Remick. It didn't matter that he was in the wrong. I had blocked his view of his lines so I must stand in another position where his Highness could view them without obstruction. I meekly did what I was told. Welles looked triumphant. His secretary brought him another cup of "tea"—which he insisted was Coca Cola but which we all knew was red wine. Not even vintage.

Peter Haskell, however, was not intimidated by Welles one bit. He bounded in the following day performing an airy speech about its being a beautiful Christmas day tra la and the snow was on the trees and frost on the ground etc. Welles boomed out in a sarcastic stentorian tone, "You read that just like a goddamn faggot."

"What did you say?" said Peter, menacingly quiet and advancing toward Welles with measured stride.

"I said you read it like—a—er—faggot. But, dear boy, I was only joking, I assure you—ha ha ha! Dear boy, I *know* you aren't a faggot— I'm sorry." His huge laugh boomed and reverberated through the drafty rehearsal hall. Some of the crew laughed with him sycophantically. Peter, slightly placated, continued the scene. Orson seemed to admire him after that and they became quite chummy. Welles obviously enjoyed people brave enough to stand up to him. He relished putting the fear of God into lesser mortals, however.

Don Knotts was not so lucky. Lee Remick and I sat in the transmission room watching a dress rehearsal on the monitor while Don had his best and funniest scene cut to ribbons by Welles. Welles insisted on restaging so that all of Don's best lines were shot on the back of his head. He insisted on cutting anything that he felt detracted from his own performance.

During the three-day studio taping, which extended to five and a half days, while another TV company stamped their feet in frenzy outside our studio door, Orson Welles read *every single line* of his part from the cue cards. Buzz Kulik tried to remonstrate with him. During the staging of each scene Welles insisted on being center stage facing the camera (and his cards). Kulik suggested that perhaps some of the other actors should get a close-up occasionally. Welles boomed angrily, "*I* am the star. This is *not* an ensemble piece. This play is about Sheridan Whiteside. The rest of the troupe are just supporting players!"

Buzz gave up and Welles did it his way. Needless to say, it was one of the unfunniest productions of *The Man Who Came to Dinner* ever. And the ratings for NBC were exceedingly poor.

I received a fine compliment from Kitty Carlisle, the widow of the co-author, Moss Hart. She came to visit during the filming and told me that I was the best Lorraine Sheldon she had ever seen—and she had seen every actress play it since the 1940s.

Although my quest had been for a father figure, not a mother figure, I was sorely conscious of the lack of a mother in my life, especially with three beautiful children to whom having a granny would have meant so much. The family unit was important to me. I missed my mother. What a pity it took me so long to realize it. I found I thought about her more and more, especially as Tara grew older. I could identify so vividly with my own childhood feelings.

My feelings for my father were not as vehement now. I realized his weaknesses and failings, but I cared about him and felt compassion for him.

He had married again and had another daughter, Natasha, when he was sixty-five. His wife was also an agent and artists' manager. Irene was about the same age as I, which was interesting. I wondered if she had ever searched for a father figure too?

But my mother's image still haunted me and I dreamed about her more often. Jackie had become enormously close to Mummy in the years before her death, and I regretted that I had not been able to do so because of leaving for America while still too young to appreciate her. A boy needs a father some of his life, but a girl needs a mother all of her life. Or is it the other way around? In any case I prefer my own version.

Ron was co-producing with David Putnam *The Optimists*, starring Peter Sellers. Putnam went on to become one of the most successful producers in Britain, his success culminating in the Oscar-winning *Chariots of Fire*. Sellers was going through the turmoil of another divorce, and was feeling rather put upon and lonely. He had adopted Ron and me as his new best friends of the month. I had known Peter since 1963 when he, Tony, Leslie Bricusse and I had made a comedy album called "Fool Britannia," which was based on the sexual excesses of certain members of Parliament and aristocrats in Britain at the time. Now Peter was down in the dumps. He had recently started a short-lived romance with Liza Minnelli. Short-lived it was indeed, for a scant ten days was about how long it took before the gilt wore off the gingerbread. Now the romance was teetering on its last legs and Peter needed someone to pour his heart out to, and we were the recipients of his confidences. At 11 A.M. one Sunday the phone rang. "Hello," said I, busily fixing bacon and eggs for the family in our sunny kitchen.

"Joanie?" said a wary voice. "It's me—Pete. What's happening? Are you and Ron up to anything today?" "No, we're staying in. Do you want to come over, Pete?" I asked, spooning scrambled eggs onto eighteen-months-old Katy's plate. "We're here all day."

"All right—yes—I'd love to." Then, dropping his voice dramatically, "Fleet Street's on to Liza and me. They've been doorstepping us all night. It's been hell. I've got to get out. I'll leave by the back entrance of the Dorchester. See you in an hour."

Shortly afterward he arrived. In deep disguise. This disguise consisted of an SS officer's uniform, complete with leather jacket liberally festooned with swastikas and an SS armband, a steel helmet covering his whole head. He drove a black Mercedes-Benz with tinted windows, obviously bulletproof. Sheldon Avenue was a predominantly Jewish neighborhood. On a sunny Sunday afternoon most of the residents took a little constitutional to nearby Highgate park with their dogs or children. The sight of a sleek black Mercedes containing a Nazi SS officer authentic down to the last swastika must have been quite a shock to them.

When the doorbell rang and I saw this apparition standing there I convulsed. "Let me in, quick. I was followed by half of Fleet Street, but I think I lost them," hissed Sellers, black leather quivering.

In the garden he regaled us for two hours with hilarious stories of his ill-fated romance with Liza Minnelli. When it was time to leave I suggested it might be better to hide the steel helmet and swastika-studded jacket. He wouldn't hear of it. With typical Sellers humor he zoomed into Sheldon Avenue, and then with right arm extended stiffly out of the window of the Mercedes proceeded down Sheldon Avenue, declaiming loudly "Heil Hitler! Heil Hitler! Sieg Heil!" in his most guttural German to the disgust of the residents and Ron's and my helpless laughter.

I finally fulfilled one of my major ambitions. To play in a Noel Coward comedy. Ron had obtained the rights to several Coward plays, among them *Fallen Angels*. We had tried, unsuccessfully, to obtain *Private Lives*. I still longed to play Amanda. *Fallen Angels* had been originally produced in New York in 1927 with the young Tallulah Bankhead and Edna Best in the leading roles. Two women, best friends all their lives and now happily, if boringly, married to dullards, had shared a passionate romance in the past with an attractive Frenchman. It was a *tour de force* for two actresses, and Tallulah and Edna made enormous successes on Broadway. Since then the play had been constantly revived, but always with older actresses in the roles which should have been played by women in their late twenties or thirties. Perhaps managements thought that only mature actresses could play these roles, as they were extremely funny, outrageous and rather camp. Hermione Gingold and Hermione Baddeley had played them, among others.

We made a deal with Sir John Woolf, the head of Anglia TV, and started pre-production. For the first time I started to become instrumental in the production side. Ron was producing, and with my casting director's hat on I suggested that Susannah York would be perfect to play Julia, and Sacha Distel, the French heartthrob, to play Maurice. This role, probably because it was small, has usually been played by some lackadaisical nonentity, but it was, I thought, extremely important to the plot that if Susannah (Julia) and me (Jane) spent three quarters of the play extolling the virtues of this wonderful Frenchman with whom we were both secretly in love, by the time the audience sees him he should be sensational.

The adaptation for television worked well. Susannah and I had good chemistry together and Sacha Distel looked suitably stunning as the devastating Frenchman. It was screened in England over the Christmas holiday and received good reviews and ratings.

"*Soak the rich!*" screamed Chancellor of the Exchequer Denis Healey in the headlines of the British papers. "Tax them till they bleed. Squeeze them dry!"

It was too ominous for us. Ron, American born and living in Europe for over ten years, could not stay. He was now president of Warner Brothers Records in the U.K.

There was nothing for it but to escape from Healey's claws. I had worked hard all my life. The possessions I had accumulated—a house, furniture, a Mercedes, jewelry, some paintings and my collection of Art Deco objects and 1920s figures—would, it seemed, be subject to an immense wealth tax each year. The newspapers editorialized that England would lose much of its creative talent by this governmental blunder, but Mr. Healey was adamant. He wanted his last pound of flesh.

With astonishing alacrity, dozens of writers, directors, producers, sportsmen and actors left England. Many Americans, U.K. residents for years, were forced to leave also.

Nevertheless I fought tooth and nail not to leave. I was desolate. Destroyed. I couldn't *bear* the thought of packing up everything once more. Taking my children from the schools and friends to whom they had become so attached, and hitting the long and winding road to Hollywood, California—again.

I adored the house on Sheldon Avenue: I had been sublimely happy at last. Why did Ron, who knew that I had been striving to put down roots for so long, insist that we uproot ourselves yet *again* for California?

I wept for days as the impending inevitability of our departure approached. It was 1975 and I was shooting a horror movie called *The Devil*

Within Her, a sort of *Exorcist*-inspired thriller, which was later moderately successful in America.

I was gaining a toehold in the fading British film industry again. The day that Ron brought the final papers to me to be signed for the sale of Sheldon Avenue at lunch in the studios I rushed to my dressing room and wept for so long that the director was unable to shoot on me for several hours. All my deepest instincts, which I usually chose to ignore, screamed at me that this move to L.A. was a *major* mistake. But inexorably we had to leave. Off we went, transporting a houseful of furniture, children, the car and the clothes. I felt like a snail who carries its life on its back.

Ben Gary's prediction for me in 1961, seventeen years earlier, was accurate again: "You will *always* be a gypsy. You will strive to have roots, but you will constantly be on the move and have to keep on putting down new roots." It was in the stars. Could Ben, I wonder, see from his grave how accurate he had been about my entire life?

"You are amazingly resilient," he had said to me. "You will always adapt, and you will always adjust to what life has in store for you. You must always work. It is essential that you be involved and creative. Nothing will ever defeat you or depress you for long. You will always have the capacity to make money and you will eventually achieve happiness because you are basically a happy person and one of life's survivors."

◆*Twelve*◆

I WASN'T HAPPY LIVING in Hollywood again however—my third permanent move there in twenty years. We bought a vast modern house with a tennis court, marble floors and a mirrored bar on Chalette Drive in Trousdale, and I started decorating. I also started the thankless task of trying to get a job. To say there was little demand for my services was putting it mildly. Joan who? Oh, yes, she's been around awhile. Must be a bit long in the tooth by now. Well, let's take a look at her. Maybe we can use her in *something.* After all, she *was* a star. . . .

Although I had endured the normal amount of career rejection in the years between 1975 and 1977, I nevertheless managed to scrape by workwise, guest-starring on TV shows like "Baretta," "Mission Impossible," "Future Cop," "Switch," "Policewoman," "Space 1999" and even "Batman," where I donned silver lamé and played the role of "The Siren" whose piercing falsetto scales could stop her enemies and even Batman himself in their tracks.

It wasn't exactly rewarding creatively, but it helped to pay the bills. Ron's career was not doing so well. He had left his good job as president of Warner Brothers Records in London and was now the head of a new film company called Sagittarius.

Sagittarius was the brainchild of Edgar Bronfman, the heir to the Seagram whiskey millions. He had taken over as chairman of the board of MGM briefly in the early seventies. He had acquired a taste for show business and had been actively involved in a few film productions in England.

Edgar was a good-looking man in his mid-forties. He had been married for over twenty years, had five children, a taste for pretty women, and his own brand of whiskey. We all became jolly buddies, double-dating with Samantha Eggar, Sue Lloyd or whoever was his lady of the moment, jetting in the Seagram private Gulf Stream jet to San Francisco, New York or Acapulco, where Edgar had a villa.

He was also a Gemini. With all his *joie de vivre*, wicked humor and almost childlike enthusiasm for certain short-lived projects, he had his dark side too. Although incredibly wealthy, he could be amazingly stingy. He seemed paranoid that women might be interested in him only for his money and not himself—a prevalent attitude among many wealthy attractive men.

But this was by the by. Ron adored, practically worshipped, Edgar. Edgar became godfather to our daughter Katy, who was born on his birthday. I liked Edgar and enjoyed his company, but there was still something about him that I instinctively couldn't trust.

I started the Hollywood rounds again. I renewed old acquaintances, friendships and contacts. I knew practically everyone in Hollywood, having arrived as a green young starlet twenty years earlier.

I plunged into the decoration and renovation of Chalette Drive with enthusiasm and a limited budget, organized Tara, Sacha and Katy in new schools, made the odd TV appearance and went back to the little wife role.

Ron was working hard at his job with Sagittarius and taking trips with Edgar whenever Edgar wanted him to.

When Edgar's eldest son, Sam, Jr., was kidnapped, it was Ron who flew to New York and stayed by Edgar's side waiting for the phone to ring and for the kidnappers to tell Edgar where to deliver the ransom money. They were as close as two men can be, both as friends and business associates.

When Edgar asked Ron and me to give his second son, Edgar, Jr., his twenty-first-birthday party at our house, Ron agreed. I pointed out to Ron that Edgar knew very few people in Hollywood and that we were being used; however Ron insisted on a big Hollywood "bash" with as many socially acceptable producers, agents, stars as I could conjure up. The planning of this elaborate party went on for weeks.

I was helped by my friend Judy Bryer. I had known Judy since she came to work for Tony Newley in 1968. He was then preparing *Hieronymus Merkin*, and although she was working for him as his secretary, she and I quickly became friends. This friendship has become stronger through the years, and she is now my secretary, closest friend and confidante, as well as being my stand-in on "Dynasty." A regular Jill of all trades. Naturally, she's a Gemini.

I cherish the relationships I have had with my women friends. It has always been tremendously important to me to have at least two or three close female friends with whom I can share so many things. Men may come and go in one's life, but girlfriends last forever, and I consider myself very lucky to have several who are in my corner when the going gets tough—which is when the tough get going.

Sadly my lovely friend Cappy Badrutt succumbed to cancer early in 1981. It was a tragedy and a deep blow to me.

I was in charge of the organization and every detail of the Bronfman party from the guest list to the table placement, the flowers and decorations, to the choice of music the band would play. It was fun but I was concerned about the cost. Ron said Edgar had budgeted the party to cost five thousand dollars, which I knew was too low, and I told him that it would inevitably be closer to eight or ten thousand. Ron assured me that Edgar would foot the bill, but I wasn't thrilled about laying out large down payments to the tent people and the caterers out of my personal bank account. We certainly couldn't afford to give a party of this magnitude.

It was a warm May night and the guest list was sparkling: David Janssen and his wife, Dani, Audrey and Billy Wilder, Dionne Warwick, director Dick Donner, soon to do *Superman,* Janet and Freddie de Cordova, Tina Sinatra, Susan George, George Segal, and many others. It was certainly a terrific party, which went on past 2 A.M.—in Hollywood a major coup.

The next afternoon I was basking in my laurels as the hostess with the mostest. The phone had been ringing all day with congratulations, and thank-you flowers were arriving from the more well-mannered guests. It was six o'clock and time to help nanny Susan DeLong get the children fed and watered and ready for bed. Ron walked with a heavy tread into our green-and-white bedroom, slightly overdecorated with bowers of palm-tree wallpaper. "Edgar's fired me," he announced wearily, his face ashen.

I could not believe it. After weeks of preparation for Edgar's son's twenty-first birthday party, after years of friendship and business partnership, after shlepping our family across the Atlantic again, his boss had *fired* him. Just like that. It was unthinkable. But it was true.

Giving a new meaning to the word "cowardly," Edgar had sent Ron a "Dear John" letter. It was probably written while we were in the middle of the final preparations for the social event of the season. Ron at least deserved a confrontation face to face—man to man. But it was not to be. Edgar had paid Ron off to the end of the month, closed up the Sagittarius film offices on Sunset Boulevard and was incommunicado to both of us for over four years.

Katy regularly received a little gift and card on her birthday and at Christmas; since Edgar's birthday was the same as hers, and since she was his godchild, it seemed the least he could do. My instincts not to move to L.A. had been right all along. Now here we were stuck with a house with a giant mortgage, three children who had recently adjusted to new schools, and neither of us working.

I was bitterly resentful of Edgar Bronfman. I had never in my life been bitter and resentful toward anybody, but now the major breadwinner of the Kass family was out of work, thanks to him.

I don't think Ron ever fully recovered from the traumatic disappointment, pain and shock that Edgar caused him. Certainly this became a turning point in our up until now happy marriage.

"My marriage is a fiasco!" I said dramatically to Stuart Emory, conductor of the workshop for the exploration of human potential called "Actualizations." It was the time of "finding yourself" and I had gone to the Biltmore Hotel with Tina Sinatra, who was also considering leaving her husband, to try and find some answers.

We had been there fourteen hours a day for two days. Sitting on hard chairs, starving, dying for a cigarette, and watching eighty other confused and unhappy people get up onto the podium to reveal the misery and failure in their lives. It was an interesting experience. Listening to the pain that came from the hearts of so many lost souls, Tina and I considered ourselves lucky that really our only major problems were the men in our lives.

Eighty pairs of sympathetic eyes and ears watched and listened while I poured out my saga of woe. I *was* unhappy. Ron had changed. Subtly, but he was no longer the man I married. He was not working creatively, and money was a big problem. Living in L.A. was difficult. Because of our financial situation we had had to sell the house on Chalette Drive and move to another glass palace on Carolyn Way. With the profits we made on the sale we were thus, according to Ron, the controllers and doyens of our money matters—able to live in a style which we were used to. I was making around $2,500 a show, occasionally guesting on episodic TV, and for the odd ten or fifteen thousand, scooting off to Spain or Italy to star in some celluloid nonsense that I sincerely hoped would never see the light of day in either the U.S. or the U.K.

This was peanuts in terms of what I had been making. I had now been an actress for a quarter of a century but still had little to show for it in terms of savings. I knew I could have lived more simply and been happier had we only been able to move back to England and turn the clock back eighteen months. Before Edgar Bronfman entered our lives. But that was impossible.

Stuart Emory, all Australian charm and intelligence, smiled at me benevolently after I had finished my piece. "Don't you realize that your husband is surrounded by the barracudas and piranhas of the business?" he said pityingly. "Don't give up, Joan, he needs you. It's been a tough time for him. Stand by him, give him support—you'll both win in the end."

He waffled on. I listened, baffled and confused. The bottom line was that he was telling *me* to be patient, that Ron would come out of his Bronfman-induced decline, and that I must be more supportive and help him over his depression. What about *my* depression? Who was helping me over that? I was physically intact, if not even better than when I was younger. I was trying to live a normal family life in an environment I no longer had a taste for. My children were at school and growing up. Ron wasn't working. We had enormous financial drains upon us, not helped by his ex-wife, Anita, who had got her claws into a bunch of money from the sale of our house and was not about to let it go. She had three growing boys to support, Ron's sons, and although he had been paying her alimony and child support she wanted more. We had lawyers coming out of the woodwork, and creditors, too. It was sinister.

I had always read with fascinated horror the stories of famous actresses who ended up living in poverty or working as waitresses to support themselves. Lonely, unloved, unlucky. Had they given up? Believed the credo that after thirty-five it was all downhill from then on? I only knew that I was now going to have to fight like hell to try and resurrect my career and my personal life, not only for myself, but for Ron and my three children.

Two weeks later Tina Sinatra separated from her husband, and I made a major and far-reaching decision: to find a suitable commercial film property for myself and put the expertise I had gathered throughout the years into getting it financed and produced.

My sister, Jackie, had written a book called *The Stud*. It had become a best-seller in England and Europe. I persuaded her to let me have the film rights. I wanted to try to set it up as an independent film. I considered myself the right casting for the rich elegant socialite Fontaine, who sets up her "stud," Tony Blake, as the "greeter" in London's hottest disco, Hobo, and uses him for her own pleasure, sexual and otherwise. It was a modern, steamy, sexy premise, and one which I felt in my bones could be the commercial vehicle to put some juice in my career, which was going nowhere. *Saturday Night Fever* had just gone through the roof with its disco background and its sexuality. *The Stud* had the possibility to do, if not the same outstanding grosses, at least reasonably well.

Meanwhile I continued, albeit reluctantly, to "guest shot." The "Starsky and Hutch" gig had been the final blow.

"Want to do a 'Starsky and Hutch' in Hawaii for eight days?" It was my agent's voice on the phone, as I maneuvered the four-foot extension cord around the kitchen, and attended to the poached eggs on the point of overpoaching, the toast about to turn black and three children clamoring for breakfast.

"Starsky and Hutch" was one of the "top ten" TV shows of the previous season. Its two stars, David Soul and Paul Michael Glaser, were the current hunks of the moment. Thirteen-year-old Tara let out a whoop of joy when I told her I might do it.

"But I haven't read the script yet, Tara," I protested, shoveling hard, soggy eggs onto blackened toast.

"Oh, Mummy, you must do it, you *must*. Maybe I'll get to meet David Soul! Oh, wow!"

"That's not the reason I would do the show—so *you* could meet David Soul," I said firmly. "I'll let you know if I'm going to do it when I've read the script, darling." This of course was a white lie—I would have to do it because we needed the money.

The script turned out to be a rather chauvinistic, slightly amusing story to be shot in Hawaii. Thick with voodoo, witch doctors and gorgeous gals, it was typical TV fodder.

I sighed—but a buck was a buck was a buck—and I was still trying hard to get *The Stud* financed.

So, in the summer of 1976 I went to Hawaii to film the two-hour episode. Paul Michael Glaser was sitting on the lawn of the location paradise we were shooting in. Palm trees waved and lush tropical plants shimmered in the hazy morning heat. He was absorbed in his script, and, although wearing an outrageously unflattering outfit of baggy Bermuda shorts, cheap printed Hawaiian shirt, red ankle socks and tennis shoes and an Andy Capp cap, he managed to look charismatic. He had a slight look about him of Charlie Chaplin and Tony Newley.

In Hawaii at the hotel Hawaii Surf sat Peter Borsari, a photographer. He was gloomily bemoaning the fact that he had been sent by the *National Enquirer* to do a story on Glaser and Soul, but they had refused.

"They are so into the vork," moaned Peter gloomily, in his Hungarian accent. "Vork, vork, vork, that's all they care about . . . no pictures, no interviews, nothing. They'd do it for the glossies—*People* or *Cosmopolitan* they'd do—but not the *Enquirer*."

I commiserated, little realizing that within five years I would be in Glaser and Soul's position vis-à-vis the tabloids and the more prestigious media. Right now, though, to get my photo in the *National Enquirer* would have been a major event.

That night at a cocktail party for the cast and crew at the hotel, I felt mature and overdressed. "We're too old to be part of this group," I joked to Samantha Eggar, who'd been cast as Charlotte. "No one's over twenty-three." David Soul joined us: tall, blond and tanned, he wore glasses and chain-smoked Marlboros. He shook his head at the army of girls parading up and down and being ogled by the crew.

"After all the effort and care Paul and I have put in trying to make this show a success, now we're doing a tits-and-ass piece," he murmured sadly.

On the first day of shooting we drove through spectacular scenery. The location was probably the most beautiful I've ever seen: an estate of over a hundred acres of lush tropical jungle garden with foliage and trees that looked as if they'd existed for two thousand years, and probably had.

The crew were setting up a scene in which Starsky and Hutch, as trespassers, were attacked by several fierce Alsatian dogs. I recalled that Paul and I had met briefly at Pinewood Studios four or five years ago when he was making *Fiddler on the Roof* and I was guesting in "The Persuaders."

"Yes! You were sitting with Roger Moore and Topol brought me over and introduced me to you, right?" I remembered that at the time I thought he had magnetic eyes.

In a coral strapless silk dress with a tropical flower behind one ear, I was handed a gun by the prop man. I asked Paul to show me how to hold it. I've often had to work with guns and I hate them—I always have the feeling a real bullet might have been left in.

I am always nervous on the first day of anything. It seems ridiculous, but I'm comforted by the thought that Laurence Olivier often feels like throwing up before a performance. Since he is also a Gemini, I feel it's a good omen.

Miss Patti, Playmate of the Month, was ensconced in a chair with "Guest Star" emblazoned on it. Hairdressers and makeup men hover. She is queening it—why not? Someone seems to have ordered the star treatment for this lady. She asks me how old I am—a question I feel should never be asked of anyone over twenty-one. I ask her to guess. She surmises thirty-five. "Around there," I reply airily. "How old are you?"

"Twenty-five," says she.

"Oh, you look younger."

"Good," she says.

A lot of the girls and crew keep telling me condescendingly how good I look, as though anyone over thirty-five is a candidate for the mortician's parlor.

Both Samantha and I asked for canvas chairs but there were none. Once Bunnies appeared, however, chairs sprouted like broccoli.

My dressing room, a two-by-three-foot space, was occupied by Debbie, who rather huffily said that there was no room for her and so the wardrobe girl put her in with me. Her clothes and makeup were strewn all over my clothes and makeup.

The wardrobe girl apologized. It's a SAG rule that leading actors do not share dressing rooms with bit players, and she promised she would move Debbie.

I felt depressed and unable to get over this feeling of really hitting bottom careerwise.

The perils of "Starsky and Hutch" were relived off the set, too. Arriving at muddy, swampy, cold and rainy locations to shoot runaway scenes in the car with the boys and the actor playing my father, everyone was uptight because of the weather.

In the car, Paul drove with my on-screen father in front, David, me and a wheelchair squashed in the back. We drove fast through gates that are supposed to burst open on impact. Three Jeeps filled with yelling stunt men pursue us hotly.

Take 2: Paul skids and we almost turn over as we plummet into a ditch. The crew rush up to see if we're OK. Charlie Picerne, the stunt coordinator, screamed angrily at Paul. "What the fuck do you think you're doing, for Christ's sake?" He was furious; Paul was furious.

Another scene: I'm in the car and the gun I'm holding inadvertently goes off when Paul swerves to avoid a truck. I horrifiedly point it at David's gut, then realizing what I've done, throw it out of the window. A print, but . . . "what's wrong?" asks David, seeing a look of alarm cross my face.

"I think a boob came out when I threw the gun!" I said.

"As long as we didn't see any nipple," says Paul. We ask. The camera is rigged to the car so no one is sure. We think it's OK. Nipples are a no-no on network TV.

Oh, the perils of TV stardom: At the base camp, as David sits reading his script, a lady tourist comes up and asks him wheedlingly if she can take a photograph. A crowd has gathered instantly, as we're on a main road. He politely says no. She insists. "It's for my daughter. Please." He tells her if he poses for her he'll have to pose for everyone else, and he's studying. She is pushy. He yells at her. She laughs and takes his photo anyway, while he's yelling. "Oh, my daughter will love it, she'll just love it," she cackles. David sighs. I don't envy him.

The perils of stunt men: Down on the pier, I climb into a camera boat with the crew, Samantha, Paul and David. All of us are festooned with cameras as this is going to indeed be a stunt worthy of a feature film.

Anticipation and excitement are in the air as the two camera boats position themselves. This stunt can only be filmed once.

After an hour of suspenseful waiting the director cries "Action." The black Cadillac comes speeding down the coast highway at what I consider an excessive speed of forty-five miles per hour. It drives up fast onto a specially constructed small ramp. I hear a laconic grip remark, "It'll never hold up," and over into the murky green water, head first, fall four doubles dressed as Starsky, Hutch, me and my father. There is a gasp from all on board. The car is supposed to land flat on the water and sink. It has been specially weighted for such an effect, but with stunts anything can happen.

But soon four little heads appear. Everyone bursts into spontaneous applause and cheers as they realize the stunt was successful.

Candy, my double, told me to be careful of "our" dress. Hers had come off completely in the water, leaving her topless. I told the wardrobe girl.

Her attitude was nonchalant. "Nothing we can do. You worry about such silly things," she sniffed. Ah, the caring attitude of TV people. It wasn't important that the dress I had put on had shrunk from cleaning and was now four inches above my knees. "It'll never show," she said, bored to tears by it all. Brought up as I was in an era when every detail of an actress's wardrobe was of immense importance, I found it appalling that the matter of a skirt length's being five inches out of whack was inconsequential to her. God, I hated TV. I vowed this would be my last episodic guest shot.

I prepared for the "wet" scene. We were in the middle of the ocean, shooting the scene following the car stunt, our characters having just been rescued from the ocean depths.

For three hours we sat in the boat, soaking wet. I had cleverly left my makeup ashore. It was baking hot. We filmed my final close-ups with me teary and bleary-eyed, sunbaked, makeup-less, my dress falling precariously every time I moved.

My shoulders were in an agony of sunburn. I requested some towels but they never arrived. Sunburned and soaking wet, we finally raced back to shore, arriving at the wharf to find the whole crew gone, and not a towel in sight. Stoically dripping, I walked barefoot the five hundred yards to my trailer, a bedraggled wreck. My enemy, the wardrobe girl, handed me a small towel. Silently I thanked her. It was time to move on in life.

Ron was now involved with Peter and Burt Kameron in a production company called Triple K; they had all invested money in it but Ron was not bringing home the bacon. Although Tony Newley was paying me $1,250 a month for Tara and Sacha, that was not enough to support them. We considered selling the house on Carolyn Way and moving to the Valley. This would mean the kids changing schools *again*.

I had, by lying vehemently about my age by ten years, fought for, and got, the part of the glamorous call girl, Avril, in NBC's big miniseries "The Moneychangers" with Kirk Douglas and Christopher Plummer. For this I had been paid the magnificent sum of five thousand dollars. I was considered lucky to have got it. True, true—I was. Hollywood was not noted for its benevolence toward actresses over thirty unless they were into character roles. See the over-thirty-fives dressed too cute and young at restaurants and parties, desperately trying to turn back the clock.

Looking objectively at the rushes of "The Moneychangers," and also in my mirror, always situated in the harshest northern light possible, I saw a woman who could pass for twenty-eight but was in fact past forty.

After the "Starsky and Hutch" gig, when Samantha Eggar suggested I should apply for unemployment benefits I was shocked. "I've seen Rudy Vallee there," said Judy Bryer. "Many actors go. You're entitled to it, after all. You've paid all your taxes and contributions." Thus persuaded, but dubious, I reluctantly set out one sunny afternoon in 1976 in my gold Mercedes to the Department of Unemployment on Santa Monica Boulevard. Judy had suggested I go there rather than the office in Hollywood, so that I wouldn't be recognized.

I wasn't keen to go at all. I had been a working actress for over twenty years now and it seemed somewhat an anticlimax, to say the least, to be on the dole. Not how I had foreseen my life at all. No way. I hadn't really wanted to be dripping with diamonds, sables and Ferraris; on the other hand, I loathed the state of constantly hovering on the brink of serious financial problems.

I had just been the hostess at the opening of a new English boutique on Sunset Boulevard. My Mercedes overflowed with flowers. I was wearing an expensive chiffon dress, a matching turban and a few gold and diamond trinkets. I tore off the turban and stuffed the jewels in my purse after I hit Sunset Boulevard to the fond farewells of my friends and the paparazzi. Putting an old trench coat over the four-hundred-dollar chiffon, a creased scarf on my head and a pair of *extremely* dark shades over my eyes, I pulled the Mercedes into the unemployment office parking lot, next to a battered '64 Chevy.

I stood in a slow-moving line for forty-five minutes trying to look as nondescript as possible. In Charles Jourdan shoes and with two inches of expensive flowered chiffon peeping out from beneath the raincoat, I realized I looked slightly out of place, to say the least. Most of the people standing around were Hispanic or black, and they seemed as if they definitely could use the money. No one looked like an actress just popping down to the dole so she could afford to pay the maid. I began to feel guilty.

"Name?" asked the bored, gum-chewing clerk when I finally reached her desk. "Er, Kass—Joan—er, Kass," I whispered nervously, hoping that two Puerto Rican gentlemen eyeing me from behind and discussing my merits in Spanish, of which I knew a smattering, couldn't hear me.

"Maiden name?"

"Collins," I croaked conspiratorially. Rivulets of sweat ran down my back. It was 93 degrees—hardly the weather for Aquascutum raincoats.

"Joan Collins?" shrieked the desk clerk with suspicious delight. "Didn't you used to be her?"

"Yes," I mumbled, silently cursing Samantha, who had sent me on this little trip with airy assurances of how easy it would be. "I still am her," I muttered ungrammatically, aware of the slight buzz of excitement emanating from the queue behind me.

"I just saw you on 'Policewoman' last week," yelled the clerk with unbounded glee. "What are you doing down *here?* Aren't you working?"

"Hey, Debbie," she called excitedly to her co-worker. "Hey, Debbie, look, it's Joan Collins!"

"Joan who?" said Debbie, peering at me. I pulled up my collar to hide my face, now crimson with embarrassment.

"No, I'm not working at the moment," I replied with as much dignity as I could muster, aware of the entire roomful of people now riveted to the little scenario unfolding before them. It was probably pretty dull standing in line down at the Santa Monica unemployment office every week.

"Er, things are a bit slow now—I'm resting," I explained, using the actor's timeless euphemism. Twenty pairs of eyes and ears clocked the action. A few more embarrassing questions were fired at me. Had I been trying to get a job? Yes—my agent had started refusing my calls, pretending he wasn't in. I knew the ploy. I used to do it with my father when he had a performer he wanted to avoid. "Tell so-and-so I'm out," he'd hiss as I answered the telephone and dutifully lisped, "No, Daddy's out and I don't know where he is," to some anxious singer or clown desperate for work.

Other questions. Had I tried getting another job other than acting in the six weeks I'd been out of work? Well, no. Waiting on tables was not my style, and I couldn't type worth a damn. Eventually I escaped. Humiliated and clutching not the $120 I had expected, but a chit that entitled me to that amount two weeks later when the Department of Unemployment had checked me out with Social Security—thoroughly.

"Can I have your autograph, please?" asked a small black boy as I opened my steaming car, now filled with the scent of a hundred flowers dying for a drink. I signed and fled.

Wending my way through the Santa Monica traffic toward the charming but at this moment heavily mortgaged home in Beverly Hills, I made a vow. I would never get myself in this situation again. I *must* work. If I couldn't cut it as an actor, then I would write or do interior decoration. I couldn't abide the humiliation of receiving a handout. I had started modeling at sixteen so I wouldn't ever have to ask my father for money; I had certainly never asked for any from my husbands. I had to succeed now by myself. I couldn't accept that this was to be the way my career would end.

To hell with my agent. He didn't give a damn whether I worked or not. A hundred other actresses were in his stable. It was all up to *me*. No one was going to extend their efforts on my behalf. I had to be the mistress of my destiny. If I didn't want to be broke, I had to pull my finger out and start thinking of a suitable project for myself. A viable and commercial project that would ensure my future as well as my children's. And *The Stud* was the catalyst.

If I thought I had been rejected as an actress, it was nothing to the rejection I received as a producer trying to get financing for *The Stud*. Producers I had known all my life turned me down flat. Lew Grade, Nat Cohen, Plitt Theatre Chain, Sam Arkoff . . . the list went on, but I persevered.

I convinced Jackie to write her first script from the book. It was good. It was hot and it was right for today's market. I knew, I just *knew* in my bones that if I could get it made, it would not only reactivate my career but could be a commercial success as well.

I was shlepping *The Stud* all over on both coasts, but I still needed a job. I got one. More than I bargained for, to say the least. *Empire of the Ants,* An H. G. Wells classic (so they said), to be shot in Florida.

This was physically the most difficult picture I had ever done. The Florida swamps in November are dirty, dark and dank—infested with crocodiles, rats and other creepy crawlies too unspeakable to think about. But we needed money, so off I trotted, along with Robert Lansing, Jacqueline Scott, Robert Pine, John David Carson, Albert Salmi, and nine or ten six-foot plastic ants, the brainchildren of Mr. Bert I. Gordon, our director.

The story of a group of people trapped on a remote Florida island infested by giant man-eating ants who stalk their hapless victims one by one and then devour them was not going to win any of us Oscars. In fact it seemed more of a certainty that this film would guarantee none of us would ever get a job again—such was the quality of the story, script and direction. As it eventually turned out, most of us went on to rather better things: Bob Lansing to star opposite Elizabeth Taylor in *The Little Foxes,*

Robert Pine to play a continuing role in "Chips." But in November of 1976 we considered ourselves lucky to be working at all.

After a week of slogging through the swamps, sometimes knee-high in slimy water and freezing weather, we were all thoroughly fed up. The only way we could go to the loo was if one of the principal ladies (i.e., Jackie or me) insisted on it. A motorboat would whisk us from the swamps to the mainland, wait, then whisk us back to where we were shooting again.

We became so irritated by this that with much coercing from the cast —who persuaded me that *I* make the demand since I was the so-called "star" of this epic—we insisted on having a portable loo on the huge open camera barge that was our headquarters while shooting. Several days later it arrived. And there it sat in all its glory on the barge . . . no doors, no privacy. It caused much hilarity, and after a bit more yelling and screaming by Jackie and me a makeshift curtain was encircled around it—but we still preferred the speedboat ride back to the mainland to using it.

One windy morning, the wind almost hurricane-like in its intensity, I left the motel at 6 A.M. to go to the location. The door of the unit station wagon was held open for me by one of the many teamsters we had on the crew, but he let it go as soon as I entered the car. The wind slammed the door shut into my face with hurricane ferocity. Blood gushed from my eye and I screamed for help, but no one could hear. My teamster friend had disappeared, it was pitch-dark and the wind was blowing at seventy miles per hour.

Eventually I wrestled open the door and staggered into the lobby of the motel where some of the cast and crew were assembled. Someone screamed.

I was a sight straight from one of the more gruesome horror movies I'd had the pleasure of starring in. Blood was pouring from a gash in my eyebrow. It had already become a bump the size of an egg. How I wasn't killed or brain-damaged by the force of the door was a miracle. I was left with an unsightly black-and-blue eye that took the makeup department half an hour to conceal. And they were unable to shoot on me other than in extreme long shots for four days.

I was not thrilled to be told one day that since our stunt doubles hadn't arrived from L.A., we were to do the canoe-capsizing stunt ourselves. I was horrified, in fact.

"We're putting stunt people out of work," I expostulated to the director, ever mindful of Gene Kelly's warning some years before.

Bert Gordon poo-poohed my fears, intimating I was a bad sport, difficult and uncooperative. Since the rest of the cast seemed resigned to their fate, I had no choice but to go along with it or be called a first-class prima donna bitch and therefore lessen my chances of ever doing another horror flick for A.I.P. again.

I took off my knee-high boots and threw them to the wardrobe girl, safe on the security of the big barge. One or two crocodiles still lurked at the edge of the swamp in spite of the prop men's having fired blanks from their rifles to frighten them away, and the crew's using them as target practice by aiming their midmorning bagels at the sinister greenish-black hulks.

"Action!" yelled Bert. Two frogmen crouched under the raft, pushed it over, completely capsizing it, and four petrified actors fell into the swamp. The water was absolutely disgusting, foul green slime. It probably hadn't moved in two thousand years and it was thick and warmish. I tried to keep my head above the loathsome liquid while acting convincingly terrified. I swam as fast as possible to the sanctuary of the camera barge. Under the water my legs and feet became entangled in the submerged giant roots of a swamp plant. I thought of swamp snakes and kicked with all my might, trying to untangle my legs from this moving mass of God knows what. I crawled onto the barge like a beached whale, blood oozing from at least a dozen cuts on my legs and from a gash over my eye. I'd swallowed some of the putrid water and felt definitely ill.

The makeup people immediately poured bottles and bottles of pure distilled water over us, and produced eyedrops, eardrops, nosedrops and throat spray, which they insisted we use immediately. The motor launch arrived promptly to rush us to a nearby hotel; we were told to shower *immediately* we got there. The women were given douche kits by the nurse and instructed to use them. "That water is a major health hazard," said the nurse, busily trying to patch up my legs as the launch carried us, wet and shaking, to safety. "You could get serious infections from it. I told them not to let you all go in. They wouldn't listen."

Within two days the cuts on my legs started festering. Some looked so bad I joked I was getting gangrene, but it wasn't fun. We still had three weeks of shooting left, like it or not.

Each day the wounds on my legs were dressed and bandaged. On top of the bandages were tied brown plastic garbage bags, attached with camera tape, which was wrapped round and round my legs until they looked mummified; and over these, the tan leather boots. I looked and felt a wreck, convinced I was scarred for life, and was never so delighted and relieved as when the last day of shooting arrived and it was finally my turn to be asphyxiated by the giant queen ant. Six cast members had already gone to the big anthill in the sky; only four of us were left.

We had miserably spent both Thanksgiving and Christmas in this hellhole, and were desperate to get out and back to L.A. for New Year's Eve.

We were shooting in a sugar refinery in a tiny town in Florida. The smell of the cane being melted was so strong and sickening that everyone wore masks the entire time we weren't actually shooting.

By now I had been turned into a zombie "ant robot" by some forgettable plot twist and was standing in line at the kiosk where the queen ant was to blow her magic breath on me so I would become even more of a zombie and do her ant bidding. As I stood face to face with this ludicrous creature, Robert Lansing burst in with guns blazing and a flare. The ant expired and fell on top of me, exuding lethal ant gas. How would Alexis have coped? I have sometimes asked myself.

The sight of this grotesque papier-mâché insect face and flaying tentacle legs—which were actually attached to moving sticks held by prop men—was so hilarious that every time I had to expire with the giant ant on top of me I burst into gales of giggles, which quickly subsided when Mr. Gordon said if I didn't stop we wouldn't get out of Florida until January 2. Perish the thought!

And that, I am happy to say, was my last horror picture. At least in terms of ants.

Wherever I went, there went the script of *The Stud*, becoming more dog-eared and worn every day.

It was at the Cannes festival in May of 1977, where I had gone at the request of A.I.P. to promote *Empire of the Ants*—and finding little that was noteworthy to say about it—that I finally struck oil.

I was seated at Hilda and Sam Arkoff's annual luncheon at the Carlton Hotel next to a man who Hilda told me was a distributor of B flicks in England, interested in getting into full-time production. A likely prospect, thought I.

I tentatively offered my by now slick opening ploy. "Would you be interested in making a commercial movie from my sister Jackie's best-selling novel *The Stud* with a disco theme and erotic love scenes, etc., etc. . . . ." I droned on enthusiastically. I knew these words by rote now.

"As a matter of fact, I would. That's just the kind of movie we're interested in producing," said burly George Walker, ex-boxer and now head of Brent-Walker.

"Have you got a script?"

"Just happen to have it at my hotel, the Majestic, next door." I smiled as sweetly as I could. "Would you like to read it?"

"Yes," said Mr. Walker. "Can you come to dinner at the villa tomorrow night and we can discuss it then?"

"I think I'm free," I murmured, barely containing my enthusiasm.

Within a week the project was set. Brent-Walker loved it. No fools they. They wanted to start shooting within two or three months. Ron and Oscar Lerman, Jackie's husband, would co-produce. I would star, with the proviso I do some tasteful nudity. Yes, I could do that. I'd done it in Italy already. This was no longer the dark ages. Look at Diane Keaton in *Looking for Mr. Goodbar*, Jane Fonda in *Barbarella*, Glenda Jackson in *Women in Love* and dozens more. Actresses of far greater stature than I had stripped to the buff for films. It was even becoming rather boring. Certainly no big deal as far as affecting their careers was concerned.

I thought the sex and eroticism would sell the movie. So did Ron. So did Brent-Walker. A vast publicity campaign masterminded by Ron started in England. "Over forty and she takes her clothes off!" screamed Fleet Street in fascinated frenzy. I decided I wouldn't let it bother me, although it seemed the press picked on me constantly. We had supposedly finished with racism and sexism. Now I thought it was time to end ageism.

I knew how I looked (objective I always was). What was this barrier about being over forty? Did over forty have to mean over the hill? Not in my book it didn't. And not in the book of the man in the street in England either. *The Stud* became a giant success in England—the biggest British moneymaker other than the Bond films for years.

I became a household name, face and body in Britain yet again, although I was still virtually unknown in the States, my early films forgotten, thank goodness.

Since my aspirations to become a "star" had always been minimal, this wasn't of too much concern. What was of concern to me was that my personal life was falling apart again.

Although Ron and I were residents of the States and had again traded in our glass-and-chrome modern Italian house on Carolyn Way for a mock Tudor mansion in Beverly Hills, I had been forced to spend a lot of time in England, shooting and promoting *The Stud*. Katy, at five, was at a stage in her schooling that presented no problem in switching to a British school. However, Tara and Sacha at fourteen and eleven were at a more difficult stage of their education. I did not want them to leave their California schools and change to English ones just because this was where my bread, careerwise, was suddenly being buttered. Tony and I discussed this amicably. We decided that Tara and Sacha should stay with him and his new wife and child while I was working in England.

The children decided that life at the Newleys' was more settled than life at the Kasses' and opted for living permanently with Tony. This caused me much heartache. I adored my children, even if I was not the "typical mum." I believed in the quality of my time with them and not the quantity. I could have said "Forget it" to my new career, but unfortunately I was becoming the breadwinner in our family, and apart from the fact that I was enjoying my work, it was now an absolute financial necessity that I continue it.

And so I did. Back to California for a highly forgettable movie called *Zero to 60* with Darren McGavin—off to South Africa and an even more forgettable one with Richard Harris called *Game for Vultures*, with a script so full of complications that none of us understood it at all. Since "Fallen Angels" had been quite a hit on Anglia TV, Sir John Woolf, the head of the company, asked me to appear in one of the anthology series they were currently making. Called "Roald Dahl's Tales of the Unexpected," they were dramatized half-hour versions of some of Dahl's cleverest short stories. Dahl was an expert storyteller, his tales always ending with a macabre or ironic twist of fate. I was asked to star in "Neck," the story of a glamorous, ruthless aristocrat married to a bumbling fool whom she cuckolds with various handsome young men who come to their grand country manor for weekend visits. The only person who has the slightest control over her is the butler Jelkes, played by Sir John Gielgud.

I was delighted at this casting. I had been an admirer of John Gielgud's since my student days at RADA, when three of the most promising students had been selected to visit Sir John and Pamela Brown at the Queen's Theatre where they were appearing in Jean Anouilh's *The Lady's Not for Burning*. After a few days of shooting on "Neck" I reminded Sir John about this meeting—I had been one of the students chosen—but, understandably, he did not recall what had been a red-letter day in my student life.

Sir John, as the cast deferentially referred to him, was exceedingly charming and witty, with exquisite manners and the ability to recall in minute detail the most interesting anecdotes about every actor and actress he had ever worked with. Since this was 1978 and he had started his career in the 1920s, he had fifty years of memories with which to regale us. "Neck" was directed by Christopher Miles, brother of Sarah, and also starred Michael Aldridge, Peter Bowles and a young actor called Paul Herzberg, who so admired Gielgud that he kept a small notebook into which he inscribed Sir John's every bon mot.

Although we were shooting at Greystone Manor, a stately home in the midst of the Norfolk countryside, we were staying at the rather tacky English seaside resort of Great Yarmouth in a small beachfront hotel.

My first meeting with Sir John took place one windy fall morning in the unit car outside the hotel, just across the road from the amusement pier. Cockney mums and dads in beach gear with assorted children and dogs and buckets and spades and picnic baskets struggled down to the beach, oblivious to the great actor who sat in solitary splendor smoking cigarettes in the front seat of the car.

"Good morning," I mumbled shyly, falling into the back seat, a morning wreck as usual in faded jeans and T-shirt.

"Good morning, my dear," he twinkled, turning his head around and extending a well-manicured hand. He was dressed impeccably in that elegant but slightly faded style that becomes actors of the old school. Gray flannel trousers, highly polished shoes—years old, but obviously of the best quality—a tattersall shirt, tie, pullover and a good tweed jacket. Elegant. So unlike most of the actors with whom I've worked, who usually look like slobs in the A.M. Never at my best at the crack of dawn, I tried to keep up my end of the conversation during the twenty-minute ride to Greystone Manor. He, unfazed by my mumbles and ineffectual chat, told several amusing anecdotes, culminating in a Noel Coward-ish "Very flat, Norfolk," when I remarked at the prettiness of the surrounding countryside. I enjoyed his company, and our off-set chats which, as long as they were not too early in the morning, were extremely stimulating.

One day a reporter was interviewing me—it was a beautiful, mild autumn day and we were seated in canvas chairs in the garden of the manor. The journalist asked the usual boringly predictable questions, finishing off with his *pièce de résistance,* "So how old are you *really,* Miss Collins? We never seem to read the same age twice for you in the papers."

At this point, Gielgud, who had been reading *The Times,* peered at the journalist frostily over his spectacles and in biting tones informed him, "Never ever ask any lady over twenty-five, particularly an actress, how old she is, young man."

"Why not, *sir?*" asked the hack sarcastically.

"In my day," said Sir John reprovingly, "it was considered unutterably bad manners to even *discuss* a lady's age, let alone ask *her* about it. How do you think the great actresses of the past could have played Juliet, Ophelia or indeed any of the heroines or leading roles had the public known that they were over thirty, forty—sometimes even fifty? Illusion, young man, illusion. The public should never know too much about an actor or an actress."

The reporter slunk away, chastened, and I thanked Sir John for his support. Considering the negative attitudes associated with age, I always believed that an actress should have the right of privacy on that subject. If an actress looks twenty-five but is in fact thirty-five, there is no reason why she should *have* to play the latter age on screen. Unfortunately, with the press and public mania for knowing ages, this becomes almost impossible nowadays.

Gielgud also gave me some insight into an actor's ability to project other areas of himself. I had given him a copy of a script I was interested in doing, asking him to read the part of a retired Italian gardener living in a home for old men. He returned the script to me, regretfully declining the part on the grounds that it was too much of a stretch for him to be believable in the part.

"But you're such a marvelous actor, you can play any part," I exclaimed.

"Not true, my dear. Look at my hands. They are not the hands of an ex-gardener." I looked at them. They were definitely upmarket hands. "Ralph Richardson could play this part very well," he said. "He could look like a gardener."

"I could play a *gentleman* fallen on hard times, of course—but you must remember that usually an actor is the victim of his or her own physicality, and one must take this into account when choosing the roles one does or does not accept."

I nodded. He continued, "You, for example, could never play an unattractive woman, because you bring to every role your physical presence and it would be difficult for you to play against that, unless you used a great amount of makeup and costumes to disguise the fact."

It was not until four years later that I finally had the chance to get away from my usual physical image when I played the wicked old witch in Showtime's "Faerie Tale Theatre" production "Hansel and Gretel."

And then came *The Bitch*. Whenever I'm asked if I've ever had any regrets in my life—which I don't—the one that might possibly come to mind is why, oh why, did they give it that damn-awful exploitive title, which stuck to me like flypaper through the popular English press for years.

I begged Brent-Walker not to use the title. Cajoled and pleaded to no avail. *The Stud* had skyrocketed—*The Bitch* should do even better. They were wrong.

Made in 1978, a year after *The Stud*, *The Bitch* was a washed-out carbon copy. In their eagerness to reap more financial goodies at the box office, Brent-Walker went into production with an unsatisfactory and, in fact, unfinished script, an unknown Italian leading man whose voice was so weak that he had to be entirely dubbed, and a mediocre director. My wardrobe wasn't even finished.

Ron and Oscar were again the producers. I pleaded with Ron not to start the film before some more work had been done on the script, which it needed desperately—but even he couldn't prevail on Brent-Walker to either change the title or alter the script. They controlled the purse strings and the creative product. And George Walker had been known to yell "Fuck creativity—that doesn't sell tickets. Tits and ass do!"

Ron was certainly an expert persuader. We had many screaming fights about what I considered unnecessary nude scenes for *The Stud* and *The Bitch*. Film nudity was OK by me in certain instances, but not when it was so deviously gratuitous. But he couldn't sway big beefy George.

There had originally been a clause in my contract for *The Stud* to shoot a sequel if Brent-Walker wanted to, but I was extremely unhappy about it. I knew I had exploited myself in *The Stud*, but I had always felt that with a couple of exceptions the film had been done with a certain amount of taste and was certainly entertaining. It captured a part of the late seventies disco scene in London as well as saying a goodly piece about women and their sexuality. One of the reasons *The Stud* was both highly successful and highly controversial was that Fontaine thought like a man, and she used men in the way men had been using women for years. But *The Bitch* was gross exploitation. It did me no good at all, and in fact my name became the butt of many a TV comedian's jokes.

I sat next to Kirk Douglas on the Brent-Walker yacht in Cannes. It was May 1979, festival time again. A light aircraft was trailing a banner all over the Côte d'Azur: "JOAN COLLINS *Is* THE BITCH," it proclaimed, puffs of little white smoke trailing it.

"You made it, kid. That means you're a star," said Kirk, whom I had known since I arrived in Hollywood.

"Oh, Kirk, I think it should say 'Joan Collins *as* The Bitch,'" I protested. "I hate the stigma of 'Bitch.' It's really degrading. After all, how would you like to see 'Kirk Douglas *Is* the Murderer,' for example?"

He thought about this and agreed that perhaps I did have a point. A point, yes—clout with Brent-Walker, no. And they still owed us all money from *The Stud*.

To the outside world I had everything. A handsome loving husband, three beautiful children, career success and money. But there was trouble in my paradise.

I had suspected for some time that Ron had been taking some kind of drugs. His moods changed drastically. Sometimes he wouldn't eat dinner or stop fidgeting during mealtimes. He often stayed up until dawn and then slept all through the day.

I was aghast. A close friend's husband had wrecked his life and almost hers through his abuse of drugs. I had a healthy fear of them. In fact, I loathed and detested any kind of drug taking, and I found people who depended upon them weak and stupid.

I had instilled in my children from an early age the horror that drugs can bring to people's lives. There is no question that they wreck. They ruin. They destroy.

I had vaguely sniffed some white powder at a party in St. Tropez in the sixties, had become high as a kite, and had a post-nasal drip for three weeks. That was the first and last time I would ever try *that*.

I'd also puffed once or twice on the odd joint passed around at parties, but I thought the whole business was infantile. I preferred to be in control of myself. The crazy blurred feeling of fake pleasure and happiness that a drug high gives was not my scene.

I had been upset about Tara and Sacha living with Tony. I missed them terribly. I had expressed my feelings to Ron, who had been sympathetic and understanding. Sometimes I wept for hours. I was embarrassed at the British press's attitude toward me because of my nudity in *The Stud*. It hurt. I didn't understand their mixture of sarcastic bitchiness and grudging admiration.

What about *my* pressure and stress? I wasn't about to let anyone other than my closest friends know what hell I was living through.

I was now a reasonably hot property in Great Britain, so when I was approached by the prestigious Chichester Festival Arts Theatre to do a summer season there I was flattered and delighted. The theater had been in abeyance in my life for too long, and although it had always been my desire to be back on stage again, nevertheless it was difficult to be accepted, particularly since my media image was so controversial now.

The play was *The Last of Mrs. Cheyney*, a frothy 1920s light comedy by Frederick Lonsdale, originally a *tour de force* for Gladys Cooper. Simon Williams, an excellent light-comedy actor, was to play Lord Dilling, the romantic lead, and a distinguished cast gathered one dank February day in 1980 in the grimy rehearsal rooms in Shepherds Bush for the first read-through. I was filled with trepidation. These were all respected West End actors with years of stage experience behind them. I was a "film star." God forbid they believed I was a bitch, too. Oh, that epithet —how it stuck. "Film star" usually meant you couldn't act, either.

I hadn't performed on the stage since I was nineteen. It was a terrifying challenge, but one I was determined to conquer.

Several of my movie actor friends were astonished that I was taking this potentially dangerous career step. I was asking for trouble from the critics—no doubt waiting gleefully, pens poised, filled with vitriol for my performance whether it be good, bad or indifferent. "The Bitch" performing at Chichester. Some had started sniggering already.

Roger Moore couldn't understand why I would put myself in such a vulnerable position now that my movie career in England was bubbling again. But I realized that my days as a "movie star" were numbered. I wanted acceptance now as an actress. This is what I had started out by wanting. Now, thanks to the dubious distinctions of *The Stud* and *The Bitch*, I was going to be able to fulfill my ambition and, hopefully, stay on the stage forever.

That early summer of 1980 was one of the happiest for ages. Tara and

Sacha had returned to live with us. Katy was doing fabulously at school. Ron was working on various development deals for me, with himself producing. I was working at the beautiful Chichester Festival Theatre, which was challenging and exciting at the same time. *The Last of Mrs. Cheyney* was sold out for practically every performance. We were the Festival's biggest hit since John Gielgud had played there nineteen years previously.

Grudgingly it was admitted by most critics that I could act a bit. I was playing a reasonably nice woman—not a bitch, not a vamp, not a sexpot. Some found it odd I could play a role like that believably.

Because of the huge success of *Mrs. Cheyney* at Chichester, Triumph Productions decided to mount a West End production, which they wanted more lavish and more beautifully dressed than the Chichester production. The fabled ninety-year-old designer, Erté (Romain de Tirtoff) agreed to do my costumes. After a lifetime fascination with his work, I was thrilled; but he insisted we had to go to Paris to meet with him and discuss the designs.

On August 1, 1980, Ron, Tara and I went to Paris. That afternoon the unthinkable happened.

At two o'clock in the morning on August 2, 1980, in a lushly appointed suite in the Hotel Lancaster, the telephone rang. I was asleep, and so was Tara in the connecting room. Ron had gone to a movie and had just returned. I sleepily heard him answer the phone, heard him say, "An accident—Katy? How bad?"

I struggled out of sleep and he looked at me with a stunned expression on his face.

"It's Katy—she's been hit by a car. She's . . . critical . . . a head injury."

"No!" I heard myself scream. "No, no, no!" I wanted to go back to sleep and wake up again. This was a nightmare. It *must* be a nightmare. "Not my baby, not Katy!" I started to scream and thrash about. All my reason went. I became like an animal. I had no control—just unbearable agony and the frustration of being away from our beloved little girl at this dreadful time.

Tara came rushing in, terrified at the sight of her mother out of control. She tried to comfort me. I felt physically sick, and was. All the time I begged them to wake me up from this nightmare. Ron called all the airlines to try and get us out of Paris. I opened the fridge and found some miniature bottles of brandy and scotch. I drank two or three and calmed down. We had to be practical and keep our heads. We *had* to get out of Paris. We had to push specific thoughts of what had happened to Katy out of our minds and concentrate on finding a way of getting to her. Fast.

We called the hospital and spoke to a doctor. He didn't sound optimistic. He put Katy's headmistress on the phone. When the hospital or police hadn't been able to find any of our immediate family (Jackie was in Los Angeles; my brother and my father out to dinner), they called John Gold, a close friend whose children also went to Katy's school, and he had called the headmistress. She had rushed over and had been with Katy ever since, holding her hand and giving support.

She was comforting. Over the long-distance wires her soothing voice allayed our fears temporarily. She talked as if Katy was in safe hands and would be fine.

We called the British and American Embassies in Paris desperately trying to find a way to get out. They could do nothing. Neither could the concierge. Neither could British Airways or Air France. We were stuck in Paris for at least another seven hours until our 9 A.M. flight to London.

In those hours anything could happen to Katy. It was unbearable.

Icy calm descended on us. We called several friends with private planes. They were all away. Of course. It was August 2. Everyone was on vacation. I called my father in London.

"I don't suppose Roger Whittaker could come and get us in his plane?" I begged helplessly, knowing that Roger had a pilot's license.

Daddy was dubious. It was Saturday night—Sunday morning, and if Roger had had even one drink he couldn't pilot the plane. Daddy said he would try to reach him anyway.

Half an hour crept by. I lay on the sofa numb with shock and apprehension. Tara put ice on my neck and face and tried to comfort me. Ron paced up and down trying to be strong, but he was biting his nails to the quick.

At three-thirty a wonderfully calm voice phoned.

"Joan, it's Roger. Be at Le Bourget at five-thirty—I'm coming to get you!"

In the next two hours every kind of emotion raced through our minds. Elation that we were finally getting out of Paris, despair and frustration that we were not with our daughter at this critical time.

Guilt. How could we have gone off to Paris and left her—even with people we trusted?

Fury. *How* did it happen? and *why?* What carelessness allowed it? Whose fault was it?

Grief. Our baby lying in hospital in what condition we couldn't imagine. And finally the dreadful, ghastly, nagging fear that we would be too late. That she would be dead by the time we arrived at the hospital.

For two hours we paced the suite. We all comforted each other, but I was in by far the worst shape. I felt ill with shock. I kept giving myself ridiculous things to do—as when you are a child you jump across the pavement and mustn't tread on any cracks because if you don't, something good will happen. So I felt that if I threw up—was sick—Katy would live. It sounds ridiculous but some voice in my head, the old ingrained actor's voice of superstition, kept telling me to do this.

As we raced through the darkened streets of Paris in a limousine conjured up by the hotel concierge, the same voice kept telling me again, "If you make the green traffic light before it turns red, she'll live. . . ."

"No, no." I squeezed my eyes shut. I didn't want to have contests with this superstitious inner voice. I held on to Ron, who was like a rock. Very strong, very calm. Inside, though, I could see he was in agony. Katy was his only daughter. He worshipped her.

We arrived at Le Bourget airport at 5 A.M. It was still dark. The ground staff knew nothing about Roger's arrival. Tara and I paced round and round the tiny airport lounge. I chain-smoked and wept. I was in pretty awful shape. I wore a ridiculously inappropriate dress I'd bought in Paris the day before. Red-and-white candy-striped, like a tent, white sandals and a sun visor. It was what I had put out to travel in. It seemed so wrong it didn't matter.

We searched the sky for hours, it seemed. No plane. The sky started to lighten. Dawn was coming. Was our baby still alive?

We called the hospital for the umpteenth time. My brother Bill was there with Robin Guild, another friend. They assured us Katy was holding her own, but I knew they were trying to make us feel better. The more snippets of information that were revealed, the worse it seemed.

Brain injury. The meaning was not clear, but the connotation was horrendous.

Coma. Was it just a long sleep or was it, as I had heard, the closest thing to death?

I closed my mind. I did not know what to expect. I refused to think what could happen.

Tara and I paced around the tarmac for what seemed an eternity, gazing at the ever lightening sky. She was brave, my sixteen-year-old Tara. It must have been hell for her. She had the clarity of adolescence.

"Don't worry, Mummy," she kept reassuring me. "Katy's a big strong kid—nothing's going to get her. You must believe that, Mummy, you *must.*"

She gave me support as we continued the endless wait.

Ron and I looked into each other's eyes and all we saw was stark terror. We could not speak much. We held each other. We cried. Occasionally I would rush to the loo to be sick again. I have been sick only about three times in my life. It was odd. I smoked a thousand cigarettes and prayed desperately.

Roger Whittaker's plane finally landed. By this time Ron's nails were bitten to the knuckle, and I felt close to a complete nervous breakdown. I fell on to Roger's chest and burst into tears. He shook me like a Dutch uncle and told me to shape up, to think positively. He almost shouted at me and strangely it calmed me down.

We hardly spoke during the hour-and-a-half journey in the tiny bumpy plane back to London Airport. Ron and I clutched each other's hands. He was trying so hard not to give in to his terror. He was trying to be strong for me. For Katy. If there was still a Katy.

We drank coffee from a thermos flask Roger had brought. I tried to blot out my thoughts and started to pray to God. To a God I had never really acknowledged existed. Not that I believed he didn't—I was agnostic. Now I prayed for my daughter's life with all my might.

At London Airport they hastened us through Customs. Bill and Robin were waiting. Tara and I went with Bill, and Robin insisted on taking Ron in his car.

We sped through the deserted summer Sunday streets. Bill prepared me for the fact that they had cut off all Katy's hair. He kept assuring me she was going to be all right. I felt he was keeping the real truth from me by telling me this detail. We passed a graveyard. Thousands and thousands of gray and white stones. I shuddered and turned away. Tara was very quiet and I tried to comfort her. We held each other's hands tightly. She was eight years older than Katy but Katy adored her big sister and Tara loved her too.

We ran through the hospital to the intensive care unit. I don't know what I thought I was going to see, but I didn't believe what I saw. My baby was lying in a brightly lit room naked to the waist. Her long blond hair was gone. It was hacked off to the skull. She was white. Bluish-white. She was tiny. Instead of a husky eight-year-old, she looked like an infant. She had tubes in her nose, in her wrists, from under her bedsheet. She had a ventilator life-support system down her throat to keep her breathing. She was still as stone, her eyes closed, her breathing a rasp. Her left fist was clenched and bent above her head. I took her right hand in mine and squeezed it.

"Katy, darling, Mummy's here. I'm here, darling. If you can hear me, squeeze my hand. Please, Katy, squeeze my hand." From the atavistic depths of her being, from the part of her brain that was working, she squeezed my hand. I knew she had heard. I knew she would survive.

To be what, though? We did not know the answer. Ron came in a few minutes later. He too spent some time at Katy's bedside, and while he was with her I saw Dr. Lionel Balfour-Lynn, Katy's pediatrician, who had been present at her birth.

"What are her chances?" I asked.

Tears filled his eyes. "Of survival, sixty. Forty against."

I burst into sobs of disbelief. Ron came out of the intensive care unit and took me to the back door. We held each other tightly and sobbed together. We made a vow to each other. Katy *could not* die. She *would not* die. We would do everything possible to make her live. We would not accept what the doctor's prognosis was, however pessimistic. We would pour into her our love, our faith, our prayers, our strength, our optimism, our utter positivity. All this we talked about in sobbing whispers at the back door of the ICU, surrounded by shelves full of shrouds.

Five minutes later we went in to see our daughter again. I had dried my tears and Ron had dried his. She would not see us cry again. From now on what Katy would receive from us was total positive input and the firm belief that she was going to live and that she was going to recover.

Here is what Ron had to say about those early dreadful days.

"Joan was petrified and asked me to deal with the situation the woman surgeon, Dr. Hunt, was briefing us on at the request of Mr. Illingworth. Joan had talked nearly nonstop to Katy's comatose frail figure for the first 72 hours. I felt Katy knew that it was her mother's voice, a penetrating one that kept her alive during that initial 72-hour critical period. It was right to spare Joan from these things she is queasy about, even in simple situations, so she certainly could not be expected to cope with all these details.

"Dr. Hunt described in detail the surgery that would be necessary when Katy was detached from the ventilator—the machine that breathes for the patient in a life-support situation. It was a common operation—a tracheotomy, which makes a hole in the throat to assist breathing until Katy's injured brain would send the correct signals for breathing.

"Mr. Illingworth told us the operation would not be necessary as he thought Katy would breathe on her own. Dr. Hunt vigorously opposed his opinion—but Mr. Illingworth prevailed. It was therefore decided, much to my relief, and with my having to sign a document, that I, Ron Kass, was taking full responsibility in case anything went wrong. (I had a strong instinctive trust in Robin Illingworth. I know better than anyone that a cool and modest demeanor hid his incredible competence and geniuslike knowledge of the brain.)

"The decision to operate or not was going to be made at the exact time the support system was detached. If Katy could not breathe, I was to stand behind Dr. Hunt to give my on-the-spot permission for the tracheotomy to be performed.

"Mr. Illingworth was standing far enough away to not interfere, but close enough to counsel me whether or not to say, Yes, operate, or No, she is breathing.

"A team of five, headed by Dr. Hunt, had assembled its equipment, normally found only in an operating theater. But Katy could not be moved—it was too dangerous; hence the surgical team set-up in the intensive care unit.

"The tension was high.

"They slowly removed the ventilator tube while Dr. Hunt was having her final scrubdown and having her surgical gloves put on.

"As the tube finally was clear of Katy, a deep wheezing sound, like a truckdriver growling, came from Katy's throat. Then it changed to a kind of heaving. I was alarmed, as it seemed so forced and unnatural. I glanced at Robin for counsel and he had a slight smile of obvious relief on his face—just as the heaving sound lurched out to a recognizable breathing sound.

"Dr. Hunt looked slightly cross, as she is never wrong. However, Robin is never wrong either. She didn't say a word, just directed her team to gather their tools and make a hasty retreat. Gifted people like Dr. Hunt often have sizable egos. I sometimes think of how strange her lack of relief and happiness was, but Robin's expression transcended all as Katy's brain instructed her respiratory system to breathe. This was a big breakthrough, the first being her surviving the first seventy-two hours."

For six weeks Ron and I lived in a trailer parked in the grounds of the hospital. I spent every waking minute at Katy's bedside. Numb with shock, I threw myself with utter desperation into not only her survival—that had been assured after the first agonizing seventy-two hours and the removal of the ventilator—but her return to normality and out of coma as soon as possible.

Ron and I simply breathed and lived and willed life back into her. If ever I believed in *will* and faith and hope and prayer, I used every ounce of it on that child.

The doctors' grim prognosis as the weeks progressed and the continuing of her comatose state did not deter us. She was going to survive. More—she would get back to normal again.

"She may be a vegetable for life," they whispered to me. "She may never walk, let alone talk again. You'll have to put her in a home."

How many times we heard it, from doctors, nurses, interns, even friends. It fell on ears of disbelief. We *would* get her back with our strength and God's help.

Each night, while I fell into exhausted sleep for four or five hours, Ron paced the corridor outside the children's ward. Keeping his vigil, watching over Katy while she slept endlessly on.

After a few weeks, we started to piece together the tragic events of how it had happened.

Katy was staying with her best friend, Georgina, and her mother, in a well-to-do residential area in Ascot, home of the famous British racetrack. Jane had assured me she would take care of Katy like "my own," while we were in Paris.

An eighteen-year-old boy, absurdly named Collins, was traveling down the country lane, driving his father home from a medical checkup. The Collins boy aspired to be a male nurse, to specialize in neurology. His father was coming home from a physical for a heart murmur.

The nanny who had been watching the two girls had been distracted and the girls mock-chased a twelve-year-old boy who had been teasing them. Holding hands, they stepped only a few feet onto the lane, which did not look like a public street. A broken gate at the bottom of the garden led into it.

Katy was hit by the on-side fender and bumper by the Collins car and thrown against the concrete curb. The right side of her head took the secondary blow.

A woman picked up a blanket and ran out to help with the appalling scene she saw from her window. Two British bobbies, Police Constable Pollard and P.C. Burredge, were on the scene within minutes, calling into their hand-talkies for an ambulance immediately.

Georgina was screaming blue murder while Katy lay very still with a blank expression in her *open* eyes.

The first ambulance attendant, R. Morris, an ambulance-driver veteran of World War II, recognized Katy's symptoms of brain injury immediately. A second ambulance came a minute later to attend to Georgina while Katy was raced to the local Ascot hospital.

There they sheared off Katy's beautiful long blond hair and prepared for a brain probe requiring holes to be bored through her cranium.

Feeling her case hopeless, the duty doctor telephoned the Central Middlesex Hospital in Acton, a suburb of London. God was on our side; the call was received by Dr. Hussein, a Ceylonese studying under the auspices of the most eminent brain surgeon in Europe—Mr. Robin Illingworth.

Dr. Hussein sized up the problem over the phone and decided Katy could not be treated properly in the rural hospital, which lacked such sophisticated equipment as the EMI brain scan computer device. He was told she probably would not survive the trip, as Ascot to Acton is a two-hour drive, especially with the Saturday night traffic.

In the great British tradition, a call was made to the Thames Valley Police Authority. They immediately dispatched two police escort cars while Katy was being cared for by Nurse Elizabeth Reed, a specialist nurse in a special ambulance equipped with the necessary life-support system.

Nurse Reed later wrote to us how terrible she felt at the time, as Katy's chances were nil, according to her vast experience. This dreaded prognosis was to follow Katy for weeks. Everyone fell in love with this comatose little girl; however they didn't expect her to survive.

The ambulance trip, normally 120 minutes, was made in 35 minutes, thanks to the police outriders, who pulled all the stops out.

She was rushed into the brain scan room, where the first of several revolutionary devices were tested.

It was around midnight when Mr. (surgeons are called Mr. in Britain instead of Dr.—this is a sign of respect) Robin Illingworth came in from his much-needed weekend. No one knew that this eight-year-old's mother was a household name in England. All this urgency and care is what the British are all about. One can criticize them for many things but if ever I'm in another desperate situation I want a British soldier beside me. They excel in *crisis.*

When Katy was wheeled into the ICU of the Central Middlesex Hospital, the night cleaning lady, Mae, burst into tears. She told me later, "I saw this beautiful little creature come in. I've been working the intensive care unit for many years. I usually can tell when they come in whether they're going to live or die. I *knew* that heaven wanted this little beauty. I knew she couldn't survive through the night, and I've never been wrong yet. I cried then. I cried for her soul and the pity and waste of it all."

Mae told me this as she was cleaning the caravan one afternoon while I was taking my afternoon break.

"I'm so happy I was wrong," beamed that friendly black lady. "For the first time I was wrong."

"Never give up, Mae," I said. "We will never give up on our Katy, I promise you."

Bit by gradual bit, oh, such tiny moments, but so infinitely precious and full of meaning, she started coming back to us, responding to the continual stimuli we gave her. She was a miracle.

On the eighth day she opened her eyes. They were blank, unseeing, but it was a marvelous sign. Her weight had dropped drastically. When her physiotherapists worked with her she looked like a little skeleton from a concentration camp with her cropped hair and skinny arms and legs. She moaned like an animal after a few weeks. Another positive sign, meaning her vocal cords could work.

After six weeks the hospital said they could do no more for her. She was, as far as they were concerned, recovered, and they sent her home. That would be the best therapy now. Home. South Street. Her cat, Sam. Her bedroom with the red heart wallpaper and the dozens of stuffed toy animals, books and pictures of horses.

When Ron carried that little stick up to her bedroom, her eyes widened and seemed to stare with an inner joy. She knew she was home, but she still didn't speak.

Over the following months Katy's miraculous progress continued. She had to have a day and night nurse constantly. Within a week she took her first faltering steps. It was almost like having a new baby again. I went to Selfridge's department store and bought all manner of mobiles, rattles and toys to stimulate her.

Every day I would point to objects and ask Katy what they were. Silence. No sound from that sweet babyish mouth. But her eyes looked, observed, *knew*. They were the eyes of an eight-year-old, even if she still seemed like an infant.

"What's this, Katy?" I pointed to a horseshoe in her room. She had loved to ride, but it was now over two months since the accident.

A whisper. Had I heard it right? A croak. "Horseshoe." It was barely audible but it was a word—the right word. She was going to be *all right!*

The next week a sentence: "I want a drink." A few days later a smile. More days passed—a little laugh.

No tears yet. It would be six months before she would be able to cry. But her improvement continued. Slowly, oh, so slowly, but surely.

Ron and I were exhausted mentally and physically. To get through the nightmarish time, I had taken to drinking heavily. White wine, whiskey. And chain-smoking. Anything to numb the pain. What Ron was taking to get through his days I didn't want to know.

Life had to go on. Bills had to be paid. Massive bills. Therapists, physical educationalists, doctors, nurses, special beds, wheelchairs . . . the list seemed endless.

While Katy was still in the hospital, we had already decided to continue with the West End production of *Mrs. Cheyney*. Rehearsals began at the Cambridge Theatre the day she said her first word. At the press conference I was ecstatic and babbling on endlessly about how wondrous Katy was. Doing *Mrs. Cheyney* was not anywhere near as important as our darling's recovery.

The photos of me in the newspapers the next morning were pretty depressing. I looked a haggard wreck. I stopped drinking immediately and went on a diet. The years of self-discipline still worked. I was still a professional actress and I had a duty to myself as well as to my daughter. And a duty to the production.

On opening night, Katy came backstage. She had written a little note, her first since the accident. "Dear Mummy and Daddy, I love you so much."

The writing was shaky, but she had written it by herself. The effort of will and strength it took this little eight-year-old girl who had had a part of her brain so severely injured was incredible. I was so much more proud of her than of any of the many curtain calls we took that night.

In November, to celebrate how far she had come, we had a photograph taken for our Christmas card. Katy wore a green velvet dress with a white lace collar. She sat next to a giant Christmas tree with a big smile on her face, clutching her favorite stuffed animal, Lambikins. The message inside was simple:

"Our dreams came true this Christmas—we hope yours do too."

The Last of Mrs. Cheyney was not a massive success in the West End. In the fall of 1980, London theater was experiencing its biggest recession in years. All over town theaters were dark. The public didn't seem desperately anxious to see a frothy period piece of 1920s Lonsdale fluff. Where were the legions of loyal supporters who had flocked to Chichester? Goodbye, name in neon lights on the marquee—hello, episodic TV again. Oh, no!

Ron and I had rashly invested in the production with Triumph. I knew things were heading for skid row when I asked the stage manager for a bit more cash than he usually handed me on Friday night. It was a month before Christmas. Instead of the one hundred pounds advance I took in cash, I wanted extra to buy gifts.

He coughed nervously and looked highly embarrassed. "I, er—I'm afraid I can't let you have *any* money, Joan," he stammered.

"Why, David?" I asked warily. I was sitting in my dressing room, prettily decorated with green and white palm trees specially for me, courtesy the management. It was minutes to curtain time.

"Because, er—because Duncan Weldon and Louis Michaels have a clause in your contract that says if the production starts losing money, your salary is to go toward the deficit."

I was appalled. "My *entire* salary?"

He nodded. "I could lend you a tenner to buy your round in the pub." I nodded no thanks. He smiled wanly and left. I appreciated his embarrassment. It certainly wasn't his problem. It certainly was mine.

I called my agent, confused. I was the star and Ron was one of the producers, and we were losing money, so was I to be the sacrifice? I was gripped by rage.

We were closing in January in any case. The play had done quite well but it was a wildly expensive production to run and Triumph said it was losing money. Yet our houses looked practically full every night.

In the intermission my friend Barry Langford came to see me. Barry had been doing secretarial work for me and running my fan club for several years. He had come to work at the Cambridge for the run of *Mrs. Cheyney*. I asked him if our houses were really so bad and he said it didn't appear so to him. Barry began doing a head count each night so I could check with the box-office receipts each Saturday.

I smoked furiously. Was there something fishy going on?

For the next five weeks I performed every night on the stage of the Cambridge Theatre for free.

I had been begging Ron to go to L.A. and sell the house we had not lived in for over a year. Our finances, as usual, were shaky.

Six children to support between us. To add insult to injury, *The Stud* and *The Bitch* had come out on video and were hugely successful. From this we were seeing no money either.

The December video magazines featured a picture of me in black stockings, black merry widow, fur coat and chauffeur's cap with the caption "Give your dad or your boyfriend Joan Collins for Christmas!" Exploited again. Would it ever end?

Ron and I went to Equity, the actors' union, to protest and see if they could do anything about obtaining some of the money we were owed. They couldn't. We asked for an audit from Brent-Walker. They hedged. Something fishy here, too, definitely.

Although he had been amazingly supportive through Katy's injury and recovery, Ron didn't seem to me to be functioning well now. Bills and mail lay unopened on his desk. Phone calls went unreturned. Creditors came to the door. It was worrying me tremendously. As soon as *Mrs. Cheyney* closed, I flew to L.A. by myself to try to sell the house. Something had to be done.

In L.A. I realized with a heavy heart the truth about my marriage. The creditors were banging on the door in Beverly Hills too. It was awful—horrible—demeaning. I wasn't a businesswoman—I was an actress and a mother. Financial matters were too difficult for me to understand, let alone control. However, self-pity was never my forte. Action was. I called Ron and told him I wanted a divorce. To have another marital failure was anathema to me, but he had changed too much. I felt he was a different person from the man I had met and married nearly eleven years before.

The next day a close friend, a devout Catholic woman who had helped us enormously by her faith during Katy's hospitalization, phoned me from London. She begged me not to divorce or even separate from Ron.

"God gave Katy back to you but He could take her away from you if you divorce or leave Ron," she urged.

My blood ran cold. Superstitious to an extreme, I had prayed to any God who existed for my daughter's life and recovery. It was only six months since her accident. She still had much more progress to make even though she was now back at school.

My friend spoke for an hour convincingly—so convincingly that I agreed not to leave Ron. I still loved the man I had married. But where was *he*? I told Ron he had to get his act together. Work, put a deal together, take care of our finances.

I did a "Fantasy Island" for Aaron Spelling, in which I finally got to play Cleopatra. This time episodic TV didn't seem so bad. A few people asked me if I would be interested in a series. No, *no, no*. Thank you. It was back to England for me. Back to the boards—that's where I belonged now.

We sold the Beverly Hills house. We moved back to London. The children started different schools—yet again.

I did a play called *Murder in Mind* at Guildford. The night of the dress rehearsal I fell down a flight of stairs backstage that was in darkness and broke my elbow. At the hospital the doctor told me my arm would have to be set in plaster.

"You can't! I open tomorrow night. I *have no understudy!* I can't do that to Duncan."

Triumph Productions had again backed the production, but this time without benefit of Ron's and my investments or lavish costumes and sets.

"I have a responsibility to them," I told the doctor. To no avail.

Plaster-casted from forearm to elbow, I opened in *Murder in Mind,* a thriller a la *Dial M for Murder* in which I was terrorized in my house by three people masquerading as my family. I was severely unglamourized for this and had to wield an immense shotgun with aplomb and authority. I always hated guns.

Opening night I stumbled backward on the step of the stage while trying to threaten my tormentors with the gun and running backward to open the front door—using only one arm, of course. Not an easy feat.

The audience seemed sympathetic toward me. I had refused to take painkillers, I was in agony, and the discomfort of the plaster, as well as first-night nerves, didn't help.

Everyone, including my insurance man, thought I was mad to go on performing a very physical role with my arm in a cast, but I knew the play would have to close without me, and never having missed a day of work in my career, I had an ingrained "show must go on" syndrome.

In the light of future events it was ironic.

In July we went for a holiday to Marbella, Spain. It was almost a year since Katy's accident. She still had a way to go before she'd be totally the girl she'd been before, but her improvement was fantastic. She was thriving with the sunshine and the swimming.

The phone rang. Tom Korman calling—my agent in L.A. "Joanie, have you ever heard of a TV show called 'Dynasty'?" he said.

"No, never—what's 'Dynasty'?" I queried indifferently. This was my first holiday for two years and I was enjoying basking in the Mediterranean sunshine.

"Well, it's a series—sort of a soap opera, a bit like 'Dallas.' It's been on for thirteen weeks so far. Could become very successful although it's about number forty-five in the ratings right now. They want you for it."

"Oh, no way," I said vehemently. I wasn't inclined to go traipsing back to the USA again. Especially for some obscure TV series I'd never heard of.

"Joanie, you've *gotta* do it. Aaron loves you, so do the Shapiros and the

Pollacks. They want you badly. It starts shooting at Fox next week. Can you do it?"

I was silent.

"Hello, hello?" Tom was getting anxious. "Can you hear me? It's called '*Dynasty*,' Joanie . . . D-Y-N-A-S-T-Y. Dynasty. It could be a very hot show. It's a great role. Her name's Alexis. She's a bitch but witty and clever and she has some great dialogue. It could make you a very big star again. Think about it."

"OK, I'll think about it, Tom."

So I did.

The 20th Century-Fox lot again. It had been twenty-seven years since I first set foot on it. The Hawaiian villages, the Western streets, the medieval castles had long gone. In their places were giant steel-and-glass cement buildings, offices, apartments and hotels. Wide boulevards with fountains emulating ancient Roman piazzas. Masses of people scurrying to work. Theaters. Shopping complexes. Big business. High finance. Rich living.

We rented one of the most securely patrolled apartments in Century City. We took it for six months as I didn't foresee the series running much longer than that. I had watched the first thirteen episodes on video and had not been terrifically impressed. The actors were good and so were some of the plots, but I thought it was somewhat dull. In any case, I wasn't a lover of soap operas, particularly ones with a lot of action in the oilfields. But a buck was a buck was a buck, so I was back at Fox again. Older and wiser, but not wise enough.

It hadn't been easy sorting out our lives in order to do "Dynasty." There were so many pros and so many cons in going back to L.A. to appear in an "iffy" series, even if Alexis was a smashing, juicy part which I had been told every actress in Hollywood wanted to sink her teeth into.

I knew I wasn't the producer's first choice. Very few actors and actresses are ever the first choice for any role, be it movies or TV. Sophia Loren and Raquel Welch had been strong contenders. But Aaron Spelling, clever and dynamic Aaron, whom I had known since I was shooting *The Opposite Sex* when he was a hungry actor, and whose every TV show now turned to gold, wanted *me*. And what Aaron wanted he usually got.

A thousand phone calls had gone back and forth in the ten days before I left Marbella. English agents, American agents, lawyers, Katy's school, her therapists, her doctors, my doctors. Agents calling, yelling, coaxing. There were many complications. It was like a "Dynasty" plot already.

Triumph Productions, my old friends Duncan Weldon and Louis Michaels, were expecting me to do a ten-week tour of *Murder in Mind* in the provinces. Since rehearsals were not going to commence for seven weeks and it was just a provincial tour without *any* guarantee of a West End run, I wanted out. Freedom to do "Dynasty."

They had refused to let me go. Ancient Louis Michaels came to see me in Marbella, his wrinkled flesh hanging, and wearing tropical sports gear. He told me the way it was. "The only way we will *not* see you appear in our theaters is if we have your *death certificate* in our hands, Joanie dear—I've got that in writing in a telegram." He waved a piece of paper at me and collapsed into a chair wheezing and coughing.

I stared at Ron and Viviane Ventura. We were in the sunlit, lush living room in Marbella. These people wanted my *death certificate?* What was this—the British mafia? After what I had done for *them?* Going on stage at Guildford with a broken arm? Appearing for five weeks for no money at the Cambridge Theatre?

There were two dozen actresses who could play Mary in *Murder in Mind.* How could they be so unfair to me—whom they professed to like and admire? The part of Alexis in "Dynasty" would obviously mean a major boost to my career, which could eventually benefit them. Surely Triumph realized my theatrical ventures had been less than triumphs?

I offered to do two plays for them for the same money I'd have received for *Murder in Mind* as soon as "Dynasty" finished. At this point I didn't think it would run for more than a season. Forty-fifth in the ratings was pretty damn low even if it was an Aaron Spelling production—and even if he *had* done "Charlie's Angels," "Starsky and Hutch," "The Love Boat" and many other prime time hits.

Triumph threatened my union, Equity. If I walked, they insisted Equity must ban me from working in the States and ever again in England. Equity was concerned. They talked to the Screen Actors Guild. SAG was concerned. Threats were bandied about with abandon. Lawyers discussed suits and countersuits. She *must* do the tour of this play. No—she must fly to L.A. immediately and do "Dynasty." Oh, how I regretted my altruism in performing with a broken arm. If I hadn't, the play would have closed then and there. Finis.

"There will be other parts, my dear Joan," wheezed the ancient Louis. "Other roles in other TV series for you. This is not your last chance, dear."

"It's a big chance, Louis. *Big.* I *know* it. I *feel* it. Even if the gig goes for only one season, with Alexis I think I can make enough impact to be able to do better things. I'll have more box-office appeal. I'll do other plays for you, Louis—I promise."

He shook his grizzled head in despair. "No, my dear. No. We *need* you in Brighton, Manchester and Leeds."

Ron went to London to placate Equity, which was placating SAG, which was talking to Tom Korman, who was telling Aaron Spelling that all was well and Alexis-Joan was on her way, picture hat in hand—well, almost. At the family summit meeting we had decided that I definitely should do "Dynasty," in spite of all the difficulties and problems Triumph was creating. At the core of our thoughts were the feelings of the three children.

Sacha was at boarding school in England. No problem there with me going away. He could fly out on his holidays. He was fifteen, a big boy now. Tara, seventeen going on eighteen, was at college in Paris. Time to leave the nest. I had left my nest at her age. She had no objections.

Katy. Ah, Katy. Our baby. The child whose well-being meant more to me than all the money and success in the world. All her teachers and therapists and doctors agreed that to be in the sunshine of California for six months or a year would be far more beneficial to her recovery than another cold winter in London. I watched her frolicking in the pool with Viviane Ventura's kids. Tanned, laughing, still a little shaky—but it's only a *year.* Just one year, for God's sake. She's nine years old. My little miracle. Ron's and mine. But mostly her own. Her will and determination got her to where she was today. She was the one who deserved the most consideration.

"Take her," said Robin Illingworth, who had saved her life.

"You'll never work as an actress again," screamed Louis Michaels.

"Take her," said her teacher at school.

"You'll ruin your career," threatened Duncan Weldon.

"Take her," said her speech therapist.

"Take her, and you—you need it," said Cecil Epel, our family doctor.

"Sue her," said Triumph.

"Fuck it," said I, and off we went.

I was extremely nervous on my first day of shooting on "Dynasty." It was mid-August 1981, 90 degrees in the shade, and I was doing the now famous courtroom scene in which Alexis Carrington, oil tycoon Blake Carrington's mysterious ex-wife, walks into the courtroom as the surprise witness to testify against Blake in his murder trial.

The cliffhanger of the previous season had concerned a mystery woman in a large white hat and sunglasses, heavily veiled and wearing a black-and-white suit, striding into the courtroom to the utter consternation, amazement and dismay of the Carrington family and other principals. Today we were shooting a twelve-page interrogation scene between me and the prosecuting attorney. I had most of the dialogue.

I was surrounded by strange new faces of the crew and cast—some friendly, some noncommittal. I had to prove myself. To them I was some British broad come over to take America by storm. Oh, yeah—sure—let's see what she can do. I was being judged. It was par for the course.

Most of the actors were friendly and kind. They had, of course, all known each other, having worked for thirteen weeks the first season. The sole person I knew was Linda Evans, who played Krystle, Blake's long-suffering new wife. I had known Linda since she was married to Stan Herman a few years previously, when Ron and I went to parties at their beach house and hung out with the same group.

Linda had come into my trailer while I was doing my makeup that morning. "We've all done this courtroom bit," she said cheerily. "Last season each and every one of us had to go and sit in that witness chair and testify. We were all terrified!" She laughed.

"Yes, but you all knew each other well," I groaned. "I'm really nervous, Linda. It's hard to play this cool, calm, calculating bitch with butterflies jumping around in my stomach and sweat running down my back." The heat was really intense, and the hot black-and-white wool suit didn't help.

"You'll be great. I'm so happy you're doing this part. We all are. Just remember, we were all in the same place and we are all rooting for you."

I sat staring at myself in the mirror of the trailer. At 20th Century-Fox in the eighties there were no more dressing rooms with built-in bars, sunken tubs and color TVs. Not that I'd ever had one like that at Fox, but I had seen Lana Turner's and Bob Wagner's, which had been palatial.

Au contraire. Neatly lined up outside Stage 8 on the Fox lot were nine identical motor homes. When the cast were on call, we lived in these, like little battery hens, being brought to the stage to do our scenes and then tucked back into our trailers again.

My face stared back at me. I looked scared. I *was* scared. This Alexis I was about to embark upon playing was a clever, ambitious schemer who lied and manipulated people, caring little for anyone or anything except money and power. I hadn't played a part as wicked as this since Princess Nellifer in *Land of the Pharaohs.* I knew there was a lot at stake. This could—if I played my cards and my performance right—turn out to be a major career break. Or it could be just another gig.

I had no choice of the costume I was to wear. The unknown actress who had played Alexis in the last episode had worn these clothes. I must wear them now. Large wide-brimmed white hat with black ribbon and black veiling. Quite becoming. Serene yet sexy black-and-white suit, hot but chic. Dark glasses. Under the veil, I thought they looked tacky. Again I had no choice.

The second assistant, Alice Blanchard, knocked on the door. "They're ready for rehearsal, Joan." I girded my loins and my veil and walked with trembling legs onto Stage 8. It never changes. Throughout the years, backstage life on a set is always the same. Grips, electricians and cameramen working, moving lamps and props, barking orders, gossiping, swapping jokes, drinking coffee, eating doughnuts. Bejeaned and sneakered. This lot looked jovial and hardworking. They looked like they knew their business—and they did.

Bobby della Santina, the first assistant director, whom I'd met the first day I'd arrived—and who later told me I had a look of horror when he told me the gig was going to shoot for eight months—introduced me to Gabrielle Beaumont, a fellow Brit who was directing this episode. She calmed my nerves, and she told me she was glad I had convinced the producers to let me play Alexis as an Englishwoman, as there had been some talk of me playing her with an American accent. I had thought seriously about this, but realized there were no other Englishwomen on TV and perhaps the American public was ripe for a new voice. I was also very well aware that "foreigners" had never done well on American TV. With the exception of Eva Gabor in "Green Acres," no non-American had sent the Nielsen ratings spinning.

"Middle America" was a term I was to hear often during the next few months. "Middle America will not *understand* you," despaired one of the executives at ABC.

"Yes they will," I argued. "I have very good diction." I was beginning to understand finally—after nearly thirty years—that you have to stand up for your rights in this business. I really felt I now knew much better than most people what was good and right for me.

I sat in the witness stand in the courtroom and gazed nervously at my new TV family. John Forsythe gave me an engaging wink. He was a darling—a true gentleman in the English sense of the word. Gallant, courteous and fun. He had been charming to me, and he was an excellent actor.

John turned out to be one of the most charming and delightful men I have ever worked with. He has been married for forty years to the delightful Julie and they have two grandchildren, and he is without doubt one of the most attractive men I have ever met. Not only physically. His warmth and wit are overwhelming. He truly is the patriarch and the strength of the "Dynasty" cast.

We were chatting on the set the day after I had just been to a friend's fiftieth birthday party. He had been terribly depressed at reaching this milestone.

"That's right," said John. "It's a hell of a birthday. I remember I was in New York doing a play for Gore Vidal when I had mine. I was very depressed and Gore asked me what was wrong. When I told him I had just hit fifty and was now officially middle-aged he looked at me and laughed. 'Oh, no, John, you're wrong. You're not middle-aged *at all*. After all, how many people do you know who are a hundred?' "

Behind John sat "our" children, Steven and Falcon. Al Corley was very tall, very blond, very macho; Pamela Sue Martin, tall, slender and pretty, with a zest for life and fervor for new experiences, quests, causes. She refused to wear fur coats on the show, or much jewelry.

And John James—JJ as everyone called him—the resident hunk. Extremely good-looking, but sweet and nice and eager to learn. He played Jeff Colby, Falcon's husband.

JJ and Pamela Bellwood, who played the fragile, neurotic Claudia (not that day in court), became my closest friends of the "Dynasty" cast. Katy came to adore Pamela Bellwood, and at parties at my house the two of them would sit together for hours engrossed in conversation.

And last but not least, Lee Bergere—Joseph, the sinister majordomo, with whom I was to have many a fracas before he decided to leave the series after the third season because he didn't have enough to do. Too true. For an actor to play just a butler is anathema. Lee had a clause in his contract stating that he didn't have to do anything menial in his role. When one day I innocently suggested that he carry in a tray instead of the day player's doing it he was outraged. I was learning a whole new set of TV rules.

"Your name?" said Brian Dennehy, surveying the crowded courtroom with an eagle eye.

"Alexis Morrell Carrington," I said with a mixture of defiance and pride.

"Your residence?"

"I've been living in Acapulco for the past several years."

"You were the first wife of the defendant, Blake Carrington. You are the mother of his children, is that correct?"

"Yes, it is."

"Was it an amicable divorce?"

"No," I replied. "It was what you might call an *enforced* divorce."

"Would you please explain that to the court and jury?"

I took off my dark sunglasses and raised my veil slowly for maximum effect. The courtroom gasped. The ABC and "Dynasty" executives gasped at the rushes the next day. The scene was dynamic, and so was I. So they told me.

Never one to believe my own publicity, I merely smiled when my father sent me the front page of the English *Daily Mirror* with the headline "Sophisticated lady Joan is set to beat J.R." emblazoned across the front page picture of me complete with hat and veil and enigmatic smile.

The word had got out, as it usually does in Hollywood, that I was "hot." I had "impact." "Magnetism." Lots of superior adjectives were bandied about. It was said in ancient Rome—and it applies to Hollywood: "Three can keep a secret only if two are dead." There are few secrets in Hollywood, and within days I was getting heavy media interest.

I got the feeling I might be becoming a star again when John Springer, an old friend, and press agent to the stars, called me from New York in November 1981 and asked me to participate in "Night of 100 Stars" at Radio City Music Hall.

"We've got Grace Kelly, Bette Davis, Al Pacino, Paul Newman, Lillian Gish, Brooke Shields and dozens more," John told me eagerly. "We want you and Farley Granger to come on stage as 'Lovers of the Silver Screen' while we show a clip from *Girl in the Red Velvet Swing*."

A buzz of excitement about the show started about three weeks before it was to open. We heard that Grace Kelly was flying in from Monaco, Roger Moore from Gstaad, that Elizabeth Taylor would definitely be there . . . and Gene Kelly, Jane Fonda, Gregory Peck. It could be the event of the year.

I told Nolan Miller, who designed the wardrobe for "Dynasty," "I have absolutely nothing to wear, darling!" Everything had been seen dozens of times either on the show or in magazine layouts and TV interviews. Nolan wanted to create a "knock 'em in the aisles" gown. "I mean, if you're going to be with all the movie stars in the world you might as well look the best!" he said jokingly.

He had designed a gold lamé dress slit to the navel for a party scene in "Dynasty." He decided it could be fun to create a similar silver lamé gown. After all, although the fabric was $125 a yard, there were only two yards of material in the dress. And it was superb.

Carefully boxed, tissued and packed to within an inch of its life, the dress, Judy Bryer and I boarded the "Red-Eye" to New York.

The fact that I had arrived back from a quick trip to England only fifty hours earlier, had arisen at 5 A.M. to pack and then shot for twelve hours had not put me in a mood of effervescent jollity. However, we soon started to feel better the moment we got to the airport. Heavyweight stars started boarding: Larry Hagman—J.R. himself—wearing a plaid Western-style jacket, large white Stetson and pink-tinted glasses. Was this a disguise, or did he want the whole world to know J.R. flew TWA? We soon realized it must have been the former when he whipped out a large polka-dot scarf, covered his face and slept for the entire trip.

William Shatner sat in front of us and we reminisced about the "Star Trek" episode I'd worked on twelve years before. Linda Gray arrived breathlessly, straight from the set of "Dallas."

New York was having one of her rare magical days of perfect crisp winter weather when we arrived. A gaggle of early-bird fans and paparazzi with strong flashbulbs and even stronger constitutions was at the airport to meet us. I kept on my dark glasses in spite of impassioned pleas to remove them. I realized now why they called this flight the "Red-Eye."

"Larry Hagman's behind me," I said, winking, and like a covey of starlings they whooped with glee and went off in search of bigger prey.

At the luxurious Helmsley Palace Hotel we were greeted by the sight of some two or three hundred fans surrounding the entrances. The whole of Fifty-first Street had been blocked off, and each darkened limousine was being eagerly scanned for famous faces.

Dozens of burly security men stood by to escort us to the safety of the elevator. The suite overflowed with flowers, champagne, fruit and invitations. The phone rang constantly. Luisa Moor and I discussed where to meet later. After considering Sardi's, Elaine's, a party at Studio 54, where Morgan Fairchild would be crowned "Miss Valentine 1982" and various others, we opted to meet at Regine's at ten-thirty.

That night at Regine's, a veritable hanging garden of red and white balloons, paper chains and assorted heart-shaped novelties hit us about the head as we stumbled through flashing paparazzis' bulbs to the top table. I sat next to Roger Moore, which caused the paparazzi to snap eagerly away, particularly when Regine herself, resplendent in black-and-red taffeta, joined us. When Veronique and Gregory Peck arrived, more photographers hounded them. When Stefanie Powers arrived and sat next to me, more still appeared from out of the woodwork. After an hour of this we began to get slightly miffed. TV camera crews had now arrived and were pushing and jostling. We felt like monkeys in a cage, as the other patrons of the nightclub clustered around, pointing and laughing.

With the arrival of Sammy Davis, Jr., and Julio Iglesias all hell broke loose. By now there were at least twenty-five photographers, and we were blinded by the flashbulbs. Luisa Moore, in her volatile Italian way, threatened to hit one of the photographers if he didn't leave us alone. They had even followed me onto the floor to get a picture of me dancing. This appeared in a tabloid some weeks later with the caption "Joan's New

Guy." Since rumbles about my marital rift abounded, this was probably the reason. The irony was that I had never met the gentleman before!

At eleven o'clock the following morning Judy and I arrived at Radio City Music Hall for the rehearsal of the "Lovers of the Silver Screen" segment.

I was assigned a dressing room. It was rather full. In it were Bette Davis, Janet Leigh, Lillian Gish, Ruth Gordon, Ginger Rogers, Anne Jeffreys and Jane Russel. Jane Powell, Brooke Shields and Diane Keaton were also supposed to be there. Every one of these ladies had an entourage of at least two. Managers, agents, press agents, hairdressers, husbands, lovers and friends. The air was thick with cigarette smoke and gossip. Judy and I escaped to the sanity of the auditorium. Grace Kelly was rehearsing her speech and lighting one of the one hundred candles on the enormous birthday cake. I remembered when I had first met her, before her marriage to Prince Rainier. Sitting around looking bored were Liza Minnelli in a black minidress, and no makeup, Paul Newman, blue-jeaned and blue-eyed, Brooke Shields in her Calvin Kleins, and Henry Winkler, who had brought a home-movie sound camera and was happily photographing everything and everyone. As I walked up to the front of the house to sign the official poster, which was to be reproduced and auctioned for charity, I marveled at the artillery of names that had accepted the invitation of Alexander Cohen, the producer and entrepreneur who had had the *chutzpah* to organize this event that everyone had said couldn't take place.

I was honored to have been included. It seemed I was having yet another renaissance. So many of these names had played important roles in my life and in my career. Warren Beatty, Gregory Peck, Farley Granger, Roger Moore, Linda Evans, John Forsythe. . . .

Farley arrived. He looked great and we congratulated each other on how well we looked considering the movie clip they'd be showing of us was twenty-seven years old!

I said hello to Bette Davis. We hadn't met since my first Hollywood movie, *The Virgin Queen*. She had intimidated me then. She still did.

We watched "One" from *A Chorus Line* being rehearsed. The most staggering array of leading men, past and present, from theater, movies and TV strutted on stage, each flanked by a Rockette. Robert De Niro, Al Pacino, James Caan, Richard Chamberlain, Dudley Moore, Christopher Reeve, Roger Moore, Larry Hagman, Jose Ferrer, Gregory Peck, Tony Perkins, Donald Sutherland, Gene Kelly, Burt Lancaster, Douglas Fairbanks, Jr.—and Lee Strasberg, not to mention ex-Mayor Lindsay—high-kicked and moved like veteran hoofers. It was quite enthralling. We rehearsed the finale. We were all told to get up on stage to face a vast set of bleachers which were numbered from 1 to 218. It wasn't the Night of 100 Stars after all—218 stars were shining!

I stood on stage next to Elizabeth Taylor and Liza Minnelli. We waited like disgruntled beauty contenders while Alexander Cohen called out our names and then a number. The top rows of the bleachers filled up.

Finally I was called. Number 168. Next to Farley Granger and behind Ethel Merman and Warren Beatty.

"It is imperative you remember your number and the people who are next to you, behind you and in front of you," boomed out Mr. Cohen to his captive audience of fidgety celebrities.

I marveled at how disciplined and well-behaved everyone was. The public could never believe such a lack of temperament could exist. We all stood, including even the older actors, some of whom were well into their seventies and eighties, for over forty-five minutes while Mr. Cohen barked instructions. "No running backstage. There are likely to be holes in it due to the many film changes. No visitors backstage after six-thirty." Where to go, what to do, how to get there. A five-star general giving commands to his troops before battle. All paid attention. Brooke Shields passed along her autograph book for signatures. At four-thirty it was off to the hotel for a quick bath and makeup, and by 6 P.M. we were back again.

The crowds outside the hotel and lining the route all the way to Radio City Music Hall were mind-boggling in their enthusiasm. Two security men led me into the car. Hundreds of fans lined the hotel lobby and were outside the Music Hall brandishing autograph books and snapping Instamatic cameras.

"Alexis!" they screamed. "We love you, Alexis." Roger Moore patted my cheek. "Fame at last, Joanie. It's more intense on TV than anywhere else." The fans went crazy for me. It was all rather incredible to realize what had happened to me in such a short time. Altogether one of the most staggering evenings I have ever experienced.

Steve Allen summed it up when he said, "If a bomb dropped on Radio City Music Hall tonight, Pia Zadora would become the biggest star in the world!"

After appearing in only three episodes of "Dynasty" I began receiving an avalanche of fan mail. Although I had been an actress for nearly thirty years, the amount of attention I was receiving from people in the street, in stores, and especially from the media, was overwhelming. After "Dynasty" had been airing for five or six weeks I finally stopped going to supermarkets other than in disguise as my recognizability quotient was so high that it took me twice as long to shop, having to stop to answer the questions that the avid "Dynasty" watchers would fire at me.

The scene that really put the "Dynasty" ratings through the roof was the one in which Alexis Carrington, using every ounce of her feminine wiles, lures her fiancé, Cecil Colby, played by Lloyd Bochner, to her boudoir where, in the last throes of passionate lovemaking, Cecil suffers a major heart attack. Horrified, Alexis in her usual charming and delightful way starts slapping the hapless Cecil about the face in a frenzy of rage and frustration because now she might not inherit the Colby billions. "Don't you dare die on me, Cecil!" she screams at him. "We're getting married tomorrow. You can't die on me—I need you to get Blake!"

The filming of this scene was considered so daring and sexy for network TV that all kinds of precautions were necessary to satisfy the ever vigilant censors.

Network TV was not allowed to show any nudity other than an occasional chaste back or leg. Certainly simulated copulation culminating in a heart seizure for the male was excessively adventurous, even in 1982.

Care was taken that no hint of nakedness would show on the screen. I eschewed the flesh-colored leotard Breezy Brooks from wardrobe produced and instead wore a purple strapless bathing suit with matching tights and leg warmers. If Bobby Dawes, our camera operator, caught so much as a sliver of purple during our thrashing about he would have to call "Cut."

I was fairly keyed up and nervous. There had been so much secrecy, talk and preparation about this scene that I just wanted to get it over with. Not one but *two* censors had to be on the set to observe Lloyd and me as we did our heavy-breathing act.

One of them, particularly eager, insisted on sitting right *under* the camera at all times, gazing expectantly at the border of the satin sheets that just covered my purple Lurex. Whether he hoped it would slip or not I do not know. He smiled a lot though, all flashing teeth and wide expectant eyes. Every one of our producers except Aaron Spelling and Doug Cramer was on the set looking anxious.

If this scene went too far and looked too sexy, the network would refuse to use it, thus necessitating a reshoot—an expensive proposition. If the scene was too tame, it would disappoint the network, as this was to be *the* cliffhanger of the '82–'83 season.

Does Cecil die or *not?* All America would wait with bated breath for nearly six months for the truth to be revealed the following October.

Lloyd Bochner looked rueful as we tried to get comfortable in the slippery satin sheets preparatory to huffing and puffing.

"*Do* you die, Lloyd?" I asked, ever eager to know what was happening in our series. Our scripts usually arrived just a week or so before we shot, and therefore I was as curious as the public to know what the future held.

"I suppose so," said Lloyd somewhat bitterly. "My agents were informed I won't be back next season, so I suppose this is my swan song."

"Put us on a bell."

"Quiet on the set," called Bobby della Santina, the first assistant director. "Rolling."

"Speed," called the soundman. Joe Valdez, the camera assistant, snapped the clapperboard in front of our noses and called out crisply, "Thirty-three apple, take one."

"Action!" called Jerome Courtland, the director.

Lloyd and I went to it.

"Cut—I can see her suit," said Bobby Dawes quietly.

The wrecking crew of makeup men, hairdressers, wardrobe and body makeup rushed to me to repair the ravages of a fast twenty-five seconds of television smooching.

"What are you *doing* to yourself?" tut-tutted Andi Sidell, the body-makeup girl. "What's all this orange stuff all over your neck and shoulders?" She busied herself with a sponge and makeup while Breezy tried to tuck a bit of satin sheet down the front of my purple bathing suit so it wouldn't show.

"It's Lloyd's body makeup," I whispered to Andi. "It comes off all over me, and the sheets, too." I noticed the orange pancake that the prop man was trying to wipe off the satin.

Painted, powdered and perfect again, we started our ritual writhing once more.

"Aaahh aaahh, oooh!" yelled Lloyd-Cecil, clutching his chest. "It *hurts*, Alexis."

"Don't you *dare* die on me, Cecil," I yelled, and hauled back and slapped him mightily three times on each cheek.

"Cut, cut, cut!" called Jerome Courtland. "We can't see your face, Joan. Your hair's all over it."

Resignedly I was "touched up" by the "wrecking crew" again. And again. And again.

After seven takes from various angles, my voice was hoarse from screaming "Don't you dare die on me, Cecil," and my chin was raw from rubbing against Lloyd's. Out of the corner of my eye throughout the whole performance I observed the censor's teeth gleaming eagerly as he watched us with more than a hint of professional interest, I thought.

Finally it was time for Lloyd's close-up. We had finished the master shot, the two-shot, two over-the-shoulder shots and every other conceivable angle. That scene was over at last. Now I sat next to Richard Rawlings, our cinematographer. I was in Lloyd's eyeline, and I gave him the appropriate moans, groans, slapping motions and dialogue.

"Action!" called Jerome.

"Aaahh! Ooohh! Oh-oh!" screamed Lloyd, giving many readings and interpretations of these noises. He had no dialogue other than sexy moans, which then had to become heart-attack moans. He writhed around believably.

I clutched Richard Rawlings, trying hard not to giggle. Love scenes always make me laugh, and Jerry seemed to be letting this close-up on Lloyd go on forever. Finally "Cut!" yelled Jerry, and added quietly "Did you come yet, Lloyd?" The crew and the censor broke up, and Lloyd, good sport that he is, did too. The scene turned out to be everything the network and Aaron Spelling Productions had hoped for, and we zoomed to number one the following season.

As "Dynasty" started to gallop up the ratings, and the popularity of both the show and myself increased, so did my personal life plummet. I was desperately anxious to remain married to Ron for Katy's sake; at the same time I knew how destructive it was for her to hear our bickering.

"Don't *fight*, Mummy and Daddy," she pleaded. "Please stop being so *angry* with each other!"

Biting my tongue, I would hide in the bathroom or the tiny patio of this far-too-small apartment to give vent to my anger, hurt and frustration —frustration at being bound into a marriage that was no longer happy.

Only my concern for Katy and my guilt at failing once again in marriage had been keeping me in it up to now.

It was now eighteen months since her accident, and my major concern was for her welfare and complete physical and mental recovery. I knew that her recovery up to now had been miraculous. Her efforts with the various physiotherapists, tutors, piano teachers and counselors to bring her back to the perfect child that she had been before, and that I *knew* she would become again, were outstanding. She was brave and indomitable. Her school work was excellent in most subjects, but her short-term memory was still not functioning as it should, and this was giving her some problems with retention of certain subject matter. She still dragged her left foot slightly, had slight shakiness in her left hand, and her speech was a bit slow. But her diligence and hard work were paying off, and every month showed an improvement. If ever a human being deserved an A for effort, she did. In spades.

"Promise me you'll never divorce Daddy like you did Tara and Sacha's daddy," she whispered as she snuggled up to me while I lay on the bed staring blankly at the TV screen after another battle with Ron.

"I can't promise you that, baby, but I'll do my best. I'll really *try.*" I hugged her with despair in my heart. I believed in trying to be honest with my children, but this was a difficult time for Katy, and I desperately wanted not to upset her or interfere with her improvement in any way.

My closest friends saw the marriage crumbling even if I refused to acknowledge it openly. During the day I went to work on "Dynasty," to all intents and purposes hard-working and full of jokes and *joie de vivre.* At night, in the hateful Century City apartment, I called on all my acting skills to convince Katy that all was well between Daddy and Mummy.

I knew I should be taking charge of my own destiny. I knew I should end the marriage, but, as throughout all my life, a decision of such magnitude was incredibly hard for me to make. I agonized.

I vacillated. I convinced myself that Ron would eventually change. He'd get another job. He'd lose weight. He'd get himself together and work really hard. He'd become the man he used to be—the man I'd married who had been so wonderful. But I was fooling myself and making no one happy. Burying my head in the sand. Joan the ostrich.

In December of 1982 I was asked to be the mistress of ceremonies at a concert at the Royal Albert Hall in London before Her Majesty Queen Elizabeth and His Royal Highness Prince Philip. The Royal Philharmonic Orchestra was to perform the music of the Beatles. It was to be in aid of one of their favorite charities, the Royal Society for the Protection of Birds, and I was honored to be chosen to be the narrator at this wonderful event.

The Royal Albert Hall is an extraordinary building with a fascinating history. Some of the most renowned performers in the world have played there ever since Queen Victoria had it built in memory of her husband, Prince Albert.

I was even more thrilled that the organizers of the charity concert requested that Katy present a bouquet to Her Majesty after the performance.

Katy was overjoyed; she was a staunch Royalist, as was I. We debated at length about what to wear. Eventually Nolan Miller made a beautiful pink velvet gown with an antique lace collar for Katy, and a ruby velvet gown for me, with which I wore some of my more majestic "Dynasty Diamonds"—ruby-and-diamond fabulous fakes. Only the Queen would know the difference!

The "Dynasty" producers, also Royal Family fans, gave me a few days off to enable me to fly to London. In recent months the English press had been having a go at me. Rumors of our marital discord abounded, and although we continued staunchly denying it, it was hard for me to lie so blatantly. At the same time, we were not completely clear on how to break the news to Katy about our problems. Our marriage counselor had advised us at this moment to "do nothing and deny all." So be it.

I felt like a total hypocrite. Although I knew my personal life wasn't anybody's bloody business except my own, I thought it was wrong to be such an out-and-out liar. I was lying to everyone: to Katy, pretending all was well; to the press, who hounded me for "the Truth," which I constantly denied; to the "Dynasty" cast and crew, who knew nothing of my problems; but most of all to myself. I *wouldn't* face reality, *couldn't* admit the truth, the unbearable fact that marriage number three was on the rocks. I rushed around patching up little cracks, hoping the dam wouldn't burst.

The week before I arrived in London, headlines screamed that my electricity supply had been cut off in the South Street house because of nonpayment. "She ignored our requests for payment," sniffed the London Electricity Board. "She is making thousands, yet she's refused to pay the £350 she's owed us for over a year."

They had repossessed the meter from the South Street house—a house I had not lived in for two years. Naturally, this was front page news in the tabloids both in England and in the States.

Tearfully I confronted Ron. I knew *nothing* of it. The house wasn't my responsibility. He was supposed to be in charge, but obviously he wasn't anymore.

Hoping things would have simmered down, I arrived at the Albert Hall with Ron and Allan Tinkley, the manager of the concert, for rehearsals on December 13. I was excited, as I had just heard I'd been voted "Female Star of the Year" by the Hollywood Women's Press Club. Tom Selleck was voted top male star. As I stepped out of the car, a man jumped from the shadows. "Joan Collins?" he barked.

"Yes," I said charmingly, extending my hand to sign the autograph he so obviously desired.

"You are hereby served with a writ of . . ." I didn't hear the rest. I pulled my hand away and fled into the sanctuary of the Albert Hall.

The front-of-house manager arrived with the writ, which of course it was. It was for the nonreturn of a car loaned to me three years before by British Leyland in return for promotional work I was doing for them to publicize their new model, the Mini Metro. I'd been told the car had been returned months ago. It hadn't.

The newspapers had a field day. The following day, alongside lovely photographs of a delightful Queen, a demure Katy and an overawed me, were banner headlines, all along the lines of "Royal Star Joan Gets Writ"; "A Writ on Joan's Big Night"; "Bill Row, Joan Blows a Fuse"; etc. etc.

I was humiliated and embarrassed, not only for myself but for the Queen, who I'm sure was not amused by the tackiness of the whole situation.

Ron and I had another raging row, he absolving himself of most of the responsibility and me feeling abused, misused and terribly unhappy. I discovered a huge number of unpaid bills that had been virtually ignored for the past few years.

Ron's excuses that due to Katy's accident he had been unable to cope didn't wash with creditors now. The press were gleeful. I was in financial hot water. It made headlines, whether or not *I* was to blame. "They've Cut off Joan's Electricity" sold a lot more newspapers than "Ron Kass Fails to Pay Bill."

The final marital crunch came on the day Linda Evans and I were to shoot a fight scene between Krystle and Alexis. The rivalry between the two women for Blake Carrington's affections had been building all season. The bitchy, hostile scenes between the two of us, who were of such physical and emotional contrast, had caught the viewers' imaginations and contributed to "Dynasty's" soaring success. This scene was to be a high point. A knockdown, drag-out cat fight, no holds barred. Scratching, biting and feathers flying. Claws out. The cat fight to end all cat fights. ABC was gleefully anticipating huge ratings.

I, however, was filled with trepidation. I loathed physical violence. I hated fighting, and, after watching the stunt double go through the extremely complicated and choreographed fight in rehearsal, I was nervous. Linda was two or three inches taller than me and very sportive. She actually preferred doing the physical fighting scenes to the verbal ones. With me it was vice versa.

Gene Kelly had told me during the time I was going through the rigor and fears of learning to horseback ride for *The Virgin Queen,* "Never do anything dangerous on film, kid. People get paid for that. Stunt people. Don't put 'em out of work." I totally agreed.

As the day of the fight approached I became more and more apprehensive. Things between Ron and me were bad. Katy was aware of it, and so was Daphne Clinch, a friend from Chichester who had come to look after Katy for the six or seven months I had thought the "Dynasty" gig would last. She was a kind woman who reminded me greatly of my own lovely mother, and she was constantly chiding me about working too hard, having too much responsibility and not getting enough support from Ron.

The morning of the fight scene I arrived on the set nervous and slightly queasy after a restless night. As I drove to the studio, I tried not to think of the day ahead.

Alice brought a cup of coffee to the trailer while I began shakily applying my makeup. The third assistant director came in and called me over for a rehearsal. I watched the stunt doubles throw their bodies about and flail their fists with expert agility.

A spasm of searing pain racked through me. A strange, unusual feeling. I doubled over in agony. "Appendix," said someone briskly. "Heartburn," surmised another expert. "Ulcer," said another. Whatever it was, I couldn't stand up straight. I was whisked off to the nurse's office on the lot, where they examined me and advised immediate admission to Cedars Sinai emergency.

Judy came with me, and, after a thorough examination in the emergency room, punctuated by beefy policemen barging in and reporting that there was "a cadaver" in the corridor, I lay bare from the waist up, electrodes attached to my chest, trying to cover that up as well as my by now famous face.

Dr. Al Sellers, who had saved my life when I had the shrimp allergy, said I appeared to have gastroenteritis, a condition exacerbated by extreme pressure, tension, exhaustion and nerves.

Judy called our apartment several times from the hospital to tell Ron of the situation, but Daphne reported she could not wake him up.

A few hours later, released from the hospital, I stood over our bed and beseeched Ron to rouse himself. I told him I was ill and had to go to bed. He continued sleeping and would not budge. I went into Katy's bed. I realized hollowly I had to escape. There was no longer any point in continuing with a situation that was causing so much pain to both of us, and was now affecting Katy.

A few weeks later when my first "Dynasty" season had ended, I flew to London with Katy. I had accepted a mediocre film called *Nutcracker* and was relieved to be leaving Ron in L.A. We decided to try a trial separation, going to great lengths to keep the truth from Katy, the press and everyone except our closest friends. We hoped that in some magical way, being separated by a continent and an ocean would do something for our marriage. But it had disintegrated too much. After endless talks, discussions, sessions with a marriage counselor, pathetic attempts at living together amicably, and enormous emotional strain, we finally came to the conclusion that there was no other choice for the three of us but for Ron and me to separate for good.

With a long career behind me, I had never received any awards of particular significance. Not that anything I had done had been particularly meritorious, but it would have been nice. I had been voted in 1956 "Star of Tomorrow" and "Most Promising Young Actress," and in 1957 "Most Outstanding Young Actress"—and in 1977 I got a best actress award for—believe it or not—*Empire of the Ants!*—but with my usual objectivity I realized I actually did not deserve any acting awards for the body of work I had done. When in 1982 the Hollywood Foreign Press Association nominated me for their coveted Golden Globe award for Best Actress in a TV drama series, I was pleased. I didn't win—but I didn't really expect to. In 1983 I was again nominated in the same category, up against Linda Evans in "Dynasty," Stefanie Powers in "Hart to Hart," Jane Wyman in "Falcon Crest." Heavy competition. Again, I did not feel that I had much of a chance. Flattered to be nominated, I agreed to be a master of ceremonies with Wayne Rogers. When the nominees for Best Actress were being announced I stood backstage stoically, prepared for rejection.

"And the winner is—Joan Collins."

Stunned, I stood there for a second, then dashed on stage to raise my arm in a victorious gesture and hear my green chiffon Nolan Miller dress rip under the arms. I had no speech prepared—just "I would like to thank Sophia Loren for turning down the part, and everyone on 'Dynasty' from Aaron Spelling on *up!"*

Ron escorted me to the Golden Globes. We had been separated for several months but were seeing each other in a friendly way. He was more thrilled than I was. But with all the joy of winning this award I was still very sad that my marriage was dead.

Ever eager to get away from the image of being just another pretty face, I jumped at the opportunity when director Jim Frawley offered me the dual role of the wicked stepmother and the wicked witch in "Hansel and Gretel."

"Hansel and Gretel" was being produced by the actress Shelley Duvall for Showtime cable TV. They were making a series of fairy tales called "Faerie Tale Theatre" and were able to tempt some fairly important stars into appearing. Robin Williams had just starred as the Frog Prince, and Mick Jagger, Christopher Reeve, Liza Minnelli, Malcolm McDowell, Vanessa Redgrave, Tom Conti and Tatum O'Neal had been signed. It was an interesting project with which to become involved.

Certainly it was no stretch for me to play the evil stepmother who sends the two innocent young children into the forest to their doom. With a curly red wig, scrubbed face and frumpy period clothes, I easily fitted into that role. The Wicked Witch, however, was another kettle of fish completely. My makeup for this part took over four hours to apply. Thick greenish paste was applied all over my face. A false hooked nose, false chin with a wart on it, brown, snaggly false teeth, a matted long gray wig, filthy curled false nails, thick straggly black eyebrows and a large hump on my back transformed me totally. On top of this went the classic witches' gear of black dress and pointed hat. I changed my voice and my walk completely. When Katy walked onto the set she came face to face with me and said, "Where's Mummy?" This was the most challenging and difficult part I had ever performed. We shot in 100-degree weather in Griffith Park. It was so hot that my nose and chin kept on getting detached from my face because of the sweat pouring down. The makeup girl spent hours pushing and prodding it back onto my face with surgical adhesive and a sharp instrument.

I had very long speeches. Since we were shooting on video, and fast— the whole episode was shot in six days—time waited for no one. It was nonstop and extremely exhausting, but very rewarding professionally for me. Particularly so when a year later I was nominated for Best Actress for this part by the National Cable TV Association.

In my third season on "Dynasty" we went to Denver, the city where "Dynasty" is set, to shoot at the Carousel Ball. This is an annual event to aid the Children's Diabetes Foundation, and it is hosted magnificently by Barbara and Marvin Davis. Marvin, one of the world's richest men, does not do things by halves, and to guest at the ball he had flown in some of the biggest names in films, TV and politics. Cary Grant, Lucille Ball, James Stewart, Raquel Welch, Lee Majors, Dolly Parton, Robert Wagner, Diana Ross, Merv Griffin, Stefanie Powers, Henry Kissinger and ex-President Gerald Ford were just some of the famous faces on the glittering dais, along with John, Linda, John James, Kathleen Beller and Michael Nader (two new faces on "Dynasty") and me. We had already shot John and Linda arriving by limo at the ball, and then Alexis with Dex, her new lover, played by Michael Nader, driving up in a white vintage Rolls-Royce.

It was amusing to hear the vast crowd in the street outside the ballroom screaming out our names with fanlike frenzy. How would that match our normal characters in "Dynasty"?

Our crew mingled inconspicuously with the gorgeously gowned and bejeweled women, the cream of Denver society. The crew embarrassedly all wore black tie and evening dress as they scurried around trying to shoot as much footage as possible before, during and after the dinner and ball.

I was seated at the dais between my escort, Peter Holm, and Dr. Henry Kissinger. I had met Dr. Kissinger the previous year at the ball and had found him a lively and scintillating dinner companion. I was draped in a two thousand dollar gold lamé Nolan Miller gown and wearing about a million dollars' worth of Harry Winston diamonds and emeralds. Suddenly a brilliant idea hit me. Why couldn't we do a little scene between Dr. Kissinger and Alexis? Why not, indeed? John and Linda had had some dialogue with Barbara and Marvin Davis, and Marvin had introduced "Blake" and "Krystle" to Dr. Kissinger at the ball, and also to ex-President and Mrs. Gerald Ford.

Elaine Rich, our line producer, was lurking in the auditorium with the camera crew shooting all and sundry. I beckoned to Elaine and whispered my idea to her.

"Will he do it?" she said eagerly. "It would be *dynamite!*"

"One can but ask," I said, boldly approaching him. "How would you like to do a scene with Alexis, Henry?" I batted my lashes and leaned close so that a hint of Scoundrel would engulf him.

"Vot vould ve do?" He twinkled conspiratorially. "I'm not an actor, you know."

"Oh, yes you *are*, Henry. Anyone who can make the wonderful speeches that you do all over the world—and convince people that you are so *right* in what you say—has got to be a *brilliant* actor. Let's do it—it'll be fun."

Reluctantly the good doctor agreed, and after the ball we went to the VIP room where the "Dynasty" crew, led by an excited Elaine Rich, were ready for us, surrounded by a multitude of sightseers.

"Now all you have to do, Doctor," explained Phil Leacock, our director, "is cross the room and meet Joan coming from the opposite direction, and just greet each other. It won't be difficult, Dr. Kissinger. It'll just take a second—Joan will help you."

And so Dr. Henry Kissinger, ex-Secretary of State genius-in-exile—his own phrase—and statesman supreme, found himself playing a scene with TV's naughtiest villainess, after I showed him how to hit his marks.

Dr. Kissinger: Alexis—how are you?

Alexis: I'm fine, Henry, how are you?

Dr. Kissinger: I'm vonderful, Alexis, good to see you.

Alexis: It's good to see you too, Henry. Yes, we haven't met since Portofino . . . wasn't it fun!

The crew collapsed at this ad lib, and another moment of television history was captured forever on film.

Ever since *Land of the Pharaohs* I have a couple of times been so convulsed with giggles while in the midst of shooting a scene that I have been unable to continue.

One such incident happened at the end of my second season of "Dynasty" when Alexis, Krystle and Mark Jennings (Geoffrey Scott) had just escaped from the burning cabin in which someone had tried to kill Krystle and/or Alexis.

Irving Moore, who was our resident director and usually directed every alternate show, was shooting this episode. He had a wonderful sense of humor, and I was very fond of him.

We were shooting inside the studio on a synthetic grass verge next to the back projection of the burning cabin. "Mark" carried me out to where "Krystle" lay panting and coughing, gazing fearfully at the flames. I was supposed to be unconscious. I was wearing a beige jodhpur suit and a large cap that kept falling off my head whenever Geoff placed me on the ground. Although my hairdresser, Linda Sharp, had attached it to my hair with forty-three hairpins and bobby pins, it still fell over my eyes each time Geoff put me down, giving me the look of a demented ventriloquist's dummy.

Elaine Rich decided I looked much too clean for someone having been almost asphyxiated by smoke, so Melanie Levitt, the makeup girl, liberally applied black pancake to my face and hands. A little too liberally. "*Cut,* cut!" yelled Irving exasperatedly. "She looks like Al Jolson, for Christ's sake. Wipe some of it off."

By the time Melanie wiped my face down, which then became an even gray, and Linda attached my cap even more firmly with more pins, I felt the whole thing was ludicrous. I "corpsed" every time Geoffrey set me down and spoke the immortal lines, "Krystle, that cabin was locked from the *outside*—somebody *deliberately* set that fire." I laughed so much that this started Geoff and Linda laughing too. Each take, the more I called on all my willpower—not to mention fiercely biting my tongue until it hurt—to refrain from laughing, the more I found it impossible to stop. Eventually we got the scene in the can, and I tottered off, still hysterical with laughter, to the shower, where it took me half an hour to remove all the fuller's earth and black pancake makeup with which I was covered. Ah, the glamour of show business!

One of the most dastardly deeds Alexis Carrington ever perpetrated was to cause saintly Krystle to lose her unborn baby by firing a shotgun into the air near where Krystle was taking a gentle ride on a horse. I wasn't too pleased about having to do this. Alexis, though mean and evil and Machiavellian in her plots and plans, would not deliberately kill or physically hurt someone, and I felt that this was a pretty low thing even for her to do. Nevertheless, do it I must, so one fine fall day I found myself traipsing up a hill next to my massively tall son, Steven (Al Corley), to go for a little skeet-shooting session, at which Alexis is supposed to be an expert—according to the script.

I had informed the writers that I was hopeless at all forms of sport and *anything* to do with horses ("Alexis *cannot* ride!" I had said to the producers loudly and clearly from the beginning), but nevertheless they decided that Alexis, *femme du monde,* jet-setter and social butterfly that she was, was an expert at all manner of sports.

It was a freezing November morning and we were shooting at a ranch in Hidden Valley. I had persuaded the wardrobe department, albeit reluctantly on their part, to let me wear a Scottish red-and-green-plaid kilt, a long plaid scarf and a beret. They in turn talked me into wearing a red angora turtleneck sweater, which I hated. Thus unsuitably attired, and carrying a huge shotgun of which I was extremely wary, I tottered up the hill, next to Al, the six-foot-four hulk.

"You must remember, Steven," I said crisply, expertly cocking my gun to shoot a skeet, "that you are a Carrington and a Carrington does *everything* well. We swim well, ride well, play tennis well and skeet-shoot well." With this I cocked my gun into space and let off a round, and the bullet went straight through the scrim surrounding an arc lamp, which promptly exploded!

Somewhat ruffled by this, and with my fear of guns still intact, I watched as the electricians replaced the lamp bulb, and then we started another take. By this time the sun had risen high in the sky, as is its wont in Southern California. The temperature had now crept up to the mid-seventies. Bits of red angora fluff had attached themselves to my eyelashes, making everything a faint reddish blurr, and some had floated up my nose, which caused me to sneeze uncontrollably at the end of each take.

Because of this I now started blowing my lines, which I rarely do. Alf Kjellin, our Swedish-born director, was patient with me, but with the heat, the angora fluff everywhere, the *ghastly* gun over which I seemed to have no control, and the "apple box" I was balanced on to get close to Al Corley's height, I was, to say the least, frazzled.

"Thirty-eight baker take nine!" called Joe Valdez, clapping the board in front of my nose and causing me to stifle another sneeze. Take nine— oh, God, how awful. I, who usually get it in one. I concentrated hard. The heat had brought out many insects, and, attracted to my hairspray, they started buzzing around and taking little nips at me.

"Action," called Alf in his calm Swedish way.

"You must remember, Steven, that a Carrington does *everything* well. We swim well, ride well, play tennis well and skeet-shoot well."

Thrilled that I had said the entire line without a fluff, I was about to raise my gun with studied nonchalance when the butt of the gun caught in my hanging plaid scarf and I inadvertently pulled the trigger, shooting myself in the foot! Luckily the gun was loaded only with blanks, but it still stung madly and I hopped around on one foot cursing wildly.

"OK—that's a print," said Alf. "Now let's move over to the tree and have Joan shoot Linda."

Disheveled, sweaty, limping and humiliated, I put on my most evil Alexis look, and with angora fluff and insects floating like an aura around me, I raised the shotgun and shot the two blasts that caused Krystle's horse to bolt, throwing her to the ground and causing her to lose the baby. For which she and thousands of viewers never forgave me!

"Playboy layout!" What did these words mean to everyone? Some cute little nymphet taking off her all for a thousand dollars? It was pretty meaningless in that respect. As far as I was concerned, it had farther-reaching consequences. Women had been exploited for years, whether by themselves or others made no difference. The women I saw in *Playboy* and other men's magazines were young girls doing their erotic or sexy "thing." I certainly didn't consider myself to be in that category any more. I didn't even consider the possibilities or ramifications of what it meant. I was never prudish—selective nudity per se did not bother me. But Middle America, to whom all Hollywood bowed, was a different problem.

Being a woman of "a certain age," I felt that revealing what I did in *Playboy* was a definite plus for women. "A significant step for feminism," I lightly announced. I was exploiting myself—yes, indeed. But in doing so I felt I was breaking the ageism taboo that so many women feared and dreaded. Be that as it may, the December 1983 issue of *Playboy* became a sellout issue and a collector's item. I realized that it was because of me —Joan Collins—not Alexis. I hoped to prove that a woman can definitely be attractive and sexy over thirty-five, or even over forty-five, and I didn't get as much flak from this layout as I had expected. I had had reservations about it, but the admiration that I received, from *women* particularly, for doing it, was well worth the minimum amount of negativity I received. "Well, Brickman," I said to Leslie Bricusse at a party the night *Playboy* hit the stands, "I think I'm about to become notorious." "What do you mean 'about,'" joked he. "You already are, Joanie!"

❖   ❖   ❖

My life has changed radically since I started "Dynasty." The stardom that I never tried to attain as a young actress I have now. How long it will last—who knows? This is the toughest of professions. Very tough. Flavor of the month changes rapidly. Only the strongest, the cleverest and the most resilient survive—but survival is not the only objective. To live as normal a life as possible without letting the enormous pressures that one faces change one's attitudes and sense of reality, without giving in to drugs, booze, sex, flattery, the "woodwork people"—to keep one's sense of balance—is an art in itself.

If my success ended tomorrow and I no longer had the attention, the money, the magazine covers, the media interest, the fan frenzy, the paparazzi, the scripts plopping onto my doorstep, I know that I could survive and still be a happy person.

Success is not enough. Money and material possessions are not enough. Nor beauty—nor men—nor love nor lust or whatever it's called these days. The truly important things in my life now are the health and love of my children—particularly Katy, with whom I have an irrevocable bond—and the love and loyalty of my close friends who have remained by me throughout the years.

To me, a good, loving relationship is one in which two secure and mature individuals are committed to *wanting* and needing to be with one another. Unfortunately, one's needs change with the years, and couples must acknowledge this and try to change too—otherwise love can only end in disappointment. The quest for true love can take many forms, as I have discovered. The acid tests of a relationship are time and growing together toward a mutual goal that is satisfying to both parties.

My life has been full of surprises, excitement, many highs and several lows. Hard work. Many relationships. Some pain, and a lot of fun. Most of the time I have enjoyed it completely. "Life is a banquet and most poor suckers are starving to death," said W. C. Fields. I agree.

Today I must contend with the public's disparate image of me as the manipulative and bitchy Alexis. Sometimes it can be amusing, like the day Judy Bryer and I were driving down Benedict Canyon about four months after I started appearing on "Dynasty." A station wagon full of little kids about seven or eight years old drew up as we stopped at the traffic lights, and they all began waving excitedly.

"Your junior fan club," joked Judy.

I smiled generously at the sweet little things and lowered my window to bestow a wide smile and my "Queen Mum" wave on them.

"Alexis," they shouted joyfully, "we hate you! we HATE you!!!"

They jumped up and down with glee and I turned, stunned, to Judy, who was shaking with laughter. "You're the woman America loves to hate," she said. "May as well face it and go for it. It's a compliment, really." There is a bit of Alexis in me—the resilience, strength, and ambition are certainly there now. I wish I had more of her shrewdness and cleverness in dealing with business, but I am learning from her.

I have given up bemoaning "but I'm *not like* Alexis." Like it or not, that bitch goddess label will probably stick with me forever. As long as I, and my family and close friends, know me as I am, that is all that matters to me.

And there is a man in my life now. I met Peter Holm in England in the summer of 1983 when the last thing I wanted or needed was another relationship.

We have been together now for a year and a half and even though I was wary of emotional involvement, Peter has been good for me; at Christmastime 1984, we became engaged. We made this commitment because we have continued to grow closer and give each other the support we need. I would like to predict that Peter and I will live happily ever after . . . as the story books end, but I realize that there are no guarantees in life, and that the only constant is change.

In January of 1985 Peter announced plans to co-produce a six-hour mini-series for CBS called "Sins," in which I am to be the star. With "Dynasty" now the #1 show in America, this is exciting! The prospect of having control over my professional destiny is truly a thrill.

My past was not perfect. Few people *are* perfect, and I am no exception. Hopefully I have learned from my mistakes and have been able to pave the way for a peaceful and more perfect future. *Onward!*

The Early Years

My favorite picture of Mummy and me.

Oh, what a beautiful baby!

Even at age 3, I was partial to a fur coat.

The little Collins sisters—Joan and Jackie—anticipating a happy future as actress and writer.

Age 11—I was already dreaming of becoming an actress.

Still dreaming in my teen years.
Eric Jackson

My earliest "on stage."

London, 1962. Our lovely mother Elsa with Jackie and me shortly before her untimely death.

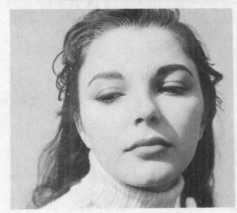

A very young, very green actress making her debut in *I Believe in You*, 1952.

J. Arthur Rank Organization

The Movie Years

With *The Girl in the Red Velvet Swing,* 20th Century–Fox launched me in a blaze of publicity that culminated in this *Life* cover.

J. R. Eyerman, *Life* magazine © 1955, Time, Inc.

My first starring movie part in *I Believe in You* with Laurence Harvey. I was terribly impressed by him.

J. Arthur Rank Organization

Montauk, L.I., 1963. The inseparable Newleys and Bricusses on vacation. Tony and Leslie were writing *Roar of the Greasepaint*. Evie and Joan were expecting Adam and Tara respectively!

Called "Britain's answer to Ava Gardner," I honestly didn't think she had much to worry about.

J. Arthur Rank Organization

Playing a novice nun wrecked on a desert island with Richard Burton in *Seawife*. We weren't allowed to kiss in the movie. Fox allowed this symbolic palm tree as a substitute.
Pictorial Parade

My first Hollywood movie, *The Virgin Queen*. I was not Bette Davis' favorite lady-in-waiting.
Pictorial Parade

Howard Hawks' *Land of the Pharaohs*. The anguished look comes from holding in my stomach. The ruby was there to satisfy the censor's stringent code.
Magnum

The Hollywood pinup factory ground out hundreds of shots like this. Here is my "pouting panther" look, usually achieved because I was bored stiff.
UPI

The Big Time at Metro! My first grown-up role as Crystal in *The Opposite Sex* with June Allyson, Dolores Gray, Ann Sheridan, Ann Miller, and Joan Blondell. Hollywood, 1956.
MGM

Warren visiting the set of *Seven Thieves,* with Eli Wallach. Hollywood, 1960.

Experimenting as a 1930s blonde for *Fallen Angels*, 1974. This amazing authentic Art Deco house in London was shortly afterwards totally gutted by new owners. What sacrilege!

My turn to visit the set. On location in New York for *Splendor in the Grass*, 1961. From left to right: myself, Warren Beatty, Elia Kazan, Natalie Wood and Robert Wagner.

Party time in Hollywood with Arthur Loew, Jr. For some reason, Errol Flynn is pretending to be a dog.

Practicing my pose for *Cleopatra*, the role I didn't get! Milton Greene is the photographer and we are on the back lot at Fox, 1961.

In Barbados with the splendid Harry Belafonte for *Island in the Sun*.

From the last of the "Road" films, *The Road to Hong Kong.* I was Dorothy Lamour's new replacement. With Bing and Bob, it was business as usual.

The laughing, dancing, drunken scene from *Rally 'Round the Flag, Boys* was Paul Newman's first, and I believe *last* attempt at hoofing.
Eric Benson

Arriving on the island of Jamaica to make *Seawife* with Richard Burton.

With Marlon Brando at a New York opening. My real romance was cropped from the photo and the gossip columns revealed Brando and me as a "new twosome."
UPI

As the sluttish alcoholic wife in Steinbeck's *The Wayward Bus* I got some excellent reviews. Many people were amazed that I could act!

My least favorite and most grueling film role, *Empire of the Ants,* on location in the Florida swamps. My legs are covered with infected wounds and I am terrorized by giant plastic ants.

Edward H. Sanderson

"Give your boyfriend Joan Collins for Christmas," screamed advertisements for the best-selling video cassette of *The Bitch*. I don't think chauffeur's caps and garter belts worn with fur coats will ever make a major fashion statement!

UPI

With Roger Moore in "The Persuaders," one of my many guest TV roles.

With Robert Mitchum in a remake of *The Big Sleep*, which was not as successful as the original.

Romances, Husbands, Children

Official engagement photo, 1961. We both look wary.
Friedman-Abels

My first husband, Maxwell Reed. But not for long!

In Rome and in love with Sydney Chaplin, son of Charlie.

Playing poker with Vivien Leigh and Warren while visiting him on the set in Rome for *The Roman Spring of Mrs. Stone*. Miss Leigh's flirtatious glances at him were not unnoticed by me.

New York, 1963. With Anthony Newley shortly before our wedding

With my darling
Katyana Kennedy
Kass, age 2 days.
London, 1972.

Mother Earth!
With my 2 beauti-
ful babies—Sacha,
6 months, Tara,
age 2. London,
1966.

Marco Schiavo

London, 1968.
Putting on a happy
family front with
Tony, Tara and
Sacha.

Happy family, with Tara and Sacha in Beverly Hills. I was content to play the little wife role and I adored my children.

Ken Whitmore

A visit to Marineland with Tony and Tara, Natalie Wood and friends.
Bob Noble

His, Hers and Ours. With my 1972 marriage to Ron Kass I inherited three more kids. From left to right: Robert Kass, Jonathan Kass, Ron, me with sweet six-week-old Katyana Kennedy Kass, my Sacha and Tara, and David Kass.

Edward H. Sanderson, *Sunday Mirror*

London, 1981. Less than a year after Katy's terrible accident, we laud "Joan Collins Jeans" together.

Bob Moody,
Scope Features

Beverly Hills, 1983. Away from the evil Alexis, Katy and I are happy together at home.

Edward H. Sanderson

The Now Years

The Alexis Look, circa 1982.

February, 1984: Showing off with 90 of the nearly 500 magazine covers on which I've appeared.
Peter Holm

As Fontaine Khaled in *The Stud*. My sister Jackie's bestselling novel became a box office hit in England. London, 1978.

John Forsythe and his "Dynasty" women: Linda Evans—*Krystle;*
Pamela Bellwood—*Claudia;* Heather Locklear—*Sammy Jo;*
Pamela Sue Martin—*Falon;* JC—*Alexis.* In spite of what you see on
the screen, we all get along...most of the time!
ABC

Krystle and Alexis at war again, inside the Carrington mansion.
1982.
ABC

Winning the 1983 Golden Globe for Best Actress in a TV Drama
Series.
Elizabeth J. Annas

A thrilling moment for Katy and me—meeting Her Majesty, the
Queen, and Prince Philip, after I had hosted a charity concert at
the Royal Albert Hall in London, 1982.

The Christmas 1983 cover of *Playboy.*
Playboy

Kay and her stable of hunks! A publicity photo for "Male Model,"
1983.
ABC·

Diamonds (in this case rhinestones) are indeed a girl's best friend in
this shot from *The Cartier Affair* with David Hasselhoff, 1984.

The Alexis Look,
circa 1984.
ABC

My first (and last)
roast. Being roast-
ed as "Woman of
the Year," with
Dean Martin and
Angie Dickinson.
Las Vegas, 1984.

Responding to some of the Roasters' more ribald remarks.

Happy Days with Alexis and Dex. Michael Nader and me in 1984.

Outside the church where Alexis married Dex. I kept on the wedding hat but changed into something more comfortable for a water break.

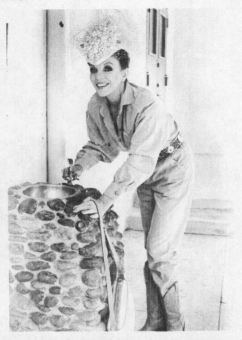

Beverly Hills, 1984. With Peter Holm launching the Joan Collins jewelry collection, shortly before our engagement.

Janet Gough, Celebrity Photo

The Alexis Look, circa 1983.

❧ *Filmography* ❧

LADY GODIVA RIDES AGAIN
GB 1951 / D: Frank Launder / with Pauline Stroud, Dennis Price, Stanley Holloway, Kay Kendall, John McCallum, Diana Dors.

THE WOMAN'S ANGLE
GB 1952 / D: Leslie Arliss / with Edward Underdown, Cathy O'Donnell, Lois Maxwell.

JUDGMENT DEFERRED
GB 1952 / D: John Baxter / with Hugh Sinclair, Helen Shingler.

I BELIEVE IN YOU
GB 1952 / D: Basil Dearden / with Cecil Parker, Celia Johnson, Laurence Harvey, Harry Fowler, Ursula Howells, Godfrey Tearle.

DECAMERON NIGHTS
GB 1952 / D: Hugo Fregonese / with Louis Jourdan, Joan Fontaine, Binnie Barnes, Mara Lane.

COSH BOY (US: THE SLASHER)
GB 1953 / D: Lewis Gilbert / with James Kenney, Hermione Gingold, Hermione Baddeley, Betty Ann Davies.

THE SQUARE RING
GB 1953 / D: Basil Dearden / with Jack Warner, Robert Beatty, Maxwell Reed, Kay Kendall, Bernadette O'Farrell.

TURN THE KEY SOFTLY
GB 1953 / D: Jack Lee / with Yvonne Mitchell, Kathleen Harrison, Terence Morgan, Glyn Houston, Geoffrey Keen, Thora Hird.

OUR GIRL FRIDAY (US: ADVENTURES OF SADIE)
GB 1953 / D: Noel Langley / with George Cole, Kenneth More, Robertson Hare, Hermione Gingold, Hattie Jacques.

THE GOOD DIE YOUNG
GB 1954 / D: Lewis Gilbert / with Laurence Harvey, Richard Basehart, Gloria Grahame, Stanley Baker, Margaret Leighton.

LAND OF THE PHARAOHS
US 1954 / D: Howard Hawks / with Jack Hawkins, Sydney Chaplin, James Robertson Justice, Alexis Minotis, Kerima, Dewey Martin.

THE VIRGIN QUEEN
US 1955 / D: Henry Koster / with Bette Davis, Richard Todd, Herbert Marshall, Jay Robinson, Dan O'Herlihy, Lisa Daniels.

THE GIRL IN THE RED VELVET SWING
US 1955 / D: Richard Fleischer / with Ray Milland, Farley Granger, Glenda Farrell, Luther Adler, Gale Robbins.

THE OPPOSITE SEX
US 1956 / D: David Miller / with June Allyson, Ann Sheridan, Ann Miller, Dolores Gray, Joan Blondell, Agnes Moorehead, Leslie Nielsen, Dick Shawn.

SEAWIFE
GB 1956 / D: Bob McNaught / with Richard Burton, Cy Grant.

ISLAND IN THE SUN
GB 1956 / D: Robert Rossen / with James Mason, Joan Fontaine, Harry Belafonte, Patricia Owens, Stephen Boyd, Dorothy Dandridge, John Justin.

THE WAYWARD BUS
US 1957 / D: Victor Vicas / with Jayne Mansfield, Dan Dailey, Rick Jason, Dolores Michaels, Betty Lou Keim, Larry Keating.

STOPOVER TOKYO
US 1957 / D: Richard L. Breen / with Robert Wagner, Edmond O'Brien, Ken Scott, Larry Keating.

THE BRAVADOS
US 1958 / D: Henry King / with Gregory Peck, Stephen Boyd, Albert Salmi, Lee Van Cleef, Henry Silva, Kathleen Gallant.

RALLY ROUND THE FLAG, BOYS
US 1958 / D: Leo McCarey / with Paul Newman, Joanne Woodward, Jack Carson, Tuesday Weld, Gale Gordon, Dwayne Hickman.

SEVEN THIEVES
US 1959 / D: Henry Hathaway / with Rod Steiger, Eli Wallach, Edward G. Robinson, Michael Dante, Berry Kroeger.

ESTHER AND THE KING
US/ITALIAN 1960 / D: Raoul Walsh / with Richard Egan, Denis O'Dea, Sergio Fantoni, Rik Battaglia, Gabriele Tinti.

THE ROAD TO HONG KONG
GB 1962 / D: Norman Panama / with Bob Hope, Bing Crosby, Dorothy Lamour, Robert Morley, Frank Sinatra, Dean Martin.

LA CONGUINTURA
ITALIAN 1964 / D: Ettore Scola / with Vittorio Gassman, Jacques Bergerac.

WARNING SHOT
US 1966 / D: Buzz Kulik / with David Janssen, Eleanor Parker, George Sanders, Stefanie Powers, Lillian Gish, Walter Pidgeon.

SUBTERFUGE
GB 1968 / D: Peter Graham-Scott / with Gene Barry, Tom Adams, Suzanna Leigh, Richard Todd, Michael Rennie.

CAN HIERONYMUS MERKIN EVER FORGET MERCY HUMPPE AND FIND TRUE HAPPINESS?
GB 1969 / D: Anthony Newley / with Anthony Newley, Milton Berle, Connie Kreski, Bruce Forsyth, Tara Newley, Sacha Newley.

IF IT'S TUESDAY, THIS MUST BE BELGIUM
US 1969 / D: Mel Stuart / with Suzanne Pleshette, Ian McShane.

STATE OF SIEGE
ITALIAN 1969 / D: Romano Scavolini / with Mathieu Carrière, Faith Domergue, Michael Coby.

THE EXECUTIONER
GB 1970 / D: Sam Wanamaker / with George Peppard, Judy Geeson, Nigel Patrick, Keith Michell, George Baker, Charles Gray.

DRIVE HARD, DRIVE FAST
US-TV 1970 / D: Douglas Heyes / with Brian Kelly, Henry Silva, Karen Houston, Joseph Campanella.

UP IN THE CELLAR (THREE IN THE CELLAR)
US 1970 / D: Theodore J. Flicker / with Larry Hagman, Wes Stern.

QUEST FOR LOVE
GB 1971 / D: Ralph Thomas / with Tom Bell, Laurence Naismith, Denholm Elliott, Juliet Harmer, Lyn Ashley.

REVENGE (US: INN OF THE FRIGHTENED PEOPLE or TERROR FROM UNDER THE HOUSE)
GB 1971 / D: Sidney Hayers / with James Booth, Sinead Cusack, Kenneth Griffith, Tom Marshall, Ray Barrett, Zuleka Robson.

FEAR IN THE NIGHT
GB 1971 / D: Jimmy Sangster / with Judy Geeson, Ralph Bates, Peter Cushing, Gillian Lind, James Cossins.

TALES FROM THE CRYPT
GB 1972 / D: Freddie Francis / with Ralph Richardson, Peter Cushing, Nigel Patrick, Richard Greene, Martin Boddey.

DARK PLACES
GB 1973 / D: Don Sharp / with Christopher Lee, Robert Hardy, Jane Birkin, Herbert Lom, Jean Marsh.

TALES THAT WITNESS MADNESS
GB 1973 / D: Freddie Francis / with Michael Jayston, Kim Novak, Jack Hawkins, Donald Pleasence, Georgia Brown, Peter McEnery.

L'ARBITRO (US: THE REFEREE)
ITALIAN 1973 / D: Louis Phillipo D'Amico / with Lando Buzzanca.

ALFIE DARLING (US: OH! ALFIE!)
GB 1974 / D: Ken Hughes / with Alan Price, Jill Townsend, Hannah Gordon, Rula Lenska, Annie Ross.

CALL OF THE WOLF (US: THE GREAT ADVENTURE)
SPANISH 1975 / D: Paul Elliotts / with Jack Palance, Fred Romer.

THE BAWDY ADVENTURES OF TOM JONES
GB 1975 / D: Cliff Owen / with Nicky Henson, Geraldine McEwan, Georgia Brown, Trevor Howard, Madeline Smith, Terry-Thomas.

I DON'T WANT TO BE BORN (US: THE DEVIL WITHIN HER)
GB 1975 / D: Peter Sasdy / with Ralph Bates, Donald Pleasence, Eileen Atkins, Caroline Munro, John Steiner, George Claydon.

THE MONEYCHANGERS
US-TV 1976 / D: Boris Segal / with Kirk Douglas, Christopher Plummer, Anne Baxter, Lorne Greene, Susan Flannery, Jean Peters.

EMPIRE OF THE ANTS
US 1976 / D: Bert I. Gordon / with Robert Lansing, John David Carson, Pamela Shoop, Jacqueline Scott, Albert Salmi.

THE BIG SLEEP
GB 1977 / D: Michael Winner / with Robert Mitchum, Sarah Miles, Edward Fox, Oliver Reed, Candy Clark, James Stewart, John Mills.

POLIZIOTTO SENZA PAURA
ITALIAN 1977 / D: Selvio Massi / with Maurizio Merli, Franco Ressel, Gastone Moschin, Jasmine Maimone, Alexander Trojan.

THE STUD
GB 1978 / D: Quentin Masters / with Oliver Tobias, Sue Lloyd, Mark Burns, Emma Jacobs, Walter Gotell, Doug Fisher.

ZERO TO 60
US 1978 / D: Darren McGavin / with Darren McGavin, Sylvia Miles, Denise Nickerson, Dick Martin.

GAME FOR VULTURES
US 1979 / D: James Fargo / with Richard Harris, Ray Milland, Richard Roundtree, Sven Bertil-Taube, Denholm Elliott.

THE BITCH
GB 1979 / D: Gerry O'Hara / with Michael Coby, Carolyn Seymour, Sue Lloyd, Mark Burns, Pamela Salem, Kenneth Haigh.

SUNBURN
US 1979 / D: Richard Sarafian / with Farrah Fawcett, Charles Grodin, Art Carney, Eleanor Parker, Alejandro Rey.

PAPER DOLLS
US-TV 1982 / D: Edward Zwick / with Joan Hackett, Marc Singer, Jennifer Warren, Darryl Hannah, Alexandra Paul.

NUTCRACKER
GB 1982 / D: Anwar Kawadri / with Finola Hughes, Paul Nicholas, Carol White, William Franklyn, Leslie Ash, Geraldine Gardner.

THE WILD WOMEN OF CHASTITY GULCH
US-TV 1982 / D: Philip Leacock / with Priscilla Barnes, Pamela Bellwood, Lee Horsley, Howard Duff, Morgan Brittany.

HANSEL AND GRETEL FAERIE TALE THEATRE
US-TV 1982 / D: James Frawley / with Ricky Schroeder.

THE MAKING OF A MALE MODEL
US-TV 1983 / D: Irving J. Moore / with Jon-Erik Hexum, Roxie Roker,
Jeff Conaway, Kevin McCarthy, Arte Johnson, Ted McGinley.

MY LIFE AS A MAN
US-TV 1984 / D: Robert Ellis Miller / with Robert Culp, Marc Singer,
Robin Douglas.

THE CARTIER AFFAIR
US-NBC TV 1984 / D: Rod Holcomb / with David Hassellhoff, Telly
Savalas.

PRIME TIME

For every actress
who has ever suffered the slings and arrows
of outrageous fortune
that are such a part of all our lives . . .
and for Daddy, who was
such a part of mine.

PART ONE

❧ *One* ❧

Chloe Carriere strode swiftly through the Heathrow departure lounge, trying with little success to escape the inquisitive lenses of the familiar throng of paparazzi. As photographers and reporters buzzed around her, several businessmen waiting for flights lowered their morning newspapers to stare at one of Britain's most famous and sexiest singing stars. "How long will you be in Hollywood, Chloe?" demanded the hack with acne from the *Sun*.

Chloe smiled, increasing her pace. Her sable-lined trench coat billowed gracefully around her newly slimmed figure. She had spent a grueling week at a health farm in Wales trying to erase the combined ravages of Josh, a demanding six-month tour of the provinces, and her first acting role in a BBC docudrama about women in prison. It had brought her down to fighting weight, and now she looked and felt great—better now in 1982 than she had in years.

"What kind of a part are you testing for?" grinned the one with the green teeth from the *Mirror*. "Is it a new television soap opera, then?"

"I don't really know too much about it yet," she hedged. "Other than that it's based on a best-selling novel called *Saga*."

"Do you want the part?" asked the one from Reuters with the adenoids and the bulging Adam's apple.

Did she want the part? What a stupid question! Of *course* she wanted the damn part. After more than twenty years of singing gigs in Britain, Europe and the States, she ached for it but she answered their questions casually: *if* she was lucky enough to be chosen for the role of Miranda Hamilton, it could turn her career around, make her a big name, maybe even a superstar. But she didn't want these little bastards—and those bigger bastards—waiting in Hollywood to look her over to know just how much she cared, how desperately she needed this role, particularly when she was only one of four or five actresses who were testing for it.

Testing for it! Demeaning, but what the hell. She knew this business was no fairy godmother. She had been up and down in it, then up and then down again, like a Yo-Yo for years. Seven hit records in two and a half decades. A fixture in the Top Ten, now suddenly, in 1982, she couldn't even make *Billboard*'s Top 100. Twenty-five years of performing, but still surviving and still sane, thank God. She gave the reporters and the photographers a smile and a friendly wave as she reached the departure gate, and as they snapped a few more frames for good measure, she hoped the photographs would be kind in tomorrow's tabloids.

In the first-class comfort of the British Airways cabin she relaxed, accepted a Buck's Fizz from the smiling steward, then changed her mind in anticipation of the forthcoming scrutiny of studio moguls, asking instead for Evian water. She waved away cashew nuts and caviar, accepted the *Herald Tribune* and the *Daily Express,* removed her cream kid boots and belt, reclined her seat to its maximum, and thought about this irresistible role.

Miranda Hamilton, in *Saga*. A story of intrigue, corruption, betrayal, ambition and lust, set against a background of great wealth amidst the opulent estates, luxurious yachts and ultramodern skyscraper offices of Newport Beach, California. A tale of men and women who loved and hated with passions larger than life. The book had been on *The New York Times* best-seller list for six months, and now they were casting for the television series. According to Chloe's agent, Jasper Swanson, they had already cast several familiar television names for various roles, but had not yet found their bitch-goddess villainess Miranda. The network wanted a glamorous manipulating bitch, a rotten-to-the-core heartless tramp, a deviously ambitious but sexily elegant woman of the world, a female so mean and gorgeous that every man watching would either want to make love to her or give her a taste of her own medicine, and whom every woman would either envy or emulate. If the show were a hit, the actress who would play her could be catapulted to ephemeral television fame, glory, and the eventual megabucks that went with that success.

But Miranda Hamilton *couldn't* be the average Hollywood blond bimbo. She had to be at least forty, preferably closer to forty-five. Survivor of three or four marriages and three or four dozen affairs, she had borne three or four children, owned three or four estates scattered throughout the world, had three or four million dollars' worth of jewels, not to mention two or three hundred million dollars in the bank. The actress picked for this plum part would certainly have to have enough in common with Miranda to be believable to the audience. They would have to hate her, and they would have to love her. Not an easy combination to achieve. She had to be a bitch, but she had to be vulnerable. She had to have fire, but she had to be warm. She had to be dominating, yet men must feel they could be the one to dominate her. And last week the producers, dynamic Abby Arafat and his partner, the equally dynamic Gertrude Greenbloom, had come up with the idea of testing Chloe.

Chloe had attracted Abby Arafat's interest at a cocktail party at Lady Sarah Cranleigh's Eaton Square flat. Just returned from a tour of Scandinavia, Chloe, unable to decide whether to reconcile with her husband, Josh, in L.A., had lingered for a few days in London, where the other person dearest to her heart lived.

She felt there was very little hope of patching things up with Josh. There was no question that she had been a loving, faithful wife to him. Yet he seemed unable to control his sexual drive with other women. He was lukewarm with her, whined if she wasn't around, yet nagged her if she was. He was a man who had almost ruined his career with his volatile temperament, so much so that record companies had been canceling contracts, and his tours were drying up. Often he would sulk for days, refusing to talk to Chloe, locking himself into his personalized state-of-the-art recording studio and mixing his own records hour after hour, day after day, week after week, blocking out everyone else around him.

The day before she had left, walking past his bathroom she saw him masturbating over a copy of a men's magazine. It had nauseated her, but she had not let him know she had seen him. If he could become aroused by a picture in a cheap magazine, why couldn't he make love to *her* properly any more? It had been weeks—no—months now since they had. Ever the optimist, she had hoped things would be different after this last separation. Obviously she had been wrong.

Chloe sighed, coming out of her reverie as the Fasten Seat Belt sign went off. Carrying her beige crocodile Morabito overnight bag, she walked to the plane's cramped toilet. Why, she wondered, with so much effort expended on design, are the toilets not big enough even to brush one's hair without fracturing an elbow? She slipped off her Gianni Versace cream silk blouse and skirt and pulled on a blue velour track suit. She ran a comb through her luxuriant black curly hair and removed her makeup to let her skin breathe, then slathered moisturizer on lavishly—flying ruined her complexion, there was no doubt about that—and strolled back to her seat.

Although aware that several of the women passengers had noticed the transformation and were checking her for cracks, Chloe didn't care. She had little vanity about her looks. She thought she looked fine without makeup, casually dressed. Not for her the elaborate lengths to which many female entertainers went to prevent the world from seeing their real faces. She smiled as she thought of her co-star in the BBC TV play she had just finished. Pandora King was a seldom-out-of-work American actress who had been appearing in supporting roles in series and movies of the week for the past ten years. Although the public never really knew her name, they always recognized her attractively foxy face and glamorous auburn hair. Pandora would arrive in a full, light makeup at six every morning, completely done, even to false lashes, and wearing one of her many Kanekolan wigs which she possessed in several styles. She would be swathed in her mink of the day, which she had in all colors, and would then disappear into her dressing room for three hours. Her makeup box was the size of a compact car and contained every device known to drugstore and cosmetic counter, from plastic fingernails to vaginal jelly. Only God and her makeup man knew what she did in that room, because when she eventually surfaced she looked little different from when she went in.

The two women had spent an amusing lunch hour going through the contents of "Pandora's box," as she called it, on a rare day when Pandora's frosty attitude toward the world, and especially toward other actresses, had thawed slightly.

Chloe wondered if a question one of the journalists had asked was true: Was Pandora also testing for Miranda? If so, Pandora herself would be the last person to reveal *that* bit of news to Chloe. She believed in giving nothing away, particularly information of a professional kind.

Arriving at Los Angeles Airport ten hours later, Chloe was whisked by limousine to the endless freeways of Los Angeles.

She grimaced as she observed the repetitive and unattractive streets and boulevards that passed endlessly. Gray smog hung heavily over the city, stinging her eyes and throat, even though the windows of the Cadillac were closed and the air-conditioning turned on full blast.

Chloe had spent a great deal of time in the past two decades living in L.A., but she still disliked the look of the city. It was so ugly, almost sordid in places, and inhabited by people who seemed to exist solely on hamburgers, doughnuts and diet sodas judging by the number of establishments that were selling those substances. New health clubs, gyms and fitness centers sprouted like mushrooms. She counted sixteen new ones. The residents obviously needed them to balance their ruinous eating habits.

Rows of faded buildings, their signs proclaiming the delights of "Yoghurt City," "The Popcorn Palace," and "Chuck's Chili Dogs," passed by. Chloe sighed. Nothing had changed in the six months she had been away. There just seemed to be more smog.

She snuggled deeper into her sable-lined coat, shivering although it was seventy degrees. She was in Los Angeles, coming home to face Josh, hoping to salvage something of their years of magic together.

When the limousine came to the end of the interweaving freeway, turning right onto the straight Pacific Coast Highway at Sunset Boulevard, Chloe relaxed, loosened her coat and opened the window to feel the cool sea breeze on her face. She loved the ocean, the mystery and power of it. She never tired of watching the greenish gray flatness of the Pacific crest into thick fierce white waves as she sat on the beach.

When they had first bought the house in a secluded part of Trancas Beach, beyond Malibu, she and Josh spent early mornings and most evenings walking along the caramel sands dodging the tide, talking about everything under the sun, laughing at the baby sandpipers, breathing the salty pure air, so different from the smoggy atmosphere that passed for oxygen in the city. They had been so happy that Chloe thought that no married couple could ever have been as gloriously and passionately devoted to each other. But that was then, and this was now, and it was time to find out if he had changed his tune in the six months they had been apart.

He was watching the box as usual, slumped in his favorite suede comfortable armchair. They kissed abstractedly, lovers whose lust for each other had lost its luster. He was dressed in rumpled navy blue cords and a V-neck cashmere sweater. His black hair was untidy and flecked with gray. Although he had known she was coming home, he hadn't bothered to shave, and she felt his splintery stubble against her soft cheek.

"I brought you some special honey from Fortnum's. It's new from Devon—they say it's wonderful." He ignored her, his body loose and relaxed as she hugged him tightly.

Was it too late for them now? she wondered, as she held the face she had adored for so many years between her hands and kissed his cool lips. In spite of his waning interest in her and his womanizing, she still couldn't believe this was happening to them. *Why* was he turning off her? After six months apart, why did he make no effort? Not even a pretense of delight in her homecoming. He didn't even bother to stand up. What had she done to make him so indifferent? Even before she went on tour, there had been too many moments in bed, their usual arena of compatibility, when she had had to coax him to make love to her. She felt like a cheap tart. Was this what ten years of marriage did to a man's libido? she wondered bitterly, as she pressed her body seductively close to his. She felt nothing. Not a bump, not a lump, not a twitch. This from a man who had a worldwide reputation as a great lover. Maybe still did. But not with her.

She turned away, pretending to busy herself with a pile of mail. Hot tears pricked the back of her lids and her throat felt constricted. How long could this continue? It was a farce. Without comedy.

"Your agent called," Josh said coolly, turning up the volume on the TV. Eyes glued to Clint Eastwood. "Call him back, says it's *important*." The last word sounded almost like a sneer. She ignored his tone, smiled too brightly. Went to the antique wooden bar to fix a forbidden vodka and ice. The health farm had said no liquor for at least a week. To hell with them.

She called Jasper from the bedroom, not wanting Josh to hear. The slightest thing set him off these days. She wanted to try and keep the peace as long as she could.

"Dear heart, I'm so glad you called," Jasper sounded pleased. "It's looking good for 'Saga,' looking very good indeed for you, dear."

"Wonderful." Chloe smiled, the vodka giving her an excited buzz.

"They will probably shoot six or seven days a month in Newport Beach," she heard Jasper saying. "The rest of the filming will be at one of the studios. Possibly Metro, maybe Fox."

"That's great, Newport is beautiful. Will we be shooting on any boats?"

"Yes, yes, dear." Jasper was often impatient with his clients' desire for details. "Listen to me, Chloe, on the twenty-fifth you're on display. Abby and Maud Arafat are giving one of their casual little dinners, just twenty or thirty of the most important people in this town. They want you there, dear girl. Best bib and tucker on. You have twelve days to prepare, so get out your new Bob Mackie. I *hope* you lost all that bloat at the fat farm, dear, bellies don't look good in Mackies."

"Yes, Jasper, I lost every ounce," she said obediently. "I won't let you down. I promise."

"You better not, dear. This one's a biggie, believe me. Could make you HUGE, dear, really huge."

"I know, Jasper. I know."

She knew what a casual little dinner for twenty or thirty meant. There were no casual little dinners in Hollywood any more. Every meeting in LaLa Land was business. Whether spoken or unspoken, potential deals simmered beneath the surface of even the simplest lunch. A gathering of twenty or thirty of the town's finest citizens at an important producer's house was often the equivalent of a summit meeting in Washington.

Knowing Abby and his partner, Gertrude Greenbloom, who would unquestionably be present too, Chloe surmised that the three or four other potential candidates for Miranda would also be attending. She knew she was only included as the lucky result of the recent fortunate meeting in London.

The slit of Chloe's black silk Valentino skirt had been just high enough to glimpse a firm, elegant thigh. Her chiseled features had a look of abandon, her hair was an aureole of black curls, and her figure was slim but voluptuous.

Abby had downed two martinis, and holding back had never been his forte. "How would you like to play Miranda? I hear you could do with a job and you've certainly got all her attributes from where I stand." His eyes scanned her body and face like a laser beam.

Chloe laughed. "Abby, you know I'm just a saloon singer."

Although she was aware that Hollywood's search for "Saga's" leading roles was a hot show business topic, she was too canny to be taken in by Abby's pitch, and yet—and yet—why not? Singing had not been satisfying for some time. The young Stevie Nickses and Pat Benatars had more appeal to the public today than a forty-year-old singer, and God knows touring was becoming more and more grueling. Maybe settling down again in California with a steady job would bring her and Josh closer together.

"Streisand said that, Garland said it, so did Liza." Abby smiled approvingly as he surveyed her. She certainly was a gorgeous woman, five feet six to his six feet two, but in three-inch black satin Maud Frizon sandals she met his eyes with ease. "They thought they were just singers too."

"I'm not really an actress, Abby. I just did one play for the Beeb, that's all." She sipped her kir while surveying him through a forest of real eyelashes. "I did get good reviews, though I'm sure you read them." She smiled a catlike beam that was one of her stocks in trade.

He started to melt. Abby was that rare Hollywood phenomenon, a producer who actually *liked* and admired actresses. He puffed on his cigar, scrutinizing her from top to toe. She had class—there was no doubt about that. And beauty, sex appeal and glamour.

"Who cares about acting? It's presence, charisma, pulling power, that's what we need for Miranda. Most of the old-time screen greats couldn't act their way out of a McDonald's hamburger bag. Look at Hayworth, Grable, Bardot, Ava Gardner. None of 'em could *act,* for Christ's sake, but they had *it.* And I think *you've* got *it,* kid, in spades—so let's give it a whirl. Come to California and we'll test you, honey. You'll be great, I know you will."

"Let me think about it, Abby—truly I will consider it." Chloe suspected that Abby's pitch, enthusiastic as it was, was probably equally strong to the other actresses he was considering. "Doesn't Miranda have to age from twenty to some ancient age? Mind you, I could probably play *that* end," she joked.

"Yes, yes," Abby said eagerly. "That will be in the four-hour movie of the week we shoot before the series starts. When first we see the young Miranda she's eighteen, and a virgin."

"Oh, no *way!*" cried Chloe with a chuckle. "I couldn't look eighteen!"

"Of course you could." He laughed at her protestations. "We've got Lazlo Dominick doing the lighting. He could make Bette Davis look twenty, for Christ's sake. You've got the aura, you've got the looks and the sex appeal. I think you've got the talent. Test for us, sweetheart, please. You won't be sorry."

"All right, Abby," Chloe had agreed. "All right. I'll test but I warn you, I'll be terrified."

"Wonderful," Abby had wheezed. "Olivier's always terrified—sign of great talent. You'll hear from us next week, sweetheart, and don't be frightened—you'll be terrific, I can feel it in my bones."

"So who else is testing?" she asked Jasper a mite too casually.

"Some of the suggestions are *insane.* Simply *mad.*" Jasper laughed. "I know it's a peach of a part, dear, and this town has gone wild about the casting. There hasn't been anything as exciting since Selznick was searching for Scarlett O'Hara, but listen to the other contenders."

"Who are they?" Chloe's voice wasn't casual now. She needed this information.

"Sissy Sharp. Now we all know she hasn't had a hit in years, needs the part badly. Wonderful actress. Zero sex appeal but she's an Oscar winner, of course."

"I know," Chloe said ruefully. "I was there, Jasper, remember? I sang the winning song. Whatever was it called?"

"Who cares?" Jasper said testily. "Nobody remembers the names of who won *last* year, let alone fifteen years ago! Sissy is hungry, dear—hungry as hell for that role. Hungry enough to test, but she's pretending she's not interested in TV, only the big screen, and they don't give a fuck about her these days. However, the good news is that Abby and Gertrude don't think she's right."

"She's not looking too good these days, is she?" said Chloe. "I don't mean to be bitchy, but I saw her on 'Lifestyles' last week; she looked, well, ravaged—like a fugitive from Belsen."

"Diets like an anorexic teenager," Jasper said bluntly. "She's crazy, she thinks she constantly rejuvenates herself with all those fad diets—not to mention the surgery. She must have had her face and her tits lifted at least three times in the past five years."

Chloe shuddered. The idea of a knife near her body terrified her.

"Then we have Emerald," said Jasper smoothly. "Now *she* is definitely a contender, Chloe, and don't underestimate her."

Emerald Barrymore. No star had ever been bigger. Not Brando, not Kelly, not even Monroe. And no one had sunk to the depths she had. Drugs, alcohol, men and scandal, all had contributed to her downfall.

"She has been the subject of more front page headlines than you have had hot dinners, my dear," Jasper continued. "But *what* a survivor. The ultimate. And the public adore her."

"And she is still a major star." Chloe heard a reverence in her voice that the mention of Emerald's name often caused.

"So's Kim Novak, dear," said Jasper snidely, "and she can't get a job either. Emerald really needs bread now. She's been desperate for cash ever since her last lover fleeced her. She wants that part desperately, and she's using all of her influence."

"Who else, Jasper?"

"Rosalinde Lamaze. Lamaze is somewhat of a slut, as we all know," purred Jasper in his smoothest English tones. "But the public love her— especially males. They would all like to fuck her tiny brains out. She's possibly a little too Latin, too ethnic for Miranda, but she has a huge fan following, even though her last three films didn't even recoup their negative costs."

Chloe took a gulp of vodka. This was indeed tough competition. Why she was even included with this group she couldn't imagine. She realized television was constantly searching for new, fresh faces—maybe that was the reason. She was virtually unknown in America now. She'd been gone so long from the charts. She could be a new face yet!

"Help!" Chloe gulped the last of the vodka. "Jasper, I'll be the *last* of that group the producers would want."

"Nonsense," the old man countered swiftly. "You actually have most of the attributes needed for the role. There are several other actresses Abby wants to test, but I assure you that Meryl Streep, Jackie Bisset and Sabrina Jones will not be interested, even though there will be a great deal of fanfare about them being considered. Now get some rest, dear. Don't worry and remember *always:* Think positively. Banish those negative vibrations."

He hung up, leaving Chloe trying to "Think positively," but still thinking her chances were slim. In the living room Josh still sat glued to the tube, oozing "negative vibrations." She poured herself another vodka. Some of his mates were on "Hollywood Squares," so he *shsshd* Chloe as she tried to tell him about her conversation with Jasper. She wanted him to cheer her up, joke with her as he used to, but he was like stone. Tears filled her eyes as she walked into the bathroom and turned on the taps in the big marble Jacuzzi tub. It had been built for the two of them. Now Chloe lay there alone, the bubbles tingling her flesh as she stared out into the beauty of the ocean and the cresting waves and wondered if she could make it work with Josh. How many more separations and reconciliations would it take before she stopped fighting for their marriage and gave them both their freedom? This had been their third separation in as many years. She remembered the first one. Two years ago. . . .

◄ *Two* ►

For eight years they had reigned as one of show business's happiest and most successful couples. But in the past year, as Josh's last three singles plummeted, Josh's behavior had finally become so outrageous and intolerable that she had to get away from him, hoping that a trial separation would make him see reason—make him see what he was losing by losing her.

Raindrops slid across the windows of the first-class railway carriage taking her to Scotland.

It was a bleak January day. Sleet scudded onto the roofs of identically dun-colored houses as Chloe's train approached the suburbs of Edinburgh. Everything looked as gray and dismal as she felt. Sheep huddled together for comfort, and the sodden meadows seemed to echo her misery.

As she poured the last of the Liebfraumilch into a thick British Rail glass, her feeling of guilt was quickly replaced by a feeling of security as the wine warmed her.

She was getting away from it all. Getting away from Josh. From his lies, his drinking, his drugs and his philandering. Getting away from her stepdaughter, Sally, a willful Beverly Hills brat, whose blazing love for her father was matched by an equally blazing dislike for her stepmother.

Chloe could never understand why Sally hated her so much. God knows, she had bent over backward to be as good a stepmother as she could, understanding only too well what effect it must have had on the little girl to watch her own mother's slow death from cancer. But in spite of her attempts to fill the maternal void in Sally's life, she only seemed to hate her more.

Sally was nearly eight when Chloe had married Joshua Brown in 1972. A scrawny, sullen-looking wisp with mousy braids, her grape-green eyes dominated a tiny, strangely adult face. She seemed to magically appear from around corners surreptitiously whenever Josh and Chloe were cuddled up on the couch watching TV, eating the lavish high teas they loved of brown bread and butter with the crusts cut off, covered with honey, being particularly cozy and affectionate with each other.

Silently the tiny child would stand, unnoticed by the lovers, staring stonily at their newlywed happiness. Josh had not always been an affectionate father to Sally, so Chloe was not taking anything away from her. But in Sally's mind Chloe was the rival for her daddy's love. Her jealousy for her stepmother turned to hatred as the years went by, and Sally grew to realize that the more she misbehaved and insulted Chloe, the more attention she received from her father.

Their houseman, Roberto, had addressed Chloe as Mrs. Brown the first week of the marriage, as they were discussing menus. Sally, who had been engrossed in a comic book, suddenly whirled violently on the frightened Filipino and screamed, *"Don't* call her Mrs. Brown! There's only one Mrs. Brown, and that's my mother!"

Sobbing, she scurried to her bedroom and locked the door, oblivious to the entreaties of everyone except Josh, who, summoned from the recording studio, arrived and finally placated the hysterical child with cuddles and as much fatherly affection as he could.

When Josh first married Chloe, to appease Sally he started to get the little girl involved in his music. She lapped it up. She took guitar lessons at eight, trumpet lessons at nine. She already played the piano, and had started singing lessons at five. Josh discussed many aspects of his music with her. She was a stern, knowledgeable critic: he had a certain respect for her ideas and opinions, and she worshipped him.

God knows there had been enough romping and giggling and wrestling and climbing on Daddy's knees and cuddling in the eight years since Chloe and Josh had married. Sally did it to distract her father from Chloe —she did everything she could to antagonize Chloe. Often she succeeded.

Chloe had tried from the beginning to conceive a child with Josh. She felt a baby would make their life together complete. But try as they might, it didn't happen. Chloe went to the top gynecologists from all over the world. There seemed to be no physical reason why she couldn't conceive; they should "just relax and keep trying," was the advice given.

She had thought that if only she could have given Josh a child, their marriage would have been better, but she knew why she couldn't. Even though her doctors said she was perfectly fine physically, she knew that something had gone wrong when she had given birth to Annabel. Chloe had been in labor for twelve hours, nearly out of her mind with pain, and the postnatal care she had received in the clinic had been minimal.

Chloe had never told Josh about her baby. At first she was afraid he would disapprove because she had given her away. Then, as time passed, she thought it best to keep the truth from him as the realization she could not have another child might have been blamed on Annabel's difficult birth.

Chloe had been twenty-one when Annabel was born. With the resilience of youth she recovered quickly from the ordeal, but the physical scars left by the pain of the difficult delivery and the anguish of having to give up her baby—her beautiful little Annabel, so close to Sally in age, but so different from her in temperament—would never disappear.

Now it was too late. Annabel had been brought up by Chloe's brother and his wife in their little red bungalow in Barnes. And nobody ever suspected. Nobody. Not the slimy Fleet Street reptiles, nor the staff at the clinic. Annabel herself didn't even know. Chloe sadly lit a cigarette in defiance of the "No Smoking" sign. No one other than her brother and sister-in-law knew about her secret child and the deep devotion she had for her.

Chloe never stopped loving Annabel. Throughout the years, whenever she saw another woman with a baby, she felt pain and bitterness that she couldn't see her lovely little girl growing up. Susan and Richard sent photographs regularly, which only made her feel worse as she saw the sweet little face, dark-eyed, like Matt, curly-haired like Chloe, laughing out at her from brief moments captured in time. On the pebbles at Brighton beach, in the family garden in Sussex, standing with Richard and some of his friends dressed in cricket clothes outside a pub, Richard proudly holding the little girl on his knee. Annabel with her favorite doll, Annabel with a kitten, Annabel with her new best friend, Annabel with her two older brothers. And growing . . . all the time growing up. Without her real mother.

Chloe kept a scrapbook of her child. Lovingly she pasted in the mementos, the photos, all the tiny notes in a childish scrawl that dutiful Susan had made the child write. Chloe sent her gifts from all over the world, and always received a grateful letter. Toys, clothes, books, souvenirs. Wherever she toured, Chloe was passionate about buying something wonderful or unusual for Annabel.

She realized that Annabel had become almost an obsession with her—and Sally noticed it. The chant of "Not *another* special present for your niece! Anyone would think she was *your* kid" made Chloe flinch.

As Sally approached her teens and became aware of Chloe's thwarted desire for a baby she often needled her with it. "You're *barren,* aren't you?" she gloated at Chloe one day as they lay by the pool trying to tan under a sun almost obliterated by a thick pall of smog. Sally was studying Elizabethan history. "Just like Henry the Eighth's daughter Mary. Barren!" She chortled gleefully, "Barren, barren, barren!" and dived into the pool, drenching the novel Chloe was reading. Eventually Chloe gave up all pretense of friendliness, and their relationship became a minor battlefield.

One spring when Chloe and Sally were in Paris, where Josh was playing at the Olympia to packed houses, Chloe had gone to Galeries Lafayette to shop, and Sally, her instinct telling her this was another chance to antagonize her stepmother, had cajoled Chloe into taking her too. Chloe picked out matching shirts and sweaters for her nephews, and then carefully chose a Christian Dior burgundy coat with a velvet collar and hat, and a matching dress, for Annabel. She was off to London to visit her brother, and was filled with excitement at the prospect of seeing her daughter. Sally, now that she was a teenager, was wearing a collection of tattered rags that were the "in" thing in Beverly Hills prep schools this year. She had sneered at Chloe's choice. "Square— *yuuck*—what a *nerd* Annabel must be," she said, examining a pile of socks in bright neon colors and stuffing a couple of pairs into the pocket of her oversized jacket while no one was looking. No matter that her father could have bought her a crate of socks—Sally loved to do the forbidden.

Annabel was a typically well-behaved, nicely brought-up English schoolgirl, the complete opposite of Sally. She had loved the outfit. She was charming, delightful and shy. After lunch as she and Chloe had walked along a leafy English lane, she confided in her "aunt" that she too wanted to be a singer one day, and had started taking guitar lessons as well.

"But you're so young," demurred Chloe. She wanted something better for her daughter than the tough life that she had chosen.

"Oh, Auntie Chloe, I love the guitar and I love singing. I love it so much." The girl had jumped up and down, her cheeks flushed, her deep green eyes sparkling.

"I play your albums all the time, Auntie Chloe. I *love* how you sing. I've never told you this . . ." She blushed and looked away.

"What, what, darling?" Chloe's throat tightened with the effort of holding back the tears. This darling girl, this sweet lovely child was her own and only baby. If only she could be with her. But she couldn't. Stop it, Chloe, she told herself. Don't rock the boat. Let's not have a True Confessions here, it will wreck everyone's life—especially Annabel's.

She listened carefully as the girl breathlessly confided her secret hero worship and admiration for her "aunt."

"When I grow up, Aunt Chloe, I want to be just like you," she chirped, her little face alive with animation.

"Oh, Annabel darling, oh, baby." Chloe couldn't stop her tears now as she knelt in the Sussex lane and hugged her daughter to her fiercely. "Darling Annabel, I will do anything I can to help you, I promise I will."

"I'm so proud you're my aunt." Annabel wondered why Auntie Chloe, normally so cool, was drowning her in tears. It was embarrassing, but grown-up people were often weird.

The sudden acceleration of the train jolted Chloe back to the present. She sighed, removing her dark glasses, which had not protected her from stares of recognition from waiters and several passengers. She looked a wreck. Two bottles of wine each evening, followed by sleepless Seconal-filled nights and a difficult tour, did not for beauty make. A week at the fat farm would take care of that. The health farm was her yearly savior. With luck, she would look five years younger again. Her cheekbones would emerge from their cocoon of bloat, her turquoise eyes, no longer dimmed with inevitable red threads of too much vodka, would brighten again, and the waistbands of her clothes would regain a comfortable ease.

She sipped her wine, trying not to feel bitter. Sally would be thrilled she was away. She could have her father all to herself. Perhaps they could share a joint and listen to his latest single, turning up the volume so loud that the Labrador whined and sought refuge in the wine cellar. Oh, they were so alike, father and daughter, two peas in a pod. Both Scorpio, both selfish, scornful, beautiful and arrogant. He was forty, she was sixteen, and they understood each other perfectly. Their close relationship made her longing for her own daughter only more intense.

❖ *Three* ❖

IN 1964, TO HAVE given birth to an illegitimate child could have wrecked Chloe's blossoming career. She was just beginning to make it as a singer; moving up from workingmen's clubs to "Top of the Pops" with new jazzed-up renditions of old Cole Porter standbys had taken her barely five years. Five years of fierce determined dedicated work on her voice, of studying Ella Fitzgerald for the phrasing, Sinatra for the nuances, Peggy Lee's husky sensual overtones. She managed to instill sexuality and meaning into the most mundane lyrics.

Every night since Chloe was still in her teens, waiting on tables, singing the occasional song when they would let her, she had gone to sleep, no matter how exhausted, to the sounds of one of her three favorite performers lulling her into the dreamless eight hours necessary for the maintenance of her second best asset, her face—hours spent applying and reapplying lipsticks, eye shadows, brow shapers, analyzing—re-restructuring with cosmetic witchery a pleasing proportion of wide innocent eyes, upturned nose, slanting cheekbones and full lips into a seductive exotic face that would not have been out of place in the fashion magazines.

She accepted any one-night gig anywhere in the British Isles, watching, learning, imitating and discarding. Eventually her talent and burning ambition to succeed turned her into a successful and popular singer, famed for her sensuality and elegance.

She had no time for men. Certainly those she met in Leeds, Glasgow or Birmingham were so dotish that rejecting their advances required little effort. But there was the occasional crooner on the same tour. Usually married, usually on the way down, whereas Chloe was—she knew it—on the way up. There was the occasional young drummer with the band and the occasional saxophonist or clarinet player, and once even the Maestro himself, the leader of the band. But all in all they were a sorry lot and in no way conformed to Chloe's ideals.

She had observed Susan, her best friend since school, now married to Chloe's brother, Richard, weighed down with the responsibility of shopping, cooking, cleaning and taking care of a toddler while pregnant again. Susan was already losing the bloom of youth and vitality that had made them the two most popular girls at school. No man was worth it, thought Chloe, worth the effort, worth the pain. And no one *had* been—until she met Matthew Sullivan.

Matt was a newspaperman. He worked for the *Daily Chronicle* as a show business journalist, interviewing has-been American stars who were flocking to London to peddle their fading wares in the thriving British film industry of the early 1960s. He drank whiskey, flirted with anything in a miniskirt and told outrageous jokes. He was a half-Irish, half-Jewish rogue, charm personified, cynical, hard drinking and careless about with whom he dallied. More often than not he could be found propping up the bar at any Fleet Street pub regaling his mates with anecdotes, rather than in his family nest in Shepherds Bush with his plain wife and their twins. His reputation as an inveterate womanizer, wastrel and life-of-the-party raconteur was well known to everyone. Except Chloe.

With fame and success on her mind, and men low on her list of priorities, Chloe, bright-eyed, full of life and twenty-one years old, was performing at the Cavern, a dingy but extremely popular disco in downtown Liverpool, much publicized recently for discovering four local lads known as the Beatles.

She had met Matt several times before at clubs up and down the less salubrious parts of northern England. He was writing about the rock scene, as his readers were interested in many of the new groups. The Beatles. The Stones. The Animals. Herman's Hermits. Chloe had been aware of his interest in her the last time they met, although he had been with his wife. They had all gone for drinks to an after-hours drinking club. Chloe was with her current clarinetist, Rick. But her interest in him was on the wane. Rick knew, and was already casting his eyes to new pastures.

Matt made Chloe laugh with juicy gossip and outrageous jokes. When she stopped laughing, she found him staring at her. Their eyes locked; he was giving her a clear message. She found herself blushing as he gestured to the dance floor.

Vic Damone was singing—something mellow and sultry. The smoky club had an aura of sexuality. Bodies swayed together, warm—sweating —moist. Matt held her confidently. Not the usual groper, she thought gratefully, although his arms around her were possessive. He had the assurance that came from knowing he was attractive, desirable, and could probably have any woman he wanted. His arms tightened as the music slowed, their bodies molded even closer. She was aware of his excitement now. She was also aware of hers. An unusual feeling for Chloe, to want a man. To really desire him. She shivered, gazing into his black eyes again. His message was clear. She felt a total melting new to her, and it frightened her. Mesmerized, she continued gazing into his eyes, holding him closer to her until his wife tapped him on the shoulder to tell him the baby-sitter had to go by twelve-thirty and they must leave.

Matt telephoned three days later. He was back in Liverpool again, minus wife. Did she feel like a drink at the Cavern after the show?

Chloe didn't hesitate. She had found herself thinking too often about his face, his hard body, his black hair—his heavy-lidded black eyes, his aggressively curved mouth. Goodbye, Rick.

Matt was pleasant and funny at the club, but they shared no

meaningful looks. Chloe began to wonder if she had imagined the physical yearning he had conveyed to her last time they had met, as she asked him back for a coffee.

When they arrived at her digs she asked him to be as quiet as possible as they climbed the rickety stairs. Her landlady didn't approve of nocturnal gentlemen callers, often a good excuse for Chloe to get rid of overly ardent swains. This time she didn't want that excuse. She wanted Matt.

When Chloe awoke the next morning, he was gone. She felt unbelievably, glowingly wonderful. She had experienced indescribable sensations last night. He had stayed until dawn, and every minute he had been with her, Chloe fell more passionately in love with him.

At least it felt like love, she ruminated, running her hands over her body that still felt his caresses. She stretched deliciously. Was six or seven hours of the most heavenly lovemaking she had ever experienced love? If not, it was better than anything Cole Porter had ever written about. At this moment, she couldn't, didn't, ever want to think about anyone but Matt. She felt vibrant, full. At twenty-one, she felt like a woman.

Annabel was conceived in London on the fine spring bank holiday weekend when Matt's wife and twins went to visit her mother in Bogner. Matt had an important article on the Beatles to finish. He asked Chloe if she wanted to stay with him for the weekend. She couldn't resist. She had fallen heavily for the irresistible combination of Irish charm and Jewish wit and wasn't about to lose any opportunity to be in his arms again for the whole weekend.

She could smell May blossom in the air as she rang the bell of the shabby front door in Shepherds Bush. In spite of herself, her breath caught in her throat when he came to the door. Although he was eighteen years older than she, Matt was an impressively handsome man. His black hair, touched with feather streaks of gray, curled carelessly around his face. His black eyes devoured her as she embraced him.

"Oh, darling, darling, I've missed you—how I've missed you," she breathed huskily, holding his body close to hers.

"It's only been a week, love, you couldn't have had time to miss me with that ball-breaking tour you've been on. Come in, come in—the neighbors will see us."

In the tiny front parlor he poured two generous helpings of whiskey into mismatched glasses and gestured to Chloe to sit down on the well-worn velveteen sofa. In a window, a yellow canary swung in its cage, the tray encrusted with droppings. Ashtrays were full of butts, files of discarded newspapers and magazines littered the floor. Take-out pizza moldered on a table next to an ancient typewriter, seven or eight half-empty mugs of congealed coffee were scattered around, and, she observed with a pang, on the piano reposed a large color photo of a plain woman and a pair of plain twins. Chloe pretended not to notice that.

"Matt, oh, Matt! It's so wonderful to see you again." She felt incredibly excited. She couldn't take her eyes off him, couldn't keep her hands off him.

"You look good, kid, you look fine." He squeezed her arms playfully and stroked the back of her neck, which sent shudders all over her body. She wanted him now—wanted him badly. But he was not ready yet.

"Ciggie?" he asked, lighting two Lucky Strikes and handing one to her.

"I'll share yours," she breathed, remembering the last time.

He took a puff of his cigarette, inhaled slightly and leaned toward her. With their lips slightly parted, hers soft and moist, new petals on a rose, his cool, yet sensual, they kissed—a kiss as soft as butterfly wings. She felt the acrid smoke filter into her mouth. She could feel, taste his lips, his tongue. He exuded a masculine smell of cigarettes, whiskey, faint sweat, but his breath smelled sweet to her. The taste of lust was in his mouth. His blazing black-fringed eyes gazed into hers as his tongue lazily traced the outline of her mouth. She saw his pupils dilate with desire. His hands softly touched her blouse, caressing the outline of her full breasts. He looked into her eyes the whole time, mesmerizing her, the fire in his eyes equaling the fire inside both of them.

"Oh, darling, darling," she breathed. "I want you so much."

"Not yet, baby, not yet." His experience made him able to hold back. She was so eager, just a kid in spite of her sophisticated songs, panting like a puppy, dying to feel him inside her. He could afford to take his time. He knew the longer he made her wait, want him, desire him totally, the better it would be for them both.

He played her like a Stradivarius. Slowly, with infinite patience, he unbuttoned her blouse and brushed first his fingers, then his mouth, against her eager nipples.

Finally, when her clothes were off, he laid her gently on the sofa, tracing a pattern of ecstasy all over her body with his tongue. She felt the hardness of him inside the corduroy of his trousers. She tried to free him, but he wouldn't let her.

Chloe thought she would die of pleasure. The only part of him he allowed her to touch was his mouth. He teased her clitoris with his tongue until she exploded. Every part of her body was afire with an intensity she had never felt before. She had never known a man to take this much time to give this much pleasure with his lips, his tongue, his fingertips.

When she felt she would go mad if he did not put himself inside her, when his touch on her clitoris made her dance to another orgasm, when she begged him, cried, pleaded, "Please darling, Matt, take me *now,* I *want* you darling, now! I want you! Please!" only then did he take off his clothes and fuse his body with hers.

It was a night unlike any Chloe had ever experienced. She had only known musicians and singers, whose chief aim was to get her pants off as quickly as possible, get themselves installed inside her immediately, pump away for a few minutes in a quick frenzy and then collapse. At best it had been only moderately exciting. She had never even approached the heights of rapture she did with Matt.

Hours later, she was limp, replete, surfeited, yet still wanting more of him as he carried her up to his tiny bedroom. There in the dark, he held her tightly, spoke to her lovingly, longingly, as he made love to her throughout the night. She clung to him, passionately whispering over and over how much she adored him, needed him, wanted him.

Unfortunately he no longer wanted or needed her six weeks later, when she informed him she was pregnant.

Chloe's obsession with Matthew had grown so much in the two months she had known him that she was now consumed by sexual passion. She could not stop thinking about his dark eyes, his body fusing with hers, his hands on her flesh, his lips bringing her to the heights of desire.

She knew his faults. Faults! There were few redeeming qualities in his character other than his extraordinary gift for love-making. He lied. She knew he lied all the time—to his wife, obviously, and to Chloe too. It was a way of life to him. Lies tripped more easily from his tongue than truths. Too much time spent in Fleet Street, no doubt. But she forgave him. She forgave him everything once he was in her bed. She could not get enough of him—but she saw him so rarely. Five times all told, including that incredible weekend. Five magical, wonderful nights that left her glowingly fulfilled, but the following day miserable with longing and the need for more of him.

But she was not to have more of him. That he made clear to her in his bluntest manner. He did not love her. He was completely honest about that, at least. He desired her sexually, he adored making love to her, but he knew himself only too well. He was nearly forty years old, he had no intention of ending his marriage; if Chloe left him, there would be other nubile young bodies around, other fish to fry. He had plenty of options and there was no way he could accept Chloe's having the baby.

In Chloe's naiveté she couldn't believe that he had made love with her so passionately and not fallen in love with her. She found it impossible to come to terms with his callousness. She cried herself to sleep for months on end.

She thought it a crime to abort their baby, their love child. Atavistic primal female instincts made her want to keep it. In spite of his denial and his dismissal, she went through to term, and in January of 1964, in a nursing home in Plymouth under an assumed name, she gave birth to a baby girl she called Annabel—it had been her grandmother's name.

She had made one difficult decision; now she had to make another. She knew she could never keep the baby. She had to earn her living, and the only way she knew how was by singing on the road again. No life for Annabel.

So Chloe's brother, Richard, and his wife, Susan, agreed to bring the baby up with their own two. They explained to nosy neighbors that Annabel was the daughter of Susan's cousin, sadly killed in a car crash in Australia. No questions were asked by the neighbors, and soon Chloe went back to work with a vengeance. She sang for her supper up and down the length and breadth of England, Ireland, Scotland and Wales. And in seven years she had risen to the top of her profession.

Chloe was an exciting singer of popular and standard songs, a performer who gave audiences more than their money's worth. And her indisputable talent, coupled with her undeniable sex appeal, enthralled audiences and critics alike. She had risen to the top in Britain, and now America was starting to make tentative overtures to her. She was considering an offer to play Las Vegas the night she first saw Josh.

❧ *Four* ❧

SHE HADN'T WANTED TO SEE the show. Having just finished a forty-city singing tour, she felt and looked exhausted. The realization had dawned on her that twenty-nine was no longer nineteen. Now she needed eight full hours of sleep every night, otherwise, goodbye face. She snapped open her compact in the warm darkness of the theater, glanced hastily at her almost flawless complexion, then looked back at Josh on stage. In spite of herself, she smiled. God, he was gorgeous!

Chloe had been instantly attracted to Josh. A surge of sexual excitement and interest she hadn't felt since Matt.

Joshua Brown was the show business king of "swinging London." Thirty years old, he was a brilliant, talented cock o' the walk and an *enfant terrible*. By virtue of his exceptional looks and innovative style, the West End was at his feet, and Chloe was no exception.

Thousands of men watching her sing her sultry songs had lusted after her, and now she was experiencing this feeling herself—lusting after the performer onstage. Why Josh Brown, of all people? This physical stirring she hadn't experienced for years—this was it. She reveled in it. She let herself bask in it. Sat back and drank him in.

Her enormous turquoise eyes widened with admiration at the athletic feats Josh performed. He was playing a 1920s silent movie star, a Douglas Fairbanks-type character. He leaped and danced about the stage and into the auditorium for nearly three hours, performing stunts of such virtuosity and sheer daring that the cheering audience gave him ovation after standing ovation.

Three days later Chloe went back again to see the show for the second time. This time, instead of being in the seventh row, she had deliberately chosen front row center. She had gone alone.

That's the man I will marry, she thought, her eyes never leaving his handsomely saturnine face, his powerful body. At the curtain call, when he stepped forward from the rest of the cast to receive a solo ovation and her palms were raw with clapping, she willed him to meet her eyes.

He bowed to the waves of applause, lapping it up, obviously loving his audience. His thick black hair fell over his tanned forehead, he was six feet tall, with a devilish face, and he personified masculinity, charm, humor and sex appeal. You name it, he had it. She could see the perfectly developed muscles of his chest ripple through his white cambric shirt open to the waist, and through his tight black trousers she could see the outline of his sex. A power bulge indeed. The cuffs of his shirt were ruffled and she noticed strong hands, hands she wanted to feel on her body. She thought about the rumors she had heard about him. Supposedly not only difficult. but the biggest philanderer in London. Well, in this business, unless you were Julie Andrews the gossips wagged their tongues constantly. Maybe it was true. maybe it wasn't. Right now she didn't care. All she felt was an unbelievable physical and metaphysical attraction.

His eyes met hers finally. They looked at her appreciatively. A clear message of interest was shown, an imperceptible nod of his head, and she was winging her way giddily backstage to his dressing room. A fourteen-year-old with a crush on Elvis.

Perry, Josh's valet and man Friday, offered her a drink as she waited expectantly in the shabby anteroom, halfheartedly looking at faded portraits of Edmund Kean and Henry Irving that decorated the peeling yellow walls. She heard him humming opera—was it Verdi? *Aida?* Could this musical-comedy singer, composer, matinee idol, jack-of-all-show-business-trades aspire to the higher level of opera? Before her question could be answered, the scruffy green velveteen curtain was flung aside and he stood there. She knew immediately he was meant for her. Forever, a voice inside her said. *Forever.* His presence overwhelmed her.

"I've loved all of your records." He wasted no time in flattering her. "Especially 'I've Got a Crush on You.' We play it all the time, don't we, Perry?" His energy was a force Chloe could almost taste.

The young man smiled admiringly at Chloe as he motioned to a stack of LPs. "Sinatra. Eila, and *you,* Miss Carriere. They've always been the young master's faves."

"Thanks," murmured Chloe, more than overcome, yet trying to act the cool sophisticate. Why, oh why did she feel, in front of this man, so weak, so *feminine,* so—let's face it, dear, said the voice inside, horny? Just plain horny. Celibacy at your age is a bit much, don't you think? Go *get* him, girl!

"I don't suppose you're free for a bite of supper?" Josh asked diffidently. They both knew the answer to that.

During dinner at a tiny restaurant in Soho they laughed and joked. He regaled her with stories of the ill-fated tour of his show and the disasters that had befallen it before it hit the West End to become the biggest musical hit in England since *Oliver.* There was no question as to where the evening would end. He had a little flat in Fulham. She had a little flat in Chelsea. They tossed a coin for it. He won.

She had thought that no man could ever surpass Matt in her bed. She had attempted a few halfhearted affairs in the past seven years, but after a while decided it wasn't worth it. She would rather be in bed with a book, or playing cards with friends, than rolling around the sheets with a stranger, trying to simulate a lust she couldn't feel. So she hadn't bothered. Idly she had thought she had probably become frigid since Annabel's birth. Luckily she was wrong!

With Josh, she was turned on even before he touched her. His curved sensual mouth brushed her lips in the elevator going up to his flat. An experienced kisser, a gentle kisser—a man who knew women, who truly liked them—she could tell by his lips, by his hands tangled in her curls, no question about that. She felt his passion building as the ancient elevator shuddered to a halt. Slowly their lips parted from each other.

Apart from the furnishings in his bedroom, very dark plain furniture, *very* large four-poster bed, the only out-of-the-ordinary feature was a large mirror on the ceiling, attached to the chrome-and-mirrored posts at each corner of the bed, incongruously covered with a blue candlewick bedspread.

"A gift from the Empire Hotel in Las Vegas," he laughed, as she looked at it quizzically. "I broke the house record there last year. They asked me if I wanted a diamond-studded Rolex, but I said I preferred the bed, so they shipped it over. It's fun."

I bet it is, thought Chloe.

Five hours later, limping to the cramped untidy kitchen for a sustaining drink, she knew just how much fun it was. Her legs felt as if she had worked out for three hours at the gym. He certainly was a wonderfully exciting lover, but oh, what fun he was to talk to as well. In between bouts of lovemaking, which at the very least equaled anything she had experienced with Matt, they talked, laughed and joked. They were so easy with each other. After hours of exploring each other's bodies with lips, tongue, fingers, she had to beg him, "Take me, please, Josh, take me." He had kissed and teased her until she was at a pinnacle of ecstasy, thinking she would die if he did not enter her. The buildup of desire made her body feel as if it were one enormous battery—a million nerve endings waiting to be ignited by his body.

When he finally started to make love to her, the sensation was so exquisite that neither of them was able to hold back. Within seconds, they simultaneously reached a plateau of such intensity that Chloe almost fainted. Afterward, as he held her tightly against his warm, muscular chest, stroked her black curls, damp now with the sweat of their bodies, she knew that he was the one. The man she had always known she would meet one day. Her forever man.

She knew in her soul that this could be the start of something big. And it *was*. They were perfect for each other. The perfect couple. They had everything in common. Their courtship was swift, their marriage three months later an occasion to rejoice. They were both extremely popular, so they had a huge flashy show business wedding at the Dorchester, attended by everyone from Peter Sellers to Sir Lew Grade, and for their honeymoon they went to Capri, where, when they weren't swimming and sunbathing, they spent most of their time in bed.

From the start Josh insisted on being totally honest with Chloe. He had told her about his many girlfriends, confessed he had never been able to be faithful to a woman for longer than a few months, but he was going to have a damn good try with Chloe. He was thirty now—time to grow up at last. He even told her about the tiny amounts of white powder he occasionally had the need to sniff to get through the exhausting show. She didn't care. She loved him. Love would conquer all. Marriage would be forever. They were ecstatically happy together, in spite of his precocious daughter, who lived with them. Although, as in most marriages, the physical side became less important with time, they had tremendous camaraderie and rapport. They laughed, loved, argued, worked together. The perfect couple, everyone said. Chloe thought their bond was of iron and she worked at the marriage, worked at their love, and it flowered and prospered.

They hated to be apart. They needed each other's support, each other's presence. Often at parties the hostess became annoyed as Josh and Chloe, who had spent all day and night together, would sit together on a sofa laughing, holding hands, engrossed in each other, ignoring the rest of the guests. Their communication was total, their commitment to each other complete. Their only area of dissent was his cocaine habit. Sometimes he wouldn't touch the stuff for months on end—then, when the pressure of work became too much, he would be at it again.

"I've been doing it since I was eighteen, for Christ's sake," he would say angrily. "It's never hurt me yet."

"It's a *killer*, Josh." Chloe always became excited and angry whenever she caught him taking it. She had seen the ravages coke, smack and speed had caused several musician friends. She hated it. It destroyed lives.

Josh made no promises to stop—only to cut down. For now, that would have to suffice, Chloe realized. After all, he *had* given up all the women. No one was perfect. Least of all herself. And they had a good marriage. A wonderful marriage. Eight years of wedded bliss. She was a lucky woman.

Then one day, she came home to the sickening truth of his infidelity.

She had told him she was lunching at the Polo Lounge with a girlfriend and then would go shopping on Rodeo Drive. By this time they had bought a beautiful airy beach house in Malibu as well as a little town house in London. They managed to combine life on both continents with comparative ease, taking the best of what each continent had to offer.

After lunch, walking out to the forecourt of the Beverly Hills Hotel to get her Mercedes, Chloe decided that the heat was so intense she could not face a trip to Rodeo Drive. Besides, her period was five days late—maybe this time she and Josh had at last made the baby they wanted so much, and at thirty-seven her biological clock was running out of time fast. She decided to head for home.

She let herself into the sunlit house quietly. There was no sound from Josh's rehearsal room, where even through the soundproofed doors she could often hear the muffled sounds of his eight-track as he endlessly mixed his next single, hoping for a new hit. Sally was at school, the housekeeper at the market.

She kicked off her shoes and walked over the soft blue carpet to their cool bedroom. What she saw there made the bile rise in her throat.

Josh had insisted on keeping the mirrored canopy from Las Vegas, had shipped it back from London. On that bed, underneath the mirror, lay a very young blond girl. Her legs were spread-eagled, her long yellow hair fanned out on Chloe's blue satin sheets. Her eyes were open, staring up into the mirror with fascination.

Kneeling over her, his black curly head between her legs, was Josh. He was doing things to the girl that were causing her to spasm with delight as she watched herself. His strong muscular hands were caressing the young girl's breasts, his thumbs massaging her nipples. Chloe knew by the movements of his body, by his deepening moans low in his throat, how much he was enjoying this.

The girl was young, fifteen or sixteen, and inexperienced; Chloe noticed that her hands, although clutched around Josh's thick penis, were not stimulating him as she knew he liked. Motionless, she stood watching the sickening tableau, the two of them so intent that they did not notice her. With horror, Chloe realized the girl was coming, her husband's head thrusting faster between the child's thighs as she bucked and moaned with pleasure.

Chloe could not stop the cries that involuntarily rose from the depths of her being. The girl screamed, and Josh turned to her, shock and horror on his face. Chloe couldn't move. In a dream she watched as the girl ran whimpering into the bathroom, as Josh picked up his terry-cloth robe and almost too casually put it on after a few minutes. The girl, now in blue jeans and T-shirt, darted sobbing out of the bedroom.

Then Chloe ran into the bathroom and wept.

Later that night Josh begged her to forgive him. "I'll go down on my knees, Chloe," he sobbed.

"You were on your knees this afternoon, you *bastard.*" Chloe's throat was raw from screaming at him, her eyes swollen almost shut with tears. "In *my* bed, you pig. You disgusting pervert. *Our* bed. How? Why did you need to do it? What did I do wrong?" She couldn't stop weeping. Couldn't bear the betrayal, the disloyalty.

"Nothing, Chloe, nothing. Christ, I don't know why, Chloe. I'd been to the bar down at the beach with the boys—had a few drinks, you *know* how it is—Chlo—"

"Yes, I *know.* I *know.*" She couldn't keep the screech out of her voice as she opened drawers and closets, throwing clothes into a suitcase blindly. "The boys, the boys—you've always got to be one of the boys, haven't you? You *bastard.*" She tried to slam the case shut. "Is *that* why you need young girls?"

She had to get away—away from him. She couldn't bear to be near him.

Hearing the row, Sally, just home from school, came into the bedroom to watch. This was better than a TV sitcom.

"Bugger *off*," her father had yelled, one of the few times he had ever raised his voice at her. Chloe knew the reason why, and it disgusted her even more—it was sick, perverted. She had recognized the blond girl as a school friend of Sally's. Sally had set the whole thing up. She knew her dad liked young "grumble," as he and his musician friends called it when there were no women around to call them male chauvinist pigs—"grumble and grunt," English rhyming slang for a particular part of the female anatomy. The girl probably had a crush on Josh. It must have been easy for Sally to arrange. She knew her father very well, knew his weaknesses. After all, he was only a man. Men were weak—Sally knew that already.

Josh continued trying to stop Chloe from leaving, but everything he said only angered Chloe even more. "Fuck you, Josh. Fuck you! Fuck you!! *Fuck you!!!*" she screamed, as she snapped the lid shut on the Vuitton case. "You *disgust* me! And I can't be with you any more—ever again." She wished she could stop weeping. "Get yourself to a shrink—you need help."

"Babe, babe, please listen—I couldn't help it. Christ, Chloe, I'm a *man*, you know—sometimes a man needs to . . ."

"Needs to what?" She turned to him, her turquoise eyes blazing with fury and hurt. "Screw a teenager? Make a groupie come? You make me sick, Josh. Sick to my stomach." She started to leave the room but he grabbed her arm and held her tight. His eyes were soft, sad—almost filled with tears. He never cried. He was a child of the Second World War years. You hardly ever cried, however much you hurt.

"I know I'm a shit, babe, but I love you. Remember that, Chloe. I've always loved you. I want you—you're my woman and you always will be. Remember that, when you sleep by yourself in an empty double bed."

She began to interrupt, but he stopped her. "I *know* you, Chloe. You're not a bed-hopper, you don't go from man to man, you won't find another man who loves you like I do. All right—so I made a mistake. A bad one. Lots of men make mistakes. You found this one out. It's terrible, I know, Chloe . . . but don't leave me, Chloe—please, please *don't*, darling."

She sobbed uncontrollably, sobbed as he tried to take her in his arms, kiss her sodden cheeks, but she wouldn't, couldn't, let him.

She pulled away. The thought of his arms around that young girl . . . his mouth, his tongue—how many other girls had there been? She felt sick. She couldn't bear to be near him. Couldn't bear his hands on her ever again, his mouth on her mouth. . . . The thought of his mouth on the girl . . .

She pulled away from him, dragging the heavy suitcase with her. She ran to the front door, climbed into her silver Mercedes and, blinded by tears and the rain that fell from the Malibu sky, she drove off into the wet California night.

Chloe immediately accepted a six-month tour of the English provinces to try and forget him. But it was not easy to forget a man you had loved with such passion, although the pain started to fade. Josh continually called her. He pleaded. He begged her to forgive him. Finally he cried, he cajoled, he sent gifts and bombarded her with roses, with messages of love undying and adoration. Until she melted and eventually forgave him. She always forgave him. Would he have done the same for her?

That had been the first time she had caught him.

The last time had been a year ago. When she discovered this second infidelity she was so hurt and confused that she had gone on a drinking binge. Vodka healed. When she came to after a week of debauchery, she decided to go to a health farm in Scotland to recuperate.

Now, together again after a six-month absence, seeing his indifference, how distant he was, she finally admitted to herself that the marriage was over. As she watched the bath bubbles slowly going flat, she thought how sad it was, how terribly sad. There had been so much that was good between them. So much love—so much investment in laughter and fun.

That was all gone now. She had to get her mind onto other things. She had to think about her career—think positively, as Jasper had said. Miranda—Miranda Hamilton. She *had* to get that part. She needed it now more than ever.

PART
TWO

❈ *Five* ❈

Sissy Sharp sank back onto her nest of pink satin and lace pillows and impatiently pushed away the head of the blond young Adonis from between her legs.

"Who?" Sissy screamed into the phone, her tiny boobs bouncing. "Luis who? He's not *right* to play my husband, for fuck's sake. You promised me it was going to be Pacino or Nicholson or that English actor —what the fuck is his name, Finney something or other—and now you tell me I'm playing opposite some fucking unknown Mexican greaseball?"

The vehemence of her yells caused the blond Adonis, whose name was Nick, to rise sulkily from the bed and skulk into a corner, where he slouched angrily in a pink art deco armchair covered with protective plastic and glared at her with ill-concealed fury.

He had been giving head to the bitch for over an hour, had her close to coming at least twice, and each time the phone rang and she picked it up. Picked it up! While his tongue was playing a concerto on her clit. This time it was her fucking agent talking about some new actor to star opposite her. Why not him?

Nick wasn't screwing Sissy for love—nor even a modicum of lust. Sissy's skinny frame, lack of frontal development and penchant for pills did not inspire him to great cocksmanship. But as the current teenager's TV delight, he was more than anxious to break into movies before he hit the advanced age of thirty. Screwing Sissy Sharp, the aging good old girl next door, was Nick's entree into the world of feature films. He hoped.

It had been Sam's idea. Sam Sharp had been married to Sissy for seventeen years, during which time they had convinced the American public that they had one of Hollywood's happiest marriages. Sam's preference for his own sex was well known in Hollywood circles, as was Sissy's sexual appetite for men twenty years her junior; but true to the Hollywood tradition of never sullying the images of their most prominent citizens, no publication had even hinted at anything untoward in the

Sharp marriage. They went their merry way, a picture of marital togetherness in the eyes of their public, while continuing to compete for the favors of the young studs who proliferated in Hollywood.

Sam and Nick worked at the same studio, where Sam had been starring in movies for thirty years. He regularly made seven hundred and fifty thousand dollars a picture, and many of the aspiring young actors on the lot.

Nick was in his second TV season, riding high. As the star of a fast-paced sitcom in which he played an undercover cop, he had teenagers in heat over his blond hair and perfect face and body. He was on the cover of every TV magazine and supermarket scandal sheet, and his love life—a succession of gorgeous starlets and models—was well chronicled. But career advancement was uppermost in his mind. The transition from TV hunk to motion picture star was tough, particularly when the powers that be considered Nick's acting ability low on his list of assets.

He knew Sissy always made sure she had casting approval of her leading man, and of any female performer who might conceivably overshadow her. She was starting her new movie in two weeks. Rumors on the street had it that everybody who was anybody had turned it down. No well-respected leading man wanted to star opposite a has-been like Sissy. But it could be Nick's big chance.

He'd allowed Sam to chat him up in the commissary one lunchtime. He'd allowed Sam to invite him to his mammoth motor-home dressing room and to share a bottle of Dom Perignon after shooting. He'd allowed Sam to unzip his jeans and expertly suck his cock. He had not allowed Sam to kiss him on the mouth. Nor had he touched any part of Sam's body himself. He closed his eyes and imagined a beautiful girl was giving him head. Men were not his scene. But he was ambitious, and he needed to get invited to the Sharps' mansion in Bel Air for dinner one night. He had been—about three months ago.

And he met Sissy at last. She looked pretty good for forty-four: skinny and bejeweled, the lines of discontent and envy not apparent behind the heavy makeup until you got close. Really close. Which Nick intended to do.

He had been seated on Sissy's left during dinner. The table was crowded with the usual overdressed dinosaurs that the Sharps surrounded themselves with socially. Median age fifty-five, thought Nick. Not an attractive woman in sight. Unless you counted Lady Sarah Cranleigh, fifty if she was a day, so covered in frilly lace, pearl necklaces, ringlets and ruffles that all that was visible was a double chin and a pair of laughing eyes.

Known in England for her penchant for young men, Lady Sarah was having a delicious time in Los Angeles. Daily trips to the Santa Monica beach yielded her a quota of gorgeous young studs of a quality hard to find in Britain. Her latest conquest, who was barely nineteen, was seated next to her, in utter confusion as to which of the three golden forks he should use on his artichoke.

Nick found Lady Sarah extremely amusing, but quite unfanciable. A true Rabelaisian character, she was devouring her food with gusto, at the same time giving the beach boy a grope and rubbing one ample, satin-covered knee against Nick's. In contrast, Sissy, ever conscious of her weight, age and appearance, was picking at her food, her tiny birdlike hands reaching often for the Venetian goblet of champagne discreetly refilled by the butler.

Nick had concentrated his considerable magnetism and charm on Sissy, aware that, at twenty-nine, he was perhaps a bit too old for her taste. He noticed her locking eyes with Lady Sarah's beach boy, who was probably more her type.

Abby Arafat, one of Hollywood's most prolific producers, was talking about his latest project, a miniseries that would spin off into a series.

"It will make *Gone With the Wind* look like a B feature," he boasted. "The budget is going to be twenty million, we'll be shooting in London, Paris, the Caribbean and Newport Beach, and with Deane directing and the right actors to play Miranda, Sirope, Armando and Steve, we're gonna blow the ratings through the roof. I know we will."

"What is this property called?" asked Lady Sarah, delicately wiping up the last of her artichoke butter with a large piece of French bread and signaling to the butler for more champagne.

"The biggest goddamn blockbusting novel since *Taipan*," bragged an excited Abby. "You must have heard of *Saga*—it's been on *The New York Times* best-seller list for six months now. Cost us two million for the rights, but what the hell! Everyone wants to play Miranda: Dunaway, Streep, Streisand. What a part! It's the greatest goddamn woman's role since Scarlett O'Hara. Miranda Beaumont Duvall Hamilton. God, what a role—a real Emmy getter."

The attention of the table had left the artichokes, and Abby had his audience.

"For Steve, we want a major male star." He looked knowingly at Sam.

Sissy pricked up her ears. As hound smells fox, so she smelled a potential part for herself.

"I didn't know you'd bought the rights to that book, Abby, darling," she trilled sweetly across the table to him, cursing silently that she had not seated him on her left instead of the blond TV star, who was obviously after only one thing—her body. Sissy was convinced that most men who met her desired her body. She had a loyal coterie of sycophants and yes-men who assured her constantly how gorgeous and desirable she was while gleefully tearing her to pieces behind her back.

"I just *loved* that book—I couldn't put it down, could I, Sam?" She smiled at her husband, who dutifully chimed in on cue. The Sharps were completely in cahoots with each other. They cared very much about their careers. Strongly supportive of each other in this respect, they cared not at all about each other's sexual flings.

The fraction of a second Sam caught Sissy's eye was enough for him to realize she wanted that role.

"So who *is* going to play Miranda?" Sam asked casually.

"Who? Who? Aha, that is going to be *the* question from now on."

Abby sat back complacently and lit a cigar despite the fact that the first course was not yet cleared and he knew Sissy loathed cigar smoke. He leaned confidentially across the table to Lady Sarah, who was far more interested in exploring Nick's thigh than hearing this boring Hollywood gossip. Really trite. So unlike London small talk. No one would ever dream of discussing his business affairs at a dinner party in England. But Americans were so crass, particularly Californians. She glanced at the young blond boy who looked totally baffled by the prospect of having to dismember the small but perfect squab just placed in front of him. She couldn't wait till dinner was over and she got him into her bungalow at the Beverly Hills Hotel. Meanwhile there was nothing to do but feign interest and enjoy the cuisine, which was not bad—not bad at all. She took a large bite of squab, oblivious to the juices that dropped onto her slightly soiled Emmanuelle dress, and leaned toward Abby, displaying a more than ample cleavage.

"Who—*do tell*—who is going to play the female lead?" she lisped eagerly. Abby drew on his cigar, aware of the interest he had created and milking it for all it was worth.

"Streisand's agent called this morning. But it's no good—as good as we could photograph her, Barbra's no beauty, and no chicken either. And if there's one thing that Miranda has to be, it is *gorgeous!*" He stabbed his squab for emphasis. "This role is too important. We can't give it to Streisand, star that she is. Miranda is a beauty—a raving beauty—and only a beautiful actress is going to play her. Maybe Brooke Shields."

"Forget her, Abby. Her mother's a pain in the ass," chimed in Arthur Van Dyk, executive vice-president of MCPC, the Makopolis Company Picture Corporation, one of the few remaining major studios in Hollywood. Founded by a shrewd Greek immigrant in 1911, it had reached its zenith in the thirties, forties, and fifties, thanks to the business acumen of its chairman, the austere Stanford Feldheimer, who had taken the studio into television production in the late fifties with great success. "Besides," he went on, "she's too young. Brooke could never age up to forty or forty-five." Sam and Sissy exchanged a fleeting glance. Although she was loath to admit her true age, nevertheless for the right role Sissy would play age sixty—or kill her grandmother.

"What we're *really* going to do—to create maximum excitement and controversy about the four-hour miniseries—is to ask the public to vote for who they think could play Miranda," said Abby smoothly with the confidence of a man whose mistakes would be paid for with other people's money.

"The public will eat it up. Great, heh?" He looked to Lady Sarah for approval. Like so many Californians, he had a healthy respect for the British aristocracy. Weren't they all related to the Queen?

"But suppose the public decides that they want Barbra Streisand or Brooke What's-her-name or other equally unsuitable people—what then?" asked Lady Sarah, bored to tears by it all, but trained in the subtle art of polite dinner-table conversation. One hand held a squab leg, the other rested on the crotch of the beach boy.

"Unknowns. We test unknowns. Dozens of them," crowed Abby, spearing his squab triumphantly.

"And—" he winked—"we'll test established stars too. Great publicity. Can you imagine? We test Bisset, Streep, Lamaze! Christ, the publicity will be *dynamite.*"

Sissy's blood froze. Lamaze! They were thinking of testing that Mexican cooze! Were they mad?

For fifteen years Rosalinde and Sissy had been one of Hollywood's favorite feuds. The thought of Rosalinde Lamaze even being considered for this plum role infuriated Sissy so much that she choked on her champagne. To control her anger she started to return the attentions of Nick's wandering fingers on her Bob Mackie beaded thigh, but her mind was elsewhere.

She wanted that role. She realized how it could revive her flagging career. All the couture clothes, the jewels, the flattery, the lavish Bel Air mansion and the ever-present sycophants could not disguise the fact that she was no longer young, no longer "hot," no longer considered for the top movies, which now mostly starred nineteen-year-olds on the heels of the hot triumvirate of Fonda, Streisand, and Lange. She tossed down another glass of champagne and gave Nick what once had been a golden smile but was now a rictus grin.

A dazzling miniseries, which would automatically spin off into a successful weekly series! It was too good to be true. She needed it, and she would do her damnedest to get it. God knows films of a decent caliber were becoming harder and harder to come by these days. Hardware films like the James Bond series, *Superman* and *E.T.* were the box-office blockbusters now. Or teenage horror and comedy films, made on low budgets and designed for the high school and juvenile college crowd, starring unknowns who looked as much like real movie stars as Lassie. The writing was on the wall. The glamorous romantic love stories she had made a career of in the sixties and seventies were finished; she must move with the times.

It was a similar story for Sam. The epic adventure stories he had made his forte in the fifties, sixties and seventies had run their course, and now were popular only with TV audiences. His last three features had been huge flops. Young audiences of today were not interested in a leading man nearly half a century old. O.K. for Newman, Redford and Nicholson —they were special. Different. Elevated super megastars. Sam was of the old school—the Cary Grant, Robert Montgomery, William Powell school of acting. Dry wit, innuendo, subtlety, glamour, romance and adventure. The kids today didn't want it. God knows, they were the only people supporting the cinema. Older folks stayed home to watch TV. And by older, that meant anyone over twenty-eight. It was too expensive to go out at night. If they had babies they had to get sitters, then buying dinner out, even if it was only hamburgers, parking and the tickets could cost close to fifty bucks for two. So they stayed home, watching the hot new TV shows like "Starsky and Hutch," "Charlie's Angels" and "Dallas," and their favorite stars of the sixties and seventies—like Sam Sharp—in the movie reruns on their own TV in their own living room.

Sam was astonished at how well his movies did in the TV ratings. The network put them on regularly in prime time opposite the rival networks' hottest shows, and invariably the Nielsen ratings proved Sam's popularity with the public. His TVQ, although he had never made a product specifically for the medium, was one of the hottest.

Although the networks and television producers always denied it, a TVQ was a popularity contest in which actors on TV were graded according to their likability quotient with the public. The public, amidst enormous secrecy, was secretly polled to name its favorites, as it was considered "unconstitutional" by the Screen Actors Guild to base hiring on the public's opinion. Nevertheless, the policy continued and those with the highest TVQ received the highest salaries. And the best parts.

Abby had made Sam a top secret hard-to-refuse offer to star in "Saga." Fifty grand an episode, thirteen episodes at least this year, and if the show was a hit, the network would guarantee twenty-three episodes next season. That was a cool million plus a year. Sam had been thinking about it but hadn't told Sissy yet.

He would play the patriarch of a large fashion manufacturing and designing family who lived in Newport Beach. They would shoot in Newport for several weeks, at least two or three times a season—a prospect most appealing to Sam, who adored the ocean and owned a ninety-five-foot sailboat. His character, Steve Hamilton, would have a devoted wife, two feuding ex-wives, and six children—a boy and a girl by each ex-wife, and a boy and a girl by the present one.

He would work a minimum of two days a week and a maximum of four. No more than ten hours of shooting a day. He would have perks galore. Approval of cast, director, scripts, his own stand-in, double, and full-time valet and cook at the studio, paid for by the company, a wardrobe of clothes made by his tailor, Doug Hayward of London, whom the studio would fly over twice a year for fittings. He would keep the clothes, naturally. There was also to be a chauffeur-driven Cadillac with smoked windows to drive to and from the studio, and his own makeup man and hairdresser to put on his pancake and his auburn toupee in the privacy of his luxurious motor home.

Yes, a veritable cornucopia of goodies. Certainly better than most actors were receiving in TV today. He was definitely considering it. Definitely. Too bad his father wasn't alive to see how big he had gotten. Not John Wayne, of course, but big.

John Wayne. "A 'real man,' " his father used to tell him on the Saturday afternoons when they would go to the cinema in Tulsa, where he had been born and raised. "That's a *man*, son. You watch how he walks and talks. He don't take no shit from no one, boy. That's what a real man is like. He's the boss—the chief, the breadwinner—everyone takes real good notice of him, you see."

Little Sam nodded, gazing in awe at the huge black-and-white cowboy up on the screen. John Wayne was a massive person, and the screen made him even more so. In fact, he did not look unlike Sam's own father, Hank. A towering granite-faced cowboy-looking man, who chewed tobacco and spat it on the sidewalk, and who got drunk with the boys in the bar every Saturday night. After he had a fight with one of them he went back to his tiny two-bedroom house, woke up Lizzie, Sam's mother, who was petrified of him, and without preamble, foreplay, kissing or hugging, fornicated with her with such grunts and groans and thumps and moans, that Sam's young ears heard everything. Heard his young mother's cries of "Oh, no, Hank, no, not tonight. I've got the curse." Heard his father's hoarse whiskey-thickened voice tell her to "shut up and raise yer nightgown, woman. I don't want to look at it, I just want to get me piece in it." Heard the stifled cries of his mother, then heard his father cursing, "Look at this, look what you've done to me, woman. Look at this blood. You're a filthy woman, and the Good Lord will punish you for having such filth between your legs."

Sam heard the slap, heard his mother's weeping long after his father's snores shook the house. He'd go sit with her in the kitchen, where, sobbing quietly to herself, she tried to hold ice on her swelling eyes.

"Don't cry, Mama—please don't cry," begged the little boy, holding his mother close.

"I'm not crying, dear." She tried to curb her tears as she held Sam close to her warmth and rocked him to her bosom. These were the tenderest moments in young Sam's life.

When Lizzie's second pregnancy was in an advanced stage, two or three weeks from delivery, Hank came home one night considerably drunker than usual.

In spite of the doctor's warning not to, he tried to have sex with Lizzie, who, after fighting him off, managed to escape next door to the sanctuary of their neighbor's house. Sam lay in his cot, scared for his mother, but relieved that tonight he wouldn't have to hear the usual panting and moaning. Suddenly, his door was pushed open and his father stood there, silhouetted against the dim yellow light.

"Wake up, son," snarled the huge man. "Wake up, I want to show you something."

Terrified, Sam pretended to be asleep.

"Wake up, I said," yelled his father. "Wake up, you little pisser."

He pulled all the bedclothes off Sam with a yank of his massive hand. Through half-closed eyes, Sam saw what his father held in the other hand. His ten-year-old senses screamed danger, but he still pretended to sleep. Anything rather than having to look at that huge red *thing* his father grasped.

"Wake up, son." Hank's whiskey breath came closer to his son's face. "I want to show you what a *real* man is like."

"Asleep are yer?—well, you won't sleep much longer now, sonny boy. I'm going to teach you the facts of life."

His huge hand lashed out. Sam jumped up to crouch, cowering, on his bed. He couldn't believe what his father was doing. His massive thing, as big as a hose pipe, red and swollen, was in his hand, and he was pulling it, pulling it hard.

"See, boy, this is a cock, boy. Look at it. This is what John Wayne and all of us *real* men have got between our legs. Let's see what you've got down there, son." With his other hand he grabbed Sam's flannel pajamas. "Well, look at that, I declare." He almost fell over laughing. "That's not a cock, boy, that's more like a little thimble, something your mother would use to sew with. *This* is a cock, boy, and if a man is not ramming it into some woman, then he's doing *this* with it." Sam watched in horror as his father jerked his hand harder and faster across himself until the boy thought it would burst. As he thought that, it did, and he watched in horror as his father let out what sounded like a wolf howl and slumped against the wall.

A few years later, a boy named Bobby took him into the boys' bathroom after school hours and, proudly bringing out a rather large thirteen-year-old penis, suggested to Sam that if Sam touched it, he would do the same for Sam. For the first time in Sam's short life, he experienced sexual fulfillment as both boys came together. He found it to be an experience of such excitement that he and Bobby met there twice a week for the next two years.

Even when Sam became a fully grown man of twenty, his penis never came even close to the size of his father's. He thought he was not a "real man" like John Wayne and his father, because, he realized reluctantly, he liked "doing it" with boys. Well, maybe he couldn't be a "real man" by his father's standards; but he soon had a chance to be a "real star."

Sam was a solid actor, one on whom the movie company could always rely. Not overly exciting, sometimes a little dull. After all, Sam had played some of the most solid citizens since God, starting off with George Washington and including Abraham Lincoln, General Eisenhower and Franklin D. Roosevelt. American heroes all. Fine upstanding gentlemen to boot. To some of the audience Sam *was* the President, so many had he portrayed.

Sam had interspersed these parts with lighter roles, for which he had been nominated for an Academy Award, though none had won. Four perma-plaqued certificates attesting to his Oscar nominations were displayed on his library walls, along with framed photos of him and Sissy with Nancy and Ronnie, Gerald and Betty, Rosalynn and Jimmy, and Jack and Jackie. A testament to almost but never. His agent had said the role of Steve Hamilton would be a shoo-in for an Emmy. It wasn't an Oscar, but it wouldn't be just a nomination this time. This time he'd have a real honest-to-goodness gold-plated statuette, almost as good as the kind he had craved all those years as he'd sat in the Santa Monica Auditorium, heard his name announced in ringing tones, and lost out with monotonous regularity to Jack Nicholson, Al Pacino, Ben Kingsley and Dustin Hoffman.

He was slightly bitter about never having won an Oscar, especially since Sissy had received one. Hers was prominently displayed on a red-

and-gold boulle table in their marble entrance hall. She kept it there, she said, because the gold in the figurine matched the gold inlay of the table so well. He knew better. She kept it there so that every damn person who came to the house couldn't fail to see it. Naturally it had been stolen a couple of times being in such an accessible place, but each time Sissy just called the Academy and they sent her another. One of the statuettes had been recovered, but Sissy, instead of sending it back to the Academy, kept it. It resided in a rather less obvious place, on a shelf opposite the bidet in her bathroom. Now it appeared she had not one but two Oscars. Bitch. He frowned. He didn't often think of his wife of seventeen years as a bitch, although to many people she most certainly was.

He was loyal to her, they had an excellent marriage, but she could be an impossible cooze. This morning she had insisted on involving him in a fashion layout she was doing for a syndicate of European magazines. Running her hands through his hair—goddamn it, how he hated having to stick his hairpiece on by himself—using him as a backdrop for her newest Norells and Blasses. When he informed her he had a one o'clock call, she had pouted sulkily, as though they were the loving couple the public imagined.

Now that she realized the potential in the role of Miranda, if he accepted Abby's offer to play the lead he would have to do his husbandly duty and try to get her a test.

He groaned inwardly. She could be the grande dame diva to end them all, but still, she was his wife. He was a loyal husband. He would try to use his influence. Otherwise, his life could become unpleasant.

Sissy had a way of doing that to people.

Sissy and Sam's party broke up early, as all the best (and worst) Hollywood parties always do.

In spite of the general public's opinion that Hollywood was a place of fun, brilliance and glamour, filled with outrageously extroverted, gorgeous people, deliciously dressed and participating in scintillating conversation, the opposite was true. The truth was that Hollywood in the 1980s was dull. The glamour girls and boys of the thirties, forties and fifties no longer existed. It was a business town now, run by company men.

Paparazzi and reporters clustered outside Sissy and Sam's home waiting to snap the stars and celebrities who were leaving were aware of this lack of star power today. That was why, when a star like Emerald Barrymore attended an event, flashbulbs exploded and the paparazzi knew they would make money tonight.

Calvin Foster waited quietly by himself, his heart pounding, but his demeanor expressionless. He would see *her* tonight. His idol, his queen: Emerald.

He was a slight young man with dirty blond hair and an absolutely forgettable face; people who met Calvin never seemed able to remember him—not even the paparazzi, with whom he spent hours, carrying a Nikon and pretending to be one of them. Only his eyes, cold, pale gray and secretive, would have attracted attention if anyone had looked closely. He knew that, which was why he usually wore mirror sunglasses.

He licked the sweat congealing on his upper lip.

The photographer from the *American Informer* was complaining that all the women had worn furs or wraps to the party and there wasn't a decent cleavage shot to be had.

"When Emerald comes out she'll have on a great dress, you'll see," volunteered Calvin, the excitement of this thought electrifying him.

"Shit—she ain't here, she's in South America or somethin'," replied the *Informer* guy.

"She's not here?" gulped Calvin. His information was usually flawless.

"Nope," said the *Informer*. "Her picture went over schedule. She ain't due back till next week."

Calvin felt emptiness engulf him. He hadn't seen Emerald for over two months now. It was true, she had been in South America recently making some low-budget adventure film with some unknown Spanish actor. The pang of disappointment was so intense that Calvin couldn't disguise it. He jabbed his fist in the air with frustration. The other paparazzo looked at him curiously as he loped off to his car, his camera bag flapping against his potbelly.

No Emerald! Damn. Damn. Damn . . .

He had been deprived of a glimpse of her beauty, her one-of-a-kind sexual glamour. No one else had it, had ever had it, like Emerald. She of the emerald eyes and the sea-green gowns. She of the golden curls and the tremulous upper lip. Emerald, the survivor of torrid love affairs with James Dean, John Garfield and Gary Cooper, among others. Close friend of Monroe, Garland and Clift—Hollywood survivor par excellence. Survivor of Valium and vodka, aspirin and anisette, casting couch and death. She'd looked them all in the face very often and said, "Fuck you." Survivor of two car crashes, one of them fatal to her husband, the other to her fiancé, six marriages, two abortions, nine miscarriages, fifty-seven mediocre movies, three Academy Award nominations, more than one hundred lovers, not all of them male, not all of them white, and numerous smear campaigns to blacken her name, starting with the one during the McCarthy era, when she was only a teenager and in no way interested in communist plots. . . .

Star of stars, oh, how he loved her, wanted her, needed her! Calvin felt the familiar heat in his loins as he slid behind the wheel of his green Chevrolet—green in honor of Emerald. Her face was everywhere in his room. He must hurry home to her.

◄ *Six* ►

Luis Mendoza slammed the door of Rosalinde's house. Her three Persian cats rubbed themselves against his ankles as he crossed the garden. He kicked them away. Luis hated animals and children. In Luis's life, only two things were important—beautiful women to make love to and Luis himself. As far as narcissism went, he made Rosalinde look like Mother Teresa. Whereas she was shrewd enough to see herself objectively as a commodity, he saw himself as simply the most handsome, most talented, most *macho* man in the world.

"The male Bo Derek," his new manager, Irving Klinger, had assured him last month as Luis had scrawled his almost illegible signature across the all-encompassing management contracts in which shrewd Irving had arranged that 40 percent of all Luis's earnings would go to him.

"The sex symbol of the eighties!" cried his new press agent, Johnny Swanson, an enthusiastic and brilliant manipulator of talent, which he brought to the attention of the world's media for only 5 percent of the talent's earnings.

"The most superb man in the world!" Rosalinde had sighed to Suzy after their first date five weeks ago. He hadn't really fancied Rosalinde—being Mexican too, she reminded him of one of his sisters. He adored blondes, but Luis Mendoza was nobody's fool. To be romantically linked with Rosalinde Lamaze was good for his image. When you were the middle son of a poor Mexican family, and from the time you could toddle had fought for pieces of tortilla with nine brothers and sisters, you grew up crafty and clever or you didn't grow up at all.

Luis Mendoza had done what most twelve-year-old boys in Tijuana did for a living. He parked cars for tourists, cleaned their car windows for the five or so pesos he was lucky to get, and sold matches, or gum, or straw bags if he had been really lucky and managed with some other hungry boys to break into a warehouse to steal a couple of cartons.

By the time his mother died he had secretly saved a thousand pesos, the equivalent of approximately eighty-four dollars, which he kept in an old sock at the back of a cupboard. It was 1968. Things were happening in the United States. Senator Robert Kennedy had just been assassinated. Luis had heard the news on the radio. The Who, a rock group from somewhere in England, were taking America by storm. A beautiful Latin girl called Rosalinde Lamaze smiled invitingly at him from billboards and newspapers all over Tijuana. She was twenty-two, ten years older than Luis, but his adolescent manhood grew hard at the thought of her juicy lips and plump round thighs. She was a girl you could dream of screwing, unlike the beautiful cool North American blondes who were beyond his reach even in his dreams.

He wanted it all, even then. He wanted to go to the United States and become a big rock star like the Beatles and make love to gorgeous women like Rosalinde, and the other one—the classic blonde, Emerald Barrymore.

One day he would have fame, success and money and make love to Rosalinde and Emerald and all the rest of the gorgeous creatures he glimpsed in the pages of the men's magazines he scanned at the newsstand. Of this he was sure.

He had been his mother's favorite. *"Guapísimo,"* she would murmur, running careworn hands through his abundant black curls. *"Niño mío."* She snuggled Luis close to her skinny frame, bloated constantly with pregnancy, and whispered endearments to him to the jealousy of the rest of her brood.

Carmelita poured the love she had once had for Luis's father into the handsome young boy—the love of a beautiful young Mexican girl who year by year grew older and uglier while her husband no longer had any use for her except as a household serf and receptacle of his occasional lust. Year by year the family increased until the frail mother, worn out at the age of thirty-seven by the birth of ten children, the poverty of her life, and the lack of love from her husband, expired peacefully in her sleep. Carmelita gave Luis her strength. She gave him pride in himself. She made him believe that he could be a king—a god—a star. These hopes and dreams she whispered to young Luis throughout his formative years, building him up, making him believe in himself, giving him the inner strength and resilience he needed to survive.

When she died, three days before his thirteenth birthday, Luis wept for the last time in his life. Now he must follow the path his mother had prepared him for.

With his thousand pesos tucked safely into his worn sneakers, and wearing one of his three T-shirts, jeans and a raveled sweater, he tried to cross the Tijuana border into the States one cold February night. Unfortunately he chose a time when Immigration was on the rampage against wetbacks. Caught by a patrol guard, he ended up spending a night in jail with a bunch of drunken derelicts, pimps and thieves, who promptly relieved him not only of his precious thousand pesos but also of his virginity. For a macho Latin boy to be disgraced and abused by foulsmelling drunks and lecherous queers, to the jeers of the other vermin who inhabited the cell, was an indignity so barbaric that Luis had nightmares about it for years. He had never liked the company of men particularly. His father's treatment of his long-suffering mother had always disgusted him. Eventually his disgust for his own sex had turned him into a loner who loved and needed the company of women.

Thirteen-year-old Luis returned to the family home the following week a sadder and wiser boy. One year later, on his fourteenth birthday, he boarded a train to Mexico City with the money he had again managed to save. He never saw his family again.

Luis was tall for his age and immensely strong and agile. His looks were such that women of all ages were his for the asking. Since the night in jail, he had made it his business not only to make love to as many girls and women as possible but had developed a peculiar passion for sadistically beating up any boy he even suspected was homosexual. He developed an aversion that bordered on the psychotic to all forms of homosexuality.

By the time Luis was fifteen, he was working as a waiter in a Mexico City nightclub. By the time he was twenty he was part of the band, singing Latin American ballads and oozing so much raw sex appeal that staid Mexican matrons groaned with ecstasy at the sight and sound of him. By the time he was twenty-two, he had conquered Mexico as Cortez had never dreamed of doing.

He was the most famous and successful singer of romantic ballads in the country. In Spain and Italy too, his records outsold those of Julio Iglesias, and his face and body endorsed everything from jockey shorts to after-shave lotion.

Adolescent girls wept when they saw him on television. They huddled for hours outside the entrance to his grand apartment in Mexico City for a glimpse of him. Luis Mendoza fever swept Latin America. At twenty-four he started making movies and became even more popular. Latin America was at his feet. But North America, the America he strived to conquer, wasn't interested in him.

"Latins have never made it big on the screen," said Abby Arafat, the arbiter of taste at MCPC Studios.

"What about Valentino?" argued Irving Klinger. "And Ricardo Montalban, he was big in the movies too."

"Yeah, but he was a has-been until 'Fantasy Island.' And Valentino was Italian."

"Look at Fernando Lamas, Cesar Romero, Tony Quinn," persisted Irving.

"People don't want to *know* from spics," spat Abby, inspecting perfectly manicured nails. "Pacino and Travolta may look a little greasy, but the world knows they're Italian, right? And Italians are O.K. So are the frogs and the limeys. But spics! There's never been one that could make it in the movies unless it was character roles. Men resent a guy who's a Mexican getting the girl. They think he should be parking cars or pumping gas."

"I'll tell you what, Abby," said Irving. "I'll test the kid in Mexico City. I'll pay for the fucking test myself, and I'll eat my fucking hat if you don't think he's got the greatest potential since Brando."

Irving rarely backed losers, and Luis Mendoza arrived in Hollywood one month later on a warm April day. He had a three-picture deal in his pocket and he expected Hollywood to be at his feet.

When he left Mexico City, hopeful of never seeing it again, he was besieged by weeping fans, harassed paparazzi, and reporters, whom he brushed off with his usual charming civility. He arrived in Los Angeles wearing a white Armani suit, dark glasses and a tan. As he moved swiftly through Immigration and Customs, there was not even a hum of interest from passengers and airport personnel.

He was one of the biggest stars in the world in Latin America, but no one seemed to know or care in California.

The going in Hollywood proved tougher than Luis had ever imagined. They snubbed him; the goddamn fucking Hollywood *pigs* ignored him. Oh, he knew why, well enough. Because he was to them just a greaseball, a goddamn Mexican wetback. What an insult. He had a legitimate green card; he was here under the auspices of the American government. He had a movie contract. Why were they so disdainful of him? Even Lamaze, that cooze, had insulted him last night. He had only screwed her because Irving said they would make a hot twosome from which he would get publicity, which might make him more popular with the American public. Sure, oh, sure. What he realized bitterly was that it was better for her career than for his to be a gossip item.

Eventually Irving got him a starring role in a picture. It meant playing opposite that over-the-hill bag of bones Sissy Sharp, but it was an American feature film at last, even though the script was lousy.

He looked in the mirror and arranged his tousled black curls more artlessly. Richard Gere, eat your heart out! Here comes Mendoza. In terms of looks and sex appeal, Gere was zero compared to Luis. He was on his way now. Nothing could stop him.

There are two kinds of people in this world, Rosalinde Lamaze decided, gazing into her magnifying mirror in the harsh north light: those who screw, and those who get screwed. And last night, she thought gloomily, she was a front-runner in category number two.

Luis Mendoza made no pretense of being in love with her. If his prowess in the bedroom was anything to go by, she was just a receptacle for his well-formed cock. So what *was* the problem? Was she losing her charms? She studied her face in the magnifying mirror, peering closely with her shortsighted eyes to get a better view. She sighed and applied Dr. René Guinot's moisturizing cream for mature skin with even more abandon to the threadlike lines that were starting to appear beneath her chocolate-brown eyes.

She was a plumpish, short, pretty woman of thirty-six, who, with the expert application of myriad cosmetic devices, exotic outfits and a number of cleverly arranged postiches and nun's hair wigs, was regularly transformed into the fantasy woman of every truck driver and construction worker from Hoboken to Hollywood.

A million men had fantasized about Rosalinde Lamaze as they reached for their wives to take their conjugal rights, thoughts of Rosalinde's tawny limbs locked around them arousing their minds and their cocks. A million schoolboys had awakened from erotic dreams with the guilty evidence of their nocturnal fantasies of Rosalinde's creamy skin, taut tits and glistening lips—a sticky little mess on their pajamas, which would be hastily rinsed under the faucet before Mother discovered it.

For fifteen years now Rosalinde had thrived on her image as a saucy, sexy Latin American goddess. It was an image that had brought her much money and many men, both of which she had used with a voracious Latin appetite.

But was she fading now? She frowned as she thought of last night, then quickly stopped as she caught sight of the furrows in her magnifying mirror. She was a study in beiges and browns. Pollen-colored skin deepened to a dark amber on her body, for she had kept her face from the sun as much as possible in the past several years. She had observed the skin disasters of women who littered the beaches and pools of Southern California like shipwrecked debris.

Her hair was as dark a brown as possible without veering to black. Her eyes were chocolate almonds and her nipples . . . She slipped the silk pareu she was wearing off her shoulders to her waist to observe the perfection of her perfectly formed, delicately tanned breasts with their thick brown nipples.

As she looked, she imagined Luis's lips on them last night, licking them to a fever before he entered her, and then a quick thrust or two and it was over. He had rolled off her, reached for a cigarette and turned his back and *gone to sleep!* He had used her like a *puta*—a whore. Her mother had been a *puta*. Some people thought of Rosalinde as one.

Unconsciously her hand reached for and cupped her left breast. It was still oily from Dr. Guinot's nourishing lotion, and the sensation was decidedly pleasant. As she caressed herself, she saw in the magnifying mirror her brown nipple hardening until it looked like a bud about to burst. In spite of her anger and sexual frustration from last night, Rosalinde felt her breathing sharpen.

To watch herself caressing herself in the privacy of her luxurious marble bathroom was a good deal more thrilling than the wham-bam-thank-you-ma'am that Luis had served her last night without a thought for her satisfaction. Angrily, she stroked herself more sensually. What would they think now, those millions of men who had lusted after her for all these years, if they could see her like this?

Suddenly she paused in the middle of arousing herself in the mirror. She left the dressing table and, stalking to her closet, took out an exquisite white ermine cloak. Throwing it on the bathroom floor she lay on top of it and looked into the mirrored ceiling of her bathroom.

She feasted her eyes on a sight most men in America would harden for. Amber skin, plump but exquisitely firm arms and legs. The face and hair were not so good, but with her shortsightedness, she neither saw nor cared; and running her hands over her own body, using the moisturizer of Dr. Guinot at two hundred dollars an ounce (an extravagance indeed), she made herself come as only she knew how to do with exquisite pleasure. She moaned, gazing at herself in the mirror as she climaxed. It excited her tremendously, and Luis was forgotten. The narcissistic pleasure she took in her body banished other thoughts. Even the ringing of the telephone did not stop her delicious frenzy. Once, twice, four, five times—the divine agony. Finally, exhausted and infinitely more satisfied than she had been for weeks, she rolled over, threw the fur wrap on the chair and answered the phone.

"How was it?" It was Polly, her agent and best friend.

"What a *disaster!*" Rosalinde was almost screaming as she reapplied the precious moisturizer to the sensitive skin under her eyes. "That bastard could barely get it up, and when he finally did, it was all over in two minutes. *Cabrón!* What a *putz!*"

"No no no, you little idiot," Polly said exasperatedly. Did Rosalinde ever think about *anything* except sex? "How was the *meeting,* dummy? Did you make a good impression on Abby and Gertrude?"

"Oh, that—oh yeah." Rosalinde slumped back in her cream satin chair, admiring her left breast as it escaped from her kimono. She grabbed a cigarette and tried to concentrate on her career, which had always come in second to her primary interest.

"Did you discuss the part with Gertrude or Abby?" Polly enunciated her words carefully, realizing that her friend and client's attention was still more concentrated on her woeful sexual fling with Luis than on an exceedingly important role.

"Oooh, yes—I did—I did make a good impression. Gertrude thinks I'm wonderful!" She beamed. "She loved me in *That Girl from Acapulco.*"

Polly groaned. "The character you played in that turkey was about as much like Miranda Hamilton as Juliet is to Blanche du Bois."

"No, no—I forgot. She saw *The Mistress*—the one I did in London."

"Ah, good, good, you were *great* in that, honey, great."

"Thanks." Rosalinde squinted, peering closely into the mirror as she found yet *another* line beneath her chocolate-colored eyes. Did they *never* stop arriving?

"Did she mention the test, honey?"

"What?" asked Rosalinde.

"The test—the test for 'Saga.' "

"Yes, she sort of did." Rosalinde was vague. She had sampled two of Luis's fine Mexican joints last night, and her mind was still hazy. The professional in her suddenly snapped back to attention. "Don't fret, Polly. Don't worry. I have an idea, *querida.* I have *every* intention of getting that part, and I *will.* I want it, and what Rosalinde wants Rosalinde *gets.*"

"Good girl." Polly knew that when Rosalinde was motivated nothing could stop her. She could be tough and strong as an ox when her mind was focused on something other than sex. In fact, when it was focused on sex she was usually stronger. "So what's your plan, honey?"

"Why *can't* you get me a fucking test for fuck's sake!" screamed Sissy Sharp over the phone to her agent.

"If you can't even get *me* a test, Dougie, I swear I'll go to the Morris office. I mean it, Doug! I truly mean it. First you get me this—this lousy Luis Mendoza, to play opposite me in this piece of shit film." She started coughing and her ever-watchful butler hastily filled her plastic patio glass with more white wine.

"Then I hear that everyone in town, I mean *everyone* except me, is testing for Miranda. You better do something fast, Dougie. I want that role. Otherwise I'm defecting to the Morris boys."

She slammed down the phone and glared into the black onyx pool where Sam was doing his usual forty laps. Part of her observed the rippling muscles of his admittedly well-shaped fifty-year-old back as he butterflied down the length. She wished she was in as good shape as he was. Maybe that's why they wouldn't test her. Too old. They thought she was too old. And I am, she thought sorrowfully to herself, allowing a tear to course down her overly tanned leathery skin. Forty-four. Shit. Even though her public relations people constantly told everyone that she was thirty-eight, the town knew the truth. Everyone always knew the truth in this town: how old you were, how much you made, how greatly in demand you were. They all knew. Jungle drums. No secrets.

Fuck this town, she told herself. There had to be a way to test! Had to. She poured more wine and stared at Sam's muscles until the phone rang. Sam had said he was going to do his best to get her a test, but he was not being assertive enough. She had to try, herself, subtly.

"Sissy, darling, have you heard the news?" purred her closest friend and confidante, Daphne Swanson.

"What news?" growled Sissy, knowing full well it had something to do with *her* part.

"They're going to test Chloe Carriere for the part—can you *believe* it, darling? A *singer* playing Miranda, and British to boot. It's too too hilarious!" Her well-modulated English diction trilled off into gales of girlish laughter.

"Who told you?" barked Sissy, rage enveloping her to such an extent that she seized a handful of Sam's cashew nut-and-raisin health mix and, throwing caution to the winds, shoved it in her mouth. She would do penance for that later, she realized—she would have to make herself do one hundred extra sit-ups. The nuts contained more calories than she usually ate all day. Sissy prided herself on weighing ninety-eight pounds. Many people said it made her look younger. Most thought she looked like a cross between a sparrow and a hawk.

"Johnny told me, darling," said Daphne, complacently munching a Godiva chocolate at her end of the telephone. She had no weight worries. Red-haired, zaftig, and at sixtyish still active in the sack. Two of her old suitors, Frank Tillie and Richard Hurrel, still were regular nocturnal visitors to her house. She was a lady at peace with herself. Her son Johnny filled her in on all the town's gossip, some of which he got directly from his agent father, Daphne's ex-husband, Jasper Swanson. "Can you *believe* it, darling?"

Sissy ground her teeth and stuffed some more health mix in her mouth. "Why her?" she sniffed. "She's not an actress. She's just a saloon singer and she's British—why would Abby want her?"

"Certainly not to screw her." Daphne laughed. "But even you must admit she's quite attractive, darling."

"Abby told me he was maybe going to test Bisset, Candy Bergen, Emerald, and maybe Sabrina Jones—what else have you heard? Who else?"

"Well," said Daphne, lowering her voice and her body into her imported downy-soft eiderdown comforter from Ireland, and dipping again into the Godiva chocolate box, "Johnny told me that Rosalinde Lamaze is *very* interested in testing."

"That Mexican trash basket," sneered Sissy. "She would be useless—hopeless. She has no class at all. What does Abby say? Have you talked to him yet?"

Daphne's mornings were always spent on the phone, where she became au courant with every piece of news, gossip and scandal from L.A., New York and London. Truly the eyes, ears and mouth of Hollywood, she was thinking of turning her expertise into something lucrative. She would, of course, continue to impart this information free to her friends, but she was considering an offer to write a gossip column in a trade paper.

"Of *course* I did. But, darling, his lips are sealed tighter than Tut's tomb. Other than Jackie, Candy, Emerald and Sabrina, he will *not* tell me who else is testing."

"Well, they've already announced *them* in the trades, so that's no news. I thought Abby told you *everything*, Daphne," Sissy said accusingly.

"He does—but, darling—" she lowered her voice—"he says he needs a star name for Miranda, so he wants the press to get really hot on this. He talks to Liz Smith and Suzy every day, darling. I'll put in a good word for you, poppet. I promise. I'll remind him you've got two Oscars." She giggled.

Sissy replaced the receiver and stared stonily at her husband, who emerged smiling and wet from the pool. He laughingly ruffled her hair, which irritated her. "You'll do anything to get that part, won't you, honey?" he joked.

"Anything," said Sissy grimly, "absolutely anything, Sam. I'd even fuck you for it." They both laughed hollowly.

The amazing thing about Sissy was that, like Rosalinde Lamaze, when she put her mind to something—really went 100 percent for it—she usually got what she wanted. She had wanted Sam all those years ago, and she had got him, even though he had seldom shared her bed even in the early days. She had wanted fame and success, and she had achieved those too.

Now the role of Miranda was her top priority and she would pull out all stops to get it.

❧ *Seven* ❧

Sabrina Jones lay on the beach and looked at the camera with an enchanting smile. The camera loved her. Everyone loved Sabrina.

She was America's newest golden girl. And golden she was. She had been renamed Sabrina by a shrewd network executive who had adored Audrey Hepburn in *Sabrina.* When she had walked into his office three years ago, she was immediately given one of the three leads in a new cops-and-robbers TV series. She didn't even have to test. Her five-foot-eight, one-hundred-ten-pound body was honey-tanned and flawless. Her tawny blond hair, the envy of every actress in Hollywood, was thick, shoulder-length, and fell into natural waves and curls without the necessity of hot rollers. She was clad in a golden mesh evening gown, which skimmed her sensational body. As she lay on the sand gazing into the camera lens the photographer shook his head in awe. There hadn't been anyone this gorgeous in town since Ava Gardner had hit it. She was sheer perfection. Those eyes! Those legs! Those breasts!

In "Danger—Girls Working," Sabrina zoomed to immediate TV superstardom. Instead of asking, as most overnight TV successes do, for more money and more perks, she had been perfectly content to stay in the series with the other two girls, accepting the reasonable increases in salary her eager bosses bestowed upon her. She was never demanding, never difficult. She loved the series, loved the crew, adored Patty and Sue Ellen, her co-stars, and had a wonderful life. She even liked giving interviews and posing for stills—a press agent's delight.

Sabrina was that rare creature, a truly happy actress, happy with her life, happy with her career, full of joie de vivre and love. A secure and loving family had given her a solid foundation for life, but at twenty-three there was one thing that had eluded her thus far—megastardom. Well, testing for "Saga" could change all that, now that her series had finished.

She turned and gave the photographer her most seductive gaze. He gulped again, clicked and immortalized her for her fiftieth magazine cover.

Sue Jacobs, her agent, was waiting for the photo session to end. "Get yourself dressed and then let's go someplace quiet for a drink," Sue said, brushing past the crewmen who were still ogling Sabrina. "We've got lots to talk about."

"How about the Polo Lounge?" Sabrina said. "I just love the Polo Lounge."

❖   ❖   ❖

Clad in a raw silk Brioni jacket, a black silk shirt and black pants, Luis strolled into the Polo Lounge and stopped dead in his tracks as he came face to face with the most beautiful girl he had ever seen in his life.

Long, blond hair, perfect golden skin, sweet innocence in her eyes, she was in deep conversation with an older woman. Luis didn't even pause. He made straight for their table.

"*Señorita,*" he said, waving away the waiter, "allow me to introduce myself. Luis Mendoza, at your service, *señorita.* You are simply the most beautiful woman I have ever seen in my life. I am stunned by your beauty. Would you share a bottle of Dom Perignon with me, *señorita—* please?"

It was not an original approach; he had used it before, but due to his magnetic looks he was seldom turned down. Few women could resist being called the most beautiful woman in the world. Sabrina Jones was no exception.

"It would be my pleasure." She smiled at him invitingly, to the annoyance of Sue, who was in the middle of trying to convince Sabrina to take a three-picture deal at Universal instead of testing for "Saga."

Half an hour later, Sue toddled home muttering, "Cock, cock, that's all they think about today." She had realized after observing the way they gazed at each other that the force of their mutual attraction was too strong to fight. She was right.

The next day Luis arrived on the set exhausted. He felt as if he had already put in a full day's work. The crew bustled around him, setting up the lights and equipment for his big love scene with Ms. Sissy Sharp. His Latin temperament was tickled by the "Ms." that Sissy insisted upon. Who was she but some over-the-hill hag, obviously so ashamed of her femininity that she couldn't be called Mrs. or Miss. "Ms." indeed. A smile crossed his handsome face as he thought of last night and Sabrina. Sabrina. What a name. What a dame. He felt his balls tighten at the thought of her. Sabrina Jones, *the* female sex symbol of the eighties. So gorgeous, so sexy, so young—every man's sublimated desire.

But not his—oh, no, indeed. No sublimated desire existed for Luis Mendoza. Sabrina was his—she belonged to him now. His Latin pride swelled at the thought of her firm tanned body close to his. They had made love for hours, their physical attraction for each other so mutual and strong that sex became ecstasy. Experience had taught him what turned a woman on, but with Sabrina lovemaking was so natural, so free, so *loving,* he didn't need any tricks. Maybe he thought he was truly in love for the first time in his life. Luis woke from his daydream with a smile as the assistant director called him to rehearse. Sissy was waiting. She looked chic. Hard and chic. Probably women all over America would copy what she was wearing in this scene. She was a clotheshorse and about as fuckable as—Luis sought the metaphor, then burst out laughing —a horse! That was what she looked like. A racehorse in drag.

Sissy frowned at him. She was a total professional, and she hadn't been in this business since she was sixteen years old without knowing it inside and out. She loathed Luis. Detested everything about him. Certainly he was handsome, and not a bad actor, but she disliked foreigners in general. That included Jews, Germans, French and Italians. About the only non-Americans she tolerated were the British, but there were so many of them around now, it would be like not accepting smog. They were there, like it or not.

She sighed and tried to smile at Luis, who strolled over cockily as the director called for a rehearsal. With thoughts of testing for "Saga" whirling around in her mind, she had difficulty remembering her lines.

"Stop it, Sissy," she said to herself sternly. "You are a star—a professional. Behave like one."

She *had* to have that goddamn part. Had to!

◆ *Eight* ◆

"The search is on!" blazed the front page of the *American Informer.* "Biggest talent hunt since *Gone With the Wind,*" screamed *USA Today.* "Who will play Miranda?" demanded *Time,* which had photographs of Sabrina Jones, Jacqueline Bisset, Emerald Barrymore, Raquel Welch, Chloe Carriere and Rosalinde Lamaze splashed across its "People" section.

Sissy was having another one of her turns. Screams of pent-up rage, long-suppressed feelings of self-doubt, were released in a frenzy of hysterics. She lay on her velvet coverlet with the three heraldic S's intertwined in elaborate Gallic gold embroidery in the middle and sobbed her heart out. Not, thought her unsympathetic maid, Bonita, that she had a heart at all, nasty bitch. Bonita bustled about dispensing Kleenex, aspirin, vodka and a stream of comforting Spanish words, while her mistress thrashed about on the coverlet, her big black mascara tears falling onto the lavender velvet.

Sam, downstairs in the study, listened with a mixture of concern and indifference. Concern, because he knew what playing Miranda could do for her career, which was definitely on a downward spiral in spite of the many movies-of-the-week she was offered by the networks, and this cheapie potboiler she was making with Luis Mendoza. Indifference, because he was finally becoming fed up with her constant hysterical, demanding and selfish outbursts.

Was she going through early menopause perhaps? he wondered, clicking a channel on his remote-control TV. She had certainly looked like hell recently—thin as a rail, dark as a prune, and with skin of the same consistency. He stopped his clicker at Channel 13 and admired the roguish looks and physique of the young Rod Dimbleby in a syndicated rerun of an old series. He certainly had what it takes in every department. Even this five-year-old rerun showed the twenty-four-year-old fledgling actor's promise. He was definitely gorgeous and charismatic. Sam felt a twinge of desire, remembering their passionate encounter in his trailer on the lot a few days before.

Sure, he realized that Rod was only doing it as a favor given for a favor gained. He wanted the role of Sam's second son in "Saga" and would at this moment turn every trick in the book he could.

Sam was aware that he could hardly enthrall for long a young man of Rod's obvious heterosexuality and sex appeal—nevertheless, he was interested enough to tell "Saga's" casting director, Dale Zimmerman, that Rod was right for the second son.

"*Saaam!*" screamed Sissy from her boudoir, arousing him from his reverie. "Come here, *Saam!*" Her voice rose to a crescendo of despair. Sighing, he clicked off the TV and loped into his wife's purple sanctuary. She was sprawled in her mauve negligeé across the bed gazing with horrified fascination at the six photographs in the magazine.

"*Look,*" she shrieked, her frizzed blond bouffant hair standing on end around her tear-bloated face. "Spic *bitch,* how could she ever be considered for *my* part?" She hurled the magazine to the floor and pressed the number 5 button of her automatic dial phone.

"Hello," said the clipped voice of Daphne Swanson.

"Did you see *Time?*" hissed Sissy. "Did you *see* it?" I can't believe that spic slut is *actually testing!* Is it true? Tell me it's a lie, Daphne, for God's sake."

"I'm sorry, darling," breathed Daphne, and in spite of her close friendship with Sissy rather enjoying her misery. "It *is* true. I don't know what she must have done to Abby—but I spoke to him ten minutes ago to confirm it for my new column. It's true, darling. She's testing. I'm *so* sorry."

She smiled in spite of herself. As a former actress, she sympathized with the grueling in-fighting that one had to be involved in to crawl up the ladder of fame and success. Such miserable bedfellows really. She was delighted she'd given it all up. None of the Swansons were actors anymore, but they were all definitely Hollywood's in crowd.

Daphne and Jasper Swanson had been stars of the British silver screen following World War Two. When this electric twosome was imported to the USA in the late 1940s, Daphne, redheaded and reckless, launched herself into a series of sizzling affairs, in some part to emulate a notorious raven-haired English duchess whom she greatly admired.

Among those with whom she had cuckolded the hapless, handsome Jasper were: Richard Hurrel, the prominent attorney, of whom it was said he bedded only major stars or the wives of close friends; Lawrence Huntington, the celebrated Scottish Shakespearean actor, who on arriving in Hollywood proceeded to cut a sexual swath through the ranks of the young and beautiful, the like of which had not been seen since the heyday of Errol Flynn; and Frank Tillie, the witty, peripatetic producer of radio soap operas. It was to Daphne's great credit that thirty years later two of the men were still her lovers.

Jasper Swanson's smoldering sensuality fired the lusts of a million Yankee virgins, and his CinemaScope career was off and running. Off and running in another direction flew the dainty Daphne. Frank, Lawrence, Richard and occasionally—very occasionally—Jasper shared the delights of her connubial bed until eventually (or was it by design?) she became pregnant and a son, Johnny, entered the world on a warm Christmas day in 1952, screaming his lungs out. Nearby, a doting father and three more-than-doting godfathers stood. Hollywood money was on Frank Tillie but no one actually knew for sure who Johnny's father really was.

When the boy was fifteen his mother, Daphne, was playing the part of the mistress of King Charles II in a boisterous Restoration comedy at MGM. It would be her last American film, even though at forty-five she was still lusty, red-haired, sexy and delectable, with a rapier wit to augment her charms. But this was 1967 and full blown forty-five-year-olds had not yet come into vogue. Johnny, however, thought otherwise, deflowered one dusty sunlit lunch hour on the Metro backlot by his mother's stand-in, Cathleen. An equally lusty, if not so tasty, forty-five-year-old, Cathleen taught him the infinite pleasures of the flesh, taught him how to please a woman as only an older woman was bold enough to demonstrate. How to kiss, to fondle—to caress. Cathleen was a fine teacher and Johnny an excellent pupil. He continued these fascinating studies, unbeknownst to his mother, for the remainder of his school holidays. He dallied with Cathleen, who with a true generosity of spirit introduced him to the likes of Deirdre, thirty-six, Maureen, thirty-nine, and Kate, forty-one. Lovely ladies all, and more than willing to play sexual coach to this precocious, erotic fifteen-year-old lad already equipped with the endowments of a full-grown man.

So Johnny had been well spoiled by these ladies, and when he came to manhood, sex was only exciting for him with mature women. Many a budding starlet and bright-eyed secretary had batted their eyelashes at handsome Johnny, but to no avail. With girls under thirty he couldn't even be *bothered* to get it up.

Daphne didn't exactly disapprove. Johnny dutifully came to dinner three times a week at her home, either before or after his current dalliance, and so there was, thank God, fat chance of her becoming—*quel horreur*—a grandmother, even though she was over sixty.

Daphne turned and smiled at Richard Hurrel, lying like a beached whale on her Irish linen and lace pillowcases. He was panting. A night with Daphne usually left him wondering if his heart would last through the next day. Even after thirty years of intermittent fornication, she was still the hottest number he'd ever had, and he'd certainly had a few, and still had, even at the age of sixty-three.

Her tumbling red curls—out of a bottle or not, he neither knew nor cared—creamy Irish skin, never abused by the California sun because, as she said, "I refuse to look like a crocodile" and abundant Rubenesque curves, coupled with a zest for life unsurpassed by many a third her age, made Daphne quite a woman. A constant parade of faithful lovers who kept coming back for more proved it.

Richard was glad of the phone break. She had been about to make a morning onslaught on him, and he knew his heart couldn't take it this time. He bounded out of bed with as much agility as a man his age could muster and, watched appreciatively by Daphne out of the corner of her eye, staggered into her marble bathroom.

"Darling," Daphne hissed into the phone, "I know the truth. I know why Lamaze is testing, but it *must* be between us."

"Why? How? What did she do—*fuck* the old fart? You know that's impossible, Daphne. If it wasn't, I would have tried."

"I can't talk now," said Daphne as Richard came into the room shaving himself with the portable shaver he always kept in his briefcase. "Let's meet for lunch—are you free?"

"Yes, of course, yes," said Sissy, mentally canceling her lunchtime exercise session.

"One o'clock, Ma Maison—I'll book."

Sissy slammed down the receiver and burst into tears. "I'm the only actress in town who's not been announced to test," she wailed to Sam. "It's so humiliating . . . I could kill myself," she sobbed as she rocked in his capable homosexual arms while he whispered comforting brotherly words in her ear.

"You'll get your test, darling. I promise you. I've spoken to Abby, I know you'll get it, as soon as the network approves."

"But suppose they *don't*," sobbed Sissy. "Then I'm truly *ruined.*"

Calvin's heart pumped fit to burst. She had *smiled* at him! Emerald Barrymore had actually smiled.

She looked past the diehard fans and the rest of the eager paparazzi pressing in on her in the parking lot of Ma Maison and smiled at *him*. He was sure of it!

When Emerald had emerged from Ma Maison, clutching the arm of that old Italian actor Vittorio somebody, Calvin's breath had caught in his throat. His hands trembled so violently that he had difficulty in adjusting the focus on his camera. She was so sexy, so beautiful, so lushly undulating, so free. He almost swooned with excitement when she turned and when, for a fraction of a second, her emerald eyes made contact with his flat gray ones. Then the other photographers got in his way, pushing, shouting, yelling, *"Emerald, Emerald,* here, here, Emerald. Turn to me, *please,* Emerald! I love you, Emerald. Emerald, just one more! Please!" She had posed and preened for the appropriate amount of time, tossing her golden curls, enjoying the attention, then jumped quickly into her limo, a glimpse of perfect leg and golden ankle-strap shoe leaving an indelible memory on his mind.

Calvin thought about the first time he'd heard of Emerald. At sixteen he had a crush on a pretty blond girl called Jenny. Everyone at high school said that Jenny was the image of Emerald Barrymore, the big Hollywood movie star. Calvin had not been aware of Emerald up to then, as he was a staunch John Wayne—Randolph Scott fan. Calvin's awkward shyness had appealed to Jenny; after he plucked up the courage to ask her, she agreed to go out with him. On their first date they went to a movie to see her favorite star—Emerald Barrymore—in *The Princess and the Pauper.*

Emerald's beautiful Technicolor face appeared on the screen, and Calvin saw the resemblance immediately. He watched her voluptuous body, clad in seductive nineteenth-century underwear—white frilly bloomers, tightly corseted waist with blue rosebuds embroidered on the bodice— and felt his adolescent cock harden. As Emerald's magnificent powdered white breasts spilled out of her lacy camisole, close enough to touch, Calvin could contain himself no longer. His sweaty, trembling hand began to inch up Jenny's thigh. She pushed him away. He tried again, nature driving him. She pushed him away again. He became more aggressive. He had heard that Jenny let other guys do it. Why not him?

Finally Jenny had enough of his insistent groping. She got up. "Creep!" she hissed, as she left the theater.

Alone, sitting in the dark, he watched Emerald's vermilion lips fill the screen and felt his cock burst in his pants.

He started spending a great deal of time locked in his bedroom, his heart pounding, his palpitating cock in one hand, a photograph of Emerald from a magazine in the other.

His infatuation with the screen goddess grew, as did his collection of her photographs, which now almost covered all the walls of his room. Eventually he plucked up courage to write to her. Within a week the dutiful studio fan-mail department sent him a glossy eight-by-ten of Emerald wearing lace décolletage, her tumbling blond tresses beautifully backlit, the photo inscribed in green ink "To Calvin, affectionately, Emerald."

Calvin, unaware that her secretary wrote the inscriptions on Emerald's photos, was overcome. Three months later he sent in another request for a picture. This time it arrived in color—Emerald in a long green satin dress slit to the thigh, her blond hair shorn in a twenties bob, a cigarette dangling smokily from her carmine lips, eyes half-closed, sheathed in mystery. "To Calvin, with all my love, Emerald" was scribbled across one milky thigh.

Calvin was never the same again.

Calvin carefully tore the "People" section from *Time*—"Who will play Miranda?" screeched the heading—and analyzed the photographs of the six beautiful women.

Saga had been America's best-selling novel for months now, rivaling *Valley of the Dolls* in sales and popularity. Miranda was a peach of a part. It could not possibly go to any of those five sluts. To Calvin, all women except Emerald were sluts. A great role like Miranda should be—must be—was destined to be—played by the greatest of all actresses, Emerald Barrymore. *She* was the only woman who could play Miranda. Emerald Barrymore, superstar, his idol, his love. No one must get in her way.

He picked up the *Hollywood Reporter*.

"Who has the inside track to play the part of Miranda Hamilton in 'Saga'? *Tout* Hollywood is talking about Rosalinde Lamaze. This columnist believes she is the only actress right for the role," glowed Hank Grant.

Calvin placed the periodical carefully on top of his desk. He took out a fresh white pad, a new ballpoint pen, and wrote carefully at the top of the page: "Project Miranda." Number One: Eliminate negative factors."

He believed in planning. He was going to make sure Emerald got that role.

◆ *Nine* ◆

WHEN ROSALINDE WASN'T WORKING, she lay around her house all day wearing nothing but her ex-husband's pajama top and a torn, stained silk bathrobe. Both had seen better days, years, actually, but it was hard for Rosalinde to throw anything out. The bathrobe had adorned her lush body in *Latin Lover,* a film made in the golden Technicolor days of the late sixties when she was a big star—which she would be again when she got the part of Miranda.

Just the night before, she had been given a lecture about her image by her sister, Maria, who was very socially attuned—much more so than Rosalinde.

"Look at Sissy," Maria had commanded as the two women sat on Maria's fern-filled patio watching "Entertainment Tonight" and sipping margaritas.

Sissy appeared on the TV screen in the lobby of the Hilton on her way to a charity gala for the Princess Grace Foundation, attended by the cream of the Hollywood crop. The families of Sinatra, Stewart, Peck, Douglas and Moore were well represented. Sissy was a vision in black Balenciaga with the yellow diamond necklace from the estate of Merle Oberon clasped around her stringy neck. Sam was clasped to her left arm as she gushingly told the interviewer how thrilled she was to support this great cause.

"You should be there, it's good for your image," Maria nagged, but Rosalinde, eating taco chips and guacamole, laughed, "Why? I don't need that sort of thing. In fact I hate it."

No, Rosalinde thought, when she became Miranda, then she would start socializing again. Meanwhile, she lay on her unmade king-size bed amidst cushions stained with the residue of last night's makeup and littered with orange peel, trade papers and nail paraphernalia. She had vainly attempted to give herself a manicure, but had dumped that in favor of an intriguing movie that had just started on Channel Z. Curling up like a kitten, sucking an orange with gusto, Rosalinde was barely recognizable as the divine diva beloved throughout North and Latin America. The phone rang several times, but she ignored it. What was an answering service for?

Rosa, her maid and also an aunt once or twice removed, knocked respectfully on the door. "What do you want?" Rosalinde snapped petulantly, her eyes pivoted to the planes of Montgomery Clift's profile as he clasped Elizabeth Taylor to his chest.

"Por favor, señorita." In spite of Rosa's being distant family, Rosalinde insisted on monarchlike respect. Rosa was weighed down with an ivory tray, a gift from a Far Eastern admirer, on which reposed Rosalinde's brunch: *huevos rancheros* covered with hot sauce, half a dozen Oreo cookies and a diet Coke.

"What's the problem?" Rosalinde sighed, glued to the couple as the camera lovingly made an eighty-degree slow pan around their rapturous faces. "If only I could be photographed like that," she sighed, and then remembered that she just had been in the new photos she had had taken for Miranda.

"The service called," Rosa wheezed, thankfully depositing the heavy tray and catching her breath. "They say they have had several nasty calls."

"So what!" snapped Rosalinde. "I'm a star, not everyone can adore me." Rosalinde's eyes never moved from the television screen.

Rosa looked frightened. "But, *señorita,* the service say, they say thees man, he want to keel you." There, she'd said it. Her obligation to the fat cow was done. Eat your Oreos and *huevos rancheros, puta,* and gain another three pounds.

Rosalinde drank the Coke from the can, ignoring the wineglass Rosa was always instructed to bring. Her eyes left the screen long enough to feast upon the steaming plate of eggs.

"Who is he, this man?"

"The service, they don't know nothing. They only want to warn you. Maybe we should call the police. He sounds like a crazy man. He calls six or seven times."

Rosalinde shrugged again. "The usual crap. Don't worry." She turned back to Liz and Monty only to find Shelley Winters's young but already pudgy face filling the screen.

"But Miss Angelica, she away, and I go off tonight to see my gran'son. Are you sure you are fine alone here?" Not that she gave a damn, but she didn't want to get fired for lack of solicitousness.

"Yes, yes, yes." Impatiently Rosalinde spooned up her eggs. "Now go away, Rosa, and leave me alone. I want to *relax.* Can't I ever relax, damn it?"

Silently Rosa left, cursing the cow. What a pig. It was bad enough when she had two or three men a week and lay in bed half the day moaning and groaning like a bitch in heat; but now men were *out* and lovely little innocent Angelica was *in*—for how long, God knows. Now

Rosalinde lay in bed longer and her moans were less frantic, more like the purring of a satisfied cat.

She knew what they did. Overcome with curiosity about the moans and screams of ecstasy, she had crept up the stairs one afternoon and applied a practiced eye to the keyhole. At first it was difficult to make out what was happening in the dim light; eventually she realized that the two women had stuck their faces into each other's most private parts and were licking and kissing each other with enthusiasm. No crevice seemed to be unexplored, and their bodies, shiny with sweat, bucked in multiple orgasms. This Rosa had only read about in the pages of Spanish *Cosmopolitan,* her mistress's favorite magazine, and she was deeply shocked and became quite faint, needing a large brandy before feeling fit enough to prepare dinner.

Her mistress was sex-mad, there was no doubt about that. A sex-mad slut. What the public saw in her Rosa could not fathom.

The following day, Rosalinde was over the moon. She'd done it! She was going to be tested! Along with five or six of the most important actresses in Hollywood. The photographs had worked. She was a genius, and so was the photographer.

She pranced around her bedroom in a paroxysm of joy as she planned the outfit in which she would lunch at Ma Maison. It was to be a celebration. A triumph of sheer cunning and audacity over established stars like Sissy Sharp, who, she knew through the grapevine, was not yet on the test list, yet desperately trying to be.

She considered the advantages of her gray silk Adolfo, very Washington working woman, against a new Saint Laurent burgundy bolero with cream silk blouse and skirt. Perhaps rhinestone buttons were a trifle much for Southern California at high noon, so she discarded both of them and decided to revert to type. It had made her millions, after all. She threw on a striped orange-and-white off-the-shoulder cotton peasant dress, several rows of chunky coral beads, and a wide-brimmed straw hat heavy with spring flowers.

In the hall she paused to tuck a celebratory white gardenia behind her ear, and with a gay "See you later, Rosa" to the maid, jumped into her red convertible and sped off down Benedict Canyon toward Melrose.

The man in the green Chevrolet followed her.

Ma Maison on a sunny Friday in early June was jumping. At the round table in the center of the patio dining area sat "The Boys." Although the cast of characters changed weekly, today most of the main protagonists were present. Richard Hurrel, having recovered from his heavy night of love with Daphne, looked dashing in a brown blazer and a brown-and-cream Cardin shirt with white collar and brown silk tie. It set off his snow-white hair and deep tan. He felt pretty good. Daphne usually had a rejuvenating effect on him—made him look and feel young again. Frank Tillie was regaling the group with hilarious stories of the latest antics of the gay male lead on one of his top seven soap opera series.

Johnny Swanson sat listening with admiration and amusement to the man who, some people surmised, could be his real father.

At the entrance, seated at a small table for two, sat Sabrina Jones and Luis Mendoza, who in a short time had fallen madly in love. They were truly a dazzling couple. Sabrina had a day off, as did Luis. She was ravishing as usual in a simple white cotton shirt and a khaki miniskirt that showed off her long, tanned legs to perfection. In her ears were tiny gold-and-diamond studs, a recent gift from Luis; around her waist she wore a thick tan leather belt with an elaborate enamel and gold buckle.

Luis wore cream linen pants and a dark blue silk shirt, open to his waist to reveal a smoothly muscled tanned chest. Several gold chains of various lengths and thicknesses, upon which dangled the talismans of superstition and virility beloved by Latin American men, glinted in the afternoon sunshine.

They were engrossed in each other—he swimming in the jade depths of her eyes, and she in the bottomless black of his.

"They seem *so* in love," sighed Lady Sarah Cranleigh, spearing the last of her asparagus, careless of the melted butter dripping onto her Victor Edelstein floral silk blouse.

"Bullshit," sneered Sissy, observing them from three tables away. "Take my word, Sarah, Luis Mendoza lives for one thing and one thing only—and that's himself." She reflected with faint nostalgia on their two-night stand during the location shooting of their movie. Brief it had been, but exciting. Luis was a thrilling lover and had been able to supply for an hour or two the sexual ecstasy she craved, but seldom received, from the post-adolescent, lackadaisical beach boys she usually sampled in bed.

But she had better things to discuss than the love life of Sabrina and Luis. She was irked that Daphne had brought along her undeniably amusing house guest, Lady Sarah. It was difficult to plot and plan with that overdressed lump of lard guzzling everything in sight. Lady Sarah had already devoured two rolls of French bread and four pieces of garlic toast with her asparagus hollandaise and was now deftly stealing croutons from Daphne's spinach salad.

Throwing pride and caution in the direction of La Cienega Boulevard, Sissy plunged in at the deep end. "How did she do it, Daphne?"

"Darling, I never would have believed that the trash basket could be so smart," said Daphne, spearing a crouton hastily, ahead of Lady Sarah's eager fork.

"Well, what? What did she do?" Sissy almost screamed, downing her vodka and Evian water and trying to remain calm.

"She went to Hana, spent thousands, poppet—absolute *thousands,* having a series of photographs taken of herself as Miranda. Brilliant photos they were, too, of course. You know Hana's work, he's the absolute best. He actually made her look nineteen. I mean, he had to put a mohair blanket over the lens, but, my God, he *did* it."

"Brilliant," agreed Sissy through gritted teeth, cursing Rosalinde's cleverness. Why hadn't she thought of that? Come to think of it why didn't her fucking PR people think of it? Four grand a month plus expenses, and they couldn't even keep her name out of the fucking *Na-*

tional Enquirer. She made a mental note to fire them and hire Rogers & Cowan.

"One photo was of her as a teenaged Miranda—she looked eighteen, I swear."

"Impossible," snapped Sissy.

"Not with Hana's lighting, duckie. He took other photos of her looking twenty-five, thirty-five, that was easy—because of course she is thirty-five." "Oh, really" sneered Sissy angrily, stuffing a large mouthful of garlic toast in her mouth. "She'll never see forty again and you know it, Daph." "Will you *listen?*" Daphne snapped. "Then forty-five, then fifty-five, and—listen to this—in the last one of the set she has been made up to look *eighty,* and that's what really sold Abby on the idea. He was so impressed with the presentation, he promised her agent, who just happens to be my ex-husband, darling, that he would definitely test her.

"And, petal—" Daphne fished in her capacious handbag and brought out an eight-by-ten envelope which she slid over to Sissy—"one of my sources managed to get hold of the photos. I thought you might be interested. Oh, but don't look at them *here,* dear."

Sissy snatched the brown manila envelope from her friend and stuffed it into her large Chanel bag. She glared at Daphne, who smiled blandly and looked around the restaurant, nodding at various acquaintances. Lady Sarah stared at Sissy with ill-disguised contempt. What a rude woman. In England she would simply not be invited anywhere.

As soon as she got home Sissy inspected the photographs. In spite of herself, she felt a grudging admiration for Rosalinde. She looked luminously young and fresh in the early photos, even if Hana had used his encyclopedia of camera tricks to make her so. And the brilliance of her attitude in the photos of Miranda at forty-five verged on sheer genius. It was a clever scheme, and there was no question in Sissy's mind that Rosalinde had leaped ahead in the Miranda Hamilton stakes.

It was so expertly simple, so obvious, so fucking clever, *goddamn* the bitch! Sissy knocked back another vodka. Bloody brilliant. It was, yes, brilliant, admit it. She, who had been in the business for twenty-seven years, should know how gullible people were. With enough chutzpah and assertiveness in this town, one could rule it easily. This round went to Rosalinde, but Sissy was not about to go down for the count just yet.

A life-sized nude of Sissy reclining on an eighteenth-century chaise à la Madame Récamier took pride of place above the gray suede couch in the combination gym and screening room.

As Sissy performed her morning workout to the music of Bob Dylan, she admired the soft angles and curves of this more than flattering picture of her painted fifteen years ago by a then unknown, but now much in demand, artist. The painting had the look to which Sissy aspired. Unfortunately, hard as she tried, the more she strove for the physical perfection of the portrait, the more it evaded her.

She was becoming dangerously anorexic-looking. Even her best friends were daring to criticize her. Her face, pulled taut from a recent trip to Rio and Dr. Pitanguy, was thin and gaunt, although there wasn't a line or wrinkle upon it. Somehow, instead of making her look more youthful, it seemed to age her. Sissy seemed not to notice. She clapped her hands with glee when she saw on her doctor's scale that her five-foot six-inch frame was down to ninety-seven pounds. She had to peer at the number with one of the thirty pairs of spectacles she left in every place where she could possibly need them.

"Perfect, perfect. Now I can wear the Grès for the test, and I won't look fat," she cried to no one in particular. She was testing for Miranda next week. Her husband had done it for her. The big pitch, and Abby had been unable to say no. Neither could the network. Sam was playing the male lead in "Saga." They could hardly not test his wife when he was so insistent. Of course she'd get the part. How could she not? After all, she was an Oscar-winning actress, star of some of the most successful films of the past fifteen years, and married to the leading man of the series. How could they not? The competition was negligible. She could beat them all, and she would—she had to!

Rosalinde Lamaze—no way. A trashy tramp, a lightweight, in spite of the amazing photographs. She was a workingman's wet dream—an aging sexpot. She couldn't be a serious contender. Emerald Barrymore? Certainly she was a legend in her own time, superstar, supercelebrity, but she was nowhere *near* the actress that Sissy was. She couldn't approach her for talent, and she was years older. Her applause and accolades had always been for her private life, which was far more interesting than the movies in which she had starred. That was what the public loved about her best—her men, her scandals, her suicide attempts. She was a tabloid celebrity, larger than life. She would overpower the rest of the cast. Surely the network was wise enough to see that?

The only fly in the ointment was that damned Chloe Carriere. She *was* a definite threat, no question about that. Sissy grudgingly had to admit that she was ideal for the role. She had the right look—that mixture of innocence and evil that everyone who discussed the part felt the actress who played it had to suggest. And she was a new face, even though she was forty—and everyone *loved* a new face. Sam tried to assuage Sissy's fears by saying that even if the network and Abby insisted on Chloe, *he* would then insist on Sissy playing ex-wife number one; he had made the network agree to that at least.

But Sissy knew that Sirope was not the plum part. Ex-wife number one was a dullard. A flaccid Goody Two-shoes role. It was Miranda Hamilton, wife number two, she wanted to play. Oh, how she wanted that role! The bitch. The wicked one. The manipulator, seductress, traitress, cunning, cool, yet with a heart of gold that she knew was buried in the pages of the "Saga" script. She could almost taste the character. Perhaps if she lost another pound?

It was the day of Abby and Maud Arafat's intimate dinner for all the contenders, and they were all rather concerned about it.

What to wear? What to wear? Chloe wondered what could she don that would knock 'em dead tonight?

Tonight, the producers—Abby and Gertrude—would see all their main contenders for the role together in one room. Comparisons could be odious, Chloe knew. Although she usually had no difficulty in choosing her outfits, tonight she was in a lather of indecisiveness. She had shopped feverishly for two days, systematically haunting Rodeo Drive and Sunset Boulevard boutiques. What facet of Miranda should she best exploit for this party?

The bitch? In that case, her high-necked black satin Valentino gown with a lace jacket sparkling with black-beaded jet bows and matching jet-and-crystal earrings should be the one.

The seductress? Ungaro's red chiffon, cut to the clavicle in front and to the tenth vertebra at the back. Clouds of red chiffon fanned seductively out from her knees to the floor, and matching red satin sandals with heels so high she could barely walk completed the ensemble. Sexy—yes —maybe too much so.

But perhaps she should just be herself, Chloe Carriere. Yes, why not? She would be just Chloe tonight. She would wear an old favorite, a gown she had worn several times before and felt at ease in. Cream silk jersey, cut on the bias, draped Grecian style over one tanned shoulder, leaving the other bare. She selected a forties faux diamond clip to fasten the draped fabric at her waist and small Bulgari diamond studs as her only jewelry. She would carry a cream enamel-and-rhinestone-studded Judith Leiber minaudière in the shape of a rabbit in her hand—a present from Josh on her last birthday, and a good luck mascot to boot. Luck! She needed it tonight.

Birthdays! She shuddered as she sat at her dressing table and swiftly applied myriad cosmetics to her face. She would be forty years old this year. Forty!!! It seemed so incredibly ancient. She couldn't believe her life had flown by so fast, her youth passed so soon. All those years so swiftly gone.

"It's not over yet, kid—not by a long shot," she admonished herself as she applied Dior lip gloss with a practiced hand. "There's life in the old girl yet." She brushed out her thick curly hair, sweeping it to one side with a tortoiseshell comb. Slipping cream grosgrain sandals, little more than tiny straps of ribbon, onto her silk-clad feet, she surveyed herself from every angle with a critically objective eye. In her three-way mirror she looked more than beautiful. She looked fabulous. Radiant. Everything was perfect tonight, except one thing was missing. Her man.

Chloe consulted her diamond Boucheron watch. He was late. Josh was recording again. He'd warned her that he might be late. The mixing of his new album was at the critical stage. Since it was already late for delivery, he *had* to get the last track finished, and he wanted it to be perfect. It was vital because this album was critical to his waning career. It had to be at least a minor hit, or, Josh knew, this time his career would be over. At his age, it *was* over as far as most of the kids who bought albums were concerned anyway. They simply didn't care about someone old enough to be their father strutting his stuff on TV, video or stage. Offers for Josh to tread the boards in New York or London were thin on the ground, too. He was slipping fast, careerwise, and no one was more aware of it than he and Chloe.

The irony was that it had taken him years, decades, to become a star. The climb up had been much more difficult than the slide down. It crossed Chloe's mind that maybe, just maybe, he might be playing around again, but she dismissed the thought quickly. She had been absolutely final about what steps she would take if he started screwing underage bimbos again. No ifs, no buts, no maybes—she would divorce him instantly.

Forget. Forget all those times she had caught him. He had promised, hadn't he? Said that now that he was over forty he thought it undignified to pull young "grumble." Told Chloe he really cared, wanted the marriage to work. He'd promised, hadn't he? The limo was waiting. He *was* mixing his tracks. It was party time. She sprayed herself with *Bal à Versailles* and left for Abby and Maud's party in an optimistic mood and a cloud of fragrance.

It definitely was one of Tinsel Town's more up-market parties, Chloe realized, as the polite young man with "Chuck's Parking" embroidered on his red jacket opened the car door for her and she glimpsed the front hall of the Arafat mansion awash with true Old World Hollywood glamour.

No photographers, either unofficial or official, were allowed inside or outside the house. This was a sure sign of social superiority. Not even George Christy from the *Hollywood Reporter* had been invited. The more important the party, the less press. It was the golden rule of Hollywood. Premieres, publicity parties, launches, wrap parties, the more press at those the merrier, but on this occasion the press was conspicuous by its absence.

The entrance hall was vast. Polished gray marble terrazzo imported from Montecatini was barely visible beneath the hems of the designer gowns of the women and the impeccably creased black trousers of the men. The seventy-five distinguished guests who sipped Cristal champagne or Perrier water ignored the lacquered eggshell walls on which hung more than fifteen million dollars' worth of paintings. They had seen it before; industry talk was far more entrancing.

An eclectic group of paintings ranging from Renoir to Fischl was displayed to perfection on walls which had been sanded a dozen times and then had seven coats of lacquer applied to create a flawless matte finish. The guests also ignored the black onyx Corinthian columns placed at four-foot intervals throughout the hallway on top of which reposed priceless Roman marble busts from the fifth and sixth centuries.

Chloe, however, could not quite ignore any of it. She found it fascinating. She had never seen such opulent grandeur. She and Josh, although they had been on the Hollywood scene for years, had not been invited to this house before. Abby and Maud Arafat believed in putting their money where their friends could see it. Their home was clearly meant to look

like that of a multimillionaire megaproducer. And see it they certainly
could. Chloe gasped at the gorgeousness of the decor, the obvious value
and beauty of the art. She accepted a glass of champagne from one of
thirty liveried servants and strolled into the living room. The room was at
least seventy-five feet long, dominated by a Picasso that was unfamiliar to
Chloe. It was obviously from his blue period and portrayed two of his
great sterile-looking athletes on the beach. The windows were over fifteen feet high, elaborately draped in cobalt blue brocade, heavy with
fringe and tassels. The doors to the garden were open, and Chloe wandered onto the terrace. There, on a lawn so thick and green it resembled
cut velvet, stood eight of the most exquisite and valuable Henry Moore
sculptures in the world. Chloe was amazed that they should be placed so
casually on the lawn.

Some of the guests were chatting on the lawn; it was a balmy California night with a light breeze blowing from the coast. Chloe thought about
the letter she would write to Annabel describing the scene. She wrote to
her at least once a week, describing with care interesting events that had
happened, and places she had visited. In return she received little notes,
for which she was grateful. Annabel, her baby. As usual, as soon as she
started to think about her daughter, Chloe became sad. She took a gulp
of champagne. "Stop it, Chlo," she said to herself. "This is business.
Concentrate on it. Sparkle, girl—sparkle." So who was there? She
couldn't help noticing that all the main contenders for Miranda were
there, in the full flower of their elaborate toilettes.

Sissy Sharp had opted for red. Reagan Red, she trilled to all who were
aware of the friendship, now, alas, long lapsed, that had existed between
Nancy and Ronald and Sissy and Sam when Ronnie was president of the
Screen Actors Guild, and Sam one of its officers. Sissy exaggerated the
depth of the friendship, dropping the Reagan name with unerring consistency. She and Sam had, in fact, recently returned from a state dinner for
the President of Yugoslavia, not one of Washington's top affairs, but
newsworthy enough for a one-liner in *USA Today*. She had regaled everyone who would listen with amusing anecdotes about the doings of Nancy,
and the funny sayings of "Dutch."

Rosalinde Lamaze, escorted by a languid stud, wore gold lamé from
Lina Lee. Rosalinde looked satisfied, the stud, tired.

Rosalinde and Chloe exchanged glances, nodding brief hellos. Chloe
thought the other woman's outfit looked cheap, but that Rosalinde herself was a remarkably attractive woman who certainly did not look her
age. With her luxuriant dark hair caught at the side with a gardenia, and
her vivacious smile, Rosalinde looked sexily gorgeous and no more than
thirty.

There was a flurry of excitement when Emerald Barrymore arrived.
She was Hollywood's child. A major star since age three, she still managed to create excitement wherever she went. Not a decent movie under
her belt in ten years, but her aura of stardom glowed undiminished.

No one loved a star more than those who lived and worked in Hollywood, and Emerald was soon surrounded by sycophants and

worshippers, none of whom, however, was prepared to offer her a decent job, save for a guest stint on an episodic TV show or perhaps a supporting role in a miniseries.

She had arrived late, as usual, being unable to decide which one of her five fabulous necklaces to wear. Her jewelry was legendary, more so because people thought she had never bought a single piece of it herself. This was actually not true. She had bought most of it herself, jewelry was a passion with her—but she wanted the public to think she was always being showered with gifts by her many lovers, and her press agent worked hard on this image.

She was with her latest husband, Solomon Davidson, a New York suit manufacturer, out of his league but determined not to show it. She sported a cabochon emerald the size of a golf ball on her engagement finger and was wearing an ankle-length sable coat—even wholesale, as Solomon had managed to buy it, the $100,000 price tag was steep. The coat was a mite too long for Emerald's five feet two, but for what she lacked in stature she made up for in hair. Back-combed to within an inch of its life, her fine blond hair stuck out in dangerous punk-style spikes. She was sheathed in a silver Norell and looked, Chloe had to admit, glorious—a true superstar.

The two contenders who everyone agreed would turn Miranda down even if they were offered the role chatted amicably. Jacqueline Bisset and Meryl Streep were far too involved with the cinema to sacrifice their careers for a part in a TV soap opera. The general consensus was that Abby and his partner Gertrude Greenbloom, as co-owners of a studio and the creators of so many great films, were demeaning themselves by turning to TV. Snobbery was still rife about the relatively young medium —so far, in 1982, very few major stars had done a series. Those who did were looked down upon by their peers. Chloe didn't care. She was not a snob—TV or movies, it didn't matter. She needed a good job—and this was the one she wanted.

A few pretty young girls with names like Sharon, Tracey and Cindy wandered around with the fixed desperate smiles of those who feel they're out of place, but realize it's good for their careers to be there. They were starlets under contract to MCPC, outfitted in beaded dresses other stars had worn in last year's movies.

The old guard clung together, as usual: Edie and Lew Wasserman, Mary and Irving Lazar, Janet and Freddie de Cordova, and Billy and Audrey Wilder. How many parties had they attended throughout the decades? How many studio heads, how many up-and-coming actors, how many hot young directors had they seen come and seen go? Still they always seemed to enjoy themselves, and the fact that they were there tonight made it an "A" party.

Chloe felt confident, even in her two-year-old Bruce Oldfield. "Better under than over, m'dear," Lady Sarah had always told her. Lady Sarah, of course, had not listened to her own advice to underdress, and was festooned with ropes of pearls the size of garbanzos, mauve organza flounces and taffeta bows bouncing in her red curls as she chatted with

Sissy. Chloe nodded to Sissy, who gave her an icy smile. They had never been friends, had little in common.

As the dinner hour approached, Chloe started to become nervous. Josh had promised to be with her tonight. She needed his moral support. It was nerve-racking enough to be at a huge formal Hollywood banquet, not to mention attending it alone. She nervously sipped her champagne, then put it down, realizing she was getting slightly high. She looked at her watch again. Ten to nine. Dinner was bound to be announced any minute. She was supposed to be seated at a table with Josh. It would be embarrassing if he didn't come. She crossed her fingers, willing him to arrive.

Another contender for Miranda, but in everyone's opinion a rank outsider because of her youth, lurked uncomfortably on the terrace, wishing she could go home.

"It's ridiculous," said Sabrina Jones to Johnny Swanson, her press agent. "I *know* I'll never get this part. I'm too young."

Johnny agreed. Twenty-three was much too young to play such a conniving woman of the world. "I'm sure Abby wants you to play one of the daughters. He knows a great hype and since you're so hot, your name means more interest in the columns." "Mmm," Sabrina said. She was miserable. She missed Luis, but Johnny had told her she couldn't bring him here. Too much emphasis on sex—not enough on career.

Chloe moved over to Sabrina and Johnny. The young man was friendly; he was witty and attractive, and, strangely, he seemed to want to pay more attention to Chloe than to his beautiful young client. Chloe enjoyed talking to him—he made her laugh in spite of her nervousness.

Johnny Swanson liked Chloe, had, in fact, fancied her for some time. She appeared to be in a daze, he thought. Was it because Josh wasn't with her? He felt sorry for her, but he admired how she was handling it. Lady Sarah approached and asked him to dance, her tongue too close to his ear for comfort. He disengaged himself in distaste. God, what a mass of amorphic flesh and frills! She didn't attract him in the slightest, even though she was the required age. "No, my little honeybunch," he said firmly. "Dance with the stallion in yonder corner who is giving you the once-over. My shoes aren't made to shuffle tonight, sugar." Lady Sarah raised penciled auburn eyebrows. "Honeybunch" indeed! She looked at the stallion, Alex. Mm, not bad, not bad at all.

Johnny moved away to continue studying Chloe. She was not easily had—the grapevine knew that. The boys lunching weekly at Ma Maison knew all about the sexual proclivities and preferences of "The Available 400," as they were called. Exchanging this information gave them many a clue as to what each lady preferred in bed. Johnny knew that Chloe's marriage had held up pretty well, but tonight it looked to be on its last legs. She was here alone. None of the boys had heard of her ever having an affair. A faithful wife was a rare bird in Hollywood. Particularly one who looked as good as Chloe. A one-man woman, faithful and around forty—just his type! She was leaning at the bar now, temporarily alone, sipping champagne, a frown between those ravishing turquoise eyes. She looked sad. Her facade was starting to crack.

"Champagne gives you nightmares," he cracked. "Hot milk's better for you. But then I suppose it depends on what you're doing in bed."

Chloe smiled faintly at his boyish charm, tried to banter back. "I hate hot milk," she said. "Reminds me of my childhood."

Before Johnny could continue his verbal foreplay the butler announced that dinner was served. The guests started to drift in from the marble hall, the manicured velvet lawn, and the Louis Fifteenth drawing room, and into the ballroom. The ceiling of the ballroom looked as if it had been painted by Michelangelo. Angels flew in formation against an azure sky with scudding white clouds. On the walls were eighteenth-century sconces in which beeswax candles burned. There was no electric light; only the hundreds of candles on the walls and on the ten tables which were set up symmetrically around the ballroom. In the center of each table reposed a Lalique bowl in which white roses, calla lilies and tiny fairy lights had been artfully arranged by Milton Williams. Liveried footmen helped the guests to find their tables.

Just as Chloe was in despair about Josh, he appeared at her side. "Hi, babe," he whispered, squeezing her arm and brushing his soft lips against her cheek. She smelled the faint aroma of tequila, and also the stronger smell of dope. "I didn't let you down, kid. I'm here—good old reliable."

"Darling, I'm so glad you came. I was getting worried." She smiled, touching the face she cared for so much.

"You knew I wouldn't let you down, Chloe." He wavered fractionally, and she knew he was high on something. His words were almost imperceptibly slurred. No one but Chloe would know he had been drinking or drugging; he was an expert at covering up, a true pro.

She did not reproach him. He had come to the party after all. For her. Don't make waves, Chloe, her inner voice said. He's here. He does love you. Be thankful.

The guests looked surreptitiously at their watches. It was ten-thirty. At ten forty-five it would be considered correct to split. Two and a half to three hours was the usual length of time guests stayed at a Hollywood party. Then they wanted to go home—watch Carson or a video, read a script, call a broad or smoke a joint. Few, other than those actors who arose at six to film, actually went to sleep at eleven, but it was such a perfect excuse to leave. There were so many parties—to stay longer than three hours would be a waste of time. Silver fork tapped against crystal goblet, and Abby had the guests' attention.

"Tonight is an important occasion for MCPC pictures," said Abby, reveling in the crowd's fickle attention focused on him.

"Our new show, 'The Great Conspirators,' has been very successful on network." Knowing looks were exchanged. A flop, everyone *knew* it was a flop, even at nine o'clock on Tuesday night when its only rivals were miserable sitcoms with appalling ratings. "The Great Conspirators" was the most dismal of failures, but Abby, a smart mover and shaker, was on to his next announcement, glossing over failure with practiced skill.

"I'm thrilled you're all here tonight, my dear friends, partners and co-workers." His eyes swept the room, meeting bland smiles, slight attention and fidgets.

"Get on with it, luv," muttered Lady Sarah, plump beringed hands tracing circles on the thighs of the hot young man she had pulled at the bus stop on Santa Monica Boulevard that morning.

"As you all know, TV is here to stay, and we're staying with it." Since the majority of his guests were motion-picture people, reaction was minimal. They still couldn't take television seriously. It was a medium for selling soap—for fading stars, and up-and-coming performers.

"We—" he nodded his head to his partner, Gertrude, who smiled encouragingly—"have decided to make *the* most exciting prime time long form series of the 1982 season. Of the next ten seasons, in fact, so successful do we think it will be!

"We have bought the book *Saga,* which as you know is the best-seller to end all best-sellers and we will start shooting the four-hour miniseries in three months, to be followed immediately by the series." He paused triumphantly to sparse applause. The guests were looking at their watches. "We are still in the process of casting, but we have some very exciting announcements to make. The part of Steve Hamilton, the Patriarch—a man of the people, a man of substance, integrity and true grit—will be played by America's favorite hero, Sam Sharp." Applause, applause. Sam was popular. Sam stood and made a self-deprecating bow, the kind that had endeared him to the American public for a quarter of a century. Sissy smiled a razor smile tinged with wifely pride.

"For the role of Miranda, the Scarlett O'Hara of the 1980s, we have narrowed our choice down to these five fabulous ladies. Please stand up, Miss Sabrina Jones." Weak applause. No one knew her here in spite of her moderately successful series. They would when her college movie was released. So far she was just hype. Sabrina looked flushed and embarrassed. Johnny gave her hand a comforting squeeze, wishing he could fancy her, but she was far too young.

"Miss Chloe Carriere!" Lukewarm applause. As Chloe took her bow in front of Hollywood's finest, she realized that she was not accepted by them at all. Certainly they would see her show in Las Vegas if they happened to be there. But she was of no real interest to them. She was just a singer. An English vocalist. Not famous. Not young. Not established. Just another performer.

"Miss Rosalinde Lamaze." More enthusiastic applause, a few murmurs of appreciation, as her bare thigh showed itself through the slit of her gold lamé skirt. Rosalinde had starred in many films that had made much money at the box office. She had been hot—could be again—so the applause was warm and almost sincere.

"Miss Sissy Sharp." Lots of applause, particularly from those who aspired to President Reagan's friendship. Sissy's flat eyes glittered triumphantly. If the reaction of her fellow guests was the criterion, she was a shoo-in! She milked it for all she could—aware that they all were pretending to love her tonight.

"And finally, Miss Emerald Barrymore." Vociferous, frenzied applause. Emerald was extremely popular, and her recent self-confessed struggle with drugs, her triumphant rehabilitation and physical metamorphosis, had touched the sympathy of the town. What difference did it make that she hadn't made an American movie in ten years? She was a survivor. A star with a capital S, and she would remain one for the rest of her life, even if she never worked again.

Josh squeezed Chloe's hand supportively. She squeezed his back and smiled. She saw by his pupils that he had been at the coke again. How long this time, O Lord? she thought. How long before his habits catch up with him and he goes off the rails and stabs me in the back again?

◆ *Ten* ◆

CALVIN NEVER MADE IT to college. Not only could his parents not afford to send him, but his grades in high school were so bad that no self-respecting university would even consider his application.

At eighteen he decided to leave the sleepy Utah town where he had grown up and head west. California was his goal, and he felt that there he would eventually attain his ultimate dream: meeting Emerald Barrymore, his idol, in person.

He didn't find it difficult to get a job. His needs were simple, and he was prepared to work hard. He found work as a packer and loader at Thrifty Drug Store on Canyon Drive in Beverly Hills. Soon he was promoted to stock clerk, and finally after five years he was allowed to deal with the public when he graduated to junior clerk behind the counter of the photography department.

There he daily came into contact with many stars of TV and the movie screen. Some of them even left their "happy snaps" to be developed, and once he had found some casual photographs of Emerald at a backyard barbecue at the home of superagent Sue Jacobs.

He bided his time. One day she would come in and he would serve her. They would become friends and then, who knows, perhaps lovers. All he had to do was wait.

When Josh was recording in L.A., he stayed in a room at the Beverly Wilshire. Watching the women on Rodeo Drive was his usual afternoon ritual. Then, trying to "pull" them. It was like big-game hunting or gambling, really, a fascinating game he never tired of. It bolstered his ego, and these days he needed that. He knew he was in a dance of death with Chloe but he couldn't help himself. It had become a sick obsession, and he knew it. In the ten days since the Arafats' party he had been snorting more cocaine than ever.

He'd woken up today at about 3 P.M. with a hangover as usual. Perry, his valet and Man Friday, had brought him the same breakfast he always had when Chloe wasn't around—a glass of Perrier and fresh lemon juice with three Alka-Seltzers fizzing in it, a cheese Danish warm with butter and blueberry jam, and half a gram of coke on a silver salver next to a fresh, neatly rolled hundred-dollar bill. The coke cleared his head. He had thought he would work today on the lyrics for the new song. But after three hours he gave up—ideas eluded him. He couldn't find words, let alone a tune, no matter how much he snorted.

He adjusted his telescope and, leaning on the penthouse windowsill, focused it on the south end of Rodeo Drive. It was just after lunch, and women and girls of all ages and sizes were spilling out of the nearby restaurants—the Bistro, the Bistro Gardens and La Scala—strolling down the elegant street, indulging in the Beverly Hills woman's favorite sport: shopping.

Josh became interested as he looked at a thirty-five-year-old Chinese woman and her adolescent daughter. They were waiting to cross the road, headed for Bonwit's. They looked around vaguely. Out-of-town from where? Hong Kong? Singapore? Not important. He grew hard as he looked at the pubescent girl's tiny nipples under her T-shirt. Her mother's were nice too. A pair of tiny Oriental porcelain dollies. He nodded to Perry. Perry was no slouch at picking up women. Over the years of soliciting for Josh, he had racked up a 75 percent success ratio, and he had a smooth line of chat.

"See the chink and the chinkette, Perry?" Josh said. "Get 'em."

From across the street where she was about to enter the Saint Laurent Boutique, Chloe stopped as she saw Perry approach two Chinese women. She felt a wave of nausea as she realized that Josh was up to his old tricks again. She could almost read Perry's lips and see the bemused expression on the women's faces as he chatted them up.

Disgusted, she turned to cross the road to the parking complex. Forget the new dress for their party tonight—they had decided to celebrate their tenth anniversary in spite of their problems.

Where did she go wrong? Was Josh just a conniving faithless philanderer, had he always been a philanderer, all through the first eight years? Had she been blind? Could he never be faithful? Or was he just bolstering his male ego? Was it because his career was on the wane, because he was frightened of getting old? Or was it drugs? Did cocaine cause him to behave in this sickening way? A forty-year-old man with the morals of a seventeen-year-old slum boy. She had wanted to understand, to forgive, but she couldn't any longer. Yes, things were looking up for her career, just as his was on the wane. But she couldn't let him destroy her now—destroy her ego along with his. How dare men think they were the only ones with a fragile ego. What presumption made them feel that women had no claims to one?

In the early months of their marriage, she had put her own career on hold. She had busied herself with newfound domesticity: cooking for her man, shopping for his favorite foods, filling his closet and hers with outfits in which they could relax around their sprawling estate in Malibu. One of their favorite pastimes was to ride around the countryside—he on his Arabian stallion, she on her favorite English mare. They would often ride through the dunes at dawn after a night of partying or abandoned love-making.

She collected records for him. He had a supercilious dislike for the efforts of Tom Jones, Rod Stewart and even Mick Jagger, all of whom he had at various times been likened to, so Chloe kept her antennae out, searching for long-lost recordings of Billie Holiday, Fats Waller and other greats of the past. Josh could listen to them all day.

He loved being cuddled as she caressed him, calling him endearing names, holding him like a baby. His eyes closed, his black tousled head would nestle between her breasts, a smile of satisfaction on his face. Her fingertips would trace a pattern across his body, touching him skillfully here, there, everywhere. Sometimes, wickedly, her expert fingers touched him intimately, transforming his soft innocence into her shaft of pleasure.

He never failed to thrill her. In all of the years of marriage she never tired of the feel of his thighs between hers, his tongue exploring her mouth, his muscular hands palpating where she liked it most, always bringing her to fulfillment.

"I want you so much, babe," he would whisper into her hair. As they entwined, all of his customary crudeness of speech disappeared in the act of love with Chloe. With her Josh became a tender, demonstrative, affectionate lover. No one was more amazed by this transformation than he— he who had never given a damn for any of the women from his indiscriminate past. For Chloe now only endearments issued from his lips. Terms of love, sweet talk, tender, loving, sincere. Chloe loved it. She loved him so much. Forever. It could only be forever.

"Stop it, Chloe," she said to herself, thoughts of their lovemaking now hopelessly interwoven with thoughts of him fucking the two Chinese women she had seen being escorted by Perry to the Wilshire. "Stop it *now,* girl. It's over. You know what you have to do. It's finished. It has been finished for years."

She drove her silver Mercedes back to Malibu, her eyes stinging with salty tears that coursed down her face. She had to get ready for the party tonight. Their anniversary party. She felt numb. Was this what a broken heart felt like?

It was four o'clock when she got home. Pop music blared from the kitchen where the Mexican staff was preparing a feast for the party. She walked to the beach and stared bleakly at the ocean. Her marriage was cracked. Josh didn't love her. She had subordinated her career, encouraged his flagging one. She had tried to breathe new life and respectability into his hell-raising image; he had not responded to her care. He was a wastrel and an ingrate.

Deny it as he might, he was a slipping, aging rock star. It didn't matter that he still looked sexy, tough and confident with his tumbling black curls, tinged faintly with gray—and only the tiniest hint of a gut, which he dieted and sweated off before each tour. No, the fourteen-year-olds *knew* he was hitting forty when they saw his face on an album cover, no matter how much retouching from the experts. Their eager hands picked at the new Michael Jackson or Rick Springfield album, ignoring Joshua Brown—he was yesterday's news, their mama's idol.

"We can't all be young forever, darling," Chloe had soothed and comforted him as he raged at the injustice of it, his insecurities mounting as his hairline receded. Try as she might, Chloe could no longer assuage Josh's self-doubt with her love. It wasn't enough for him any more. He needed fresh game to stalk. New pussy. The chase. Ah, the thrill of the hunt! He never tired of it now.

Although Josh had been notoriously successful with women, he had tried to be true to Chloe during their marriage. Chloe, loving, caring, demonstrably sexy, gave him neither reason nor motivation to stray in the early years of their marriage. But a stiff prick no conscience hath, and now he needed more reassurance that he was up to it twice, thrice, sometimes four times a session. He became petrified by his waning sexuality, a normal thing for most men his age. He had to prove himself again and again—perhaps not the same way as when he was a kid on tour with groupies—but certainly he needed to feel he was still desired by other women. His sexual interest in Chloe waned. Her all-consuming love began to smother him. Sure he loved cuddles—"the goodies" he called them—adored lying close to her as she caressed him, sang to him. She even sang *his* hits! Clever girl. He loved that. But she was too damn clingy, too damn wifely-womanly-motherly. She was smothering. Suddenly he wanted new game to hunt.

He thinks I'm his goddamned mother, she fretted, as she strode the Malibu sands in a flowing white cotton Laize Adler. Her painted toenails crunching and popping the seaweed that encrusted the shore, she puffed nervously on a cigarette, a habit she had quit a year ago.

"Damn him!" she thought two hours later as she lay back in the black marble Jacuzzi, so often the scene of their lovemaking. Only last week he had "taken" her there as she lay mesmerized listening to Lena Horne wailing "Love Me or Leave Me." It had been the first time other than an occasional "duty fuck" in six months that they had made love joyously and spontaneously. Covered with bubbles they had embraced each other in the hot foaming Jacuzzi. It was almost like the old days. Almost.

That had been a week ago. Remembering a time when they felt deprived if they had not made love once in the morning and once at night, at least, Chloe felt bitter sadness at the thought of him with the two Chinese women. What was he doing with them? She couldn't bear to think about it.

Love dies, passion erodes. The opposite of love is not hate—it is indifference. She groaned inwardly, trying to think about tonight's party, wishing she could feel indifferent toward Josh instead of this jealous sexual angst. She loved him still, she could not help herself. Oh stop it, girl—get it *together* now, get out of the bath. Think about the damn guests. Could she cancel the party now? Impossible. Half of them were home in Beverly Hills preparing their toilettes, painting their faces and nails, having their chauffeurs spit-polish the Silver Spirit or the Porsche. No, she must brazen it out tonight. There were problems with Josh's recording session, she would tell the guests with a smile. He's still at the studio. Deadlines. You know how it is. They would nod wisely. Of course they knew how it was. They were all in the business so they knew only too well.

Rosalinde Lamaze and Johnny Swanson were the first to arrive. She had dressed casually—tight white leather pants were tucked into seven-hundred-dollar Di Fabrizio cowboy boots inlaid with turquoise leather; her turquoise silk cowboy blouse was slashed to the navel; around her neck cascaded the spoils of some long-forgotten Navajo tribe, a silver, turquoise and mother-of-pearl squash-blossom necklace. A silver belt encircled her twenty-three-inch waist, and several turquoise rings adorned her dusky fingers.

Johnny and Rosalinde had been friends for years, relying on each other for "escort duty" when no one more exciting was on the horizon. Johnny was twenty-nine to Rosalinde's thirty-six, and six feet to her five feet two. He was good-looking and slim in a suave boyish way, and his cutting wit gave him a special brand of charm. For one so young, he had more than a way with both words and women. "If it moves, fondle it," was his motto. His prowess as a "stick man" preceded him, along with his colorful family history.

Rosalinde rearranged her silver neckwear and surveyed the room. Featured tonight were several bit players in both her life and Johnny's. But Eureka! There he was again, fat old Abby Arafat. The man who held the key to her future. She oozed beguilingly over to Abby, voluptuous hips performing a melody of their own as she played the game of "Oh I'm bored—I've got *sooo* many movie offers but nothing turns me on. What shall I *do*, Abby darling?" She didn't want him to know she was eager for Miranda, although she had agreed to test. She who plays it the coolest shall win the first prize. American phrase much in vogue recently.

Abby chomped on his cigar and half-listened with amusement as he surveyed the other woman he was going to test next week for Miranda. That Chloe. She was beautiful and charismatic. His eyes narrowed as he watched her in a clinging white silk Azzedine Alaïa dress, her black curls tumbling artlessly, and the definition of a well-formed breast visible as she threw back her head and laughed with Alex Andrews. Where was her hubby, Abby wondered? Why wasn't he keeping an eye on this hot number?

Alex Andrews was the latest hunk in town. Gorgeous, young, sexy, blond, virile, intelligent, he possessed every one of the qualities necessary for big screen appeal. However, it just wasn't enough to be gorgeous and young, etcetera, today, mused Abby. That had been sufficient in the thirties, forties and fifties to guarantee movie stardom; then in the sixties, those attributes almost became impediments to an actor's career. Were Dustin Hoffman, Michael Caine and Jack Nicholson gorgeous and young? No. They were actors, artists, thespians who had perfected their craft. They had charisma as well as talent. Intelligence as well as interesting looks. In the eighties you had to have it all. The public was too demanding. Gorgeous, young and sexy were minor requirements. Essential were talent, personality, intelligence and uniqueness.

Alex, studying hard with his acting coach, strived to acquire all these. But tonight he was working in a different way on Rosalinde, flashing his hooded hazel eyes in her direction, turning to give her a fine view of his twenty-five-year-old black-leather-covered buns. Alex was a pure soul, a cowboy from Indiana, with all the accompanying naiveté. "The great open spaces are in his head," quipped Johnny, ever vigilant to spot an upstart trying to break into the rarefied ranks of the "in" crowd.

Johnny was totally accepted everywhere in Hollywood: at A parties, B parties, orgies, stuffy charity affairs he was ever welcome. He wasn't an actor, and he was from a fine family, even if no one was quite sure who had sired him. But Alex was an outsider. A climber. All curls and cock. No family. No background. He had far to go, even if his agent claimed that he had the part of Steve's son on "Saga" all but sewn up.

Alex chatted eagerly with Rosalinde, trying to spark her feminine interest in him. He realized that although she was a big star, and he the male equivalent of a starlet, they were both playing the same game. He felt she was hungry. He could sense her sexual hunger in the way her round brown eyes admired the contours of his high-cheekboned face. Her plump, beringed fingers had started to flutter gently, skimming over his black silk shirt. A delicate butterfly touch. Little did he know she wasn't thinking of him. Rosalinde had Angelica on her mind. God forbid this crowd should ever find out she was a dyke. She'd be finished in this town. Men could get away with being gay; it was a man's world, let's face it—but a woman—a sex symbol be a lesbian? Perish the thought. She'd never get another job.

Abby Arafat moved smoothly through the crowd, talking to everyone. Smiling, nodding, charm personified, he was fully aware of his power tonight. Who wouldn't be? He had the crème de la crème of the acting profession at his feet, all dying to play one of the six or seven wonderful roles in "Saga."

Abby mourned the long-gone era of the true movie stars. The Hedy Lamarrs, Ava Gardners, Lana Turners and Rita Hayworths. Nubile, tender wisps of sixteen or seventeen summers plucked from high school or the cosmetic counters of the local drugstores, adored and worshiped for a few years by an adulatory yet fickle public who soon glorified another new face. That same public was unaware that the stars they paid homage to were merely the products of a slick studio build-up. Many of them were plastic models, with no heart, no guts, no reality—robots who lived by the studio's rules and behaved themselves. So they should, thought Abby. Do what the studio said. Enough already with these coozes with brains, these Glenda Jacksons, Vanessa Redgraves and Shirley MacLaines. They thought they had ideas. They wanted to produce, to direct, to have a say in their work. They couldn't be manipulated, cajoled or flattered.

None of *them* would ever play Miranda, or even Sirope. He wasn't even considering them. He needed a dame with oomph—vulnerable, soft, beautifully dressed, who oozed sex appeal—all those qualities that were unfashionable in these emancipated days of 1982. A woman of sensitivity and sex appeal who appealed to the basics in a man. A woman like . . . Chloe. His eyes glimpsed her curves again through the silky stretch fabric of her gown. Her sultry face, knowing, yet young-looking. Why not Chloe? He chomped on his cigar. Sure, she's really a saloon singer, but who says singers can't act? Look at Streisand, Minnelli, Cher. On second thought, don't, he groaned. Streisand gave him heartburn.

He moved to where Chloe was talking animatedly to Johnny. She knew she was giving off good vibes tonight. She was amusedly aware of her power over men who were attracted by her aura of vulnerable little girl, but one who knows the ropes. Several men at the party were vying for her attention as she fumed inwardly over Josh's nonappearance but desperately tried not to show it. She knew what she wanted to do, what she *had* to do for the sake of her self-respect. Dump him. End the marriage. Get the part of Miranda and ta-ta, Josh.

"Great party, Chloe," Abby intruded, reeking of cigar and goodwill. Johnny melted away. He had nothing to gain from chitchatting with this ancient relic of Hollywood about whom his dear mother, Daphne, often fondly reminisced. Aware that his dear mother had bedded half of Hollywood, Johnny was shrewd enough not to let it bother him—in fact, he joked about it, so that Daphne's escapades in bed became part of his own repertoire of anecdotes. Often he recounted a tale of Mummy and a swain with minor embellishments at the exclusive men-only Friday lunches at Ma Maison.

Suddenly Chloe saw her husband stumble in through the Aztec-carved front door. He was supported on each side by an Oriental female, and the crowd engulfed him in a shower of bonhomie as he disappeared toward the bar. He was drunk—very drunk. Probably stoned, too.

"Darling," Chloe cooed, pressing her silken body close to his. "You're just a tiny bit late, darling. Did the session go well?" She managed to combine wifely concern with womanly understanding, while squeezing his cheek hard.

"Yeah, babe, went late, real late." He pinched her perfumed ivory cheek gently. He wasn't about to tell her about his afternoon at the Beverly Wilshire. He realized he'd made a mistake. A bad one. He hadn't fucked the Orientals, although they clung to him like lint. As his head cleared and the room came into focus, the realization of the magnitude of his mistake in bringing them here hit him. Christ, if Chloe should suspect, she'd be bloody furious! She didn't seem to be.

"Why don't you have a quick shower and freshen up, *darling?*" Chloe used her sweetest tone, aware of forty pairs of potentially gossiping eyes viewing their reunion. Rumors were already rife that Josh had started catting around—and he and Chloe were, after all, on their third reconciliation in less than two years. Everyone knew Josh possessed a roving eye, and many people were surprised that Chloe had kept him by the home fires all these years. "A leopard never changes its spots," observed Abby sagely. "Never."

After Josh's arrival the party proceeded smoothly. A tiered mocha cake from the X-Rated Cake Shoppe, featuring a couple in pink-and-brown icing suggestively entwined, was served. A trio of singing telegramettes arrived and sang "Happy Anniversary" while stripping to approving cheers from the crowd. Toasts were drunk to the happy couple who had survived ten years of marriage, a record by many Hollywood standards. Chloe watched Josh with impassive eyes that hid her pain as she realized it was finally over. Goodbye and farewell to her "forever marriage." There was no use prolonging the agony. She glimpsed his tongue playfully teasing the ear of one of the women he'd arrived with, saw her stroke the bulge in his jeans, observed his hand try to sneak up the skirt of the other. Saw—and died inside.

Sally saw it all, too, and, daughterly devotion aside, felt sorry for her father. But she did enjoy seeing Chloe squirm. She could read the pain in her eyes. She saw the glances Chloe stole at Josh. She realized how it must hurt her to watch him with the two women. She didn't care. Maybe they would get a divorce and she would never have to see Chloe again. "Miserable old cow," she said, downing a beer and throwing back a tequila after it, as she had seen her father do.

Chloe circulated among her guests, laughing, charming, playing her part. Josh stayed at the other end of the stadium-sized living room, surrounded by his buddies and the two women. As he drank more, he became more raucous, more aggressive and, Chloe noticed, more unattractive. An aging, graying, middle-aged rock star trying to remain young. It was pathetic. He had been smoking dope and drinking tequila—he looked out of it. He looked over the hill, tired and unsuccessful. "He's wrong for you, darling," Daphne whispered. "Wrong, wrong, wrong. He's a lout, and a drunk and a wastrel." And a loser too, she thought, behaving like this in front of everyone.

Chloe was beyond humiliation. The embarrassment of seeing her husband in her living room with those two strange women, his obvious fascination with this Chinese mother-and-daughter act, made her ill. She felt as if she were observing everything in slow motion. One of the waiters continuously refilled her glass with champagne. She floated through the room, watching everything objectively, not caring any more about anything or anyone. She realized that Abby had left. She was thankful that a potential boss was not a witness to her humiliation. As for the other guests, she simply didn't give a damn what they thought.

"Where's the wife? Where is she then?" Josh suddenly called out, whirling on the tinier of his tiny strumpets, slapping her hands away from where they were toying with his chest hair. "C'mon, Chloe, give us a song," he bawled, grabbing Chloe's hand in his bear grip and pulling her over to the piano.

"No, Josh, no." Chloe tried to pull away from him. "No duets tonight. I can't. Don't do this, Josh, *please.*"

Josh seemed oblivious to her distress. He shrugged and beckoned to the teenage Chinese girl, who came to his side with a sly Oriental smile.

Chloe desperately wished everyone would leave. Finally, as if reading her thoughts, they started to.

Rosalinde threw back her sixth Bailey's Irish Cream and smiled at Alex. "Let's get out of here, honey pie. It's a bore," she murmured. "Got wheels?"

"Sure, sure," Alex said happily. His manager had lent him his Cadillac, not wanting his latest client to be seen at an important party in a clapped-out Mustang. Alex realized that leaving this party with Rosalinde Lamaze was quite a coup. Even if she was a decade older than he, she was a big star. He hoped there would be paparazzi outside the house, ready to take a happy snap for the *National Enquirer.* He made a mental note to have his press agent call Army and Hank tomorrow, to give them the exclusive scoop about this new hot twosome. Maybe even Liz Smith or Suzy would run it in New York. What would the folks in Indiana think!

Johnny hadn't scored tonight. Not that it bothered him. Scoring was too easy in this town. By the time a good-looking guy was twenty-nine he had usually scored so much easy pussy that, if he didn't start playing the marriage-and-divorce game, only challenges could excite him. Chloe Carriere, for instance, was quite a challenge, and Johnny thought he might throw down his gauntlet for her.

Calvin, from his hiding place, outside the house, saw Rosalinde leaving the party with Alex. He sneered to himself. What a slut! Hanging on to a stud at least ten years her junior, stroking his long blond hair, fondling him in places that Calvin knew were dirty. Filthy whore! She was scum.

Where was Emerald? Why wasn't she at this party? Many others of importance seemed to be. He had been told she was coming, but perhaps Chloe hadn't invited her—out of jealousy, no doubt. A jealous British bitch. They were all jealous of Emerald—she was so ravishing, so sweet. Vulnerable yet glamorous. None of these over-the-hill spic sluts or limey cows was in her league. None of them was fit to lick her size three satin-shod feet. She was the Queen. The Goddess. The Best.

He looked at his watch. Twelve-thirty. He saw that the Mexican tramp and the stud toy-boy were locked in an embrace in the front seat of a Cadillac.

An unaccustomed excitement suddenly engulfed him as he watched the couple fondling each other. Even though he despised Rosalinde, watching her hands roam over Alex's body aroused Calvin tremendously. As Alex finally disengaged himself from Rosalinde's hot hands, put the car in gear and moved into the highway, Calvin followed in his green Chevrolet.

After the guests had left, Chloe confronted Josh. "This was the last straw tonight, Josh. I want a divorce, and I mean it this time. How *dare* you bring those women to our house?"

"No, babe, please, *no*. Chloe, I love you, you know I do. It's always been you, babe. Always, you know it, babe." His words were erratic.

"Oh, stop it, Josh—you sound like a broken record. I can't take your cheating any more." She tried to keep the pain out of her voice. It hurt to swallow, her throat was so constricted. He had wounded her too many times now with his playing around. She had tried to pretend to herself it didn't really matter, it was just sport fucking—nothing serious. Had tried many times to forgive him. But tonight she had run out of forgiveness. "I *won't* stand for it any more, Josh," she said wearily. "We've come to the end of the road. You know we have. We *must* divorce, or I'll go mad, because I think *you* are, Josh."

" No, Chloe, no. I can't make it without you," he had begged her, gone on his knees, tears streaming down his face. He used every trick in his book to persuade her not to end their marriage. But bringing up old times only made her think of old injuries and convinced her more than ever that the marriage was over. The Oriental women were the end. It was intolerable. Whether or not he had made love to them made no difference. The fact that he *wanted* to was enough. In front of their guests, at their anniversary party, he had humiliated her terribly. Insulted their marriage. Disgraced them both. "This isn't *love* any more, Josh," she screamed, all control suddenly evaporating. "It's war—it's sick—it's horrible. The whole goddamn party saw it, and I *won't* stand for it. It's an *illness*, Josh."

She'd drunk a lot of champagne. Now it released her, released the pain. She locked the bedroom door, took two Valium, ripped off her clothes, letting them lie on the floor, and, without removing her makeup, fell into a dreamless slumber.

Josh zoomed down the Pacific Coast Highway at 75 mph in his Cadillac convertible. He didn't notice the police car behind him. His stereo was turned on full blast to his latest track, and he had just taken a swig of tequila from his leather Gucci flask. The booze and the joint he had smoked earlier were making him feel slightly better. Chloe would eventually come to her senses. She had to. He needed her. They were the forever couple, weren't they?

Then as the flashing lights of the police car pulled in front of him and the sound of the siren finally penetrated his consciousness, he realized that he was in more trouble.

He woke up covered with sweat. His black silk shirt was sodden, his gray slacks oozed moisture. Where the hell was he? His bewildered brain waves tried to connect. Was he in jail? But for chrissake, why? How dare they put him, Joshua Brown, superstar, behind bars. He started sweating even more; he needed a snort badly. He reached into his pocket for the leather pouch in which he kept his paraphernalia—the brown cube of "downtown," the glass phial of "uptown," the solid-gold razor blade, the platinum straw. Gone. Frantically he felt in his other pockets and then scrabbled on the filthy floor. "Hey, you motherfuckers," he screamed, the tendons standing out on his neck. "Bring me back my stuff, you shit-eaters!"

A black guard appeared, opened the hatch and looked at him coldly. "Shut your mouth, junkie, or we shut it for you," he spat, and slammed the hatch shut.

Josh started to tremble. He hadn't had a fix since . . . when was it? Two or three o'clock this morning—after Chloe had gone to bed and left him alone. It was now—he looked at the clock on the wall outside his cell —9 A.M.

Shit. He started to tremble violently, waves of nausea rocking him. He threw up into a bucket, then, weakened and disoriented, fell back onto the filthy bunk again. Staring at the ceiling and walls encrusted with the graffiti of a thousand derelicts, he dropped off to sleep. The pain in his head and chest faded as his dreams took over. He was a star once more. A superstar. Caesars Palace in Vegas . . . the London Palladium . . . Olympia in Paris. He had packed them to the rafters all over the world. Standing room only. Josh Brown, the most charismatic English performer the world had ever seen. He could have had any woman he wanted, and he did. But eventually he wanted only one—only Chloe. And he wanted it to last forever. The others never mattered. Why couldn't Chloe realize that? He loved her—he would always love her. He groaned.

He was allowed one phone call from jail. He called his agent, who immediately sped down to the county court with bail money. Josh was released in a blaze of bad publicity.

In the days that followed, Josh tried to contact Chloe, but she insisted the marriage was finished and she wanted out. With a heavy heart, he moved into the Beverly Wilshire, and she sent his belongings over with Perry. Chloe filed for divorce two days later on the grounds of irreconcilable differences.

Josh threw himself into finishing the album while he consumed huge amounts of tequila and cocaine and made frantic love to as many underage girls as he could. When the album was nearly finished, his agent called and told Josh he had an interesting job for him. He could and should go back into the theater. A major English impresario wanted him to write and star in a musical version of *Cyrano de Bergerac*. It was a wonderful opportunity, one he had wanted for years, for the theater had always been his first, his true love.

Two weeks after he and Chloe separated, Josh packed his bags and left for London.

PART
THREE

❧ *Eleven* ❧

THEY SAT IN THE NUMBER one booth at the Polo Lounge drinking Dom Perignon and exchanging information.

Solomon Davidson, Sol to his many acquaintances, was telling Chloe about the events at the end of his recent marriage to Emerald. Sol and Emerald had indulged in a rapid tabloid-style romantic affair, culminating after a few months in a quick engagement, a short marriage and a fast separation last week.

"Why did you wear that color?" he asked her accusingly, eying her jade-green Halston dress.

"Why—don't you like green? Don't tell me you're superstitious?" Chloe murmured, as she sipped her champagne, watching him with amused eyes.

Solomon, bon vivant and friend to the stars, and Chloe had been good friends for years. They had laughed and joked through many evenings together, and Chloe was sorry to see him still clearly obsessed with Emerald.

When Emerald divorced for the fifth time, she had immediately turned her sea-green eyes, the light in them undimmed, even though she was approaching her half century, in Sol's direction. Oh, lucky man! Oh, foolish and vain man! She had eventually crucified him on the altar of the trash magazines. He had been made to look like a bumbling fool—a poor peasant not fit to slip a bangle on Emerald's slim wrist.

Poor Sol, who reveled in his role as confidant and gofer to the famous, lost both his credibility and his lady to the snide sniggerings of supermarket pulp. But he had swallowed his pride, picked himself up, dusted himself off and ventured back into the Los Angeles social scene again.

"I want her back," Sol confided to Chloe. "I still love her."

Chloe sympathized. Josh-less now for over a month, she had shed many tears and soaked many pillowcases every night as she yearned to have him beside her.

✥   ✥   ✥

Emerald read Army Archerd's column with growing concern: "Chloe Carriere, one of the main contenders for the coveted Miranda role in 'Saga,' and Solomon Davidson, Emerald Barrymore's soon-to-be ex, had more to discuss than the heat wave in the Polo Lounge last week. Is that the love light in their eyes?"

She threw down the paper, lit a Sherman with a green malachite lighter, and with remarkably steady hands inserted it into a pale emerald holder.

Chloe was a parvenu, a Johnny-come-lately. She didn't belong. First of all, not only was she British, but she was not even an actress. She was a singer—a singer who had a couple of hits in the sixties and seventies, and then faded out. Now she had reemerged as a more-than-serious contender for her, Emerald's, role. When Emerald first heard that Chloe was testing, she thought it was a joke. Now the joke was turning out to be a serious threat not only to her part, but to her nearly-ex-husband. Not that she wanted Sol, but she didn't want Chloe to have him either.

Emerald crunched the pale emerald holder between her tiny, perfectly capped teeth. It was essential to her career that she get this role. She was no longer hot in movies. She needed this part. Doing this commercial in Australia was not a great career move.

In spite of her many marriages, her drinking problem and a penchant for carelessly throwing away her hard-earned cash on her friends and husbands, she was a true child of Hollywood, and it still loved her. She had thrived in the era in which she had grown up, become Hollywood royalty, and the ultimate symbol of survival. Many of her contemporaries had succumbed to drugs, drink, suicide or illness. How much of it caused by career failure, no one could know, or even guess.

Marilyn Monroe. Poor Norma Jean—she had never believed in herself, and it had destroyed her. Emerald and Marilyn had studied at the Actors Studio together. Milton Greene, their feisty mentor and glamour photographer par excellence, brash, knowledgeable, and crafty, had guided both their careers simultaneously in the early sixties. The girls had been close friends. Shared gowns, men, and laughs. Emerald had been devastated when Marilyn had died.

James Dean—Jimmy—darling Jimmy—her first lover. No matter that Pier Angeli, Ursula Andress, and countless others were on his fishing line that long hot summer of 1955. She had given herself to him—totally. Emerald Barrymore, eighteen years old, gorgeous, sexy, idol of millions of youngsters, had allowed James Dean, moody, unpredictable and intense, to take her much-discussed virginity.

She had adored him passionately until his death a few months later. A shortish period of mourning—after all, she was only eighteen—then Emerald was in love again. This one was more dependable, and the studio breathed a sigh of relief when they married. A young actor, up-and-coming. Unfortunately for Emerald, he was not able to come up often enough to satisfy her. And when she discovered him in bed with another man, he had to go. Divorce, more tears, more mourning. Then into her life came Stanley O'Herlihy. How destructive can one man be to himself?

Maybe Irishmen have a death wish, but Stanley carried it to new heights. He was short, middle-aged and ugly, with a thirst for whiskey and women that was practically unquenchable. Writing was the driving force of his life, and he devoted most of his waking hours to it.

He was fifty to her twenty when they wed for the first time. His lovemaking left a lot to be desired: two bottles of Irish whiskey a day did not a stallion make. After brief, unsatisfactory couplings he would retire to his desk and his fountain pen and write far into the night, leaving his radiant young bride alone and unfulfilled. He gave her a vibrator for her twenty-first birthday, with a sarcastic note. She took it to the studio and her latest leading man showed her what to do with it—and him.

For some reason, Stanley's obvious lack of interest in her charms captivated Emerald further, making her more determined to make him love her. He had told her he had never truly loved a woman in his life, and that if he did, she would certainly not be the one, as she was nowhere near intellectual and intelligent enough for him; the more he insulted her, the more besotted with him she became.

Twice she left him in frustrated rage for younger, handsomer, wealthier and more caring men—men who satisfied her sexually, who complimented and praised her, who wanted to marry her. But they were never enough for Emerald. They represented only convenient arm decorations and temporary sexual passion—they meant nothing.

She yearned for Stan O'Herlihy, who, knowing a good thing when he saw it, allowed Emerald to move back into his life time and again. She put up with his drunken rages, his foul Irish temper and his indiscriminate fornication with the trashiest of waitresses and prostitutes, women he seemed to find far more exciting than he did her. He craved kinky sex: threesomes, orgies, S and M. She put up with it until finally after two marriages and divorces and ten years of on-again, off-again connubial non-bliss, Stanley drove his Porsche into a tree, instantly killing himself and the black prostitute with him.

Emerald mourned long and loud. It was 1970; she was at the peak of her beauty and sexuality, yet now she couldn't get arrested as far as movies were concerned. Studios considered her a celebrity, no longer a serious actress, in spite of having made fifty films. After decades of success, suddenly she was considered box-office poison.

In Hollywood, socially she was still the crème de la crème, but to new hot young directors and producers she was yesterday's news. She was, after all, well into her thirties, even though her smashing blond beauty showed none of the wear and tear expected.

Eventually Emerald philosophically accepted that Hollywood had turned its back on her and she went to live in Italy. There she learned the language, starred in some low-budget but compelling Italian and French program fillers throughout the decade, married a couple of times, traveled, spent every cent she earned, and waited for the day when she would return in triumph to Hollywood.

Now as she sat in her Sydney hotel room, watching the sunset behind the facade of the beautiful white opera house shining off the harbor waters and reading a week-old copy of *Daily Variety*, she knew she *must* pull out all the stops to get this part. She would call in every one of her markers. She would do anything to get it. *Anything.*

A week later, back in her Hollywood apartment, she reclined on soft green towels and let Sven do his damnedest to her vertebrae. "God, vat kinks," he said, enthusiastically pummeling her with firm Scandinavian hands. Emerald's eyes were alight in her middle-aged, still-beautiful face. More than four decades a star and now reborn, thanks to the miracles of South American plastic surgery and a Midwestern alcohol-and-drug rehabilitation clinic. She had lost more than thirty pounds in the past year thanks to a restrictive diet of zucchini, broiled chicken and Evian water. A major consumer of alcohol all her life, she had completely cleaned out her system of the poisons and toxins that had accumulated over the years, and was now determined to conquer the new and exciting world of prime time TV.

She balanced a pale green phone on the pillow. "You know I'll test," she said. "I don't have any false pride about that, darling." Her agent, Eddie De Levigne—a diminutive, elflike figure who had been around since the days of Swanson, and whose legendary career and monetary accomplishments for his clients always paid off so handsomely that his nickname in the business was Fast Eddie—was pleased. Emerald was a smart cookie. The smartest thing she'd done recently was to fire the Morris boys and hire him. In this town where fledgling actresses become prima donnas in less time than you could say, "Who won last year's Oscar?" her attitude was refreshing. Throughout her bouts with alcoholism and drug addiction and her mistakes with men, Fast Eddie had waited in the wings for her to come to her senses so that he could pick up her pieces and put them together again, as only he knew how. He was an agent in the proper sense of the word, not a faceless gray-flannel-suited cipher like so many of the boys at the conglomerates. Fast Eddie cared— and he got results.

Sven finished kneading her back, packed up his equipment and left. With a groan of pleasure, she strolled, unself-consciously naked, into her mirrored closet to survey her dozens of green outfits.

Emerald almost exclusively wore green, and, occasionally, white. For films she wore other colors, but in private life, all she ever wore was pistachio green, grass green, pea green, or olive green—every imaginable shade of green hung in the hundred feet of her spacious walk-in closet. She selected a mint-green Ungaro blouse with matching gabardine culottes, clasped her everyday emerald pendant around her reconstructed throat and left for Eddie's office to discuss strategy.

Fast Eddie did not mince words. Although Emerald was at the moment his favorite client, he always called a spade a spade. "This Carriere dame is the favorite, kid," he rasped. "No doubt about it. I talked to Gertrude today and she gave it to me straight. Abby loves her, so does the network, and they always have the final say, as you know."

"Shit." Emerald sat up straight, her gorgeous eyes flashing. "That

English nobody. How *can* they prefer her to me? I'm a *star*. She's a nightclub singer. What can we *do*, Eddie?"

"The best we can, kid, the best we can,' said the little man wisely, frowning through his massive spectacles. "Listen, kiddo, we've just gotta persevere. I've told 'em you're the best, the biggest star, the most gorgeous and the most talented. I'm gonna give 'em all I can, kid, and you've gotta help me."

"Oh, I will, you know I will, Eddie darling."

"Give 'em your best shot on the test. You're a damn fine actress kiddo. in spite of all your rotten movies and your stupid marriages."

Emerald winced. True, the critics didn't love her, but the fans did They adored her. Producers and directors loved her too, but didn't give her jobs. They gave them to Anne Bancroft, Sally Field and Jessica Lange. "Saga's" Miranda Hamilton was the key to a whole new career for Emerald, and she was determined to get it.

The network, Abby, and Gertrude finally decided on a date to test their finalists for Miranda. Scripts were sent. Wardrobe women went on the hunt for costumes. Early nights for the five actresses became de rigueur. The town waited for the results eagerly.

The day of the test dawned to uncharacteristic California weather. Rain in great gray sheets had bucketed down on the highways and boulevards all night, leaving the Los Angeles area sodden and drab.

Chloe was awake at 5 A.M. She gazed with alarm at the six-foot waves pounding the foundations of her Trancas house and wondered if, as usual, the hills around Malibu Canyon had collapsed under the weight of the rain and become impassable. What then? Maybe she could make it over the Ventura freeway and cut through to Hollywood Boulevard via Franklin Avenue. She wasn't due at the studio until seven-thirty. Throwing on an old chenille robe and snuggling her feet into oversized bunny slippers, she went down to the kitchen. As she waited for the coffee to percolate and the Highway Patrol to answer the phone, she inspected again the call sheet for today's test.

There they all were, the final *six* names that had been approved by the network, by Abby and by Gertrude.

So Pandora had managed to get a test, too, Chloe mused. Or was she going to play the other ex-wife? Either way it was not a bad idea. She had a sharp, dark, foxy face, was a good actress, the right age—oh, dear, more competition for Miranda.

As she sipped coffee, then showered, she mulled over her chances compared to the other five actresses.

Sabrina Jones was no competition. Everyone including Sabrina knew she was wrong. She was a red herring. A publicity shill used by Abby to garner media coverage and hype the public's interest.

Pandora King? She would probably get the other role of the first wife, since according to the call sheet she was testing for both roles. She was a respected actress, but a second-stringer, and always would be.

Rosalinde Lamaze? Too ethnic. Whatever the networks might say, however much the producers denied it, it was doubtful that this very important leading role would go to Rosalinde, because of her Mexican origin. It wouldn't jell with the total Anglo-Saxon feeling and look that Chloe knew Abby and Gertrude wanted for the show.

Chloe's main competitors were Sissy and Emerald—she had absolutely no doubt about that. Sissy was the better actress, plus being married to Sam would give her a strong edge. But Emerald was still such a megastar that Chloe was surprised she had agreed to test. Still, what the hell—they were all only actresses, weren't they? Bakers must bake, painters must paint, and actresses must act. That was their life.

Ah, well, may the best woman win, she thought as she dressed in jeans, a flannel plaid shirt of Josh's, and her Burberry raincoat that had seen many a rainy day in the provinces of England. She drove her silver Mercedes swiftly through the pouring rain without encountering anything other than the occasional stalled car. Highway Patrol had managed to keep Malibu Canyon open, thank God. Huge men, sweating in spite of the freezing rain, shoveled the sliding mud as it threatened to cover the Pacific Coast Highway. Once on the Hollywood freeway, she relaxed and put the tape of the scene that she had committed to memory into her tape deck.

The English-accented voices, hers and that of Lawrence Dillinger, her acting coach, filled the Mercedes. Chloe listened objectively. Would she be too British for the network? There seemed to be no foreigners on prime time TV right now except Ricardo Montalban, and he was a character actor. The darlings of the tube were all-American as apple pie and very *young.* Charlie's Angels were all in their twenties—and the Dallas Dollies were certainly a lot younger than the group who would assemble on Stage 5 today.

True, Suzanne Pleshette, Stefanie Powers and Angie Dickinson had all starred in prime time shows recently. They were close to, if not over, forty, but they were also 100 percent American. Chloe wondered for the umpteenth time if her British accent would hamper her chances.

She rolled down the window as she approached the guard at the studio gate. He wore a clear plastic cover over his policeman's hat, and barked at her in an unfriendly way, "Name?"

"Carriere," said Chloe. "I'm here to test for 'Saga.' "

"Oh, yes—report to makeup, Stage Five." He peered into Chloe's face, letting raindrops drip from his visor down her neck. "Don't I know you? Didn't you used to be Chloe Carriere, the singer?"

"I still am," said Chloe calmly, having endured this type of conversation with strangers for the past six or seven years.

"Well, I'll be damned," said the cop, smiling now. "I used to *love* your records, Miss Carriere—played them all the time when I was in high school." Chloe winced. *High school!* The man was at least forty-five judging from his weatherbeaten face; he was older than *her* high school!

"How do I get to Stage Five?" she asked, politely cutting him off before he had a chance to get effusive.

"Turn left at Ladies' Wardrobe . . . see that cross light? . . . then make a right at Stage Seven and then another right past the Administration Building and you'll run right into it. Good luck, Miss Carriere." He saluted her goodbye and Chloe, obeying the five m.p.h. speed limit, drove to Stage 5.

She parked in a visitors' parking space as a young girl with waist-length blond hair ran eagerly up to her. "Hi, I'm Debbie Drake, the trainee second assistant director on 'Saga.' If you'll just follow me, I'll show you to your dressing room, they're not quite ready for you in makeup yet."

In a seven-by-seven-foot shoe box called a dressing room Chloe regarded the lilac satin peignoir in a clear plastic bag hanging on one of the metal hooks hammered inexpertly into thin, cracked plywood. A pair of satin shoes dyed to match was placed carefully on the one piece of furniture, a brown couch. Next to the shoes lay two envelopes of Caress panty hose, one Beige Glow, the other Tawny Tan, and three pairs of rhinestone earrings of various sizes. They winked at her in the light from the flyspecked lightbulb hanging shadeless from the ceiling of this cell. There was a tiny dressing table with a cracked mirror in which she could see herself only if she hunched down two feet. There was a rickety chair, and covering the yellow-and-black linoleum a threadbare rug with "Property of MCPC Studio" stenciled on it in fading black.

What a dump, thought Chloe à la Bette Davis, hanging her raincoat on the one other hook behind the door. But you've seen worse, she said to herself. *Much* worse! The English provinces—nothing could ever be more disgusting than that rat hole infested with cockroaches she had dressed in while appearing at the Alhambra Theatre, Basingstoke, in 1968. Compared to that, this was a palace.

Too restless to just sit, Chloe stared out of the tiny window. She found she could almost see into the window of the large trailer with "Makeup" stenciled in lipstick red on the door. She wished she could see what was going on in there.

Makeup was a hive of activity. Although it was already seven-thirty, Sabrina's face was not yet finished. Ben was applying peach blusher on her lids and cheeks, while Barry, the third assistant, fretted in the doorway.

"How much longer, Ben?" he asked the bearded giant with the delicate fingers.

"As long as it takes, Barry."

"And how long is that—*pray?*" Barry fumed. Ned, the first A.D., would jump on him if the actors weren't ready on time. Today with all these divas and old-time stars coming in to test, it was an assistant director's nightmare. He realized that a one-and-a-half-hour makeup and hair call, which when discussed at the production meeting had seemed ample time to get each actress ready, was not nearly long enough. The youngest and most beautiful of all, Sabrina—every time he looked at her he swallowed hard, she was so gorgeous—spoke to him sweetly.

"I'm ready now, Barry." She flashed him the world's most breathtaking smile and Barry inwardly swooned. Having just recovered from a year-long crush on Jackie Smith, which had caused him many sleepless nights, he did not want his eager heart to plunge again. Barry continued to worship from afar.

Robert Johnson, the actor known as "A.N. Other" on the call sheet, had been hired today to play opposite all six of the leading ladies. He had been a minor TV star in the fifties in Steve McQueen's TV series "Wanted: Dead or Alive," and his conversation was peppered with references to "Steve and I," as in "When Steve and I went cycle racing in 'fifty-two . . . When Steve and I went sailing . . . When Steve and I pulled those broads in Acapulco. . . ." He leaned against the door, trying, unsuccessfully, to engage Sabrina in some sexual eye contact.

Sabrina wished that this good ole boy would stop undressing her with his hot eyes, but she was too polite to say so. She smiled pleasantly as he rambled on about his adventures with Steve.

In the next chair sat Rosalinde, her hair in soft pink rollers, a black-and-white-striped cover over her shoulders, while Nora, the other makeup person, deftly applied frosted eye shadow to her lids. Nora did not approve of frosted eye shadow. It looked common, and it caked into the crinkly crevices of the eyelids of anyone over twenty-five. Certainly it looked wonderful in the current Revlon ads, on their eighteen-year-old models' flawless baby skins, but on Rosalinde it looked hard and old.

Rosalinde held a hand mirror while she applied lashings of thick black mascara. She hummed gently to herself along with the samba music from the radio she had brought along. She had also brought boxes of chocolates for all the hair and makeup crew and a magnum of champagne for the director of photography, which she had given him with a kiss and a sly "Now, darling, you promise you'll give me the key light only directly *above* the camera, *yes?* And don't forget the eye light too, darling."

Lazlo Dominick, who had lit every top actress in Hollywood since Fay Wray, knew all the tricks in the book. He winked at her and agreed. He would have lit her that way anyhow, but the champagne was a nice thought, so perhaps he might give her a little more care than the others. He whistled inwardly when Sabrina Jones, dressed in a pale peach satin negligee, drifted onto the set. What a looker, he thought as did the rest of the crew, who all stood a little taller and watched their language. Sabrina's innocence, freshness and niceness brought out the best in men. The director, another old Hollywood hand, Marvin Laskey, discussed the scene with her and tried to put her at ease. Since she was already at ease, secure in her beauty, fully aware that since she was completely wrong for this part she would not get it, Sabrina gave him her dazzling smile and her full attention.

"They're ready for you in makeup now, Miss Carriere," said Debbie brightly. Chloe walked the ten yards from the tiny shoe box to the vast shoe box that housed the makeup department. The rain had stopped, and a rainbow shimmered in the lightening sky. A good omen, she thought as she stepped into the room. The first person she bumped into was Rosalinde.

"Chloe—*chica*—Chloe, how are you doing?" Rosalinde noted that

Chloe didn't look bad, considering her face was totally nude of makeup, and she had pulled her hair straight back. She looked severe, somewhat sexless. No wonder Josh had strayed, though: Rosalinde.

Chloe tried to be polite as she slid into the black leatherette chair and let Ben examine her face. She observed that even though everything was muddy from the rain, Rosalinde was wearing high-heeled black strappy sandals through which her toenail polish showed chipped and discolored. She recalled Sissy's sneering at "the Mexican trash basket," and smiled to herself.

"Hurry *up*, for Christ's sake. We're late enough already," Sissy yelled to her chauffeur. Harry merely shrugged. If they were late, it certainly wasn't his fault. He had been told to be at the Sharps' Bel Air mansion at eight, and he had been there on the dot. Madame had appeared at eight twenty-five, cursing like a truck driver, expecting him to get her to the studio in the pouring rain in five minutes. Well, he wasn't about to risk life and limb to do it—neither his nor the old cow's. He kept to the 35 mph speed limit and to his usual careful driving in spite of her furious shrieks to get a move on.

Having read and reread the call sheet the night before, she had hardly been able to sleep, so enraged was she that there were now no less than *six* actresses testing. SIX!! It was ridiculous. Although she had used every contact she had in this town to get this test, she was filled with bitter rage that she was actually lowering herself to do it.

"Do you realize how *demeaning* it is for me to test—especially with that Mexican slut in the running?" she had spat at Sam as he relaxed in his armchair attempting to watch a ball game on TV.

"Yes, dear, I do," said Sam, imperceptibly pressing the up volume on his remote. "But you wanted to test, Sissy. You used enough pressure on Abby to get this test. You can't back out now, dear. You will look foolish."

One thing Sissy Sharp did not relish was looking foolish. She glared at her husband, who was totally involved in the Lakers game, and flounced off to bed in quest of an early night; but sleep eluded her in spite of three Valium and eventually a Mogadon taken in desperation at three o'clock. She tossed and turned all night, her mind in a whirl about the test and her competition. At half past six she eventually nodded off.

Bonita, her maid, had brought a spartan breakfast on a white wicker bed tray into her bedroom promptly at seven. "*Buenos días, señora,*" Bonita whispered, drawing the drapes to reveal the sodden palm trees, which dripped relentlessly over the six-acre estate.

Sissy mumbled, turned over in bed and, ignoring the glass of hot water with lemon juice and the sliced pineapple, continued to sleep.

Only when Sam, leaving for his twice weekly squash game, woke her for the second time did Sissy jump out of bed, overturning the wicker tray onto the Porthault sheets and screaming blue murder at everyone in sight, including her Pekingese dogs.

Now, swathed in a new sable cape, with matching crepe de chine blouse, gabardine trousers and polished boots, an Hermès silk scarf covering her hair and immense Ray-Bans covering her bloodshot eyes, she perched on the edge of the backseat of her Rolls and yelled at the driver to hurry.

"Yes, your name?" said the cop at the gate. Sissy glared at him venomously through the smoked glass of the Rolls.

Peasant, didn't he go to the cinema? If she got this part, he would be fired immediately.

"Ms. Sissy Sharp, testing for 'Saga,'" said Harry deferentially, with a wink at the cop. Sissy gritted her teeth. Harry was in the firing line now.

"Oh, of course. Hi, Sissy." The cop smiled familiarly, waving them on.

Sissy gave her dressing quarters a sharp inspection. Knowing that most TV actors are given cubbyhole dressing rooms or tiny trailers, she had insisted on borrowing her husband's lavish motor home, supplied by the studio, for the test. It was fully furnished with a bed, a stove, a television set and a makeup mirror surrounded by flattering pink lights.

Sissy had been used to making films in the days when stars were given the delicate treatment they expected—treated like hothouse orchids, fawned over by everyone. The age of television had spawned a new bunch of overly young and eager, or over-the-hill but grateful, stars, who didn't care a hell of a lot if they had to dress in a garage, they were so thrilled to be working. Then, if their show became a prime time hit, they became excessively demanding. They would then insist on every sort of perk from a cellular telephone to a private sauna, and, in the case of some female stars, on days off for their menstrual periods, and breastfeeding privileges for the infants they often insisted on bringing to work with them.

Each season, network executives observed with a mixture of dread and greed the rise to stardom of obscure actors or actresses. Eager to work initially for a reasonable salary, they soon become complaining, dissatisfied autocrats who, believing their own publicity, wielded their newly gained power over the studio, the producers and the network. The networks liked to create stars, but not superstars. "The bigger the stars, the more the public loves 'em, the bigger the monsters they all become," Abby said ruefully. This happened a couple of times each season. The public's obsession with new fresh faces on the box guaranteed that new TV stars were born each year.

"We've *got* to keep them in their place, dammit," cried Gertrude. "I *insist* that we make everyone on 'Saga' equal—equal salaries for all."

"Impossible," Abby interjected. "We've got young kids and established stars. You can't give 'em all equal salaries—don't be a fool."

"Well, we must *try* to keep equality in other things then," said Gertrude implacably. "There will be no fancy-shmancy dressing rooms, Abby. No free gowns, no unlimited phone bills. No privileges other than the privilege of working for *us* on 'Saga.'"

"Try it, Gert." Abby smiled cynically. "Just try it, hon. It'll never work, you know it. We've already set a precedent with Sam Sharp. He's getting a goddamn limo, a massive motor home, Doug Hayward flying from London to make his fucking suits. It's a wonder we don't have a unit cocksucker in his contract to keep him happy on his lunch hour. God knows what else. Do you *really* think our other stars aren't going to want the same?"

"Sam Sharp is a highly respected motion picture star. He has *earned* his place in the sun," insisted Gert. "He has a 'favored nations' clause in his contract. No one can get a salary within fifteen thousand of his."

"Yeah, we're not paying him peanuts, thanks to you, Gert," said Abby, angrily lighting his third cigar of the day. "Fifty grand an episode for a new show for an over-the-hill actor is *steep*, baby, it's *steep*."

"Abby, the character of Steve Hamilton is highly important to the success of 'Saga.' You *know* that," Gertrude said stiffly. "If he is not the quintessential patriarch with inbred qualities of leadership and a dynamic force, *we have no show*. In Sam Sharp we have all of these qualities. They are built into his character throughout the years of playing all of those fine Yankee gentlemen. Plus of course his TVQ is tremendous. His last three films did at least a Nielsen forty share in prime time."

"Yeah, and bombed at the box office," said Abby flatly.

"He's a major star," insisted Gertrude.

"He's a has-been," sighed Abby.

"We *need* him," persisted Gertrude.

"O.K., O.K. Maybe you're right, Gert. Maybe he *is* a star, but he's also a fucking faggot. How are we going to keep *that* out of the garbage magazines?"

"Very easily," said Gertrude. "Since he has pulled the wool over the public's eyes for thirty years, there is no reason he cannot continue to do so. *Particularly* if we cast Sissy as Miranda."

"What? Sissy? That shriveled cooze? Oh, c'mon. She's *wrong*, the wrong woman for Miranda. I'm only testing her as a favor to Sam. She could never play Miranda. Miranda is sexy, feminine, voluptuous. Sissy's too—too—" He fumbled for the word.

"Hard?" asked Gertrude.

"Yeah. Hard, ball-breaking hard. She lacks—"

"Sex appeal?" murmured Gertrude.

"Yeah. Miranda's gotta have tons of the old SA."

"She's a brilliant actress, Abby," said Gertrude.

"Yup—in the right role, tremendous. I don't deny that, but I don't know many guys who would want to get it up for her."

"Well, let's think about her for Sirope, then?" said Gertrude.

"Sirope! For Christ's sake, the woman's supposed to be the fuckin' Virgin Mary. She's Ingrid Bergman before Rossellini, Doris Day with Little Red Riding Hood thrown in. We need a *saint* for Sirope. And there ain't many saints in this city, particularly forty-year-old ones."

"Let's try her," said Gertrude with a wheedling smile. "I think she'll be wonderful. A bitch playing a saint—it's inspired casting, Abby."

"Oh, God, Gert. She's all wrong."

"Abby, Abby—what can we lose? She's a fabulous actress, she still looks good—she's got that tired angelic look. A bit of a pain, I admit."

"A *bit?*" Abby threw in. "I know ten directors who would rather direct the shark in *Jaws* than work with her. But O.K. O.K.—O.K.—if you think it could affect the Sam Sharp situation she'll test. She's testing for both parts."

"Right?" said Gertrude, knowing she'd won. "It's the test that counts, isn't it, Abby?"

Sissy had decidedly mixed feelings about testing for both Miranda and Sirope. She couldn't decide whether the network was paying her a compliment or hedging their bets. She sat on the brown suede sofa in Sam's motor home, looking at the bottle of Dom Perignon in an ice bucket, the six-ounce can of Sevruga caviar and the Lalique dish containing grated egg, brown bread and finely shredded onion.

"Welcome to a star, Love, Abby and Gertrude" was written on the gilt-edged card. A Baccarat vase full of calla lilies and cream roses reposed on the mahogany coffee table with another note: "Rooting for you, my darling, Your Sam."

She grimaced. *Why* did he always send her calla lilies? They were only for funerals. God knows she had told him often enough she detested them, even told his florist, but still they arrived on every occasion where floral tributes were appropriate. Lilies and cream roses. How boring!

The orchid was much more attractive—a cymbidium in a plain stone pot. The card simply said, "Kill 'em." It was from Robin Felix, her new agent—a man who knew very well how to keep his clients, and his temper, unlike her ex-agent, Doug. Sissy as a client was a lucrative proposition, but sometimes without a doubt she was simply the most difficult of any female stars Robin had ever handled. However, he felt she had the inside track to the role of Sirope—which he knew she was right for, and he was going to be right there when the big TV bucks came rolling in.

"Ready for you, Miss Sharp." Debbie was deferential as she knocked at the door of the motor home. Sissy was the only actress testing today occupying one. The others were all in the egg boxes. "Can I get you something to eat or drink?"

"No, thank you, my dear," said Sissy grandly. "I never eat or drink before a performance. Just see that the prop man puts a bottle of Perrier water and a packet of Dunhill cigarettes next to my chair and make sure that chair is right next to the one of the lighting cameraman, Mr. Dominick."

"Right away, Miss Sharp," chirped Debbie, scampering away.

Sissy entered the makeup room by one door as Rosalinde exited the other. Ben was putting the finishing touch to Chloe's face. She looked radiantly exciting. This was a completely different face from the pale, washed-out visage of this morning. Witchy, bitchy, sexy, exotic, yet soft—Ben had done his work well, although Chloe had the basic beauty to let his craft express itself.

She looks common, thought Sissy, who believed any woman weighing over one hundred pounds, with a chest measurement of more than thirty-three inches, common. Common and overweight. The ladies nodded briefly and then ignored each other as De De, the body makeup girl, dabbed Beige Blush pancake onto Chloe's cleavage.

When Chloe finally walked onto the set at ten-thirty, her palms were sweating. Sabrina and Rosalinde had finished their tests and had left. The crew was taking a coffee-and-doughnut break. Robert Johnson came up and smilingly reintroduced himself.

"Last time we met was at a party at Steve's, when he was married to Ali. I was the guy that went on the cycle race over the Trancas dunes with him. You were cheering us on like crazy—remember?"

Chloe didn't, but she made all the right noises.

The director came in to discuss the scene.

Chloe half-listened. She had her own ideas about this character— definite ones. And she was going to play it her way.

Pandora King strolled into the makeup room to give Chloe a quick hug and an effusive "Hello, darling!" Pandora was sharp, a good trouper, with no side to her. Except for her enormous makeup case, which went with her everywhere, she was just like a rather acerbic woman next door.

"Darling, darling, we *must* have lunch and discuss this *insanity.* I'm testing for both roles—isn't it a riot?" She laughed, showing strong white teeth and too much gum. Even though she hadn't been made up yet, she wore a light layer of base, lip gloss, blusher, eye liner, and a tousled blond wig. She was not a beautiful woman, but she made the best of herself and would never be caught dead without her face on. "Ready, Miss Carriere?" Debbie popped her head around the door. "As soon as you're dressed, they'd like you back on the set."

Chloe stood in the center of the magnificent set, feeling more relaxed. Milton, the test's director, had staged the scene much the way she had envisioned it. Now it was time for her to perform to the ultimate. Robert stood behind the camera ready to give her lines off. "O.K., ready, darling?" asked Milton. "Yes, fine. I'm ready." Ben dusted her cheeks with a puff, Theo fluffed out her thick dark curls, Trixie fussed with the lace around her shoulders, Hank brought a tape measure to her nose and called out a number, Lazlo held a light box to her face and called instructions to a shadowy figure twenty feet up in the gantry. Big John and Reggie rearranged lights behind her head.

"O.K., Chuck, take it down a tad," called Lazlo to the figure in the gantry.

"Right," called Chuck. Now they had all left. Chloe was alone with the camera to record her emotions, her passions. Alone even though seventy-five men and women stood idly by observing her—judging her. Alone. It was time to show them.

"Aaaaand—*action*," yelled Milton.

" 'I never loved you, Steve,' " said Chloe to Robert calmly, feeling the fire of Miranda building inside her. She remembered the last time she had talked with Josh. *The last time.* She used the emotion that came welling out of her. " 'To me, you were someone to be used, because you always used me. Someone who could get me what I wanted—what I needed.' "

" 'I don't believe you, Miranda,' " said Robert quietly, with dignity.

" 'It's true, Steve. As God is my witness, it's true. How could I love you when I *knew* you killed Nicholas?' " Her eyes were filling with tears now. Real tears. She felt her throat aching, and she had to use her actor's control to stop the tears from carrying her away.

" 'That's a damn lie and you know it.' "

" 'Oh, no, Steve. I have the proof. You see, I was there that night, when you thought you were alone with Nicholas.' " Chloe took a step toward the camera and started to build her intensity. Her nerves felt raw. For two pages she gave the scene everything she could, every nuance, every emotion. Her experiences of life added to her fire. She berated Robert, scorned him, declared that her love for her dead lover, Nicholas, would never end, and that she would hate Steve until her dying day and would do anything to destroy him. Throughout the scene, she thought of Josh. It was Josh she was pouring out her heart to. Josh who had destroyed a part of her that was hollow now, empty—miserable. She thought of how she had loved him with so much passion, of how she could love him again if only . . . if only . . .

When she finished the scene, sweat was dripping down her robe and tears down her face. Milton yelled out in delight, and several crew members broke into spontaneous applause. "And *print!* That was fabulous, darling, absolutely *fabulous*. You're great! We don't need another one."

"Check the gate," yelled Hank.

"It's O.K.," the operator, Bill, said. "Thank you, darling, thank you," Milton enthused. "You were wonderful, you brought tears to my eyes." He bent his head and whispered, "I hope you get it."

Gratefully Chloe walked off the stage. Her coterie of helpers had deserted her and gone off to attend to the next testee. She got out of the lilac negligee herself, combed her hair free of the sticky hairspray and ripped off the false eyelashes. As she finished dressing, she saw through the mirror that Emerald and Co. had arrived.

Emerald never traveled light, never alone, and never on time—a reaction to her childhood as a baby star, when she had had to get up at five each day and live her day by the call sheet. When she was thirty and her contract finally expired after twenty-seven years of living by the clock, Emerald vowed she would never do it again.

She was forty-five minutes late, which for her was almost punctual. She looked great. Her blond hair was freshly bleached, framing her chiseled, newly tucked face, and her figure was as curvy as it had been in the fifties. Behind her marched a battalion of her troops: her personal assistant and man Friday, Rick Rock-Savage, her manager and agent, Eddie De Levigne, and her public relations man, Christopher McCarthy. Eddie was large and nasty, and Christopher was small and sweet. Together they balanced each other out. Christopher's main job was fending off the dozens of calls and inquiries that still came into his office each week for Emerald's availability to do interviews, talk shows, attend openings, appear at charities and attend premieres. Public interest in her had never waned, although she could not get a decent movie job in the States.

Emerald greeted everyone in makeup and hair like an old friend; she had worked with them all through the years, and they adored her.

"I *want* this job, Ben," she said seriously to the bearded giant. "Make me look better than any of them."

"I'll try, darling. I'll do my very best," said Ben, looking at her with professional objectivity.

"How was the English girl's test?" asked Emerald a mite too casually.

"Oh, er, good. She was very good." Ben didn't have the heart to tell her that Chloe had been great; it could affect her performance. "But I gotta tell you, darling, we had a gal in here this morning prettier than Lana in her heyday. We can't beat *her,* 'cause she's just a baby, but I guarantee we'll beat the others."

"I need this job, Ben." Emerald looked into her old friend's eyes. "Do your damnedest for me, you hear?"

She smiled the dazzling smile that had graced a thousand magazine covers and sank into the black leather chair.

❖ *Twelve* ❖

For the six women, the following days were not easy. Only Sabrina banished thoughts of the role from her mind. She had been offered a feature movie in which she would play a seventeenth-century virgin transported by time warp to a modern-day college campus. She was more interested in that. The part would pay her two hundred thousand dollars, and could make her a major movie star. Then she would be ready to play opposite Al Pacino or Richard Gere, she hoped. She was continuing with her acting classes, while her nights were filled with love and Luis.

"TV is for old actors," she confided to Sue, her agent. "Movies are where it's *at,* and that's where I wanna be!" Each of the six women had her own individual method of getting through the agonizing waiting period, since it was going to be at least three weeks before the network executives made their decision.

Pandora went to Las Vegas to visit her current boyfriend, a young Borscht Belt comedian, where she spent her time in bed with him or engrossed at the blackjack table.

Chloe stayed at the beach house. She took long walks along the coast, contemplating her future if she failed to get the part. The marriage with Josh was over. Lawyers had taken over the question of the divorce settlement. When necessary, she and Josh spoke by phone; the conversations were like those of casual acquaintances. He told her about his new record; he said he was working hard on the new scenario for his London play.

After dinner she went straight to bed, restlessly switching channels, comparing herself to Farrah, Jackie, Cheryl, Stefanie and Angie, which only made her more depressed.

One day Johnny Swanson called to invite her out. What the hell? she thought. He seems like a nice guy. Who cares if he's ten years younger than I am? The older woman-younger man couple is all the rage these days.

Johnny came to the beach house in a black Porsche 911 Turbo. Of course he *would* have a black Porsche, thought Chloe. It was the ultimate phallic symbol. As she climbed in and looked around the sleek car, she was amused by the way Johnny had fitted it out like a mini-office. Next to the driver's seat was the latest-model cellular phone with automatic dialing for twenty-five numbers. A microphone above the sun visor assured Johnny that he could always hear and be heard on the phone, even while going through tunnels. A highly complex stereo system with four speakers installed in strategic spots amplified Chloe's own mellow voice as she heard a recording of herself singing "From This Moment On."

She smiled, flattered in spite of herself. He certainly knew how to charm. He'd then put on her own favorite recording—an old album of Cole Porter and Gershwin classics. He was definitely very classy, very smooth, and as she looked at his profile, blond hair artfully curling over a black polo neck, very attractive.

In the back of the car was a small TV set, attached to the back of one of the seats, and a well-stocked bar plus a miniature fridge.

"Drink?" offered Johnny, turning left on the Pacific Coast Highway.

"No, thanks—it's illegal in the car," Chloe replied, remembering Josh's recent trouble. "The police are tough on you if you're caught."

"No sweat, sugar, my uncle's the chief of police down here." Johnny laughed. "Here, have one of these instead." He offered her an expertly rolled joint.

" No, thanks," said Chloe, feeling rather old-fashioned. In spite of her years around musicians and rock stars she still hated druggies.

She hadn't been out on a "date" in a long time—since before Josh— over ten years. She felt strange. Strange and archaic. Johnny didn't seem to be fazed that she didn't want a toke, and he chatted amiably until they arrived at a picturesque restaurant nestled in a tiny street behind Topanga Canyon. The owner knew him well, greeting him effusively, and Johnny seemed at home there, even knowing the names of most of the waiters.

Throughout dinner Chloe felt herself warming to him. Despite his brash exterior he was delightful. Witty, charming, lively, handsome—a veritable cornucopia of male goodies. His sense of humor reminded her of Josh—a youthful Josh. So he was young—so what? thought Chloe, feeling abandoned and young herself after they had drunk two bottles of champagne. Twenty-nine wasn't *that* young.

Arm in arm they walked into the cool California night. "Look—stars.

Maybe the world is coming to an end," Johnny said. "I haven't seen stars in California for years."

"Where's the smog? L.A.'s not L.A. without it." Chloe laughed. She felt ebullient, as if a weight had fallen from her shoulders. She liked Johnny more and more, even though she knew his reputation with women. Well, she was a mature adult now, not a naive young woman as she had been with Josh. She was not going to be hurt, whatever happened.

This they would play by *her* rules.

As the black Porsche pulled into her driveway, she invited him in for coffee.

"Never touch it," said Johnny, as he opened her door in his gallant English public-school manner. "I'll take a cognac though. Or an Armagnac if you have it."

They sat before the flickering fire, sipped Armagnac and talked. She had turned the lights off, and through the big picture window the sky was filled with a million stars. They started exchanging pieces of the jigsaw puzzle of their lives that might one day, if their relationship progressed, form a complete picture.

His lips eventually touched hers, and she found herself responding. His mouth was insistent, seductive, sweet. His hands touched her face, then fluttered to the buttons of her silk blouse. It had been a long time since Chloe had been caressed. It was all too sweet, all too tender.

She tried to draw back as a vision of Josh came to her.

This was wrong, wrong, wrong. Johnny was too young for her. It was too soon after Josh. She wasn't ready. He would tell the boys at Ma Maison. He would boast about her. *Josh,* her inner voice screamed silently. Josh, oh, Josh, I don't want this. I don't. I want you. She tried to put the brakes on, then realized how ridiculous it was. A forty-year-old woman acting like a girl. Necking like an adolescent. Smooching as though she were sixteen again. "No, I can't. I'm sorry. I just can't, Johnny." She pushed his tender, insistent mouth away, and his hands, which were expertly but gently pulling on her skirt now.

"Why *not?*" His voice was hoarse; he became more insistent. He kissed her again and again. He seemed to know where she wanted to be kissed and his lips were there, turning her into a furnace against her will.

She had no answer. She felt weak. She wanted him. She hadn't been with Josh for months now. This, their third separation, looked as though it would be their last. She certainly wasn't in love with Johnny, but he was attractive and she found him sexually appealing.

Why not? She felt surges of desire building within her. She wanted him to take her now. She felt the hunger of her sexual need.

Suddenly it didn't seem worthwhile to fight him any more. Go with it, she thought. To hell with tomorrow. To hell with Josh. To hell with what people think. With thoughts of Josh filling her head and her heart, she let Johnny Swanson take her to bed.

◦　　◦　　◦

During the difficult weeks of waiting, Emerald went on a social whirl. Ever popular, she accepted every party, every luncheon, every premiere. She emptied her diminishing bank account on dozens of new outfits. Her business manager despaired, but she smiled deliciously and continued to spend.

Sissy punished her body religiously. She lost three more pounds on a magic new diet of Chinese seaweed, rice cakes and kiwi fruit. She spent her mornings jogging, doing yoga and exercising, and her afternoons on the phone with Daphne and Robin Felix, her agent, discussing her chances.

Rosalinde Lamaze spent a great deal of time in her sunny little kitchen indulging in two of her favorite pastimes: cooking and watching soap operas on Channel 8, the Spanish station. At the moment she was preparing refried beans and rice, which smelled delicious. She couldn't wait to devour them with her young niece, Angelica, and later devour Angelica. The two of them sat in the breakfast nook eating beans and rice as, enthralled, they watched Lolita Lopez, great Mexican star of the fifties, emoting in *Mis Niños y Mis Hombres,* a favorite of the Spanish-speaking community of L.A.

Rosalinde was happy just pottering in her house. She was a simple woman at heart. Simple in everything but sex. She had become bored by the sexual embraces of her numerous lovers over the past few years. The weight of their thick bodies, their heavy breathing, their sweating hot flesh, their smells of alcohol and tobacco had started to repel her.

Recently, each time she had let a man make love to her, she had tried to feel *some* sort of excitement and had felt nothing. When she failed to respond, she impatiently sent them away, finding sensation with her fingers. That too, soon began to pale. When Angelica, her cute little eighteen-year-old niece, came to stay, she found to her delight that they had a lot more in common than a love for refried beans and Channel 8 soap operas.

These days nothing could compare to the enthralling nights she spent exploring and being explored by the delicate body of the young Angelica.

When Chloe's agent called and said that Dionne Warwick had suddenly been taken ill and couldn't perform at the Las Vegas Empire Hotel, Chloe jumped at the opportunity to fill in for her. She would be getting away from Johnny, who was pestering her now, wanting what she didn't have to give him. She realized that her attraction to him was diminishing more rapidly than she even dreamed was possible. What had been for her a minor fling to get her over Josh had meant more to him, and he was insistent on seeing her more than she wanted to see him.

"Singing again will get your mind off the waiting, duckie," said Jasper soothingly.

"You're right, Jasper, this waiting is too much even for my nerves of steel," Chloe said gratefully.

"Can you leave the day after tomorrow?" He sounded anxious. "Be ready for a nine o'clock show."

"What?" gasped Chloe. "Jasper, I know we're both British and can do anything, of course, but *darling*, I haven't rehearsed. I haven't even sung a note since the last tour ended."

"That was only two months ago, my dear," Jasper chimed in smoothly. "If you can take the company plane from Burbank on Thursday at one o'clock, you can be rehearsing in the Copa Room at three. You can sing your little heart out for four hours. Surely that's enough for a silver-throated talented nightingale like you, my love?"

"Bullshit, Jasper!" Chloe smiled in spite of herself. "Actually, though, it could be rather exciting; at least it will give me something to do to take my mind off that bloody *test*."

"Good girl, clever girl." Jasper's voice was soothing. "I have the hotel over a barrel moneywise, darling. Not quite what Dionne was getting, naturally, but forty-five grand a week, how does that grab you, my love?"

"It will keep the wolf from the door and help me at Valentino for a while." Chloe was mentally going through her wardrobe. "O.K., Jasper, I'll see you at the airport. I must pack now."

Chloe filled her suitcases swiftly and efficiently. Twenty years on the road had enabled her to pack what was necessary in minimum time. She surveyed her rack of beaded evening dresses critically as she skimmed through other racks, selecting and eliminating with an expert eye. She packed a red bugle-beaded Bob Mackie slit to the thigh, with a "Merry Widow," also beaded in red, and another in black lace, a silver lace and nude chiffon Nolan Miller, accented on the broad padded shoulders with exquisite appliquéd flowers, went in along with a sleek black silk jersey Chanel, the flute-shaped sleeves trimmed in black fox. A white lace Valentino dotted with pearls and rhinestones, his masterful cut accenting the simplicity and purity of the long, slightly fitted gown, completed her selection of stage gowns. Chloe surveyed them while waiting for her maid to bring her black wardrobe skips and tissue paper.

Next she surveyed her two racks of short, informal evening outfits, dresses and suits that she changed into after the show, when she would either go out to dine or cut a swath through the casinos of the Vegas strip. Three Saint Laurent suits and three Bruce Oldfields, two or three Coveris, one Donna Karan, and her favorite dress, a black lace point d'esprit, designed by herself and made by Freddy Langlan. Was that enough for two weeks? God forbid she should ever be seen offstage in the same outfit more than once. Suppose Sinatra was performing at Caesars? Barbra would certainly be there, too. Las Vegas was a small community. They would all be at the same parties every night. Be prepared. Better too much than too little.

She hastily picked out two more short dresses, a Karl Lagerfeld and an Anthony Price, and gave instructions to Manuela to pack the correct accessories, which were neatly stored in appropriate boxes under each dress. Chloe was exceedingly organized about her clothes. Each outfit she considered an investment, and she took great care of them.

She scooped up an armful of assorted sweaters, shirts and skirts, threw them on the bed and went to her jewelry drawers. An entire chest of small drawers contained her extensive collection of costume jewelry. Not for her the responsibility of real jewels. With the exception of her sapphire-and-diamond ring and a diamond Boucheron watch, she only wore faux jewels. Her collection was fabulous, extremely expensive, and much admired.

Manuela had finished packing the theatrical gowns and accessories in the black skips, and was now filling her burgundy ostrich suitcases.

Johnny had called this morning murmuring something about meeting Richard Hurrel at the gym, then lunch with "the boys" at Ma Maison.

As Chloe rolled her hair and rapidly applied makeup, she tried to ring him at the gym. He was not there. Ma Maison expected him at one-thirty. She left a short message with his secretary.

"Where you going?" Sally appeared at the door without knocking, as usual. She was sporting a new punk hairdo and her usual sarcastically belligerent attitude.

"What are you doing here?" Chloe asked as evenly as she could.

"I'm picking up some more of my things. Dad bought me an apartment in the Wilshire Towers. I'm decorating it myself." She fingered one of Chloe's Gallé vases carelessly.

"I'm doing it modern, of course. State of the art. High tech."

"How nice," said Chloe pleasantly, wishing the girl would stop touching her things and leave.

Sally's hair had been shaved two inches above her ears, and what was left had been dyed into jet-black and silver stripes and sprayed with a lacquer so strong that seven- and eight-inch spikes stood up all over her head. Her lipstick was purple, as was her eye paint. She wore an incredible outfit—a purple vinyl skirt, barely covering her pubis, silver thigh-high leggings over silver crocheted tights, and an immense lavender mohair sweater which almost covered the skirt. Around her neck was a five-inch statue of Christ on the Cross attached to a tarnished silver chain, and she appeared to have pinned what looked like black bats in her hair. From one ear hung a black rubber snake, the kind sold at toy stores for fifty cents, in the other was one of Chloe's most expensive Dior rhinestone earrings. She seemed high, although it was barely 11 A.M.

"Where are you off to then?" Sally opened and closed the drawers of Chloe's lingerie cabinet, picking up and discarding some of her step-mother's most intimate apparel as she spoke.

"Vegas." Chloe gritted her teeth in disgust, determined not to rise to the bait that Sally always threw to her.

"Got a gig then?"

"Yup, two weeks at the Empire, in Vegas." Chloe concentrated on combing out her hair, observing Sally opening her bathroom cabinet and casually inspecting the contents. She seethed, but she could hardly throw a teenager into the street.

"Oh, well, I suppose you better get on with your singing career," Sally said with a sneer. "It doesn't look like you're gonna get the part, does it?"

Chloe was calm as she finished her face, ever determined not to let this snotty kid get to her. "Why do you think that, Sally?"

"It's in the trades today, haven't you seen it yet?"

"No. Why don't you tell me what it said, dear? I have a plane to catch."

"It's in Army's column—he said that Rosalinde Lamaze is a shoo-in." She left the room and returned with the paper. "Here."

Chloe glanced at it briefly, her heart sinking.

"It's just conjecture," she said briskly, checking in her Hermès alligator bag for her lucky mascots.

"Sure." Sally grinned, revealing a small diamond inserted in her front tooth. "Well, good luck in Vegas then, Chloe. See ya."

Chloe noticed that she had appropriated a vial of Valium, a mauve chiffon scarf and four silver bracelets before she left.

"Limo's here, Miz Carriere." Manuela buzzed her. "He's comin' up now for the bags."

"Send him up," said Chloe. "I'm ready." And with a deep breath she walked swiftly down the stairs.

Rosalinde read the piece and smiled. Her new press agent had proved his point.

She had agreed to sign with his firm at three thousand dollars a month if they got her into Army Archerd's important trade column within the week. Well, they had done it. They were worth the three grand. She called her business manager and told him to send the check.

She glanced at the other side of her bed. It was empty. Angelica had gone to visit her sick mother in Mexico City for the weekend. Three days to work on a tan, thought Rosalinde, luxuriating in her crumpled flowered sheets. And who knows, maybe I *will* get the part. God knows she had said enough Hail Marys, confessed to sins she could barely remember, and lit an extra thirty candles to the Virgin Mary and baby Jesus last Sunday in church. If religion and superstition could guarantee it, she should get Miranda.

Calvin read the item in the gossip column again and again. Cold rage gripped him. What kind of people were these Hollywood morons? Didn't they know a true star when they saw one? How could they *possibly* pass over the most beautiful, talented actress in the world? How could they even *consider* that trumped-up Spanish tart, Rosalinde? It was an outrage. A slur and an insult to Emerald.

Calvin was out every night now with the amateur and professional paparazzi, who hung around outside Spago, Morton's and Chasen's like a pack of wolves, whenever they heard through the grapevine that a party, an opening or a premiere was going on.

He had seldom been disappointed in the past two weeks—Emerald was having one of her social bouts. Desperately insecure about the results of the test, she was hitting the high spots of Tinsel Town with a vengeance.

Emerald had gradually started falling off the wagon. She was furious with herself for her lack of willpower, but she simply couldn't help it. She needed to forget about that damn test. Forget how much she needed that part. Forget the fact that in spite of her mansion and the fabulous jewels, she was almost flat broke. Forget she was well along in her forties and not good marriage material after so many failures. She threw herself into social life with gusto, yet was completely unaware of the slight, sandy-haired, pale-eyed man who watched her every movement. Each restaurant, each party, each opening she attended, Calvin was there, looking through his lens at Emerald, holding his breath at her beauty, capturing her flesh, her blond loveliness forever with each click of his shutter.

His room now was a positive shrine to her. Every wall was covered with posters from her films. More than two hundred plastic frames contained her image, many of the pictures taken by him. Huge scrapbooks also filled with her pictures were piled in the bookshelves, along with seventeen of the books that had been written about Emerald's movie career and her even more exciting private life.

He even had one of the Emerald dolls that had been so popular with every little girl in America in the 1930s when she was a baby star and box-office champion. The doll was three feet high, with big round sausage-shaped flaxen curls and huge green saucer eyes fringed with thick auburn lashes. The little painted mouth formed a perfect Cupid's bow, and tiny porcelain hands had fingernails that were painted pale pink. The doll had come in a white carrying case, complete with three changes of costume, from a lime-and-white striped bathing suit with a tiny rubber cap and a miniature terry-cloth robe to a frilly green party frock. There was also a little green enamel mirror with comb and brush which could be used to comb the Emerald doll's curls.

Sometimes Calvin sat and did his doll's hair. He would talk to her as he manipulated the nylon curls with his rough hands. "You *are* Miranda, my lovely girl," he would croon to the painted face as he turned the curls around his fingers. "No one, but *no one,* can be her except you." Lovingly he would change her clothes, pausing often to examine and stroke the smooth, sexless body of the doll. He would put the tiny cotton socks on her perfect feet, then the little black patent-leather Mary Jane shoes.

He loved this doll. But he loved the real Emerald even more.

◆ *Thirteen* ▶

Rosalinde glanced again in the rearview mirror of her BMW. It seemed stupid to be paranoid about this car that appeared to follow her from La Scala to her home on the summit of Mulholland Drive. The car pulled ahead of her and vanished around a corner at high speed. Stupid, but all the same, the voice of reason warned her, as she drove up the long, winding canyon: "Watch out, *querida*."

John Lennon's sweet voice poured forth "Imagine" from her tape deck. She thought about his death—so recent, so sudden, so . . . It could happen to *me,* she thought—it could happen to any of us. To Robert Redford, with his notions about solar energy and conservation. Or to Jane Fonda, with her radical ideals and impossible exercises. To anyone some fanatic became phobic about. To *her,* for no reason at all except that she was a star. She shivered, despite the warmth of the car, as she drew up outside her Mulholland mansion.

Why did I buy a bloody mansion? she asked herself as she sat in the car staring at the ominous outlines of her home. And *why* wouldn't I even consider having a bodyguard? Everyone was getting one these days.

The house looked like something out of Edgar Allan Poe on this windy night: a gray stone facade, thick black clouds, winds of fifty mph. There was a Santa Ana blowing, and the palm trees swayed violently in the gale. Strange objects—birds? leaves? debris from some unknown holocaust?—scudded around the house. Her house. Wrested from the fangs of a crazed ex-husband and his ravening Beverly Hills lawyer. Court fights, acrimony, tabloid headlines. Thanks to some brilliant legal manipulations, eventually it became *her* house. Was it worth it, though, this big pile of pewter-colored brick, ersatz nineteenth century, with the latest twentieth-century plumbing?

She cut the engine. It was suddenly still. The wind had dropped with characteristic California suddenness. It was a silent night all right, but far from holy—a silent and venomous night. She felt suddenly fearful.

Calvin sat in the attic observing Rosalinde's hesitation from the tiny window.

He heard her close the car door—her footsteps had a deceptively casual sound—and insert her key into the front-door lock. He heard her call out halfheartedly, "Rosa, are you back?" proving she had given her housekeeper the night off. The door closed. She was inside. Inside the house with him. Just the two of them, he thought, locked in together. . . .

Soon the TV clicked on in her bedroom. He heard her flushing the toilet as he crept down the stairs and put his ear to the bedroom door.

"Hi, Angelica." She was talking on the phone. "I know this is crazy, but I'm spooked tonight." Calvin smiled to himself. "I miss you, *querida mía.* Come home to me soon."

Rosalinde was smiling as she hung up the receiver and popped a chocolate into her lush mouth. As Calvin pushed open the door of her sanctuary, she looked up, startled.

"What do you want?" Suddenly her voice was a dry rasp. The pupils of her beautiful brown eyes dilated to points of fear, and her hands brought the creased comforter up to her body as if she could protect herself with it.

Calvin could sense the animal terror in her as he stood at the door. He felt himself controlling the situation. Controlling her with his presence.

"Nothing," he replied slowly. "I don't want anything at all." He stood very still, taking in the surroundings. Everything was pink. She sat cross-legged, a crumpled pink comforter pulled up to her waist, a flimsy silken wrapper barely concealing her abundant body. Behind her dark nimbus of curls were piles of pillows embroidered with sayings: "A hard man is good to find"; "Happiness is having you for a friend"; "I come alive at five." Stuffed animals cluttered the bed, even an old Snoopy.

Calvin jumped as he felt a silken ghost brush his legs and saw a white Persian cat spring off its mistress's bed. The cat crouched under the dust ruffle, peering out. The two of them stared at Calvin with eyes of dread.

Rosalinde swallowed. She thought of what she had read in magazine articles about rapists. How to talk them out of it, be assertive. The stories she had read had said to be ballsy, tough, let him know she was stronger than he, that he could not get the better of her.

"Get the fuck out of this room, you creep!" she shouted in a voice that called upon all of her acting ability. "How *dare* you come in here? You're trespassing. I'm calling the police."

Frantically she tried to remember where she had put the panic button. Bel Air Patrol had been absolutely specific when they installed the latest fail-safe burglar alarm. First and foremost, they had instructed her, *always* turn on the alarm when leaving or entering the house. She realized she had ignored *that* advice tonight, as she had ignored the second warning: *Always* keep the panic button on your person while in the house. When activated, it would send a signal straight to police headquarters, and help would arrive within eight minutes. So they said. She knew it was more like fifteen or twenty minutes because she had pressed the panic button by mistake a couple of times. She *must* keep this maniac talking! Where, oh *where* was the damn panic button? she cried silently to herself.

One hand clasped her robe around her throat as the other crept beneath the rumpled sheets, magazines, pillows and scripts in search of the alarm.

She looked at her bedside table. The pink marble top was obscured by the paraphernalia of her bedtime pastimes. A half-empty wineglass, two coffee cups with congealed contents, an apple with one bite out of it, piles of letters, fan mail, photographs of herself, baby oil, ashtrays overflowing with butts, even, she noticed, a roach. What she would give for a puff now!

This wasn't, *couldn't* be happening to her! Suddenly, she caught sight of the panic button, half hidden under the pile of mail. Time to talk. Time to deal with this madman—for he looked mad, his face soaked with the perspiration that flowed down his forehead, his eyes dilated. He's even more frightened than I am, she told herself—but it didn't help.

Calvin licked his lips. He could taste the warm salt of his sweat. The bitch was talking. It was hard to understand what she was saying, the pounding in his head was so intense, like a hammer. Her lips were moving but he couldn't hear her. As she spoke, her robe parted more. He glimpsed her breasts, her navel, and that other thing. The thing that disgusted yet excited him. Her hand stroked a stuffed teddy bear. He wanted her hand to stroke *him*, but at the same time the thought repelled him. He loathed her femaleness. Hated her moist red mouth, her high, brown-tipped breasts. As she talked, her hand was moving to the bedside table. What was the bitch doing? She had something in her hand, now what was it. A radio? A tape recorder? She continued talking to him. Smiling, looking pleased with herself. Bitch Cow. Whore. She almost looked as if she were tempting him as she sat on her satin sheets, robe open, stroking her bear and trying to smile.

Suddenly he heard her words: "You know you're quite a good-looking guy. What's your name, honey?"

Honey! She was calling him "honey"! What kind of disgusting slut was she? When a man breaks into her room she calmly invites him to seduce her! She was a slut, a tramp. That the network was even *considering* her for the same part as Emerald was an abomination. *She* was an abomination, he told himself. He walked toward her slowly. The pounding started in his head again. He saw only her actions—her seductive smile, her calm voice. As he came close to her her smile faded. A whimper escaped her.

"Don't hurt my face, please," she said in a feeble, little-girl voice.

"Your face?" The fact that she cared so much about it made him want to smash into it. "What face?" He picked up a large bronze statue and brought it down with all his force on her upturned, pleading face.

"No, please, no!" Blood streamed from her forehead. "I'll do anything. You can take me, do what you want, but please, please don't kill me, don't, don't, I beg you."

"Whore!" he screamed as his hands encircled her white throat, slippery now with her blood. "Bitch!"

The cat jumped fearfully away, its back arched as it tried to get out of the room, but the door was closed.

When Calvin had finished with her he gazed at her voluptuous nude body splayed on the satin comforter. In spite of himself the urge to ravish her was so strong that he hated her even more for this feeling she aroused. She was stretched out in such a way, her blank celluloid stare and limp flesh curiously erotic, that he could not help himself. The white cat cowered in fright, low yowls emanating from its throat as it watched Calvin perform the ultimate horror. As Calvin finally drew away from the still body he heard police sirens in the street.

By the time the police reached the house he was gone. Only the white cat hiding under a sofa was witness to what had happened.

Chloe stared horrified at the headline: "ROSALINDE LAMAZE SLAIN— RAPED." She put down the paper, shaking her head in disbelief: Rosalinde dead, horribly murdered. It was unbelievable. What was even more horrible was the message scrawled obscenely in lipstick across the body: *"You won't be the last."*

Chloe shuddered, pushing away the poached eggs and grapefruit juice the hotel waiter had placed before her.

The TV set was tuned to the local Las Vegas news program. She switched channels with the remote to hear more. After every program there was another news flash with more reports about Rosalinde's death. Clues, inside information, close friends and family, fans with tear-stained faces talking to the TV cameras about their dead darling.

Chloe was genuinely upset. Although she had not known Rosalinde well, the woman had been a guest at her house only a few weeks ago. She wished she could call Josh to talk about it. He had always been her best friend. They had always been able to laugh, to cry, to discuss everything. . . . But Josh was now the past. She looked at the Cartier clock next to the rumpled burgundy sheets. Not rumpled by passion—just by yet another sleepless Las Vegas night.

It was 1 P.M. It would be 9 P.M. in London. Even if she did call Josh— which she shouldn't anyway, her lawyer had forbidden it—he would be out. He'd be down at one of his haunts, the wine bars in Chelsea or Soho, hanging out with the boys, his drinking and womanizing buddies. No doubt he'd contacted them all again, started up where he'd left off before he married Chloe. He'd be buying them champagne, getting drunk, telling jokes—and all the boys would be hanging on to his every word. After all, he was a star. But he loved the camaraderie of his own sex, the jokes about women, the drunken anecdotes.

Forget Josh, she sighed to herself as the phone rang. It was Johnny Swanson with the latest Hollywood gossip. He wanted to talk about Rosalinde's murder. "They found a book of matches, apparently from some bar in downtown L.A., someplace Rosalinde would never go. Must be the killer's."

"How do you know?"

"Uncle Van. He's a buddy of the L.A. Chief of Police. He says they'll find this nut case soon."

"I hope so." *You won't be the last.* It had an ominous ring to it. Chloe shivered.

"Anyway, sugar pie, I miss you, and I'm thinking of you," said Johnny affectionately, not mentioning the evening of fun and frolic he had indulged in the previous night with a sultry Brazilian actress in town overnight to plug her new movie. "I'll be up to see you next weekend, sugar, O.K.?"

"O.K., Johnny, I'll look forward to that." She sat on the rumpled bed and looked at her heart-shaped face in the mirrored canopy above it. Would it always remind her of Josh? *Damn* him!

She picked up the phone and gave the hotel operator a London number. Time to talk to Annabel. Darling Annabel, her baby, who always made her feel so good. . . .

Rosalinde's sister Maria held the wake at her Beverly Hills mansion. Maria had married a successful movie producer, Emanuel Siegal, taking immediately to Beverly Hills like a duck to water. The wake lasted five days. Chasen's catered continually at a cost of over ten thousand dollars. Chuck Pick supplied valet parking from noon to midnight, three hairdressers from the Beverly Hills Hotel were in constant attendance, servicing Maria, the young, grief-stricken Angelica and a host of Rosalinde's cousins and aunts who appeared from Mexico and downtown Los Angeles.

Practically every major producer, director, agent and star in town came to pay homage to the woman at whom they had often sneered when she was alive, although, to be fair, they had grudgingly admired her indisputable spirit and the box-office pulling power that had made millions of dollars for many of them.

Rosalinde would have been proud to know who attended her wake. Many of the same people who would barely have crossed the commissary to say hello to her in life cried crocodile tears and mouthed platitudes about her. Despite her on-screen success, Rosalinde had never been socially accepted. There had been something a little tacky about her. Certainly truck drivers, blue-collar workers and college kids had adored her, but in spite of her sister's efforts, she had never made a social impact. Not that she needed to. Her richly varied sex life and her career had been all-consuming. She had merely shrugged when Maria had tried to get her more socially committed.

As the turnout at Rosalinde's wake showed, Hollywood still loved to mourn its celebrated dead in style, as though to make up for the long-gone wonderful parties of the thirties, forties and fifties; with each decade, Hollywood's sparkle had dimmed. Nevertheless, a carnival atmosphere prevailed in the Siegals' antique-filled yellow living room featured only last month in *Architectural Digest*. Manny had never stopped moaning about the cost, but he wasn't moaning now, Maria said to herself, proudly watching Hollywood's famous at her groaning buffet.

Comedian Buddy Bridges, with a week off between Vegas dates, was a daily visitor, regaling everyone with a stream of patter so blue that he would not dare to do it on Carson, or even in Vegas. The word had spread that the Siegals' was *the* place to be—that week.

Even Sissy, crocodile tears, crocodile shoes and matching handbag, went to the wake. She made her entrance complete with tiny pillbox hat with point d'esprit veil on Friday evening, the day before the funeral. She had been informed by Daphne, who had hung out at the Siegals' daily, receiving the juiciest gossip she had obtained all year, that "tout Hollywood" was there. Indeed it was, and Sissy had herself a productive time culminating in a discussion with Menahem Golan of a possible three-picture deal with Cannon.

The funeral at Forest Lawn was a frantic mix of hysterical fans, munching junk food and snapping stars with their Instamatics, and eager paparazzi, heedless of the immaculate grass and flower beds, pushing and shoving for their respective tabloids. Sweaty cops, boiling in ninety-degree heat, tried to keep order. A small group of soberly clad mourners, Rosalinde's closest friends and family, attempted to retain dignity in the face of the pandemonium. Four burly TV camera crews pushed heedlessly through the gaping crowds, their cables tripping up those too busy gawking to look where they were going. A few blocks down the tree-lined boulevard, four TV trucks manned by efficient technicians recorded the scene for the jaded appetites of their nightly news viewers. The only thing that mattered to them was getting the best footage. To that end, people were pushed, lawns were mangled, tempers frayed. Celebrity funerals rated at least fifteen or twenty seconds on prime time news and garnered good ratings, particularly if there was an interview with a major name.

Chuck Waggoner, anchorman from CBS News, an old and experienced hand, had covered most of the major Hollywood funerals of the past twenty-two years. He looked serious and trustworthy, wearing a somber gray suit, as he stood to the side of the chattering crowd, while the cortege and coffin came slowly out of the church and up the hill to Rosalinde's green and sunny final resting place. It was her wish not to be cremated. She had been shocked when the loveliness of Marilyn Monroe was incinerated nearly twenty years ago. Although barely seventeen at the time, she had told Maria that when she died she wanted to be buried in a beautiful sunny place, Maria had remembered, and as the big oak-and-bronze nine-thousand-dollar coffin was lowered into the ground, and cool earth covered it, she wept for her little sister who had loved the sun so much.

Calvin, wearing a Universal City T-shirt and bermudas, and sucking on a frozen Kool-Aid, stood outside the church with the rest of the paparazzi and fans. He was filled with a strange joy, a feeling of euphoria. He smiled and chatted with the other photographers, who were a bit surprised at the gregariousness of this usually reticent little man.

He felt almost godlike. He had done it! He had paved the way for his idol to get the part. Surely the network would pick her now! Emerald. His goddess.

He pretended to photograph the other stars as they drew up in their mourning clothes, posing briefly for the photographers. Sabrina Jones came with Luis Mendoza. They looked stunning together, arm in arm, both dressed in charcoal gray. Her blond unteased unpinned unbleached hair blew in the warm Pacific breeze. Luis's curls fell darkly over his forehead, accenting his brooding Latin eyes. The photographers surged forward to snap them. Calvin stayed back. He was waiting for *her* to arrive. He knew she would. And she did.

Emerald looked exquisite clad in a silk jersey dress of such a dark green it was almost black, a demure inch below her knees; she wore black hose with seams and a large black straw hat on her platinum hair. She was escorted by Sol, hastily summoned from New York for escort duty. Sol was more than happy to oblige, as the torch he carried for her still burned brightly.

"You'll get that role, Emerald my love," whispered Calvin to himself. "Miranda *is* you! Only you can play her." If only she could know what he had done for her, he thought. But he wasn't finished yet. . . .

✧   ✧   ✧

Sissy watched the news coverage at six o'clock, grudgingly admiring Emerald's stunning yet sober outfit. She sneered at Luis, Latin-smooth as ever. What a prick, she thought, sipping Perrier and chewing a sliver of lemon peel.

She had just finished her massage. Her skin felt taut and tingly. She was always relaxed after Sven's hard Scandinavian fingers manipulated her bony frame.

A few years ago Sven's hard Scandinavian cock had manipulated her too. It had been an erotic experience, especially exciting since her door had been left slightly ajar and she knew that Sam was on his way back from the studio and might discover her at any moment, flat on her back on a portable massage table, covered with baby oil, legs in the air, a large blond Swede installed between them.

That had been the first and last time Sven had gifted her with the pièce de résistance of his famous Swedish massage. Not that he wasn't good at it, but Sissy preferred toy-boys, and Sven, at thirty-seven, was too old for her taste.

"The best stud in town, dear, is the silent Swede," Daphne had confided to Sissy at Ma Maison one day at lunch as they became nostalgically drunk on champagne supplied by Patrick Terrail while celebrating one of Daphne's many birthdays. "Ten years ago, dear, more or less, I never remember dates, we had a little thing, or rather a big one." She giggled as Patrick poured more champagne and threw in a strawberry for good measure.

"Darling heart, he was divine, truly divine, and what is more, he doesn't *talk*, no ceaseless chatter about business, politics or *golf!*" The dreariness of masculine conversation had never appealed to Daphne. Masculine company was important, men were important, too, for their proper functions, which for Daphne were money and sex, but she preferred the company of her own sex to share her most intimate thoughts, and the thing she adored perhaps even more than sex—gossip!

The fact that Daphne had now been able to parlay her considerable talent for the innuendo, the whispered secret, the rumored affair into a lucrative syndicated column had also given her some new influence in town, which she was beginning to relish.

Now, snuggled in a white terry-cloth robe from the Ritz, Sissy read Daphne's latest column. She owned a selection of terry-cloth robes taken from every major hotel in the world, a habit she had developed when the studio picked up the tab.

"Vivacious and free-loving Rosalinde Lamaze will be sorely missed by her scores of loyal friends and millions of fans. Our town honored the sexy raven-haired spitfire at the fabulous mansion in the heart of Beverly Hills of her sister, Maria, and brother-in-law, Emanuel Siegal. Emanuel told me confidentially that Dustin Hoffman will definitely play Toulouse-Lautrec in his remake of *Moulin Rouge*, which Manny will film in Paris next spring. His lovely and grieving wife, Maria, confided in spite of her sadness that they were looking forward to their vacation on the Côte d'Azur at the fabulous Voile D'Or Hotel, where they would be meeting their good friend Adnan Kashoggi on his gorgeous boat, *Nabila,* and attending Lynn Wyatt's annual birthday bash. And reed-thin, divine-as-ever Sissy Sharp, elegant in Bill Blass black, lamented the loss of the talent and beauty of Rosalinde. Sissy had just returned from a sneak preview of her new picture, *Lady Be Bad,* which opens nationwide next week, and is tipped to be a big one.

" 'Luis Mendoza will be a major star after this film is released,' confided the ever-generous Sissy.

"They sure don't make 'em like Sissy any more. A true star in the old Hollywood mold. Glamorous, talented and considerate. And one of the leading contenders for the most coveted and talked-about role of Miranda in 'Saga.' "

Sissy reread the article, pleased that Daphne had been so kind to her. That's what friends were for. She picked up her Sony cassette recorder and left a message for her secretary to send a basket of orchids to Daphne.

And then there were three, she mused. Three actresses who would be right for Miranda Hamilton.

Poor old Rosalinde, you will not be missed by me, she thought spitefully.

The amateur British bitch and that talentless, passé Hollywood celebrity ex-baby star, Emerald, were her only remaining competition. There surely could be no contest in the minds of the powers that be at the network that she, Sissy Sharp, acclaimed actress and Academy Award-winning star, was the only right choice to play Miranda.

◆ *Fourteen* ◆

THE DAY AFTER ROSALINDE's funeral Emerald woke up feeling sad. She had liked Rosalinde, who, although younger, had been a close friend in the early seventies.

Emerald remembered the smoldering summer when they both had found themselves staying at the Byblos in St. Tropez. Emerald was between husbands and recuperating from filming in Spain during which time she had not only fucked her two leading men but also the lighting cameraman—a good trick that guaranteed to get a girl great closeups. Rosalinde was on the prowl, taking her pick of the dozens of tanned, gorgeous young men who strolled the beaches, bistros and discos looking for distractions.

The two women had fun together. Emerald's sexual appetites were not as eclectic as Rosalinde's, but when Rosalinde, flushed from lovemaking with some Gallic stud, regaled her with the stories of her exploits, she would get hysterical with laughter as they ate croissants and drank café au lait on Emerald's tiny balcony overlooking the Mediterranean.

Emerald had been her idol since she was a schoolgirl in Mexico, and it thrilled her to have her idol right there.

Emerald enjoyed playing the sophisticated older woman, dispensing advice and wisdom with the breakfast croissants. "There's nothing wrong at all with having a passion for men. I've loved a few myself, but I married or lived with most of them. Your mistake, my darling, is you're just too open about it."

"I know." A frown creased Rosalinde's pretty face. "I hear what they have called me sometimes. The Mexican Open! What an insult! Did they call Errol Flynn or Warren Beatty such names? They loved women like I love men. Oohh! Look at him!" Rosalinde suddenly leaned over the crimson bougainvillea to observe a young man bouncing on the hotel diving board. He had rippling muscles, a deep tan and a more than respectable power bulge. "Mmm, *very* nice. What do you think, Emerald?"

"Sure is, why don't you go get him?" Emerald laughed. "And I will see you at the Tahiti for lunch." When they met at lunchtime, Rosalinde, as always, had caught her prey. She was twenty-six years old, gorgeous, and a movie star few red-blooded males could resist.

Emerald sighed, remembering those days. She was sad. When she was sad only two things could cheer her up—shopping or a visit to Bekins.

She phoned good old Sol, and he drove her to a large ugly building on Western Avenue. Emerald had told him about Bekins Storage but he had never been there with her.

The staff knew her well. "Good afternoon, Miss Barrymore," the man at the desk said respectfully. "Everything is ready for you."

In an ancient freight elevator they ascended to the third floor and walked down corridors lined with cardboard, metal and wood crates and containers of every possible size.

"Here we are," said the guard as they came to a large padlocked door. "Shall I leave you, Miss Barrymore?"

"Yes, please," said Emerald.

The man left, bowing deferentially.

Sol couldn't believe his eyes. The room was lined with dozens of cardboard dress cartons. The lids had been removed and the contents were revealed, glittering and sparkling in the harsh neon light.

Emerald's dresses. Her costumes. Every outfit she had ever worn onscreen and off was stored there, each carton neatly labeled. "Isn't it wonderful, darling?" Emerald's eyes lit up with an ecstasy that was almost evangelical. "Aren't they beautiful?" she whispered as she caressed silks, chiffons, satins, ginghams, every possible fabric ever created.

Sol nodded, amazed. Emerald had mentioned that she kept a "few things in storage," but the extent of her collection was incredible.

"Look, darling, look, my first movie," she breathed.

The box was labeled *"Little Miss Marzipan.* 1940. Columbia."

Emerald took out some of the tiny spangled dresses, almost in a trance. "I was six years old," she breathed. *"Six* years old." She sighed. "Look, here I am with Mr. Douglas and Miss Goddard. Look, wasn't I *adorable?"* She took out a few eight-by-ten stills from a cardboard folder taped to the inside of each carton and showed them to Sol. She had indeed been a little cutie—her hair a mass of golden curls, chubby dimpled cheeks, Cupid's-bow mouth. In the photo she wore the frilly white spangled dress she now held and stroked. Her mind drifted back over forty years as she gazed at the smiling faces of Melvyn Douglas and Paulette Goddard, who had played her aunt and uncle.

"They wanted me to be a musical star in that, and I *was,"* she said softly. "I sang and danced, and no one could ever *believe* I was only six years old. They thought I was a twenty-five-year-old midget, can you *believe* it, Sol?" Her laughter rang out, and, looking at her, Sol could almost see the tiny sweet little girl she had been.

"Miss Goddard was *so* wonderful to me," whispered Emerald. "She showed me how to put on eye shadow and rouge. She used to let me use her perfume. It was so strong, so sexy. 'Je Reviens' it was called. She had it sent from Paris, bottles of it. She even gave me my own little bottle."

"Do you still have it?" asked Sol, his brash New York manner slightly subdued by this new strange Emerald.

"Of *course* I do." She flashed her jade eyes. "Look, come with me." She took him into the next room, which was filled with smaller cartons similarly labeled. She opened the first one. It contained dolls, teddy bears, tiny tap shoes.

"Look!" Triumphantly she retrieved a tiny navy blue bottle, empty now. She held it to her nose and sniffed deeply.

"I can still smell it. 'Je Reviens.' I wore it for ten years after that. Paulette, I mean Miss Goddard, was *so* kind to me. I loved her, really."

She went back into the first room to a carton labeled, *"Daisy Did It,* Fox. 1951." Out came crinoline gowns like those then worn by teenage prom queens. "Janet Leigh and I were the stars of that." She carefully opened the manila envelope. "Look at this *coverage!* We made the cover of every single fan magazine at least three times in 1951. Look Sol, *look!* Every teenage girl in America wanted to look like us."

Sol looked at the two blond smiling girls wearing sneakers and shorts, windblown at the beach, and another shot of them in matching strapless formals standing beside a young Robert Stack.

"See, I even made the cover of *Life."* She showed him a black-and-white cover of a laughing young Emerald kneeling in a white two-piece bathing suit on the beach, head thrown back, yellow hair blowing, not a care in the world.

"There's another one—*Look* magazine—now *that* was *hard* to get on. Milton Greene took this picture." A serious, pouty young Emerald gazed thoughtfully from the cover of *Look,* wearing a chaste high-necked blouse and a thick leather belt that gave the illusion of an eighteen-inch waist.

"Jesus, why do you keep all this stuff, Emerald?" Sol was confused. A man of simple tastes, he was of the disposable generation—if you don't use it, throw it away. He thought it strange that Emerald kept all this. "It's junk, honey."

"Junk? Junk! You stupid son of a bitch! This is Hollywood history! No one has this, *no one.* Mary Pickford, Gloria Swanson, Greta Garbo, Joan Crawford, Liz Taylor, Lana Turner, *none* of them kept their things, none of them cared enough about this wonderful business of ours to keep their clothes, their accessories, for posterity. Do you realize what this will all *mean* to film historians in a hundred years, Sol?"

Sol nodded, humoring her. He couldn't understand the fascination of a bunch of out-of-date gowns and old movie magazines and stills. Who'd want 'em?

"1962. Look, Sol. I made *Les Amies de Montmartre* in Paris. It was my first French film. With Alain Delon. He was unknown then, of course. I was the star. I was the biggest star in France then. Wasn't I gorgeous?"

"You still are, hon," said Sol, gazing in fascination at a 1960s copy of *Paris Match* where Emerald, teased platinum hair, high white boots, a black micro-miniskirt and fishnet stockings, was leaning on the balustrade of the Pont-Neuf over the Seine next to a glowing-faced dark-haired beautiful young man whom Sol recognized as the young Alain Delon.

"I played an English rock star." Emerald laughed. "Just look at the stuff we wore then. I bought it all on Carnaby Street and Kings Road. Oh, it was such *fun* in those days, Sol. The Parisians hadn't seen anything like my clothes. I wore the shortest miniskirts in Paris—in the whole of France, in fact. Look!" She brought out a hanger on which hung six or eight small skirts made of leather, felt and denim. Each one of them was no longer than thirteen inches and contained only about half a yard of fabric.

"Jesus, you wore those?" Sol swallowed. "They must have seen your cooze every time you crossed your legs."

"Sol, really. I had matching *panties,* look!" Under each skirt hung a pair of pants the same color as the skirt. "With Courrèges flat high-white boots, I looked like a teenager, even though I was nearly thirty. See." She shoved another bunch of eight-by-ten glossies into his hand. "London and Paris in the swinging sixties. *God,* did we have fun."

There was Emerald with Brigitte Bardot on the quay in St. Tropez, both of them in gingham shorts so short that the cheeks of their round brown derrières were almost revealed; there was Emerald sitting with Belmondo in Paris, wistfully sipping coffee at a Left Bank café. Emerald had long blond bangs and she wore a French beret. There was Emerald in London with Mick and Bianca, with John Lennon at a Bob Dylan concert, both of them in identical flat black leather caps and granny glasses, and with Michael Caine, Terence Stamp, and England's most famous model, Jean Shrimpton, dining at Club del Aretusa. They all looked young and eager and joyful. "The sixties." Emerald sighed fondly. "The best of times—and the worst of times for me." She picked up another batch of photographs.

"Here's me and my Lord." She laughed, showing him a formally posed black-and-white wedding picture. "Lord Lichfield took the pictures. Princess Margaret came, so did the Duchess of Argyll and the Duke of Westminster. All the English aristocrats came. The crème de la crème of England. It was at St. Mary's church in Mayfair. I was Lady Haverstock for, oh, at *least* two or three years."

Sol laughed. Emerald always joked about her many marriages, filled with delight and expectation as each nuptial day approached. She always started out as a devoted, dutiful wife, until her expectations were unfulfilled and the husband turned out to be a human being after all. None of Emerald's six marriages, other than to O'Herlihy, had lasted longer than three years, but, ever the optimist, she continued to walk blushingly down the aisle.

"Didn't you marry *twice* in the seventies?" queried Sol.

"Yes, the English lord and my Italian count—'the cunt,' my friends all called him." Emerald smiled and went to a carton marked 1971, which was filled with lacy, flowery garments—floating sleeves, embroidery, and ethnic trimmings. "In 1971, I became La Contessa Calimari for seven and one half magic months—which I spent mostly lying in the sun in Franco's marble villa in Ibiza, while he cruised for young boys. And when I say young, darling, I mean *young*. He married me as a cover-up. Let's face it, an American movie sex goddess is about the best cover-up you could have for a practicing Italian homosexual. We were annulled. The Pope did it, of course."

"Of course," Sol said. "Who else?"

"Sol?"

"Yeah, hon."

"I don't know why I'm doing this. I never brought anyone here before. Maybe you think it's strange, but—" her voice started to break, but she controlled it—"it's all I *have*, really."

"You got *me*, hon. If you want me, of course," said Sol, who would have remarried her in a flash if she'd have him.

"No, Sol. You're sweet, but this place, these boxes of possessions, *they* are my real life, Sol. They are more real than any of the men, any of my marriages. This is the *real* Emerald Barrymore. This warehouse is where she lives."

She sat down on one of the cartons, sobbing violently. Sol felt helpless. She had never opened up like this to him before. Emerald Barrymore, Movie Queen Supreme for over forty years, had a heart just like any other broad. He didn't know what to do.

Up to now, theirs had been a friendly marriage and divorce based on physical attraction and convenient availability. Emerald often needed an escort. She liked going out, was bored being "walked" by gay men friends. For Sol, it was a dream come true when he finally met the gorgeous girl whose picture he had pasted on the wall of his locker while he fought the Koreans. But that dream had lasted considerably less time than her others. She had worn his Van Cleef and Arpels emerald-and-diamond wedding ring for only three months. But thank God, they were still friends. Now he could be the strong shoulder she needed to cry on.

And cry she did. "If only I could have had children," she sobbed, as mascara ran down her cheeks in blue rivulets "Sol, I wanted to have kids more than anything in the world, when I was thirty."

"What happened?" he said, stroking her fine platinum hair, the roots showing grayish brown.

"Between the abortions the studio insisted I have and the damn fucking *pill*—too many years on that goddamn pill, Sol, that's what happened. I stopped when I married his lordship. I really wanted to give him an heir, someone to play with Princess Margaret's son when they grew up."

She dabbed her wet lashes with a tiny hanky trimmed in lace. Sol didn't know anyone else who carried a hanky, let alone a lace one.

"So, go on, hon."

"I got pregnant by his lordship three times in two years. I lay flat on my back, hoping, but each time I lost it. Finally his mother gave him an ultimatum. Emerald can't have children, get rid of her. You must have an heir to the title. Well, anyway by that time, I was bored to tears with that horsy 'Hooray Henry' British crowd, but I was sad. I was so sad, Sol." She blew her nose on the tiny hanky violently.

"So then?" asked Sol. He couldn't believe what she was telling him. She never had confided in him during their marriage.

"Oh, so then, I bought the dogs!" She laughed hollowly. "I had the dogs, and I got fucked a lot, and I fell in love a lot, and I got engaged a lot, and I kept getting pregnant, and I kept losing them until my gynecologist took me into his office the day before my fortieth birthday, by which time I'd been pregnant *eleven* times in ten years, and told me I could *never* have a child, and to stop fooling myself. Forty was too old anyway."

"Nonsense," Sol said kindly.

"For motherhood," Emerald said bitterly. "I was an aged primipara every time I got pregnant. Cute, isn't it? An aged primipara! Ugh! So I got rid of all the equipment."

"What equipment?" Sol was bemused.

"The *female* equipment, darling. The tubes. All the stuff that makes you moody and unpredictable twelve or thirteen times a year, and which arrives unexpectedly as you've put on a new white skirt and you're sitting at a formal dinner with the Ambassador of God-knows-where and the host is gay, so you know you can't find a tampon in *his* bathroom, just Vaseline and amyl nitrate."

She smiled sadly. "So that's when my career packed up. My gyno must have told *tout* Hollywood I was no longer a *real woman*." Anger crept into her voice. "No more offers for poor little Emerald. And I still had my 'fabulous' life style to support. That's when I did the pornos."

"They weren't *pornos*, for Christ's sake, Emerald. They were fuckin' *art* films, and you know it."

"To you they were art films. To me they were pornos."

"So you showed your tits," he argued.

"And my ass, too."

"You got a great ass, kid," he said, affectionately squeezing it, wondering if she might consent to a quickie among the crinolines.

"They *were* great photos though, weren't they, Sol?"

"Yeah, oh, yeah, babe." He remembered, as had thousands of men, her revolutionary pose for the exceedingly serious yet erotic Italian film *L'innamorata.*

"There's the picture, Sol. It's five years ago now. Do you think I look any different?"

She was holding up an eleven-by-fourteen color photo from *L'innamorata.* She wore a Gestapo officer's hat set at a rakish angle on cropped blond curls, and a black Nazi uniform, the jacket of which was open to reveal a medium-sized but perfect bosom.

It was a sensational photo, more so because Emerald had been forty-three years old at the time. It had got her the cover of *People, Newsweek* and a spurt of new movie activity, mostly in Spain, Germany and France.

"Now you know why I must play that part in 'Saga,' Sol. I *swore* I'd never do TV, swore it on Momma's grave, but time is running out, and my only assets are my face, my body and my fame."

"You're still beautiful, hon, beautiful," Sol soothed.

"I have exactly two hundred and fifty thousand bucks in the bank, which, with *skimping*, will last me a year, if I'm clever. I have the house in the hills . . ."

"That's worth a couple of mil," Sol said, "easy."

"Maybe *one,* tops. I have furs galore, loads of fabulous jewels; if I sell those then maybe I can get by for another year, and then what? *Then what,* Sol? What does Emerald Barrymore do for an encore?"

"Marry me again, sweetheart. Marry me."

"No, I can't. I'm sorry but I don't love you, honey. You're adorable, funny, sweet, but I *must* feel passion. I've always had to feel passion, and I can't pretend. You know it, and I can't fake it."

Amidst the paraphernalia of Emerald's forty-year career, they gazed at each other sadly. "Now you know why I *have* to have that part, Sol," she said, gripping his hand. "I've been an actress for forty years. I don't know how to do anything else. I *want* this role, I want acceptance in this town by my peers. I want the money, the fame, the magazine covers again, Sol. If I don't get them, I'm on the scrap heap forever. I'm too tired. I'm too old . . ."

"No, hon, you're not."

She stopped him. "If there's one thing I know, it's Hollywood. Yes, I'm still a star to the public, but everyone in the business, every goddamn producer and agent in this whole stinking, rotten town thinks I'm a washed-up has-been, Sol, and, damn it, it's not going to stay that way. I'm going to play Miranda if it kills me. I'm going to do everything I can, and I'll be a *real bloody* star again! I can't and I won't settle for anything else."

He nodded sadly. It was only too true. "Let's get the hell out of this place, kid," he said.

◆*Fifteen*▶

Nothing had changed in Las Vegas, Chloe realized, as she surveyed her companions in the casino elevator. Fat thighs in tight shorts, shriveled old ladies whose hair had been permed so often it looked like gray-blue cotton wool, hookers and businessmen. Chloe never failed to wonder at the beefiness of the Vegas visitors. Maybe they had too many milk shakes and doughnuts, too many snacks. Certainly the fattest were the ones who drank diet soda with their food. A woman sucking an ice-cream cone dripped it onto Chloe's suede shoes, and she grimaced.

Her suite at the Las Vegas Empire was as lavish as ever, even though the "damask-and-silk" hangings on the wall and windows were 100 percent polyester and felt like glazed cardboard to the touch, and the "velvet" sofa was hard as a rock. The black acrylic bathtub with ersatz gold faucets was wide enough for two; it had a thin black plastic pillow at one end, in case two wished to sample the delights of the Jacuzzi. She sat on the eight-foot-wide burgundy crushed velvet-covered bed and looked up at her lonely reflection in the beveled mirrored ceiling. She remembered the last time she and Josh had played the Empire, how they had shared this suite, the shiny black tub, the same bed, watched themselves in that same mirror. . . .

Josh always loved looking at their two bodies entwined together on wine-colored sheets, her ivory legs encircling his bronzed ones. He was never more aroused than when they were together in Las Vegas, and he took her sometimes three or four times a day, his ardor fired by the sight of their bodies in the mirror. She sighed as she removed her De Fabrizio suede pumps. Stop thinking about Josh, she admonished herself. Stop thinking about what was. Get yourself together, girl—you've got a show to do.

In a cramped motel room in downtown Las Vegas, Calvin unpacked his canvas holdall and regarded the contents. There it was. The knife. Its flat bluish metal reflected his flat bluish eyes, which gazed blankly out the window at the high blue Nevada sky. They didn't see the bare sandy vista shading into the distance, interspersed with a few sickly palm trees and shaggy bushes. All they noticed was the sign that dominated their view. A huge billboard announced:

CHLOE CARRIERE

July 16–27
$25 early show $20 late show
For show reservations call 732-8800

THE LAS VEGAS EMPIRE
AMERICA'S #1 ENTERTAINMENT SPOT

Slowly Calvin picked up the phone and dialed 732-8800. Under the name John Ryan he booked a booth for the following night. It was time to get her.

Later that evening, as she sat in the dressing room, her hairdresser fixing white sequinned flowers in her dark hair while she painted her face with trembling hands, thoughts of Josh tormented her. She could hear the crowd out front, laughing at the opening act—Shecky Greene.

She remembered four years ago, in this same dressing room, begging Josh to stop taking the drugs that were destroying his career and their marriage. The bouquet of medication he needed for support had become a nightmare. He usually awoke at four or five in the afternoon and got a vitamin shot for his voice from the local Vegas quack. Then he took three uppers, a large snort of coke and a Coca-Cola. He'd stop at the crap table for a couple of hours if Chloe was having a massage or a manicure. If she was around, he'd want to have sex. In spite of his drugging, he was still incredibly virile. He was her husband, and she adored him in spite of everything. An hour before their show he would get another shot for his voice, swallow a decongestant with codeine, two uppers, and take another massive snort of coke. Just before he went onstage he took a Dilaudid, a legal drug twice as powerful as heroin. His beautifully tanned and muscular body in a white silk shirt open to the waist and black pants showed off his tremendous sex appeal. He still had "it" for the female Las Vegas patrons. Old and young, they found him wildly attractive. After the show, in which he sang for the first forty minutes, she for the second forty, they then harmonized and vocalized together for fifteen more minutes. They gazed into each other's eyes, singing ballads, love songs and point numbers with sophistication and sexy undertones that drove the audience wild. Afterward, his trusty doctor took his blood pressure, and if it was over 140 gave him a pill to come down, after which he'd take another snort of coke. Fortified by the applause, by the onstage empathy and rapport with each other, they then received visiting friends, acquaintances and business associates in their dressing room with the mirrored bar and wood-burning fireplace.

Later they would go to dinner with friends in the Rib Room; then he would hit the tables until dawn. Before he went to sleep, Josh took two Quaaludes, a blood-pressure pill and a Demerol.

It was too much. Much too much. She had lectured him long and often, but he maintained he was not addicted, he could handle it, he needed it to work. "Cut the crap, Chlo," he'd say. "It's not hurting me."

The extraordinary thing was, it didn't seem to—then. But gradually his habits began to erode his performances, then his life.

The owners of the Vegas casinos soon got the message. He was becoming irresponsible, unreliable. Slowly the Vegas gigs, the years of the big money—seventy-five, one hundred grand a week—started to drift away, and then they had to start doing the tours. Oh, those tours! Numbing.

Soul-destroying. Milwaukee, New Haven, Idaho, Atlanta, Connecticut, Kansas. Weeks, months of one-night stands.

It was a killer. It had killed his career and their marriage. Now she only had herself to take care of. She looked at her face, finished now. The matte complexion, the fuchsia-gloss lips, the smoky eyes. Her black lace over nude chiffon Bob Mackie original clung to every contour of her thoroughly toned body. She looked in fighting form.

The band was playing her intro now. She heard applause for the well-known songs—*her* songs.

It was time to perform.

Although Chloe hadn't played Vegas for four years, her opening was a huge success—she still had many fans. To her surprise and delight, Sammy and Altovise Davis, Milton and Ruth Berle, and Steve Lawrence and Eydie Gormé had shown up the first night to wish her well. Pandora had been there too. Her romance with the young comedian was on the wane. He spent more time at the tables than he did with Pandora. She was philosophical.

"Honey, romance is like a bag of groceries, the more you put in, the heavier it gets."

Chloe laughed as the two of them lay by the pool at the Empire the next morning, watching the constant action.

"Another ship will cross my horizon, honey," Pandora drawled, rubbing Bain de Soleil on her slender legs. "Men are like buses; if you wait long enough, another one will come along."

"The way you look, darling, it won't be long either," said Chloe, admiring her friend's slim body in her white maillot.

"Phone for you, Miss Carriere," trilled a tiny page as he plugged a phone into an invisible outlet and handed it to Chloe.

"Hello, darling, it's Jasper," he said in his impeccable English accent. Chloe smiled.

"Hi, Jasper, what's happening?"

"I think you're the number one front-runner for Miranda, my pet. I spoke to Abby and Gertrude this morning. They *and* the network feel that you gave the best test. They feel certain that they want you for Miranda."

"But they're not completely sure yet, right, Jasper?"

"Right, petal. You know how it is. So stay calm, dear, do the show, and I'm sure by the end of the week we'll have a firm answer."

"Good." There didn't seem much else to say.

"Oh, and Robert Osborne has you as his lead item in the *Reporter* today, said that you were the main contender for Miranda. Just thought I'd let you know."

"Thanks, Jasper, keep in touch, love." Chloe hung up feeling elated.

Pandora was deep in conversation with the straight half of the magic act that was currently breaking all records at the hotel. "You know The Great Geraldo, don't you?" she breathed, her eyes alight with new found interest.

The Great Geraldo inclined his head with European gallantry, revealing dyed black roots and an inch of flab hanging over green Ralph Lauren trunks.

"*Enchanté, madame.*"

"Excuse me a second, I'm going to buy the trades." The Great Geraldo bowed in gallant Continental fashion, as Chloe, avoiding oiled mahogany bodies, walked into the cool darkness of the lobby.

She was indeed the lead gossip item in the *Hollywood Reporter:* "Abby Arafat and BCC network seem to agree that the perfect choice for Miranda Hamilton on Abby's new series, 'Saga,' is Chloe Carriere, now headlining *sans* Joshua Brown at the Las Vegas Empire until July 27th. Catch her if you can, folks: this gal is hot!"

Chloe was pleased. This was no public relations plant. She didn't have a press agent. Maybe the item was true.

> "*It had to be you*
> *It had to be you*
> *I wandered around*
> *and finally found*
> *somebody who—*"

Chloe was in good voice, relaxed and confident. The nerves of the first few nights had evaporated, and she was surprised at how much she was enjoying this gig.

She looked radiant in a silver lace Nolan Miller gown. The spotlight sparkled on the tiny rhinestones scattered on it, and her face seemed to reflect the glow. The house was packed. The audience liked her, and appreciative applause greeted the end of each number.

In a back booth, huddled alone with an unaccustomed whiskey to bolster his courage, Calvin watched her every move.

Bitch. Where did she get that confidence? How *dare* she flaunt herself in that gown, that silken dress so sheer that the audience could see the outline of her breasts and twat. She was an English whore; she would pay dearly for it. He swallowed the whiskey, feeling the unfamiliar taste burn his throat. He stared at her malevolently as she came down into the audience singing her signature tune, "Everyone's Gotta Love Someone," weaving gracefully through tables full of polyester-clad tourists who reached out to touch her radiance. She took their hands, looking warmly into their faces, sharing her joy with them.

"Cunt." His lips tightened as his hand tightened on the knife in his pocket. His fingers itched to slash the bitch's face. He groaned. He was getting hard. Why did this happen *now?* When he hated this woman so much, why did his body betray him?

He tried to distract himself by observing the faces of the audience, eyes glued to her glittering feline figure as she threaded her way through the packed tables in the moving spotlight.

"Get a load of the guy in the booth," Jake Walker whispered to his partner, Hank Gillis.

A plainclothes security man, with fifteen years in the casino business and ten years as a state cop behind him, Jake prided himself on his instincts. But Hank wasn't listening to him. Jake nudged his partner again.

"Ssh!" Hank hissed. He was mesmerized by Chloe, gazing at her as she slowly advanced through the audience. Maybe she'd reach out and touch him. Oh, boy! "Shut up, Jake, I'm in love," he said.

Chloe was getting closer now. She paused at a table of excitable Japanese tourists. *"Everyone's gotta love,"* she breathed, clasping the hands of a young Japanese girl, who blushed with excitement.

Calvin's breath caught in his throat. He'd planned it brilliantly. This booth was next to the exit. One quick move, and even before the blood could come spurting out of her throat, before anyone realized what had happened, he would be in the casino mingling with the crowd. It was almost midnight on a Saturday, and the room was packed. He could disappear easily into the crowd. He was disguised in a red wig and horn-rimmed glasses, which he intended to dispose of later.

She was edging nearer. Would she come to him? Yes, of course she would. Last night he had observed both her shows. She always performed to the last row. The time was nearly ripe. The knife was burning on his lap. His hands were soaking wet as he wiped them on the red linen napkin. Red, the color of the blood that would soon be splashed all over that silver dress. He hadn't had an erection like this for a long time. He groaned. He needed relief.

Chloe was so close now, he could almost smell the scent she wore. It was pungent, musky—in spite of himself he liked it.

All eyes were on her except for the pair that was fixed on Calvin.

As Jake watched him with instinct honed by years of experience, he knew something was very wrong with this man. *"You gotta love, love, love . . ."* Chloe sang, thrilled by the love and happiness the audience brought to her and she gave back to them.

"Love, love, love," the audience sang back happily. All except Calvin, his eyes glazed, and face sodden with sweat. Jake watched his eyes, then his hands, waiting for any move that would tell him his suspicions were correct. When Chloe was only yards away Calvin's hand reached for the knife. Jake moved into the booth next to him. Calvin froze.

Jake flashed his badge. "Freeze, motherfucker," he said, as, with expert pressure on the man's hand, he extracted the knife. It was certainly a lethal weapon, a deer-hunter's knife, eight inches long, five inches past the legal limit. Sharp as a bayonet.

"This is a concealed weapon. You planning on going hunting?" he snarled to the trembling Calvin, as Chloe sang her way past the booth on her way back to the stage. Terror gripped Calvin. Sweat dripped from his brow onto Jake's hand, which held his wrist in a viselike grip. No one noticed the two men. All eyes were on Chloe's undulating figure. As thunderous applause rang out, Jake's attention was momentarily distracted.

With an animal cry and a madman's sudden strength, Calvin whipped his left arm into Jake's face, leaped over the table and sprinted toward the exit.

"Stop him!" Jake yelled to the uniformed guards at the entrance. "Stop that man!"

Calvin screamed in frustration and pain as the hefty guards grabbed him and tussled him to the ground. His wig fell off, his glasses crashed to the floor. Chloe's reprise was forgotten as the audience, distracted by Calvin's screams, got up to see what was happening.

Chloe froze in fear as the chattering crowd thronged around her, pushing her in their panic. The same people whom she had enthralled only seconds before now shoved her out of their way. As she started to move up the steps to the stage, she lost her footing and tripped. A hand reached out from the crowd to steady her and helped her onto the stage. The band was playing another tune now, the bandleader having signaled the orchestra to play something upbeat.

"Are you all right, Madame?" Chloe looked gratefully into the eyes of a tall, dark man, who put his arm around her protectively.

"I'm fine . . . no, I'm not. I . . . I feel faint. What's happened, do you know?"

"Come with me," he said, leading her backstage, past gossiping bare-breasted showgirls in ostrich feathers who were oblivious to the commotion out front.

In her dressing room, Chloe sat on the couch as he poured her a glass of water. Then, silently, he half-filled a brandy snifter with cognac and passed it to her.

"Do you know what happened?" she asked again.

"Drink, don't talk. Drink the brandy," he commanded.

Chloe felt a surge of gratitude to the stranger who obviously understood how disoriented she was and wanted to help.

"Oh, God," breathed Chloe. "What was that man *doing?* Who was he?"

"I don't know." Chloe recognized an accent. French, Italian? She couldn't tell.

"Thank you for helping me. Please excuse me, I'm a bit rattled."

"Understandably so, Madame. May I introduce myself? I am Philippe Archambaud, *à vôtre service.*" He made a slight but formal bow and gave her a smile that enhanced his attractiveness.

"Las Vegas is a long way from France." Chloe felt better as she sipped the brandy, felt it warming her.

"I'm here on a working vacation, to experience and write about what we call 'The American Scene.' I'm doing a series of articles for *Paris Match.*"

A *journalist!* Chloe groaned inwardly. She never trusted journalists. They were her *bêtes noires.*

Her maid came in and said the police would like to talk to her. Philippe stood up. "I shall go now." Philippe pressed her fingers swiftly to his lips. *"Tout à l'heure, Madame Carriere."*

"Au revoir, et merci," Chloe said, admiring his physique, his

impeccably cut dark suit, beautifully knotted, subtle tie, and noticing that he had written something on a book of matches which he now put into her hand.

"I shall be here for the rest of the weekend. If you would like, perhaps we could have a coffee together. If you are free, of course."

He bowed again, in the manner of a cultivated Frenchman, and left her dressing room as two policemen entered.

The interrogation was short. Although the officers seemed sympathetic, there was an edge to their concern that made Chloe feel almost guilty, as if the incident had been her fault. She was glad when they left. There was nothing she could say to help them. She had only seen the man for a second or two. She had no enemies.

Her maid bustled about. Would madame like another drink, a cigarette? No, madame would not. Madame knew what she needed tonight.

She felt lost, lonely, cold. She wanted to be close to someone. She picked up the match book that Philippe had left, and looked at it. "Philippe Archambaud. Room 1727."

What an attractive name. What an attractive man, she thought. And opening her handbag she put the match book firmly inside.

She would spend the night as she had spent the last forty nights—alone.

PART FOUR

❧ *Sixteen* ❧

CHLOE LOOKED AT HER WATCH. This was the day. Jasper Swanson had promised to call her with the news as soon as Abby called him. It was three o'clock. He should be back from his Friday lunch at Ma Maison. It's gone to Sissy, thought Chloe, staring at the ocean. Better accept the offer to tour Europe for three months. It was preferable to doing episodic TV guest shots on "Charlie's Angels" and "Policewoman," both of which she'd politely declined in the three weeks since she had been back from Vegas. Were they *ever* going to make a decision? It was almost the end of summer. "Saga" would start shooting in two weeks—what were they waiting for? She pulled on a black one-piece swimsuit and a white terry-cloth robe. To hell with waiting. To the ocean—a long swim, a glass of iced tea, then off to the Bill Palmer Salon to have Tami give her a manicure and Dino give her a new coiffure. *Forget* about Miranda! The phone rang. Twice. Three times. She picked it up on the fourth ring.

Chloe heard Jasper's excited tone. "You have it, my love, you have it!"

The excitement in his voice infected Chloe. "Oh, Jasper, I can't believe it! Are you sure? Are you positive?"

"Yes, yes. Of course I'm sure, my love. The network *adored* you. They said there really was no contest. Your test was by far the most exciting. Gertrude said you *are* Miranda!"

"Oh," bubbled Chloe, "Jasper darling, you're a magician. How could they have chosen me over Emerald, who is such a huge star . . . and Sissy, such a great actress? I simply can't believe my luck. Why did they wait so long?"

He laughed. "They received a million dollars' worth of publicity by stringing it out. Dear girl, the network isn't stupid, you know. You have a quality, Chloe. You may not even understand what it is. If you start to realize what it is, and if you start to analyze it, you may lose it, so don't think about it, that's my advice, dear."

"What do you mean?" asked Chloe. The enormity of what had happened was just beginning to penetrate.

"I mean you have got *star* quality, toots." His British voice became more serious. "Abby and Gertrude knew it right after your test. They just had to convince that bloody-minded network that you were the right woman for the part."

"And they did. Oh, God, Jasper, I'm so excited I could scream! We must celebrate."

"All right, we'll hit the town tonight. Put on your best bib and tucker." Jasper had been in the business for nearly thirty years but he had rarely heard a performer so happy to get a job. "Spago, Chasen's, Ma Maison— what is your pleasure, Milady?"

"Oh, all of them!" Chloe laughed. "Spago for champagne, Chasen's for chili and Ma Maison for dessert."

"You're on, toots." He added knowingly, "Now you must watch out, my love. Watch out for the woodwork people—the ones who didn't want to know you before, who will try to become your best friends now. You will be *swamped,* dear, with new 'best friends.' "

"I will watch out, darling, of course I will. By the way, how much will I be getting?"

He paused. "Weeell, my love, that's a *teeny* bit of a problem. I mean, let's face it, we *know* you're a cabaret star. For a singer you're quite big."

"Bottom-line it for me, Jasper darling."

"Fifteen an episode."

She was astonished. "Fifteen! Oh, Jasper, that's *peanuts.* I don't mean to sound ungrateful but I know that Sam Sharp is getting fifty, why only fifteen for me?"

"My dear, you know this business. They want you, but as far as the U.S. of A. is concerned, you're an unknown."

"I just sold out the house in Vegas," remonstrated Chloe.

"For goodness' sake, Chloe, be reasonable! After all, we are *both* British. We know you did well in Vegas, but they've got ten other cast members to pay. You are not a star yet. Oh, by the way, they've cast Sissy as the other wife, Sirope."

"Sissy! How odd, when she tested for Miranda. Why?"

"Well, Abby needs star power for this role. And Sissy needs a decent job. That is why they can't pay *you* what you deserve, dear. Sissy is still a star, and she will be paid like a star. In this town, my love, a star is a star is a star."

"O.K. You know how much I wanted this part. And I'm certainly glad I got it. But what happens if I become a big star too, Jasper? Will I get a raise?"

"My love, the sky will be the limit then, no question about it, I'll see to it that they triple your salary if you get a high TVQ, I promise you, my love. *Triple* it."

"Fine." Chloe beamed. "Then I accept. Not that there was any question, really. You knew I would."

"That's my girl. You've always been smart, Chloe. My limo will pick you up at eight. Don't forget, watch out for the woodwork people."

"I won't forget, Jasper, I promise."

✧   ✧   ✧

"No—no—no! I *can't believe* it!" screamed Sissy to her agent. "How dare they give it to that no-talent saloon singer? How *could* they?"

In spite of herself, large black tears rained mascara from her eyes. She clutched a towel around her nonexistent breasts and signaled to Sven, the Swedish masseur, who had been doing his best with the kinks in her neck, to bring her a cigarette.

"Shit! Shit! Shit!" she screamed in frustration and rage as she sat up on the portable massage table inhaling smoke deeply into her lungs. Screw cancer, she thought to herself bitterly. "I'm finished, *ruined* by this foreign *cow.*"

Sven lit a Camel and stoically sat studying the latest issue of *Body Building* he had taken from his briefcase. His calm Scandinavian features betrayed nothing of the pity he may or may not have felt for Sissy—sad sight that she was, with her overtanned skin, overdieted body, and overdyed hair, sobbing in rage on the telephone.

"How can I hold my head up in this town ever *again?*" she yelled to Robin, her hapless agent, on the other end of the phone. "How? Tell me?"

Robin was obviously trying to placate her because she remained silent for a while. "Well, I'll think about it," she muttered. "That wife is nowhere near the role that Miranda is, but if I did accept, of course they *would* build the show around me more, wouldn't they?"

She listened again, dragging heavily on her cigarette. Sven observed the lines etched deeply above her thin lips, the result of thirty cigarettes a day, which no number of face-lifts could erase.

"Forty thousand an episode? Hmmmm." She was getting visibly calmer. The lines in her face softened a little.

Sven looked up from his magazine.

Sissy finished her phone call with an "I'll think about it. I promise I will. Call me tomorrow," and hung up. She smiled. The deep wrinkles and the bitterness in her face seemed to vanish. When she smiled she lost ten years, and could look almost girlish. "Come here, Sven," she commanded in a husky, sensual voice.

The beauty of Sven was that he was terribly discreet and definitely heterosexual. None of the ladies who had partaken of his munificent Scandinavian charms had ever had cause for complaint. He aimed to please, and he did. He also never passed up an opportunity. If the lady wanted it, he could and would supply it. In spite of his total lack of interest in Sissy as a person, her body or her sexuality, Sven uncapped a bottle of baby oil and, slowly removing the towel from her body, commenced work on the famous pièce de résistance of his repertoire.

When Sue Jacobs told Sabrina that she hadn't gotten any of the roles, Sabrina had been pleased, and she signed for a new movie immediately.

✧   ✧   ✧

But Emerald, Miss Tricky One, was something else, and she had to be placated.

Emerald was upset when she had lost Miranda to Chloe—very upset indeed. She had spent one entire morning weeping alone in her bedroom, her hysteria mounting along with her insecurities, then called Eddie back.

"Why Chloe? Why not *me?*" she demanded. "Who is she anyway? Can she act? Is she a megastar? I *still* am!" she yelled, looking closely into her superstrong magnifying mirror to see if the tiny scars from her jaw job were visible.

Fast Eddie sighed. The bigger the star, the harder they fell, and the more difficult it was for them to accept it.

"They *loved* your test, kiddo. Abby and Gertrude thought you looked fantastic, and your performance was great—magic, kid."

"Terrific!" spat Emerald, catching sight of yet another line under her wide green eyes. "But Eddie, dear—if it was so fucking magical, why didn't I get the fucking part?"

"Chloe fits the role better, that's all, kiddo. They wanted a new face, they always do." Eddie was right. They wanted someone they hadn't seen for years with their morning coffee in every gossip column and on their TV screens with another newsworthy scandal, marriage, engagement or divorce. It was obvious that the American public, although they still admired Emerald, found her a larger-than-life character. They could never disassociate the persona of Emerald Barrymore, superstar, from the character she played. This was Abby's, Gertrude's, and the network's opinion. Emerald would off-balance what they wanted to be an ensemble piece.

Eddie tried to explain this to a furious Emerald, but in the middle of the conversation, Emerald hung up on him with a harsh "Fuck you and your fucking agency! Eddie, I'm firing you!"

Emerald took a deep breath and a long, harsh look at her own assets. She still possessed beauty and sex appeal, and she was famous. She hired the best agent in town—Jasper Swanson—who, never one to let a star fall by the wayside, immediately found her a low-budget movie in Australia. It was directed by the very hot, very up-and-coming young black filmmaker Horatio George Washington.

"Australia? Again? Why not?" Emerald said. "I want to be as far away as possible from Chloe Carriere when she becomes a star."

❧ *Seventeen* ❧

Perry brought Josh his breakfast along with a copy of the *Hollywood Reporter* which he had thoughtfully highlighted in red for his master to read.

CHLOE CARRIERE TO PLAY MIRANDA IN SAGA

Josh, in L.A. to record a hopeful new single, read the piece with a mixture of elation and sadness.

She'd done it. His little Chloe had the role she craved. He wanted to congratulate her, send her her favorite flowers, a little note. He picked up the phone to call Perry, but then out of habit punched in their private number at the beach house. It hadn't changed.

She answered on the third ring.

"Chlo, I'm so happy for you, luv. I just heard the news. Congratulations."

"Thanks, Josh." Chloe couldn't keep the happiness out of her voice. He had called—and in spite of her denial to herself, she still cared. "It's sweet of you to call."

She had heard it in his voice. He cared too. In spite of his other women, his boozing, his drugging, his newfound bachelor freedom, his voice brought such happy memories flooding back. He wanted to see her, wanted to hold her close to him again.

"Well, I'd like to buy you a bottle of champagne, babe. I don't suppose you're free for dinner tonight?"

She hesitated for a moment, then, "Yes, I am. I think I'd like that, Josh. Where shall we go?"

Possibly as a result of her getting the part, Josh and Chloe reconciled again, for the fourth and—Chloe hoped—final time. Her lawyer had groaned in annoyance, saying he had never in thirty years of practice known a woman who changed her mind as often as she. Josh had said he was definitely going to go to a psychiatrist and solve his problems.

For the last two weeks everything had been more or less rosy, thought Chloe as she surveyed herself objectively in a tiny spotted mirror of what was laughingly called a star's trailer.

Ben had done a good job. Good old Ben. Discreet makeup, excellent hairstyle, chic, definitely *non*-Hollywood. Simple black Chanel suit, expensively elegant enough to make the other actresses's clothes look like those of a hausfrau. It was Chloe's own suit. Last week she had categorically rejected in disgust the studio's safe little tweed suits with mink collars and rhinestone buttons. Asserting her dramatic rights, she had requested a high-fashion look. All the actresses on most of the other prime time soaps wore silk blouses, gabardine trousers or skirts. For evening scenes, they dressed in low-cut silk jersey dresses with spaghetti straps from Holly's Harp or Strip Thrills. Chloe was determined to create a look that no other actress had featured since the glamorous days of Dietrich, Turner and Crawford.

She had stressed the glamour image in all her interviews. "I am *not* the woman next door," she insisted over and over again. "Miranda is a mysterious woman of the world, and that's what I shall look like. She wears couture clothes and lives a jet-set lifestyle."

There had been some flak at the front office when Abby and Gertrude heard about the way she wanted to portray Miranda, but after viewing some tests, they were ecstatic.

"Gorgeous, she looks simply gorgeous," glowed Gertrude, congratulating herself for having had the strength to reject Sissy's frenzied pleas of longtime friendship, reminders of all the things *she* had done for Gertrude when they had been starting out in New York together a century ago.

"Fabulous. I *love* her. She looks mean and bitchy and evil, but underneath it there's something about her that you can't help liking," Abby said.

"You're right, and she's a good actress too," said Bill Herbert, "Saga's" executive producer. "She'll be big, very big. What are we paying her, Abby?"

"She's a steal, a *steal.*" Abby was excited. A bargain always appealed to him. "Only fifteen grand an episode, and by looking at these tests she's worth at least twice that."

"Don't let her get too full of herself," warned Gertrude, ever the pragmatist. "This is an *ensemble* piece, remember, everyone's equal."

"Bullshit," said Abby, getting to the point as usual. "She and Sam will be the stars of 'Saga'—I can see it."

"Any actor or actress is dispensable," Gertrude continued. "Don't let us *ever* forget that, fellows. If we do, we let the inmates run the asylum. Look what happened to the movie business!"

They all took a moment to think regretfully about how the movie business had been disrupted by upstart actors and actresses who had started their own production companies, taking over the reins and the power. Redford, Beatty, Reynolds, even Goldie Hawn, had taken off and, in control, were calling themselves producers. And, of course, some of them had become successful, which made it even worse.

"Well, it'll never happen in TV." Abby broke the silence.

"Oh, yeah? What about Lucy? She owned a frigging *studio,* for Christ's sake! How about Mary Tyler Moore?"

"Mary was a figurehead. Her husband was the power. TV is safe. Actors act, producers produce, directors direct, and that's the way it's going to be in *my* company, all the way down the line. On 'Saga' no one is more important than the producer and the product." Abby was adamant. They nodded in agreement.

"Run those rushes again," he ordered. They watched earnestly as Chloe's face filled the tiny screen.

"She's got it," breathed Gertrude. "I just hope she doesn't realize it too soon. Once she does, we won't be able to hold her back."

Chloe walked onto the set of "Saga" exuding a confidence she did not feel. She was exhausted; she had spent half the night—when she should have been preserving her looks for the camera that never lies—in screaming arguments with a drunkenly abusive Josh.

His new single, "Rainbow Girl," instead of gliding slowly but surely up the charts, as he and his advisers had predicted, had failed to make even the Top 100. It was received coolly by DJs from Coast to Coast.

His hopes of making a three-minute video of the song, an innovation still in its infancy, had been dashed when Polygram's president brushed him off. "I gotta be brutally frank: The rock-video market is aimed at kids —and by kids we mean eleven to twenty." He shrugged. "Josh, these are the *children* of your fans, y'know what I mean?" he added, with a hint of malice.

Josh had taken his fury out on Chloe, and now sat in front of the giant TV in their "playroom" off the master bedroom drinking brandy from a tumbler and flipping channels every few seconds. The volume was on full blast, and the constant changing of the channels was driving Chloe mad.

She tried not to get rattled as she busied herself with the myriad details she had to attend to before going to work the first day on what was probably the biggest career move of her life.

She puffed furiously on her twentieth cigarette, trying to study dialogue already committed to memory. Her hair was wrapped in a towel while the conditioner worked, and she tried with shaking hands to give herself a manicure.

She had dieted and exercised for weeks now, and was down to a fighting weight of one hundred and ten pounds. Ideally she would have wanted to rinse out her hair, dry her nails and fall asleep by nine o'clock with a glass of wine, which beat sleeping pills *any* time. That would give her eight solid hours of beauty sleep before she had to arise at five to get to the studio by six.

Perfect. Simply perfect. To make this break work for her, she had to be prepared. Mentally, physically and emotionally. TV was a tough, competitive arena. There were several prime time bitches out there, waiting for Chloe to come out of her corner; they were sharpening their claws, ready for battle. "I'll chew her up and spit her out in little bits!" one of her TV rivals had sneered to Daphne Swanson, who couldn't wait to print it in her column. "After all, I *am* ten years younger and four inches taller." Chloe had smiled at the insecurities of this actress, obviously terrified she was going to slip in the ratings. The truth was, Chloe planned to give them all a damn good run for their money. She would make Miranda unforgettable. She hadn't spent the past twenty years of her life singing to and observing the jet set in their natural habitat without getting a head start on the character of Miranda. Witty, scintillating, glamorous and naughty—Mirandas were everywhere in the *haut monde,* the international jet set.

"Chloe, Chloe, when's dinner, for Christ's sake?" Josh yelled from the playroom, interrupting her reverie.

"Well, darling," she placated, "you said we didn't need a live-in cook any more after Manuela left. Can't you find something in the fridge?"

The old row about having a live-in housekeeper was about to start. Chloe disliked cooking, and certainly did not intend to learn on the eve of her new job. Josh had always tried to instill a bit of old fashioned prefeminist guilt in her by insinuating that a "real woman" always cooked. His mother cooked. His sister cooked. Even Sally cooked. Why couldn't she?

"What kind of a wife *are* you?" He was still clutching the brandy bottle as he lurched into the room. He tried to smile in a winning way—the way that always warmed her heart.

"Ha, indeed, and what kind of a husband are you?" She tried to banter with him. "Don't start, Josh, darling, please," she said calmly, trying to ignore him as she unwrapped the towel from her hair.

He grabbed her, twisted her around to face him. The brandy was strong on his breath and his pupils were dilated. Her heart sank. Brandy and cocaine. A bad mix. He was out of it. She had seen it before, and it was not a pretty sight.

"I've got to rinse this off. If it stays too long on my hair, the hairdresser won't be able to work with it tomorrow." She shook herself free and escaped into the shower.

"I don't care. I want dinner, and then I want you." He loomed in the doorway, yelling over the noise of the shower. "C'mon, Chlo, let's open up a coupla cans of beans and fry some eggs like the old days. Chloe, c'mon, luv." His tone had changed to flirtatious charm, hinting of romance, a prelude to what had once been their mating call in his voice. In spite of herself she found him exciting. In spite of a six-o'clock makeup call and first-day nerves, the residue of their long-time passion still stirred her.

She stepped out of the shower and wrapped herself in a terry-cloth robe. What the hell. She returned his embrace. Two poached eggs and a can of beans didn't take long to fix, she decided. If we make love, he'll fall asleep instantly, and then I can get some rest. . . .

Afterward she snuggled against him trying to recapture old feelings of satisfaction and comfort, and longing for sleep. But he started complaining again. He moaned about his career being on the wane while hers was taking a turn for the better.

She let him ramble on about his frustrations with show business, about the unfairness of a record industry that failed to appreciate his talent, and about the stupidity of his fickle fans.

"Darling, please go to sleep," Chloe mumbled, her glass of white wine having done the trick. "I've *got* to sleep, Josh."

"Damn it, Chloe, you don't *give* a shit, do you?" he accused. He sat up in bed, snapping on the lights and the TV at the same time. "You just care about yourself and *your* bloody career, not about mine. You're a selfish bloody bitch."

There was no stopping him. Chloe closed her eyes, trying at least to rest them, and resigned herself to a bumpy night. Finally she went to the chilly, narrow bed in the guest room.

The final separation was easier than Chloe had expected. She had returned unexpectedly one day from the studio and found him making love to another fifteen-year-old girl. They were in the Jacuzzi, no less, using *her* foaming bath oil and with *her* favorite Lalique champagne glasses balanced on the edge of the tub, massaging each other with *her* one hundred and fifty-dollar-an-ounce body lotion.

She couldn't even be bothered to fight any more. Numb with pain, shock and disappointment, she locked herself in the guest room, swallowed two Valium and went to sleep in spite of Josh's night-long crying outside the door.

There was a limit to anyone's endurance, and Chloe had reached hers. The next day she called her lawyer. It was the end—absolutely. Reluctantly he agreed to take on the case again.

Josh didn't fight her. He moved to his favorite suite at the Wilshire. Tactful Perry arrived, quickly packed twenty suitcases of clothes, tapes and electronic equipment, and Josh was out of her life. "No sweat, babe," Josh said with a smile as he kissed her goodbye—kissed eleven years of their life goodbye.

"Still mates, O.K., Chlo? We'll always be mates, won't we?"

She nodded dumbly. Her throat hurt with the effort of trying to stop the tears from running down her cheeks. Damn him, how dare he be so cool, so casual, so chummy. Would she *ever* get over him completely?

She slammed shut the heavy Aztec-carved doors and walked out onto the balcony. It was a sensational beach day. Seagulls swooped, joggers jogged, the cobalt seas washed the seaweed-encrusted shoreline. A perfect Trancas Sunday. She was alone: her marriage ending, a TV career beginning, big things ahead. But she was now forty, an age considered scrap-heap ten or fifteen years ago. Thank God for Jane Fonda's changing so many people's attitudes about aging women. They should build a shrine to her.

But today she felt her age. Felt old, washed-out, sad.

Sunday stretched ahead emptily. So, for that matter, did Monday, Tuesday and the rest of the week. The months and years seemed to lie ahead of her with nothing to fill them, except "Saga." Was a TV career that important to her? So many of her recent years had been dedicated to just being with Josh. He had filled her life, fulfilled her for much of the time, too. And now it was truly over. Dammit, *why* couldn't she stay happily married? Not for her the bed-hopping and assignations that filled the lives of so many of her acquaintances. It didn't thrill her. Her thrill was being with one person. All she wanted was one guy. One faithful man to be with, to share her life with. Why couldn't she have it?

So now what? She had the TV series, but she did not have—would never have—what she wanted most. A child. A baby to hold and hug and be Mummy to. A bit late now, sneered her inner voice. Your biological clock has ticked itself out. Her baby, Annabel, her best-kept secret, was now a long-legged, independent eighteen-year-old, living happily in London with an equally independent boyfriend, blissfully unaware that the famous Chloe Carriere was her mother. Chloe wrote to her every week, called her as often as she could, and thought about her every day. Annabel suspected nothing. Chloe felt such love for the tomboyishly beautiful girl so like herself at the same age. Independent, enthusiastic, ambitious. God, she prayed she wouldn't get hooked on a man like Matt or Josh.

"Good to see you, Auntie Chlo," Annabel beamed whenever they saw each other. She was always rushing somewhere, long auburn hair flowing, guitar thrown over her shoulder, off to some rendezvous to play her music with her friends. "Must dash, luv, see you *soon*, promise." Oh, yes, Chloe's sister-in-law sympathized with her, but if Chloe had been stupid and ignorant enough to get pregnant by Matt in the days when it was such a stigma, she must now bear the consequences of her actions. Besides, Annabel was Susan's child—legally adopted, much loved. And no one would ever know the truth.

PART
FIVE

◆ *Eighteen* ▶

IN THE LATE FALL of 1982 "Saga" went on the air. Sam Sharp played Steve Hamilton, the gruff, manly patriarch of the Hamilton clan. Chloe played Miranda Hamilton, his silkenly sexy ex-wife. Pandora King played the cool, sophisticated Judith Hamilton, ex-wife number two, and Sissy Sharp played Sirope, the saintly current Mrs. Hamilton.

With assorted young actors playing a variety of sons, daughters, nephews and nieces, mistresses and lovers, within six weeks the ensemble soap opera became the biggest hit of the 1982–83 season. And Chloe Carriere was well on her way to becoming the household name that everyone had predicted.

"It's a total bummer," confided Larry Carter, over a year later, as they sat in the studio commissary at a quiet corner table. He ate an Abby Arafat Sandwich, while Chloe munched on sliced apple and avocado to keep the pounds off.

"I mean, how do you think I feel taking over from Alex? It's a break, I know, but, hell, he's one of my best friends."

"Yes, but he didn't conform to the system, darling," said Chloe. "He bucked the system, Larry. You know he was always giving interviews, knocking the show, making fun of it on Carson and Merv. They won't stand for that. You know it."

"True," he said gloomily.

"Saga" had been on the air for one and a half seasons. It had become a gargantuan hit, greater than any other prime time soap opera in history. It had catapulted Chloe to stardom and fame she had never believed possible. Now there were Miranda Hamilton dolls, Miranda Hamilton makeup, Miranda Hamilton T-shirts, greeting cards, and even car-bumper stickers with "Let Miranda Live!"—referring to the courtroom scene in which Miranda had pleaded for her life after being wrongfully accused of killing one of her many lovers.

Magazines were clamoring for Chloe. So were gossip tabloids desperate for any skeletons in her cupboard to reveal to their readers. She started with diet and beauty magazines, fan magazines and fashion spreads. But soon she graduated to interviews in *People, US* and prestigious foreign publications like *Paris Match* in France, *Holá* in Spain, *Oggi* in Italy, and the Sunday *Times* Magazine in England. After that she started getting covers. Over an eighteen-month period, she was on the cover of more than two hundred magazines worldwide. "Saga" had done great things for Chloe and for its other stars. All except Alex Andrews.

He had played Steve and Judith's evil son, Cain, in the first thirteen episodes, but he had become deeply embarrassed by some of the clichéd dialogue and situations his character was involved in. He had started to bad-mouth the show in every interview he'd done, and he talked disparagingly on the set and in the makeup room about how stupid TV viewers were to be interested in such a puerile piece of crap.

It didn't take long for his bad-mouthing to reach the ears of Abby and Gertrude. He was called on the carpet in their palatial suite of offices— offices which could easily contain the living spaces of all the actors' trailers in "Saga"—and told to cool it or else he would be replaced.

"We simply will *not* tolerate disloyalty to our show." Gertrude's normally high color dramatically increased, and her normally placid voice had turned shrill.

Abby said little. His huge bulk seemed totally in proportion with his massive imported black onyx desk, bare except for a color photograph of him and Maud with President Nixon, one of his closest friends. It was tacitly understood that Gertrude was the spokesperson for the show when dealing with difficult actors, the schoolmarm telling off the naughty little boys and girls. Spank their bottoms, scold them sternly, and tell them to run away and behave. Alex was embarrassed. At twenty-three, he considered himself intellectually superior to both of these doddering relics who knew absolutely nothing about art, whose idea of cultural fulfillment was watching a Bertolucci movie at Sue Mengers's house. But he was also an actor who had to eat, and he had not bankrolled himself sufficiently to relinquish the role of Cain.

Gertrude's diatribe lasted twenty minutes, in spite of three phone calls from a panic-stricken Ned, who needed Alex back on the set.

"So don't let it happen again," hissed Gertrude, her face now as flame-colored as her frizzed red hair. "We're a family here—a happy, productive family. We support each other, we *don't* bite the hand that feeds us."

"Yes, Gertrude, of course. I'm sorry, it won't happen again," he promised, hating his hypocrisy.

"Well done, Gert," Abby said after the actor left, tail between his legs. "Mustn't let them get away with it."

"We never will," she said strongly.

Two weeks later, while in New York for the weekend, Alex found himself drinking with some newly acquired Actors Studio friends at the Russian Tea Room. They were all unemployed, all secretly jealous of his prestige and the bread Alex was making, but they goaded him about what crap "Saga" was, told him it was demeaning for a serious actor to be on it.

"The worst thing I have *ever* seen; it's an insult to the intelligence," said the small wiry-haired actress with a cast in one eye whose lack of talent and looks guaranteed that she would remain unemployed in her chosen profession forever. "Doncha get sick to your stomach when you have to say those ridiculous lines?" said Tiger Lily, a beautiful Oriental actress who was having a tough time getting a job performing in anything other than porno films.

"The acting is the pits, man. The motherfuckin' *pits*," groaned Mack, who washed dishes at Sardi's at night and auditioned in vain during the day. "Quit! Become a *real* actor, man. Cut the crap. Come and live in New York where the action is, where an actor can have respect for himself. Where real talent is appreciated. Get back on the boards, man—the theater. The real thing . . ."

Gertrude was in the middle of watching "Saga" when the call came in.

"Fuck you—fuck your motherfucking shit show—it stinks. *You* stink. Let me out!" screamed drunken Alex.

She wasted no time. Without taking her eyes off the screen and Chloe's lovely face, while making a mental note to tell the hairdresser that Chloe's bangs were getting too long, she dialed Abby's house.

The news was on the street by the next afternoon. Alex had been dropped like used Kleenex. His scenes had been canceled and new scenes with other actors substituted. A scene was written in which everyone wondered about his disappearance, then discovered that he had gone to Australia on a quest for his real father.

Two weeks later, Larry Carter was cast to replace him.

There was no explanation to the viewers as to why Cain had a different face, was ten years older and spoke with a British accent.

Larry's hair, dyed black, was the only concession that the producers made to the public. Such was the popularity of "Saga" that viewers bought it without a murmur and the show continued from strength to strength each year.

Her message service called Chloe with a wake-up call at 5 A.M. "Good morning, hon, it's five o'clock. Are you up?" said the sympathetic voice of Gloria.

"Mmm, yeah—I am." Chloe groaned, glancing at the digital clock on the bedside table. She slipped out of bed and into her lavish bathroom/dressing room, where she plugged in the electric coffee-maker which sat on top of a small fridge next to her "Who Says Life Begins at Forty?" mug. She did ten minutes of fast sit-ups and push-ups while the water heated and her bath was running, and she watched the news on CNN. Twenty minutes later, scrubbed, showered and shampooed, and wearing a comfortable velour track suit, she jumped into her Mercedes and drove to "The Factory," as the cast and crew affectionately called the studio.

MCPC Studios was a dull gray windowless building on the less attractive part of Pico Boulevard in Los Angeles. It bore about as much resemblance to the public's idea of a movie or TV studio as a prison did to a nightclub.

In her tiny dressing room, Chloe switched on Channel 5 to watch the local news, listened to the messages on her answering machine, and, sitting before the lightbulb-framed mirror, applied her TV makeup with swift, practiced strokes. She preferred doing her own makeup when it was feasible. It was a little bit of time she had totally to herself—the only time she would have during the long twelve-hour day ahead.

Theo, her hairdresser, put hot rollers into her thick, dark curls, as she studied the scenes for the day. Debbie, the second assistant, brought her breakfast on a Styrofoam plate, with plastic fork, paper napkin and apple juice in a can, the whole covered by aluminum foil. At seven o'clock she went down to Stage 11 for the first rehearsal of the day. Gina, her secretary, arrived with a clutch of eight-by-ten fan photos, and they discussed Chloe's schedule of social events and interviews for the next two days.

Today they were shooting a party scene in which all the cast were present. Sissy and Sam huddled together in a corner as usual, talking their heads off privately. For a married couple whom everyone knew had no sex life they certainly spent enough time gazing raptly into each other's eyes and having in-depth conversations. Today both wore designer jeans and plaid shirts and great wads of Kleenex were tucked into their collars to protect their clothes from the orange makeup the TV cameras required. Sissy's behind was so flat now, it looked as if it had been cut off by a bacon slicer. Her thin blond hair was uncombed. It had suffered from the strong TV lights and from constant setting with hot rollers of the past seasons so she now wore a soft blond wig while shooting.

Chelsea Deane, Chloe's favorite director, was directing this episode. The thirty-fifth. There were only nine episodes left before the end of the year. Ratings couldn't have been higher, nor could the spirits of everyone involved in the show. " 'Saga,' Prime Time Hit Show," the assistant director cheerfully answered the stage phone, which rang constantly. There were eighty extras today, dressed in 1920s costumes for a costume ball. Three cameras were being used for the opening shot of the Hamilton mansion in which Sam, as Steve Hamilton, and Sissy, as the third Mrs. Hamilton, stood in the doorway to greet their guests. The crew sat around desultorily gossiping, munching bacon-and-egg sandwiches or doughnuts, sipping coffee. There was a hum of conversation as the actors rehearsed the first scene of the day. Chloe, Pandora and Sam usually referred to the script while they rehearsed, as they had not yet memorized the lines. Sissy was always word perfect, not only with her own lines but with everyone else's too. Woe betide any actor who dried. She had no patience and would blow her top.

After rehearsal Chloe went back to her dressing room. A heavily beaded gold flapper dress that had been designed for her by Rudolpho, "Saga's" resident designer, was hanging in the wardrobe.

"God, this is heavy," she gasped, as Trixie, her dresser, helped her into it. "It must weigh at least twenty pounds."

"Thirty," said Trixie laconically laying out long chandelier earrings, diamanté bracelets and golden shoes. "We weighed it. It's broken two hangers already."

"Great," said Chloe. "My shoulders already feel like I've been pulling a plow."

"You must suffer to be beautiful," deadpanned Trixie, as they heard the sound of Sissy yelling down the corridor, "Trixieee, where the hell *are* you?"

"Ah, the dulcet tones of our divine diva." Trixie smiled and winked at Chloe. "Maybe I'll catch that skinny ass of hers in the zipper. That'll *really* make her yell!" Sissy was generally detested by cast and crew alike, but seemed oblivious to it.

In the hairdressing room, Theo combed out Chloe's hair and fixed golden ostrich feathers into it on a tight beaded band across her forehead. In the next chair sat Larry, while the other hairdresser, Monica, applied a layer of black pancake makeup to the bald spot that had started to appear recently on his scalp.

"Great, huh?" said Larry ruefully. "My only consolation is that Prince Charles has one too."

"And he's younger than you," Chloe teased.

Larry grimaced. At thirty-five he was playing twenty-five, and it was becoming more difficult. He had to watch his weight constantly, as did all the actors to maintain their youthful appearance for the camera that never lied. Most of the crew gained several pounds each season, due to the long, boring hours and the ever present trestle table loaded with snacks and coffee that the producers laid on for them all day long. But the camera added five to ten pounds to an actor's appearance, so the cast tried to keep away from the junk food that was always on display. Often, however, at the end of the day all willpower lapsed, and to Pandora's and Chloe's dismay their tight-fitting costumes now and then would have to be let out in the waist or hips. This never happened to Sissy, however. Dieting was her religion.

"Ready, Chloe?" chirped the ever cheerful Debbie. "Stage eleven, mush, mush, woman."

On the stage, eighty extras were being organized by Ned, the first assistant director, as Chelsea Deane painstakingly rehearsed a scene in which Chloe and her latest lover, played by Garth Frazer, arrived to greet Sissy and Sam.

It was a short scene but difficult to shoot because the extras, or "atmosphere" as they preferred to be called, had to move around in front of the principals without blocking the camera when the actors spoke their dialogue. The extras had to look animated, talk and laugh, yet were only allowed to mime so that the sound operator would pick up only the principals' dialogue.

After five takes Chelsea yelled, "Cut and print." The performers sat in a semicircle in their green director's chairs amidst a tangle of cables and arc lamps, relaxing for the eight to fifteen minutes it took to relight the scene for each of their close-ups. Theo and Ben fussed around Chloe's hair and face and Trixie worried about the bugle beads that kept falling off Chloe's bodice. She tried to sew them back on but finally gave up with a sigh. "I don't think it'll show on camera." Chloe tried to remain cool, calm and collected even though at 10:30 A.M. the temperature outside was hovering in the mid-nineties and the studio wasn't much cooler. According to weather expert Doctor George on Channel 7, it was due to hit a hundred today.

Chloe felt her face sting under the heavy makeup. The strong lights washed out the performers' features to such an extent that excessive makeup was necessary to give definition to their faces. Sissy sat fanning herself with an antique fan she was convinced had once belonged to Lily Langtry. Garth, Chloe's TV lover, sat next to her, sweat pouring down his orange-tinted face.

Garth Frazer had blond, thinning hair and was only five feet nine, short compared to the other actors, most of whom were at least six feet. He had to wear high lifts inside his shoes, which gave him a curiously tipped-forward look, as though, if pushed, he might tumble over like Humpty-Dumpty. Chloe surreptitiously inched her chair away to escape his breath. Garth had obviously indulged the previous night in a fine Italian dinner laden with garlic. Little thought had he given to the fact that he would be locked in passionate embraces today with Chloe. But the more she moved her chair away to escape his breath, the closer he leaned, explaining to Chloe, as if she didn't know, the finer points of the scene they were going to perform.

Chloe was amused by his pomposity as he informed her what *her* motivation in their scene should be. Certainly he had been the star of two or three reasonable Movies of the Week, and had done a fairly respectable long-form series on prime time, but Lord Olivier he was not. She was beginning to resent his condescending attitude toward her and the rest of the cast and crew.

"I know you've only been acting for three years, darling." He smiled, revealing the most awful capped teeth she had ever seen. How much longer could she tolerate this buffoon? Her "beauty crew"—Trixie, Theo, De De and Ben—sat nearby, observing, containing their amusement. Gina came over with a pile of mail to try to help Chloe escape as he droned on.

"So you see, darling, *that's* how I see Miranda and Charles's subtext in the scene, don't you agree?" said the blond actor earnestly.

"Mmmm, yes, of course," muttered Chloe. She knew her character better than he knew his, and she certainly knew her lines. He had been having serious trouble with his dialogue for the last four episodes. This was becoming a problem, as they were falling behind schedule. It cost them money, and if there was one thing the producers hated it was spending extra money. But Garth was seemingly unconcerned; he was a boorish puffball, a conceited egotist, in short, a fairly typical example of a mediocre prime time TV actor who had hit it lucky and whose success had gone straight to his head.

Mumbling "Excuse me," Chloe let Gina lead her away.

Several hours later the time had come to do their love scene. Chloe groaned inwardly.

"Ready for you, Chloe," said Ned, as Ben packed Max Factor powder onto her face to stop the shine.

"O.K., my darling, let's go for one, shall we?" said Chelsea, still as hearty as a sailor on leave.

The lighting cameraman instructed the gaffer to move the lights more to the left. The sound man instructed the boom operator to adjust the proximity of his mike to the two actors because he was picking up too much echo. The camera assistant whisked a tape measure up to Chloe and Garth's noses and did some computations in his head, which he jotted down. Trixie fussed with Chloe's beads, Theo fussed with the feathers in her hair, which were starting to molt and fall onto her eyelashes. Ben outlined her lips for the fifteenth time that day with peach lip gloss. Bobby, the second makeup man, with a sigh of resignation mopped Garth's face with a wet chamois dipped in witch hazel, then mopped it with Kleenex before adding a thick coat of powder.

One of the secretaries from Bill Herbert's office arrived on the set with her entire family from Arkansas. They stood, mouths agape, directly in Garth's eye line. One of them fiddled with an Instamatic camera, and they whispered loudly among themselves with excitement.

Chloe signaled to Ned to have them moved, but before it could be done Garth blew his top.

"Get those people out of my eye line, *please*," he yelled. "What is this, feeding time at the fucking zoo?"

"Calm down . . ." Chloe started to say.

"We're trying to do a goddamn scene here, not be stared at like monkeys in the motherfucking zoo, for Christ's sake."

In unison the crew silently raised their eyes to the heavens. They had been suffering Garth's overbearing airs and graces in silence for months. Sissy they tolerated. Sissy was a big star, a central part of this show, their bread and butter. Garth had no such clout. This was basically Chloe, Sissy and Sam's show, in spite of the constant insistence by Abby and Gertrude that it was an ensemble piece.

Garth's makeup man once more attended to his sweaty face, and Chloe wondered if he was on coke. She had never seen so much sweat.

"O.K., kids, let's 'ave a go, shall we?" Chelsea Deane was calm on the surface, but seething inside. This ignorant poofter was getting to him. "What a no-talent numbnuts," he had confided to Chloe the previous week, after directing a scene in which Garth blew his lines no fewer than eight times.

"I know, I know, darling, he's a pain. Why they cast him instead of Colin Bridges I'll never know."

She and Chelsea exchanged glances of understanding. "O.K., kids, *action!*" Chelsea stood next to the camera watching intently as Chloe and Garth started the scene. Garth immediately blew his first line.

"O.K., we go again," said Chelsea, as the beauty crew trotted in to mop up. Ned called for the red light. The third camera assistant brought in the clapper board. "Thirty-three take two," announced the sound man. "Rolling."

"Action!" yelled Chelsea.

"I love you, Miranda," breathed Garth/Charles as he gently bent his blond head to Chloe's dark one. They were seated together on a chaise longue in the Hamilton mansion.

"I've never loved anyone as much as I love you." Chloe felt nausea assail her at his garlic-laden breath.

"Oh, Charles, why do you say one thing, yet mean another?" Chloe moved her head away as far as she could without getting out of the careful lighting setup. There was a pregnant pause. Chloe tried to fill it with a girlish sigh. Garth had dried again.

"Sorry about that, love," he said calmly. "Heat's got to me."

Chloe gritted her teeth. Trixie and Gina threw her sympathetic looks. The crew tried not to look affected.

"Thirty-three take fourteen," cried the camera assistant briskly an hour later, as he snapped the clapper board exceedingly close to Garth's nose. The crew were seething inwardly now, and they felt sorry for Chloe, who was extremely uncomfortable. It was over a hundred degrees on the set. The heavy beaded dress, the molting ostrich feathers, this ghastly actor with his awful breath and the sweat that poured from his brow onto her upturned face were a nightmare. Chloe had had enough. She had really had her fill this time.

They finally finished the master scene, and after Chelsea covered it with medium shots and close-ups, Chloe went to her dressing room and called Gertrude's office. "I need a meeting with you, now," she said. "And it can't wait."

After seeing the abysmal rushes, Abby and Gertrude realized they had to find a new love interest for Chloe, and soon. She had rebelled for the first time in three and a half seasons. She told them she needed a strong, assertive man for her character to play opposite, a real macho man with strength, masculinity and sex appeal. They knew she was right.

An emergency meeting was called with Bill Herbert, Chloe and Jasper Swanson in attendance. Sitting in Abby's oak-paneled office they discussed the possibilities. Who was available, who wasn't. Who would do TV, who would think it was demeaning.

"Burt Reynolds," suggested Chloe optimistically. "There's a real man, and his movies haven't done well recently."

"Ha!" said Abby. "He's features, honey, *features.* He won't do TV."

"Timothy Dalton," suggested Jasper, ever one to get a fellow Englishman a job.

"Timothy who?" rasped Gertrude. "Never heard of him."

"He's good. He's an excellent Shakespearean actor. He's going to be hot," insisted Jasper.

"Well, not on 'Saga,' " said Abby. "I saw him in that Mae West film years ago. Nah—next."

"You'll be sorry," said Jasper. "Timothy's going places, he'll be big."

"Let him be big somewhere else," said Gertrude. "We need a macho guy with a name."

For two frustrating hours they played the casting game. Then Jasper played his ace. He'd been waiting for the right moment. The moment when Tom Selleck, George Hamilton, Robert Wagner, James Farentino, Alain Delon, Michael Landon, Peter Strauss, Martin Sheen, Jeff Bridges and Gregory Harrison had all been considered and, for one reason or another, dismissed.

"How about Luis Mendoza?" he suggested.

Luis sat across from Jasper at Ma Maison twiddling his thumbs. It had been three years since his movie with Sissy, a bomb if ever there was one. The producers couldn't even sell it to cable TV. Movie offers since then had been thin on the ground for Luis. If it hadn't been for his passion for Sabrina, he would have gone back to Mexico, where he was a superstar and his records still outsold Julio Iglesias's. In spite of his looks and his belief in his talents, Hollywood refused to take a singing Mexican seriously. He had hired the best public relations firm in town to promulgate his image as a serious but sensual actor. He had fired Klinger and hired Jasper Swanson as his agent. He had been considered for movies with Bo Derek, Kim Basinger and Kathleen Turner—but he had had no firm offers.

He was now nearing thirty, and, with his black lustrous curly hair and slanting, heavily lashed brown eyes, handsomer than ever. He and Sabrina were the most beautiful and photogenic couple in Hollywood; the paparazzi went wild whenever they went out publicly, which was not often. They preferred to stay at the beach making love, lying in the Jacuzzi that was fitted into the deck outside their house, drinking wine and talking about their future.

Recently, though, the charms of Sabrina had begun to pall for Luis. Sabrina, gorgeous and loving as she was, had become a tiny bit boring. Occasionally, to his horror, he found that he was unable to respond to her amorous advances. Pretending headaches, exhaustion or lines to learn, he would retire to his study, where he sat pondering why his libido, of which he had always been justly proud, seemed to be deserting him. He recalled hearing the macho men of his youth discuss their *amigos* who "couldn't get it up"; now he, too, seemed to be joining their ranks. Although it had only happened a couple of times in the past month, it was enough to turn Luis's hot Latin blood cold.

In the nearly three years he and Sabrina had been together, he had been more or less faithful to her, which for a Latin man was unusual. They had made love at least once or twice a day. Now his equipment was letting him down, a fate worse than death.

Preoccupied with his troubles, Luis was barely listening to Jasper.

"I think you should do a series," Jasper was saying as he expertly slipped the band off a Davidoff cigar, lighting it with a kitchen match from a Victorian silver box he carried.

"A series? *Ay, mamá,* I was offered a series last month. The stars would be me and a talking car. No, thanks."

"I don't mean *any* series." Jasper was impatient. "I'm talking about 'Saga,' the series of the moment, the hottest show in town."

"So what? It's already cast with Sam and Sissy—ugh!" He grimaced remembering their ill-fated movie and even more ill-fated short-lived affair.

"What do you think of Chloe Carriere?" asked Jasper, puffing on the huge cigar with enjoyment. At his age, a cigar gave more comfort and pleasure than sex.

"Chloe Carriere, she's a dish, a bitch too, I hear." Luis laughed. "I hear she cuts off her leading men's balls and fries them for breakfast like *huevos rancheros.*"

"Not true, Luis," said Jasper gravely. "Not true at all. Chloe is actually a very nice girl who has become a victim, of sorts, of her own publicity."

"But she's gone along with it, hasn't she?" persisted Luis.

"Dear Chloe, she is a wonder, I'll admit," laughed Jasper. "She's waited a long time for this break, so she's making the most of it. To get to the point, Luis, Abby Arafat and Gertrude have made us an offer that is hard to refuse."

"What is it?"

"Two years on 'Saga' with an option for a third. Twenty-five thousand an episode for the first year, forty thousand for the second, and the third negotiable, of course."

"Hmm, I can make more than that on a tour of Spain in a month," said Luis.

"Luis, old boy—" Jasper was more serious now—" 'Saga' is a hot show this year, next year too. If they're lucky, they may even go to six or seven years. Chloe Carriere is a hot actress. They want you for her lover, husband, boyfriend, whatever. This will make you the household name in America you've been dying to be. Let me tell you something, old boy, about the film scene. Nicholson and Redford find it hard to get the right roles and stay up on their movie pedestals today. TV is making the stars now. Take this part, Luis. Make every woman in America cream in her knickers when you come on the screen, and you can write your *own* ticket in two years' time. Look at Selleck—he made it on TV, and now he's got more movie offers than he can handle."

Luis considered the Englishman's advice. It was true. TV was where it was now. With a few exceptions, there were no big movie stars any more. TV stars were the current royalty of show business, invited to the White House, curtsying to the Queen, on the covers of major magazines.

"Maybe I should do it. Let me think it over."

"Do that, old boy. You have twenty-four hours to make up your mind; then they will go in another direction."

Luis frowned. "Don't threaten me."

"I'm not, old boy, I'm not. I simply believe this is a major career move for you."

"I told you I'll think about it," said Luis.

✧   ✧   ✧

It didn't take Luis long to accept the offer, and a few weeks later, locked in a passionate embrace with his new on-camera lover, Chloe, it didn't take him long to become a macho man again. He felt his manhood rising against the filmy chiffon of her nightgown. They were entwined under lilac Frette sheets on the set. Dozens of men and women barking orders and busying themselves with the thousand and one duties necessary before the camera could roll on the love scene unfolding in front of them milled around the bed. Luis started to sweat, something he normally didn't do. How *could* he be aroused by Chloe? She was far too old for him, and he hated her crisp British manner. She seemed always to be secretly laughing at him, and although she was friendly and charming, he hated her coolness and her lack of deference toward men in general.

Chloe looked startled at the feel of Luis's normally lackadaisical cock twitching against her thigh.

She looked into his eyes as they lay together while the camera assistant brought the measuring tape to each of their noses, and gave Luis a conspiratorial wink. Luis managed a weak smile as he willed his defiant member to subside.

Why, for God's sake, why now with Chloe? Why not with soft, adoring, gorgeous young Sabrina?

"O.K., kids." Chelsea Deane beamed his cockney charm. "I'm givin' you a lot of space here to really 'ave a go at it. I really want you to melt those TV screens. We've got a lot of leeway, so let me see if all the stuff they write about you in the papers is true, eh, luv?" He grinned at Chloe and she smiled back. Chelsea had a great sense of humor, something sadly lacking in most of the producers and directors of the show. He and Chloe insulted each other outrageously on the set, sometimes joking and kidding around until the crew broke up and Chloe had to go to her dressing room to try to recover from the giggles.

"*Aaand* action!" shouted Chelsea.

After the passionate love scene was over, there was silence from the crew. Trixie gave a terry-cloth robe to a stunned Chloe. Luis had been amazing. His ardor, inflamed by his sudden unexplainable desire for Chloe, had almost caught her up in the passion of the moment.

"Blimey, kids, that was *hot!*" said Chelsea admiringly. "Print it—we don't even need coverage. Hey, Luis, you were great, man. Like just great!" Proudly Luis accepted compliments from various crew members and retired to his trailer as lunch was called.

Debbie Drake, the pretty young second assistant director, brought him his usual chef's salad, iced tea, and apple pie with ice cream. "Anything else you want, Luis?" she said brightly, standing silhouetted against the bright California noonday sun in the doorway of his trailer, her taut breasts outlined by the simple white T-shirt she wore. She had a cute rear end enhanced by faded blue jeans. Her face, unadorned by makeup and framed by long blond hair caught up in a ponytail, was pretty in a wholesome all-American way.

"Yes, *querida*—I want you," he said huskily, giving her the benefit of the famous dark eyes that had caused maidenly hearts to flutter throughout Latin America.

"Oh," gulped Debbie, having witnessed the love scene earlier. Oh, well, uhm, why not? she said to herself. Let's see if it's true what they say about Latin lovers. With a sharp kick of her sneakered foot, she pushed the door of his trailer shut and, pulling her T-shirt over her head, joined Luis on his sofa bed.

The following week Luis fucked Pandora. Although he had never been interested in older women, Pandora's brisk manner, coupled with a truly magnificent bosom, captivated Luis's imagination. His conquests seemed to improve his ardor for Sabrina. He found himself able not only to have some of the most interesting lunch hours he had ever had, but also to achieve new heights of passion with Sabrina. It was clear it couldn't last. All of a sudden Luis Mendoza was having his cake and eating it too.

His sudden fame astounded even himself. After appearing on the TV screen in "Saga" only twice, he had received tons of fan mail. Women found his macho, slightly cocky good looks a total turn-on. He was suddenly the flavor of the month throughout the whole United States. Editors besieged Christopher McCarthy, the PR man for "Saga," with requests for cover stories, photo sessions, interviews, anything and everything to do with Luis.

Before he knew what had hit him, Luis was on the cover of *US, People, USA Today, GQ,* the *American Informer,* the *National Enquirer,* the *Star,* the *Globe* and even the corner cover of *Newsweek.* It was heady stuff. Intoxicating. Luis had never been modest, and his Latin pride swelled even more at the sudden attention and admiration he was receiving.

Sabrina didn't like it. It wasn't that she was jealous. With her wholesome all-American beauty, she was in demand herself, building a solid foundation for a film career that she hoped would flourish for years. But she didn't like Luis's preening himself all day long, constantly combing his shiny black hair, working on his rippling muscles and admiring them from all angles in the three-way mirror in *her* dressing room. This was when he wasn't lying by the pool obsessively working on an already perfect tan, a sun reflector handy to catch every last ray. Their love life was still good, but there was something missing in their relationship now, and she didn't know what it was.

◆ *Nineteen* ◆

I N A WEATHERED HOUSE on a small cul de sac in Santa Monica lived Sam Sharp's very good friend, Freddy.

A designer of ladies' clothing, Frederick Langlan was not in the class of Bob Mackie or Nolan Miller—his Hollywood gowns were more in the seven-hundred-dollar price range than the seven-thousand—but he had a loyal show-business clientele of not only wealthy, frugal women, but also of young TV starlets on the way up who wanted to look fabulous but couldn't afford Bob's, Nolan's or even Neiman-Marcus's prices. Wives of B-picture actors on a tight budget but with a full social schedule, girl-friends of studio executives, older actresses who did occasional guest shots on "Love Boat" and "Magnum" and wanted to look their best, all were habitués of Freddy's rococo salon by the sea.

He painstakingly designed an "original" Frederick Langlan for each one, an original that bore more than a passing resemblance to the exqui-site creations of Valentino or Jacqueline de Ribes in the current issues of French or Italian *Vogue*.

To the ladies, it didn't matter. They were secure in the fact that there was no chance of the catastrophe that had happened recently at a Beverly Hills charity ball. The wives of two of "Saga's" producers, who had each blown nine thousand dollars on a gorgeous Galanos gown, appeared at the ball wearing the same dress. If looks could kill, Mr. Abby Arafat and Mr. William Herbert would have been widowers. Hollywood chuckled with delight when the *Beverly Hills Tattler* ran front-page photos of the two women side by side wearing the identical dresses.

As they waited for Freddy, Sabrina Jones and Daphne Swanson sat in cozy chairs in his anteroom flipping through the *Beverly Hills Tattler* and laughing at the photographs of the two women.

Freddy drew aside the silver lamé curtains to his anteroom and swept in, followed by a cloud of pale gray organza and a torrent of the latest gossip.

"My dears, have you *heard* about Emerald's new boyfriend?" he said, giggling, as he lowered the neckline an inch and a half on Sabrina's creamy silk jersey to reveal more of her fabulous bosom, a sight guaran-teed to get her, if not into the "People" section of *Time* magazine, at least into "What the Stars Are Wearing" in the *Beverly Hills Tattler*.

"I thought she was still seeing Solomon. Who is it?" Daphne inter-rupted her inspection of a box of Cadbury's milk chocolates which Freddy's flight steward friend had brought him from England. Daphne prided herself on being the first to know who was sleeping with whom—often stale news by the time the couple in question finally did it. With her network of spies in every restaurant, studio, boutique and hotel between Palm Springs and L.A., she usually knew, before the fact, the first time the eyes of potential lovers locked.

"My dear, it's *too* camp." Freddy said through a mouthful of the pins with which he was outlining Sabrina's bosom. "You *know* she's doing that movie in Italy?"

"Yes, yes." Daphne impatiently lit a Dunhill, ever true to all things British.

"Of course we all know it's a turkey, if I ever heard of one, and she's playing opposite that has-been Italian star, what's his name?"

"Fabiano Frapani." Sabrina whispered the name reverently. A has-been indeed! The greatest actor ever to come out of Italy. So what if he was pushing sixty—with talent like his, who cared?

"Weell," said Freddy slyly, enjoying drawing out this scrap of gossip. "You *know* who's directing, don't you?"

"Ouch!!" He had inadvertently pierced Sabrina's priceless left nipple with a pin.

"Oooh, *sorry,* dear, mustn't tamper with the merchandise. Do you want me to kiss it better?" He giggled, though both women noticed he was somewhat less effervescent than usual.

"It's all right, *go on.*" Even Sabrina, usually bored by gossip, as those whose lives are full mostly are, was intrigued by tales of Emerald's escapades. Almost three generations had now been titillated by them, yet interest in her private life still persisted.

"Horatio's directing, right?" Daphne was offhand. Although she knew who was fucking whom, minor details like who was directing whom usually escaped her.

"Yes indeedy. Horatio George Washington." He stopped, becoming involved with the extent of the slit in Sabrina's skirt.

"To the thigh or to the crotch, dear? What do you think?"

"The thigh, please. I'm *not* Cher."

"So what about Horatio George Washington?" Daphne was impatient. "He's married to Edna Ann Mason, they just had a baby. Oh, dear, I *must* send her flowers."

"Dear, he and Emerald have been at it like rabbits ever since they met when she went down under nearly three years ago."

"How do you *know,* Freddy?" snapped Daphne, annoyed that her sources from Italy had not filled her in on this one.

"It's been in the English papers. Dempster's column, as a matter of fact. Now you've *got* to believe Nigel Dempster, haven't you, darling?"

"Not necessarily," Daphne snapped. "How do you know this for an actual fact?"

"Sorry, dear, can't reveal me sources." Freddy leaned back on his heels, surveying the perfection of Sabrina in his copy of a Halston. "We all know Emerald has always liked a touch of the tar brush, and Horatio *is* a famous colored man, isn't he?"

"Black," corrected Daphne. "We say 'black' now, Freddy dear, not 'colored.' "

"Black, shmack, he's no more *black* than you and me, dear," sniffed Freddy. "More the color of those chocolates, I'd say. But that doesn't matter at all. I think the fact he's married makes it a bit, well—"

"Tacky, darling?" finished Daphne.

"Yes, I suppose."

"Well if the American papers get wind of this, *if* it's true, of course," said Daphne unzipping her dress and struggling into her organza, "she will be in a lot of trouble with Middle American backlash."

"I don't understand," said Sabrina during the conversation as she threw on a faded denim shirt. "He's married to Edna. *She's* white, *he's* black, no one cares about that, so why should it be such a scandal if

Emerald sleeps with him? I mean DCOL: *Doesn't Count on Location,* right, Daphne? Isn't that what you told me once?"

"Absolutely," said Daphne breathing in for dear life and pressing her flesh over her rib cage as Freddy attempted to zip her into the new dress. "Dammit, Freddy, why did you make it so *tight?*"

"Duckie, face it, you've gained," said Freddy, patiently opening up the seam.

While Freddy worked, Daphne explained. "Edna is a, well, *proper* actress. I mean no one is really interested in what she does and with whom she does it. She could stand naked on the Empire State Building jerking off King Kong and it wouldn't even rate a mention in the trades, let alone the tabloids. She's too boring, too good, too mumsy. So the fact that she's married to a black director, even if he is only milk-chocolate-colored does *not* interest the public. Edna is Edna. Solid, dependable, dull. But Emerald is Emerald, and *everything* she does, even if she sends back an overdone steak at Hamburger Hamlet, is of enormous interest to the public because of her *charisma,* darling. . . . *Aaah,* that's better, Fred." Daphne breathed a sigh of relief as Freddy finally managed to do her up.

"Telephone, Meester Langlan." The maid came in tentatively, in awe of Sabrina's beauty and Daphne's assertiveness.

"Who is it? I'm busy." Freddy was fussing with the frills around Daphne's still appealing cleavage. Daphne was determined to outdo Lady Sarah in the frills department at next week's gala dinner in aid of cancer research. Her gown was an exact copy of the latest Zandra Rhodes.

"Eet's Meester Smeeth," the maid said hesitantly.

Daphne looked knowingly at Sabrina.

" 'Scuse me, dears, be right back." Freddy disappeared into his tiny cubicle of an office.

"Now you *know* who Mr. Smith is, don't you, darling?" Daphne said smugly.

"No," said Sabrina. She was wondering if she should take out a full-page ad in *Reporter* and *Variety* when the sequel to her college movie was released. Her press agent wanted her to, so did her agent, but her boring business manager said she couldn't afford it. What a drag. She was making over two hundred thousand a movie, and he said she couldn't *afford* a measly nine hundred bucks for an ad to enhance her flourishing career. Where did all her money go, for goodness' sake? she wondered. Nobody in Hollywood ever seemed to have the "fuck-you" money they craved.

Her rented furnished house at the beach cost three thousand a month, the cost of which she shared with Luis. Her car was leased. She had few good clothes; those she had were made by Freddy, who always gave her a good deal because she was the freshest, most beautiful of all his clients. Where *did* the money go? Her reverie was interrupted by Daphne's whispering, "If you don't know who Mr. Smith is—I shall tell you, dear."

Sabrina neither knew nor cared. Her interests were mainly limited to her career and Luis. Both were full-time jobs, especially Luis, who seemed distracted these days. They certainly weren't making love as often as they used to.

Daphne went on, "He's Sam Sharp, of course. They've been having a thing for *years*."

"Oh." Sabrina looked at Daphne, who was obviously pleased with imparting this bit of spice to one of the few who didn't know about it. "How interesting." Golly, she was bored by gossip.

"What's going on?" said Freddy to Sam, who almost never called during Freddy's work hours. They met, when possible, twice a month in Freddy's art deco-filled apartment above his shop.

"I haven't been feeling well, Freddy, and I'm working late. I can't make it tonight. Thought I'd let you know because we're on location and the damned cellular phone doesn't work when we get beyond a twenty-five-mile radius of L.A."

"Never mind, poppet," said Freddy, slightly relieved to be on his own tonight. Now he could meet that pretty young sailor who was on leave for a week, and who drank at the King's Head in Santa Monica every night. They had locked eyes a few times, and Freddy thought it time to move in before the others did. "Next Tuesday, O.K.?" Sam asked.

"Of course, luv."

"Later, then." Sam was terse on the phone. Terror at the possibility of his gay lifestyle being discovered became stronger with each passing year.

After Sam hung up on Freddy, he stretched and surveyed himself in the bathroom mirror of his luxurious trailer, which was now proceeding at a brisk clip down the Ventura freeway.

Not bad, not bad at all. He was fifty-three now, a vigorous, athletic, macho-looking fifty-three. If only he didn't feel so weak . . . maybe it was time for a checkup.

❦ *Twenty* ❧

"WHAT DO YOU THINK of them?" asked Emerald shakily. The emerald-and-gold bracelets winked on their dull black velvet bed.

"Beautiful, simply beautiful," Vanessa Vanderbilt breathed. "I must have them. How much?"

"Well, a bargain at thirteen thousand," Emerald said tentatively. "Don't you think?"

Thirteen thousand dollars. Vanessa mentally calculated the profit she could make from Emerald's bracelets. "Too much, luv. Nine thousand, take it or leave it."

And Emerald had to take it. It had been more than three years now since she had failed to get the role of Miranda. In that time things had gone from bad to worse. Everyone knew who she was, but as usual no one wanted to employ her. She still spent money as though it were 1957 and tried to live the way she had then.

But it wasn't 1957. She was no longer in her twenties and America's favorite sweetheart, with suitors galore, a lucrative contract and money to buy enough gems to fulfill all her girlhood fantasies.

It was 1985, and in spite of the face-lifts, the other plastic surgery and the celebrity, she was in big trouble.

The six films she had made in the past three years had been worse than B. They were F—F for Failure. Emerald would now go anywhere for a movie. Anywhere she would be paid at least twenty-five thousand, anywhere they would agree to pay for an expensive suite at the best hotel near the location, anywhere she would be assured of five hundred a week in expenses, anywhere she would get to keep her wardrobe.

She didn't care if the movie was good, bad or indifferent. She had to keep up her lifestyle; she could not drop her standard of living.

Although she had traded her Beverly Hills mansion for a smaller house, it was still a little jewel in the hills of Beverly. But it cost. It cost her every penny she made. Unable to cope alone, without a steady man in her life, she took solace in vodka. Lots of vodka. Vodka with orange juice in the morning, vodka with ice on the set in a water glass; then bottle after bottle of Dom Perignon throughout the afternoon and night, whether she worked or not. And then after dinner, 90 proof Armagnac. Her drinking pattern would make strong men reel.

As the movies got worse, she hid her pain with other substitutes. The occasional odd joint at first. Then the snort. The blessed white powder that gave her such a lift. That made her feel young, successful, full of life and love again. It was expensive, and she was now selling her jewelry to get it.

Vanessa Vanderbilt sounded tougher than she looked. Underneath her hard business exterior, she was generous and sympathetic. But dog will always eat dog, as Daddy had taught her. Only the most cunning survived in this world. There was no room for compassion in business. "There's a bunch of fuckin' barracudas out there, me luv!" Daddy had instilled this dogma in her from the time she was four. "Watch that little arse of yours *all* the time, darlin', otherwise the sharks will have it for their tea—mark my words."

Vanessa, dutiful daughter, did just that, soon becoming more cunning and manipulative in business than Daddy ever had. Oil-rich sheiks, Arab arms dealers, superstar entertainers, American politicians—Vanessa knew many, and she used them before they used her and abused her.

"Everyone's a user. Don't ever forget that, my little love," Daddy had said. "If they're not a user, then they're a loser, and you're bloody well better off not havin' doin's with 'em, darlin'." Thus spake Luke Higgins, the oracle of Petticoat Lane, as he cheerfully dispensed cockles and whelks from his stall every Sunday, worked in his secondhand furniture

shop Monday to Friday, and Saturday taught his brood of eager kids the facts of life. Every Saturday morning in his cluttered shop off Petticoat Lane, a stone's throw from the Elephant and Castle, where Vanessa attended the local comprehensive school, Luke Higgins wheeled and dealed. This enabled Vanessa to grow up not only knowing the value of a pound, but also that of a dollar, a yen, a franc and a ruble.

Perhaps "fence" was too strong a word for Luke, as he managed to stay a hair's breadth away from the law by dealing only in property stolen from another country. Interpol, although often hot on a scent, never managed to trace it to Luke, who was in his own words "a crafty bugger" who always looked out for number one. Possessing a streak of Robin Hood's philosophy, he was a good-looking cheerful chap, with ginger wavy hair, matching mustache, and rippling muscles in his wiry body, and he always gave the poorer of his clients a break when they needed to sell something legitimately. But to those from Italy, France and Germany who passed their stolen goods to him, he showed no mercy.

The jewelry, cameras and other objects he received were the fruits of petty thievery on the French Riviera or the ski resorts of Gstaad and St. Moritz—also minor baubles that ladies had not bothered to put into their safes when they locked away their forty-carat diamond rings and half-million-dollar diamond necklaces. This was daytime jewelry, fun jewels: gold chains, Cartier or Piaget watches, one-carat diamond earrings, the odd charm bracelet. So wealthy were these women that they usually didn't even report these losses to their insurance companies, since it would only increase their premiums. A five-thousand-dollar Bulgari gold chain can easily be replaced, so can a Cartier watch—and it's *so* much fun to do it.

Through Luke's capable hands had passed some up-market, not overly expensive merchandise, which he managed to dispense via dealers in the antique markets of Portobello Road, Bermondsey and Kensington.

Luke had an enjoyable life, a pretty Jamaican wife who adored him and didn't give him a lot of lip like some of those uppity black women from Nigeria and Uganda. In return, he was a good father, a good provider and an excellent teacher, and his four children learned well from him.

Vanessa broke away from the family fold at eighteen to become a model. Having seen photographs of a gloriously elegant Gloria Vanderbilt in American *Vogue,* and becoming intrigued with all that her family represented, she changed the name Higgins to Vanderbilt, Vera to Vanessa. Higgins was too evocative of the East End to suit the lifestyle she craved.

In the 1960s Vanessa, a bubbly cocktail of her father's red curls and Irish charm and her mother's warm brown Jamaican skin, black eyes and sweet personality, became a minor success as a model, but a major one on the London social circuit.

Modeling was soon behind her, as she accompanied princes, rogues and rock stars on their travels. A diamond earring here, a Buccellati bracelet there, mink coats and fox wraps galore, Vanessa was in heaven.

The Jet Set life was hers. Gloria Vanderbilt, watch out, she mused, here comes Vanessa Vanderbilt snapping at your heels.

She was courted and admired and made love to by wealthy and powerful men, but none of them ever fell in love with her. She sailed in their yachts, cruising in extravagant 180-foot vessels. She drove in their Ferraris, their stretch Mercedes, their antique Bentleys. She pocketed their crisp dollars, pounds, or francs and shopped—as much as her heart desired. Vanessa was desirable, an alluring toy for rich men to play with. Year after year she flaunted her pert café au lait body on luxury yachts in Portofino and Monte Carlo, basked by the pools in marbled villas in Marbella and Sardinia, grazed the boulevards of the Rive Gauche, Fifth Avenue and Rodeo Drive in search of ever more outrageous clothes to add to her vast wardrobe. She was a happy woman. So happy in fact that she celebrated this happiness with her favorite pastime—eating.

Vanessa would rather make a reservation than make love. Often during the act of love, she would think excitedly about the snack she would order after this tiresome tussle was finished. As the rich and powerful of the world buried their heads and their members in her fragrant alcoves, aroused by her moans of ecstasy, they never imagined that her lust was not for them, but for food.

Usually Vanessa kept a little snack next to whatever bed she happened to be occupying—perhaps a biscuit tin with a picture of the Queen on it, full of Mars Bars or Swiss milk chocolate, on which she would happily munch afterward, while her lover lay spent beside her. Soon, as she ripened like a watermelon in the noonday sun, she started to lose her lovers. The Americans went first, then went the English, then the French left. Soon the Italians and Germans lost interest, until eventually the only men left who desired her were Arabs.

Vanessa didn't care, so happy was she with her life of luxurious opulence and the friends she still had in abundance. Friends of both sexes adored her. She was fun, the first to make fun of herself, including her battle with the bulge.

In vain Vanessa tried to diet. Jane Fonda videotapes littered her rooms, but she had absolutely no willpower. She simply could not resist caviar with sour cream, veal chops with *pommes frites, mousse au chocolat,* everything delicious—not to mention the wines that accompanied her feasts and the liquor-filled chocolates, mints and savories that followed.

To her current beau, an Arab sheik, she was manna from Allah. A Western woman who loved to eat was as rare as teeth on a hen in London. Most of the "models" and starlets he entertained ate like birds. Vanessa was more than just a hearty eater. She matched him in gluttony.

"Another baby lamb," he would roar with delight as they squatted on the floor of his suite at the Dorchester Hotel, while his personal chef from Kuwait prepared delights from the Sinai desert, desserts the like of which could not be found in any cosmopolitan restaurant in the Western world.

Vanessa leaned her plump little cheek on Samir's big plump shoulder, and, spooning pâté into a piece of pita bread, popped it affectionately into his mouth. It was so wonderful. Such a wonderful life. Samir was so generous with money and presents, so attentive when she needed him—which was not often, as she was far happier eating and shopping. Unlike many Arabs, he had charm, manners and, thanks to a Harvard education, the cutest American accent.

Sex bored her, and she found "The French Way" positively repugnant. The only way she could tolerate it was to pretend she was eating an ice-cream cone. When Samir had to go to Kuwait, he left Vanessa in his permanent suite at the Dorchester with a generous supply of money and his company's American Express and Visa cards made out in her name.

She heard about his murder on breakfast television news in bed one morning as she devoured her fifth croissant with raspberry jam and Devonshire cream.

Things did not go well for Vanessa after that. Since she was not mentioned in Samir's will, his money and estate went to his three wives and eleven children in Kuwait. All that Vanessa possessed, apart from clothes and jewels, were two company credit cards. Her father's teachings having had good effect, she immediately went to the Bond Street antique shops and art galleries and bought as many objects of value as she could until the credit dried up. Although she still had a pretty face, Vanessa's weight now hovered around the 200-pound mark; she no longer appealed to any of the eligible rich or powerful men in London or Europe. They preferred their women sleek, like their boats, their planes and their automobiles. Pretty butterballs with cheerful personalities did not interest powerful, eligible men, not even as temporary arm decoration. For the occasional one-night stand, maybe—but most of the men of her acquaintance were not interested by Vanessa sexually at all.

Vanessa had to face the unhappy fact that her days of using her looks to earn a living were over.

She was thirty-two. She had enjoyed *La Dolce Vita* to the hilt. Now it was time to go legit.

She started selling her own jewelry and the paintings and objects she had acquired after Samir's death. She had an abundance of items from fourteen years of grateful donors. Her father gave her a few pieces and she started attending auctions and estate sales in England. She had a clever eye both for a bargain and a good jewel, and in three years she had built her traveling jewelry emporium into a lucrative business. Often she did business with many of the men she had bedded, and since she was such a likable and loyal friend, her business prospered, and now she was on a trip to L.A.

"Would you like the box?" Emerald asked Vanessa. Looking at the red leather Cartier container with the embossed gold edging, Vanessa nodded. "Yes, but I'll wear them," she said, scribbling a check. "I like them so much, I'm keeping them for myself—temporarily, that is."

Emerald looked longingly for the last time at her bracelets. She loved them. She adored all her jewels. If a man wasn't buying them for her, she bought them for herself. Now they were going. And no one, it seemed, would be buying any more for her. Ever.

٭   ٭   ٭

After selling her bracelets to Vanessa, Emerald headed for a bar she knew in West Hollywood. She ordered vodka stingers. Five in a row.

The barman looked at her curiously. She looked vaguely familiar, but he knew better than to engage in conversation anyone who obviously had a lot of problems in life. This woman looked as if she had more than most. Obviously she had been quite a looker in her day. Now the blond hair had gray roots and hung in uncombed snarls around a face devoid of makeup, but in which he could see vestiges of what might once have been aristocratic cheekbones, a sculptured nose and luscious lips. Her eyes were hidden behind tinted glasses, and she wore a shapeless tweed jacket and sweatpants that hid her body. On her feet were scuffed high-heels. She smoked Luckys, lighting each one from the last, rejecting offers of a light from the men who occasionally looked at her, perhaps catching the animal scent of her former glory. She stared straight ahead, barely moving except to lift the glass to her pale mouth.

Draining her fifth stinger, Emerald motioned shakily to the bartender for another.

"Lady, I think you've had enough, don't you?" The bartender tried to be kind. He had observed her coming back from the ladies' room. This broad could hardly walk.

"I'm fine. Give me another," she snapped.

"I can't, lady. I'm sorry."

"Screw you, buster!" snarled Emerald.

"Look, lady, there's a law in this town. I can't serve drinks to a person who's obviously had too many. I don't want to lose my license."

"Fuck your license," mumbled Emerald, getting up from her stool and lurching to the door. "Fuck your license and your crappy bar." She looked around the bar at the dozen men staring at her. None of them recognized her. "Fuck you, all you bastards," she exclaimed and, slamming the door, staggered onto Olympic Boulevard.

The next day, when she came to, she pulled herself together and went to visit Daphne Swanson.

"To be frank, love, I need a job—any job. I'm not proud. I'm down to my last few trinkets. I sold my favorite bracelets yesterday, the ones Stanley gave me for our wedding. You know how much he meant to me."

"I know, dear, I know. I remember it well, even though it was thirty years ago."

"Twenty-eight," said Emerald crossly. "And I *was* only twenty."

"Of course," Daphne agreed, smiling inwardly. Why did they all try and lop off the years when the town knew to the month what year they were born—and to the thousandth how many bucks they had in the bank?

"You know everything that's going on, Daphne. There must be *something,* somewhere, coming up that I would be right for. I mean, I *am* Hollywood royalty." She laughed lamely.

"I know, duckie, you were—I mean, of course you are," soothed Daphne. "But dear heart, you must realize that movie stars of your generation are, well, a bit *passé.*" She bit into a marron glacé, grimaced at the sweetness of it and fed it to the Pekingese nestled close to her on her pink down comforter.

Emerald bit a hangnail and lit up a Lucky Strike. God, she'd love a drink. She'd love a snort, too. What time was it? 11 A.M. Oh, well, it was 7 P.M. in London—cocktail time, civilized time. Her friends in Eaton Square and Chelsea would be drinking martinis now, or champagne.

"Do you want a drink, dear?" asked Daphne, reading her mind.

"Oh, I don't think so, yet . . . well, maybe just a Bloody Mary."

"I'll join you," said Daphne, graciously coming down to her level. "Then we'll have lunch at the Ivy. Burt Hogarth is lunching there today."

"What is Burt doing these days?" asked Emerald.

"Darling, *really!* I know you've been away, but don't you know anything that's going on in this town?"

"No," said Emerald vaguely. "I've been in Italy for the past five months, remember."

"You'd better wise up, dearie, or get off the merry-go-round," said Daphne, accepting the Bloody Mary from her maid. "This is 1985, dear. If you want to stay in this business, you better get into television fast, because *that* is where it's all happening today. Even Burt Hogarth knows that—that's why he's doing TV after all those hit movies."

Emerald drank her Bloody Mary, feeling the quick buzz vodka always gave her, the false sense of hope and optimism it inspired.

Daphne continued, "Burt Hogarth is producing a prestigious and *very* ambitious series, darling. Not the usual potboiler schlock. It's called 'America: The Early Years.' I think the title tells the story, dear. I know they are casting now, major names, darling, major. They've already signed Sir Geoffrey Fennel and Olivia Grosvenor from the National Theater—remember her Juliet? God, she was wonderful! But if Burt could see you, see how good you still look . . ."

In fact, Daphne didn't think Emerald looked good at all. The face-lift had not been much help, though her glamour was still there under the bloat, the bags and the gray roots. Having read the script, Daphne realized that actually Emerald might be a long shot for the part of Evelyn, the lusty, adventurous pioneer woman who comes from the old country to a new frontier town in the America of the 1880s. Against all odds she makes herself and the new town a force to be reckoned with throughout the nation. It was going to be the most important new series on prime time for the 1985–86 season—the most talked about series, in fact, since "Saga."

The fact that Burt Hogarth, film *Wunderkind,* was taking a temporary leave of absence from his dazzling film career as writer, producer and director of seven worldwide box-office blockbuster movies was a major and unprecedented event for television. Already all the rival networks were concerned enough about "America: The Early Years" to be approaching top talent from both film and theater to prepare projects to pit against it.

"So, shall we lunch or shall we not, dear?" Daphne asked. Emerald nodded. Daphne picked up the phone and made a reservation.

"Now go home and change into something glam and sexy, darling," Daphne instructed. "I'll meet you at one and you'll work your magic on Mr. Hogarth. He'll be entranced, I'm sure of it."

It hadn't worked out quite that way. Emerald had gone home and taken several Valium washed down with vodka to calm her nerves. In her muddled state, remembering Daphne's "glam and sexy, darling," she had chosen a highly unsuitable lime-green lace cocktail dress, too *décolleté*, too short, simply too much, in fact.

She was late, as usual, as she pulled up outside the Ivy, and instead of hitting the brake, her foot slipped onto the accelerator, smashing her Mercedes into the open door of Abby Arafat's brand-new maroon-and-black Rolls-Royce Corniche—all in full sight of the amused lunch bunch and a couple of cops.

When her agent, Eddie—she'd come back; he'd known she would—finally bailed her out, the media had a field day. Her secret life of drugs and booze was openly discussed in newspapers, on television and in every drawing room and office in Los Angeles. Tongues wagged, and what they said was not complimentary.

"You've fucked up royally, kiddo," said Eddie in no uncertain terms. "You have *blown* your career. No studio, no network, no producer will ever touch you now."

Emerald wept. She couldn't help it. Forty years of stardom! Is this how it ended? "I'm not a lush, Eddie, I'm not an addict either, you know I'm not," she sobbed into a lime-green hanky.

"Do I?" He looked cynical as he peered at her through his giant magnifying spectacles. "You certainly looked like one, kiddo, when I sprung you from that vile prison." He shuddered at the thought of seeing Emerald in her ridiculous short lace dress, facing the harsh California sunlight and the hordes of press and paparazzi. "You looked the pits, woman."

The photos had not been pretty. They had made the front pages of every tabloid from Tokyo to London—a weary, disillusioned, bloated and blowsy woman looking older than her fifty years. Over the hill. Used up. No use to anyone anymore.

Calvin had been in jail for nearly three years. Most prisoners doing time for possession of a deadly weapon were paroled sooner, but Calvin had blown his chance for that by his uncooperative behavior and attacking a guard who had tried to have sex with him. He sat in his cell and reread the article in the *American Informer* for the umpteenth time.

"As Chloe Carriere soars to superstardom on the hit prime time show 'Saga,' so the sad, once superstar, legendary actress Emerald Barrymore fights the twin battles of depression and dope. Picked up for drunken driving in Hollywood last month, the once-beautiful star is now practically destitute and unable to get a decent job in Tinseltown. How different would her life have been if *she* had won the coveted role of Miranda? Chloe Carriere now queens it in Hollywood while Emerald Barrymore is a broken woman."

His Emerald. *His* beautiful, indestructible Emerald, was being ruined by this English bitch! He looked at the calendar again. The date was engraved on his memory. April 24, 1987. That was the day he finally would be paroled. That was the day the bitch would die!

Burt Hogarth studied the clippings his assistant had placed on his desk.

Certainly the woman looked awful. In that short low-cut dress she looked ridiculous. Booze and drugs had finally caught up with her as they do with everyone who abuses them. Her skin was stretched too tightly across her neck, and her cheeks were bloated, but there was an undeniable strength beneath the vulnerability there—a softness underneath the tacky veneer that appealed to him. "Let's test her," he said to his assistant.

"*Test* her!" The young man looked at Burt in amazement. "You can't *test* Emerald Barrymore, she's a superstar—a legend in her lifetime, even if she's the town joke this week."

"She tested for 'Saga,' didn't she?" Burt knew his Hollywood like a great white hunter knows the plains of Africa. " 'Saga' is schlock, we know that, but she wanted it. Badly, I hear. That was three years ago, and she's done nothing decent since. From what I hear she's hungry."

"Maybe we should take a look at that 'Saga' test?"

"No. I want to shoot my own. As far as I'm concerned, Emerald Barrymore is an over-the-hill aging *ex*-star who *could* be right for this role, and if she is, it will be the best thing that happened to her since Rin-Tin-Tin rescued her from the train track. So get her fucking agent on the phone and set up the test. The network is trying to ram Angie Dickinson down my throat, but as much as I like Angie, she's not right. So we test Miss Barrymore, and hope for the best."

"*Another* test! Oh, Eddie, why? I mean, I've made fifty-two fucking films for Christ's sake. I tested for 'Saga' and lost. Can't they look at *that* test?"

"No, kiddo," Eddie said coldly, looking straight at her. He was tough with his clients when they got out of line; hence they respected him all the more. Apart from Emerald no client had ever left him, was his boast, but he had dropped several.

"The 'Saga' test was over three years ago, dear. Hollywood has a short memory. As far as the network shooting 'America' is concerned, you are a convicted drug addict and a drunk."

"No, Eddie, that's not true!" cried Emerald.

"It's the truth that hurts, kiddo. Face it, my dear, you were the family favorite of the forties, the flavor of the decade of the fifties, the sexpot of the sixties and seventies. But it's 1985 now. You've been around a long time. It's time to get your act together or get out of the rat race."

"I love this business. It's my *life*," cried Emerald.

"Good. Then test," said Eddie bluntly. "Test and you'll get the part. Trust me." The tiny man suddenly smiled a rare smile. "The ironic part, kiddo, is that the network is throwing all of its biggest guns into 'America,' they are going to pit it head to head against 'Saga' next season. They're sick and tired of having 'Saga' the number one prime time show week after week. This is war, toots, total war."

"I've always loved a battle." Emerald smiled, beginning to feel more like her old self.

"I know you do, duchess, and one of the things that is going to make this battle even more interesting is that if the series succeeds—which it will, of course—you will be Chloe Carriere's main rival on television. 'The Battle of the Bitches!' I can see the headlines now." His elderly eyes twinkled mischievously behind the huge glasses.

"I thought you adored Chloe, Eddie."

"Of course, kiddo. I *do* adore her. She's my friend even if she isn't my client. She's made it big, and it hasn't changed her. I wish she could be happier in her personal life, though. I think she's still carrying an ember for her ex. That's the trouble with all you girls." He looked scoldingly at Emerald. "Unless you have a man in your life, you don't seem to be complete." Emerald shrugged. "But competition is healthy, kid. Makes the juices flow. Emerald Barrymore versus Chloe Carriere. For this event *I* want to have a front row seat. And so will the public, I guarantee it."

◀ *Twenty-one* ▶

CHLOE AWOKE AT SIX o'clock. It was still dark outside, and "cold and damp," as Lena Horne sang it was in California. She staggered down to the kitchen to make a strong cup of Nescafé with three teaspoons of honey for energy. She showered, jumped into jeans, T-shirt, shirt, sweater, jacket, scarf and woolly hat. Despite what the world thinks, it really is *icy* in California in the early hours. Since the temperature changed from forty to eighty-five degrees during the day, she always dressed in layers.

The teamster driver waited for her in the minibus for the seventeen-minute drive to the studio. While he drove, she tried to study the scenes for the day, a total of eleven pages of dialogue—mostly a diatribe by Miranda.

After more than three years, the dialogue had begun to bear a dreadful similarity to the dialogue of last week's episode, and those of the weeks and months before. The actors seldom changed, the sets didn't change, only the costumes were different, which represented the only proof that this was another episode. In her tiny shoe box of a trailer, identical to those of the other ten actors, the makeup man had laid out the tools of his trade. The trainee A.D. brought her another cup of coffee. She turned her radio to FM KJLH (Kindness, Joy, Love, and Happiness—*the* survival station) and to the songs of Al Jarreau and Lionel Richie and applied her makeup while studying lines, drinking coffee and eating an orange.

At 7 A.M. Debbie, the second assistant director, summoned her to the set. Half made up, hair in rollers, script in hand, lines still fuzzy and only half-learned, she, with Sissy and Sam, blocked the first scene of the day.

Then it was panic and rush to finish hair and makeup and run lines with Ostie, the dialogue coach.

Trixie, the wardrobe assistant, entered the trailer carrying six outfits in plastic hanger bags and a large Neiman-Marcus shopping bag full of shoes and purses.

"Rudolpho thinks you should wear the black, but the director says that the set's too dark and you'll fade into the woodwork, so I brought the red for the first scene, hon."

"O.K." Chloe squinted at her face in the three-way mirror. Losing a pound or two wouldn't hurt. Weight always went straight to her face, and then her cheekbones disappeared.

"What do you want for lunch?" Debbie popped her head in the door. Chloe grimaced. Lunch! How could she know at 7 A.M. what would titillate her at one in the afternoon?

"Give me a tuna on rye and apple juice, darling," she said, turning to Trixie, who was rummaging through a four-foot-high black chest of drawers—Miranda's jewel box—which stood on the floor.

Pearls, diamonds, rubies, emeralds and gold baubles trickled through her fingers.

"I think the Chanel pearls would look hot with this outfit," said Trixie, critically laying them on the elegant suit. "Or do you want to wear that Kenneth Lane gold chain?" "Anything you say, luv," agreed Chloe. She trusted Trixie's excellent taste in accessorizing the nine or ten outfits she had to wear each week.

"How about the Givenchy earrings? They look fabulous."

"Don't you think they're too big?" said Chloe distractedly, working on her lashes.

"Hon, nothin's too big for 'Saga,' surely you know that!"

After Chloe put on the tight red suit, Trixie stood back surveying her handiwork and tugged at Chloe's skirt, which was beginning to feel uncomfortably binding around her waist.

"Got a little extra there today, huh?" Trixie was used to her female stars' fluctuations in weight. Even two pounds made a difference when each outfit was fitted like another skin.

"Thanks, darling. You're not exactly Twiggy today either." They smiled at each other, used to the banter that kept them sane at 7 A.M.

Chloe bumped into Pandora on the short walk to Stage 2. Pandora was wearing a gray flannel Thierry Mugler suit, the shoulders of which were so exaggerated that she looked like a football player. Her red wig was styled in a 1940s page-boy, and she wore fuchsia lip gloss and gold eye shadow. She looked hard and chic.

"Hi, there What did you think of the show last night?"

Pandora was a friendly soul with no ax to grind with anyone. She was no great shakes as an actress, but she was sweet and professional, and knew that she was lucky to be pulling down twenty-five grand an episode in one of the hottest shows on prime time.

"I thought your courtroom scene was excellent—really good." Chloe never praised unless she meant it.

"Thanks, honey, it was a well-written scene. What did you think of *her?*" She gestured toward Sissy, already sitting upright in her director's chair, Kleenex folded down the neck of her turquoise suede dress, smoking the first of her eternal cigarettes through a holder and dispensing a stream of invective to all who came her way. "Watch out, someone got out of bed on the wrong side today," Pandora said.

"What else is new?" Chloe laughed.

Sam stood on the set sipping coffee from a Styrofoam cup and chatting to the crew. He was popular with all of them, making genuine efforts to communicate, to joke, trying to make up for the bitchiness of his wife. The crew felt sorry for him. "No wonder he's a fruit," Maxie, the teamster, muttered to Chloe one day. "With a cow like that for a wife, I'd like boys too."

Like everyone else, Chloe despised Sissy and adored Sam. She gave him a peck on his heavily made up cheek, which was becoming alarmingly thin these days, she noticed.

He was not looking well. His normally luxurious brown mustache looked unkempt and bedraggled. The thick brown toupee he always wore looked strange and lopsided, as though it was too big for him. Maybe it was because he was in pajamas and a dressing gown and made up to look ill that he didn't look good. They were shooting a scene in which Sam/Steve was in a coma in a hospital bed, while his three wives, one current and two ex, stood around his bed willing him to live.

"Here's your coffee, darling."

"Hi, Vanessa." Chloe smiled at her new personal assistant.

Since stardom had been hard to handle with just a secretary, she had started to look around for a personal assistant to help her with the hundreds of requests for interviews and personal appearances, to sift through the thousands of pieces of fan mail and to read some of the torrent of scripts that were sent.

Vanessa Vanderbilt had become vaguely bored with her jewelry business. Fine jewels at the price she could afford to pay were not easily available these days, and Vanessa had been looking around for something more stimulating. One day she and Chloe had found themselves seated next to each other on a flight from London after one of Chloe's visits with Annabel. Chloe complimented Vanessa on her beautiful emerald-and-diamond bracelets, and Vanessa replied that they were for sale. Surprised and thrilled, Chloe wrote out a check for twelve thousand dollars, in defiance of her business manager, and slipped Emerald's lovely jewels on her wrists. The two women toasted the transaction with champagne, and after the third glass started to let their hair down. They discovered they had tremendous rapport. They laughed, told intimate stories of their lives, and found they were soul sisters. Before the plane landed, Vanessa had agreed to a trial run of three months as Chloe's personal assistant. So far it had been a success. The two women got along like a house on fire, much to the envy of Sissy, who could never bear to see happy business relationships around her, particularly between two women. She was unable to keep any assistant, and few of her domestic staff, longer than a few months.

"O.K., let's try a rehearsal," called Ned, the first A.D.

The four actors walked onto the "Saga" set. Sam stripped off his dressing gown and gratefully lay down in the bed. Thank God he had nothing to do in this scene except groan. He felt he could do that realistically enough. Last night had been ghastly. Sissy had been in one of her more vile moods. Her jealousy of Chloe was fueled each day by various items in magazines or gossip columns. Last night her fury was released when she read the piece in Army Archerd: "Chloe Carriere's career goes from strength to strength. The hottest female on TV has been signed to produce and star in her own miniseries 'Ecstasy' in conjunction with Hammersmith Productions. Shooting will commence in London and Madrid during Chloe Carriere's third hiatus from 'Saga.' "

"Damn that woman!" Sam barely had the strength to duck as Sissy threw the trade paper across the room with such force that the tropical fish swimming lazily in their five-thousand-dollar aquarium, tastefully set into the polished granite above the authentic wood-burning fireplace, hastily disappeared behind their painted rocks.

"Damn that bitch. *Why*, why does she get her own fucking miniseries? What's *wrong* with my agent?" she railed, pouring a generous shot of Smirnoff into a Lalique tumbler.

Sam lay on a tan leather sofa quietly trying to watch a video of a John Wayne movie and feeling weak and ill.

Now Sam lay in a hospital bed on Stage 2, feeling worse. During a break in the shooting the three women couldn't stop talking about an item in today's Army Archerd column about "America: The Early Years." The columnist waxed enthusiastic about the new prime time series and the excitement in the industry about Burt Hogarth's masterminding of it.

"I heard he was interested in Emerald Barrymore for Evelyn," said Pandora, tolerating having Theo comb out her red wig for the umpteenth time.

"Really!" sneered Sissy, dragging on her cigarette holder. Her brown birdlike hands were tipped by scarlet claws that matched the slash of her thin lips. "Are they going to be able to get her out of bed and off the bottle long enough to get her in front of the cameras?" She laughed maliciously.

Pandora and Chloe ignored the remark, but Sam managed a weak smile. He was not feeling good. He *must* find time for that checkup.

"Now, now, honey," he remonstrated to his wife. "You know Emerald's had a run of bad luck. Let's hope she gets that part. She's a nice gal. She needs it."

Hmmm, Sissy calculated to herself, if Emerald *did* get it, there might be some advantages. Emerald might knock that snotty British bitch off the front pages and the magazine covers. Chloe's success was beginning to become more of an irritant every day. Chloe was becoming an obsession with Sissy. An obsession of hate. Only one person felt that hate more strongly.

Calvin lay on a rough gray blanket in his cell trying not to listen to the disgusting conversation of his cellmates. They were talking about sex as usual. That was all they ever talked about. Occasionally baseball or football was discussed, now and again a new inmate would cause a brief flurry of interest, but basically every man in that jail was obsessed by one subject. Sex.

Calvin's cellmates were discussing in intimate detail the merits of the current *Penthouse* pinup. The woman's legs were spread wide, showing a view only a gynecologist usually saw. The men were turned on. Calvin knew what would happen next. After three years he knew only too well. They would do things to each other, pretending it was the woman in *Penthouse*. Sometimes they would do it to Calvin, even if he resisted. He knew that. It had happened the first day he arrived in this jail. With sickening regularity it had continued. Calvin was not classically handsome, but he was reasonably young, had fair skin and a firm body. The rest, the men's imaginations took care of.

Prison was a seething cauldron of the suppressed sexual desires of nine hundred potent men cooped up in the prime of their life with nothing to do except fantasize about sex.

Calvin tried to feign sleep but it was no good. Kolinsky, the big twenty-three-year-old Pole with the dark hair, bad teeth and huge thing, came over to him.

"C'mon now, Calvin, old buddy. Time to have a good time with yer ole friend here."

Calvin knew if he rebelled he would get beaten. The guards turned a blind eye. Sometimes they themselves sampled some of the tastier young "virgins" first. As he braced himself for Kolinsky's onslaught, he blanked out his mind until all he could think about was his hatred for Chloe Carriere, how she was to blame for this, and that he had only fifteen more months of this horror.

◆ *Twenty-two* ◆

SINCE HER FINAL SPLIT with Josh, Chloe's love life had become a topic of great interest to the supermarket tabloids and gossip columns, and they printed every bit of dirt they could on her.

More than a casual chat with a man at a party, and she was reported to be having an affair with him. More than two dates with the same man, and she was engaged. More than six, and elopement and marriage were imminent. Since her split with Josh she hadn't been serious about anyone. She and Johnny spent the occasional night together now and then and dated on and off, but it was not a deep relationship. He had plenty of women on his string. With the AIDS threat hovering uneasily on the horizon, she was not about to risk her life for a casual encounter, however attractive that encounter might be. Three years of stardom and celebrity were beginning to take their toll. She was becoming snappy, irritable and uninterested in anything except "Saga."

"You need a man, dearie," observed Daphne at lunch one day. "A *good man.*"

"Yeah, and they're hard to find around these parts," Vanessa added.

Chloe, tight-lipped, was drinking Perrier on the rocks and picking at her cuticles.

Daphne was insistent. "You don't look happy."

"I don't need a *man* to make me happy," snapped Chloe, lighting a cigarette and wearily signing another autograph.

The table at which she sat with Daphne and Vanessa was in a corner of the studio commissary, but it was still the focus of all eyes. Fans came in droves to do the studio tour. The top draw was a visit to the "Saga" set. It didn't matter that the actors were filming scenes that required concentration. Abby and Gertrude, realizing they had a gold mine in "Saga," allowed tourists to roam free on the lot and provided a friendly studio tour guide to accompany them.

"You know, Vanessa, I don't mean to be paranoid but do you see that woman with the Instamatic over there?" Chloe said. Vanessa looked over to where a nondescript woman, dressed in a drab gabardine pants suit, sat looking around the commissary, her eyes too often returning to Chloe.

"What about her?" asked Vanessa.

"She gives me the creeps. I *swear* she's press. I've seen her here several times. She was even lurking on the set listening to me talk to Annabel on the phone last week."

"You're joking?" Vanessa was alarmed. She was very protective of Chloe.

"No. She was hanging around by the coffee machines chatting with the craft service guys and the teamsters. I thought she was a hairdresser from the cop show on the next sound stage; then I saw her make notes in a book. Check her out, Van."

"O.K., Boss Lady," said Vanessa. She glanced at the woman, who looked away quickly. Chloe was right. She did look like press. British press, too, probably from one of the scummier daily rags.

Magazines and tabloids had now printed every major and minor detail of Chloe's past life ad nauseam. They had interviewed her school friends, teachers and co-workers. Rick, her old lover from her provincial touring days, had sold his "kiss and tell" memoirs of their "stormy affair" to the *Sun*, and reporters constantly called Richard, Susan *and* Annabel for any scraps of trivia on Britain's by now most famous actress. Chloe lived in terror of the press's discovering that Annabel was really her daughter. One of the gutter tabloids had gone to Somerset House, the British register of births and deaths, and had printed her birth certificate, so that none of its readers could have any doubt how old she was. What was to stop them from snooping around and finding out that on January 15, 1964, a baby girl, father unknown, mother, Chloe Carriere, age twenty-one, occupation singer, had been born in a nursing home in Plymouth? Chloe had nightmares about how it would affect Annabel's life.

She hated the fact she was becoming cynical and paranoid, but the relentless onslaught on her personal life, by both the media and the fans, had clouded her normally sunny disposition. The work was hard. Just the act of keeping her hair, makeup and clothes pristine twelve hours a day, while the crew sweated in T-shirts and sneakers, was an effort.

It was tiring to smile all the time at the fifty or sixty visitors a day who plucked up courage to speak to the Queen Bitch in person. God forbid she slough one off. Every fan lost was multiplied a hundredfold in viewing audiences, scolded Gertrude. "Offend one fan, and they'll tell ten friends who'll tell ten more."

"Be nice to them on the way up," warned Jasper. "You may be the flavor of the month now, but they'll all be there waiting on the way down —and there *will* be a way down, luv. That's for sure. Every actor has his shelf life. With some—the Cary Grants, the Katharine Hepburns—it's fifty years or more. With others—*especially* TV stars—it can be fifty months, or weeks, even days. The public is . . ."

"Fickle! I know, Jasper. You've told me a million times. I *know* they are."

"Good girl. Remember it now. Don't become bigheaded."

"I won't," she almost screamed. "I'm just trying to be *me*."

She had no time for men in her life. On a rare day off she was involved in interviews and photograph sessions. And fittings with Trixie and Rudolpho took hours of thought and concentration. She had to know lines, have script conferences, have a weekly manicure and pedicure, she had to exercise regularly, she had to have facials, keep up with current fashion trends. All in all, there wasn't enough time in the day even to read a newspaper or get a decent night's sleep, let alone get involved with a man.

"If only the public realized what a bloody grind this so-called glamour job is," sighed Chloe, acknowledging the signal from Ned that her fifty minutes for lunch was up.

Lunch gave her indigestion. Everything was always rush, rush, rush. By the time she left the set, exchanged the beaded décolleté gown or some other fashionable outfit for a track suit, walked to the commissary, waited for a tuna salad and Perrier to arrive, exchanged a few stories with Vanessa and Daphne, who sometimes came by, it was time to return to the set. "Heigh ho, heigh ho, it's off to work we go. Just like the seven dwarfs." Vanessa laughed.

"I think, dear, you need a man, for therapeutic reasons if nothing else, and I happen to know just the one. Perfect for you, and *very* handsome, darling." Daphne never let up; she kept pushing the subject each time they had lunch together.

Vanessa giggled. She adored romance and intrigue. "Who is he, any-one we know? I'd like her to get laid too. She's becoming a pain in the neck to me." Vanessa smiled at Chloe teasingly. She adored her, even though they sometimes clashed. And Vanessa had become indispensable to Chloe for social arrangements, business meetings, clothes problems. Vanessa was Chloe's confidante and doer—a far cry from her days as an Arab potentate's mistress, but more interesting, certainly.

"Laid! What's that? I can't remember that experience. Isn't it some-thing mortals do?"

"Next Saturday night, darling, dinner *chez moi*." Daphne loved playing Cupid. "This man is French, and he is seriously sexy."

"Oh, an import!" Vanessa beamed at Chloe. "Someone who hasn't fucked all your friends. Ain't *that* good news?"

Chloe recognized him as soon as he walked into Daphne's living room. Although she hadn't thought about him in more than three years, she remembered the chemistry she had felt that awful night in Vegas. She shuddered. She still had nightmares about it.

Philippe Archambaud smiled his Alain Delon smile, revealing perfect teeth. He looked romantically Continental in a dark blue suit and a con-servative tie, in sharp contrast to Daphne's beau, Richard Hurrel, who was a sartorial disaster in a cyclamen blazer with matching ascot, and to Luis Mendoza, who hadn't really bothered, because when every woman in America wants your body, all you need is a black silk shirt, tight white pants, and a tan. Philippe was handsome, tall, with brown wavy hair, dazzling eyes. He was also quiet. Not your actual comedian, thought Chloe, having sat through his rather pedantic discourse on French poli-tics during dinner.

She remembered Josh's colorful English charm—how he had en-tranced her with his wit and humor. There had been so much passion and togetherness between them in the first seven or eight years. Where had it gone wrong? Why? Forget about it. She pushed those thoughts from her mind and concentrated on Philippe. Yes, he was extremely handsome. Yes, he was exceptionally charming. Yes, he certainly paid her attention and was very flattering. And why should he not be? She was at this moment the biggest female star on TV. For how long, of course, no one could predict. . . .

"When can I see you again, Chloe?" Philippe's hand traced a tiny path down her spine. She suddenly felt the remembered stirrings of desire—absent now for so many months. "Tomorrow?" His eyes—what color were they? Gray? Green? Blue? Chameleon eyes—they sent a clear message of ardor. In spite of herself she was interested.

"Well, tomorrow is Sunday. I have *tons* of dialogue to learn, a new script to study, and . . ."

"Darling!" Vanessa interrupted, reddish curls bouncing, cleavage brimming over her creamy antique lace blouse. "*No* excuses, I think you should take him to the beach house," she whispered through gritted teeth, her tiny satin pumps giving Chloe a sharp dig in her shin.

"And Richard and I will come too. Don't *worry,*" said Daphne joining in as she saw Chloe start to demur. "I know you don't have staff on Sunday and you *hate* to cook. Richard will stop at Nate 'n' Al's tomorrow and get their Scottish smoked salmon, bagels and cream cheese. We'll have a picnic on the beach. Won't that be fun, dear? Just like England."

Richard groaned. At sixty-five he felt a mite too old for picnics on the beach, let alone hopping down to Nate 'n' Al's on Sunday with the Beverly Hills jet-setters. But Daphne was the boss in their relationship, so he tried to muster a smile.

"All right," said Chloe, seeing Vanessa's enormous grin. "We'll *all* have a picnic."

"With champagne!" Daphne added.

"*Naturellement,*" Philippe said with a smile that was definitely beginning to affect Chloe. "I will bring it."

"Dom Perignon," Vanessa warned. "One *only* drinks D.P. on a picnic."

"Of course, it will be my pleasure." He bowed slightly, his eyes not leaving Chloe's.

Here we go again, she thought.

It was a short, fast courtship. Philippe's physical charms captured Chloe so quickly she didn't know what had hit her. For a woman who had always insisted on wit and conversation in her relationships with men, suddenly it didn't seem to matter this time.

They started seeing each other every weekend, then every other night, then every night. Soon he had moved many of his things into Chloe's houses at the beach and in Beverly Hills. After a couple of months they decided it was foolish for him to waste money renting an apartment he hardly used, and he moved in.

Philippe still wrote stories for *Paris Match, Jour de France* and an occasional article for *Oggi* or *Tempo.* That kept him reasonably busy during the day. Since he was good with figures and a dab hand at analyzing the stock market, Chloe let him invest some of her money. He did so well and made her such consistent profits in the market that finally she fired her business manager and let Philippe handle her finances full time.

"Darling, he *is* adorable, but he is, well . . ." Vanessa tried to warn her friend a few weeks after her whirlwind affair with Philippe had begun.

"Dull? Boring? Opinionated?" Chloe laughed. "I *know*, Vanessa. I'm not so stupid. I realize that he isn't Einstein. I don't know what it is—he seems to have my number, though." She thought of last night and the passion they had shared until she had wearily risen at five to leave for the studio.

"Well, whatever it is he's doing to you, it seems to be doing you good," said Vanessa. "You haven't looked so well in a long time."

Chloe blushed. Her nights, mornings and afternoons with Philippe had been amazing. The man was a fountain of energy. When he wasn't making love, he wanted to hold her in his arms, stroke her hair and tell her how wonderful she was. It was unusual for a man of thirty-nine to be so openly affectionate. And Chloe *liked* it, and liked him. More and more.

She still thought about Josh. Occasionally he phoned her from England or wherever he was. The first play he had done had been a disaster. Then he had disappeared for a year, and she had no idea where. One rumor was that he had emigrated to Australia, another that he was living with a pair of seventeen-year-old twins. Writing music. Entertaining in piano bars, men's clubs. Finally, out of the blue he'd called her.

"Hello, Chloe, my little love. How are you?"

She couldn't believe the way her heart still fluttered when she heard his voice. Like a stupid schoolgirl, she scolded herself, after their short but sweet conversation.

He told her he'd been working in Australia, touring the outback. There was no mention of teenage twins. And she didn't ask. He was working on cruise ships now. It was fun, he said. He had a lot of fans still. Middle-aged matrons and their paunchy consorts who remembered the young Joshua Brown of the 1960s. Remembered his songs. Gave him the applause he craved. He was off to sing his way around the Caribbean for the next few months on another cruise ship.

"Is it really fun?" Chloe had asked, feeling in some bizarre way guilty about her own immense success and his slide down the ladder. "Are you enjoying it, Josh?"

"Sure, it's great," he lied. "All the fun of the fair, darlin'. Lots of booze, lots of laughs, lots of birds." Chloe couldn't suppress a wince. The thought of Josh with another woman in his arms still gave her a jolt.

"Hopeless! You're *hopelessly* old-fashioned and out of date," said Vanessa after Chloe recounted her conversation with Josh. "I don't think you really know anything about men, do you, Chloe?"

Vanessa, having spent eighteen years studying them, was somewhat of an expert and was often amazed by Chloe's romantic naiveté.

Chloe changed the subject. Talking to Josh had rattled her. She wanted to hear from him again. Their divorce still wasn't final. It had been dragging on for two years now. Her lawyer kept trying to get her to sign the final papers. Then, when Josh disappeared, even his own lawyer couldn't find him.

Philippe was now pushing Chloe to get the divorce finalized. He wanted to marry her, but Chloe wasn't at all sure. She was mad about Philippe physically; it was almost as if he had put a spell on her. But the communication she'd shared with Josh was missing.

Perhaps she expected too much, she told herself, as she drove down drab Pico Boulevard to MCPC Studios. Oh, well, you can't have it all. You can. You can. You can, her inner voice whispered back. You *can* have it all, Chloe. You can and you *should*.

"Saga's" success had been so immense and extraordinary that every TV company and network had jumped on the bandwagon to imitate it. One rival network had put out an imitation, "Abraham's Family," a near-clone of "Saga," another had tried with "Arizona Empire," but both had fluttered briefly and then expired.

"Imitation is *still* the sincerest form of flattery," beamed Gertrude at a meeting with a worried Abby. "We have nothing to fear, Abby. Just look at our ratings." She was right. "Saga" had consistently been one of the top five shows for the past four seasons. Saga clothes, Saga jewelry, Saga dolls, Miranda and Sirope dressed in tiny facsimiles of Rudolpho's beaded gowns, were everywhere. The world was aglow with Sagamania. The world loved Chloe and Sissy. And Sam and Pandora. They loved them all. Saga bedspreads, plates, candles, shoes, blouses and ties—department stores bulged with them.

"About the only goddamn things they haven't put the Saga name on are condoms," laughed Pandora to Chloe on the set as Christopher, the diminutive public relations man, approached Chloe with the blueprint of the new advertisement for two Saga perfumes she, along with Sissy, would endorse.

One would be called "Wicked" and feature Chloe looking provocative on the package. The other would be called "Woman," and would feature Sissy looking as warm and sincere as her talent would allow.

In the four years the show had been running, Sissy had indulged in two mini face-lifts, one eye job and a breast implant. She still dieted relentlessly and looked like a hawk in real life, but she was a good enough actress to breathe life into the saccharine role of Sirope. She personified Mother Earth: sweet, long-suffering and kind, putting up with the problems of her TV children and the machinations of her TV husband's ex-wives. Chloe, on the other hand, personified the wicked, manipulating, sex-hungry bitch.

The public had taken the two women to their hearts, never quite sure if they were in reality the characters they played on the screen.

"You're sitting in my chair," snapped Sissy to Chloe. "Oh, sorry," said Chloe eying the three empty canvas chairs that Sissy could have parked her scrawny behind on if she had chosen.

What Sissy did choose to do was to needle Chloe and the rest of the cast at every possible opportunity. With her newfound success, she had become impossible. Even faithful Sam, who had been loyal to her for years, found it hard to swallow her arrogance. She was rude to the crew, who loathed her. She was envious and spiteful to the cast, refusing to rehearse, abusing any actor who forgot his dialogue, and never deigning to read off-camera lines even for Sam. She hassled the producer to get better story lines for herself, she changed her dialogue constantly, confusing the other actors, and then became furious with them because they couldn't understand what she was doing.

Recently she had started snorting a line of coke first thing in the morning to get her through the tedious days, another line at lunchtime, and one more halfway through the afternoon. At home each night she complained bitterly to Sam about the fact that the lighting cameraman preferred Chloe and Pandora to her, that the director was an untalented ruffian, her trailer not as big as Sam's. Sissy overreacted to the merest slight. Cocaine was turning her into a paranoid schizophrenic. If the public that admired her so much had known the truth, she would have been standing in the unemployment line on Sunset Boulevard.

"So what do you think of the new script?"

Chloe was surprised Sissy bothered to ask her opinion. She never had before. "It's O.K. What do you think?"

"Trash, fucking trash. They keep writing like this, we'll be off the air next season." Sissy was nervously running her fingers up and down her satin-clad thigh. "Doris, bring me a cup of coffee—for Christ's sake, *hurry up.*"

Chloe felt sorry for Sissy. She couldn't really hate a woman whose insecurities were so obvious, and she often defended her while the rest of the cast tore her to pieces and mocked her. It didn't really help, because Sissy hated Chloe more than anyone else in the show.

If Chloe made the front page of *USA Today,* Sissy would scream at the network public relations people until they got the same coverage for her. In fact, the women got an equal number of national magazine covers. With a show as hot as "Saga," the magazines knew a good way to sell copies was to put Sissy, Chloe or Pandora on the cover.

"Oh, did you see this?" Sissy had a glint in her eye as she passed Chloe the latest copy of the *American Informer.*

"CHLOE CARRIERE IN LOVE CHILD MYSTERY," the headline blazed.

Chloe almost fainted when she read it. She pretended a casual glance, aware of Sissy watching her with a glint in her eye.

"Interesting, isn't it?" Sissy smiled her cobra smile. "Any truth to it, Chloe *darling?*" She attempted a confidential girl-talk tone, which Chloe found even more offensive than her bitchy needling. "You can tell *me.*" She leaned closer and Chloe saw the deep crow's-feet under her eyes and around her lips that even three face-lifts hadn't managed to erase.

"The usual pack of lies, Sissy—you know that." She couldn't resist a dig. "You remember the story they had about Sam being gay a few months ago? Ridiculous, isn't it?"

Sissy's jaws clamped shut and her flat gray eyes gave up their pretense of charm. "Doris, where's that fucking coffee, for Christ's sake. Hurry it up."

Chloe moved away. The story she had dreaded had finally appeared. She saw Sissy display the tabloid's cover with waspish glee to several of the crew and groaned inwardly.

At home Chloe studied the tabloid article with mounting horror.

"Secret Love Child Chloe Hasn't Seen In 20 Years," blared the headline. "Chloe Carriere—superstar of the soap opera 'Saga'—has a secret that will haunt her to her grave. Twenty-one years ago she gave birth to an illegitimate child. The *Informer* can exclusively reveal that this young girl, Annabel, lives happily in the English countryside with Chloe's brother, Richard, and his wife, Susan, unaware that her real mother is television's most famous bitch."

"Oh, my God—Annabel!" She threw the offending scandal sheet onto the floor and picked up the phone with a shaking hand.

"Hello, Daphne—Daphne, darling, I didn't wake you, did I?"

"No, no, of course not, dear, I'm wide awake. What's happening in your life?" Daphne pushed Richard aside, and brought out the tape recorder she kept next to the bed.

It was not often that she received a call for help from Chloe. Chloe received so much unfavorable personal publicity that she rarely bothered to do anything about it except shrug it off.

"Have you read the *Informer* yet?" Chloe asked desperately.

"Yes, dear, I have."

"It's a bunch of lies, Daphne, you *know* that."

"Of course I do, dear. Everyone in town who reads that revolting garbage knows it." But they love it, Daphne thought, *everyone* reads it at their executive desks, at their hairdressers', or borrows it from their maid, avidly reading the lies and innuendo about everyone else. "Stop it, Richard," she hissed. Being rejected had excited him more than usual, and he was exploring Daphne's abundant thighs with his tongue.

"Daphne, people are actually beginning to believe all that stuff about me being a bitch. I don't mind that, but this story is terribly upsetting for my niece."

"I know, dear, I know it's a pack of lies. Ignore it, you're bigger than all of them, don't you ever forget it."

"I always ignore it—maybe that's the trouble."

"So what can an old friend do, dear?" said Daphne, having slapped Richard away and tried to settle him comfortably in the crook of her arm like a big floppy doll.

"Tell them to print a retraction as soon as possible."

"I'll do what I can for you, I promise, dear," said Daphne, her attention distracted by Richard's halfhearted administrations as she hung up.

Chloe picked up the vodka and poured a generous slug into her orange juice as the phone started to ring. She let the answering machine pick up, listened, heard the nasal tones: "Hello, it's Mike Russel here from *The News of the World.* I'd like to speak to Miss Carriere about . . ."

Wearily she switched it off. Tomorrow this American tabloid story would be in all the English papers. Annabel would see it. Uppermost in Chloe's mind was how her daughter would react. Her darling Annabel, who thought of Chloe as her aunt. What would she think? How would she feel, knowing she had been lied to all her life? She had to be devastated.

Whatever her reaction, Chloe had to see her face to face. *Now.* There was no putting it off. She had to tell her the truth.

She called Gertrude. "You've read the story?"

"Yes, of course. Is it true?" rasped Gertrude.

"It is, Gertrude. As far as I'm concerned I don't give a damn what the press write. But this has to be the most ghastly shock for Annabel. She had no idea that I was her mother, that Susan and Richard were not her real parents. I *must* go to England, Gertrude, immediately. Can you shoot around me? Please. It's urgent."

"Darling." Gertrude's voice was cool. "You *know* we can't. We're coming to the end of the season, you're in *everything.* This has to be the best cliff-hanger ever, because 'America' is starting up against us next season. Can't it wait?"

"No!" Chloe was desperate. "No, it can't. It's my daughter's *life,* Gertrude. Isn't that more important than the show, for heaven's sake?"

"Frankly, honey, it isn't. I have every sympathy for you, I promise we'll get the publicity people to do the best they can to help you out of this mess, but we simply *cannot* and *will not* cater to the whim of an actress in this way."

"Whim!" Chloe almost wept. "Gertrude, this is the most important thing in my life!" She started to tell her the real story, but Gertrude cut her off.

"I'm in the middle of a dinner party, honey—now don't you worry," Gertrude tried to soothe her. "I don't think bad publicity will harm you. After all, you *are* a bitch."

"I'm not!" Chloe screamed. "I'm an actress and a good one too, which is why they all think I'm a bitch. Please let me go, Gertrude, please, just for the weekend. I must sort it out. Annabel needs me—I have to explain everything to her myself. I *can't* do it on the phone."

"I'll have to speak to Abby," Gertrude said crisply. "I'll see what I can do. I've got to run now, my guests are waiting." She hung up.

"Damn you!" yelled Chloe, tears welling up. "Damn you all! I'm bloody going anyway." Lifting the receiver, she called Vanessa. "Get me on tomorrow night's British Airways flight to London, Van, and call a meeting here tonight with Christopher. I've got to face the music."

"I'm going, Abby," she said calmly the next morning, as she sat across from the huge man in his immense office.

He had been more sympathetic to her than Gertrude. "We're going to let you go so that you can sort this unfortunate story out," he said. "It makes you look bad in the public's eye. If you just ignore it, the public will think you're a bitch. So although there really isn't a stigma about the illegitimate aspect, I think the public have got to know the truth. You owe it to them, if not to the girl." He chewed on his cigar and surveyed her kindly. When the chips were down, Abby usually came through for his stars. He liked Chloe and he knew she was nothing like the hardhearted vixen she portrayed.

"Go, sweetheart. Give a press conference in London for the media, that's important, but more important is the kid—how's she taking it?"

"I don't know," said Chloe, fighting back the tears. "I can't get through —they've taken the phone off the hook, and I can't reach her at college. It's really hard, Abby. This girl is the most important person in my life." Tears started to flow down her cheeks. Abby, a sentimental man in spite of his hard exterior, felt his throat tighten and hastily passed her his handkerchief before he started to bawl too.

"Now, now, sweetheart," he said gruffly. "No tears, please, you'll only hold up production while they fix your makeup. Go back to the set; we'll release you by four-thirty so you can catch the flight to London and sort things out."

Before the story broke, Annabel had been a well-adjusted young woman at college, studying to be a musician. She had been outgoing and happy, as well, in her home life in a secure family atmosphere. This did not stop the Fleet Street vipers, who fell upon the scandal like vultures. Anything about Chloe was news. This was huge, and they would play it up to the hilt. The glaring headlines shrieked their news daily.

"Chloe Abandons Love Child," screeched the *Sun*.

"Selfish Soap Queen Gives Baby Away," the *Star* squawked.

"Oh, Chloe, Chloe, how could you be so heartless? Where is your sense of moral virtue, your motherly instincts? Foolish woman. Do diamonds, furs, Hollywood mansions, and swimming pools make up for a child's life? For a baby you bore, and then gave away to your relatives while you pursued your career, chasing shallow fame and the frivolous good life and leaving your own flesh and blood to be brought up living a lie? . . ." Every tabloid drooled on. It was a hot story and they milked it for everything it had. It was nauseating, thought Chloe.

She read the articles on the plane to London, more horrified at each one as she wondered how Annabel would take all of this. Vanessa was with her, excited about going back to London. Some of Chloe's fame had rubbed off on her and she had become something of a celebrity in Petticoat Lane, where her family still lived. Philippe was there too, sitting next to Chloe, asleep and snoring. He had been supportive of her when the news broke, and had insisted on coming along.

"What does it matter, sweetheart, what they say about you?" he had asked. "They all think you're a bitch anyway." He had infuriated her with his French pragmatism, and they had finally had a tearful argument.

The press were out in force at Heathrow—dozens of them including TV cameras and news. As soon as she stepped off the ramp, they were all over her, pushing, yelling and snapping her as she strode down the drafty Heathrow corridor, head held high. She wore a simple tan cashmere overcoat belted snugly against the London chill. A smooth-tongued BBC reporter thrust his microphone into her face, demanding a statement. The woman from ITV insisted on a quote too. NBC and ABC were there, as well as her parent network BCC, and news crews from Europe and Australia.

"Wait a minute. *Wait a minute* everybody!" Christopher, "Saga's" diminutive press agent, was flushed scarlet with the effort of trying to control the excited crowd and the press. "Miss Carriere is *not* going to make any statement at this moment. As you all know, we have called a press conference at the Ritz Hotel at four o'clock. Miss Carriere will then talk to all of you in detail about—recent events."

Chloe smiled through clenched teeth as three policemen, two officials from the airline, Vanessa, Philippe and Christopher tried to force a way through the throng of photographers, journalists and rubberneckers.

This was going to be tougher than she had expected. They had stayed up late the previous night planning their strategy. Make it work, please God, breathed Chloe. Make it work.

◆ *Twenty-three* ◆

Annabel's protected private world had suddenly become a public nightmare. Her face was splashed over the front pages of the tabloids. Her fellow students gossiped about her at college. Why hadn't Auntie Chloe—no, it was Mummie Chloe now, wasn't it?—told her the truth?

The gutter press started bombarding the neat terraced house in Barnes with phone calls, and Annabel's family went into shock. It became unbearable. When they were "door-stepped" by dozens of journalists and photographers from all over the world, they turned the house into a fortress. They took the phone off the hook, kindly neighbors brought in food, and the family waited and prayed it would all be over soon and that the media circus outside would go away.

But it wouldn't. The reporters dug themselves in, waiting for action, and soon it arrived in the person of Chloe as they knew it would. When she arrived at the house she was inundated by a thousand intrusively crude, curious questions. Flashbulbs popped so rapidly in the afternoon gloom that she was almost blinded. Christopher, his diminutive height no barrier to his strength as he maneuvered her through the jabbering throng, was red-faced by the time the door was opened by a pale, worried-looking Susan, who hurriedly ushered them into the narrow hall.

She, Richard and Chloe exchanged affectionate greetings and muffled words of encouragement, then Susan took Chloe aside, motioning toward the closed door of the living room. "She's in there," she whispered, as Richard took Christopher through to the kitchen.

"She's taking it very hard, Chloe. I've tried to tell her it wasn't your fault, that it was the way the world *was* then and that you did your best, but it seems that the more I say, the more upset she gets."

"Thanks, Susie." Chloe smiled at her sister-in-law and squeezed her arm appreciatively, remembering those long-ago days when they were schoolgirls, remembering the whispering, the giggling, the sharing of such delicious secrets when they were twelve and "best friends" forever. And now here they were whispering secrets again. "I told her you were coming," said Susie, "but she didn't say anything."

"It's all right, Susie. I have to talk to her, I know how difficult it must be for her." Chloe pushed the door open.

Annabel sat in the living room slumped on a flowered chintz sofa. Mother and daughter looked at each other. This was the moment Chloe had been dreading. Her throat was so tight she had difficulty swallowing, and she had developed a nervous tic in one eye, probably because she had not had a wink of sleep in the barely three days since the story about Annabel had broken. She looked at her daughter with love, but Annabel's eyes were cold, flat and detached.

A fire crackled in the grate. It was a cold March afternoon, and although only four o'clock, it was almost dark outside. The green velveteen curtains were drawn and the windows tightly closed, but even so, the hubbub and chatter of the press outside could still be heard.

Chloe had come straight from Heathrow, and as she stood in her tan suede boots and matching cashmere overcoat, she felt horribly Hollywoodish and overdressed in this simple, cluttered living room. On the piano and mantelpiece were photos of her and the family. In one corner sat a ficus plant Chloe had sent Richard for his birthday, in another, a plastic trolley held bottles of whiskey, gin, vodka and liqueurs. How she would love a drink, she thought fervently, but this was not the time.

Her daughter, her beautiful, joyous daughter, had turned away from her, her eyes hard.

"I suppose you expect me to fall into your arms and all will be forgiven," Annabel said sarcastically in her clear young voice.

"No, of course I don't, Annabel, I would never expect that of you. You deserve an explanation, and I'm going to do the best I can to explain everything."

Chloe took off her coat, tossing it onto an armchair opposite the sofa on which her daughter was curled up, her normally cheerful expression a hard mask. Her curly dark hair was caught up with a bright yellow plastic comb, which matched the yellow sweater she wore over worn blue jeans torn at the knees, and cowboy boots. She was truly a lovely young girl who looked so uncannily like the young Chloe that an outsider seeing them together would have known instantly they were mother and daughter.

Susan had left a tray of tea and shortbread biscuits on the walnut table in front of the fire. There were two cups and an earthenware vase with a few early daffodils from the garden. The silence seemed endless. Annabel glanced at Chloe, then turned away again, drawing deeply on her cigarette and gazing into the fire.

Chloe tried to swallow. She knew she couldn't speak, say any of the thousand and one things she needed, wanted, to say until she had a sip of tea. Her throat was so dry it hurt. "Would you like a cup of tea, darling?" Her voice sounded too bright, theatrical, her newly acquired transatlantic accent all wrong in the calm Englishness of this room. "No, I wouldn't," the girl's voice was low. "What I *would* like is an explanation, *Auntie. Now.*" Sarcasm didn't become her. She was unused to problems; hers had been a happy life, full of laughter and fun.

"I know, darling, I know and I—I want to explain. I really do. But I'm a bit dry from the plane." Chloe managed a wan smile as she poured the tea with a shaking hand.

"Go ahead," Annabel said coldly as she looked away from Chloe again and into the fire.

Chloe sipped the scalding liquid gratefully. "Annabel, you must realize this is not easy for either of us."

"You bet it isn't. God, how I despise liars." She looked at Chloe defiantly. "I hate the fact that you *all* lied to me all my life—every one of you lied. Mum lied, Dad lied, *you* lied. Why couldn't you have told me the *truth,* for God's sake, or at least told me I was illegitimate when I was old enough to understand what that meant?" she said bitterly. Chloe noticed that her nails were bitten to the quick, and she was clenching and unclenching her hands as she twisted a damp handkerchief in her palms.

"I want to know, *why* didn't you tell me? *Why?*" Her voice was accusing.

"I'm going to be honest with you," Chloe said with a calmness she did not feel. "But the events I must tell you about belong to a different era almost, a totally different morality, a period of time I know may be hard for you to comprehend, darling, but please try."

The girl looked challengingly at Chloe. "I'm *all* ears—" that sarcasm again. Her hostility was a barrier, she prickled with rage. This was harder than Chloe had thought it would be.

"I was twenty-one years old, about the age you are now, so I'm sure you can understand maybe a tiny bit what that was like," Chloe began slowly.

"Of *course,*" Annabel said coolly.

"I fell in love for the first time in my life," Chloe continued. "He was married, but I didn't care. I was completely infatuated with him—totally besotted. I couldn't think about anything or anyone else. He became an obsession." Chloe stopped, lit a cigarette, her hand shaking.

"*Please* don't smoke. Mummy hates people to smoke in the house." Annabel's voice was icy, and now her face seemed even more full of hatred for her mother. Chloe started to protest that Annabel had just extinguished a cigarette, but decided that was not the issue here. She swallowed. Her foot started to twitch; seemingly it had a life of its own. The tic in her eye flickered madly. She had to tell her everything.

Annabel was her child. Even if it meant the end of the relationship they had had up to now, she would tell her every detail, all the reasons. Painstakingly, haltingly, Chloe described her bittersweet affair with Matt. Her hurt feelings when he had suggested an abortion. Her pain when he rejected her. "I couldn't destroy that part of us that we created together. I simply couldn't, it was too precious. If ever there was a true 'love child,' it was you, darling." Annabel didn't answer, but at least her attention had turned away from the flickering fire and to Chloe.

"It was a different time then. The world had just come out of the moralistic fifties," said Chloe. "Women were still second-class citizens; it's hard to believe, I know, but it was years before the sexual revolution. Before the sexual equality we have now. It was a time when nice girls didn't have sex, didn't take lovers. I was in show business, which had a different morality to most people's, so those attitudes never really applied to us. But Matt told me he was through with me when I became pregnant, and I simply didn't know what to do. I was at my wit's end. The only way I knew to earn my living was to sing. I had to support myself because my father was dead and my mother made very little money working in a shop."

"I see." Annabel leaned forward, her eyes still cold, and took a sip for the first time at the tea that Chloe had poured for her. "Go on."

"I wanted to have you, Annabel. I wanted to have my baby so much. I couldn't do what some of my girlfriends did when they became pregnant, go to some butcher on a back street, get it cut out, destroyed. I simply couldn't. I wanted you, Annabel. Can you understand that, darling?"

Annabel didn't answer and Chloe continued, trying to be as factual as possible. Trying not to get too emotional, trying to hold back her tears, both for the memories and for the hostility emanating from the girl she loved so much.

"There was no doubt in my mind, Annabel, that I couldn't destroy that life. Your life. My agony was knowing that an illegitimate child in 1964 would have ruined what little chance of a career I had, and that the child would grow up living with the stigma of 'illegitimate.' And it was an enormous stigma then—it really was.

"It would have been a nightmare trying to bring you up properly. It was difficult enough being a young single girl on the provincial nightclub circuit in England, what with one-night stands, bus and truck tours, standing in railway stations for hours in the middle of the night waiting for milk trains to take you to Wigan or Sunderland or Skegness. Having a baby along to look after would have been absolutely impossible. Singing was my only way of making a living, and if I'd kept you I would have had to give that up. Can you understand that?"

Chloe's eyes were blurred with tears, but Annabel's expression did not soften.

"Whatever your cheap, self-serving excuse, Mummie *dearest*, nothing can change the fact that you *didn't want me,* you didn't have a place for me in your life. You abandoned me. You simply didn't care, and you didn't have the *guts* to tell me before, when you could have. You had to wait until some *rotten* newspaper spilled the beans. Don't give me all that crap about loving me. You never loved me—you never cared at all. All that mattered was your bloody *career*. The limelight—the bright lights." She looked as if she was going to cry; all the pent-up hostility and anger of the past three days came bursting out as she let loose a tirade of fury at her mother.

"What kind of a woman *are* you?" she screamed. "Selfish, thoughtless —you never gave a thought to what might happen when you went jumping around in bed—a married man's bed," she said in disgust. "While his wife was away. I think that's nauseating.

"Oh, I *know* all about the sexual revolution of the sixties, women thinking they could fuck around like men. We're not like that today," she said accusingly. "Young women today think a bit more before we jump into bed, we *try* to be responsible, we take precautions, we have a bit of a social conscience. We are not promiscuous bitches in heat." Her voice was rising now in evangelical fury. She was the new generation of sexually educated young women—the AIDS generation. Look before you leap, and don't leap unless you're very sure it's safe.

"Annabel, I was *not* promiscuous, so stop it, stop it *now*." Suddenly Chloe was very angry. "I've had enough of this."

Annabel looked up, startled at the change in her mother's attitude.

"Stop being so judgmental. It's no good your going on at me, telling me what a terrible, lousy person I was. It's too late for that now, Annabel. We have to understand each other and to accept the past—make the best of it."

She lit a cigarette in spite of Susan's "no smoking" ban and continued, calmer now.

"I'm not going to excuse my behavior in 'abandoning' you, as you say, to be brought up by my brother and Susan. It's a fact that I *cannot* and *will not* apologize for any more. I did what I had to do. I still believe that it was the best thing for you too, whether or not you think so now. You have had a very happy life. They adore you like one of their own. They think of you as their child—can't you realize that?"

Annabel looked at Chloe, her green eyes unfathomable, but Chloe thought she saw a spark of understanding.

"I've come six thousand miles today, Annabel, to tell you the truth. Yes, it's painful. Yes, it's horrible. Yes, it's unfair. I know these last days have been difficult for you; they've been no picnic for me either. But think about this—" She put both hands on her child's shoulders and she could feel her trembling under the thin yellow sweater—"I *could* have aborted you."

Annabel shuddered and moved angrily away from her mother. "Thanks for that," she said flatly. "I suppose I should be thankful, but knowing you now, you were probably too much of a coward to do it."

"Damn it, Annabel, don't *be* like this," Chloe exploded. "I love you. I have *always* loved you and I have never gone to sleep at night without thinking of you—but I needed to make a success of my career. I *wanted* to be a singer. It was my life. If I had acknowledged you, I would have had to live with the scandal of having given birth to an illegitimate child. That would have meant *no career*. I would have been finished. I would have had you, yes, but I would have had to give up my dreams, *my life.*"

"I understand dreams," said Annabel quietly—no trace of sarcasm now. "They make life worth living."

"I want you to remember, I *chose* to have you." Chloe was calmer now. "Susan and Richard were wonderful parents to their children and they welcomed you as one of them. I knew you would be in a loving home with a devoted family, two big brothers, that you would have a stable, happy life. So I made that decision—a decision I've thought about every single day of my life since."

She paused. The memories were so painful: Matt's rejection of her and their baby, the agonizing sleepless nights when she found out she was pregnant, the frenzied discussions with Susan and Richard, the constant tears, trying to contact Matt, hearing his voice telling her he wouldn't see her again, he didn't want any "aggro." She was a big girl who knew what she had been doing. It was her problem. Hers alone. Yes, it *definitely* had been; he had done nothing. He considered it had nothing to do with him, so Chloe had dealt with it alone.

Annabel leaned her dark curly head on the back of the green sofa and bit into a shortbread biscuit as she looked at Chloe. She still felt angry, but her rage and turmoil were softening with comprehension.

"What are you thinking, Annabel?" Chloe asked, trying not to sound too eager.

"Oh, just a saying the kids are using at college." A faint smile illuminated her sweet face briefly. " 'Life's a bitch—and then you die.' " Chloe smiled tentatively. Oh, how she wanted Annabel to understand and accept what had happened. She wanted to comfort her, wipe the unshed tears that must be shed from those clouded eyes. She remembered holding her at the hospital when the nurse first put her in her arms. Remembered the funny wrinkled little face, the warmth of that tiny body close to hers. Remembered how with a fierce primal urge she had wanted to keep this infant with her forever. She remembered cuddling her daughter for hours in that stark hospital room with its acid-green, peeling paint. Annabel had rarely cried. Sometimes when she awoke and gazed up at Chloe with wise infant eyes, Chloe had felt the purest love she had ever felt for another human being.

Now Chloe looked into Annabel's eyes, so troubled now, and longed to hold her again, to stroke her hair, to tell her how much she loved her. But this was not the time. Not yet. Maybe tomorrow. Maybe next week. Maybe, God forbid, it would never happen; maybe Annabel would never forgive her, never accept what she had done.

Chloe had said what she had to say, done what she had to do. Now it was up to her daughter.

"Ladies and Gentlemen—" Chloe cleared her throat. This was *terrifying*, probably the most difficult audience she had ever had to face. No, she thought, telling Annabel had been worse. A battery of microphones and cameras was massed in front of the podium where she stood, palms damp, sweat rolling down her back, drenching her simple beige crepe de chine blouse. A sea of hostile faces confronted her. God, there must be at least one hundred of them! She panicked. Could she pull this off? A great deal depended on it. Most important were her daughter's feelings, but the public's opinion of her concerned her too. She was sick of their thinking of her as an inhuman bitch goddess.

Out of the corner of her eye, she observed Annabel giving her a tremulous smile and a "thumbs up" sign. She began:

"Twenty-one years ago . . ." then—Oh, my *God,* who was that? In that sea of journalists, she recognized a face. It couldn't be—it couldn't! She took a deep breath and looked at him. He was staring at her with a vestige of that sexy smile she had found so irresistible so many years ago.

Matt Sullivan! Her selfish, sexy, self-absorbed lover, Annabel's father. Her first real love. Chloe was shocked, mesmerized into immobility. His black eyes, still remarkably sparkling, gazed mockingly into hers, as though the people around them didn't exist. He still exuded sexual confidence, amazing in a man of his age; he must be over sixty, she thought. He had lost most of his hair, but there was an animation about him that made him still attractive. A cigarette clung to his lower lip, as it always had—and what was that in his hand? A notebook! How could he? He was taking notes—he was obviously still a reporter. Apparently he didn't have what it took to become the editor of one of those sleazebag rags. At his age he was still just a hack, competing with twenty-five-year-olds. She felt sorry for him. For what gutter tabloid did he work now? Chloe tried desperately to pull her thoughts together and continue her speech. He must *know* that Annabel was his baby. Their love child. This was sick. The last time they had met, twenty-one years ago, he had told her to get lost. How could he be here now?

She swallowed, directing her attention to another part of the room and the other journalists.

"Twenty-one years ago, I was very naive," she began tentatively. "I was starting a career as a singer, and singing was my life. At least I thought it was." She glanced momentarily at Matt, who was looking at Annabel with an unfathomable expression.

"One day I fell in love, for the first time." The press scribbled wildly— oh, the headlines tomorrow!

"He was a married man, much older than I. I know it was terrible to have an affair with a married man, but I fell in love—very much in love." The truth was the only thing that could save her. This was tough, but she couldn't stop now. "Don't let the bastards get you down, dear," Vanessa had warned her before she had walked to the microphones.

Chloe told them the full story. How she hadn't been able to bring herself to have an abortion—to kill a life born of love. How her brother and sister-in-law, a secure and lovely family unit, had agreed to take the baby and bring her up with their own. How her career had meant so much to her and how, in 1964, giving birth to an illegitimate child could have wrecked her career and hurt the child irreparably.

Chloe realized she had their rapt attention now. Some of the more emotional sob sisters of Fleet Street were almost teary-eyed as Chloe finished her speech. She noticed Jean Rook giving her an encouraging smile.

"I know that many of you believe I have sinned, but my transgression was one of innocence and ignorance and love for my unborn child. Later I realized it would be terribly upsetting for my daughter to find out that her parents were not who she thought they were. I didn't want to upset her. She had a stable family, she was adored by her parents and her brothers. I kept the secret for the sake of my daughter's happiness, not for mine, and I sincerely hope you will all believe me."

They all seemed to. But first they had to ask their nosy Fleet Street questions. How did she feel when she found out she was pregnant? Did she feel guilt about having an affair with a married man? And, finally, who was he? Who was the man whom Chloe had been so passionate about? What was his name? Where is he now? They were really curious about this—desperate to know. She told her only untruth then, but she knew that if she did not tell a lie the investigative reporters would go to work. It wouldn't be too difficult to find some bartender, one of her musician friends, somebody who had seen her and Matt together in Liverpool, Manchester or Newcastle back then. So she lied. "He died," she said simply, "in a car crash in Marbella, just before the baby was born." They seemed satisfied with that, although Annabel looked sad. "And now, ladies and gentlemen," she said, her voice tight with emotion, "I would like you to meet my daughter." As Annabel joined her mother on the podium, the press went wild. Annabel's resemblance to Chloe was unmistakable. The same walk, the same cheekbones, the same eyes, the same dark curls. They posed for the cameras for five minutes until Christopher had to beg them to stop.

Later, Chloe, answering questions, surrounded by a group of female writers from the more conservative women's weeklies, suddenly felt a tap on her shoulder. "Good girl, I'm proud of you, Chlo." Matt spoke to her as if they had last met yesterday, instead of twenty-two years ago.

She looked at him long and hard. Strange—even though he was almost old now, the feelings he had created in her could still flicker faintly. "Thanks, Matt," she whispered. Memories came flooding back.

"She's a beauty—just like her ma." He gave her a wink, then drew her aside, brushed his lips against her cheek and whispered, "I loved you, Chlo. I didn't realize it then. Too young, too ambitious—too selfish, I suppose."

Too drunk, too often, Chloe thought without malice. "I don't think you loved me, Matt. You never told me you did. Please—don't say it now. I know it's not true," she said.

"I, well—you were just a kid, I was married. Still am." He was rueful now. "I'm a fucking grandfather. Can you believe it, Chloe? A grandfather!"

She could believe it. He was old enough. Still, her heart wondered, "Why did he desert me when I loved him so much?" For years she had thought about him. His memory had never been fully erased—not until she met Josh.

"I'd like to see you again, Chlo." His whisper was urgent. "I'd like to get to know her, too. Spend some time together."

"No, Matt. No." This time it was Chloe's turn to reject him. She remembered the endless phone calls to his office, a secretary telling her he was out to lunch, off, away, not in, not available—all of the stock secretary's lines.

Not that revenge was sweet—that had never been Chloe's way—but seeing him again had closed their chapter forever. "Goodbye, Matt," she whispered, brushing his old man's cheek with her well-preserved one. "Take care."

"Goodbye, darlin', and good luck. You did it, Chlo! You made the buggers do you right this time!"

She watched him go, and to her surprise saw that he was crying.

Within the month the whole incident was forgotten when Prince Charles and Princess Diana announced that she was expecting again.

Emerald had tested well, she decided. Banishing her usual glamour, she had thought of herself as just a working actress, and got on with it. The crew applauded when she finished. Afterward she went straight home to her penthouse in Century City, took off her makeup, told the answering service to ring through only if Eddie De Levigne called, and went on a bender.

For three days she lay on her bed drinking straight vodka. If she didn't get this role, she was determined to drink herself to death. What would be the use of going on? It was difficult enough to survive in this business. She couldn't *not* continue to enjoy her lavish lifestyle. She had sold all of her jewels that were worth anything, except one necklace. This she wore, with a tattered white terry-cloth robe, for the three days she lay in bed mindlessly switching TV channels and drinking vodka from the bottle.

She didn't talk, she didn't cry, she didn't think about anything. She was in limbo, waiting to be put out of her misery forever—or to rise to new heights.

The call came on Wednesday morning. "Eddie De Levigne on the line," said the voice of Gloria at her service.

"Hi, Eddie. What's up?" The actress in her managed to banish any hint of drunkenness from her speech. She didn't even slur her words.

"You've got it, kiddo," he said excitedly. "God knows, Emerald, you're a lucky woman, after the fool you made of yourself. Jail and all. But Hogarth loves you. He's had to practically suck cock at the network to get you for this."

"Why?" she demanded. "I'm still a big star."

"Christ, Emerald, the truth, kiddo, *is* you've been in the game too long. The network knows it, the studio knows it, even the great unwashed public knows it."

"I'm big—*huge* in Europe," Emerald said proudly. "I get mobbed when I walk down the Via Condotti."

"So does Pia Zadora, dear. So what? Listen, Emerald, Europe is a *very* small piece of the action, and frankly, I don't see Zeffirelli banging on your door—even if you are big on the Via Condotti."

"He couldn't," she giggled. "He doesn't like girls."

"You are not a *girl* any more, kid. Face it, Emerald, however many studs you take into your bed, you are a middle-aged woman who is rapidly losing her pulling power—on *and* off the screen."

"You don't have to rub it in, Eddie," she moaned. "I can still look good, though, and you know it." She understood he was being harsh to her as a warning. This was her last chance.

"They want you in wardrobe next Tuesday. Eleven o'clock. Be punctual, toots—for a change. And they start shooting in a week. You're a lucky woman, Emerald," he added gently. "Don't screw it up."

She knew he was right. In the intervening five days, she stopped drinking, cold turkey, lost eight pounds, spent two hours at the gym every day, bleached her gray roots back to their golden glory, and arrived in wardrobe punctually on Tuesday morning, almost as good as new.

Nobody else, she told herself, could have done it.

PART
SIX

◀ *Twenty-four* ▶

Josh yawned, stretched, and threw out his arms.

" 'Ere, watch it," the little redhead with the thin frizzed hair groaned sleepily.

Not again. Self-disgust flooded him at the memory of last night's performances, on and off the stage. The opening night. The party. The people.

The Manchester Hippodrome was a far cry from Broadway and Las Vegas, where he had once done sellout business.

Show business was brutal, as all who chose it as their profession knew. Ultimately no one gave a shit. Every cliché was true: dog eat dog; jealousy thrives; adulation on the way up, indifference on the way down. Josh was on the way down, and he knew it. Self-pity and nausea attacked him simultaneously, and he groped for the paraphernalia to prepare his first fix of the day.

He lit the match under the spoon and watched the white powder dissolve into brownish syrup. After it hit him he turned to inspect the tiny girl by his side. Christ, this one was *really* young stuff. He lifted the sheets up. No more than fourteen or fifteen by the look of her. Even for him, this was younger than usual. He liked them in full bloom, just past puberty, in their first flush of womanhood—sixteen or seventeen was usually the age he preferred. Once he had been lucky enough to find sixteen-year-old twins. They couldn't do enough for him, unlike this little creature, who had lain back uncomplaining while he tried to whip up a fever for both of them. He had failed miserably. Maybe he was getting too old. But the forties weren't old these days. Tom Jones was still around, so was Julio Iglesias, and Jagger—Mick, the idol of all of them—was creeping up the old 4-0 ladder. Not to mention McCartney, Rod Stewart and David Bowie. Forty wasn't fatal—or was it?

" 'Ello," the little thing said. God, she was *tiny*. Maybe she was even younger than fourteen. Innocent gray eyes gave him a tentative smile. She hurriedly skipped out of bed, hoping he wouldn't try and do again what he'd done so boringly last night.

Why did I do it? she wondered. He's old enough to be me dad. No, on second thought, he was possibly old enough to be her granddad. Her dad was thirty-two—Josh must be at least fifty. She dressed quickly, rehearsing tales with which to regale friends at school. Joshua Brown, big stud, big star. Her mum's favorite crooner. She had grown up to the sounds of his plaintive ballads on her mum's stereo. Her mum had had a real thing for Josh. Used to talk about him for hours. Boring old fart, she thought. Couldn't fuck his way out of a paper bag. Had a hard time even getting it up. Uncle Fred was much better. She struggled into black lace tights, green Lurex socks and, mumbling something about being late for school, skipped away.

Josh was relieved. Now he must get it together. Meet the press, then face the cast at rehearsal, discuss the reviews. Oh, God, the reviews. He was in no hurry to do so. During his final ballad last night, he had observed a steady trickle of customers edging out the exit doors. The applause had been meager at the final curtain. The stage manager had been hard-pushed to milk two curtain calls.

After the show last night, a supercilious pockmarked journalist from a down-market tabloid had cornered him at the party. Josh, conscious of the power of the press, was always ready to fraternize with them. He needed them now, if this show was to succeed, but basically he loathed their guts. Maybe this reptile could serve a purpose, though. Josh bandied wisecracks and charm for four full minutes before the reptile asked him the oh so familiar question he dreaded. "So what's Chloe *really* like?" Josh played dumb. The hack plodded on. "You were married to her for over ten years—is she *really* like Miranda?"

Chloe. That woman was ruining his life with her goddamn TV series and her "over forty" fame. Some kind of fucking Joan of Arc for the blue-rinse brigade. She thought she was hot stuff now. Showing off her body in those magazines, bragging about how women over forty were just as sexy as twenty-year-olds. Balls. How could she know? She wasn't a man. Young, firm flesh was what most men were interested in. They were wrong, these feminists with their "Look at us, we're over forty and aren't we wonderful" crap. Didn't they *know*, didn't Chloe realize, for Christ's sake, forty was *past* it?

It was pathetic. It was O.K. for him to be over forty—he was a man. But everywhere these days were these ball-breaking broads with their diets and exercise books, their hit records and their box-office pulling power. Tina fucking Turner, Jane fucking Fonda. And now Chloe.

To add insult to injury, only yesterday she had been on the front page of the *Daily Mirror* with Macho Man Luis Mendoza. "SOAP'S HOTTEST LOVERS" screamed the headline, and the story chronicled how Chloe and Luis were making the screen ignite with their passionate love scenes and volatile chemistry.

"Not since Petruchio tamed Katharina the shrew have a pair of lovers excited audiences so much," drooled the article.

"Luis Mendoza is the sexiest, most electrifying leading man to hit the TV screen since Tom Selleck. Already movie companies are standing in line to offer him contracts. All America is at his feet, thanks to 'Saga' and the combustibility of Luis and Chloe Carriere."

Josh had smiled bitterly, trying to hide his jealousy from the reptile. "Oh, Chloe . . . Yeah . . . Great . . . She's a great girl. Deserves her success. Yeah, really. I'm happy for her." Bullshit. The words, uttered for the umpteenth time, stuck in his throat, and he had to excuse himself to go to the men's room for a snort.

Sally had looked after him worriedly. He was too pale. The show had not been good. She had seen the audience's glazed faces as the subtlety of *The Private Life of Napoleon and Josephine* went over their heads.

Poor old Dad. She had tried to cheer him up in the way she knew he loved—had looked around and seen the tiny redheaded teenager gazing admiringly into the space her father had recently vacated. She wandered over to her. "How'd you like to meet him?" she offered casually. "Ooh, not 'alf," squealed the girl. It was easy for Sally to succeed in anticipating her father's wants and needs—though "thanks" was not a word that was featured in his vocabulary these days. But Josh should certainly see that Sally cared very much for him.

Josh, relieved that the girl was gone and feeling better as the cocaine took effect, dressed and left for a press luncheon at the Metropole Hotel.

A Fleet Street hag, invisible venom dripping from her ballpoint pen, pretended to give Josh her rapt attention. She was asking the inevitable questions again about Chloe. The practiced answers flowed easily from Josh's lips as he tried to hide his chagrin. Would they never stop interrogating him about her?

"Phone, Dad." Sally was at his elbow, steering him away. The hag seemed satisfied. She had her story. She would make up the rest. She always made it up. That was why she was called "The Barracuda of Fleet Street."

She had already written the story before meeting Josh today. It was titled "The Fallen Star."

"He was once a superstar in America and all over the world. Now he ekes out a meager living playing suburban theaters in Britain. Joshua Brown, once the idol of millions, is now a broken man—a broken man full of broken dreams. His beautiful ex-wife, Chloe Carriere, has become a mega-soap star on American TV while Josh barely makes ends meet touring in mediocre musicals." The article continued in this vein. This was tremendous stuff. The public would eat it up. They adored a rags-to-riches story, but when it was rags to riches and back to rags again, they loved it even more. And Josh was a natural, with his bouts with drugs and alcohol, jail sentences, drunken rages, affairs with young girls—they all made great copy. The public longed to see him fall on his face.

The female barracuda had the perfect set of photos to accompany the story. Josh in 1965, all white teeth, tumbling black locks and shiny satin trousers, holding the mike as if it were his cock, and giving the camera his wildest, sexiest look next to a recent photo of Josh hunched up in an overcoat and scarf, pale face, graying hair, spectacles, glancing suspiciously over his shoulder, surprised by the camera's flash and, hanging on his arm adoringly, a girl easily young enough to be his daughter. Before and after. How the mighty have fallen. Eat it up, all you readers! Two nice photos of Chloe. Chloe in 1962—wide-eyed innocence, black hair in neat bangs, a chaste miniskirt and knee socks. And there was Chloe now—sheathed in Rudolpho bugle beads, white fox and diamonds, lying seductively on a satin chaise, with a knowing and successful look on her painted face. Perfect. The hag cackled. She had never liked Josh anyway. Too bigheaded by far. He had reaped what he had sown.

Chloe read the piece on Josh a week later. In spite of herself she felt sad for him. Why had he allowed himself to fall so far? He had had it all. If he found himself a decent agent, went to a psychiatrist, gave up drugs and bimbos and really concentrated on his work, on his music, he could have it all again. Maybe. Maybe not. Nothing in this business was easy.

She sighed and looked at Philippe, who lay next to her in their huge bed with the art deco padded satin headboard and lilac silk sheets. He was watching MTV, his favorite station.

Chloe thought it odd that a man of forty could become so hooked on the gyrations of Madonna and Michael Jackson. But he watched Music Television all day long when he wasn't working on her accounts or writing an article for *Paris Match*.

Philippe was always in the house. He was on a marriage kick again after seeing the article about Josh in the British tabloid.

"When are you going to get the final papers signed, *chérie?*" he asked, massaging her shoulders in the seductive way she loved. "Why don't you get them? Then we can be married. Get rid of Josh, *chérie*, it's time."

Oh, no, here he goes again, thought Chloe. Not wedding talk again. They had been living together for a year, but he kept going on about marriage. It was unusual for a man. And much as she adored him, she didn't feel like making a lifelong commitment. Josh was always at the back of her mind.

As tactfully as possible, Chloe gave him once again her anti-marriage speech. It didn't placate him and he sulked for the rest of the day to the sound of MTV turned up full blast.

Chloe left for the studio attempting to forget Josh's predicament and Philippe's sulks. She called Jasper from her car phone. "What is the decision?" she asked. "Has the network come up with the raise for next season, Jasper? We're on our last episode of the season. We've only got another five days to shoot."

Jasper had met with Abby in the big man's sumptuous office at the beginning of the season. Abby's reputation as a producer who couldn't tolerate insubordination in actors and others who worked for him was legendary. To the world he played Mr. Always Understanding, but in reality he was ruthless if anyone dared step out of line. Several members of the company had been fired for demanding more money.

Jasper had transmitted Chloe's discontent with the fact that after four years on "Saga," contributing to its success in the ratings, and having become one of the most copied, admired and hated women on TV, she was still receiving far less salary than Sam and Sissy. Abby would not hear of an increase for Chloe. Through gritted teeth he spelled it out: "Tell her if she wants to continue working in this town she'd better not make waves. If she doesn't conform, if she gives us *any* trouble, she'll be *out*. We'll kill her off; write her out. We won't be blackmailed, Jasper, not by her nor any of them. She's making forty thousand a week—that should be enough for an ex-nightingale from provincial Britain."

He added with a shark's smile: "Tell Chloe I'll expect her at my 'Man of the Year Award' dinner at the Beverly Hilton next Tuesday, Jasper. She's seated at my table. She'd better be there."

A command from the emperor. Abby wore his power easily. It confirmed his self-worth. God knows his wife, Maud, didn't care about it, unless it was his *net* worth. Abby was not going to let any actor, producer or director get the better of him, and he was not above deliberately humiliating any of them. Chloe would never forget what he had done to Pandora King last season.

Pandora had been late on the set too many times, made fun of "Saga" too often on talk shows, and complained and moaned on the set about the poor dialogue she was getting and how her costumes were not as expensive as Chloe's and Sissy's. Abby and Gertrude were becoming thoroughly sick of her.

Pandora, along with the rest of the cast and crew, had attended the wrap party at the Beverly Hills Hotel for "Saga" to celebrate the end of shooting. Everyone was in an "up" mood, and it should have been a joyful occasion. Nine months of hard work were over. A three-month hiatus lay ahead of them. They could all do what they wanted. For the crew, this usually meant getting another job as quickly as possible, since they couldn't afford to be out of work for that long. For the three best-paid actors, Sam, Sissy and Chloe, it meant they could choose from the fat pile of scripts that their agents had waiting on their desks or go on an extended vacation. The rest of the cast were at the mercy of whichever producer or network chose to give them a job.

After dinner and the gag reel—a twenty-minute compilation of actors and crew doing inadvertently funny things, breaking up, tripping, choking, giggling or generally making fools of themselves—Gertrude and Abby went to the podium and introduced all the cast, each of whom was invited to the stand and to say a few words.

First Sam, as the most senior member of the cast, made his usual charming speech. He sounded good, even though he was beginning to look old without his thick orange makeup.

Vanessa whispered to Chloe, "He's lost so much weight, his teeth seem to be getting too big for his mouth!"

Sissy flounced on, thin as bone, brittle as glass, wearing a gray taffeta strapless dress that made her shoulder blades look like chicken wings.

Then came Chloe, looking strained after another petty row with

Philippe. He had refused to come to the wrap party, so she had to ask Ostie, her dialogue coach, to escort her.

Abby then called upon Pandora:

. "And now we are going to hear from a lovely lady and a talented actress who, regrettably, will not be back with us next season. Please all give a great big round of applause to Miss Pandora King."

Pandora's blood froze. *Not be back next season?* They couldn't. They wouldn't. Not after she had just turned down a firm offer from Disney for a half-hour sitcom. She had suspected for some months that her days on "Saga" were numbered. That was the way the cookie crumbled in TV Land. Her fan mail had been getting sparser, and it seemed that the fewer letters she received, the fewer lines she had to learn. She was a realist and had been excited about the Disney series, looking forward to the challenge of a new project. However, after speaking to Abby, her agent had told her that she would definitely be back on "Saga" next season with a hefty raise. Abby had assured him they all adored her. She shouldn't have believed a word of it. Now the sitcom at Disney had gone to another actress, and the bastard was firing her in front of the entire cast and crew. She swallowed her pride, aware that her face was aflame, and went up to the podium to say the few words she had carefully prepared but which now seemed horribly inappropriate.

After her speech, Chloe squeezed her arm sympathetically as they stood next to each other on the podium. It could have happened to any of them. In their hearts, all of the cast breathed a sigh of relief that this season, at least, they had escaped the hangman's noose. During the shooting of thirty episodes of the third season, Chloe had tried to remain calm and not get upset when highly paid guest stars were brought in for seven or eight episodes to "bolster the ratings"—which were already high. Neither the network nor Abby nor Gertrude had any qualms about paying these often fading stars twice the amount they paid Chloe.

"It's my fault for coming in so cheap at the beginning," Chloe told Vanessa bitterly, having just played a scene with a "famous name" who had blown his lines fifteen times in a row and who was getting sixty thousand dollars an episode.

Two days before shooting ended, Chloe received Jasper's news that her raise had once again been denied. Backed by Philippe, she grimly decided she had to take a stand before the next season began. Since she had not received the twenty thousand-a-week increase she felt she warranted, she informed Jasper that she would quit the show.

"I mean it, Jasper," she said. "I'm off to the south of France and I'm not coming back unless you can get them to change their minds."

They didn't.

Although the network wanted Chloe to remain on the show, Abby and Gertrude were adamant. No raise. In their eyes, Chloe had committed the cardinal sin. Self-righteously they announced that Chloe had attempted to blackmail them. People who would cut each other's throats for a project, who lied, cheated, schemed and manipulated, were up in arms over Chloe's deed. During the hiatus, which had been shortened from the usual three months to six weeks by the network's desire to have "Saga" back on the air in late October, Jasper tried to negotiate a compromise with Abby, Gertrude and the network executives. To no avail.

They dropped her. They wrote her out of the first episode, giving her dialogue to other actors, and they sent her the news by cable.

Cold rage gripped Chloe when the cable arrived. "The producers of 'Saga,' MCPC, and the BCC Network hereby inform Chloe Carriere that, effective today, her services as a performer in the television series 'Saga' are no longer required." It was signed "Abby Arafat, President of MCPC."

She had been lying by the pool, basking in the warm Mediterranean sunshine, when Philippe handed her the cable.

"How *can* they even consider doing this to 'Saga' even if they don't care about me?" said Chloe, amazed at how they would cut off their nose to spite their face.

"It's suicidal," Philippe agreed. "Everyone knows how popular Miranda and you are. You're the only reason anyone watches the damned trash in the first place." It was four o'clock on the Côte d'Azur. It would be 7 A.M. in L.A., Chloe thought. The cast would be rushing to finish their makeup and hair to be on the set for rehearsal. Sissy would be putting her wig on while gulping down her vitamin pills and protein drink for the grueling day ahead. Sam would be resting. The younger actors would be gossiping in the hair and makeup rooms.

Chloe felt a touch of melancholy. The view of the Mediterranean from the house was more beautiful than any in Beverly Hills or Malibu, but the thought that she might have blown her hard-won career made her worse than melancholy.

"Drink?" Philippe asked. She nodded and he went to the bamboo bar, poured cassis and Dom Perignon over ice into a tall glass and brought it to her.

She drank it gratefully. "All I did was ask for what I deserve, Philippe. No more, no less."

"I know, *chérie.*"

"They all think I'm really a bitch," she said bitterly, a sliver of self-pity in her voice. She gazed at the turquoise waves, oblivious to the seminaked flesh that paraded unself-consciously up and down the *plage*. Young and old, perfect and not so perfect, downright ugly—it was of no importance on the French Riviera. They all showed it off. "Don't brood, *chérie,*" he said, leaving her to go surfing.

Her eyes scanned the bay. White yachts rocked gently on their moorings as their owners sat sipping cool drinks and watching speedboats piloted by tanned young men and bare-breasted girls dart between them. Floating on the waves like multicolored butterflies were the gaily hued striped sails of the wind-surfers. It was a view Chloe never ceased to admire as she lounged in her beach chair luxuriating in the laziness of watching other people hard at play.

The telephone rang.

"Chloe, my dear, you *must* be back for the second episode or you will never work in television or movies again." Jasper's long-distance voice was faint. "They mean business, Chloe. You cannot fight them. I have done everything I can, dear, *everything,* but I must tell you that I have never seen Abby so resistant. He's *very* angry with you."

"I thought he loved me," sighed Chloe. "He told me so often enough."

"He does, in his way, he does. But I think it's more than resistance to you and the raise. It's Sissy's influence. I think if you come back, though, you just may get your raise, my darling."

"What do you mean?" Chloe was puzzled.

"I found out that Sam has points in the show. It's supposed to be a deep, dark secret, but I found out. He originally signed only a two-year contract, and when it was up, the only way he'd agree to stay was if he got a financial interest in the show."

"Ah!" cried Chloe. "All is clear. It *is* Sissy, then."

"Right, darling, Queen Bitch herself. She *will not,* as part owner of the show, allow you to have a raise, and she will rip Sam's balls off if he agrees to give you so much as one cent more."

"Damn her," said Chloe sadly. "Why does she hate me so much?"

"Jealousy, my pet. You get more fan mail, more attention. You're more popular, your role is more exciting *and,* of course, you're better-looking. Don't fight it, toots, jealousy is a fact of life in this town. And don't take it personally, either. If it wasn't you playing Miranda, Sissy would loathe whoever it was. She's that kind of woman."

Chloe sighed. "I know, I've worked with her all these years. She's not a lot of laughs, believe me."

Jasper continued, "The network told me in deepest confidence that if you come back, *they* will give you the twenty thousand out of their own pockets. But Sissy and Sam must never know. . . . Ignore the cable, Chloe dear. Come back Tuesday. I promise you within two months you will have your raise."

"All right, all right, Jasper—I'll come back. Just as you knew I would, darling."

Jasper was pleased. He liked Chloe. The fact that she hadn't saddled herself with the usual slew of personal managers, business advisers and tax-shelter specialists meant she had probably saved more of her earnings than most actresses in her position. Clever girl. Not only that, but she steered clear of booze, dope and the swingers scene. By Hollywood standards she was almost square.

Chloe hung up, her feelings still unsettled. She felt ill-used. The tone of the cable, the way she had been so swiftly written out of the premiere episode, gave her a sense of mortality that made her uneasy. I'm dispensable, like Kleenex, she thought.

She watched Philippe on his wind-surfer as he maneuvered the small craft across the waves, brown curls clinging to his head. His body was tanned, lean and athletic, although he did little exercise. Emotionally he had been a rock, a difficult rock sometimes, but a rock nonetheless that she could lean on. And he handled her finances and her business affairs, and most of the time she was content with him, although he could be stubborn, and he had incredible mood swings which turned him from Prince Charming into male chauvinist pig. His conversation was quite limited, too. She sighed. The more she knew Philippe, the less substance there seemed to be in him. But the more the fabric of their psychological relationship weakened, the stronger the physical side became.

She shivered in spite of the Mediterranean sun. He pushed her so often for marriage. *Why?* She was extremely wary. The pain Josh had inflicted on her had not gone away completely.

Josh. Poor Josh. Brilliant, funny, self-destructive, complex Josh. Where was he now? And what was he doing?

◀ *Twenty-five* ▶

EMERALD WAS THE FIRST big name to be cast in "America." She would play Evelyn Alexander McFadden, the female lead, the lusty, beautiful proprietress of a hotel saloon in the little Midwestern border town. But Burt Hogarth was having trouble casting the male lead. He had approached some of the most prestigious actors in England for "America," with no success.

The network was anxious to start production by early July. They wanted the series ready to start airing in October of 1986. They had decided to program "America" opposite the so far invincible "Saga," which had been the ratings winner practically every week for the past four years.

It was generally agreed by the producers of "America" that the competition between Emerald Barrymore and Chloe Carriere would excite the viewers' interest. And they had shrewdly cast Pandora King, recently dumped by "Saga," to play the second female lead.

The only problem that remained was finding a strong English leading man to play opposite Emerald—a man who would not be overshadowed by her star power. Sir Geoffrey Fennel had bowed out in favor of doing Mercutio at the National. They approached Pierce Brosnan, Roger Moore and Michael Caine. All turned it down. The part of Malcolm McFadden called for a forty-to-fiftyish actor to be the heroic, tough and sardonic husband of Evelyn/Emerald. He had to be strong, sexy, masculine, have a sense of humor, ride a horse, fence, and be in peak physical condition.

Ten days before shooting commenced, the producers, having interviewed and tested dozens of actors and watched hundreds of miles of videotape, were still no closer to finding their male lead. Shooting was set to start the day after Independence Day. July Fourth was "America" Day, but no suitable leading man had been found.

❀   ❀   ❀

Josh lay in bed sweating. Pulses he never knew he possessed hammered in his skull and his tongue was a slab of decaying meat. The phone wouldn't stop. It kept on interrupting his dream—or was it a nightmare?

He and Chloe—young again. In love again. Kids, in the 1960s walking down King's Road laughing like teenagers. He never failed to have her in gales of laughter. She laughed a lot, and he wondered if she still did. He wondered if Philippe made her happy.

In his dream, he was hugging her so tightly he could feel his hardness against her thigh. Then people started to tug at him, pulling her away, as her expression of joy turned to fear. "Chloe, Chloe—" he tried to call her name, but the words wouldn't form. "Josh," she screamed, as hands, eager, excited hands, grabbed at her body and hair, tearing at her clothes. Then hysterical voices started yelling her name. "Chloe! Chloe! Miranda! Miranda! We love you! We love you!" Faceless fans pushed Josh away. He staggered and fell to the pavement, watching as they overwhelmed Chloe, pulling at her clothes, pulling them off, grabbing chunks of her hair and her flesh, tearing at her with their fingernails and teeth, huddling over her now as she lay bleeding on the pavement. She was screaming for help, but Josh couldn't move.

As the dream continued, he saw her body supine on the ground. Fans crawled over her like ants: kissing, biting, ripping her flesh, sucking her everywhere as she screamed with horror. He couldn't stop them. "Fuck off, Granddad," yelled a punk with green hair who was about to plunge himself into Chloe. "Fuck off or I'll ram this up yer arse." He shoved Josh viciously and he fell against the wall watching helplessly as the fans ravaged his Chloe.

He woke up screaming her name. Finally he heard the sound of the ringing phone echoing Chloe's cries.

"What? Who is it?" he yelled hoarsely, needing liquid, anything to ease his throat. The voice on the phone was friendly.

"Josh, dear boy, it's Jasper Swanson. How are you, old boy?"

"Fine, fine, just great, Jasper. How's yourself?" He tipped a half-empty wineglass to his cracked lips and felt the sour liquid moisten his parched tongue. "What's up, Jasper?"

"Well, dear boy, I don't know whether you'll be interested or not because I know the tour is going so well. . . ."

Fucking liar, thought Josh. The fucking *world* knows it's a flop. What's the old fart going on about? "Not that well, Jasper." He might as well be honest. "I mean, if another gig came along I could be tempted."

"Naturally, dear boy, naturally, which is why I'm calling you at this unearthly hour. You've heard of the book, *America: The Early Years?*"

"Yeah, of course, who hasn't?" He sat up, dying for a smoke. The ashtray was full of butts, the pack empty.

"Well, it's going to be a very important series. I think I have convinced them that you would be perfect for the part of Malcolm McFadden—the lead opposite Emerald Barrymore. Would that interest you, old man?"

There was silence as Josh digested this.

"Hello, hello, Josh? Are you there?" Jasper's time was money, and he was always impatient. He was a great agent, and he knew it. Some said he could sell the Vatican to the Pope, so good was he at his job.

"Yeah, yeah, I'm here." Josh lit one of the butts. The smoke seemed to clear his fuddled brain. "It's a soap opera, isn't it?"

"Well, I suppose you could call it that, but it's a very prestigious series. Burt Hogarth is the producer, and he is one of the most important men in Hollywood, let's face it, and of course Emerald Barrymore is still a major star."

"She hasn't worked in a while, has she?"

"Neither have you, dear boy." Frost crept into Jasper's voice. "I think you should face the fact, *young man*," he said with a hint of sarcasm, "that Hollywood is not clamoring for the services of fifty-year-old English ex-pop singers."

"Hold on, old boy, I'm nowhere near fifty," said Josh, "and I was *never* a pop singer."

"This role could make you an important star again, Josh. Everyone knows you have talent, but we all know your—well—your problems. I've had a damn difficult job convincing the network that you don't drink now, and are certainly *not* doing drugs." Disdain colored his tone. Jasper despised both drug addicts and alcoholics. "They have bought my idea of Joshua Brown as Malcolm. It's a hell of a role, old boy, and a stupendous break for you. They will pay twelve thousand an episode this year, and twenty-five thousand next season. They will supply you with two first-class tickets from London to L.A., and first-star billing after Emerald. And they want you in Hollywood for costume and camera tests the day after tomorrow. We'll go through all the other details then."

Josh's mind reeled. "My musical—what about the show? We've got another week here, then Leeds and Manchester, all the provinces."

"Your show is a flop. You know it. I know it. Even the British public knows it. The network is prepared to discuss a payoff with the theater owners. They will spring you, in fact. What do you say, Josh? This could be a major comeback for you, something you cannot turn your back on."

"Of course I'll do it," said Josh excitedly. "I have to—you know it. Book me into my old penthouse at the Wilshire. Can you get three plane tickets, first class?"

"No." Jasper was cool. Starting his demands already, was he? "If you need to bring two other people we can exchange the two first-class into three club. Remember, Josh, you are not a star in Hollywood. You cannot make demands—yet."

"Yeah, well, O.K. Change the tickets. It's just that I need to bring Sally, and Perry, my valet."

"Done, dear boy, done. Now, congratulations. I know you are not going to regret this. I'll be in touch tomorrow."

Josh lay back on the bed feeling euphoric. Hollywood! A major TV series with a major star! Emerald Barrymore. Publicity. The studio machine in action for him. The big time—it could be the big time for him again. It could be. It *would* be.

He leaped out of bed, energized with excitement, not needing the fix he'd been subconsciously thinking about.

"Look out, Chloe, babe, here I come!" he yelled.

Chloe went back to work on "Saga." Due to pressure from the network, Abby and Gertrude had relented. They had wanted to make an example of Chloe, show the rest of the cast and actors in their other shows what would happen to a star who demanded more money. Although they had bragged that they could do without Chloe's contribution to "Saga," they hadn't considered the network's reaction.

"Get her back on this show," Irving Schwarzman, president of the network, told Abby. "Give her the fucking raise—she deserves it, for Christ's sake. *Get her back*." Despite Abby and Gertrude's protestations that the inmates would end up running the asylum, they were overruled. Chloe came back twenty thousand dollars a week richer.

But her life with Philippe was becoming somewhat confusing. He had often been loving and affectionate; at the same time he was constantly arguing with her about getting married. His own bourgeois ideas and his even more bourgeoise French mother were pushing him. His mother thought that at forty he was too young to be living with a forty-three-year-old woman. She wanted grandchildren. He was her only child and she was nearly eighty.

Philippe hoped he could persuade Chloe to get married and then persuade her it was still possible for her to have a child. Now that he had seen her with Annabel, he realized how maternal Chloe could be and was determined to have a baby with her.

That was his plan, but it clearly wasn't Chloe's. Marriage to Philippe and babies at her age—ridiculous.

"Ursula Andress did it," he sulked. "She had a child at forty-four. Many women do; it's possible, you know, *chérie,* and you would be a wonderful mother."

"Why, Philippe? *Why* do we need marriage and a baby? We're happy the way we are—why spoil it?"

"You treat me like a stud," he replied sulkily. "You use me like men used to use a woman. You pick my brains and use my cock. You're just a user, Chloe."

"That's not true and you know it," she said angrily. "Look, we're together, we live together. I love you. Please, darling, *don't* make me get married. I've done it once. It doesn't work for me."

Annabel was living with them for the summer in the guest house. Both women were happy with each other. Their relationship was excellent and they spent hours together in deep conversation. Philippe felt annoyed and left out, and was sulking more than ever. Annabel swam in the pool, tended the rose garden, and scattered the pillows she beautifully embroidered all over the house. Making them was her hobby, that and playing her guitar.

Having Annabel around was good, the show was doing well, but Chloe often awoke in the night with nightmares. Sometimes in her nightmare she would see the face of the man with the knife whom the police said had wanted to harm her that night in Las Vegas. She wished they had never shown her his picture, that blank, emotionless face. When she awoke in the middle of the night, Philippe's strong arms and calming voice enfolded her. She needed him to fend off the demons that haunted her.

There was no question Sam was not feeling up to par. He had lost an alarming amount of weight and couldn't seem to force himself to eat anything. During the day's filming he often became exhausted and had to lie down to rest. He first noticed the ugly red patch when he felt an itching on his chest. Forcing himself to look in the mirror, he saw with a sinking dread what he had feared, what he had tried never to allow to enter his conscious thoughts—a red patch, scabby and swollen, the size of a quarter.

Bile rose in his throat. It couldn't be. It *couldn't.* Since the wild days of his youth, he had indulged in very few homosexual affairs. He had been more-or-less faithful to Freddy. Good old dependable Freddy. They were almost like a married couple—except a married couple who only do it occasionally have a tendency to do it with other people. He remembered Nick. He groaned. What about Freddy? Had he been with anyone else?

While the cat's away, the mice go down to the nearest gay bar. Did Freddy do that still? With AIDS the latest scourge? A rapping on the door announced that Sam was needed on the set in four minutes. He went back to the set, convincing himself it was all in his imagination, but he told his secretary to make a doctor's appointment as soon as possible.

He sat opposite Dr. John Willows, who looked grave.

"I'm sorry to have to tell you this, Sam." The doctor coughed. He was embarrassed. He'd known Sam for thirty-five years, but his homosexuality was a topic they had never discussed.

"What? What? Tell me for Christ's sake, John. Is it AIDS?"

The physician nodded. "I'm . . . I'm afraid so, Sam. We tested your blood twice to make sure there was no mistake. I'm very sorry." The doctor looked down at his mahogany desk, at the framed photograph of his wife, his grown-up children and his grandchildren. He thanked God he had always been faithful to her—for more than thirty years now. Thank God he hadn't given in to the temptations that had occasionally crossed his path. But what could he tell this aging TV superstar whose gaunt, lined face suddenly looked much older than fifty-five? How to help him?

"I'm afraid there's no cure just yet, as you know." He twiddled with the pencils on his immaculate desk.

"We can, of course, treat the carcinoma with ointments and antibiotics, but eventually the patches will get worse, I'm afraid."

Sam felt the room swimming before him. His career was in ruins. He had caught the plague—some likened it to the bubonic plague—the Black Death. And as with the plague there was no cure for this scourge of the eighties.

"How long." He gulped for air. "How long do you think I have before it'll be obvious?"

"Hard to say—months, maybe years. I'm not an expert, Sam. You know we've only been really aware of this disease for a few years, but it's spreading. My God, it's spreading."

"Will people have to know from you? Do you have to tell them?"

"Of course not, of course not." The doctor's voice had a heartiness he didn't feel. God, Sam was the seventh person he'd seen this month who had contracted the virus. It was terrifying.

"Listen, sport, if you need counseling about this, there are experts who know how to deal with the problem."

"Christ, no!" Sam was shocked. "I can deal with it myself. My career will be shot if a word of this gets out. You do understand that, don't you, John?"

"Of course, of course I do. Don't worry, Sam. No one will know, but . . ." The doctor looked at his watch. He had a waiting room full of patients. "You better check your contacts, your recent ones, that is."

"Damn it, John, I've only had one contact."

"Yes, yes, of course. Well listen, sport, come in next Tuesday and we'll get you set up with all the right stuff." He was desperate to end this. Nothing he could do. He was just a doctor seeing these pathetic men, trying to help them. He managed a sympathetic smile as he walked Sam to the door.

Only eight more months left. Eight months before he was out of this fucking hellhole. He had made no friends. No one in jail wanted to be friendly except when they abused him sexually.

In his cell each night, Calvin took out the magazines he'd accumulated. *Penthouse. Playboy.* All the magazines were old issues, but he didn't care.

He looked at them, gloating with excitement. In these magazines, the full-bosomed girls in their black lace underwear, with their open legs, all had one face. Emerald Barrymore's. Calvin had cut pictures of his idol from other publications and carefully pasted her head onto the bodies of the lush young creatures in his magazines. His Emerald. His queen.

He had been upset when he had seen the photographs of her in the tabloids emerging from jail. What infuriated him even more was the piece written at the time in the *American Informer.*

"If the part of Miranda Hamilton in prime time's hit series 'Saga' had gone to Emerald Barrymore, who lost the role to British singer Chloe Carriere, would Emerald have come to this pathetic end, living like a down-and-outer and with no trace of her former beauty left?"

Calvin had scrunched the paper up into a tight ball and thrown it into a corner of his cell. It was all *her* fault, that black-haired witch, that no-talent nonentity. It was because of Chloe Carriere that his Emerald was in this state. All because of her. She would suffer for it. When he got out of here she would really suffer for her sins.

Sam stalked into Freddy's workroom and went directly to the bar. Satin and lace, half-finished beaded frocks for fashionable starlets littered the sofa and table. Fashion magazines from Italy, France and England were piled on the floor. An orange cat lay on the windowsill basking in the hot Santa Monica sunshine. Outside, Sam could see suntanned teenagers oiling themselves, surfing, eating hot dogs and laughing. Laughing. Ha! Would he ever laugh again? Could he?

"Who've you been fucking, you lousy little faggot?" he demanded, as he knocked back a whiskey and poured another.

"No one, no one, I *swear*. My love—I've been faithful."

"Tell me the *truth*," Sam screamed. "Who? *Who?!* I know you did, I know it. I've got fucking AIDS, for Christ's sake, and you've given it to me, you bastard."

"Oh, God, no, no, you can't—oh, my good Lord. How could it happen?" Freddy threw himself onto the pile of fabrics on the couch and burst into tears.

"Don't fucking give me the fucking tears routine, you motherfucking queer." Sam could not contain his rage. The cat looked up, decided this was the wrong place to be and padded to the kitchen with dignity.

"Only once," Freddy sobbed. "Only once, darling."

"Don't call me darling." Sam's voice was hoarse. "Where? When? Who with?"

"Oh, God, Sam, I love you, you know I do. Oh, my God, I don't know why, I swear I don't know how but . . ."

"Yes, go on." Sam's lips tightened into a thin line. There was so much anger in him he thought he would explode. His face was crimson and his heart was beating so fast he thought he might have a heart attack.

"It was two years ago." Freddy wiped his bloodshot blue eyes with a scrap of one-hundred-dollar-a-yard Fortuny silk. "At the bathhouse."

"The fucking bathhouse! Shit! Go on, who with?"

"I don't remember," whined Freddy.

"Remember!" Sam grabbed him by his mauve cashmere sweater and leaned his face close to Freddy's. "Fucking *remember,* or I'll fucking kill you."

"Oh, Sam . . . Sam. It was awful, awful I couldn't help it. I was drugged. God knows why I did it. It's you I love. You know I do."

"Shut up, shmuck. I want *details*. All the details."

Gulping back his tears, Freddy tried to explain.

His friend from the airlines had arrived one night from Acapulco. He had brought a new kind of dope with him.

"Acapulco gold is a Marlboro compared to this," Hugh had told him, grinning from ear to ear.

They had smoked two joints, becoming so high that they didn't know what day it was—which was when Hugh suggested they visit the bathhouse. Since Sam had become Freddy's lover, bathhouses were strictly off-limits. But the dope had taken effect—Freddy no longer cared.

The place was jumping with the usual Saturday night insanity. The two men had showered and gone into the sauna room. Freddy, a handsome short blond man of thirty-nine, was usually highly sought after. Although he had saved himself exclusively for Sam for the past few years—except for a very occasional and discreet fling, that is—the dope had made him feel not only high but also extremely sexy. He was approached by the three gorgeous young studs he had observed oiling themselves on the beach this morning. He lay back as the boys attended to him expertly. It was mind-blowing. Ecstasy. Three or four other men stood around watching.

"Don't stop," begged Freddy. "I want more." By this time the other men were excited too. The first one rolled off Freddy and another took his place. Then the next, then the next. Freddy couldn't get enough of this incredible feeling. He felt like a satyr. The dope had made him insatiable.

"More," he begged, and they were only too eager to oblige.

Freddy's joy continued into the morning hours. But his shame lasted considerably longer.

"So that's it, my love," he said sadly to Sam. "That's what happened. I couldn't help it. I'm sorry. It won't ever happen again, I promise you."

"Too fucking late." Sam was weary now, disgusted with Freddy's story. "I've got AIDS. And you've probably got it. We're both going to *die*, Freddy, you know that, don't you?"

"Oh, God, what can we do?"

"Nothing." Sam sat heavily on the sofa, his anger spent. "There's nothing we can do now, Freddy, except wait."

Sam lost more weight each week. He had cleansed his system as much as possible, cutting out red meat, sugar, alcohol, salt and preservatives. He lived on the healthiest possible diet, slept ten hours a night, exercised, prayed, thought positively—and was terrified.

The hideous red scabs were gradually spreading all over his body until he could no longer bear to look at his flesh. He refused to allow his "Saga" dresser to help him when he changed. He lived in constant fear of being found out. He couldn't even confide the dreaded secret to Sissy. He didn't trust her—he didn't trust anyone.

His private line rang one lunch hour when he was restlessly trying to nap in his trailer.

"Sam, how are you? It's John Willows."

"Oh, hi, John. I'm . . . I'm fine." He tried to muster a cheerfulness in his tone.

"Well, Sam, I've got some good news and some bad," the doctor said, trying to sound heartier than he felt. "Which do you want first, old man?"

"The good," said Sam.

"Well, old man, it looks like we've arrested the virus—in your case. I wouldn't say you were in remission exactly, but the tests we did on you last week showed a slight but definite improvement. I think this new experimental drug from France could be working."

"Great, great, that's wonderful news, old boy. Wonderful!" He felt instantly better. Arrested the virus! That meant he could maybe last for years, decades even. He smiled a genuinely happy smile for the first time in months.

There was a pause as John Willows cleared his throat—an embarrassed silence.

"And so what's the bad news, old man? Nothing could be *that* bad after what you've just told me."

"Well, old boy, I've just had a call from the clinic."

"What clinic?" asked Sam.

"The clinic where we sent your blood to be tested," said Dr. Willows, treading carefully.

"So—so what, what's so bad about that?" barked Sam.

"I have to level with you, Sam, this is terrible for you, I know, but when we sent your blood in to be tested, I told my assistant to put a phony name on it."

"Yes! Yes!" Sam sat bolt upright, almost screaming now. "So what happened?"

Silence.

"She did it, didn't she?" His voice rose to such a crescendo that Sissy, trying to nap in the trailer next door with earplugs in and eye mask on, sent her maid over to tell him to shut up.

"Fuck off!" Sam screamed at the woman as she knocked tentatively on his trailer door.

"I'm sorry, Sam," continued the doctor. "She didn't. She goofed. She's new, it was her first week here, fresh out of nursing school. Your name was on the blood sample we sent to the clinic. And there's a problem now. The problem is—"

"*Whaaat*—tell me what the fuck the problem is. I'm making a fucking series here, I can't shilly-shally around listening to you all day. *Tell me!!*"

"O.K., O.K., calm down, please. This is pretty embarrassing for me."

"Embarrassing?" Sam shrieked, out of control.

"I'm very sorry to tell you, Sam, that the clinic's confidential log book containing the names of all the individuals carrying the virus has been stolen."

"Stolen. *Stolen.* Who the hell would want to steal it?" Suddenly Sam thought he might black out. He groped for one of the cigars he hadn't touched in three months and tipped a bottle of Evian water to his lips.

"They think it's been stolen by blackmailers," the doctor said quietly.

"*Blackmailers!*" Now he knew he was going to faint.

"In fact, the police are pretty sure of it."

"Oh, my God, I'm ruined. I'm fucking ruined!"

"Well, if it's any consolation to you, old man, there are hundreds of others on that list who could possibly be ruined too. Prominent lawyers, politicians, doctors and actors. You're not the only actor in town who has

AIDS, you know. It's rampant here. In San Francisco it's a nightmare. It's bankrupting the city."

"Jesus Christ, Jesus Christ, Jesus H. Christ," Sam kept repeating.

"I'm sorry, Sam. Look, I'll talk to you tomorrow. I—I have a few more calls I must make. You do understand?"

"Sure, John, sure, sure." Sam hung up and, head in hands, sat stonily until Sissy walked in.

"What is it, darling? You look positively *vile*. And why have you started that filthy habit again?"

Sam didn't answer. Sissy was wearing a fawn 1930s fitted suit, with a beige fox collar and muff, and a ridiculous Cossack hat. Her blond hair, teased to within an inch of its life, fuzzed out around the hat. Her eyes were shaded by eyelashes like awnings, her lips a thin crimson slash.

"Sam. Answer me, Sam," she snapped, used to his jumping to attention when she spoke.

He looked at her—at her angular hard body, her bony sparrow's face.

"Get out of here, Sissy, right now," he growled.

"Sam—I—"

"Get out, you cunt," he screamed. "Out, *out,* out of here. I don't want to see your bloody face again. Get out of my dressing room." The uproar caused two assistant directors and a couple of stand-ins to come over and gape at the normally charming, even-tempered star.

"Mr. Sharp, Mr. Sharp, calm down, *please.*" Debbie Drake shooed the others, including a furious Sissy, out of the trailer and slammed the door behind her.

"I'm sorry, sir. Is there anything I can do for you?"

"Nothing, dear, nothing. I'm sorry. Give me half an hour, Debbie, and I'll be back on the set. Tell Chelsea to shoot Sissy's close-up first. I just need a little time to myself, dear."

"Of course, sir, of course. We will give you as long as you need," she said, and tactfully left him, closing his trailer door quietly.

◀ *Twenty-six* ▶

Horace Reid, editor of the *American Informer,* flipped through the pages of the thin book with mounting excitement. What a coup! This list was dynamite. It was mind-blowing. And to top it all it had come into his hands anonymously. He hadn't had to pay a brass farthing for this unbelievable and incriminating item. It would have cost at least thirty thousand dollars if he had had to buy it.

"Six actors, three of them household names, four politicians, two writers. It's *dynamite.* The hottest thing we've ever had. We'll have the sellout issue of all time when we print this list. We're gonna take TV ads, the works." The ugly little man smirked with glee at his assistant, as he wondered fleetingly who hated someone on the list enough to do this.

"We'll leak it a little bit at a time, I think," said Horace, picking his teeth with a paper clip. On the walls behind his desk were framed some of the more memorable best-selling front-page stories of the past decade:

"Marilyn Monroe a Lesbian." That had sold over eight million copies.

"I was Elvis' Love Child." Close to eight and a half million there.

"President Kennedy's Assassination: Masterminded by His Own Family." Another biggie.

Since leaving Australia and becoming editor of the *Informer* ten years ago, Horace Reid had turned the tabloid into a gold mine. He left no stone unturned to obtain the most intimate, degrading and damaging stories on celebrities: stars, politicians, British royalty. His assistant shook his head. "It's definitely an original. If anyone else *does* have it, we go to press first, don't we?" He smiled, revealing jagged yellow teeth.

"Look at these names," Horace said gleefully. "Look at 'em. It's a dream come true! I don't even know which name we should devote the bulk of the story to."

"I think it's obvious, don't you?" the other man said crisply. "Sam Sharp's the one. I mean . . . Star of 'Saga Has AIDS. What a story! We'll sell ten million."

"You bet your bollocks, sport," chortled Horace Reid in his thick Australian accent. "That poor old poofter is finally going to pay for his sins, and we're going to have our best-selling issue ever. Whoopee!"

"Saga's" diminutive PR man, Christopher McCarthy, called Sam in his trailer a few days later.

"Sam, I'm a little worried."

"Why, what's up now?" Sam replied irritably. He was like a cat on hot bricks these days, even taking to snorting a touch of cocaine each morning to get him out of his terrible black depressions.

"I've heard a rumor," began Christopher tentatively. "I know it's ridiculous, it couldn't *possibly* be true—and you can sue the arse off them, of course—but I've heard that the *Informer*'s cover story for next week is the most disgraceful they've ever had. And I'm afraid it's about you."

"Me? About me?" Sam's words were a whisper. This couldn't possibly be true. So *soon?* It was impossible. "What about me?" He sat down. He felt nauseated.

"Well . . ." Christopher was embarrassed, but he was a good press agent so he had to get it out. It was his job. "They say you've got AIDS. I *know* it's ridiculous, Sam."

"It *is* ridiculous, it's disgraceful. Outrageous." Sam summoned up all his theatrical talent to make his outrage believable.

"It's disgusting," sighed Christopher. "They're unscrupulous bastards, those supermarket rags, absolute scum. Nevertheless we've got to fight this all the way, Sam. I think we should set up some interviews immediately: Oprah Winfrey, Carson and the morning news program. Then *People*, I'm sure, will do a cover story. I'll call Suzy, Liz Smith and the trades.

We'll kill this whole thing. Defuse the story right away. Show them how great you look. This is a vicious smear campaign and we *cannot* let those bastards get away with it, right, Sam?"

"Right," Sam said wearily. He had slumped onto the couch, shakily trying to pour whiskey into a tumbler, but his hand was trembling so much that he dropped it.

"Are you *sure* about this story, Christopher? Are they *really* going ahead?"

"I'm afraid so. In fact, I'm positive," said Christopher grimly. "It's unfair, Sam. It's the pits. I'll keep you posted. Don't worry about anything. I'll set up the interviews, and prepare a statement for the press to go on the wire service immediately."

"Do that, Chris," said Sam softly. "Do that. I'd appreciate it."

Chloe and Sissy were having a heated argument on the set with Luis Mendoza. He stood arrogantly, arms crossed, in his black silk shirt and white linen trousers, gold chain adorning his neck, challenging the two divas of soap. It was rare for Sissy and Chloe to agree about anything, but in this case they had no choice. Luis was becoming a conceited oaf. His astonishing success had swelled his head and ego to such an extent that few people could handle him any longer.

This argument, about Luis's motivation in the scene, raged while the crew stood around watching. When the shot rang out, everyone thought it was from the cop series on the next sound stage. It was only when Debbie Drake, calling Sam's trailer, didn't get an answer, and so went to investigate, that they discovered what had happened. The hero of the United States, the actor who had so brilliantly portrayed Lincoln, Eisenhower and FDR—America's "real man"—had killed himself.

Calvin was glued to the television set in the prison common room. A second celebrity funeral in four years, and he was missing it. Soon there would be a third—and he'd be there that time. His lips parted in an animal snarl as he saw Chloe, escorted by Philippe, descend from a black Mercedes, dressed in dark gray and looking sad.

You're next, *madam!* he said to himself. Trumped-up bitch. She *deserved* to die.

"It's a nightmare, a fucking *nightmare*," ranted Abby, stomping up and down the Aubusson carpet in his football stadium of an office. "What the hell are we going to do?"

Gertrude's cuticles were picked to the quick. Her normally well-groomed frizzy hair hadn't been combed for twenty-four hours, and the network was in a furor. Sam's suicide was tragedy enough; but when the *American Informer* came out with its AIDS cover story on him, it was crisis time.

Hate mail for Sam started pouring into the offices of the producers, and especially to Sissy.

The grief-stricken widow had retired to the seclusion of her Holmby

Hills mansion for ten days, emerging only for the funeral, a fragile ninety-five-pound figure sheathed entirely in Oscar de la Renta black, wearing a veil as thick as a beekeeper's.

She had cried herself to sleep for ten straight nights. She missed Sam more than she had ever thought she could. But there was something else. So little was known about AIDS—could he somehow, even though they had not had sex together for years, have given it to her?

To those privileged to see the early rushes, "America: The Early Years" looked as if it was going to become a gigantic hit. The chemistry between Emerald and Josh was electrifying. Both were vibrant, dynamic and attractive. Sparks sizzled in their scenes together.

Emerald became seriously attracted to Josh, completely infatuated with his intelligence, his masculinity, his sensitivity and his fabulous sense of humor, listening to his anecdotes and jokes for hours. Josh loved having such an appreciative audience, but unfortunately he did not feel the slightest desire for her. He liked her—she was a competent actress and still a looker. Yes, she was in peak condition, all traces of the blowzy hag leaving jail just a few months before obliterated by a strict regimen of early nights, no dope, no alcohol and lots of exercise. But she was not his type, and he was going through a period of celibacy.

Emerald was happy in her work. She enjoyed "America," enjoyed being Queen Bee again, but she needed, wanted a man, and her luminous green eyes were firmly focused on Josh Brown. They spent a great deal of time together both during and after work, but however much Emerald practiced her feminine wiles on him, Josh was simply not biting. He did not want to become involved with her. She was a man-eater, an extremely demanding female in her relationships with men. He liked her but was not prepared to be her next man. He didn't want or need that. What he *did* need was to concentrate on his career, on keeping fit, steering clear of booze, broads and drugs, and making this the best damn show on prime time. In everyone's mind was the desire to beat "Saga" in the ratings. The network, the actors and the producers were all doing their utmost to make their show the best. And it was.

Long before the first episode of "America" aired, those who had seen some of the rushes were raving about the quality of the production and the performances of the cast, particularly Emerald and Josh. Emmy talk was bandied about. Eventually Chloe heard about it.

On Chloe's instructions, Vanessa had visited the set of "America" to check out the rumors and see what was going on. Vanessa had made a lunch date with Pandora King. Standing on the sidelines, watching Burt Hogarth direct, Vanessa realized this wasn't the usual hurried TV direction—this was feature time.

Each episode of "America" cost twice as much as "Saga." The network executives were tearing their hair out, but Hogarth had been given carte blanche on this production, and only if he failed to deliver in the ratings could they change anything. Until then, they realized they had a gem on their hands even if it cost a fortune. They would not rock Burt Hogarth's boat. "America" had more class than "Saga." It was masterly, artistic, stylish yet with a rugged outdoor realism depicting pioneer America. They were banking on the fickleness of the viewing public to switch gradually from "Saga" to "America."

Vanessa stood quietly in a dim corner of the set watching Emerald and Josh rehearse. The rumors of their magnetism together were obviously true. Not only did Josh look more attractive than ever, but Emerald was as ravishing as she had been at thirty-five. It was astonishing, since she was fifteen years older than that, give or take. Granted, face-lifts and other plastic surgery and platinum hair can do a lot for a woman, but Emerald had an undeniable glow about her, particularly when she was close to Josh and looked at him with the eyes of a woman in love. As a screen pair they sizzled.

Vanessa knew that she would have to report this news to Chloe, who still cared for her ex-husband in spite of their separations. The rumors that Emerald and Josh were having a passionate affair and were crazy for each other were upsetting her in spite of herself. Neither Emerald, Josh nor the network publicists denied the story. It was great publicity for the show. From the look of the two of them together on the set, Vanessa was pretty sure the rumors were true.

Poor Chloe. Vanessa sighed. She disliked Philippe, and Vanessa knew that Chloe was becoming bored with him, despite her assurances that their love life was as good as ever.

Wait until Chloe sees the "new" Josh, thought Vanessa. He was a changed man: more at ease, more in control, more manly and wittier than she remembered. He really was quite wonderful. His potential had come to fruition. Mmm, thought Vanessa. If I still liked men, I might even go for him myself.

There was no point in telling Chloe she had any chance of getting him back. He was obviously as crazy about Emerald as she was about him. Vanessa watched them as, arm in arm, they strolled toward the coffee machine, deep in conversation.

Chloe listened to Vanessa and died a little. So it was true. Oh, well, she thought regretfully, how could Josh help but fancy Emerald? According to Jasper, she was as beautiful and desirable as she'd ever been. Josh knew that Chloe was living with Philippe. She hadn't even called him in the months he'd been back in California.

Stop thinking about Josh, she chided herself. Think about *Emerald.* If her looks and acting are as stunning as Vanessa, Jasper and half the town says they are, and the series is as brilliant as people think, "Saga" could be in serious trouble, and Chloe's reign as Queen of Prime Time could soon be over.

"Saga's" ratings started to slip badly three episodes into the new season. It was as though the public's love affair with the show had ended with Sam's death. As "Saga's" ratings dropped, "America: The Early Years," which had come into the Nielsen poll with a 20 share in the first week, started to accelerate. As each week it picked up one or two more ratings points, "Saga" dropped a couple. "America" was on the way up as "Saga" was on the way down.

At a meeting in the offices of Gertrude and Abby, the creative forces of "Saga" had come together to try and devise some new angles and clever story lines *fast*.

"Who got the most fan mail last month?" barked Abby to Bill Herbert.

"Chloe," replied Bill, consulting his notes. "Between ten and twelve thousand a month. That's more than any other series star, and she's been holding that average for over four years now."

"Who's next?" Abby was impatient. He already knew Chloe got the most.

"Well, it used to be Sissy, but since Sam . . . er . . . left us, it's dropped considerably. Actually, Luis Mendoza's mail has increased tremendously, especially after his first love scene with Chloe."

"We should definitely feature him more," murmured Gertrude.

"Make him more important. Now we've lost Sam, we need a strong male character. You know it was Sissy and Sam who stopped Luis from getting a meatier story line. So let's build him up, make him our main male focus."

"He's strong all right." Bill grinned. "I've never seen so much erotic fan mail from women. You can't believe the things they say they'd like to do to him."

"Give him more screen time," said Abby curtly. "More love scenes, strong emotional scenes with Chloe."

"Make him the male lead," said Bill.

"Exactly," Abby replied. "Build him up. We've got to regain our ratings from 'America.' They're fucking destroying us. The network is pissed. They want to see some action." He turned to the show's three scriptwriters. "Now get to work, boys, write some juicy scenes, for Christ's sake. Otherwise we'll *all* be out of a job by the end of the season."

Josh looked at the magazine Perry had brought him. "From Has-been to TV Stardom." The cover of *People* magazine heralded the favorable article inside.

Josh's smiling face was on the cover. It was the face of a handsome, sexy, confident man in his forties. His hair, showing few traces of gray, was pushed casually forward to disguise the fact that his hairline had receded slightly. His tanned face had a few lines around the eyes, and wrinkles here and there, but they suited him. They were the lines that appeared on a face that laughed a lot. It was the face of a man at peace with himself, who accepted his age, was comfortable in his own skin.

Josh had gone through many changes since his latest comeback. He had learned from his past mistakes. In addition to giving up drugs completely, he had cut his drinking to a minimum and no longer chased young girls. With a newfound success in middle age, he lost the need to prove himself between the sheets with women young enough to be his daughters. A psychiatrist had helped, too.

He had the occasional girlfriend—usually a woman over thirty, but lovemaking now was secondary to what he wanted from a woman. Conversation, wit and humor, shared values, friendships were his requirements now. He looked for these in the women he dated, but although they had some of the qualities he admired, none had them all—he realized he had found them all together only in Chloe. Often he dreamed about her—about their life together before his career had started to go foul, before little dollybirds had loomed too large in his life.

In sessions with Dr. Donaldson, he realized what a shit he had been to her, how wonderful she had been to him.

Why, why did I screw it up? he often asked himself. The best goddamn woman I ever had and I fucking ruined it. Shit!

He sometimes fantasized that he and Chloe had reconciled, were together again as they once had been. He had never met a woman with whom he had enjoyed life so much, whose humor was on his own wavelength, who so completely understood him. God, what he'd put her through. How many reconciliations had they had? He couldn't remember. He'd been too heavily into nose candy and nymphets at the time. Trying to bolster his flagging career. Sticking his prick into whoever asked for it, and some who didn't.

And Chloe had known. But she had been there for him until it had become unbearable for her.

He heard she was happy with Philippe. He was glad for her, although it gave him a pang every time he saw pictures of them together. Occasionally they bumped into each other at a social or industry function—the People's Choice Awards, the Emmys, or a Beverly Hills screening room. She was always on Philippe's arm, smiling and friendly. Chloe was not one to bear a grudge, and she was genuinely happy for Josh's success.

If it was a scientific principle that no two objects can share the same space at the same time, then Chloe knew there was not enough room for Philippe in her life. She still thought subconsciously about life with Josh, although conscious thoughts of him were banished from her mind with military precision. But her dreams were peopled with images of their life as it had once been. Her weekdays were filled with "Saga" work, "Saga" minutiae, time-consuming problems with script revisions, dialogue changes, costuming, set politics. The public could never imagine what a hard, unglamorous drudge grinding out a prime time TV series could be. Her weekends were spent in a mindless daze drifting about the house without makeup, in a track suit, lazing, with Philippe ever attentive nearby.

Philippe's idea of a fun-filled evening was to watch three videos back to back, make love a couple of times and dine on takeout pizza in bed. Chloe, exhausted from her unrelenting pressure of work, enjoyed this at the beginning of the relationship, but she soon began to realize that culturally and conversationally Philippe was dull. True, he filled the present need in her life for companionship without effort, intimacy without commitment, closeness without true emotional involvement—and she was fond of him. He demanded little of her except her presence, and since she was usually so exhausted after work, for a while this was welcome.

But on the rare occasions when they made the social rounds of the Bel Air circuit, he often succeeded in embarrassing her by his lack of depth and obliviousness to anyone other than himself or Chloe. It was, nevertheless, flattering to be so adored, thought Chloe as she observed Philippe lolling sleepily on a Regency satin couch at one of Daphne's star-studded soirees. Around him thronged two dozen of Hollywood's most famous and scintillating individuals, the women resplendent in designer dresses, designer jewelry and designer cosmetic surgery, the men all distinguished, whether they were six feet four and hirsute or five feet two and bald.

Chloe's friends had all made genuine efforts to conduct a civilized conversation with Philippe during the eighteen months that he and Chloe had lived together. All had eventually decided that it was a waste of time. He had little to say, no opinions to speak of, and other than his obsession with Chloe and his dashing good looks, none of them saw what she could find remotely interesting about him. Chloe found herself thinking the same thing as she touched up her makeup in Daphne's powder room. They had often quarreled about his lack of enthusiasm and his lack of interest in her friends, but he refused to compromise, making no attempt to ingratiate himself, leaving Chloe embarrassed by his dullness, and her women friends changing place cards in desperation at dinner parties so as not to sit next to him.

Chloe sighed as she adjusted the sleek lines of her black silk Donna Karan dress. The thought of sitting on the sofa attempting to talk to Philippe, who would try to make an early getaway so that he could watch another video and try and jump on her for the third time that Saturday, was not enthralling. The man was insatiable, and she was wearying of his incessant sexual demands and lack of communicativeness and empathy.

"Bored, let's face it, duckie, you're *bored stiff* with him, aren't you?" Daphne interrupted Chloe's reverie, red curls springing animatedly around her chubby Cupid's face, as she entered the room with her usual gusto.

"I mean, he really *is* dull as dishwater, dear. Good-looking or not, I know you can do so much better. Don't you think it's time to dump him? I know this *divine* Italian marquis who is coming to town next week. Dying to meet you, duckie. If not you, then Linda Gray is his second choice. What do you think?"

She plucked off a few loose beads on the bodice of her old, but still serviceable, Norman Hartnell frock, and squinted at her abundant curves with satisfaction. At well over sixty-five, she was still a good-looking, sexy woman. She knew it and it had been proven many times throughout the past four decades by the number of stars who had shared her bed.

The walls of her tiny guest loo were decorated from floor to paisley-tented ceiling with photographs of Daphne in the company of many of

Hollywood's and Europe's most famous celebrities. There were over one hundred framed pictures dating back to the late 1940s when Daphne and Jasper Swanson had descended to the shores of Malibu and the hills of Beverly fresh from their respective successes in England—his at Gainsborough Studios, where he had starred in a dozen swashbuckling adventure films, and hers initially through a contract with Sir Alexander Korda, who had tried unsuccessfully to turn her into a clone of either Vivien Leigh or Merle Oberon. When the realization hit Sir Alex that red curls, a perky smile and a thirty-nine-inch bust cannot compete with alabaster skin, smoldering black hair and a sylphlike body, he sold her contract to Ealing Studios, where she did rather better in black-and-white comedies with Alec Guinness and Jack Warner.

Chloe looked at the attractively saturnine face of thirty-six-year-old Jasper and vibrant thirty-year-old Daphne laughing arm in arm with the Oliviers and Sir Ralph Richardson on the lawn of Highgrove one long-ago summer afternoon. In another photo, Daphne gazed fondly into the faces of a handsomely togaed Richard Burton and a Grecian-draped Jean Simmons on the set of *The Robe,* a CinemaScope epic in which Daphne had played a small part. Daphne was smiling and laughing in many other photos in the company of what were, the gossips said, some of her many lovers. Errol Flynn, Gary Cooper, David Niven, William Powell— Daphne had been rumored to have bedded them all, but would neither confirm nor deny to even her closest chums which, if any, of those illustrious lads she had tumbled with.

"Let's just say all my lovers have been well-endowed," she would laughingly reply to anyone inquisitive enough to ask. "Both *above* and *below* the belt, I require the utmost stimulation. Big cocks are not enough. I need big brains too.

"Take a look at him, duckie." Daphne pointed with a long vermilion fingernail at a photo of herself with a young, very handsome blond boy taken on a film set in about 1950.

"That's the sort of man you should meet, dear heart." She sighed. "Dusty Lupino. He was a big star and one of the best lovers I ever had. I taught him a great deal too—even though he was eighteen and I was—ah —eh—over thirty. He's rich as Croesus now, duckie, and *still* only fifty-six. His business manager got him out of the movie business and into real estate when you could still buy half of Rodeo Drive for under a million. He's never looked back, and still looks divine, even if he is a bit of a recluse."

"Darling, darling! *Stop.* I *know* what you're saying. Philippe is not right for me. I'm aware of that. I'm not as much of a fool as everyone thinks, Daphne darling. Yes, we squabble. Yes, he's not very stimulating or entertaining. But for *now,* Daphne, dear, I'm living with him, and when we end it, which, as you say, and as I *know,* is inevitable, I shall then cast my eyes further afield, but *not yet,* my dear." She bent and kissed Daphne's Coty-perfumed cheek. "Not yet. I can only handle one man at a time."

"What a quaint, old-fashioned girl you are," sighed Daphne in mock exasperation as they went back to the party. "But remember, dear, when you *are* ready to dump him, all your friends will be rooting for you."

"O.K., creep, time to get the fuck out of here." The guard picked at a boil on his chin. "Better not try anything again, creep. You'll be in a lot of trouble if you do. Now git!"

Calvin ignored the man. He was free. Free at last to go where he wanted—do what he wanted. He had to find her now. Track her down. Make her suffer, as he had suffered over the years.

Although he had read in the tabloids that Emerald had the lead in the new series, "America: The Early Years," it continued to infuriate him that Chloe Carriere was such a huge star in "Saga," which was still a phenomenal success. He couldn't stand Chloe. He loathed her arrogance in that part. He detested her trumped-up English accent. He despised everything about her. Most of all he hated her because she was the reason his beloved Emerald had hit rock bottom. She had to be punished.

❖ *Twenty-seven* ❖

"AND NOW, LADIES and gentlemen, it's America's Favorites!" The crowd applauded frantically. Whistles and shrieks of appreciation greeted the master of ceremonies as he announced the nominees in each category.

Chloe and Philippe had arrived late. They smiled for the phalanx of fans and paparazzi who were gathered like a flock of sheep outside the Santa Monica Civic Auditorium. She held his tuxedoed arm, looked into his smiling face, smiled for the cameras—Mr. and Mrs. Togetherness, a portrait of bliss, even though they weren't wed.

Tonight was an important night. These January awards, both for films and TV, were considered the harbingers of the Emmys and the Oscars later that year.

Chloe wore a magnificent Christian Dior white taffeta dress, which cinched her waist and pushed up her bosom. Her black hair was piled high with diamanté combs, and around her neck was a beautiful Georgian rose diamond necklace that Vanessa had found for her.

As she and Philippe settled themselves, with whispered apologies, at the "Saga" table, where Sissy, Luis, Abby, Gertrude and Bill Herbert were already seated, Chloe glanced around the auditorium. Josh was smiling at her. She smiled back. After all, he was her ex-husband. "We must be polite, dear," said Sissy snidely. She was dressed from shoulders to toes in yellow bugle beads that matched her hair. The six-month period of mourning was over and she was playing the merry widow with a good-looking young actor on her arm.

"Pour me some wine, darling, will you?" Chloe murmured to Philippe.

"You drink too much," he whispered too loudly. Surreptitiously she looked over at Josh again. He was with Emerald, who looked dazzling in a mint-green silk jersey Empire gown, the bodice embroidered in four-leaf clovers.

"How cute!" sneered Sissy. "She needs all the luck she can get: Tyne Daly is the hot favorite tonight."

It was a night of extreme competition. "Saga" and "America" were competing with "Hill Street Blues," "Dynasty" and "Cagney and Lacey" for best dramatic TV series.

Chloe, Sissy, Emerald, Tyne Daly and Sharon Gless were up for best actress in a dramatic TV series. Josh and Luis, Daniel Travanti and Larry Hagman were nominated for best dramatic actor.

The tension was palpable as one by one glittering stars of screen and TV paraded their finery onto the stage either to present an award or accept one.

Chloe, having won the past two years, was less concerned than the others about the coveted crystal statuettes. She felt that Tyne or Sharon Gless definitely deserved one for their consistently fine work in "Cagney and Lacey."

Emerald was desperate for the award. "America: The Early Years" was only in its first season, but it was a huge success—now neck and neck with "Saga." Winning would be a major step for her and complete her comeback.

Josh didn't really care. He had quickly joined the rarefied ranks of mature TV leading men and it would not mean anything to his career one way or another. What *did* mean something to him, although he was reluctant to admit it, was the beautiful black-haired woman in the white gown sitting two tables away.

Goddamn it, Josh, he said to himself for the hundredth time, why did you mess up that relationship? How the hell could you have let that woman go? You loved her, she adored you. . . .

Emerald pulled at his sleeve and whispered animatedly into his ear, but he hardly listened. He was watching Chloe out of the corner of his eye, across a room filled with some of the most beautiful women in the world. His Chloe. His forever lover, gone now forever. He watched her bend her dark head to Philippe's brown one, smile at something the Frenchman said, and put her pale hand on his arm in the loving gesture he remembered only too well. She raised her hand to Philippe's hair and ruffled it. She used to do that to me, thought Josh fiercely. They certainly looked happy, gazing into each other's eyes, fingertips touching. There was something about the tall Frenchman that Josh didn't like. He envied his relationship with Chloe, but there was something else that he couldn't quite put his finger on. It was a quality many people felt about Philippe. He made them uneasy.

Josh came out of his reverie to hear the nominations for best actress being announced.

Emerald had a hand on his knee, which became more viselike as each name was called. She was about to cut off his circulation. He could see her moist cyclamen lips parted in anticipation, longing. She was lusting for this award, this accolade to symbolize her return to the top of the heap.

He glanced at Chloe, who looked cool, calm and collected. Sissy's face wore a fixed smile. She too was dying for this award. She had won it the same year she won the Oscar. It was time again. She deserved it. Hers was a performance—an acting tour de force. She was a wonderful actress; everyone knew it. Certainly for someone of her rancorous nature to bring such believability to the cloying role she played proved she indeed had considerable talent.

The "Cagney and Lacey" actresses looked self-possessed. Their show was a hit, too. This award wouldn't affect it—or them—much. It would just be icing.

"The envelope, please." Don Johnson was presenting this award. "And the winner is . . ." He paused, looking mischievously at the audience, milking the moment.

"Once again, Miss Chloe Carriere!" A shriek of delight came from the fans and audience high in the gallery of the auditorium. Almost as loud was the cry from Chloe, who threw her arms around Philippe in a bear hug that almost strangled him, blew kisses to everyone at her table and, in a flurry of white taffeta, ascended the stage to make her acceptance speech.

In the gallery, Calvin's fury turned his face scarlet. It was Emerald, the Goddess, who deserved this honor. She truly deserved it. Not this second-rate British bitch. How *dare* she take Emerald's award?

His binoculars focused on Chloe's slim figure as she addressed the audience and the millions of TV fans. She expressed her happiness, thanked the cast, the crew, Jasper, blew a kiss, wept a little and was escorted triumphantly off the stage by Don Johnson, holding the statuette high above her head.

Calvin turned his binoculars on Emerald. She had removed a tiny lace hanky from her rhinestone Judith Leiber purse and was blowing her nose. *She was crying!* Chloe Carriere had made his darling weep! Bitch!

Josh was trying to comfort Emerald when the award for best actor was announced. "And the winner is Joshua Brown for 'America: The Early Years,'" Angie Dickinson announced with a big smile. Calvin ignored Josh's hasty departure to collect his award and continued to focus his attention and his binoculars on his lovely Emerald. He hated to see her hurt like this. Chloe, done up like a dog's dinner in virgin white, would pay for this. The time was coming for Miss Carriere. Oh, the time was coming *soon.*

In the eighth week of the fall season, "Saga" was rated the number two show and "America" number one. One week later the ratings were reversed: "America" was number two, "Saga" number one. The following week, "America" held its lead but "Saga" lost a couple more ratings points, dropping to number six.

Panic reigned at MCPC. Advertisers started to cancel the time slots on "Saga," which they now thought were overpriced. They preferred to sell their products on the rival network where, with more viewers tuned to "America," their goods would sell better. The network was giving Abby and Gertrude a hard time. They must make the shows more exciting, more dramatic, meatier, so that they could regain their lost audiences. Gertrude and Abby screamed at the line producer, Bill Herbert, they screamed at the writers, they screamed at the actors and crew. An emergency conference was called with Sissy, Luis and Chloe, to pick their brains for fresh story ideas. Everyone seemed to be becoming desperate to get back their place in the sun.

Chloe was not too concerned. She had always realized that the flavor of the month had to change. She still felt loyal to the show and enjoyed it, but she was looking forward to accepting other offers of miniseries and movies, singing again, making a video for MTV.

Luis hoped "Saga" would be canceled. He was hot for movies now. Jasper had three sizzling offers for him in the spring. In one he could even star with Sabrina. He felt he had done enough TV, although he had been in "Saga" little over a year. He wanted to move on, become a real movie star.

Sissy, perennially discontented, wanted to stay with "Saga." Since she now owned her own *and* Sam's points in the show, she was making a fortune. She would make even more when it went into syndication.

After losing the America's Favorites award to Chloe, Emerald had gone on another bender. Increasingly frustrated and upset by Josh's lack of interest in her as a woman, she had again sought solace in liquor. Try as she might, she could not get him to play her game. He had told her frankly, "Look, Emerald, I think you're great. You're a terrific woman, beautiful, fun to be with. I just don't think of you that way." Emerald bit her lip until it almost bled. Rejection from a man was hard for her—it had happened so rarely. Was this a portent of her future?

They were in Josh's car outside her house, having just returned from a screening and dinner at Corinna and Freddie Fields's house. Emerald had had many glasses of champagne and, feeling frisky, she tried to embrace Josh, but he had drawn away from her.

"Please, Emerald. I want to be your friend, I've told you that so many times. It's better that way."

"Why?" Emerald almost yelled. "Why just *friends?*" She spat the words. "We've got so *much* going for us, Josh. I don't have anyone in my life right now and I don't think you do . . . do you?"

Josh didn't answer. He lit a Marlboro and stared out at the starless sky.

"Do you, Josh? If you do, tell me and I'll . . . oh, hell, I'll get over it." A tear slid down her matte-complexioned cheek and dripped onto her green satin Enrico Coveri lounging pajamas. He remained silent, smoking, his strong profile etched against the door of his Porsche.

"Are you in love with someone?" she asked again, so persistently that he turned to her and said quietly, "Yes, Emerald, I suppose I am. I am 'in love,' as you say, with someone else."

"Who is it?" He was silent. She *had* to know. "It's Chloe, isn't it?" She felt bitterness. "It's your ex-wife, isn't it?"

"She's *not* my ex-wife—not yet—and, yes, well, you're right. I haven't quite got over my feelings for her."

"Oh, my God! Have you been seeing her?" Emerald took the cigarette from Josh's hands and took a deep drag.

"No, absolutely not. She's living with Philippe Archambaud. But I'd like to."

"Damn, shit, hell!" cried the diva as she jumped out of his car and ran into her house in tears. *How could he reject her?* Emerald Barrymore. World-renowned beauty, idol of millions. Legendary sex goddess. How *could* he? She couldn't understand it. Not when she was looking so good and was so successful. She realized she was acting ridiculously but she couldn't help it. She loved him. Why couldn't he love her back?

Josh started his car and drove off. No point trying to calm her now. It was a difficult situation. He wanted to keep their working relationship a good one. It seemed that might be a little harder now. Oh, hell, he thought, I'd better send her flowers tomorrow.

His driving away infuriated Emerald even more. "Damn you," she muttered and climbed into her Mercedes to follow him down the canyon to the bright lights of Santa Monica Boulevard.

The police picked her up four hours later, hopelessly drunk, without a driving license, and weaving her car in and out of the Sunset Boulevard traffic. It took four cops to subdue her enough to get her into the police car, and a passing Japanese tourist with a camera made a fortune from the photographs he took of her and sold to the *American Informer* for a cover story.

Her second sojourn in a jail cell garnered even more publicity than the first. Out-of-control drunken TV actors were not what viewers wanted. Drunken actresses were even more of a turnoff. When the torrent of unfavorable press came out, turn off they did.

The ugly front-page photograph of Emerald fighting the police who arrested her harmed "America's" ratings enormously. Public sympathy turned against her. The ratings started to plummet and soon "Saga" rose like a phoenix from the ashes back to the number two spot again.

Calvin reread the article in *Daily Variety*. " 'Saga' boffo in ratings war once more gains five points." His lips clenched in fury. He had just returned from another fruitless attempt to find out Chloe's new address, having failed to gain entrance to the "Saga" studio where he knew she would be. He had bought a map to the movie stars' homes from a crone sitting under a faded umbrella in the boiling sun on Sunset Boulevard and staked out the vine-covered house on Blue Jay Road identified as hers for two weeks. But he never saw Chloe either coming or going. Three times the police had moved him on. Then, not wanting to arouse more suspicions, he had kept away for a few days. Eventually he struck up a conversation with the young housekeeper after bumping into her "accidentally" at Hughes supermarket one morning. She was pretty, with long blond hair and a cute Scandinavian accent. Casually he had asked what it was like working for Chloe Carriere, the famous TV star.

The girl had laughed at him as she threw packages of frozen peas into her basket. "I vork for Dr. Sidney, the famous plastic surgeon." She giggled. "I don't think he even knows Chloe Carriere, unless he did her face."

Calvin went back to the map-selling hag and screamed at her for selling false information.

She shrugged. "Listen, fella, half the names on that list are dead. The other half has moved. I don't print it, I just sell it. So fuck off, fella, otherwise I'll stick this to ya." She revealed a switchblade gleaming under her torn dress. Calvin backed away from the old witch. He had other fish to fry. He had to find Chloe's address.

On Hollywood's biggest night, Academy Awards night, Mary and Irving Lazar threw their celebrated annual Oscar party at Spago. Every major name from movies and TV attended. The women wore their most gorgeous gowns and the men were equally elegant.

Irving Lazar—"Swifty" to his friends and foes—circulated through the well-dressed throng, dodging TV cameras and paparazzi and having a word and a joke with everyone.

Chloe sat at a corner table with Philippe and Annabel. She was glad Irving had invited Annabel to attend as it was a very insular Hollywood party—superstars and megacelebrities only. Annabel was again visiting from London. She and Chloe had developed a very close relationship.

Philippe didn't say much. Chloe sighed. When you ran out of things to say to each other, it was a sure sign of serious trouble in a relationship. She knew the relationship was more than just sour, yet she didn't have the heart to end it.

Across the room a battery of flashbulbs popped as Emerald and Josh entered Spago. Emerald looked radiant again in a jade-green velvet gown with deep décolletage. All traces of the drunken harridan of last month were erased. She certainly can pull herself together in a hurry, thought Chloe. Emerald was smiling glowingly as she gazed at Josh, who returned her look affectionately.

Chloe turned away. They seemed in love, so happy. She glanced at Philippe, who was eying a new redheaded vamp at a nearby table, brought in to boost "America's" ratings.

Emerald and Josh were being seated at a table in the center of the room. Oh, Lord, thought Chloe, Josh is right in my eyeline. He was indeed positioned in a such a way that when she turned her head to the left she was directly facing him.

He came over to her table as soon as he saw her, gave Philippe a manly handshake, Annabel a hug, and Chloe a kiss on the cheek. She shivered when she looked into his eyes. He was, if anything, more attractive than ever; there was a quality of tenderness and compassion about him now that he had never possessed before.

Soon it was time for everyone in the room to become absorbed in the large TV screens which had been set up at strategic points throughout the restaurant. Chloe could not concentrate on who was winning, on the delicious pizzas with smoked salmon and caviar, on the vintage champagne. She kept sneaking glances at Josh.

This is idiotic, she said to herself. Stupid. A grown woman, a *middle-aged* woman at that, mooning like a schoolgirl.

During one of the commercial breaks, as she and Annabel were in the powder room, Emerald swept in.

The two women eyed each other. Although they had attended a number of Hollywood parties, it was the first time they had been alone together since "America" had begun. The only other person in the room was Annabel, who was now in the cubicle.

"Hello, Emerald." Chloe smiled, extending her hand.

Emerald didn't take the proffered hand. She simply stared, stunned with jealous anger as she realized that the sensational diamond-and-emerald bracelets encircling Chloe's wrist were *her* bracelets. Her favorite jewels, the last to be sold to Vanessa to keep the wolf from her door. Bitch! Chloe now possessed her bracelets *and* her man. It was just as many people said of her in this town—Chloe was a nouveau-riche conniving bitch, and Emerald detested her.

Suddenly she leaned against the door, facing Chloe with a strange expression. Chloe realized she was more than a little drunk.

Fishing a phial of scent from her purse, she turned to the mirror.

"So now I know," said Emerald, her speech slurred. "Now I *really* know."

"Know what?" Chloe applied fragrance rapidly behind her ears, wishing Annabel would exit so they could leave.

"What he sees in you, of course," Emerald hissed.

"Who is *he?*" Chloe said, her voice betraying little of the emotion she felt.

"Josh, of course." Emerald gave a brittle laugh. "He loves you, don't you know that? He's never *stopped* loving you. Aren't *you* the lucky girl?" She staggered to the mirror, pretending to be busy combing her hair but Chloe saw that her eyes were blurred with tears.

"How do you know that?" In spite of herself she had to ask. Was it true? Could Josh still care as much as she did? Nonsense. It was nonsense, Emerald was stoned out of her skull.

"He told me." Emerald looked at Chloe's reflection in the mirror. "He *told* me he loves you. Always has. Big deal. Who cares? *I* certainly don't. We're just friends—good friends—and that's how it's gonna be." She turned away to inspect her painted face, dismissing Chloe with a shrug of jade velvet Giorgio di Sant'Angelo shoulder pads.

Annabel came out and Chloe grabbed her arm as they quickly left the ladies' room.

"I *heard,* Chloe. I heard it all," said her daughter. "Do you think it's true? Do you think Josh is still in love with you?"

"I don't know, darling. I really don't. She's drunk."

"Well I hope he is," said the girl, affectionately squeezing her arm. "You know how I feel about Philippe."

The two went back to the festivities. For the rest of the evening, Chloe tried to avoid Josh's eyes, but as winner after winner appeared on the TV screen and made their speeches, she heard none of them. All she could think of were Emerald's words.

"Give that bouquet of flowers the archer." Chelsea Deane was peering through the viewfinder on the set of Chloe/Miranda's boudoir.

"The what? What is he talking about?" prop man number one asked prop man number two.

"Beats me, Stu, ask him. These limeys sure have a strange way of talking."

"Sorry, Chelsea, what d'you mean?"

"*Archer,* that's slang for Get rid of it," Chelsea yelled with exasperation.

"What the hell's an archer?" yelled the prop man.

"Oh, Gawd, sorry, thought I was at Pinewood for a sec!" Chelsea smiled his captivating cockney grin. "Spanish Archer—*El-bow,* get it?" The two prop men scratched their heads.

"*Elbow* the flowers—get rid of 'em," Chelsea said with an up-and-down movement of his elbow, irritated by the man's obtuseness. Chloe gave him a sympathetic glance from where she sat with Vanessa and a coterie of makeup, hair and wardrobe assistants. She was trying to run through her lines with her dialogue coach, while the girls gossiped around her.

"O.K., first team, ready for you," called Ned.

"Second team can relax."

The couple who had been standing in the middle of the set for the past fifteen minutes while the crew set up the camera and lights went off to the coffee stand. Chloe and Luis took their places. They walked through the scene for marks only. After every move, the camera assistant used his tape measure to judge the distance from their faces to the camera.

God forbid it should be a millimeter out of focus in dailies tomorrow. Gertrude and Abby would scream blue murder, and if it happened more than twice, heads would roll, in particular, the camera assistant's—so he was a careful fellow.

It was freezing cold on the set today. As usual, the heating had gone on the blink. The studio was over fifty years old, freezing in the winter and boiling in the summer.

"That's when they put the bleedin' 'eatin' an' air conditionin' in," said Chelsea acidly. "Fifty bleedin' years ago."

The crew all wore sweaters, parkas and scarves, but Chloe had on a low-cut black chiffon dress. The only thing she had to keep her warm was four hundred dollars' worth of Kenny Lane rhinestones around her neck.

They shot the master. They had to do it four times because once an airplane could be heard on the sound track, the second time a visitor coughed in the middle of Luis's impassioned "I love you, Miranda," and in the third Chloe caught her heel in the carpet.

Eventually Chelsea printed the fourth take. "All right. That's a print. Let's go in for coverage. We'll do Luis's close-up first, Chlo, you can relax, darlin'."

Brad, from Abby and Gertrude's office, came on the set and handed around a piece of paper with last night's ratings score on it.

Chloe was glad to see that last night they had taken their time slot by a good margin and had got a thirty-one share that would definitely put "Saga" among the top ten prime time shows this week.

"How did 'America' do last night?" she inquired.

"They're doing *very* well," enthused Brad, even though they were on the rival network. "Very well indeed. They're a big hit. Of course, Josh winning the award helped. The public have certainly taken to your ex, haven't they?"

Chloe was glad for Josh. She had sent him a cymbidium plant and a congratulatory note after he won. She wondered how he was. She hoped he was happy. She wished *she* were happier and wished she could do something about the information Emerald had drunkenly given her. Trouble with Philippe again. Another ridiculous row over nothing. *Why* was he so spiteful? Recently he had started to ridicule her. He called her "Diva" and "Megastar." What was wrong with him?

"Darling, you'll never *guess* who I saw today!" Red hair hidden by pink rollers, Daphne sat next to Chloe under the dryer at the Bill Palmer Salon, ready for a good gossip.

Chloe put down her magazine and smiled at her friend. She never failed to be amused by Daphne, whom she basically thought kind and funny, although a bit of a chatterbox.

"Joshua Brown, darling—looking, I *must* say, very, very fanciable indeed." Chloe's heart skipped. Jungle drums started beating whenever she heard his name.

"Where?" She casually lit a cigarette. "Where did you see him?"

"At his new house at the beach, darling. I interviewed him for *TV Faces.*"

"How was it? I mean, how was he?" Chloe was interested, intrigued. Damn it, she thought, I wish I weren't.

"Wonderful," gushed Daphne. "Darling, he is *so* divine, full of the old S.A. What a man! I mean, my knees were so all of a tremble I could barely balance my pad in my lap."

"You don't use a tape recorder?"

"Of course I do, dearie. The pad is for background, you can't record *that.* Color of sofa, what he was wearing, that sort of thing."

"What *was* he wearing?" Chloe was curious in spite of herself.

"Blue shirt," Daphne said breathlessly. "Open, very simple. Very sexy. He's got a wonderful body, Chloe."

"I know, dear. I was married to him, remember?"

"How could I forget?" Daphne laughed. "Anyway, darling, we had this terrific *in depth* conversation. He told me *all* about his drinking and drugging—how it destroyed him."

"Did he tell you all about his schoolgirls?" Chloe asked sarcastically.

"I'll get to that," Daphne said crossly. "Don't interrupt, dear. Anyway he told me that *he* was the one who ruined your marriage because of his drug taking. He said what a wonderful woman you are—the best ever." Daphne smiled as she saw Chloe blush slightly.

"Anyway he was going on about you when his valet or whoever came in with a *terribly* important call from South America—something to do with a film he's going to do out there next year, so he excused himself and went and took the call."

"And?" Chloe was more than interested.

"Well, darling, he'd left the door to his inner sanctum open. I absolutely couldn't resist—I peeped in, and *what* do you think I saw?"

"What?" Chloe smiled. She liked this.

"One whole wall, darling, is covered, I mean literally *covered,* with photos of you."

"Come on—you're joking."

"No, darling. I mean it. There must be twenty pictures of you. You alone, you with him, you and Annabel—even your wedding photo." She leaned forward to give Chloe a conspiratorial nudge. "I think he still loves you, dear, I really do. This is obviously his most private room. Oh, and there was also one of your records on the stereo—your last one, the love ballad." She leaned back triumphantly under the dryer as she waited for Chloe's reaction.

"Well, Daphne, what a regular little Sherlock Holmes you are. That *is* interesting, darling, but I'm not interested in him. What's over is over."

"Nonsense," said Daphne. "You never got him out of your system. If you had, you would have signed your final divorce papers *and* you would have married Philippe by now."

"I'm allergic to marriage," said Chloe sincerely. "I'm not good at it."

"You were *very* good at it, dearie, for all the years you were married to Josh. You looked the other way when he was unfaithful. You ignored his drug problems. You put up with a lot of naughtiness from him. You were too easy with him and too forgiving, dear. Treat 'em mean, keep 'em keen!"

"I know, I know. Look, Daphne, don't go on. I told you, it's over, I'm happy with Philippe," she said crossing her fingers. She hated to lie.

Daphne's dryer buzzed. "I must dash now, darling. I'm doing a cover story for *US* on Sabrina Jones."

"Come to dinner next Saturday. Philippe's barbecuing," called Chloe.

"Love to, duckie," said Daphne, aware that she had stirred certain unexpressed feelings in Chloe.

Alone for a moment, Chloe sat very still, one thought continuously turning over and over in her mind. Emerald had told her the truth.

Calvin had finally managed to find a way to get onto the set. He had struck up a friendship with Debbie Drake, the assistant director. He had observed her every day after work, going into the bar across from the studio. She usually sat and drank a few beers with the crew before getting into her little red Mustang and driving home to Westlake. He spent several days sitting at the bar observing her. She was a friendly soul, and it was not difficult to become acquainted with her. He cultivated their camaraderie over the weeks, although it made him feel disloyal to Emerald. Her hair was long and pretty and she had a nice smile and a pleasant personality, but Calvin didn't care about the girl one bit. All he wanted was to win her confidence and friendship enough to gain access to the "Saga" set.

One day he casually mentioned that he would like to visit the set as he was a great admirer of Sissy Sharp. Debbie, ever anxious to please, arranged a visitor's pass for him.

One fine spring afternoon, when the temperature hovered in the nineties, Calvin Foster entered the "Saga" set for the first time.

❄ *Twenty-eight* ❖

PHILIPPE, HIS FACE FLUSHED, stood before Chloe. His cream crocodile shoes contrasted with his immaculately creased dark-brown trousers. He was impeccably turned out, as usual, even though it was seven in the morning and the temperature was stifling.

Chloe, with a slight hangover from the previous night, was attempting to get ready in her dressing room. She was already half an hour late. It was unprofessional to be late, and it threw the assistant director into a flap.

"*Chérie,* we have *got* to talk about this video offer. I thought you *wanted* to get back into singing again." He kept waving the contract in front of her as she zoomed around the room trying to dress, clean her teeth and brush her tangled curls.

"Look, Philippe, I *can't,* I simply *cannot* discuss it now. I'm terribly late, can't you see?"

"We must agree on this deal, *chérie.* You're *always* too busy these days —putting things off, procrastinating. Now, sweetheart— *calm* down—sit down and let's read the contract together for a minute."

"Philippe, listen to me, damn it!" Her rage, the rage she was saving for Miranda's scenes with Sirope today, had built up so much she could no longer control it.

"*I have to leave now!* I have a hangover. I've had four hours' sleep. *Please*, Philippe, let me go to work." Her face was flaming, the heat and anger making her heart skip several beats. Could women in their forties have heart attacks? she wondered fleetingly. "We'll have to talk later, Philippe. Tonight, I promise you."

"O.K., O.K. You never listen to me, I'm just a dog. Forget the video deal—we'll just forget it, see if I care. I was doing it for you, but you never appreciate my efforts, *Miss Diva*."

She felt she couldn't bear another day of his sulking. "Darling, look, I know the video deal is important. I don't want to forget it, let's discuss it at the studio after work, before we go to Jasper's dinner, O.K.?" She gave him a fleeting kiss and as much of a smile as she could muster.

"O.K., O.K., we always have to fit in with your plans," he grumbled, semi-placated by Chloe's affectionate gesture.

"Well, I *am* the one who has to be a 'Saga' slave," she said, throwing on a scarf and sunglasses and noticing in her full-length mirror that she needed to lose three pounds again. "Come to the studio about sevenish, darling. It will be quiet then, we can go over the contract thoroughly without being bothered. Bye now, darling, I *must* go."

Shooting went slowly. The sudden heat wave had affected cast and crew alike, and, as usual, the air conditioner was not working properly. It seemed to Chloe that the temperature in southern California was never temperate. It was always either too hot or too cold, and at the ancient studio the heating and air-conditioning units were, as usual, inoperative.

Tempers were frayed. Chloe had even had a tiff with Chelsea Deane, whom she adored. Sissy was more vicious and back-biting than usual, and the crew was glum. But when Bill Herbert brought the overnight ratings to the set, everyone brightened up—they had gained three places in last week's ratings, and now were one place above "America."

Wearily, Chloe sat in front of the portable makeup table and powdered her face for the twentieth time. She looked and felt exhausted, and there were dark circles under her eyes that even the thick TV makeup couldn't hide.

Calvin had been lingering on the periphery of the studio floor all day. A shadowy figure in his reddish wig, baseball cap and sunglasses, he had been observing Chloe's movements intently from the moment she had arrived. He noted how nasty she was when she walked off the set after a row with the nice little English director, phony tears running down her face.

He watched her pack of sycophantic bitches—Vanessa, Trixie, De De —go to her trailer to placate her, listen to her demands, bring her tea, aspirin, cigarettes. Cater to the slut.

He overheard Sissy tell her girl Friday, Doris, what a selfish arrogant cow Chloe was. How she couldn't act her way out of a paper bag, how she only got her role because she had slept with Abby Arafat.

"Ugh, Abby is so gross, can you *imagine* four hundred pounds of heaving flab on your bones," they giggled together in mock horror.

Calvin picked up a discarded copy of the *American Informer* and read that Chloe had simultaneously just been voted by their readers:

A. One of the most admired women in America.

B. One of the most hated.

There was no doubt how Calvin would have voted. Those who voted as he would have would thank him when he finally disposed of her.

He had failed before in Las Vegas, but this time, nearly five years later, he knew he was going to succeed. He felt it in his bones. His hands tightened over the handle of the seven-inch switchblade in his pocket. He had experimented on a couple of stray dogs. It had slit their throats extremely efficiently.

This was the third day he had hung around the set waiting for her. He hoped to get her that night in the parking lot. She had given up being driven by a studio driver since she had bought that flashy red Ferrari. He would wait for her in the back seat of her car. She never bothered to lock it. Stupid bitch.

"O.K., it's a wrap," called Ned. "Same time tomorrow everyone. Goodnight." Gratefully, the crew started packing up their equipment. It was 6:45 P.M. and already dark outside. It was not a late day, as TV shooting went, but most of the crew would still have to be back at six the following morning.

Chloe flopped onto the chintz couch of her tiny trailer on the sound stage. Wearily she removed her earrings and necklace. "I'm too tired to dress," she said to Trixie, and sat in her silk robe while Trixie put away her Miranda clothes and Vanessa poured her a much-needed glass of wine.

"Do you want me to stay with you, love?" asked Vanessa protectively.

"Not tonight, darling, Philippe's coming over with a contract to look over. I'll see you tomorrow." She managed a wan smile.

"Bright and early!" chirped Vanessa, who never seemed to get tired. "Don't forget to bring your blue Saint Laurent blouse."

Outside, on the dark sound stage, Calvin waited. He was hidden behind a flat with "Miranda's Bedroom" stenciled on it. He saw the two women leave the bitch's trailer, saw the last of the crew members trundle away their equipment. It was quiet now on the set except for a hint of thunder in the stale air. Stealthily he crept to the window of the trailer and looked in.

She was sitting at the dressing table in a red dressing gown, leafing through some papers. She was sipping wine and smoking. What a whore! He crept to the door. Pushed. It was unlocked. Careless slut.

With a gasp, Chloe turned to confront the intruder. Who was he? He smiled, a horrible grin. "Good evening, Miss Carriere."

"Who are you? Get the hell out of my dressing room before I call security." She felt fear immobilize her.

"Don't you remember me, Miss Carriere?" he mocked as he took off his sunglasses and baseball cap, then slowly peeled off the red nylon wig.

Oh, my God! Chloe almost fainted. It was he, dear God. The man the police said had tried to kill her in Las Vegas. They had let him out. Why?

"What are you doing in my dressing room? What do you want?" Her voice exuded a confidence she didn't feel. Although she was petrified, her hand went to the phone, but he grabbed it first.

"I want to talk to you, Miss Carriere. You remember me now, don't you?"

She didn't answer.

He put his face close to hers. *"Don't* you remember me, bitch?"

"Yes," her voice was a whisper. "I do."

Close your eyes and he will go away. It's a dream, a nightmare. It isn't happening. Where is Philippe? He's supposed to be here at seven. Oh, God, where is he? Why isn't he here?

"We are going to talk now. I want to talk to you, Miss Chloe *Mega*star *bitch,* but first I've got a little *present* for you."

He unzipped his jeans and revealed it, an angry red, rigid penis, which he held with filthy callused fingers. In his other hand was a knife, its blade glimmering in the bright lights of her dressing room mirror.

He was inches from her, that revolting object in one hand, the knife in the other. She picked up the glass of wine and in a desperate move threw it in his face. He gave a hoarse shout, blinded momentarily by the wine. His hands went to his face and he dropped the knife. In that split second, Chloe darted between him and the bunk bed in the tiny trailer and escaped onto the sound stage.

It was dark, except for the glimmer of a dim work light high above on the gantry, but she knew this stage like the back of her hand. Knew the location of the four exits. She had to get to one of them, find a guard. She realized it was futile to call out. No one would hear her on this sound-proofed stage. Her high heels smashed into the pitted bare floor as she tripped over a cable and fell to the ground. She turned, sobbing, and saw the man silhouetted against the light of her trailer. Animal sounds issued from his throat. She could see the knife and his flaccid penis hanging outside his jeans.

She tried to stand up and, with a sob, realized she had wrenched her ankle. Gasping with pain and fear, she tore off her shoes and limped across the network of cables to the library set of "Saga," trying to reach the Exit sign.

"Bitch. Whore. I'm gonna get you, you fucking *bitch!*" She heard him crashing through the cables behind her as her stockinged feet felt the soft Persian carpet of the library. Only fifty more yards. The green Exit sign was like a beacon. She hobbled past the arc lamps lined up like sentries, past the coffee wagon. Where was the guard? Where was Philippe? She was weeping with fear, unable to move any faster.

Suddenly she felt Calvin's hands clawing at her back. She tried to throw him off, but he had her. She smelled his sweat as he threw her onto the brown leather couch in the library and straddled her.

It was hard again, that revolting red thing. Her silk robe had fallen open and she was naked underneath, except for sheer black tights. He sat across her thighs, his erect penis pressing into her stomach, the knife at her throat.

"This is it, Miss Carriere. This is the end of the line for you. You *slut!*" He spat at her as he took his knife and slowly slit her tights from waist to pubis. Terror engulfed her as she struggled, but his knife was digging into her chin, drawing blood.

"*Don't!* Don't move, bitch. If you want to enjoy this—and you *will* enjoy it, won't you, don't you dare move, you ugly slut. I've read about how you enjoy doing it with everyone—everything—men—dogs—horses —right, bitch! Right? I heard all the filthy stories about you in prison, you whore." He slapped her face repeatedly as he tried to force himself inside her.

Death was preferable to this, thought Chloe. Instant death was infinitely preferable to being raped by a homicidal maniac. With superhuman strength, screaming for help, she threw Calvin off her body kicking out at his groin as hard as she could. On her knees she started to crawl toward the door.

Outside the stage, Philippe thought he heard muffled cries as he slammed his car door shut. It was almost impossible to hear anything coming from the soundproofed stage, but he sensed danger.

He pushed open the heavy doors and stopped in his tracks as he saw the horrific tableau before him. A nude Chloe huddled on the carpet, her face a mask of mute terror. Inches from her stood a man, his upraised hand holding a knife poised to strike.

Calvin looked up at Philippe, startled. For a second the tableau was frozen, then Philippe moved and Calvin's hand sliced through the air and the blade tore through Philippe's shirt.

Chloe's ears were ringing with the screams, but she could no longer tell whether they were hers, Philippe's, or the madman's.

They always watched the early-morning news on the tiny portable TV in the makeup room.

Emerald sat in one chair, her lovely new face having a delicate layer of Max Factor base applied to it. She looked at herself in the mirror, seeing again, with eyes that had with the passing years lost some of their clarity, the face of a beautiful thirty-five-year-old.

Josh leaned back in his leather-and-chrome makeup chair, eyes closed, thinking about the next scene while his face "had the polyfiller applied," as he joked to the makeup man.

The TV announcement of the attempted murder of Chloe, and Philippe's death, jolted them out of their respective reveries.

"Christ! I must call her," he cried out, springing out of the chair and into his dressing room. Chloe's phone number, the one he had obtained from Daphne but had never used, was busy—constantly busy. In frustration, he dialed and redialed.

"You are needed on the set." Emerald came in without knocking. "I wouldn't call her if I were you," she said jealously. "The woman has just lost the man she loved. The last person she wants to hear from is her lovesick ex-husband."

Josh put the phone down. He asked Perry to send Chloe a basket of white roses and tulips, and wrote a note of condolence. The next day he left with the unit for a week of location shooting in the San Gabriel mountains.

Emerald traveled in the limo with him. She looked at him coldly as he sat, shoulders hunched in his woolen sweater, deep in thought, ignoring her. She bit her lip and settled back angrily into the fake leather upholstery.

She would try to get him out of her system. She would. She must. She had just met a new man, a stockbroker from Houston. He was rich, twice divorced, gray-haired, but still reasonably attractive. Maybe he was finally the one. The one she had been searching for all her life yet could never find—would never find. She opened her compact to gaze at her face again. Yes, it was still gorgeous. It had not changed in the half hour since she had last looked. She still had "it." Beauty, charisma, fame, power. She was a superstar again. She had the world in the palm of her hand. Didn't she?

The radio was playing soft, romantic music. "The greatest thing you'll ever learn is just to love and to be loved in return," crooned Nat King Cole.

Josh listened to the words. That had been one of the songs he and Chloe had sung together in Vegas in the seventies. It had brought the house down.

He remembered her turquoise eyes, how they had glowed when they looked into his, as they harmonized those words, oblivious to everyone and everything in the smoky saloon except each other.

❧ *Twenty-nine* ❧

PHILIPPE'S FUNERAL MADE front pages all over the world, getting almost as much coverage as those of Rosalinde and Sam. "Saga" was hotter than ever, even if tragedy was the reason. Abby and Gertrude were ecstatic. They were now consistently ahead of "America" in the ratings.

But Chloe was melancholy and depressed. She lived because Philippe had died. She mourned for him, for the love they had shared. She forgot his sulks, his stubbornness. She chose to only remember the happy times.

It was a hot Saturday afternoon in June of 1987. Chloe walked slowly along the beach at Malibu, her little terrier dog panting at her heels. In two weeks, the fifth season of "Saga" would end. What then? What would she do with her life in the three-month hiatus that stretched ahead of her? Should she accept one of the movie offers she had received? Or should she take a trip round the world with Annabel, who had been such a comfort since Philippe's death? Annabel had flown in from London to be with her mother as soon as she had heard the news, and she had not left her since. She was in the beach house now preparing Chloe's favorite dinner.

Chloe kicked a stone along the water's edge as she contemplated her future; the little terrier bounded joyfully after it.

"Good afternoon, Chlo. What a day, huh? Makes you glad to be a Brit in California." The familiar voice interrupted her thoughts.

"Josh—what are you doing in this part of Malibu? I thought you lived in town." She was thrilled to see him.

The reflection of the sun sparkled in his eyes. His black hair, flecked now with gray, was tousled, a little too long, a little untidy. She had always loved it like that. Her eyes sparkled back at him, drank him in.

"I took a house just down there." He gestured past where toddlers were playing and teenagers were now throwing a ball to Chloe's dog, pointing to a small redwood shingle house. The house had a little chimney from which smoke was rising. It looked cozy, faintly English, and had hollyhocks growing outside.

"What a sweet house," said Chloe.

What a sweet face, he thought as he looked into her turquoise eyes, at the tan freckles dusting her upturned nose. She was wearing jeans and a plain white T-shirt. Her hair was tied in a ponytail and she wore no lipstick on her pale, full lips. He wanted to hold her in his arms, to kiss away the pain that he saw in the depths of those eyes.

"I got your flowers and note," she said softly. "Thanks, Josh." He squeezed her arm gently. There was no need to say more. The sun was shining, the waves were lapping at their bare feet, and she was here.

"How about a cuppa?" he asked.

"English tea? I'd love some. Do you have Earl Grey?"

" 'Course I do, luv—you don't think I'd drink *American* tea, do you, in *bags* with string hanging out of it? It's revolting. I've even got a new china teapot from Harrods, *and* scones and cream."

"Biscuits?" Chloe smiled as they slowly sauntered across the sand to the little gray house. "Do you have any English bickies?"

"Do I have bickies?—I most certainly do." He looked at her with raised brows and a mischievous smile. "Name your brand, babe, and I've got 'em. McVities chocolate digestive. Custard creams, ginger snaps and Scottish shortbread from Fortnum's." Chloe smiled as he went on. "And brown bread and butter, with the crusts cut off. All your favorites, Chloe, all the ones you've always loved."

"What about sugar?" She liked this. She liked him. She more than liked him, she loved him—she'd never stopped. She knew it. The flame flickered stronger. "I hope you've got proper sugar."

"You bet I have, darlin', none of that saccharin sweetener stuff or brown crystals—turns the tea a funny color. Proper sugar. Lumps, of course. White. Even if it is bad for you, I don't care. I'm English—I like my tea how it's meant to be." They looked at each other for a very long moment, then walked slowly along the wet sand.

The tide lapped their bare feet, and they laughed as they rolled up their jeans. A phalanx of seagulls swooped in the distance in perfect formation. The little dog chased them, wagging his tail, frolicking in and out of the waves. The Malibu ocean was flat, like deep blue velvet brushed the wrong way. The late afternoon sun burnished the gentle swell with golden reflections. "And is there honey still for tea?" she murmured softly.

Josh's arm encircled Chloe's waist, her head folded into his shoulders, and her hand found his and held it very tightly.

LOVE

&

DESIRE

&

HATE

For Robin
With all my love

They are not long, the weeping and the laughter
Love and desire and hate:
I think they have no portion in us after
We pass the gate.

ERNEST DOWSON *Vitae Summa Brevis*

❖ *Prologue* ❖

THE CHIEF INSPECTOR of the local police didn't like movie people at all. He disliked them disrupting his happy playground of a town when they were shooting, and he hated it even more when one of them died.

There was only one thing worse than a death on location and that was two deaths; now there were three.

This last tragedy appeared to have been an accident. An old wooden cable car carrying the unfortunate man had crashed down to the rocky beach, killing him instantly. For the third time in as many months Chief Inspector Gomez had been awakened from an untroubled sleep to attend to the needs of this ill-assorted group of actors, producers and technicians, who now stood ashen-faced on the beach by the light of a sickly moon, the light Pacific breeze ruffling the chiffon and silk of the women's dresses.

He began by asking them some well-chosen questions.

The young *wunderkind* director, the first to have reached the body, told Gomez that without exception every member of the cast and crew had loathed the dead man—but:

The legendary leading lady protested that he had truly been a gentle man beneath his ruthless exterior.

The underaged, overly sexed ingénue kept repeating over and over, "Death comes in threes," in her whispery French accent, while her spinster chaperone wept, feverishly wringing her hands.

The award-winning screenwriter blew her nose and latched on to the comforting arm of a young policeman, explaining to him exactly what she thought had happened, as the distinguished English character actor with the plummy voice announced that in his opinion the contraption had always been a death trap.

The dashingly handsome star said nothing, but he wondered where his mysterious fiancée had disappeared to.

Just as Gomez was deciding to send everyone away, a young police officer ran up and urgently whispered in his ear.

"One moment," the Chief Inspector called out. "One moment, please." Then he proceeded to speak quickly in a low voice.

He told his shocked and attentive audience that a preliminary examination of the cable car wreckage indicated that it had been no accident.

"It is murder," he said.

But of course one of them already knew that, because one of them had an excellent reason to kill.

As they stared at each other in stunned silence, no one noticed as the last of the amber beads which had been clutched in the dead man's hand rolled slowly into the warm sea.

PART
ONE

❦ *One* ❦

Inès awoke in the Ritz Hotel beside a snoring Italian officer, with waves of pain shooting through her body. Outside the windows of the sumptuously decorated Louis XIV bedroom she could see the chestnut trees which were just beginning to blossom, and feel the cool spring breeze on her aching body. Inès adored Paris with a passion which could not be extinguished by the multiplying throng of Nazi uniforms continually parading up and down the streets, the constant ache in her belly from lack of food or the brutal men she had to serve.

She turned to look at the sleeping man next to her. By the skin on his body he appeared to be quite young, but his face, even in sleep, was cruel and insensitive, and his short bloated body bordered on the grotesque. She shivered with revulsion, remembering his so-called lovemaking last night with horror. *Merde*—what this monster had done to her.

She had met General Scrofo two days before in the Café Flore on the Left Bank, when she went to observe *la vie de bohème* which appeared on the surface to continue much the same as usual. Artists, writers and students still sat sipping drinks on spindly iron chairs outside the bustling cafés. There was always good conversation, laughter, and gentle plumes of cigarette smoke. Only the men in gray and green uniform who also sat sharing the friendly ambience indicated that Paris was an occupied city.

As Inès sipped her coffee, the hazy afternoon sunlight glinted on her golden hair, dappling her cheeks, emphasizing the bloom of her youth. Picasso was sitting at a nearby table surrounded by his usual group of sycophants and beautiful models, and his mesmerizing black eyes stared with an artist's interest in Inès direction as he puffed on his yellow Gauloise while luxuriating in the adulation of his admirers. Inès felt she could understand the fascination that this middle-aged, balding man held for the young women with him—were it not for the more pressing attentions of the Italian at the next table, she would have answered his silent black-eyed call and joined his adoring coterie. But General Scrofo advanced on her in his heavily flirtatious manner, an appointment was made and the die cast.

The following evening she walked to her rendezvous with the General, from the boulevard Malesherbes, past the place de Wagram and across the river Seine. The boulevard Malesherbes, one of the longest streets in Paris wound past the *marché* at the Porte de Champerret, where the few remaining scraps of food and clothing were available.

Inès stopped for a sip of water from one of the bronze drinking fountains, the legacy of the English nobleman Sir Richard Wallace. Many Parisian streets boasted these charming yet functional sculptures. In the early 1870s, at the end of the Franco-Prussian War, Wallace had given them to the city which he loved, a token of his admiration for the bravery of its citizens in surviving the siege of the Prussian army. Inès hoped that in the 1940s the citizens of Paris would manage to survive the invasion of the Germans and Italians with equal courage.

Inès had been grateful for the water last night; the air was humid and dusty, and she was not looking forward to what awaited her. But it was her job—just a job. Yves always told her she must think of it only as that. Inès passed only a dozen or so cyclists and a few pedestrians on the boulevard. There were no cars for private citizens in Paris now. Only the sinister black Mercedeses of the Gestapo or the SS sped by, their darkened windows hiding the evil that lurked within.

Inès slowed her pace, thinking of all the enemy officers she and her friends had entertained at the Ritz and other Parisian hotels. Inès and Jeanette had often shared tricks together, joking hollowly about their profession, which was one of necessity. If they did not sell themselves, they had no other skills with which to survive. Yves told Inès he was unable to support her now. She was trapped in this life but made the best of it, hoping it would not last forever. When the war was over everything would change.

One day Yves informed her that Jeanette's body had been pulled from the Seine, brutally beaten. Inès was always aware that this could happen to her, too. The Nazis—and their allies, the Italians—were cruel, vicious men to whom whores were just toys to be used for whatever perversions they desired. Inès realized she was lucky to have escaped a similar fate.

Although Yves had forbidden it, Inès had gone to see Jeanette's body in the morgue, staring horrified at the once-pretty young girl, at the bruises that covered her bloated body, the deep cuts across her breasts and belly. Inès heart beat faster with fear.

The night she died Jeanette had left the night club L'Éléphant Rose with a group of drunken Italians. Jeanette had wanted Inès to come with them, but Yves had a better trick for her that night and Inès always obeyed Yves. Even though he was a pimp, he was a kind man, with a wicked sense of humor, and she paid him the respect he deserved. Lucky for him she did, otherwise it could have been her broken body lying in the morgue. It was Russian roulette with these enemy monsters. The girls had to do whatever they desired, never sure when they would turn into sadistic beasts.

Inès was determined to survive this war, survive the Germans, the Italians, the rationing, the privations and, most of all, survive the indignities she suffered. She was going to make something of herself one day: what, though, she did not yet know.

As she entered the most beautiful of all Parisian squares she paused to admire the perfection of the octagonal place Vendôme. Honey-colored stone buildings were perfectly enhanced by the black and gilded enrichments of their balustrades and the gray-green of their sloping roofs. The stone gargoyles above the doorways of some of the buildings seemed to be jeering at her with their lolling tongues so she did not linger. Running lightly up the red-carpeted steps of the Ritz, she was directed to General Umberto Scrofo's suite by a contemptuous middle-aged concierge.

Although he had to serve Nazi generals, SS militia, Gestapo officers, majors, captains, and generals of Hitler's and Mussolini's armies with smiling servility, the concierge despised them all. Disapproval of Frenchwomen who fraternized with the enemy was all too visible on his craggy face as he watched the young prostitute going into the lift to the second floor and God only knows what degradation from General Scrofo. She was little more than a child. The concierge shrugged. It was none of his affair—he too knew the meaning of survival. These days it was every man, woman and child for themselves.

She was by no means the first underage girl whom he'd directed to Scrofo's quarters in the past two years. The thirty-year-old General liked nubile, Nordic-looking blondes, and this girl looked a suitable partner for tonight's revels.

"Come in, *cara*," said the General, surveying her with a cold smile. "And close the door." He was standing behind a marble-topped table and pouring pale amber liquid into a delicately fluted, gold-rimmed glass which, he had been assured by the most important *antiquaire* on the fabourg St.-Honoré, was from a set of glasses owned by Talleyrand himself. Inès noticed that many of the decanters on the table glittered in the soft peach lights, as only very expensive objects do, and her eyes opened wide with wonder as she took in the expensively furnished lavish room.

"Have some champagne," he commanded, taking in her slim figure, blue eyes and golden hair. Yes, she was as freshly beautiful and young as he remembered from their brief meeting in the café. Her face was devoid of makeup and she looked virginally innocent. He ran a thick tongue across his sweating upper lip and, putting his hand casually in his pocket, felt himself hardening.

She would do. She would do very nicely indeed. He had chosen well. Now he would play with her, taunt her, in the piquant way he liked best.

"What is your name, *cara*?" he asked in a reassuring tone, watching her look of appreciation as she sipped the vintage champagne.

"Inès Dessault, sir," she said, looking admiringly at an eighteenth-century ormolu-and-bronze clock on the ornately carved marble chimney-piece as it struck nine times.

"Inès, a pretty name for a pretty girl. Come over here, Inès, take off your coat, I won't bite you." He laughed softly. He loved to tell them that he wouldn't harm them. A trusting look would come over their silly little faces and he could see their bodies visibly relax. No matter that they knew that he and his allies—Hitler's Master Race—had seized their country, pillaging it for every piece of treasure which France possessed. No matter that they all knew of someone, somewhere, who had been taken away in the middle of the night to some unspeakable place. A sliver of kindness from the enemy, a flicker of feigned affection, and the idiots smirked like gullible puppets. Stupid. They were all stupid, the French. Men and women. They thought their culture was without equal, that their pictures, their sculptures, their boulevards, their architecture, were supreme. Arrogance was inbred in them. Herr Blondell, who each day supervised the collection and shipping of dozens of works of art to Germany, said that soon all that the Gallic fools would have left of their beloved culture would be their boulevards, their parks and their chestnut trees. All their priceless treasures—the furniture, the greatest artistry which the sixteenth, seventeenth and eighteenth centuries had to offer—the paintings, sculptures and objets d'art from Versailles, the Louvre and the Jeu de Paume, the accumulation of hundreds of years of collective genius, all would be gone. These riches would be secured in the Fatherland, owned by the Master Race—with the exception of a select little hoard which Umberto Scrofo was cunningly keeping for his own future, safely hidden in a cellar in the rue Flambeau.

Inès slipped her thin coat off thinner shoulders. The red silk dress was new, Yves had given it to her only last week. She didn't ask where he had found it, it had obviously been stolen, but it was of good quality and she recognized the couturier's label—Worth.

"Sit down, Inès Dessault," Scrofo instructed, gesturing towards a crystal bowl filled with a gritty-looking black substance unfamiliar to her. "Have some caviar."

Caviar! Inès had heard of it, but this was the first time she had ever seen it. The taste was strangely salty but not unpleasant, and she was always hungry these days. She wondered if she might be appearing too greedy, but the General didn't seem to care. She sat on the edge of a blue moiré bergère, eating hungrily. He certainly was a strange-looking creature, this officer. No more than five foot three, he had a wide squat body and an enormous, almost bald head which seemed out of all proportion. His uniform was thickly encrusted with medals and insignia, and he wore several rings on his stubby hands, which Inès did not think was quite correct for an officer. She saw the General's hand making circular motions in his pocket and smiled to herself. She knew that like so many enemy officers, he probably had a sexual problem. With the unforgettable atrocities which they witnessed at the front, the men often needed outlandish tricks to arouse them. A flash of thigh or breast was not enough. They needed titillation, stimulation, something to goad them to excitement. Yves had taught her how to do that, often practicing with her in his big soft bed. Yves . . . whenever she thought of him, she was filled with love.

All her friends told her how lucky she was to have a pimp like Yves Moray—a man who loved her, even though he took her money. A man who never beat her, or abused her as so many of the other *maquereaux* did to their *poules de luxes*. A man whose warm kisses and caresses made up for the heartless and cold-blooded screwing which she endured from her clients. A man who made her laugh with his magic tricks both in and out of bed.

Deliberately, with ingenuous, practiced ease, Inès sat balanced on the edge of the bergère, her slender legs parted just enough to let the General see where her silk stocking tops ended and her slim white thighs began. She wore no panties and her stockings were secured with a pair of red satin garters, a flea-market bargain from last week.

She saw the General's eyes search for a more erotic sight, and she reached for the caviar, dipping her finger in it and sucking it slowly, her eyes never leaving his. Slowly she allowed her red skirt to slide up past her thighs so that Scrofo could see part of her golden mound. Nonchalantly, Inès dropped her other hand to the blond fuzz, touching herself gently, and saw the small bulge in his trousers become more pronounced. This was going to be a piece of cake. With luck she would be out of here in half an hour, off to L'Éléphant Rose, leaving this lout satiated and snoring happily. There she would be reunited with Yves and they would sit together giggling at poor old Gabrielle when she sang her latest songs to the idiotic Germans who drank each night until they were sick.

She moved her index finger rhythmically, becoming slightly aroused in spite of her lack of interest in the officer. Good. That would make it better with Yves tonight. She would tell him everything. Describe the reactions of the General staring in fascination at her sex under the red dress, laugh about the bulge throbbing in his trousers like a little mouse. She would tell him what it felt like when the General took her, and how she felt with him inside her. Yves would get tremendously aroused and he would possess her so violently, yet so passionately, that they would come together in a burst of rapture. She shuddered with expectation, feeling herself moisten with desire. Well, so much easier for this great brute to shove it in. Why doesn't he hurry up?

She smiled up at him sexily as Yves had taught her, then put a triangle of toast covered with caviar in her mouth, sucking it with relish while keeping her other hand busy.

He was ready now. She could tell. His breath was coming in shallow gasps, one hand fumbled with the buttons on his trousers; the other brought the glass to his lips, draining the last few drops.

"Go in there," he ordered huskily, gesturing towards the bedroom. "Get undressed but leave your stockings and shoes on. Do you under-. stand?"

Inès obeyed, feeling lighthearted. Soon it would be over. She had him hooked now.

She lay back on the cool linen sheets of the four-poster bed, admiring the blue-and-gold ceiling. A magnificent chandelier hung in the center, the cut crystals tinkling faintly in the breeze from the open windows. Her hands sensuously cupped her breasts as she continued to stimulate herself. It was, she had to admit, rather exciting, making love with the enemy. It was something that she would never admit to Yves, but when one of the more handsome German officers took her, if he was gentle, she would find herself responding to his moans of delight, and several times her orgasms had been almost genuine. But not tonight. Tonight she was saving her genuine passion for Yves. This Italian was a grotesque pig-faced creature. She must use her erotic expertise to finish him off quickly. But not too quickly, otherwise he might feel cheated and make her wait for an hour or two until he felt ready again.

Umberto entered the room, still wearing his uniform. His hands were behind his back, but his rigid penis was sticking out of his unbuttoned fly, and he looked so ridiculous that Inès had to stifle a giggle. Most men looked ridiculous with their cocks stuck straight out in that silly way. But Scrofo looked even more so because his organ was small, about the size of a ten-year-old boy's. This didn't seem to bother him though as he strutted into the bedroom, the cigar in his mouth almost twice the length of the thing sticking out of his trousers. He removed his trousers and shirt swiftly, then leaning against the Louis XIV commode next to the bed he gestured to Inès to start on him. She concentrated on Scrofo's small, stiff penis, imagining it to be Yves'. Her soft fingers stroked the stretched skin seductively, and she started to caress his wide white thighs, her mind far away.

The slashing pain as Umberto suddenly brought a whip down with stunning force onto her naked back was completely unexpected.

"Whore! French whore!" He laughed harshly as he cracked the whip against her shoulders with all his force, and Inès screamed in agony.

"Yell all you want, Mademoiselle. These walls are completely sound-proofed, and no one would come to rescue you even if they heard you. Suck me, bitch!" he commanded, his face a mask of sadistic pleasure as he slashed her again. Inès tried to obey, moving as best she could while he rained blows down on her, screaming obscenities.

"Sir, please *don't*," she begged, trying to move away from him. "You're hurting me."

"That's the idea," he leered. "I love hurting whores, especially French whores."

He grasped a fistful of Inès' long blond hair. "What are you?" he asked hoarsely, his eyes slits of brownish-black ice.

"Inès Dessault, sir," she whimpered softly.

"*What* are you, I said," he roared. "You know what you are, don't you, Inès?"

"Yes sir."

"Then tell me, slut. Go on, tell me what a whore you are."

"I'm a whore," she whispered as tears coursed down her cheeks. "I'm a—a—whore . . ." She hated herself, hated him, but she was thankful because the beating had stopped.

"Of course you are, Inès. You're a disgusting little slut—a horrible rotten creature, and this is what a whore like you deserves." He threw her roughly onto her stomach, forcing himself into her from behind with a moan of pleasure, his hands pulling her hair back so brutally she felt her neck would break.

Inès screamed as fresh pain engulfed her.

"Tell me again, slut." His breath was coming faster now as he held her around the neck by her hair. "Tell me what you are."

"I'm a whore," she whispered weakly, her tears raining on the pillow.

"Again," he demanded harshly, the stubble on his chin scraping her back. "Say it *again*, Inès. Tell me what you are, I like to hear you say it."

"A whore. I'm a whore," she wept.

"And a stupid one too," he sneered. Suddenly he stopped and she collapsed onto the mattress, sobbing with relief. She heard him opening a drawer, and raising her head from the pillow saw that he had removed a terrifying object from it.

"Roll over," he commanded harshly. "On your back, and open up those legs."

Eyes wide with fear, Inès obeyed, staring in horror as he strapped onto himself a rubber contraption shaped like a giant penis.

"No," she screamed. "Oh no, no—please don't—you can't." She tried to roll away but he grabbed her hair and in spite of her struggle started to force the hideous object inside her. She screamed but he clapped his hand over her mouth, hissing.

"If you don't shut up I'll ram this down your throat, and then you'll be a dead whore as well as a stupid one."

Pain came and went in great waves as Inès closed her eyes, praying for this excruciating suffering to end. She had never felt such agonizing degradation.

At last Scrofo's moans were becoming faster and Inès knew it must be ending. His hot breath scalded her shoulders and his saliva dripped onto her face.

"Yes, yes, you *whore!* You filthy French *cow*—you disgusting bitch. This is for *you!*" With a scream of satisfaction, the General gave a final vicious thrust, at the same time punching Inès in the face so violently that she lost consciousness.

He was born in Calabria, the toe of Italy, of a mother drunken and negligent and a father ignorant and weak, in the year before the outbreak of the First World War. It was a bitter winter night when Umberto Scrofo was pulled into the world. His mother had suffered agonizing labor for more than forty-eight hours before she was finally delivered of a child with a head out of all proportion to its tiny writhing body. The horrific ordeal and massive loss of blood left her only half alive.

Carlotta was barely twenty-three and the youngest of six children, all of them married and all with several children of their own. The already large family was growing fast, with many mouths to feed and precious little income with which to do it. The pitifully small amount of land which her father cultivated for vegetables had not only to feed his brood, but also to produce enough to sell at the market for necessities.

Carlotta never cared about her only child. Although it was no fault of his, he had injured her so badly during his birth that lovemaking was painfully uncomfortable for her afterward. Umberto's father loved his son, but as soon as the boy grew old enough to know which of the men on the farm was his father, Alberto was conscripted into the Italian army and the family did not see him for three years.

Carlotta called Umberto her little pig, her runt, and mocked him constantly. Full of resentment, she never forgave him for the pain he'd caused her, or for the loss of her sex life. She began to drink great quantities of rough wine all day long, and being an aggressive young woman, would often pick fights with anyone who cared to have one.

Sofia, Umberto's grandmother, also had little time to spare for the ugly boy with the huge head, and his cousins soon followed the example of their elders. By the time he was six Umberto was treated virtually as an outcast by the family, and was the butt of all their jokes.

At the age of seven, left in charge of his aunt's new baby girl, he decided to amuse himself one afternoon. He started sticking pins into the baby's bare bottom, never quite enough to draw blood, but enough to make the infant scream long and satisfyingly. This amused Umberto enormously, and he found that tormenting creatures smaller and weaker than himself gave him real pleasure. He once put a stray cat that he'd caught into a pot of water on the stove, watching it scream in agony as he boiled it to death. But he was discovered doing this, and Alberto pulled down his pants and thrashed him so soundly in front of the whole family that in the future he became more careful. Umberto was so humiliated by the incident that he allowed his sadistic impulses to lie dormant for several years.

At the age of twelve, while peeing with three of his male cousins in a field, the eldest, Pino, a strapping lad of seventeen, pointed to Umberto's penis and with peals of laughter screamed, "*Guarda* the little acorn! Cousin, your little *cazzo* hasn't grown a millimeter since you were seven. Hey, look at Benno here." He pointed to seven-year-old Benno, whose little penis pointed bravely into the ditch as he aimed his stream.

"*Guarda, guarda!*" Pino screamed with laughter, "Umberto's got the tiny little dick of a seven-year-old."

The other boys crowded around eagerly to peer at it, all of them proudly fingering their penises, which seemed to Umberto's eyes to be exceptionally long and thick. He cringed, and his cock cringed with him. It was very small indeed, but he hadn't really taken much notice of it before. Now it had become a thing of scorn, a freakish object for others to mock.

The boys soon told all the male members of the family of their discovery (the women would never have tolerated such vulgarity) and the news spread fast among the rest of the village men. Umberto Scrofo had a tiny penis the size of a bambino's, and they never let him forget it. The ignominy and shame remained with him always.

Its size had never increased. He tried excessive masturbation, as one of his kinder cousins helpfully suggested that this practice might help it grow, but that only made Umberto interested in girls and sex, which caused him even more frustration.

At sixteen he attempted to make love to the plain young daughter of a neighboring farmer. She was known to be easy and to "put out," but when she saw his childish equipment she started to rock with laughter, saying, "That's the most ridiculous excuse for a cock I've ever seen—it's no bigger than a thimble. I wouldn't even feel it inside me—take the pathetic little thing away, it's no good to any woman."

Poor Umberto. It wasn't until he was drafted into the Italian army in the spring of the following year that he began to come into his own. From then on—as promotion followed promotion—he never looked back, knowing that in time he would find a solution for his humiliating inadequacy.

◆❧ *Two* ❧◆

Yves Moray had found Inès when she was a weeping ten-year-old waif. Thumb in mouth, dressed almost in rags, she was standing outside a shabby block of flats where her prostitute mother had broken her neck by falling drunkenly down the stairs.

Yves the Magician, as he was called, had known the mother, Marie, but only slightly, since she was far too old to be in one of his *poules de luxe*. A fleshy blonde, she was only thirty when she died, but already well past her prime. The frightened girl, her mother's sole mourner at the burial, was another story. She would be a rare beauty. Yves could see the potential in her tangled honey-colored hair and in her innocent yet somehow carnal slanting blue eyes. But her personality was cold, frightened, uncommunicative. Little wonder. Marie had been short on maternal instincts, and Inès had been left to fend for herself since she was a toddler. Yves took the frightened girl under his protective wing, since there was no one else who could do so, or would want to. He saw in her a kindred spirit for he too had been orphaned as a child.

In the first weeks that Inès lived in the sanctuary of his house she never smiled. Yves opened up his sorcerer's basket for her, fascinating her by his sleight of hand with cards, his hocus-pocus with colored scarves, his skill with the juggling of oranges. But the little girl would just sit there watching him wide-eyed, sucking her thumb with a sad solemn expression.

One day Yves was smoking a cigarette and found the child's eyes fixed upon him as usual. "How about this one, Inès?" he said, and popping the lit cigarette inside his mouth with his tongue, he stared at her bug-eyed until two long streams of smoke issued from both ears.

At that Inès let out a shriek of pure laughter that didn't stop until tears ran down her face. Yves picked her up, hugged her tightly and from then on the ice was broken. Inès had smiled, and whenever her beloved Yves was near her she smiled a lot.

Yves was gentle and kind with Inès. He sent her to school, gave her warm clothes and enough food to eat, and loved bringing happiness to her sad little face. Within a year she was wildly infatuated with him, following him around whenever he was home like a devoted puppy, but he realized that Inès was really frightened of men. The only men she had ever known were the coarse oafs who had paid churlish court to her mother. Louts from back streets, they bought Marie's body for a few francs, often abusing her too. Many was the morning when Inès had awoken to the sound of her mother's whimpers as she examined the black eye or swollen lips that one of her "gentlemen" had given her. Eschewing Inès' timid offers of assistance, Marie would usually give the girl a cuff for her consideration.

Sometimes Marie would be lucky enough to land herself a "Mic," but usually he would be some heartless pimp from the alleys of Montmartre who would take all of Marie's earnings, spending it on whiskey, other women and scented hair pomade in exchange for the loveless lovemaking that he would provide for her.

As she got older, each of Marie's successive pimps seemed to become more avaricious, odious and unkind. Marie seemed to attract men who treated her badly and beat her, and often when they had drunk enough absinthe they liked to beat Inès too. The child grew to hate her mother and the vile men who punished them both, but there was little she could do about it.

At the time her mother died, Inès had never known a kind word from a man. She knew well what a pimp was and what he did. She saw how harshly they treated their women, and she knew in her childish heart that none of them was worth a sou. But Yves Moray proved a different customer altogether. Younger than the usual *"macrous"* that Marie had suffered, he had a roguish smiling face made even more appealing by a nose that turned up into a pair of curved nostrils which seemed to flare like a horse's whenever he laughed. His hair was pale brown, soft and curly, and when it was wet it clung to his head in tight Grecian curls. His eyes were a merry hazel, full of life and amusement, and when he laughed, which was often, they crinkled enchantingly. Inès used to stare at him covertly as she studied at the kitchen table at night. Some of his select stable of girls would sit adoringly at his feet while he regaled them with magic tricks, stroked them fondly like kittens and made them feel special and cherished. All of the girls worshiped Yves, not only for his kindness, amiable winning nature and impish smile, but for his fascinating conjuring act. He could juggle six oranges at a time without dropping one, as the girls whooped him on with cries of glee. He could do magical card tricks, making the ace of spades or the king of hearts disappear into thin air, and then "discovering" it under one of the girls' skirts. This would cause such shrieks of laughter that Inès would look up crossly from her housework, wishing that she was part of the enchanted circle at Yves' feet. He had all manner of bewitching tricks to enthrall his whores. For it was important to Yves to enthrall. Since the age of ten his childhood and early youth had been spent on the streets of Montmartre performing the conjuring tricks and magic he had learned at his father's knee. By the time he was seventeen girls flocked around him, mesmerized by his cheeky charm. It wasn't long before he gave up his life of street busking and let the girls take care of him. With Yves the Magician there was never a dull moment.

Soon he had cast a spell over the child Inès, and in her preadolescent way she tried to attract him. She wanted him to love her. Craved his affection. He was the father she had never known, the benign kindly laughing uncle she had always wanted, the lover she needed to captivate and make her own. But although Yves found her appealing, she was too young, so he made her wait for him for more than three years. Made her wait until she thought she would die for want of him. Made her wait as she sat sulkily in the front parlor of his house in the respectable Parisian suburb of Neuilly, listening while he made love to Francine or Olivia or Anna, or to any of the others. Sometimes she would eavesdrop on the sounds of his lovemaking, her ear against a thick tumbler pressed to the wall between their two bedrooms. Weeping bitterly, she listened to the sounds of the man she worshiped as he made love to other women, and sometimes she touched herself clumsily, finding a kind of relief.

Inès was precocious in both face and body. On her fourteenth birthday, standing before him rose-colored and golden, she stood on tiptoe to kiss his lips thanking him for the small presents he had bought for her.

She particularly loved a slender bracelet of amber and silver beads which he had found in an antique shop off the rue Jacob. As he fastened the filigree clasp around her slender wrist, he could almost smell the scent of musk emanating from her as she breathed, "Oh, thank you, Yves." The smile of an innocent Venus made her look even more seductive. "It is the most beautiful bracelet I have ever seen—I will never take it off. *Never.*"

Inès was wearing her simple school uniform, a white blouse with a wide collar, a dark blue serge tunic, pleated, sturdy shoes and long woollen socks. Her hair fell halfway down her back, curling in delicate tendrils around her oval face. With her clear blue eyes and golden skin, she looked like one of Botticelli's angels. Yves was a man who truly appreciated women, even though he exploited them. He examined her: the seductive, knowing look on her face that predicted delights in store for him; her budding breasts, whose rose-tipped nipples were hardening under the blouse. The parted pale lips seemed aching to be kissed. His eyes narrowed as they met the shy gaze that told him what she desired. She was ripe, she was ready, it was time. Finally Yves the Magician allowed Inès, the teenage seductress, to conquer him.

They made love for hours in the warm, soft darkness of his bed. She knew how it was done—she had been in the room often enough when her mother had been at work.

Ever since Inès had reached the age of awareness—five or six—she had watched what Marie had done with her men. Some of them liked her mother's style so much that they came back week after week, for months, even years. So although Inès was technically a virgin, her mother had been an excellent teacher of the erotic arts. With a natural instinct as well as lessons learned from hours of observation, she gave Yves the most enthusiastic lovemaking that he had ever had. From that time on, Inès had shared Yves' bed nightly; he soon found himself entranced by this child with the gorgeous face, magical body and sexual tricks of an experienced courtesan, and he managed to teach her even more.

Six months later, with the advent of war, pandemonium ruled France. Several of Yves' regular girls fled Paris, and he had little choice but to put Inès to work. She started off at a nightclub owned by Gabrielle Printemps, L'Éléphant Rose.

As the daughter of a whore, Inès wasn't really too upset. Yves loved her, she worshiped him, and she didn't really care much about anything else. Being a professional prostitute was only a job. She didn't like it, she didn't dislike it. It was just the obvious and inevitable way of her life.

The men she slept with meant nothing; her mind was far away when they possessed her body. She knew they could never possess her heart because that belonged totally to Yves, her wonderful, magical Yves. She was his completely, and whatever other men did with her could make no difference to her devotion to Yves.

Their mutual passion was pure and strong, symbolized, Inès thought, by the shimmering amber-and-silver bracelet strands which encircled her wrist and represented the eternity of their love.

❧ *Three* ❧

As THE MORNING LIGHT began to flood into the bedroom Inès regained consciousness. Her head throbbed painfully. The linen sheets were encrusted with blood, her blood, and the pain all over her body was so intense that she wanted to weep. She had to escape from this loathsome creature who snored next to her, she had to get away immediately—but he had not paid her yet. No matter, she would take the money herself. God knows she'd earned it.

Please let him stay asleep, she thought as she crept from the bed, wincing in agony. His trousers lay on the floor where he had thrown them, next to the discarded whip and the disgusting false penis. She still ached from the numbing pain of it. Quickly she searched through his pockets but there was no money in them. Glancing at the snoring man, she tiptoed into the marble bathroom, where, in the full-length mirror, she saw her bruised and tear-stained face, her shoulders and breasts covered with welts and cuts, the dried blood on her thighs. Flinching in pain, she squatted over the bidet, washing herself with scented soap. It was then that she noticed the thick wad of francs lying by the side of the marble washbasin, next to his razor and toothbrush. There were a lot of notes, more than she usually made in a month. Should she just take what she was usually paid or all the money to make up for the atrocities Scrofo had done to her? "Take them all," she whispered to the reflection of the pale wounded girl who looked out sorrowfully from the mirror. "You deserve them, Inès."

Hastily she seized the banknotes, just as the Italian lurched into the room. Seeing what she was doing, he grabbed her hair and smashing her head against the marble wall with all his strength, screamed "A whore *and* a thief, huh? There's only one way to treat scum like you—give you more of what you had last night."

Inès saw with dread that he held that disgusting rubber object in his hand and that he was erect again. He forced her over to the washbasin, all the time mouthing his litany of filth. Oh, my God, he was going to do it again. He couldn't, he simply couldn't. It was unbearable.

"Please don't," she sobbed. "Please, please stop—you can't do this again. Please, you can't. I promise I'll come back when I'm better. I am in so much pain—such pain, look, I'm bleeding."

"Good." His grin revealed sharp yellow teeth and she could smell the reek of garlic and stale champagne, see that his eyes were bloodshot and wild. "The way *you* want it, I only do with *proper* women," he gloated. "Italian women, *good* girls, ladies, not French harlots like you. I only do it like *this* with *scum.*" He bent her over the basin, and his small penis stabbed into her with the dull pain of a blunt knife. "We will do it like *this*—and then we will do it again with *this*," and he brandished the repulsive plaything in front of her. "My little rubber friend. You like him, Inès, don't you? I know you liked him last night."

"No!" screamed Inès. "No! Please!" As if in a dream, her eyes suddenly focused on an old-fashioned cut-throat razor which was lying open on the marble counter. Without thinking, the terror and pain so excruciating, she picked up the razor and lashed out blindly behind her. She heard the General scream in anguish and then a great crash as he fell to the floor. Inès gasped when she turned and saw what she had done. The blade had sliced across his throat as cleanly as a seamstress cuts into a length of cloth. Blood bubbled from the wound and his eyes rolled back in his head. There was no doubt that he was dying. Ghastly rasping sounds issued from his throat even though his tiny penis still stood lewdly erect, like some defiant flagpole. Stricken into immobility, she watched as his huge bald head, spattered with the blood that pumped from his throat, lolled sideways onto the floor.

Inès gazed at the dead man, panic-stricken. She had killed an Italian officer of the occupation. What on earth was she going to do?

✧   ✧   ✧

Frozen with fear, Inès didn't know how long she stood staring at Umberto Scrofo as blood poured from his neck and mouth onto the shining marble tiles. In the mirror, she saw a terrified girl whose blond hair hung over her face in matted snarls, whose eyes were wild and who had blood on her hands. She had to get out.

It was seven o'clock. How long before one of the General's aides would call for him? He was bound to have army matters, maneuvers, something to do, he was an important part of the war machine. He had told her that at the café. Her mind raced with possibilities. She could just leave, after she dressed in the red frock and shabby coat which she had worn the previous night. The concierge had barely looked at her when she arrived. He wouldn't remember her—would he?

Her fingers rubbed her chafed wrists, raw from Scrofo's brutal treatment, and she ran them under the warm tap water. Then with a shock she realized that her lucky bracelet was missing. Fear made her limbs tremble uncontrollably as she rushed into the bedroom, throwing back the bloodied sheets, searching desperately for her precious beads. The bracelet—her talisman—anyone who knew her would instantly recognize the fine strings of amber and silver beads which she always wore. If they discovered the bracelet, it would only be a question of how long before they found her. In a frenzy she dropped to the floor, crawling about on hands and knees, but the bracelet wasn't there. Tears rolled down her face, stinging her cut lips, her bruised cheeks. Then she remembered: she hadn't been wearing it last night! The clasp was loose and Yves had promised to take it to be mended. Thank God, oh, thank God.

Back in the bathroom she grabbed the wad of notes—they were well paid, these Italians—then ran back to the bedroom and flung on her clothes. She had retrieved everything except one red garter. So what? Every whore in Paris wore red garters. They couldn't possibly trace her with that—could they?

She shoved the other garter and her stockings into a pocket and cautiously opened the suite door, looking down the deserted corridor. Her heart beating painfully, she tiptoed down the passage towards the back stairs, hoping to find the staff entrance. As she crept down she heard laughter and a door opening, and hid herself around a bend in the stairway as several chambermaids came chattering down the long hall to begin their shifts. Entering a changing room in shabby dresses, they emerged in starched blue-and-white uniforms, and sped off to begin their work.

Inès' heartbeat was so loud that she imagined the chattering girls might hear it. She wondered what sort of security the hotel would have at the back entrance. Would they, like many hotels, have guards who must check the staff out for possible theft after every shift? Would the employees have to carry identity cards which proved they worked there? It was almost more of a risk than to leave by the front entrance—nevertheless it was a decision she must make.

She looked at her wristwatch, another present from Yves. It was nearly seven-thirty, over half an hour since she had sliced the razor across the General's throat. She shuddered at the thought of how the authorities would punish her if they ever caught her. Execution would be the least painful death she could expect for someone of her age and looks. They would no doubt inflict on her the most sophisticated tortures, after the inevitable multiple rapes. Death would be a blessing. No, she was determined that this would not be her fate, this was not the way she had envisaged her life. In spite of her past, in spite of the ignominy of her profession, Inès possessed innate pride and belief in herself. She was determined to escape. The stream of arriving girls had now slowed to a trickle. Two more exhausted, gamine-faced young women, little more than children, arrived, then there was a lull; it was now or never.

Mustering all her courage, Inès strode purposefully into the small room in which the maids changed. None of the girls even looked at her, so busy were they dressing and gossiping. Keeping her head down, she moved along to the last shabby overcoat hanging on the row of hooks. Below each hook was a locked wood-and-wire netting cage in which the girls kept their handbags and walking shoes. Their identity cards would, no doubt, be in those handbags.

Inès put on the tattered overcoat, which was too long for her. There was a flimsy scarf in the pocket, and thankfully she tied it around her matted hair. All she needed now was another girl's identity papers. Stealthily she pulled at several of the little hatches on the wire cages, but they were all securely locked. Never mind, she had her coat and scarf, and most important of all, she had courage. Tightening the belt on the overcoat, she followed two chattering chambermaids who were going off shift. They clattered down granite steps to a small foyer inside the door leading to the rue Cambon. A Ritz security guard sat at his desk, cigarette drooping from a tired mouth. Behind him stood a Nazi officer staring at the wall with a look of deep melancholy.

Hans Meyer was usually one of the most zealous and thorough of guards. This morning, however, his mind was elsewhere. The previous night he had received a letter from his fiancée in the Fatherland: she had fallen in love with his own father—a widower for many years—and they would be married by the time Hans received the letter. She was very sorry, of course, wartime stress and all that, but c'est la vie, and she hoped Hans would try to understand. He had been so full of rage that he had drunk himself into a stupor and was now suffering the worst hangover of his life. He took no notice of the prattling maids who were emptying their handbags onto the trestle table for the guard to examine. His father! His beautiful twenty-two-year-old flaxen-haired Fräulein was going to marry his bald-headed sixty-year-old father. Between bouts of nausea, he plotted his revenge, totally ignoring the guard's cursory examination of the girls' belongings.

Inès emptied her handbag onto the table and the guard halfheartedly flicked through its meager contents. Lipstick, mirror, comb, a door key, a few francs. The wad of two thousand francs was well hidden in her shoe.

"Okay, you can go," said the guard. "Next."

Praying the German soldier would not question her lopsided walk, Inès bundled her possessions back into her bag and strode out into the golden Parisian sunshine.

Free! She was free. But how long could it last?

◆*Four*◆

THAT SPRING OF 1943 the Gestapo seemed to be everywhere in Paris, and they were a sinister sight. They lurked in black Mercedeses wearing heavy leather overcoats, with the dreaded swastika emblazoned on their sleeves. They smoked harsh cigarettes, looking with dead eyes at everyone who passed.

They always pounced at night. Small groups of men, their cold eyes insensitive to human suffering, sometimes accompanied by ferocious Alsatian dogs straining at their leashes, would come to their victims' homes without warning. The dogs could root out "enemies of the Reich" hidden anywhere—in cellars, cupboards, even concealed behind walls.

Every night the Gestapo discovered groups of hidden Jews, herding them into trucks to be sent to God knows where. All French Jews had to wear badges, on which JUIF was printed in yellow letters, and none of them ever knew when they could expect to hear the dreaded sound of barking Alsatians, the staccato rap of the SS at their front doors. Every Jew lived in fear, but all of them did their best to disguise it.

Polished leather jackboots glistening, gray uniforms bristling with insignia, the long, dark shadow of the Third Reich fell across the entire Jewish population of France that spring. But although every patriotic citizen detested the sight of the enemy soldiers, with true French spirit they tried to live as normally as possible. The Nazi soldiers, their coarse faces framed by ugly helmets, leather straps tight under their chins, were ruthless, completely without mercy. They had been trained a long time in Germany for this moment and they treated the French nation with undisguised contempt.

Agathe Guinzberg had spent the last of her teenage years hiding in a basement in Montparnasse. The house was owned by Gabrielle Printemps who also owned L'Éléphant Rose, the club next door, a favorite haunt of enemy officers and their floozies.

Gabrielle lived with her grandfather, mother and crippled eighteen-year-old brother, Gilbert. By chance, that particular evening when the Gestapo arrived to arrest the Jewish Guinzberg family, Agathe was at the Printemps' house, reading to Gilbert. When the Printemps family saw what was happening across the street, they made Agathe hide down in their basement. Peeping through lace curtains, Gabrielle saw Agathe's family pushed unceremoniously into the back of a truck. There were three little girls under twelve, two boys of about fifteen and sixteen, and their mother and father. The commandant didn't seem to realize that he should be taking a family of eight *Juden* off to await deportation to the camps. He was weary. This was the fourteenth family they had "collected" that night. He knew that there should be several children, and indeed there were, so that was that, he had filled his quota for the night, now he could go off and enjoy himself.

The truck took the Guinzbergs, with all the other Jewish families to a makeshift camp outside Paris. There they joined several hundred other families and were soon put on a train to Buchenwald, from where none would ever be heard of again.

Hidden in the Printemps' cellar, eighteen-year-old Agathe slowly learned to adapt to living alone among the spiders and the cockroaches; with the mildew and the stench of drains; with the rats, the mice and the unspeakable horrors of her fertile imagination. She had been given a supply of candles but was told to use them sparingly. Her only substantial meal was delivered by Gabrielle in the morning, when the last drunken footsteps of the enemy echoed down the cobblestone streets. Only then did Agathe allow herself to light a candle, eat her food and spend the next few precious hours reading in the recesses of her tomb. Occasionally a brief note from Gabrielle accompanied the food—the latest news of the war, good or bad, or perhaps a concerned query about her welfare. Gabrielle was terrified to the point of paranoia about talking to Agathe. She believed that walls—even floors—had ears, and consequently kept conversation to a minimum. Agathe was able to wash only once a week, when Gabrielle would send down a basin of lukewarm water, and soon her clothes hung on her sparse body in filthy tatters. Whenever her head itched so much that she could hardly stand it, she would pick the lice from her scalp, cracking their bodies between her thumbnails like peanuts.

Agathe's mind began to inhabit a world of its own as each day drifted into endless night. There was darkness all the time except for the blessed candles; it was bitterly cold and damp; but at least she had some comfort —the books.

If her body suffered from lack of nourishment, her mind did not. Gabrielle's grandfather had been a bookseller who specialized in rare books, and the cellar was crammed with leather-bound volumes of Balzac, Molière, Racine and Victor Hugo; poems by Byron, Shelley, Voltaire, Baudelaire and Robert Browning; and escapist adventure stories by Alexandre Dumas and Rider Haggard—all piled high in the damp cellar. Better mildew on the precious volumes, Grandfather had said, than for them to fall into the hands of the Germans. Throughout her numberless lonely nights, Agathe read hundreds of books as she prayed for the occupation to end.

Agathe had studied ballet since she was a child—her ambition was to be a prima ballerina. To retain her sanity, she would often practice, whirling and bending frenziedly in the darkness, humming the music of

Swan Lake and *Giselle,* her mind full of the glory that could be hers when she was released from captivity. Unable to count the days to her freedom, for she had no idea when it would be, she was a prisoner without parole—a jailbird with no end to her sentence.

Gabrielle had given Agathe her own rosary and crucifix when she first went into the cellar. Despite being Jewish, Agathe took comfort in the amber beads, constantly caressing them, praying for her deliverance.

Sometimes she scribbled plaintive notes to Gabrielle: "How much longer will the war last?" The reply would always be the same: "Not much longer, child, I hope. Have faith, we are all praying for it to end soon."

Every night Agathe heard the raucous laughter of German and Italian officers who patronized the nightclub next door, the shrill, high-pitched shrieks of their young whores, and Gabrielle's husky voice singing to them. As rats and cockroaches scurried around her feet, and her body shook with the cold, she began to learn the true meaning of hatred.

Early one evening before the club had opened, the Gestapo came to the house for a routine search. While Gabrielle and her family were being questioned, two Alsatians sniffed around the bedrooms, the front parlor and the kitchen. Agathe could hear the sound of boots clattering above her, and froze. The cellar opening was covered by a sheet of metal set into the floor of the scullery, camouflaged by cracked linoleum. Agathe trembled on her filthy bedding in the blackness beneath them, but remained undiscovered because the dogs were far more interested in the appetizing scent of meat in the larder, and barked enthusiastically.

Whenever Gabrielle passed a platoon of soldiers in the street she shuddered and looked away. Each time she took a plate of food down to Agathe, she wondered fearfully how long it would be before the girl was discovered and Gabrielle's own family were persecuted for hiding her. But as the months and then the years passed, she began to realize that Agathe had been forgotten by the Nazis; she no longer existed.

As the Jewish population continued to be systematically exterminated, as the hunger pangs of France grew more severe, the French Resistance worked on.

Maurice Grimaud was the best forger in France, the unrivaled expert in counterfeiting identity papers and passports. A highly valued member of the Resistance, he fraternized at L'Eléphant Rose several times a week, playing the jovial drunk, the buffoon, making the hated enemy laugh. The Germans enjoyed his idiotic antics, encouraging him to sit at their tables to joke with them. Since liquor loosened tongues, he picked up enormous amounts of information which was invaluable to the Resistance.

Maurice was a man of so many faces who had so many hiding places that the Gestapo were never able to track him down because they had no idea who he really was. He was a master of disguise, an expert in calligraphy and counterfeiting, and his efforts on behalf of the French Underground were legendary. He had nine lives and had not yet lost one.

He was a generous old friend of Gabrielle's. She was becoming extremely worried about Agathe, and decided to talk to Maurice about the girl. The last time Gabrielle had shone a torch on Agathe's face, she could hardly believe what she saw. Agathe was wasting away to nothing, her hair had turned lint white, her face was so thin that her cheekbones stuck out like pieces of jagged glass, and the deep hollows around her eyes were those of a forty-five-year-old woman. Her appearance had changed so radically that Gabrielle decided that, with new identity papers, she could be released from the cellar. No one would ever recognize her. Gabrielle also thought that if the girl died—and with Agathe looking so frail and ill this was not a remote possibility—getting rid of the body would be a great problem. Besides which, Gabrielle needed someone to work behind the cash desk at her club. Agathe could work for what she ate, and sleep on a cot in the parlor.

Thanks to Maurice, Agathe soon possessed an authentic-looking set of identity papers, passport, birth certificate and even a complete set of school reports going right back to kindergarten. They were masterpieces of his art and Maurice was proud of them.

When Agathe was finally helped out of the cellar and took a few faltering steps into the backyard, the faint autumnal sun was such a shock to her system that she fainted. She weighed barely ninety pounds. Her skin was as pale as mountain snow and her black hair had turned completely white. She looked so different from the plump, laughing teenager who had disappeared nearly two years ago, that even the neighbors who had known her before gave her no glance of recognition.

In the following months Agathe sat silently behind the cash register at L'Éléphant Rose, watching the Germans and the Italians fraternize, observing how they abused the French whores. Her hatred for every one of them grew like a cancer in her weakened body.

Traitors. Those girls, so young and pretty, were despicable traitors who betrayed their country and their people by consorting with the enemy. She hated all the Frenchwomen who hung over the soldiers and officers, laughing with them, fondling their bodies, kissing their cruel lips. No one ever gave *her* a second glance and Agathe realized bitterly that her prettiness was gone forever. Although she was just twenty she looked fifty, and though she ate heartily her body remained almost skeletal. Silently each night she sat in the tiny glass-walled booth at the back of the nightclub, to all intents and purposes immersed in the accounts. Her silver hair and pale skin glowed spectrally in the dim lighting and she constantly fingered her rosary as she simmered with a quiet but consuming rage and a desperate desire for revenge.

❧ *Five* ❧

"Y ou did what?" Yves' eyes narrowed and the color drained from his face.

"*Chérie,* it is *not* possible. Why did you have to *kill him?* What he did couldn't have been *that* terrible, surely?"

"It was, Yves, it was torture. You have no idea of the pain and the horrible things he did." Inès tried to control her hysteria, sipping at the whiskey which a rabbit-faced waitress at L'Éléphant Rose had brought her. "I *had* to do it, Yves—I had to, he would have killed me if I hadn't, he threatened to kill me. I know he would have—I know." Tears streamed down her cheeks.

Gabrielle, with a murmur of sympathy, passed her a handkerchief. *Merde,* what slime these men are, she thought. She had seen the bruises and cuts on Inès' body and looked pityingly at the girl who, in her grief, looked little more than a child.

They were sitting in a dimly lit back booth of L'Éléphant Rose. Although it was eight-thirty in the morning, the club had only just closed. Yves' brain raced with the problems they all now faced. Whatever Inès had done, no accusing finger must ever be allowed to point at the club. It was much too valuable to them all and too many lives would be put at risk. Even though most of its habitués were the enemy, the club was still one of the most important cores of the Resistance in Paris. The enemy must never know that the killer of an Italian officer had in any way been assisted by *le Maquis.*

"Thank God you met him in the café and not here," Yves said. "Did anyone see you with him? Anyone at all?"

"No, no, I don't think so—he was sitting at a table alone—it all happened quite quickly. He knew very well what I was when he picked me up. I was wearing that low-cut green dress. We only spoke for a moment or two before he propositioned me. And told me to meet him last night at the Ritz." She started to cry again and Gabrielle poured her another shot of whiskey. "I should've gone and sat with Picasso," sobbed Inès. "He smiled at me too."

"Shut up, Inès," snapped Yves. "The concierge last night—do you think he saw you?"

"I can't remember." Inès did her best to recall the events of twelve hours ago, which already seemed like an eternity. "I don't think he looked up at me when I asked for Scrofo's room number—but you never know with concierges, do you?" More tears ran down her face and her shoulders heaved with sobs. Gabrielle squeezed her hand sympathetically.

"No, I suppose you never do." Yves' voice was grim. "But since you *did* speak to the concierge, the Gestapo are sure to question him. There are probably no more than two or three hundred blond teenaged prostitutes in Paris. It's only a matter of time before they trace you, line you up for the concierge to identify—and then accuse you. Don't forget, they will find fingerprints."

"Yes—yes, of course," Inès groaned. *Why* hadn't she thought to clean the marble surfaces of the bathroom, the handle of the razor, the champagne glass? It was too much to think about. She felt dizzy and nauseous. All she wanted was to sleep in the safety of Yves' arms. She wanted him to stroke her hair, comfort her, tell her that everything was going to be all right, promise that he would take care of her, as he always had done.

"Come. We must go to see Maurice right away," Yves said decisively. "We have no time to lose."

After four days the scandal and gossip about the murderous attack on the Italian General began to die down. No suspect had been found, and the concierge at the hotel had a conveniently patriotic memory block about the prostitute whom he had seen going up to Scrofo's room. No one else had seen Inès at the Ritz that night, and there were simply no clues as to the identity of who had slashed the General's throat.

While Yves and Maurice decided what to do with her, Inès was hidden in the same cellar where Agathe had lived for so long. When Gabrielle came down to cut and dye her long blond hair, she told Inès that plans and arrangements were under way to smuggle her over to England.

"He was a complete bastard, that Italian General. I heard about him," Gabrielle said as she fluffed up Inès' newly dyed shoulder-length dark hair.

"You would not *believe* the disgusting things he did with some of the girls." Her voice was full of bitterness. "They say that *he* was the one who killed Jeanette. Everyone who knew him, even his so-called friends in the army, seems happy that he's gone. I think you did us all a big favor, *chérie.*"

"When will Yves get me out of here, Gabrielle?" Inès said plaintively. "I'm so lonely and frightened. There are hundreds of spiders and rats and cockroaches. I have the most terrible nightmares—I keep on seeing Scrofo's face—I just can't sleep. I'm scared." Inès began to cry, but Gabrielle grabbed her hair, bringing the girl's face close to hers.

"Listen, little girl," she whispered fiercely, "you are very lucky. *Whatever* that swine did to you, you *are* a whore, and it's your *profession* to serve and satisfy men, even pigs like him."

Inès winced as Gabrielle continued: "We are all risking our lives every day for you, you ungrateful, selfish child. And as for being frightened, we had to keep Agathe down here for nearly two years, and she never complained. You're lucky to have a man like Yves who loves you—even if he is only a pimp," Gabrielle told her. "Not many little whores are so lucky. And to let you know how *really* lucky you are, my friend Maurice has been working day and night for you on your identity papers. Tonight—"

she leaned forward—"tonight, you have a nice surprise coming, and you don't deserve it."

"Hmmm, good. Excellent. Very convincing."

Yves admired the worn French passport, the set of bound school reports dating back over ten years and the ragged identity card with Inès' photograph. They were all made out in the name of Inès Juillard, and they appeared completely authentic.

"From now on, that will be your name," Yves told her. "You must forget that Inès Dessault ever existed. She is gone forever."

They had been cycling through the leafy country lanes of Normandy towards the coast of Calais, where they were to meet their contact. Now they were lying under a huge chestnut tree and the afternoon sun dappled Inès' dark brown hair with highlights of burnished gold. They felt almost safe while they ate their frugal sandwiches and drank from a bottle of rough red wine. In the distance they could see some farmers toiling in the fields, and it seemed that country life was going on much as usual.

Inès leaned forward to kiss Yves. He wore scruffy peasant clothes, with his hair cropped and a three-day stubble on his cheeks, but his magnetism stirred her more than ever.

"Yves," she whispered, her tongue tracing his lips. "Oh, Yves darling, I love you so much." Her hands caressed him inside the coarse cloth of his shirt as his lips hungrily responded to her delicate kisses. She stretched out like a cat on the soft grass surrendering herself to his touch.

Danger made their coupling sweeter. The smell of the sweet crushed grass mixed in her nostrils with the scent of Yves, the warm familiar smell which Inès loved beyond all others.

Their bodies fused, fueling each other's fire. This man was the only person in the world Inès had ever truly loved, and she knew she could never love another.

Too soon he looked at his watch, saying briskly, "It's three o'clock, *chérie*—we must go or we will never be in Calais by eleven."

He spoke almost lovingly to Inès, although he knew he had never completely loved anyone in his life. He had decided that it was necessary that he accompany her to England, for if the Italians ever discovered who had murdered Umberto Scrofo, life for those who had anything to do with Inès would become very unpleasant indeed. Like the Gestapo, they were not particular about whom they tortured, or how they did it, and a murderess's pimp could expect no mercy from Mussolini's men.

An old blue-and-white rowboat was waiting for them in a small cove down the coast from Calais, exactly where the Resistance had said it would be. In it were three men who were also, for one reason or another, being smuggled out of France by the partisans.

As Inès sat hunched in the tiny craft, watching the French coast recede, she breathed the fresh sea air gratefully, feeling more free than she had for days. The four men rowed vigorously. It was a fine, spring night with little wind and few cross-currents, so they made the crossing in good time. Four hours later Inès blinked in wonder as she saw the magnificent chalk cliffs of Dover appear, dimly lit by weak moonlight.

As soon as the boat beached, the men hauled it quickly up onto the pebbles, covering it with fishing nets and clumps of seaweed and waited for their contact to arrive. As they had been told to expect, a man cautiously approached them through the darkness, mumbling a few words of welcome. The contact handed them a brown paper parcel which contained five English ration books made out in fictitious names, identity cards and some crumpled pound notes. There was also a timetable for the local trains, and four different addresses in England.

Inès and Yves eagerly peered at their own particular address:

Madame Josette Pichon
17 Shepherd Market
London W1

"Shepherd Market." Inès rolled the name on her tongue, savoring the Englishness of it. "How pretty it sounds. Oh Yves, do you think there will be lambs and chickens and a maypole with ribbons on it in the middle of the village square?"

"Hardly, *chérie*." Yves chuckled at Inès' naïveté. "England is suffering in this war almost as badly as France. Night after night German planes bomb London to hell and back. From what I've heard, Shepherd Market is right in the center of everything. We'd probably have been safer in Paris."

"I don't care where I am, *chéri*," Inès sparkled, "as long as I'm with you, Yves. That's all I want."

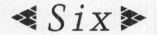

Six

LONDON 1943

"OH, DAMMIT, NOT AGAIN," Phoebe mumbled to herself. She had just crawled into bed, shattered after another long night of toil at the Windmill Theatre, where "We never close" was the famous motto. "Not another bloody air raid. Will it *never* end?"

Half asleep, she pulled on her warm dressing gown and fluffy sheepskin slippers. Carrying a Thermos of hot tea and a bag which contained her worldly essentials and went everywhere with her, she staggered down seven flights of stairs into the scant comfort of the crowded air-raid shelter.

Along with the other occupants of her block of flats she tried in vain to doze while the sound of exploding bombs echoed through the darkened and shuddering shelter, babies cried and children whimpered with fear. As soon as the All Clear had sounded, the weary group picked up the bits and pieces of their lives and ventured shakily back to their flats . . . until the next night.

Phoebe sighed with exhausted relief as she let herself in, and throwing herself onto the bed slept the dreamless sleep of the innocent. She had survived yet another night of Luftwaffe air raids, yet another night of earth-shattering, deafening noises as the anti-aircraft guns blazed and the German bombs blitzed the city to hell.

In the morning she listened to the BBC as the solemn tones of Alvar Lidell broadcast the extent of the damage to the city. Over seventy buildings had been partially or completely destroyed, fifty-two civilians killed and more than twice that number injured. His voice was grave as he recited the death toll, and Phoebe switched off the wireless. She couldn't bear to hear such bad, sad news.

After patiently queuing in her local teashop for a cup of strong tea and a sticky bun with some scant raisins in it, she picked her way fastidiously down Great Portland Street towards the West End. The streets were covered with shrapnel and debris, but thankfully none of the buildings that she passed had collapsed. Most of the bombing had been concentrated near the river, from where she could see a tall gray pall of smoke rising above the chimneypots of Oxford Circus.

Phoebe's natural exuberance managed to flourish even in war-torn London. At twenty-three she had the robust curves, creamy skin and willful red hair inherited from her forebears—stalwart country men and women from the north of England, not afraid of hard work and deprivation. Hardy British stock, they had all been survivors, and she was going to survive this bloody war, even make the best of it. She wasn't going to allow herself to get depressed. She had a job to do at the Windmill Theatre: to entertain the boys—the boys in blue, the boys in khaki, the boys in green, even the boys in white. They were all on leave, all with weary, jaundiced eyes that spoke of dreadful war experiences—which their raucous laughter belied. The showgirls would give seven performances today, as they did every day. They would change their costumes no less than forty-nine times—seven changes in each show—and some of them would even bare their breasts for the soldiers to gawk at.

Phoebe's thick Cuban heels clacked down Regent Street, daintily avoiding the street cleaners who were trying to sweep up "Jerry's garbage." In spite of the nightly air raids, Piccadilly Circus was always a hive of festive activity. The statue of Eros, God of Love, had been removed from the center of Piccadilly to a safe haven. Allied military men of every nationality milled about in a maelstrom of color and movement, and dozens of young women mingled on the pavement, chatting to them animatedly. There was a carnival atmosphere in Piccadilly Circus, a desperate gaiety on the faces of the crowds as if to say that the war could not affect them.

No matter that for many servicemen leave was over tomorrow, and they were off to fight in North Africa or Burma or Salerno. It was party time all the time in London, especially in the West End and particularly at the Windmill Theatre.

Phoebe walked past Lyons Corner House, where two long queues stood waiting patiently for it to open, and hurried up Shaftesbury Avenue.

Entering the stage door, she stopped as she saw one of the best-looking young men that she had ever laid eyes on, talking animatedly to the stage doorkeeper. Thick, dark brown hair in unruly waves, jet black curved eyebrows, a handsome, slightly saturnine face, and a nose and cheekbones which were almost a living replica of Antinous, the youth so beloved of the Emperor Hadrian. Navy blue eyes met hers briefly, then turned away without the remotest flicker of interest as he continued chatting to the old man.

The stranger was dressed in a gray Prince of Wales checked three-piece suit, a pale blue shirt and an extravagant tie. A light gray homburg was tipped rakishly over his eyes as he leaned toward the doorman, charm oozing from every pore.

"But look here, old chap, just tell the boss that I've had *years* of experience in variety. Manchester Hippodrome, Gaiety Theatre, Liverpool, the Alhambra in Brighton. I've topped the bill at all of them. And," he whispered conspiratorially, "I've got the best repertoire of blue jokes this side of Blackpool Pier—I've had 'em rolling in the aisles, old chap, everywhere. Here." He handed the disinterested man a typewritten résumé which was glued to the back of an eight-by-ten smiling photograph of himself. "What's your name, old chap, by the way?"

"Fred," said the doorman unsmilingly.

"Julian Brooks is my name—comedy's my game." Julian gave Fred the benefit of a smashing smile with a perfect set of even teeth, framed by a small, beautifully trimmed Ronald Colman moustache.

"Why aren't you in the army then?" asked Fred, looking suspiciously at the photograph which the young man was waving at him.

"Flat feet, old boy. Not very honorable, but there we are."

Phoebe felt a tingle of excitement as her eyes connected again with the stranger's for a fraction of a second.

"That's why I'm so anxious to do my bit for our boys, old chap. I've got comedy routines that will have 'em splitting their sides. They'll go back to fighting Jerry with a big smile on their faces—and so full of piss and vinegar, the Hun will run like rabbits." He smiled engagingly, but to no avail. His charm fell on stony ground with the stage doorkeeper.

"Nah, sorry, mate." Fred pushed the photograph back at him. "We're not 'irin' anyone, guvnor's orders, and even if we wus—I ain't the one wot does it, so piss off—and go peddle yourself somewhere else." He picked up the *Daily Mirror,* immersing himself in Jane's cartoon exploits, leaving Julian standing there in disappointed frustration.

Phoebe stepped forward. Mustn't let this one get away—handsome, still young, obviously not about to be posted to foreign parts, to become cannon fodder like some of her ex-lovers had been stupid enough to do.

"Hello, I'm Phoebe Bryer," she gushed, holding out a well-manicured hand. "I work here. May I help you?"

"You most certainly may." Julian looked at the tumbling Titian curls, fresh complexion, sparkling eyes and luscious curves. What a cutie this one was, he thought, a delectable dish indeed. Sending out availability signals, too. Perfect.

"I think you just might be able to help me, Miss Bryer," he said, his Royal Academy of Dramatic Art accent smooth as silk and twice as seductive. "Perhaps you would allow me the honor of buying you a delicious cup of tea and a sticky bun at the little coffee shop on Shaftesbury Avenue?" He looked her up and down with the requisite amount of lust and Phoebe felt her cheeks start to tingle.

"It would have to be after the next show," she said excitedly. Not again, Phoebe, said her warning conscience. It's much too soon after Jamie—whoa, my dear, slow down. She gave Julian a sweet but saucy smile. "We break at noon, but only for half an hour, I'm afraid, so you'd better be on time."

"Wonderful. I'll meet you here on the dot. Okay?" He smiled again, and she noticed the dimple in his chin.

"Okay," said Phoebe with a maidenly blush. "I won't be late."

Fred put down his newspaper and, with a meaningful look at the clock, announced, "Curtain's up in fifteen minutes, duckie, and from the look of yer, you'll need all that time to put yer slap on." He gave Julian a baleful glare and snorted, "Time to move orf the premises, laddie, let the little lady get to work," and buried his face in his tabloid again.

"Noon, then, it's a date." Julian winked at Phoebe and, tipping his hat rakishly, left her with a waft of Brylcreem in her nostrils and romance in her heart.

❖ *Seven* ❖

JULIAN BROOKS HAD BEEN packed off to a prep school on the south coast of England at the age of eight. He had been short for his age, and, being an only child, was shy and nervous around other children.

Amid the hustle and bustle of Victoria Station he clutched his much-loved teddy bear tightly, weeping quietly as his mother, fair and pretty under her aigrette-feathered hat, bestowed a dry peck on his wet cheek, and bade him a fond farewell for the duration of the three-month autumn term.

In the railway carriage with five other sniffling eight-year-olds all trying to control their misery, an equally sad Julian gazed unseeingly at the damp Sussex countryside while the train sped on.

With the exception of his austere mother, women were rather a mystery to Julian. His father had been killed at Arras in 1917, two months before Julian was born, and his mother and nanny had taken sole charge of him since his birth. He had been deprived of the companionship of an adult male and was terrified at the idea of living with over a hundred other boys. He wanted to be with his mother and his beloved nanny; he had dreaded going away to boarding school.

But school turned out to be much better than he'd expected. He found he could head off the teasing the boys gave him because of his lack of stature by making jokes about his height, sometimes even drawing attention to his lack of inches before they did and sending himself up about it. Soon he progressed to imitations—Charlie Chaplin, W. C. Fields, Buster Keaton, Harold Lloyd—regaling the dormitory each night with his impressions of these and other favorite stars, making his classmates laugh so loudly that Matron would bang on the door, issuing fierce threats.

When he was thirteen he was sent off to Eton College, where much against his will he developed a passion for Wilson Minor, who occupied the room next to his. Because of his strikingly beautiful face Julian was soon nicknamed "Looks" Brooks by the older prefects, a nickname which would stay with him for the rest of his life. He became much in demand as a "fag," running errands, picking up jars of Marmite or honey from the village stores and delivering notes from the prefects to boys in other houses. Some of these boys of seventeen or eighteen made no secret of their desire to have Looks Brooks for themselves, but Julian always deflected their passes with a quip or a one-liner. He was popular in the rooms of the older boys at night, where he would happily perform turns from the cinema and music hall, and regale them with his vast repertoire of filthy jokes.

One hot day in June, Simon Gray, a tall, eighteen-year-old senior boy in Julian's house, who had been making unsuccessful passes at Julian for some time, sent him off to deliver a note to his current lover.

The boy's house was over two miles away, an exhausting run on a boiling hot afternoon. On the way, Julian sat down for a rest in the shade of a great Dutch elm, fanning himself with the envelope which soon came unstuck in the heat. Curiosity never having really killed the cat, he opened it, reading, to his horror: "Darling boy, isn't Looks Brooks *divine!* And I've been having him regularly for the past six months! Maybe when we meet next Tuesday, we can both have him *together* . . . Eternally mad for you, Simon."

Julian's heart jumped and he could feel a deep flush spreading over his face and neck. That he could be discussed like a tart or a piece of meat came as an ugly shock. He and Wilson Minor always referred disparagingly to boys who "did it" with each other as poofs or queers. That he should be thought of as "one of those" was infuriating.

Wilson was as blond, blue-eyed and delicately skinned as Julian was dark, heavy-lidded and exotic-looking. They had, of course, experimented sexually with each other, as most boys had at English public schools. The odd, unspoken fumble or mutual masturbation when too much beer or

Pimm's had been drunk was never to be discussed by the light of day. But a poof? Him? Julian Looks Brooks—never in a million years! He would rather die than have people think that of him.

Twenty minutes later, as Simon's lover read his note, Julian saw a look of sly interest creep across his face. Licking his lips, the prefect examined the boy from head to toe with lascivious eyes, which made Julian's face blush the color of poppies. Sauntering to his desk, the prefect penned a quick reply to his paramour. Julian naturally read it on the way home: "He is certainly divine, darling, but I'd much rather have you. Next Tuesday *comme toujours*—eternally yours!"

Julian started worrying about his feelings towards his best friend. Although not exactly platonic, they never spoke of their mutual attraction or their love for each other; it was a "manly relationship," but one that now, obviously, had to end or Julian would be thought of as a poof. He couldn't bear that, not to mention the fact that the shame would probably kill his mother.

From then on, Julian became the most sports-mad boy at school and even more of a clown. Although he adored Wilson, he felt that these feelings were wrong, so he ended the relationship abruptly, much to Wilson's shock. Every holiday he arranged to spend with boys whom he knew had sisters and female cousins, and at fourteen he started on his magical primrose path of the seduction of the fairer sex. Since he suddenly grew several inches in height between the ages of fourteen and fifteen, he had little difficulty in persuading even the most virginal of damsels to allow him at least a discreet kiss. From then on, such was his sex appeal and charm that it was usually easy to persuade them to go even further.

When Julian was twenty he had the distinction of being not only the most handsome boy at the Royal Academy of Dramatic Art, but also the finest actor, easily the most popular student, and the man who had the most success with women.

At twenty-one he went into a repertory company where he deliberately and systematically seduced every female in the company whether she was young or old, pretty or pretty ugly.

He loved sex. He liked to prove himself, adored feeling his masculinity conquering the weaker sex. He learned everything he possibly could about women. Seducing them was too easy. His looks were so arresting that with just a little smooth chat any chickie could be cajoled into the feathers before she even knew what was happening. Julian excelled at the superfuck. He flew his conquests to the moon and back again on a surging sea of sexual rapture which none of them had ever experienced before. He was a true Don Juan, the peerless romantic Romeo, Casanova in corduroy trousers. Irresistible to women, he would go to any lengths to ignite them, to make them his forever.

Phoebe had little difficulty in arranging an audition for Julian. After all, her uncle was one of the Vivienne Van Damm's major shareholders. (Indeed, this was how she had obtained her own job, despite having limited experience in singing or dancing.) The Windmill Theatre was short on smart young comics with a clever patter and genuinely good jokes. The servicemen, who all loved to watch the long-legged, full-bosomed Windmill Girls dance, preen and posture, also wanted to hear raunchy, dirty, close-to-the-knuckle humor, delivered by someone who wasn't their father's age.

Julian was extremely funny. His repertoire of jokes ranged from droll, dry, almost too subtle humor to those which were so incredibly and disgustingly filthy that some of the younger soldiers were quite shocked.

Julian and Phoebe lost no time in slipping between the sheets together. Phoebe was considered fast. At twenty-three she had enjoyed at least a dozen affairs and she was uninhibited and natural in her lovemaking. Men were to be toyed with, to be enjoyed, and Phoebe enjoyed them well and often.

As for Julian, he soon realized he had fallen into a pot of honey. Although his chosen profession was acting, he had not had a legitimate theater role since leaving Maidstone Rep. Despite this he was convinced, as indeed was Phoebe, that his day as a leading man would eventually dawn. Until then he was happy to be the resident comedian at the Windmill Theatre all day and to share Phoebe's cozy bed all night. He allowed her to think that he had fallen in love with her. He knew that was what all girls wanted to believe, although he himself had never managed to fall in love with anyone for longer than a week. He had happily fucked his way through RADA and Rep, and although now apparently settled, he still managed discreetly to seduce almost all girls at the Windmill while living with Phoebe. This was further tribute to his palpable sex appeal, spellbinding charm and expert manipulation of the female sex.

Everyone thought Phoebe was the perfect mate for Julian. They shared a similar sense of humor, and possessed huge ambition. When Phoebe suspected Julian of bedding her friends and co-workers, she wasn't prone to bouts of jealous nagging like his previous girlfriends. She just looked the other way, pretending not to see. Her mother had given her that piece of valuable advice. Their lovemaking was a source of delight and, despite the war, they enjoyed their life together immensely.

Yes, they were a good couple, well suited. Everyone said so. Julian should marry her.

◆ *Eight* ◆

HYDRA, GREECE, 1944

HE WAS HUNGRY, terribly hungry, but Nikolas couldn't remember when he hadn't been hungry. His body was pitifully thin, the flesh drawn tightly across his olive-skinned cheekbones, his stomach was concave and his ribs showed through his shabby shirt.

He was standing on a parched grassy hill high up on the island of Hydra while the black-robed priest droned on. The sea was a dark blue mirror, and the Peleponnese Mountains of the Greek mainland just a smoky haze in the distance. The body of the last of his baby sisters was being laid to rest in her pathetic grave. His mother leaned heavily on him, her thin frame draped in black, her eyes reddened by endless tears.

But Nikolas Stanopolis would not cry. At sixteen he was the head of the family. It had been less than a year since his father had been executed along with eight other Greek fishermen who had been accused of aiding and abetting the partisans in the mountains. Nikolas would never forget that terrible day.

Down in the port where a few fishing boats bobbed lazily, pulling gently at their moorings, he had watched a group of men in the center of the square being savagely beaten with rifle butts until their faces turned to pulp. The entire population of Hydra had been forced to watch and then see them shot. What made the event even more horrible was that the Italian soldiers who had carried out this atrocity and many others seemed to derive brutal satisfaction from seeing these wretched men die. The soldiers joked with each other, laughing as their prisoners screamed in agony.

Silently, in a ragged circle, the population of Hydra had stood watching. There were three hundred or so black-shawled women, the young almost indistinguishable from the old, so wizened and weak were they from lack of food and the cruel deprivations of the island's occupation. A few puny children scampered about, even the horrors of war powerless to suppress their antics. A dozen adolescents stood transfixed with horror, and a handful of toothless old people shook their wrinkled heads as they watched yet another execution with a stoicism born of longevity and passive resistance.

Nikolas had clasped his arms around his mother, trying to give her support and comfort as she leaned against him, burdened with grief. His mother was thirty-four but looked more like sixty—worn out with fear and the torment of watching her children suffer and die. At her breast was the youngest of her brood, a little girl who weighed no more than twelve pounds though she was nearly a year old. The nourishment she received from Melina's shriveled breasts would not be enough to sustain her for much longer.

There was hardly any food left in the village. No goats, no pigs, not even any donkeys—the villagers survived only on what they were allowed to forage from the sea.

Within a year, Nikolas' last brother and sister would die slowly and painfully, along with almost a third of the island's children.

The Hydriots were a simple but proud race, used to hard work, and their island had given them a good living for several hundred years. Such was the determination and resilience of its inhabitants that Hydra was the only Greek island which had never before fallen to an enemy. Even the Turks had found it impossible to conquer a hundred years earlier.

The Germans had stolen all the available food to feed their armies fighting in the Afrika Korps. Crops were seized, sheep and goats slaughtered, olive groves and orchards laid waste. The Nazis had battles to fight, and little or no feeling for starving women and children.

When the Germans left in 1941 the Italian army came to garrison Hydra. As it was considered a backwater post—it was eleven miles long and sparsely populated—the dregs of the Italian army were sent. Louts from Sicily and Naples who could barely read before the war issued orders, made rules and used their tyrannical power to instill more terror in the islanders than the Germans had ever done.

Benito Mussolini was their revered leader and their idol. No matter that he was so self-conscious about his puny height that he insisted in all official photographs that he be photographed from below; every halfwit in the Italian army blindly worshiped Il Duce.

Nikolas' thoughts of his father's terrible death were interrupted by a chilling shriek from his mother. Her baby's pathetic little coffin was placed in the grave and she slid to the ground in a spasm of grief. Melina's worry beads slipped from her feeble grasp as the priest gravely offered her a shovel to sprinkle the first spadeful of dry earth onto the tiny driftwood box.

Wailing in sympathy, three women helped the weeping Melina back to her feet. The priest's voice droned on, ignoring the women's sobs. He had become so conditioned to grief that he was almost immune to the agony of his starving villagers. He couldn't count the number of children he had buried in the past two years. The poor Stanopolis woman had lost four as well as her husband. But at least she still had the boy, and at sixteen, although painfully thin, he was tall and had the resiliency of youth. At least Melina had someone to depend on: recognizing the look of defiance in his face, the priest felt instinctively that the boy would survive. He brought the simple service to a close, and watched as his congregation shuffled wearily away.

Almost doubled up with grief, Melina, escorted by the three women and Nikolas, slowly made her way to the sanctuary of the cool stone walls of her little hilltop house. The small group of mourners climbed the steep cobblestone steps of the narrow winding street, and one by one entered the shuttered darkness of the Stanopolis house. The women fussed over Melina while Nikolas went to his room, his eyes prickling with the stinging tears he had tried so desperately not to allow his mother to see.

Opening up the chipped blue shutters, oblivious to the beauty of the olive and almond trees which grew outside his window, he thought of vengeance. Vengeance on the Germans, vengeance on the Italians. But most of all, vengeance on the commanding officer of the Italian garrison, the fat pig who now ruled Hydra without justice and without mercy, and whom the locals called "Gourouni."

Nikolas fidgeted fiercely with his mother's translucent yellow worry beads, which he'd picked up at the graveside, passing them back and forth between his fingers. He leaned out to gaze at the highest point of the island, where all the glorious eighteenth-century mansions stood, built by rich shipowners. Gourouni had chosen the most beautiful and imposing of them to be his official residence.

He was the undoubted cause of the recent crop of executions, the cause of the deaths of Nikolas' father, his brothers and sisters. Nikolas thought him filthy, depraved, corrupt scum, a travesty of Mussolini. All of the villagers silently mocked the squat fat figure as he preened and postured in his ludicrous musical-comedy uniforms thickly encrusted with gold braid, glinting with stolen medals.

In his exquisite neoclassical villa, set in lush gardens of grape, olive and pine trees, was the plunder from a dozen of the wealthiest Hydriot mansions, and from the fabled temples of the surrounding islands of Spetsai and Aegina. Rare paintings, tapestries, sculptures and eighteenth-century furniture which would hardly have been out of place in Versailles filled the villa, which he proudly believed to be the finest in all Greece. Some of the luckiest villagers were employed as gardeners, cooks and housemaids.

Elektra Makopolis was one of the latter. Exactly the same age as Nikolas, she had lived next door to him all their lives. Occasionally she managed to smuggle a loaf of bread or some fruit or cooked meat out of the Commander's fortress. She would share anything she pilfered with the Stanopolis family, as there was no one left of her own. Her father had been deported to a labor camp by the Germans, and soon afterward her mother had starved to death. A young Italian lieutenant with a grain of sympathy in his heart heard about the wretched girl's predicament and found her a job in "the Palace" where she worked hard polishing marble, cleaning furniture and scrubbing floors. Everything Elektra knew about the Palace she had described to Nikolas in minute detail. Every atrocity which she saw committed by Gourouni she reported to him . . .

There was a faint tap at his bedroom door and Elektra appeared.

"Nikolas," she whispered, "I've brought you some cake and hot coffee."

Coffee! How had she managed to find coffee? Nikolas didn't want to ask. She had stolen it from Gourouni's villa, knowing full well the penalty if she were ever found out. He swallowed the bitter liquid and wolfed down the delicious honey cake greedily.

The two of them leaned out of the window and Elektra ran a hand through Nikolas' untidy curls. He tried to muster a smile. He loved her and she loved him. It was all very simple. Both their families had known for years that one day they would be united by the marriage of Nikolas and Elektra, and now it was inevitable that it would happen.

"He showed a movie last night," whispered Elektra. "Some of us sneaked into the projection booth to watch it. Oh, Nikolas!" Her lovely young face glowed with excitement. "It was so wonderful—you cannot believe what an exciting film it was. American, of course, with a wonderful little girl with ringlets who sang and danced. She was tiny, maybe six or seven years old—but so clever, and so pretty. I wish you could have seen it, Nikolas, you would have loved it—I know how much you love movies."

Nikolas was passionate about films. Before the war, he had gone to the open-air cinema to watch his idols. He was mesmerized by the brilliance of film directors like Alfred Hitchcock and John Ford, and he studied their techniques, returning time after time to see their work.

But there were no longer any film performances for the villagers. Now the only place movies were shown was up at the Palace where Gourouni somehow always managed to procure the latest offerings from Hollywood.

Elektra looked at Nikolas. His eyes were riveted on the Commander's citadel: it seemed to glow with a fiery light as the late-afternoon sun reddened its white marble walls to the color of blood, and the hated Italian flag flapped gently in the faint breeze.

They both thought of the toadlike creature who now inhabited the house. A sadist who regularly sent innocents to their deaths, who tortured men for pleasure, all the while accumulating the spoils of war.

"He's probably busy stuffing his ugly face." Nikolas' voice was full of hatred. "Guzzling meat and wine, thinking about which movie he'll show tonight. He's a murdering monster. He shouldn't be allowed to live."

"Nikolas, guess who made the film?" Elektra tried to change the subject. Whenever Nikolas started talking about Gourouni, it was difficult to get him to stop. He seemed to have an obsession about the man. "My American uncle, you remember him? The one who went to America years ago, before we were born—the one who has done so well." Her face beamed with pride. In the past, her mother had often talked of her eldest brother, the brash young man who was always so ambitious, so determined to leave Greece, to succeed in the new country, and who had finally triumphed there.

"Spyros!" she said proudly. "Spyros Makopolis. I recognized his name at the beginning of the film. It was in *huge* letters—'Produced by Spyros Makopolis.' Isn't that wonderful?" Her smile was radiant. "He's from Hydra, Nikolas, and he produces films in Hollywood." She leaned towards him, fingers gently stroking his face. "If he can do it, Nikolas—so can you."

"One day—if ever this war is over—we will both go to Hollywood and I will make such wonderful films that the whole world will want to see them," said Nikolas bitterly. "But not before that sadistic pig is dead." His voice rose in passionate rage and he looked again towards the mansion and thought of the destruction of Gourouni, and how only fools underestimated the pride of the Greeks.

It had been a convivial evening. The film, the latest offering from the MCCP studio, was excellent, and the female star was a ravishing creature, blonde and ripe, who looked no more than eighteen. Both the Commander and his aide-de-camp, Major Volpi, found her so appealing that thoughts of her juicy charms lingered pleasurably.

The wine had been excellent. A Château-Lafite '29, two cases of which had been discovered last week in the cellar of one of the Hydriot mansions.

The Commander stretched and yawned as he unbuttoned the gold buttons of his skintight blue uniform. He admired his reflection in the narrow eighteenth-century gilded mirror which was hung on his dressing room wall in the most flattering light. He was a *bella figura,* no doubt about that. His resemblance to his idol Mussolini seemed to be increasing, particularly now that he had completely shaved his head and always copied Il Duce's latest uniforms in the most painstaking detail. The one he now wore was impressive, of the finest gabardine, one of many made for him by a good Greek tailor on the island.

Never mind that the uniform he should be wearing as Commander of Hyra was a drab gray. The stupid villagers knew no better, and as for his soldiers, with the exception of Volpi, whose palms were more than well greased with silver, they were a bunch of dolts.

The Commander undid the heavy gold buckle of his wide leather belt, then took off his jacket and shirt and tossed them onto a brocade-covered Jacobean bergère.

The dim peach lamp on the armoire illuminated his face and torso with a soft flattering glow. He smiled at his reflection admiringly, his small eyes almost disappearing into the pads of fat surrounding them. The bald bullet head, sensual lips and strong chin were pleasing to him, as were the hirsute barrel chest and thickly muscled forearms.

The only thing about his physical appearance that didn't please him was the thick keloid scar that traversed the base of his Adam's apple in a clean three-inch line. He always attempted to conceal it with his high-necked uniforms. The rumor on Hydra was that someone had tried to kill him, that he had hovered between life and death in a Parisian hospital for several weeks, and only the attentions of the finest throat specialist in France had saved his life and his larynx. Now he could talk only in a harsh, rasping whisper, which further added to his terrifying demeanor.

He fingered the scar gingerly. They had never found the girl who had slashed his throat with his own razor and left him for dead on the cold marble floor of his bathroom.

He had survived that bitch's murderous attempt only by overwhelming physical strength and will to live. But even though the throat surgeon had done a brilliant job in saving both his life and his voice, Umberto Scrofo would never be satisfied until he found the girl who had almost killed him, and paid her back a thousand times over for her crime.

◆ *Nine* ◆

NIKOLAS LEANED HIS HEAD against the whitewashed stone wall of the tiny balcony and sobbed. His beloved mother, the last family link he had left, was dying, withered by starvation, her heart broken.

Melina lay on her bed, weakly fingering her rosary, mumbling over and over again the names of her dead husband and children. She had simply lost the will to live. The light had gone out of her warm brown eyes, leaving them expressionless and dead, and she weighed less than ninety pounds. She had even refused to eat the small fish which Nikolas had managed to catch by spending some fourteen soul-destroying hours in his boat. Two of the village women attended her, their faces stoic masks of suffering.

Nikolas was in total despair, his mind numbed by misery and privation. All he could do was pray that his mother wouldn't die. He went back into his room and opened the drawer next to his bed. From beneath a meager pile of shirts and socks, he took out his knife. It was in a brown leather sheath, shiny and new. He had found it yesterday as he was cleaning his nets on the beach. One of the soldiers had obviously dropped it, and Nikolas had quickly put it in his pocket, hoping he was unobserved.

Now he slowly pulled the shining blade out of the holder and watched the dying moon's reflection shimmer on the polished steel. He ran a thumb gingerly down the cutting edge, feeling the sharpness of it. How he would love to plunge this blade into Gourouni's fat stomach and wrench it until his entrails spilled onto the ground like a gutted fish's.

Nikolas knew he would take great satisfaction in watching that sadistic swine wriggle in his death agonies. He imagined the Italian's face contorted in agony, pleading for help, but he was interrupted in his fantasy by the sound of his mother weakly calling his name. Quickly replacing the knife in its hiding place he ran downstairs to kiss her and to bid her a tender good-bye. It was time to fish now, to catch the only sustenance left for them.

He strode purposefully down to the harbor, his thoughts still full of Gourouni.

Although it was not yet five in the morning there was a bustle of activity in the tiny fishing port. Nine or ten fishermen, all either under sixteen or over sixty-five, were carefully arranging their yellow and cream nets in the bows of their boats, preparing their lines for today's catch.

The bare bulbs in Dmitri's beach bar glowed yellow, giving a jaundiced look to the hard faces of the Italian guards who lounged about, paying no attention to the fishermen, thinking only of when their watches would end. Some looked so drunk that there was little chance of their protecting anything, should the Allies have picked that moment to invade Hydra. But there was no likelihood of that. The Allies had no strategic interest at all in the remote little island. Dmitri gave Nikolas a friendly *"Yassou"* as he poured him a small cup of thick, sweet coffee and pushed a tiny piece of honeyed baklava across the counter. The boy drank and ate gratefully, pleased that Dmitri always managed to have coffee and cake in his bar. In return, he hoped to bring Dmitri some *pompano,* red mullet or sea bass, although the fish had not been jumping recently. Even at the nearby islands of Mykonos, Spetsai and Poros, it was as if all sea life knew there was a war on and wanted no part of it.

Dmitri leaned conspiratorially towards Nikolas, with a glance at one of the snoring Italians.

"I listened to the wireless last night," he whispered, making a great show of wiping some glasses with a grubby rag. "It's going to all be over soon, Nikolas, very, very soon."

One of the sleeping soldiers gave a loud snore which made Nikolas jump nervously.

"They say it's only a matter of weeks before the war is over. And they say that the Allies will win for sure. They've really got the Boche going now."

The boy drained the dregs of his coffee. "It's incredible news, Dmitri, I hope it's true."

"It's true," whispered Dmitri excitedly. "Believe me, Nikolas, it's true. The Allies have got these pigs on the run. Keep your fingers crossed, Nikolas—maybe this time next week we'll be free, we'll have our island back again."

Nikolas nodded his thanks to Dmitri with an excited conspiratorial smile, and set off to fish, feeling more lighthearted than he had for months. Soon the war would be over. Soon the Hydriots would be rid of their murdering oppressors and it would be time for the villagers to forget. But Nikolas knew he could never forget his hatred for the Commander.

Umberto Scrofo read the terse orders on an official paper which had arrived during the night by messenger from his commanding officer.

Propped up in his ornately carved Venetian bed between the finest linen sheets to be found in all Greece, he was surrounded by old master paintings of erotic scenes. A richly colored tapestry had been draped carelessly over an elaborate Henri Jacob daybed against one wall, and a set of four magnificent sculptures—which might have been by the hand of Michelangelo himself—lurked in the shadows of the four corners of the room.

But this particular morning Scrofo derived none of his usual pleasure from any of them.

As soon as he read the message he leaped furiously from his bed onto the pale Aubusson carpet, mouthing profanities at the hapless officer who had brought him both the message and his chamberpot. He aimed into the delicately painted receptacle, held in the trembling hands of the young lieutenant, while launching into another wildly vituperative verbal attack. The scar on his neck throbbed as it always did whenever he was angry. He bounced around in his short silk nightshirt so much that the unfortunate youth could barely manage to keep the pot under the General's Lilliputian organ.

Barking out orders in his rasping voice, Scrofo darted about his bedroom, flinging objects into gaping leather bags which had miraculously appeared, wrapping precious artifacts and bronzes in thick velvet cloths, helped by a handful of clumsy gray-uniformed soldiers.

The message received that morning had galvanized him into a vindictive rampage. So he was supposed to evacuate the island immediately, was he? And leave behind all the priceless booty which he had so painstakingly collected? He would see about that! He wasn't going to leave any of his treasures on this pitiful excuse of an island.

Squeezing into a black uniform which had grown too tight with the many months of excess, and pinning on as many medals as time permitted, he clattered down the marble staircase in his high tight boots.

"I want every last one of the islanders here at once," he barked in his strained croaking voice to Major Volpi. "Go into the village and round them all up now. Every man, woman and child. *Now.*"

"Very well, sir," said Volpi, saluting smartly while privately thinking what an oaf this Commander was. But who was he to cast stones? Before the war he had been in prison for murder; now he was a favored citizen, a much admired soldier.

"The sick ones too?" he inquired.

"Every one of them," snarled Scrofo. "Every single one of the inhabitants."

He paced feverishly around the magnificent villa appraising the pictures, statues and furniture which filled it, taking mental stock. It seemed to him that his plunder was smiling at him in a most pleasing way, bathed as it was in the gentle morning sunshine. Peerless treasures of only the highest quality—all his, all stolen. His dream had been eventually to take his treasures back to Italy, and once ensconced there he would become a respectable *antiquaire*, selling beautiful things to collectors and competing with the best art dealers of London, New York and Paris. That dream would now be shattered unless he could get everything packed, crated and transported down the three hundred or so cobbled steps to the harbor at once. His plan was to load them onto a hidden yacht, sail over to Albania, and from there, on to Italy. He would take only four trusted accomplices with him, whose pockets had already been well lined with gold bullion. And he was well prepared. Up from the cellar came the soldiers carrying wooden crates, cartons and great quantities of packing materials. At once his troops set to work, wrapping and crating the pictures and sculptures as fast as they could.

Soon the villagers arrived. Small children, old men and frail women were divided into makeshift working groups to pack up Gourouni's loot.

Melina had been pulled from her sickbed by a posse of soldiers. Now, almost too weak to walk, helped by the devoted Elektra, she was commanded by Volpi to wrap a collection of exquisite enamel-and-gold Fabergé eggs. Even in their weakened and dazed state, the women were stunned by the beauty of the jeweled snuffboxes, the richly gilded and inlaid furniture, the brilliant colors of the eighteenth-century paintings and the golden flesh tones of the Rembrandts.

Melina's eyes were so clouded that she could hardly see. Her hands were trembling so much that it was practically impossible for her to hold onto anything. The soldiers moved among the women, yelling at them, giving them a sharp punch if they didn't seem to be working fast enough. The frightened children had been given the task of crating up Scrofo's collection of extremely rare first editions of Dante, Goethe, Shakespeare and Tolstoy, and the little ones stumbled about with frightened eyes as they tried to handle the precious volumes without damaging them.

Suddenly with a startled cry, Melina let slip a crystal egg encrusted with seed pearls and precious stones. With a noise like a gunshot the priceless treasure shattered on the marble floor.

Everyone stopped what they were doing, to stare at the wretched woman, but Melina's eyes were so glazed with despair and fever that she felt no fear as the dreaded Gourouni approached her.

"Do you see what you've done, you stupid idiot!" he rasped, his face scarlet with fury. "Idiot. *Idiot! IDIOT!*" He cracked his pistol down on her skull with the full force of his rage. Melina felt no pain as blood coursed down her waxen face. She felt nothing as she lay in a crumpled heap and the enraged Scrofo rained blow after blow on her face and head as he screamed abuse.

"Back to work," Scrofo screeched as terrified children ran crying to hide under their mothers' skirts. "Back to work or you'll suffer the same fate. And no one had better break anything else."

Some of the villagers crossed themselves while several people moaned quietly or openly wept. Quietly Elektra asked permission to remove Melina's body and Volpi nodded a curt affirmative. She wrapped the pitiful, wasted shape in her long black shawl and two other women helped her to take Melina out into the bright sunshine, where with tear-stained faces they laid her gently down in the cobbled courtyard.

When Nikolas returned to the harbor at sundown he was pleased with his catch. It was the best for a long time—almost half a kilo of whitebait, several red mullet and a couple of plump pompano. They would have a feast tonight. Dmitri was sure to give him some olive oil and some potatoes and tomatoes, maybe even a small bottle of wine, in exchange for a few fish. He, Elektra and his mother could then celebrate the imminent end of their island's occupation.

As he hauled his boat up the pebbled beach, a weeping black-shawled

Elektra, her long hair ruffled by the breeze, ran to him and threw herself into his arms.

"Nikolas, oh, Nikolas, I'm so sorry."

"Sorry—for what? What is it, Elektra?" He was suddenly apprehensive. Elektra was usually a strong, resilient girl. Toughened by the harsh life of the island, she retained an innate gentleness which inspired devotion in all who knew her.

Sobbing quietly into Nikolas' shoulder, she told him of his mother's death.

Nikolas' face hardened. He had known his mother could not survive much longer, but the war was nearly over—surely then she would have recovered? He tried hard not to weep. He would never forgive Gourouni for this—never.

"Where are all the soldiers now?" he asked harshly.

"Gone. Every last one of them. They sailed this afternoon. We burned their flag when they left," she told him. "All of their flags."

"Did the bastards murder anyone else before they left?" Nikolas asked as Dmitri came out of his bar bringing him a glass of brandy.

Dmitri put his arms around Nikolas, trying to comfort the boy whom he loved like a son.

"No," Elektra said gently, her hand stroking Nikolas' cheek. "No one else. Oh Nikolas I'm so sorry."

Nikolas drained his brandy, the unfamiliar burning sensation fueling him with unaccustomed power. Seeing the forlorn faces of his friends, he was filled with such anger that his fury almost had a life of its own. He needed to kill. He wanted to plunge his knife into the Italian pigs, killing them all, but especially he wanted to put his hands around the throat of that diabolical Commander and squeeze the life out of him. He wanted to watch him die before his eyes. Wanted to hear his slug-like lips beg for mercy. As he felt the knife in his pocket, Nikolas knew he had the power of death in his fingers and knew too that his hatred would eventually give him strength to do what he had to do.

"One day—one day—one day," he muttered harshly, fingering at his mother's beads furiously as though they were the tendons of his enemy's neck. "I'll kill him if it's the last thing I do in my life. I shall find that murdering bastard and make him suffer more than he ever dreamed possible. By the time I have finished with Commander Umberto Scrofo, he'll be begging me to kill him, I swear it."

❧ *Ten* ❧

LONDON 1944

Iఢɴᴇ̀s ᴡᴀs ᴘᴇʀꜰᴇᴄᴛʟʏ ᴄᴏɴᴛᴇɴᴛ living in London, although she missed Paris. The tiny flat in Shepherd Market on the top floor of an old Georgian house was cozy, and its leaded-glass windows trapped every ray of the pale London sunshine. Often she sat on the window seat, looking out over the tops of the plane trees in Green Park, her mind far away, thinking about Paris. Were the Gestapo still searching for her? Nightmares about the dead Italian General still disturbed her sleep, but Yves' arms were always there in the night to soothe her fears when she would wake screaming and drenched in sweat, and in the morning he would make her laugh again with some of his magic tricks.

Yves kept up with news of the French occupation through the newspapers and wireless while Inès devoted herself to mastering the English language and keeping house for him. She would spend her mornings trying to buy food with ration books which allowed them only the barest essentials. Casseroles were hard to make with four ounces of meat, and it was impossible even for a French girl to make an omelet for two with just one egg.

Yves had contacted some of the names he'd been given, intent on building himself a new life in London. He was often out all day, while Inès listened to the wireless and sang as she cleaned and dusted the flat, relishing her new domestic role. For the first time in her life, she was living a normal existence and she worshiped Yves more than ever.

She struck up a friendship with Stella Bates, a redheaded girl who lived on the floor below. Often they would shop together, carrying their string bags in search of groceries, sugar, butter or jam—all commodities in short supply and for which coupons from their ration books were necessary. Stella regaled Inès with amusing stories of her life. She was a successful prostitute, with few qualms about her profession. A couple of years older than Inès, she had an attractive body and a flaming halo of red hair which ensured that she rarely spent her evenings alone. She was also very funny, and even Yves was amused by her cockney repartee.

He had recently brought up the matter of Inès' returning to "work," a subject she hated to discuss. She didn't want to be a prostitute anymore. Her intense love for Yves made the thought of being with another man an anathema, and the experience in Paris was still far too vivid. But Yves was becoming more insistent. Money was always short, they had rent to pay. He couldn't make enough on the black market to keep them both, and he wasn't qualified for anything but menial work or his clever tricks.

"I'm not a good enough magician for the music halls, *chérie,*" he laughed. "It's up to you to start making some money for us." But Inès resisted, hoping against hope that Yves would get some sort of job, maybe even marry her, so that they could continue this proper life that she was relishing so much.

Eventually Yves convinced her that she must become the breadwinner or they would both starve. So she confided most of her life story to Stella, without mentioning that she had killed a man. Stella gave her sage advice.

"It's time to stop trollin' the streets, darlin', you're *much* too classy for that. I've got a really nice, exclusive clientele now, duckie—references only—so, just give me the word and I'll fix you up with one of my classy titled gents. No kinky stuff, I promise you."

Inès grimaced, but Yves was hungry and demanding. She had no choice but to become a whore again. But at least this time it would be with English gentlemen, not enemy louts.

London was swarming with servicemen of all nationalities and a party mood prevailed. Even though the Blitz continued as the German bombs hit their targets with monotonous regularity, London's nightclubs still had a carnival atmosphere which made people forget that a war was going on. The favorite haunt of partygoers, the Café de Paris, had sustained a direct hit the previous year, killing at least forty revelers, but the wartime festivities continued unabated.

The following night Stella invited Inès to go to a nightclub with her. "I've got a date with a very nice gent an' a couple of friends of 'is, and they're anxious to make whoopee, luv—so come with us, we'll have a lovely time, I promise."

Inès reluctantly told Yves, who insisted that she go.

"You must start working, *chérie,*" he said heatedly. "We need the money. You know we do."

"I know," said Inès gloomily. "Oh, Yves, how much longer will I have to do this? I hate it. I hate it more and more."

"Not much longer, *chérie.*" Yves smiled, stroking her luxuriant hair and nuzzling her neck in the way that always gave her excited shivers. "When the war is over we will be able to go back to Paris, I will get a job there, I promise you, and you can stop this life. Now be a good girl and get some good clients tonight."

After dressing carefully in her one good black dress with a wide belt which accentuated her narrow waist, Inès stood balanced on the tiny kitchen table while Stella first painted her bare legs with dark pancake foundation and then carefully drew a line down the back of her calves with a stub of eyebrow pencil.

"There," chuckled the redhead when she'd finished, pleased with her handiwork. "Now duckie, if you can get a hold of one of these Yanks tonight you won't 'ave to do this anymore—it'll be nylons, nylons, nylons all over the bleedin' place, not to mention chockles and cigarettes and all sorts of lovely goodies. But tonight we concentrate on the toffs."

"OK," said Inès gloomily. "You're the boss Stella."

The Bagatelle was in a gala mood, packed with revelers. As Inès followed Stella she admired the baroque decor of the fashionable nightclub.

A wide red-carpeted staircase swept grandly into the bar, the walls of which were covered in great golden mirrors. On scarlet velvet chairs dozens of well-dressed vivacious young women sat engrossed in conversation and flirtation with a variety of men, many in uniform, some in black tie. Paul Adams' band was playing the catchy current hit tune, "I Left My Heart at the Stage Door Canteen," and Inès felt her pulse beat faster to the rhythm of the music. She was suddenly quite excited to be on the town again. Her months in London had given her a passable command of English, which she was eager to practice, and in spite of her trepidation about the evening the animated atmosphere started to whet her appetite for a good time.

Stella's date was an educated, jovial titled man in his thirties, up from Shropshire and determined to paint the town red. Champagne flowed, as did his jokes, which Inès found mostly incomprehensible but which had Stella bent double with hilarity. The club was dark and smoky and the tiny lights with their pink pleated shades on each table cast a flattering glow on everyone's face.

Stella was in top form, her cockney humor fired by the atmosphere, trading wisecracks with Lord Worthington, whispering to Inès that he was a real live lord. " 'E's in some top position at the Foreign Office, a real toff," she said when he went to greet some friends who had just arrived.

"And bloody generous 'e is, too, luv—gave me a tenner extra last night, and sent me over a pound of bacon and a pair of nylons this morning—look!"

Proudly she extended her slender legs for Inès to admire the new nylon stockings.

"Ssh, 'ere 'e comes," warned Stella as Lord Worthington returned with two younger men in tow.

"I've brought over a couple of chums, my dear. I hope you don't mind if they join us—Charlie and Benjie. Introduce your friend, will you, old girl? I'm off for a pee."

Charlie, who was short and plump, turned out to be the Honorable Charles Brougham and Benjie, who was tall and skinny, was Viscount Benjamin Spencer-Monckton. The two young men ensconced themselves on either side of Inès, both seemingly spellbound by her cleavage.

"What a splendid accent you have," murmured Charles, his hand brushing against her knee, his eyes on her breasts.

"Yes, it's absolutely spiffing. French, are you?" breathed Benjie.

"Yes." Inès smiled demurely, not altogether displeased by the young men's interest in her. Lord Worthington had now returned and was howling with laughter at another of Stella's bawdy jokes. Inès thought her two titled admirers were not bad-looking in a bland English way, attentive and well mannered, even though both were quite drunk. They were infinitely preferable to the portly pomposity of Lord Worthington.

"Would you care to dance?" Benjie asked as the band began "Moonlight Becomes You."

"I'd love to," Inès smiled. "I haven't danced in a very long time."

As they wended their way through the throng of swaying bodies, Inès suddenly stopped dead in her tracks, an all too familiar fear gripping her. She shook her head as if to dismiss the hallucination. Surely it couldn't be? It simply couldn't. Benjie was pushing her politely to move on, and she edged past the man's table with mounting dread.

Cold black eyes met hers for an instant, and she froze again. How could he be here in the Bagatelle in London when almost a year ago in Paris she had killed him? What was Umberto Scrofo doing in London? An Italian general from Mussolini's army sitting at a ringside table as bold as brass, with a bottle of champagne in front of him and flanked by two blond hookers. It was impossible.

But there was no mistaking the tiny vicious eyes, that huge bald head, the cruel mouth. Mesmerized, she stood before his table unable to move a muscle. The man's eyes caressed her body for a second, then swiveled back to the two blondes, and Inès was swept into the middle of the packed dance floor, trembling violently as Benjie took her in his arms.

"Are you all right, old thing?" he asked solicitously. "You're shaking like a leaf. You look like you've just seen a ghost."

"I think I have," Inès whispered, holding on to him tightly, willing her heart to stop beating so wildly. She looked over again at the table where she thought she'd spotted Scrofo. A fat, bald man was sitting there, shoulder to shoulder with two buxom blondes, but it certainly wasn't Umberto Scrofo, of that she was now absolutely positive. She laughed out loud, a great burst of hysterical relieved laughter. How stupid she was, what a silly fool, with her over fertile imagination. Of course it couldn't have been Scrofo—he was dead. But in those horrific dreams which haunted her subconscious so many nights, he was very much alive. She could still clearly recall every last detail of the grotesque Italian, and just glimpsing a man with similar features or a similar shape was enough to plunge her into a turmoil of fear and anxiety. Inès knew very well that her imagination had always been too vivid for her own good, and she breathed a great sigh of relief that it had been no more than her fancy which had conjured him up. Scrofo was dead and gone—forever—and that was that.

As Inès' waves of panic subsided and the orchestra started to play the romantic "Bewitched, Bothered and Bewildered," she decided to concentrate her attentions on Benjie's erect penis which was begging for notice as it prodded insistently against her thigh. She smiled up at him, slyly acknowledging it, and his pale, almost transparent gray eyes, fringed with sandy lashes, looked away from her shyly as he blushed.

Poor bashful man, she thought sympathetically. He was obviously unused to being in such close proximity to a woman. To make him feel more at ease she rested her head lightly on his shoulder and placed her hand gently on the back of his neck as the romantic music washed over them. She started singing, "I'm wild again—beguiled again, a simpering, whimpering child again—bewitched, bothered and bewildered am I."

Benjie's breathing became more erratic, and as the dance ended, he bent his sandy head to hers, whispering self-consciously, "May I see you again, Inès? I know it's a bit of an imposition because you've probably got a boyfriend and all that, but I do find you terribly attractive."

Inès smiled. He was titled and rich, personable, from a good family. Yves had been telling her for weeks that she had to start work again. This young man seemed kind, and cultured. If she had to continue her career as a prostitute, she could do a great deal worse than become the mistress of Viscount Benjamin Spencer-Monckton. After all, there was a war on.

Even though the war was at its harshest peak and nightly blitzes devastated London, Benjie took Inès on a social whirl such as she had never known before. Although he must have known she was a professional, he treated her like a girlfriend whom he wanted to woo. His manners were impeccable, and Inès became caught up in the time of her life.

The night after they met he took her to a film at the Odeon Leicester Square and then next door to his favorite nightclub, the 400, where he seemed to know everyone, and everyone knew him. The intimate private club was jammed with young aristocrats and society figures. Some of the men were in uniform, some in black tie, a few of the more conservative even wore white tie. They were a high-spirited, jolly crowd bent on merrymaking, and Benjie and Inès moved from group to group as he introduced her to his friends. They were so young, these men, Inès thought. Babies, some of them. No one could see there was any fear or trepidation in the men's hearts by their behavior. The abandoned pleasure-seeking and frantic revelry made each night like a New Year's Eve spree. Many of the young people at the 400 seemed madly in love, and there was a great deal of petting and smooching on the congested dance floor.

"More people get engaged here than anywhere else in London," Benjie shouted to Inès, a twinkle in his pale eyes, as they danced to the music from the new Broadway musical *Carousel*.

Benjie's elusive hardness started to poke again at Inès' thigh, and she smiled up at him as she sang seductively, "If I loved you, words wouldn't come in an easy way."

"Lovely," breathed Benjie, holding her so close that his protuberance almost made her wince. "You have a lovely voice, Inès, in fact everything about you is lovely."

"Thank you," she smiled. "You are very sweet, Benjie."

The following night he took her to dinner at the Gay Hussar in Greek Street, then to the Berkeley, where they danced the night away to Ian Stevens and his peppy music. As usual the place was swarming with pleasure-seekers of every nationality. The band played many of Inès' favorite tunes, and she hummed and sang them to an enraptured Benjie. He particularly liked her version of "This Is a Lovely Way to Spend an Evening," and insisted that the band play it several times.

Afterward they walked home through Berkeley Square as the birds were singing their morning song and the soft fingers of dawn were creeping across the plane trees.

"Tomorrow?" he asked softly as they arrived at Shepherd Market.

"Yes," she whispered, wondering when and if he was ever going to kiss her.

"We'll go to the Savoy with Charles and his girlfriend, Henrietta," said Benjie. "Black tie. I'll pick you up at eight." With a dry kiss on her cheek he tipped his hat and walked away off towards Curzon Street.

"Well," asked Yves sleepily from the bed as she came into his room. "Has it happened yet?"

"Not yet," sighed Inès, flopping onto the bed and into her lover's warm arms. "Not yet, *chéri*. He's English, this may take a little more time than usual. I think he needs to get to know me first."

"Hmph," snorted Yves. "He better hurry up It's all right for you being wined and dined every night, but this poor Frenchman is starving to death. Oh, *mon Dieu*, I would *kill* for a steaming cup of *café au lait* with three teaspoonfuls of sugar, and a hot croissant dripping with raspberry jam."

"You'll just have to live on love," teased Inès, kissing his lips. "Until I break down Benjie's British reserve, love will have to do, my darling."

Inès was running out of evening clothes. Indeed she was running out of any clothes at all. Her clothes cupboard, like their food cupboard, was practically bare, and she had so far worn the same secondhand black dress on every date with Benjie. In desperation she asked Stella if she could borrow something, and the girl threw open her wardrobe door for her friend.

"Whatever you like, luv—take anyfink." She smiled generously. "We're about the same size—'cept I'm a few inches shorter an' a bit more flashy than you luv."

That was an understatement, thought Inès. Stella's wardrobe was crammed with brightly colored frocks decorated with all manner of beads, buttons and bows.

"What about this?" Inès reached into the darker recesses of the cupboard and pulled out a pale gray crêpe dress, the bodice trimmed with gunmetal bugle beads.

"Ooh, that was me mum's!" shrilled Stella. "'Er only good frock it was, she got it from a lady she did a good turn for. It's a bit too drab for me, dearie. It would look good on you though. So you can 'ave it—it's a present."

"Oh, Stella, *thank* you," cried Inès. "You're the best friend I've ever had in the whole world."

Inès tried on the dress. It was the first full-length gown she had ever worn, and it accentuated her height and slim, curved hips. Bias-cut, with short puffed sleeves, the skirt ended in a fan-tailed pleat which Inès almost tripped over as she tried to walk across the room.

"You'll 'ave to practice with that, luv," laughed Stella. "You'll look a bit of a burk if you come a cropper on the dance floor in front of all those la-di-das. You need some matching shoes too. C'mon, let's go to Dolcis. For seventeen and six you can get a nice pair dyed to match—it'll look such a lovely outfit then, an' I'll teach you how to walk with the train."

"But I haven't *got* seventeen and six," wailed Inès. "Stella, I don't have more than a few shillings."

"I'll treat you to the shoes." Her friend grinned. "I've 'ad a very good month, dear, thanks to the Hon. Charlie Boy—you can do the same for me, dear, if I ever go through a dull period. Look out, Oxford Street— 'ere we come."

Inès had enough clothes coupons in her ration book for the shoes which Stella bought, and enough coupons left over for at least two more dresses. She had only bought a few things since arriving in England, but although she had the precious coupons she had no cash.

After their shopping trip Stella came to Inès to inspect the contents of her wardrobe.

"Oh, dearie me, duckie, you'll never be successful on the game wearin' that little lot," she said disparagingly, flicking through Inès meager supply of clothes. "Tell you what, as soon as the Hon. Benjie manages to get his noble pecker up, we'll go on a little shopping spree, you and I—at least Yves can get you some clothing coupons on the market, can't 'e?"

Inès nodded.

"Good," said the redhead. "Never forget Inès my friend, money maketh the man, but clothes, my dear, most definitely maketh the girl."

They dined at the Savoy Grill amid soft lights and the soothing melodic sounds of Carrol Gibbons' Orchestra. Like everywhere in London it was packed with eager diners and even more eager dancers. The five-course menu was delicious and Inès wished she could smuggle some leftovers to take to Yves.

"Damn good spread for five bob, don't you think, Charlie?" asked Benjie.

"Absolutely spiffing, old boy. Soup—fish—meat—sweet—savory, excellent, just as it should be. Let's order a bottle of claret, shall we?"

Inès looked around. She felt ill at ease with Henrietta, a debutante from a titled family who had merely sniffed when introduced to Inès, looking her up and down rudely before turning her head dismissively. Inès had blushed. She wondered if Charlie had told Henrietta that she was a tart. She hoped not, but Henrietta seemed to avoid any kind of conversation with her, hanging on the two men's every word.

They were on the fish course when the air-raid siren went off. Its harsh, familiar sound caused a sudden silence in the room. Almost at once their waiter was at the table.

"Won't you please follow me, ladies and gentlemen," he said in a smoothly assured voice. "Your dinner will not be interrupted, I promise you."

Bemused, Inès followed the waiter down several flights of stairs. The entire roomful of people trooped in an orderly manner to the basement, where almost a facsimile of the Grill Room met their eyes. Dozens of tables were laid with sparkling white cloths and highly polished knives and forks. They were ushered to their table where their dinner and the dancing continued as if nothing had happened, until the All Clear sounded and everyone went back upstairs to the Grill.

"Is this normal?" Inès asked Benjie.

"Oh, yes, my dear," he said airily. "The Savoy is completely organized so that if the bloody Blitz interrupts their sacred dinnertime, they have everything prepared to continue business as usual in the basement. Good idea, what?"

"Absolutely spiffing," smiled Inès.

The following week went by in a haze of nightclubs, bars, theatres and restaurants. Inès was taken by Benjie to the Milroy Club in Mayfair, where they listened to the melodic piano playing of Tim Clayton, and to the Orchid Room in Brook Street, where the maitre d'hôtel, Jerry Marco, greeted Benjie like a long-lost brother. He insisted they try a new drink from New York called the Bronx. It was a potent mixture of gin, orange juice and Curaçao, and Inès drank so many of them that she found herself getting almost too forward with Benjie. He drew away from her swiftly and she realized he needed to make the first move.

"I think I'll stick to champagne or white ladies in the future," she groaned to an impatient Yves the next morning, giving him one of the rolls she had smuggled out of the restaurant.

"I don't care what you drink, *chérie,* as long as you make some money soon," he sighed. "This poor *macrou* has an ache in his belly that only a good meal will dispel."

"I'm trying," said Inès. "I'm really trying, Yves."

A few nights later Benjie took her back to the Bagatelle again with Charlie and Stella. Edmundo Ros was playing torrid Latin American music and the sexy beat excited both girls.

"C'mon, let's do the conga," yelled Stella excitedly, grabbing Charlie's hand and leading him onto the packed dance floor.

"Come on, Benjie, let's do it too," said Inès, trying to pull the young viscount up.

But Benjie was too embarrassed and inhibited to attempt the conga, even though several of his friends were part of the long line that wound through the club whooping and shrieking. He was drinking pink gins dripping with angostura and occasionally he would put a match to the mixture, watching with childlike glee as it ignited.

"Whew, that was a good one," exclaimed Stella, out of breath and laughing as she came back to the table, her red hair in disarray and her lips bare of their usual scarlet slash. She leaned towards Inès conspiratorially as she reapplied her lipstick with a heavy hand.

"It's a whoopsee-do and up to the chandelier with *that* one, dearie!" She gestured towards Charlie, who had a satisfied expression on his face as he adjusted his trousers.

"What do you mean?" asked Inès.

"I mean, dear, 'e's like the bleedin' Eiffel Tower in 'is private parts.

Ready, steady *and go*—whoa—whoa—I won't 'ave to work too 'ard to-night, luv, I guarantee—it'll be an easy bit of goosey-gander. 'Ow're you doing with yours, ducks? 'As 'e 'ad the 'orn yet?"

Inès shook her head regretfully and looked at Benjie. Was he ever going to make a move? A week had gone by without any sort of pass. It was definitely time for her to try to seduce him before Yves wasted away to nothing. If Benjie wasn't going to play, maybe she should look around for someone else. There were plenty of available-looking men around, a lot of cute young Americans too. It shouldn't be too difficult to find one who wanted her, they all seemed to give her the eye and wolf whistles whenever she walked by. Yes, maybe she should go off with one of these good-looking Yanks. At least she'd get paid, and probably even get some nylon stockings, and tins of fruit, too, if she picked a generous one. But she decided to give Benjie one more chance.

After they left the Bagatelle she realized that Benjie was quite drunk. Hailing a taxi, she bundled him into it.

"Shepherd Market," she told the driver. "And quickly, please."

In her flat, in the bedroom next to the one she and Yves usually shared, she threw herself on him with excited cries and appropriate moans, and eventually succeeded in getting his clothes off him, and into bed. Once there, however, she immediately realized that he might have a few sexual problems. He seemed not able to rise to the occasion.

"Oh, dear, naughty thing—where's he gone?" giggled Benjie, pink with embarrassment. "He was certainly there on the dance floor the other night. Why is Willie being such a bad boy?"

"Don't worry," soothed Inès, applying expert pressure to the limpness lying crumpled forlornly against his thigh. "Willie will be back, I guarantee you."

"I say, that's wonderful," said Benjie a few moments later, a twitch betraying the return of his amorous appetite. "I rather like that!"

"Thank you, *Monsieur*," Inès smiled, working diligently with delicate expertise. "We aim to please."

"Go on," whispered Benjie hoarsely, "don't stop, Inès—it's awfully good." But unfortunately, with the exception of that one tiny initial spasm, the viscount's noble cock remained sadly flaccid.

"Don't worry, *chéri*." Inès was all sweetness and understanding. "I will take care of it—just relax. Don't do anything, Benjie, just enjoy this." Yves had shown her how to turn clients on when this happened—as it so often did.

There were several traditional methods of arousing a limp cock, and Inès decided she would try them all. After all, if Viscount Spencer-Monckton was to be an important client she had to please him. Enough to get a good remuneration. Maybe if she was really good she'd get a tenner. First she attempted the ice in mouth then the hot-water method. This succeeded only in making Benjie squirm and giggle like a ten-year-old, and diminished his manhood even more. She then gave him the ever popular ice-cream-cone treat. Although genuine ice cream was a rare commodity in wartime London, Inès improvised with a few ounces of her precious jam ration. But it was all to no avail. Benjie's cock was so soft, so shriveled with terror that it seemed to want to go to ground in his scrotum.

"He's a naughty little fellow," sighed Benjie, mortified. "Maybe you should smack his bottie."

Ah, a clue at last, Inès thought and leaping into action she commanded in a menacing tone, "Turn over, Benjie."

He eagerly obeyed and his pink skin started to redden as Inès began smacking his small, tight buttocks.

He murmured into the pillow, his cultured voice sounding as high-pitched as a five-year-old's, "I've been *so, so* naughty, Nanny, *such a bad boy.*"

"Then the naughty boy must be spanked," Inès said sternly, biting her lip to stop her giggles.

"Ooh no, Nanny," cried Benjie, "you can't spank me—it'll hurt."

"Oh, but I can," said Inès gruffly. "Like this, you bad boy. You naughty, naughty little boy."

Harder and harder she pummeled him, his moans of delight muffled by the pillow, his writhing bottom proof of his growing excitement.

"You are a wicked, terrible creature," she admonished, slapping away at his skinny shanks. "Nasty little boys must be punished." Slap—slap—slap. "They must be beaten until they beg for mercy."

"Punish me—oh—*please*, Nanny," Benjie groaned in ecstasy. "Oh, Nursie, tell me what a bad boy Benjie has been."

"Bad boy—boy *méchant, petit garçon.*"

Inès' palms stung, and her breath came in gasps. She was desperately trying to stop laughing. But then she started to become strangely excited herself. She had rarely inflicted pain on a client before, and suddenly she was finding it exhilarating. She picked up Yves' ivory shoehorn from the bedside table, and rained a series of sharp blows with it on Benjie's now scarlet bottom.

"Ooh, ooh, Nanny, you punish me so well," groaned the naughty boy. "But now I'm going to punish *you* with my big nasty sticking-out stick, Nanny dear, so turn over, it's Benjie's turn now." With that he rolled over, confronting Inès with an enormous smile and a matching penis.

"Lie down now, Nan▮ quietly," Benjie whispered authoritatively. "Don't let Mummy hear what I'm doing—you must keep quiet. You've been such a *naughty* Nanny that now Benjie must punish you with this."

With that he thrust into Inès, riding her with joyful, throaty cries while his pale patrician face with its refined features contorted in ecstasy.

"That's right, Nanny, you deserve this. Benjie's got you where he wants you now, and you—you—you better not tell—Mummy or Daddy, oooh—ahhh!"

Half an hour later, after a glass of vintage port and some digestive biscuits which Yves had managed to find, the viscount was ready again. This time Inès improved her dialogue, finding acting talents which she never thought she possessed as she embellished the bad-little-boy/naughty-nanny scenario. Benjie was in seventh heaven, and Inès found herself feeling curiously maternal towards him, even somewhat protective. When he left at dawn he put a pile of crisp white five-pound notes on the dresser and Inès was delighted.

After stocking up on essentials to feed the hungry Yves, she and Stella took Oxford Street by storm. She had twenty pounds and enough clothing coupons for four new dresses.

"Gor blimey, luv, he's bleedin' generous for an 'onorable," said Stella enviously. "Twenty-five quid 'e gave you?"

Inès nodded.

"Your you-know-what-twat must be lined with gold, duckie, that's all I can say," snickered Stella as they admired the dresses in the windows of Bourne & Hollingsworth. "Lord Worthington only gives me a tenner, and the Hon. Charlie the same. Whatever did you do to get twenty-five quid?"

Inès said nothing, changing the subject as she spotted a dress she liked in the window. "Ooh, look, Stella—it's lovely, is it not?" She was admiring a dark brown satin frock with a sweetheart neckline edged with pink silk. It had a large pink bow at the daring décolletage, three-quarter-length sleeves with a little bow at each elbow, and an intricately draped skirt.

"Mmm," Stella sniffed disparagingly at it. "It's a bit drab for my taste, ducks, but I s'pose it would look good with your 'air."

"What's the price?" Inès peered at the tag.

"Thirty-seven and ninepence," said Stella. "That's a bit of all right—it won't break our little bank. C'mon, ducks, let's get you glamorous."

After they had bought the brown dress, and then a black one, and another pair of shoes, and some new earrings, Inès started to feel frugal, but Stella was insistent. She liked Inès and enjoyed helping her.

"We've got to do somefink about yer boat race," she said, dragging a reluctant Inès down Regent Street towards Swan & Edgar in Piccadilly Circus.

"My what?" asked Inès, almost colliding with a handsome City gentleman who tipped his hat, smiling at her charming figure laden with packages.

"Yer boat race, dearie—yer face."

"What's wrong with my face?" asked Inès defensively.

"Look, duckie, I always call a spade a spade—well almost always," said Stella. "Frankly, ducks, you're gettin' a bit too long in the tooth to go around with the scrubbed virgin look."

"I'm just eighteen," said Inès indignantly.

"I know, I know, and I'm King George's auntie," said Stella. "It don't matter 'ow old you are, dear—the bloom's startin' to go orf—you know what I mean? You've been on the game for four years now since you was fourteen, so it's time to tart yourself up—get a nice sparkling new look. 'Ere, now get a load of that—ain't they pretty."

They stopped at the cosmetics counter in Swan & Edgar, one of the few places that still sold bits of makeup in London. A long queue of eager young women craned their necks eagerly to look at the desirable, hard-to-obtain articles, and Inès looked into the glass showcase full of lipsticks and rouge pots with excitement.

"Do you think it will suit me?" she asked anxiously after she had parted with a precious half crown for one scarlet lipstick which smelled of candle wax, and a small pot of brick-colored rouge. The makeup was rationed, one to each customer, but some of the girls, after making their purchases, quickly slipped to the back of the queue again to buy some more.

"You'll look the Queen of bleedin' Sheba by the time I've shown you what to do," Stella smiled. "We need one more thing now."

"What's that?" asked Inès as Stella hustled her down Piccadilly towards St. James's Street.

" 'Ere we are," Stella said proudly, as they arrived at the exclusive gentlemen's bootmaker, Lobb. "By appointment to 'is bleedin' Majesty 'imself—come on, Inès."

Inside the shop she pointed to a tin of black boot polish displayed discreetly on the polished oak counter.

"We'll 'ave one of those," she told the salesman who looked them up and down disdainfully. Two obvious tarts if he ever saw one, although the dark one was sexy in a foreign sort of way.

Inès gave the man sevenpence for the boot polish, and the two women rushed home giggling like schoolgirls. Stella was going to give Inès a lesson in makeup.

"Now you're the dark and sultry sort," Stella told her. "Me, I'm the outdoor type, with a talent for indoor games!" She opened the tin of shoepolish and began to paint it around Inès' pale blue eyes with a little brush. "Now no peeking." She doused Inès' face with white powder, dabbed a generous amount of lipstick on her pale lips, and stroked her cheekbones lightly with rouge. She fiddled with her long hair with curling irons for half an hour, and then allowed Inès to look.

"An' *voilà, chérie,* or whatever you say in Froggie land," exclaimed Stella triumphantly. "*La grande transformation*—Cinderella into Hedy Lamarr."

Inès looked at herself in amazement. The woman who stared back at her in the cracked dressing table mirror looked like a Hollywood vamp. Dark red lips in a pale, almost translucent skin, contrasted brilliantly with her light blue eyes. They glowed with a sultry sparkle, the heavy shadowing of black boot polish exaggerating their luster and depth to great effect. Her dark hair was parted in the middle and fell to each side of her face in asymmetrical waves and curls.

"*Mon Dieu,* is that me?" breathed Inès.

"You bet it is, dearie," chuckled Stella. "And I'll tell you somefink for nuffink. When the Hon. Viscount Benjie sees you tonight, dearie, 'is little wee willie winkie is going to get as 'ard as a bit of Brighton rock. He'll be N-S-I-T tonight, I betcha."

"What does that mean?"

"Not Safe In Taxis, dearie," sniggered Stella. "Now throw some of this over yourself tonight, luvie." She handed Inès a small bottle of perfume in a distinctive geometrical bottle.

"Chanel Number Five," whispered Inès reverently. "Where did you get this, Stella?"

"Never you mind, luv, never you mind," said Stella mysteriously. "All I know, duckie, is that once old Viscount Benjie-poo gets a whiff of this, 'is dickery-dickery will be up 'igher than a bleedin' barrage balloon."

"His what?" laughed Inès.

"Dickery *dock,* dearie," said Stella in mock exasperation. "It's rhymin' slang, see. Don'cha know what dickery dickery dock means?"

"Oh, yes, I get it." Inès smiled. "Okay, Stella, I think I'm ready to go to the rub-a-dub-dub tonight."

"You're learnin', girl, you're learnin'."

Soon Inès had Benjie and several of his society friends totally under her spell, and her career as one of London's most beautiful and successful courtesans was well and truly launched.

Inès entertained her viscount three times a week. He preferred to visit her in the evening after dining at his club.

She hardly saw Yves except on weekends when her bluebloods returned to their country estates from London. Yves was pleased with the money she was now making, and she saved up her own sexual thrills, or at least most of them, for weekends with him. Although she did occasionally become aroused by some of her clients, Yves was her man, their sex life was as torrid as ever, and he still made her laugh like no one else could.

Inès was happy. The money rolled in, enabling them to afford more luxuries from the black market. Her clients occasionally brought her expensive presents and always treated her like a lady when they were not treating her like a nanny. She loved Yves and he seemed to love her. Everything was almost too good to be true.

Since clothes coupons were hard to come by and Yves had found several bolts of beautiful prewar fabric, Inès decided to learn to sew. Yves bought her a secondhand sewing machine and she quickly learned to love dressmaking. Although fashion magazines were hard to come by, Inès went to the cinema often, and she would copy the gorgeous clothes the Hollywood glamour queens wore. She particularly liked the gowns Esther Williams wore in *A Guy Named Joe,* and Lana Turner's in *Slightly Dangerous.* She gave the first dress she made—a floral print in shades of cyclamen and dark blue—to Stella.

"You're a real chum, you know that, duckie," the redhead said, her eyes shining gratefully. "No one's ever given me anything before, unless I've 'ad to give out to get it—if you know what I mean. Thanks, Inès, I really appreciate it."

Inès smiled. Stella was the first real girlfriend she had ever had, and she valued the friendship tremendously.

"Oh, by the way, duckie, I've been meaning to ask you this." Stella was admiring her reflection in the new dress. "You are taking care of yourself, aren't you?"

"What do you mean?"

"Against the old you-know-what. Against falling in the family way—you're doing something, aren't you?"

"Well, not really." Inès started to blush. "Yves always has said I'm too young to get pregnant so I just cross my fingers—"

"You little fool." Stella was cross now. "Yves is even more of a bloody burk than I thought. Right, my girl, I'm making an appointment with Dr. Wright in Weymouth Street first thing tomorrow. We're getting you fitted with a good old Dutch cap."

When one or the other of them was not entertaining clients, Stella and Inès were inseparable.

Inès taught the redhead how to sew on her old Singer machine, and the two women spent many afternoons devouring fashion magazines, searching for new styles to copy.

Under Stella's tutelage Inès learned the intricacies of cosmetic witchery. How to put up her hair with three pins and a lick of glue, and where to find the precious dye to keep her blond hair the dark brunette that she now preferred. She learned jokes and songs, for Stella was a cheery soul who liked a sing-along with the wireless. Stella knew all the popular songs of the day, and taught Inès the lyrics to most of them. She also taught her how to do the conga, the rhumba, the jitterbug and even the Lambeth walk, and they practiced them together to Stella's old gramophone with girlish squeals of laughter.

The two of them often went to the cinemas in Leicester Square to see the Hollywood musicals that were being churned out of the studios to fulfill the needs of a public which craved light entertainment.

Sometimes they window-shopped together in Oxford Street and Bond Street, admiring the expensive things that were far beyond their means.

Inès was thrilled to have a female companion in London. Since Jeanette had been murdered she had had no one with whom to share confidences and dreams. She simply adored having a best friend. Stella was like a kind older sister to her and made life much more fun.

But after a time, Inès' close and sisterly relationship with Stella seemed to cool. Suddenly Stella never had time anymore for their shopping trips or for the intimate chats on personal philosophy and life which had become so important to Inès.

Stella had told Inès that she was terribly busy with her afternoon clients, and since Inès' clients visited mostly at night, they gradually started to drift apart.

"Yves, Yves, darling," Inès called excitedly as she opened the front door of their flat. "I'm home."

She was happy. A naughty weekend at the Viscount's country house with plenty of giggles and spanking had ended abruptly when a telegram arrived, announcing that his dragon of a mother was returning home a day early from a trip to their Scottish estate. It had thrown him into a complete tizzy. Frantically, Benjie bundled Inès into his Bentley, drove her to Godalming station and put her on the London train with a cursory peck on the cheek and a thick wad of clean white fivers in her bag.

She hummed to herself as she walked into the hall of the flat. It was only two o'clock on a Sunday, and the beautiful summer afternoon stretched ahead for her and her lover.

"Chéri!" she cried, dropping her suitcase and running through the small drawing room towards his bedroom. "I'm home. Get up, lazybones. I've had a reprieve from his lordship, isn't that—" Her voice trailed off as she opened the bedroom door, to see the two of them curled up together, asleep like kittens in a basket.

She couldn't see the girl's face, only the long, carrot-red hair which fanned out over Inès' favorite antique linen pillowcase; that pale freckled arm thrown possessively across the muscular shoulders of her man. Inès' stomach churned and her legs started to buckle.

Her loud intake of breath stirred them into sleepy wakefulness.

"Oh, my Gawd," Stella muttered glumly, picking up a transparent black chiffon robe. "Christ all bloody mighty. Sorry, luv, you know 'ow it is, I'm reelly sorry." She disappeared into the bathroom and Inès heard the sound of water running. She felt as if a fist had thudded against her heart, smashing it to pieces.

Yves lit a cigarette with a great show of indifference. It dangled from his lips as he stared at Inès dispassionately, both arms behind his head, the smoke rising into his curly brown hair. His hazel eyes were narrowed, giving her no clue to his feelings as he said, "Why didn't you tell me you were coming home?"

"I thought you loved me, Yves," she said, her voice choked with tears. "How could you do this? And with Stella—my best friend—how *could* you?"

"Chérie, I did love you—I did. I *do* love you." He dragged at his cigarette, searching for words. "I love you like a—friend—like a sister . . . like my own daughter."

"What are you saying?" Inès was stunned. "What we do together, Yves, is hardly what a brother usually does with his sister."

"I know. I know. Look, Inès, I have to be honest. I know you'll understand, but things happen. *C'est la vie,* I suppose." His voice was low and sincere. He evinced no sign of guilt, no pang of remorse; he seemed cool, and too collected.

Inès sank slowly into the armchair at the foot of their bed, staring into the face of the only man she had ever loved, her broken heart fluttering wildly. She felt sickened.

"I know this is hard for you, Inès, but four years is a very long time for a man like me to be with one woman. I think I've taught you a lot, and I love you, *chérie,* but I must admit my love has been more . . . more— well, paternal, lately."

"No!" cried Inès. "No. Yves, it's not true—what are you saying?"

"I'm leaving you," he said flatly. "I must. I was going to tell you next week—I'm going back to Paris. I want to go back." He paused, taking a deep drag on on his Gauloise. "And I'm taking Stella."

"Stella? You're going with *Stella*?" Inès could barely speak from the shock and pain. "*Why?* Why with her? Do you love her?"

"No," he admitted, frowning. "Not at all—it is hard for me really to love, Inès. You know that. But certainly it is—well—more than brotherly love at the moment. I think Stella will do quite well in Paris now that the occupation is over, there will be a lot of work for her. And you are doing fine here now, you have good clients—plenty of them—you will become more successful, make more money. You don't really need me anymore."

"I do," she sobbed. "I need you—there's never been anyone for me like you; there never will be."

"You'll find someone," he said coolly. "A girl like you—you'll find a new man."

"You bastard, you two-timing *macrou*. I loved you. How could you do this to me with that . . . *creature*?" She was becoming hysterical now. The thought of losing Yves was insupportable. It couldn't happen, he was her life.

The sound of running water ceased abruptly. Inès knew that Stella was probably listening at the bathroom door. Stella—her best friend. She was filled with pain and rage and grief. Suddenly memories of the Italian she had murdered came flooding back. She almost wished that she could find that same razor, slice it into Yves and Stella, kill them both, the ache in her heart was so palpable.

"Yves—oh, God, Yves," she cried despairingly. "You've broken my heart today, just as if you'd smashed it into the ground. You've destroyed me, Yves—completely destroyed me." Fresh tears filled her eyes but he stopped her.

"Listen to me, Inès . . . I always thought you should make something of yourself. But I'm not the man to be with for that. You'll be better off without me, *chérie*, I know you will. You're young, beautiful—too beautiful to be a *poule de luxe* forever. You'll make a life. Find a good man—not a pimp, a *macrou*. Someone to really love you, because I know for damn sure I'm not the one for you."

Inès stared at him. "You are," she sobbed. "You are, Yves, you're all I've got, all I've ever had. All I want."

"Stop it, Inès—stop it, please, *chérie*. It's over, can't you see that? Where's your pride? It's over between us; you must understand that now."

"I'm going for a walk," Inès said in desperation, running her fingers wildly through her hair. "When I come back, I hope you and that—that—red-haired *whore*"—she spat the word, even though her voice was almost cracking with the effort of holding back her tears—"will be gone."

"*Chérie*, I'm sorry . . ."

"Good-bye, Yves," Inès said in a tiny, broken voice. "And good luck in Paris—*au revoir*."

She strode from the room, her head held high, clutching desperately to what remained of her pride, her throat aching with unshed tears. She was not yet nineteen years old and she was completely alone in the world once again.

✧   ✧   ✧

After Yves and Stella left for Paris, Inès wept bitterly for days, pounding her pillow in frustrated anguish, crying Yves' name throughout the long wakeful nights. But she was young and resilient, and after a period of both intense rage and grief-stricken mourning, she slowly began to entertain her clients again. It was, after all, her only livelihood, and to live in war-time London was expensive. She frequented nightclubs, jazz clubs, bars and restaurants, hoping to meet a man for whom she could feel something—anything. She wanted to find love—she desperately wanted to stop her life of whoring before it was too late.

She had been a prostitute since the age of fourteen, and though it had meant little to her then, lately she had begun to feel more and more contempt for men's lust; disgust as their sweat dripped onto her; loathing as she mechanically pleasured them with her mouth. She was so erotically expert in what she did that all her clients were completely enthralled by her. But she hated it, and she started to hate them too.

She wanted a real boyfriend, someone with whom she could build a proper life, marry. She wanted to raise a family who would receive all the love and attention from her that she had never had from her mother. She wanted to become a normal woman.

As the weeks and months passed, as Inès searched for the elusive commodity called love, she realized that to find the type of man she sought she must become worthy of him.

She began an extensive course of self-improvement of both her mind and body. Every morning she exercised vigorously, the window open to all the sights and smells of Shepherd Market. Then she meditated, as she had learned to do from an ancient book written by an Indian seer. She tried to cleanse her thoughts of her clients, their depravity and kinkiness, to fill her mind with purity. She started going to church, praying for her soul and the souls of the men who used her. She found an inner peace in the teachings of Christ and in the Desiderata. She was convinced that she would one day shed the decaying skin of prostitution and become a member of the human race again. She knew she had to.

She spent almost all her afternoons at libraries and museums, letting great works of art fill her with wonder. She read voraciously—philosophy, religion and art history; she went to the theater, to concerts and to the opera. She studied the newspapers, becoming so well informed about current affairs and world events that she started debating with some of her clients. Much to their amazement and delight, they soon found that the mind of this beautiful whore was almost as fascinating as her face, her body and her incredible sexual skills.

Sometimes, so involved would both become in a discussion of Buddhism or poetry or the work of some new artist that a client would forget the original intention of his visit, and sipping dry sherry, they would argue fiercely and debate long into the night.

Inès was pleased with her progress. The frightened whore-child, ignorant of everything but men's desires, was gone forever. Instead, a woman of intelligence, beauty and knowledge was emerging, a woman of whom a man could be truly proud.

❧ *Eleven* ❧

LONDON 1945

I̲t̲ w̲a̲s̲ f̲i̲n̲a̲l̲l̲y̲ o̲v̲e̲r̲. Six long and bloody years of hell ended on a warm May night, and all London seemed to be in Trafalgar Square celebrating the German surrender.

No one was in a more joyous mood than Phoebe and Julian, for it was a double celebration. They had finally been married in Caxton Hall Registry Office the previous weekend. Julian had been reluctant, but Phoebe was pregnant. Ever the gentleman, Julian "did the right thing."

Now, along with thousands of other revelers, they danced, laughed, cried with joy around the fountains in the square. The sky was illuminated by a dazzling fireworks display, and everyone was singing "Rule Britannia," "God Save the King" and other patriotic songs in drunken, tuneless delight. Groups of French sailors with their pompommed berets tipped over their eyes drunkenly chanted the "Marseillaise" as they tried in vain to stay on their feet.

In the grand houses of England the armistice was being welcomed with lavish parties. Rare vintage wines and spirits were uncorked. Exotic tinned fruits, hams, cheeses, quail eggs, pheasant, sides of beef and delicacies not tasted since the outbreak of war adorned the groaning tables. Even the most stingy of the aristocracy had on this occasion given in to the black marketeers and were sparing no expense for this glorious celebration.

The ordinary citizens, the common people—the backbone of Great Britain—had taken to the streets to celebrate together. Thousands of them had gone to stand outside Buckingham Palace and cheer the King and Queen as they waved from the balcony. The crowds stretched down the Mall to Trafalgar Square, where servicemen in uniform frolicked in the shallow, cold water of the fountains alongside boys and girls, middle-aged mums and dads with their floral skirts or flannel trousers hitched uninhibitedly over their knees.

A few brave souls tore off their clothes in a frenzy of exhibitionism, posturing before the cheering crowds. Some of the younger people were so carried away with excitement that they openly made love on the backs of Landseer's colossal lions, guardians of Nelson's Column. Dozens of church bells rang out as the crowd formed circles, dancing the knees up, the conga, the rhumba, even the Highland fling.

Bottles of champagne and beer were tipped to laughing lips as groups of giggling young girls ran around hugging and kissing anyone who took their fancy, sometimes even those who didn't. Every car had its headlights on and its horns blaring, and every municipal and government building was brilliantly lit. It was the bacchanal to end them all, the party of the century. But in all the crowd's jollity there was a frenetic desperation, for many had lost loved ones or possessions and homes during the war.

"I love you, Mr. Brooks," Phoebe yelled above the din.

"I love you too, Mrs. Brooks." Julian laughingly kissed his wife's full lips, then was unceremoniously pulled away from her by a teenage soldier.

" 'Ere, give us a kiss too, lovely," said the boy with a cheeky smile, and Phoebe obliged him with a smacker.

"Strumpet." Julian looked at the vermilion lipstick smeared across Phoebe's laughing face.

"Scoundrel!" she giggled. "And, speaking of which, look at *that!*" They observed a naked young woman being powerfully serviced by a French soldier whose trousers were around his ankles, while another young soldier hung on to his arm and vomited into the fountain.

"Charming! What a delightful sight. I think I've had just about enough of this party, old girl. Let's go home and celebrate being married in a rather more traditional way." Julian slid his hand over her full bosom.

"Naughty boy—people looking." Phoebe slapped his hand away coyly.

"Who cares?" laughed Julian. "The war's over, darling—it's finally over."

"Okay, let's go home to make love, celebrate our new baby, celebrate *life,* my gorgeous husband. That's the only proper way to end a war."

"There's a bloke 'ere to see yer—says 'e's from a film studio or somefink." The stage doorkeeper poked a grizzled head around the door of Julian's minuscule dressing room, where the young comedian was taking a catnap between shows. It was tough work performing seven times a day and night. All right for Phoebe and the showgirls. They just had to wander across the stage, tits up, feathers erect, perform a little bit of a song and dance, and look sexy and pretty.

Julian had to think up amusing, hilarious and original monologues night after night, day after day—and after eighteen months it was becoming more and more difficult.

Before he could say anything the door was pushed open by a man in his late forties wearing a double-breasted black cashmere overcoat, a black homburg and gray suede gloves. He walked into the room and removed his hat. His nose was full and fleshy, and his lips were those of a gourmet—a man who appreciated only the finest in food, wine and, no doubt, women. His eyes were masked by thick-rimmed, dark-lensed black spectacles, and his skin was deeply tanned. He exuded an aura of supreme self-confidence, that of a man used to giving orders which would be instantly obeyed, of making decisions that would always be right, and of always having the very best of everything which life had to offer.

"Good evening, Mr. Brooks. My name is Didier Armande."

Julian stood up immediately, impressed and excited. Didier Armande —*the* Didier Armande. Probably the most important and influential film producer in Britain. Julian knew it was he who had produced the unforgettable *Romeo and Juliet,* the extraordinary *Woman of Baghdad* and the revolutionary epic *The Life and Times of Louis XIV.* It was he who had discovered not only the legendary Elaine Roche, the gorgeous Maxine Von Pallach and the dashing Jasper Swanson, but had helped his own sister—the sultry and mysterious Ramona Armande—to reach the heights of international and Hollywood stardom, in his avant-garde production of *Mata Hari.* What on earth was Didier Armande doing here in this tatty dressing room? And what could he possibly want with Julian Brooks?

"May I sit down?" The older man's faint accent gave the impression of culture and education.

"Of course, of course." Hastily Julian brushed a pile of his discarded clothes from a small chair.

Mr. Armande sat down, his silver-topped ebony cane resting lightly between his knees. Taking a leather case from the pocket of his overcoat, he proffered what was surely the first Havana cigar Julian had seen since before the war.

Havana cigars! Where the hell had he managed to find such a luxury? It was hard enough in austere Britain to find a packet of Woodbines, let alone a cigar. Julian accepted one, and Didier coolly lit both cigars with a heavy-looking gold lighter, into which the initials D.A. had been set in small diamonds.

"I know you don't have much time," he said, glancing at his slim platinum wristwatch, whose shape and design were of faultless taste, "but I have watched you perform for the last few days and I wanted to express to you my most sincere congratulations."

"Congratulations? Whatever for?" Julian was mystified. All that he'd done recently was to trot out some old gags, fumbling in his memory for a bit of business or some material that he could remember from other comedians' acts—anything with which to raise a laugh from that sea of servicemen who sat enthralled each night by the tawdry glamour of the Windmill.

"You are indeed a comedian *par excellence.*" The man inhaled deeply on his cigar, filling the tiny room with a haze of delicious blue smoke. "You made me laugh even when I'd heard the same joke before."

"Thank you." Julian was pulling himself together, feeling more secure with the compliments. "That's most kind of you to say so. I was always told that the hardest thing for any comic to do is to make the same audience laugh twice at identical material."

"Exactly, my dear fellow. It is an art, a true art. However, I realize from watching you carefully that you possess much more than just a talent to amuse, as dear Noël is so fond of saying. You were an actor, were you not?"

"Yes, I was. Still am, really. Now that the war is over, I hope to go back into acting, but so many of the reps are still closed."

"Perhaps you won't have to go back to repertory." Didier Armande inspected the glowing tip of his cigar carefully. "Have you ever thought of making films?"

"Films! Well, no, actually I haven't, I've always done theater."

"I'll get straight to the point." Didier leaned forward, his hands resting casually on his cane, on which Julian could see an eagle, its wings spread, emblazoned with some kind of writing.

"My company, Goya Films, will shortly be making a film about Charles the Second, and the fascinating relationship that he was reputed to have with one of his illegitimate daughters."

Julian leaned forward, almost tipping his chair into Armande's.

"You bear a most striking resemblance to some of the portraits of Charles the Second," Armande said. "Similar coloring, even bone structure. It is uncanny, actually, quite amazing."

"Oh," said Julian feeling at a loss as Sammy, the call boy, poked a cheery carrot head around the door.

"Five minutes, matey," he chirped.

Didier Armande handed Julian a white card engraved with his name, that of Goya Pictures, an address and a telephone number. "If you would be interested in screen-testing for the role of King Charles, please have your agent call my office within the next two days. You may want some time to think it over."

"Oh—no. No, I don't need any time, I'll do it—I mean, I'll test. I'd love to test, absolutely love to!"

"*Très bien,* Mr. Brooks, good news indeed. I shall have my people call your agent."

"Great, great, that's wonderful. Oh, God, I'm sorry, but I don't have an agent." Julian felt embarrassed.

"You have no agent?" Didier raised black brows eloquently—an actor without an agent? How odd. Even if agents didn't seem to do much, they were a necessity when things got rough.

"Well, no—you know how it is at the Windmill—nonstop work, nose to the grindstone all the time, never even have time to write a letter. Actually I was really waiting until the war ended to get an agent, and I just don't seem to have got around to it yet."

"Very well. That is of course no problem. If you will be so kind as to give me your telephone number at home, my people will contact you in order to make the necessary arrangements."

Didier Armande rose, pulling tight suede gloves over his muscular hands, which were the only thing about him that seemed less than elegant.

"*Au revoir,* Mr. Brooks, until we meet again at Pinewood Studios, I hope." He extended his hand to Julian, who clasped it firmly.

"May I inquire what the film is to be called, sir?"

"It's called *The Merry Monarch.* The script was written by the Academy Award-winning writer Irving Frankovitch, and it will be directed by Francis Lawford, who I'm sure you must know. We fully expect the actor who plays the King to be nominated for the Oscar next year. It's a hell of a role, Mr. Brooks, a hell of a role, and one for which you were born."

Julian Brooks and his career were both thriving. He looked wonderful as Charles II. His own hair was covered by a shoulder-length wig of lustrous tumbling black ringlets, and a delicate moustache enhanced his gorgeous face. He swashbuckled his way through the film: fighting, romancing, dueling, perfectly cast as the suave, vain, highly sexed and romantic King. The story was based less on historical accuracy than on the fertile imagination of the American writer Irving Frankovitch, but it was exactly the kind of romantic epic for which postwar film fans yearned, and Julian was the kind of romantic hero female fans lusted after.

Goya Pictures' publicity department moved in on Julian, typewriters and cameras clicking. When not wearing his seventeenth-century costume, Julian was dressed by the wardrobe department in a variety of well-cut threads so that Didier's number one stills photographer, Curly, could snap to his heart's content.

Bronzed by the wizardry of the makeup department, Julian posed for hours, self-conscious in the freezing stills studio, wearing bathing trunks or rolled-up blue jeans, tennis shorts or sometimes only his Restoration doublet and hose from *The Merry Monarch* and a bare chest. And the chest had better be bare. Modesty, also known as the Production Code Administration, or the Hays Office, regarded a hairy chest as a major cause of moral corruption. Therefore, on the morning of every stills session, Julian's pectorals would be painstakingly shaved by the makeup man and covered with deep bronze makeup which was then topped off with a thin sheen of oil. This made his chest glisten like polished mahogany, and many a maidenly heart beat faster when she saw her favorite in all his masculine glory smiling out from the magazines. Beefcake was big business, and Julian epitomized it totally.

Before *The Merry Monarch* was even released, publications all over the world were clamoring for more and more photographs of Looks Brooks. The fewer clothes he wore, the more his fans seemed to like it. It did not matter that as yet none of these fans had even seen him on the silver screen—he was a world-famous star before his first film had been released. He bared almost his all whether he liked it or not: on a beach, tossing a medicine ball, swinging an ax with convincing dexterity, pulling a rope, flying a plane, riding a horse, always dressed in appropriate gear. Once the crafty Curly even had him wrestling with a giant rubber alligator. Julian found this endless posing and shaving of his chest tedious, to say the least, but Phoebe, ever the pragmatist, and a teeny bit envious of all the attention he was receiving, encouraged him to do anything and everything which the studio asked.

"You want to be a star—well, this is how it's done," she told him bluntly.

After having miscarried their baby, Phoebe had made Julian's career ever more her concern. Not satisfied with the simple domestic life of their new flat in Cadogan Square, she appeared constantly on the set, watching over him jealously from the sidelines as he played love scenes with a succession of glamorous actresses. She inwardly seethed when he embraced them, her innate common sense beginning to founder in a sea of envy. Phoebe was not as pretty as she had been. Lines of discontent had started to form on her face, and her voluptuous body was becoming soft and flabby.

Superficially she reveled in her husband's success, but she began to have serious acting ambitions herself. These had lain dormant until Julian started riding the crest of success, and now she too wanted to bask in the spotlight of fame. Several times she subtly suggested to Didier Armande that she would be right to perform opposite Julian or even play a second lead, but Didier diplomatically laughed off her aspirations, pretending that he didn't really understand.

"One star in the family is enough, my dear," he would say, patting her plump, powdered cheek. "Our boy needs to be taken care of, Phoebe, and you do that so beautifully it would be a great pity to do anything to prevent the golden goose from laying his lovely valuable eggs."

Phoebe bit her lip and kept quiet, but the more famous her husband became, the more the long green fingers of jealousy gripped her heart.

Julian's career thrived. When he wasn't acting he gave interviews. He confided his life story to *Picturegoer* and *Picture Show Illustrated*, *Photoplay* and *Look* magazines. He laughed and joked with the cameramen and crew as he posed beside boats, planes and cars with the all-important macho stare. He chatted long distance to the twin witches of Hollywood, Hedda and Louella. He was becoming the most popular actor in England, but he still considered movies as just a means to an end. His ultimate ambition was to do classical stage roles, with aspirations to the crown of Olivier himself.

"There's no doubt about it, no doubt at all—the man's got star quality," Didier muttered to his assistant, delighted with his personal choice of a leading man after seeing the first rushes of *The Merry Monarch*. Didier stared at the last frame of Julian's beautifully lit, handsome face gazing into the camera with tears in his velvet eyes, the black poodle curls and rakish feathered hat accentuating both his innate masculinity and a brooding sensitivity.

"Run them again, Johnnie," Didier commanded, slipping back in the gray plush chair, eyes half closed to bask again in Julian's aura. "Run them again."

"Star quality," he murmured softly to himself. "If you've got it, you don't need anything else—except perhaps a little bit of luck."

◆*Twelve*◆

HYDRA 1945

Nikolas Stanopolis stared at the thick blue envelope in astonishment. It carried a U.S. airmail stamp, and in the top left-hand corner was printed importantly:

MCCP Studios
7700 Melrose Avenue
Los Angeles, California

On the back of the envelope was a name that made Nikolas' heart leap with excitement, SPYROS MAEOPOLIS, PRESIDENT. With trembling hands he handed the letter to his wife, Elektra. It was addressed to her, but she smilingly handed it back to him.

"No, no, Nikolai, *you* open it."

He ripped open the letter, reading it with mounting elation:

MY DEAR NIECE ELEKTRA,

I was happy to receive news of Hydra, but so sorry to hear about your dear departed mother. My heart is very heavy at her passing, but I shall think of the good days when we played together as children in our sunlit paradise of a village.

My congratulations on your marriage to Nikolas Stanopolis. He sounds like a fine young man, and his interest in the business of filmmaking is most interesting.

If you are able to make your way one day to Los Angeles, I would be happy to see Nikolas as you have suggested, and perhaps give him an opportunity to work at this studio if he seems suitable.

Please remember me to Dmitri Andros at the old bar in the port —I am happy to know the old man survived the war and remains in good health.

I am enclosing a little gift which may help you if you decide to come to America.

Be happy, my dear young niece,

Cordially,
Your Uncle Spyros

"Oh, my God—Elektra, this is fantastic, wonderful news—America! He wants us to come to Los Angeles! Hollywood! Elektra, do you know what this means?"

"Yes, yes, Nikolai my love, I do." Elektra's face shone with joy as she looked up lovingly at her husband. "And look, Nikolai—look at this." Triumphantly she waved the check at him. "He's sent us money. My uncle is a truly wonderful gentleman."

"Money?" Nikolas grabbed it. "How much?" He looked at the unfamiliar writing on the check.

"Five hundred dollars!" Elektra gasped. *"Five hundred dollars.* That is a *fortune,* Nikolai. Now we can go to America, my darling, we can both go to Hollywood, and you can make great films."

But the passage to America was not as easy to negotiate as Nikolas and Elektra had hoped. A few days later, having changed the five-hundred-dollar check into drachma, Nikolas took the weekly ferry from Hydra to Athens to make preparations for their trip. His first disappointment was finding out that it was extremely difficult for a Greek national to visit America, and it involved a considerable amount of red tape. Then, in the offices of the new Olympic Airlines, he discovered that two airline fares to Los Angeles cost more than twice the amount that Mr. Makopolis had sent, and with a heavy heart Nikolas returned to Hydra to break the news to his wife.

"Never mind, Nikolai. You must go first to America, make Uncle Spyros give you a job, then in a few months I can follow you there."

"But I need you with me," said Nikolas sulkily, "I won't go without you, Elektra."

"No, Nikolai. No. You must go," the girl said firmly, pouring out two glasses of wine. "It will be too difficult for us if we both go now. You will be worried about me—about where we shall live—about too many things. First you must go and make money, then I will follow. Now eat your supper before it gets cold."

Nikolas marveled at his young wife's understanding, as she raised her wineglass in a shy toast. "To America, Nikolai, and to us."

Nikolas Stanopolis arrived at Los Angeles airport on a cold November night in 1945. Shivering in his thin cotton jacket, he stood outside the busy terminal, wondering what he should do. Why was it so cold? He had been told that California weather was warm, sunny, like the weather of the Greek islands. Well, they'd been wrong, those fools who had told him this. It was freezing; a light rain was falling, and a foggy, choking, dark mist wafted in from the Pacific.

Everyone seemed to be busy rushing somewhere, as if they had a purpose, knew exactly what they were doing, where they were going. Nikolas waited forlornly outside the terminal where the giant four-engine plane had brought him from New York. He felt lost and homesick as he thought of his beautiful Elektra, of his beloved Hydra, thankfully now slowly recovering from the war and the atrocities committed by Umberto Scrofo.

Scrofo—whenever he thought of that odious Italian, he felt blinding rage. One day he would find him and make him suffer as his mother, father, brothers, sisters and so many others on Hydra had. The desire for revenge consumed him almost as much as his desire to succeed in the film business. He had no clue as to where the Italian was living now: whether in fact he was still alive, but that did nothing to assuage his two burning ambitions.

Nikolas' English was limited, picked up mostly from an old man on Hydra who had once worked in London and from the movies, but he spoke enough to communicate his predicament to a porter. The man wore a red cap and a blue shirt and he had the black, shiny hair and olive skin of a fellow Greek; but he was Spanish, having himself only recently arrived from Barcelona. He took pity on Nikolas, escorting him two blocks to the sign DOWNTOWN BUS and chatting to him in a mixture of Spanish and English.

Nikolas stood shivering behind two round, gossiping women, not unlike the women of Hydra. When the bus arrived he gave the conductor five dollars, but became confused when asked for his destination. "Downtown," he said in heavily accented English. "Downtown L.A., please, sir."

The man shrugged, giving him a handful of change. "Downtown's a big place, kid," he said. "Whereabouts downtown?"

Nikolas had been given the name of a hotel by one of the Greek officials in New York. So he said proudly, "I'm going to Roosevelt Hotel, Hollywood Boulevard, in Hollywood, sir."

He was on his way.

The following morning Nikolas Stanopolis presented himself in a state of high excitement at the imposing entrance of MCCP Studios.

There was a flurry of activity around the high wrought-iron gates, but the uniformed guard told him bluntly, "Get lost, buddy, you're too early —no one's in the administration offices yet."

Nikolas pleadingly brandished his letter with the offer of employment written by Spyros but the gum-chewing guard barely raised his eyes from his copy of *Variety*. He barked something unintelligible in a harsh voice, but the body language was clear. Nikolas would not be able to get in, nor could he hang around the gates.

"I said, get lost, buddy," snarled the cop. "Git outta sight. *Now*."

In desperation, Nikolas crossed the road to sit on a bench plastered with advertising signs. Here at least he had a front-row view of the studio, and could see a good deal of what went on behind the iron gates. For several hours he sat completely fascinated, watching all manner of people come and go.

The costumes of the extras particularly enthralled him. Cowboys and Indians, peasants and soldiers, cops and robbers all milled about, fraternizing with one another. At eleven o'clock a group of beautiful showgirls, their long California legs encased in flesh-colored fishnet tights, trooped out from a huge building marked Stage Three.

Nikolas sat up, his eyes widening. These were women such as he had never seen before. The women of Greece wore modest, all-enveloping clothes—even Elektra covered herself from neck to calf. The thought of her body started to excite him as he looked longingly at the showgirls.

These women were crimson-lipped, their hair was marceled yellow, flame red or jet black. Hips swaying provocatively, they sashayed around the courtyard, laughing, smoking cigarettes, drinking Coca-Colas straight from the bottle. He saw the studio employees, men in work shirts and denim trousers, eyeing the girls lecherously as they passed, some of them making, he was sure, suggestive or lewd remarks at which the girls just laughed. Nikolas was shocked. Although he had seen women like this in movies, he was amazed that they could prance about half naked in public so brazenly, placidly ignoring the men who flirted with them.

One particular girl caught his eye. She was lissome, with luxuriant black hair tumbling halfway down her back, where it was caught up with scarlet feathers. Although slightly shorter than the other girls, she possessed the most magnificent breasts he'd ever seen, which were more than half exposed in their gold lamé bra.

Nikolas felt dry-mouthed with desire. How he missed Elektra. It had been more than a week since he'd last seen her, she who gave her body to him joyously yet modestly every night, every morning, and sometimes even in the afternoon. This buxom girl in red feathers reminded him slightly of Elektra, and shaking his head he walked down the boulevard, trying to rid himself of carnal thoughts, concentrating again on the problem of how to pass through the hallowed studio gates.

Spotting a telephone booth, he scanned his dog-eared letter to read the number, but unfamiliar with even a Greek telephone, it took him ten minutes and as many nickels and dimes before the number rang and a cheerful-sounding voice chirped, "MCCP Studios, good morning."

"Spyros Makopolis, please," said Nikolas, his Greek accent making his words practically incomprehensible to the telephone operator.

"Who?" she squawked.

"Spyros Makopolis." He enunciated each syllable carefully, as beads of sweat trickled down his forehead. The noon sun was at full blast and the kiosk felt like a furnace.

"Hold on a minute," the voice snapped.

"Mr. Makopolis' office." Another female voice, this one mellow and cool, was on the line. Gratefully Nikolas spoke in Greek, hoping that the voice would understand him. Several times he repeated his name, and the halting English words "My wife's uncle. I am nephew of him."

Finally the woman seemed to understand, but after her crisp "Just a moment, I'll see if Mr. Makopolis is available" the line went silent again.

For several more minutes Nikolas stood sweating in the cramped booth as occasionally voices came on the line instructing him to insert "Five cents, please." He was praying for Mr. Makopolis to answer before he gave up the last of his coins.

Suddenly the cool female voice was on the line again. Nikolas couldn't understand her, but he hoped salvation was at hand as she said, "I'm putting you through to Mr. Makopolis now, sir."

Then a deep friendly Greek voice came on the line: "Nikolas, Nikolas my dear boy, where are you?" Spyros spoke in Greek, his voice warm and welcoming. When Nikolas told him he was only across the street the old man said happily, "Come, I must see you now, Nikolas—I will leave a pass for you—come to see me right now." With enormous relief Nikolas knew then that everything was going to be all right.

However, things did not go as smoothly as Nikolas had expected. Instead of immediately giving him a job on a film set, as he'd hoped, Spyros Makopolis was blunt with him.

"There is no way that you could work on a film now, Nikolas."

"Why not, Uncle? You said you could give me a job."

"Well for one thing, you speak hardly any English, which, of course, will eventually be remedied," said Spyros. "For another, our unions are tighter than a rat's ass and newcomers to technical jobs are unwelcome, to say the least." Nikolas looked confused. "Listen, son—listen to me," said the old man. "The war has just ended. Young servicemen are pouring back to the States from Okinawa, Bataan and Anzio. A lot of these soldiers, sailors and marines worked at the studios before the war; now they find their jobs going to younger men, or sometimes to even older ones, who don't want to give them up." Spyros sighed. "And they're all having tricky times. All the studio heads are trying to repatriate and reinstate the men who fought for us. There's hardly any room for new blood, Nick."

Nick looked crestfallen and Spyros patted him comfortingly on the shoulder.

"Another major problem all the studios are facing is that they aren't sure what the public now wants to see at the movies."

Nick's face was puzzled. "Movies—they just love any movies, Uncle."

"No, my boy. Postwar audiences are tougher, much more discriminating than they were. The harsh realities of daily life are difficult. Appetites have become cloyed by the bland diet of musicals, comedies and lightweight films; audiences are demanding more robust fare. It's a problem, Nick—a big fat problem, my friend."

The old man was right. Escapist movies had been churned out during the war by every studio to boost the morale not only of the armed forces, but also of those who by reason of sex, physical disability or age had stayed at home to keep things running. "Serious" pictures were in vogue now. Some were blatant copies of Roberto Rossellini's *Open City,* a harshly neorealistic film about Rome during the war. Films about GIs returning to civilian life were extremely popular. *The Clock* with Robert Walker and Judy Garland, *Hail the Conquering Hero* with Eddie Bracken, and *I'll Be Seeing You* with Joseph Cotton and Ginger Rogers had all done well at the box office.

"Now MCCP is making its own neorealistic pictures, of course," said Spyros proudly. "We're on that bandwagon. And we're also making Westerns, gangster movies and musicals. We hope to entice whole new audiences into the cinemas, Nick, after all the studio is humming with

activity. We've got eighteen pictures shooting, twenty-two in post-production, and at least eighty in the development stage."

"That's wonderful, Uncle," said Nick, relieved. "Then you must have a
job for me?"

The old man sighed and fidgeted with some scripts on his cluttered
desk.

"I'm gonna do my best, m'boy," he boomed. "But you're gonna start at
the bottom, son—just like I did."

To Nikolas' disappointment the only position which Spyros Makopolis
could find for his nephew-in-law was one of the lowliest jobs on the lot—
in the mail room. But at least it was a job, a well-paid job, and Nick was
going to take the opportunities he was given and run with them. He was
ambitious, not only for himself and Elektra, but also for his secret plan.
The foul cloud of hatred that hovered in his subconscious had to be
expunged and there was only one way to do it.

◀❖ *Thirteen* ❖▶

LONDON 1945

THE END OF THE WAR meant little to Inès. It would hardly change her life
at all.

Every evening, and many afternoons, she received one of her gentlemen callers. She now had an elite clientele, consisting of several of the
most illustrious men in Great Britain. Unconcerned that by being a prostitute she was breaking the law, she was dedicated to self-improvement
and to money. The money was her key to escaping from this life, and she
saved every penny she could in her goal to live normally one day. She
loved to hear the rustle of the crisp five-pound notes which men gave
her. She squirreled them away in a copy of Stendhal's *Love,* thinking the
title ironically apt. She had painstakingly cut out a square center section
of the book, into the hollow of which she fitted her takings. *Love,* she
thought with a wry smile, was only to be found in her bookcase, along
with *Who's Who, Burke's Peerage, The Diaries of Samuel Pepys* and
dozens of richly illustrated books on art, British history, the great houses
and collections of England, and biographies of influential men and
women.

Every Friday at lunchtime, elegantly dressed in one of the outfits she
herself had made, she would take her thick wad of notes to Coutts Bank
in the Strand, ceremoniously handing it over to the clerk, who would
credit it to her ever-growing bank account. It had been Yves who had
opened an account for her at the prestigious bank whose customers numbered not only members of the Royal Family but some of Inès' own

clients. How Yves had managed this was still a mystery to her, since a client's breeding was often as important to Coutts as his wealth.

It gave her enormous pleasure, when shopping in the exclusive Burlington Arcade or in Bond Street shops, to pay for her purchases with a Coutts check. Certainly none of the salespeople would ever have imagined that this poised young beauty was a common prostitute. She looked, dressed and behaved like a lady. Although only nineteen, Inès possessed the manners and sophistication of a woman far older; she now prided herself on a quiet elegance which spoke of breeding and old money. It was one of the attributes which most intrigued her clients when they took her to dine at the 400, the Caprice or the Coq d Or. In her perfectly cut chic clothes she seemed to belong in these places far more than many of the English matrons in their frumpish prewar dresses. As she snuggled into the womblike comfort of these establishments jealous glances were often thrown her way. Inès had the Frenchwoman's innate understanding of clothes, and was always beautifully and stylishly dressed in outfits mostly created by herself. During the day she lived the life of a woman of leisure. Sometimes she strolled up Shaftesbury Avenue on her way to the Queens Theatre or the Globe to see the latest play by Terence Rattigan, Noël Coward or Emlyn Williams, passing the Windmill Theatre, where she would glance at the front-of-house photographs of the seminude showgirls and the leering comics.

Now she never thought of herself as a whore, but as a courtesan, and had improved herself to suit her new role. She had decided to keep her once-blond hair dark. It framed her pale, high-cheekboned face with its slanting blue cat's eyes and sculpted chin. She had grown taller in London, her body svelte and toned, her legs those of a thoroughbred, her breasts magnificent. Underneath all her elegance, her mound of golden pubic hair was trimmed to a heart shape, which further fascinated her devoted clients.

Courtesan. She liked that word. A courtesan was a woman who shared the fantasies of a man's secret life, who knew everything about his occupation and all that it entailed. She knew about his wife, what that particular woman liked in bed, and what she didn't; she knew which schools his children attended, and even what they wanted to be when they grew up. She knew what wines he preferred, how dry he liked his martinis, how strong his whiskey and soda. She knew his favorite foods and sometimes, for a special client, she would prepare them for him perfectly. She knew which books he read, which plays he'd seen, in which sports he participated, what politics he favored, but most important of all, she knew what excited him in bed.

Inès was quick to discover what a man liked sexually. Most of the time it wasn't anything that he couldn't get from his wife, except that from what she'd discovered, most English wives were not keen on oral sex. Thanks to Yves this was one of Inès' specialties. Most women wanted to please their husbands but often didn't have the time, energy or knowledge.

A sexually inept female is a turnoff to most men, and Inès became accustomed to hearing many clients complain that their wives just "lay there like stone and never responded." She could bring a man to orgasm within minutes. When men kissed her breasts, or her mound of Venus, running their fingers and tongues into her most intimate places, arousing her, they made her body shake with lust, for Inès had become an accomplished actress. She made sure her clients thought that they were exciting her, and that excited them more than anything else. They kept returning to her, often referring their friends to her. But Inès was careful about whom she entertained. She had never forgotten the perversions of the Italian General, and in her cozy, well-decorated flat she interviewed prospective clients carefully, questioning them as strictly as a duchess employing a chambermaid.

Politicians, members of Parliament, aristocrats, industrialists, men of finance, power and position, these were the men she entertained. Credentials were essential. Most of them became entranced with her, more than one proposing matrimony, but although Inès was ready for that, she knew she had to fall in love. Visions of true love haunted her. She still thought about Yves, dreamed about him, his laughter, his magic, his crinkly eyes and his soft hair. And she also dreamed too often of the Italian whom she had killed that April morning, awakening with a scream on her lips, vividly reliving the horror. She never allowed a man to spend the night with her during the week, and only for her most special clients would she consent to spend a weekend away. In her search for love she found all men lacking, and the more she saw of their weaknesses and foibles the less she felt she would ever meet the right one for her.

Armistice night she spent alone, in front of her sewing machine, working on a velvet Maggy Rouff suit which she was copying from *Vogue*. Inès felt more truly alone than she ever had before. All her clients were with their families and friends, and she had no one with whom to share this momentous night. Not a man, not a woman friend, not even a cat. From her windows she could hear the boisterous sound of revelers outside singing, laughing, hooting with joy.

On the wireless the excitement in the voice of the normally severe BBC commentator was contagious. The BBC was broadcasting from every European capital, so that their listeners could hear how the rest of the free world was celebrating victory.

She sat quietly working, listening to a French-accented voice describing the frenzy of the Parisian crowds. When the announcer started to describe with poetic reverence the beauty of Notre Dame Cathedral completely lit up, glowing like an exquisite gothic fairy-tale castle, and surrounded by French patriots singing the "Marseillaise" at the top of their lungs, tears ran down her face for the very first time since Yves had left.

"Paris," she whispered, as her fingers deftly cut cotton and threaded her needle. "Paris. I wonder if I will ever see you again. I wonder if there's anything left for me there anymore."

❖*Fourteen*❖

CALABRIA 1945

UMBERTO SCROFO RETURNED to his native village in Calabria a very rich man. With his spoils of war he was able to purchase the land to build an enormous house on the highest part of the mountainous region. The terrain was harsh, rocky, difficult to farm, but since the whole region was so desperately poor and even more so as a result of the war, Umberto found no shortage of peasant labor to cultivate his unproductive land.

Because of his now enormous assets and possessions, he was able to wield great power in Calabria. Not, however, as great as the power of the Cosa Nostra; they still ruled the lives and destinies of those around them with total and unquestionable authority. But Scrofo had more than enough power to guarantee him the serenity he longed for.

Inside his new fortress he had built a screening room where he reveled in his passion for the latest Hollywood movies. Most nights he sat alone in the velvet-tented room watching carefully, admiring the beauty of the young blond actresses he desired: young virginal types like Bonita Granville, June Haver, Mary Beth Hughes were his great favorites. Girls who gave the illusion of being fresh from puberty. Often, as he watched them, his Lilliputian penis would stiffen and he would pleasure himself.

Since his "accident" with the French whore in Paris, he had rarely indulged in sex. He had found the olive-skinned, black-haired women of Hydra unappealing, preferring his own secret fantasies to coupling with them.

In addition to the Hollywood films, he possessed a large collection of blue movies imported from Scandinavia. The cool Nordic beauties who frolicked naked in sauna baths and pastoral streams could always arouse him.

As he rested his overstuffed body on an overstuffed couch one afternoon, he looked up from the Christie's catalogue he was flicking through and saw, tending his flowerbeds, a young blonde of exquisite beauty. She looked up, caught his eye, then blushed and looked away. Scrofo found her beauty and innocence exciting. It was the first time in years that he had felt such a strong desire for a woman, and it stimulated him into action.

On making inquiries he discovered that she was the niece of his gardener. Her parents had been killed in a road accident and she had been adopted by the gardener and his wife. Her name was Silvana, and she was seventeen years old.

Umberto insisted that the girl be given a job inside the house as parlor-maid. It would be her job to dust and clean some of the treasured objets d'art that glittered on the tables and in the display cabinets of his villa.

Every day Silvana performed her tasks happily, humming quietly, a smile playing around her gently curved, soft pink lips, blushing whenever she caught Umberto's intense stare.

Soon he became obsessed by the girl, his thoughts full of her breasts, her innocent gray eyes, the way her body undulated underneath the plain blue calico house dress. He ordered another uniform to be made for her by one of the village women—the costume of a French maid, just as he had seen in so many movies. Silvana was embarrassed to be seen in it, but Signor Scrofo insisted, and, after all, he was her respected employer.

One afternoon Silvana shyly entered Umberto's drawing room with a timid knock on the door. She was wearing sheer black hose, a short frilly black skirt, a white organdy apron and, perched on her abundant yellow curls, a little mobcap such as might be worn by an eighteenth-century maiden in a picture by Boucher. As she knelt to dust the legs of a console table, Umberto could see her lacy panties, and he caught a tantalizing glimpse of succulent white thighs above black stockings.

He strode to the double doors, quietly closing and locking them. Silvana was busy cleaning around the gilded crevices, and cried out in fright when Umberto crept up behind her, grabbing her breasts through the flimsy silk of her blouse.

"No, please, no, Signor," she whimpered, her frightened eyes exciting him so much that he thought his tiny cock would burst through his trousers.

"Yes, yes, my dear, yes, *now*," he rasped, his harsh wheezing voice thick as he ripped open her blouse, exposing her mouth watering, rose-tipped breasts. "I must have you *now*, Silvana—I must. Be a good girl now—I won't hurt you."

Her terrified screams continued to inflame him as he wrestled her down onto the flowered Aubusson carpet. The velvet curtains were drawn against the afternoon sun, and the thick stone walls were as good as soundproof.

Umberto's gross body pinioned her to the floor and no one heard Silvana's cries as he raped and sodomized her throughout the afternoon. Blood ran down her face and back as he beat her, and after a while she mercifully lost consciousness. She reminded him of that French tart in Paris, and this drove him to hurt her more.

"Whore," he said viciously, slapping the girl's unconscious face. "Cheap whore, you deserve this."

At last he was finished; Silvana lay slumped in front of the fireplace, her uniform in tatters, her face bruised and puffed from weeping and his beatings, her body covered in blood. Umberto looked at her coldly as he zipped up his trousers. Her eyes opened, looking at him pleadingly. She was disgusting to him now. No longer desirable—a discarded toy.

"*Signor*—help me, please," she said, crawling across the carpet, her words muffled by her swollen lips.

"Get out," Umberto said curtly, mopping his hairless sweating head with a silk handkerchief and rearranging his clothes.

"*Out*—now." He turned away from her, pouring himself a brandy with a gratified smile. "I've finished with you, little slut."

So—he gloated to himself. He could still perform, and very well too. This was the first time in over two years that he had done something like this with a woman. Ever since that creature in Paris had robbed him of most of his sexual desire with her vicious attempt on his life. But that little whore hadn't succeeded. He was still a man, a stallion, a stud, in spite of the tiny penis which had caused so much mirth in the girls he had attempted to make love to when he was young.

And he was still young, was he not? He preened in the mirror, his eyes not seeing the bloated features, the thick lips, the short, scarred neck. All he saw was a facsimile of Benito Mussolini—a soldier, a patriot, a man of power, irresistible to women. Alas now dead, hanged by his own people in disgrace. But Umberto was too pleased with himself to dwell on Mussolini's untimely death. He felt his sexual vigor to be in full and potent flower again. He was ready to take other women now. Many others. He didn't give a thought to Silvana; she meant less than nothing now that he had had her. But perhaps she had a pretty friend, a sister, or a cousin? He would find out.

The following night as Umberto lay asleep in the canopied Empire bed which was reputed to have once belonged to Napoleon, the locked bedroom doors burst open, and four men, hats pulled low over their eyes, surrounded him. They said nothing as they pulled him roughly out of bed, nothing as he called out hoarsely for his servants. Where were they, why didn't they answer him? Where were all his bodyguards? His entourage of lackeys? But no one answered his screams for mercy, and the house was dark and silent as a tomb as the men bustled him roughly down the marble staircase, out across his manicured lawns, ghostly green in the moonlight, down to the rough pebbled beach.

Whimpering with terror, the scar on his neck throbbing, the soles of his feet bleeding from the jagged rocks, Umberto was experiencing a fear unknown to him before.

His hands and feet were tied tightly together with rope and he was tossed roughly into a small fishing boat resting on the shoreline. The four men climbed into another boat and began towing Umberto's tiny craft out to sea, into the notoriously dangerous currents which swept down the coast. They grinned in the reflected moonlight, but their eyes were dead.

"What are you doing to me?" Umberto choked, feeling his throat constrict. "Where are you taking me?"

"We're sending you to die, scum," the leader snarled. "Die pig, alone and scared. If you live to come back to this place ever again, we'll find you and we'll kill you in a way that will make you wish you had never entered this world—you have our word on that."

One of the men then unhooked the tow rope and the swift current started to carry Umberto farther and farther out to sea. "Why? Why are you doing this?" he bleated. "What have I done?"

"This is for Silvana," the tallest man shouted harshly. "We are her blood brothers. If you return to Calabria we will cut off your balls, stuff them in your mouth, and then kill you—and you'll be begging us to do that by the time we're finished. Antonio Rostranni has given us his blessing to do so, and he wants to watch." The men laughed coarse, loutish laughter, and Umberto froze. Rostranni, the most feared name in the whole of southern Italy. The Padrino himself; the Mafia chief whose word became unquestioned law. If the girl Silvana was indeed related to someone in the Cosa Nostra, he could consider himself extremely lucky that they hadn't slit his throat while he slept.

The boat was swept farther out to sea, and the four men sat motionless, staring after it. Umberto then noticed the oars, an earthenware jug of water and some dry biscuits, provisions for an existence of a few days, if that, and only if he could find a way to remove the ropes which tied his wrists together so tightly that his arms were starting to go dead.

"Where am I to go?" he whispered. "I can't survive in this boat. How can I save myself? Where do you want me to go?"

"Go to hell," the leader jeered as the two boats drifted farther and farther apart. "You belong with the perverts there, with the other scum, go to hell, pig."

There was much rejoicing in the small Calabrian village when the hated Umberto Scrofo suddenly disappeared. Although foul play was suspected, not a single one of Umberto's numerous servants had either seen or heard anything the night that he had mysteriously disappeared. In spite of extensive police investigations, no trace of him could be found. Several months later the remains of a small fishing boat were found washed up on the northern shore of an Italian beach. It was smashed to pieces and contained only a few tattered scraps of what the police identified as Scrofo's clothes. With that evidence, Umberto Scrofo was then declared officially dead.

His palatial mansion was sold, and his magnificent possessions were divided between the remaining members of his family in Calabria. The cousins, aunts and uncles who had mocked and despised him as a child found themselves the heirs to the glorious pictures and booty which he had scavenged from Paris and Hydra.

A funeral of sorts was held, which the family attended, but no one could have been said to mourn him. Very soon he was completely forgotten by everyone in the world except for Inès Juillard and Nikolas Stanopolis. Neither of them could ever forget him.

PART
TWO

❧ *One* ❧

Elektra knew that life wasn't going to be easy for her in America. Nikolas had sent for her about three months after he'd arrived, and now she was almost beside herself with excitement as she caught a glimpse of his tall wiry body leaning against a pillar inside the arrivals hall at L.A. airport.

"Nikolai, oh, my darling Nikolai—I can't believe it's really you—" she said ecstatically as she threw herself into her husband's open arms, which were not as warmly welcoming as she'd expected them to be.

"What's the matter, Nikolai?" she asked tentatively as he pulled away from her embrace with apparent embarrassment.

"Elektra, I'd like you to meet Errol," he said in Greek, gesturing towards an enormous black man wearing a burgundy uniform, trimmed with an excessive amount of gold braid.

"Welcome to L.A., Missus Nicky," beamed the man as he stood to attention. "Sure are glad to have you here—our Mr. Nick he's bin pinin' away, he never stops talkin' about you."

"This is Errol—Uncle Spyros' chauffeur. Uncle Spyros has lent us his personal car today. He wanted you to have a special welcome to this wonderful country."

Elektra nodded in silence, wishing that Nikolas had come to meet her alone. The chauffeur seemed pleasantly friendly, but Elektra was shy, and she had wanted to be reunited with her husband in private.

A cheerful porter carried her only shabby piece of luggage through the jostling crowds as they all walked out to the sidewalk, where Elektra's mouth opened wide with amazement. Waiting at the curb was the longest black car she had ever seen. There were no vehicles of any kind on Hydra, and she had hardly seen any cars before except on occasional trips to Athens. She looked fearfully at the busy street where cars, buses and taxis sped by at terrifying speeds, and laughing pedestrians seemed to defy death as they dashed between them.

"Come on, Elektra." She thought that Nick's voice seemed to have a more authoritative edge to it than before. "Hurry up, stop gawking, we must get to the house before dark. Aunt Olympia has prepared a Greek feast to welcome you."

Clumsily Elektra climbed into the cavernous backseat of the Cadillac, conscious that her skirt had bunched itself up well above her knees. Blushing furiously, she pulled it down and huddled in a corner, looking anxiously out the rear window to see if the porter had brought her suitcase.

Nick jumped in effortlessly, and gave her a brief hug. He held her hand, talking to her excitedly in their own language for a few minutes, but then he became involved in a long conversation with Errol in English. The men were laughing loudly as Errol seemed to be telling some kind of amusing story. Elektra leaned her head back onto the lush leather upholstery, closing weary eyes. She hadn't slept for days. It had been a long and exhausting trip to California, but she was here at last on the other side of the world. She hoped it wouldn't take long to become as settled and Americanized as the loving husband who had left her only three months ago.

Olympia Makopolis was a warm, motherly, comforting woman so like the women of Hydra that Elektra felt immediately at home with her. In spite of her husband's enormous wealth and position in Hollywood, Mrs. Makopolis still insisted on cooking and preparing everything herself, and her vast dining table was laden with familiar dishes from their homeland. Great plates of taramasalata, dishes of baby shrimp, squid and pompano, *tzadziki,* vine leaves stuffed with meat and rice, succulent baby lamb with eggplant, crisp lettuce tossed with diced pieces of goat cheese, *bourekia* wrapped in pastry, and freshly baked bread, mixed with the powerful aroma of freshly chopped garlic in the *skordalia* sauce—a sauce so overpoweringly pungent that it was considered bad manners to eat it before a social event unless everyone was having it. Jugs of cooled white wine had just been put on the table when Olympia heard the crunch of the limousine on the graveled driveway.

"Welcome, my dear Elektra, I'm *so* happy to see my cousin's daughter at last," said Olympia, embracing Elektra warmly and feeling an immediate rush of affection for the shy girl.

"Come, come—we eat right away—you must be starving." She looked approvingly at Elektra's full-bosomed and rounded figure, in such contrast to the greyhound-sleek body of her very pretty niece Vicky Zolotos, who was Americanized to within an inch of her life.

"Vicky, this is Elektra, my wife," said Nikolas proudly.

"I'm thrilled to meet you, honey, Nicky has talked about you *so* much," gushed Vicky, her long shiny blond pageboy, tightly belted green gabardine suit, and tiny matching hat tipped over one ravishing turquoise eye making her appear to Elektra like a fashion plate straight from the pages of *Vogue.*

Elektra cringed. She couldn't understand a single word the girl said, even though Nicky, who seemed to possess such newfound confidence, quickly translated.

"Vicky also works in the mail room at the studio," he said rapidly. "Her father is one of Uncle Spyros' board members—she's just out of university—her mother is Greek and she's a cousin of Uncle Spyros. She's been helping me learn English and we're both slaves of the studio system, aren't we, Vicky?" He flashed a confident grin at the beautiful girl who made Elektra feel hopelessly drab, dowdy and old-fashioned. Elektra's long serge skirt, sensible brogues and heavy lisle stockings were hardly a match for this American beauty's slim nylon-clad legs, sculpted bosom and perfectly made-up face. Although she thought that they must be about the same age, Elektra felt hideous and inadequate beside her.

Olympia had lived in California for nearly thirty years, but she was still a simple Greek woman at heart. Seeing Elektra, so small, frightened and awed by the sumptuousness of these alien surroundings, reminded her of herself three decades ago, and Olympia made up her mind to help this girl to make the difficult adjustment to the American way of life.

Later that night, as Nikolas gently undressed his wife, whispering passionate endearments to her in the language she understood, Elektra felt herself beginning to relax at last. The tension in her knotted muscles began to ebb away as her husband's sensual fingers slowly caressed her. Gently his hands encircled her breasts and his fingers as gentle as butterfly wings touched her nipples, causing gasps of joy to spring from her throat. Nikolai, her husband, the only man she had ever been with—the only man she could ever love—was still hers. He loved her. Now she knew that she had nothing to fear in America.

Nikolas Stanopolis, with a natural aptitude for languages, had learned English surprisingly fast. Now not only could he read and write with few mistakes, but he had become a master of American slang, almost a necessity in the movie business.

But for Elektra, adjusting to American life was a struggle. Everything confused her—the language, the hectic pace of Los Angeles, the motorcars, and the airplanes which shattered the afternoon peace of her siestas. The gadgets in her kitchen might as well have come from another planet, and the fast, streamlined supermarkets all made her feel a hopeless wreck. She felt stupid, dumb, completely alien to this modern world.

In spite of Olympia's patient coaching, and in spite of the beautiful, bright and breezy Vicky coming to dinner several times a week to help her with her English, Elektra couldn't manage to grasp more than a few words. Desperately she studied phrase books and dictionaries, read magazines and newspapers, but her brain, already befuddled with trying to cope with electric cookers, washing machines and refrigerators, and trying to cook with tinned and frozen ingredients foreign to her, simply couldn't cope. Nikolas, Vicky and Olympia insisted that she listen to the news programs, plays and variety shows on the radio, but the foreign language was still a foreign language to her. She tried gallantly to make herself understood at the enormous Food Giant supermarket on Canon Drive where Olympia had insisted she shop. Numbly, pushing her shopping cart around the endless aisles stacked high with colorful products, none of which she'd ever heard of, she was jostled by confident wholesome women in crisp shirtwaist dresses, their faces made up, their hair coiffed into soft curls or covered by a becoming hat. Elektra couldn't even begin to think of shopping for new clothes, even though Nick asked her when she was going to get rid of her dowdy dresses.

"Why don't you buy some new clothes, honey?" he asked her one night, grimacing as he saw the overcooked meatballs and eggplant croquettes which she'd done her best to prepare on the incomprehensible modern cooker. "We can afford it; I'm making good money now."

They were sitting at a shiny yellow Bakelite kitchen table in one of many little bungalows Spyros reserved for his nearest and dearest. There was a tight enclave of Makopolis relations living on the land which bordered his estate. Vicky Zolotos lived in one with a female cousin, Olympia's three sisters lived in another, and Spyros' uncle and aunt lived next door to them. Unfortunately for Elektra, all of these Greek immigrants seemed to have had no difficulty at all in learning English. They chattered away effortlessly, switching back and forth between English and Greek with the practiced ease of people who had totally adjusted to both cultures.

Nikolas was glued to Jack Benny on the radio, laughing at his jokes until tears ran down his face while Elektra silently ladled the hardened, lumpy meatballs onto his plate.

"You used to cook these so well in Hydra," he said during the commercial break. "What happened?"

"I'm sorry," mumbled Elektra, close to tears. "I just can't get this cooker to work."

Nikolas took another bite, and made a face. "You've got to adjust to the modern world, Elektra, this is 1946, the war's over now, the men are all back, everyone is competing in America for jobs—position—everything. You've got to compete too, Elektra—you must—you've got to try."

"I can't." She slumped down at the table with her head in her hands, starting to weep. "I just *can't* learn English—I can't cook with this stove —I don't fit in here, Nikolas. I don't belong in America. I want to go home—back to Hydra. That's where I really belong."

Nikolas stroked her hair sympathetically. He loved her very much, but he couldn't help but compare her simple rounded peasant looks to the glamorous women he came into contact with daily at the studio. Vicky was always flirting with him, joking in that sassy cute way so many American girls seemed to have. He liked it. He liked Vicky too, and why shouldn't he? After all, she was his distant cousin, albeit a couple of dozen or so times removed.

"Try, Elektra—please try—for my sake," he said, tuning back into another wisecrack from Jack Benny and Rochester.

"I'll *try*, Niko," sobbed Elektra despairingly, "I will, but I don't think I'll ever succeed. I don't have the ear."

"You must be patient, and try harder," said Nick firmly. "You *must*, Elektra—for us—for our family. Our future is here, Elektra—in

America, in Hollywood—with these people. I'm going to become a director one day—Spyros has promised, I'm going to be a great director. This is our life here now, Elektra, and we're never going back to live in Greece. Never!"

Elektra nodded, trying to control her welling tears. "I know," she said sadly, thinking of the mountains, the sea, the beauty of her island. She felt a great lump in her throat and her heart was heavy as she realized that they might well never see Hydra again. "I will try," she whispered. "I'll really try, Nikolai."

And she did. She studied for hours each day. Olympia became a mother hen to her, and Vicky, if not quite like an older sister, at least helped her with her wardrobe.

"You've gotta get out of those dowdy duds, kiddo," she insisted. "You look like a total frump—it's time for you to get hip." She dragged Elektra off to Saks to sharpen her image in spite of Elektra's protestations that they simply couldn't afford to buy such expensive new clothes. But Vicky took no notice at all and they returned from their shopping trip laden with boxes and bags full of pretty cotton shirtwaist dresses, slim Capri pants, frilly blouses and shorts, most of which Elektra vowed that she'd be too embarrassed to wear.

Vicky laughingly contradicted her. "Honey, when the weather gets hot here you're gonna *live* in those shorts, and you'll wonder how you could ever have put on those old fuddy-duddy long black skirts."

After a very long time Elektra finally managed to learn to speak English, albeit falteringly, but she never felt completely comfortable with it. She still read, with pangs of homesickness, the Greek newspapers and magazines which were sent regularly to Olympia Makopolis. She never really found any American friends, preferring the company of Olympia and her three sisters to the wives and girlfriends of Nikolas' co-workers. But she both worshiped and respected her husband, and to her he was king.

As for the luscious Vicky, she still terrified Elektra with her stylish clothes, glossy pageboy and fast talk. Elektra suspected that she would never feel at ease with her. She still felt left out when Nikolas and Vicky chattered together for hours about the film business, sharing industry gossip and jokes together in the American slang with which they both seemed so comfortable.

Elektra's happiness flowered completely the year after her arrival in Los Angeles only when the first of her beautiful babies was born. Then she was in her element, taking care of little Alexis totally, eschewing the nannies and nurses which Vicky and Olympia recommended. To Vicky's shocked amazement, Elektra breast-fed the baby until he was more than a year old and she was already pregnant with her second.

I will never become Americanized, particularly now with my baby boy and girl to look after, thought Elektra, looking at her bonny plump reflection in her dressing table mirror. She didn't have time for sessions at the hairdresser or for afternoons browsing at Saks or Magnin. She was perfectly happy in their little bungalow with her lively children and her beloved husband, who alas, wasn't there as much as she would have liked. He was becoming more and more involved with his work at the studio, and although he was a good husband and a loving father to the babies, Elektra knew that work was fast becoming the most important thing in his life.

Elektra woke up gasping and choking, unable to breathe. It was pitch dark in the bedroom and strong hands were clamped around her neck trying to squeeze the life from her. The figure was on top of her, the wiry fingers so tight around her throat that had she not awakened she knew it would have been only a matter of seconds before she was asphyxiated by this maniac. She tried to scream for help but no sounds would come. Where was Nikolas? Where was he? And how had this intruder got into their bedroom?

Elektra fought for her life, hearing nothing but the harsh breathing of her assailant. She knew she had to attack his eyes before she lost consciousness but his body was strong and pinned her to the bed. She struck out blindly with the remains of her strength where she thought his eyes were and to her horror heard the man exclaim as her fingernails raked his flesh:

"You bastard. You fucking scumbag—this is it, pig. I've got you now and I'm going to kill you."

In panic Elektra heard her husband's voice screaming this litany of hatred at her. Nikolas trying to kill her. Oh, dear God, thought Elektra as unconsciousness threatened to engulf her. God, no. How could he do this? Her gentle, kind Nikolas. Was he mad? Weakly she tried to cry out, but realized that she was completely powerless. She was going to die. She was going to die at the hands of her husband—the man she loved. She could feel the last thread of consciousness breaking . . .

"Mama—Papa—what are you doing?"

The bedroom light suddenly illuminated little Alexis standing at the door in his pajamas, his eyes wide with fear as he saw his father straddling his mother, hands gripping her throat.

"No, Papa, no," the boy screamed, running to the bed and tugging at his father.

As if from some great distance Nikolas heard his son's voice and opened his eyes which had been tightly closed in rage. When he saw what he had been doing to his wife he stopped with a scream of terror.

"My God, Elektra, oh, Jesus, what have I done?"

The baby girl now toddled into the bedroom holding her teddy bear and crying, wakened by the noise.

Elektra moaned and drew deep, gasping breaths into her aching lungs.

"God, Elektra! Oh, God, are you all right?" cried Nikolas. He was weeping now with the horror of what he had done. The two children were crying and his beloved wife was groaning in agony.

"I—I'm all right, Nikolas," Elektra managed to say as she tried to sit up.

He pressed a glass of water to her white lips.

"God, I almost killed you." Nikolas looked like a man possessed. His hair was disheveled and his whole body was shaking.

"Go back to bed, children, Mama is all right," Elektra managed to croak. "Everything's going to be all right now."

"It was a nightmare," cried Nikolas after he had tucked the children safely back in bed and sought the sanctuary of Elektra's arms. "I thought you were Scrofo," he wept. "It was a nightmare, Elektra, I didn't mean it. You know that, don't you?"

"Of course," she soothed. "Of course I do, Nikolas."

"I thought about Mama's death," he said softly. "Then I saw him and I tried to kill him, but it was *you!* Oh, God, Elektra, can you ever forgive me, can you?"

"Of course I can—of course," she soothed again.

"The dream was so vivid," he murmured, his body still shaking, and sweating. "Where do you think he is now?"

"You mean Scrofo?" she said gently, holding him safely.

"Yeah, Gourouni—the bastard. Commander Umberto Scrofo."

Nick's eyes began to gleam with rage again in the dim light from the bedside lamp.

Elektra was surprised that he was still so obsessed with Scrofo. They had been in America for nearly four years. Surely his anger must be waning by now?

"Don't think about him, Nikolai," she murmured. "That's all over now —it's all in the past."

"Mother of God, Elektra—here we are in America, in this nice house with my good job—the American Dream." His face was contorted with fury. "And that fucking piece of scum is probably still alive somewhere." He pounded the pillow with all the force of his frustrated anger. "The murdering bastard is still alive, do you realize that? Do you?"

Elektra tried to calm him down again but he was like a wild man.

"Sshh, you'll wake the babies again," she admonished. "Stop thinking about Scrofo, Nikolai—you must stop—you'll make yourself ill."

"Elektra." He turned to face her, his eyes wide and full of passion. "I said it that day on Hydra, but I *know* it now—one day I'm going to find that bastard—and I'm going to kill him with my bare hands."

"Sshh—no, Nikolai, no." She tried to hold him but he leaped out of bed and stood before her—a naked avenging angel.

"I swear it—I swear it on the lives of our children—on the memory of my mother—I'm going to find Umberto Scrofo and I'm going to kill him if it's the last thing on earth I do."

Ever the nepotist, Spyros Makopolis had taken Nikolas and Elektra to his bosom. He often invited them to join his family at their table, which was always groaning with Greek delicacies. At work he pushed Nikolas for promotion after promotion. From the mail room he went on to become a gofer in the publicity department; from there he became assistant to the assistant editor in the cutting rooms. He stayed there for nearly four years until he understood everything there was to know about editing, splicing, dubbing and the entire technical process of filmmaking. Finally he graduated to the floor itself. Third assistant director, second assistant director, first assistant director, location manager, production manager, and finally, joy of joys, Spyros called him into his office one day to announce the promotion he ached for more than any other: director.

Spyros sat behind a desk covered with scripts, puffing on his ever-present Havana.

"Take a look at *that,* kid," he beamed, throwing a bound blue script at him. "Something special, something real cute and zany."

Eagerly Nick caught it, but his face dropped as he saw the title. *"Bobby Soxers in Space?"* Nick looked astonished. "What's this, Uncle—do you want me to give you a budget breakdown on it?"

"No! No!" the old man boomed out. "No, my boy, I want you to *direct* it."

"Direct *Bobby Soxers in Space?* My God! You've gotta be kidding, Uncle." Nick didn't know whether to laugh or cry. For years he had been yearning to direct a feature film—any feature—but *Bobby Soxers in Space?* Even he had his pride. The title was a complete joke, and the content probably much worse.

"My boy, I won't lie to you," Spyros said with a sigh. "Not to put too fine a point on it, our studio is in deep and rising shit."

"How can it be? According to the trades, our last five movies grossed millions. Is that a lie?"

Spyros nodded sadly. "Alas, my boy—the publicity department did a sterling job in telling the world that our last five films did well. I must admit, however, it's not true. In fact it's a fucking lie."

He paused, dabbing his florid face with an enormous silk handkerchief, choosing his next words with care. "Understand, my boy, that after the war, MCCP could do no wrong—no wrong at all.

"Spyros Makopolis could do no wrong, either," he continued. "As the major stockholder, president and chief executive in charge of production, I was the golden boy to all the bankers and brokers."

Nick listened, aware that his uncle was under intense strain. This was obvious from the puffy liverish bags under his eyes and in the way he leaned heavily on the vast desk to relight his cigar.

"What happened, Uncle?"

"Television happened," Spyros spat out bitterly. "Tee bloody Vee is *destroying* the film business, Nick, *ruining* it. Do you realize that after the war, *ninety* million people a *week* went to the cinema? You know how many go now?" he asked accusingly. "Three years ago, in 1950, only *sixty million* people a week. Down to only sixty million. It's terrible, Nick, just terrible, and it's getting worse all the time."

"But it's not just our studio——it's all of them, surely?" asked Nick.

"Yeah, yeah—Zanuck, Warner, Cohn—we're all in the same kind of shit. Our jobs are hanging by a thread, Nick. If this decline in movie-going continues, by the end of this decade movie studios as we now know them will be practically extinct."

"But I don't understand. Surely this space movie is just another piece of shit," Nick said. "Who the hell is going to see something like that?"

"It's something *different!*" cried Spyros excitedly, getting up from behind the desk to throw a beefy arm around his nephew's shoulders. "Something new, something zany, crazy—a novelty for the kids that adults will love, too. They'll love it, Niko, I know it. Now look, I know it's low budget, but if you can bring this picture in for one hundred fifty thousand, kid, I can guarantee it will gross at least ten times that. We'll bring it out for Easter vacation—the college students will love it. You'll be a hero, my boy, a hero." He patted Nick benevolently and smiled broadly at him. "Especially to me."

"But, Uncle, why do you want *me* to direct it when I've never directed before? I mean, I'm honored, sure, but what about Weston or Ratoff, surely they'd be better?"

"I have to be honest with you, Niko—none of them will touch it with my left testicle," Spyros admitted. "Only a newcomer can do this movie, Niko. Someone fresh, young, with new ideas. Someone who understands the youth market. It's a break for you, kid, a big break."

No one would touch it? This was bad, very bad. Nick had expected to start by directing low-budget films, yes, but hopefully more of the quality of *The Window* or *Laura*. With *Bobby Soxers in Space,* he could quickly become the laughingstock of the business; then he'd never be able to get a decent movie to direct. Hollywood was a tough, snobbish town where you were only as good as your last film. If that film was a turkey, or, even worse, a lemon, no one was likely to take another chance on using you again.

"Do I have to do it, Uncle?"

"Yes, yes, you can *make* something of this, boy—I know you can," growled the old man. "This is your big break, Nick. I could give it to one of the young contract directors but I'm giving it to *you*. It's not a bad script, it's cute. You can shoot it in Death Valley with a non-union crew and some of our contract players—it'll only take four weeks. If you do well, there'll be other scripts—I promise you, Niko. For the sake of the old country, for your mama, for all of us Greeks who must stick together —you direct this picture and there'll be plenty more, I promise you. Plenty. You've got the talent, boy. Just do this for me, and for the studio."

That night, with a heavy heart, Nicky began to read the ridiculous script. Hidden beneath the tired old clichés, the heavy-handed humor and the wornout gags, there were grains of originality—a modern twist which might well be hilarious. If he could get a decent rewrite from one of the contract hacks who wasn't a lush, use some of his own ideas—and he was never short of those—and get a couple of halfway decent actors, maybe *Bobby Soxers in Space* could turn out to be the sow's ear which became the silk purse.

❖ *Two* ❖

Fㅇㅇ seven consecutive years Julian Brooks had been one of Britain's top box-office stars, each film propelling him to even greater cinematic glory. The fans simply could not get enough of him. His films were nearly all in the romantic adventure genre, and men and women alike doted on them.

His first film, *The Merry Monarch*, had been the precursor of his swash-buckling roles, and he'd continued to play a succession of brave adventurers and heroes on locations as far away as the Sahara Desert, the Amazon and the South China Sea. Didier Armande had signed him to a viselike contract, and in spite of the fact that almost every major studio in Hollywood wanted him loaned to them, Didier simply would not let Julian Brooks go. He was unquestionably England's number one male star, he was Didier's discovery, and the shrewd producer was going to get his pound of flesh each and every year from the watertight seven-year contract. Not only that, but Phoebe wasn't at all keen on going to Hollywood.

"Better a big fish in a small pond than vice versa," she snapped whenever the subject came up. "Here you're a star, there you'll just be one of the players on C. Aubrey Smith's cricket team."

Julian was in his element for the first two years of his contract. Mr. Christian—Beau Geste—Chopin—Sir Walter Raleigh—he played many of the great romantic leading men, and he also starred opposite some of the world's most desirable actresses. For even if Didier was not keen to lend them his most important star, American studios were more than happy to allow their beautiful contract actresses to cross the Atlantic to star opposite Julian Brooks. Soon there were few leading actresses whom Julian had not played opposite, and not only played opposite on screen, but off screen too.

He seemed irresistible to practically all women. For Julian, making love to each new leading lady was as easy as tying his Charvet tie. The actresses were all more than willing, and he was more than eager to please, as long as there was always complete discretion. That was the only provision in Julian's liaisons. He insisted that no breath of scandal should leak out to the gossip columns or magazines. He always made it quite clear before an affair began that he was happily married, and not prepared either to hurt his wife or damage his marriage. Many was the Hollywood siren who, having sampled the delights of Looks Brooks' lovemaking techniques was loath to let him go when their director had called the final "cut."

"Not since Gary Cooper," one actress told her friend who was off to London to play Roxanne to his Cyrano, "not since Coop has *any* guy made me come so many times and *so* deliciously." She shivered with pleasure at the memory.

"That good, huh?"

"Yeah—better than Sinatra—much better than Flynn."

"What does the wife think about all these shenanigans?" inquired the friend—Candida Willow, one of MCCP's most promising young stars.

The redhead tossed her titian pageboy. "Oh, she doesn't care. He doesn't flaunt it—he lets you know it's just a fling—but oh, boy, what a fling! Honey, you're in for *some* treat, I'm telling you."

"You mean his wife doesn't *know?* She doesn't even suspect?" asked Candida, big blue eyes wide with disbelief.

"Sure she knows. But she's so busy huntin' at Harrods 'n' Hartnells 'n' hobnobbing with the gentry, that she turns the other cheek—know what I mean?" The redhead winked and Candida giggled.

"Well, I'm certainly looking forward to getting to know this Mr. Brooks," said Candida. "But I won't sleep with him, because I *don't* have affairs with married men—besides, you know I'm in love with Gerry."

"Just wait till Looks turns on the charm," laughed the redhead. "You won't be able to resist those navy blue eyes, honey. Take it from me."

"Well, maybe *he'll* fall in love with *me*," smiled Candida, confident in her twenty-two-year-old glory. "Then the shoe will be on the other foot."

"Forget it, honey—everyone's tried—Ava—Lana—Liz—they all got nowhere with our Mr. Brooks. Wham, bam and thank you so *terribly terribly* much, ma'am—that was absolutely delightful—I'll see you on the next picture."

"We'll see," laughed Candida. "I'll send you a postcard from Jolly Olde England and let you know what happens—you know I love nothing better than a challenge."

While Julian pursued his career and his leading ladies, money continued to roll in, and Phoebe became no slouch at spending it. Aware of Julian's little flings, she was equally aware that he would never leave her, and she proceeded to spend, spend, spend with zest.

As Julian's fame grew, so did their accommodations. By 1953 they had moved seven times, and now lived in a beautiful Queen Anne house in Connaught Square just behind Hyde Park. But Phoebe was already preparing to upgrade again, and had her eye on a large country mansion only a few miles away from Sir Laurence and Lady Olivier. The Brookses now numbered among their intimate friends the Oliviers, Ralph Richardson, John Gielgud, Noël Coward and practically every other major film and theatrical name in England not to mention many choice members of the aristocracy and a couple of minor royals.

In spite of Julian's looks, sex appeal and fame he was so funny and self-deprecating, so down to earth and nice, that all the men liked and admired him, while their wives simply adored him. Some of them lusted after him fiercely, often making it quite apparent, but Julian would never have an affair with the wife of a friend. Only actresses and single women not in his set were his province. Consequently he continued to enjoy the reputation of the man's man that he'd always had, while remaining supremely attractive to all women.

When two years of his seven-year contract with Didier had expired, he agreed to sign for two more, but only if he were allowed to appear in a West End play every eighteen months. This gave Phoebe the chance she had been waiting for and she cajoled and persuaded her husband to finally cast her opposite him in some of the classics in which he performed.

She was hardly a staggering actress, her only previous experience on the stage having been in skits at the Windmill, but she tried hard and she still looked quite attractive. Buxom, creamy-skinned, and with abundant red curls and a sparkling personality, she appeared reasonably successfully with him in *The Taming of the Shrew, Present Laughter* and *The Importance of Being Earnest.*

They had just finished a successful three-month limited run at the Aldwych. Julian was now preparing to go to Normandy to play the lead in a film of *Cyrano de Bergerac,* but this was going to be the first time that he had not played a romantic part. He was keenly anticipating the challenge of playing a character part, a character who, for once, does not get the girl.

He had decided to take his black Bentley across the English Channel to the Normandy location. He enjoyed long drives and was expecting Phoebe to fly over to join him the following weekend. They were dining together at the Caprice. It was a quiet Monday night and the softly lit peach walls of the elegant restaurant reflected the orange highlights in Phoebe's dyed hair as she nibbled and sucked noisily on a fat asparagus stalk.

"Darling, I've decided not to go with you to Normandy," she said, her lips glistening with melted butter, a trickle of which was running down her chin. Julian leaned across and wiped it off with his damask napkin.

"Why not?" he asked, popping a piece of pâté de foie gras into his mouth while Phoebe repaired her lipstick.

"Darling, how can I *possibly* go to Normandy in the middle of the season?" She bared capped teeth in what she assumed to be an ingenuous girlish beam, but which at thirty-three was beginning to look a little frayed around the edges.

"I mean, next week is the Derby, two days later the Cavendish wedding, then the Oliviers are having that big birthday party for Michael, and I promised that I'd help Vivien with the decorations." She paused for a sip of wine as Julian looked across at her with raised eyebrows.

"Do I detect a mild dose of social-climbing fever here, my dear? Nothing before has ever kept you from visiting me on location. How on earth will I manage without you?" he asked, his irony totally missing its target.

"Oh, darling—I *know.* Do understand, my pet—please." She patted his hand with the absentminded gesture a nursemaid might make to her charge, and prepared to tackle the beef Wellington with sautéed potatoes which a waiter placed before her. "It's just that it's a terribly bad time now, what with redecorating the house, all these parties, and then the charity. The actors' charity, you remember, darling, you're on the committee. Surely you're going to fly back for that, aren't you, pet?"

"Phoebe, how *can* I?" he asked exasperatedly. "I know it's for a very good cause and so forth and I know we're both on the board but I'm in practically every damn shot of *Cyrano.* I can't *possibly* get away in the middle of the week, even for a charity."

"Exactly," crowed Phoebe triumphantly. "So I'll have to be there to represent you—the Rahvis girls are making me the most divine gown—completely covered in beaded topaz flowers, darling—you'll love it, it matches the topaz necklace and bracelet you gave me for the opening night of *Shrew.*"

"Mmmm." Julian was not listening. He picked at his roast chicken, his mind absorbed in his forthcoming characterization. He really didn't care whether Phoebe was with him or not on location. She was just a habit, always around like some annoying lucky mascot. He'd even become used to her complaints, which were becoming more frequent since she'd struck up an apparently close friendship with Vivien Leigh. Although Phoebe considered Vivien to be her best friend, Julian knew that she was little more than another one of the actress's sycophants. Phoebe was neither intellectually stimulating nor amusing enough to be an intimate friend of the scintillating actress.

"So you won't be coming to Normandy at all then?" asked Julian, not really caring what his wife's answer would be.

"Well, I'll *try* and pop over for a few days, darling," trilled Phoebe. "But don't forget there's Ascot—we're expected every day in someone or other's box or in the Royal Enclosure. The Denhams are having that big lunch for the Aga Khan, then Lord Cheltenham and the Countess of Rathbone have taken a huge tent for Ladies' Day, and of course, Binkie's special outing—Noël and Gertie are *definitely* coming to that—I couldn't *possibly* not be there, darling."

"To represent me, I suppose?" said Julian with even more sarcasm.

"Of course, darling," she answered, yet again missing the barb as her mind whirled with the dozens of new outfits that were even now in the process of being created for her by Norman Hartnell, Rahvis and Jacques Fath.

"What I *will* do, darling, is when I have to go to Paris for my fittings, I'll pop up to Normandy and see you for a few days—how would that be, pet?"

"That would be just dandy, dear," said Julian, signaling to the waiter and at the same time noticing that Phoebe had spilled gravy down her creamy lace cleavage. She was becoming quite sluttish recently, and many a couture gown had been spoiled by her greed and lack of dexterity at the dining table.

"Well, good. Then that's that, dear. You'll be fine without me, you'll have all your cronies with you, won't you?"

"Yes, of course," he said, thinking fondly of his makeup man, his dresser and his stunt double who always accompanied him on every picture.

"Then I don't really have to worry too much about you, do I, darling?" smiled Phoebe, dabbing with a damp napkin at her Hartnell lace collar. "You'll be quite all right then?"

"Don't give it another thought, my dear—I'll be perfectly all right." Julian smiled, signing the bill with a flourish. "I'll be perfectly fine."

Indeed, as it turned out, Julian was more than perfectly fine. As soon as his navy blue eyes connected with the sexy yet innocent blue eyes of blond Miss Candida Willow it was instant and spontaneous combustion.

Phoebe heard no rumor of the affair until three-quarters of the way through the filming. She had been so heavily involved in her social whirl that she had been able to think of nothing but society balls, garden parties and weekends with the Oliviers. She did not bother to stop off in Normandy when in Paris for her fittings, as Paris suddenly had a little flurry of *petite saison* before the *haut monde* rushed off in opposite directions to Deauville and the Riviera. So Phoebe's Parisian friends stole the time that she had earmarked for her husband. Not that said husband minded one whit. He was quite content living with his entourage in a charming farmhouse far from the bright lights of Paris, London and the Riviera. He was adoring playing Cyrano, the tragicomic figure with the enormous nose who loves the gorgeous Roxanne in vain. And the gorgeous Roxanne herself, Miss Candida Willow, was so hopelessly in love with him and, in addition, such a sweetly adorable girl, that Julian's cup was, if not exactly running over, most definitely full to the brim.

It was one of those idyllic summer film locations, shot in the wilds of the French countryside in which everything went completely according to plan from start to finish. The director was a poppet, the actor who played Christian was talented and affable, and Miss Willow was even more enchanting than her name, everything which a man could want in a temporary paramour.

The crew, many of whom had worked with Julian before, were, as always, well aware of what was going on, but such was their loyalty to Julian that no breath of scandal concerning the two lovebirds was allowed to leak into general circulation.

Phoebe breezed in and breezed out of the location one brief weekend between attending the Oaks at Epsom and the Henley Regatta. Julian dutifully performed his marital obligations with eyes closed, although for the past several years Phoebe had been a less than enthusiastic partner, but Julian persisted because he was still hoping that they would have a child. They had now been married for eight years, and except for being pregnant when they were married, Phoebe hadn't conceived since. Now at thirty-three her biological clock was rattling on very fast indeed, but Julian's sincere longing for a child far outstripped her own. Although she pretended to want a baby, and indeed did nothing to prevent its possible conception, she lost no sleep about her failure to conceive, having plenty to occupy her in other ways.

They were in his trailer and Phoebe was preparing to leave for the airport. "Well, darling, I'll see you in London in a few weeks then," she trilled, adjusting her new Dior cream straw hat which overflowed with silk strawberries and violet ribbons. Julian thought that it clashed rather alarmingly with her red hair, whose color had become more pronounced with each passing year, but things of that nature never seemed to bother Phoebe. She loved vivid colors and strongly believed that they suited her vibrant personality.

"Yes, dear, enjoy Cowes, won't you—give my love to Larry and Viv and the gang," he said, abstractedly examining his huge rubber nose in the mirror of his portable trailer. It was terribly hot today, and the rubber prosthesis applied so painstakingly this morning by Tim, the makeup man, was in grave danger of peeling off around the edges. Damn—he had a close-up to do after lunch and that would mean that Tim would have to come back again with his bottles of glue and his orange sticks and fiddle about for hours to attach it again properly. It was most important that this nose look perfectly authentic. The new film system— CinemaScope—showed up every tiny pore, each and every crow's foot. Every minute detail of a face was magnified a thousand or so times. Nothing would appear more ridiculous than for Cyrano's enormous snout to look like little more than something a circus clown might wear. It was desperately humid in the cramped little trailer, and with his heavy plum velvet tunic and breeches, yards of lace ruffles and two-pound wig, sweat was streaming down Julian's forehead, threatening to wash the nose away completely.

"Timmy," he shouted, "get in here right away and save this fucking nose. I think the bloody thing's about to slide off my damn face."

"Well, I'm off then, pet," said Phoebe, typically oblivious to his problems. "The limousine has to get me to the airport by three—I suppose if we leave now, I'll have plenty of time to catch the plane?"

"Yes, yes, yes," snapped Julian—why wouldn't the bloody woman leave and let him get on with his bloody job, for Christ's sake? This nose was killing him—it was made of solid rubber, smelled absolutely foul and seemed to weigh a ton. Now the tip was beginning to droop, making it look even more ridiculous.

"Bye, dear—bon voyage." He blew her a vague kiss, as he yelled again, "Tim, Tim—where the bloody hell are you?"

"Right here, guv—sorry, just finishing me dinner." The makeup man rushed in, almost colliding with Phoebe, who was floating out in her white silk frock like a ship in full sail. With a final wave to her husband she left, and Julian sighed with relief. Closing his eyes, he allowed Tim to probe about under his false nose with orange sticks covered with cottonwool and acetone.

"Hell, Tim, this elephant's trunk is bloody uncomfortable, you know. In this damn heat I feel about to explode."

"Well, you know what me dear old mum always said, old sport." Tim grinned, deftly picking tiny bits of rubber out of the gaping cavern of Julian's rubber nostrils.

"I can't say that I do, Tim," groaned Julian, squinting at his grotesque reflection in the mirror. "What did the dear old thing say?"

"You've got to suffer to be beautiful, duckie."

That night in his cozy rented farmhouse, Julian slouched comfortably on the sofa, his arm around the delicate white shoulders of Candida Willow. Candida was gently nibbling at his ear while he leaned his head back and they listened to extracts of *La Bohème* on the old-fashioned radio gramophone.

He was exhausted from the long day's shooting, and also from a whole weekend with Phoebe which had not been without its usual share of squabbling. Now he was looking forward to some languid stress-relieving lovemaking with his delectable co-star, and then a long restful sleep.

"Julian, let's get married," the delectable star suddenly whispered, between licks, into his ear.

"What—what did you say, darling?" Julian sat suddenly bolt upright, all hopes of a relaxing evening dashed.

"I said I want to marry you, Julian—I love you—I've never loved anyone like this before. You love me too—don't you, darling? Let's do it —please, please."

Pleading eyes turned to meet his, eyes which looked so radiant and gorgeous on the huge CinemaScope screen, but which now welled with huge CinemaScope tears.

Julian was dumbstruck. Surely she must know the way this game was played? He was married. This was just a location romance—he'd told her that when they'd begun their affair. Why on earth was she carrying on like this? Lovey-dovey, getting all emotional—talking marriage babble? Oh, hell. Women—women—women—damn the whole bloody lot of them, he thought, Henry Higgins was right. His mind desperately searched for a way to get himself out of this situation with his dignity and her pride intact.

"Darling heart, you *know* that's impossible," he said sincerely, making the effort to appear serious and lovingly understanding, in spite of his growing exhaustion.

"Why—why? You don't love Phoebe. You couldn't. I saw her today. She looks like an old tart," spat Candida tearfully. "I saw her with you all weekend—it almost *killed* me." She burst into sobs, spattering her angora sweater with tears. "The thought of you together—in bed—oh, oh, oh, it was terrible."

"Were you spying on me, darling heart?" scolded Julian gently. "That's very naughty, you know. Very, *very* naughty."

"Yes—yes I was," wept the girl, her tears flowing unabated. "I couldn't *help* it. I looked through your bedroom window one night. I saw her in her nightdress—she's *fat*. How can you *possibly* prefer her to me?"

Julian maintained a dignified silence as his mind raced. Candida peeking into the bedroom windows like some Peeping Tom—what sort of a woman was she?

"She's not *right* for you, Julian. I can tell. I watched you. You're like

chalk and cheese together. You must know she's not the woman for you
—you can't possibly love her. She's so old, how can you?" Fresh tears
erupted and he automatically handed her his handkerchief.

He didn't answer her. The heartrending strains of the last act of *La
Bohème* were moving on to their inevitably tragic end, the finale in another sense of an almost perfect evening which Candida was now ruining.
"Look, my darling girl," he said, gently wiping the tears from her cheeks,
marveling as if for the first time at how fresh and beautiful she was, "I
don't want to hurt you, dear, but I *cannot* and *will* not marry you—*ever*.
Do you understand that? It simply isn't possible, dear."

"No," said the girl churlishly, picking up her glass of wine and tipping
the contents down her throat. "I don't understand. You *told* me you loved
me, Julian—you know you did—didn't you? Were you lying?"

It was Julian's turn to be churlish now, and he knocked back his
brandy with frustration. Of course he'd told her he loved her; it was all
part of the game, dammit—a game he'd been playing for years now. She
must know the rules. You always told them that you loved them when you
were making love to them; it simply wasn't gentlemanly behavior not to
—but one never, ever spoke of love when out of bed. All his other
mistresses had understood it perfectly well. Why didn't this little fool, for
God's sake?

"The picture finishes next week." Candida sounded desperate now,
tears still dripping from her eyes with a persistence which unnerved him.
"I can't live without you, Julian—I can't go back to America, my darling
—I need you and I want you. I want to be with you always—forever and
ever." She threw herself onto his chest, her body shaking with sobs that
were verging on hysteria. Julian heaved a long inward sigh, and held her
shaking shoulders tightly.

Throughout the long and sleepless night Julian talked reassuringly to
Candida. He explained patiently all the reasons why it was impossible for
them to marry. He told her that she must be a big grown-up girl, and that
she must accept that their relationship must end when filming stopped.
By the time they attempted to sleep as he held her comfortingly in the
big four-poster bed, Julian thought that he'd successfully calmed Candida
down, and had at last made her see reason. He was wrong.

When Julian woke up to Tim's knock and his cheerful "Five thirty,
Julian—time to open those baby blues, chum, coffee's on the way up" he
found that the other side of the double bed was empty. He moved an
exploratory foot over to the other side, finding it not only empty, but
cold. Candida had obviously accepted what he'd said to her, and decided
to make a dignified exit during the night. So much the better, he thought.
He hated scenes and confrontations, and much as he had liked Candida
and adored making love to her, he knew that she was just another one
of his flings. She was a charming child, an adorable sex kitten, but if he
were ever to leave Phoebe, a thought which had certainly crossed his
mind from time to time, then the woman for whom he might consider
sacrificing his marriage would have to have a great deal more character,

intelligence and personality than some cute but limited California cupcake. He swung his feet to the cool wooden floor and padded into the bathroom.

Nothing could have prepared him for the appalling sight which met his eyes. Lying in the old-fashioned splay-legged bathtub, floating as peacefully as Ophelia in the rushes, was Candida Willow. One slim arm was hanging over the rim of the tub and the dark red slash in her wrist was making a rich crimson pool on the floor. Her eyes were closed and her head was submerged almost up to her nose.

"Christ Almighty—*Candida*—Oh, my God—*Candida!*" Julian leaped towards the girl, sweeping her up into his arms, aware that the bathwater was the color of rosé wine. "Tim—*Timmy!*" he called at the top of his lungs. *"Get in here, for God's sake!"*

Within seconds Tim, who was carrying a tray of coffee and croissants, rushed into the bathroom and dropped the lot as soon as he saw the ghastly tableau "Jesus Christ, guv—why the fuck's she done this?" he asked as they hastily carried the girl to the bed. Julian applied mouth-to-mouth resuscitation while Tim swiftly and efficiently shredded pieces of Julian's discarded white shirt into strips to stem the flow of blood from her wrists. Candida had slashed both of them with a razor blade which lay bloodied on the bathroom floor.

"Is she alive?" breathed Julian hoarsely.

Tim nodded. He had been in the ARP during the war and had had more than his fair share of dealing with serious injuries during the Blitz.

"Just about," he said grimly. "But she lost a lot of blood—we've got to get her to a hospital and pronto—otherwise she'll snuff it, guv, 'n' then the shit'll really hit the fan."

"Oh, my God," whispered Julian. "Oh, God, the poor silly little girl."

"If I were you, guv, it's *me* that I'd feel sorry for," said Tim bleakly. "The girl'll probably recover, but if this gets around, you'll be in deep deep shit. You won't be winnin' any popularity contests after this little lot, I'll bet my bottom dollar on *that.*"

Somehow the studio managed to keep it out of the newspapers. Candida was young and strong, and by pure luck Julian had discovered her just in time. She would only have had two days' more shooting before her role was completed, and Didier Armande's imaginative publicity machine concocted a story about a sudden appendicitis attack which had made it necessary for her to be flown back to America immediately. Candida stayed in the local Normandy hospital for a few days and then her mother and father arrived with a lanky young lawyer from Pasadena called Gerry, who turned out to be Candida's fiancé.

"We're engaged," he drawled, having managed to steal an hour away from his bedside vigil to watch some of the shooting.

"How long have you two been engaged?" Julian asked, as Tim raised an eyebrow at him.

"Oh, two years now. We've been going together since high school, but Candy—that's her real name, Candy Wilson—the studio thought

Candida Willow suited her better—well, Candy wanted to wait to get married until she'd forged her career—made a success, you know?"

"I know," said Julian, scratching his great itching nose, which was starting to droop again in the heat.

"Well, that's all changed now," said Gerry brightly. "She's decided, for the best, I think, to give up all this acting stuff and come back and live in Pasadena with me. We're gonna get married next spring."

"Congratulations, mate," said Tim, busy once again with his orange sticks in the crevices of Julian's nose. "She's a nice little gal—we've enjoyed having her, 'aven't we, guv?" He winked at Julian cheekily, his face inches away.

"I hope you'll both be very happy," said Julian sincerely, trying to ignore Tim. "Candida is a lovely girl, very lovely indeed."

"I know," said the young man, "I'm a real lucky guy." And he looked over in surprise at Tim as the makeup man gave a snort of suppressed laughter.

Although the general public was never allowed to hear about Candida Willow's suicide attempt, before long the entire show-business community from Paramount to Pinewood knew the whole story. Julian's charm and sex appeal were magnified tenfold, and he became almost a living legend. Nothing creates so much excitement as a woman trying to kill herself for the love of a man, and Julian found himself in even more demand both as an actor and as a lover.

He had felt guilty and responsible for Candida's suicide attempt, and had tried to visit her in the hospital, but was told that only her close relations were allowed to see her. He sent her a letter and three dozen white roses, and tried to put the incident out of his mind.

Candida's recovery was swift. As soon as she was out of intensive care, and the doctors said she could travel, the studio rented a private plane and packed her and her entourage back to California.

Julian never did get the chance to talk to her, and his letters to her in California were always returned unopened. He decided to be a great deal more careful with his love affairs in the future. And he did try. But Looks Brooks found it hard to change. In a matter of weeks, he was continuing on his path of casual philandering once again, and Phoebe was continuing to squander even more of his money.

Although Julian never mentioned Candida's suicide attempt to Phoebe over the telephone from France, the West End jungle drums were not long in relaying the news to her. It was one of the two Hermiones who imparted this particularly succulent piece of gossip to her while the women were lunching together at the Savoy Grill. It was all Phoebe could do to hold down her *sole bonne femme*, while Hermione rattled on about the wretched girl's suicide attempt.

"In Julian's bathroom, if you please! And I gather that the whole thing has been kept under wraps by Didier's film company. My dear, can you imagine *what* would happen if the story ever got out?"

"I certainly can," said Phoebe grimly, pecking at a piece of melba toast in a vain attempt to diet. "The newspapers would destroy Julian."

"I know I shouldn't really be telling you all this, darling," purred Hermione, her evident relish for relating the sorry tale to the injured party seemed to increase her already healthy appetite for plump roasted grouse, mounds of mashed potatoes and Brussels sprouts, all of which were washed down with copious amounts of dry Chardonnay. "But although they say that the wife is always the *last* to find out, I think you *should* know, my dear. You deserve to hear the truth, don't you agree?"

"Absolutely," croaked Phoebe, almost choking on a fishbone. "Damn it, this thing is supposed to be filleted," she snarled. "Tell me everything, Hermione, everything you know."

"Well, we all *know* what Julian's always been like—don't we?" giggled Hermione coyly, intimating by a flicker of false lashes that she also might have been among the lucky ones to have partaken of Julian's charms.

Phoebe stared at her with exasperated sarcasm. "What *is* he like, Hermione, dear? Do tell me."

"You're such a clever girl, Phoebe, that I'm sure that he's never managed to pull the wool completely over your eyes—not *quite,* has he, my dear?"

"Never," snapped Phoebe, trying to pour some more Chardonnay into her glass but spilling it onto the linen tablecloth. She felt a deep flush of humiliation creeping over the collar of her fuchsia silk dress—now almost a perfect match for the color of her face. "I'm not stupid, Hermione—I've always known he played around, of course, all men do—especially actors."

"Of course you have, dear, we're women of the world, we've always known. Well, there's nothing you can do really, I suppose, except pretend that absolutely nothing has happened, put on a happy face as it were."

"I always do that," Phoebe said icily. "Turn the other cheek, all that sort of stuff—what the eye doesn't see . . ."

"The heart doesn't grieve over," finished Hermione with a patronizing chuckle. "Exactly, dear. My mother taught me that too. Funny isn't it? It gets you through life pretty well—especially with the way most men are."

"What do you mean 'most'?" said Phoebe viciously. "They're all alike, Hermione. You must know that better than anyone, surely?"

"Really? I don't quite see the point of that last remark, Phoebe." Hermione raised a questioning penciled brow. "What exactly do you mean, dear?"

"Well I suppose it's bad enough that everyone knows that Julian has been pathologically unfaithful to me for years," said Phoebe, lighting a cigarette, and allowing a cloud of smoke to drift across her luncheon companion's face. "But at least he's unfaithful to me with *women.*"

"And just *what* are you implying?" asked Hermione, looking suddenly irritated and defensive as she shifted in her chair, fanning at the cigarette smoke with a lace-bordered handkerchief.

"*Really,* Hermione dear, is it honestly necessary for you to be quite so naive?" Phoebe laughed lightly, enjoying the look of growing discomfort on Hermione's heavily powdered face, into which she blew another cloud of smoke.

"What I mean is that although *my* husband has been busy screwing lots of young girls, *yours*, my dear, has been equally busy with lots of young boys!"

"Absolute nonsense!" Crimson spots now appeared on each of Hermione's normally porcelain-white cheeks. "That's utterly ridiculous—it's a slanderous lie, Phoebe, and you know it."

"Oh, do come off it, Hermione. You can dish it out but you obviously can't take it. Your precious Basil is as queer as a seven-pound note—you know it, I know it, everyone in the bloody business knows it—even the press knows it, for God's sake, so don't pretend to me that *you* don't know. You just make yourself look even more of a laughingstock."

"Well, I don't believe it, and even if it were true—I don't care—it doesn't matter. Basil loves me—he simply adores me," stammered Hermione. "He worships the ground I walk on."

But Phoebe was too fast for her. Leaning forward she hissed with calculated vehemence into the other woman's face, "Listen, Hermione, Julian may cheat on me, but he's a man—a real *man*—and although he fucks other women he *always* comes back to me—*me*, do you hear? He makes love to *me*, and I'll have you know he does it bloody well—now, duckie, can you say the same for your Basil?"

Hermione glared back at her, speechless. Some of the other people in the restaurant had turned in their direction, watching with great interest the two well-known actresses in heated discussion.

"Well, I was only trying to help," said Hermione huffily, patting the frizzy curls beneath her flowered hat. "After all, that's what friends are for, isn't it? I was just trying to let you know, my dear, that you have many many friends who are fully behind you, while you're going through this perfectly horrible situation."

"Thank you, Hermione." Phoebe signaled for the bill. "But probably not *nearly* as many as dear Basil has had behind *him!*" With a flourish she signed, leaving an unnecessarily large tip and, brushing her friend's cheek with her own, said through clenched teeth, "Thanks for all your interesting advice, dear . . . I'll think about it, and I dare say I'll see you both at Binkie's on Sunday."

By the time Phoebe got back to Connaught Square she had worked herself into a complete fury. Ignoring her butler, who opened the front door, she raced up to the master bedroom and throwing her hat, gloves and handbag on the bed, stood in the middle of her Colefax and Fowler chintz extravaganza seething and shaking with rage. That smug bitch. The vicious back-biting cow. How dare she give advice on how to handle Julian and his affairs when everyone knew that *her* husband was camper than a row of tents, and more than likely hadn't made love to her in years. How could he want to anyway, when he had to look at a face like hers. She paced up and down the room, puffing furiously on one cigarette after another. There was no way she could stop Julian's philandering, she knew that. She had allowed him to get away with it almost since the first day they'd met at the Windmill. He knew that and she knew that he knew that she knew. She could hardly make him stop now—it was far too much of a habit for him. But obviously his affairs were heating up, becoming more than just meaningless flings. This little harlot—starlet—trying to kill herself for love of him meant that Julian must have made romantic promises to her, maybe even heartfelt protestations of true love. She gritted her teeth. God, if he'd started to do *that*, then her days as Mrs. Julian Brooks could really be numbered. Before she even knew anything about it he could make some girl pregnant—become all broody, and ditch her to become the daddy he'd always wanted to be. Maybe she should really try to have a baby. She pulled a face—the idea was utterly repugnant to her. Motherhood in any of its aspects definitely didn't appeal to her. But perhaps she should attempt that ultimate sacrifice. After all, she thought, Julian was getting to that vulnerable age for a man, when the right woman could steal him away from her if there wasn't a tiny little Brooks junior to cement their bond.

"Not while I'm still around and breathing," muttered Phoebe, and with a great burst of energy she disappeared into his dressing room.

A week later Julian returned to London to find Phoebe not at home to greet him as was her wont. Everything in the house seemed perfectly normal but when he went upstairs into his dressing room and opened the heavy mahogany doors of his wardrobe, he was greeted by a sight which, to a man who prided himself on his sartorial elegance, was one of ultimate horror. Three dozen or more Savile Row suits hung, perfectly separated by a precise three-inch space, dark to the left, lighter cloth to the right, but every last one of the jackets had been cleanly cut off at the elbow, and all the trouser legs had been chopped off at the knees. Julian let out a howl as he fumbled through the rest of his costly and extensive wardrobe, and found to his horror that his Turnbull & Asser shirts, his beloved Charvet ties, Huntsman cashmere and vicuña coats, and dinner jackets and tailcoats from Kilgour, French & Stanbury, had all been systematically and very deliberately slashed to ribbons. Everything was completely ruined, nothing was salvageable, not even any of his dozens of silk boxer shorts. Phoebe had taken a vicious petty revenge, and Julian, realizing the penalty had now been paid in full for his potentially fatal indiscretion with Candida Willow, knew that he should try to toe the marital line—at least for the moment.

In its autumn issue, *Life* magazine named Julian Brooks as The Most Handsome Man in the World. They featured him on a full-color cover in his costume from *The Devil Is a Man*. He was standing at the tiller of a ship, wearing blue jeans, and a black shirt open to the waist revealed the glistening muscles of his broad chest to their best effect. His head was thrown back, and he was laughing into the wind, which was blowing his unruly hair back off his famous noble forehead. The article and accompanying photographs inside the magazine painted an idyllic portrait of

Julian and Phoebe as happily married lovers living in intimate connubial bliss in Connaught Square, and sharing the theatrical limelight in the West End. They showed photographs of the two of them seen enjoying a joke at Ascot in the company of Noël Coward and Sir Crispin Peake, and they even printed a picture of Phoebe in the kitchen of their house, wearing a simple dress and to many people's great amusement, a modest apron, as she stirred a steaming casserole at the stove. In the background Julian held one of their many Persian cats and smiled fondly at her. The text was syrupy. The female writer had evidently fallen heavily for Julian, and the article was a paean of praise to his charm, talent and physical beauty. Phoebe had dozens of copies of the magazine sent over from America, as it was hard to find in London, and sent them to all their friends. She even put one in an Asprey's silver frame on top of the grand piano.

Even though they were in the middle of rehearsals for *Hamlet* Phoebe still found time to give an interview to one of the more sympathetic journalists from the *Daily Express*. She was delighted when she read the text of the article which appeared a month before they were due to open, and which helped make the box-office grow. It was headlined "If he cheated on me—I'd kill him" and in it in no uncertain terms, Phoebe warned the women of the world to keep away from her man.

"I know very well that because Julian is regarded by many as the handsomest man in the world, women will always be chasing him," gushed Phoebe in the article. *"But I also know that he's completely faithful to me, and to me alone. Oh, yes, of course I've heard all those silly rumors about his flirtations with his co-stars when he's away on location, but Julian just can't help but be charming and helpful to everyone he works with. It doesn't really mean a thing. We've been married for over eight years and our marriage is as sound and loving today as it ever was. No woman could ever come between us, and if anyone did try to steal him from me—I'd kill her."*

Several copies of the *Daily Express* were passed around the dingy hall in Camberwell where *Hamlet* was in rehearsal, and the cast couldn't help giggling when they read about Phoebe's bravura performance in the paper.

"My dear, she acts so much better for the tabloids than she does on the stage," exclaimed Sir Crispin Peake at the local pub during a lunchtime break.

"Frankly, if she carries on giving the newspapers these perfectly *wonderful* pieces of fictionalized nonsense, she'll be able to make far more money writing penny-dreadfuls than Julian makes as a film star."

❧ *Three* ❧

Often when the mistral whistled tirelessly through fragrant hills of cypress and pine, Agathe Guinzberg would bring out her scrapbook. Unlike the more docile winds of the sirocco, on whose hot breezes the scent of Africa wafted, the mistral was a demon wind. The shrill clattering of the rigging continued ceaselessly on the many vessels moored in the tiny harbor of St. Tropez, and the larger boats heaved against each other with a sound like the groans of ravening beasts.

But Agathe could disregard it all as she slowly and deliberately turned the pages of her album to gaze at the face of the man she adored. If the mistral became fierce enough to whip the village women's long skirts above their knees, to whisk the kerchiefs from their heads, and force old men to chase through narrow lanes after their black berets, then the loudest church bell would toll three times. When Agathe heard the bell ring out from the old tower she felt relieved, as this was the signal that there would be no school today.

Then she would sigh with pleasure, snuggling back under her goosefeather quilt as she leafed through her scrapbook and imagined herself with the man who so enriched her life. Julian Brooks and Agathe were dancing together, in glorious Technicolor, their bodies melting into one, as the orchestra of the Paris Opera played Tchaikovsky's *Romeo and Juliet*.

Agathe had thrilled to Julian's romantic exploits and escapades in *The Merry Monarch* and the many other films which had made him the most glamorous leading man in England, and now she seemed to live only for those moments when she saw him on the screen.

There were dozens of photographs of him, cut from *Ciné Monde, Ciné Revue* or *Jours de France*, which she had pasted into her thick scrapbook. Although he was England's biggest star, the French still preferred their actors home-grown, so Gérard Philipe, Jean Gabin and Fernandel were the masculine faces most frequently featured in French magazines. But nevertheless Agathe still managed to find quite a few pictures of her idol. Here was Julian clipped from the cover of *Paris Match* wearing a blue turtleneck sweater, tweed jacket and—his trademark—a fedora tilted at that rakish angle she adored. He was leaning against an oak tree, an ironic smile on his face, his thick dark hair tumbling over his forehead as he gazed into the camera with the tantalizing expression which Agathe and millions of other female filmgoers worshiped. She knew it was ridiculous for a woman of thirty-one to have such a passion for a film star, but she didn't care. To her he epitomized all that was romantic, gallant, quixotic and mysterious—he was her life.

Reverently she turned to another page where Julian, suavely dressed in white tie and tails, with his hair slicked back, clasped the eighteen-inch waist of some ravishing actress. They gazed into each other's eyes, appearing deeply in love, while a remarkable authentic studio moon shone down brightly on their enraptured faces. Agathe sighed. She really didn't like looking at photographs of Julian with other women. She preferred to look at him alone, bounding out of the waves onto some beach, his chest bronzed, wet and glistening, wearing a pair of tight-fitting white shorts. That kind of picture always gave her a strangely thrilling feeling in her loins that she knew was wrong.

At thirty-one Agathe was still a virgin who had never been involved with a man romantically. Sometimes at night as she looked at Julian's photographs an overwhelming heat would make her tingle so much that she would touch herself guiltily as she had done in the cellar years before. But her sense of relief was always followed by such feelings of shame and self-disgust that she would feverishly turn the amber beads of her rosary, begging forgiveness from the Virgin Mother. Those beads and her prayers had been her comfort and salvation when she had been hidden beneath Gabrielle's house for eighteen months, and Jewish or not, she still treasured them.

The shutters outside her window banged loudly and monotonously against the ivy-clad, pink-painted granite of the little house. The terrible force of the wind was tearing the jasmine and mimosa, so carefully nurtured by Aunt Brigitte, from the lattice-covered wall. Even the Nazi occupation hadn't been able to make her aunt's mimosa perish, but now the pale blossoms were falling to the ground like confetti.

"Agathe!" Aunt Brigitte's cross voice interrupted Agathe's reverie, and with a sigh she slid the album under the safety of her mattress.

"Close those shutters, Agathe," her aunt shouted, her voice sounding feeble against the howling of the wind. "Now!'

Agathe opened her window to reach the shutters, and the wind caught her long white hair, whipping it around her face in a blinding swirl. She gripped the heavy shutters, pulling and locking them firmly with the rusty catch.

Her aunt peered into the bedroom with a suspicious expression on her lined face, then went off muttering under her breath. Aunt Brigitte was a faded woman of sixty-four, whose thinning hair and sad demeanor mirrored all the suffering and loss of the war years, including the death of a much-loved husband. Now all she had left was this strange niece whom she'd inherited when the war had finally ended, and with whom she had nothing in common. Aunt Brigitte had escaped Paris just in time and had fled to the south of France and relative safety.

When the repatriation of families decimated by the Nazis began, Agathe had been reunited with the last surviving member of her family. She had insisted that Agathe come to live with her, and secured a job for her at the local school, where she was able to use her ballet training to teach the young girls.

Aunt Brigitte always looked as if the troubles of the whole world rested on her thin shoulders, and Agathe often wondered if her grim-faced aunt had ever been carefree and happy even as a girl. She sometimes studied the yellowing black-and-white photographs on her aunt's dressing table, pictures of the extensive family which no longer existed. How many of them there once were, and how pitifully short their lives had been. Agathe particularly loved one picture of the father she had known for barely eighteen years. How handsome Papa was, with his tanned, intelligent face and his thick black curls. His arms were holding the beautiful young girl who had been her mother, whose eyes were laughing and filled with joy. They had obviously been madly in love. Agathe sighed. Would she ever fall madly in love? Or was she destined to spend the rest of her life as a childless spinster, a ballet teacher, whose only joy was collecting photographs of a man she would never meet?

Well, there would be no school today, the mistral had conveniently seen to that. The whole day now stretched ahead of her—hours of emptiness which somehow had to be filled.

She decided to take a walk into the village—maybe the new edition of *Ciné Monde* was out, perhaps even with a photograph of Julian which she hadn't yet seen.

In her favorite café on the quay, the locals sat about glumly sipping their glasses of Provençal wine or cognac, staring out at the churning gray sea with grim resignation. Each day of mistral was a day of work lost, so the fishermen's families would eat little tonight. In spite of the wind, the blazing sun glittered on the rolling mass like shattered diamonds, and the air was fresh and tangy.

In the distance she could see boats bobbing even more furiously in the waters of the normally protected port. The Mediterranean had whipped itself into a foaming frenzy, and now golden sand swirled like clouds of smoke through the narrow streets. It seeped through even the most tightly closed doors and windows, while the wind screeched incessantly.

Agathe yearned to leave St. Tropez, to go somewhere, anywhere, away from the stern prying eyes of her aunt.

She sipped her coffee, gloomily thinking that judges in the south of France tended to be lenient in their sentencing if a crime, even murder, was committed during the mistral. They blamed it on "mistral madness," because the unrelenting winds had often been known to drive people quite literally mad. Mad—maybe that was why she had no friends. Everyone in St. Tropez thought she was slightly mad; she herself thought it a miracle that she wasn't, in fact, insane. If only everyone knew what she had been through during the war, perhaps they would be more friendly towards her. She had no friends of her own age, nor indeed of any age; and men friends, as Aunt Brigitte said, were all a waste of time. "All that giggling and gossiping, going to cafés and dances. You have responsibilities, *chérie*—no time for such nonsense."

As she stared out to sea Agathe began to daydream. Visions of a soft meadow came to mind, where wildflowers grew in great tangles and a gurgling stream ran nearby; there she wandered hand in hand with a friend, a lover perhaps, sharing hopes and dreams and confidences. Not that Agathe liked men, they frightened her. Only with Julian did she feel she could come into her own. The unattainable Looks Brooks. Unattainable, like all her dreams.

❧ *Four* ❧

"DOMINIQUE. DOMINIQUE! Regarde ici." The girl, pigtails flying, raced along the cobbled back street of St. Tropez, excitedly waving a piece of paper. "Dominique. Stop—*please,* you must see this," she called breathlessly to her friend, who stubbornly strode on ahead, a knapsack full of books resting easily on her sturdy shoulders.

"Not now, Genevieve," Dominique said impatiently. "You know I'm late for class and Madame will give me hell again. *Merde,* that's the second time this week M'sieur has kept me late for talking in his science lesson. I think he must hate me." She increased her pace as Genevieve, two months younger than the sixteen-year-old, and a few inches shorter, hurried to keep up with her.

"Look, Dominique. Look at this, please, you are *such* a stubborn idiot," the girl said firmly, thrusting her prized scrap of paper in front of Dominique's enormous green eyes. "They have been giving these away outside the school, at the patisserie and the butcher's shop and all over the village. Some Americans have come down from Paris and they are looking for someone—" she said secretively, her freckled face attempting a look of mystery—"someone like you."

"Oh, Genevieve, you're *so* naive." Dominique broke into a run as she heard the church clock strike three and realized she should already be in her leotard, ballet shoes and tights. Madame Agathe would even now be flouncing into the chilly practice room, dispensing sarcastic comments to the disgruntled group of twelve schoolgirls who all strived for the perfection which, alas, Madame Agathe had never achieved herself. But Agathe thought Dominique showed some promise, and she encouraged her constantly, helped her, grilled her, instructed her, perhaps seeing in her the young ballerina she herself might have been if it hadn't been for the war.

"If you won't look at it yourself, then I'll read it to you," squealed Genevieve, keeping up with her taller friend's strides with difficulty.

"Okay, okay, I'm listening," said Dominique, "but read it fast, Genevieve. Between Madame Agathe and M'sieur Millet, they'll finish me off. *Merde—les salopes.*"

"Listen." Genevieve blushed at Dominique's language, although she had heard it often enough before.

" 'Wanted to audition for American film: classical ballet and jazz-trained girls aged between fifteen and twenty. Must have some acting experience and be willing and able to travel to the United States to work. Bring dance clothes, sheet music of one classical and one modern dance piece. Ten A.M., Saturday, March fifth. Théâtre de Comédie, boulevard des Anglais, Nice.' "

"Tiens!" Dominique stopped dead in her tracks and, snatching the paper from her friend, stared at it in wonder. "Do you think this is some sort of joke, Genevieve? Maybe the boys from the parish school have printed this up to make us look like fools. We all turn up in our tutus full of great expectations, and that bunch of spotty creeps will be waiting there to giggle at us." Most of the young girls who lived in St. Tropez hated boys, or at least pretended they did. Refined young ladies had nothing in common with uncouth teenage louts, avoiding them as much as possible. Boys seemed interested only in *boules,* darts, football and wrestling with each other in the meadows of the surrounding Provençal countryside. Girls were a total mystery to them—just boring fragile creatures to be teased mercilessly.

"I don't really think it is a joke," Genevieve insisted. "Dominique, you simply *must* go!"

"Genevieve!" gasped Dominique. Her eyes were sparkling, her long hair, tied into a ponytail, glistened like black swansdown in the fading afternoon sun, her sensual gamine face radiated excitement. "This is *fantastic—amazing!* An *audition*—right here in the south of France."

"Well, not exactly right here," Genevieve pointed out pragmatically, peering again at the paper. "To get to Nice will take the best part of four hours on the bus. I suppose you could take the train, but Papa says it was only Hitler who managed to get the trains running on time, and that now they're even *more* hopeless than they were before the war."

"Never mind, never mind, never mind," cried Dominique, breaking into a run. "Even if I have to leave at *five* in the morning, I *must* go to this audition. Genevieve, *quelle chance!* I could meet Gene Kelly or Fred Astaire! I could even become a *Star.* Well, maybe," she said as her friend giggled. "Look, I must run now, I'm so late—but thank you, Genevieve. Thanks!"

In the cloakroom Dominique quickly changed. Hearing Agathe already instructing the dance class, she burst in flushed and rosy, her heart pounding with excitement at the prospect of her audition, and was scolded for her lateness. She tried to execute the complicated pirouettes and *jetés* that Madam Agathe was showing her pupils, but she couldn't keep her mind focused. It kept returning again and again to the audition. A Hollywood movie! Hollywood! America! Dominique had often fantasized about becoming a Hollywood star. No matter that she was French: so were Leslie Caron and Zizi Jeanmaire!

Sweat trickled down the neck of her tight cotton leotard, and her legs felt hot and sticky in their thick lisle tights.

"Pay attention, Dominique," Madame Agathe snapped, banging her slender silver-topped cane down hard on the parquet floor. She always

carried this cane when she led the class; it gave the impression of authority which she needed to control the group of overexcitable adolescent
girls.

Most of the girls made fun of Agathe behind her back—of her white
face and hair, her gaunt body in its shapeless clothes, her eyes which
possessed such a fierce flame of discipline that they seemed to burn right
into anyone who made a mistake.

"Those who can, *do*. Those who can't, teach," Genevieve had once
told Dominique—another of her father's observations. Dominique now
stood, head bent, chastened because Madame Agathe was giving her a
tongue-lashing for lack of spontaneity, in front of the whole class.

"I'm sorry, Madame," Dominique said, close to tears. Madame could
be very cruel when she wanted to be, her criticisms always hitting the
mark with brutal accuracy. "I'm very sorry."

"I want you to stay behind after class, Dominique," Madame said
brusquely. "We will go over this *again*—the solo you were *supposed* to
have practiced this weekend. Obviously your ballet homework has not
been done, so you will have to do it *now*."

"Yes, Madame," Dominique mumbled, exchanging a quick look with
another girl, who shrugged sympathetically.

Sometimes Madame's tongue was so razor sharp that the girls joked
that if she swallowed it she'd slit her own throat. There was no doubt that
Madame could be quite a tartar. Her quiet, inhibited exterior concealed
a savage temper and a fury with life which lurked just beneath the surface.

At last the class was over and the other girls filed out. Dominique
stood alone and silent, while Agathe lectured her and then went on to
demonstrate some of the steps. Suddenly Agathe showed an infinite patience; kindness radiated from her eyes, which were no longer burning
points of suppressed rage, but warm and understanding.

Dominique felt a wave of pity mingled with affection for this woman
whom the village children all rudely called "the mad old maid," and she
decided to confide her plans for Saturday's audition. Excitedly she told
Agathe how much she wanted to go.

"*Chérie*, this is very, very exciting," Agathe breathed, a faint pink flush
coloring her pale cheeks. "Certainly it is a very important opportunity.
You must be good. You must be more than good. Dominique, you must
be the absolute best."

"Yes, Madame." The girl nodded, her eyes bright, her legs suddenly
no longer tired. "Will you help me?" she blurted out. "I need to practice
much more, I know I do. Oh, Madame—" she looked at Agathe, her
young face flushed and joyful—"Oh, Madame, I want this—I want so
much to go to Hollywood—can you imagine?"

"Yes, yes, I will help you," Agathe said simply. "I will rehearse you
now and for the next three days before the audition, and you must practice at home too," she said sternly. "It will take much hard work, but you,
more than all the others in class, have the talent, the potential to succeed."

"Thank you, Madame, oh, thank you," Dominique breathed, thrilled by her teacher's rare praise. "I will kill myself working, I promise you."

"And I will take you to the audition myself," Agathe said, looking fondly at her lovely young pupil. "We will work very hard now, *chérie*, and on Saturday morning you will be prepared, and . . ." She paused, her dark eyes twinkling now with an unaccustomed pleasure. "And you will be the best, Dominique. You will be given the part, you will go to Hollywood—and who knows, perhaps I will even go with you."

Dominique was so overexcited after her afternoon of intensive rehearsal and about the upcoming audition, that after an early supper with her parents and three young brothers, she took her bicycle and rode into the center of St. Tropez.

The sign "Gaston's Glacés" emblazoned in purple on a small yellow ice cream wagon looked so inviting that she propped her bicycle carelessly against a tree in the Place des Lices, and sauntered over to investigate.

"I'll have a *framboise*," she said, fishing for change in the pocket of her shorts. "Double, please."

"It's on the house," Gaston said, not only giving her an extra scoop of ice cream, but also the benefit of perfect white teeth in a beautifully tanned face.

She smiled back. "Merci, *M'sieur*."

He admired her gamine face, sparkling green eyes and long tanned legs. She had an aristocratic accent, but her attitude seemed modern and free—not like the snobbish young tourists from England and Scandinavia who usually bought from him.

Gaston instantly decided that she was a prize not to be missed and that there was no time to lose. He quickly locked the door of his wagon and matched her stride as she wandered into the tiny square.

"I'm Gaston Girandot," he volunteered. "I own the joint."

"So I gathered—I'm Dominique du Frey," she said, licking at the melting pink ice cream.

"Daughter of the banker?"

"Yes," she said, watching him slyly out of the corners of her slanting eyes. *Tiens*, but he was very good-looking, better-looking than any of the boys at school.

"My parents have a patisserie on the Avenue Bazoche," he volunteered.

"I think our cook buys from them sometimes," said Dominique, looking up at him through thick black lashes with an expression which was both challenging and shyly sensual.

"Would you like a cup of coffee?" He felt gauche for the first time in his nineteen years. Because of his good looks, girls usually made advances to him, but it was different with this one. She was cool and, although very young, seemed quite sure of herself.

"Yes," smiled Dominique, "I'd love one."

In the outdoor café, drinking espresso and smoking Gauloises, they talked until nearly ten o'clock, when Dominique, noticing the time, jumped up. "Ooh, I must go, I have to practice my ballet again tonight. Madame wants me to practice three times a day. She says practice makes perfect."

She smiled her kitten smile at him. "Will I see you again?" he stammered.

"Of course," said Dominique, wise beyond her years. "You know we will, but probably after my audition. I must work like a dog now." She extended a slim hand, *"Au revoir*, Gaston Girandot."

He kissed her hand solemnly, gazing into her face as if he had just discovered a priceless treasure.

"Tomorrow—Tango Beach, eleven o'clock?"

She nodded shyly. "Maybe, Gaston—maybe, but I cannot promise." With a smile that took his breath away, she climbed onto her bike and pedaled off into the darkness, leaving him with stars in his eyes and a thumping heart.

That night, lying in her bed, Dominique thought about the beautiful boy and about the power she felt she had had over him during their brief meeting. Power. Power over men. It was an exhilarating sensation that she was experiencing for the first time. She didn't particularly like the local boys but this one was so good-looking, with his dazzling white smile, tanned face and tight black curls that she thought she might make him the exception.

The following day, after a hot morning of vigorous ballet practice with Madame Agathe, she decided to go down to Pampellone for a swim and some sunbathing. She pedaled fast over the two miles of hilly road outside central St. Tropez, arriving in good time at the beach and she wondered if Gaston would be there. There seemed to be only a few people on Tango Beach. The pale yellow sand was clean, and several sailboats and motorboats zoomed about on the sea, which was flat and invitingly deep blue. About a dozen empty wooden sunbeds covered by yellow-and-white-striped mattresses were lined up on the beach waiting hopefully for occupants. She paid the mahogany-skinned beach boy a few francs, and he settled her up near the sea, stuck a parasol in the sand, and brought her a small slatted wooden table on which he set a glass of Coca-Cola. She took off the short cotton sundress which she was wearing over her bikini and lay back on the mattress, letting the glorious rays fall on her body. Closing her eyes behind her sunglasses she was almost asleep when she felt a gentle touch on her shoulder.

"Bonjour," said Gaston Girandot, squatting down on the sand beside her, his brown muscular body gleaming with Ambre Solaire, a shy grin on his face.

"Bonjour, Gaston," she smiled up at him through her glasses.

"What a perfect day," he said.

"Yes, it was so lovely after my practice I decided I needed a swim."

"So what are you waiting for?" said the boy. "Come on, Lazy Bones— get up, let's hit the water. I'll race you."

Laughing and protesting, Dominique allowed Gaston to pull her up, and they dashed into the warm inviting Mediterranean where they swam and frolicked until they were both starving. In the tiny thatched outdoor restaurant where bamboo tables with yellow checked cloths were laid for lunch, the sun filtered through the bamboo blinds which protected the diners from its fiercest rays, throwing striped shadows across Dominique's and Gaston's smiling faces. They ate salade niçoise, provençal chicken with fried potatoes, and *tarte tatin,* washed down with a robust Beaujolais Nouveau. They talked and giggled all through lunch, watched over benignly by the portly proprietor who had known them both since they'd been children.

"Why have we never met before?" asked Dominique, feeling completely satiated by the delicious lunch, and exhilarated by Gaston's company.

"I've been at college in Aix-en-Provence for the last three years," he said. "Before that we probably saw each other here—at the beach." He bent his head until it almost touched hers. "I didn't notice you then, nor you me—but if you'd looked the way you do now I certainly would have."

Dominique blushed and lowered her eyes. She was experiencing such new exciting feelings with this boy, that later when he brought his mattress next to hers on the beach and they were lying half asleep, their bare shoulders almost touching, Dominique knew that she would like to see more of Gaston Girandot—much much more.

In her chaste, narrow bed Agathe was unable to sleep. She was too excited by Dominique's news. She had herself read one of the notices which had been distributed in the village and had experienced her own quiet thrill. When Dominique had spoken to her after class, she had felt that the forthcoming audition might be the key to an escape from her own dull life.

If the girl won the audition, if she were given the part in a Hollywood film, *she,* Agathe, could go with her. Why not? Dominique's parents had heavy responsibilities. Her father was a locally important banker. Her mother was tied down by three young sons, and visibly pregnant again. If . . . if . . . *if* . . .

Agathe was too agitated to sleep, the possibilities of the future too exciting. She turned on her light and took out her scrapbook to gaze lovingly at the handsome face of Julian Brooks. Would she meet him if they went to Hollywood? Maybe not; he was a British star, who worked in England. She knew he had never been to America. But the joy, the freedom to leave her bourgeois and claustrophobic life in St. Tropez, to go out into the real world, to go to America! Everyone wanted to go to America. The golden land of opportunity, where all men—and women— were equal. Agathe would find friends there, a new life—she knew she would.

The past years had not been kind to Agathe. Nothing in her life of freedom could ever minimize the damage of her time in that cellar, and after that her years in L'Éléphant Rose. Watching the traitorous whores fraternizing with the monsters who had destroyed her family, her life, her future, had been purgatory. But worst of all was her deep sense of self-loathing.

She felt that she was hideously ugly. Whenever she looked into a mirror and saw the gaunt white spectre reflected there, she remembered how she had been as a young girl. Almost as pretty as Dominique. Well made, a little plump, with dark sparkling eyes and blue-black glossy hair. Pretty and far more talented. She had never been vivacious, but her quiet charm had its own appeal.

It was gone now forever. All of it—her talent, her looks, her appeal. She had heard the whispered taunts of the village children: "Old maid." "Ugly witch." She saw her aunt's disapproval of her. Brigitte's pursed lips and lack of communication with Agathe revealed clearly enough what her aunt thought of her. But Agathe had no money. What else could she do? Where could she go? Only into her imagination, where she walked in fragrant meadows, hand in hand with laughing friends, or with Julian Brooks—only there was she always happy.

Unless Dominique du Frey could win that audition . . . and perhaps give her the key to a new life in America.

❖ *Five* ❖

Inès had returned to visit Paris nearly two years after the end of the war, and found sadly that she cared little anymore for the beloved city of her birth. She thought her fellow countrymen brusque and cold, although she had to admit they had reason to be. So many of them seemed bitter and resentful about the long Nazi occupation, and now they faced a relentless day-to-day struggle to rebuild their broken lives. All seemed involved only with themselves and their families. Food, a national obsession, was still in very short supply, although the grand hotels and better shops were well stocked and open for business as usual.

After her years in London, Inès felt as if she didn't really belong in Paris. She missed the English sense of humor, missed her pretty flat in Mayfair. She revisited a few familiar haunts to look for old friends, but her only real friends had been Yves, Gabrielle and the rest of her "family" from L'Éléphant Rose. When she went to the old familiar club in Pigalle she found the building shuttered and locked with an *A Vendre* sign on it.

She made inquiries of the neighbors and learned, to her horror, that Gabrielle and many of the girls who had worked at the club had been condemned as traitors and collaborators when Paris was liberated. They had been publicly humiliated in a nearby square by having their heads shaved, being stoned and abused by the local patriots, and then ostracized completely. All of them seemed to have vanished without a trace, and Inès' efforts to track them down were fruitless.

Why hadn't the neighbors and Free French defended them and put the record straight? Told them of the sacrifices these women had made during the war? It was too unfair. They had all done so much for the Resistance from the headquarters at L'Éléphant Rose, and to be punished in such a brutal way was hideously unjust.

But Paris still held so many memories for Inès, both good and bad, that she found it difficult to tear herself away. Just wandering through Montmartre, Pigalle and the glorious narrow streets of the Rive Gauche brought a rush of nostalgia. She knew that there was nothing left for her here anymore, but she felt she couldn't leave just yet.

One day she sat at one of the rickety iron tables outside the Café Deux Magots, which was packed to capacity. Tourists, laughing students and a sprinkling of old men wearing the shabby black berets indigenous to France, and who could nurse a cup of coffee or a glass of red wine for hours, all sat watching the comings and goings at the Boulevard Saint-Germain. Inès sipped at a glass of cognac, remembering that day when she'd sat almost at this very same table and been propositioned by the odious Italian General Umberto Scrofo. What would have been her fate if she had not kept that fateful appointment which had ended in his death?

Would she have been condemned as a traitor and sent away in disgrace? Or would she have simply remained in Paris working as one of Yves' girls? Yves. At the thought of him her heart lurched in spite of herself. Did one ever get over the infatuations of youth? It had been nearly three years now since he'd left her, but whenever she thought of him it was still with a pang.

She stared out into the busy street, and her eyes suddenly focused on a thin man, a grubby beret perched sloppily on his untidy brown curls, a cigarette hanging from his lips, who was walking slowly down the Boulevard Saint-Germain. It couldn't be, it couldn't.

"Yves! *Mon Dieu,* Yves!" Inès jumped up, the people around looking at her irritably as she stumbled through the tables and chairs to the street and grabbed his arm. It was almost as if she'd willed him to appear.

"Yves—it's you—it's really you!" Inès' eyes shone, her face was flushed and glowing as the man swung around and turned to face her.

"My God—Inès!" Yves smiled slowly and she noticed that his teeth had become yellowed from too many Gauloises, and there were deep lines around his eyes.

"What the hell are you doing in Paris?"

"I came to see the sights," said Inès breathlessly, "visit old friends—except that there don't seem to be any old friends around anymore. But now I've found you." She saw that his cheeks were gaunt and unshaven, and that the collar of his blue shirt was grubby. "D'you have time for a cup of coffee with me?" she asked eagerly. "I'd love to talk to you."

"Of course," he said. "I don't have anything else to do. I have all the time in the world, *chérie.*"

They weaved their way back to her table, and he ordered coffee and Armagnac for both of them.

"But you'll have to pay for it." He winked at her wryly. "I'm a little short today."

"Of course," Inès smiled brightly. "So tell me about yourself, Yves. What are you doing? Are you still with Stella?"

He shook his head, lighting another cigarette from the stub of the old one. His hands were shaking, his fingernails dark with dirt, and the index finger of his right hand was deep yellow with nicotine stains. Yves had always been extremely fastidious, and Inès was startled by his transformation.

"Stella—poof—she's gone."

"Oh." Inès didn't know whether to feel a frisson of triumph over an old rival. Certainly this Yves, this man in the shabby overcoat with a three-day growth of stubble, was by no means the handsome dandy she'd always remembered him to be. "Why did she go?" she asked.

"A better offer." He laughed bitterly. "A better *macrou*. Someone who gave her more thrills in bed."

In spite of herself Inès felt herself blushing. Yves had always been a superb lover if nothing else.

"That's ridiculous—you were wonderful in bed—why should she leave for that?"

"*Merci, chérie,* but *malheureusement* a little problem arose when our great country was liberated." There was no mistaking the bitterness in his voice now, and she saw sadness in his eyes as he threw back his brandy and signaled to the white-aproned waiter for another.

"Do you really want to know what happened to me, Inès?"

"Yes," she whispered, "I do—tell me—please, Yves."

"You won't like it," he said bluntly.

"I don't care—tell me—tell me everything."

"When Stella and I came back here from London in 1944 the war was not yet over, you remember—although Paris had been liberated by the Americans. We found a flat, near here actually, and Stella went back to work. She was a good worker but times were bad, food was short." He paused and Inès leaned forward to hear his voice, which had become quieter. "I got involved in the black market. I was doing it in London, you remember, and I still had some contacts here."

"Yes, I know." Inès took a sip of brandy, listening intently, watching Yves' dead eyes growing more impassioned as he continued his story.

"One night a truckload of champagne was coming into Paris from Epernay. I'd arranged with my contacts to buy it—ten million francs, almost all the money I had, but New Year's Eve was on the way and there was a growing demand for all the best champagnes and wines; everyone wanted to celebrate. Don't forget that even though people had suffered during the war, many of them made a great deal of money from it."

"Yes, I know that. Go on, Yves," she coaxed. He'd stopped, the pallor had returned to his face and his hands were now shaking badly. She pushed her Armagnac across the table to him, watching as he drained it immediately.

"I was supposed to meet Gino, you remember Gino? He was one of my most trusted boys, at eleven o'clock on the Quai d'Orsay. He was driving the truck, I had the money. I gave him the cash, then I drove the truck on to my warehouse. I distributed the cases to the clubs and restaurants through my boys—and then I went home—"

He stopped again and Inès saw it was becoming more difficult for him to continue.

"Then what happened?" she coaxed. He didn't answer, lighting another cigarette, his hands as frail and shaking as an old man's. Both their glasses were empty, and she motioned to the waiter to bring more brandy.

"I don't know why I'm telling you all this." He gripped her hand suddenly, his bloodshot eyes those of a frightened animal. "You won't like it, Inès."

"I don't care, Yves—please—please tell me—you must—maybe I can help you."

"Help me—ha!—that's rich—that's very funny indeed." The waiter brought the brandies and Yves downed his in one gulp. His hands stopped shaking and he continued. "Three nights later, while Stella and I were asleep, they came for me."

"Who—who came for you?" whispered Inès.

He shrugged. "Them—the boys—the mob—who knows? It was a set-up, and I was the patsy. They dragged me off in the middle of the night." His voice dropped to a whisper and tears began to roll down his face. "They took me to a warehouse—somewhere near Les Halles I think it was, I could smell the stink of the fish." He stopped, the muscles in his neck quivering.

"And then," Inès prompted quickly.

"The bastards accused me of watering down the fucking champagne. They accused me of fixing it to make a bigger profit. Do you know what, Inès? It wasn't champagne at all in those bottles, it was some kind of cheap colored fizzy water. Someone—and to this day I don't know who—palmed three hundred cases of fake champagne off on me and they blamed me—the scum blamed *me*, Inès."

He was sobbing quietly, unashamedly now.

"So what did they do to you?" Inès almost didn't want to hear the answer.

"Guess?" He looked up at her with a cynical smile. "What's the worst thing you could possibly do to a pimp?"

"I—I don't know," said Inès, mesmerized by this pathetic wreck of a man whom she'd once loved so desperately.

"They castrated me, *chérie*." He put his face very close to hers and grinned horribly. "They made me into a eunuch."

"Oh my God, Yves—no, it's not possible." Inès felt faint as Yves' calloused hands clutched hers tightly on the iron table.

"They cut off my balls and they told me that was the *lightest* penalty that they usually gave to someone who tried to doublecross them. Emasculate them, turn them into a *nothing.*"

Inès' head has swimming. This couldn't be—this couldn't have happened to Yves. Yves who had lived for making love, who had taught her everything she knew about it.

"Mon pauvre Yves, I don't know what to say—I'm so sorry, so terribly sorry." She was crying now and took out her handkerchief to wipe her eyes, oblivious to the curious stares of people at other tables.

"Don't be sorry, *chérie,* I hadn't exactly been Prince Charming in my life, I probably deserved it."

"No! No! No one could deserve that," said Inès in horror. "It's barbaric —did you go to the police?"

"Police?" He laughed bitterly. "You must be joking, *chérie,* they knew what my game was. They despise black marketeers. I got as much sympathy from them as Adolf Hitler would have got if he'd been bleeding to death in a concentration camp. They took me to the hospital, of course, sewed me up. It's not serious, you know—being a eunuch. It doesn't endanger your life or anything, but it sure as hell fucks up your sex life." He laughed again, a hollow dead sound, and lit another Gauloise. "A dead cock. A neuter. It makes you a laughingstock, but people pity you, too."

"So what did you do? What do you do now? How do you live?" Inès stammered, her face flushed and hot.

"I have a few friends left," he said. "I do odd jobs, this and that, betting on the horses, fencing a few bits and pieces, nothing too expensive, of course. I'm okay. I'm fine." He smiled, trying to reassure her, and Inès could see that the Armagnac had done its work in making him more confident. He had obviously become completely dependent on alcohol. Now he sat up straight, his hands no longer trembling, his gaze direct. "Stella left, of course, like a poxy rat deserting a ship—I can't say I blamed her. She liked a good fuck, did Stella, and she couldn't get it from me. Well, *chérie*—that was more than two years ago—I suppose we all have to play the cards that fate deals us—that was a shitty hand for a *mic* to get but I've coped with it. I've tried. What about you, have the gods been good to you?"

"Oh—I'm—well, I'm fine actually," mumbled Inès, her mind still reeling from his revelations. "Pretty good, really."

"Got any good clients?" he asked. "Rich mugs?"

"Yes, oh, yes—very good—I mean—yes, they're all right." Inès felt stifled, even though it was cool outside the café.

"I bet none of them can do this," exclaimed Yves and he flicked his tongue into his mouth with the burning cigarette on it, closed his lips and stared at Inès with the wide-eyed comical look that had so entranced her when she was a little girl. As she watched in dismay, two long puffs of smoke came out of Yves' ears.

Inès felt she had to escape. She wanted to run—run like the wind. She wanted to go back to her hotel and weep bitter tears for her erstwhile lover, who smiled, pleased with himself as he stubbed out the damp cigarette and looked to her for approval. She smiled weakly and he grinned back.

"Good, *chérie*, that's good. You always were a clever little *poule de luxe*, Inès, one of the best, you deserve to do well."

Suddenly Inès wanted to leave Paris right now. She felt sick, dirty, sullied. She wanted to cry for this sad little man she had loved so much, for the friends she had lost. As if reading her thoughts Yves leaned towards her, brushing her cheek briefly with dry lips.

"*Au revoir, chérie,*" he said briskly, arranging the beret on his graying curls. "I have to go now. Thanks for the drink." He stood up, the sun shining on his lined face, and Inès could see clearly how much he'd changed, how the years had taken their toll. "Good luck, Inès."

"*Au revoir,* Yves," she whispered. "Good-bye."

He tipped his beret, and as he walked off down the Boulevard Saint-Germain, his shabby overcoat flapping around his thin body, Inès silently thanked God that her heart was no longer in Paris, that her life was in England now.

The next day Inès stood outside the Ritz Hotel in the Place Vendôme, staring up for one last time at the window of the room where she had killed Umberto Scrofo. She was on her way to the airport back to London, and she knew now that Paris held nothing for her but sad, bad memories.

During the next few years in London Inès became more and more disenchanted with her life of prostitution, even though her clients were all rich and reasonably attractive. The frightened, ignorant teenager had matured into a sophisticated, chic woman of the world who suspected that true love existed only in novels and women's magazines. The pain of Yves' betrayal had never really healed and she had not found a man to inspire feelings of truly belonging to someone body and soul.

As the years passed and her savings grew, Inès gradually eliminated most of her clients, keeping only a few of her most powerful and influential customers. Apart from Viscount Benjie, for whom she had a special affection, a series of mentors had kept her—in particular three rich, middle-aged Englishmen. One was an aristocrat who had come out of what he called a "good war" with a chestful of medals to prove it; the other two were more bourgeois men of the City, securely married industrialists who between them appeared to own half the home counties.

They had given Inès money—though not an enormous amount, since "old" English money is never thrown around by those who possess it. But what they had given her that was infinitely more precious than cash, expensive trinkets, or the occasional visit to Deauville, Cannes or New York, was knowledge—an understanding of politics, of stocks, bonds, equities and market prices. They had imparted secret share tips to her, and insider advice on futures. An overheard phrase in a business telephone conversation at her flat, an artfully veiled question or two from her, and she would call her stockbroker to buy coffee beans, nickel, tin, gold or silver. Knowledge is power, and Inès learned fast. Her portfolio grew, as with a shrewd Frenchwoman's understanding of financial matters she made it her business to protect her future.

Inès became resigned to never finding her own man, to never falling in love. She supposed it was her fate never to settle down in security with a safe husband and two-point-three children. One day soon, however, she would have enough money to stop working and to retire. What would she do with herself then? It was a thought she did not like to dwell on. Her flat was filled with expensive, beautiful objects, and revealed no clue to her profession. But there was no one to admire her pretty things. No one to share her life when she would finally end her "career."

Inès had felt little emotion for any man since Yves—only a vague fondness for them, an almost niecelike attitude. To her, men were all the same: mostly selfish, sexual animals. The more they used her for their pleasure, the less she felt for them. Week after week, month after month, year after year, as she plied her sexual trade, she yearned for a romantic love which, in her heart, she believed did not exist.

She had met many eligible men—young men, handsome men, clever and ambitious men, some with great futures. None of them had moved her one iota. She tried desperately to fall in love, to feel some small part of the passion, ecstasy and joy which she'd known with Yves, but she felt nothing. Sometimes she wondered cynically if it was Yves' magic tricks which had so entranced her and that at heart she was still eleven years old.

Then one afternoon she went to a matinée performance of *Pygmalion* at the Aldwych Theatre. There on the stage was a tall handsome actor with curved black eyebrows and a face like an archangel. His dark hair was severely brushed back, tortoiseshell spectacles were perched on his aristocratic nose, and a deerstalker hat sat on his head at a jaunty angle. From her seat in the stalls, surrounded by the rustle of chocolate wrappings and the excited murmur of the matinée matrons, she could sense his innate sensitivity spiced with roguish masculinity and humor.

His name was Julian Brooks, Looks Brooks, the Idol of the Odeons, as he was known in the tabloid press, and not since Yves had Inès seen a man who so captured her heart and her imagination. When he was on stage, Julian entranced her with his charisma and waspish sexy charm. Her eyes never left him for a second. She perceived in him a quality of warmth and wonderful fun that she knew was real, and not just the actor playing a part. Inès knew that she had to meet this man.

Inès did not miss a single matinée performance of *Pygmalion* for the remainder of its run, and she made it her business to find out every scrap of information she could about the man who had started to inhabit so many of her waking thoughts.

❖ *Six* ❖

As JULIAN BECAME A BIGGER and more glittering star, Phoebe had gradually changed into that kind of dreadful snob which only a middle-class Englishwoman can be. She loved two things beyond all else: money and social position. Her main interest in Julian's career, other than landing herself a plum part, was the position in society and the wealth which it could bring them. She rarely spoke to any of the cast or crew with whom Julian worked, choosing only to speak to stars and important directors. The artistic side was of no interest to her; she couldn't have cared less whether her husband was starring as Othello or Charley's Aunt. She loved being Mrs. Julian Brooks, close friend of the Oliviers and the Redgraves. She loved the life of a star's wife: the society rounds of Royal Ascot, Wimbledon, the fourth of June at Eton, Cowes, Henley; charity balls and weekends at country houses with the aristocratic and the famous, as well as gleaming black limousines and accounts with all the best couturiers and shops. Fueled by Julian's success, her acting ambitions came into full flower when she had forced him to cast her in his plays. She would have made his life quite intolerable had he not given in to her. Appearing on stage with Julian gave her even more cachet with her friends, and naturally she always insisted on having above-the-title billing: not just a star's wife, but a star in her own right.

But at this moment she was absolutely furious with Julian. She had in fact been fuming ever since he'd categorically refused to allow her to play Eliza Doolittle in *Pygmalion.*

At thirty-five, she looked at least a dozen years too old to play the part of the waiflike cockney flowergirl, not to mention the indeterminate number of excess pounds which gave her the look of a well-padded matron.

"I'm perfect for the part, *perfect,* you always *said* I was," Phoebe yapped. Lipstick was smeared on her front teeth, and her heavy makeup did nothing more than bring the deepening lines of discontent on her face into sharper focus. The henna which she used so liberally to brighten her fading locks glowed garishly in the thin afternoon light which filtered into Julian's dressing room at Pinewood Studios. He was in the last stages of shooting *The Buccaneer,* another swashbuckler for Didier Armande, and in the middle of intense casting and preproduction sessions for a stage production of *Pygmalion.* Exhausted after two long months on such a physically demanding movie, he had been trying in vain to take a nap on the daybed in his dressing room when Phoebe burst in, dismissing his dresser with a typically waspish "Get out. I don't care if he *is* asleep—I'm his bloody wife!"

"Phoebe, for God's sake," Julian pleaded, looking up bleary-eyed at his once desirable wife, now an outraged, overweight virago who stood before him, hands on hips.

"How *could* you have cast that *slut* Louise James as Eliza?" she said, spitting venom. "She's *hideous*. She can't act and she's *far* too old!"

"She's twenty," Julian said simply. "She won a Tony award on Broadway last year, she's been acting since she was eleven, and, what's more, she happens to be very pretty."

"*Pretty?*" Phoebe screeched. "You call that baggage pretty? She's got a face like a . . . like a cheap china doll. *I'm* your wife. How about some loyalty to me, *me!*"

"Phoebe, please. Please do be reasonable." Julian was trying hard not to lose his composure, not to say his temper. He had an important emotional scene to play this afternoon, and Phoebe's rages were far from helpful. "You're just too old for Eliza, can't you see that, dear?"

"No, I bloody can't." She started to cry the crocodile tears which Julian had grown to know so well. "I'm the same age as Vivien. She plays young girls."

"Look in the damned *mirror,* for Christ's sake. It doesn't *lie,* you know. You're almost thirty-six. You *can't* play an eighteen-year-old, Phoebe, you just can't, and that's that."

"I *can,*" she wept. "Oh, Julian, *please please* let me. I'll lose some weight, I'll be so good . . . Look at my reviews for *Present Laughter—* they said I was enchantingly young and vibrant."

"That was several years ago, old thing." Julian knew he had to remain adamant; Phoebe was doing everything she could to manipulate him, and he couldn't allow the balance of power in their marriage to shift in her direction. God knows she tried all the time. It was always an uphill struggle, but he had to remain in control. He believed in the dominance of the male, and just as importantly, the strong professional standards he wanted maintained.

"Nearly five years ago, Phoebe," he went on, "and the role of Joanna was of a woman of the world. Eliza's almost a *child.* I'm sorry, but it's done now. I've cast Louise, and the announcements go out to the press tomorrow."

Phoebe stopped crying and looked at him warily. "I see," she sighed, wiping her smudged eyes with a mascara-stained handkerchief. "Just like that—humped and dumped. Thanks a bunch."

"Don't be so bloody ridiculous, Phoebe. You've got a damned good life. I try to give you *everything* you want. You've been in practically every one of my plays but you're just not going to be in this one. So let's finish this stupid argument, and for God's sake let me get some sleep."

Phoebe thoughtfully fingered her huge Kashmiri sapphire-and-diamond ring from Garrard's, then adjusted her gold-and-pavé diamond choker from Van Cleef & Arpels and toyed with the buttons of her beige cashmere Jacques Fath couture suit. These were all too familiar signs to Julian that she was plotting something. He threw himself back on the couch with a sigh, his body craving rest. He'd been up since five that morning. Phoebe had insisted that they go to the opening of *Ring Around the Moon* the night before, and afterward to yet another of Binkie Beaumont's lavish parties. He had slept for only three hours and was shatteringly exhausted.

"I'm so tired, Phoebe," he said simply. "Would you mind leaving me now? I need a bit of a doze—got an important scene this afternoon."

"Oh, yes, I'll leave, all right," she said frostily, pulling on her beige suede gauntlet gloves trimmed with mink and shrugging her new sable jacket from Bergdorf Goodman of New York City over her hefty shoulders.

"I'm not exactly happy with you these days, Julian. I don't think I'm going to enjoy being around London while you're rehearsing with that talentless trollop."

Julian sighed again. What now? Which threatening ploy did she have in mind this time? Was this bitch never satisfied?

"Last night at the party Hermione was telling me that she wants to take a little trip," she went on. "I think I'll join her. I'm sure we'll have a lot of fun together; Hermione's so amusing."

"Wonderful, dear," Julian sighed, closing his eyes, praying that she would now leave. He heard the assistant director knocking at his leading lady's dressing room next door.

"Where will you and Hermione go?" he asked, more out of a sense of politeness than interest.

"Around the world," Phoebe snapped, striding to the door. "It's expensive, of course," she added with smug satisfaction. "About ten thousand pounds for the best hotels, restaurants and so on. But since I'll be bored being around here with you and that James girl, probably fucking like rabbits, I know you won't mind too much forking out. Oh, by the way—" she stopped at the opened door—"don't forget—you've promised me Ophelia. *That* I will never give up. *Never.*" She sailed out, slamming the door just as Julian's dresser appeared carrying his usual wake-up cup of espresso.

"Everything okay, guv?" he asked sympathetically, seeing the evident strain on Julian's face.

"Fine, Freddie, fine. Thanks, old boy. Tell Tim in makeup I'll be over in five minutes."

Ophelia my arse! he thought tossing down the bitter but reviving espresso, and pulling on his black leather boots. The way Phoebe looked now she'd be a more likely contender for Gertrude. Maybe even Gertrude's mother if there was such a part. He was in a black mood when he stomped into the makeup room, only to be greeted by a warm smile from his current leading lady.

That evening, after shooting had finally ended, Julian was a most welcome visitor in the dressing room of his gorgeous, pouting co-star,

Rebecca Chamberlane. There he released all his anger and pent-up frustration, leaving them both so delightfully sated and fulfilled that their liaison continued right up until the movie was finished.

❧ *Seven* ☙

NICE

"Jesus, what a bunch of dogs." Bluey Regan leaned back in his seat in the darkened auditorium of the old theater in Nice. He studied the lineup of forty-seven nervous teenage girls who huddled together on the stage in their skimpy black leotards, mended tights and shabby ballet shoes.

"Not a decent body among them," he muttered to Nicholas Stone, the talented young director who was leaning forward in the seat next to him, staring intently at the girls. He was whispering something rapidly to his secretary, who was writing as fast as her limited shorthand would allow her.

"They've got no *tits*, Nick," complained Bluey. "Not one of 'em has anything more than a thirty-two A-cup. *That's* going to look *real* great in an off-the-shoulder period gown, in glorious Technicolor, up there with Julian Brooks trying to act as if he wants to screw her brains out."

"Shut up, Bluey," Nick snapped. "Haven't you heard? We're doing the sixteenth, not the eighteenth century. She's supposed to be a princess and she'll be dressed in something loose. Just *forget* tits for a minute, if that's remotely possible for you. Just look for raw talent, photogenic faces, the innocent but sexy quality of these girls. If you don't want to watch, go for a walk, go get laid, go get lost! I'll weed 'em out myself."

"Yeah, well, remember, you're the Charlie who's gonna be directing her."

"Yeah, and I know what I'm doing," said Nick implacably. "If you stay, keep your mouth *shut*, Bluey. When I want your advice I'll ask for it, and tits are no big deal in this case."

"Okay, okay," Bluey said, slumping back in his seat. He looked again at the group of terrified girls, muttering one last disparaging remark loudly enough for Nick's French secretary to hear.

"Please do not forget, *Meestair* Regan, that we have only come out of a war—an occupation—less than nine years ago," the woman said frostily. "These young girls 'ad very leetle to *eat* when they were babies and that is why they are so small—the *contraire* of your well-fed *American* girls."

"Well, I guess a few good American steaks, fries and chocolate malts would fatten 'em up. Get 'em lookin' as good as Marilyn Monroe and

Jane Russell quicker than you can say Metro fuckin' Goldwyn Mayer, right?" Bluey smiled lazily, offering the woman some chewing gum.

"Quite," said the Frenchwoman, refusing. "But I don't think any of these girls are quite that type of *mademoiselle*. They are all French— *typiquement française*—and you will find, very proud of it, *Monsieur!*" She turned away from him, unable to disguise her extreme dislike for Nick's leathery assistant.

A frail redhead in a burgundy leotard and tights which did nothing for her coloring stepped forward on stage, shyly handing her sheet music to the pianist. She performed the dance of the dying swan from *Swan Lake;* it was technically perfect but had no passion at all. Shaking his head, Nick Stone whispered to his secretary to dismiss her. She was the fifteenth applicant they had seen so far. This was going to be much harder than he'd anticipated.

An hour later, Bluey was snoring loudly when Nick nudged him excitedly. "Take a look at this one," he whispered. "Now *she* is much more the type I had in mind for Isabella. What do you think?"

Bluey sat up, watching with a critical eye as Dominique danced a fandango from *Carmen* with such style and barely suppressed sensuality that both men found themselves aroused and intrigued.

"Hot damn, she's *good*," breathed Bluey. "Fucking good, eh, Nick? And getta load of those legs. Looks like the kid's got star quality if ever I saw it."

"Yeah, she sure does," Nick agreed, scribbling notes and tossing them into a folder. "She's sure one helluva dancer, helluva looker too. Maybe she's the one, Bluey."

"About time too," said Bluey. "At least this hasn't been a complete waste of time."

At the back of the auditorium, Agathe clasped her hands joyfully as she saw how well her pupil was performing. All of her extra rehearsals had paid off. If there was any justice in the world, Dominique must get the part, be off to Hollywood, away from this Provençal backwater. And with a little luck, Agathe would be going with her.

"Well, what d'you know." Bluey stared with mounting admiration at Dominique as she finished her second audition piece, a perfectly executed version of Eleanor Powell's tap dance from *Broadway Melody*.

She had thrown a short skirt around her black cotton leotard which accentuated her tiny waist and small, firm breasts. Her long hair was loosened and it seemed to float in the air like soft black tendrils around her flushed face.

All but five of the girls had been dismissed. They sat watching cross-legged in the wings, cardigans and shawls draped over their shoulders, grudgingly admitting to each other that Dominique was very good, far better than any of them. She was more than good. She had a magical presence, a powerful charisma, a sweet gamine quality which could change like quicksilver into smoldering sensuality.

Dominique had now finished, and stood flushed and shaking with

nerves, in the center of the vast stage. She waited, trembling, as the two
men approached her.

"Very nice—*very* nice indeed," Nick said. Since his recent success he
had become partial to the suave Fred Astaire school of dressing. He wore
cream gabardine slacks with an open-necked pink shirt and a navy blue
polkadot cravat. Even with his black curly hair greased down, it still
looked wild, accentuating his boyish good looks. At twenty-seven he now
had two major movie hits under his belt in less than a year, and he was
considered one of the hottest of Hollywood's new generation of directors.

Bobby Soxers in Space had been the teenage cult movie of 1953,
grossing over twenty million dollars at the box office, and giving Nick his
first taste of the critical acclaim which he'd longed for. His second movie,
a screwball comedy, had done equally well with critics and audiences
alike, although the original script had been fairly mediocre. But Nick had
a magic touch with film. He understood and respected it, he revered it,
he could see the whole film in his mind's eye before he even shot it. He
was sizzling in Hollywood, MCCP's golden boy, Spyros Makopolis' favorite, and now for his third film they had given him the prize plum of the
year to direct: *The Legend of Cortez.*

After shaking Dominique's hand, Nick handed her a stiff white card
with his name engraved on it in bold black letters.

"Come and see me this afternoon at three o'clock at the Carlton Hotel
in Cannes. Can you get there all right, honey?"

Dominique almost fainted. She barely managed a nod and a whispered
"Oui, Monsieur, I can. May I bring my chaperone?" She nodded towards
the dim figure of Agathe shrouded in gloom, far beyond the footlights.

"Of course." Nick smiled at her. She certainly was adorable. Sexy,
fresh and sweet too. "Bring your mother and father, your grandmother
and all your aunts and uncles too, if you want. We are going to talk
business, young lady, and I think you're going to like what I have to say."

Dominique smoothed back her waist-length hair so that it framed the
perfect oval of her face as she shyly looked up at Nick through her forest
of lashes with green lynx eyes.

"Merci, M'sieur Stone," she whispered in a girlishly sexy voice, which
both men immediately realized would be another major asset to her. But
those eyes. Nick found himself entranced by them, and Bluey's experienced gaze roamed over her young body like a gourmet before a feast.
Gorgeous—yes, she was gorgeous all right. A tasty young dish to set
before a king—or in this case an explorer.

In the darkness of the auditorium Agathe smiled to herself. She sensed
the reaction of the two men to her pupil but clenched her fists in spite of
her pleasure in Dominique's performance. It was always the same with
men. Show them a young, pretty girl and they turned to putty. Once a
woman was no longer young, no longer pretty, no one would bother to
give her a second glance. In spite of her good wishes for her young pupil,
Agathe felt a twinge of jealousy. If it hadn't been for the war, that could
have been her up there.

❖ *Eight* ❖

IN THE SPRING of 1954 an American film company came to Rome to shoot a frothy escapist movie featuring two famous stars of the thirties. Ramona Armande and Gregory Mendelson were playing a middle-aged couple who find both adventure and autumnal love in Rome, amid its romantic beauty and its broken stones.

The film company had been setting up lights and equipment in a small piazza for a scene between Ramona and Gregory. It was unusually hot, and the stifling room above the café, which had been provided for Ramona's relaxation, was becoming uncomfortably warm.

She decided to walk a little, to explore the endlessly fascinating side streets of Rome, where each shop seemed to hold even more eye-catching, exquisite treasures than the last. Ramona adored collecting, and the more bizarre the objects the better they could be shown to advantage in her exotic house in Acapulco. She looked the height of chic in a beautifully tailored cream linen belted suit from Balenciaga, and a large beige straw hat, laden with silk lilies of the valley, perched on her shining black hair. Dark sunglasses covered her famous amber eyes, but even with them the sun was so blindly strong in the piazza that she squinted against its brightness.

"Principessa, where are you going?" asked Tinto, the first assistant director, with a concerned expression on his permanently anxious face as he hurried after her.

"Don't worry, Tinto my dear." Ramona smiled in the charming manner with which she always managed to endear herself to the crew. "I'm just going for a little stroll down the shaded side of the Via Babuino. I shan't be gone for more than half an hour and by that time you should have finished lighting the set, *si?*"

"*Si, Principessa,*" smiled Tinto, admiring the slim straight-backed figure as she wandered off up the cobbled and sun-dappled street. She was still a beautiful woman, even though there was no question that she would ever see fifty again.

Ramona strolled slowly along the hot dusty street enjoying the faint breeze which gently ruffled her hair. Each little shop was a treasure trove of beautiful things, and she lingered in several of them, admiring an eighteenth-century painted lace fan with an ornate silver gilt handle, then a pair of 1920s emerald-and-diamond ear clips, and finally a beautifully sculpted bronze figure of a muscular youth throwing a discus. But it wasn't until she found herself outside the last shop in the street that she caught her breath. The ivory-and-ruby bracelet which lay on a black velvet cushion in the window was truly breathtaking. To her experienced eye it was of museum quality, with its sugarloaf cabochon rubies surrounded by brilliant-cut diamonds all set into a wide cuff of creamy ivory. Immediately intrigued, Ramona opened the door and stepped into the cool, darkened interior. An extremely ugly fat man who reminded her of a toad sat behind the glass counter examining a diamond bracelet through a loupe. He looked up at her, and as the bright sunlight from the street only illuminated her as a silhouette, he did not immediately recognize her.

"May I help you?" he inquired, his voice sounding harsh and uncultured. Ramona thought she detected the southern accent of a Neapolitan or a Sicilian, certainly not the refined tones of a Roman gentleman.

"Yes—the ivory bracelet in the window—I'd like to see it, please."

"*Prego*—sit down, *Signora.*" The man gestured towards a carved eighteenth-century bergère, which she noticed was of superb quality, like everything else in the shop.

Ramona looked around her admiringly at all the shelves and cabinets which were full of jewels, small enamel and gold boxes, carved figures and other objects d'art. Obviously he was a man of taste in spite of his grotesque and off-putting appearance and that curious rasping voice.

"There—it is ravishing, is it not?" He placed the cuff gently on a velvet pad, watching her carefully as Ramona reverently picked it up.

"Beautiful—it's absolutely stunning," she breathed, removing a glove and admiring the bracelet on her slim wrist. "Such quality. How much?"

"Ah . . . for you, *Signora,* a very special price indeed," beamed the *antiquaire,* having recognized her when switching on the desk light. "Only ten million lire to you, *Signora.*"

"It's superb," breathed Ramona, "truly beautiful—ten million, you say?"

He nodded encouragingly. His tiny eyes were slits, his hands clasped across his imposing stomach. But Ramona noticed how the excellent quality and cut of his suit managed cleverly to disguise so much of his bulk, and that his watch and cufflinks were from Cartier.

"I have an idea," she said as she leaned forward, removing her sunglasses to give him the full benefit of the amber lynx eyes which had captivated so many audiences for more than three decades. Their magic obviously still worked, for she saw him swallow, and a faint pink tinge begin to suffuse his sallow complexion.

"This bracelet looks wonderful with this dress, don't you think?"

He nodded, quite captivated by the extraordinary glamour and mystery of the woman.

"We're in the middle of shooting a movie down in the Piazza Barbarini—" Ramona clasped his arm with her delicate scarlet-tipped fingers like an excited child. "Let me wear it in the next scene. The production manager will be there to see to the insurance and all of that sort of thing—and—" she positively glowed as she continued—"when we've finished filming this afternoon, *Oggi* is shooting a photo layout of me all around Rome. You know the sort of thing, throwing coins into the Fontana di Trevi, wandering around the Forum and the Piazza di Spagna. If I was wearing this bracelet, I should *insist* that the magazine give your shop a credit for it in the article—then perhaps the price might be a little less?" She smiled ingenuously, pleased with her little plan, and he couldn't help but smile back. She was certainly an enchanting woman. A woman of the world—no doubt at all about that—but with a childlike charm which he found quite irresistible.

He pretended to heave a great sigh and then shook his shiny bald head from side to side. "The Signora drives a hard bargain." He smiled. "But as it is you, Madame Armande, such a great, great star—" he gave a little bow in her direction and Ramona acknowledged it by inclining her head regally—"I can see no way in which I could refuse you—with one proviso, of course."

"Which is?" asked Ramona, unable to tear her eyes away from the glorious cuff and the diamonds which glittered brilliantly on it in the dim light.

"That I might be allowed to accompany the Signora on her trip around Rome this afternoon, perhaps even to show her some sights that she has not yet seen—then perhaps—if she would permit—to have the honor of escorting her to dinner tonight at Taverna Livia?"

Ramona studied him. He would certainly be an unprepossessing escort —short, fat and ugly. But she found that he had a certain kind of charm, and obviously from the exquisite contents of his shop, he had an enormous knowledge of art and a great eye for beautiful things.

She was becoming bored by the fawning Italian gigolos who had found their way to her suite in the Grand Hotel. Bored too by the labored huffing and puffing of her co-star Gregory Mendelson during their occasional bouts of lovemaking. They had indulged in a torrid affair some years ago, when he had been a desirable stud and the idol of millions, but unfortunately time had been unforgiving, not only to his hair and waistline, but also to his sex drive. Although he'd made a valiant effort to satisfy Ramona in bed for old times' sake, their perfunctory couplings had become less than gratifying for them both.

"Very well." She inclined her head to him again. "I should be happy for you to accompany me—and delighted to accept your invitation to dinner." She glanced at her wristwatch. "Oh dear, now I must go—it's time for the filming to start, I mustn't be late. Won't you join me, *Signor?*"

Pulling a bunch of keys from his pocket and carefully locking the door of his little shop behind them, the jeweler followed Ramona out into the blistering Roman sunshine.

He picked her up at the Grand Hotel at nine o'clock. His car was an open black Lancia, and his portliness was again adroitly disguised in a midnight blue shantung suit from Caraceni. He was wearing a white silk shirt from the Burlington Arcade, and a fairly garish crimson tie. If it weren't for the ugliness of his face and body and the cloying cologne in which he seemed to have bathed, he would indeed have cut quite a *bella figura*. As it was, he complemented Ramona, who was elegance personified in a champagne lace cocktail dress which nipped her tiny waist into a handspan, and gave her a cleavage that Miss Marilyn Monroe would envy. Around her neck was a simple diamond necklace from Fulco, and on her wrist she wore the beautiful ivory-and-diamond bracelet. They made an arresting couple as they walked through the lobby of the hotel, and several people turned to stare in genuine admiration at Ramona's style and presence.

He couldn't help feeling pleased with himself. He had never gone out with a woman as ravishing and as famous as Ramona—in fact no beautiful or even pretty girls would even give him a second glance unless plenty of lire changed hands. But Ramona seemed not to care about his lack of height or looks. She seemed more interested in his knowledge of jewelry and pictures. As they drove in his open car through the streets towards the quieter outskirts of Rome, she covered her hair with a chiffon scarf and listened carefully to the replies he gave to her many questions.

Ramona was an excellent listener, a natural expert in finding out every detail about a person's past. With a subtle and well-chosen question or two, she tried hard to piece together her escort's life story. As they sat at a table outside the elegant restaurant in the balmy night air, sipping champagne from heavy Venetian glasses, Umberto Scrofo told Ramona Armande everything that he thought she should know about his past life.

Umberto had been an extremely lucky man. When the Mafia thugs had left him to fend for himself in the tiny rowboat off the coast of Calabria, it had been a moonlit night and the sea flat and calm. Without the aid of a compass, and with more luck than skill, he had managed to drift around the cape of Calabria, the southernmost part of the Italian mainland, and through the Straits of Messina. There he had been found floating by a fisherman out in his boat who had rescued him and taken him, half dead, to his home in a tiny Sicilian village. When Umberto had recovered he contacted an old army friend, not a member of the Cosa Nostra, who had, with the help of a few gold coins, taken him to Rome.

Always prepared for any eventuality, Umberto had made it his habit to sleep with a money belt around his waist, in which he kept some ancient gold coins and a small fortune in loose diamonds, emeralds and rubies. The Mafia gang had luckily neglected to give him a full body search when they broke into his room, so he was a rich man when he arrived in Rome to begin yet another new life

After a few months he opened an antique shop on the Via Babuino with many of the precious things that he had stolen from the French and the Greeks, and had shipped to Italy for storage during the war. Because so many of his pieces were from lesser-known museums and the great houses of France, he soon owned one of the most beautifully stocked antique shops in Rome.

He shrewdly released only a few selected items from his looted plunder onto the market each year, being extremely careful not to attract the attentions of Interpol, who were still on the lookout for the thousands of works of art that had been stolen during the war.

The gold rings and bracelets of all the unfortunates who had been tortured and sent to their deaths during his regime had provided an excellent income for him. He still had many of the silver and gold icons, enamel vases, alabaster figures and candlesticks pilfered from the Greeks, and from France he still had what he referred to as "my pictures." Among these were masterpieces by Manet, Van Gogh, Renoir, Cézanne, and three large and highly important cubist canvases by Picasso. These were all kept secured in an underground vault in his new house close to the Piazza di Spagna, waiting for the rainy day when he might need to sell them.

Umberto was a rich man, but a bored one. The pleasures of the flesh no longer titillated him much unless they were of a truly bizarre nature, and it was becoming tedious sitting in his shop day after day. He certainly didn't need the money. What he really needed was something to stimulate him, but apart from sex, he could not think of anything.

But when he stepped into the Piazza Barbarini that sunny day and saw the huge arclights glittering down from the iron girders, saw the hustle and bustle of the film company, the glamour and enthusiasm which everyone seemed to have, he realized at once that at last he had found the answer to his long days of ennui.

It was during the making of *One Sunday in Rome* that Umberto and Ramona became firm friends. Umberto, who had always been intrigued by Hollywood, began to be even more interested by the fascinating business of filmmaking, and he became a regular fixture on the set. He met the producer, Henry Hornblower, an over-the-hill grizzled Hollywood legend, almost ready to be put out to pasture, but still full of gutsy anecdotes and stories about the days before talkies were invented. He met the director, a brash young whiz kid well on his way up the ladder, ambitious as hell and absolutely sure both of himself and of his talent; and he met the money men, the mysterious financiers who had managed to raise the money for the movie like conjurors. He expertly picked all their respective brains, convinced that he too could find the money to both finance and produce a film in Italy. And why not? It was now an open city for filmmaking, the very hub of the movie industry in Europe.

All roads truly led to Rome in the early 1950s. The Via Veneto was a constant hive of activity, as busy as the terrace of the Carlton during the Cannes Film Festival. Every table at Doney's and the other cafés was packed with producers, financiers, writers and entrepreneurs, as well as a heavy sprinkling of Italian and American movie stars. The Via Veneto was the place to be seen, to be noticed, to clinch a deal.

It was hard to tell the difference between the aspiring starlets who table-hopped from group to group with calculated charm and the prostitutes who plied their timeless trade up and down the Veneto. Both groups were equally attractive in their tight low-cut dresses, bouffant hair and made-up faces.

Everyone seemed to have a movie which they wanted to make or were about to shoot, and everyone had a deal or a contract ready to be signed. Rome was Little Hollywood on the Tiber, and movie people from around the world were flocking in hordes to the Eternal City.

When Umberto confided his plans to Ramona one evening as they were sitting at the Café Doney, sipping *crème de menthe frappé* through long pink straws, she turned to him in surprise and exclaimed, "Why Umberto, I never knew you were interested in this crazy business. When did all this happen?"

"Well, a long time ago, I suppose," he laughed, eyeing a sloe-eyed blonde slowly cruising the street looking for some action. "During the war we used to see many American movies—some with you in them, my dear." He kissed her hand gallantly, his downcast eyes in fact following the progress of the young blonde's swaying buttocks up the pavement. "Those were always my particular favorites."

"How sweet of you, my dear Umberto, how very very kind you are."

"Not at all, my dear. But you are so much more beautiful in life than you ever were on the screen."

She laughed girlishly. "Now, Umberto, don't go too far, my dear, after all I am nearly forty, you know." She lied with a smile, as he smiled back, playing along with the joke.

"Forty or not, you are lovelier than *any* of these girls walking here tonight."

Another tall slender blonde, wearing a figure-hugging red sheath dress which was cut completely down to the vee of her bottom, tossed her hair and winked at Scrofo as she swayed past their table. He feigned indifference, but remembered her well from the week before. She'd been very hot indeed. He still had her number somewhere. Tonight he would call her—later. Much as he liked and admired Ramona he did not find her sexually attractive at all, and he was only too aware that the feeling was mutual. So much the better. Business and lust never made good bedfellows.

Ramona was well aware of his eyes on the red-sheathed blonde, but pretended not to notice. Removing a black Sobranie from her platinum Boucheron cigarette case, she carefully placed it between her vermilion lips and waited for him to light it, which he did immediately with a heavy gold lighter.

"Umberto, I have a little proposition for you," she said, leaning forward confidentially, allowing him to peek down her white chiffon décolletage—if he felt so inclined.

"What is it, *cara*?" He smiled at her, aware that at the surrounding tables everyone was whispering about her. He was pleased when a couple of paparazzi snapped photographs of them deep in discussion, and he posed casually, without looking at the cameras. There had already been several photographs of the two of them together in the Italian magazines, and she had also been snapped in his shop for the *Oggi* layout. The gorgeous bracelet on her wrist had created so much publicity for his business that he now had to have an assistant working in the shop.

"What is your proposition, *cara?*" he asked after the paparazzi had moved off in search of fresh prey.

"I have a wonderful script that was written for me last year. It's an art film of a kind, but it also has so much scope for action and spectacle," she said excitedly. Umberto's face was impassive as he sipped at the sticky *crème de menthe.* "My brother Didier in London has some backers who could put up more than half the money, and we're looking for the rest, and also for someone to produce the film. That someone could be you, Umberto," she said, her voice rising so that an American posse of journalists at the next table stared at them curiously. "Would you be interested?"

"I could be—in fact I could be very interested indeed, my dear." Umberto tapped his cigar into the ashtray, his heart beating fast with unexpected excitement. But he did not want Ramona to know how truly he wanted to grasp this key that she was offering him.

"Tell me something of the story—what's it all about?"

"It's called *La Città Perduta—The Lost City,*" she told him excitedly, "and it's wonderful, Umberto, just wonderful—it'll probably win every award at all the festivals next year—it's tough—gritty—and very modern."

"And I'm sure there's a great part in it for you," he smiled, his mind racing.

"Naturally." She smiled archly, puffing on her cigarette. "I would play a grandmother. A young one, of course, darling," she giggled, "poor, destitute, hungry, who has a teenage daughter with an illegitimate baby all living together in Rome. It's the story of her courageous struggle to build a life for them all after the war."

"It sounds promising," he said, chewing on his cigar.

"It certainly does. I'm not a complete fool, Umberto—I know that there are younger, prettier, more bankable actresses than me out there today. They're the ones who are getting the pick of the roles, girls like Grace Kelly, Ava Gardner, Marilyn Monroe. I'm no longer among the top boxoffice stars anymore, I'd be the first to admit it, but I still do love to work."

He patted her beautifully manicured hand, adorned as it was with the staggering forty-carat diamond which he knew was a present from her husband, the mysterious Prince Kasinov, and told her, "You're *Numera Una* with me, *carissima,* and if this movie is half as good as you say it is— I would like very much to become involved with it."

Ramona beamed at him. "Wonderful, Umberto, wonderful. I have a copy of the script back at the hotel—I'll give it to you to read tonight."

"One thing," he asked, "how much money did your brother say that you're looking for from the other side?"

"Oh, peanuts, darling, only peanuts," trilled Ramona. "I will work for virtually nothing, of course, just a percentage of the profits. We will cast an unknown girl for the daughter, and this new young director on *Sunday in Rome* is very talented; I'm sure we could get him for a song. So the above-the-line is minimal. I would say about four hundred thousand dollars—"

"Excuse my ignorance, *Principessa*, but what does 'above-the-line' mean?"

Ramona laughed lightly and said, "That is the salaries for the stars and the director, Umberto. I suppose we would need about one million dollars total financing, certainly not much more." She looked at him, batting sooty eyelashes. "A million dollars isn't really too high a price to pay to get into the movie business, is it, Umberto, darling?"

"Not if it means working with you, *carissima*," said Umberto, a sudden burst of adrenaline making his heart pound. The movies! At last. Umberto Scrofo, a film producer—no longer an obscure antique dealer, but someone truly to be reckoned with again. A wheeler-dealer. A force. A *bella figura*. "What about the film's promotion and distribution—all of those kinds of things?" he asked. "I know absolutely nothing about all that, you know."

"Oh, Didier will take care of that—I'm sure. He's the expert of the family. He wants to do everything to help me, and I know he'll want to help you too." She smiled dazzlingly, raising her glass to him, her face looking amazingly young and joyous in the light of the Via Veneto streetlamps. "To *La Città Perduta*," she breathed, "and to a long, happy and profitable association with you, Umberto."

And Umberto Scrofo clinked glasses with the beautiful star and smiled triumphantly.

❖ *Nine* ❖

ST. TROPEZ

Even though Dominique had many things to do before she left for America she found her mind whirling with thoughts of Gaston Girandot. After she had told the thrilling news that she was going to Hollywood to star in a film to Maman, Papa, Genevieve and all her relations and friends, she felt she must tell him too.

It was a humid evening when she pedaled her bicycle once again to the Place des Lices and saw with a lurch of pleasure the little van with its gaily painted slogan, GASTON'S GLACES.

Leaning out of the hatch onto the ledge where he was serving a couple of lanky teenage boys was Gaston Girandot, more handsome than ever, and Dominique was thrilled to see him.

"*Bon soir*, Gaston." She smiled innocently as she slid five francs across the shallow wooden counter. "I would like a double *framboise*, please."

"Dominique, *quelle surprise!*" His white smile and tanned face made him look more than ever like James Dean, screen idol of all the girls and boys in France. "I haven't seen you for ages—I expected by now you would be flying off to Hollywood, giving Leslie Caron a run for her money." He winked at her and slid the coin back. "This is on the house."

"*Merci*," smiled Dominique, licking her ice cream with a pert pink tongue as her eyes searched the boy's face for signs that he was still interested in her. They were certainly still all there, and his eyes burned into hers so steadily that she felt a hot blush start under the bodice of her blouse and spread to her cheeks.

She turned away and started to walk across the little square to where the old men were smoking Gitanes and playing *boules* outside the Café des Lices.

"Where are you going?" He was beside her, slowing his stride to match hers. "Would you like to go for a ride on my new motorcycle?"

"Oh, Maman would *murder* me if she knew I went on a motorcycle," squealed Dominique, the forbidden thought of it nevertheless filling her with excited anticipation.

Gaston sensed it. "Come—come with me," he said in a suddenly pro-prietorial manner, and taking her arm, steered her out of the square and down one of the narrow cobbled streets. "There," he said, proudly ges-turing to a shining green machine parked boldly next to the gendarmerie. "Isn't she a beauty?"

"Beautiful," breathed Dominique, hearing her mother's voice instructing her that she must *never* accept rides with any men. Especially on scooters. "Absolutely *ravissant*."

"We can go for a little ride now, come—" he said, quickly jumping astride the black leather seat and patting the space behind him invitingly.

"Oh, no—I *can't*. Dominique was of two minds now. He looked even more like James Dean as he sat astride the machine, smoke from the cigarette in his mouth making his eyes half close in a sexy way that she found extremely tempting, his blue jeans tight across his muscled thighs.

"Come on," he said insistently, "don't be scared, it won't bite you—neither will I."

"Oh, all right," said Dominique tentatively, sliding onto the pillion. "But only for a little while, Gaston. I *must* be home by ten-thirty, prom-ise?"

"Right," said the boy as the motor sprang to life, and she clutched him around his waist with both hands as he guided the motorcycle carefully down the stony streets. "We'll go to Tango Beach," he said, "it's not too far."

The beach was dark and deserted and only a sliver of pale moon illuminated the black sand.

"Goodness, it's so dark," Dominique shivered. Instead of feeling ner-vous she was experiencing thrilling new sensations in the pit of her stom-ach. The ten-minute ride with her arms and head nuzzled into Gaston's cotton shirt had excited her, her mouth was dry with anticipation of an unknown which she felt sure she was going to like.

He turned off the engine and they sat for several minutes listening to the almost-silence. Dominique was sure that he could hear the thumping of her heart mixed with the faint lapping of the waves. A soft breeze ruffled her hair, and all was very still.

Without words Gaston took her hand and they walked across the sand to the water's edge. Simultaneously they flopped onto the sand, still slightly warm from the afternoon sun, and for a long moment sat staring up into the star-littered sky.

"It's beautiful, St. Tropez, isn't it?" breathed Dominique, conscious of Gaston's muscular arm resting lightly on her shoulder.

"Beautiful," he said softly, "but not nearly as beautiful as you, *chérie.*" His head turned to her and she saw the pupils of his eyes were so dilated they almost hid his irises. *"Mais tu es belle, Dominique,"* he whispered. *"Trop belle—trop, trop belle."*

His lips were on her hair now, searching for the softness of her neck.

"No, Gaston, no." Dominique heard her faint yet unresisting voice as his soft lips gently bit her neck. "No."

"Yes," he said insistently. "Yes, Dominique, yes, yes." He bent her body back slowly onto the warm sand, and she could feel the cool water of the sea lapping at her feet as his mouth traced a pattern of exquisite pleasure around her lips. His tongue was delicate, probing, sensitive. It seemed to know where she wanted it to go. Her mouth opened to his kisses and she felt the heat of desire starting to burn through the thin cotton of her skirt. She shivered as waves surged over her feet, and she felt his hands move to the buttons of her blouse.

"No—Gaston, not here," Dominique said, almost starting to giggle with nerves. "We're right in the middle of the beach, what if someone comes along?"

"No one is going to come here at night, little goose," he said. "But I suppose you're right. Let's go up to the restaurant—we'll be safe there—come." He helped her to her feet and they ran towards the dark outline of the beach bar.

It was pitch dark in the interior and smelled of cooked garlic and herbs, a warm, comforting smell. Gaston held Dominique's hand tightly as they fumbled their way through the stacked tables and chairs to the back of the bar. Piled against the wall were dozens of the striped mattresses that were used for sunbathing during the day.

"Here," said Gaston as he helped her clamber up onto the top one. "Up here, Dominique—it's nice here."

"I feel like the princess and the pea in that fairy tale," giggled Dominique, feeling incredibly grown up, nervous and excited all at the same time. "Lying on top of so many mattresses—ooh, Gaston, I hope we don't fall off."

"I won't let you," mumbled the boy, his hands busy with the tiny buttons of her blouse. "Don't worry, Dominique, my darling, I will protect you. I promise."

With the scent of Ambre Solaire filling her nostrils and the gentle sound of the sea in the background Dominique abandoned herself to the fervent kisses and caresses of the young ice-cream vendor with a sigh of pleasure.

From then on they met several times each week, and Gaston taught Dominique many new delights. Their silent private world at the back of the beach hut was a haven of pleasure where Dominique amazed Gaston by her sexual ardor and enthusiasm. She had no prudery or false modesty. Her only fear was that she might become pregnant, but he protected her from that. She was a willing, wanton partner, and as he often told her, "made for love."

When the crisp telegram finally arrived from MCCP studios informing Dominique that it was time for her to leave for Hollywood to prepare for the filming of *The Legend of Cortez* the young lovers wept copiously.

"I won't forget you, I promise," cried Dominique, clinging to Gaston in the comforting darkness of their love nest. "I'll write every day—every single day."

"I will, too, my darling," said the boy, desperately trying not to weep. "I will not stop loving you, Dominique, and I will be waiting for you when you come back from America."

A few days later Gaston Girandot stood on the upper level of the white concrete terminal at Nice Airport, watching Dominique and Agathe board the huge Air France four-engine airliner which was taking them to New York. Dominique was dressed formally in a new black-and-white checked suit with black shiny buttons on the jacket and a tight black belt. The skirt was full and mid-calf length, and she wore a small felt hat on the back of her flowing hair which was tied with black grosgrain ribbon. Around her neck was a white Peter Pan collar trimmed with a small black bow, and in her white-gloved hands she carried a black patent boxy handbag which matched her high-heeled shoes. She looked grown-up and sophisticated as she posed prettily at the bottom of the airplane's steps for a lone photographer from *Nice Matin*.

In the background Agathe, the chaperone, smiled proudly at her young charge. At last they were off. After months of waiting they were being summoned to the magic land of Hollywood. In little more than twenty-four hours they would be there, and maybe some of Agathe's dreams would finally come true.

❧*Ten*❧

LONDON

THE APPLAUSE WAS DEAFENING. Even by Julian's standards, it was an unusually enthusiastic and tumultuous first-night ovation, and he reveled in it. Handsome and romantic in black cotton tights and a loose white linen shirt, he held hands with the woman beside him, smiling at her with well-concealed fury, bowing yet again to the thunderous applause. The bloody bitch had been upstaging him all evening. Each time he had turned to her during their scenes on stage, Phoebe had managed to remain two or three steps behind him, thus enabling the audience to see all of her, but only three quarters of him. He was the star, after all—Julian Brooks *was* Hamlet. Ophelia was just a supporting role, and the redheaded witch was trying to muscle in on his territory to beef up her part.

But what was even more galling was that he knew that the Oliviers and Johnny Gielgud were in front, watching what Phoebe was doing. No doubt they were having a good laugh at his expense. "Ophelia upstaging Hamlet—what *is* the theater coming to?" they would be saying. "Julian must be going *mad*, darling."

True, he had promised his wife some seven years ago that if he ever played Hamlet, she would be his Ophelia, but she'd been more than two stone lighter in those days. He had finally given in wearily after her vastly expensive trip of revenge with Hermione. To play Ophelia she had lost fifteen pounds, and with a three-foot-long, curly auburn wig and brilliantly cantilevered costumes, she wasn't altogether terrible. Certainly not Vivien Leigh, but not Sophie Tucker either. Julian had naively thought that by letting Phoebe share some of his glory, it might help their marriage. But on the contrary, it only served to show her up as the mediocre actress she undoubtedly was, and make him look a complete fool for having cast her. To top it all, their marriage was now practically in name only.

He was reminded of the story about the flamboyant actor-manager Sir Donald Wolfit who, on a tour of the English provinces, stepped towards the footlights after his curtain call, announcing to the audience in stentorian tones, "Thank you, dear people, for your most kind reception tonight given to our play. Next week we shall be presenting here at the Alhambra Theatre, Shakespeare's *Othello.* I myself shall be playing the stately Moor, and my lady wife shall give her Desdemona."

A voice from the gallery called out, "Your wife's an old ratbag."

There was a very long pause. "Nevertheless," continued Sir Donald, "she shall *still* be playing Desdemona."

That was him and Phoebe, thought Julian, knotting his dressing-gown cord savagely. He was the star and she the ratbag, and an upstaging ratbag to boot.

Even though they took eleven curtain calls, he was still seething in the dressing room, as he roughly wiped makeup from his face.

"Now look here, Phoebe, I've had just about enough of your continual upstaging. Dammit, how many times have I told you that in my 'Get thee to a nunnery' speech, you *must* stay downstage. Are you *deaf* or something?"

"Oh, I *know* you did, dear," fluttered Phoebe, as helpless as a leopard in a jungle. She sneered at him in the fly-specked mirror, rubbing a touch of the powder and paint from her cheeks and removing a smidgin of eye shadow with the corner of a Turkish towel. After all, there was no point in wasting perfectly good cold cream to take this lot off, when she would only have to put it all back on again for the party. Besides, she was too lazy. Excited by the first-night fever, she ignored Julian's exasperated tirade as she primped and fussed with her carroty curls in preparation for the tidal wave of backstage visitors. Even now, she could hear them coming down the drafty stone corridors of the Haymarket Theatre. They'll put a stop to Julian's nagging, she thought.

Vivien and Larry, Johnny and Ralphie, Noël and Sir Crispin, and the two Hermiones all burst into the dressing room together in a rush of excited praise. "Darling, you were *divine*—simply *marvelous,*" gushed one of the Hermiones to Julian, who stood in the middle of the cramped dressing room in his navy blue-and-crimson Charvet dressing gown, modestly accepting the sincere compliments of his peers, along with a glass of champagne from his dresser.

"Best Hamlet I've seen in *years,* old boy," said Larry, patting him on the shoulder. "Really bloody good." Then he bent down, whispering conspiratorially, "Better than Alec's last year—much better."

"Not really, Larry." Julian smiled broadly, luxuriating in the praise from the supreme actor's actor. "But thank you very much."

"Dear boy, you were good; very, very good indeed," said Noël, a twinkle in his Chinese eyes, an ivory cigarette holder clenched between his teeth. "I've never seen you better—you must do more of the Bard, dear boy, although I hear Hollywood's crooked little bejeweled finger has been beckoning you—right, dear boy?"

How did he know that? Julian wasn't really surprised. Noël knew everything that went on—not only in the West End, but on Broadway and even in Hollywood. He was a walking cornucopia of fascinating theatrical gossip.

Another call from Julian's Hollywood agent had, in fact, come only yesterday. His agent was insistent that Julian make a film in America. He had missed the boat twice before and it was high time he didn't miss this one. Selznick had wanted him to play Rochester opposite Joan Fontaine in *Jane Eyre* but Didier had dithered for so long that the part had gone to Orson Welles. Three years ago they had wanted him again, this time to play opposite Joan's sister, Olivia de Havilland, in *My Cousin Rachel,* but

he had been in the middle of a Restoration epic with Margaret Lockwood, so the role had gone to Richard Burton. Now Hollywood was
beckoning again—with a juicy contract and Didier's blessing, lots of
lovely dollars and a peach of a part: the title role in *The Legend of Cortez*.
It was a difficult decision and Julian felt torn. Although *Hamlet* was only
playing for a limited run, Phoebe was pregnant for the second time. He
was delighted, but she wasn't happy about it at all—not that she was ever
happy about much unless it involved spending money or hobnobbing
with high society. It was almost an immaculate conception, as Julian had
hardly gone near her at all since *Pygmalion*, but for Phoebe it was a
trump card. Rumblings of incipient miscarriages and morning sickness
kept him in line. She was hardly two months into her pregnancy, but she
was more difficult, tetchy and discontented than ever.

"*Hollywood!* Over my dead body," she had barked at him that morning as she lay in bed in a maribou bedjacket, which always made her
sneeze, while she cooed and caressed one of their five cats. "We can't
leave the cats, and I *hate* Americans and their perfectly dreadful food—
hamburgers and chili dogs—ugh, it makes me retch to think of it."

"Phoebe, what bloody difference does it make?" Julian roared, standing before her in his striped pajama bottoms, his face covered with shaving cream. "What the blazes—we'll import a bloody cook from England.
We'll have fucking bangers and mash, boiled beef and carrots—whatever
you want, Phoebe, but for Christ's sake, don't make me give up this big
chance, *my* big chance, just because you don't like bloody Yankee food."
Phoebe started to splutter, but he shut her up.

"If we go to Hollywood, I'll do this three-picture deal for Spyros and
then we'll come back to London, I promise you. Then we'll buy that
fucking house in Sussex, if that's what you want."

"The one near the Oliviers?" Phoebe asked eagerly.

"The one near the Oliviers," said Julian resignedly.

"I'll think about it," Phoebe pouted, pulling the green-and-pink
chintz-covered eiderdown up to her chins. "I'll let you know after the
opening tomorrow. I must rest now. Doctor's orders. Please leave me
alone." She closed her eyes dismissively as Julian Brooks, matinée idol
and leading male star of the British screen, stood helplessly in yet another fury of frustration.

Now, surrounded as he was by the *crème de la crème* of the theatrical
profession, Julian tried once again to control his anger towards his tiresome wife. Tonight he was a great success; that was all that mattered at
the moment.

"Darling heart, *go* to California, you simply *must*," said Vivien, her
beautiful cat's eyes alight in her perfect face. "But *do* come to Notley
Abbey next weekend before you go."

"I could think of nothing I'd rather do more," Julian said with a smile.
That should placate Phoebe. She wouldn't have too much morning sick-
ness down there, he was sure of that. Not with Larry and Viv and Johnny
G., and Noël and Binkie Beaumont for company. She'd do her best to be

the life and soul of the party, and she certainly always could be if she felt like it.

"Hollywood can be *the* most ghastly bore, of course, but the *money*, darling—you can't, you simply *can't* turn it down," said Sir Crispin Peake, ever the pragmatist. "Take it and run, my dear. I've just bought an enormous house near Windsor and the most ravishing little Renoir you've ever seen, and both with my last paycheck. You must come down and stay, if you ever manage to tear yourself away from Notley Abbey!" He winked as he was sucked into the crush of well-wishers.

"The British invasion, darling, that's what they call it," croaked Hermione One. "Hollywood simply adores the Brits, dear—they all play cricket at dear Aubrey's every Sunday in white flannels, and eat cucumber sandwiches at every opportunity."

"It's nothing to be ashamed of—we've *all* done it," said Vivien, looking over at her husband. "Even Larry, and he fought against it like a *dervish*, darling—didn't want to go at all, did you, pet?"

"No—but once we went we had a glorious time. The weather is divine, the work conditions excellent, and the natives are really quite amusing—aren't they, darling?" said Sir Laurence, smiling fondly at his wife. "And the women are terribly pretty."

"So are the men." She smiled back at him slyly.

"Go, dear boy, go, you simply simply must," said Noël. "Let's face it, England is just a backwater these days, and who can ignore all that lovely green lolly?"

"Certainly not Phoebe," answered Hermione impishly as Phoebe glared at her, and Sir Crispin stifled a snigger. "She loves a buck, don't you, dearie? Cannot say no to ye olde filthy lucre, never could, even when she was a Windmill cutie."

"Well, now I think it's time for us all to go to the Ivy," announced Noël, sensing a sudden chill in the atmosphere. "Let the revels begin, my children, it's fiesta time. Let us eat, drink and become very, very merry indeed, and toast dear Julian's grand success."

The first-night party in the Edwardian back dining room of the Ivy bubbled with the aristocracy of film and theater. Conversation was brittle and brilliant. The expensive smell of cigar smoke wafted through the air, mingling with the dozens of scents worn by the glittering women, and Julian modestly accepted congratulations and praise from friend and foe alike.

Everyone was exquisitely dressed. In the theatrical world of the 1950s, actresses were not afraid to look the part of the glamorous stars that many of them were. The rainbow colors of their taffeta, satin and velvet gowns were perfectly complemented by all the elegant men in their black dinner jackets and crisp white shirts.

Television was not taken at all seriously by anyone in the profession. Even actors who appeared in films were looked upon with a certain disdain by their more respected thespian brothers and sisters, which was part of the reason why Julian had decided to play *Hamlet*. He wanted the respect of his peers, which he knew he would never earn by toiling in his romantic potboilers for the screen. But he equally wanted, and Phoebe needed, the large sums of money which he made from his screen career.

Phoebe's outgoing personality was spilling over, as were her enormous breasts, which bounced like two pale sponge cakes, half in and half out of her Norman Hartnell ice-blue dress. She circulated tirelessly, passing on snippets of theatrical gossip and naughty jokes with gusto. She was totally without diplomacy as she told vicious and hurtful stories about everyone. Many disliked her for it, but Julian was so popular that they put up with Phoebe's bitchiness and backbiting for his sake.

As the clock struck midnight the star of the evening suddenly found himself alone at the bar, with only a glass of Dom Perignon for company. He lit a cigar with his gold lighter—a present from Phoebe when he had played Othello at the Old Vic, opposite her far too curvaceous Desdemona. Slowly he became aware of a subtle scent and a pair of magnetic eyes staring at him.

He turned to meet the cool gaze of a tall young woman who was leaning elegantly against the bar, staring at him with barely disguised interest. She was beautiful in a sultry way, but there was an aura about her which spoke of much more than beauty. There was danger in her eyes, a look that signaled trouble for any man who got too close. She looked to be in her mid-twenties, with shoulder-length dark brown hair, and a thick fringe which seemed deliberately to draw attention to electric-blue eyes. They were boldly outlined in kohl and drawn in that doe-eyed slant which Audrey Hepburn had made so fashionable. Her lips, curved, full and sensual, were painted a deep, glossy scarlet; she now parted them, placed a cigarette between them and waited with a faint, expectant smile. All the while her eyes never left his.

Like all good actors, Julian always picked up his cue. In an instant he was at her side, gold lighter at the ready.

"*Merci.*" Her voice was low, husky, evocative of endless evenings in smoky clubs and long nights of love. He was instantly captivated. "You were excellent tonight," she smiled. "The best Hamlet I've ever seen. Better than Guinness. Maybe even better than Olivier."

"Thank you, *Mademoiselle,* you are really too kind. But I'm afraid you have the advantage of knowing who I am, while I don't know you."

"Inès," she replied softly. "Inès Juillard."

"A beautiful name for a beautiful woman." Julian couldn't help the cliché. He felt himself blush and noticed the girl's faint smile, but there was warmth there, and a sexual interest he could feel. Usually when he felt mutual attraction this strongly he went after it immediately. Having had many affairs during his marriage, he fully intended to have as many more as he wanted. No matter that Phoebe was finally pregnant, that was not going to stop him, particularly with this gorgeous creature who was oozing sexuality and fascination.

Suddenly he wanted Inès Juillard very much. He wanted to touch and caress her long, slim curves, wanted to feel those elegant hands with their short, unpainted nails rake his back, wanted to strip that severely chic clinging black dress from her body, feel her breasts against his chest. All those thoughts passed rapidly through his mind in the time it took for him to inhale his cigar, and for her to brush the ash from her cigarette.

Inès, of course, read them all instantly. She had been around men long enough to understand them completely, and since she had been intrigued by and attracted to Julian ever since she had seen him in *Pygmalion,* she was thankful that he obviously found her desirable. But she needed to be clever here. Very clever indeed. He was devastatingly good-looking, charming, famous, fascinating—and married. Looks Brooks— the most handsome man in the world. Every woman must be after him— some, so they said, had tried to kill themselves for love of him. She must make herself extra special, more than special to him.

"When can I see you?" Julian whispered urgently, as he saw out of the corner of his eye a particularly vicious gossip columnist who was bearing down on him. "I want to see you soon, Inès—as soon as possible. Please."

"Grosvenor 1734," she whispered, wafting away like some beautiful black wraith in a fragrant cloud of scent. "Call me during the day, any time. *J'attends,* Julian, *j'attends.*"

Julian could hardly wait. He had to see Inès Juillard. He rang her the next morning, she gave him her address in Shepherd Market, and he was out of the Connaught Square house and into a black cab before Phoebe had even opened an eye from her hangover slumbers. He knew that she'd have a fit when she saw her notices; he definitely didn't want to be around when she read them. The critics had not been kind to her, and although they praised Julian's Hamlet, they castigated him as producer for casting his wife in such an unsuitable role.

He was perfectly turned out in a camel cashmere belted overcoat, his caramel-colored fedora worn at its usual angle, so it was not surprising that the cabbie recognized him.

"'Ello, Mr. Brooks." He smiled genially. "Good reviews, guv. Didja see 'em? Even James Agate liked it." London cabdrivers loved celebrities, often letting them travel for nothing in exchange for an autograph.

Julian smiled his thanks dismissively. He didn't want to talk to the cabbie. He only wanted to think about Inès. For the first time in years his interest in someone else overshadowed his interest in his reviews. His anticipation was electric. He felt like a small boy on Christmas Eve. He had not been able to put her out of his mind since last night. The cabbie took the hint, allowing Julian to be alone with his thoughts until they arrived at Shepherd Market.

Inès opened the door wearing a black polo neck sweater and a full black-and-white checked skirt cinched with a wide patent-leather belt around her tiny waist. She was ravishing, yet with a sweet vulnerability that he found incredibly refreshing. Her skin was devoid of any makeup, but her face glowed serenely, her complexion fresh and clear.

Julian noticed that on the walls of her flat hung exquisitely framed neoclassical drawings by Delacroix, Ingres and David. He thought he also recognized some early drawings by Boucher and Fragonard. The furni-

ture was good, some of it very good, and there were spring flowers everywhere in blue and white pots. This was obviously a woman of considerable taste and style as well as great beauty.

Inès was playing him as gently and carefully as a fisherman landing a
prize salmon on a slender trout rod. Finally he was in her flat. Julian
Looks Brooks. The Idol of the Odeons in person sitting on her sofa,
sipping espresso from one of her Sèvres cups, his eyes looking at her with
steady desire.

She gave him no clue to her profession, gave him none of herself,
either—not that day, nor the next, nor even the following week. For
more than a month she refused to even let him kiss her. It wasn't until
he'd convinced her that he was mad with love for her that she finally
allowed him to possess her. And, of course, she made him think it had all
been his idea.

He had suggested that after his Saturday performance they drive to his
tiny cottage in the country. Phoebe had bought it in an uncharacteristic
flash of country-life fever but had visited it only once, preferring the
streets of St. James's and Piccadilly to the muddy lanes of Gloucester-
shire. He had talked Inès into it, and she finally reluctantly agreed.

Once there Inès concocted a gourmet feast on the old-fashioned
cooker, produced a bottle of distinctive claret, and cuddled up to Julian
after dinner in front of the roaring log fire with innocent seductiveness.

She knew the time was ripe for him to seduce her, and she resisted
him girlishly until finally she succumbed to his ardent kisses. But once
they were ensconced in the downy soft featherbed, Inès took the initiative, amazing Julian by her athletic ardor.

They made love all night long, and it exceeded his every expectation.
It was an experience beyond his wildest fantasies.

Although Julian had had dozens of affairs, they had been mostly with
English or American women, usually actresses, none of whom could exactly have been called passion flowers. They had moaned, groaned,
writhed and performed with all the appropriate wiggles, thrusts and the
"Oh, my *God*, darling, it's so good," but he had always felt that there was
something important missing in his lovemaking with all of them. They
gave their bodies enthusiastically enough, but he knew that their hearts
were seldom truly in it.

With Inès it was totally different. The white heat of her passion
seemed almost to scorch him, and he never wanted to stop. He knew it
was real, he could feel that hers was not a performance, that it was just
for him. Her skin drove him wild. It was the color of crushed pearls, and
smelled like jasmine. When she wrapped her amazingly long slim legs
around him, whispering eroticisms in that husky French voice of hers, he
would become like a man possessed. He'd never been with a woman like
her before. Few had specialized in the sexual arts and crafts which Inès
had been perfecting since her teens. She was a walking mantrap, desire
and lust incarnate. A wonderful wanton with such incredible sexual skills
that even the sophisticated and worldly Julian was dazzled by them. That
long weekend in the cottage as he tried to doze after yet another blissful

session of lovemaking, she would take his sleeping cock in her mouth as gently and delicately as a snake would swallow a small mouse. She was insatiable and tireless, her tongue an instrument of pure pleasure, a lethal weapon, as were her mouth and lips, which she used to take him to the highest stratosphere of pleasure, from where he never wanted to return.

More than anything, Julian felt that her passion truly matched his. Her lust and physical need for his body were as strong as his for hers. After their affair started it was nothing for them to spend the entire morning together, and then the whole afternoon in her soft bed, until it was time for him to go to the theater. They made love at least three times a day, and at nearly thirty-seven, Julian became possessed with the sexual energy of a seventeen-year-old. He sometimes had odd pangs of fear that expending so much of his precious essence might somehow interfere with his performance on the stage, but in fact it seemed to do just the opposite. His Hamlet soared to new heights each night, and audiences cheered and applauded him until the rafters of the Haymarket Theatre seemed to shake. He often told her that, like Cleopatra, she never made his appetites for her cloy, but instead made hungry where most she satisfied.

Of course Phoebe soon suspected that another affair had begun. She had miscarried their baby again and, although secretly relieved, was making an enormous show of her misery. When Julian made a halfhearted attempt to make love to her one night, simply because he thought he should, Phoebe rejected him huffily.

"Don't point that tired old thing *near* me," she hissed. "You must wait at *least* three months. The doctor says I mustn't have sex until then, so just go and jerk off in the bathroom, like a good boy, or whatever else you've been doing." She bit viciously into another chocolate biscuit.

His wife's attitude suited Julian perfectly. He was totally consumed by thoughts of Inès, his angel, his gorgeous French beauty, his *grand passion*. He was her slave, completely besotted, and not only sexually. He had never felt such pure joy in a relationship with a woman, and soon he began to realize that he could no longer imagine his life without her.

Inès had still given Julian no hint of her true profession. At twenty-nine she knew that her years of successful and financially rewarding whoring were rapidly coming to an end. Julian was handsome, rich, successful, and a wonderful lover. She knew that he was the man for her, but she also knew that he lived by the usual convenient double standard, like so many Englishmen. He had been a philanderer and womanizer most of his adult life, which she was able to accept. However, she soon found out that her own past life needed to be practically perfect to please his curiously exacting moral values—he would never be able to accept the fact that she had been a whore. That was the one thing she would never be able to tell him. However much in love he was, she was sure that should he find out, their relationship would be destroyed.

Inès was in a difficult position. The chances of Julian's discovering the truth about her past were fairly slim, since most of her clients would be terrified of exposure themselves. She had stopped seeing all of them as soon as the romance with Julian began, telling them she was going away for a long time. She had concocted a thin web of lies about her life which Julian unquestioningly believed, and she prayed that he would never discover the truth.

She had told him that her parents had been killed in a car crash in Paris when she was very young. She had been brought up by a maiden aunt in Yorkshire who had died when Inès was twenty, leaving her this flat, some pretty and valuable bits and pieces, and enough money to live well on. He had believed her. In spite of his own promiscuity, Julian was extremely old-fashioned. He couldn't even think of Inès with another man. She had admitted to having had three boyfriends, but had refused to go into details about any relationships, saying that he mustn't be jealous of past loves.

Having completely sexually and emotionally enslaved him, and tangled him up in her beauty's web, prying him away from his wife was her next problem. And it was a major problem. Phoebe would not let Julian go without a fight. Even though she was no longer in love with him and the marriage was little more than a sham, she loved her life as Mrs. Julian Brooks and all that went with it. Phoebe was a tough, single-minded woman, both shrewd and clever. But perhaps not quite as shrewd and clever as her rival.

Inès had hinted at marriage but Julian had not been enthusiastic—why should he be? Phoebe always turned a blind eye to his affairs, realizing that they would all eventually come to an end and he would return to the marital fold.

And she was right, of course. Inès knew that there was a certain time between a man and a woman when the desire for each other was so strong that marriage was inevitable. If it didn't happen at that time, then it never would.

Julian seemed to be completely hooked now, and Inès knew the time was propitious to give him her ultimatum.

"Marriage, Julian darling," she said calmly as they sat by candlelight at her lace-draped dining table eating *coq au vin* from Spode plates. "We must get married."

"Darling girl—my angel, it's impossible, I've told you," Julian demurred. "Phoebe will never let me go, we both know that. Angel, can't we just stay the way we are? I'm so happy like this, Inès."

"No, Julian," said Inès firmly, aware that she was treading the trickiest of ground, but shrewdly knowing she had to do it. "In that case I can't continue seeing you."

"Of course you can, my angel," said Julian confidently. "We love each other too much, Inès, how could we bear to be apart from each other?"

At that moment Inès knew this was going to be much tougher than she had expected. She worshiped Julian, wanted desperately to marry him, to be with him forever. There was only one way to get him now—she had to play a brilliant game, and for high stakes. Julian was a rare prize.

The following day Inès withdrew from Julian's life completely. She packed a small suitcase and disappeared for a week without telling him. The she sent a brief note to the theater telling him she was in the country and only giving him her telephone number.

Instantly he was on the telephone, begging to see her.

"No, Julian, no. I cannot see you again," Inès said firmly, her heart pounding with longing for him. "I love you too much to go on like this without marriage. We must forget each other, *chéri.*"

"No!" roared Julian, beside himself at the thought of losing her. "You can't do this, Inès, you simply can't. I've been going mad without you. What's your address? I'll come and see you, angel. Now, I simply must."

"No," said Inès softly. "No, Julian. It's marriage or it's over between us. We have been together now for seven months. If we don't marry I must get on with my life. If it has to be without you—so be it."

She hung up, leaving Julian staring blankly at the telephone. He knew she was right, of course, his marriage with Phoebe was a farce. Divorce. He would divorce Phoebe and marry Inès. That was the inevitable way it must be. Why not. He loved her. She was everything he desired and admired in a woman.

It had been a tough ultimatum for Inès. Please God, let it work, she prayed. Please God. She wanted to be with Julian forever. She had to be.

When Julian finally confessed his passionate affair to Phoebe, and his desire for a divorce so that he could marry Inès, Phoebe went berserk. Ranting and raving, she threw all her valuable painstakingly collected Chelsea and Bow porcelain at her husband in a furious barrage that lasted for hours. She threatened Julian with the most dire consequences if he left her.

"I'll create a scandal that will *ruin* you. That Candida *bitch* trying to commit suicide will be *nothing* compared to this," she screamed, her face ugly and puffy, her bloodshot eyes swollen with tears. "You'll *never* be Sir Julian Brooks now. Not with a divorce behind you."

"My dear girl," Julian said, trying to remain calm as he brushed bits of broken china off his sleeve, "I don't give a damn what you do. And I don't give a damn about becoming a knight. I'm an actor and that's all I bloody well care about."

"You're not an *actor,*" Phoebe spat out contemptuously. "You're just a joke. When you first came on the screen as Charles the Second with that dead poodle on your head, everyone screamed with laughter. Everyone says you can't bloody act to save your bloody life."

"Thank you, Phoebe," Julian said quietly, "for those few kind words. Your undying loyalty is most touching."

"That French *whore*—I suppose *she's* loyal."

"Yes," he sighed. "She is."

"Does she know you're a pansy?"

Julian paled. Since his passing attachment to Wilson at school, he'd gone out of his way never to do, say or appear as anything other than the most masculine of men. But he had once in the early days of their marriage confessed to Phoebe his fondness for the boy. Like the elephant, she never forgot.

"And what's that supposed to mean?" he asked coldly.

"Nothing." She shrugged, realizing her barb had found its mark. "Nothing at all, Julian."

Phoebe had never suspected it herself, but maybe this man with whom she'd lived for nearly eleven years did have some homosexual tendencies. She always thought that Julian flirted with Sir Crispin Peake when they laughed and teased each other. Unfortunately, she had no proof. Pity—that would have been the perfect stick with which to beat him. He couldn't have put up with the stigma of being thought of as queer.

Julian's seemingly genuine love for this other woman enraged Phoebe. Whatever was wrong with their marriage, it was no worse than that of many other theatrical couples. Phoebe had always assumed that, like other couples they knew, she and Julian would last forever, conveniently if not romantically. Now he'd turned her whole world upside down all for the sake of love. *Love!* What a joke, she thought viciously. There was no such thing, it was all as Noël said, a very bad joke.

Julian tried to pacify Phoebe with offers of huge sums of money. He offered her the house, the furniture, the paintings, all of the possessions which they had carefully collected during their years together. He would give her everything in exchange for his freedom to marry Inès. But Phoebe refused.

It was Inès who at last found the answer. She had been thinking and analyzing the problem long and hard. She came to the conclusion that Phoebe would give Julian his freedom in exchange for a cut of his future earnings—for life. She suggested he offer Phoebe ten percent. After mulling it over for twenty-four hours, Julian confronted his wife with the more than generous proposition.

"Twenty percent," Phoebe fired back. "Forever and ever."

"Fifteen," sighed Julian wearily.

"Oh, all right, you mean son of a bitch," sniffed Phoebe. "Fifteen it is, then—for life dear, don't forget. Till death us do part, *lovey*."

"Done," said Julian, feeling as if some intolerable weight had been lifted from his shoulders. He was free at last. Free of Phoebe. Free to be with his perfect Inès for ever. Free to fly to Hollywood.

❧ *Eleven* ❧

ROME

UMBERTO SCROFO STRUTTED onto the soundstage at Cinecittà Studios, his cigar jutting from fleshy lips, his step self-assured. He was overseeing the final days of shooting of his film *La Città Perduta*. The word was out on the streets of Rome, on the Via Veneto, on the beaches of Ostia and

Fregene where the film people gathered, even in the cutting rooms of the rival Scalera Studios, that Umberto Scrofo, this newcomer to their ranks, had a hit on his hands—and it was all his own work. Well, not quite all his own—after all, the script had been written by Irving Frankovitch, and Didier Armande had helped raise most of the money, but it was Umberto's name on the film, and everyone knew it.

He smiled with smug satisfaction as he stood watching carefully from outside the enchanted circle of arc lights, inside which his actors were performing. He had a proprietorial feeling towards his actors. It was as if they belonged exclusively to him. Not that they did; they had all, in fact, cost a fortune. Even Ramona had eventually demanded a salary, albeit minor. It hadn't been easy. Whoever told him that to break into the Italian film business was a breeze was a fool. He'd had to fight hard to get this script off the ground. Ponti, De Sica, Fellini and Visconti seemed to have rented all the studio space and hired every decent technician and piece of film equipment in Italy. He'd fought the American film companies as well. They had come to Italy in droves after the war, with falling stars of the 1930s and 1940s, plowing millions of dollars into crap, pure crap, and getting a guaranteed release, just because some faded Hollywood has-been's name was above the title and it was an American picture. Umberto had watched the Italian film industry thrive since the war, and with it the fortunes of the filmmakers, and he wanted to thrive, too. Oh, how he longed to succeed, how he yearned for Hollywood to beckon to him, and one day soon it would, of that he was certain.

◆*Twelve*◆

Dominique loved Hollywood and Hollywood loved Dominique. Each morning on her way to the studios, she gazed with childlike excitement through the windows of her chauffeur-driven limousine, wondering what joys this day would bring. She adored California. She thought that hot dogs, hamburgers, drive-in movies, Hula-Hoops, the Santa Monica beaches and the California sun, which always seemed to be shining, were the best things ever. She especially adored the camaraderie with the other actors and dancers at the rehearsal studio. She laughed at their quick repartee even though she didn't quite understand it, as she studied hard, learning English, and the sensual dance she would perform in *The Legend of Cortez*. She loved the exciting bustle of MCCP's commissary, watching the comings and goings of the stars, but best of all she liked television, especially *The Jackie Gleason Show*, *Cavalcade of Stars* and *The Milton Berle Show*. There had been no television in St. Tropez, no hot dogs, no film studio commissary, no excitement at all—except for Gaston. Now she never wanted to go back there ever; California life was nothing less than terrific. She belonged here.

Gaston had written her several impassioned letters and she had sent both him and her family pages and pages of exciting news, but as each day passed, St. Tropez, her family and Gaston Girandot seemed farther and farther away. Soon she had almost forgotten what he looked like.

Only the memory of those nights on Tango Beach brought his image back to her. She imagined them lying together on the striped beach mattresses with the smell of Ambre Solaire in her nostrils, remembered how thrilling it had been. But it was all work work work now, no time for romance—which was just fine with Dominique. The studio wanted to make her into a new star and she was more than willing to help.

The only tiny fly in her ointment was her chaperone. With her eerie, bleached-looking skin, silver hair, those burning black, sad eyes in her haunted face, Agathe made most people uncomfortable. There was so much suffering in her face, such sorrow in her eyes, no joy in her life. Her clothes were old-fashioned, dark, dowdy—and far too heavy for California. Her manner was quiet and almost lethargic. What Dominique and others didn't realize was how thrilled Agathe was to be in Los Angeles; she was simply incapable of showing it.

Dominique, on the other hand, was bursting with vitality. In Levi's and plaid shirt, with her long hair in a ponytail, she had become hooked on the American way of life, its fashions and customs. She was almost beside herself with anticipation on this steamy November afternoon as they headed towards the studio for her first costume fitting.

"Oh, Agathe, I'm *so* excited I can hardly breathe! My first fitting—what do you think it'll be like?"

Agathe made no reply as the car pulled into the studio lot. She was, as always, mesmerized by the extras walking about. Today they were dressed in *fin-de-siècle* winter costumes, incongruous in the heat and humidity.

They drove down several winding streets, each of which had a completely different character, towards the wardrobe department. Here was a New York nineteenth-century tenement which connected to an exact facsimile of a part of London's Eaton Square, complete with perfect replicas of Regency houses, plane trees and laburnum shrubs. Here a cobblestoned French medieval village, the narrow houses with strings of washing hanging between them looking so authentic that both women suddenly felt a pang of homesickness for St. Tropez. This led to the wardrobe department, which was simply an unpretentious clapboard building with brown paint peeling from its drab exterior.

While Dominique was being fitted, Agathe explored the department, awed by the multitude of costumes housed there on endless racks, ranging from Roman togas to thousand-dollar beaded evening gowns. After the fitting Agathe suggested an uplifting visit to the Los Angeles Museum of Art, but Dominique had other plans. One of the dancers had told her about a new nightclub on Sunset Boulevard where all the young actors and dancers hung out. It was the ultimate in cool, she'd been reliably informed, and she was dying to go there to jive the night away.

"I'm exhausted." She smiled at Agathe, feigning a yawn. "I want to sleep for fifteen hours. Drop me at the hotel, then you take the car on to the museum. But I must sleep. Agathe, *ça va?*"

"All right," muttered Agathe, thinking how sophisticated Dominique had become after only a few weeks in Hollywood. The typically French schoolgirl seemed to have blossomed overnight into a genuine American teenager, complete with a mouthful of chewing gum, and all the right slang. Why was the girl so at ease while Agathe herself felt like a fish out of water?

"Now don't you worry, Agathe," Dominique said as the car pulled up outside the Château Marmont. "I'm going straight to sleep with a glass of hot milk, and I'll see you in the morning bright and early." Blowing a kiss to Agathe, she ran lightly up the steps of the hotel, giggling to herself. Poor old Agathe, it wasn't too difficult to pull the wool over *her* eyes.

Agathe stared unseeingly ahead of her as the driver edged into the heavy Sunset Boulevard traffic. She felt a terrible envy of her charge boiling up inside her, an envy which spread like some fast-acting drug through her veins, and she hated herself for it. Maybe it was because Dominique was so young—almost the same age as Agathe had been when she was banished to that cellar; or maybe it was because Dominique had her whole life before her, a joyful, exciting life filled with promise. At thirty-one Agathe felt that her own life was as good as over except for one thing: the prospect of meeting the star of *The Legend of Cortez,* Julian Brooks. When she had heard that he was to play the lead, Agathe had almost swooned. The prospect of finally seeing her idol in the flesh was so overwhelming that she had to lie down to stop the terrible dizziness. Now she waited each day, hungry with anticipation until the moment when she would finally meet the one man in the world that she knew was her destiny.

Dominique dressed carefully in the height of hip teenage fashion: a black sleeveless sweater, pencil-tight blue jeans, a wide black belt cinching her waist into an impossibly small eighteen inches, and red ballet pumps. She outlined her eyes with a heavy black pencil and carefully arranged her bed with pillows and towels to appear as if she were sleeping in it if Agathe came snooping around. She crept down the back stairs of the hotel to walk the eight blocks to the Rock 'n' Roll Club.

Although it was only nine o'clock, the small, smoky dive was already crammed with people, all young, all out for a good time.

As she waited for her friends to arrive, Dominique stood at the bar sipping Coke, and surveying the dancers bopping and jiving beneath the flashing colored lights. A good-looking black boy whose muscles bulged out of his short-sleeved yellow shirt, and glistened under the prisms of light, swaggered up to her.

"Wanna dance?" he asked in a bored, cool voice, extending a calloused brown hand without even looking at her. Dominique was thrilled. She had never danced with a black boy before; indeed, until only recently she hardly ever danced anywhere but at dancing school. This kind of dancing —close, grinding, primitive—was all new to her.

"Sure, love to," she drawled, trying to sound cool and bored herself.

"How old are you, girl?" the boy asked as he threw her out on the floor to the rhythm, catching her expertly and twirling her back to him.

"Sixteen," Dominique answered, feeling excited. This boy smelled different from other boys. There was an aroma of musk and sweat about him. He smelled of the West Indies—as she imagined them to be.

"What's your name?" she asked.

"Cab. Yours?"

"Dominique."

"Hi there, Dominique, I guess you're French, huh? And sixteen, huh?" He winked at her as he pulled her back to him. Then as the music changed he started to hold her close and she suddenly felt something large and hard against her thigh. "That's old enough then, ain't it?" he breathed, his lips close to her ear.

"For what?" Dominique asked, almost stumbling to the unaccustomed new slow beat.

"For a smoke, hon. Ya done it, ain't ya?"

"Oh, sure," drawled Dominique. "I've done it loads of times."

Dominique sensed danger, but was stimulated by it. The lights were flashing. The Dirty Dozen was playing a hot beat with pounding expertise, and the crowd seethed with sensuality and youth. The black boy— well, brown really—was deliciously different. Agathe would *kill* her if she knew, and so would her mother. She would be dead meat but it was deliciously thrilling.

"How old are you?" she yelled above the din.

"Twenty," he said, flashing snow-white teeth. "An' I've seen it all, hon. I want to show some of it to you, too—c'mon." The band finished, and as the teenage audience whistled and clapped enthusiastically, Cab grabbed Dominique's hand and led her through the surging throng out through the kitchen to the back door.

In a narrow alley, Dominique leaned breathlessly against a brick wall, watching Cab remove a few things from his pocket. Tobacco, cigarette papers, matches. It was so dark that she couldn't really see what he was doing but when he lit up, inhaling deeply, she could smell a sweetish, pungent odor which made her think of an exotic jungle.

"Take a drag on this, kid—an' let the good times roll!"

He drew deeply again on the cigarette, and Dominique watched, fascinated by his glittering dark eyes with their thick black eyelashes, and by his fleshy pale mauve lips.

She was tingling with anticipation and her high was already halfway there before she even took her first pull of marijuana.

"*Ooh la la.*" She coughed as acrid smoke hit her lungs. "What *is* this?"

"Jamaica Joy, babe," Cab said, taking the joint from her fingers and passing her a flask which he'd taken from his back pocket. "It's the best—

it's crazy, man—real cool stuff. Now take a swig of this an' you'll feel better than you ever felt in ya whole life, girl."

Dominique tipped the flask to her lips, almost gagging at the harsh taste.

"Wow, what's that?" she gasped.

"Gin, of course, kid. Good old mother's ruin." He looked at her with amusement. "It won't hurt ya. You wanna feel real good, doncha, kid? Cool, crazy and real real good?"

"Mmm. You bet." Dominique nodded. Suddenly she certainly was feeling good. She was feeling excellent. She was experiencing a great rush of love for the whole beautiful world, for California, and especially for this exotic dusky animal who stood before her puffing on his magic weed and looking at her with glittering black eyes full of some secret amusement.

He passed her the reefer again and she drew it down deeply into her lungs, feeling the drug explode in her head like a Catherine wheel. It burned her throat with its bitter aftertaste, but it felt wonderful, delicious. Her head was as light as a puffball; it seemed to be stuffed with feathers, balloons, and those little globes of gossamer lightness which grow in summer meadows, carried by breezes to other pastures. It was as if her head were one of those puffballs, and if Cab's face came a millimeter nearer to her, his lips would blow it away, breaking her cottonwool skull into a million specks of dust. But she wasn't in a meadow. She was in the dank back alley of a club on Sunset Boulevard in Hollywood, surrounded by the putrid stench of dustbins and the raucous sounds of rock 'n' roll.

As if from a great distance, she saw Cab's enormous lips approaching her. Closer and closer they came, unattached to anything, like some figment of Alice's imagination in her Wonderland. He had no face, just those great mauve lips, coming towards her closer, closer—so close that her eyes crossed, trying to keep them in focus. The lips were moving, saying something, but she couldn't hear what it was.

They looked terribly funny, those enormous lips, suspended in space, in time, moving rapidly, yet with no sound coming from them.

Then suddenly, the lips were on hers, but they were not alone. A wet snakelike tongue darted from between them, entering her mouth like a reptile slithering into its lair. The slimy, slippery serpent filled her mouth with its mushy wetness as the enormous lips tried to suck her mouth into its cavern.

"No, no, *stop*—I can't breathe!" Dominique spluttered, the tongue still probing her mouth and the great lips continuing to scour her face like a wet mop over a kitchen floor.

"Don't." She pushed him away hard, looking at him with distaste.

"What were you *doing?*" she gasped. "That was horrible!" Despite her new and unaccustomed sense of power over men, Dominique was not experienced in repelling unwanted suitors. When Gaston had kissed her it was delicate, tender, his tongue exploring her mouth with gentle ardor. This boy was rough, pushy, crude. She hated what he was doing.

The lips opened, revealing teeth as big as tombstones. "That's good, kid, that's really, really good." The lips covered the teeth now, and the big black head bent closer to hers as two huge hands grabbed her shoulders.

"You're messin' around with things ya don't know nothin' about, little girl." Her head lolled from side to side as he shook her shoulders roughly. "I give ya a joint and whadda I get? Eh? Horrible—ya say—*I'm* horrible. That's great, isn't it, eh? I don't give 'em for nothin', ya know. Whadda I get then, what's *my* reward for givin' ya a good time? C'mon, tell me—what?" He started shaking her so hard that tears came to her eyes.

He tugged her head back by her hair, clapping a sweating palm over her mouth. "Now you better keep away from me in the future, girl," he hissed in her ear. "I know your kind of motherfucker. Pretend you've got the jungle fever, then ya chicken out." He slammed her against the brick wall until she hardly had any breath left in her body. "I'll have the world out on you, so don't be hangin' 'round here no more if ya know what's good for ya." With a final vicious shove at her, he strutted splayfooted back to the club, muttering "Cock-teaser" under his breath. Loud blasts from the rock band escorted him down the alley.

A few minutes later, Dominique limped her way down Sunset Boulevard towards the hotel. The whole experience had been far from pleasant, but she had felt stimulated by the danger and the knowledge that the menacing boy desired her. He had been crude and offensive, but the delicious sensation she had felt when she smoked the reefer still lingered. She knew that Cab's warning or not, she would go back to the club again. But next time she'd go with friends.

When she reached Agathe's door she heard the sounds of the television on. She crept silently into her own room to ruminate on this latest episode in her California adventure. "The perils of Dominique," she chuckled as she locked her door and took out her diary. "What a gas."

Agathe stared intently at the television screen. Wearing a highwayman's mask, a loden-green frock coat adorned with silver buttons and a black velvet tricorn hat pulled low over his forehead, astride a rearing black stallion with the muzzle of his flintlock pistol pointed at the beautiful, terrified face of Margaret Lockwood, was Julian Brooks. Agathe was riveted. She was watching one of a series of romantic swashbuckling films which Julian had made in England after the war, but it still held up. Agathe thought it was marvelous. How handsome he was, how dashing. She could barely breathe as Julian leaped down from his stallion, flung open the door of the carriage and pressed his lips to those of the frightened heroine.

"*Quelle merveille,*" breathed Agathe, her excitement mounting as their kisses intensified, and Miss Lockwood was swept with a passion which Agathe shared. How wonderful to have the lips of that man who looked like a Greek deity pressed against hers. She could almost feel the electricity between them, as her hand went to her mouth and her own lips opened to the barren dryness of her thumb. "Julian," she moaned softly, closing her eyes to everything but his television voice. "Oh, Julian, *Je t'aime. Que je t'aime, mon amour.*"

◆*Thirteen*◆

IN A HUGE MANSION hidden high in the canyons of the Hollywood hills, the legendary Ramona Armande was preparing for another evening out. A battalion of maids, hairdressers and *visagistes* hovered in reverential silence around the ivory-and-silver Ruhlmann dressing table at which the great star now sat, fastening diamond-and-emerald pendant earrings to her plump earlobes.

The pale, raven-haired woman had been a legend and a star for so long now that much of her early life was shrouded in mystery. Such was her exquisitely romantic past, which she'd read about in countless fan magazine interviews for some thirty years, that Ramona now believed each romantic word. The fact that she and Didier and their parents, Rachel and Eli Levinsky, had fled Hungary during the First World War, was not to be found in any of her biographies. The Levinsky family had been fortunate to find some relations in the East End of London, and Eli had continued as a fishmonger while she and Didier had been sent to the local school to learn English and the British way of life. Names were changed and both children's lives went on to great success.

Though small in stature, Ramona had a strong character. Woe betide the hapless menial who might misunderstand his mistress's commands at any time, but especially during her elaborate three-hour *grande levée*. Misunderstanding an order from the Princess would cause the unfortunate wretch to receive a withering look from her fabled amber eyes, fringed in lashes long and thick as spider legs, and a few well-chosen phrases from her were more than enough to terrify even the most insensitive.

In her vast bedchamber, lamps were kept dimmed to their lowest wattage to flatter her white, fine skin which was always covered with a special foundation created especially for her by Mr. Max Factor himself. It helped to camouflage the tiny wrinkles which, in spite of all the creams and potions which she applied every night, were multiplying over her precious face. What did it matter that her milky skin wasn't as perfect as it had been in the days of silent movies? She was still a star, and one who had every intention of remaining in the firmament, and she expected to be treated like one. Ramona was a true child of Hollywood, who knew the tricky ropes as well as Mr. Zanuck, Mr. Warner and Mr. Cohn. Tonight she was going to beat them at their own game.

"Bring me my diamonds, Maria," she commanded in the distinctive voice which had been her salvation when talkies had arrived. When many of her compatriots were being laughed off the screen because of their unsuitable voices, Ramona's dulcet tones had, thanks largely to her English education, appealed to the public, and her career had continued to flourish.

She thought about some of her contemporaries who had failed, as she studied her reflection in the three-way mirror. Poor old Jack Gilbert. Audiences had shrieked with laughter when they heard his voice. The great lover who had bedded so many stars of the silent screen and broken so many famous hearts, abandoning their beautiful owners to sob for him into their lace pillowcases, thought only of Greta Garbo, his one great passion. Garbo, Ramona thought, gritting her teeth—she'd certainly managed to pass the talkies test with flying colors. If it were possible, the public's love affair with her had grown even stronger when they all heard her first husky utterance: "Gimme a viskey, ginger ale on the side, and don't be stingy, baby." Audiences all over America had screamed with excitement, and Garbo had become the greatest star of all time.

Ramona frowned as she thought of her former arch-rival. Annoyingly, she was still continually in the American public's eye, as she slithered from yet another transcontinental train or transatlantic liner sheathed in a long coat, floppy felt hat, and always wearing those stupid sunglasses, stage-whispering, "I vant to be alone."

Ramona knew very well that this catchphrase was just another publicity ploy. She knew that Garbo really secretly loved the interest which her self-conscious mystery provoked. Garbo thrived on it. The more she "vanted to be alone," the less, of course, she was allowed to be. It was irritating and infuriating to Ramona, but Garbo was still continually in the newspapers and magazines, despite not having made a single appearance on celluloid for more than ten years.

Plucking a Lalique scent bottle from the massed ranks of expensive objects cluttering her dressing table, Ramona sprayed herself with a cloud of Shalimar, while her maid attached a diamond-and-tortoiseshell comb to her sleek black chignon. Ramona clasped the magnificent emerald, natural pearl and European-cut diamond necklace around her well preserved throat and surveyed herself critically. "Perfect," she breathed to herself, "perfect." She was ready at last, as ravishing as she could possibly make herself.

Tonight was another Hollywood party, this time to welcome the distinguished English actor Julian Brooks into the enchanted circle of Beverly Hills. He would be with Inès Juillard, the woman for whom he had left his wife, the woman all Hollywood was eager to meet. Their romance had been conducted discreetly because of his impending divorce, and few, if any, photographs had as yet appeared of the loving couple. The party was to be at the house of Spyros Makopolis, president of MCCP and one of the most important men in town. Ramona was determined to look more beautiful than ever before, fresh from her recent success in her new Italian movie. Tonight she would show the elite of Beverly Hills that

Ramona Armande was still a star of the greatest magnitude—still someone very much to be reckoned with.

In the Aubusson-carpeted drawing room of her mansion, Ramona's escort for the evening and the producer of her new but as yet unreleased film, Umberto Scrofo, sat admiring her collection of Impressionists and sipping champagne while he waited patiently for her to finish dressing. This was his first trip to Hollywood and he was in a fever of anticipation about tonight's A-list party.

He couldn't wait to belong and to take charge once more.

"Spyros' house is lit up like a bloody Christmas tree!" Julian Brooks observed. It was true. Every window blazed with light, and the white Palladian-style villa, set in manicured lawns among tall cypress trees, had been strung with thousands of colored fairy lights, reflecting something which few Californians ever saw.

"Snow! *Mon Dieu!*" Inès exclaimed, leaning closer to the limousine window. "For goodness' sake look, Julian—it's snow! How could we have snow here? It's been over seventy degrees today."

Julian looked down at the thick sparkling expanse of virgin snow which carpeted either side of the long, winding driveway, and smiled at Inès, who was staring at a gargantuan jade-green Christmas tree, some thirty feet high, which was completely covered with sparkling baubles of every imaginable color.

The door to their limousine was flung open by a parking valet who was dressed, much to his own embarrassment, as one of Santa's elves. Most of these boys were out-of-work actors, so they managed to conceal their embarrassment fairly convincingly as they politely helped the glamorous guests from their cars with "Good evening, ma'am, sir, and a very merry Christmas to you."

Inès stifled a giggle at the sight of Spyros' impeccable English butler, Sanderson, now dressed in the unlikely costume of Santa Claus. His solemn face hardly matched the jolly seasonal red outfit and white beard. He had in fact refused point-blank to wear the costume, even threatening to resign, but Mr. Makopolis had finally persuaded him to don it in the way that he persuaded everyone to do anything: with money.

"This could never happen in England or France, could it, darling?" Julian whispered, squeezing Inès' hand as they exchanged amused glances. Inès was amazed. Ten years of associating with aristocrats and people of culture and breeding in London had given her a definite knowledge of what is done and what is not done. So far, what she had seen of the overdecorated Makopolis mansion had been frightful. A butler dressed as Père Noël? *Quelle horreur!*

"But, chéri." Inès was still puzzled. "Today I was sunbathing by the pool. How can it snow here at night?"

"Fake, my darling, fake," Julian laughed. "I'm quite sure that old Spyros had the prop department whip up this little concoction."

"But how?" A sophisticated woman of the world as far as most things were concerned, Inès found the ways of Lotus Land a total mystery. "You cannot make snow, Julian. How can you?"

"Crystals and cottonwood," he explained. "Must have cost the studio prop department a bloody fortune. Good old Spyros, he's an amazing old coot."

"But why would he want to do that when it is so pretty here without it?"

"One-upmanship, my darling," Julian said. "Next year everyone in Hollywood will have their driveways and lawns covered with *fausse neige* —and dear old Mr. and Mrs. Makopolis will be crowing to themselves because they were the first on the block to think of it."

Julian took a slim flute of champagne from a footman, this one ludicrously dressed as Rudolph the Red-Nosed Reindeer, and winked at Inès. Already half the female guests were eyeing him covertly and looking enviously at her. Muted chatter without beginning or end flowed throughout the room as Spyros and Olympia Makopolis bore down on Julian and Inès with overflowing bonhomie. Taking them in tow, they introduced them to the rest of the famous guests, all of whom were dying to meet "the new Olivier," as Julian had recently been dubbed by the MCCP publicity department, much to his embarrassment.

Ramona Armande stood to one side, talking to her brother and Umberto Scrofo. Didier was carefully eyeing his protégé while Umberto stared at the beautiful woman Julian was escorting. Ravishing, she was absolutely gorgeous. He couldn't see much of her face but her creamy décolletage was quite mouthwatering. Umberto appreciated rare beauty, and this woman was A-first class. He hoped he'd get a chance to meet her later on. She was obviously cultured; they could talk about paintings.

Didier thought Julian had done well—extremely well—since the time of their first meeting in his dingy dressing room. Didier always recognized those who possessed star quality, and those who did not. Julian Brooks had it in spades, and it had been polished and honed throughout the years until it radiated from him almost palpably.

In the years that Julian had been under contract to Didier's company, he had achieved precisely what had been planned for him. He had become unquestionably the biggest star in England. And this in spite of his bitch of a wife who, Didier thought, had always been an impediment to Julian. Phoebe and her social climbing, her pathetic attempts to become some kind of aristocrat, and all those damn cats of hers had not helped Julian's career. Happily, thanks to Inès, Phoebe was ancient history. All that the loving couple were waiting for now was the decree nisi. Once that obstacle had been cleared, they would be free to marry.

Inès observed the chattering throng in Spyros' vast drawing room, admiring so many faces which she'd seen in the movies since childhood. All the women were impossibly glamorous, groomed like prize fillies in the parade ring before a race. Their toffee-tanned, sleek bodies, even some of the plumper producers' wives, were corseted, girdled and brassiered to within an inch of their lives, and there seemed to be no such thing as a gray head of hair.

A sea of décolletage bobbed around. Breasts of all shapes, sizes and shades, many pushed up with underwiring and Merry Widow corsets, spilled seductively over the colorful satin, chiffon, lamé and lace gowns of Hollywood's most illustrious women. And their jewels! Inès had seen jewels like this only in the Tower of London or on the Queen of England.

But if Inès was fascinated by the women of Hollywood, the entire Hollywood community was more than curious to meet the woman for whom it was said Julian had given up everything but his talent. Despite the attempts of Julian and Didier to keep the terms of his divorce settlement quiet, the news had soon become common knowledge in the business. There were few secrets in the tight-knit community—none in fact —and everyone at the party knew every detail about Julian's divorce.

The women grudgingly agreed that Inès was very beautiful. The slim column of champagne silk worn with a simple string of pearls, the long, dark brown hair, unteased, unsprayed, uncurled, and the fine porcelain complexion with barely even a hint of cosmetic enhancement were in sharp contrast to the flashy looks of so many of them. Dark red lips and smoky kohl-shadowed eyes were her only makeup.

"She's so French," breathed one buxom starlet to another as they teased, sprayed and painted in the green marble splendor of the Makopolis powder room.

"Yeah, she just oozes class, don't she?" said starlet number two, painting an already pouting lower lip into a cyclamen moue.

"I bet she's from a *real* top-drawer family," breathed the first girl, inserting a hand deep into her cleavage to push up her breasts until her chin could almost have rested on them.

"Yeah—aristocratic all right. She sure didn't have to work to make out like we've had to."

"Yup," said the first, spraying a generous amount of Evening in Paris into her ample cleavage. "She's a real lucky dame. I bet it all came real easy to that one. Just as easy as pie."

"Ah, there's Julian," Shirley Frankovitch said as soon as she saw the English star. "Damn, he's great-looking, isn't he, Irving? No wonder they call him the handsomest guy in the world."

Her husband, a lugubrious man of nearly sixty, nodded. Early in his career he had written several fictional masterpieces and been hailed by the literate as the natural successor to Hemingway. Upon his meeting Shirley Horowitz, however, ten years his junior and ambition her middle name, his brilliant literary style had gradually been eroded by her demands and influence.

Ignoring the plays and novels of genius which were fermenting inside him and which his publishers begged him to write, he had become her mentor. He was in fact so besotted by her that it was *her* writing career which had become his obsession, while his own had taken a backseat.

In 1946 Shirley had had her first book published—a novel which had owed a great deal to Irving's literary talent and a certain amount to her own fertile sexual imagination. *Valentina,* the tale of a gorgeous courtesan in eighteenth-century France, had become an overnight best-seller all over the world. Soon Hollywood had beckoned, wanting Shirley to write the script for the movie. Shirley craved a Hollywood career, and who was Irving to argue?

They had taken the train to the West Coast from New York and installed themselves in the Garden of Allah. For six months they had partied with Hollywood's finest, between bouts of serious writing. The fruits of their labors—Shirley's *Valentina,* a dreadful yet successful movie, and Irving's infinitely better *Silence of the Damned*— both became box-office smashes.

Irving then went on to have enormous Broadway and London successes with his two plays about distinguished political-historical figures, while Shirley then wrote *Valentina and the King* and two more smash-hit sequels to her carnal heroine's adventures.

With Shirley's bawdy portraits of seventeenth- and eighteenth-century heroines, and Irving's critically acclaimed scripts, the Frankovitches soon earned a reputation for really knowing their onions when it came to historical melodrama. Who better than they to write the screenplay for *The Legend of Cortez,* which was being heralded as the greatest historical epic since *The Ten Commandments?*

Shirley licked her lips in anticipation of meeting the star of their movie. Julian was catnip to women, a fact she appreciated only too well. After all, she had been quite a swinger herself for a while, although her own unspectacular looks had now turned to bloated flesh. But Shirley appreciated male beauty, aware, always, of the unlikelihood of her fantasies ever turning into reality. After all, a girl could dream, and it was Shirley's dreams which translated so convincingly onto the printed page.

There were so many people at the party that it was impossible for Julian and Inès to meet them all.

Every important star, director, producer and studio head had been invited, along with a spicy seasoning of contract starlets of both sexes. By nine o'clock there was such a heated crush in the three enormous reception rooms that Olympia Makopolis insisted that dinner be served at once.

Fifty tables covered with lamé cloths and each laid for ten people had been set up inside a giant red-and-white striped tent in the sprawling back garden. The walls of the tent were draped in evergreens, ivy and red poinsettias, and hundreds of tiny lights twinkled down from the ceiling, interspersed with more than ten thousand red roses suspended in silver mesh baskets. A vast eighteenth-century rock-crystal chandelier, some five feet in diameter, blazed down on the guests from the center, casting prisms of light on their expectant faces.

Spyros was known to give wonderful parties, but this one was set to top them all, it seemed.

A groaning buffet table, covered with scarlet satin and decorated with holly and silver lamé ribbons, held huge Baccarat crystal bowls of beluga caviar, silver salvers of lobster, baby crayfish, *foie gras* with the finest black truffles, smoked salmon flown in from Scotland, quail eggs and a profusion of exotic salads. At the opposite end of the tent a twenty-piece band in red dinner jackets played Gershwin and Cole Porter, and over a hundred waiters and waitresses, all dressed as fairies or elves, took the guests' orders from individual menus, written in exquisite calligraphy, which rested in front of each place card. Money was no object at the Makopolis house; after all, the studio was paying, and they were in the black this year.

Inès was seated between Spyros and the scintillating Cary Grant. Across the table Julian had Olympia Makopolis on his left—not much fun in the witty repartee stakes—but to his relief vivacious Rosalind Russell had been placed on his right and she kept Julian amused with a stream of fascinating and hilarious anecdotes.

In the center of each table an enormous cornucopia overflowing with Christmas goodies—tiny wheelbarrows filled with miniature Santa Clauses, jack-in-the-boxes, Raggedy Ann dolls, gift boxes, fairies, pixies and candy canes—spilled over in elegant yet ordered disarray onto the silver lamé tableclothes. In front of each guest was a present, a hallmarked silver Tiffany frame, wrapped in sky-blue paper and tied with silver ribbons and sprigs of holly. In the frame was a photograph of the smiling and paternal-looking Spyros Makopolis, Mrs. Makopolis, and their five children, all looking stiffly self-conscious.

"Hollywood, darling," mouthed Julian with a wink across the table to Inès as she opened her package. "Take it as it comes."

Inès sipped her heavily scented wine and smiled inwardly. So this was what it was really like. This was the Hollywood that the fans revered and the movie magazines gushed about; the magic place which intrigued everyone who went to the cinema. She would have to learn to like it, in spite of the incredible excesses of vulgarity she'd seen tonight, but she knew she could like anything as long as Julian was by her side. As long as she could be Mrs. Julian Brooks. How long—oh, Lord, how long would it be before his final decree was granted in London?

Across the sea of faces and noise, seated at a table of less important guests, the other newcomer to Hollywood gazed around in impressed delight. Umberto Scrofo fingered the scar beneath his tight collar uncomfortably. As usual, when he was excited or ill at ease, it itched and burned like the devil. He fought the strong desire to rip open his collar and scratch it fiercely. Tonight he must behave like a gentleman even though he felt out of place. He'd felt like a country bumpkin when introduced to Grace Kelly, Marilyn Monroe and so many other stars. He was so overawed that his conversation dried up and he knew he was making a *bruta figura*. He was angry with Ramona Armande, who seemed to have deliberately ignored him from the moment they arrived. She flitted from group to group, laughing her affected laugh, stopping often to huddle with her brother. The two were known to be inseparable when Didier was in town, inspiring the nickname the Magyar Mafia. He noticed angrily that Didier had been seated at the top table with Julian Brooks, while Ramona was at an adjacent table far away from Umberto. Insulting bitch.

One of these days, I *will* belong there, at the number one table, he thought, maneuvering a dollop of caviar into his mouth. When these Hollywood people see my finished masterpiece, I'll be courted and admired the way Julian Brooks is with that woman who isn't even his wife.

He had caught another glimpse of Inès profile earlier as her dark hair swung around her shoulders and she smiled at Julian. There was definitely something familiar about her—something which struck a strangely responsive chord in him. He'd wanted to get a closer look but she and Julian were surrounded by Gary Cooper, Errol Flynn and Clark Gable, all laughing, sharing secrets that men who looked as they did always seemed to share, so he couldn't get near them.

Umberto exchanged a few remarks across the table with Irving Frankovitch, who had written his superb script for *La Città Perduta,* then tried to listen to the boring babble of the woman next to him, a fat, overdressed monstrosity in a purple tent covered with flowered sequins. She had obviously tried hard, but failed miserably to pull herself together for tonight. Face powder in an unsuitable shade of orange caked the pores of her sweaty face, and her gray hair was frizzed and sprayed into an unfashionable style. But his jeweler's eye noticed that she was wearing a magnificent parure of diamonds and sapphires, obviously of extremely high quality, so she must be someone. Everyone here seemed to be someone.

He was becoming bored by her chatter, as he disliked ugly women, and it was only when Irving Frankovitch spoke to her that he realized she was Frankovitch's wife. While Irving was in Rome writing, Shirley had stayed in New York, so Umberto had never met her. Ah, this was much better. Shirley Frankovitch was a force to be reckoned with. A brilliant writer, an important woman in this town. He decided to cultivate her. She could help him with his plans of glory.

Shirley had been drinking steadily. Four or more glasses of Krug before dinner, and three glasses of Stolichnaya with her beluga had been downed faster than a sailor on shore leave. She had signaled to her waiter, good-looking even though he was dressed as an elf, to keep her wineglass topped up. By the time Spyros was making his introductory toasts, she was feeling no pain. Irving had tried to stop her drinking but she reprimanded him sharply. She felt good—she liked the way she felt when she'd really blasted a few.

Shirley hadn't been a heavy drinker when she was a teenager, but as she grew older and Mr. Right hadn't crossed her path, drinking had somehow become second nature to her. She had less than fond memories, in the days when she'd been a struggling writer in New York, of getting drunk night after night—always in the company of men, none of whom could ever have been remotely considered the answer to a maiden's prayer. Shirley had been so shy, insecure and intimidated by almost everything and everyone that she tried to lose herself in the romantic worlds which she created in her writing. But in sober reality, constant rejection was more the order of the day. Rejection from the publishers, rejection from the men. Only a diet of pink ladies, dry martinis and champagne cocktails could instill in her the illusion that she really mattered. Through her haze of alcohol she was able to amuse some of her male drinking partners enough to end up in bed with one of them occasionally. But the following morning she would always wake with a throbbing hangover. Sometimes she would find herself slumped across crumpled linen sheets in a shiny penthouse in uptown Manhattan, but more often than not her puffy eyes opened to a peeling fly-specked ceiling in some dingy midtown bedroom. There the object of last night's lust, typically some bleary-eyed blue-jawed brute, would avoid looking at her, which made her feel even cheaper.

It would have been stretching it to have called Shirley attractive, but she was eager to please, longed to be loved, and had good legs and big breasts. When the lights burned low and the hour was late, many men would lose their former powers of discrimination through drink, and slake their lust with Shirley. She always knew that she was never the first, second or even the third choice of her passing parade of paramours, but she never let her bitterness show. Instead she made every effort to become the life and soul of whatever party, club or bar she happened to find herself in. As she knocked back cocktail after cocktail, the skirts of her evening dresses hitched steadily higher as the evening progressed, revealing a tantalizing glimpse of garter belt and white thighs to entice the boys.

Occasionally, one of the boys would prove to be more than just a one-night stand, his attentions lingering towards her for a week or two, even for a month, but these liaisons always seemed to wane rapidly, and the shapely legs, the thirty-eight-inch bust and the increasingly bawdy repartee were never enough to sustain any permanent interest.

By the time Shirley Horowitz met Irving Frankovitch, she was pushing thirty-five and filled with an inner discontent and anger with a life which she felt had dealt her a rotten hand. Irving, however, the unassuming, unattractive, but brilliant writer from Hoboken, fell heavily and totally under her spell. He thought Shirley was the wittiest, funniest and sexiest woman in the world. The fact that his experience of women was severely limited, due largely to his shyness and unassuming looks, did not bother Shirley at all. Finally she had hooked herself a man.

Both sets of parents in Brooklyn and Hoboken breathed a communal sigh of relief when their respective only children were finally married in a burst of post-austerity glory. At the strictly Jewish wedding where the guests tucked into mountains of smoked salmon and sturgeon, potato *latkes*, wedding cake and expensively imported French red wine and champagne, Shirley became very drunk indeed. When Irving had finished his wedding speech, she rose, her veiled headdress of orange blossoms askew on her mouse-colored hair, and drawled triumphantly to the assembled throng.

"I know that all of you probably think that Irving doesn't look like much, but at least he's all mine, so hands off, girls, I've staked my claim."

Some of her girlfriends giggled, but a disapproving murmur echoed from the older members of the Frankovitch clan, and Shirley's mother raised a warning eyebrow at her daughter. But the bride, taking another few sips of champagne, would not be halted. Swaying from side to side, her massive breasts pushed up so high by her underwire bra that they seemed on the point of an escape attempt, she hiccuped loudly several times, then said, "Yeah, I know he's got a body like a shrunken little runt, but he's a real tiger between the sheets, girls—real hot stuff." The younger members of both families screamed with laughter, as the parents, uncles, older cousins and aunts sat rigid with disapproval, and Irving's normally sallow face flushed deeply as he lowered his head in embarrassment. Clutching her new husband's hand, fueled by the laughter and the sea of upturned smiling faces around her, Shirley couldn't stop herself. Grabbing Irving's glass of wine she downed it in one gulp and screeched.

"You may all think he's got a face like a big rabbit too what with those big ears and that funny twitchy pink nose of his, but let me tell you, girls—" her voice dropped to a conspiratorial stage whisper—"I'm delighted to tell you he sure as hell fucks like one!"

Shirley let out a screech of delight as she threw back another glass and almost everyone except Irving's parents screamed with laughter. The new bride could feel great waves of love washing over her, as the laughing faces looked up at her with admiration. She reveled in it. Taking no notice at all of Irving's pained discomfort, ignoring the furious stares of his parents, Shirley threw her enraptured audience a final outrageous tidbit:

"Confidentially, girls . . ." She steadied herself with her hands on the table, whispering in such a way that the hundred guests had to lean forward to catch her every word. "Between you 'n' me—he's the greatest little sex machine I've ever known, and believe me I've known more than my fair share, much *much* more. He can go *all* night 'n' every morning and although his little *schlong* may not be up to very much in the size department, what he lacks in inches he sure makes up for in staying power, he can *shtup* the night away, girls, and the afternoons too."

Her audience was in the palm of her hand now and Shirley had never had such a good time. Heedless of the disapproving maiden aunts shepherding the juvenile members of the party out of the room, oblivious to the guffawing waiters, some of whom had rushed from other parts of the hotel to hear her, she turned to her flushed and shell-shocked bridegroom and planted an enormous open-mouthed kiss on his gaping lips. "This little *putz* is the greatest *shtupper* I've ever known, and I've known a helluva lot!"

The whole room burst into applause, except for Irving's horrified father who was fanning Irving's deeply shocked mother with his fringed *tallith.* They were unable to comprehend why their precious only son had married such a vulgar drunken slut. A small gaggle of wide-eyed nephews and nieces stood snickering at the door, not understanding what Aunt Shirley had said, but knowing from the reaction of their elders that, whatever it meant, it sure was hot stuff.

That night, in the privacy of the honeymoon suite, Irving gave vent to his anger and burst his bride's balloon of happiness.

"You behaved like a cheap tart, Shirley," he told her, a pulse beating in his neck, the only physical sign of his shame and rage. "Worse than a street-corner tramp. I know that isn't the *real* you, which is why I forgive you, but I beg you, *please,* honey, you must stop drinking—it doesn't suit you, Shirley, and it's so undignified."

"Why should I?" snapped Shirley, tossing her orange-blossom head-dress to the floor and gratefully unfastening the tight ankle-strap sandals which had been pinching her feet for hours. Irving was a spoilsport. He was bringing her down from an all-time high. Why was he trying to ruin everything now when everyone had adored her this afternoon?

"It's degrading," he said mildly. "It makes you look foolish, Shirley."

"Foolish, shmoolish, what the fuck—who *gives* a damn—they *loved* me—all of those people—all our relatives, and friends—even Mom and Dad. They never gave a shit about me before but they were laughing their heads off—did you see 'em laugh, Irving? Didja?"

"Yes, I did, Shirley," said Irving patiently, noticing that Shirley was calming down, becoming herself again as the effects of the lethal alcohol wore off. "I did see them laugh, but they were laughing *at* you, honey, not *with* you. There's a difference—don't you see that, honey?"

"No, I don't. I had a great time, Irv, and you're bringing me down now."

Shirley flounced into the bathroom, her eyes bright with hot tears, and slammed the door. Then Irving heard her violently throwing up, and shrugged. He was a kind and patient man, who loved this woman, his new wife, recognizing many of her fears and insecurities. But the *Beaujolais Belligerence* she evinced when drunk would have to go. He would see to it that she stopped drinking. He felt sure he would be able to handle her now that they were married.

Irving glanced over at Shirley as Spyros started talking. No doubt about it—she'd had much more than a snootful. From the way she was glaring at everyone, she looked about to explode at any moment. He sighed, mentally fastening his seat belt for the bumpy ride which looked now to be inevitable.

After dinner Spyros introduced Julian, who rose with a modest bow to enthusiastic applause from the guests. How Hollywood loved a true thespian from the British theater. The *crème de la crème* of the cinema always felt inferior, somehow insignificant, beside an actor who regularly performed the classics on stage. With all their fame, looks and wealth, many of these stars were desperately insecure about their abilities and envied Julian his impeccable theatrical reputation.

Many also respected his brave stand against Phoebe. Few of them would have given up a perpetual slice of their earnings, a house and all its contents, just for the love of a woman. Consequently Inès was the object of enormous conjecture and gossip, most of which subsided as she passed her test with flying colors. Her beauty and style couldn't be faulted on any level. Those who talked to her found her charming, witty and cultured, not bitchy in the slightest.

Julian started to speak now, his melodic baritone entrancing the guests with a particularly amusing and self-deprecating joke at which the crowd roared its approval. Inès looked at him, admiring his poise and his velvet voice.

Shirley glanced around the room irritably. Every eye seemed riveted on Julian or on the woman across him. No one was looking in her direction. Why not? *She* too was a Star. A star writer and a star novelist who had written the script that had enticed Julian to America. *She* had single-handedly kept MCCP afloat through the lean, tough times after the war when audiences didn't know what the hell they wanted to see. But they'd all gone to see the movies she'd written, hadn't they? Especially the *Valentina* series. If it weren't for writers, nothing would ever happen in this town. No one seemed to appreciate how important they were to the movie product. No one.

"He's a lucky guy to have a woman like that," Irving said admiringly.

"And what's so great about her?" Shirley slurred belligerently. "She looks like a cold fish to me."

Irving ignored her as Julian told another joke and the rapt faces laughed again.

God damn it. Suddenly Shirley realized furiously that she wasn't even at the top table. Shit, shit, shit. What a bummer. Okay, so she was seated with Zanuck and Orson Welles—neither of them exactly *schleppers* in the business—but she still took it as a personal insult. After all she'd done for Spyros, this was his appreciation. Voices inside her seemed to be having a furious argument as they battled for supremacy. Good little Shirley was telling off bad little Shirley, but bad little Shirley seemed to be winning. Shirley knew she was losing control. Her head felt stuffed with cottonwool, her mouth dry. She quickly slugged back another glass of champagne, looking around the room with a challenging expression.

Irving's eyes were glued to Julian. Or was it Julian's French mistress he was staring at? Shirley squinted, trying to figure out *who* held her husband's attention. Yes, she was right, bad Shirley thought triumphantly. He was staring at the stuck-up Frenchwoman who looked as if butter wouldn't melt in her cocksucking mouth. Irving should be looking at her —her, *her!!* He was *her* husband, for Christ's sake. If he loved *her*, he should be paying attention to her.

Angrily, Shirley stuck a Lucky Strike in her mouth, turning to Irving for a light. He ignored her. He's ignoring you, Shirley, said the bad voice. As if you were nothing, no one, a fucking stranger!

"Gimme a light, Irving," she snapped, so loudly that Julian paused momentarily in his speech to look over at her.

Irving gestured that he had no matches, ignoring her again as his attention returned to Julian. In a fury, Shirley scrabbled through the cornucopia in front of her for matches. Some of the guests began to notice the disturbance and to make shushing noises. There were no matches in Santa's goodie box, and no one was smoking at Shirley's table.

"Fuck, fuck, *fuck!* Where are the motherfucking matches?" she screamed.

Julian stopped speaking as every head turned towards her and collectively Hollywood tut-tutted its silent disapproval of the bleary-eyed writer. Empty glass in hand, unlit cigarette dangling from slack lips, she was obviously completely, unbecomingly smashed.

Julian resumed his speech as Shirley's cute-looking waiter-elf dashed forward and struck a match for her. Inhaling deeply, she watched the sycophantic faces as they turned again in unison to listen to the actor's speech. What bullshit, she thought. They're all full of shit, every single one of the motherfuckers.

No longer giving a damn what anyone thought, Shirley suddenly stood up and said in a sarcastic, belligerent voice, "Everything that you say is absolute bullshit, your lordship. Everything in this room is bullshit—everyone in Hollywood is just a piece of *crap!*" She belched loudly, weaving violently as Irving grabbed her and pulled her into her seat.

"What the *hell* are you doing?" he whispered furiously. "For God's sake, behave yourself, Shirley. You're way out of line and making a complete fool of yourself again."

Everyone was looking at her now, some even standing up to get a better view. The whole damned tent—five hundred pairs of curious eyes were staring at her in shock, yet with the secret pleasure that tomorrow they'd all have something really juicy to gossip about.

That's the way it ought to be, Shirley thought, pleased with herself as she greedily downed another glass of champagne. They *should* be talking about her. Then she hiccuped so violently that the glass of champagne she was drinking spilled all over the front of her sequined tent dress. When the pretty waiter rushed forward to try to help her, he tripped over a piece of loose grass-green carpet and landed head first in Shirley's ample cleavage to shrieks of shocked laughter from the guests. Then, to add to Irving's intense embarrassment, Shirley's humiliation and the rest of the guests' hilarity, the two of them plummeted in slow motion to the floor, the tiny waiter in his elf's costume almost disappearing into the massive folds of Shirley's caftan.

Hollywood, of course, hushed up the story and closed ranks, as Hollywood always attempted to hush up the scandals and peccadillos of its darlings to the outside world. Nothing at all appeared in the press. But telephone wires hummed the next day throughout the Hills of Holmby and Beverly as chattering tongues broadcast the delicious news of Shirley's scandalous behavior to friends and acquaintances who'd neither had the luck nor the clout to have been invited to what must have been the party of the season.

Exaggerations abounded. By the end of the week, the story had been completely blown out of proportion. Not only had Shirley Frankovitch been completely drunk, but she'd ripped off her dress, danced half naked on the table, then pulled the waiter under the table, where she'd tried to give him a blow job. Olympia had become hysterical and had to be given a sedative by Dr. Zolotos. And Spyros had threatened Shirley that he would never use her again on a movie and fired both her and Irving from *Cortez*. Tittle-tattle and scandal. How the town loved it—revelled in it. Gossip, power and the movie business, these were the three ingredients that made its world turn and its inhabitants thrive.

On the way home from the party Inès couldn't stop talking and laughing about the party and the excesses of vulgarity she'd seen.

"Don't worry, darling," Julian smiled. "It's not always quite as tawdry as that—actually, many people who live here do have the most wonderful taste. Some of the most knowledgeable private art collectors in America live here. Many of them are even actors, believe it or not."

"Who?" inquired Inès. "I would like to meet them, Julian. Some of the pictures I saw on Mr. Makopolis' walls were absolute fakes. Anyone could see that. The original of the Renoir above the fireplace in the library is in the Louvre! How can Mr. Makopolis be so gullible?"

"Good old Spyros. He knows everything about the movies but not much about the art world. Tell you what, darling. Next week we'll go and see Eddie G. Robinson or Vincent Price, they both know everything about pictures and have marvellous collections."

"Mmm, I'd love to." Inès rested her head on Julian's shoulder as he drove them through the darkened empty streets of Beverly Hills towards their hotel. "But all I want to do now, *mon amour*, is to go home and make love with you."

"You've got yourself a deal, *Mademoiselle*," said Julian gravely. "And you are not allowed to go back on your word."

❧ *Fourteen* ❧

EVEN THOUGH IT WAS DECEMBER it was a boiling hot day. Dominique was playing volleyball on the Santa Monica sands with a group of shrieking teenagers, mostly boys, leaving Agathe with little to do but lie in the sun —something which she hated—or to eat lunch, which she'd already done. She decided to go for a walk. She wandered down the asphalt pavement which bordered the beach, thinking, thinking, thinking, oblivious to the cars speeding past, to the high, bright sun, indeed to anything at all except the vision of Julian Brooks which now filled her thoughts constantly.

They had met at last. Well, not exactly met. She had been having lunch in the MCCP commissary with Dominique and Kittens, the costume designer, when he'd come over to introduce himself. Agathe felt a deep flush suffuse her entire body as he stood chatting charmingly at their table. The flush seemed to rise from between her legs and engulf her until she felt that her face was a scarlet mirror in which he could read all her most secret thoughts.

She hardly dared to meet his eyes; she just listened to his melodious voice as he spoke and laughed with Dominique and Kittens. The easy camaraderie the three of them seemed to share goaded Agathe into a silent jealous frenzy. Julian stood so tall and easy, one hand casually resting on the back of Dominique's chair, while the girl giggled up at him, chattering nineteen to the dozen. Agathe had frozen. She had been unable to meet his eye even for a second or two, conscious of the sweat which trickled down her back, the flush on her face and the horrible, embarrassing tingling in her groin. He could sense it—of course he could sense it. That was why he was ignoring her, wasn't it? Julian tipped his hat to the women as he left, and Agathe felt herself relax. Dominique's face was flushed and happy as she bit into her hamburger.

"Golly, he sure is cute for an old man, don't you think, Agathe?"

Kittens nodded in agreement.

"I'm sure I don't know what you mean," said Agathe stiffly.

"He's terribly good-looking," sighed Dominique, then leaning towards her chaperone, she whispered, "I hear that practically every actress he's ever worked with has fallen for him!"

"Don't say things like that, it isn't right for young girls like you to have thoughts like that," snapped Agathe. "Eat your lunch."

Dominique grinned to herself. If Agathe only knew what thoughts she did have, the poor old thing would probably have a nervous breakdown.

Inès woke up to the Beverly Hills sunshine, which streamed into the hotel room through the cloudy muslin curtains. She was nauseous and her head felt fuzzy. Strange, as she usually was able to handle champagne. Julian had left early for the studio's Malibu ranch for the first of his stunt-riding lessons. It was essential to be an expert horseman, and the end of the eight-week instruction period would hopefully guarantee that Julian would be able to deal with a horse better than the grizzled handlers at the ranch.

The telephone rang, the shrill sound making her head throb. It was Julian calling from the ranch.

"Darling." His voice was warm. "How are you feeling?"

She lied and assured him she was feeling fine.

"Good, good. Darling, I've just bumped into Flynn down here at the ranch. He's asked us to dinner tonight at Romanoff's—will you be up to it, angel?"

"Of course, *chéri.* I liked him so much when we met last night. And I've always wanted to go to Romanoff's."

"Good. Okay, I've got to run, my love. God, my arse is so sore from the damn horse. They must have been supermen in those days to ride without saddles."

"I'll kiss it better when you come home." Inès murmured, laughing.

"Can't wait, darling. See you later—dinner's at eight. We'll meet Errol there."

After a lazy, relaxing day, Inès dressed carefully for dinner, in a black *peau de soie* cocktail dress with a full mid-calf skirt. Her only jewelry was Julian's simple diamond engagement ring, small diamond stud earrings and her lucky bracelet, but she looked ravishing and Julian couldn't stop telling her so.

Romanoff's was on Rodeo Drive. One of the most famous restaurants in the world, it was owned and run by Prince Michael Romanoff, a self-styled exiled Russian prince with impeccable manners and immense charm. Because there were no top tables at Romanoff's—hence no Siberia—he managed to have half of Hollywood dining there regularly without ever offending any of their fragile egos. Stars always sat where Prince Michael put them and never complained.

He now stepped suavely forward to greet Julian and Inès as they came through the thick glass doors into the foyer. Every table was in full view and most of the diners looked up as they entered. Though small in stature, Prince Michael was big on personality. Inès could feel the power behind his twinkling brown eyes as he charmingly kissed her hand murmuring to Julian, "Looks, m'boy, you've done it again as usual—what a ravishing gel—French too—excellent. I'm very happy for you, m'boy—come, Errol's waiting."

He led the way down the carpeted stairway while everyone in the room stared at Inès and Julian. It was as if the restaurant had been designed for people-watchers. None of the booths was high-backed, so one group could easily chat to another at the tables on either side and behind and could see everything else that was going on.

Julian nodded hellos to Cary Grant and Darryl Zanuck as they wended their way to the table where Errol Flynn sat beside a pretty girl who looked young enough to be his daughter.

Prince Michael took their drink order in his clipped English accent, then, clamping his cigarette holder firmly between his teeth, left them to greet the ravishing Grace Kelly, who was standing at the top of the stairs with a handsome escort.

The room buzzed and then went silent as every detail of Grace's hair, makeup and outfit was analyzed by the women, while every man marveled at her beauty. Inès thought she was breathtaking. She deserved her title of Hollywood's reigning princess. She was flawless, besides being a highly talented actress.

It was an exhilarating dinner, and Errol was in top form, although drinking heavily. His young companion spoke little, content to giggle shyly at his jokes, most of which she didn't really understand, and to eat everything put before her. Errol embroidered on the fracas created by Shirley Frankovitch at Spyros' party the other night, and had everyone in stitches.

Several studio executives stopped by the table, ostensibly to pay their respects to Errol, but after a perfunctory greeting to him, they seemed far more interested in Julian. By the end of the evening his pocket contained half a dozen cards from some of the most influential men in town, with instructions to call them as soon as possible.

Flynn was not given even one card. Although only in his mid-forties he was almost finished in Hollywood. He had been a great star, but he was now considered box-office poison, having outraged moral Middle America with his amorous antics, his philandering with underage girls, his drunken brawls, and his "I don't give a damn" attitude. Studio publicists had been unable to hold down the lid on his scandalous behavior, and he'd become Hollywood's whipping boy—almost a pariah. But he was wonderfully charming, Inès thought, full of humor, and a truly great raconteur. He must have been glorious-looking once, she decided.

When Inès went to the powder room, the peach-mirrored haven was empty but for one girl whose enormous overly tanned cleavage swelled out of an unfashionably short tight white lace dress which cupped her too-plump derriere in a most unflattering way. Her big lips were painted with thick pink gloss, and her mane of platinum hair heavily teased. Inès realized that the girl had gone to enormous trouble to try to look as much as possible like Jayne Mansfield, one of the town's leading sex symbols. The starlet was a true Hollywood cupcake. She eyed Inès simple black Balenciaga dress admiringly while she applied yet more hair spray to her platinum helmet.

"I saw you the other night at the Makopolis party," she confided in a friendly way, removing another cosmetic necessity from her pink plastic and rhinestone bag, bending over so far that Inès could see her nipples. "I just *love* the way you dress. It's so chic—so French!" she gushed.

Inès murmured a thank you. What a pitiful girl—professional, obviously; Inès could always recognize one of her own. And this one was on the brink of losing her looks. Poor thing, Inès hoped she'd been clever enough to put some money away. She wondered who'd had the bad taste to bring such an obvious tart to Romanoff's. She soon found out.

Outside the powder room a tall, thin man stood waiting. He turned to Inès, and with a shock which electrified every nerve in her body she recognized him immediately. She tried to move away, but it was too late, he had seen her, and he pounced.

"Inès! Hello. Well, goodness gracious me. What the blazes are *you* doing here, old girl?"

"Benjie." Inès' voice was a hoarse whisper. "What a surprise. Oh, dear, I'm terribly sorry, Benjie, but you must excuse me—I have to go back to my table—they all want to leave." She moved away, but Benjie grabbed her arm, and with growing horror she saw that they were now in the foyer of the restaurant, in full view of the whole room. What was Benjie doing here? He never left London except to go to the country or Monte Carlo. Beverly Hills was Non-U to his set.

"Oh, no you don't—I'm not letting you get away again. I've *missed* you, Nanny." He bent his head closer as she tried to edge away. She could smell the gin on his breath which had always made him desperate to play his kinky sex games.

"Benjie's missed Nanny, vewy vewy much." He was lapsing into baby talk now, much to Inès' discomfort. "Benjie's been bad, a vewy *naughty* boy—needs Nanny to spank him *hard*," he whispered, looking pleadingly at her, his long, bony fingers still holding tightly onto her arm. She could hardly put up a struggle in front of Hollywood's elite. He would never dare behave like this in London at the 400, the Café de Paris or any of the haunts that he and his friends frequented. Benjie had always behaved with the most impeccable manners everywhere in London, the perfect English gentleman. Only when he'd been in bed or drinking heavily, which was obviously what he'd been doing tonight, did his aristocratic demeanor lapse.

The door to the powder room opened and the Barbie Doll minced over, patting her hair. Benjie loosened his grip on Inès' arm as he greeted his platinum-haired companion.

"Well, it's been very, very nice to see you again, Inès," he said with a sly smile, taking the blonde's arm in a proprietary way. Inès was even more amazed. In London he would never have allowed himself to associate publicly with such an obvious tart.

"We must get together, I'm here until Sunday at the Bel-Air—where are you staying?" he asked.

"Oh—er—with friends," Inès said. "They're waiting for me. I must go —good-bye, Benjie."

At that moment Prince Michael came over to escort the couple to their table, but before he walked away, Benjie, sotto voce and with a wink, said, "Do give my very best regards to *Nanny!*"

Inès felt her face flame, truly shaken by this unexpected encounter. Her past seemed to be catching up with her already. Benjie had recognized her instantly, of course. With her pale matte face, red lips, kohl-rimmed eyes and distinctive long, dark bob, she would always stand out in a crowd. Most women today wore their hair in a curly, short poodle style, or in a gamine cut. Inès had not changed her look for nearly ten years.

She walked unsteadily back to her table, and Julian watched her curiously. She seemed flustered, and Inès was a woman who was rarely flustered.

"Wasn't that old Benjie Spencer-Monckton you were talking to?" he asked. "I remember meeting him once or twice at White's in London."

"Yes, it was," she said, taking a long cooling sip of ice water as she saw, to her dismay, that Benjie and the starlet-tart were being seated in a booth almost opposite theirs.

"You've never mentioned him," Julian persisted. "How do you know him?"

"I don't," Inès lied. "I mean, not really. We met at a weekend house party in the country once. I'm surprised he even remembered me." She laughed, the sound ringing tinnily in her ears, her eyes scanning Julian's face for any sign that he might not believe her. But he'd obviously accepted what she'd said. This time.

The blonde looked over at Inès, smiling amiably through lipstick-smudged lips. No doubt she was questioning Benjie about Inès, just as Julian was questioning her about Benjie. Would Benjie tell her the truth? He wouldn't dare—surely? They had been too fond of each other. But if he did tell this hooker that Inès had also been a whore; if he told her of the perverse games that they had played together, the occasional *ménage à trois* they'd had with some of his friends; if these stories began to circulate in Hollywood and Julian heard of them, her life with him would be finished. Inès couldn't bear to think about it. She didn't know what Benjie was doing in Hollywood nor what he was now whispering to the giggling girl. All she felt at that moment was the imminent danger that she might lose everything.

Inès' premonition proved horribly accurate. Later that evening, after having said good night to Errol and his girlfriend, who had decided to join another table of friends, she and Julian were standing outside the restaurant, waiting for their car to arrive. Suddenly Inès went rigid with fear. This was too much, much too much. It simply couldn't be true, it just wasn't possible.

Escorting a sable-clad Ramona Armande from Romanoff's was a short, bald paunchy man. Even though she only glimpsed his profile, Inès recognized, to her unspeakable horror, the loathsome face which had haunted her dreams for so many years. That squat body, the thick neck, that bullet head—she could never forget him. Eleven years had gone by, along with most of his hair. He was much fatter now, deep lines had etched themselves into his forehead and between his nose and mouth. His fleshy lips were thinner and pulled into a grimace which he no doubt thought was a charming social smile, as he leaned towards Ramona to whisper in her ear.

But he was dead. She'd killed him, hadn't she? She had washed his life blood from her hands with the perfumed soap at the Ritz. Wiped it on the soft white towels. But there was absolutely no doubt about it at all. It was the face she knew from her most terrifying nightmares. It was undeniably Umberto Scrofo. The man she thought she'd murdered in the Ritz. The man who had worn the uniform, bristling with medals, of an Italian general. The man who'd forced her to have brutal, sadistic sex, who'd degraded and beaten her so violently that the thought of his repeating those vile acts had made her kill him.

She had always believed that she'd killed him. But if he were dead, how could he possibly be here, standing outside Romanoff's on Rodeo Drive in Beverly Hills? Was she going mad? Was this another nightmare? Some horrible, sickening hallucination? Or was this reality?

Inès felt about to faint. Her palms were soaking wet and her heart pounded like a piston. Her sense of panic was so suffocating that she could hardly breathe. Umberto Scrofo, here, alive, in the all—too—gross flesh.

She turned her back, facing Julian so that the man couldn't see her features. Would he recognize her? She prayed he wouldn't. Surely she'd altered physically a great deal since Paris in 1943—but had she changed enough?

"I want to look like this." Inès handed the hairdresser a photograph of Grace Kelly that she'd cut out of *Look* magazine, and watched him expectantly.

"But you look so great the way you are," the hairdresser said in amazement. "Why d'you wanna change, honey?"

"Please, just do it," said Inès simply. "I want to, that's all."

The hairdresser shrugged indifferently. He would never understand dames as long as he lived. Here was an original beauty, distinctive, classy, a real elegant European lady, who wanted to change herself into another Kelly clone. Well, he thought, at least she didn't want to look like Marilyn Monroe, the other great flavor of the fifties. So what, he'd do it, he was getting paid to do hair, not to be a psychiatrist.

Inès buried herself in a book while he mixed his colors, and she didn't watch as he cut and colored her long dark hair. Only when the hairdresser had finished his work did she look at herself critically in the mirror. It was uncanny—the transformation from a dark-haired, sultry, European-looking sophisticate to a distinctly American-looking rose was extraordinary. She was almost unrecognizable but, happy to see, still beautiful. Her hair was cut into a short bob which skimmed her earlobes, with a low parting and soft waves around her forehead. The new color was masterful. A pale ash gold, almost the color of champagne, not the bright yellow gold of her teenage years, but a subtle, classic color with delicate bronze highlights. The style and shade were different enough to separate her from her past and anyone who had known her then.

Inès spent the rest of the afternoon at the Elizabeth Arden salon, completing her transformation. She invested in a complete new range of cosmetics, powder blue eyeshadow, light lipstick, pale rouge, and a new wardrobe for the upcoming Acapulco location. Pastels, frothy chiffon and light cotton gowns in pink, powder blue, lemon yellow. She would no longer wear those favorite severe blacks and whites of past years. She would be transformed. A new life. A new image. A new Inès.

Inès Juillard the courtesan was now dead. She was going to be Mrs. Julian Brooks in only a few weeks. No one from her past would ever be able to recognize her now, nor could they ever hurt her again, of that she felt sure.

❧ *Fifteen* ❧

Umberto Scrofo sat glumly in his Hilton suite waiting for the telephone to ring. He had called every single studio head since he had been in California, trying to arrange a meeting or a screening for his film. Not one of them would even take his calls. He was always sloughed off to one of their assistants who, with smoothly insincere voices, gave Umberto a dozen excuses as to why their bosses were too busy to see him.

"So what if the picture stars Ramona Armande?" Spyros Makapolis had growled to his second-in-command. "Who cares? She's an old has-been. She's been around longer than Garbo, for Christ's sake—and no one's interested in some goddamn Italian art film, even if it is supposed to be better than Rossellini's."

"Mr. Makopolis will let you know," the silken-voiced secretary had informed Umberto. And so indeed would Mr. Zanuck, Mr. Warner, Mr. Cohn and Mr. Schary. All had given him the cold shoulder, the frozen mitt. He was feeling unspeakably frustrated.

Didier Armande, who had been responsible for most of the financing, had seen a rough cut of *La Città Perduta* and had thought it a minor masterpiece. But although he was a powerful film producer in England, Didier didn't have the same clout in Hollywood, and even he couldn't persuade the tycoon moguls to attend a screening.

Umberto scratched furiously at the thick keloid scar on his throat until it was almost raw. Even the underage prostitute whom a bellboy had procured for him the night before hadn't managed to alleviate his rage. He had pummeled into her pale quivering body until she had cried out with pain, and he had to slap her across her sniveling face until she was silent. But he had never tried to do again what he had done with that little blond whore at the Ritz all those years ago, or in Calabria with Silvana. The revenge that had been meted out to him had been too terrible. How he had survived either attempt to destroy him had been a miracle. Whenever his secret erotic senses told him what he wanted, where he was headed, he always managed to stop in time. Thoughts of parched and starving days adrift in a fishing boat filled him with dread, and the memory of the blond tart's terror-stricken face as she slashed his razor across his throat would haunt him forever. The authorities had never found her. Was she still alive? Probably, but if she was she would now be some broken-down old strumpet selling her poxy, raddled body in the back alleys of Montmartre for a few sous. It must be eleven years ago, but he had not forgotten. He would never forget, he thought, as he once again scratched at his constant reminder of her.

He looked out at the fine blue December sky, but couldn't see too much of it. All his attempts to get one of the best suites at the Beverly Hills Hotel, the Beverly Wilshire or the Bel-Air had failed miserably. Money didn't talk in Hollywood. Power and fame did. Umberto had a great deal of money, but no one here knew or seemed to care who he was. He had only managed to get this suite at the Hilton which had no view at all and was decorated in a revolting shade of orange, by heavily bribing the man at the front desk.

He decided to go for a walk down Wilshire Boulevard to take some air. He had loved walking in Rome recently. There he was somebody. People stopped him in the cafés, glad to see him. *"Ciao,* Umberto, *come sta?"* they asked, eager voices showing their respect and admiration. On the Via Veneto he was the new king of the movies, ever since the word had spread about *La Città Perduta.* Here he was treated like a piece of shit. He put on a green mohair cardigan, similar to one he had seen Dean Martin wearing at a golf tournament. Tying a poison-green paisley scarf around his throat to hide his scar, he put on large dark sunglasses and a pristine panama hat, so new that it shrieked vulgarity.

He sauntered down Wilshire Boulevard towards the Beverly Wilshire Hotel, smiling at the few pedestrians who ignored him. He passed the shining red-lacquer door of the Elizabeth Arden beauty salon and idly looked into the windows at the displays of delicate lingerie, casual sports-wear and cosmetics.

When the red door opened and a waft of subtle perfume caught him, he turned to see a delicate profile, a waterfall of shining champagne hair and a tall, lithe body dressed in powder blue. The woman walked briskly, disappearing in the direction of I. Magnin. Puzzled, he stared after her. He knew that woman, he was sure of it. There was something terribly familiar about her. He had thought he'd recognized someone like her at the Makopolis party too—but that girl had been a brunette. This one was a classic blonde. But she struck a definite chord. Now where had he seen her before? He shrugged. It wasn't important. What was important, all he cared about now, was getting Zanuck, Makopolis or Jack Warner to see his movie. If they didn't he might as well get out of this ghastly place and go back to Rome.

PART THREE

❖ *One* ❖

THE ABOVE-THE-LINE CAST and technicians began dribbling into Acapulco
early in January. Set designers, architects, carpenters, painters, plasterers
and prop men had already been there for four months creating the grand
and elaborate sets needed for *The Legend of Cortez*. The film's plot,
which didn't even pretend to be historically accurate, given that this was
a CinemaScope epic, was fairly thin. In 1518 Hernando Cortez and his
fellow adventurer Francisco Pizarro were sent by King Charles V on a
mission to find gold. Their expedition landed in Mexico with only six
hundred men. At first Cortez was received by Montezuma—who was to
be the last Aztec emperor—like a god, but Cortez repaid this honor by
imprisoning him and later by conquering his entire empire.

When Cortez' men attempted to leave Montezuma's capital, then
called Tenochtitlán, the Aztecs finally rose up against him. They unsuccessfully fought Cortez and his troops in a pitched battle, largely because
so many of Montezuma's men deserted and went over to the side of the
Spanish invaders.

The Aztec emperor died in prison, leaving Cortez to win the heart
of his fiery, beautiful daughter, and they supposedly lived happily ever
after.

But Spyros Makopolis needed a much stronger plot than that. Historical epics were in vogue, the bigger the better. Chariots, togas and ruins
were fascinating audiences everywhere, as long as the historical facts
were beefed up; and Irving and Shirley Frankovitch had been hired to try
to glamorize the life of Señor Cortez. They had started diligently re-
searching and writing early in 1953, spurred on by Makopolis' offer of an
unprecedented hundred-thousand-dollar advance plus seven percent of
the gross profits. The following year, the studio sent teams of scouts all
over the world to find the most suitable yet cheapest locations for this
four-million-dollar Technicolor CinemaScope extravaganza. MCCP had

high hopes for a box-office bonanza and were sparing no expense to achieve it.

Location scouts had returned from months of all-expense-paid trips to dozens of exotic places to inform the studio, that with its thirty-eight lush beaches, dozens of gorgeous tropical bays and lagoons, clear, calm water and incomparable sunsets, Acapulco was the most perfect location for the movie.

After Irving and Shirley had written their first two drafts in New York and their third in Los Angeles, they arrived in Acapulco to give it the final polish. The couple now sat on the vine-covered balcony of their Villa Vera suite, sipping *piña coladas* in the humid dusk and waiting for the new arrivals.

"Here comes Julian with his fiancée." The perpetually inquisitive Shirley was able to get a good close-up view of the couple with the help of a strong pair of binoculars.

It was obvious, from the proud looks she gave him and by the way in which she held his arm, that Inès Juillard, svelte in champagne linen, was utterly devoted to Julian Brooks. He looked a little overheated for such a handsome star, Shirley thought. Under his cream panama hat beads of sweat shone on his matinée-idol brow, and his usually crisp moustache appeared to be wilting.

Inès spotted the glint of the binoculars in the reflected sunlight, looked up and then smiled at Julian. She wondered who could be watching them. No, not them, *him,* Julian; he was the star, the one the world was interested in. She knew that the studio and the Frankovitches had gone to considerable lengths to make the part of the buccaneer-adventurer Cortez to fit Julian, who at thirty-eight was now at the height of his masculine beauty.

Although the split from Phoebe had taken its toll on him financially, in the time Inès had been living with Julian she believed that he had found true contentment. He really loved her. More than he had ever loved anyone before. But he was, after all, an actor, so if he ever did stray a little, she knew that she would have to turn a blind eye. Her years as a courtesan had taught her that so many men were just like little boys. Sex was a sport, a hunt and a challenge to them. Even when they loved their wives madly, the best of men thought little of sexual infidelity. Unfaithfulness had been accepted in Europe as a fact of life for centuries, and intelligent wives had always ignored it. Inès had played brilliant sexual games, intrigued Julian with her quick mind, her knowledge of art, politics, music and finance. She had also woven a bond of sexual magic that made him feel as he never had with any other woman before.

Now, with the new year Inès would soon start a whole new life as Mrs. Julian Brooks. She was now nearly thirty years old. Beautiful, intelligent and desirable. To make her situation completely perfect, she suspected that she might be pregnant. Julian had often spoken of his desire for a child, and although they were not yet married she felt confident that he would be thrilled if her Los Angeles doctor confirmed her suspicions.

Julian smiled at his bride-to-be. She was the perfect woman for him in every way.

It never ceased to amaze him that after a grinding fourteen-hour day at the studio or on location, fencing, riding or performing his own difficult stunts, she could make his homecoming an event. An ice-cold martini would be waiting, made just as she heard his car coming up the winding driveway of their house. Exquisitely but simply dressed in the latest fashions from Paris, coolly elegant, she always managed to reveal a glimpse of something which would be guaranteed to arouse him. Perhaps the curve of a perfect breast through some transparent chiffon, or a creamy shoulder emerging from the depths of velvet, or her gorgeous legs through a split satin skirt. She would rub the back of his neck to relieve his tension, her cool fingers caressing his tired muscles. From this massage, Inès could always gauge his mood. She could tell if he'd be receptive to lovemaking or not; he almost always was. They would bathe together in the cool marble bathroom, in the shower which had powerful yet soothing jets positioned in strategic places, where she would wash his tired body with scented Guerlain soap.

As she kneaded his cock gently and lovingly with the soap, the tips of her nipples would brush lightly against his chest and he would harden; then her tongue would make its way into his mouth, as the strong jets burst into power, and she would position his body where the water would touch him most pleasurably.

She never seemed to mind that her makeup and hair were ruined by these few blissful moments. The only thing which truly mattered to her was giving pleasure to her man. Sometimes she left him, still tumescent after the soaping and the kissing, to withdraw to her bedroom to anoint herself with various oils and moisturizers. Usually he would come and take her as she stood in her curtained dressing room, possessing her fiercely, with stallion speed. But often they would linger in the shower. Before it was over, and when he was almost bursting with pleasure, she would take him to one of the many places that she'd designed for love. She knew all the answers to a man's tired libido and used them cunningly. Afterward, she washed him gently, leaving him to doze on cool linen sheets while she prepared dinner, which she would take to him on a tray. While he ate she would watch him. If he wanted to talk, she chatted away. If he craved silence, she would be as quiet as a mouse; if he wanted to study his dialogue, she would read a book. She was the perfect woman who wanted to be the perfect wife: a tigress in the bedroom, a sophisticated lady everywhere else. The only thing about her which displeased him was the new color of her hair. He had adored her long thick dark brown hair, loved twining it around his hands like silken ropes. This new style, although soft and becoming, made Inès somehow lose the aura of strength and individuality. It made her look more ordinary.

Never mind, it was probably only temporary. Her Grace Kelly style would be nothing more than a passing phase, and before long she would once again return to being his ravishing brunette. But whatever color

Inès' hair might be, it didn't ever seem to stop men staring at her admiringly wherever she went.

Many men coveted Inès, sensing her almost palpable sexuality. But she belonged to him. Whatever relationships she had had in the past, they were now meaningless. She had told him about her only three lovers, refusing to go into any detail at all in spite of his pressing insistence. She was a clever woman. Julian knew that the more she told him the more he would jealously want to hear about her past. For Looks Brooks, Inès had no past. Her life had only begun when he met her.

◆ *Two* ◆

Umberto Scrofo sat in his drawing room in Rome, surrounded by some of his favorite furniture, pictures and sculptures; he was picking his teeth with a paper clip and reading an airmailed copy of *Weekly Variety*.

La Città Perduta—The Lost City, in English—was a massive success. He had been right to insist on a European publicity tour with Ramona and the rest of the cast. *La Città Perduta* had received a phenomenal boost, and despite the actors demanding perks like grand hotel suites and limousines, it had all paid off handsomely. The picture was a smash hit in Europe. It was his first taste of cinematic success, and he was immensely pleased with himself.

His young housekeeper entered the semi-dark room which was shuttered against the afternoon sun, her manner subservient.

"May I get you something, Signor Scrofo?"

"Yes," Umberto snapped in his croaking voice, wondering why she always sounded so fucking apologetic. "Iced coffee with plenty of sugar, and don't spill it on the tray like you did last time."

"Yes, *Signor*," the girl bobbed and hurriedly disappeared. Signor Scrofo terrified her, but she wanted to keep this job. It paid well and her large family needed the money.

Umberto sighed. He was bored, and Umberto disliked being bored. It was about time for another visit to Signora Albertoni's apartment in the Via Sistina. *She* never bored him. Not when she stood tall and Aryan in long black boots and black silk stockings, a lacy suspender belt cutting into the flesh of her strong thighs, her blond hair flying around her flushed face, as she let him whip her with any one of the assorted implements which she kept for her clients' pleasure.

Five minutes later the housekeeper fluttered in nervously. "It's the telephone for you; I think it's America." When she smiled her face looked almost pretty. America. He knew how she'd love to go to America. So would he. He yearned for it. Maybe he would, now that the picture was a success.

When he'd been in L.A., Umberto had signed with the William Morris Agency, unconcerned that they represented almost three hundred producers worldwide, but his ego was big enough to stand the competition because he knew he had produced a great picture. Everyone in Rome had said so, and Umberto was a man who had never lacked a highly developed sense of his own worth. Even though he was ugly, he thought himself irresistible, witty and cultured. It was everyone else's stupidity that they couldn't seem to see it.

He opened one of the shutters and glanced outside at the tourists milling about on the Spanish Steps, cursing to himself that they were ruining his beautiful neighborhood with their loud voices and their cameras.

Gia brought him the telephone and he heard the crackle of the long-distance line as Abe, his agent, came on the line.

"Hi, Umberto, how ya doing?"

"I'm doing fine, Abe, just fine. What's the latest news on the movie?"

"Picture's doing great business in Europe as you know, Hubie baby. I'm sure you've seen *Variety*. We've had some interest in you here too," he said.

"Really?" Umberto lit his cigar, his fat face beaming. "Any of the majors?"

"Well, not exactly the majors, but there's been some independent interest—Roger Corman, for instance."

"Roger Corman!" Umberto spluttered. "He makes horror films, for Christ's sake—I'm beyond that now. I told you, Abe, that after *La Città Perduta* I want to produce something in Hollywood—haven't you been trying?"

"We're trying, we're trying," said Abe in the Hollywood agent's usual semi-placatory tone which they used on actors and producers alike. It didn't really matter a fig to Abe whether Umberto Scrofo made a film in America or not. Producers grew on palm trees in Hollywood; they hardly needed to import them from Europe.

Umberto's film was a success in Europe, but it had caused little excitement in America. It couldn't even get distribution. Abe, overworked and underpaid, was not about to go out of his way to push Scrofo. He was just one of thousands of William Morris clients, and this was simply a bread-and-butter call.

"If you read the European grosses in *Variety*," Umberto asked, "why don't you tell everyone about them, for fuck's sake?"

"Yeah, yeah, we told 'em it's a great picture, real great. We're tryin' to get it to Cannes for the festival, you know. I just want you to understand that we're working hard on a whole lot of things, Umberto," the agent said easily. "A whole bunch of things. Something could happen very soon, believe me. Just keep the faith, sweetheart, keep the faith."

"I am a good producer, Abe, maybe even a *great* producer," Umberto said coldly. "Not only *Oggi* but *Gente* and *Tempo* said I am the new De Laurentiis—and those putzes in Hollywood—Makopolis, Cohn, Zanuck — they wouldn't even go to *see* my movie."

"I know, I know, Umberto baby," said Abe soothingly. "Just be patient, something'll come up—something big—so hold on for a little longer, be patient, we'll get a picture for you soon. Listen, I gotta go now. We'll keep in touch. *Ciao* for now, baby."

"*Ciao,* Abe," said Umberto crossly as he banged down the receiver. He swallowed his iced cappuccino with a scowl. If this picture was so big in Europe, why wasn't America interested? It had become his obsession to make an American film, to be an important man in Hollywood. To be up for an Oscar, to go to parties at Jack Warner's, Ray Stark's and Charlie Feldman's. He had adored the Makopolis Christmas bash. It was a stinging blow to his ego that the excellent reviews for *La Città Perduta* hadn't led to anything in the States. But he wasn't going to sit around and feel sorry for himself. He had three European projects on the boards, and he was dedicating himself passionately to them.

"Fuck America," he said to himself, rubbing the itching scar on his neck. "Who needs them? I'll stay here." Better a big fish in a small pond . . .

He gazed now at a beautifully lit Manet which hung on the pale gold damask-covered wall. This picture always gave him enormous pleasure, although the blond girl in it vaguely reminded him of that whore who'd tried to kill him at the Ritz. Maybe he'd find her one day. Then he would exact the revenge he'd dreamed of so often. Meanwhile, he had motion pictures to make.

❧ *Three* ❧

"I COULD LIVE like this forever," chuckled Bluey Regan. "Who needs the movie business when you've got a boat?"

The Irish-American Bluey Regan had been an assistant director since the talkies began. As he would constantly remind people, there was nothing he didn't know about the picture business. Full of life, always cheerful, he was a director's dream, and Nick Stone valued him immensely as his right-hand man; what Nick didn't know, Bluey would.

Nick agreed with Bluey. It was perfect. Nothing was more exhilarating than the camaraderie between men on a boat.

It had been thirty-six hours since they'd left the Los Angeles marina on a cold, misty morning. The seas were a sulking, churning mass in which a hundred-foot ketch had great difficulty maneuvering just to get out of the port. The *Jezebel* with its crew of five had traveled some fifteen hundred miles in this bad weather. In spite of Nick's Greek boyhood as a fisherman and a love for the sea which matched Bluey's, he had succumbed to bouts of *mal de mer.* But this was all behind them now; the icy gray Californian Pacific had gradually turned blue as they sailed closer to the tropics. Both men were bronzed, fit and muscled as they stood at the helm taking turns to steer, caught up in an easy flow of jokes and conversation.

Bluey was forty-eight, with hair bleached yellow-white by the sun, and wrinkled skin sunburned to the color of caramel. His blue eyes danced with humor; he was never happier than when sailing on a trip like this. He was in a state of total relaxation tinged faintly with the anticipation of the work ahead.

Nick was less sanguine. Against his will, he'd been persuaded by Bluey to make the trip down to Acapulco by boat. Much as he adored the sea, his first instincts had been to fly down, as he had much to do and many decisions to make before shooting started.

But his first assistant had been adamant. "Heck, Niko, it takes almost as long to fly to the damned place as sail. First, you've gotta drive to Tijuana on that shit road that takes at *least* six or seven hours. Then you grab a broken-down, two-engine plane left over from *Wings*—Richard Arlen's probably still the pilot. When you finally get to Mexico City, ya gotta stay overnight, and there's so much crazy fuckin' night life there you'll end up with a hangover the next day that'll make your teeth fall out, which is when you'll have to take Aero Nervoso de Mexico, or whatever the fuck it's called, and boy, oh boy, will you be needing a handful of their sick bags then, kid."

Nick could feel himself smiling as Bluey went on.

"I'll tell you the truth, Nick, you won't get me on *any* plane that hasn't got a good ole American pilot in the cockpit with at least five years' service in the US of A Air Force." He smiled beguilingly. Nick was laughing now.

"Come with me on the *Jezebel*, kiddo—you'll have four days to relax, work on the script, you'll arrive in *great* shape, and I promise I won't keep you up drinking all night."

The crew, all Bluey's buddies, doubled as bodyguards, companions or valets when they weren't being stewards or cooks. Bluey's "boys" had been together for years, so the atmosphere was that of a close fraternity, in which practical jokes and laughter were the order of the day.

Nick was worried about his line producer, Zachary Domino, who hadn't been well recently. Zack was sixty-eight and tired. With more than fifty years' experience, starting as a runner on some early Chaplin films, graduating to camera assistant on Mary Pickford features, then assistant director in the twenties with Clara Bow in *Red Hair* for First National Pictures, he was an excellent, knowledgeable and tough producer. He understood every aspect of the movie business and Nick was looking forward to learning a great deal from him. In fact he needed him badly. This was Nick's first major blockbuster movie, and everyone, not only in the studio but in Hollywood, would be carefully watching the results of this one. If it was a flop, he would be back to directing *Bobby Soxers in Space,* and then only if he was lucky. If MCCP lost its bets on *Cortez* he would probably never work again.

So Nick was understandably edgy about *Cortez*. He knew many people at the studio didn't want him to direct it, considering him more of a boy-wonder cult director, in spite of the fact that the two pictures he'd directed had been box-office successes. There were so many other directors they preferred. George Cukor had been first choice, followed by David Lean and Fred Zinnemann. But dear old Uncle Spyros, waving his nepotism like a tattered flag, had insisted on using Nick, and since he was the ultimate arbitrator, the studio had had to capitulate—for the moment.

MCCP's administrators couldn't believe that Nick was capable of handling this huge assignment. He was only twenty-seven. This picture needed a man of immense experience, a director used to dealing with thousands of extras, handling fragile star temperaments, coping with the thousand decisions which needed to be made daily on a picture this size. They didn't believe that Nick could do it, and they were waiting to be proved right. But Spyros had great faith that Nick would do an excellent job on this film, particularly with Zachary Domino as line producer to help him. Good old Uncle Spyros—he'd come through at last.

Bluey threw an affectionate arm around his friend's shoulder as he expertly handled the tiller with the other.

"What's the matter, Niko?"

"I just hope Zack holds up," Nick replied quietly. "I read the doctor's insurance report, Bluey. He smokes sixty a day, drinks like a fish, and he's had a heart murmur for years. But he's still one helluva great producer and we need him with us on this."

"Don't worry, kid, Zack's a *fighter*— tougher than an army boot with rusty nails in it. He'll have whipped everyone in shape, kicked their fat asses, and got all the wheels in motion on location by the time we arrive. Stop worrying, Nick—everything's gonna be okay."

On the flights all the way from Los Angeles, Dominique had kept up a nonstop stream of excited chatter. Her girlish enthusiasm increased the closer they came to Acapulco. The trip had taken almost two days and Agathe felt that she would scream if Dominique didn't stop babbling. The girl had bought every single movie magazine at the airport, and had scanned them all intently for any photographs of the stars who might be in *Cortez* or vacationing in Acapulco while they were making the movie there.

Agathe's head was splitting with one of the migraine headaches which were becoming more prevalent lately, but despite her telling Dominique that she was feeling terrible and needed to be quiet, the girl didn't stop to draw breath.

The noise of the plane's engines exacerbated Agathe's headache and she had absolutely no interest in looking at the celebrity photographs which Dominique insisted on pointing out to her.

"Look—*voilà*—Julian Brooks. Ooh, wow, Agathe, he is *magnifique*, *n'est-ce pas?* A really cool guy."

Agathe snatched the magazine out of Dominique's lap. Magnificent was an understatement, she thought. He was a god; a giant among men, a true living Adonis. The pit of her stomach churned as she feasted her eyes on his glorious dark perfection. His arm was around some woman, probably his latest leading lady.

"The fiancée," Dominique said, jabbing the photograph with her finger. "He's now engaged. She's beautiful too, don't you think?"

Fingers of ice curled around Agathe's heart. Fiancée? Julian was engaged? Agathe stared at the woman, who was in profile, her long dark hair almost obscuring her face, but from the way Julian was looking at her they were obviously mad about each other. Who was she?

Viciously Agathe threw the magazine back to Dominique. *"Tais-toi, Dominique,"* she snapped. "I'm not interested in these movie stars. Rest now and stop all this chattering, you've got important days ahead of you."

She closed her eyes and tried to sleep, but a jealous disappointment gripped her whenever she thought of Julian and the new woman in his life. How could Julian be marrying someone else *now*, now that Agathe was so close to being with him at last? How could he be doing this to her?

❦ *Four* ❧

As soon as he arrived at Villa Vera, Nick called Elektra, who was thrilled to speak to him. He unpacked, showered, changed and within twenty minutes was sitting in one of the hotel suites, which had been turned into a production room. His entire production staff were assembled around a table—art directors, set designers, costumiers, assistant directors, stunt coordinators, editors, the writers—that baleful-looking New York couple, the Frankovitches—and most important of all, Zachary Domino, Nick's line producer. Zack's eyes were weary, his shoulders stooped, and he chain-smoked Camels with nicotine-stained fingers.

"How are you feeling, *amigo?*" Nick asked.

"Not so hot today." Zack's smile was halfhearted. "But don't worry, I think it's just a touch of Montezuma's famous revenge. He's probably mad at us for doing his life story."

The crew all chuckled, except for the costume designer, Kittens.

"Montezuma's revenge doesn't last for three weeks, Zack," she said anxiously, then aside to Nick, "He's been feeling bad for a while, Nicky. We've been worried."

Nick clenched his fists. Jesus, he'd only been in the place for an hour and already everyone was worried about the main cog in his wheel.

"I *told* him to take Pepto-Bismol and not to eat salads," said Shirley Frankovitch impatiently. "But he wouldn't listen, would he, Irving?"

"No, dear," said Irving. "He wouldn't." Irving spoke little, his mind spinning constantly with new and different ideas for characters and situations in *Cortez*. Half the time he paid no attention to Shirley at all. Her embarrassing drunken antics at Makopolis's party had caused him to become more aware than ever of what a vulgarian his wife was. He didn't like to think about it, so he chose to ignore her most of the time.

Irving glanced out of the window of the second-floor suite. The sky was the softest blue, tinged apricot by a sun which was beginning to sink behind one of the hills. Irving sipped his drink, imagining what the effect of coconut milk on the taste buds of his hero would have been when he first reached La Roqueta island. He looked at the palm trees, their branches which were vivid green swaying softly in the breeze. Abundant foliage grew in the hotel courtyard. Acapulco was a luscious tropical paradise, and the variety and beauty of its plant life were a continual source of wonder to Irving. He wasn't really listening to Zack, who had been talking about some of the multitude of technical problems which they'd discovered in transporting their equipment on to La Roqueta.

Irving was brought back to reality when Zack announced that the studio wanted the scene in which Cortez first makes love to the beautiful princess to be much more erotic, albeit within the bounds of censorship. The MCCP top brass insisted on sex, lust, sensual romance. Barrages of telephone calls and cables were constantly arriving from Hollywood. They wanted more sex and they wanted perfection. Now it was up to Irving and Shirley to make the script the best goddamn script of the decade. As writers, they could only do so much—because once the script fell into the hands of the actors and directors, God only knew what damage could be done to "great" dialogue. The Frankovitches were old campaigners on the Hollywood trail. Irving had seen two of his scripts destroyed by studios and others badly butchered, so he and Shirley intended to be around all the time, even though a writer on a shooting set was as welcome as a nun in a whorehouse.

The heat in the production office became more oppressive as the sun sank lower. The room was stifling, and even the ceiling fan made little difference. The men were all shirtsleeved but sweat glistened on their faces; Shirley wore a muumuu, one of many which she had bought at the local market. Shirley adored a bargain, and clothes here cost a fraction of what they would in New York or Beverly Hills. The muumuu was the perfect solution for her figure as her weight had ballooned in the past months.

She glanced at Zachary Domino, wondering how on earth he was going to survive the eighteen weeks of tough location work around beaches, mosquito-ridden swamps, forests and rivers.

Zack lit another Camel in spite of doctor's orders. In Los Angeles he had visited his doctor for the usual studio checkup. Dr. Zolotos had assured him that he was in fairly good health for his age. "Just remember to take a salt pill every morning, never drink the water—in spite of what the Mexican government may say, it's poison! Stay away from raw fruit and vegetables, especially lettuce, don't exert yourself too much, and stop *smoking!*"

Easier said than done. When you were line-producing one of the major motion pictures of the decade—quite impossible. Zack was practically living on cigarettes and coffee. He sipped some salty-tasting mineral water. Everyone at the meeting was smoking, no one giving a thought to what they were doing to their lungs or heart. Zachary inhaled deeply, trying to contribute to the discussions.

Across the table, Shirley's cunning, laser-beam eyes glared at him. There was no love lost between them. He thought her a pushy shrew and a lush who constantly and irritatingly interfered during production meetings. Zack tried patiently to explain to the Frankovitches that their latest rewrites would be much too expensive to shoot.

"Money, money, money—that's all you ever fucking *think* about, Zack," shrieked Shirley. "This is *art,* you fucking moron. *Art!* Who gives a *shit* about money."

"We don't *need* two hundred and fifty extras watching Cortez and Princess Isabella strolling along the seashore." Zack tried to remain calm. "It's supposed to be lyrical, romantic. We don't *need* a bunch of fucking voyeurs standing around them just staring." He raised his voice, his efforts to stay calm failing. "I'm taking them *out*—do you understand, *out. No extras.* And that's that—*finito.*" He hated shouting matches, but knew he had to win this point, otherwise the Frankovitches would walk all over him.

Nick nodded his approval. "I agree totally. I'm sorry, Shirley. Zack's right we don't need any atmosphere in that scene, so that's that."

Shirley was not about to give up her two hundred and fifty extras without a fight. *No one* messed with Shirley Frankovitch. She was a star writer. She looked over to Irving for support, but he just shrugged. Although Irving possessed infinitely more talent than she, he'd subjugated it much too often to her pleading banshee wails, sly feminine wiles, and insidious whining.

It meant a great deal to Shirley to win. She wanted *her* script to be the one that was shot. She wanted the studio to know that *they,* the fabulous team of Shirley and Irving Frankovitch, were the most brilliant writers on the Hollywood scene. But it was evident that at this lengthy production meeting they were not winning. Many of their most daring and innovative ideas were being shot down—by both Nick and Zack. The meeting, like the room, was becoming increasingly heated. Expletives were bandied about and the air hung heavy with the smell of hostility, sweat and cigarette smoke.

Irving raised a laconic eyebrow in Shirley's direction. They would thrash this out later, privately. He sighed, remembering fondly his rapport with Umberto Scrofo during the shooting of *La Città* in Rome a year ago. Irving had praised Umberto to Shirley highly—he had been sympathetic to everything that Frankovitch had wanted—and Umberto Scrofo had been more than eager to cultivate the most important screenwriter in Hollywood

Even though Shirley had made a fool of herself at the Makopolis party, it hadn't stopped Scrofo from wining and dining the Frankovitches during his Los Angeles trip. Shirley found Scrofo amusing. She liked his acerbic wit and bitter comments, which perfectly matched her own cynical attitude to the world. She thought that his *La Città Perduta* was excellent and had invited Spyros Makopolis to a screening, but at the last moment the old Greek had canceled and she had been unable to get him to reschedule.

Scrofo agreed with Shirley that the script was absolutely the most important ingredient in filmmaking and that everything and everyone else was secondary. It didn't matter if the movie had the most shimmering stars or the most elaborate sets, if it wasn't on the page the public wasn't going to see it on the screen.

Nikolas Stone shifted uneasily in his chair. His instincts were turning out to be right. Shirley Frankovitch was a meddling bitch, and her husband was a pathetic, pitiable excuse for a man. He thought their script was good in parts, but too overwritten, too flowery, too excessive. He envisioned a simple tale of adventure and discovery, of the battle of wills between Cortez and King Montezuma. He wanted a simple sensual love story between Cortez and Princess Isabella. He wanted to show the untouched beauty of the Mexican country, the incomparable lagoons, the ravishing sunsets. He wanted to reveal real people with real emotions, ambitions, passions. The Frankovitches didn't seem to want this at all. Their script was one gargantuan battle after another, an endless array of wounded, bleeding men being dispatched by the point of the hero's sword; scenes of sticky passion so trite that they'd be out of place in a shopgirl's weekly. And now, the sight of Zachary, his most important support, obviously unwell, was not a promising omen.

Suddenly Zack called a halt. The production office had become so unbearably hot that tempers were frayed to boiling point.

"Let's sleep on everything, boys and girls," he said quietly. "We've still got a few days before shooting starts to sort out our problems. Tomorrow, ten A.M. sharp, we'll have a read-through with some of the cast. Until then, let's get some rest."

Inès was suffering a mixture of jet lag and morning sickness which seemed to continue well into the early evening of their arrival. She was sleeping so soundly that Julian decided to accept Nick's invitation to dinner on the terrace of a restaurant away from the Villa Vera. They wanted to escape from the prying eyes, the clacking tongues and the electric tensions which always fill the air before a movie begins. The cool veranda looked down to the curve of Acapulco Bay where the ink-black water seemed striped with thin slivers of luminous silver.

A faint breeze blew in from the sea as they dined on *ceviche*—raw fish marinated with onions, lemon and avocado, charcoal-grilled prawns, and a great deal of tequila and beer. They chain-smoked as Nick shared his problems with Julian, who listened attentively, becoming increasingly aware that Nick was facing some serious hurdles.

"If Zachary is totally on your side," he said, "then what's the difficulty? You're the director—he's the producer—you've both got the final say, after all. Tell the Frankovitches to get stuffed."

Nick stared at him with a worried frown. "I don't know," he said. "I just can't figure it out. I don't think Zack's up to par, and that bitch Shirley is out to have his balls for *huevos rancheros* on her breakfast tray. I want to make this film as realistic and as modern as possible. I want the audience to *identify* with Cortez. Oh I know he's a sixteenth-century man but I want him to be a man of the moment—a today kinda guy. I know that's what audiences are looking for now. They've had too much escapist crap, musicals, biblical epics. They've gotta believe this man is made of the same flesh and blood as them. I just hope the studio isn't going to try and sabotage it. I think the Frankovitches have got enormous pull with Spyros in spite of the bitch getting plastered at his party. Jesus, Julian, some of their new dialogue is unspeakable—a couple of the scenes are straight out of Grand Guignol!"

Julian smiled. "I don't believe they're as bad as you think, Nick. I got the rewrites earlier this evening, but I'll look them over again tonight. So what are you going to do about all of this?"

"Tonight, my friend, I'm going to get very drunk." Nick drained his tequila with a wicked smile. "Then tomorrow, like Scarlett O'Hara, I'm gonna think about it, and work my ass off to get it right. Maybe it's just my old Greek instincts working, pal, but I'm worried."

◀*Five*▶

Dominique arrived at the Villa Vera the following afternoon. She looked around her luxurious hotel room and giggled, "What a dump," à la Bette Davis in *Beyond the Forest*. She pranced to the window and gasped. Thick pink-flowered bougainvillea curled around the stone terrace, the ocean glittered invitingly, and the brilliant cobalt sky, which shaded to a bluish gray as it met the curving hills surrounding Acapulco Bay, made the view breathtaking.

Her portable record player was in her luggage, along with her much-treasured box of records. She flipped through them, finally choosing one of her favorites, Edith Piaf singing "La Vie en Rose," then lay back on the sofa feeling gloriously grown-up and romantic as she thought about Gaston's latest love letter and the naughty things he wrote.

Feeling a sudden surge of energy, she got up to look through her suitcases for something to wear to the pool. The studio had provided her with plenty of clothes for the many photographic layouts they expected of her. Dozens of coordinated summer costumes had been carefully packed in layers of tissue paper by the wardrobe department and she rifled through them, humming happily.

Putting on a tiny pink gingham bikini with a matching short skirt, she grabbed a straw hat and her script and skipped down the stone steps towards the inviting swimming pool. Thankfully, Agathe was sound asleep, as the tropics didn't agree with her, and she was exhausted after the long flights from Los Angeles and Mexico City. Dominique loved being on her own, particularly when she had new pages of her script to study. It was just after two o'clock, and most of the Villa Vera residents were at lunch. There was nobody at the pool except for a lackadaisical Mexican boy removing crumpled, damp towels from the deck chairs.

Placing her towel on a chaise longue, Dominique put on her sunglasses, perched her straw hat on top of her head and gazed contentedly around. Gorgeous, there was no question of that. The pool was edged with tiny blue-and-white square tiles and looked truly inviting. It was set into reddish-pink, rough-hewn stone, and surrounded by huge pots of flaming bougainvillea. Their color was dazzling—lilac, mauve, fuchsia, cyclamen, shocking pink—a riot of reds and purples. Beyond the pool lay a garden dominated by tall palm trees, whose thick leaves gave shelter to a wide lawn and tropical flowerbeds. Floating on the pool were dozens of white, red and yellow hibiscus blossoms. A tulip tree, its flaming red torchwood branches standing like bayonets, shaded most of the far end of the pool. Farther away were sharp spires of banana trees, hibiscus bushes, frangipani and an occasional banyan tree with its huge, ancient twisted roots, an ideal shelter for the birds that flew about happily in the jasmine-scented air.

In spite of the heat, Dominique could feel a refreshing breeze as she lay under her umbrella. A smiling waiter appeared, asking in Spanish if she wanted a drink, Latin eyes drank in her lissome body, and a flash of lust crossed his adolescent features. Dominique was getting very used to men responding to her sex appeal. She asked for a Coke and lay back comfortably, the *Cortez* script in front of her. The only sound was the splashing of water into a small stone pool around which enormous velvet-winged butterflies hovered and danced. The sound was soporific and soothing.

From down on the beach, came the music of mariachis and the gay chants of a Mexican band. She'd heard that Acapulco night life was exciting, although nothing compared to that of Hollywood. She knew that Lana Turner, Tyrone Power and Errol Flynn were all staunch aficionados of Acapulco, coming here regularly. Perhaps she might even meet them.

From his secluded terrace on the first floor Julian Brooks looked down at Dominique as she buried her glossy head in the script.

In the time he had been with Inès he'd been as dutiful and loving as any man could be, never tempted once by the many offers to which his striking looks and fame made him subject. Inès was attentive, beautiful, kind—what more could he want? What more, indeed, he thought—except now the sight of Dominique's ravishing face, waist-length black hair and honey-colored limbs was suddenly a powerful stimulant. Most intriguing of all was her undeniable resemblance to Inès. She seemed like a younger version, with the same appealing mixture of sensuality and innocence. Odd, perhaps, but this similarity made Dominique an object of great interest to Julian.

He pulled his panama hat down farther over his eyes, watching intently as she stood up and peeled off her tiny skirt, revealing a bottom so round and peachlike in her bikini that he caught his breath.

Stretching unself-consciously, unaware of her admirer up on his terrace, she ran her fingers through her hair, removed her sunglasses and dipped her feet in the pool. The sun, filtering through the leaves of a palm tree, dappled her shoulders. Thinking about the bathtub scene she would have to film next week, and not wanting any white marks on her shoulders, she slipped off the straps of her bikini top. Then looking around to make sure no one was near she undid the hooks, tossing it to the edge of the pool, then slid slowly into the water until it barely covered her breasts.

Julian's mouth was suddenly dry. This was one of the most erotic little scenes he'd witnessed for a long time. He was, after all, only a man—a fact which the discomfort inside his immaculately cut linen trousers confirmed. He thought he'd seen few more glorious sights. This golden-skinned goddess, almost naked in a swimming pool, wet black hair flowing around her shoulders, was deliciously and enchantingly exciting. . . .

Out of the corner of her eye, Dominique had become aware that she was being observed. She lazily splashed water over her shoulders, enjoying the coolness on her sun-kissed skin. She realized that it was Looks Brooks who was watching her beneath his panama hat, and as she started to sing "La Vie en Rose" in her best Edith Piaf voice a secret smile crossed her beautiful face.

❧ *Six* ☙

Agathe was unable to sleep. A full moon shone through the bamboo window slats, and the ceiling fan did little but churn the sluggish air. She was roasting, her cotton nightgown soaked with sweat, her mouth like cardboard. The carafe next to the bed was dry as a bone. She got up to get some water from the bathroom tap, then remembered all the dire warnings she'd been given about not drinking the water. Searching through her valise, she found nothing to drink except a bottle of cough syrup

Slipping off her nightgown, she threw on some shorts, a short-sleeved shirt and rope-soled espadrilles. Grabbing the room key and a handful of pesos she glanced at the seductive moon suspended over the black sand, closed the door quietly and ran down to the lobby. It was empty except for a fat concierge dozing over a copy of *Hola*. She asked him in French and English where she might find something to drink, but he understood nothing until she spoke the magic words Coca-Cola. His greasy face, slippery with sweat, perked up as he jabbered away in Spanish, pointing across the road to the beach.

There was little traffic on the road. She heard the occasional *fut-fut* of a motorcycle, and in the distance mariachis playing. From some nearby houses came exciting-sounding Spanish love songs which made her senses quicken. How she'd love to dance to that music. How she would whirl and twirl—if only Julian could be with her too. She could show him how well she danced. He must have arrived in Acapulco by now.

The beach was deserted, the sand pockmarked with a thousand footprints. There were a few thatched-roof beach huts on the sand, around which abandoned chairs and tables were clustered. A few yards away, a larger hut boasted a flickering neon sign saying something incomprehensible in Spanish. She would surely find a drink there, she thought, as she made for the light.

Four tough-looking Mexican men sat at a cigarette-scorched table, playing cards. Behind them were several tired hookers, their black hair and exotic Spanish dresses only emphasizing their state of fragile weariness. At the bar stood half a dozen truculent-looking men, most of them drunk. Agathe blushed, wishing she'd worn a bra and panties underneath her skimpy clothes. The barman looked less ferocious than the others and she quietly asked for a coke.

Unsmiling, he passed her the bottle and a damp, chipped glass. She drank fast, eyes downcast, and asked for another, while hostile eyes stared at her.

She asked the barman if she could take the bottle with her, then, throwing some coins onto the zinc-topped bar, casually walked out, pretending not to hear remarks in Spanish from which she could make out the words *guapa* and *linda*. In spite of herself she felt flattered that the men had noticed her and admired her feminine charms. It had been a long time since anyone had.

Enveloped by the sultry night, her thirst satisfied and her adrenaline pumping, Agathe didn't feel like going back to the hotel yet. It was barely midnight. She would take a stroll along the beach.

In the distance she could see the lights of the town, and some brightly lit boats. She walked slowly along the shoreline, enjoying the sensation of the cool waves lapping at her feet, catching the scent of jasmine and the salty tang of the sea. She thought about the upcoming film with excitement. As Dominique's chaperone she knew that she was only a tiny cog in the wheel of *Cortez*, but still, she was important. Everyone was important, because she knew that filming was a group effort. But the most thrilling thing of all was that she would be near Julian Brooks. She wondered if she would see him soon, so that they could talk of mutual interests—of art, philosophy, religion. She knew that he must be a man of superior intellect to match his superior looks. She fingered the small crucifix which she always wore around her neck. The tiny amber beads on the fine silver chain were her talisman—her luck. Superstitiously she believed that if she didn't wear it, something unspeakable would happen to her.

Lost in reverie, Agathe did not hear the muffled footsteps approaching her. Coarse hands grabbed her from behind and another pair clamped themselves over her mouth. There were two men—or three?—she couldn't tell. Their arms seemed to be everywhere. As wiry as she was, there was no way she could overcome their combined strength, try as she might. She heard hoarse drunken voices mocking her and, with a surge of fury, brought the bottle in her hand up behind her with all her strength. She heard a satisfying crack as it connected with a nose, and with a yelp, one man was out of the fray, blood pumping from his nostrils. But two still held her. One of them yanked at her blouse viciously as the other tried to pull off her shorts, but they had loosened their grip on her mouth and she started screaming desperately for help.

In the moonlight she could see the sharp stubble on the men's chins, their bloodshot eyes; smell their unwashed bodies, the beer on their breath. There was no doubt what they were intending to do. They threw her on to the sand, tearing off her shorts and shirt. She tried to crawl away, as she heard them unzipping their trousers. She was a thirty-one-year-old virgin, this couldn't be happening to her. Not after everything she'd been through in her life.

"No, *mon Dieu, no,*" she sobbed as one of the men tried to force his sweating bulk on top of her naked body. With a dancer's dexterity she twisted away, scrabbling sideways over the sand like a demented crab. With trousers around their ankles, both men were at a momentary loss, which gave her the edge. Screaming for help, she ran as fast as she could across the slippery sand. Their heavy footsteps were coming closer, gaining on her. However fast she ran, they were stronger and quicker. She knew she couldn't outrun them, it was a losing battle. She heard them cursing harshly, yelling with drunken rage as they were in danger of losing their prey—she could almost feel their blood lust. Where was everyone? Oh, sweet Jesus—was there no one to help her?

Four hundred yards away pleasure boats bobbed gently in the bay. She saw their lights, heard faint music, the gentle laughter of women. Civilization, but still too far away. She must get to the boats before these animals caught her—she had to. She felt a hand grab her nude back, but slick with sweat, she twisted free. The thundering feet ran faster, she could smell the sour, garlicky stink of their last meal.

Julian was the first to hear the faint cries. He'd spent the evening with Nick and Bluey on the *Jezebel,* discussing the continuing problems: Zack's health, Shirley's subversive bitchery and various studio vendettas. Inès had decided to give Julian an evening out with the boys, but now he was eager to get back to her. Straining his eyes across the darkness he thought he saw a naked girl being chased by two men.

"Good God," he whistled, running down the gangplank, calling out for Nick and Bluey. "Damsel in distress, boys. Let's go."

As he got closer, Julian saw it was that weird Agathe woman, Dominique's chaperone. What the blazes was she doing on the beach at this hour?

With Nick and Bluey hot on his heels, Julian launched himself at the nearest ruffian. The trio made short work of Agathe's attackers with a few well-placed kicks and punches. It was over in a matter of seconds, and the Mexicans ran off shouting empty threats.

Agathe sank to the sand, trembling with fear and shame, trying in vain to cover her naked body. Tears streamed down her face, and she was covered with painful cuts and bruises.

"Here." Julian took off his shirt and handed it to her. "Put this on. We'll go back to the boat. We've got first aid stuff there."

She put it on quickly, thankful that it was long enough to cover her thighs. Nick went off to retrieve her clothes as Julian helped her down the beach. She looked at her watch—only five past twelve. Everything had happened so terrifyingly fast. What would those men have done to her if Julian had not saved her? She couldn't bear to think of it, or of what he must think of her. He must think her insane.

"You must be insane," he said with a gentle smile, putting his arm around her trembling back. "What on earth were you doing on the beach at night? Don't you know how dangerous it is?"

"I was thirsty," she said in a small voice, realizing how ridiculous it sounded. "I went to a bar."

"Well"—he smiled—"that doesn't exactly explain a helluva lot, but come on board. You need a stiff drink, my dear."

Julian helped Agathe onto the deck of the *Jezebel*. She seemed so frail and vulnerable with that ice-white hair and skin; she obviously needed protection. Any woman stupid enough to wander alone at night on a Mexican beach could hardly be called mature. Old-fashioned feelings of responsibility stirred in him as he ushered her into the main cabin. She collapsed onto the sofa, trying to get her breath, and Julian strode over to the bar. He poured her a large drink which she sipped gratefully, the amber fluid warming her comfortingly. He smiled at her and she smiled shyly back. What would Dominique say if she heard about her midnight stroll? She'd surely think she was no longer either fit or responsible enough to be a chaperone. Now she was just a frightened waif, dirty and bruised.

"Why don't you take a shower?—Clean up, you'll feel a lot better," said Bluey. "C'mon, I'll show you where the head is."

"Thank you," said Agathe, blushing as Julian's eyes smiled sympathetically into hers again.

Invigorating needles of water tingled on her aching body, and she scrubbed away until she felt completely clean. Bluey's rough towels smelled strongly of camphor but they felt good; she was relieved to rid herself of the sand, the sweat and the touch of those filthy, grasping hands. She pulled on her shorts, managing just barely to secure them with the loose top button, and Julian's shirt. There was a brush on the dressing table, and she tried to tame her tangled hair. She looked at herself in the mirror. Better. Although still frightened, at least she was no longer a total wreck. She padded back into the salon where Bluey, Nick and Julian were sitting with large drinks at a table strewn with yachting magazines and books. Julian stood up.

"Come and sit down, Agathe," he said benevolently. "You look done in, poor dear. Drink up."

Agathe took another sip of her drink, grimacing at the strength of it.

"Bluey's special remedy." Bluey winked at her. "Good for what ails you, sweetheart—seasickness, tummy upsets, first-day nerves on the set, whatever it is, the Bluey Special will cure it."

"What is it?" she asked tentatively. Though she rarely drank anything alcoholic except for an occasional glass of wine, she was beginning to like the taste.

"Ah-ha, that's a secret," Julian said, smiling at her. She was such a strange, quiet girl, but she seemed sweet, and terribly innocent, with her soulful eyes and tragic face. Certainly not his type, though he realized from the way she was gazing at him that she could probably fall for him much too easily. Agathe seemed so demure—she even wore a little crucifix around her neck. But he could sense that there was something lurking beneath the surface, something odd about her—what was it? Oh, Lord, he could almost see the look of love growing in her eyes. It made him nervous. He'd never been in the business of encouraging lovesick women in their fantasies. That he saved for the screen.

"Drink up," he said looking at his watch. "It's nearly one o'clock. We've all got to get up early for the reading tomorrow. And we don't want anyone to find out about what happened tonight, do we?" He winked conspiratorially at Agathe who smiled nervously.

"Oh, no, they would think I was such a fool—everyone warned me about going out alone. Please promise you won't tell anyone."

"I promise, Agathe, so do the boys," Julian said, his voice so gentle it seemed to her almost like a caress. "It's our little secret, Agathe." And she felt herself flush with pure happiness.

Agathe was too excited to sleep. In her humid room she hugged a pillow to her aching body and, closing her eyes in a kind of ecstasy, relived the enchanted hour that she'd spent with Julian. It had almost been worth being attacked, she mused, to have had her idol's attentions so intently focused on her. Her pulse fluttered as she remembered how his firm brown hand had gently stroked her hair away from her forehead. His shirt. She still wore the blue cotton shirt which he'd so gallantly taken off and given to her. It smelled of him—of his Turkish cigarettes, the faint and far from unpleasant smell of his sweat mingled with a subtle trace of his after-shave.

She rubbed the loose shirt up and down her body, between her legs and across her breasts. She began to feel feverish as his face filled her imagination; in her mind, his eyes gazed into hers with tenderness and love. His bare chest streaked with rivulets of sweat was next to hers now . . . his muscular arms encircled her shoulders, his lips kissing her hair. She felt herself rising to peaks of pleasure which she'd never known before. Rocking from side to side, eyes tightly closed, with Julian's shirt squeezed between her legs, her body stiffened into a series of shuddering and glorious spasms of release as she breathed his name over and over again in the darkness.

◆ *Seven* ▶

Zachary Domino had achieved something which Hollywood believed to be impossible. He had a secret mistress for more than five years.

He and Ramona Armande had enjoyed their on-again-off-again clandestine affair. It suited them both. He was single, and even though Ramona was married, her husband was absent so much that few people had ever seen him in the flesh. Hollywood had always been intrigued by Ramona in all of her thirty years on the scene, but no gossip had ever surfaced about her. No one really knew exactly how old she was, but she was certainly well into her fifties. Her face was almost unlined, however, her body lithe, and her sexual vigor that of someone half her age.

She and Zack were in her extraordinary villa on a hill high above Acapulco Bay, their privacy guaranteed by a highly efficient security system of guards and German shepherd dogs.

She had cooked dinner for him herself: chicken enchiladas, and his favorite—refried beans with tortillas, which she believed had aphrodisiacal qualities. She had given him a good claret to drink and a fat Havana cigar to smoke after dinner. Now they were discussing the film and especially her part in it. She was unhappy with her role and had accepted it only because parts for women her age were rather thin on the ground. Playing Dominique's mother deeply rankled with her.

"I've been a star," she complained. "One of the biggest stars in the history of movies. It's a *scandal* that all I play now is a supporting role." She spat the "supporting" from between her lips as if it were a piece of tobacco from the end of a cigarette. "I had a wonderful part in my Italian film—wonderful. I don't expect to play leads anymore, but I wish I had more to do in this one, Zack, really I do."

Zachary gently stroked her arm, looking hopefully towards the bedroom. He didn't feel like getting into yet another discussion about Ramona's career. He wanted to change the subject as quickly as possible. He wanted to get laid, then go home to his own bed and study the script again. He wanted to get his rocks off and not listen to the woes and complaints of an actress. Staying overnight with Ramona was taboo, on the off-chance that her husband might appear unexpectedly. He had had a bitch of a day. Between the appalling Shirley Frankovitch's continuous whining over the script, Irving supporting her with threats of returning to New York, Sir Crispin, who was playing King Montezuma, having a tantrum over his wig, the studio screaming about everything under the sun, and the postponing of the first day's shooting until the script problems could be worked out, he'd had a bellyful.

"Hell, let 'em go," he'd insisted wearily to Nick earlier when both Frankovitches had flounced out of the room, slamming the door. "We've got a halfway decent shooting script, we'll bring in someone else from Hollywood to rewrite certain scenes if it's necessary. We don't need 'em. Fuck the Frankovitches. They're more trouble than they're worth." Nick had agreed with him; the two men were formidably strong allies, God knows they needed to be.

Now Zack sighed. He desperately needed to forget all his problems in the arms of his sultry mistress. As if anticipating his needs, she looked at him seductively and glided gracefully into her vast white bedroom. He quickly followed.

After they finished making love, Ramona rose immediately from her bed and padded across rose-colored rugs to her marble bathroom. There she deftly massaged Zachary's semen into the skin of her face and neck, an invaluable beauty tip which her friend Mae West had taught her years ago.

"Forget all those expensive face creams and fancy lotions, hon," Mae had drawled. "If guys are good for only one thing, it's that essence they produce. Don't forget, honey, they use us, we can use *them—I've* been doin' it for years—and my skin's gorgeous, ain't it?"

Ramona smiled as she thought of raunchy Mae while Zack lay on the bed smoking his usual après-sex Camel, watching the tropical fish darting about in the aquarium which covered one entire wall of the bedroom. He idly wondered about the whereabouts of Ramona's husband, the White Russian Prince Ivor Kasinov who was even more mysterious than his wife. Why was he always so often away on business? No one had any idea what business the Prince was involved in, but he seemed to be colossally rich in cash and other assets—one of which was this magnificent mansion and its precious contents. Scheherazade was a palace in the tropical jungle. Made of onyx, marble, glass and stone, all supported by marble Corinthian columns brought from Italian quarries at phenomenal expense, the villa was like a Visconti film set.

Ramona had been married to Prince Kasinov for more than a decade. After the war she had returned to Hollywood from making a movie in Vienna with the diminutive Prince in tow. Hollywood bowed and scraped to both of them, impressed with Ramona's pedigree prize, and she had queened it in Beverly Hills for several years until the Prince had decided to move to Mexico for unexplained reasons. She then became the most celebrated society hostess in Mexico, an invitation to one of her parties being most coveted. She was throwing a gala next week to launch *Cortez*. Dozens of Hollywood celebrities would be flying in, as well as the society and show-business press of the world.

Other than her intimates—of whom there were few—everyone who knew Ramona never called her anything but Princess. Unless she was working on a film, when she became democratic. In some small way this compensated for the decline in her movie career, as did her glittering parties and, of course, her lavish photo-layouts in all the best magazines. She was determined that this party would be the most dazzling to date, an event to remember.

Looking at the Cartier clock on the bedside table, Zack saw it was time for him to leave.

The key technical crew and main actors were congregated in one of the assembly rooms of the Villa Vera for the ten o'clock read-through. All were punctual, but Zack had not yet appeared, which was unusual, as he was always the first to arrive. The room was dominated by a huge oak table around which everyone could sit comfortably. A silver urn dispensed coffee, and there were ash trays and bottles of mineral water on the table. Nick glanced at his watch nervously; it was nearly a quarter past ten. He wanted to give a short motivating rah-rah speech to everyone, but he needed Zack's support. Where was he?

"I think I'll call him," Nick said to Bluey. "He's *never* late—he's probably overslept."

There was no answer from Zack's room and Nick looked over at Bluey with concern.

"I don't understand this at all," he muttered. "It's not like him."

"Hang up. Let's start the reading anyway," Shirley rasped. "We don't need to wait for him. C'mon, Irving and I have written a coupla new scenes—we want to read them to you."

"No, we can't do that, we must have him here, we need him. It's just not right," Nick replied.

He looked over at Shirley, whose shrewish face was puffy and shiny with perspiration. God, she was a malevolent bitch, and a drunkard into the bargain—a lethal combination.

Julian was chatting with Agathe, whose eager black eyes never once left his face; although she was blushing she still managed to retain a pinched, cold look, icy in spite of the heat.

Dominique sidled up to Julian, green eyes sparkling, perfectly shaped breasts seeming to point deliberately at his chest. "Did you sleep well, Julian?" she asked with a sly grin.

"Like a log." He smiled, aware more than ever of her resemblance to the young Inès. It was truly striking. They were the same height, had the same oval face, small nose, sensual lips—but this little girl was years younger. Jail bait. "Don't even *think* about it, Julian," said his conscience. "It could never be worth it in a hundred years."

"I'm so excited," Dominique sighed. "This is going to be a *thrilling* film, *n'est-ce pas?* And I'm so honored to be playing opposite you, Julian." She was giving him the sexual come-on. He had never been wrong about female vibrations before, and this one was only a teenager! But what a teenager. He remembered the sight of her luscious body in the swimming pool and his eyes flitted appreciatively over her breasts, barely covered by a flimsy pink blouse. "Yes, it certainly is going to be exciting," he said. He felt that disturbing stirring again, and moved away from her to the safety of the coffee urn.

"And, I'm looking forward to working with you, too, Dominique, my dear," he said as he poured himself a cup of coffee while the girl smiled secretly and Agathe glared at her jealously.

"I'm going to Zack's room—find out what's going on." Nick banged down the phone. "I'll be right back," he said, and strode out.

The cast and crew started to gossip and chatter. Dominique monopolized Julian's attention again discussing the script, and completely cutting Agathe off from the possibility of any further conversation with him. She went to the window to stare sulkily at the view and to relive last night with Julian on the boat. Suddenly the telephone rang harshly. Bluey answered it.

"Oh, my God, Jesus Christ—no, I don't believe it." Bluey's face hardened and he leaned against the wall for support. The room became hushed. "I'll be right there. Have you called the doctor?"

"What on earth's the matter, old boy?" Julian asked.

"It's Zachary, he's—er—not well, it seems." The normally unflappable assistant director was trying not to sound flustered. "I'm going up to see if I can help."

"What do you mean, 'not well'?" Julian insisted. "What's wrong with him?"

"I don't know, I'll go and see. Don't worry, I'll be right back," he added as he raced out.

The group began muttering. This sounded ominous. A film crew has a sixth sense about one of their own, and they realized something must have happened to Zachary. Something which could affect the movie.

His face the color of chalk, his eyes open, blank and staring, Zachary Domino was lying on the bed. He had obviously tried to get up because of the strange angle of his body, but he hadn't been able to make it.

"He's dead," said Nick numbly. "Oh, Christ."

"Jesus," Bluey gasped. "How the hell did it happen?"

"I don't know," sighed Nick. "I suppose it must have been his heart." He felt for Zachary's pulse but there was nothing, even in the heat the body was cold. He'd obviously been dead for some time—maybe several hours.

Julian came in, immediately followed by the frantic hotel manager, who crossed himself, raising his eyes to heaven when he saw the corpse. Death was terrible for business in the hotel trade. He wondered if they might be able to hush it up. They wouldn't be able to rent this room for a while, that was for sure.

"Oh, God," Julian groaned when he saw Zack's body. "Poor old chap."

Nick nodded slowly, staring at Zachary, his eyes brimming with tears. He had seen his mother, father, baby brothers and sisters, almost all of his family, in death, and he had always tried not to weep, but somehow the sight of this stalwart old man, who had meant so much to him, who had helped him and guided him, touched Nick deeply. Tears ran down his cheeks as he heard Bluey's shocked voice saying, "Well, Jesus H. Christ! Who the hell is going to produce this fucking movie now?"

❄   ❄   ❄

Shirley Frankovitch was immediately on the telephone to Spyros Makopolis, but he had already heard the news half an hour earlier and had called an emergency meeting of the MCCP board.

"We need a new line producer down here right away," she said in her gravelly voice. "I've just had a *great* idea, Spyros, it's simply *great.*"

"And what's that?" Spyros asked. He'd always had a soft spot for Shirley. Her films had made the studio pots of money. She was smart, despite being a woman, an ugly and occasionally drunken one at that, but he admired her talent, especially her undoubted ability to make the coffers of the box office rattle.

"Umberto Scrofo," Shirley said triumphantly. "He produced *La Città Perduta*, the film Irving wrote in Rome last year. He really is a *wonderful* producer, Spyros darling, very talented. Irving can't speak highly enough about him. You met him at your party, remember? He came with Ramona. He's intelligent, cultured; he has innovative, brilliant ideas. He's great with budgets, understands cast and crew, and I think you can get him cheap."

"Well, I was thinking of Gregory Ratoff," Spyros said after a slight pause. "But I'm told he's shooting in Egypt. We've already contacted the agents for Spears Farnsworth and Jack Hall, but they're both probably booked. We can't afford to waste any more time, Shirley. It's already costing us more than ten thousand dollars a day just to keep everyone in Acapulco. Our studio has no acceptable producers available at the moment."

Shirley shot back with a triumphant "Well, let's use Scrofo—take a chance on someone new for a change—someone who isn't part of your family." She realized she had probably gone too far with that but Spyros answered as if he hadn't really been listening.

"How do you know if this Scrofo guy is free?" he asked.

"I spoke to him last week in Rome," Shirley lied. "He's a good friend of ours, Spyros, he's available, and I *know* he's ready to do an important American movie. You did see *La Città,* didn't you, darling?" she asked, knowing he hadn't.

"Sure, it was great." It was his turn to lie, and, covering the receiver, he hissed at his assistant to find a print of *La Città Perduta* right away.

"And he brought it in for under a million," Shirley persisted. "With that amazing cast—Mendelson, even Ramona." A sarcastic tone crept into her voice. She was not enamored of Ramona Armande; indeed, she didn't like actors in general, considering them shallow, vain creatures whose only interest was getting as many close-ups of themselves as possible. Her only exception was Julian Brooks, whom she admired in spite of herself.

"Give this guy Scrofo a call," Spyros conceded. "If he's available, have him telephone me at my office immediately. We've got to get moving on this, Shirley, this delay is gonna cost us *thousands*—and the stockholders are gonna blow their stacks."

"Right away, Spyros my darling," crowed Shirley. "I'm on the blower to Italy now."

Shirley hung up, a victorious smile splitting her pumpkin face. This is it, she said to herself. Signor Scrofo, you better be good to us now. This is a gift I've given you—a fucking *gift*. And picking up the telephone, she instructed the operator to place a call to Rome immediately.

It was six o'clock in Rome. The vast apartment was chilly and Umberto Scrofo was freezing. His southern Calabrian blood never seemed to have adjusted to the cold Roman winters. He picked up the telephone receiver after only two rings.

"*Pronto*," he snapped. He'd been receiving a good many unpleasant calls recently, perhaps because of the excessive nudity in his movie which had caused some offense to the Catholic community. The shrill tones of Shirley Frankovitch crackled down the transatlantic line.

"Umberto, it's me, Shirley, Shirley Frankovitch. Do you remember me?"

"Of course," he said gallantly. "How could I forget you, Shirley?"

"I have some *great* news for you, Umberto. Tell me, are you working on anything right now?"

"Well, there are a few things in the pipeline, Shirley my dear, many things actually," Umberto hedged, glancing at the small pile of dreadful scripts on his desk. "But I must confess, nothing definite—nothing I'm really excited about at this moment."

"How about coming to Acapulco and taking up the reins of our movie *Cortez*?" Shirley asked excitedly. There was a pause as Scrofo digested this.

"Hello—Hello, Umberto, can you hear me?"

"*Cortez?* The Makopolis film with Julian Brooks? Of course I've heard about it, but I thought Zachary Domico was producing."

"He's dead," Shirley stated triumphantly. "He died this morning. Heart attack, they think. I've spoken to Spyros about you coming down here to produce it, Umberto, and he seems keen. Are you free? Can you do it?"

"Well, yes, yes, I am free actually, I certainly am." Umberto couldn't keep the eagerness out of his voice. "E— how sad about Zachary, he was a fine producer." The realization of what this could mean to his career was hitting Scrofo like the rush of cocaine, and excitement made his voice even harsher than usual.

"Then call Spyros Makopolis right away. Here's the number—Crestview 77933. Get your ass on the first plane out of that Eternal fucking City," cackled Shirley, "and fly on down to Acapulco. We've got work to do, Umberto. Lots and lots of work."

"*Ciao*, Shirley—and thank you, *cara*," shouted Umberto. "I shall be there *subito*." As he replaced the receiver his heart was beating so erratically that he thought it might stop altogether, and all his dreams would be ended before he even clambered on the first rung of his stairway to

Hollywood success. Quickly he dialed the international operator but was frustrated to find all circuits to the United States were busy.

He took his solid-gold pen, an "end of picture" gift from Ramona, and started to doodle on a pad. PRODUCED BY UMBERTO SCROFO. Somehow that didn't look right now. Not that there was anything wrong with Italian names. On movie credits they hadn't hurt Carlo Ponti or Federico Fellini, but there was something . . . well . . . unpleasant about *his* name. Scrofo—in English it sounded like "scruffy," or "scrofulous," a bad connotation. No, it wasn't right for an above-the-title important Hollywood producer; he needed something better.

He doodled some more, leaving out the S. CROFA, CROFF, CROFT. Croft—now that was a good surname. It sounded vaguely Scottish to him. Croft. It reminded him of a charming cottage in the Scottish Highlands that he'd visited once. Umberto, of course, he would change to Hubert. Hubert Croft. Excellent. One thing was missing, though. He thought of the producers who were his idols: David O. Selznick, Jack L. Warner. Darryl F. Zanuck. A middle initial—that's what he needed. He would take the *S* from Scrofo. Hubert S. Croft. Now that was a fine name for a fine Hollywood producer. He tried the international operator again and this time he got through to Spyros Makopolis.

He was on his way at last.

◄*Eight*►

As THE DAY of her party dawned, Ramona woke up in her shimmering white bedroom with an appalling headache, Zack's tragic death still fresh in her mind. Her maid brought her breakfast in bed, along with a copy of the *Acapulcan News.* It was crammed with gossipy details of tonight's lavish celebration for *Cortez.* According to the society reporter, this would be the most spectacular society event here of the whole year. Lana Turner and Linda Christian were flying in from Hollywood, and so were Errol Flynn, Ava Gardner and Gilbert Roland. Miguel Alemán, until recently the President of Mexico, had also promised to attend as had many prominent dignitaries and politicians from America. The festivities would begin at sunset because Acapulcan sunsets were of such particular and extraordinary beauty, and probably not end till the equally spectacular dawn came up.

Ramona had hired two bands to play: one dance band from Mexico City, and a strolling group of mariachi players called Los Paraguayos who would play Mexican folk songs.

Ramona regularly made "the ten best hostesses in the world" list in the glossy magazines, and for this occasion she determined to live up to her reputation in spite of her sorrow over her secret lover's death. A small army of servants had been up since dawn, scrubbing, scouring, polishing and sweeping the vast areas of marble, glass and stone. The two swimming pools were to be covered with a floating veil of flowers, hundreds of imported white roses, costing thousands of dollars, and so much more unusual than jasmine or hibiscus, would float in her brilliantly lit pools tonight.

The fiesta was going to cost a minor fortune, but Ramona wouldn't be footing the bill. Although the Prince indulged her every financial whim, her childhood in Hungary had left her with a solid respect for the value of money. Didier, who had himself started at the bottom of the film ladder before finally becoming the most powerful producer in England, had taught her all she'd needed to know about finance. His advice was: "Never pay for anything yourself if you can get someone else to pay for it." Didier had scolded her when he'd discovered that she'd been buying her own stockings and gloves for a movie in which she'd only had a small role. "Always charge *everything* you can to the production—that should be your credo." Ramona had learned well from her brother, so when Zack had approached her to give the *Cortez* launch party, she'd agreed, provided, of course, that MCCP would be footing the bill.

Pragmatically unsentimental, Ramona wasn't going to allow Zachary's death to spoil her day. To her, there was no point in mourning too long after the departed had been sent off in a civilized manner. It had been three days since Zack's funeral. That was long enough; the show must go on.

She dressed quickly in a cream cotton caftan. Catching her sleek hair back with a tortoiseshell comb and leaving her skin bare of makeup, she began her long list of household checks.

Everything must be perfection tonight, not only to impress the glamorous guests, but because she was looking forward to again seeing her friend Umberto Scrofo, Zachary's replacement as producer. Irving Frankovitch had let slip last night that it was to be him, but that Umberto had insisted on changing his name. Not only had she enjoyed working with Umberto in Rome last year, but he'd also been an interesting and knowledgeable escort. She had played one of the starring roles then. Now she hoped that Umberto might be persuaded to build up her role in *Cortez*, something Zachary hadn't been prepared to do in spite of their relationship.

Scheherazade was a vast, multilevel mansion modeled after an Arabian mosque. From the top level, which was some ten stories high, an old white wooden cable car with creaky metal gear teeth and thin wire pulleys ran down the side of the house to Ramona's private beach. Although antiquated, the cable car always had regular safety checks, and all visitors to Scheherazade used it to take them down to the secluded beach.

This top level was a huge open terrace paved with diamond-shaped mosaic tiles. A fountain gushed in the center and palm trees and tropical plants grew in luscious profusion. There was an enormous white marble bar, and here and there, as if resting at some oasis, stood a dozen or more white stone camels.

On the second level were six guest bedroom suites, nestled together in an intimate group around their own swimming pool.

Down winding steps lined on each side by jungle foliage, through sparkling white arches so bright that they dazzled the eye, was the unbelievable vista of the main salon. From here there was a panoramic view of the Pacific revealed in all its glittering glory, for where the south wall should have been was only the peerless beauty of the sea. Around the salon snaked the main swimming pool, its very edge the horizon. Were it not for the marble figures at the edge of the pool, pool and sea would appear as one.

A large golden snail with *trompe l'oeil* butterflies painted on its shell guarded the entrance to the grotto, where revelers were often serenaded long into the night.

Set into the wall was a huge shell of shimmering pearl big enough for a small woman to sit in. Ramona had done that herself once for Zack, wearing just a pair of golden stockings and a smile. He'd been quite insatiable that night. Poor Zack.

At the bottom of more steps was her own private beach—the only private beach in Acapulco—and Ramona used it with pleasure and great pride.

It had taken Ramona and her Prince five years to construct Scheherazade—five arduous years during which the most brilliant architects and designers from Mexico, New York and Paris had created this fantasy masterpiece. Now the perfectionist Princess Ramona reigned supreme, secure that it was the grandest house in Mexico.

Nicholas Stone shaved with his customary speed. He hated wasting time on shaving and showering and other mundane things. His mind constantly whirled with every tiny detail of his movie which would finally begin shooting on Monday morning. The jet-set party tonight held no interest for him. Parties of any description were just not his scene. He was a simple man, and having to make small talk with the *beau monde* was not his idea of a good time. He had tried to telephone the new producer, Hubert S. Croft, the night before, but had been informed by the hotel operator that Mr. Croft was sleeping off his arduous trip from Rome and was not to be disturbed under any circumstances.

He had, however, spoken to Elektra and his children, and in spite of a bad connection he could hear the warmth in their voices which always brought him such happiness. He knew it was time now to pick up Bluey at his boat and, grabbing his keys, he glanced briefly into the mirror and made a face of resignation at the boring evening that stretched ahead of him.

In complete contrast to Nick, the newly christened Hubert S. Croft spent a great deal of time on his toilette. Unfortunately, his beautifully cut cream-colored suit from Caraceni of Milan did nothing to minimize his bulk, and his sallow complexion was not enhanced by a striped voile shirt with a tight white collar. He had hoped that the midnight blue silk tie would give him the look of respectability and authority that he craved. It was most important that he make the right impression tonight.

He knew how much was at stake. With a big Hollywood film to produce, he needed to earn the trust of the director, encourage the actors, ingratiate himself with the crew and show everyone that he knew exactly what he was doing. He'd succeeded in Rome; he would succeed in Hollywood at last, and he had excellent ammunition in that he believed in himself. He also had strong allies already in the Frankovitch team and Ramona Armande—a good set of cards in his hands. Very good indeed.

He flicked back what little remained of his hair and doused himself with the pungent French cologne which he'd worn for so many years. Inserting a pair of gold links set with enormous sapphires into his cuffs, he wondered if his favorite sapphire stickpin might not be a little too fancy for the tropics. He was already sweating profusely, even in the relative cool of the hotel room. He hoped it would be cooler at Ramona's party. He must make a *bella figura* tonight—he had to let the cast and crew know who was boss. And the first person he must convince of this would be the young hotshot director, Nicholas Stone.

Inès looked in the mirror and put the finishing touches to her makeup, liking what she saw. She was glowing. A one-shouldered sarong dress of pale green silk complemented her elegant figure. It was clasped at the shoulder with a jade-and-ivory brooch which Julian had given her just this morning, on receiving a letter from Dr. Langley in L.A., confirming her pregnancy. Tiny jade studs gleamed in her earlobes, and her hair was tied with a simple emerald-green ribbon. On her wrist she wore as usual the delicate amber-and-silver bracelet given to her by Yves. She never took it off; it was her lucky mascot. The only night she had not worn it was the night she had killed the Italian General with his own razor. She shuddered. Forget about that night, she told herself. Why was it so hard to forget?

Julian, casually immaculate as ever, tanned and handsome, looked her up and down approvingly.

"Darling, are you sure you're up to tonight?" he asked. "I'm worried about you. You know how we both feel about the baby, I don't want you to risk overdoing it."

"Don't worry, my love," she said, coming close to him, touching his cheek with her gentle fingers. "I feel fine—it's just a touch of morning sickness and Dr. Langley told me that almost every woman suffers from it, particularly with the first baby."

"I hope you don't get it with our next one," said Julian sincerely, cupping her face in his hands and gazing lovingly into her eyes. "And the ones after that. You know how much I love you—want you—want to be with you all my life, don't you, my angel?"

"I do, darling—I really do," Inès whispered, her heart full of love for him.

"This is going to be a tough film for me, darling—I just need to know that you'll be as understanding as ever—and that you'll always, always be here with me."

"You'd better believe it, Mister Brooks," Inès replied with a big smile. "Looks, honey, you ain't *never* gonna get rid of this particular woman."

"And I never want to—ever," he said, his expression so penetrating and sincere that Inès looked surprised.

"Julian—darling—what is it?" she asked. "You seem so worried suddenly—why? What's the matter?"

"I don't really know," said Julian, moving away and looking out the window at the dark blue velvet of the sea.

"Everything's so perfect, Inès. Almost too good to be true. Everything. You—the two of us together—the baby—I just couldn't bear anything to go wrong, ever."

"Nothing's going to go wrong, silly," said Inès lightly, thinking that it was so unlike Julian to voice this kind of thought. "Phoebe has agreed to your terms, we can be married as soon as the decree comes through—the baby's fine, and Dr. Langley says he sees no reason why I can't have *lots* more—so why are you so suddenly worried, darling?"

"I'm not—I'm not, forget it." He scooped her up in his arms and kissed the soft fragrance of her neck. "I'm just behaving like a stupid superstitious actor before the show starts. Come on, old girl, let's get off to this dreaded gala."

She kissed his cheek, feeling the rush of pleasure from the knowledge that she was going to have his child.

He smiled back at her tenderly. She was the woman he wanted to be with forever. He loved her so much—but how he wished that these new and alarming erotic images of Dominique would stop coming into his head whenever he made love to the woman who was not only carrying his child but who was soon to be his wife.

After Dominique had awakened from her afternoon siesta she stood under the shower, letting the tingling cold water revive her. She was looking forward tremendously to this evening. She loved parties, the new thrill of dressing up, painting her face, designing her hair in some daring new style. She loved to flirt—and now, she especially loved to flirt with Julian. Julian Brooks. So famous and charming—and the handsomest man in the world.

She knew she had his male libido in a spin. She smiled to herself as she sat at her dressing table fiddling with her lipstick. Although her face hardly needed any cosmetic assistance, playing with paints and brushes gave her more time to think. Looks Brooks liked her. She smiled like a cat while she applied Revlon's Fire and Ice to her full lips. He more than liked her—he desired her, too. She'd become aware of that when she'd spotted him watching her in the pool. On the few occasions that they had met since, it was increasingly obvious to her how he felt.

Dominique was beginning to understand how desirable she was, how much power her youthful beauty gave her. She loved it. So Looks Brooks wanted to play, did he? At sixteen she was hardly an expert in the game of love, but she was going to try and experiment. She'd enjoyed her affair with Gaston in St. Tropez very much. But she'd had to come to America for this film just as she was really beginning to enjoy his lovemaking. What would it be like to make love to Julian?

That Julian was both engaged and in the middle of a divorce didn't bother her at all. Love was all only a game, wasn't it? she thought as she clipped on a pair of big golden hoop earrings. After all, Inès was French too, and Frenchwomen understood about these things. So she wouldn't mind if Dominique flirted with her fiancé—it was all part of the game.

Dominique chose a short strapless dress from her wardrobe. The waist was tightly cinched and the hemline high, which drew attention to her splendid legs. Her hair was dry now, and she brushed it until it tumbled in uxuriant splendor down her bare back.

She knocked on the door of the room next to hers. "Ready, Agathe?" she called out in her breathy little girl's voice with its newly acquired American accent. "Let's hit the road, baby."

Tonight she was determined to have a wonderful time and perhaps to captivate Julian Brooks even more.

Irving and Shirley put the finishing touches on their respective toilettes. He felt comfortable in a pair of loose cotton trousers and an old shirt; he cared little or nothing about his appearance; his only concern was his work.

Shirley fussed miserably in front of the mirror. The new caftan she was wearing, in its bright shades of orange and yellow, did nothing to disguise her ballooning girth. She was allergic to the sun so her face was white, and her salt-and-pepper hair clung to her head in tight, old-fashioned curls, giving her an uncanny, but hardly becoming, resemblance to Harpo Marx. She had done her best with her makeup, as she wanted to look as good as possible when she met Umberto Scrofo again. Or Hubert S. Croft—she didn't care what he wanted to be called. He'd rung the day before, informing the Frankovitches that now that he was making an American film, he wanted an American name. Since only Irving, Shirley and Ramona knew him as Umberto Scrofo, he would appreciate . . . must insist, actually . . . that they never refer to him as anything but Hubert S. Croft. Hell, she'd call him Donald Duck if it would help their cause. Croft was sure to be the Frankovitches' ally, the man to reinstate those violent battle scenes and those lyrical pages of prose to the shooting script. Zachary Domino and Nicholas Stone had callously sabotaged it; now Scrofo would be their savior. He would be as strong and authoritative as he had been in Italy, even inspiring fear in some of the cast and crew. That was good. That was how a producer should be—respected. A hard task-master. He would make this truly a Frankovitch film, not one for which the critics would praise only the director and the actors, leaving the writers unappreciated, as usual. Shirley smiled grimly as she pinned an emerald brooch to her caftan. Oh yes, she'd call him anything he wanted as long as he helped the cast and crew of *Cortez* to realize the true worth of the Frankovitch team and give them the respect and glory which they so richly deserved.

◆ *Nine* ◆

Ramona was a vision of composed loveliness as she waited for her guests in the center of her marble entrance hall. Wearing a slim column of white silk crepe, her ebony hair caught up with a diamond comb from the estate of the Prince's family, enormous pear-shaped diamonds glittering on her ears, and several diamond bracelets on each wrist, she was coolly elegant, but exuding that charming effervescence which is the mark of every good hostess.

Agathe and Dominique were the first to arrive, Agathe in a long matronly floral dress in which she appeared uncomfortable. Her normally expressionless white face was awestruck. Not only was she a guest at one of the most talked-about houses in the world, but soon her idol would be here. He would smile at her. They would chat wittily. He would see how bright she was, how cultivated.

She accepted a glass of mineral water and was content just to sit on a divan watching the fabled sunset and waiting for Julian's arrival.

Dominique sashayed around, looking older tonight than her sixteen years. Tanned to a golden honey-color, she mixed gaily with the arriving guests, chatting and joking with genuine camaraderie and charm.

Agathe envied her. Where had she found that poise, that sophistication, that ease with people? Just a few months ago she was a French schoolgirl; now she was a woman of the world, an actress—glamorous and confident. She made Agathe feel even more like some insecure country bumpkin.

Soon the marble floors echoed to the chatter and laughter of the jet set, Hollywood stars, local celebrities and politicians. Bluey and Nick were both impressed by the sheer scale of the house.

"Jesus H. Christ," whistled Bluey. "I've seen some pads in my time, but this takes the cake, cherry, icing and all."

Nick nodded. In spite of having lived in America for ten years, he was still unaccustomed to the palatial, often vulgar residences of the high-living Hollywood stars, directors and producers, but this extraordinary villa was more lavish than any he'd ever seen there. His director's eye was enthralled by the beauty of the landscaping, the exotic pictures, sculptures and other objects, the depth and dimensions of all the rooms. He set off on his own to examine them more closely.

The usually jaded photographers from *Life*, *Look*, *Vogue* and the movie magazines—*Photoplay*, *Modern Scene* and *Motion Picture*—were so excited that they jostled and pushed each other to take pictures. There were stars galore to fill both their columns and their lenses. Lana Turner, with her new husband, Lex Barker, had arrived; she, with her silver-blond hair, was more tanned than the Mexican waiters, and he was as handsome as any film star had a right to be. Hedda Hopper and Louella Parsons had sent only their stringers, but influential, fast-talking Walter Winchell from New York and Harrison Carroll from the Los Angeles *Herald-Examiner* had arrived in person, and now mingled with the chattering crowd, whose voices competed with the music of the strolling mariachis.

As the sun dipped into the horizon, the guests gathered at the end of the huge terrace to view its fading glory. Even the waiters stopped work to admire it, for to the Mexicans it is the symbol of eternal life. There were appreciative gasps as the sun made a dramatically rapid exit to the west, casting a soft apricot glow over everyone and everything. It was such a magnificent sight that spontaneous applause broke out. The mariachis played more wildly and the margaritas began to stir everyone's blood with fiesta excitement.

No one noticed the entrance of Hubert S. Croft as he stood at the top of the tall marble staircase and watched the partygoers as they oohed and aahed at the sunset. He gave a sneering smile. They all seemed so childish.

Ramona was the first to see him; she hurried over to greet him effusively. "Hubert, my dear Hubert, I'm so happy to see you again. You look very well." She was careful to use the new name which he'd insisted on.

Hubert took her hand and with European gallantry bowed his head over her fabled forty-carat diamond. "Ramona my dear, you are more ravishing than ever—and what a superb house. Magnificent, my dear, magnificent."

Ramona beamed as Hubert accepted a margarita from a passing waiter; then she whisked him off to be introduced to her other guests.

Across the sea of laughing faces, Inès froze in horror. No. Not again. Not here in Acapulco. Was this a dream or a ghost? Why was he here? Her eyes were riveted to the short, paunchy man who strutted around shaking hands and smiling and who in turn was being greeted with friendly smiles by everyone. But of course he must be some friend of Ramona's; she had seen them both outside Romanoff's last month.

As the man came nearer to her she could see the unmistakable face and squat body which had haunted her dreams. His fleshy lips were at this moment pulled into an expression which he imagined to be a charming social smile, but which made him look like some grotesque gargoyle. But there was no doubt at all that this was the face from her past. Inès clung to Julian's arm; her heart hammering as Umberto Scrofo advanced towards her with an ominous tread and with that ghastly smile plastered on his hideous face.

There was nowhere to hide.

❖   ❖   ❖

"*Bon soir,* Julian," Dominique said, licking pink glossy lips and smiling up at him seductively.

Julian beamed. "Dear girl," he said heartily, "you look very pretty tonight, very grown up—doesn't she, Inès?"

"Thank you, Julian," Dominique smiled, her attention focused totally on him. She completely ignored Inès even though she was arm in arm with her fiancé. "And you look very—what is the word?—dashing. Yes, that's it, you look very dashing tonight, Julian."

Julian laughed, again finding himself uncomfortably bewitched. Damn, damn. This child-woman was irresistible.

"Would you have a few minutes to discuss something with me, Julian?" Dominique went on, her eyes now downcast shyly. "There's a scene that I didn't quite understand and I would so appreciate your advice about it."

"Well, this *is* a party, my dear. Perhaps tomorrow—" demurred Julian.

"I don't think I could sleep tonight for worrying about this, Julian," Dominique implored, looking up at him, again beseechingly with her Circe-green eyes. "It is so important to me, this film. And I am only a beginner, you can teach me so much, Julian."

Julian shot a quick look at Inès, but she was staring out towards the main salon with a curious blank look on her face. Probably admiring the decorations, he thought.

"Excuse me, darling—I hope you don't mind. Dominique and I are just going over to the edge of the pool to discuss a scene."

She nodded, not speaking, and Julian let go of Inès arm and allowed Dominique to lead him into the shadows at the base of a nearby palm tree. By God, she was having an amazing effect on him. He was becoming aroused just by the soft touch of her fingers on his hand. What was wrong with him—was he mad?

"Now which scene is it, Dominique?" he asked sternly, annoyed with himself as he felt his cock starting to harden.

"This one," she said simply, opening her pouting mouth to his, running a tongue full of silent promises across his dry lips, and pressing her yielding body to his. Before he had a chance to respond, she pulled away, looking up at him with a kittenish smile. "I thought that perhaps *this* should be how we did the first kiss after my dance, the firelight scene— what do you think, Julian?" She looked at him in mock innocence while she gently dabbed at her lips with her handkerchief, then wiped his with it.

Julian was dumbstruck. He had always thought that he understood the workings of the female mind, at least as well as, if not better than, the next man. But Dominique was so much more unpredictable than any other woman he had known—even Inès. She was flaunting her sexuality tonight like bunting strung across a pleasure boat. She was a pubescent jade, a wanton child-woman—and God, he desired her.

As Julian stood there dumbstruck Dominique reapplied her lipstick, whispering conspiratorially, "Think about it, Julian, *chéri.* It should be a tender moment, don't you agree? I mean, really sexy but sweet, like Liz and Monty in *A Place in the Sun. N'est-ce pas?*"

Before the spellbound actor could reply, the teenaged minx disappeared into the shadows with a roguish smile, and an embarrassed and tumescent Julian stared after her, alarm bells ringing in his ears.

Inès prayed that Scrofo wouldn't remember her, or that her scarlet face would not betray her. She had tried to disappear into the crowd, but after Julian had finished his talk with Dominique he had found her in the marble bar and taken her over to meet the new producer, who was with Ramona.

"Inès, my dear, I should like you to meet Hubert Croft—Hubert, this is Mademoiselle Juillard, Julian's fiancée," said Ramona.

"How do you do, Mademoiselle," said Scrofo in a rasping harsh voice. *"Enchanté."*

"Hubert is our new producer," beamed Ramona. "And we are very lucky to have him."

Inès felt faint and put her trembling hand on Julian's arm for support.

Producer? Umberto Scrofo was Zachary's replacement? It simply wasn't possible.

"How do you do," Inès mumbled. She knew she had to say something. She felt her knees starting to buckle, and only Julian's steady arm prevented her from swooning. So she hadn't killed him after all.

In horrified fascination she stared at the rim of a pink puckered scar which was only slightly concealed under his flashy shirt. *She* had caused that scar. It was because of her that his voice was a grating whisper.

For eleven years she had believed that she had murdered this man, who was here shaking her hand with a ghastly smile on his brutish face. This was certainly no ghost who held her gaze and rasped, "You're a very lucky man indeed, Mr. Brooks."

Umberto drank in Inès' loveliness with no visible sign of recognition, although he'd held her gaze for perhaps a second longer than necessary. But that was something Inès was used to. Her beauty often caused men to react in strange ways. Croft shook hands with Julian, expressing his delight at being on the movie and his admiration for Julian's fine work in the past. Then his eyes began flitting back to Inès. Faintly she could smell the same sickly after-shave that he'd worn that night at the Ritz. She wanted to flee to the other side of the room, to escape his probing stare, but Julian held her hand tightly. Her heart thumped so hard she felt sure someone would notice. How in heaven's name had Umberto Scrofo ended up here? Why had he changed his name? How on earth could he possibly be producing Julian's movie? But most of all, why wasn't he dead?

As if reading her thoughts, Hubert turned to look at her again with a penetrating stare.

"You're a very beautiful woman, Mademoiselle Juillard." He had barely a trace of an Italian accent. "Very beautiful indeed."

"Thank you," she murmured, gulping at her margarita, the salt that encrusted the rim of the glass stinging her lips. She looked at Julian for help, but he was busy talking to Hedda Hopper's stringer, who was scribbling in a notebook.

"Have we not met somewhere before?" His beady black eyes roamed over the contours of her breasts. "You look familiar."

"I don't think so," Inès said quietly, trying to move away, "I'm sure I would have remembered." Hubert took a step closer and yet another wave of his familiar cologne hit her. She felt her stomach churn.

"I never forget a face. Never." His eyes searched hers as he suddenly sensed her fear. Who was this woman? He felt sure he knew her from somewhere. But where? What was the story of this beautiful creature? He must find out. He would make it his business to find out. Hubert always needed to know every detail about everyone with whom he worked—knowledge gave him power.

"Where are you from?" he probed.

Inès felt as if she were going mad. She had murdered him, hadn't she? She remembered all too vividly the look on his face, the blood covering the bathroom floor, the hue and cry in Paris when they'd searched for his murderer. Her flight to England to escape certain death. Surely, though, there was little chance that he would recognize her today. She looked so very different from the skinny teenage prostitute of wartime Paris. She was now an elegant, chic woman of the world, in her prime. But she *had* tried to kill him. No one could ever forget a face seen in those circumstances, could they? But her face wasn't the same—or was it? The style and blondness of her hair were different, her cheekbones were more pronounced, she was taller, sleeker. She was *not* recognizable, she told herself.

But she knew she could not lie to him about her nationality. Everyone knew where she was from.

"London," she murmured. "I'm from London."

"London?" he said in surprise. "But you cannot be, you are French, are you not?"

"Yes," said Inès quietly. "I am."

"She lived in London for twelve years," smiled Julian, turning away from the reporter, his actor's instincts sensing tension. "That's where we met, isn't it, darling?"

"Oh really," Umberto smiled, still staring at Inès. "Where were you born, Mademoiselle Juillard?"

"France," she whispered.

"France?" he said, raising an eyebrow. "France? France is a very big country. Which part of France, Mademoiselle Juilliard?"

"I was born in Lyon," she lied.

His eyes narrowed. "Lyon, really?"

"Yes." Then, more boldly, "Lyon. Have you ever been there?" She could barely keep the loathing from her voice.

A smirk crossed his slug-white face. She was *avverso* towards him, was she? He was used to that. It certainly wouldn't be the first time someone had disliked him on sight. He couldn't place her, but it seemed that she was most anxious to hide something from him. "Lyon, hmm?" He looked carefully at her again. "I was never in Lyon, but I know that I'll remember where it was that we met; it's sure to come back to me. As I say, I never, ever forget a face, or where I saw it."

He smiled craftily and strolled out onto the terrace to rejoin his hostess.

Ines felt as if she'd been kicked in the stomach. Julian had been right in thinking that everything was almost too perfect. She had to get away. Julian was holding court in one corner of the vast room. She needed to be alone, to have time to digest Scrofo's presence here.

As soon as Scrofo left her, she ran down the stone steps which led to the beach, and stood on the toffee-colored sand, staring out to sea with unseeing eyes. She was now sure that Scrofo would inevitably remember her as the whore who had slashed his throat. She shuddered at the word: *whore.* How would it affect Julian's career if the world found out that his fiancée had been a Parisian prostitute and a failed murderess? A woman who had serviced the enemy during the war? She couldn't bear even to think about it, or what it would do to their relationship.

However much he professed to love her, Julian would dump her immediately—she knew that. Although she believed that he truly loved her, she knew that Julian Brooks simply couldn't handle the ramifications of marrying a woman with such a sordid, even criminal, past.

No, her life would be totally ruined if Julian were to discover any part of her past. Ruined. His divorce was supposed to be final in two months. They must marry soon, before her pregnancy became obvious; before he had time to learn the truth. If he did, it would be the end. He would leave her, she knew. Oh, he would be kind—he would give her money, which she did not need. She had invested wisely and could provide for herself. She would be left with nothing of his except his child. No one even knew that she was pregnant. If they found out, that would no doubt cause another scandal, but not nearly as ignominious as the one Umberto Scrofo could cause.

Inès sat down on a rock, her mind spinning. What could Scrofo possibly want from her? She was no threat to him. But if he recognized her he would want his revenge, naturally, and from the way he stared at her it was only a matter of time before he did. She cursed the fact that her first name had never been changed.

She placed her hand comfortingly on her still-flat stomach. Sweat trickled down the inside of her thin silk dress and she took off her shoes, putting them on one of the rocks which lay like beached sea monsters on the sand. Across the bay in the dusk she could see a speedboat weaving about, filled with laughing people. The sea was flat and oily, without the slight wind that usually came from the bay. A fisherman suddenly emerged from the water in the crepuscular light, a baby octopus impaled on his rusty spear, its saclike pink body hanging down limply like the scrotum of an elderly man. Inès shuddered. She had seen too many of those. The thought of ever again having to make love to any man except Julian was anathema.

She paddled her feet listlessly in the tide in the hope of cooling down, but the water was too warm, only making her feel stickier. She bent down to splash some water on her flushed face. Her mind was crowded with thoughts of the embarrassment, the humiliation, the indignity if her past were to be discovered. Julian would never be able to forgive her. He was the traditional public school English gentleman just as much as he was an important star. He'd sacrificed his marriage and a great deal of money for Inès, but she knew he wouldn't be willing to sacrifice his future. Her female instincts warned her that she was in grave danger. She had to do something drastic about Umberto Scrofo before he tried to ruin her life all over again.

Agathe had been looking forward with mixed feelings to the party. She usually felt out of place and ill at ease at social gatherings, but as Dominique's chaperone she had had to go. At least there was the presence of Julian to look forward to.

She sensed his arrival at once, almost smelling him across the room, the same scent she cherished in the fabric of his blue shirt. She had kept it hidden away under her mattress, and slept with it entwined around her body every night.

He was even more handsome than the last time she'd seen him, more sexually arousing to her just from across the room than during her fevered nights when her thoughts were constantly of his body curled around hers, their two mouths one. He was wearing a white shantung suit of exquisite cut, and the palest of blue silk shirts open at the neck to reveal the dark curly hair of his chest. His hair tumbled over his bronzed brow as he laughed into the face of the woman by his side—laughing joyously, intimately, with a slim ash-blond woman in a green sarong, his hand casually resting on her one bare shoulder.

Agathe drew in her breath with a gasp. The hair was different. The style, the sophistication had not been there. But there was no one from those wartime days Agathe could *ever* forget. What was Julian doing with that tart Inès?

How could he be with that slut-child who'd slept with half the Gestapo in Paris? Surely *she* wasn't his fiancée?

They were being greeted by everyone like an emperor and his consort, but Inès was no empress, Agathe thought. She was a cheap whore and a traitor to her country. Why was Julian, who deserved only the pure and the good, engaged to this . . . this personification of evil? The bitch must have put a spell on him, for it was impossible for a man so wonderful, so kind, so magnificent in every way to want to take a whore as his wife.

Agathe remembered the magazine photograph which Dominique had shown her on their flight to Acapulco. The woman with Julian had been in profile and had been dark haired so it was no wonder that she hadn't recognized her, but there was no mistaking the traitor now, even though she was blond.

The past came flooding back to her. This was the tart who'd killed an

Italian officer. They had hidden her in the same cellar next to L'Éléphant Rose where Agathe had been made to stay for so long. But Inès had spent only a few days there before becoming hysterical. She had no stamina; she was weak and evil. Of course they had all rallied around the girl. Her pimp Yves, old Gabrielle, all of them who hadn't raised a finger to help Agathe until she was almost *dead* had done everything for Inès the whore. False passports, changing her name, coloring her hair, sending her off to the safety of England, spoiling the little bitch. Agathe had never heard anything about her again after that. But now, here, engaged to the man Agathe worshiped, was Inès Dessault, smiling at the world as if she owned it.

Bluey and Nick watched the sunset from the second level of Scheherazade, and Nick enthused, "It's the most goddamn gorgeous thing I've ever seen in my whole life, far more beautiful than the sunsets in Hydra. I want to be able to have this sort of look in the last battle scenes, Bluey —it could symbolize the tragedy of Mexico—the dying sun, the sun that the Mexicans so revere—dead and dying soldiers lying in the sunset when the battle's over—" Nick rattled on excitedly about the pathos and symbolism of the sunset, but Bluey, having seen it far too many times to wax lyrical, only noticed his margarita was finished.

"C'mon, let's get a refill, kiddo," he said. "There'll be plenty more sunsets, believe me."

Nick looked back at the amber sky, ideas fermenting in his mind as he reluctantly returned to the party. He had to capture this on the screen— had to.

The mariachi music in the main salon was only slightly louder than the conversation and laughter, now that all the guests had become more relaxed with one another. Nick and Bluey strolled to the bar, and Ramona, like a sliver of moonlight, drifted over to them.

"Darlings, our new producer has arrived. I've been looking everywhere for you. You must come and meet him."

"Of course, I've been waiting for this," said Nick as Ramona led him through the jostling crowd. "It's about time."

In the middle of a small group, consisting of Irving and Shirley Frankovitch, Dominique and Agathe, stood a short, overweight man, his back turned, wearing an expensive-looking tailored suit.

"You haven't met Hubert, have you?" Ramona smiled.

The man turned around to face Nicholas, whose heart almost stopped beating as he stared into the stony black eyes of Umberto Scrofo, his nemesis: the man who had murdered his mother.

Nicholas stood transfixed while introductions were being made. As if by remote control, he shook the sweaty hand of Gourouni, the man who'd destroyed his entire family in Hydra more than a decade before. His mouth was so dry that to speak was out of the question. He knew that no sound would come out of his throat. He couldn't even hear what anyone was saying, so loud was the pounding in his ears. He could only see the toadlike face of the man he'd vowed to himself he would destroy one day. Granted, with the passing years, with the fading of excitable youth, his burning hatred and desperate desire for revenge had diminished. But now, face to face with Scrofo on this tropical night in Acapulco, it surfaced again with deadly vehemence. And it was all he could do to hold back from throwing himself at the fat swine and screaming out that he was a murdering bastard who deserved to die. But he held his tongue and said nothing.

He knew that he must appear to be behaving stupidly. Ramona was looking at him quizzically, and Scrofo was eyeing him with a strangely patronizing expression. Through the fog in his brain, Nicholas heard the Italian say, "I'm delighted to meet you, Nick, we will make a great picture here, I know it. I like most of the script and we've got a terrific cast, haven't we? We need to meet before the others tomorrow morning so I can give you a few of my ideas."

Nick knew a remark was expected of him, but he was unable to reply with even the simplest platitude. He nodded, muttering something unintelligible under his breath.

Hubert Croft scrutinized the young director coolly. His appearance had so often alienated him from people that over the years he'd found ways in which to camouflage the rejection, including doling out saccharine doses of charm and heavy-handed wit. But this Nick Stone, the *wunderkind* of the 1950s cinema, was behaving in a particularly strange manner. Was he drunk? Had tequila taken its inevitable toll so early in the evening? Hubert smiled saying, "When I saw your first picture, Nick, I knew you had talent—anyone who could make something witty and fresh out of *Bobby Soxers in Space* must be a genius."

"Mmm, thanks," mumbled Nick, his throat so dry it was painful to speak.

"And your next movie was a work of art too—brilliant. I'm proud to be working with you, Nick—really thrilled."

Nick's gut instinct was to take the fat Italian's neck between his hands and squeeze the life out of him. He felt that he was no longer in Acapulco, but back in war-torn Hydra, a sixteen-year-old boy whose brothers and sisters had died in starving misery, whose father had been bludgeoned to death in front of all the villagers by Scrofo's men, whose mother had died at Scrofo's very own hand, and whose friends and relations had been either starved or tortured to death.

Less than a minute had passed when Bluey pressed a fresh margarita into his hand. Nick drained the glass, his eyes never leaving the Italian. Bluey looked at him in mild surprise. Nick seemed in a trance, like a man lost in a dream. His face was drained of color and he appeared to have lost both his tongue and his composure. Bluey cracked a joke as he was introduced to Hubert, who flashed him a beaming smile, glad to have his attention diverted from the dumb Greek director.

Mumbling some excuse about feeling ill, Nick desperately wanted to escape. This meeting was so unbelievable that he simply couldn't cope with it. He had to be alone. He had to have time to think. He must telephone Elektra. He was just about to leave when there was a sudden farfare from the mariachi band, and Ramona, grabbing him firmly by the arm, announced that dinner was served. Nick was trapped. The Princess's arm was like a handcuff as she led him down the winding onyx staircase to the main terrace.

The tables were set exquisitely. In the center of each of the round tables for ten, all covered with gold lamé tablecloths, a thick, gold-painted palm frond was embedded in a gold pyramid-shaped container which was in what looked like fine golden sand. Circled around the sand were a dozen tiny flickering lights which cast a flattering glow on the faces of the guests. On either side of the pyramid, two sleepy-eyed ceramic camels nestled against each other. The knives and forks were of solid gold, as were the saltshakers and the peppermills, which were also shaped like camels.

Ramona considered herself an expert at the tricky art of *placement*. The first three tables were the most important, and table number one was naturally presided over by Ramona herself. She had placed Hubert on her right and, to his dismay, Nick on her left. Next to him was Shirley Frankovitch, which made Nick's spirits sink even lower. He actively disliked this pseudo-intellectual, mean-spirited woman, who thought herself some kind of literary giant, but who owed most of her success to her husband.

"Good evening, Nicky," she said to him sarcastically as he sat down. "Gorgeous party, isn't it? Ramona's got so much class, doncha think?"

Nick nodded briefly to her, signaling to a waiter to fill his wine glass. He needed to get drunk tonight—very drunk indeed.

Next to Shirley sat Julian, who was also not overly fond of the blowsy writer, but as if to make up for this, Ramona had thoughtfully placed Dominique on his left. Between Dominique and Inès sat the American ambassador to Mexico, who drank much and talked little.

To her utter distress, Inès found herself sitting only four places away from Umberto Scrofo's penetrating stare. The only guests between her and the vile Italian were Teddy Stauffer, owner of the Villa Vera, self-styled "Mr. Acapulco" and leader of local society, and beautiful Gene Tierney, "Laura" herself.

The celebrities, press, cast and crew at the other tables all seemed to be having a much better time than those at Ramona's. A movie company works and plays hard, and tonight was supposed to be playtime, but as an experienced hostess, Ramona wondered why on earth there was such a chilly atmosphere at her table. She chatted away animatedly with Hubert, who responded with his usual heavy-handed wit, but Nicholas Stone, she thought, was being little more than downright rude. His morose eyes never left his plate, and he gulped the Château-Lafite 1929 as if it were lemonade.

"You are as ever looking glorious tonight, *Principessa*." Hubert smiled oilily, raising his hand-blown Venetian goblet in a toast to her. "More ravishing than ever."

"Why, thank you, Hubert dear." If Ramona could have managed a maidenly blush, she would have summoned one up, but her thespian gifts were not that munificent. "You are so kind."

"Tell me, my dear, who is the woman who is engaged to Julian? I think I know her from somewhere."

"Oh." Ramona seemed disappointed that the conversation had so quickly turned away from her. "Julian met her in London, Hubert. She's French, from quite a good family I understand—orphaned before the war and brought up by an aunt somewhere."

"Hmm." Hubert sipped his wine, regarding Ines covertly as she attempted conversation with the ambassador. "Attractive woman, I'm sure I've met her before."

Ramona gave no answer, and Hubert realized that he had committed the cardinal sin of discussing another woman's merits too glowingly in front of his hostess, who was now attempting conversation with a sullen-looking Nick Stone. Croft leaned across Ramona to join in the conversation.

"I think one of the things we must do, Nick, is to build up the role of the queen, don't you agree?"

Nick nodded, unable to speak, still convulsed with fury. The nerve of the slime. Script and character changes already, and he'd only been on the picture ten minutes.

"Oh, Hubert, do you really mean it?" Ramona glowed, her amber eyes shining like a teenager's. "I've got *so* many ideas about my character—do let me tell you some of them."

"I'd love to hear them, my dear," said Hubert. "Tell me everything you would like us to do, I'm sure we can work it out to everyone's satisfaction."

Across the table Inès picked at her food, trying not to watch as Umberto Scrofo stuffed his odious face, occasionally dropping bits of food down his tie. Every few minutes her eyes would catch his, which were observing her carefully, asking silent questions about her identity.

She was beautiful, Hubert thought, seemingly aristocratic and elegant —meeting her would surely have left an indelible impression on him. She looked about twenty-eight or thirty, which meant that if he'd known her in the past, it must have been about ten or twelve years ago when she was in her late teens. And since he had visited London briefly in 1946— maybe he had met her there? Ten years ago he'd been on Hydra. She certainly hadn't been there. Twelve years ago, however, he had been in Paris. Could he have met her there? No, it was impossible, she would have been too young. He barely listened as Ramona prattled on, giving him ideas and suggestions about how the script could be vastly improved by making Princess Isabella's mother a more interesting character. He hardly heard her, he was concentrating on unearthing the mystery of the enigmatic beauty who sat opposite him, so pale and quiet.

Lyon—Lyon—Lyon? He'd never been to Lyon in his life, but he knew this woman.

Julian was unaware of Inès' distress because Dominique had decided to play footsie with him. She had slipped off a shoe, and her bare foot caressed his ankle as she gazed into his eyes, finding his desire for her incredibly stimulating. Julian looked towards Inès, but she seemed so totally oblivious to everything going on around her that he decided he might as well play Dominique's little game with her. After all it meant nothing. She was just a young girl testing the new waters of flirtation. He could easily handle her.

◆ *Ten* ◆

B y the time they had returned to their hotel, Inès was feeling dreadful. Throughout the evening the continual gaze of Umberto Scrofo had haunted her. After dinner, when the guests drifted down to the lower terrace to dance, she had wanted desperately to leave, but Julian was dancing with Dominique, deep in conversation, so she hadn't wanted to interrupt him. Inès understood that actors filming together needed to spend time getting to know each other. Since Dominique was so young and completely inexperienced in the world of movies, Inès was sure that, being the true professional, Julian would want to help her as much as possible.

She was just coming back from the powder room when a damp hand clutched at her bare shoulder.

"Why do you always seem in such a hurry to get away from me, dear lady?" Hubert said. "Let us dance together."

"I'm afraid I'm not feeling very well," she said, pulling away from his grip. "I don't want to dance."

"Then let us sit this one out," he said, firmly taking her arm and leading her to a carved ivory seat close to the dance floor. "I want to talk to you." Scrofo appeared to possess that formidable inner strength which came from being used to having his orders carried out without question.

"I remember you now," he said suddenly, with a basilisk stare.

She looked back at him, struggling to keep her eyes expressionless. "How could you? We've never met."

"Oh, but we have, my dear Inès." His voice was rancid oil. "We most certainly have." He paused, waiting for her to react, relighting his cigar, surveying her through narrowed eyes. Inès didn't flinch, willing him not to remember.

"Of course you look quite different now. Almost twelve years makes a great difference to a pretty young girl." He smiled, waiting for her reaction. She found it hard to stop her glass from shaking and her stomach felt as if it had turned to stone.

"Well, if you won't remember, then I shall have to remind you," he said ominously. "I'm sure you recall a certain hotel room in Paris in 1943?"

Her expression was impassive. "I'm afraid I don't. What are you trying to imply? This conversation is getting us nowhere—excuse me."

She made a move to leave, but he was too quick for her and his hand shot out to grab her arm. She felt the unforgettable frisson of cruelty in his viselike fingers.

"I told you I never forget a face. I never forget a name, either. Foolish of you not to have changed it; Inès is an unusual name—so beautiful that you decided that you wouldn't change it when you gave up your occupation. *Whoring!*" His lips were close to her ear now as he spat out the word; she saw the undisguised hatred which had turned his sallow complexion florid.

"Mr. Croft, I don't know what you're talking about. Please, let me go. My fiancé is waiting for me."

But she was unable to extricate herself from his tight grip. As if in a dream, she saw the dancers whirling around the floor, the band playing, guests laughing. She heard the faint hum of the nighttime insects, smelled the soft scent of jasmine—but all she could think of was the torture of this man's vicious attack on her, and how she had repaid him for it.

"Ah, yes, I can see you remember now, don't you?" His teeth split his face like a Halloween pumpkin. "You don't need to answer, Inès. Your silence is enough; besides, as I told you, my memory never fails me. You were that little tart who came to service me at the Ritz Hotel, weren't you? And then you tried to kill me, didn't you?"

Inès felt she was in a nightmare from which she could never wake up. Less than twenty yards away, the man she loved so passionately was dancing with his leading lady. She wanted to be close to him, to hold him, to be Mrs. Julian Brooks, as soon as possible. She wanted to escape. That was all she wanted—but this reptilian creature held her rigidly in his grip. To get away from him she would have to create a scene.

"So, Miss Prim and Proper, Miss Fiancée of the Star, Miss *Murderess.*" He blew a cloud of blinding cigar smoke into her face. "So here we are—together again." He obviously hadn't changed much in all these years. He was still a monster.

"What is it you want from me?" Inès whispered.

"Nothing, my dear, absolutely *nothing*— yet. I just want you to be aware that I know who you are, Inès . . . whatever your name has become. I remember you very well. You were a young prostitute, obviously you'd been one for some time. You were good—very, very good." He licked his lips in recollection. "And then you tried to kill me, didn't you?" He bent his face so close to hers, that she could see the tiny broken veins on his nose and the stubble on his chins, smell that sickening cologne.

"You nearly succeeded, too—bitch!" His fingers held her upper arm so tightly she knew that by tomorrow their imprint would still be there. "I almost died because of you, you lousy whore. Look—" Quickly he loosened his tie, pulling open his shirt to reveal the thick scar at the base of his Adam's apple. Inès gasped. The wound was three or more inches long, pinkish-white, shiny and raised.

"I was in that fucking military hospital for week after week after fucking week." He pulled her nearer to him, his saliva almost hitting her face, and Inès thought the whole room must be watching them now. Then he smiled—a rictus grin. "I shall have my revenge for this," he hissed ominously as he straightened his tie. "I've waited a long time to find you, young lady, and you are going to curse the day you ever met me."

Inès shuddered. "I don't know what you're talking about, Mr. Croft," she said defiantly. "Whatever happened to you was a long time ago, and it had nothing to do with me."

He was even more loathsome than she'd remembered. With a wrench she managed to pull her arm away, just as the dance number was ending and Julian sauntered over, his arm casually around Dominique's waist.

"I'm so tired, darling," Inès whispered, moving into the safety of her fiancé's arms. "Can we go home now, please?"

"Of course, we'll go now, darling. Goodnight, Dominique." His eyes held Dominique's for a fraction longer than necessary. "Hubert, good to have met you, I expect we'll talk tomorrow." Arm in arm he and Inès strolled away to say goodnight to their hostess.

Umberto Scrofo's eyes stared after them. However much she might deny it, he was positive that it was she. He knew it was. The whore from Paris.

So he'd finally found her. The girl who'd tried to kill him—the skinny slut he'd dreamed of meeting again—of doing the most unspeakable things to, of punishing her. Well, her punishment must wait—but only for now. Priorities. The *Cortez* film had to be number one on his list—and Mademoiselle Inès Juillard was going to be of great help to him in that particular direction, whether she liked it or not.

Inès slept fitfully, visions of the sadistic Scrofo tormenting her subconscious. She tossed and turned, thrashing in the humid darkness, crying out in her sleep. Julian held her close, whispering comforting endearments, feeling waves of love for her. He tried to make love to her during the night, to calm her unspoken fears, but for the first time in their relationship, Inès refused him. Julian, slightly piqued, tried in vain not to let his thoughts turn to fantasies of Dominique.

"I'm sorry," Inès said shakily. "I'm really sorry, darling. I . . . I . . . don't feel well; I don't know what's wrong with me, Julian, but please understand, my darling."

"Of course, my darling," said Julian soothingly as he held her closely. "I understand."

He drifted back into an untroubled sleep but she lay awake throughout the night, staring up at the ceiling, thinking only of her enemy.

The following morning Inès found patches of blood on the sheets. Horrified, she called her gynecologist in Los Angeles, but it was Sunday; he was out playing golf. Inès crawled back to bed, suggesting to Julian that he go off for the day by himself.

"I'll be fine, darling," she assured him. "I just want to rest."

She didn't tell him about the hemorrhaging. She only hoped that if she rested, it would stop.

Again she didn't want to make love.

Julian was as edgy, restless and nervous as are most actors the day before a production starts. Inès' second rejection of him, this time giving him no reason other than saying that she felt unwell, made him even more restless. Julian was a highly sexed man, and he needed an outlet for the eve-of-picture tension which was building inside him.

He was quite nervous about this film. Even though he had made so many films in England, this was his first American production, and there was much at stake.

He looked down at Inès who lay white and drawn on the pillow, a faint sheen of sweat on her normally cool forehead. "Are you sure you're all right, Inès?"

"Oh, yes, fine, just fine, darling," she murmured weakly. "Just exhaustion from the party."

"Well, I think I'll water-ski after the production meeting," he said. "Are you sure you don't mind being alone, my love?"

"No, I'll be perfectly all right," she said, not wanting him to leave at all, yet needing her solitude to think. "Have a wonderful day, darling—don't fall off the slalom. I'll see you tonight."

She blew him a kiss as he left the room, but he didn't return it, and Inès slumped sadly back on to the crumpled pillow, thinking that Julian's strange premonition of last night was coming horribly true.

❖ *Eleven* ❖

ALTHOUGH IT WAS BARELY eight o'clock, the secret breakfast meeting was in full swing. Irving and Shirley Frankovitch and Hubert Croft sat on the shaded balcony of Hubert's suite, the glass table in front of them piled high with scripts, revisions, budgets, coffee cups, tropical fruit, breads, assorted jams and preserves.

Hubert ate continuously as he talked. When he wanted to make a point, he would jab his finger in the air and gesticulate wildly. Whenever he did this, his resemblance to Mussolini was quite remarkable, thought Shirley, picking at another piece of fruit, Hubert's appetite inspiring her own.

"The main problem, as I see it, is that Nicholas Stone appears to have drastically changed the original script as *you* have written it." He glanced at Shirley. "It was a brilliant script, Shirley, my dear—you did your usual stunning job, absolutely brilliant."

"Every new suggestion we had—every idea—everything clever and innovative—Nick has shot down in flames," Shirley said bitterly, pleased by Hubert's praise. "It was a great script, wasn't it, Irving?"

"Bluey is Nick's main ally," Irving chimed in. "Between the two of them and Zack Domino, who had the total support of the studio, we were completely outflanked."

"No longer." Hubert smiled. "No longer, my dear friends. I've read both scripts—the one you wrote, which Zachary Domino and Nick Stone tried to ruin, and the one of which Nick approves. There is no question in my mind as to the one which possesses the greatest merit."

"Ours!" snapped Shirley, slipping another sliver of papaya between sausage lips.

"Yes, indeed. To that end, we now need to get the studio, and the rest of the cast on our side."

"Of course," Shirley and Irving both agreed.

"Ramona Armande is no problem," Hubert said. "She can, and will, be an excellent ally, as well as being an excellent actress of course."

"But she hardly has a part," Shirley frowned.

"I think we can possibly improve her role," Hubert said smoothly, "without damaging your script at all." Shirley looked dubious, as Hubert continued.

"The little girl—Dominique—what has been her reaction to both scripts? I tried to speak to the young lady last evening but she seemed to have other things on her mind."

"You bet," Shirley smirked. "Looks Brooks' cock is on that young cookie's mind, and it'll be in certain other places besides her mind soon enough, I should think."

Irving shot his wife a disapproving look. Sometimes her gutter language repelled him.

"Really? Very interesting." Hubert made some notes in his brown leather folder. "Tell me more."

Irving sighed. He didn't believe the Julian-Dominique gossip which was circulating already. Shirley had been babbling on about seeing the young actress draped all over him the night before. She rarely missed anything; and her observations gave her a kind of vicarious pleasure, as her sex life with Irving was negligible these days. He tried hard, but basically he wasn't interested anymore.

"His fiancée is a very beautiful woman—why should he want to stray?" Hubert fingered his scar, images of Inès' elegant limbs flashing across his mind

"He's an actor." Shirley shrugged. "You know actors—all cock and no confidence, most of 'em." She again ignored Irving's disapproving look and pushed some more papaya into her mouth. "He's famous for putting it into anything that's playing opposite him. Several of his co-stars have even tried to kill themselves over 'the handsomest man in the world,' " she sneered.

"I see. How do you find *his* allegiances then?" Hubert was still scribbling his notes. "Whose side is he on?"

"Middle of the road," said Irving. "He likes some of our stuff and some of Nick's. He's difficult to sway because he goes for the scene that he feels will be of benefit to the film; he's not nearly as much of an egomaniac as Shirley likes to make out, he's a team player."

"Hmm." Hubert prodded his teeth with a toothpick while he studied a yellow bird perched at the edge of his table, which was pecking happily at the remains of the food, but his thoughts were evidently elsewhere.

"Nick is on the phone *constantly* to the old man in Hollywood. He's some kind of nephew, y'know, and being Greek, of course, they all stick together," Shirley said sarcastically.

"Naturally." Hubert was not surprised. He remembered the fierce family loyalty of the Greeks when he'd commanded Hydra.

"And Sir Crispin?" he asked, referring to the world-famous and much-loved English actor who was playing Emperor Montezuma. "What about him?"

"Oh, just the usual full of shit, faggoty Old Vic actor-knight, who thinks he knows everything," Shirley said waspishly. "Always sounds to me like he's got his mouth full of plums. So far, he's kept a low profile though. Too busy making goo-goo eyes at beach boys. I think he rather fancies our Mr. Brooks, too, so he'll probably agree with anything the great movie star wants."

"We have to get *all* the actors on our side, then there will be no contest with the scripts," said the Italian. "The studio will have to go along with the majority, otherwise we will have nothing but unrest and trouble on the set. That costs money, and you know how the studio hates wasting money."

"Right," said the Frankovitches in unison.

"But how are you going to do that?" Shirley asked. "There's a production meeting with Nick in two hours. He'll fight our script, he always does."

"Leave it to me," Hubert said, Inès' pale face flickering across his mind like some old black-and-white movie. "Leave it to me, my friends— I'll find a way to shoot *our* script, believe me, that I guarantee."

At the official production meeting Bluey fidgeted uncomfortably—he hated confrontations. The only scenes he enjoyed were the ones he viewed from behind the cameras. But Nick needed him. Nick looked odd today. His olive skin was a greenish white, and his normally smiling mouth was clamped tighter than a rattrap.

The oily Italian, whom Bluey had disliked on sight, sat flanked by the Frankovitch team on one side of the table. As a trio, they'd be hard to beat in an ugliness contest, he mused. A war of words was in progress which was becoming even more heated as the tropical sun came beating through the windows.

Hubert Croft held two scripts before him, one red, one blue.

"I will make no bones about it, Nick," he rasped in that gravelly wheeze Nick remembered so well. "This script—" he held the blue one high above his head in a boxer's gesture of victory—"*this one* is magic, pure cinematic *magic.* I read it last night and I cried tears of happiness that I was *privileged* enough to be involved in a project that uses the talents of these two wonderful people who wrote these brilliant words."

Irving and Shirley beamed and nodded like ventriloquists' dummies as Bluey gave an audible groan.

'It's really up to the studio which script we shoot, isn't it?" Nick kept his voice crisp and businesslike, belying his fermenting fury at this man's astonishing audacity. One Italian art film unreleased in America was all he had under his too-tight belt—Nick had checked that out last night— and he was now giving orders like the Mussolini clone he'd always felt himself to be. The hairs on the back of Nick's neck rose as he thought of Scrofo on Hydra, remembering the squat body stuffed into the ridiculous medallioned musical-comedy uniforms, prancing and puffing his way around the island, creating havoc and hatred wherever he went. But he mustn't think about that now—he couldn't. He must get his film made the way *he* wanted it.

If this movie failed, he would be blamed. Not the loathsome trio of the Frankovitches and Scrofo, not even the stars. No, it was *his* ass, Nick Stone's, that was on the line, and all his years of yearning, struggling to be a decent film director, would end up on the scrap heap. God, *why* had Spyros agreed to send this toad, this scowl on legs, to Acapulco? He had telephoned the old man last night and had been told to "shut up and do your job—that's what you're being paid for." So much for family loyalty. With a film as expensive as *Cortez,* someone would have to be the whipping boy if it failed, and he knew that it would be he alone up there on the sacrificial altar.

The script Nick wanted was gritty, historically accurate, with battle scenes which showed the true horror of war. His love scenes were sensually realistic, not the lovey-dovey treacle syrup of the Frankovitches. And his dialogue was pithy and modern, in contrast to theirs, which was stilted and flowery.

Tomorrow they would shoot the first scene of the movie, where Cortez and his men greet Emperor Montezuma on the shore. Nick wanted to shoot Cortez and a small boatload of sailors arriving to greet the emperor, who would only have a handful of warriors with him. The Frankovitch script had six hundred extras with Cortez, and several hundred men on shore with Montezuma. It certainly wasn't going to be easy, but that scene was going to be shot *his* way, or not at all. Let them fire him, he'd go back to the mail room if he had to.

As soon as the production meeting was over Nick hurried back to his room to try again to telephone Elektra. She was his rock, his sanity, and she was wise, not so much in the ways of the modern world, but in the simple ways which really counted. Wise about life, about people, about relationships. Her brand of wisdom was the wisdom of centuries, handed down from generation to generation by the power of the family, by which all Greeks still lived. All international telephone lines had been down yesterday and he had spent a frustrated night, needing to speak to her.

"Elektra." He was so delighted to hear her voice that he immediately started talking rapidly in the Greek she still preferred, even after nearly a decade in America.

"What can I do, Elektra? They're all ganging up on me, I know it—I can't stand it, darling—I'm about ready to walk off this picture even if Uncle Spyros sends me back to work in the mail room."

"No, Nikolai." Elektra's voice was quiet but insistent. "You cannot do that. You have worked too hard for this opportunity—you cannot let it go, Nikolai—and you mustn't."

"But you don't understand, Elektra," he said despairingly. "You don't know who's producing this film."

"Who?" she asked.

"Scrofo," he said grimly. "Umberto Scrofo."

"*What?*" cried Elektra. "No, Nikolai, don't be ridiculous. It's not possible—Scrofo's dead—you remember we heard that he'd died in Italy years ago?"

"Well, he isn't dead," said Nick bleakly. "I'm afraid the bastard's very much alive. He's here, and he's about to make my life a complete fucking misery. I want to *kill* him, Elektra—every time I look at his monstrous face I think about what he did to my mother and I feel this urge to crush the life out of him."

He started to sob into the telephone as Elektra tried to soothe him.

"No, Nikolai, *stop it,* you cannot allow Scrofo to win. First of all you *must* go ahead with the film—you must, you have to—for us, for Uncle Spyros, for the children." She paused as she heard her husband's voice down the long-distance wires, still quavering but more in control.

"I know, Elektra—I know I've got to do it—but how in the bloody *hell* can I possibly work hand in glove with that murdering, thieving piece of scum? How can I?"

"I know it's going to be difficult," she said softly. "I know it will be hard for you to forgive him for what he did to your mother."

"Forgive him—*forgive Gourouni!* That slimy motherfucker! Forget it!" hissed Nick. "I'll never forgive him—how can I? I thought that maybe my hatred had died, Elektra—I thought now that I'm older I could never have the same kind of thoughts I did about that bastard when we were on Hydra. But I was wrong, completely wrong—my hatred was only dormant. It never died."

"How, Nikolai, what do you mean, you were wrong?" she asked fearfully.

"I want to kill him." His lips were very close to the receiver and she heard the intensity in his voice as he spat out the words. "I want to kill him, Elektra, and I'm going to kill him."

"No, Nikolai, don't talk like that." Elektra was afraid as she remembered how he'd tried to strangle her in her own bed. Sometimes her husband's Greek temper and hot blood got the better of him. "You mustn't do anything foolish, Nikolai," she pleaded. "Please don't."

Talking to his wife had made him feel suddenly better, more in control, stronger. "Don't worry—don't worry about it now, Elektra. I'm not going to do it at this moment. I'll make this damned movie, I'll eat crow

—I'll even work side by side with that filthy scum—but when it's *over* with—I swear to you, Elektra, Umberto Scrofo will be a dead man."

It was lunchtime and as Julian walked along the burning sands to Caleta Beach, where the local water-skiing instructors were chattering like magpies beneath cool thatched huts, he thanked God that the production meeting was finally over. Frankly, he didn't really care if Cortez had six men or six hundred with him when he arrived in Mexico. Characterization was the most important thing to him, and the Frankovitches, Croft and Nick had nothing to say about that.

He ordered a *cerveza,* a local beer, instructing Angelito, the boat boy, that he wanted to go skiing right away.

"Oh, *Señor.* I'm sorry," said Angelito. "The Señorita Dominique, she book me for this afternoon."

"Well, what about you, then? Are you free?" Julian asked another boy irritably.

"I's fine with me, *Señor,* fine" smiled Miguel, the proud possessor of a perfect set of gold-capped teeth which must have cost him a year's pay. "My boat ees good—we ski well together, *Señor."*

Suddenly there was a ripple of excitement from all the beach boys as Dominique arrived. Seeing Julian, she gave a little squeal of joy and rushed over to kiss him, letting her firm breasts crush against his chest through her flimsy *pareo.*

"I'm *so* happy to see you, *chéri,"* she gushed. "Why don't we ski together?"

"Well, I—I've just booked Miguel." Julian actually heard himself stutter.

"Oh, don't be silly," cooed the peach, flashing Julian an irresistible smile that would no doubt bewitch her future film audiences as much as it bewitched him. "We can ski together, we're both alone." She grabbed him by the hand and led him down the hot golden sands.

"You can teach me how to para-ski—they say you're so good at it." She smiled mischievously. "Come on, let's go."

Inès' doctor called her back from L.A. after lunch, ordering complete bed rest.

"Complete, you understand? That means you do not *move.* You stay in bed. You get up to go to the bathroom, but that's *it. No* sex for a fortnight, no moving about at all for at least a week."

"Oh, no." Inès was dismayed. "But the film starts tomorrow, and Julian wants me to be on the set all the time, or at least nearby, and well—you know Julian is a very sexy man," she said, feeling rather embarrassed.

"Well, I'm afraid Julian has little choice," said the doctor brusquely. "He can have you, or he can have this baby, but certainly not both. I warn you, Inès, if you exert yourself in any way, you could lose this child. I told you it was going to be difficult for you to conceive, you're lucky that you did; if you want this baby, be a good girl, stay put."

He prescribed pills through a local doctor and Inès asked the concierge to pick them up for her; then she lay back, trying to relax. She felt feverish, her head was a furnace, her mouth parched, but the more she drank, the more thirsty she became. She tried to lie still, but her knees were trembling with fear as she felt warm blood trickling slowly from her—blood that might be her baby.

She couldn't lose this baby that Julian wanted so desperately. Conceived in love, it would be so adored, she couldn't lose it. She drifted into a light, feverish sleep from which the deafening jangle of the old-fashioned telephone next to the bed woke her.

She instantly recognized the chilling tones.

"Mademoiselle Juillard," inquired the gravelly voice.

"Yes?"

"I know you're alone because I saw your husband on the beach this morning, going water-skiing with our beautiful young star."

"So? What do you want, Mr. Croft, I'm resting." Inès' voice was frigid. She refused to let him intimidate her. She was strong, a survivor. Her experiences with men, Scrofo in Paris, Yves' cavalier departure from her life, her perverse English aristocrats, had made her vow that she'd never allow any man to abuse her again. She was a woman of the world, engaged to a famous man, beautiful, secure, happy and pregnant. So she'd tried to kill an enemy officer years ago. So what? What could Umberto Scrofo possibly do to her now that could affect her life? She knew full well what he could do. But would he dare?

If Umberto let it be known to the cast and crew that she'd been a whore, and that he had been one of her clients, they would realize, if they didn't already suspect, that he'd been one of Mussolini's bloodiest generals. Many of the film crew had fought on the beaches of Anzio, Dunkirk and the Pacific, in the deserts of North Africa, or over the skies of Great Britain. The war had ended scarcely ten years ago, but many people still treated Germans, Japanese and Italians with antipathy, particularly if they thought that they had been actively involved in it. No, Signor Scrofo would make a bad mistake with everyone if it was discovered that he had been a high-ranking officer in occupied Paris. She held a good hand of cards in her well-manicured fingers—she could bluff him out.

"Since you're alone," continued the hateful voice, "I must insist upon seeing you. It is for your own benefit, Mademoiselle Juillard."

Inès groaned. "Listen to me. I'm unwell. My doctor has told me I must rest, which is exactly what I'm trying to do. If you feel you have any business with me, please state it on the telephone."

"Mademoiselle Juillard, right now I'm downstairs in the lobby of your hotel." Umberto's voice held more than a hint of menace. "I will take up no more than five minutes of your precious time, but I must see you." The "precious" held an insulting innuendo. "There are several people standing around here, including some crew members of *Cortez*. I do not think, Mademoiselle Juillard, that you would want them to hear what I have to say to you, do you?"

"Very well," said Inès with a deep sigh. "Room seventeen, on the second floor." And she banged down the receiver.

❀   ❀   ❀

Julian and Dominique lay back comfortably on their brightly colored towels as the tropical sun tanned their bodies. The boat was a relatively crude affair, but Angelito was an expert at maneuvering it. Acapulco Bay was peacefully calm, and the boatman made a smooth circuit before turning towards La Roqueta Island.

Julian found Dominique's proximity, as she snuggled next to him, unnervingly erotic. Her eyes had cast a spell on him again, and her curved, honey-colored body, in the tiniest bikini, was driving his cock mad. He usually made love to Inès at least once a day; being deprived yesterday and this morning had made him acutely aware that the damn thing had a mind of its own, especially when it was near Dominique. His erection was becoming so obvious that he edged away from her before he made a complete fool of himself.

"Angelito, I want to ski around the bay," he ordered. "Stop the boat, I'll jump off here." The tiny craft slowed down and Julian leaped over the side into the sparkling water, thankfully feeling his erection subsiding.

Angelito threw him a ski and the rope. Julian signaled to the boy, with a jerk the ancient boat sputtered and accelerated, and Julian rose from the water on his slalom like an arrow. Dominique cheered, admiring his marvelous physique. She thought that Locks Brooks possessed a body and a face which even a Greek god would envy. His week of rest and rigorous morning workouts had brought him back to perfect shape. His hair was now slicked down flat to his head by the wind and water as he gestured to Angelito to go faster.

There were only a few luxury pleasure boats in the port and around the bay, but many speedboats and tiny sailing boats. Angelito steered the boat past the "morning" beach, where laughing brown children played together in the waves while their weary fathers stared blankly out to sea. Mothers, aunts, sisters and grandmothers ceremoniously laid out the Sunday lunch on the beach for the one day the family all spent together. The children, many of them naked, since bathing suits were a luxury few Mexican families could afford, waved excitedly at the passing speedboats.

They zoomed past the "afternoon" beach, the more tourist-oriented area of Acapulco, where under straw hats overweight vacationers from cruise ships sampled the pleasures of this new resort. Sipping *piña coladas*, they oiled themselves as the tropical sun turned their bodies various shades of scarlet. On the shore, Julian could see the skeleton of the new Hilton Hotel, its iron girders an eyesore. If those hideous high-rise hotels start being built along this shore, it will only be a matter of time before this glorious place is ruined forever, he thought. Saltwater stung his face as he criss-crossed over the wake several times with professional panache, until he finally let go of the rope and waited for the boat to pick him up.

"Bravo," cried Dominique. "Oh, Julian, you're brilliant. Where did you learn to ski so brilliantly?"

She leaned over the bow of the boat, looking so sexy that it would have been hard for any male over the age of seven not to have been affected by her. Julian had noticed the bulge in Angelito's trunks when the boy helped Dominique into his boat, brushing his arm unnecessarily against her lightly tanned shoulder. She was an incredibly sensual girl, a little minx who was learning—too well—the art of driving men crazy.

Angelito looked questioningly towards an island of mustard-colored rock shaped like a fat man sleeping after a good lunch. Julian nodded, and the boat sped across the bobbing waves.

One o'clock was early for lunch at La Roqueta, and few people were there. The jovial *patron* offered them the most secluded table in the restaurant, his eyes goggling at the sight of Dominique in her virtually transparent *pareo*. Angelito's brief words in Spanish gave him the low-down on Julian, the big movie star.

"Let's have the biggest, strongest, most Mexicanish drink in the house," Dominique said, a mischievous glint in her eyes.

"What a marvelous idea," Julian laughed, already half drunk with her charms. "Let's have two each."

Soon they were sipping, through straws, from coconut shells in which pineapples, bananas, three kinds of rum, tequila, brandy and fruit juice had been expertly blended.

"Mmm. Delicious." Dominique smiled. "Better than a chocolate malt any day."

The tropical air on his skin, the sense of well-being and exhilaration from water-skiing, and the sight of this delectable female all left Julian feeling incredibly virile and young. Not even the most exotic lovemaking with Inès had ignited him in this way; he felt like a slow-burning coal which had either to be doused completely or be allowed to burst into leaping tongues of fire. He didn't understand himself at all. He didn't want to.

He downed both of his drinks fast, then blurted out, "God, you're so beautiful. I know this sounds strange—and I know I shouldn't say this—but I want to kiss you, Dominique." All inhibitions seemed to have flown and he watched the slow smile spread across her exquisite face.

"It's what I want too, Julian," she whispered huskily. "So much."

Her total lack of pretense and archness was so unlike the ways of the women he usually met that Julian felt like a schoolboy again. That delicious innocence which hadn't yet learned to say *no* when desire was saying *yes* made her sensuality more erotic than if she were lying naked in bed beside him.

After several more strong drinks and a lunch of plump grilled shrimps, lobster and rice, Julian and Dominique set off to explore the tiny, almost deserted island. Only the restaurant, now half filled with tourists, was evidence of any habitation. Julian felt as if he were going to burst. The touch of Dominique's hand on his arm was sending electric shocks of desire through his whole being, as they strolled around the rocks and out of sight of the few tourists.

Dominique felt a shiver of excitement and anticipation as they rounded a corner where an ancient banana tree shaded a small beach.

Julian stopped, held Dominique's lovely face between his hands and let his mouth gently explore hers. Her lips were petal-soft, more yielding than any he had ever kissed before. They were innocent, naive, the lips of a little girl—then as her tongue came to claim his, they became wantonly erotic. It was the mouth of a woman who knew exactly what she wanted and knew how to get it, and knew instinctively where all the pleasure sources lay. His hands dropped to the ribbons of her bikini top. How he longed to hold these glorious breasts, to trace their contours, exploring with fingers and tongue, to watch her excitement increase. But Dominique was not quite ready to grant his wish yet.

Moving away from him, she took a bottle of suntan oil from her straw bag and, leaning against the trunk of the banana tree, started to rub it slowly into her shoulders and chest. Her head thrown back, her eyes closed, Julian watched, mesmerized, as her bikini top started inching down and her rosy nipples became visible. Her breathing accelerated as she started to massage them with the oil. They glistened in the sunlight, her nipples, like pink shells, now erect. Julian moved towards her, but she stopped him with a gesture, continuing her erotic caresses—the ones that Gaston had taught her last summer. Her top was off now; her fingers had worked their way down to her flat stomach, to the band of her bikini bottom. Julian was now dizzy with desire as the vision shimmered before him in the heat. Soon she was completely naked, abandoned, leaning against the tree, her skin glistening, and her eyes signaled that now it was time.

Dominique's fingers entwined in Julian's thick brown hair as his tongue and lips pleasured her breasts and his own fingers encircled her soft but muscled rear. She gave little whimpers of ecstasy as she stripped him of his shorts, aggressively pulling him down onto the hot sand, oblivious to discomfort. She took his cock into her mouth as Gaston had taught her, and he felt the eruption start to rise deep within him, an explosion which took every ounce of his concentration and willpower to control. Her catlike eyes smiled up at him as her lips anointed him and she slid warm, hard, bursting skin in and out of her hot mouth.

He had to take her now—he could wait no longer. He forgot Inès—forgot their love, their baby, their marriage. All he could think of was this enchantress. Gently he lifted her from him, moving until his body lay on top of hers for a magic second or two, then with a groan of pleasure he entered her. She was a more than willing partner, moistly receptive. Their sweat mingling, lips and tongues entwined, her eyes wide open, smiling, willing him on, he plunged into her, his face contorted in fierce ecstasy as he set the rhythm of their passion. She could feel an imminent and unfamiliar convulsion building inside her.

"I love you," she whispered, "I love you, Julian. I love you," truly meaning it as she cried out his name in joy.

As the sound of speedboats hummed in the distance and the waves lapped near their bucking bodies, the lovers orgasmed together with cries which seemed to echo around the whole bay.

And from far away, the lone passenger in a small motorboat focused his telescopic lens and clicked the shutter of his camera again and again.

With her silk kimono sticking uncomfortably to her moist skin, Inès lay on her bed in agony listening to what the detestable Scrofo had come to say. "Please, get to the point, Mr. Croft," she said weakly, lighting a cigarette. "I must rest, it's my doctor's orders."

"Then you shouldn't smoke." His tone was irritatingly patronizing. "Especially since you are pregnant."

"How do you know I'm pregnant? No one here knows. Besides, it's none of your business."

His voice was steely. "I know everything, I'm the producer of this film and I make it my business to know everything about everyone." But he smiled inwardly. It had been an educated guess, but it had hit its mark. "Don't forget that, ever—don't underestimate me either, Mademoiselle Juillard."

"Well, what's your business with me? I have nothing to do with your precious film, so what do you want?"

"You have *everything* to do with the film. You're the fiancée of the star. It seems that the great star doesn't much like the excellent script which Mr. and Mrs. Frankovitch, writers of the highest proficiency and artistic merit, have written. He and Bluey Regan were quite difficult with me this morning." His pig eyes drilled into hers. "And the Greek, Nicholas Stone, the so-called *wunderkind* director who has directed only two films, he also does not like the script."

"But what does all this have to do with me?" Inès cried. "I hardly know Nick Stone or the Frankovitches."

Scrofo's body oozed over the edge of the chair in which he sat while staring at her contemptuously. She felt a terrible stab of fear. How could this man not inspire terror, with his evil smile, twisted mind and grotesque body in his vulgar and self-conscious clothes. He looked ridiculous in his powder-blue safari suit, his hairy arms bulging out of the short sleeves, and the military-style gold buttons which looked about to burst from their buttonholes as they strained across his gross belly. In spite of herself a look of revulsion came into her face as she noticed the silk scarf knotted loosely around his neck, and the hideous scar for which she had herself been responsible. But he'd made her do it, there was nothing else she could have done. She shuddered at the memory of the agony and humiliation Scrofo had caused her, and a cold fury came over her as she pictured herself as that young girl in Paris. How could she ever forget the pain? Dr. Langley's sinister words suddenly came back to her: "You're a healthy woman, Inès, and there's no reason why you shouldn't have a beautiful baby, but you've obviously had a very bad time with someone. You have some scar tissue, you must have been injured once."

"Could it affect the baby?" Inès had asked tearfully.

"Not if you're careful. But you've suffered quite a bit of damage to your womb and cervix—and I'm not saying it necessarily will, but it *might,* affect your pregnancy unless, as I say, you're very careful."

Now as Inès stared back at Scrofo with undisguised loathing in her eyes, she suddenly understood. Of course, this man was the very reason why she was lying here in her bed of pain, bleeding, unable to move, all because of those monstrous and perverted acts which he'd inflicted on her years ago.

Scrofo moved from the wicker chair to stand at the end of Inès' bed, his brown boots clattering on the marble floor, his slug-white face covered with a thin film of sweat. Inès could hear luncheon being served and happy Mexican music from the patio below. She looked out at the beautiful day, at the sun-flecked cottonwool clouds. How she wanted to be outside, anywhere but here, alone with this horror.

"So," he said, his voice now becoming venomous and threatening, "I'll spell it out for you, you murdering whore." Involuntarily he fingered his scar, his lips twisting in that familiar and repulsive way she could never forget.

"Nobody knows anything of your past here, do they? Not even your precious fiancé?" He looked at her menacingly. "Do they, Inès? Prostitute, whore, streetwalker—from what age? How old were you when I had you? Thirteen? Fourteen?"

Inès felt her brain fill with a kind of red mist. She was reliving the nightmare—she could almost feel the razor in her hand as she'd sliced it across his yielding throat. She felt her stomach contracting in intermittent spasms of pain. Warm blood had made her thighs slippery. She made an immense effort to calm herself.

"It's none of your business, Scrofo! Tell me what you want of me, for God's sake." She stubbed out her cigarette, lighting another immediately. The bed was now wet with blood, but she couldn't move. There was a buzzing in her head. This spectre from her past was going to ruin her future, her perfect future.

"I'm not going to say anything more to upset you now." He looked at her in mock pity. "You're white as a sheet, you don't look at all well. You should get some rest, so I'll get to the point and then leave you in peace. I want to tell you just one thing. As I have told you, I have discovered that nobody either in America or on this film—and most certainly not Julian Brooks—is aware of your sordid past. I'm going to need your help at certain strategic times during the filming. I know you discuss the script with your fiancé, I know he depends very much on your advice. When I tell you—" he leaned towards her menacingly—"I repeat, when I tell you that I want Julian to prefer scene A to scene B, I want you to coerce him, exert every particle of influence that you have on him to see that he accepts my choice. *Do you understand?* If you *don't* comply with my wishes, well, let's just say there'll be very serious consequences."

She nodded silently. She would have agreed to anything just to get this creature out of her sight.

"All right, I will. I promise," she whispered, holding back her tears.

"Good, then your secret, as they say, will be safe with me, Inès my dear." He waddled over to the door. "The first two scenes will be arriving

this evening. Be sure you insist that Mr. Brooks prefers the first one."
And with that he closed the door behind him.

With an animal sound, Inès staggered to the bathroom, seeing, to her horror, that her blood was streaking the marble tiles scarlet.

"Oh, no," she cried. "No, no. Oh, please, God, no!"

◆ *Twelve* ◆

A FTER THE INCIDENT with Croft, Inès had spent the rest of the afternoon attempting to recover. When Julian returned from his afternoon with Dominique, she was able to greet him with a semblance of normality. Caught up in her own personal trauma, she failed to notice that Julian was somewhat distant, lacking his usual affectionate attentiveness.

But he was still extremely concerned about her condition, even though she assured him that Dr. Langley had said that, as long as she was careful, all would be well. Julian was secretly relieved that lovemaking was forbidden for at least two weeks.

It would give him time to think, and to savor the enchanted afternoon he'd spent with Dominique, who had visited him in his dreams last night. He awoke, covered with sweat, and to feelings of guilt and horror, mumbling her name. But Inès was sleeping soundly, a pill helping her to expunge the memory of Scrofo's threats.

Julian was worried and ashamed of his behavior with Dominique. He tried hard to analyze what spell she must have cast over him, but he couldn't. Their lovemaking that afternoon had been both wonderfully exhilarating and quite exceptional, but maybe it was because she was so young, just a schoolgirl really, and the added spice of being outdoors and the possibility of being discovered had made it all the more thrilling.

He sighed heavily, looking at his frowning face in the bathroom mirror. "You're a rat, Julian Brooks," he mouthed to himself. "A dirty rotten rat. What the fuck are you doing?" He gazed at himself for a minute or two but his reflection gave him no answers. Throwing cold water on his face, he walked back into the bedroom and settled down to study his dialogue for tomorrow's scenes.

In the morning, while they breakfasted on their terrace, Inès and Julian chatted desultorily. This was to be the first day of shooting, and he seemed preoccupied. There was a dull ache in the pit of Inès' stomach—whether from a possible miscarriage or the fear of Scrofo's threats, she didn't know. She only knew that for the first time since they'd met she was pleased that Julian was going out. The previous evening she'd done her utmost to persuade him that the scene in script A was so much better for him as an actor than the scene in script B. Appealing to his ego seemed to have succeeded and she thought she'd managed to convince him, even though he went off with both scripts in his haversack.

She was left alone with her thoughts, and with only the sounds of the seabirds for company.

Nick tried hard to overcome his first-day nerves as he stood in the bay, starting to block the first scene of the morning when Cortez, Pizarro and the r men arrive on the shores of Mexico for the first time. Cortez was to be greeted by Emperor Montezuma and his warriors, while his beautiful daughter, Princess Isabella, stayed modestly in the background.

Dominique had been enveloped by the wardrobe department in thick folds of embroidered linen. She had little to do in this scene but play the virgin maiden, eyes appropriately downcast as she sees bold Cortez for the first time.

She tried to catch Julian's eye as she was sitting on her canvas chair under a large umbrella planted in the sand. It was only eight in the morning, but the heat was already overpowering, encased as she was in the yards of itchy fabric, with an enormous hank of false hair under her headdress, which weighed a ton. She cooled herself with a woven straw fan and sipped ice water as her makeup crew buzzed around her.

Suddenly an aide came running down the beach waving two telegrams —one for Nick and one for Croft. When Croft had read his, a triumphant look came into his face. He knew victory was his now.

Julian had called him late the night before, informing him that he preferred the first script. Croft had also had a short telephone conversation with Dominique, who'd been anxious to do whatever Julian wanted. Sir Crispin too had agreed.

Now there would be a more audience-pleasing spectacle, more pomp and circumstance, more crowd scenes, more bloody battle scenes. Croft and the Frankovitches would make *Cortez* a much more important movie —a worthy successor to *The Robe*, *Quo Vadis* and the other epic blockbusters of the fifties. The actors would glitter and shine like thirty-carat diamonds in a Van Cleef & Arpels setting.

Nick stared in silence at his own telegram, which was also from his uncle. He'd lost.

Spyros Makopolis had made it abundantly clear. He and the vice-presidents of MCCP, having carefully reviewed the relative merits of the two scripts, had been unanimous in their verdict. The most bankable script was definitely the Frankovitch one. That was the one they wanted Nick to shoot, that was the one he was going to have to shoot.

They wanted pageantry, histrionics, lavish spectacle and violent battles. The Mexican extras were paid so little that it wouldn't make much difference to the budget if the film company used sixty or six hundred of them. They were even now being outfitted in the uniforms of sixteenth-century sailors and warriors, while two hundred and fifty others, stripping to the waist, were having wads of black hair attached to their scalps and skimpy loincloths draped around their hips.

"You've won, you leprous bastard," Nick hissed, grabbing the Italian's arm with furious strength as Scrofo's livid face stared back at him in triumph.

"You may have won this round, pigface, but don't you *dare* tell me where I should put the extras or the actors or any piece of fucking furniture in any scene. Don't you dare tell me how to direct my actors— they'll say the motherfucking lines *my* way, and if you put your fat face near any one of my crew, I'll slam it into that rock until it's mincemeat."

Dominique pricked up her ears and watched with the rest of the cast and crew in amazement as Nick and Hubert Croft battled it out at the water's edge.

Next to her sat Sir Crispin Peake, his noble brow beaded with sweat which trickled out from under his large black wig. He now put aside his *Times* crossword to watch the argument between the two men. He never liked to miss anything, and he and Julian exchanged knowing glances.

Sir Crispin adored Julian, and they'd been in several West End plays together. He had agreed to appear in this film only for a substantial salary. Although his *King Lear* had been a great success with the London critics, the public, alas, had not flocked in any great numbers to see it. He'd accepted this job partly in order to save face but, as he was fond of remarking, also to "keep Tony in gold taps." Tony was his handsome young live-in companion, who was constantly redecorating their two enormous houses.

As befitted his position as one of Britain's theatrical knights, he'd been given his own personal dresser, the ubiquitous Alf, who busied himself bringing "His Nibs" all that was required for his rarefied English blood to better withstand the tropical climate. Even now in the ninety-degree heat, Sir Crispin was sipping a hot cup of Lapsang souchong tea from a delicate china cup, as he held a Friebourg Treyer cigarette between his elegant fingers. A Chinese paper fan was doing little to cool him, and his patrician features were flushed.

Scrofo's much more plebeian features were also flushed as he strode about on the sand, waving his arms and shouting at Nick in his throaty squawk, his voile shirt already wringing wet and his few remaining strands of hair stuck to his scarlet scalp. He was exhausted. Unable to sleep last night due to a combination of heat and excitement, he'd been up at dawn, awaiting confirmation from Spyros Makopolis that the studio would agree to shoot the Frankovitch script. And he had! Success was his.

Nick and Bluey now found themselves outflanked, outnumbered and outvoted.

Umberto started to speak, but Nick's fingers, which were still holding onto his arm, dug tighter.

"You don't remember me, Gourouni, do you? But I remember you—I remember you very fucking well no matter what you call yourself now I'd never forget you, never. I'll do this fucking script the way you and those two scumbags and the fucking studio want me to. I'll have the thousand fucking extras and the goddamn battle scenes and the charge of the fucking Light Brigade." The whole beach was now riveted by the screaming fury of the normally soft-spoken young director. He towered over the squat Italian, and even though the crew couldn't quite hear any of the words, the body language was unmistakable.

'But just watch it, you pasta-loving prickhead," Nick spat out venom-ously. "Watch your fat ass. I'll play *everything* by the rules, but it's gonna be *my* film, the way I want it, with or without a crowd of extras standing around scratching their balls." With a snort of contempt he released Scrofo's arm and the Italian stumbled, almost falling over.

Taking his well-fingered Greek worry beads out of his pocket, Nick started turning them in his fingers rapidly while calling, "Okay, Bluey, let's go. I want first team and all the extras for a line-up—*now!*"

As the Pacific ebbed around Umberto's handmade shoes, he was torn between elation and blinding rage. Yes, he'd won. He was going to pro-duce a film with all the brilliance which he'd put into *La Città Perduta,* but the angry young director had berated and humiliated him in front of the entire cast and crew, made him look idiotic—weak—foolish. And God, how he hated to look a fool, for people to laugh at him.

Stone's hatred, Scrofo thought, was out of all proportion to their short working relationship. They'd known each other only for a few days. Since Nick was Greek, Umberto wondered if perhaps he'd lived on Hydra during the time of his command. So what? The Greeks were all so stupid. All those peasants had gone to their deaths without protest or resistance, whether it was by starvation, torture or firing squad, like silent and obedi-ent sheep. He had no respect for any of them. Reluctantly, however, Scrofo had to admit that even though he'd humiliated him, this Greek had balls.

"Well done," Ramona said admiringly. "Well done, Hubert my dear." The sun was glittering on her heavily embroidered costume as she gushed, "I'm *so* glad we're going to shoot the Frankovitch script, darling, I *much* prefer it."

Umberto knew she preferred it only because she had a few extra scenes to play, but he smiled his thanks, even though he was seething, and conscious of the entire crew looking at him out of the corners of their eyes—probably laughing at him, he thought.

"Now, Hubert, I have an idea." Ramona linked a braceleted arm through his while they strolled across the beach towards the setup. "That wretched hotel where you're staying has no air-conditioning and such terrible service, I'm sure you didn't sleep much last night. You didn't, did you?"

Umberto shook his head.

"I'm in that huge house all by my little self," she said coquettishly. "I have more guest rooms than I know what to do with. You'd be *far* more comfortable staying there with me. You can have the whole second level of rooms for your offices and secretary, and of course we're only five minutes from the Villa Vera. What d'you think, Hubert dear, would you like that?"

"I should like that very much indeed. Thank you, Ramona my dear," he said. "You're very thoughtful, as usual."

"Wonderful," Ramona beamed. "I've also asked the little French girl, Dominique, and her guardian, to stay." She leaned confidentially towards him. "It's not safe for young women to walk alone at night in Acapulco anymore. I heard that the chaperone was attacked and almost raped on the beach only a few nights ago."

"Really?" Umberto raised his eyebrows, looking towards the ghostly, waiflike figure of Agathe who was hovering near Dominique. Who could possibly want to rape *her*?

Since there were never any secrets on a location, the entire crew seemed to know the story of Agathe's narrow escape from the thugs in the bar. And some of the boys were already taking bets as to when Julian would pack Inès off to Europe so that Dominique could move in on him lock, stock and eyeliner. It seemed to be even money on that.

❖ *Thirteen* ❖

Sᴜ Cʀɪꜱᴘɪɴ Pᴇᴀᴋᴇ ꜱᴛᴀʀᴇᴅ down the beach at Dominique's tanned dancer's body as she played around at the water's edge with several of the younger male crew members. They had been shooting for over a week now, and she was friendly with all of them.

"Surely that child must be jail bait?" he asked Ramona, who sat sipping iced orange pekoe tea with him beneath the shade of an enormous striped umbrella.

"Of course she is," smiled Ramona, who had become more than a little maternal towards Dominique. "But I'm quite sure she's still an innocent, Crispin; after all she is only sixteen and she comes from a good family in France."

Sir Crispin slowly nodded his head, which was heavy with the plaited hair of a dozen Chinese maidens.

"I wouldn't believe that for a second, my dear. And what's France got to do with it?" he asked, watching the squealing and giggling Dominique being chased into the waves by one of the better-looking stuntmen. "She certainly has oomph, but she looks as if she likes to do a great deal more than just frolic in the waves."

Ramona took off her sunglasses in order to get a clearer view of the laughing nymph at the water's edge.

"Nonsense, Crispin, Agathe guards that girl like a tigress. She couldn't *possibly* be anything but a virgin. There's no doubt she's destined for stardom, wouldn't you say? With that face and that unbelievable shape— how could she not be?"

"I wouldn't know, my dear, she's not really my type," Sir Crispin replied with an ironic little smile. He looked quizzically into Ramona's painted face. She really was a creature of cosmetic myth.

'My dear, it was your star which surely shone the brightest when the Hollywood dream factory was at its zenith. Now, of course, the star system, as we both used to know it, is fast disintegrating," he said.

"It most certainly is," agreed Ramona. "And the studios are signing fewer and fewer contract players each year; the big stars are now all trying desperately to be independent."

"Out of the dozens that they do sign, how much longer after the initial burst of fame do you think their moment of celebrity will last?" Sir Crispin asked dryly.

Ramona made no reply as she thought about her own long and eventful career, remembering herself at Dominique's age.

"What, I wonder, does *her* future hold," the old knight speculated, almost to himself. "Is she a Cinderella girl who will return to St. Tropez in a few years to become just another *femme de ménage?* Or will she become an addict of all the hoopla and idolatry, and throw herself away on a succession of unworthy men?"

"She'll hardly do *that*, Crispin," laughed Ramona. "She's so ravishing that they'll be standing in line to escort her. She's not a girl to lose her head over a man."

"Humph," said Sir Crispin enigmatically as Julian joined them, hot and sweating from the scene he'd just been shooting.

"Jesus, it's a scorcher," he gasped, ripping off his velvet doublet and pulling open his shirt to the waist. "How you stand that bloody wig on your head all day, old boy, I'll never know. Why on earth don't you take it off?"

"My dear fellow," Sir Crispin answered drolly, "this hideous object is attached to my poor scant-haired scalp by at least a pound of the most foul-smelling glue. I can assure you that its removal every evening is absolute torture, dear boy, worse than anything which could have been thought up by Torquemada and his frightful Spanish Inquisition."

Ramona and Julian both laughed as Julian's dresser brought him a cold glass of beer, which he tipped to his lips, watching the object of his new passion, who was still cavorting in the waves.

Sir Crispin turned his beady eyes towards Julian, paying particular attention to the muscles of his golden chest, which quivered deliciously as he swallowed his beer. Sir Crispin was always attracted to a magnificent male body, and few he'd ever seen were as magnificent as Looks Brooks'. Julian always reminded him of a breathtaking Bernini sculpture of Apollo that he'd once seen in a museum in Rome.

"Dear boy, we were just talking about yon vestal virgin," he said waggishly. "I was saying to Ramona that I thought she was *no* stranger to the world of the championship blow job. What do you think, Julian?"

Julian almost choked on his beer, and to his horror felt himself blushing.

"Now, now, Crispin, we'll have none of that," he said with a splutter as his dresser sprang forward to mop his velvet breeches.

"Crispin, you're terrible," chuckled Ramona. "Dominique's just a baby. How can you say such things?"

"It seems to me that the younger they are, the more sex they always want," said Sir Crispin authoritatively.

"Well, I suppose you should know, old chap, shouldn't you?" Julian winked, grinning at Ramona.

Suddenly Dominique let out an ear-piercing shriek as one of the men she'd been fooling around with jumped on top of her in the water.

"Our baby is growing up fast," observed Sir Crispin, his eyes glittering with amusement from behind his sunglasses. "And, my dears, if *she's* a virgin then *I'm* Edith Evans."

"Now you come to mention it, you've actually developed an uncanny resemblance to Edith recently," Julian teased, trying his best to ignore Dominique, who was now completely soaked, her long hair flying in the wind, as she was chased repeatedly across the waves by two large and excitable members of the camera crew.

"Yes, I think it must be the wig," laughed Ramona.

"That mass of hair, old chap, is identical to the one Edith had to wear as Cleopatra," Julian said, tears of laughter coming into his eyes.

"But I have bigger breasts than she has," Sir Crispin said archly, reveling in his audience's laughter. "I remember going to see a matinée of Edith's Cleopatra," he reminisced. "My dear, the audience consisted of three old ladies and an Afghan hound, and the Afghan hound appeared to be having the most fun."

They laughed again as Dominique, like a giggling dervish, streaked towards them, hotly pursued by her group of admirers.

"Julian, oh, Julian, help me please!" she squealed in mock terror as she threw herself down into his lap.

"These men, they're teasing me so much," she said, nestling her wet body against his warm chest. "Please help me, Julian," she said plaintively, peeking up at him through her wet, sooty eyelashes which partially hid the secret message contained in her eyes. "Please!"

As Julian felt an embarrassing erection stirring, he quickly but playfully tumbled her off his knees and onto the sand.

"What do you think you're doing, young lady?" he scolded. "Nick told me the next scene is with you and all of us, and here you are messing about in the waves. You're a very naughty girl."

Dominique pouted prettily up at him.

"Most unprofessional, dear girl," said Sir Crispin, wagging an admonishing finger. "Never keep them waiting on the set, my dear—better you wait for them—as alas we've all been doing for *hours.*"

"Okay, okay," laughed Dominique, cheekily grabbing Julian's beer from him and taking a large sip. "I'm going—I'll be ready in less than ten minutes, I promise, you know how fast I can be."

"We'll take your word for it," murmured Sir Crispin, noticing with a frisson of pleasure that Julian was rearranging the crotch of his trousers. He congratulated himself for not having missed the stimulating sight of Julian's sudden and impressive erection. "Oh, well," said Sir Crispin blithely, "where there's youth, there's bound to be gaiety—isn't that true, Julian dear boy?"

"Absolutely," Julian agreed, finishing his beer and casually picking up his script to cover his lap.

"She's certainly a bright and spirited young maiden, our little *mademoiselle*." Sir Crispin smiled. "I daresay she'll break many a heart before we're all much older."

The small house party usually dined quietly each evening on Ramona's second terrace. Shooting finished at sundown, and after Umberto had attended a series of production meetings in his offices, spoken to Hollywood half a dozen times, and screamed at everyone who'd crossed him that day, a calm, civilized dinner would be served.

Dominique adored living in Ramona's palatial mansion; it was as if she'd found herself in some great big beautiful doll's house. Agathe was quietly impressed by some of the pictures and sculptures, and she lived in constant nervous anticipation that Julian might be invited to dinner.

When Ramona first extended a dinner invitation to Nick, the young Greek asked her bluntly, "Will Croft be there?"

"Why, yes—of course he will," answered Ramona, somewhat flustered by Nick's burning brown eyes. "He's one of my houseguests."

"Then thank you very much for the invitation, Princess," he said, "but I don't intend to spend any more time in the company of that creature than is absolutely necessary."

"I see," said Ramona, raising penciled brows, not seeing at all. "In that case perhaps it would be better if I didn't invite you again."

She seemed so piqued that Nick, always trying to be the diplomat and also a genuine admirer of Ramona, said, "Please don't take it personally, Princess. You know, as well as the whole crew does, that there's no love lost between Croft and me. In fact we loathe each other. Please try to understand, will you?"

"Of course," said Ramona graciously. "But I hope that one day you may change your mind."

He smiled grimly. "If the toad is guaranteed not to be there, then I'd be delighted to dine with you, Princess."

"It's a date," smiled Ramona, mentally removing Nick from the guest list which she kept permanently in her head.

Sir Crispin Peake, whose eccentric English humor livened up the sometimes somber gatherings, was one of Ramona's favorite guests. Attractive young diplomats from the American embassy, visiting socialites, film stars and politicians would also often be asked. Ramona's table was famous, and invitations from her were in demand, but to Agathe's disappointment Julian never came to her dinner parties.

Ines had become virtually a prisoner in her hotel suite. Dr. Langley had insisted that she spend the next seven months in bed if she really wanted to have this baby.

"Just get up for the wedding day. And *no sex.* Not even necking," he told her continually.

Although Julian had been extremely understanding about her condition, Inès knew there was a limit to a man's sexual altruism. She was torn between her love for him, and wanting to show it, and her longing to have his child. Every night they were together, and he studied his script while she lay in bed trying not to feel sorry for herself, trying to make bright and interesting conversation. But it was difficult to make interesting conversation when she spent every day flat on her back staring at the ceiling. Although Inès tried hard, she had the ominous feeling that Julian was drifting away from her, his mind on other things. She knew that the movie was arduous and that there was a good deal of tension on the set. What Inès didn't know was that each lunch hour and practically every day after shooting, Looks Brooks and Dominique were making passionate love behind the locked doors and curtained windows of her trailer.

◆*Fourteen*◆

THE STUDIO WAS ECSTATIC about the first week's rushes. Nick was doing a masterful job of injecting an intimate, realistic style into the Frankovitches' overly melodramatic and flowery script. The result was a brilliant contrast with the sixteenth-century grandeur and pageantry. The studio believed it was going to create a new look in film, and they were eagerly planning other historical epics for Nick to direct.

Each day Agathe would sit on the set quietly watching, saying little. The crew hardly ever spoke to her. With her strangely forbidding looks and manner, and her stiff and correct English, it was almost like trying to communicate with a wax mannequin. She rehearsed Dominique in her lines and watched over her while she daydreamed constantly of Julian.

Since Agathe's experience on the beach she regarded all men, with the exception of Julian, with great suspicion, but she was totally blind to the smoldering affair that was going on between him and Dominique. To her, Dominique was nothing more than a schoolgirl. Granted, she was an actress now and in a major motion picture, but she was still a child, a girl who knew nothing of life. Agathe's mind was a kaleidoscope of images of Julian. She couldn't keep her eyes off him when she sat on the sidelines at the beaches, lagoons and mountains, watching the shooting. Through her dark glasses and with a hat tipped over her forehead she would observe his every gesture, his every movement.

The fact that he was friendly, even flirtatious, with Dominique was attributed by Agathe to the natural closeness that all film people seemed to develop with one another. How she envied them that. The easy jokes, the sarcastic familiarity which bordered on a kind of rudeness, seemed to bird them all closely together.

The only person who spent any time with her, other than Dominique, was Sir Crispin Peake. He often sat beside her underneath a striped umbrella, regaling her with long-ago anecdotes and tales of the British stage. Agathe thought him tedious, since she found it difficult to understand his theatrical humor, but she tried to sit near him because Julian adored him and would always come over to talk to him between setups. With his doublet off, his chest gleaming with a faint sheen of perspiration, he would laugh his head off at the old knight's stories and captivate Agathe still more. After those days when she sat with Sir Crispin and Julian, Agathe's nights would be gloriously erotic and she would pleasure herself frantically.

One day, when no one was near, she purloined another of Julian's shirts from his trailer. It was of white cambric, one that he'd worn in a dueling scene. The wardrobe woman had several doubles of it, and this one had been ripped. As it couldn't be used again, Agathe didn't consider that she was stealing. She was just borrowing something of Julian's which would bring him even closer to her. She could almost feel his body next to hers when she lay with it at night.

As for that prostitute fiancée of his, Inès, she never appeared, although rumors were rife around the unit that she was pregnant and confined to bed. Pregnant! Agathe didn't ask Julian if it was true; she hardly dared talk to him at all, because she always blushed so furiously that she felt sure he could read her thoughts. But she was filled with bitter rage that this magnificent man could have sown his seed in the body of that traitorous whore.

◀ *Fifteen* ▶

DOMINIQUE NOW BELIEVED that she was madly in love with Julian. Two weeks of abandoned lovemaking made her want him all the more. When they were together on the set it was as if an electric current flowed and crackled between their bodies. Her eyes glowed whenever she was near him, and their sexual combustion on the screen was so visible that rapturous telegrams were sent from Hollywood to Nick congratulating him on creating and capturing such magical chemistry on film. The screen almost melted the first time Julian and Dominique kissed. Gasps of amazement rippled through the screening rooms, as many of the normally hardbitten executives sighed with vicarious pleasure.

"More love scenes! These two are hotter than even Gable and Leigh, Clift and Taylor. Write more," went the gist of the telegrams which were fired off to Nick and Hubert Croft.

✧   ✧   ✧

"More love scenes!" cackled Shirley, crouching over her ancient type-writer, a cigarette dangling from between her lips. "What a pity we can't shoot the hot ones going on in that hussy's trailer every lunchtime. I'll give 'em more love scenes—we'll scorch the screen with 'em."

Irving didn't bother to answer. He ignored Shirley when she was being a bitch. She was so obviously vicariously enjoying the steamy affair which was being played out right under everyone's noses that he thought he would give her the job of writing the new romantic scenes between Julian and Dominique that the studio craved. He was sitting at the other end of their Villa Vera sitting room with a yellow legal pad on his lap as yet again he rewrote the ending of the film.

Nick had not given up. Even though MCCP was still insisting on shooting the original Frankovitch script, Nick was such a perfectionist that he was constantly harassing the Frankovitches into changing a line here—making a scene better there—polish, polish, polish. Irving admired and respected his persistence, and he'd grudgingly had to admit that Nick was almost always right. Croft and Shirley were usually unanimous in *their* criticism and denunciation of all Nick's ideas, and the battles between them still raged on, but now with Irving more often taking Nick's side of the argument.

Shirley rat-tat-tatted away on her typewriter, spinning out the erotic scene in which the young Princess Isabella has to perform a dance for Cortez before they make love. She wondered what she could possibly do to make it really hot—"to melt their zippers" as she put it—to make it sexier than anything that had ever before been seen on the screen. She thought of some of the recent films: *The Robe* had been far too pure in its content, as had been *The Ten Commandments*, and even *Miss Sadie Thompson* with Rita Hayworth. Everyone in Hollywood had made such a big song and dance about her, but the movie had turned out to be as tame as a pet parrot.

"*Gilda*—now that was a sexy film," Shirley said out loud.

"What, dear?" Irving asked.

"The dance Hayworth did in *Gilda*—you remember, 'Put the blame on Mame, boys'—erotic, wasn't it?"

"Very," he replied. "But a little out of period for us, dear. We're trying to stay in the sixteenth century—*Gilda* was 1947."

"Hmmm." Shirley tapped at her teeth with a pencil. "What about Ava in *Pandora and the Flying Dutchman?*" she yelled across the room to him. "She sure lit up the screen in that scene where she swims out to the Dutchman's schooner in the nude."

"That was a great scene," recalled Irving, "and it really was shot in the moonlight too—on actual locations in the Mediterranean, I believe."

"Yeah, yeah, yeah—I'm gonna use it," said Shirley, tapping excitedly on her machine. "It'll be great, just great, Princess Isabella's gonna swim out to Cortez' boat in the nude," she said gleefully. "She's gonna climb on board, in the nude." Now she was becoming even more gleeful. "And then she's gonna do her hot little dance for Señor Cortez in the—"

"Don't be ridiculous, Shirley, you *can't*." Irving was shocked and irritated at his wife's stupidity. "The Hays Office will have all our asses. We can't have any nudity on the screen.'

'Oh, yes we can." Shirley picked up the telephone from her desk and barked at the hotel operator, "Get me Hubert Croft."

'We can and we will, Irv," she went on. "The studio'll love it—we can shoot it two ways—with and without veils." She cackled and shrieked into the phone. "Hubert—Shirley. Now listen, I've just had this great idea—can you come over and see us right away? Right—okay. You're just gonna *love* this scene, Hubert—yeah, I'm quite sure."

Julian was in a stupor of erotic tension. He hardly knew what had hit him. He adored Inès, worshiped her. His divorce from Phoebe would be final in a month, and his marriage to Inès had been planned for the following week. This was what he still wanted in his heart. But he knew that he somehow had to get Dominique out of his system. To do this he had convinced himself that if he made love to her as much and as often as possible he would grow tired of her. But the more wildly they made love, the more he wanted her. He simply couldn't get enough of this teenage temptress who reminded him so much of a younger version of the woman he really loved.

For him, Inès' illness was a blessing in disguise, although he suffered pangs of desperate guilt which made him drink more than usual. But Dominique's glances full of promise, her creamy lusciousness, her sensual touch, caused him to think of nothing but his hunger for her. One morning during shooting she deliberately teased him by repeatedly moistening her lips with her little pink tongue. This caused him a painfully embarrassing erection which lasted until she allowed him to take her, in a blazing burst of passion, in her dressing room during the lunch hour. They'd both been in full costume, but he'd plunged into her in such a frenzy of abandonment that the thin plywood walls had begun to rock, and many of the crew grinned knowingly at each other.

"Location romance, my foot," said Tim. "I ain't *never* seen the guvnor like this before—he's gorn, 'ook, line n' sinker."

Dominique loved it. She had found her ultimate power in the discovery of sex. This famous and gorgeous star, engaged to another woman, was hers to twist around her finger as much and in as many ways as her heart desired, and there was absolutely nothing he could do about it.

"It's quite impossible, Dominique. I could never allow you to do this scene—it's disgraceful, disgusting. Scandalous." Two red dots burned on Agathe's pale cheeks as she confronted Dominique with the new blue pages of script which had been delivered that evening.

"Don't be such a square, Agathe." Dominique yawned. "What's such a big deal about it? Why should I mind about a bit of nudity, it's perfectly natural—bodies are nothing to be ashamed of."

"It's immoral," spluttered Agathe. "It's—it's—disgraceful—it's demeaning and cheap—swimming out stark naked to a man—" her voice rose almost an octave—"then climbing onto the boat and dancing naked in front of Julian Brooks." Her tone had become so hysterical and outraged that Dominique looked up at her in astonishment.

"What do you care, Agathe—as long as I don't? I can't see what's the big deal—aren't you overreacting?"

"I'm your chaperone, young woman, in case it's slipped your mind," huffed Agathe. "I am supposed to look after your welfare, your morals, and help you sustain the values instilled in you by your parents."

"Bull," said Dominique rudely. "My parents didn't instill any values in me."

"That's a lie and you're a wicked, wicked girl to say so," Agathe shrieked. "I know your father. He's one of the most respected bankers in St. Tropez—*mon Dieu,* what will he say when he sees you prancing about in the nude? *Quelle borreur.*" She crossed herself and rubbed the little crucifix she always wore.

"Stop being such an old fuddy-duddy, Agathe," said Dominique. "Look—just take a look at this girl—she's French too, and her parents are *petit-bourgeois* too, just like mine." She threw over a copy of *Cinémonde,* the French magazine that she'd been reading.

Agathe picked it up and gasped at the photograph. A beautiful young blonde lay on her stomach, her hair covering the curves of her breasts, but her bare buttocks were prominently exposed and she was staring into the camera with an alluring and provocative smile.

"*Mais c'est porno*—what is the world coming to?" gasped Agathe, shocked to her foundations.

Dominique shrugged. "That's Brigitte Bardot," she said as if that were enough. "She's a couple of years older than me, maybe eighteen or nineteen, but that's what they're doing in France now—that kind of movie. They're shooting it now with a young director called Roger Vadim. It's called *And God Created Woman.*"

"I don't care if it's called *And God Created Shit,*" hissed Agathe in an unusual burst of blasphemy. "I'm going to see our producer right now and tell him I will never *allow* you to shoot this disgusting scene! *Never,* do you hear?"

Dominique shrugged. Agathe certainly seemed to be under a great deal of nervous tension recently. She wondered why.

Hubert Croft was trying unsuccessfully to take a nap when Agathe burst into his room unannounced and with only a perfunctory knock at the door. He'd taken off his shirt and trousers and was dressed only in his voluminous underpants and an undershirt when his visitor appeared.

"How *dare* you send Dominique this filth," she yelled, brandishing the pages of the scene under his nose. "I cannot permit my charge to perform this degrading act. She's my responsibility and *I forbid it.*"

"And what does your so-called charge have to say about it?" asked Hubert sarcastically, shrugging his bulk into a terry robe, complete with

Ramona's royal crest embroidered in red and gold on the breast pocket. "I'm sure she probably doesn't mind the idea in the least."

"That's not the point—she's a child and she knows no better," Agathe replied stiffly. "I'm the adult who's responsible for her and I *will NOT*, indeed *cannot*, allow her to reveal herself in such a debasing and disgusting fashion. It's abominable, I'm calling her parents tomorrow to tell them what's happening. She's underage, you people shouldn't even suggest that she do it."

"Sit down, *Mademoiselle*," said Hubert calmly. He gestured to a turquoise suede armchair, and Agathe sank into its depths, quite out of breath and fanning herself with the offending pages.

Just the thought of Julian seeing Dominique totally naked filled her with such conflicting feelings that her whole body was tingling. Her Julian—her love—watching Dominique perform this wanton dance wearing nothing but a smile. It was bad enough when she'd had to watch them making love for the screen. She had sat on the sidelines, out of sight, dry-mouthed with lust while the two of them kissed and caressed each other with such a passionate frenzy that she'd felt the moisture welling up in the most secret and private part of her body. It had almost been unbearable watching Julian hold that immature child in his strong arms, seeing his lips devour hers, her breasts pressed to his muscular chest, his arms holding her tightly. It had been a bittersweet sensation, particularly as Nick had insisted on shooting the love scenes from several different angles. She had suffered, oh, how she had suffered the pangs of jealousy and desire. She'd been unable to control herself, and had crept away to Dominique's empty trailer to relieve herself in the only way she knew. Whispering Julian's name, biting her lips until they almost bled, rubbing herself furiously with his scarf—another purloined object—she came to one torrential orgasm after another.

"Now, Mademoiselle Guinzberg," said Hubert, lighting a cigar and closely observing her through his narrowed eyes, "this is all a lot of nonsense. You know that, don't you?"

"I certainly don't," she huffed peevishly. "Dominique is only sixteen— I'm her guardian and—"

"Shut up, Mademoiselle Guinzberg," snapped Hubert. "Sit down and stop behaving like a two-faced bitch."

"What—what did you call me?" His sudden orders stunned her into confusion and anger.

"I said you're behaving like a two-faced hypocrite," he continued. "Do you think I don't make it my business to know what's been going on?"

"I don't know what you're talking about," gasped Agathe.

"Don't pretend to be as stupid as you look," snapped Hubert. "Listen to me for a minute before you start telephoning the girl's parents or the police or the fucking coast guard." He sucked on his cigar and pinioned her to the chair with his look of contempt. She squirmed uncomfortably, aware of the power of his penetrating stare. God, he was ugly. The crew, who all seemed to dislike him, made jokes about him all the time, and had christened him "the Toad." He looked like a great bulbous toad now as he sat hunched in the dark green robe, his bald head glistening with sweat, and stubble like black sandpaper covering his several chins.

"Don't for one minute think that I don't know *everything* that's going on in this film unit," he said slowly. "I mean *everything*."

"And what's that supposed to mean?" Agathe tried to sound resolute, but there was no question that Croft not only repelled her but also terrified her. She disliked any kind of confrontation, and she was starting to wish that she'd never come.

"I know what you think, Mademoiselle Agathe Guinzberg." He leaned forward, staring so intently into her eyes that she had to look away. "I know your every thought when you're on the set watching Julian Brooks work."

"What—what do you mean?"

"You love him, don't you, Agathe?" He leered. "You're passionately in love with him, and you lust after his body."

"No—no, I don't, it's a lie, a monstrous lie."

"Nonsense, woman. I've *seen* you—I miss nothing, you know." Hubert's cigar had gone out, and he relit it with an elaborate gold lighter. "I've *seen* the expression on your face when you sit under the umbrella with Sir Crispin and Julian—I *know* what's going through your mind, *and* your body."

"You don't—you couldn't," said Agathe fearfully.

"Don't be a cretin, woman." He smiled triumphantly, knowing that his next revelation would prove the killer for her. "I've seen your book—your precious scrapbook. Did you think you could hide anything from me?"

"No!" cried Agathe. "You couldn't have."

"Oh, but I could, and I have. A lovely book, Agathe, so beautifully assembled, and with such affection. I must congratulate you on such a comprehensive selection of photographs of our dear Mr. Brooks." He laughed unpleasantly. "It's certainly been well thumbed, your scrapbook."

"How did you find it?" whispered Agathe, shame for herself and hatred for the Toad both rising in her like lava.

"I searched your room, you fool." He smiled again. "I had a suspicion you might have something like that—I needed to find it. You didn't conceal it very well, Agathe. Under the mattress—ha!—very original. Any one of those stupid maids who work here could have found it, even though it was well wrapped up—in one of Julian's shirts, if I'm not mistaken." His eyes gleamed.

"No," she said softly. "No. No, that's my property—it's private—private. You're trespassing."

"Now, Mademoiselle Guinzberg, I'm going to forget totally that we ever had this little conversation, but only if you go away right now like a good woman and allow Dominique to get on with her work. If you choose to make a scene, call her parents, or do anything of that kind, I will personally see to it that everyone on this picture, including Julian Brooks himself, gets to know of your pathetic, pitiful obsession with him. Do I make myself clear?"

She nodded, her eyes burning with tears.

'And of course if Dominique's parents ever find out that the very person they trusted to look after their precious daughter is no more than a sick, sexually obsessed *pervert,* you will be undoubtedly thrown off this film in less than the time it takes to shout 'Action'—I do make myself clear, don't I?"

She nodded again, still unable to speak, and rose to leave.

"Not a word of our meeting here tonight will you breathe to anyone, Mademoiselle Guinzberg. And we shall all continue to be one big happy family. Do you understand?"

His eyes never left her as she walked slowly to the door, her shoulders slumped, her head bowed in defeat. Pathetic creature, he thought, feeling an unaccustomed emotion—pity. He would spare telling her about Dominique's roaring affair with Julian—the shock would probably kill her.

◆ *Sixteen* ◆

IT WAS A CLEAR moonlit night when Nick decided to shoot Dominique's nude swimming scene, followed by her seductive dance for Julian. The studio had become terribly excited when they had heard about it. It was breaking nearly all of the Hays Office censorship codes. Spyros Makopolis knew that in the new and dangerous territory they were entering, the studio was creating a precedent for future erotic scenes in movies. If the censor passed the scene in *Cortez*—without cuts—it would open the floodgates for other productions to shoot bare-skinned actresses and the public would demand more and more titillating scenes.

After arduous discussions with the Hays Office, with Scrofo, the Frankovitches and with Dominique herself, Nick had finally figured out a way to shoot it which would make it not only erotic and sensual, but would not actually show any censorable parts of Dominique's body. Only in long shots or in silhouette would the outlines of her beautiful figure be seen. To be completely safe, the following night they were going to shoot the identical scene all over again, this time with Dominique in a primitive bikini

Agathe spoke little as Dominique prepared for her first swimming shot. She stood completely and unself-consciously naked in front of Agathe, who had to avert her eyes while the makeup girl applied waterproof makeup to the girl's nipples. Her breasts were firm and up-jutting, her nipples dark pink. The makeup girl was trying to mask their color with the sponge so that the camera would not be able to see them from the boat, some two hundred yards away in the lagoon.

Dominique rather enjoyed the sensation of the soft sponge on her breasts, but her mind was filled with thoughts of what she and Julian would do together to while away the time tonight between shots. They both had cabins on the boat, and she knew that as soon as they finalized the first take, and he had glimpsed her glistening nude body rising from the sea, climbing up the side of the boat, he would feel a desperate urge to take her. She shivered at the delicious expectation, already becoming aroused by the thought of their passion taking place so close to where the crew would all be working.

She admired her reflection in the full-length mirror. Her belly was flat and tight, and at the base of her pubic triangle of black hair the wardrobe woman had pasted a small piece of flesh-colored fabric, not as a concession to her own modesty—which didn't exist—but to protect the footage from the potential wrath of the censor.

There was a sharp knock at the door, and Bluey's voice boomed out, "How we doin', Dominique?"

"I'm ready," she said happily, tossing her hair over her shoulders and smiling again at her gorgeous reflection. Agathe stole another look at her charge. The girl was exquisitely formed, there was no doubt at all about that. She seemed to have matured in the few months since she'd left St. Tropez; now she was no longer a schoolgirl but a ripe young woman in full flower. Agathe felt a surge of jealousy engulf her again as she imagined how Julian would feel when he saw the naked girl for the first time. She shuddered. She didn't *want* to think about that.

The wardrobe woman tied a large multicolored sarong around Dominique, who then tripped down the beach to where a small tent had been erected on the sand.

Nick was there waiting to meet her. "All set, Dominique? You look terrific, darling—how do you feel?"

"Great, Nick, great—I'm so excited, ready for anything."

"You really don't mind the nudity, you're absolutely sure?"

"Of course not." She laughed. "We all look the same without our clothes—it means nothing to me, Nick, less than nothing. I do think it's better for the scene too, more—how-you-say—*érotique, n'est-ce pas?*"

"Erotic, right." He grinned, admiring this girl's frankness and her refreshing joie de vivre. They'd made the right choice with this one, no question—she was a born star, and her sexuality seemed to gain in power each day. "Okay, now I'm going to get on the boat. Wait in the tent until you hear me call 'Action.' Then you come out slowly—look around you—to see if the guard is watching. When you get to the edge of the water you drop your scarf, and wade out very, very slowly into the sea. All the time you look towards the boat with an expression of anticipation. You're longing to see Cortez. Let me see how you're going to do it."

She rehearsed for him in the tent, and when he was satisfied with everything he gave her a big kiss on the cheek.

"You're gonna be great, break a leg, kid, and if you get a cramp in one while you're swimming, just yell—we've got divers all around—you'll be quite safe."

'I know." She smiled. "I'm a strong swimmer, Nick. Don't forget I live in St. Tropez."

He smiled to himself as he sat back in the speedboat which took him out to the majestic sixteenth-century schooner, whose masts towered impressively. If his instincts were correct, this was going to be quite some scene.

The crew were busy setting up on deck, and as he went over to consult with his lighting cameraman, he was accosted by Croft.

"I need to talk to you, my friend," the Italian said in an unexpectedly amiable tone, putting his hand on Nick's arm.

Nick pulled his arm away as if it had been stung, saying, "Okay, let's go down into my cabin then."

In his claustrophobic cabin, Nick nodded towards a chair for Croft to sit in. Ignoring the Italian, he stood with his hands on his hips thinking through his script with a frown.

"It's about this nude scene we're going to shoot," Umberto began.

"What about it?" Nick's voice was sharp. "The studio has agreed to this scene in principle, so what's the problem, Hubie baby?" He couldn't keep the sarcasm out of his voice, nor could he bear to look at the abhorrent creature who sat puffing on his stinking cigar.

"I want to know exactly how you're going to shoot it, to protect Dominique's modesty," said Umberto. "She's young—she shouldn't be out there flashing her snatch at the crew without a stitch on. I want to know that you're all going to behave like gentlemen."

Nick raised his eyebrows. "Since when did you become the moralist?" he sneered. "Since when did *you* know anything about gentlemen and their behavior? I didn't realize you were so concerned about protecting Dominique—I assumed that you had other ideas about her."

"And what do you mean by *that*?" snarled the Italian.

"Oh, nothing, nothing," said Nick, innocently glancing at his script. "You've got a cock too, Hubie baby—haven't you?"

"Listen, asshole." Umberto rose, his huge bulk, enveloped in clouds of cigar smoke, seeming to fill the tiny cabin. "Let's not have any more cracks about *me*—I'm still the fucking producer on this fucking epic whether *you* like it or not, you Greek shithead. *Here*." He threw a crumpled telegram on the desk. "Read that."

Nick picked up the scrap of paper and read: "Hays Office most concerned STOP Despite them having agreed to pass nude scene it is essential that any shots filmed, repeat, any at all, must have no salacious content vis-à-vis body position or exposure of the girl STOP They unaware Dominique is a minor STOP Be very careful STOP Picture so far is great but we need this scene so get it right STOP Regards Makopolis."

"I've already had a copy of this," said Nick, throwing it back to Umberto. "I've spent all today and yesterday on this boat with the operator, the lighting cameraman and with Dominique or her stand-in. We've carefully gone through every fucking frame. Any time there's the minutest possibility that we might see a flash of tit or any of her other bits, we've always got a piece of sail or some scenery to cover it—does that satisfy your prudery, Hubie baby?"

"What about the crew—will they be able to see any of her body?" Umberto asked persistently.

"Of *course* they'll be able to see her!" exploded Nick. "But they're fucking professionals, for Christ's sake, not a bunch of Peeping fucking Toms." Like you, he almost added, but he badly wanted to get rid of the Toad. The sight and sound of the man always put him into a blinding fury, and he had to get to work right away. There was a great deal to be done tonight.

"Well, I'll be watching the whole time to see that you do *exactly* what you're supposed to," said Umberto, his eyes glinting at Nick like chips of coal. "And no one had better take advantage of that girl."

Least of all you, asshole, Nick thought to himself, but all he said was, "Right, have you finished now, Hubert? Are you satisfied?"

"One thing you should know about me, Nick," sneered Umberto, his face close to Nick's, "I'm *never* satisfied." With that he stalked out, slamming the cabin door.

Nick shrugged and made a couple of notes in red pencil on his script. This was just another typical day with Hubert S. Croft. Every day he tried to make trouble, and every day he succeeded in infuriating someone in the crew or a member of the cast.

Nick looked out of the cabin's minute porthole which faced the deck and saw Hubert talking angrily to one of Dominique's wardrobe women who was looking back at him with patient irritation. Nick grinned. He'd seen that particular look on practically every one of the crew members' faces. They all loathed Scrofo. He put the Italian out of his mind as best he could and, as he strode purposefully back onto the deck, concentrated his attention on the forthcoming scene.

"Ready, boys?" he called to his two camera crews, both set up for different angles on the deck.

"Okay—ready, Nick," they shouted back in unison.

"Right—let's *go!*"

The clapper boy snapped his wooden sticks in front of camera one, then again in front of camera two. The sound operator called, "Rolling." Nick then shouted the magic words through his loudhailer: "Aaand— *Action!*"

Also on deck, out of sight just behind the camera crews Umberto Scrofo stood, a pair of powerful binoculars pressed firmly to his porcine eye sockets. He didn't want to miss a single second of this spectacle. Naturally he'd thought Dominique a lovely little creature since the first moment that he'd laid eyes on her, but she had resolutely and continually ignored him. If he ever tried to talk to her, she would only reply in monosyllables and with barely disguised boredom.

As she paused at the shoreline Dominique looked steadily towards the anchored boat. Slowly and with an infinite yet natural sensuality, she unloosed her flimsy sarong and let it fall with a faint whisper to the sand. The full moon illuminated her flawless breasts and gave an ethereal beauty to her whole body. She looked like a dark and less modest version of Botticelli's Venus rising from the waves. She was a divinely created masterpiece, the personification of youthful and feminine perfection.

"*Madonna mia*," muttered Scrofo, the lump in his throat almost as uncomfortable as the one in his trousers. "*Che bellissima ragazza—bellissime.*"

He was far from alone in his admiration for the naked beauty who was milking her moment at the water's edge to the very utmost. Slowly, sinuously, she walked into the cool black waters. Pausing momentarily as the ocean lapped around the tops of her thighs, she gazed again with a look of undisguised desire at the deck of the boat where Julian was waiting for her.

"My God, what a dame," whispered Bluey to Nick, who stood transfixed, just gazing at her. "That's the fuckin' body of a fuckin' angel if I ever saw one."

Nick didn't bother to answer. The tableau was so exquisite in its simple timeless beauty that he felt he wanted to drown himself in it. Dominique took another two or three steps, and, as the water covered her waist, she gave a tiny cry and dived under the surface, to reappear seconds later with her hair streaming out behind her like black seaweed. She swam impressively and strongly towards the boat. The close-up camera was filming her face and shoulders, but the operator was concentrating on trying not to reveal any glimpses of her breasts.

"Fantastic," he murmured under his breath to his assistant, who was constantly adjusting the focus as Dominique swam closer and closer to the boat. "Fan-fuckin'-tastic."

Julian was standing between the two cameras, so that as Dominique swam within thirty yards of the boat she could see him clearly. She gave him a smile of such devastating innocence, seductively tinged with voluptuous adult longing, that he could feel his mouth becoming dry, and his cock in anxious anticipation of the delights in store for it later, began its irresistible rise.

Finally she arrived at the rope ladder which hung over the side of the boat, and grasping it tightly climbed on board. For an instant she stood absolutely still, posing, allowing the cameras to capture the electric sensuality that emanated from her. Then with a passionate sigh she murmured, "Oh, Hernando, my love," and threw herself into Julian's open and welcoming arms.

"Cut," shouted Nick. "Beautiful, Dominique—absolutely beautiful— we don't need to do another one; that was perfection, darling—just great. Relax for an hour while we get set up for your dance—dry yourself off, have a hot drink. We don't want you catching cold."

The wardrobe woman had already draped Dominique with towels and a terrycloth robe, and she wrapped herself in them, twisting a towel around her wet hair like a turban. Julian stood nearby while her posse of helpers fussed around her, and she felt she could almost see his hardness through the material of his breeches. She shooed away her entourage and stood very still as he approached her.

"Can I buy you a drink?" he whispered.

"You could," she breathed. "But I'd rather you make love to me."

In the privacy of his tiny cabin, neither could control their desperate impatience. Julian sat on the bunk fully clothed, and she stood shaking between his legs—more from lust than from the effects of the cold water — as he slowly unwound the towels from her damp body.

They could hear the crew up on deck preparing for the next shot, and the gentle slap of the waves against the hull. A dim yellow lamp glowed from the table in the cabin, and as the towels fell away from her breasts it bathed them in a warm, golden light. His mouth went to each one in turn, licking and gently biting them until she threw back her head and cried out for him to stop—then his hands caressed her hips as he unwound the towel from her waist, laying bare her buttocks and her sex. He stroked the soft firmness of her muscled rear as his lips dropped down to her silky mound and his tongue found the exact place for which it longed.

She moaned softly as it probed her gently and softly. He now knew well how to please her, and in only a matter of seconds she came, her hands tangled in his thick hair, as he continued to massage her nipples gently with the palms of his hands.

Then she was on him like a wild creature and his cock leaped out at her as she unbuttoned his trousers. It seemed to her harder and larger than it had ever been before. Lovingly she put as much of it in her mouth as she could, rhythmically sucking it until he almost burst. Then she put him inside her, and rode him, gently at first, but gaining momentum until together they became two bodies but one flesh.

Bluey went to knock on Julian's cabin about an hour later.

"Is Dominique in there by any chance?" he said with mock innocence.

"*J'arrive*—coming right out," called Dominique happily, blowing her lover a kiss, and leaving him lying back on his bunk completely sated.

Nick was ready to rehearse the dance scene, so Dominique put on a leotard to run over it until Nick was completely satisfied that it was perfect. Umberto stood beside the cameras, cigar jutting out from his mouth, saying nothing, but his very presence making everyone uncomfortable and distracted.

The cameras were positioned in such a way that the areas of Dominique's body which were censorable were always masked by parts of the boat's equipment and rigging. It was a highly complicated and difficult shot and it took almost all night to get it. They needed to do more than fifteen setups with the three cameras to make quite sure that no mistakes were made.

Dominique was in her element. She found the idea of dancing naked in front of forty men, including her lover, enormously exhilarating. Each time that Nick yelled "Cut—it's a print—next setup" she and Julian would slink away to one or other of their cabins. No one disturbed them. Even though everyone knew exactly what was going on, and although lewd jokes and comments were bandied about by the crew, nothing was ever said within earshot of the two principals.

"Maybe we should call her the Submarine," joked Bluey to the camera operator.

"And why's that?"

"Because she's always going down," laughed Bluey, nodding towards Julian's cabin.

Julian was lying on his bunk after the fifth setup. They'd been shooting Dominique's dance for over six hours now and he was exhausted. Not from the dancing, as all he had to do was watch, but because Dominique was so sexually demanding. Every time they came back down to the cabin, she would want to make love again. She was in such a high state of excitement that it was becoming infectious. All the crew could feel it radiating from her, and almost every one of the men had a pleasurable discomfort in his loins as they watched her, each with his own fantasy.

Her body glistening with water in the lamplight, she leaned against the cabin door, eyeing Julian, who was lying back on his bunk.

My God, they'd done it four times already tonight. Surely she couldn't —wouldn't—be able to do it again, he thought—not after all that swimming and dancing. But he was wrong. Her robe dropped to the floor once more, and he could almost see her pulsing to receive him.

"Dominique, don't you think we've had enough for one night?" he said weakly, but only too aware that in spite of his physical exhaustion his expectant cock was rising yet again.

"Certainly not," she crooned, leaning against the mahogany door, looking like some wanton maiden, her hair falling shiny and wet around her full breasts.

"I want you to want me again, Julian—I want you again, my love—I want you now." She was touching herself now, in a way which she knew would drive him half mad with desire. Massaging her nipples gently between her fingers, she then slipped one hand down to between her legs, two fingers beginning to slide in and out of her moist pink sex.

"Of course I want you," he said, his voice made hoarse with passion. "I want you too damn much—you're an enchantress, you know that—a little witch, and you're driving me mad."

"I want you, Julian," she moaned, still leaning against the door, her fingers now moving so rapidly, and her breathing so fast that he could see that she was about to come again.

He watched spellbound as she did, crying out his name.

"*Je t'aime, Julian, je t'aime, mon homme.*" He saw her whole body quiver with her own ecstasy.

"Come over here," he said huskily. "My God, what have you done to me, Dominique—what have you done?"

"Nothing," she whispered, "nothing at all." Her eyes were wide with rapture as he immersed himself into her once again.

"I've just made you love me—*j'espère*— because I love you, Julian, I always will."

❊   ❊   ❊

As Julian walked from his cabin to the upper deck where the crew were filming he saw a man silhouetted against a pile of rigging in the shadows. He paused for a second, his actor's instincts sensing something unusual.

Thinking himself unseen, Hubert Croft was leaning against a furled sail, his eyes fixed on the distant, dancing figure of a naked Dominique. One of his hands was moving fast and furiously in the pocket of his baggy linen trousers, his eyes were half closed and his breathing harsh.

"What the devil do you think you're doing, Croft?" hissed Julian.

The Italian abruptly ceased what he was doing and stared at Julian.

"Well, well, well, if it isn't our Mr. Brooks come to check up on his Lolita," he sneered, seeming neither ashamed nor embarrassed to have been caught masturbating almost publicly. He removed his hand slowly from his trouser pocket, looking at Julian with a mocking smile.

"Jesus Christ, Croft, you're acting like a bloody pervert," said Julian in disgust. "If any of the crew saw what you were doing you'd be thrown off the set."

"Let you *not* be the one to cast stones, Julian old boy," said Croft, mimicking Julian's impeccable English in his grating voice. "If any of the men saw what *you* have been doing with that little slut—deliberately flaunting herself in front of them—you would not be thought of any longer as the second coming of Olivier, but rather a pathetic aging Lothario."

"I'm not going to bandy words with you, Croft," said Julian, feeling his face burn. He knew what the crew were all thinking about Dominique and himself. He couldn't blame them, either. "It's none of your damn business."

"Oh, but it *is* my business," smirked Scrofo. "And my dear chap, much as I, the producer of the film, admire your performance on the screen, your performance *off* it proves that you are nothing but a vain, shallow actor, attempting to retain your youth through having repeated sex with that innocent girl."

Oh, sure, thought Julian. Dominique was about as innocent as a basketful of adders. Where she had learned her siren skills he didn't dare think.

"I'm wanted on the set, Croft," he said tensely. "I'd prefer not to linger any longer in this conversation. Frankly it's making me ill."

"Not as ill as Mademoiselle Inès is going to feel when she reads yesterday's *Herald Examiner*," said Scrofo.

"Oh? And what, pray, is so interesting about that?"

"Read it and weep," said Scrofo, "as will your fiancée, no doubt. As I told you before, Brooks, don't throw stones—you'll only get mud on your shoes."

He chortled harshly as he waddled back to the set, and Julian stood quite still. What could possibly be in the newspaper that might affect Inès? He groaned silently. He knew only too well what it could be: some gossip about him and Dominique. It wouldn't be the first time that he had been grist for the gossip-mongers' mills, but, by God, if it hurt Inès . . .

He walked quickly back to his cabin where his makeup man was busily sharpening eyebrow pencils.

"You haven't by any chance got a copy of yesterday's Los Angeles newspaper, have you, old chap?" he asked Tim casually.

"Naw, guv, you know I only read the comics," said Tim cheerily, blotting Julian's sweating face with Kleenex. "But some of the boys get it, guv. I'll see what I can do."

"Thanks, Tim, I appreciate it," sighed Julian, wishing this night were over. Talking to Croft always left him with a sour taste in his mouth.

Tim went around to the crew asking for a copy of yesterday's paper, while Kittens was retailing to the wardrobe women, in excited indignation the fact that she had seen Croft peeping voyeuristically at Dominique's nudity and playing with himself at the same time. Within an hour the entire unit knew what their producer had been doing, and their dislike of him reached new heights.

The following night the whole scene was shot again, this time with Dominique clothed in a series of veils. These worked perfectly well when she was in the water, but as soon as she was out of it, the see-through chiffon clung to her curves in the skimpy bikini underneath in such a suggestive way that Hubert again cornered Nick in his cabin after the very first shot. The crew were then treated to a screaming match between the two men that could have been heard far away in the highest guard tower of Ramona's villa. Eventually the two protagonists emerged, both grim-faced, to consult further with Agathe, Kittens and the wardrobe woman.

It appeared that Hubert thought Dominique's nipples were clearly visible through the flimsy, saturated material, the censor would be forced to use his sharpened scissors, and the scene would be a write-off.

Dominique was summoned away from Julian's cabin where the two were about to indulge in yet another amorous session. She stood sullen and pouting in her cabin, fuming that she'd had to leave her lover, as they fussed around her. Nick was furious, but he did see that Umberto had a point. During Dominique's dance the wet fabric rubbed itself against her breasts and excited her already prominent nipples until they became clearly visible from several yards away. It was impossible for the camera not to see them in all these shots unless they could somehow be camouflaged.

"I really don't see what all this *fuss* is about," sulked Dominique, longing to get back to Julian. "*All* women have breasts, I can't understand why you Americans are so prudish about showing them?"

Everyone ignored her as Kittens and the wardrobe woman conferred in hushed voices. Eventually the men were shooed out of the room while the women performed various experiments to try to conceal Dominique's pert papillae. But the more they pressed on flesh-colored pads and stuck them down with strong surgical adhesive, the more her nipples seemed to swell, pushing through the material like two acorns.

Dominique felt impatient, hating the whole infuriating performance. She was already in a state of advanced sexual arousal, and having her breasts poked and pushed only encouraged it. She just longed to be back cuddling up to Julian and feeling him inside her again.

Eventually the women were satisfied with their handiwork and Dominique was dismissed. She rushed back to Julian's cabin, where her lover waited, his erection long since deflated. When he saw Dominique's breasts covered with a curious network of masking tape, Band-Aids and flesh-colored silk, looking something like a cubist collage, he threw back his head and roared with laughter.

"What's so funny?"

"Darling heart, I'm sorry but they do look strange—like two perfect little peaches all bandaged up!"

"Not so little, thank you very much—I think you're a very rude man," said Dominique, giving him her most seductive smile. "And now, since you're not allowed to touch them"—she bounded friskily onto the tiny bunk bed—"I'll just have to play with this soft old thing." With that she took some moisturizer from the shelf next to the bed and began massaging the liquid on his slumbering cock. In no time Julian was back at full stand and he groaned ecstatically as she gently lowered her body onto him once again.

Dominique's sensual dance had excited practically all of the male crew members to such an extent that for the next few nights the whorehouses of Acapulco did a roaring trade.

Hubert Croft had found himself tremendously aroused by the girl's erotic dance. Although he had no feelings one way or another about Julian Brooks, thinking him merely a conceited but handsome actor who had just been lucky, Umberto felt angry and jealous that Dominique seemed so crazy about him. His only consolation was that the whore Inès seemed to be getting what she deserved. He knew the bitch was on the verge of a miscarriage, and it pleased him enormously that her fiancé was blatantly two-timing her with a girl young enough to be his own daughter.

The night following Dominique's dance scene, Ramona's small house party dined as usual on her candlelit terrace. Dominique was extremely tired, as well she might be, thought Scrofo, excusing herself soon after dinner to retire to her room.

Half an hour later, Hubert tapped at her door.

"Go away—please," the girl called out sleepily. "I'm asleep."

"I have to talk to you, Dominique," said the producer. "It's extremely urgent."

"*Merde,*" he heard her mutter as she opened the sliding opaque glass doors to her bedroom.

"What do *you* want?" she asked sulkily, loping back into her room to sprawl sleepily on the edge of the bed. She hadn't bothered to put a robe on, and was wearing just a tiny baby-doll nightdress of sheer white cotton edged with *broderie anglaise* and blue ribbon. Umberto could see her matching panties as she looked up at him with bored resignation.

He never felt quite sure of himself in her presence. She seemed to possess the assurance of an adult, and never seemed intimidated by him, unlike so many others on the film.

"I think that your liaison with Julian Brooks must stop," said Hubert stonily, feeling the familiar tingling in his groin.

She laughed contemptuously. "It's none of your business, Mr. Croft. Whatever Julian and I do off the set has *nothing* to do with you."

"But it most certainly has, my dear," he said frostily. "Please *don't* forget that you're still a minor, and as producer of this film *I* am the one responsible for your welfare."

"Agathe is responsible for all that," yawned Dominique, leaning back cross-legged against the zebra-striped headboard, a challenging expression on her sulky face.

"And she doesn't know a thing about your sordid little affair, does she? You've been very clever, Dominique, very clever indeed. But if Agathe had been aboard the ship last night she would certainly have known about it Everyone else does."

"So what?" said Dominique. "I'm doing nothing wrong."

Umberto's breath started to quicken and lowering her eyes, Dominique saw to her dismay a small distention in his trousers. She raised her eyes quickly—*merde*, the pig was getting excited. *Quelle horreur.* She uncrossed her long tanned legs and tried unsuccessfully to pull her nightgown down a little more.

"If you told Agathe about it she wouldn't believe you anyway. She thinks I'm a blushing virgin—just like she is."

"And of course you didn't allow her on the ship to watch your dance, did you?" said Umberto ominously. "So she could see your disgusting behavior."

"Well, that was her idea," Dominique shrugged. "She had a migraine or something—she just wanted to go to bed."

How very convenient for Agathe, thought Umberto. She was obviously unable to bear the sight of her idol making love to this minx. "What does she think happens when you go into Mr. Brooks' locked trailer at lunchtime?" Umberto was genuinely curious.

"She thinks we're practicing our lines, of course, or maybe even having lunch," laughed Dominique. "Rehearsing—and that's exactly what does happen," she added defiantly, disconcerted because the fat man's expression had become more intense.

He took a step nearer the bed.

"That's what we were doing last night Hubie—and you have no proof of anything else."

"Oh, don't I?" sneered Umberto. "What about these?" From behind his back he produced a large manila envelope which he threw on the bed. "Open it."

Slowly Dominique undid the flap, pulling out several black-and-white photographs.

Her hands flew to her mouth. "What are these? Where did you get them?"

"I'm sure you know perfectly well what they are," sneered Scrofo. "They are some photographs of you and Mr. Brooks which I took on the beach the day you were fornicating together in front of anyone who happened to be passing. *Slut,*" he hissed. "French slut."

He suddenly felt totally omnipotent, as finally Dominique looked up at him with genuine fear in her eyes.

"What are you going to do with them?"

"That rather depends." Scrofo advanced slowly towards her, his bulk ominous in the semi-darkness of the room. "It depends on how nice you are to me."

"Nice? *Mais, c'est une blague! Non—non!*" Dominique tried to scramble across the huge bed, but despite his size Umberto was too fast for her. He grabbed her ankle and pulled her towards him as she screamed for help.

His huge body pressed her down onto the bed, and he clamped his hand over her mouth. *Merde,* the pig was strong, she thought with mounting panic, as she thrashed around trying to throw him off. To her disgust she became aware that he was trying to unzip his trousers with one hand as he moaned his litany of lust to her.

"Don't scream, Dominique—just be a good girl, a nice girl, you'll like it, I know how much you like it—you'll like it with me too—I'm good— just as good as Brooks." She tried to squirm away from him, but he was so heavy that she was pinned like a butterfly to a specimen board.

"Be a good girl now," he rasped, his mouth close to her ear. "A good nice little girl, and I won't show the photographs of you fucking Julian to your chaperone—because if I *do*"—his hand tightened sadistically over her face—"she will make sure that your parents hear about everything that's happened, and you'll be bundled back to St. Tropez in disgrace, faster than it would take you to unzip Julian's fly."

Dominique tried to scream out, but it was impossible with his clammy hand pressed hard over her mouth. She tried to raise her strong dancer's legs to kick him in the stomach before he could manage to force himself into her, but his sheer weight made it impossible.

Momentarily she lay still, the realization of what could happen paralyzing her. Agathe. Would she report back to Maman and Papa? Surely not—Dominique could twist Agathe around her little finger, the woman was always in such a daze.

Umberto continued to drone on in his horrible rasping voice, his erect penis pressing itself against her bare thigh. "Just be a good girl, Dominique—just be good, my dear, and when I've finished I will tear up all the pictures and you won't have to worry about anything anymore."

"No, get away!" she screamed with a sudden surge of strength, struggling more forcibly as a rough hand grabbed at the elastic around her panties and began to pull them down. The pungent smell of his vile cologne assailed her nostrils, and she threw her head from side to side as his bulbous lips drew closer.

At that moment there was a knock at the door and Agathe's shrill voice called out, "Dominique, are you all right?"

Dominique's eyes widened with relief, and triumphantly she looked into Umberto's bloated face. For a second he froze, then the knock came again.

"Dominique, I said, are you all right? I thought I heard you call out? Answer me, Dominique, otherwise I'll call the guards."

Umberto bent his gross head and whispered, "I'm going to take my hand off your mouth—and you better say you're all right or *I can promise you that you'll regret it*— right? No tricks now."

She nodded and gradually he released his hand. After a deep breath of air, she shouted towards the door, "Agathe, oh Agathe, thank God it's you. I've had such a scary dream—I feel so frightened."

"Let me in, *chérie*," Agathe ordered, worriedly rattling at the locked door. "Right now."

"No, no, don't come in," Dominique called, gloating exultantly at Umberto's face which was grotesquely contorted in anger and panic. "I'll come out to you—I want to sleep in your room tonight, Agathe. I've had such an awful nightmare."

"Of course, *chérie, viens,* hurry up. I'll take care of you."

Triumphantly Dominique rolled away from under the Italian and scampered over to the door, grabbing up a dressing gown and stuffing the photographs into a pocket.

"You haven't heard the last of this," Umberto whispered hoarsely as she glanced over at him from the door. "No one ever gets the better of me, you little slut—no one."

Dominique made no answer as she slid open the glass doors and fell into the security of Agathe's arms.

"Oh, Agathe, it was such a horrible nightmare," she sobbed, tears of relief running down her flushed cheeks.

"Hush, hush, don't cry, *chérie*. I'll take care of you, *ma petite,* come—come with me."

With her arms enfolding the shaking girl, Agathe led Dominique into her room and locked the door behind them.

Umberto Scrofo listened carefully to his telephone caller, blue jowls creasing into a wider and wider smile, as he heard the news which made him so pleased.

"In Paris, you say—you found him in prison?" He listened again and then laughed. "French drunks—I've seen 'em—they're all the same. They'd sell their grandmothers for a glass of absinthe. How much does he want?" He frowned when he heard the reply. "One hundred thousand francs, that's ridiculous—I wouldn't pay him nearly as much. Offer him ten thousand."

The caller continued to jabber on, and Umberto's demeanor became increasingly ebullient. "Tell him to call me himself—no, better not—the poor bastard probably can't afford it. I'll call him. What did you say his name was?" Umberto scribbled down a name and a telephone number in Paris, saying softly to himself as he hung up, "Yves Moray, how very, very interesting."

Julian had been in a turmoil of guilt since his two nights of frenzied sex during the shooting of Dominique's nude scene. He knew only too well that everything he was doing with Dominique was completely and utterly wrong, but his body recently seemed not to belong to him anymore. It was nothing more than a series of raw nerve endings, all connected to his cock, which swelled expectantly each time he found himself near her.

They had made love for hour after hour in the cabin and now he could barely walk. Last night he'd arrived back at the hotel just as the gray fingers of dawn were creeping over the hills.

When he staggered into the bathroom he started thinking of their lovemaking, and immediately became hard again. He stared at himself in the mirror in shocked self-disgust. He was either Superman or on the way to becoming certifiable, and although this amazing virility which Dominique inspired had enslaved him, he knew that he was in the throes of a selfish obsession which could well destroy his relationship with Inès forever.

He had tried to obtain a copy of the newspaper Croft had mentioned, but no one had it or seemed to have read it, so he dismissed it from his mind, thinking that it was obviously just some cheap ploy to annoy him. Croft was not worth worrying about. He was a low life whom Julian found intensely disagreeable. He knew Inès disliked the Italian too. She had told him so after Ramona's party. Did *anyone* have a good word or kind feelings for Hubert Croft? Obviously not.

In the bedroom Inès awoke from a drug-induced slumber as she heard Julian in the shower. Dr. Langley had sent her pills to help her sleep at night, because she was so inactive with nothing to do all day except read, or stare at the view, that to sleep at night had become more and more difficult.

"Are you all right, darling?" she murmured when Julian quietly slipped into his side of the big double bed. "You've been working so hard lately, such long hours, I've been worried about you."

"I'm fine, just exhausted," he whispered, a painful pang of guilt hitting him like a physical blow. "Please don't concern yourself about me, sweetheart, just worry about yourself and our baby. Goodnight, my darling." He kissed her gently on the forehead and turned over, pretending to sleep.

Inès stared into the darkness of the room. Her finely tuned instincts told her something was wrong. She knew all about Julian's sexual past and the succession of liaisons with every single one of his leading ladies. Surely he wasn't having an affair with a sixteen-year-old girl? Not now, when the two of them were in such harmony together, and she was finally giving him the child that he'd always wanted. Surely he couldn't contemplate doing such a thing—could he?

Although not an analytical man or one to share confidences, Julian felt he had to talk to someone or else go mad. He decided to confide his problem to Nick Stone, whom he believed to be discreet, a man he could trust. The day after the dancing scenes were wrapped, filming finished early. Also Dominique wasn't around to bat her eyelashes coquettishly and bewitch his cock into a state of perpetual tumescence, so on the way back from location he asked Nick, "Fancy a drink, old chap?"

"Good idea—how about hitting La Perla? We can watch the divers— and I don't know about you, but I feel like diving into several margaritas," said Nick. He was in high spirits about the film, although his hatred for Scrofo was smoldering away just beneath the surface. He tried hard to control it, but Umberto seemed capable of inflaming his anger with only the slightest provocation.

At La Perla, Julian and Nick sat at a corner table, away from the tourists. As soon as they had ordered, Julian began to unburden himself.

"I don't know what the hell to do, Nick," he said. "I'm truly up the proverbial shit creek without a paddle."

Several young muscular Mexican boys were crawling like spiders up the steep rocks behind him as they prepared to perform their famous death-defying dives into the ocean far below, but the two men ignored them.

"I presume you've noticed what's been going on?" said Julian.

Nick smiled ruefully. "Kiddo, you might as well have stood on the Empire State Building and yelled it out," he said. "I guess you mean you and the girl?"

"I certainly do," said Julian glumly. "The girl. I can't get enough of her, Nick. I don't want to do this, but I can't stop myself. Christ, I'm thirty-seven years old, for God's sake—old enough to be her father. I hate myself for it, but she's honestly bewitched me."

Nick listened sympathetically, glad that he didn't suffer similar problems with women—maybe that's what comes of being too handsome, he thought. Julian had always been romantically incontinent, but who could blame him with the way women had always thrown themselves at him? "Do you love Dominique?" he asked.

"Hell, *no*—of *course* I bloody don't. I'm *madly* in love with Inès—at least I think I am—that's why I'm in such a bloody state about Dominique. Every time I'm *near* that little minx, I just have to have her. I think I'm going mad—I think I'm going stark staring bonkers, Nick."

"Of course, you're not," said Nick. "You're not crazy, Julian—you're a man just like the rest of us."

"A man doesn't behave like this," said Julian bitterly. "A man is faithful to the woman he loves, especially when the woman is as wonderful as Inès, and lying flat on her back all day long to save our baby."

"So why *do* you do it?"

"She's a witch—I've told her as much," breathed Julian. "A siren; a Circe. She's springtime—she's innocence—and she's unbelievably sexy.

Sex with her is *incredible,* indescribably amazing. She's *sixteen,* Nick, and she makes love like—like a goddess. I want her whenever I'm near her— she's like a drug and I've become a complete addict."

They ordered more margaritas, and watched as the first of the Mexican divers took off like a swallow from the peak of the high rock, hitting the water at the exact moment when the seventh wave crashed into the shallow gully. As the boy's head appeared triumphantly above the water and the assembled patrons cheered and applauded, Julian leaned forward.

"I want to end it, Nick, but every time I manage to make that decision I see her again and this bloody thing"—he pointed angrily at his crotch— "changes my mind for me, and what's more, so does the rest of me."

Nick laughed. "Then I guess you do have a problem—I can't really help you. I wish I could. I can only say that every man on this film would give his balls to fuck Dominique."

"Even Sir Crispin?" laughed Julian.

Nick smiled. "Perhaps not him, but I've talked to the guys—I've heard what they say about her. It isn't just you, Julian—you're not alone. She's a mantrap, she's like a walking aphrodisiac. Every single guy has got the hots for her, and the more they see her the more they want her—and how they envy you! I think she's just sex appeal personified, it's like some kind of gift."

"That's for damn sure," said Julian ruefully.

"Monroe, Brigitte Bardot, they're gonna have to look to their laurels when our kid hits the screen," said Nick. "I think she'll be the biggest female star that Hollywood's had for years."

"Yes, well, that doesn't exactly solve my problem," said Julian, "which is simply that the woman I love is off games until our baby is born, while I *cannot* stop being self-indulgent and fucking this nymphet. Wherever and whenever I can."

"Listen, Julian," said Nick. "I'm not a man of the world, I'm nowhere in your league—I'm just a simple Greek guy who happens to be happily married and wants very much to stay that way. But let me give you a bit of advice."

"What is it?" said Julian. "For God's sake, I'll do anything that will help me to get out of this mess."

"There's only one way," Nick said simply. "If you really love Inès you've gotta pretend Dominique doesn't exist. You're an actor—you can do that, can't you?"

Julian looked skeptical.

"Cold turkey," said Nick. "It's the only way, Julian, the only way to do it."

Inès sat on the hotel balcony numb with shock. A slim manila envelope, addressed to her, had been placed on her breakfast tray that morning. A wave of nausea had engulfed her when she'd opened it. Blurred black-and-white photographs, taken with a telescopic lens, revealed a couple entwined on a beach.

There was no mistaking Julian's back, just as there was no mistaking the slim, sensual legs and long black hair of Dominique, her body hidden from the camera by Julian's. Inès was aghast as she read the enclosed press clipping from Harrison Carroll's Los Angeles gossip column.

Mr X, the handsome but not yet divorced matinée idol, has been "oh-so-close" with the beautiful but very young Miss Y, while they toil together on a tropical location. This column is concerned as to how attractive Miss Z, the fiancée of the former, must be coping with the situation.

Who could have hated Inès enough to send this disgusting, loathsome piece of gossip, take these perverted photos? She knew the answer only too well. There was just one person in the world odious enough to want to hurt her so much. Umberto Scrofo.

What was Julian doing? One blissful year together, a baby on the way, a wonderfully romantic life, the most fulfilling happiness she had ever known, and Julian had started to cheat on her. Why? What was he getting from Dominique that he could not get from her? She knew the answer to that, if she knew men. Gloomily she stared out of the window. He was getting sex, and plenty of it. But was it just sex, or was it something more?

She mustn't let Julian suspect that she knew of this affair, or behave any differently towards him. Any change of attitude from her would cause him to ask questions that she didn't want to answer. Certainly he had been no less affectionate or considerate towards her in the past few days, even though lovemaking had been forbidden. What did he say about that to Dominique, a girl not quite seventeen? Did he confide in her the truth that his love life with Inès was suddenly nonexistent because of her pregnancy? Or did he lie to her, saying Inès was cold, unaffectionate, did not give him what he wanted? Inès knew that old routine. Her past lovers had often told her how disappointing their wives were in bed.

Her hands cupped her still-flat stomach. Dominique—young, French, beautiful. Maybe she should take some small measure of comfort in the fact that Dominique was so like herself—Julian had remarked on the amazing resemblance between them when they had first met the girl.

It was all because of Scrofo that she had not had enough time to spend with Julian. Scrofo, who had made her so involved in his script problems. Scrofo, who had made her life so miserably stressful recently, and Scrofo, who had abused her so brutally as a girl, causing her to suffer the pain of imminent miscarriage. If only she had succeeded in killing him, none of this would be happening.

Inès fingered her lucky bracelet of amber and silver. That loathsome creature was ruining her life. She had to do something about him. But what? He was the producer of her fiancé's movie, he had power and influence, she was just the girlfriend. But she had survived Scrofo's monstrous humiliation before. She would again—she had to.

Without doubt it was he who had sent her the vile photographs, planted that sickening blind item. Could he also possibly have contacted the dreaded *Confidential* magazine too, telling them of her past? Knowing his sick mind, that would obviously be his next step.

A pair of tropical birds was singing outside her balcony, chasing each other around the lush foliage. Beyond the palm trees Inès could see the hard red tennis court, hear the thwack of ball against catgut, the excited cries of the players.

This is a war, but one neither of you will win, she thought. I've been in plenty of battles before and I have come out of them intact. She smiled grimly to the empty room.

You, Mademoiselle Dominique, even though you are more than a dozen years younger than me, and a little sex bomb to boot, will be quite easy to eliminate. Scrofo, however, would be another problem entirely. Until he was out of her life she would never have the secure future she craved.

❖ *Seventeen* ❖

RAMONA ARMANDE'S DINNER PARTY for Dominique's seventeenth birthday was a command performance for all the principals in the cast. Filming had been going well, and everyone seemed to be in high spirits as they gathered on the starlit terrace to toast the girl. But Dominique herself was in a sullen mood. She had been given a horrid shock when Julian arrived with Inès, who had pleaded with Dr. Langley to allow her to go to this party. Inès had decided that she must fight fire with fire. Even if that meant a possible risk to the baby, it was better than losing Julian to that pubescent Jezebel.

Julian had expressed guilty surprise when Inès told him that the doctor was allowing her to get up and do a little more, but he was delighted to see how gorgeous she looked when she was dressed and ready. More ravishing than ever—more desirable. He knew that sex was still out of bounds for them but he realized how much he truly loved her.

"I love you, Mrs. Brooks," he whispered as they walked arm in arm into Ramona's marble-and-crystal palace. "I can't wait to be married to you."

She smiled up at him radiantly as they strode into the room, the two of them a perfect picture of togetherness. Inès, pale but ravishing in a Balenciaga sheath of apricot chiffon, a color which complemented her luxuriant champagne-colored hair, Julian, as heart-stoppingly handsome as ever, in a black voile shirt and white linen trousers.

Dominique drew in her breath sharply and gritted her teeth. Her fingernails cut deeply into the palms of her hands, and she was flushed with fury. How could Julian show up with *her*? Why hadn't he told her that he was coming to her birthday party with Inès? She was supposed to be bedridden. *Merde.* This would certainly ruin her party. Particularly since the horrible Hubert Croft, who she had tried to keep away from the past several days, kept glaring at her with a secret disgusting smile. She shuddered. She hated that man. He was a sick monster, and she wished he was dead.

As for Hubert Croft, he thought himself quite a *bella figura* tonight in his overly tight black silk trousers and his white frilled Mexican shirt. But he too was also extremely surprised to see Inès. Surprised and angry, even though she'd been doing exactly what he'd instructed her to do. The six or seven times that he'd ordered her to persuade Julian to choose a particular scene, she had always managed to convince him to do it.

Hubert had been delighted that she was ill and no doubt tortured by the possibility of a miscarriage. Serves her right, the murdering whore. He'd put her out of his mind recently, concentrating all his attention on overseeing the movie and on keeping the studio in Hollywood up-to-date on what was happening.

Now here she was once again, the picture of elegance, dressed up like a fashion plate, hanging on to the arm of her famous fiancé, and smiling as charmingly as if butter wouldn't melt in her slut-mouth. His lips closed in a grim line as he observed Inès' perfect composure across the terrace. Surely she must have received the photographs he'd sent? It was meant to be his little joke, just to make her suffer more as she lay in bed day after day. Obviously the joke had misfired, because here she was looking radiant and carefree, and gazing at Julian as if he were Romeo, and she his Juliet. He'd like to wipe that sweet smile off her face. Oh, how he wanted to hurt this woman who had almost managed to put an end to him. He fingered his scar, which had started to itch again. Well, it wasn't too late—not at all. There was a week left to go on the movie, still time left to give Mademoiselle Inès Juillard a real taste of what she deserved.

Ramona was also thrown into a tizzy. She had a superstitious dread of thirteen people at her dinner table and Sir Crispin had brought his boyfriend, Tony, who had unexpectedly flown over from London. There was little she could do about it other than cross her fingers, pray to the blessed Virgin and nervously twist her elaborate necklace of gold-and-amber beads. She had placed the guests with her usual care tonight, with some help from Agathe, who had become friendly and helpful to her in so many ways. Ramona was pleased with her natural ability to bring shy people out of their shells.

Ramona drifted off to her winter dining room, where the glittering table for twelve twinkled with crystal and silver. Polished mirror placemats reflected the white lilies and hothouse roses which had been flown in specially on her private plane only that morning from Mexico City. Thirteen for dinner. Damn, damn, damn. She didn't want to make a fuss, but she felt it was a terrible omen. She ordered her butler to set another place, and after a few deft arrangements was satisfied that all would be well, though she hoped that no one else would notice the unlucky number.

Dinner proved a great success, and no one paid much attention to Dominique's barely disguised sulking. The oysters Mornay were delicious —several people asked for more—and the roast partridge, flown in from England, was a triumph.

"I'd like to make a toast," Nick said, raising his glass of vintage Krug. "To our new young star. Happy birthday, Dominique—we all love you, darling." He had been persuaded to come to Ramona's, just this once tonight, by a prettily pouting Dominique. He could hardly refuse.

Inès winced as everyone raised their glasses to Dominique and an enormous pink birthday cake, ablaze with seventeen long sparklers, was wheeled in. Dominique cut the cake prettily, posing flushed and excited for photographers from *Look* and *Photoplay*. She looked over at Julian, who smiled back at her coolly.

Hubert Croft made a pompous speech in his croaking voice, then Sir Crispin said a few amusing and well-chosen words, and finally Julian was cajoled into speaking. He rose, not one person at the table missing the irony of this situation: Julian and his two mistresses, both hanging on his every syllable. After he had finished a brief simple toast, finding it difficult to meet Dominique's wounded stare, there was a sudden silence. To break the tension, Irving Frankovitch decided to stand up and take the limelight.

"To a young actress of charm, talent and grace beyond her years," he began. "We are delighted—" Suddenly, a spasm of pain contorted his face; he weaved slightly and then slumped back into his chair, breathing heavily, his face ashen.

"I'm terribly sorry, but I don't feel at all well," he wheezed as Shirley rushed over to him.

Suddenly Inès too felt a wave of sickness, and she had a terrible feeling that if she did not leave the table at once she might embarrass herself dreadfully.

The baby, oh, the baby, she thought, as she felt the familiar and agonizing empty sensation deep down in the pit of her stomach. She looked towards Julian pleadingly, who was shocked at her pallor. Damn. He had told her he didn't think she could come out, but she had assured him that the doctor had said she could. Now she was the color of chalk and looked on the verge of collapse. He started to help her from the room when there was a piercing scream from Shirley Frankovitch as her husband fell heavily forward onto the table, his bald head smashing down on a Limoges plate of birthday cake with a sickening crash. The entire table was now in an uproar as all the guests started up, their faces greenish white, dashing for the bathrooms, some collapsing onto the floor with groans of pain.

Ramona was in a panic. "What on earth is happening?" she called to her dumbstruck butler, who couldn't seem to move. It was exactly as she had feared. The curse of thirteen at dinner was coming true with a vengeance.

"For God's sake, call a doctor," Nick shouted, unable to control the great tide of sickness which engulfed him. "Get an ambulance."

The stunned butler and waiters all stood rooted to the spot with fear, as if by moving they too might be infected by this terrible plague.

"We've all been poisoned."

Inès had no recollection of collapsing, no memory of the drive to the hospital, the trip in Ramona's private plane to Mexico City, or the long, complicated and dangerous operation which had been performed to save her life.

When she finally regained consciousness, it was several days later. She lay in a narrow white room, tubes and needles connecting her to various drips, and a pale, frantic Julian standing at the foot of her bed.

"Darling, oh, my darling, thank God," he cried softly, covering her arms and face with solicitous kisses. Then he held her face between his warm and reassuring hands, kneeling on the floor next to her bed, gazing at her with wonder, sadness and, most of all, with love.

"I thought I'd lost you, my angel. I thought you'd gone." His tired eyes were tearful, and Inès saw the exhaustion in his face.

"What happened?" She heard her own voice as if from a great distance. "We were at the party, then I can't remember anything. What was it, Julian? What happened?"

"Food poisoning," he said. "We all got it, everyone who was at the dinner. Some had it worse than others. You were one of the unlucky ones, I'm afraid."

"Where am I?" She looked out of the window, expecting to see palm trees and luxuriant foliage, but seeing only the concrete slabs of a city.

"Mexico City, darling—the best hospital in Mexico. Ramona sent us here in her plane. Oh, God, Inès, you nearly *died*. It's made me realize what a total fool I've been, what a bloody, stupid fool. I'm sorry, darling, I'm so sorry." He started to weep tears of both remorse and relief.

"Don't, darling, please don't." She lovingly stroked his hair and touched his tear-stained cheeks. She had never seen him cry before. Then her hands went to her flat stomach.

"The baby?" Her eyes were pleading now, filled with tears. "I've lost the baby, haven't I?"

He nodded sadly.

"Darling, listen." He sat on the bed, holding her close to him, filling his voice with optimism. "Please don't think about the baby—it's tragic, I know, but you're young, you'll have another baby, the doctor said so— many babies." He put a hand to her trembling lips, holding her closer as she started to sob.

"No, Inès, no," he said firmly. "*Stop* it. Please don't feel self-pity. It really could have been so much worse."

"How?" She tried to stop crying, but found she couldn't. "How much worse?"

"Irving Frankovitch is dead."

"Oh, God, no!" Inès' hand flew to her mouth. "How? Why?"

"According to the autopsy it was those bloody oysters Mornay we all ate. Apparently they were flown in from Mexico City the day before, but they were all rotten." He shook his head. "God, darling, you can't believe how sick everyone was. I've *never* seen anything like it, but poor old Irving didn't stand a chance. The old boy sort of crumpled up, collapsed in agony, and just died in front of us before the doctor could even get there. Sir Crispin got it very badly, too, but he's a tough old bird—he seems to have recovered now."

"And Dominique, how is she?" Inès tried to keep her voice expressionless as she watched Julian's reaction carefully.

"About the same as the others, I suppose," Julian replied simply. "I haven't spoken to her." This was the truth. "The only person who didn't get sick was Ramona."

He wanted to stay off the subject of Dominique. He had been burdened with even more guilt and shame ever since the dinner party. He had seen his weakness for what it was: purely and simply the lure of flesh, the lust of a greedy, selfish lecher who cares nothing for anyone or anything other than himself. An aging man making love to a teenager. He felt ridiculous and weak.

He despised himself for his affair with Dominique, for allowing it to get out of hand, for stupidly allowing it to become a subject for common gossip. He now realized that he would hate himself forever if he did anything to hurt Inès. But he *had* hurt her—he could clearly see the pain in her face which she was trying so hard to disguise.

"Why not Ramona?" Inès' voice sounded weak. "Why didn't she get sick?"

"She hates oysters—never eats them at all," Julian told her. "It was a stroke of luck that she didn't—she was able to organize the panicking servants, telephone doctors and arrange the ambulance and the plane for you. God, darling, it was ghastly."

"It must have been." Inès' eyes started to close. She felt so tired, but still clung tightly to Julian's hand. "I don't remember . . . I must sleep now, darling. Do you mind?"

He kissed her pale forehead. "Of course not. Sleep tight, angel," he whispered. "I love you, Inès—so much. I'll be right here when you wake up. I'll always be waiting for you, my love. Always."

Dominique had tried continuously to contact Julian. She, like the others, had suffered from the particularly virulent bout of salmonella food poisoning, and it had left her feverish and vomiting for twenty-four hours, frail and listless for several days.

The doctor had advised Hubert Croft that it would be unwise to shoot in the tropical heat while the actors were still in such a weakened state. The insurance company in L.A. had screamed their heads off, but the doctor remained adamant. The only people he would allow to work were Ramona, who had not been affected, and Julian, who had barely touched the oysters so had suffered little. But there were no scenes in *Cortez* which involved Ramona and Julian alone, so the crew and technicians sat idly by in the cafés and on the beaches, drinking beer and tequila punches and playing cards, while the insurance company fumed and Umberto weakly croaked out his instructions and sent long telegrams from his sickbed to the studio.

When Dominique hadn't been able to reach Julian, she had presumed he was just too sick to answer the telephone. But when Agathe reported that he had gone to Mexico City to be with Inès, Dominique was beside herself.

She stayed sobbing for hours in her room, not eating, playing Edith Piaf records of love and betrayal, miserably unhappy that Julian had not contacted her, not even sent her a note, a flower, anything. So this was the pain of rejected love which Piaf sang about. Well, she was certainly experiencing it for herself and she hated it—her heart felt empty and hollow and she had no appetite at all.

Whenever Agathe or Ramona called to see if she was all right, she sent them away, then buried her head in the pillow, weeping until she felt that she had no more tears left. Even Hubert Croft came to visit once, knocking at the door, but she had screamed "Fuck off" to him with such a volley of hysterical fury that he hadn't returned.

She had heard from Ramona about what had happened to Inès, and the thought that Julian was with his fiancée made her sick with jealousy. After discovering the name of the hospital in Mexico City she had instructed Ramona's operator to place a call.

When she heard Julian's voice on the crackling line, her knees started shaking.

"Julian," she whispered. "Oh, Julian, *mon amour,* is that you?"

"Dominique?" His voice was hushed as he stood in the corridor outside Inès' room. "Dominique—how are you?"

"Oh Julian, Julian—how *could* I be? I'm *terrible,*" she cried, starting to weep softly into the telephone. "I've missed you so much, but I didn't hear anything from you—nothing, nothing—oh Julian, what is happening to you—to us?"

There was a long silence before Julian answered.

"Dominique, what I am going to say to you is going to hurt you very much, I know, but I have to say it—I must say it now, otherwise I'm being a coward—and I *am,* Dominique—I've been the most terrible coward and I despise myself for it."

"What do you mean?" she asked, a feeling of panic rising within her.

"We cannot go on, Dominique," he said. "We can't—we just can't—it has to end."

"No," she moaned. "No, Julian, you can't mean it—I will *die*—I *swear* it—I'll kill myself."

"Hush, silly little girl, you'll do absolutely no such thing." His voice had a stern authoritative tone—almost fatherly, she thought bitterly.

"I was going to tell you properly, Dominique, when I returned to

Acapulco, I was going to tell you face-to-face—not like this on the telephone. But now that you have called, I must confess."

"Confess what?" she whispered. "What, Julian, *mon amour, l'amour de ma vie?*"

"Stop it, Dominique," he said. "Darling child—and you *are* a child, Dominique—I don't want to hurt you, I *never* wanted to hurt you—I loved you—in my fashion."

"I know you did," she breathed. "I know that—when you made love to me I knew how much you loved me."

"But it's not going to *work*, Dominique," he said firmly. "It *can't* and it *won't*."

"Why?" she asked. "You love me—you said it many times. Why can't it work?"

"Because I'm in love with Inès," he said simply, "and my life, my future is with her. I know that this is hard for you to understand, Dominique—and God knows I feel like a first-rate bastard for telling you like this, but even before the food poisoning I was going to tell you that it was all over between us. Our affair, my darling girl, must end."

"No, Julian, it's not true!" she cried.

"*Please,* Dominique darling—*please try* to understand. I know you're young. You're a baby. I'm twenty years older than you. You need to be with someone of your own age. It could never work. I don't want to hurt you but this must be the end." He could hear her sobs but he continued, "Please understand, darling girl, please."

"No," she sobbed. "I can't—I won't understand."

"You must," he whispered. "You *will*, my darling child. I know you will. Now be a good girl—go back to bed and tomorrow you'll start forgetting all about me—good-bye, my darling."

"Never," said Dominique, tears running down her face. "I'll never forget you, Julian, how can I?"

But there was nothing more to be heard from Mexico City. The line was dead. Sobbing, Dominique threw herself on the bed, buried her head in her pillow and finally cried herself to sleep.

And some three hundred miles away in a stark hospital room, Inès quietly closed the door, a faint smile on her lips, having listened to all of Julian's conversation.

Dominique eventually decided that weeping over Julian wasn't worth it. Her pragmatic French brand of common sense took over, and she decided that she had been a complete fool to fall in love with a man the same age as her father. Yes, he had been a wonderful lover, he had taught her a great deal about sex, but then so had Gaston. Perhaps now was the time to put their lessons into practice.

Two days after speaking to Julian over the telephone she had recovered, and her natural youthful energy returned. She put on her beach clothes, and knocking on Agathe's door, called that she was heading for Caleta Beach to go water-skiing, did Agathe want to come? The door was slightly ajar so she pushed it open wider and saw, to her surprise, Agathe fast asleep on the bed. She was wearing a man's dirty white shirt, an old rag was bunched up under her chin, and a large album crammed with what looked like press clippings and photographs lay on the floor next to the bed.

"Agathe," Dominique said softly, "want to come skiing with me?" There was a groan from the sleeping woman, so Dominique shrugged, closed the door and skipped off to the beach.

She was seventeen, gorgeous and a budding movie star. The world was hers for the taking. Young men whistled wherever she went, and she smiled back at them. There was nothing for her to feel sad or down about, nothing, not even Julian Brooks. He was a middle-aged man, she was young—young and free and beautiful. She could have her pick of men.

She took one of Ramona's jeeps to drive to the beach. The soft breeze blew her hair across her face, and she could smell the tang of the ocean and the aroma of tacos cooking in the little beach restaurant. As she came nearer she could hear mariachis playing and see teenagers dancing and enjoying the glorious day. She parked the car, conscious of the many eyes watching her. Dominique always enjoyed people staring, and she swung her hips in her snug shorts as she walked.

She quickened her stride as she saw a tall, tanned boy with yellow curls looking at her, smiling invitingly with eyes that were bluer than the sea.

"Hi. Wanna Coke?" he asked as soon as she entered the bar. She nodded. When he brought it over to her, she noted with some interest his strongly muscled arms and sculpted chest. How firm and deeply bronzed they were. In contrast, she noticed that he had tiny golden hairs like down all over his arms. Very pretty indeed, she thought. How exciting to have those arms around me. He was good-looking, too. Not the handsomest man in the world but young and sexy and very virile.

"An' then maybe you an' I can go water-skiing?" He grinned lazily, and Dominique smiled back.

"Would you like that?" he said.

"I love water-skiing," she told him. "I know *just* the place to go." And her eyes strayed down to the bulge in his shorts.

Agathe awoke just when Dominique closed her door. At first she didn't know where she was, and then it all came back to her. In the week since the salmonella outbreak, she had thought of nothing else.

Fool. She was a fool and an idiot. She had failed to do what she had planned so carefully. It had been a faultless scheme—the perfect murder which she had read about long ago in one of her books in the cellar in Paris, but it had backfired badly. Her plot had killed the wrong person. Agathe hadn't really spoken more than a dozen words to Irving Frankovitch—a nice enough man, now dead because of her ineptitude.

She had bought some oysters at the local market some days before Dominique's birthday party, and had hidden them in a windowsill just outside her room. The day of the party she had helped Ramona and the servants set the table and had supervised the staff as they brought in the first course of oysters Mornay. Unknown to them, she had inserted an eyedropper into the rotting oysters and dripped a tiny drop of their poison onto each fresh oyster. One of the bad ones, however, as well as some slightly poisoned oysters, she put on the plate intended for Inès. The Mornay sauce, Agathe assumed, would disguise the taste of the rotten oyster, and Inès would die soon after she swallowed it.

But Sir Crispin had unexpectedly brought a friend, and Ramona had not consulted Agathe about changing the place settings. Irving Frankovitch had eaten the oysters meant for Inès. Agathe's *soi-disant* perfect murder was ruined.

She had bungled it badly, very badly indeed. It was Inès who should have died . . . Inès the whore . . . the murderess . . . the traitor . . . the enemy slut. Agathe's hatred for her was so intense that it was almost like a burning coal in her chest. She moaned, clutching Julian's tattered shirt to her lips, sniffing the cotton fabric, trying to find a taste of him, his scent, his essence, his sweat.

Where is he now? she thought. With *her,* in Mexico City, planning their wedding day, the birth of their baby, their life together in London? *No!*

Agathe sat bolt upright in Ramona's silky lime-green-sheeted bed, staring at an enormous painting of some huge butterflies of all shades and varieties. She was trembling violently, both from the aftereffects of the self-inflicted food poisoning and from pure hatred. She looked around the silk-paneled room decorated with every species of butterfly imaginable. Her heart was beating so fast she thought it would burst, and she pounded her fists on the mattress in an uncontrollable fury.

First the woman had been Inès Dessault. Then Inès Juillard and within the next few weeks she would be Inès Brooks—Mrs. Julian Brooks. "No . . . no." Agathe was crooning softly now, feverishly turning her amber rosary around her neck. "It can't be. It can't happen. She will *not* marry him. She cannot. She *will not.*"

Two people now seemed to be in possession of her psyche, each battling for supremacy. There was Agathe Guinzberg the prim chaperone, the spinster ballet teacher—polite, quiet and well-mannered. And then there was Agathe the devil, the woman who slaked her lust for Julian Brooks every night on her bed, in the green onyx bath, on the floor . . . whispering his name, rubbing herself fiercely with his shirt, kissing his photographs, moaning with infatuated madness.

She could not stop herself anymore. Just the thought of him made her ache until only the rough touch of his shirt could ease the burning between her legs.

Last week, when she had sat on a canvas chair next to Sir Crispin, watching Julian laugh, studying the tiny beads of sweat on his muscled chest, right there in the chair she had felt the waves rise within her. She could almost feel him entering her as she squeezed her thighs together tightly until she reached a plateau of pleasure which had been unknown to her a few weeks ago.

It was as though a dam had burst inside her. She couldn't stop. Six, seven, eight times a day, whispering her love's name, she reached more and more tumultuous orgasms. But once—oh, God, just once—she wanted *him* to make love to her, to fuse that magnificent body with hers. She yearned for that.

Agathe was still technically a virgin and had only a vague idea of what a naked man even looked like, but last week, she had even stolen one of the phallic-shaped candles Ramona kept for her winter dining room, and now this, too, was used to pleasure herself.

Thirty-one years of frigidity exploded into lust as Agathe found herself on a merry-go-round of erotic enslavement without a partner to satisfy her. Julian belonged to her. He was her destiny—her man—she had to win him away from Inès. He had to know how much Agathe loved him—how they were meant to be together.

Despairingly, she did it again now, almost viciously—chafing, hurting herself with the blue shirt which was now not much more than a tattered rag. Afterward, exhausted, she tried to think. She *had* to think, she knew she must try to end this obsession with Julian—his face, his body, his eyes, his cock which she had glimpsed once, outlined by yellow bathing trunks when he was playing ball in the water with some of the crew.

She knew that what she was doing and what was happening to her was a sin, but she was no longer in control of herself.

She rang for some coffee and papaya, and while unsuccessfully trying to read the *Acapulcan News,* she thought again of how her plan had failed. It had been a good plan—an excellent plan, but the next one had to be absolutely foolproof.

◆ *Eighteen* ◆

THERE WERE ONLY a few days of shooting left, and Inès began to feel better both physically and emotionally. Although saddened by her miscarriage, she was assured that she could have more children, and there was the consolation that the experience had brought her closer to Julian again. He had confessed his affair with Dominique, apologizing so profusely and so fiercely that Inès forgave him. Now she could visit the set to watch him work again, and she went every day, trying not to be intimidated by Scrofo and his cold, deadly stare.

Much to Scrofo's chagrin, the sexual electricity between Julian and Dominique had fizzled out completely. He had tried to cause a chasm between Inès and Julian by sending her the scandalous photographs he had bribed a local photographer to take the day Julian and Dominique had gone to the island. The pictures were excellent but his ploy hadn't worked, for Inès and Julian were still together. Stupid bitch, she had forgiven him. To take a man back into her bed when she knew he'd been fucking another woman—she didn't deserve to be happy.

Scrofo followed Inès one night when she took a solitary walk along the beach, away from the shooting; then he cornered her.

"You think you're safe now, don't you—whore," he said, his eyes gleaming a sulphurous yellow in the humid darkness as he grabbed her arm, holding it too tightly.

"Let go of me, Scrofo," Inès said calmly, realizing that no one was around to help her.

His grip became more viselike as she repeated, "Please let me go."

"I'll let go of you when I'm good and ready, whore," he hissed. "You got my little present, I presume?"

"If you mean those filthy photographs—yes, I received them. And I tore them up," she said coldly.

"Of course—of course you did. You didn't want to look at snaps of your fiancé making love to his underage paramour, did you?"

"Look, Scrofo, why are you doing this? I did *everything* you asked of me."

In spite of herself Inès felt hot tears stinging her eyelids. Still weak from surgery, she detested this man so much that the mere touch of his hand filled her with loathing.

"*Every* scene that you sent to Julian I persuaded him to do—for weeks I did that, Scrofo. Surely that's enough for you?"

"No—it'll *never* be enough," he croaked. "It's a small price to pay for *this.*"

He pushed his neck closer to reveal in ghastly detail the puckered scar tissue. She could almost see the surgeon's stitches in his flesh.

"*You* did this, bitch, and you must be punished. I need to punish you much, much more—and you will be when the magazine comes out. You certainly will be." He laughed triumphantly. "That will make you squirm."

"What magazine?" she asked.

"Ah, that's *my* little secret," he gloated. "But the whole of America, in fact the whole of the world, will see the pictures of Dominique and your fiancé screwing each other—censored of course," he sneered. "Then the whole world will know about you and your whoring past."

"How will they know? How—what have you done?" cried Inès. "Whatever I did to you . . . whatever happened was *years* ago. Can't you forget it, Scrofo—leave me in peace? Why do you need to do this now? Why?"

"I can *never* forget, slut—never," Scrofo said savagely. "But it isn't just me who's contributing to your downfall. I have an expert witness to your sordid past. One who knows you well. Better than Julian—better than anyone in fact."

"Who?" breathed Inès. "Who is this person?"

"Yves Moray," chortled Scrofo, relishing his moment of victory. "Your ex-pimp. Your ex-lover—the one who deflowered you. My people found him in Paris last week."

"No, it's not possible," whispered Inès. "You couldn't have."

"Oh, but it is, it's very possible. The world is really a very tiny place," sneered Scrofo. "Look at us, Inès my dear—who would ever think that you and I, who met in such unfortunate and squalid circumstances in Paris, would be here together in beautiful Acapulco making a film?"

His brutal hand held her arm so tightly that she could feel the bruises his fingers were making.

"Where did you meet Yves?" she asked, her voice shocked into a thready whisper.

"Oh, I didn't meet him—I didn't even see the man. It all happened quite by accident, a fortuitous coincidence for me. He was arrested in Paris for fencing some stolen jewelry. At the police station he was babbling on in an alcoholic stupor and pleading his innocence—his complete innocence—of the theft, but of course he was such a pathetic drunken bum that no one believed him, so they threw him in a cell. And guess what, Inès?" He bent his face close to hers, leering with vindictive glee. "There was a photograph of you and Julian in a magazine that another prisoner had; poor Yves started bragging that he knew you. In fact he knew you extremely well—because *you worked for him when you were fourteen years old!* He said he was your pimp and you were his little baby whore, and he taught you everything he knew."

"No . . ." sighed Inès. "It's a lie."

"Oh, no, my dear—it's no lie," said Scrofo, relishing his power. "One of the prisoners happened to be an old army acquaintance of mine, a Signor Volpi who knew that I was producing a film with Julian Brooks. He contacted me and told me the whole fascinating story, and then I phoned your old boyfriend Yves. Of course he told me everything. It's amazing what a drunk will do for a few hundred francs," he remarked contemptuously. "Well, the rest, as they say, is history. It makes a wonderful story, Inès—rags to riches, tart to movie star's wife—and then *fini.*" He looked at her pityingly. "Enjoy the short time you have left with your fiancé, Mademoiselle. Because when he reads the truth about your whoring past, your life with Julian Brooks will be finished."

On the way down to the beach from his trailer, Nick was stopped by the harsh sound of Scrofo's raised voice. What was Gourouni doing now? Who was he trying to intimidate? He drew closer into the shadows to watch and listen, silent as stone. Scrofo obviously had some sort of sick hold on Inès. Nick heard the vicious blackmailing threats and his lips tightened in anger. Scrofo was vermin. He didn't deserve to breathe the same air as decent people.

Nick was just about to go over and help Inès when he heard Bluey's voice yelling on the loudspeaker from farther along the beach: "Nick, where the hell are you? We're ready for rehearsal, pal, get your butt down here pronto."

At that the Italian released his grip on Inès' arm, pushing her away from him so violently that she stumbled and fell to the sand.

In Nick's mind Inès suddenly became his mother, cowering on the ground while the monster Gourouni towered over her, ready to kill. The tableau was so real, so terrifyingly graphic that Nick wanted to scream out at the top of his lungs. Nick was going to kill the murdering slime now. He had to.

As he started to race towards them the tableau suddenly dissolved. Inès had clambered to her feet and run down the beach and Scrofo had turned, laughing, strutting off in the opposite direction. Nick's hand clawed at the knife in his pocket and he started to follow Scrofo.

"Nick! For Christ's sake, where are you? It'll be dawn soon. Hurry up." Bluey's amplified voice brought Nick back to the present. He shook his head as if to clear it as he watched the squat figure of Gourouni disappear into the night, then he walked rapidly down to the set, with more loathing than ever in his heart for Scrofo.

The following evening in the production office at Scheherazade, Scrofo attempted to tell Nick and Bluey that Inès had been a prostitute. Bluey looked at him with disgust.

"That's a helluva thing to say," he spat. "You've got a dirty mind, Hubie baby."

Nick however, suddenly became violently angry.

"Listen, you suet-faced prick," he roared as he gripped the Italian's fleshy shoulders and pushed his face close, "don't you ever, *ever* talk about a lady—*any* lady—like that around me, or in front of *anyone*, do you understand, you motherfucker?"

Suddenly Umberto was genuinely terrified as Nick's hands were now around his neck, his voice hoarse with hatred as he squeezed the adipose, scarred flesh of Scrofo's throat.

"You rotten scum," he bellowed. "You *dare* to talk about whores. *You're* the whore, you lump of shit. What you did to those people. What you did to them . . ." His voice started to crack as his grip tightened, and Scrofo's eyes were beginning to pop out of their sockets, his face turning crimson.

The vision of his mother filled Nick's brain. Her quiet beauty and goodness snuffed out by his bastard. He was going to kill him now, at last. He'd rid the world of this filth.

Nick's eyes were closed and his hands, clamped around Scrofo's neck, began to squeeze even harder.

Bluey could see that Hubert was losing consciousness.

"For Christ's sake, quit it, Nick. He's not worth it," Bluey screamed as he tried to pry his friend off the wilting Italian. The transformation of a man who was usually so controlled in spite of all the difficulties on the set, calm in emergencies, hardly ever losing his cool, was as alarming as what he was actually doing.

"*Stop* it, Nick, for God's sake stop it! You're only hurting yourself," Bluey yelled. "Get hold of yourself, man—you must."

Nick released Scrofo's neck as Bluey's voice penetrated his consciousness and he slumped into the chair, his breathing shallow, his face still contorted with rage. Bluey realized that Nick could have killed Umberto if he hadn't intervened—and the Italian thought so too. His pudgy hands gingerly massaged his scarred and now bruised throat where the livid red marks of Nick's fingers were imprinted.

"Jesus, kid. Jesus Christ, slow down," Bluey said and quickly poured him a stiff scotch.

Nick tossed it down, his burning eyes fixed on Scrofo.

"Get out of here, you fucking pig," Nick spat, his voice hoarse and shaking. "I'm making a fucking movie. I'll do what the fucking studio tells me to do on the set but don't *ever* talk about that woman or *any* woman in front of me again or I'll squeeze your fat neck until your eyeballs come out of your head. I mean it, pigface—get out of my sight. *Now.*"

Bluey poured another whiskey as Umberto, badly frightened and quite the opposite of the *bella figura* he fancied himself, nervously slunk out of the office. I will have my revenge, he thought. When these idiots see what comes out in *Confidential* they will realize I am right about the French slut. They'll know she's a murdering whore. That will be my first revenge on her. After that—who knows? His mind boiling with ideas about how to ruin Inès, he limped off through the dark corridor to his room.

"I hate that motherfucker," Nick breathed. "It's only a matter of time before I kill the bastard."

"Hey, hey, kiddo, *quit* it, will ya?" Bluey tried to soothe Nick. "We all know he's a complete asshole—a phony who knows as much about the movie business as my left testicle. Don't let him get to you. You're doin' great. The studio loves the dailies, you're keeping your head above water, and the picture's on schedule and even on budget. We've only got a few days left. You're a whiz kid, so calm down, will ya?"

Nick nodded, the whiskey clearing his head a little. "Gotta get some sleep, Bluey." He pulled his worry beads out of his pocket and swung them morosely while he gazed out of a window at the sliver of new moon palely reflected on the still, black water. Then he picked up his bulky script, and walked decisively to the door. "I'm sorry, Bluey. It's a good thing you stopped me. I was out of control—I was gone, man, gone."

"Get to bed, kiddo," Bluey said. He looked worried. "Big scene tomorrow. You gotta give it your best shot. Forget Hubert, Nick, for God's sake."

"I can't forget him, Bluey—I've seen that face too many times. I've seen it in my dreams and in every fuckin' nightmare I've ever had."

"What are you talkin' about, man?" asked Bluey. "You only met the motherfucker a few months ago."

"Oh, no," Nick said harshly. "He's haunted my life for more than ten years."

"Jesus." Bluey was silent as he stared at Nick's grim face. "What has he done to you, kid? Whatever he did, it couldn't have been that bad."

"He murdered my mother," Nick said simply. "He killed her and I'm going to kill him."

◆*Nineteen*◆

Inès had been undecided about whether or not to watch Julian and Dominique shooting their tenderly erotic final love scene. The two actors had not worked together since Dominique's birthday party, and when they saw each other again there had been a noticeable coolness between them. Inès had heard through the gossip grapevine that although she now had a new boyfriend, Dominique was still furious and hurt that Julian had ended the affair. Inès understood how the girl must feel; Julian had not conducted himself at all well.

"Do you want me to come to the set tonight?" she asked casually as she lay back on the bed in the twilight dusk, watching Julian prepare to leave.

"It's entirely up to you, darling." He found it difficult to meet her eyes. Julian was in a quandary. He hadn't spoken to Dominique since he terminated their affair, and felt like a cad because of explaining the situation to her only on the telephone, but the circumstances had never seemed right to face her directly. He had been working hard on the exhausting battle scenes, and in his free time had thrown himself into his reconciliation with Inès. They had been utterly inseparable as he comforted her over the loss of their baby.

He was secretly dreading his lovemaking scene with Dominique. It was tricky enough to have to simulate making passionate love to a girl with whom you had recently ended a blazing real-life affair, but even more galling was knowing that he had not behaved at all like a gentleman towards her, and he was angry with himself.

Now the thought of Inès watching their fervent kisses and caresses embarrassed him.

With her natural intuition, Inès understood completely. "Darling, don't worry," she said, smiling. "I'm expecting a call from the doctor in Los Angeles. The results of those blood tests should be in. I think I'll just stay here, drink margaritas and watch the sun set."

"No, I really think you should come, darling. Yes, yes, really, I want you there," Julian said firmly, moving next to her on the bed, gazing into her glorious eyes. "Please come, darling. I need you. You know it's over between Dominique and me, you do believe me, don't you?"

"Of course I do. All right, I'll come, later tonight," Inès agreed, brushing a strand of hair off his forehead, then kissing him lovingly. "I'm not worried about you and Dominique. And I'll stay well in the background. Don't worry, my darling; I won't make a fool of myself, I promise."

Julian gave her a rueful look as he picked up his script and blew her a kiss.

"I love you, Inès. You're magnificent. I'll see you later."

Inès stared at the closed door for several minutes, trying to analyze how she really felt about watching Julian and Dominique making love. Did she mind? Did it bother her, knowing that the whole crew would be watching her reaction? And the odious Scrofo, who had gone to such pains to blackmail her, gloating—looking at her for any signs of weakness.

She shrugged as she sauntered into the bathroom. It didn't bother her anymore. She believed that Julian was completely over his infatuation. If his verbal assurances were not enough, his passionate declarations of love, even though lovemaking was still forbidden, reassured Inès that he was hers, and hers alone As far as others were concerned, she really didn't give a damn what people thought If they chose to gossip and tittle-tattle, she would be above all that. The only person who made her skin crawl, whose very presence in a room made her squirm with loathing, was the sluglike Scrofo. She had to do something to stop this terrible story coming out in the magazine. She had tried hard to talk to Scrofo the day after he'd threatened her, begging him not to print it, but he had merely laughed, telling her, "You have a couple more months of the good life left, Inès. The magazine is holding the story until just before the release of *Cortez* It will be great publicity for the film—huge coverage. Make it an absolute surefire box-office blockbuster, don't you agree? Those pictures of Julian and Dominique making love—so sexy—so titillating—everyone will race to see the film. We'll be a runaway hit."

Sickened, unable to reply, she had walked away. There was still some time left to stop the story from being published, but it would be common gossip in Hollywood long before that. As soon as Julian heard, he would question her. Of course she could lie, but she would have to tell him the truth, the whole sickening ghastly truth. Inès shuddered.

Next week, as soon as she and Julian arrived in Los Angeles, they were going to be married. The final decree had been issued, and she would be Mrs Julian Brooks at long last. She had to stop Scrofo from printing the truth about her in that magazine. She had to—but how?

Agathe sat beside Dominique in her small, stuffy trailer by the water's edge. She was going through tonight's dialogue with her, but her heart wasn't in it.

On the sofa was a week-old copy of *The Hollywood Reporter*. The lead item in the gossip column had caught Agathe's eyes the instant she sat down:

Wedding bells will ring out at last for Julian Brooks and the lovely Inès Juillard. The happy couple will tie the knot next week at the home of Spyros Makopolis after an arduous three-month stint in Acapulco on *Cortez*, the legendary Julian's first American film. Congratulations to the two of them.

A white-hot flame was burning in Agathe's head and she couldn't concentrate on anything Dominique was saying or doing.

Makeup girls and hairdressers bustled around the young star as she sat having pancake makeup applied to her chest and shoulders. She seemed as usual to have no modesty; she was bare to the waist, calmly allowing the body makeup girl to paint her exposed flesh.

She had few words to learn except "I love you" and "My father will never understand." Kisses and burning passion were the main ingredients of the scene tonight as Cortez and the princess would be rolling around naked on the sandy beach in the moonlight. Dominique had been given a flesh-colored body stocking to wear to save the censors' blushes. Her nude dance scene had been approved by the Hays Office but there was still a limit to the amount of licentiousness which they would allow on screen.

Dominique thought about how it would be to make love with Julian again. Always during their scenes together he had wanted her afterward, and their combined passion had rocked the flimsy walls of the trailer. But Inès had never been around then. Now she was on the sidelines watching all the time, never taking her eyes off her fiancé. Dominique sighed. There was little chance of a reconciliation with Julian, she realized. But she had seen the flash of desire in his eyes when they had kissed during rehearsal, though it had gone as quickly as it appeared and he was again the ultimate professional—the actor—coolly removed, pleasant, trading japes and jokes with the crew, polite and considerate towards her. Dominique knew she had lost him, but after all she had Frankie. Her new boyfriend was a member of the crew, American, young, blond, a most attentive suitor and a good lover. Not as good as Julian but certainly younger.

Agathe, her own passion for Julian still raging, couldn't have cared less by now that her young charge was having an affair. Nothing mattered to her anymore. She tried hard to act as normally as possible around the crew, hoping that no one would notice that she was thinking about Julian all the time. No one did.

There was a knock on the door and Frankie loped in, a broad smile on his face.

"Oooh!" Dominique said, pretending to be shy and half-covering her breasts. *"Méchant garçon.* You surprised me—give me a kiss."

They kissed lingeringly, neither noticing that Agathe had slipped out of the trailer as soon as the boy entered it—she needed her fix. A glimpse of Julian, maybe even a word from him, it was all that she lived for these days.

As the new moon slid behind a puff of darkened cloud, a lone figure sped quickly down the hundred or more stone steps that descended at one side of Scheherazade. The guard dogs were silent; the figure knew at exactly what time they were taken on their rounds, and had timed the arrival at the cable car perfectly to avoid the watchdogs and their handlers.

Swiftly the figure squatted by the side of the wooden carriage and, removing a few small tools from a pocket, made some slight adjustments to the machine's gear box. It took only a few minutes; then, with a furtive glance around, ears strained for the slightest sound, the figure disappeared into the thick tropical foliage which surrounded the vast estate.

Now, as the moon reappeared from behind the clouds, it was reflected in the small puddle of amber beads which had been dropped behind the padded seat of the wooden cable car.

They had decided to shoot Dominique and Julian's love scene on Ramona's private beach, well away from the prying eyes of Acapulco tourists. Part of the beach was brilliantly lit by a dozen arc lamps, which were placed around the area on which the stand-ins for Julian and Dominique were lying on the sand entwined in each other's arms.

Nick paced up and down nervously, a cigarette hanging permanently from his lips, talking to his lighting cameraman and to Bluey. Sometimes he glanced over to where Scrofo stood, half concealed behind an arc lamp, as usual speaking to no one but occasionally staring over at Nick with hatred.

Nick stared right back at him. How could this man have become such a monster, he wondered. What in his childhood had created such a sadistic beast? There had to be some reason for his venom, for the evil that seemed to radiate from him. He looked over again, but Scrofo was gone.

Nick shrugged as he went over to where his unit bustled about chatting quietly. They were all thankful that for once the Toad was not hanging around the set to irritate them. All the crew, and most members of the cast, had suffered from Croft's foul mouth during the past few months. All of them despised him, and few made it a secret.

Shirley Frankovitch's reports on his acumen as a line producer had been totally exaggerated. The charm, diplomacy and respect she had glowingly talked of were all sadly lacking. His knowledge of the mechanics of filmmaking was rudimentary, and his alienation of the crew and the actors was remarkable in its totality. Things were always more calm on the set, and certainly Nick was easier to work with, when the fat Italian wasn't around.

Farther down the beach Julian sat in his canvas chair wearing a light seersucker robe over his flesh-colored bathing suit. He flicked through the pages of his dialogue casually, looking up as Inès came to sit beside him, smiling as he put his hand lightly on her shoulder.

The moon shimmered on the flat ocean, with only a slight tide disturbing the shoreline as Inès put her hand on his, and they both stared out at the sea.

One of Ramona's houseboys suddenly appeared and tapped Inès on the shoulder, handing her a scribbled note.

"Excuse me, darling," she said. "The doctor's calling from Los Angeles. I must go up to the main house to take the call."

"I hope the results from the tests are okay," said Julian.

"I'm sure they are," Inès smiled. "I'll be right back, darling."

Julian blew her a kiss and admired her slender body as she walked across the beach to the cable car.

It sat at the base of the jagged rocks, its plain white wooden frame strangely out of place against the splendor of the exotic, sumptuous surroundings.

Inès got in and pressed the third button. With a shuddering creak the ancient contraption started its gradual ascent up the side of the steep rocks to the house. It seemed to be going much slower than usual, Inès thought; it shook and trembled all the way up, and there was an odd sort of rasping sigh from the pulleys as they dragged the groaning machine up to the third level.

The third floor was in complete darkness. Inès stepped from the cable car onto the white marble floor, her flimsy sandals echoing hollowly as she made her way to the main production office.

The room was pitch black. Inès shivered even though it was a humid night. She switched on the light, went over to the telephone and told the operator to put through her call from Los Angeles.

"There's no one on the line for you, *Señora*," the operator said.

"But there must be. I just received a message that my doctor was calling," Inès told her.

"No, I'm sorry. No one has called you at all tonight, Miss Juillard. It must be a mistake."

Puzzled, Inès replaced the receiver and sat thinking for a moment before she went to the door. As she reached it she saw in the hallway the shadow of a horribly familiar squat figure strutting slowly between the marble pillars of the terrace. She stopped. The last person she wanted to see or talk to was Umberto Scrofo. She did not want to be cornered by him again. Not at night, in the empty darkness of the villa.

Suddenly Scrofo stopped in his tracks, turning around swiftly as if he had heard something. He was like an animal, Inès thought, he had the instincts of a beast.

She could smell his cologne, that foul, cheap scent which seemed to hang in the night air like a noxious vapor. Even the odor of his body lingered after him.

After a few seconds Scrofo continued on his way, obviously heading for the cable car. Inès saw him press a button, then heard the familiar loud creaking as the machine began its laborious, strained descent.

The funicular had not gone more than a few feet when there was a harsh rending noise, a cacophony of screeching wires and pulleys exploding out of their sockets, and a hideous animal scream from Scrofo as the white wooden carriage was ripped from its moorings and began to fall down the sheer cliff.

Inès ran to the cable car's top landing and to her horror saw the cable car smashing its way down, down, down to the bottom of the rocks. All the way Scrofo screamed in terror. Inès could see as if in slow motion the hated bullet head, the great yaw of a gargoyle's mouth opened in the agony of his inevitable death as he plummeted to the ground.

Scrofo tried to hang on until the last impact. When his body was thrown twenty feet through the air, it landed on the rocks like a smashed doll. All that he had managed to clutch for support was a small row of broken amber beads, and the tiny crucifix which hung from them.

❧ *Epilogue* ☙

HOLLYWOOD. ONE YEAR LATER

For over a year the whole of America had been bombarded with hype on MCCP's latest, greatest and soon to be released blockbuster, *The Legend of Cortez*. It was a rare newspaper or magazine indeed which had not featured some story, photograph or article on one or other of the principals in the movie. *Cortez* mania gripped the nation, and MCCP was crossing its corporate fingers that the publicity machine had done its work well enough to guarantee that every box-office register would be working overtime.

Although the new stretch-version Cadillac was fitted with the latest in air conditioning, the hot California night still made the air hang heavy inside the perfumed darkness of the car. There were six of them in the limousine—Nicholas and Elektra Stone, Dominique with a handsome escort, and Julian and his wife.

She was concerned that the excessive and controversial publicity which he had received might adversely influence the critics. Julian was being hailed as the greatest English actor since Olivier, and his name had become a household word long before most of the American public had even had a glimpse of his talents. Hubert S. Croft's death and the scandal of Inès' past had been universal gossip for months after the incident. The death of the Italian producer was as juicy a piece of news as anyone had heard for years.

Julian held his wife's hand, smiling at her reassuringly. He had seen a rough cut of the movie, and although self-critical to an extreme, he realized that his performance had been electrifying. He had brought to his stereotyped role a swashbuckling magnetism, combined with a sensitive naturalism, which had been nurtured and polished on the London stage. The word was out in Hollywood that he was about to become as big a male star as Gable. The stacks of offers which poured into his agent's office ensured him a place in cinematic history, but his thoughts, in fact, were less on tonight's premiere than on his next challenge. He was going back to his roots to star in *Coriolanus* on the West End stage. He felt that he'd already spent enough time on the Hollywood scene, even though the result so far had been just two films, but he had only two more pictures to make for MCCP. When those were finished their baby,

David, would be almost three years old, and they had decided to settle down in one place to give the child the security of an ordered life.

"Did David mind that you didn't stay with him until he went to bed?" Julian asked.

"Oh, no, darling. I think he must somehow have realized how important tonight is to his daddy." She thought lovingly of month-old David's beautiful smile as she handed him to his nanny after giving him his bottle. Julian was her life, but David ran a close second, and she adored her two men passionately.

She sighed happily. She felt she was a lucky woman.

"Oh, look," Dominique pointed excitedly to a small art-house cinema they were just passing on Sunset Boulevard. *"La Città Perduta*—wasn't that Hubert Croft's Italian film?"

Everyone peered through the tinted windows of the limousine to where the flickering neon sign spelled out the names of the cast and that of Umberto Scrofo as producer.

"Honey, don't remind us of *him*—that's all over and forgotten," Dominique's escort told her. "It's yesterday's news."

Nick stared out blankly at the cinema. Hubert S. Croft, Umberto Scrofo. The man whose ghastly image had haunted him for so much of his life. Dead now, but the memory of him would never die. Nick could never forget the horrors of those war years on Hydra, the countless atrocities which Scrofo had committed, culminating in the brutal murder of his mother.

"It's a year ago tonight," Nick said quietly.

"What is?" Dominique asked.

"It's one year exactly since Scrofo died." Nick's voice was so soft that the others had to strain to hear him.

"Oh, my God, so it is, you're absolutely right," breathed Julian. "God, only a year."

"As far as I'm concerned that bastard finally got what he deserved," Nick said harshly.

"Poor Agathe," Dominique muttered. "I wonder what she's doing now."

"Rotting behind bars in some Mexican jail." Julian's voice was uncharacteristically unsympathetic. "She was a madwoman, completely certifiable. If Croft or Scrofo, or whatever his name was, hadn't died that night, it would have been Inès for certain."

"And all for the love of you, Julian," Dominique teased. "All for the love of you." She flashed him her sultry gamine smile as she snuggled closer to her escort.

There had been several men in Dominique's life in the past year. As an eighteen-year-old star with a brilliant future, she was more gloriously sexy than ever and reveled unashamedly in her sorceress ways. She smiled at Julian, who smiled back uncomfortably. They were friendly now, but she knew she would never get over their passionate romance until he belonged to her again. How could she? It had been the ultimate and perfect love for her—and she wanted it to happen all over again. It was a once in a lifetime affair, never to be forgotten.

But something which none of them would ever forget was that night—that terrible night in Acapulco exactly one year ago.

When the Acapulco police arrived at Ramona's villa, Inspector Gomez had begun his slow interrogation of each of them about Hubert Croft's "accident." He strongly believed it to be murder, and questioned everyone with painstaking care. By the time he turned his attention to Agathe, the woman was trembling violently, her face shining with sweat, and she was wringing her hands in a frenzy.

Before the Inspector could question her, she fixed her eyes on Inès and crooned softly, "It's all her fault. She made me do it—didn't you, Inès?" Her eyes seemed to burn into Inès who was suddenly dry-mouthed, unable to speak. "Yes, you did," Agathe spat. "You forced me to do it. I killed Hubert Croft. *I* did," she hissed. "But I didn't mean to. I meant *her* to die. She—*she* should have been the one who ate the poisoned oyster, not Irving." She took a step toward Inès, who stood absolutely still, rooted in shock. "Inès Dessault—Inès Juillard, the *whore*. She should have been in the cable car."

"What? What did you say? Why did you kill him?" said the Inspector, scribbling furiously as the others watched Agathe's transformation in amazement. The mouse was turning into a she-wolf, and it was not a pretty sight.

"Because of *her!*" she screamed, saliva flecking the corners of her lips; her eyes wild and bloodshot "The enemy whore—why didn't you die? Why—why? You should have. I planned it so well—so perfectly."

Dry keening sobs racked her emaciated body and her hands became claws as she suddenly tried to pounce on the spellbound Inès. Two burly policemen grabbed her by the arms, trying to hold her as her sobs became heaving cries of pent-up rage and frustration.

"The wrong person died. Hubert wasn't a saint but he didn't deserve to die like that—the filthy slut should have died. I arranged it for *her*. Why didn't she die?"

Julian was stunned. Whore—Inès? Enemy slut? What was this demented woman saying? His arms tightened around Inès, who was staring at Agathe, a faint flicker of recognition dawning in her eyes.

Oh, God, Inès thought. Another one—another creature from the past come to destroy my life. But who was she? Inès desperately racked her brain to try to recall when she had known this woman.

Agathe screamed hysterically, "You didn't know she was a famous Parisian prostitute, did you, Julian? Did you?" She laughed, her face a mask of hatred.

Inès' face paled and she felt the rigid body of Julian moving away from her. Then suddenly she remembered.

"Oh, my God," she whispered. That wispy, strange girl she had seen only once or twice at the cash register of L'Éléphant Rose during the war. She had never even seen the girl's face properly, but now she

remembered all the stories they'd told about her. Those years of privation when the Jewish girl was hidden down in the cellar; how her hair had
turned completely white; how when she got out she had despised not
only the enemy but all the girls who fraternized with them.

Inès took a step towards the babbling woman whose face was a twisted
mask of pain and vengeance. She seemed barely human now. "Please
stop, Agathe," Inès pleaded. "Don't. I beg you, *don't! Please*. Why are
you saying these things? They're lies. You mustn't do this—you *can't*."

"I can—oh, but I can and I *will*." Agathe's smile was vicious, her laugh
a crone's cackle. "Now that *he* knows what you were—what you *are*—he
won't want to marry you anymore—will you, Julian?"

Suddenly she burst away from the restraining grasp of the two policemen and rushed towards Julian, crooning, *"Mon amour—mon amour."*
One skinny arm clamped itself around his neck, while the other yanked
feverishly at the knot of his robe, trying to pull it open.

"My God, Agathe, what the hell are you doing? Stop it!" Julian was
strong, and he held her at arm's length in a tight grip, staring into her
demented eyes.

"Tell me what you meant about Inès," he said, his voice steady and
menacing. "Tell me, Agathe."

Inès sank on to a couch, hiding her face in her hands. It was over now.
All over. Now the truth would finally be known. To her lover, the man
whose child she had carried—whose wife she was going to be. It was
finally finished. And ironically not by Scrofo, but by a woman she hardly
knew. Her whole life lay in ruins around her. Julian would never forgive
her for her past and her deception. How could he?

"Yes, yes, Julian, of course I'll tell you—I want to tell you *everything*."
Agathe licked at her dry lips, her eyes darting gleefully between Julian
and Inès, reveling in the attention of the whole group who were riveted
to her every word with horrified fascination. She was center stage finally,
now they would watch *her*, listen to *her*, while the arms of the man she
worshiped held her tightly.

"Paris. It was Paris—at the nightclub L'Éléphant Rose during the war
—she fucked them—all of them—the Boche, the Gestapo, the SS, the
Italian pigs. Soldiers, officers, she didn't care who she did it with. She
danced with them—she laughed with them and she let them *all* fuck her.
Do anything with her. They gave her money which she threw around,
showing off to everyone. She loved the life of a whore, didn't you, Inès?"
She glanced over at Inès' slumped figure and, with a contemptuous
laugh, continued, "Then one night she went too far. She killed a man
with his own razor, she cut his throat. At least she thought she did—
didn't you, bitch?" Again, she looked towards Inès huddled on the couch,
the humiliation of having her past laid bare rendering her mute and
immobile.

"*Who*—who did Inès kill?" Julian's voice sounded hoarse, cold and
tired. Inès could tell now as he looked at her that he hated her. Her
dream was just another nightmare.

"*SCROFO!*" Agathe screamed. "Umberto Scrofo—the Italian

General, the fat one with all the medals. The one who called himself Hubert Croft here. She was his girl—his doxy He made love to her *many*, many times in Paris. Then she tried to murder him—but you didn't succeed, did you?" She sneered at Inès. "What a pity for you, whore. You didn't succeed just like I didn't succeed in killing you—but maybe I've done something even better. I've *ruined* you, and your precious life with Julian, because he's *mine—MINE!*" With that she lashed a bony hand across her dress, tearing off the buttons to reveal her shriveled breasts.

"Kiss me, Julian! *Mon amour.*" Eyes closed, she tried to squirm closer to him, but Julian held her away from him, an expression of disgust on his face.

"I've been waiting for you, *mon amour*, my Julian," she cried despairingly, her eyes now open and pleading. "Waiting, my love. I know you want me too, it's our destiny to be together."

As Agathe tried to press her writhing body against his, the Inspector signaled to the two policemen, who grabbed her, pulling her away from Julian. Ramona put her shawl over Agathe's half-naked body, her eyes mirroring the pity she felt for this poor wretch, and the rest of them turned away in shocked embarrassment.

Julian stood quite still, his tanned face ashen.

Nick went over to him. Unable to find anything to say, he put his hand comfortingly on Julian's shoulder. Dominique drew closer to the two men, her childlike, inquisitive eyes riveted to Inès, who still hadn't spoken.

Ramona was comforting Shirley, who was weeping quietly. "Irving, my poor, poor Irving. That mad bitch killed him too, that bitch. Oh, Christ."

The rest of the cast and crew stood stiffly like extras in a crowd scene, huddled in the background, staring at Julian, Agathe and Inès in fascination. They sensed that something even more dreadful was about to happen in this frozen tableau. All the principals were silent except for Shirley's muffled sobbing, and the faint sound of waves sighing on the shoreline was the only background noise.

Then Julian spoke in a dark, threatening voice which sent a shudder through Inès. "Is all this true, Inès? Is what Agathe said the truth?"

How could he? How *could* Julian ask her that question in front of everyone? Couldn't he leave her with even a shred of self-respect? Inès had waited to find the man of her dreams for many years. Now he stood before her with dozens of people as witnesses, about to denounce her for what she had been, and for what she had done in what seemed a former lifetime.

Julian asked the question again, his voice even icier than before. The electrified silence of the onlookers intensified his theatrical presence. He was center stage—the leading actor—and all the supporting cast seemed to be waiting with bated breath for the inevitable drama to unfold.

"I asked you if what Agathe has said is true, Inès," he said for the third time, his voice raised. Inès could hear the suppressed rage, see it in his posture, his attitude. His fists were clenched, his eyes narrowed, his regal head proud. The king was demanding obedience from a subject.

"Answer me, Inès!" he roared authoritatively. "Say something."

Inès raised her head to look unflinchingly into Julian's cold eyes, struggling to keep her face impassive. She had too much pride to cry, though her throat ached with pain. The man she loved was demanding a public confession from her, demanding that she reveal her past to him—to all of these people—because of what he considered to be *his* divine right.

Slowly Inès rose to her feet and the crowd held its breath in anticipation. There was silence as Inès stared defiantly at Julian, a slight breeze stirring her dress. He took an angry step towards her, roughly brushing aside Nick's restraining hand.

"I said *answer* me, Inès, I want the truth. *Now.*"

Inès' voice was only slightly louder than the whisper of the breeze. "Julian, oh, Julian, the camera isn't turning. You don't have to perform now."

"How dare you!" The power of his voice caused the sleeping parrots in the trees to awaken and raise a cacophony of screeching. "Don't *preach* to me, Inès. Answer my question. That's all I ask of you."

"Not here—not *now*." Her eyes never left his face. "No, Julian. No. I can't and I won't."

She turned, light as gossamer, and walked swiftly from the great marble hall into the welcoming darkness of the night, the tears that she had held back almost choking her.

Nick grabbed Julian's arm as he tried to follow her. "No, Julian, no, let her go. She's right. This isn't the time or the place. Leave her alone, you must."

Weeping with despair, Inès began flinging her clothes into suitcases. One of Ramona's drivers waited outside the hotel. She was leaving Acapulco. Leaving Julian. Leaving behind her perfect future. She was going —to where? She didn't know; she knew only that she had to escape. Hastily she pulled off her silk dress, putting on a skirt and jacket. She snapped her suitcases shut, oblivious to the pieces of stray fabric which trailed from their sides, and rang down for a porter.

The door opened suddenly and Julian walked into the room. He had changed out of his robe into trousers and a shirt. His face was pale, his eyes full of pain.

They stared at each other. He looked down at the closed suitcases, at her traveling clothes, at the defiant hurt expression on her beautiful face.

"Why are you leaving me?" he asked.

"Why?" She smiled weakly. "Oh, you know why, Julian. It's true what Agathe said—not all of it—she exaggerated—but I *was* a prostitute in Paris, and I *did* try to kill Scrofo or Croft or whatever he called himself."

"My God." He shook his head and sat down heavily on the bed. "But *why,* Inès? Why in God's name did you never tell me before? You must have known that one day I'd find out."

"I just hoped that you wouldn't. I suppose I didn't think you could bear to hear the truth. Yes, I was a whore," she said quietly, "but only because of circumstances. You see, my mother had been one, and probably my grandmother before her."

She looked at him but his expression remained enigmatic. She sighed.

"It was an easy, almost normal way of life to me. Julian—I was very young when I started, an adolescent, and I really knew no other life. Perhaps I was too greedy; maybe in London I should have stopped being a prostitute, taken a proper job in a shop or an office, and found a man, any man, to marry. I shouldn't have cared whether I loved him or not. I should have just married him for security and to have him take care of me."

She looked at him, her eyes huge with tears. "That's how it's supposed to be for a woman, isn't it, Julian? No one said you had to be in love to be married—but to me, to marry someone I didn't love was an even worse kind of prostitution."

Julian said nothing, his face still expressionless, as Inès continued, "I loved you so much—I *do* love you so much, that I couldn't run the risk of probably losing you. I know you, Julian. Don't forget that. I know how you think, how most men think. You have double standards regarding men and women. You would have left me if you knew, I know you would. You wouldn't have been able to bear what people would have said, the malicious gossip, the scandal and all the whispering that would have gone on behind your back."

"No, Inès." He took a step towards her and she thought she could see tenderness gradually coming back into his face. "It isn't true. I would have understood, and I would have forgiven you because I *love* you. You are—you always have been, always *will* be, the only woman for me in my whole life. Don't you know that?"

She stared at him uncertainly. "But my past? Doesn't it bother you— surely you must mind?"

"Mind—mind? Of *course* I bloody mind, you silly little goose. But what can I do about it? Nothing. It happened, it's part of what has made you the person you are, the woman I love, the woman I want to marry and spend the rest of my life with. Inès, you forgave me for Dominique —a far worse thing. How could I not forgive you, my darling, how could I not?"

"But you were so angry in front of everyone—it was so humiliating. I was mortified, Julian."

"I'm sorry, my darling. I'm truly, truly sorry. What more can I say? I hate myself for hurting you, Inès. You've been hurt too much in the past."

His arms reached out for her and she found herself wanting to melt into their safe refuge.

"God knows I've been a bastard to you, worse than a bastard."

"It's all right, darling," she murmured. "It's all forgotten."

"None of it really matters to us anymore," he whispered, taking her in his arms, and the breath left her body in a great sigh of abandoned relief. "It's all forgotten, my love. All over now."

"Thank God," Inès breathed. "Thank God, everything's out in the open. I'm glad you know the truth, Julian. I think our life together would have become impossible if I had always to pretend."

"You're right, my angel." Julian smiled lovingly at her. "You're absolutely right, it's never any good to pretend. That's only for actors."

Long before their limousine arrived at the theater, the occupants could see the dozens of searchlights crisscrossing the thick blackness of the sky and hear the excited shrieks of the eager fans in the bleachers greeting each arriving celebrity with approval.

"Here goes," Nick said, adjusting his black bow tie. "This is what we've all been waiting for. It's sink or swim time, boys and girls."

The women took out their powder compacts to check their perfectly made-up faces for the last time. All of them were silent with their own particular thoughts of what tonight's premiere would mean to each of them.

For Elektra it meant that Nikolas would finally achieve his lifetime's desire: to be acknowledged as an important director in the American cinema. He had expunged the memory of Gourouni from his mind in the past year and was filled with optimism about the future.

Dominique was being hailed as the brightest, most exciting new star in Hollywood, and the studio was considering casting her opposite Julian in his next film.

Inès smoothed the folds of her ice-white velvet gown. Turning her perfect profile away from her husband, she looked out the window into the night, the encroaching cheers of the fans suddenly provoking thoughts of the past. She thought how lucky she was—so very lucky. Luck had saved her from the vengeance of the Gestapo after the incident with Scrofo. If it hadn't been for luck, she too might have lived those years of torment that Agathe had endured, which had slowly driven her mad. If she had been forced to exist in that cellar, would her life have been any different from Agathe's? Could *she* have remained sane?

Inès really couldn't blame Agathe for what she had tried to do. The ravages of war and evil had created a certain kind of madness in almost everyone who had survived it.

As the white limousine drew up outside the brilliantly lit theater, the crowd's cheers built to a tumultuous crescendo.

"Ready, darling?" Julian gently squeezed Inès' white-gloved hand.

"Ready," she said with a brilliant smile. "Ready for anything, darling."

From the darkness opposite Dominique looked across at them and a sly and secret smile flickered over her beautiful face. One day, she thought, one day soon, Julian, you will be mine again, I know you will. I can feel it in my bones.

About The Author

JOAN COLLINS made her stage debut in London's West End at the
age of nine and has appeared in over fifty feature films and over
300 hours of television, and is world-renowned for her portrayal of
Alexis in the series, "Dynasty." In addition to her acting career,
she continues to delight her millions of fans with her bestselling
fiction and nonfiction that has been translated into many different
languages.. Her newest bestseller in England, *My Secrets*, will be
published in the United States this year. Joan Collins is also the
mother of three children, Sacha, Tara, and Katy.